Constructing
JESUS

Constructing
JESUS

Memory, Imagination, and History

DALE C. ALLISON JR.

Originally published in the United States of America in 2010
by Baker Academic, a division of Baker Publishing Group
P. O. Box 6287, Grand Rapids, MI 49516-6287

First published in Great Britain in 2010

Society for Promoting Christian Knowledge
36 Causton Street
London SW1P 4ST
www.spckpublishing.co.uk

British Library Cataloguing-in-Publication Data
A catalogue record for this book is available from the British Library

ISBN 978–0–281–06358–1

1 3 5 7 9 10 8 6 4 2

Printed in Great Britain by Ashford Colour Press

Produced on paper from sustainable forests

For Chris Kettler

Friends, although absent, are at hand.

—Cicero

Contents

Preface   ix

Abbreviations   xiii

1. The General and the Particular: Memories of Jesus   1

2. More Than a Sage: The Eschatology of Jesus   31

   Excursus 1: The Kingdom of God and the World to Come   164

   Excursus 2: The Continuity between John the Baptist and Jesus   204

3. More Than a Prophet: The Christology of Jesus   221

4. More Than an Aphorist: The Discourses of Jesus   305

5. Death and Memory: The Passion of Jesus   387

6. Memory and Invention: How Much History?   435

Bibliography   463

Ancient Writings Index   535

Author Index   567

Subject Index   583

Preface

This is my fourth and, I hope, final book on the historical Jesus. I never intended to produce more than a single slim volume. But one thing led to another, or rather one book to another. After the publication, in 1998, of *Jesus of Nazareth: Millenarian Prophet*, I received invitations to speak further on the subject, and I ran across responses to my work that called for clarification and commentary. And so, in 2005, another book was born, *Resurrecting Jesus*. The process then repeated itself—more invitations to speak, more clarifications to offer, more rejoinders to issue. The upshot has been two more books, one being *The Historical Christ and the Theological Jesus*, which appeared in 2009, the other being the present volume. That, however, should be the end of the line. Although the subject remains hypnotic, I have contributed more than my fair share of pages to this limitless field of controversy. It is time to move on to other things.

Chapter 1, which outlines and offers justification for the method I adopt throughout the rest of the book, is a much expanded version of a lecture delivered in the spring of 2009 at Yale University, to the department of religious studies. Thanks go to Dale Martin for making the arrangements and for his attentive hospitality.

Chapter 2 is an attempt to present, one last time, my case for Jesus as an apocalyptic prophet. Although it is the culmination of a series of contributions I have made to the subject over the past three decades, it also and more particularly grows out of a paper presented in April of 2007 at Princeton Theological Seminary for a symposium organized by James H. Charlesworth. The questions and comments that followed that address have helped me to improve greatly the present product. I wrote additional sections of chapter 2 in anticipation of a presentation for the annual meeting of the Jesus Seminar in March of 2010.

Excursus 1 is my attempt to rethink, in the light of a fresh review of Jewish materials, the meanings of "kingdom of God" in the Jesus tradition. It is intended to reinforce the major conclusions of chapter 2, as is excursus 2, a lightly revised version of portions of an article originally published as "The Continuity between John and Jesus," in the *Journal for the Study of the Historical Jesus* 1, no. 1 (2003): 6–27. I thank Brill and the editor of that journal, Robert Webb, for permission to use copyrighted materials.

Chapter 3, on the genesis of Christology, presupposes the results of chapter 2 and is entirely new. It gives me the opportunity to address an exceedingly controversial matter that, despite my keen, long-standing interest, I have heretofore written about only in passing. I have tried hard not to repeat what others have said before, and because of this I have even at points allowed myself the freedom to speculate well beyond the evidence; nonetheless, some recapitulation on this topic, as on others in this volume, has proven inevitable.

Chapter 4 builds upon two previous studies. In *The Jesus Tradition in Q* (Trinity Press International, 1997), I observed that some of the literary features in the Sermon on the Plain appear also in extracanonical parallels to Luke 6; and in *The Intertextual Jesus* (Trinity Press International, 2000), I argued that the middle portion of that sermon is largely a rewrite of Lev 19 and attendant traditions. The present volume offers me the chance to bring my earlier claims together and to unfold their large implications for the history of Q's inaugural discourse.

Chapter 5 applies the method introduced in chapter 1 to a famous crux: how did Jesus face his death? My intention is not only to suggest an approach to that fascinating question but also to contribute to our understanding of the origin and evolution of the pre-Markan passion narrative.

Chapter 6, which addresses a fundamental issue too often neglected, reproduces the plenary address for the annual meeting of the Central States Region of the Society of Biblical Literature, held in Saint Louis on March 29, 2009. I happily thank Brad Chance, Milton Horne, and Steve Patterson for the invitation and their welcome on that pleasant occasion.

This volume as a whole is testimony to my conviction that the means that most scholars have employed and continue to employ for constructing the historical Jesus are too flimsy to endure, or at least too flimsy for me to countenance any longer. I learned the discipline during an era when everyone was taught to employ the so-called criteria of authenticity. We were to find Jesus by, first, isolating individual units and then, second, running them through a gauntlet consisting of multiple attestation, dissimilarity, embarrassment, and so on. After many years of playing by the rules, however, I have gradually come to abandon them. I have decided that knowing the old directives has been of much less help than promised. I am trying something else. This book is the result.

My wife, Kristine Allison, and my administrative assistant, Kathy Anderson, read through the entire manuscript. Chris Kettler, Nancy Klancher, Joel Marcus, and Mike Winger commented on portions of it. Their eyes have caught seemingly countless errors both large and small, and their questions have led me to revise some of my judgments—all, no doubt, for the better. I am most grateful to them, as also to James Ernest, who helped me first form the vision for this book and who, along with Wells Turner in the editorial process, greatly improved it.

I dedicate this book to my longtime friend Chris Kettler, who has had the good sense and good fortune to spend most of his life in my favorite place, among some of my favorite people. He understands: history is not theology.

Abbreviations

General

ad loc.	at the place discussed	*pace*	contrary to the opinion of
a.k.a.	also known as	par.	parallel
apud	according to, in the writings of	p(p.)	page(s)
bis	twice	Q	*Quelle* (German for "source"), putative source of the sayings of Jesus appearing in Matthew and Luke
col.	column		
diff.	differs from		
esp.	especially	R.	Rabbi
fol.	folio	RecLng	long recension
frg(s).	fragment(s)	RecShrt	short recension
Gk.	Greek	repr.	reprint
ibid.	in the same source	rev.	revised
idem	by the same author	s.v.	under the word
inv.	inventory number	v.l.	variant reading
Lat.	Latin	v(v).	verse(s)
n.d.	no date		

Ancient Texts, Text Types, and Versions

LXX	Septuagint	Tg.	Targum
MT	Masoretic Text	Θ	Theodotion

Modern Editions

NA²⁷   *Novum Testamentum Graece*. Edited by [E. and E. Nestle], B. Aland, K. Aland, J. Karavidopoulos, C. M. Martini, and B. M. Metzger. 27th rev. ed. Stuttgart: Deutsche Bibelgesellschaft, 1993

Modern Versions

KJV   King James Version
NRSV   New Revised Standard Version
RSV   Revised Standard Version

Papyri

P.Flor.	Papiri Fiorentini	P.Oxy.	Oxyrhynchus Papyri
P.Heid.	Heidelberger Papyrussammlung	P.Vindob.	Einige Wiener Papyri

Hebrew Bible / Old Testament

Gen	Genesis	Neh	Nehemiah	Hos	Hosea
Exod	Exodus	Esth	Esther	Joel	Joel
Lev	Leviticus	Job	Job	Amos	Amos
Num	Numbers	Ps/Pss	Psalms	Obad	Obadiah
Deut	Deuteronomy	Prov	Proverbs	Jonah	Jonah
Josh	Joshua	Eccl	Ecclesiastes	Mic	Micah
Judg	Judges	Song	Song of Songs	Nah	Nahum
Ruth	Ruth	Isa	Isaiah	Hab	Habakkuk
1–2 Sam	1–2 Samuel	Jer	Jeremiah	Zeph	Zephaniah
1–2 Kgs	1–2 Kings	Lam	Lamentations	Hag	Haggai
1–2 Chr	1–2 Chronicles	Ezek	Ezekiel	Zech	Zechariah
Ezra	Ezra	Dan	Daniel	Mal	Malachi

New Testament

Matt	Matthew	1–2 Thess	1–2 Thessalonians
Mark	Mark	1–2 Tim	1–2 Timothy
Luke	Luke	Titus	Titus
John	John	Phlm	Philemon
Acts	Acts	Heb	Hebrews
Rom	Romans	Jas	James
1–2 Cor	1–2 Corinthians	1–2 Pet	1–2 Peter
Gal	Galatians	1–2–3 John	1–2–3 John
Eph	Ephesians	Jude	Jude
Phil	Philippians	Rev	Revelation
Col	Colossians		

Apocrypha and Septuagint

Bar	Baruch	Sir	Sirach
1–2 Esd	1–2 Esdras	Tob	Tobit
Jdt	Judith	Wis	Wisdom of Solomon
1–4 Macc	1–4 Maccabees		

Old Testament Pseudepigrapha

Ahiqar	Ahiqar	Ps.-Phoc.	Pseudo-Phocylides
Apoc. Ab.	Apocalypse of Abraham	Pss. Sol.	Psalms of Solomon
Apoc. Adam	Apocalypse of Adam	Sib. Or.	Sybilline Oracles
Apoc. El.	Apocalypse of Elijah	Syr. Apoc. Dan.	Syriac Apocalypse of Daniel
Apoc. Sedr.	Apocalypse of Sedrach		
As. Mos.	Assumption of Moses	Syr. Men.	Sentences of the Syriac Menander
2 Bar.	2 Baruch (Syriac Apocalypse)	T. Ab.	Testament of Abraham
3 Bar.	3 Baruch (Greek Apocalypse)	T. Adam	Testament of Adam
		T. Ash.	Testament of Asher
4 Bar.	4 Baruch (Paraleipomena Jeremiou)	T. Benj.	Testament of Benjamin
		T. Dan	Testament of Dan
1 En.	1 Enoch (Ethiopic Apocalypse)	T. Gad	Testament of Gad
		T. Isaac	Testament of Isaac
2 En.	2 Enoch (Slavonic Apocalypse)	T. Iss.	Testament of Issachar
		T. Jac.	Testament of Jacob
3 En.	3 Enoch (Hebrew Apocalypse)	T. Job	Testament of Job
		T. Jos.	Testament of Joseph
4 Ezra	4 Ezra	T. Jud.	Testament of Judah
Gk. Apoc. Ezra	Greek Apocalypse of Ezra	T. Levi	Testament of Levi
		T. Mos.	Testament of Moses
Jos. Asen.	Joseph and Aseneth	T. Naph.	Testament of Naphtali
Jub.	Jubilees	T. Reub.	Testament of Reuben
L.A.B.	Liber antiquitatum biblicarum (Pseudo-Philo)	T. Sol.	Testament of Solomon
		T. 3 Patr.	Testaments of the Three Patriarchs
L.A.E.	Life of Adam and Eve		
Let. Arist.	Letter of Aristeas	T. 12 Patr.	Testaments of the Twelve Patriarchs
Liv. Pro.	Lives of the Prophets		
Mart. Ascen. Isa.	Martyrdom and Ascension of Isaiah	T. Zeb.	Testament of Zebulun
Pr. Jos.	Prayer of Joseph		

Dead Sea Scrolls and Related Texts

CD-A	Damascus Document[a]	CD-B	Damascus Document[b]

Mur 24	*papFarming Contracts*	4Q300 (4QMyst[b])	*Mysteries[b]*
1QH[a]	*Hodayot[a]*	4Q377 (4Qapocr-Pent B)	*Apocryphon Penta-teuch B*
1QM	*War Scroll*	4Q381	*Non-Canonical Psalms B*
1QpHab	*Pesher to Habakkuk*	4Q385 (4QpsEzek[a])	*Pseudo-Ezekiel[a]*
1QS	*Rule of the Community*	4Q386 (4QpsEzek[b])	*Pseudo-Ezekiel[b]*
1Q28a (1QSa)	*Rule of the Congregation*	4Q398 (4QMMT[e])	*Halakhic Letter[e]*
1Q28b (1QSb)	*Rule of Benedictions*	4Q399 (4QMMT[f])	*Halakhic Letter[f]*
4Q161 (4QpIsa[a])	*Isaiah Pesher[a]*	4Q400 (4QShirShabb[a])	*Songs of the Sab-bath Sacrifice[a]*
4Q164 (4QpIsa[d])	*Isaiah Pesher[d]*	4Q403 (4QShirShabb[d])	*Songs of the Sab-bath Sacrifice[d]*
4Q174 (4QFlor)	*Florilegium*	4Q405 (4QShirShabb[f])	*Songs of the Sab-bath Sacrifice[f]*
4Q175 (4QTest)	*Testimonia*	4Q417	*Instruction[c]*
4Q181 (4QAgesCreat B)	*Ages of Creation B*	4Q426	*Sapiential-Hymnic Work A*
4Q185	*Sapiential Work*	4Q427 (4QH[a])	*Hodayot[a]*
4Q203 (4QEn-Giants[a] ar)	*Book of Giants[a] ar*	4Q471b	*Self-Glorification Hymn[a]*
4Q225 (4QpsJub[a])	*Pseudo-Jubilees[a]*	4Q491 (4QM[a])	*War Scroll[a]*
4Q242 (4QPrNab ar)	*Prayer of Naboni-dus ar*	4Q504 (4QDibHam[a])	*Words of the Luminaries[a]*
4Q243 (4QpsDan[a] ar)	*Pseudo-Daniel[a] ar*	4Q509+4Q505 (4QpapPrFêtesc)	*Festival Prayers[c]*
4Q244 (4QpsDan[b] ar)	*Pseudo-Daniel[b] ar*	4Q511 (4QShir[b])	*Songs of the Sage[b]*
4Q245 (4QpsDan[c] ar)	*Pseudo-Daniel[c] ar*	4Q521	*Messianic Apocalypse*
4Q246	*Aramaic Apocalypse*	4Q525 (4QBéat)	*Beatitudes*
4Q252 (4Qcomm-Gen A)	*Commentary on Genesis A*	4Q554 (4QNj[a] ar)	*New Jerusalem[a] ar*
		4Q558	*Vision[b] ar*
4Q264 (4QS[j])	*Rule of the Community[j]*	4Q559 (4QpapBib-Chronology ar)	*Biblical Chronology*
4Q285 (4QSM)	*Sefer ha-Milḥamah*	11Q5 (11QPs[a])	*Psalms[a]*
4Q286 (4QBer[a])	*Blessings[a]*	11Q13 (11QMelch)	*Melchizedek*
4Q287 (4QBer[b])	*Blessings[b]*	11Q19 (11QT[a])	*Temple[a]*

Targumic Texts

Frg. Tg.	Fragmentary Targum	Tg. Onq.	Targum Onqelos
Tg. Isa.	Targum Isaiah	Tg. Ps.-J.	Targum Pseudo-Jonathan
Tg. Neof. I	Targum Neofiti I		

Mishnah, Talmud, and Related Literature

b.	Babylonian Talmud	*'Ed.*	*'Edduyot*	*Pesaḥ.*	*Pesahim*
		'Erub.	*'Erubin*	*Qidd.*	*Qiddušin*
m.	Mishnah	*Giṭ.*	*Giṭṭin*	*Roš. Haš.*	*Roš Haššanah*
t.	Tosefta	*Ḥag.*	*Ḥagigah*	*Šabb.*	*Šabbat*
y.	Jerusalem Talmud	*Ḥul.*	*Ḥullin*	*Sanh.*	*Sanhedrin*
		Kelim	*Kelim*	*Šeqal.*	*Šeqalim*
'Abod. Zar.	*'Abodah Zarah*	*Ketub.*	*Ketubim*	*Soṭah*	*Soṭah*
		Kil.	*Kil'ayim*	*Sukkah*	*Sukkah*
'Abot	*'Abot*	*Ma'aś.*	*Ma'aśerot*	*Ta'an.*	*Ta'anit*
'Arak.	*'Arakin*	*Meg.*	*Megillah*	*Tamid*	*Tamid*
B. Bat.	*Baba Batra*	*Menaḥ.*	*Menaḥot*	*Tem.*	*Temurah*
Ber.	*Berakot*	*Mo'ed Qaṭ.*	*Mo'ed Qaṭan*	*Yebam.*	*Yebamot*
B. Meṣi'a	*Baba Meṣi'a*			*Yoma*	*Yoma (= Kippurim)*
B. Qam.	*Baba Qamma*	*Ned.*	*Nedarim*		
		Pe'ah	*Pe'ah*	*Zebaḥ.*	*Zebahim*

Other Rabbinic Works

'Abot R. Nat.	*'Abot de Rabbi Nathan*	*Sipra*	*Sipra*
Mek.	*Mekilta*	*Sipre*	*Sipre*
Midr.	*Midrash*	*Sop.*	*Soperim*
Pesiq. Rab.	*Pesiqta Rabbati*	*Tan. d. El.*	*Tanna debe Eliyahu*
Pesiq. Rab Kah.	*Pesiqta de Rab Kahana*	*Tanḥ.*	*Tanḥuma*
Pirqe R. El.	*Pirqe Rabbi Eliezer*	*Yal.*	*Yalquṭ*
Rab.	*Rabbah*		

Apostolic Fathers

Barn.	*Barnabas*	Ign. *Pol.*	Ignatius, *To Polycarp*
1–2 Clem.	*1–2 Clement*	Ign. *Rom.*	Ignatius, *To the Romans*
Did.	*Didache*	Ign. *Smyrn.*	Ignatius, *To the Smyrnaeans*
Diogn.	*Diognetus*		
Hermas, *Sim.*	Shepherd of Hermas, *Similitude*	Ign. *Trall.*	Ignatius, *To the Trallians*
		Mart. Pol.	*Martyrdom of Polycarp*
Ign. *Eph.*	Ignatius, *To the Ephesians*	Pol. *Phil.*	Polycarp, *To the Philippians*
Ign. *Magn.*	Ignatius, *To the Magnesians*		

Nag Hammadi Codices

Dial. Sav.	III,5 *Dialogue of the Savior*	*Thom. Cont.*	II,7 *Book of Thomas the Contender*
Gos. Phil.	II,3 *Gospel of Philip*	*Treat. Res.*	I,4 *Treatise on Resurrection*

New Testament Apocrypha and Pseudepigrapha

Acts Andr. Mth.	*Acts of Andrew and Matthias*	*Gos. Pet.*	*Gospel of Peter*
		Gos. Sav.	*Gospel of the Savior*
Acts John	*Acts of John*	*Gos. Thom.*	*Gospel of Thomas*
Acts Paul	*Acts of Paul*	*Inf. Gos. Thom.*	*Infancy Gospel of Thomas*
Acts Pil.	*Acts of Pilate*		
Acts Thom.	*Acts of Thomas*	*Pist. Soph.*	*Pistis Sophia*
Apoc. Paul	*Apocalypse of Paul*	*Prot. Jas.*	*Protevangelium of James*
Apoc. Pet.	*Apocalypse of Peter*		
Apos. Con.	*Apostolic Constitutions and Canons*	*Ps.-Clem. Hom.*	*Pseudo-Clementine Homilies*
Ep. Apost.	*Epistula Apostolorum*	*Ps.-Clem. Rec.*	*Pseudo-Clementine Recognitions*
Gos. Naz.	*Gospel of the Nazarenes*		
Gos. Nic.	*Gospel of Nicodemus*		

Greek and Latin Works

Adamantius

Dial.	*Dialogue (De recta in Deum fide) (On True Faith in God)*

Ambrose

Exp. Luc.	*Expositio Evangelii secundum Lucam*

Ambrosiaster

Comm. Rom.	*Commentary on Romans*

Aristides

Apol.	*Apology*

Aristophanes

Ran.	*Ranae (Frogs)*

Artemidorus

Onir.	*Onirocritica*

Athanasius

Vit. Ant.	*Vita Antonii (Life of Antony)*

Augustine

Civ.	*De civitate Dei (The City of God)*
Doctr. chr.	*De doctrina christiana (Christian Instruction)*
Ep.	*Epistulae (Letters)*

Exp. Gal.	*Expositio in epistulam ad Galatas*
Serm. Dom.	*De sermone Domini in monte (Sermon on the Mount)*
Trin.	*De Trinitate*

Babrius

Fab.	*Fabulae Aesopeae*

Basil of Caesarea

Comm. Isa.	Commentary on Isaiah
Reg. br.	Regulae brevius tractatae (Shorter Rules)

Bede

Comm. Acts	Commentary on Acts

Cassiodorus

Exp. Ps.	Expositio psalmorum

Chrysostom

Hom. 1 Cor.	Homiliae in epistulam i ad Corinthios
Hom. Eph.	Homiliae in epistulam ad Ephesios
Hom. Jo.	Homiliae in Joannem
Hom. Matt.	Homiliae in Matthaeum
Hom. Rom.	Homiliae in epistulam ad Romanos
Leg.	De legislatore

Cicero

De or.	*De oratore*

Clement of Alexandria

Paed.	Paedagogus (Christ the Educator)
Prot.	Protrepticus (Exhortation to the Greeks)
Quis div.	Quis dives salvetur (Salvation of the Rich)
Strom.	Stromata (Miscellanies)

Commodian

Inst.	*Instructiones adversus gentium deos pro christiana disciplina*

Cyprian

Dom. or.	*De dominica oratione*

Cyril of Alexandria

Comm. Isa.	Commentary on Isaiah
Comm. Luke	Commentary on Luke
Hom. Luke	Homilies on Luke

Didymus of Alexandria

Fr. Ps.	Fragmenta in Psalmos

Dio Cassius

Hist.	Roman History

Diogenes Laertius

Vit.	Vitae philosophorum (Lives of Eminent Philosophers)

Ephraem

Comm. Exod.	Commentary on Exodus

Epiphanius

Pan.	Panarion (Refutation of All Heresies)

Eusebius

Dem. ev.	Demonstratio evangelica (Demonstration of the Gospel)
Hist. eccl.	Historia ecclesiastica (Ecclesiastical History)
Mart. Pal.	De martyribus Palaestinae (The Martyrs of Palestine)
Onom.	Onomasticon
Praep. ev.	Praeparatio evangelica (Preparation for the Gospel)

Gregory of Nyssa

Vit. Mos.   Vita Mosis

Haymo of Halberstadt

Exp. Rom.   Expositio in epistulam ad
                 Romanos

Herodotus

Hist.   Historiae (Histories)

Hippolytus

Comm. Dan.   Commentarium in
                 Danielem
Haer.   Refutatio omnium hae-
                 resium (Refutation of All
                 Heresies)

Horace

Ep.   Epistulae (Epistles)

Irenaeus

Epid.   Epideixis tou aposto-
                 likou kērygmatos (Dem-
                 onstration of the Apos-
                 tolic Preaching)
Haer.   Adversus haereses
                 (Against Heresies)

Isho'dad of Merv

Comm. Luke   Commentary on Luke

Isocrates

Ad Nic.   Ad Nicoclem (Or. 2)
Aeginet.   Aegineticus (Or. 19)
Demon.   Ad Demonicum (Or. 1)

Jerome

Comm. Eph.   Commentariorum in epi-
                 stulam ad Ephesios libri III
Comm. Gal.   Commentariorum in epi-
                 stulam ad Galatas libri III
Comm. Matt.   Commentariorum in
                 Matthaeum libri IV

Vit. Paul.   Vita S. Pauli, primi
                 eremitae

Josephus

Ag. Ap.   Against Apion
Ant.   Jewish Antiquities
J.W.   Jewish War

Justin

1 Apol.   Apologia i (First Apology)
2 Apol.   Apologia ii (Second
                 Apology)
Dial.   Dialogus cum Tryphone
                 (Dialogue with Trypho)

Lactantius

Epit.   Epitome divinarum insti-
                 tutionum (Epitome of the
                 Divine Institutes)

Livy

Hist.   History of Rome

Longinus

Subl.   De sublimitate (On the
                 Sublime)

Marius Victorinus

Comm. Gal.   Commentary on Galatians

Oecumenius of Trikka

Frag. 1 Cor.   Fragmenta in epistulam i
                 ad Corinthios

Origen

Cels.   Contra Celsum (Against
                 Celsus)
Comm. Jo.   Commentarii in evange-
                 lium Joannis
Comm. Matt.   Commentarium in evan-
                 gelium Matthaei
Hom. Jer.   Homiliae in Jeremiam
Hom. Jos.   Homiliae in Josuam

Hom. Luc.	Homiliae in Lucam
Hom. Num.	Homiliae in Numeros
Mart.	Exhortatio ad martyrium (Exhortation to Martyrdom)
Princ.	De principiis (Peri archōn) (First Principles)

Paschasius Radbertus

Exp. Matt.	Expositio in evangelium Matthaei

Pelagius

Comm. 1 Cor.	Commentary on 1 Corinthians
Comm. Eph.	Commentary on Ephesians
Comm. Rom.	Commentary on Romans

Petronius

Satyr.	Satyricon

Philo

Abraham	On the Life of Abraham
Alleg. Interp.	Allegorical Interpretation
Confusion	On the Confusion of Tongues
Dreams	On Dreams
Drunkenness	On Drunkenness
Embassy	On the Embassy to Gaius
Flight	On Flight and Finding
Giants	On Giants
God	On God
Good Person	That Every Good Person Is Free
Hypothetica	Hypothetica
Moses	On the Life of Moses
Posterity	On the Posterity of Cain
QG	Questions and Answers on Genesis
Rewards	On Rewards and Punishments
Spec. Laws	On the Special Laws
Virtues	On the Virtues
Worse	That the Worse Attacks the Better

Photius

Frag. Gal.	Fragmenta in epistulam ad Galatas

Plato

Phaed.	Phaedo
Phaedr.	Phaedrus
Theaet.	Theaetetus

Pliny the Younger

Ep.	Epistulae

Plutarch

Alex.	Alexander
Mor.	Moralia
Pomp.	Pompeius

Pseudo-Justin

Quaest. et resp.	Quaestiones et responsiones ad orthodoxos

Quintilian

Inst.	Institutio oratoria
Rhet. Her.	Rhetorica ad Herennium

Sedulius Scottus

Comm. Matt.	Commentary on Matthew

Seneca

Ben.	De beneficiis
Ep.	Epistulae morales

Severian of Gabala

Frag. 1 Cor.	Fragmenta in epistulam i ad Corinthios

Sextus

Sent.	Sentences

Socrates Scholasticus

Hist. eccl.	Historia ecclesiastica (Ecclesiastical History)

Suetonius

Aug.	Divus Augustus
Cal.	Gaius Caligula
Dom.	Domitianus
Vesp.	Vespasianus

Tacitus

Ann.	Annales
Hist.	Historiae

Tertullian

An.	De anima
Apol.	Apologeticus (Apology)
Bapt.	De baptismo (Baptism)
Carn. Chr.	De carne Christi (The Flesh of Christ)
Marc.	Adversus Marcionem (Against Marcion)
Or.	De oratione (Prayer)
Pat.	De patientia (Patience)
Praescr.	De praescriptione haereticorum (Prescription against Heretics)
Prax.	Adversus Praxean (Against Praxeas)
Scap.	Ad Scapulam

Theodore of Heraclea

Comm. Matt.	Commentary on Matthew

Theodoret of Cyrus

Comm. Col.	Commentary on Colossians
Comm. 1 Cor.	Commentary on 1 Corinthians
Comm. Gal.	Commentary on Galatians
Comm. Heb.	Commentary on Hebrews
Comm. Rom.	Commentary on Romans

Theophylact

Comm. Luke	Commentary on Luke
Comm. Matt.	Commentary on Matthew
Exp. 1 Cor.	Exposition of 1 Corinthians
Exp. Eph.	Exposition of Ephesians
Exp. Rom.	Exposition of Romans

Thomas Aquinas

Comm. Eph.	Commentary on Ephesians
Comm. Gal.	Commentary on Galatians

Thucydides

Hist.	History of the Peloponnesian War

Xenophon

Hell.	Hellenica

Other Ancient Works

CMC	Cologne Mani Codex
Keph.	The Kephalaia of the Teacher

Secondary Sources

AAJRP	American Academy of Jewish Research Proceedings
AASF	Annales Academiae scientiarum fennicae
AB	Anchor Bible

ABD	*Anchor Bible Dictionary.* Edited by D. N. Freedman. 6 vols. New York, 1992
ABR	*Australian Biblical Review*
ABRL	Anchor Bible Reference Library
AGJU	Arbeiten zur Geschichte des antiken Judentums und des Urchristentums
AJEC	Ancient Judaism and Early Christianity
AJSR	*Association of Jewish Studies Review*
AnBib	Analecta biblica
ANF	*Ante-Nicene Fathers: The Writings of the Fathers down to A.D. 325.* Edited by A. Roberts and J. Donaldson. Revised by A. C. Coxe. 10 vols. Repr., Grand Rapids: Eerdmans, 1978
AnGreg	Analecta Gregorianum
ANRW	*Aufstieg und Niedergang der römischen Welt: Geschichte und Kultur Roms im Spiegel der neueren Forschung.* Edited by H. Temporini and W. Haase. Berlin, 1972–
ANTC	Abingdon New Testament Commentaries
ANTJ	Arbeiten zum Neuen Testament und Judentum
AR	*Archiv für Religionswissenschaft*
ASNU	Acta seminarii neotestamentici upsaliensis
ATANT	Abhandlungen zur Theologie des Alten und Neuen Testaments
ATLAMS	American Theological Library Association Monograph Series
ATM	Altes Testament und Moderne
AYB	The Anchor Yale Bible
BA	Berichte und Abhandlungen
BBB	Bonner biblische Beiträge
BBR	*Bulletin of Biblical Research*
BCNH	Bibliothèque copte de Nag Hammadi
BDAG	Bauer, W., F. W. Danker, W. F. Arndt, and F. W. Gingrich. *Greek-English Lexicon of the New Testament and Other Early Christian Literature.* 3rd ed. Chicago, 2000
BDF	Blass, F., A. Debrunner, and R. W. Funk. *A Greek Grammar of the New Testament and Other Early Christian Literature.* Chicago, 1961
BECNT	Baker Exegetical Commentary on the New Testament
BETL	Bibliotheca ephemeridum theologicarum lovaniensium
BHM	*Bet ha-Midrasch.* By A. Jellinek. 6 vols. Leipzig: C. W. Vollrath, 1853–77
Bib	*Biblica*
BibInt	*Biblical Interpretation*
BibSem	Biblical Seminar
BibTS	Biblical Tools and Studies
BIS	Biblical Interpretation Series
BJRL	*Bulletin of the John Rylands University Library of Manchester*
BJS	Brown Judaic Studies
BNTC	Black's New Testament Commentaries
BR	*Biblical Research*
BRev	*Bible Review*
BS	*Beth She'arim.* Vol. 2, *The Greek Inscriptions.* By M. Schwabe and B. Lifshitz. New Brunswick, NJ: Rutgers University Press, 1974
BT	*The Bible Translator*
BTSc	Biblisch-theologische Schwerpunkte
BTSt	Biblisch-theologische Studien
BU	Biblische Untersuchungen
BZ	*Biblische Zeitschrift*
BZAW	Beihefte zur Zeitschrift für die alttestamentliche Wissenschaft
BZNW	Beihefte zur Zeitschrift für die neutestamentliche Wissenschaft

BZRG	Beihefte zur Zeitschrift für Religions- und Geistesgeschichte
CahRB	Cahiers de la Revue biblique
CBET	Contributions to Biblical Theology and Exegesis
CBQ	*Catholic Biblical Quarterly*
CBQMS	Catholic Biblical Quarterly Monograph Series
CBR	*Currents in Biblical Research*
CBT	Cultures, Beliefs and Traditions
CCCM	Corpus Christianorum: Continuatio mediaevalis. Turnhout, 1969–
CCSL	Corpus Christianorum: Series latina. Turnhout, 1953–
CEJL	Commentaries on Early Jewish Literature
CGTC	Cambridge Greek Testament Commentary
CIJ	Corpus inscriptionum judaicarum
ConBNT	Coniectanea neotestamentica or Coniectanea biblica: New Testament Series
ConBOT	Coniectanea biblica: Old Testament Series
CRINT	Compendia rerum iudaicarum ad Novum Testamentum
CSCO	Corpus scriptorum christianorum orientalium. Edited by I. B. Chabot et al. Paris, 1903–
CSEL	Corpus scriptorum ecclesiasticorum latinorum
CSHB	Corpus scriptorum historiae byzantinae
CSHR	Chicago Studies in the History of Religion
CTJ	*Calvin Theological Journal*
CTQ	*Concordia Theological Quarterly*
CV	*Communio viatorum*
DBM	*Deltion Biblikon Meleton*
DCLY	Deuterocanonical and Cognate Literature Yearbook
DHRP	Dissertationes ad historiam religionum pertinentes
DJD	Discoveries in the Judaean Desert
DJG	*Dictionary of Jesus and the Gospels*. Edited by J. B. Green and S. McKnight. Downers Grove, IL, 1992
DSD	*Dead Sea Discoveries*
EB	Echter Bibel
EBib	Etudes bibliques
EC	Epworth Commentaries
EDNT	*Exegetical Dictionary of the New Testament*. Edited by H. Balz and G. Schneider. 3 vols. Grand Rapids, 1990–93
EH	Europäische Hochschulschriften
EKKNT	Evangelisch-katholischer Kommentar zum Neuen Testament
EPRO	Etudes préliminaires aux religions orientales dans l'empire romain
ErIsr	*Eretz-Israel*
ETL	*Ephemerides theologicae lovanienses*
ETS	Erfurter theologische Studien
EvQ	*Evangelical Quarterly*
EvT	*Evangelische Theologie*
ExpTim	*Expository Times*
FAT	Forschungen zum Alten Testament
FB	Forschung zur Bibel
FRLANT	Forschungen zur Religion und Literatur des Alten und Neuen Testaments
FZPhTh	*Freiburger Zeitschrift für Philosophie und Theologie*
GCS	Die griechische christliche Schriftsteller der ersten [drei] Jahrhunderte
GNS	Good News Studies
GP	Gospel Perspectives
GTA	Göttinger theologischer Arbeiten

GTF	Greifswalder theologische Forschungen
HBS	Herders biblische Studien
HBT	*Horizons in Biblical Theology*
HCOT	Historical Commentary on the Old Testament
HDR	Harvard Dissertations in Religion
HNT	Handbuch zum Neuen Testament
HR	*History of Religions*
HSCP	*Harvard Studies in Classical Philology*
HSem	Horae semiticae. 9 vols. London, 1908–12
HSM	Harvard Semitic Monographs
HSS	Harvard Semitic Studies
HTKAT	Herders theologischer Kommentar zum Alten Testament
HTKNT	Herders theologischer Kommentar zum Neuen Testament
HTR	*Harvard Theological Review*
HTS	Harvard Theological Studies
HUCA	*Hebrew Union College Annual*
HUT	Hermeneutische Untersuchungen zur Theologie
HvTSt	*Hervormde teologiese studies*
ICC	International Critical Commentary
IDB	*The Interpreter's Dictionary of the Bible.* Edited by G. A. Buttrick. 4 vols. Nashville, 1962
IDBSup	*The Interpreter's Dictionary of the Bible: Supplementary Volume.* Edited by K. Crim. Nashville, 1976
IEJ	*Israel Exploration Journal*
IMJ	*Israel Museum Journal*
Int	*Interpretation*
ISFCJ	International Studies in Formative Christianity and Judaism (University of South Florida)
ITS	International Theological Studies
JAOS	*Journal of the American Oriental Society*
Jastrow	Jastrow, M. *A Dictionary of the Targumim, the Talmud Babli and Yerushalmi, and the Midrashic Literature.* 2nd ed. New York, 1903
JBL	*Journal of Biblical Literature*
JBT	Jahrbuch für biblische Theologie
JC	Judaica et Christiana
JCR	*Journal of Contemporary Religion*
JECS	*Journal of Early Christian Studies*
JEH	*Journal of Ecclesiastical History*
JIGRE	*Jewish Inscriptions of Graeco-Roman Egypt, with an Index of the Jewish Inscriptions of Egypt and Cyrenaica.* By William Horbury and David Noy. Cambridge, 1992
JIWE	*Jewish Inscriptions of Western Europe.* By David Noy. 2 vols. Cambridge, 1993–95
JJRS	*Japanese Journal of Religious Studies*
JJS	*Journal of Jewish Studies*
JJSoc	*Jewish Journal of Sociology*
JQR	*Jewish Quarterly Review*
JR	*Journal of Religion*
JRS	*Journal of Roman Studies*
JSHJ	*Journal for the Study of the Historical Jesus*
JSJ	*Journal for the Study of Judaism in the Persian, Hellenistic and Roman Period*
JSJSup	Journal for the Study of Judaism: Supplement Series
JSNT	*Journal for the Study of the New Testament*

JSNTSup	Journal for the Study of the New Testament: Supplement Series
JSOTSup	Journal for the Study of the Old Testament: Supplement Series
JSP	*Journal for the Study of the Pseudepigrapha*
JSPSup	Journal for the Study of the Pseudepigrapha: Supplement Series
JSQ	*Jewish Studies Quarterly*
JSSR	*Journal for the Scientific Study of Religion*
JTC	*Journal for Theology and the Church*
JTS	*Journal of Theological Studies*
KAV	Kommentar zu den Apostolischen Vätern
KBANT	Kommentare und Beiträge zum Alten und Neuen Testament
KD	*Kerygma und Dogma*
KEK	Kritisch-exegetischer Kommentar über das Neue Testament (Meyer-Kommentar)
LCL	Loeb Classical Library
LD	Lectio divina
LHB	Library of Hebrew Bible
LNTS	Library of New Testament Studies
LRC	Library of Religion and Culture
LS	*Louvain Studies*
LSAAR	Lund Studies in African and Asian Religions
LSJ	Liddell, H. G., R. Scott, and H. S. Jones. *A Greek-English Lexicon.* 9th ed. with revised supplement. Oxford, 1996
LTT	Library of Theological Translations
MBCBSup	Mnemosyne, bibliotheca classica Batava: Supplementum
MdB	Le Monde de la Bible
MTS	Marburger theologische Studien
Mus	*Muséon: Revue d'études orientales*
NCB	New Century Bible
Neot	*Neotestamentica*
NGS	New Gospel Studies
NHMS	Nag Hammadi and Manichaean Studies
NICNT	New International Commentary on the New Testament
NIGTC	New International Greek Testament Commentary
NJahrb	*Neue Jahrbücher für das klassische Altertum*
NovT	*Novum Testamentum*
NovTSup	Novum Testamentum Supplements
NTAbh	Neutestamentliche Abhandlungen
NTG	New Testament Guides
NTL	New Testament Library
NTOA	Novum Testamentum et Orbis Antiquus
NTS	*New Testament Studies*
NTTS	New Testament Tools and Studies
NV	*Nova et vetera*
OBO	Orbis biblicus et orientalis
OECT	Oxford Early Christian Texts
ÖTKNT	Ökumenischer Taschenbuch-Kommentar zum Neuen Testament
OTL	Old Testament Library
OTP	*The Old Testament Pseudepigrapha.* Edited by J. H. Charlesworth. 2 vols. Garden City, NY: Doubleday, 1983–85
OTS	Old Testament Studies
OtSt	Oudtestamentische Studiën
OtSt	*Oudtestamentische Studiën*
PAPS	*Proceedings of the American Philosophical Society*

PG	Patrologia graeca [= Patrologiae cursus completus: Series graeca]. Edited by J.-P. Migne. 166 vols. Paris, 1857–66
PGL	*Patristic Greek Lexicon.* Edited by G. W. H. Lampe. Oxford, 1968
PGM	*Papyri graecae magicae: Die griechischen Zauberpapyri.* Edited by K. Preisendanz. Berlin, 1928
PIBA	*Proceedings of the Irish Biblical Association*
PilNTC	Pillar New Testament Commentary
PL	Patrologia latina [= Patrologiae cursus completus: Series latina]. Edited by J.-P. Migne. 221 vols. Paris, 1844–65
PNMES	Publications in Near and Middle East Studies (Columbia University)
PNTC	Pelican New Testament Commentaries
PO	Patrologia orientalis
PRSt	*Perspectives in Religious Studies*
PS	Patrologia syriaca. Rev. ed. I. Ortiz de Urbina. Rome, 1965
PTMS	Princeton Theological Monograph Series
QD	Quaestiones disputatae
RBL	*Review of Biblical Literature*
RCatT	*Revista catalana de teología*
REJ	*Revue des études juives*
RestQ	*Restoration Quarterly*
RevB	*Revue biblique*
RevQ	*Revue de Qumran*
RHPR	*Revue d'histoire et de philosophie religieuses*
RHR	*Revue de l'histoire des religions*
RM	Die Religionen der Menschheit
RNT	Regensburger Neues Testament
RRelRes	*Review of Religious Research*
RRJ	*Review of Rabbinic Judaism*
RSO	Religion and the Social Order
RSR	*Recherches de science religieuse*
RTR	*Reformed Theological Review*
SBA	Stuttgarter biblische Aufsatzbände
SBEC	Studies in the Bible and Early Christianity
SBL	Studies in Biblical Literature
SBLDS	Society of Biblical Literature Dissertation Series
SBLEJL	Society of Biblical Literature Early Judaism and Its Literature
SBLMS	Society of Biblical Literature Monograph Series
SBLSCS	Society of Biblical Literature Septuagint and Cognate Series
SBLSS	Society of Biblical Literature Semeia Studies
SBLSymS	Society of Biblical Literature Symposium Series
SBS	Stuttgarter Bibelstudien
SBT	Studies in Biblical Theology
SC	Sources chrétiennes. Paris: Cerf, 1943–
SCI	*Scripta Classica Israelica*
SCJ	Studies in Christianity and Judaism
ScrHier	Scripta hierosolymitana
SemeiaSt	Semeia Studies
SESJ	Suomen eksegeettisen seuran julkaisuja
SHBC	Smyth & Helwys Bible Commentary
SHR	Studies in the History of Religions
SJ	Studia judaica
SJLA	Studies in Judaism in Late Antiquity
SJSHRZ	Studien zu den jüdischen Schriften aus hellenistisch-römischer Zeit
SJT	*Scottish Journal of Theology*

SKKNT	Stuttgarter kleiner Kommentar, Neues Testament
SNTSMS	Society for New Testament Studies Monograph Series
SNTSU	Studien zum Neuen Testament und seiner Umwelt
SNTW	Studies in the New Testament and Its World
SO	*Symbolae Osloenses*
SocRel	*Sociology of Religion*
SOTSMS	Society for Old Testament Studies Monograph Series
SSN	Studia semitica neerlandica
StA	Studienhefte zur Altertumswissenschaft
STDJ	Studies on the Texts of the Desert of Judah
StPB	Studia post-biblica
Str-B	Strack, H. L., and P. Billerbeck. *Kommentar zum Neuen Testament aus Talmud und Midrasch.* 6 vols. Munich: Beck, 1922–61
StSin	Studia Sinaitica
SUNT	Studien zur Umwelt des Neuen Testaments
SVTP	Studia in Veteris Testamenti pseudepigraphica
SWBA	Social World of Biblical Antiquity
TANZ	Texte und Arbeiten zum neutestamentlichen Zeitalter
TAPA	*Transactions of the American Philological Association*
TB	Theologische Bücherei: Neudrucke und Berichte aus dem 20. Jahrhundert
TBN	Themes in Biblical Narrative
TDNT	*Theological Dictionary of the New Testament.* Edited by G. Kittel and G. Friedrich. Translated by G. W. Bromiley. 10 vols. Grand Rapids, 1964–76
TDOT	*Theological Dictionary of the Old Testament.* Edited by G. J. Botter-weck and H. Ringgren. Translated by J. T. Willis, G. W. Bromiley, and D. E. Green. 14 vols. Grand Rapids, 1974–
TEH	Theologische Existenz heute
TF	Texte zur Forschung
ThBT	Theologische Bibliothek Töpelmann
ThG	*Theologie der Gegenwart*
ThGl	*Theologie und Glaube*
THKNT	Theologischer Handkommentar zum Neuen Testament
ThQ	*Theologische Quartalschrift*
ThTo	*Theology Today*
TJT	*Toronto Journal of Theology*
TLG	*Thesaurus linguae graecae: Canon of Greek Authors and Works.* Edited by L. Berkowitz and K. A. Squitier. 3rd ed. Oxford, 1990
TLZ	*Theologische Literaturzeitung*
TQ	*Theologische Quartalschrift*
TRSR	Testi e ricerche di scienze religiose
TRu	*Theologische Rundschau*
TS	Texts and Studies
TS	*Theological Studies*
TSAJ	Texte und Studien zum antiken Judentum
TSS	Theological Seminar Series
TU	Texte und Untersuchungen
TynBul	*Tyndale Bulletin*
TZ	*Theologische Zeitschrift*
UNT	Untersuchungen zum Neuen Testament
USQR	*Union Seminary Quarterly Review*
Vat. gr.	Vaticani greci
VC	*Vigiliae christianae*

VCSup	Vigiliae christianae Supplements
VD	*Verbum domini*
VT	*Vetus Testamentum*
VTSup	Vetus Testamentum Supplements
WBC	Word Biblical Commentary
WBS	Wiener byzantinistische Studien
WMANT	Wissenschaftliche Monographien zum Alten und Neuen Testament
WPC	Westminster Pelican Commentaries
WUNT	Wissenschaftliche Untersuchungen zum Neuen Testament
ZBK	Zürcher Bibelkommentare
ZDMG	*Zeitschrift der deutschen morgenländischen Gesellschaft*
ZNT	*Zeitschrift für Neues Testament*
ZNTh/JHMT	*Zeitschrift für neuere Theologiegeschichte / Journal for the History of Modern Theology*
ZNW	*Zeitschrift für die neutestamentliche Wissenschaft und die Kunde der älteren Kirche*
ZPE	*Zeitschrift für Papyrologie und Epigraphik*
ZTK	*Zeitschrift für Theologie und Kirche*

1

The General and the Particular

Memories of Jesus

I wept for memory.

—Christina Rossetti

The frailty of human memory should distress all who quest for the so-called historical Jesus. Even were one to hold, as I do not, that eyewitnesses or companions of eyewitnesses composed the canonical Gospels, our critical work would remain.[1] Personal reminiscence is neither innocent nor objective.[2] Observers habitually misperceive, and they unavoidably misremember. As Thucydides remarked long ago, "Different eyewitnesses give different accounts

---

1. A notable recent attempt to link the canonical Gospels closely to eyewitness testimony is Richard Bauckham, *Jesus and the Eyewitnesses: The Gospels as Eyewitness Testimony* (Grand Rapids: Eerdmans, 2006). Although he is, in my view, overly optimistic about the reliability of the tradition, and although I believe that the Gospels are further removed from eyewitness testimony than does he, Bauckham engages some of the modern scientific literature on memory. For discussions of his book, see the multiple review articles in *JSHJ* 6, no. 2 (2008); *NV* 6, no. 3 (2008).

2. According to C. D. Broad, although "George IV used to say that he remembered leading a charge at the Battle of Waterloo, . . . there is every reason to believe that he was never within a hundred miles of the battle" (*The Mind and Its Place in Nature* [London: Kegan Paul, Trench, Trübner, 1925], 231). For an entertaining collection of eyewitness fictions, see Malcolm Muggeridge, "The Eye-Witness Fallacy," *Encounter* (May 1961): 86–89. For an introduction to the topic of self-deception from a psychological point of view, see Roy F. Baumeister, "Lying to Oneself: The Enigma of Self-Deception," in *Lying and Deception in Everyday Life* (ed. Michael Lewis and Carolyn Saarni; New York: Guilford, 1993), 166–83.

of the same events, speaking out of partiality for one side or the other or else from imperfect memories" (*Hist.* 1.22).

Because human memory "leaks and dissociates,"[3] all of us are, to one degree or another, fabulists, even when we try not to be.[4] As modern research abundantly documents, memory often leads us astray.[5] Among its many sins are the following, all of which matter for sober, honest study of Jesus:

1. To recollect is not to play back a tape. Memory, at least long-term memory, is reconstructive as well as reproductive[6] and so involves imagination.[7] This is how it can come to be that, with the passage of time, memories often move from a participant's viewpoint to an outsider's viewpoint; that is, we often recall events as though we had been a spectator off to the side.[8]

Remembering is not like reading a book but rather like writing a book.[9] If there are blanks, we fill them in. If the plot is thin, we fill it out.[10] As we constantly revise our memoirs, we may well recollect what we assume was

3. Sue Halpern, *Can't Remember What I Forgot: The Good News from the Front Lines of Memory Research* (New York: Harmony Books, 2008), 4.

4. On the phenomenon of confabulation, which all of us engage in routinely, see William Hirstein, *Brain Fiction: Self-Deception and the Riddle of Confabulation* (Cambridge, MA: MIT Press, 2005). For a convenient, brief overview of the subject, see Helen Phillips, "Mind Fiction: Why Your Brain Tells Tall Tales," *New Scientist* 2572 (October 7, 2008): 32–36.

5. For general introductions to the fallibility of human memory, see Alan Baddeley, Michael W. Eysenck, and Michael C. Anderson, *Memory* (New York: Psychology Press, 2009), 317–42; Daniel L. Schacter, "Memory Distortion: History and Current Status," in *Memory Distortion: How Minds, Brains, and Societies Reconstruct the Past* (ed. Daniel L. Schacter; Cambridge, MA: Harvard University Press, 1995), 1–43; idem, *The Seven Sins of Memory: How the Mind Forgets and Remembers* (Boston: Houghton Mifflin, 2001); John Henderson, *Memory and Forgetting* (London: Routledge, 1999).

6. "Reproductive memory refers to accurate, rote production of material from memory, whereas reconstructive memory emphasizes the active process of filling in missing elements while remembering, with errors frequently occurring" (Henry L. Roediger III and Kathleen B. McDermott, "Creating False Memories: Remembering Words Not Presented in Lists," *Journal of Experimental Psychology: Learning, Memory, and Cognition* 21 [1995]: 804).

7. The classic work is F. C. Bartlett, *Remembering: A Study in Experiment and Social Psychology* (Cambridge: Cambridge University Press, 1932).

8. See William F. Brewer, "What Is Recollective Memory?" in *Remembering Our Past: Studies in Autobiographical Memory* (ed. David C. Rubin; Cambridge: Cambridge University Press, 1996), 27–28, 37.

9. I borrow this analogy from John F. Kihlstrom, "Memory, Autobiography, History" (online: http://socrates.berkeley.edu/~kihlstrm/rmpa00.htm [cited 18 November 2009]). Gayle Greene observes, "Memory is a creative writer, Mother of the Muses . . . maker of stories—the stories by which we construct meaning through temporality and assure ourselves that time past is not time lost" ("Feminist Fiction and the Uses of Memory," *Signs: Journal of Women in Culture and Society* 16 [1991]: 294).

10. See Halpern, *Can't Remember*, 66. Ulric Neisser offers this analogy: we work with memories in the way that paleontologists work with bones: from a few pieces of bone, we reconstruct the original animal (*Cognitive Psychology* [New York: Appleton-Century-Crofts, 1967], 285).

the case rather than what was in fact the case;[11] and as we confuse thought with deed, we may suppose we did something that we only entertained doing. In addition, we regularly mingle related or repeated events,[12] so the memory of a single occurrence is often composite, "a synthesis of experiences,"[13] the upshot of "an abstractive process based on selective attention"[14] or "schematic processing."[15] When asked, for instance, to recall last year's Thanksgiving, people typically borrow details from what they otherwise know about the holiday in general. In this way, one event blends in with other events.[16]

2. "Postevent information often becomes incorporated into memory, supplementing and altering a person's recollection,"[17] so much so that people can "remember" events that they never experienced.[18] Just hearing about a purported incident can lead us to believe that we actually saw it, a phenomenon sometimes dubbed "retroactive interference."[19] In like manner, even when we have beheld

11. See Roediger and McDermott, "Creating False Memories," 803–14; Michael Ross, "Relation of Implicit Theories to the Construction of Personal Histories," *Psychological Review* 96, no. 2 (1989): 341–57.

12. Craig R. Barclay, "Schematization of Autobiographical Memory," in *Autobiographical Memory* (ed. David C. Rubin; Cambridge: Cambridge University Press, 1986), 82–99; Marigold Linton, "Transformations of Memory in Everyday Life," in *Memory Observed: Remembering in Natural Contexts* (ed. Ulric Neisser; New York: W. H. Freeman, 1982), 77–91; Ulric Neisser, "John Dean's Memory: A Case Study," *Cognition* 9 (1981): 1–22.

13. Elizabeth Loftus, "Our Changeable Memories: Legal and Practical Implications," *Nature Reviews: Neuroscience* 4 (2003): 231.

14. Richard Luftig, "Abstractive Memory, the Central-Incidental Hypothesis, and the Use of Structure Importance in Text: Control Processes or Structural Features?" *Reading Research Quarterly* 19 (1983): 29. See further B. R. Gomulicki, "Recall as an Abstractive Process," *Acta Psychologica* 12 (1956): 77–94.

15. George A. Bonanno, "Remembering and Psychotherapy," *Psychotherapy* 27 (1990): 177. See further John D. Bransford and Jeffery J. Franks, "The Abstraction of Linguistic Ideas," *Cognitive Psychology* 2 (1971): 331–50.

16. Schacter, *Seven Sins*, 14–15. For a summary of the secondary literature on "relatedness effects" in memory, see Henry L. Roediger III and Kathleen B. McDermott, "Distortions of Memory," in *The Oxford Handbook of Memory* (ed. Endel Tulving and Fergus I. M. Craik; Oxford: Oxford University Press, 2000), 151–53.

17. Elizabeth F. Loftus, James A. Coan, and Jacqueline E. Pickrell, "Manufacturing False Memories Using Bits of Reality," in *Implicit Memory and Metacognition* (ed. Lynne M. Reder; Mahwah, NJ: Lawrence Erlbaum Associates, 1996), 197.

18. In addition to the classic treatise by Hugo Münsterberg, *On the Witness Stand: Essays on Psychology and Crime* (New York: Doubleday, Page, 1909; online: http://psychclassics.yorku.ca/Munster/Witness [cited 18 November 2009]), see the extensive review of the literature in C. J. Brainerd and V. F. Reyna, *The Science of False Memory* (Oxford: Oxford University Press, 2005). For briefer, helpful overviews, see Elizabeth F. Loftus, "Make-Believe Memories," *American Psychologist* 58 (2003): 867–73; Elizabeth F. Loftus and Daniel M. Bernstein, "Rich False Memories: The Royal Road to Success," in *Experimental Cognitive Psychology and Its Applications* (ed. Alice F. Healy; Washington, DC: American Psychological Association, 2005), 101–13.

19. Stephen J. Ceci et al., "Repeatedly Thinking about a Non-event: Source Misattributions among Preschoolers," *Consciousness and Cognition* 3 (1994): 388–407; Lynn M. Goff and Henry L. Roediger III, "Imagination Inflation for Action Events: Repeated Imaginings Lead to

something for ourselves, our own memory, under social pressure, may conform itself to the expectations of others or to their erroneous recall.[20]

3. We are apt to project present circumstances and biases onto our past experiences, assimilating our former selves to our present selves.[21] We may, for example, assume that we once believed what we have believed only of late and distort our recall accordingly.[22] "Surely it must have been like this" readily becomes "It was so."[23] Similarly, our moral judgments may amend our memories. We may confuse what we think ought to have occurred with what did occur.[24]

Illusory Recollections," *Memory and Cognition* 26 (1998): 20–33; Elizabeth Loftus, "Planting Misinformation in the Human Mind: A 30-Year Investigation of the Malleability of Memory," *Learning and Memory* 12 (2005): 361–66; Elizabeth Loftus and J. E. Pickrell, "The Formation of False Memories," *Psychiatric Annals* 25 (1995): 720–25; Stefanie J. Sharman, Maryanne Garry, and Carl J. Beuke, "Imagination or Exposure Causes Imagination Inflation," *American Journal of Psychology* 117 (2004): 157–68; Ayanna K. Thomas and Elizabeth Loftus, "Creating Bizarre False Memories through Imagination," *Memory and Cognition* 30 (2002): 423–31; Giuliana A. L. Mazzoni, Elizabeth F. Loftus, and Irving Kirsch, "Changing Beliefs about Implausible Autobiographical Events: A Little Plausibility Goes a Long Way," *Journal of Experimental Psychology: Applied* 7 (2001): 51–59.

20. Saul M. Kassin and Katherine L. Kiechel, "The Social Psychology of False Confessions: Compliance, Internalization, and Confabulation," *Psychological Science* 7 (1996): 125–28; Elizabeth F. Loftus, "Illusions of Memory," *PAPS* 142, no. 1 (1998): 60–73; Henry L. Roediger III, Michelle L. Meade, and Erik T. Bergman, "Social Contagion of Memory," *Psychonomic Bulletin and Review* 8, no. 2 (2001): 365–71; Roediger and McDermott, "Distortions of Memory," 157–58; Lawrence Wright, *Remembering Satan* (New York: Alfred A. Knopf, 1994). Bartlett already recognized that "social organization gives a persistent framework into which all detailed recall must fit, and it very powerfully influences both the manner and the matter of recall" (*Remembering*, 296).

21. This is known as "hindsight bias" or the "bias of retrospection." See Deborah Davis and Elizabeth F. Loftus, "Internal and External Sources of Misinformation in Adult Witness Memory," in *Memory for Events* (vol. 1 of *Handbook of Eyewitness Psychology*, ed. Michael P. Toglia et al.; Mahwah, NJ: Lawrence Erlbaum Associates, 2007), 206–7, 218; Scott A. Hawkins and Reid Hastie, "Hindsight: Biased Judgments of Past Events after the Outcomes Are Known," *Psychological Bulletin* 107 (1990): 311–27; Linda J. Levine, "Reconstructing Memory for Emotions," *Journal of Experimental Psychology: General* 126 (1997): 165–77; Barrett J. Mandel, "Full of Life Now," in *Autobiography: Essays Theoretical and Critical* (ed. James Olney; Princeton, NJ: Princeton University Press, 1980), 49–72; G. B. Markus, "Stability and Change in Political Attitudes: Observed, Recalled, and 'Explained,'" *Political Behavior* 8 (1986): 21–44; A. E. Wilson and M. Ross, "The Identity Function of Autobiographical Memory: Time Is on Our Side," *Memory* 11 (2003): 137–49.

22. Markus, "Stability and Change"; C. R. Brewin, B. Andrews, and I. H. Gotlib, "Psychopathology and Early Experience: A Reappraisal of Retrospective Reports," *Psychological Bulletin* 113 (1993): 82–98; R. M. Dawes, "Biases of Retrospection," *Issues in Child Abuse Accusations* 1 (1991): 25–28; George R. Goethals and Richard F. Reckman, "Recalling Previously Held Attitudes," *Journal of Experimental Social Psychology* 9 (1973): 491–501.

23. John Robinson comments, "Anything that alters the way a past experience is interpreted would alter what a person remembers from that experience" ("Perspective, Meaning, and Remembering," in *Remembering Our Past* [ed. Rubin], 209).

24. David A. Pazarro et al., "Ripple Effects in Memory: Judgments of Moral Blame Can Distort Memory for Events," *Memory and Cognition* 34 (2006): 550–55.

4. Although time's passage may add perspective, memories are not evergreen; they become less and less distinct as the past recedes. Weeks, months, and years dim lucidity, reduce detail, and diminish emotional intensity.[25] Output does not match input.[26]

5. Memories are subject to sequential displacement. We often move remembered events forward and backward in time.[27] "Temporal judgments . . . appear to be highly reconstructive."[28]

6. Individuals transmute memories into meaningful patterns that advance their agendas.[29] Collectives do likewise.[30] We remember publicly in order to

25. Introspection alone reveals that memories become "dim," "unclear," "simplified." See Brewer, "What Is Recollective Memory?" 23–24. Note also this remark by Bertrand Russell: "Memory is trustworthy in proportion to the vividness of the experience and its nearness in time. . . . Thus there is a continual gradation in the degree of self-evidence of what I remember, and a corresponding gradation in the trustworthiness of my memory" (The Problems of Philosophy [New York: Oxford University Press, 1959], 115–16). Emotion matters because memory of a particular event can improve when one's emotional state during recall is congruent with what it was when the event transpired (see Alan Baddeley, Human Memory: Theory and Practice [Boston: Allyn & Bacon, 1990], 390–97). But note this generalization by Daniel Reisberg and Friderike Heuer: "Emotion improves memory for some sorts of material and undermines memory for other material. Emotion seems to slow forgetting. Emotion creates an interesting species of intrusion errors in recall testing" ("Remembering the Details of Emotional Events," in Affect and Accuracy in Recall: Studies of "Flashbulb" Memories [ed. Eugene Winograd and Ulric Neisser; Cambridge: Cambridge University Press, 1992], 185). For a survey of the issues, see Daniel L. Schacter, David A. Gallo, and Elizabeth A. Kensinger, "The Cognitive Neuroscience of Implicit and False Memories: Perspectives on Processing Specificity," in The Foundations of Remembering: Essays in Honor of Henry L. Roediger III (ed. James S. Nairne; New York: Psychology Press, 2007), 353–77.

26. See H. Schmolck, E. A. Buffalo, and L. R. Squire, "Memory Distortions Develop over Time: Recollections of the O. J. Simpson Trial Verdict after 15 and 32 Months," Psychological Science 11 (2000): 39–45; Michael Schudson, "Dynamics of Distortion in Collective Memory," in Memory Distortion (ed. Schacter), 346–64. Charles P. Thompson et al. observe, "Event memory is initially highly reproductive but becomes increasingly reconstructive with lengthening retention interval" (Autobiographical Memory: Remembering What and Remembering When [Mahwah, NJ: Lawrence Erlbaum Associates, 1996], 204).

27. Norman R. Brown, Lance J. Rips, and Steven K. Shevell, "Subjective Dates of Natural Events in Very Long-Term Memory," Cognitive Psychology 17 (1985): 139–77; George D. Gaskell, Daniel B. Wright, and Colm A. O'Muircheartaigh, "Telescoping of Landmark Events: Implications for Survey Research," Public Opinion Quarterly Review 64 (2000): 77–89.

28. So Thompson et al., Autobiographical Memory, 204. Morris Moscovitch remarks, "Temporal order . . . is conferred on recovered traces only on retrieval" ("Confabulation," in Memory Distortion [ed. Schacter], 246).

29. Memories are "transmuted re-creations," part of "our continued efforts to make coherence of our own lives, to synthesize past and present so as to face the future" (Steven Rose, The Making of Memory: From Molecules to Mind [New York: Doubleday, 1992], 307). For a valuable illustration, see Laura A. Smoller, "Miracle, Memory, and Meaning in the Canonization of Vincent Ferrer, 1453–1454," Speculum 73 (1998): 429–54.

30. Ever since the work of the French sociologist Maurice Halbwachs in the 1920s, there has been a large literature on social or collective memory, most of which emphasizes the social frameworks and social interests of memory. For a convenient introduction to Halbwachs, see

persuade, to justify ourselves, and to explain current circumstances.[31] In other words, memories are a function of self-interest, and we instinctively revise them in order to help maintain "a meaningful sense of self-identity."[32]

Alfred Adler wrote, "There are no 'chance memories': out of the incalculable number of impressions which meet an individual, he chooses to remember only those which he feels, however darkly, to have a bearing on his situation."[33] Utilizing the past to promote current interests—the classical form critics saw this on every page of the canonical Gospels—leads to alteration, because those interests, a component of which is often entertainment, cannot help affecting both the content and interpretation of what one retrieves from memory.[34] Susan Engel offers an effective example:

his book *The Collective Memory* (trans. Francis J. Ditter Jr. and Vida Yazdi Ditter; 1950; repr., New York: Harper & Row, 1980). For a helpful bibliography, see online: www.phil .mq.edu.au/staff/jsutton/Socialmemory.htm (cited 18 November 2009); and for overviews of the discussion, see Jeffrey K. Olick and Joyce Robbins, "Social Memory Studies: From 'Collective Memory' to the Historical Sociology of Mnemonic Practices," *Annual Review of Sociology* 24 (1998): 105–40; Schudson, "Dynamics of Distortion." Particularly important works include Eric Hobsbawm and Terence Ranger, *The Invention of Tradition* (Cambridge: Cambridge University Press, 1983); Michael Kammen, *Mystic Chords of Memory: The Transformation of Tradition in American Culture* (New York: Alfred A. Knopf, 1991); Jacques Le Goff, *History and Memory* (New York: Columbia University Press, 1992); Edward Shils, *Tradition* (London: Faber, 1981). For some necessary corrections, see Noa Gedi and Yigal Elam, "Collective Memory—What Is It?" *History and Memory* 8 (1996): 30–50; Wulf Kansteiner, "Finding Meaning in Memory: A Methodological Critique of Collective Memory Studies," *History and Theory* 41 (2002): 179–97; for the larger cultural currents that have led to the boon of studies on social memory, see Kerwin Lee Klein, "On the Emergence of Memory in Historical Discourse," *Representations* 69 (2000): 127–50. Recent attempts to apply theory of social memory to religious history and/or early Christianity include Jan Assmann, *Religion and Cultural Memory: Ten Studies* (trans. Rodney Livingstone; Stanford, CA: Stanford University Press, 2006); Markus Bockmuehl, *Seeing the Word: Refocusing New Testament Study* (Grand Rapids: Baker Academic, 2006), 161–88; Alan Kirk and Tom Thatcher, eds., *Memory, Tradition, and Text: Uses of the Past in Early Christianity* (SBLSymS 52; Boston: Brill, 2005); Anthony Le Donne, *The Historiographical Jesus: Memory, Typology, and the Son of David* (Waco, TX: Baylor University Press, 2009); idem, "Theological Memory Distortion in the Jesus Tradition: A Study in Social Memory Theory," in *Memory in the Bible and Antiquity: The Fifth Durham-Tübingen Research Symposium* (ed. Stephen C. Barton, Loren T. Stuckenbruck, and Benjamin G. Wold; WUNT 212; Tübingen: Mohr Siebeck, 2007), 163–78; Rafael Rodríguez, "Structuring Early Christian Memory: Jesus in Tradition, Performance, and Text" (PhD diss., University of Sheffield, 2007).

31. Ross, "Implicit Theories."

32. Greg J. Neimeyer and April E. Metzler, "Personal Identity and Autobiographical Recall," in *The Remembering Self: Construction and Accuracy in the Self-Narrative* (ed. Ulric Neisser and Robyn Fivush; Cambridge: Cambridge University Press, 1994), 129.

33. Alfred Adler, "Early Recollections and Dreams," in *The Individual Psychology of Alfred Adler* (ed. Heinz L. Ansbacher and Rowena R. Ansbacher; New York: Harper & Row, 1956), 351. All therapists know that what one recalls of the past says much about one's present state.

34. See Levine, "Reconstructing Memory"; Wilson and Ross, "Identity Function." One of the results of recent work is that we tend to report our past selves as inferior to our present

Think back to some charged event in your own life. Perhaps the first fight you had with your spouse. Now imagine telling that story to your mate, many years later at the celebration of your twenty-fifth wedding anniversary, telling it to the divorce lawyer, telling it to your children now that they are grown up, writing it in a humorous memoir of your now famous life, or telling it to your therapist. In each case the person you are telling it to, and the reasons you are telling it, will have a formative effect on the memory itself.[35]

Just as we take on different roles for different occasions,[36] so too do we shape our memories according to the varied settings in which we find ourselves.

7. Groups do not rehearse competing memories that fail to shore up what they hold dear. Approved remembrance lives on; unapproved remembrance expires.[37] Communities, like individuals, systematically forget.

8. When, as in the canonical Gospels, memory becomes story, narrative conventions inescapably sculpt the result.[38] Storytellers, needing to bring order out of life's chaos, are wont to impose upon their materials a neat beginning, a coherent middle, and a resolution that satisfies. They also tend to stereotype and to cast characters as protagonists and antagonists, heroes and villains.[39]

9. Although we are inclined to trust vivid, subjectively compelling memories more than others, such memories can be decidedly inaccurate.[40] No

selves: "As . . . time increases, people become more critical of their earlier selves" (Wilson and Ross, "Identity Function," 140).

35. Susan Engel, *Context Is Everything: The Nature of Memory* (New York: W. H. Freeman, 1999), 12. This brings to mind *Rashomon*, the 1950 Japanese film directed by Akira Kurosawa, in which one event is seen through four pairs of eyes, each with a very different recollection of what really happened.

36. The classic work here is Erving Goffman, *The Presentation of the Self in Everyday Life* (New York: Doubleday, 1959). For Goffman, the self changes as it plays varying roles.

37. See James Fentress and Chris Wickham, *Social Memory* (Oxford: Blackwell, 1992); also an illuminating article by Jan Assmann, "Ancient Egyptian Antijudaism: A Case of Distorted Memory," in *Memory Distortion* (ed. Schacter), 365–76.

38. "The structure of discourse affects the structure of recall, which in turn affects the structure of later recall" (David C. Rubin, introduction to *Remembering Our Past* [ed. Rubin], 2). See further Jean M. Mandler and Nancy S. Johnson, "Remembrance of Things Parsed: Story Structure and Recall," *Cognitive Psychology* 9 (1977): 111–51.

39. For a recent attempt to relate this fact to the canonical Gospels, see Le Donne, "Theological Memory Distortion."

40. On the topic of "flashbulb memories"—vividly detailed, personally significant memories that are supposedly like a photograph and resist deterioration—see, in addition to Winograd and Neisser, eds., *Affect and Accuracy in Recall*, the recent collection of essays *Flashbulb Memories: New Issues and New Perspectives* (ed. Olivier Luminet and Antonietta Curci; New York: Psychology Press, 2009); and for a more popular presentation, Helen L. Williams, Martin A. Conway, and Gillian Cohen, "Autobiographical Memory," in *Memory in the Real World* (ed. Gillian Cohen and Martin Conway; 3rd ed.; New York: Psychology Press, 2008), 63–70. Despite the famous and influential paper by R. Brown and J. Kulik, "Flashbulb Memories" (*Cognition* 5 [1977]: 73–99), it has turned out that "flashbulb memories" show as many reconstructive errors as more ordinary personal memories; they are distinguished not by their accuracy but by their

infallible inner voice or sense can consistently adjudicate the accuracy of our recall.[41]

Given what we now know about human recollection, given that "the past is produced in the present and is thus malleable,"[42] one researcher, Elizabeth Loftus, has opined, half seriously, that our lawcourts should administer this oath to witnesses on the stand: "Do you swear to tell the truth, the whole truth, or whatever it is you think you remember?"[43]

The fallibility of memory should profoundly unsettle us would-be historians of Jesus. We have no cause to imagine that those who remembered him were at any moment immune to the usual deficiencies of recall. When we additionally reflect on the common errors of human perception[44] and the human proclivity for tall tales,[45] and then take full cognizance of the strong ideological biases of the partisan sources that we have for Jesus as well as their frequent differences from each other, doubts are bound to implant themselves in our souls, send out roots, and blossom. Even where the Gospels preserve memories,[46] those

---

perceived accuracy (so Jennifer M. Talarico and David C. Rubin, "Confidence, Not Consistency, Characterizes Flashbulb Memories," *Psychological Science* 14 [2003]: 455–61). Compare these remarks by Antonietta Curci: "Reconstructive factors determine the intrinsic nature of the phenomenon" ("Measurement Issues in the Study of Flashbulb Memory," in *Flashbulb Memories* [ed. Luminet and Curci], 27); and Jennifer M. Talarico and David C. Rubin: "FBMs are distinguished from ordinary memories by their vividness and the confidence with which they are held. There is little evidence that they are reliable different from ordinary autobiographical memories in accuracy, consistency, or longevity" ("Flashbulb Memories Result from Ordinary Memory Processes and Extraordinary Event Characteristics," in *Flashbulb Memories* [ed. Luminet and Curci], 92).

41. See Moscovitch, "Confabulation"; Matthew G. Rhodes and Larry L. Jacoby, "Toward Analyzing Cognitive Illusions: Past, Present, and Future," in *Foundations of Remembering* (ed. Nairne), 379–93.

42. So Olick and Robbins, "Social Memory Studies," 128.

43. Elizabeth F. Loftus, "Memory Faults and Fixes," in *The Best American Science and Nature Writing 2003* (ed. Richard Dawkins and Tim Folger; New York: Houghton Mifflin, 2003), 127.

44. See Daniel J. Simons and Christopher F. Chabris, "Gorillas in Our Midst: Sustained In-attentional Blindness for Dynamic Events," *Perception* 28 (1999): 1059–74, and their subjoined bibliography.

45. Those of us who remember our dreams know that human beings are well practiced at creating fictions. Dreams are not historical narratives. They tend instead to be unreal, a strange mixture of remembered people, half-known places, and exotic events. We seem to be wired to compose, at least when asleep, unhistorical tales. One cannot but wonder whether all that incessant practice at creating fictions might not spill over into real life.

46. Which, I will argue, they do; note Schacter's comment: "It is unlikely that a memory system that consistently produced seriously distorted outputs would possess the adaptive characteristics necessary to be preserved by natural selection" ("Memory Distortion," 25). Compare these remarks by Gillian Cohen: "In daily life, memory successes are the norm and memory failures are the exception" ("Overview: Conclusions and Speculations," in *Memory in the Real World* [ed. Cohen and Conway], 389); and Patricia J. Bauer: "Although memory is at times fraught with error, at other times it is amazingly accurate" (*Remembering the Times of Our*

memories cannot be miraculously pristine; rather, they must often be dim or muddled or just plain wrong.[47]

This is, of course, common opinion, even when uninformed by modern studies of memory.[48] Recognition that the Gospels, just like the writings of Josephus,[49] are not storehouses of auditory and photographic reproductions, and that their

---

Lives: Memory in Infancy and Beyond [Mahwah, NJ: Lawrence Erlbaum Associates, 2007], 44). Mnemonists and those with eidetic memory are the proof of Bauer's remark; see Earl Hunt and Tom Love, "How Good Can Memory Be?" in *Coding Processes in Human Memory* (ed. Arthur W. Melton and Edwin Martin; Washington, DC: V. H. Winston, 1972), 237–60. Even for those not thus gifted, memory can be especially reliable when handling atypical events that one personally participated in, found mentally engaging, experienced as emotionally intense, and then later rehearsed. See Bauckham, *Jesus and the Eyewitnesses*, 319–57 (although my conclusions regarding the canonical Gospels often differ from his).

47. Paul Rhodes Eddy and Gregory A. Boyd come to a different conclusion via a number of observations: postmodern skepticism about the possibility of human knowledge has fueled doubts about the reliability of memory; ideologically driven theory has welcomed the recognition of how malleable and unreliable human recall can be; excessive cynicism about memory negates the very possibility of human knowledge, including knowledge derived from scientific experiments; oral history can be quite reliable; many experiments on human memory have had a built-in bias that skews the results toward inaccurate recall; extrapolation from experiments on modern individuals to traditional oral communities is hazardous; the pre-Gutenberg world much valued memorization; when memories are shared, they can be all the more reliable (*The Jesus Legend: A Case for the Historical Reliability of the Synoptic Jesus Tradition* [Grand Rapids: Baker Academic, 2007], 275–86). Despite the apologetical agenda, there is justice in some of these observations. Yet they are aimed at what Eddy and Boyd label "hyperskepticism," which is not my position (see the preceding note). I do not contend that the evangelists were, in effect, amnesiacs. On the contrary, throughout this book I urge that their traditions often remember Jesus. I nonetheless remain persuaded of the sound empirical basis for the unsettling generalizations that I have made about memory and of their direct relevance for studying the Gospels. One can be suitably cautious without adopting "hyperskepticism." There is a middle way.

48. See the still useful remarks and cautions by Ferdinand Hahn, "Methodological Reflections on the Historical Investigation of Jesus," in *Historical Investigation and New Testament Faith: Two Essays* (Philadelphia: Fortress, 1983), 36–50. In addition to Bauckham (see n. 1), a few New Testament scholars have begun to pay attention to modern studies of memory; see, for example, the interesting work by April D. DeConick, "Human Memory and the Sayings of Jesus: Contemporary Experimental Exercises in the Transmission of Jesus Traditions," in *Jesus, the Voice, and the Text: Beyond the Oral and the Written Gospel* (ed. Tom Thatcher; Waco, TX: Baylor University Press, 2008), 135–79; also Armin Daniel Baum, "Experimentalpsychologische Erwägungen zur synoptische Frage," *BZ* 44 (2000): 37–55; Bockmuehl, *Seeing the Word*, 161–88; John Dominic Crossan, *The Birth of Christianity: Discovering What Happened in the Years Immediately after the Execution of Jesus* (San Francisco: HarperSanFrancisco, 1998), 59–89; Robert K. McIver and Marie Carroll, "Experiments to Develop Criteria for Determining the Existence of Written Sources, and Their Potential Implications for the Synoptic Problem," *JBL* 121 (2002): 667–87; Michael Winger, "Word and Deed," *CBQ* 62 (2000): 679–92. The older and still useful article by W. S. Taylor, "Memory and the Gospel Tradition" (*ThTo* 15 [1959]: 470–79), which takes up the work of Bartlett (see n. 7), seems to have had little or no impact upon the field.

49. On the problem of Josephus as a historical source, see Steve Mason, "Contradiction or Counterpoint? Josephus and Historical Method," *RRJ* 6 (2003): 145–88. Josephus is notorious for contradicting his own autobiographical statements.

recollections must be mixed with much else, explains why scholars have long employed and sought to refine criteria of authenticity, their winnowing forks for separating the ecclesiastical chaff from the pre-Easter wheat. These criteria have, for decades, been much discussed and much deployed.[50] Regrettably, we have good reason to be cynical about them all and about all their refinements, which sometimes presume a crude distinction between Jesus and the churches.[51] This is not the place, however, to rehearse yet again my criticism of how others have proceeded.[52] My present contribution lies elsewhere. I wish, throughout this book, to explicate my conviction that we can learn some important things about the historical Jesus without resorting to the standard criteria and without, for the most part, trying to decide whether he authored this or that saying or whether this or that particular event actually happened as narrated.

The Big Picture

We all know from introspection that our long-term memories, which are "constantly evolving generalizations,"[53] tend to retain "whole events, whole faces,

50. For a helpful review of some of the issues, see Gerd Theissen and Dagmar Winter, *The Quest for the Plausible Jesus: The Question of Criteria* (Louisville: Westminster John Knox, 2002). John P. Meier's multivolume work, *A Marginal Jew: Rethinking the Historical Jesus* (4 vols.; New York: Doubleday, 1991–2009), relies heavily on these criteria. In my view, this hampers the project's utility, which otherwise is considerable.

51. On the challenge of distinguishing Jesus from the church, see Dale C. Allison Jr., *The Historical Christ and the Theological Jesus* (Grand Rapids: Eerdmans, 2009), 22–30.

52. I first expressed serious reservations about the standard criteria in my book *Jesus of Nazareth: Millenarian Prophet* (Philadelphia: Fortress, 1998), although there I tried to redeem them. I have now abandoned that ambition. For my reasons, see my essay "How to Marginalize the Traditional Criteria of Authenticity," in *The Handbook for the Study of the Historical Jesus* (ed. Tom Holmén and Stanley E. Porter; 4 vols.; Leiden: Brill, 2009), 1:3–30. Among them are the following: (1) That Jesus said X or did Y is of itself no reason to believe that we can show that he said X or did Y; conversely, that he did not say X or do Y is of itself no reason to believe that we can show such to be the case. The criteria, moreover, do not contain within themselves any promise of what percentage of the tradition can be traced to its source. In practice that percentage turns out to be small. (2) Our criteria have not led us anywhere near a consensus on anything of importance. "Although there is widespread agreement that Jesus was a Jew, no agreement exists as to what kind of Jew he was" (so, rightly, George Aichele, Peter Miscall, and Richard Walsh, "An Elephant in the Room: Historical-Critical and Postmodern Interpretation of the Bible," *JBL* 128 [2009]: 396). (3) Some criteria can favor the authenticity of a unit while other criteria favor the inauthenticity of the very same unit. (4) The criteria are not strong enough to resist the wills of their users, who tend to make them do what they want them to do; subjectivity still reigns. See also the skepticism of Klaus Berger, "Kriterien für echte Jesusworte?" *ZNT* 1 (1998): 52–58. For an alternative and more traditional view, see Gerd Häfner, "Das Ende der Kriterien? Jesusforschung angesichts der geschichtstheoretischen Diskussion," in Knut Backhaus and Gerd Häfner, *Historiographie und fiktionales Erzählen: Zur Konstruktivität in Geschichtstheorie und Exegese* (Neukirchen-Vluyn: Neukirchener Verlag, 2007), 97–130.

53. Israel Rosenfield, *The Invention of Memory* (New York: Basic Books, 1988), 76.

whole conversations, not the sub-plots, the features, the words that make them up."[54] As our recollections become increasingly tattered and faded, they are disposed to retain, if anything, only the substance or "gist" of an event.[55] We may forget the words and syntax of a sentence yet still remember its general substance or meaning.[56] We construct memories of people and events in the same way we reproduce maps from our heads: we omit most of the details, straighten the lines, and round off the angles, thereby creating a sort of minimalist cartoon.

Who has not more than once thought, "I can't recall the exact words, but they were something like this"? As one researcher has put it, "Verbatim/perceptual traces fade more quickly than 'gistified' traces."[57] It is the same with the images in our heads. We may recollect visiting the Parthenon, but unless we are that rare, one-in-a-billion individual with a photographic memory, we will not be able to close our eyes and count the number of its columns.[58] Similarly, those who have been robbed will not forget being robbed; yet, as the critical study of criminal lineups has demonstrated, this circumstance does not ensure that witnesses will correctly remember what the robber looked like.[59] This is because, in the words of one authority,

54. Henderson, *Memory and Forgetting*, 28–29.

55. John Bradshaw states that long-term memory "is normally semantic, whereas memory for syntax is attained only if there is a societal expectancy for total accuracy in a given context, or a request is made by the speaker, or the hearer concludes that total recall for a small part of a discourse is vital to his own purpose in listening" ("Oral Transmission and Human Memory," *ExpTim* 92 [1981]: 304). There is a parallel here with social memory. Although "not stable as information," it can be fairly stable "at the level of shared meanings and remembered images" (Fentress and Wickham, *Social Memory*, 59). We should not forget, however, that human beings exhibit a tendency to retain not only patterns of meaning but also, when this is possible, patterns of sound, especially rhyming schemes (see David C. Rubin, *Memory in Oral Traditions: The Cognitive Psychology of Epic, Ballads, and Counting-Out Rhymes* [New York: Oxford University Press, 1995]).

56. See J. D. S. Sachs, "Recognition Memory for Syntactic and Semantic Aspects of Connected Discourse," *Perception and Psychophysics* 2 (1967): 437–42. On the synthesizing of ideas from multiple sentences, see Bransford and Franks, "Abstraction of Linguistic Ideas." Even when we memorize texts and repeat them through the years, we introduce changes. I have recited Keats's "On First Looking Into Chapman's Homer" throughout my life. Recently I checked my current memorized version against the original (very short) poem with this result: Keats's "realms of gold" had become "lands of gold"; "Yet did I never" had become "Yet never did I"; "Till" had become "Until"; "into his ken" had become "within his ken"; "eagle eyes" had become "eagle eye"; and "star'd at the Pacific" had become "gazed at the Pacific." In each case my memory had retained the meaning but not the precise wording.

57. Stephen J. Ceci, "False Beliefs: Some Developmental and Clinical Considerations," in *Memory Distortion* (ed. Schacter), 96.

58. At present only three living individuals are known to have hyperthymestic syndrome, which means that they have near perfect autobiographical memory going back to childhood.

59. Patricia A. Tollestrup, John W. Turtle, and John C. Yuille, "Actual Victims and Witnesses to Robbery and Fraud: An Archival Analysis," in *Adult Eyewitness Testimony: Current Trends and Developments* (ed. David Frank Ross, J. Don Read, and Michael P. Toglia; Cambridge: Cambridge University Press, 1994), 144–59.

With passing of time, the particulars fade and opportunities multiply for interference—generated by later, similar experiences—to blur our recollections. We thus rely ever more on our memories for the gist of what happened, or what usually happens, and attempt to reconstruct the details by inference and even sheer guesswork. Transience involves a gradual switch from reproductive and specific recollections to reconstructive and more general descriptions.[60]

Maybe it is a bit like Plutarch's description of the oracle at Delphi (*Mor.* 397C). The voice, Plutarch tells us, is not that of the god; neither is the diction nor the meter. The deity gives only the inspired vision, which the oracle then translates into her own ideas and speech. Perhaps, in like fashion, memories are our visions, more or less vivid, which we interpret and elaborate.

Scientists, incidentally, now have some credible explanations as to why evolution has sculpted our mnemonic capacities so that they do better with the general than the particular. One proposal, in the words of Daniel Schacter and Donna Addis, is that "remembering the gist of what happened is an economical way of storing the most important aspects of our experiences without cluttering memory with trivial details."[61] Another plausible suggestion, which could coexist with the first, is that we look to the past in order to navigate the future. Again in the words of Schacter and Addis,

> Future events are not exact replicas of past events, and a memory system that simply stored rote records would not be well-suited to simulating future events. A system built according to constructive principles may be a better tool for the job: it can draw on the elements and gist of the past, and extract, recombine and reassemble them into imaginary events that never occurred in that exact form. Such a system will occasionally produce memory errors, but it also provides considerable flexibility.[62]

Whatever the explanation as to why memory fares better with generalizations than specifics, everyone knows that when two cars run into each other, witnesses may well differ on the details. And yet, observers of such an accident will remember that cars collided. They can recall the central fact, upon which

60. Schacter, *Seven Sins*, 15–16. Baddeley observes that our memories are "reasonably free of error, provided we stick to remembering the broad outline of events. Errors begin to occur once we try to force ourselves to come up with detailed information from an inadequate base" (*Human Memory*, 310).

61. Daniel L. Schacter and Donna Rose Addis, "Constructive Memory: The Ghosts of Past and Future," *Nature* 445 (2007): 27.

62. Ibid. This scientific hypothesis was anticipated by Jorge Luis Borges, "Funes, the Memorious," in *Ficciones* (trans. and ed. Anthony Kerrigan; New York: Grove, 1962), 107–15. Borges's piece is about a man with a perfect memory who "is not very capable of thought," for "to think is to forget a difference, to generalize, to abstract. In the overly replete world of Funes there were nothing but details" (p. 115).

they will accordingly agree, even though they may be mistaken about any number of particulars, which is why their stories will contradict each other.

Matthew 10, Mark 6, and Luke 9–10 come to mind. The tradition purports that Jesus, when he instructed apostles for mission, prohibited some things and allowed others. The texts, however, diverge on the specifics. Mark 6:8–9, for instance, has Jesus permitting a staff and sandals. Matthew 10:10, to the contrary, has him forbidding those. Likewise, the accounts of the Last Supper concur to an extent: Jesus, at a meal shortly before his death, broke some bread and said, "This is my body"; he further took a cup and said something about "blood" and "covenant." Beyond that, however, the discrepancies are notorious. The textual disparity, no matter what the historical facts, should not surprise.

Given that memory is "fuzzy,"[63] that we remember the outlines of an event or the general import of a conversation better than the details, that we extract patterns and meaning from informational input,[64] it would be peculiar to imagine that, although their general impressions of Jesus were hopelessly skewed, Christian tradents somehow managed to recall with some accuracy, let us say, two or three of his similitudes or parables and a handful of one-liners. A memory is

> far more generally than is commonly admitted, really a construction, serving to justify whatever impression may have been left by the original. It is this "impression," rarely defined with much exactitude, which most readily persists. So long as the details which can be built up around it are such that they would give it a "reasonable" setting, most of us are fairly content, and are apt to think that what we build we have literally retained.[65]

All this is why fictions may convey facts; an accurate impression can take any number of forms. Even a work as full of make-believe as the *Alexander Romance* sometimes catches the character of the historical Alexander of Macedon. Similarly, tales about an absentminded professor may be apocryphal and yet spot-on because they capture the teacher's personality. The letter

---

63. There is in fact a school of thought that promotes what it calls "fuzzy-trace theory." See Valerie P. Reyna and C. J. Brainerd, "Fuzzy-Trace Theory: An Interim Synthesis," *Learning and Individual Differences* 7 (1995): 1–75; Valerie F. Reyna and Farrell Lloyd, "Theories of False Memory in Children and Adults," *Learning and Individual Differences* 9 (1997): 95–123. Note that E. P. Sanders uses "fuzzy" with regard to details in the traditions about Jesus (*The Historical Figure of Jesus* [London: Penguin, 1993], 290).

64. Maryanne Garry and Devon Polaschek comment, "Very few scenarios repeat exactly, so our memories work mostly by extracting the essence of those scenarios" ("Reinventing Yourself," *Psychology Today* 32, no. 6 [November/December 1999]: 66).

65. Bartlett, *Remembering*, 176. Compare, from the perspective not of the cognitive science of memory but rather the study of oral tradition, this remark by James A. Notopoulos: "In prose, memory of the oral word preserves the ideas rather than the words" ("Mnemosyne in Oral Literature," *TAPA* 69 [1938]: 493).

can be false, the spirit true. One student of human memory has justifiably asserted that "the gospels are more likely to be deeply true than superficially exact."[66]

If general impressions are typically more trustworthy than details, then it makes little sense to reconstruct Jesus by starting with a few of the latter— perhaps some incidents and sayings that survive the gauntlet of our authenticating criteria—while setting aside the general impressions that our primary sources instill in us.[67] The larger the generalization and the more data upon which it is based, the greater our confidence.[68] The more specific the detail and the fewer the supporting data, the greater our uncertainty. We should, after reading Thucydides, be assured that there was indeed a Peloponnesian War, even if we may well wonder about many of the details in his account. If, however, we were to doubt that there was a Peloponnesian War, how could we not be dubious of all the details?

The modern study of memory moves me to differentiate myself from those who, proceeding by subtraction,[69] presuppose that we can learn about Jesus chiefly on the basis of a handful of parables and a small collection of aphorisms deemed, after a critical sorting, to be authentic.[70] Such scholars also believe that nothing stands in the way of interpreting those parables and aphorisms contrary to the general impressions that the tradition, in toto, tends to convey (not to mention contrary to their present literary contexts, which, although secondary and artificial, often remain our best guides to what Jesus might

66. Bradshaw, "Oral Transmission," 305–6.

67. Crossan (*Birth of Christianity*, 59–89) has similarly recognized the vagaries of memory, but he arrives at conclusions much different from mine, partly because he privileges overlaps between Q and the *Gospel of Thomas* and sometimes puts a great deal of weight on individual sayings as well as his own tradition histories.

68. With reference to the study of Jesus, Theissen and Winter maintain, "We are more certain about general statements about Jesus' life and teaching than about judgments on many individual items" (*Quest*, 200).

69. The method goes back as far as the eighteenth century and Hermann Samuel Reimarus (see *Reimarus: Fragments* [ed. Charles Talbert; Philadelphia: Fortress, 1970]), who sought to find the historical Jesus by looking in the Gospels for "a few remaining traces" of the truth that had "unintentionally" survived the fabricated overlay of the ecclesia (p. 135).

70. Note Aharon Oppenheimer's critique of Peter Schäfer's book *Der Bar Kokhba Aufstand*:

For each subject . . . the sources are broken down into their components, each of which is treated in isolation. It is doubtful that such dissection is justified. . . . The possibility of using it [the Talmud] for historical research depends largely on combining various sources from different works. Disregarding such combinations and handling only isolated sources necessarily reduces the possibility of extracting historical meaning from them. If Schäfer wanted simply to prove that certain sources have no historical meaning for the period of the revolt, he should have shown that in regard to those sources in combination, and not contented himself with rejecting them one by one. (Review of *Der Bar Kokhba Aufstand: Studien zum zweiten jüdischen Krieg gegen Rom*, by P. Schäfer, *JSJ* 14 [1983]: 218–19)

have meant).[71] If, to illustrate, Jesus was a "secular sage" little concerned with "the last things," as the Jesus Seminar collectively determined,[72] then the Synoptic tradition, which everywhere depicts a *homo religiosus* and a man who frequently promotes an eschatological vision, is mnemonically defective in a massive way, so much so that we probably cannot justify using it to investigate the pre-Easter period, in which case we cannot persuade ourselves that Jesus was a secular sage uninterested in eschatology. Here skepticism skewers itself.

There is, happily, another path. The first-century traditions about Jesus are not an amorphous mess. On the contrary, certain themes, motifs, and rhetorical strategies recur again and again throughout the primary sources; and it must be in those themes and motifs and rhetorical strategies—which, taken together, leave some distinct impressions—if it is anywhere, that we will find memory.[73]

71. Some scholars, operating with something like a hermeneutics of suspicion, assume almost as a matter of course that editorial contributions distort the tradition. Might those contributions not rather sometimes rightly interpret it? Richard Horsley remarks:

> Purposely isolating sayings from their contexts in the ancient texts . . . effectively discards the primary guide we might have as historians to determine both how a given saying functioned as a component in a genuine unit of communication (a speech or a narrative) and its possible meaning context(s) for ancient speakers and hearers. With no ancient guide for its meaning-context . . . interpretation is determined only, and almost completely, by the modern scholar, who constructs a new meaning-context on the basis of other such radically decontextualized sayings. ("Prominent Patterns in the Social Memory of Jesus and Friends," in *Memory, Tradition, and Text* [ed. Kirk and Thatcher], 62–63)

On the basis of what we now know about social memory, Rodríguez has come to a similar conclusion: "The programme of atomising, decontextualising, and recontextualising snippets of the gospel tradition in order to critically reconstruct the 'historical Jesus' has been exposed as culturally and historically inappropriate" ("Early Christian Memory," 223). See further Rafael Rodríguez, "Authenticating Criteria: The Use and Misuse of a Critical Method," *JSHJ* 7 (2009): 152–67; Winger, "Word and Deed."

72. Robert W. Funk, Roy W. Hoover, and the Jesus Seminar, *The Five Gospels: The Search for the Authentic Words of Jesus* (New York: Macmillan, 1993); Robert Funk and the Jesus Seminar, *The Acts of Jesus: The Search for the Authentic Deeds of Jesus* (San Francisco: HarperSanFrancisco, 1998). On p. 287 of the former, Jesus is called a "secular sage" who used "secular proverbs," and on p. 201 we read that in debate his "responses were more secular than legal in character."

73. Recently, Gerd Theissen and Annette Merz ("The Delay of the Parousia as a Test Case for the Criterion of Coherence," *LS* 32 [2007]: 49–66) have redefined the criterion of coherence so that it comes very close to what I am suggesting here. They write, "Elements which recur and correspond to one another in different independent currents of tradition and forms (and are thus numerously attested), may be due to an effect made by the historical Jesus" (p. 54). See also Theissen and Winter, *Quest*, 234–39. For related points of view, see Nils A. Dahl, "The Problem of the Historical Jesus," in *Jesus the Christ: The Historical Origins of Christian Doctrine* (ed. Donald H. Juel; Minneapolis: Fortress, 1991), 95; Martin Dibelius, *Jesus* (Philadelphia: Westminster, 1949), 28; A. E. Harvey, *Jesus and the Constraints of History* (Philadelphia: Westminster, 1982), 4–5; John Knox, *Jesus: Lord and Christ* (New York: Harper, 1958), 114–15; Ragnar Leivestad, *Jesus in His Own Perspective: An Examination of His Sayings, Actions, and Eschatological Titles* (Minneapolis: Augsburg, 1987), 18; Gerhard Lohfink, "Die Naherwartung Jesu," in Gisbert Greshake and Gerhard Lohfink, *Naherwartung, Auferstehung, Unsterblichkeit:*

In this, Jesus is like the historical Socrates, who is often thought present not in this or that aphorism but above all in some of the philosophical interests and rhetorical strategies that recur in Plato's early dialogues.[74]

I am not, I should emphatically add, urging that all the stories in the Gospels must be unhistorical (I am far from being so skeptical) or that our sources fail to preserve some aphorisms of Jesus (again, my doubt is scarcely that large). That is, I am not, a priori, deciding how much history is or is not in the Gospels (which, in any event, is unfeasible, given how often my mind shifts on the issue). Rather, I am making a point about method, about how we may proceed, and contending that the historian should heed before all else the general impressions that our primary sources produce. We should trust first, if we are to trust at all, what is most likely to be trustworthy. This requires that we begin, although we need not end, by asking, "What are our general impressions?"

We—I include myself—have been, in part because of form criticism, hypnotized by tradition histories of this isolated logion or that individual pericope, histories that are, more often than we care to admit, just guesses, however educated they may be.[75] Our hope, if we summon any, should be less in our

---

Untersuchungen zur christlichen Eschatologie (QD 71; Freiburg: Herder, 1975), 41; John Riches, *Jesus and the Transformation of Judaism* (New York: Seabury, 1982), 53; Marinus de Jonge, *God's Final Envoy: Early Christology and Jesus' Own View of His Mission* (Grand Rapids: Eerdmans, 1998), 36; Eduard Schweizer, *Jesus, the Parable of God: What Do We Really Know About Jesus?* (Allison Park, PA: Pickwick, 1994), 16; James D. G. Dunn, *Jesus Remembered* (Christianity in the Making 1; Grand Rapids: Eerdmans, 2003), 330–35, 405. I agree with Walter Schmithals ("Gibt es Kriterien für die Bestimmung echter Jesusworte?" *ZNT* 1 [1998]: 63) that although we cannot demonstrate that Jesus must have uttered any particular saying attributed to him, nonetheless we can recover the basic outlines (*Grundlinien*) of his proclamation. The earliest example of someone arguing this way known to me is Friedrich Loofs, *What Is the Truth about Jesus Christ? Problems of Christology* (New York: Charles Scribner's Sons, 1913), 120–45. Unfortunately, Theissen and Winter (*Quest*), in their comprehensive review of the criteria of authenticity, neglect Loofs entirely.

74. Another parallel, which in so many ways begs for the attention of historians of early Christianity, lies in the sources for the life and teaching of the founder of Hasidism, the Baal Shem Tov. These are notoriously problematic. The letters attributed to him may be pseudepigraphal, as may his supposed last will and testament. This leaves us with only secondhand sources, above all the *Shivhei ha-Besht*. This collection of stories was not published until fifty-five years after the Besht's death, and it is full of fantastic legends and motifs from folklore. It is, however, hardly devoid of authentic memory. Although no one has devised credible criteria to determine what words the Besht actually uttered or what stories have some basis in fact, we still can use the book to say some very important things about him. This is because the various tales are not a heterogeneous jumble. Despite coming from a variety of individuals, some of whom knew the Besht, certain ideas or themes reappear again and again in the many stories. It is in these, if it is anywhere, that we can learn something of what he was all about. That is, without deciding that any particular saying or event is authentic, we still can know that he emphasized that the divine is everywhere, know that he criticized asceticism, and know that he believed that the zaddik should not withdraw but rather should dwell among the common people.

75. See further Allison, *Jesus of Nazareth*, 27–31. The hope of Martin Dibelius (*From Tradition to Gospel* [New York: Charles Scribner's Sons, n.d.], 290) that "formal criteria" might

aptitude at authenticating solitary pieces of the tradition than in the prospect that our primary sources are not bereft of some substantial and substantially reliable broad impressions. For if those sources do not in large measure rightly typify Jesus' actions, give us some sense of his situation, accurately exhibit some habitual themes of his speech, capture the sort of character he was, and so on, then what hope is there? If the chief witnesses fail us in the larger matters, we cannot trust them in the smaller matters either, and we are not clever enough to make up their lack. To imagine otherwise, to pretend that we are as dexterous at doing history as Sherlock Holmes was at solving crimes, is to deceive ourselves.

An Illustration

Before turning to the eschatology of Jesus (chap. 2), I will illustrate my approach. (I say "approach" not "method" lest I imply a specious objectivity.) Consider the following traditions, which display a family resemblance:[76]

1. The temptation narrative, in which Jesus bests the devil (Matt 4:1–11 // Luke 4:1–13 [Q]; Mark 1:12–13)
2. The exorcism of a mute demon (Matt 12:22–23 // Luke 11:14–15 [Q])
3. The saying about Satan being divided (Matt 12:25–27 // Luke 11:17–19 [Q]; Mark 3:23–26)
4. The declaration that Jesus casts out demons by the finger/Spirit of God (Matt 12:28 // Luke 11:20 [Q])
5. The parable of binding the strong man (Matt 12:29 // Luke 11:21–22 [Q]; Mark 3:27; *Gos. Thom.* 35)
6. The exorcism of an unclean spirit in a synagogue in Capernaum (Mark 1:21–28)
7. The passing editorial notices of successful exorcisms (Mark 1:32, 34, 39; 3:22; Matt 8:16)
8. Jesus' authorization of disciples to cast out demons (Mark 3:15; 6:7 [cf. 6:13]; Matt 7:22; Luke 10:19–20)
9. The healing of the Gerasene demoniac (Mark 5:1–20)

---

exclude "subjective judgment" in evaluating the historicity of the Jesus tradition has proven vain. Critical portraits of Jesus today differ from each other as much or more than ever. I agree with Richard Bauckham: attempts to authenticate "each saying or story individually" have been "doomed to failure. We simply do not have the means to sift the tradition, unit by unit, in this way, even if there may be a few cases in which it is possible. The results have been so disparate as to confirm that the method is fundamentally flawed" ("Eyewitness and Critical History: A Response to Jens Schröter and Craig Evans," *JSNT* 31 [2008]: 225).

76. For what follows I am indebted to C. H. Dodd, *History and the Gospel* (New York: Charles Scribner's Sons, 1938), 92–110. Dodd's observations about method seem to me more important and useful than many subsequent discussions.

10. The casting out of a demon from the daughter of a Syrophoenician woman (Mark 7:24–30)
11. The healing of a boy who has a spirit that makes him unable to speak (Mark 9:14–29)
12. The story of someone other than a disciple casting out demons in Jesus' name (Mark 9:38–41)
13. The healing of a mute demoniac (Matt 9:32–34)
14. The report of Jesus' vision of Satan falling like lightning from heaven (Luke 10:18)
15. The account of Jesus healing a woman "whom Satan bound for eighteen long years" (Luke 13:10–17)
16. The autobiographical comment "I am casting out demons and performing cures today and tomorrow" (Luke 13:32)
17. The announcement that the ruler of the world has been driven out (John 12:31; 16:11 [cf. 14:30])

If there is no obvious objection—and I do not see one—we might sensibly gather from these materials, which include parables, prophetic declarations, stories of exorcism, and editorial asides, not only that Jesus was an exorcist but also that he and others saw his ministry as a successful combat with the forces of Satan. I doubt that we can ascertain the origin of most of the traditions listed above. I judge #13 (Matt 9:32–34) to be a redactional doublet of #2 (Matt 12:22–23; Luke 11:14–15), and I deem the story of Jesus' temptation in the wilderness (#1) to be a legend;[77] but I simply do not know—because the arguments I have heretofore scrutinized are insufficiently persuasive and because I am unable to devise better ones—if the pigs ran off the cliff and into the sea (#9) or if Jesus really declared that he had seen Satan fall like lightning from heaven (#14). In my judgment, obtaining such knowledge, or even just enough knowledge to make a wise or safe bet, is beyond human ability.[78]

Yet, failure in these and other particulars means little for my purposes. Whatever one makes of the individual units, at least some of which are hard to think of as historical, and which in every case are at best "mixed products"— that is, indebted to the churches as well as to Jesus[79]—what matters is the

77. On the latter, see Dale C. Allison Jr., "Behind the Temptations of Jesus: Q 4:1–13 and Mark 1:12–13," in *Authenticating the Activities of Jesus* (ed. Bruce Chilton and Craig A. Evans; NTTS 28/2; Leiden: Brill, 1999), 195–214. There I argue that the story is a fiction that nonetheless communicates facts about Jesus.

78. In this connection, we should keep in mind the problem of "relatedness effects": we regularly and unconsciously tend to fill in the memory of an event with memories of closely related events (see p. 3). This implies that if someone had indeed witnessed Jesus conducting exorcisms on multiple occasions, later recall of one incident for the purpose of storytelling would likely have involved, to some degree, conflating details from several incidents.

79. The Gospels are not literary wrappers to be removed so that we can espy a preecclesiastical Jesus. See Hahn, "Methodological Reflections," 149–50. Note also this observation by Alan

larger pattern. According to the sources as a whole, Jesus was an exorcist who thought of himself as successfully combating the devil. How should we account for this fact? I would argue, if demonology were our subject (which it is not), that in this particular our texts remember rightly.

Modern medical experiments supply an analogy to my approach. Even a perfectly devised double-blind, randomized trial counts for little if taken by itself. What matters is replication. And for highly controverted issues, what finally matters is meta-analysis, the evaluation of a large, bundled number of individual studies, including those with possible design flaws. The tendency of the whole is what instills conviction, not any one trial or single piece of evidence. Why should it be any different with research about Jesus? We should, at least initially, be looking at macrosamples. We are rightly more confident about the generalities than about the particulars. We are more sure that Jesus was a healer than that any account of him healing reflects a historical event, more sure that he was a prophet than that any one prophetic oracle goes back to him. When the evangelists generalize, in their editorial comments, that Jesus went about teaching and casting out demons, these are, notwithstanding the redactional agendas, the most reliable statements of all.

Scholars commonly have conducted business as though all this were true. They have, for example, rarely disputed that Jesus taught about the king-dom of God, despite the failure of that theme to pass the criterion of double dissimilarity.[80] The reason must be that ἡ βασιλεία τοῦ θεοῦ is so frequently attested.[81] This is a question not of multiple attestation—a particular saying

---

Kirk and Tom Thatcher: "The dynamic nature of . . . [the] interplay between past and present complicates attempts to isolate so-called authentic elements of memory from their interpretive reception in any given unit of tradition. The notion that traditional materials embedded in the Gospels can be analytically and cleanly separated into two piles—authentic remembrance and fabricated elements—is predicated upon questionable views of the operations of memory and tradition" ("Jesus Tradition as Social Memory," in *Memory, Tradition, and Text* [ed. Kirk and Thatcher], 34).

80. Cf. Acts 8:12; 1 Cor 4:20; 15:50; Rev 11:15. Even here, however, there are doubters; see Ernst Bammel, "Erwägungen zur Eschatologie Jesu," in *The New Testament Message* (part 2 of *Studia Evangelica II–III: Papers Presented to the Second International Congress on New Testament Studies Held at Christ Church, Oxford, 1961*, ed. F. L. Cross; TU 88; Berlin: Akademie-Verlag, 1964), 3–32; Charles Hedrick, "Parable and Kingdom: A Survey of the Evidence in Mark," *PRSt* 27 (2000): 179–99.

81. Note these observations by Jürgen Becker: refusing to acknowledge the kingdom "as Jesus' central concept, or even denying it to him altogether, would involve going against the unanimous witness of the synoptic tradition. We would then have to explain how the wealth of evidence and the unanimity among the witnesses came into existence" (*Jesus of Nazareth* [trans. James E. Crouch; New York: de Gruyter, 1998], 100–101); by James D. G. Dunn: "It is hardly possible to explain" the data regarding the kingdom of God "other than on the assump-tion that Jesus was remembered as speaking often on the subject" (*Jesus Remembered*, 384); and by E. P. Sanders: "It is beyond doubt that Jesus proclaimed the kingdom. We know this not from analyzing any one saying or group of sayings, but from noting the ubiquity of the theme 'kingdom'" (*Jesus and Judaism* [Philadelphia: Fortress, 1985], 139).

or event being independently attested in two or more sources—but rather of what one might call "recurrent attestation," by which I mean that a topic or motif or type of story reappears again and again throughout the tradition.[82]

Clarification

Tom Holmén, in discussing my sponsorship of recurrent attestation, has asserted that the motifs that it highlights tend to be rather general. "Consequently, the knowledge yielded by the criterion will usually remain on quite a general level. The composite picture of Jesus based solely on such knowledge, again, will turn out nonspecific and cursory."[83] Holmén is not rejecting recurrent attestation—he indeed recognizes that the other criteria that he defends "cannot regularly be expected to provide arguments of equal strength"[84]—but is observing that, by itself, it will not take us very far.

I am of another mind. Recurrent attestation yields much more than Holmén imagines, for not all the regularly attested themes and motifs are nonspecific and cursory. I offer this book as the proof. Nevertheless, I agree with Holmén to the extent that recurrent attestation is not sufficient unto itself. It supplies, as I hope to show, much more than a minimalist foundation. It is not, however, everything. As I stated earlier, although we may well begin by asking, "What are our general impressions?" we need not end there.[85]

My approach does not deny that constructing one's historical Jesus requires additional considerations, nor that, on occasion, and despite all the difficulties involved, we can give some decent reasons for thinking that Jesus did this or

82. This line of reasoning often appears in the critical literature even though it has not been recognized as a standard criterion. In addition to the quotations in the preceding footnote, note the following remarks by David E. Aune: "While it may be difficult to argue that this or that particular saying is 'historical' or 'authentic,' . . . the sheer number of such aphorisms together with their persistent attribution to Jesus makes it certain that Jesus regarded himself and was regarded by his followers and later Christian generations as a Jewish sage and teacher of wisdom" ("Oral Tradition and the Aphorisms of Jesus," in *Jesus and the Oral Gospel Tradition* [ed. Henry Wansbrough; JSNTSup 64; Sheffield: JSOT Press, 1991], 240–41); by John P. Meier, on Jesus as a miracle-worker: "The material seems simply too mammoth and omnipresent in the various strata of the Gospel tradition to be purely the creation of the early church" (*Marginal Jew*, 2:618–19); and Gerd Theissen and Annette Merz: "There is no reason to deny that Jesus preached judgment. The tradition of this is too broad" (*The Historical Jesus: A Comprehensive Guide* [Minneapolis: Fortress, 1998], 269).

83. Tom Holmén, "Authenticity Criteria," in *Encyclopedia of the Historical Jesus* (ed. Craig A. Evans; New York: Routledge, 2008), 47. Holmén is responding to my article "How to Marginalize the Traditional Criteria of Authenticity."

84. Ibid.

85. Nothing prohibits those less skeptical of the criteria of authenticity from employing them in connection with what I have called "recurrent attestation."

said that. In the following chapters I will, for instance, contend that he likely appointed a symbolic group of twelve disciples, and that presumably he was the chief contributor to the sayings collected in the central section of Luke's Sermon on the Plain; and I have no trouble affirming his likely authorship of several moral aphorisms (see p. 24). Further, although I regard tradition histories as very fragile things, they sometimes are unavoidable, and I do not altogether forswear them.[86] Chapter 4 of this book, which presupposes not only the Q source but also that we can sometimes decide whether the Matthean or Lukan version of a saying is more primitive, is testimony to this conviction. Above all, I believe that once recurrent attestation highlights a theme or motif, we should seek to interpret that theme or motif in the light of early Judaism, and in such a way that helps us make sense of what we otherwise know about Christian origins. If we can credibly do all that, we are likely getting a glimpse of Jesus. In any event, espying a pattern is not enough; we need to account for it sensibly.[87]

Perhaps it will prove useful to compare briefly my approach with that of E. P. Sanders in his influential book *Jesus and Judaism*. Convinced that "scholars have not and . . . will not agree on the authenticity of the sayings material, either in whole or in part," Sanders opts to pursue what he thinks of as "more secure evidence."[88] He begins with what he believes to be facts about Jesus and the aftermath of his ministry, from which he seeks to develop a "good hypothesis" about Jesus' intention.[89] Sanders does not resolutely refuse to pass judgment on the origin of the logia in the tradition. He does, for instance, argue at length that Jesus said something much like Matt 19:28. But authenticating isolated sayings is at the periphery of his work. Persuaded, quite rightly, that the bulk of the words attributed to Jesus have "been subject to change in ways that cannot be precisely assessed,"[90] he prefers to hang as little as possible upon our ability to decide what Jesus really said and instead to interpret the facts about Jesus within the context of early Judaism.

I share the decision by Sanders to start somewhere other than sayings supposedly authenticated by our criteria. One reason for my reluctance to rely on these criteria is as follows. As I have, over the years, repeatedly worked through the materials, they have sorted themselves into three piles. Some logia obviously betray themselves as secondary because they are redactional or promote purely ecclesiastical convictions. Jesus' rationalization for his

---

86. Here I am in league with David Catchpole (*Jesus People: The Historical Jesus and the Beginnings of Community* [Grand Rapids: Baker Academic, 2006], 55–60), who dissents from what he refers to as "neo-conservative, anti-critical procedure."

87. Here I heartily agree with Eric Eve, "Meier, Miracle, and Multiple Attestation," *JSHJ* 3 (2005): 23–45.

88. Sanders, *Jesus and Judaism*, 4–5.

89. Ibid., 18–22.

90. Ibid., 15–16.

baptism in Matt 3:15 and the commissioning narrative in Matt 28:18–20 come to mind. Other logia almost certainly are historical because church invention is wildly implausible, such as the prohibition of divorce found in Paul, Q, and Mark. Those two piles are, however, very small. The vast majority of sayings—for example, the parable of the rich man and Lazarus (Luke 16:19–31), the command not to let the left hand know what the right hand is doing (Matt 6:3), and the parable of the wicked tenants (Mark 12:1–12)—are neither obviously of pre-Easter origin nor manifestly post-Easter inventions. They should be classified as "possibly authentic," which is the same as "possibly not authentic."[91] The same holds, I believe, for most of the stories that the Synoptics tell about Jesus. Our ignorance, despite all our endeavors to undo it, remains substantial.[92]

In addition to being persuaded that the standard criteria much more often than not leave us with an uncertain verdict, I am haunted by what we now know about the frequent failings of human memory. This instills modesty and reinforces my conviction that the historicity of most—not all—of the events associated with Jesus and the origin of most—not all—of the sayings attributed to him will always fall woefully short of demonstration. We see him as in a mirror darkly. The attempt to espy more, which is the quest of the historical Jesus, can deliver only this or that scholar's reconstruction, which is always an inadequate cipher, constructed by inference, out of indirect knowledge. Usually, the best we can credibly do, in my judgment, is set our general impressions within the framework of facts that we can reasonably establish.

So I agree with Sanders in at least two respects. First, I doubt anyone's ability to demonstrate that Jesus composed or did not compose very many of the sentences attributed to him. Second, I concur that we should proceed by abduction—that is, by inference to the best explanation, always looking for a Jesus who makes the most sense of the available facts and what we otherwise know of Judaism and nascent Christianity.[93] To my mind, however, the chief facts are not just those that Sanders enumerates—Jesus was a Galilean who preached and healed, submitted to the baptism of John, confined his activity to Israel, and so on—but prominently include the themes and motifs that recur in the early traditions.

91. For thoughts along this line, see Eckhard Rau, *Jesus—Freund von Zöllnern und Sündern: Eine methodenkritische Untersuchung* (Stuttgart: Kohlhammer, 2000), 69–74.

92. What Joel Marcus has written concerning the Last Supper seems to me to hold good for most of the Synoptic tradition: "Categorical pronouncements about historicity are out of place, but so are categorical pronouncements about fictitiousness" (*Mark 8–16* [AB 27A; New Haven: Yale University Press, 2009], 963).

93. This last point corresponds in part to the notion of "historical plausibility" in Theissen and Winter, *Quest*: items that we attribute to Jesus should be contextually plausible within Jesus' Jewish world and should help explain things that we know about early Christianity.

Reasons for Proceeding

To this point, my discussion has been mostly hypothetical. I have urged that we are more likely to find the historical Jesus in the repeating patterns that run throughout the tradition than in the individual sayings and stories. Do we, however, have cause to believe that the sins of ecclesiastical recall did not thoroughly corrupt everything, so that the larger patterns are misleading?[94]

C. H. Dodd maintained that when we have made due allowance for the distortions of the tradition, "it remains that the first three gospels offer a body of sayings on the whole so consistent, so coherent, and withal so distinctive in manner, style, and content, that no reasonable critics should doubt, whatever reservations he may have about individual sayings, that we find reflected here the thought of a single, unique teacher."[95] I understand this comment, with which I am, on most days, sympathetic. I find it very difficult to come away from the primary sources doubting that I have somehow met a strikingly original character. I seem to have a permanent and vivid impression of who he must have been. Dodd's words, however, constitute not an argument but an opinion, albeit an informed one; and my own conviction is inevitably a personal, subjective response. What else might one add?

I can think of no line of reasoning that is not, in the end, strictly circular. Nonetheless, there remain some observations that, though they do not firmly establish anything, remain suggestive, observations that may encourage those of us who are otherwise inclined to side with Dodd.

94. I will not attend here to the objection that the large number of miracles in so much of the tradition testifies to its thorough corruption. I have discussed that matter elsewhere (Allison, *Historical Christ*, 66–78), arguing that a miracle story, just because it is a miracle story, is not necessarily late and unhistorical; that we have no reason, whatever our philosophical or religious disposition, to deny that people could have perceived or remembered Jesus doing miraculous things, or even a large number of miraculous things; that whether or not divinely wrought miracles or paranormal events ever transpire, many have believed that they do, and many have thought themselves to be witnesses of events resembling those in the Synoptics, including the so-called nature miracles. See further Russ Llewellyn, "Religious and Spiritual Miracle Events in Real-Life Experience," in *Religious and Spiritual Events* (vol. 1 of *Miracles: God, Science, and Psychology in the Paranormal*, ed. J. Harold Ellens; Westport, CT: Praeger, 2008), 241–63; William P. Wilson, "How Religious or Spiritual Miracle Events Happen Today," in *Religious and Spiritual Events* (ed. Ellens), 264–79.

95. C. H. Dodd, *The Founder of Christianity* (London: Fontana, 1973), 33. Compare this judgment by W. K. C. Guthrie regarding another problematic figure: "Reading our authorities on Socrates gives a vivid impression of a highly individual character whom one feels one knows not only as a thinker but as a whole person. . . . This feeling of personal acquaintance gives a certain encouragement (may I even say a certain right?), when a particular philosophical point is in question, to say: 'No, I can't imagine that Socrates himself would have put it like that,' or 'Yes, that is just what I should have expected Socrates to say.' If this sounds an impossibly subjective criterion, I can only say that, provided it is based on a reading of all the sources, I do not believe that any better one presents itself" (*Socrates* [Cambridge: Cambridge University Press, 1971], 30–31).

The first is that a few items in the tradition, like some of the sayings in the rabbinic tractate 'Abot, look as though they were composed precisely in order to lodge themselves in memories. Whoever first charged, "Hate your father and mother," managed to create an unforgettable, hyperbolic revision of "Honor your father and mother." And whoever first said, "Love your enemies," formulated an equally sparkling gem. To hear this counterintuitive rewrite of "Love your neighbor" is to remember it. The same is true of "Render to Caesar the things that are Caesar's, and to God the things that are God's" as well as the parable of the good Samaritan and a number of other arresting items in the tradition. All this suggests that somebody near the font of the tradition was adept at minting strikingly memorable sentences and stories. We have, admittedly, no proof that Jesus authored any of the materials that, once heard, are hard to forget. So doubt we will always have with us. At the same time, all the relevant items are attributed to him, not to anyone else, and I know of no explanatory advantage in assigning them to some anonymous contemporary or contemporaries of his.[96]

Second, it is more than a safe bet that Jesus was a teacher and, beyond that, an itinerant one.[97] This means that he was not like a modern pastor who, facing one and the same congregation week in and week out, must constantly strive to concoct new and different things to say. Jesus instead was more like a seasoned professor teaching an introductory class for the umpteenth time, who can rerun the same lectures year after year because the students are always moving on. Although one needs new words for an old audience, one can recycle old words for a new audience. An itinerant is likely to reuse more or less the same materials again and again.

This matters because, as the proverb rightly has it, repetition is the key to learning (cf. b. 'Erub. 54a; b. Sanh. 99a–b); and if, as our sources abundantly indicate, Jesus was accompanied in his travels by committed supporters, such supporters must, with time, have become familiar with his standard repertoire.[98] People who repeatedly heard him utter a series of similar sentences over a period

96. Other formal features of the tradition may also have served to preserve memory. For parallelism, see below, pp. 316–46, 374–86. On triadic structures, which, along with parallelism, are prominent in the mishnaic tractate 'Abot, see C. Leslie Mitton, "Threefoldness in the Teaching of Jesus," ExpTim 75 (1964): 228–30. For the possibility that alliteration, assonance, and paronomasia marked some of the Aramaic sayings of Jesus, see Joachim Jeremias, New Testament Theology: The Proclamation of Jesus (New York: Charles Scribner's Sons, 1971), 27–29. Yet we should be careful here because, as Werner Kelber points out, in ancient and medieval settings mnemonics could "allow for, indeed thrive on, hermeneutical inventiveness and compositional freedom in performance" ("The Case of the Gospels: Memory's Desire and the Limits of Historical Criticism," Oral Tradition 17 [2002]: 60). Kelber also notes that "mnemonic storage existed in the interest of inventio" (p. 79).

97. For the evidence, see Dale C. Allison Jr., Resurrecting Jesus: The Earliest Christian Tradition and Its Interpreters (New York: T & T Clark, 2005), 31–32.

98. They would also have experienced "spaced learning," which means acquiring the same or similar information over time as opposed to all at once. See David A. Balota, Janet M. Duchek, and Jessica M. Logan, "Is Expanded Retrieval Practice a Superior Form of Spaced Retrieval?

of weeks or months would presumably, at some point, have gained a decent grasp of what he was about and, presumably, even have been able to recite some of his aphorisms.[99] We may also safely wager that if Jesus was in any sense remarkable—and surely he was already becoming a legend in his own lifetime—his admirers must already have been saying things about him.[100] Why imagine that the widespread curiosity on display in so many of the apocryphal Gospels was utterly alien to Jesus' own contemporaries? Notoriety after death usually follows notoriety before death. All of which is to say: even prior to Easter, a group of people almost certainly repeated words of and stories about Jesus.[101]

My third observation is less secure than the first two but nevertheless worth pondering. Our sources not only have Jesus moving from place to place with a band of sympathizers but also tell us that some of those partisans, on at least one occasion, went out on their own, extending his ministry through their own activities, including preaching. Attesting to this are Matt 10:1–23; Mark 6:7–12; Luke 9:1–10; 10:1–17, and Paul seems to have known some form of the missionary discourse.[102] Beyond that, a few passages in the Synoptics have followers of Jesus minister without him present (e.g., Mark 9:14–18; Luke 9:52). None of which, it must be conceded, comes close to establishing that our sources here have the facts right. Still, if Jesus was a man with a mission, it would have made perfect sense, in a world without mass communications, and especially if he was in the grip of eschatological expectation, for him to have enlisted others to help him spread abroad his urgent appeal. Surely he "would have neglected no available means to give his message the widest possible circulation."[103]

A Critical Review of the Extant Literature," in *Foundations of Remembering* (ed. Nairne), 83–105.

99. See Winger, "Word and Deed," 686. Maybe Bradshaw's formulation is apt: "Jesus' message was *caught, not taught*" ("Oral Transmission," 307).

100. See Ferdinand Hahn, "Die Verkündigung Jesu und das Osterzeugnis der Jünger," in *Bekenntnisbildung und Theologie in urchristlicher Zeit* (vol. 2 of *Studien zum Neuen Testament*, ed. Jörg Frey and Unliane Schlegel; WUNT 192; Tübingen: Mohr Siebeck, 2006), 20; David Friedrich Strauss, *The Life of Jesus Critically Examined* (trans. George Eliot; ed. Peter C. Hodgson; Philadelphia: Fortress, 1972), 85; Ulrich Wilckens, *Geschichte des Wirkens Jesu in Galiläa* (part 1 of *Geschichte der urchristlichen Theologie*; vol. 1 of *Theologie des Neuen Testaments*; Neukirchen-Vluyn: Neukirchener Verlag, 2002), 136 n. 12. Would the Romans have crucified Jesus if he had no following?

101. On the importance of socially motivated narratives for maintaining memory, see Ulric Neisser et al., "Remembering the Earthquake: Direct Experience vs. Hearing the News," *Memory* 4 (1996): 337–57; see also Steen F. Larsen, "Remembering without Experiencing: Memory for Reported Events," in *Remembering Reconsidered: Ecological and Traditional Approaches to the Study of Memory* (ed. Ulric Neisser and Eugene Winograd; Cambridge: Cambridge University Press, 1988), 326–55.

102. See Dale C. Allison Jr., "The Missionary Discourse, Q 10:2–16: Its Use by Paul," in *The Jesus Tradition in Q* (Harrisburg, PA: Trinity Press International, 1997), 104–19.

103. Burton Scott Easton, "The First Evangelic Tradition," *JBL* 50 (1931): 149.

When we imagine that Christianity's missionary impulse was not born solely of post-Easter circumstances, and that Jesus was not alone in broadcasting his message, what follows? One inference is that the principle of the disciple being like the master (Matt 10:24–25; Luke 6:40; John 13:16; 15:20) must have been in effect, so that, just as the Synoptic missionary discourses report, to join in Jesus' ministry was to repeat to some extent what he proclaimed.[104] As Luke 10:16 has it, "Whoever listens to you listens to me." Nothing else makes sense. What else were they to say? So then, if their message was his message, his speech must have entered their speech. If he spoke repeatedly about the kingdom of God, they must have followed suit. And if he spoke repeatedly about God as a loving father, they must have done likewise. In other words, it is plausible that some people were already teaching, which means in effect rehearsing, parts of the Jesus tradition before their leader was gone. Once more, then, we see how the later ecclesiastical traditions could have grown out of pre-Easter memories and pre-Easter recitals.[105]

104. For a detailed argument along this line, see Rainer Riesner, *Jesus als Lehrer: Eine Untersuchung zum Ursprung der Evangelien-Überlieferung* (WUNT 2/7; Tübingen: Mohr Siebeck, 1981), 453–75.

105. See further Heinz Schürmann, "Die vorösterlichen Anfänge der Logientradition: Versuch eines formgeschichtlichen Zugangs zum Leben Jesu," in *Der historische Jesus und der kerygmatische Christus* (ed. H. Ristow and K. Matthiae; Berlin: Evangelische Verlagsanstalt, 1962), 342–70. My discussion, one might object, overlooks the work of Birger Gerhardsson, who has posited something akin to a rabbinic model for the transmission of the Jesus tradition: much as disciples memorized the teachings of their rabbis, so Jesus' disciples laid up his words in their memories (see four works by Gerhardsson: *Memory and Manuscript: Oral Tradition and Written Transmission in Rabbinic Judaism and Early Christianity* [trans. Eric J. Sharpe; ASNU 22; Lund: Gleerup, 1961]; *Tradition and Transmission in Early Christianity* [trans. Eric J. Sharpe; ConBNT 20; Lund: Gleerup, 1964]; *The Origins of the Gospel Traditions* [Philadelphia: Fortress, 1979]; *The Reliability of the Gospel Tradition* [Peabody, MA: Hendrickson, 2001]). For all I know, Gerhardsson is partly right. I have only a vague sense of how early Christians passed on the words and deeds of Jesus; and as I suspect that practices differed from place to place and from tradent to tradent, I do not deny that, in some quarters, some authorities—perhaps members of a small scribal school—may have deliberately studied and memorized traditions. The rabbinic data do, after all, take us close to Jesus' time and place. Even so, I see no evidence of a formal academic or school-like setting in the pre-Easter period. In addition, Gerhardsson has always stressed the flexibility of both the rabbinic and early Christian traditions, emphasizing that even memorized texts were regularly revised, altered, expanded, and so forth. Given this, and given that our sources are in Greek and so can at best be translations of Aramaic sentences, and given the creativity necessarily involved in first recalling and then formulating stories about Jesus, and given the countless significant variations among the Synoptics themselves, between the Synoptics and John, and between all four canonical Gospels and the *Gospel of Thomas*, surely the methodological cautions of the present chapter are warranted. It is not as though tradents learned words by rote, repeated them mechanically, and, so to speak, saved all commentary for the margins. Rather, Christian interpretation must have recalled, formulated, and revised everything from the beginning.

Objections

Because I have sought to relate my approach to the Jesus tradition to contemporary cognitive studies of memory, one might protest that it is hazardous to move from psychological studies of moderns to historical conclusions about ancients, for recollection is a function not just of biology but also of culture. Might it not be that ancient memories, less assisted by paper and altogether bereft of electronic support, were generally more retentive than their modern counterparts, which technology has enervated?[106] Again, I have read that in traditional Chinese culture, where becoming old is not such a bad thing and indeed typically honored, memories often stay intact better than in contemporary North American culture, which constantly conditions us to believe that recall recedes as age advances.[107] It appears, then, that memory is not just a hard-wired given. Its capacities vary not only from person to person but also from place to place and from time to time. Is it wise, then, to make generalizations and draw inferences about first-century Christians on the basis of studies of modern people?[108] Are my doubts and cautions unwarranted?

It would be idle to deny that human memory is, in certain respects, a variable, not a cross-cultural constant. My approach does not, however, assume otherwise, only that the sins of memory cataloged above are not confined to our time and place, and especially that the distinction between detailed memories and more generalized recall is applicable to ancient Christian texts. On neither score is there cause to hesitate. The Bible is full of injunctions not to "forget"—שכח in Hebrew, ἐπιλανθάνομαι in Greek[109]—which entails that people often did forget. Beyond that statement of the obvious, who would be so bold as to claim that first-century memories did not lose details with the passage of time[110]—the

106. Julius Caesar asserted, "The assistance of writing tends to relax the diligence of the student and the action of the memory" (*Gallic Wars* 6.14). Many ancients, most famously Plato (e.g., *Phaedr.* 274e–275a), held this sentiment, the truth of which is almost self-evident.

107. See Becca Levy and Ellen Langer, "Aging Free from Negative Stereotypes: Successful Memory in China and among the American Deaf," *Journal of Personality and Social Psychology* 66 (1994): 989–97. By contrast, people in Western cultures tend to have earlier autobiographical memories than people in Eastern cultures. See Mary K. Mullen, "Earliest Recollections of Childhood: A Demographic Analysis," *Cognition* 52 (1994): 55–79.

108. See Martin Hengel, "Eye-Witness Memory and the Writing of the Gospels," in *The Written Gospel* (ed. Markus Bockmuehl and Donald Hagner; Cambridge: Cambridge University Press, 2005), 70–96. In arguing against what he labels "radical anti-historical scepticism" (p. 88), Hengel contends that "the memory of ancient people was . . . better than that of people today who suffer from constant information overload and stimulus satiation" (p. 86). Eddy and Boyd (*Jesus Legend*, 281–83) make a similar point, as does Donald Hagner, "How Well Was Jesus Remembered? What Model of Oral Transmission Is Most Persuasive?" in *Remembering Jesus: Essays in Honor of James D. G. Dunn* (ed. Scot McKnight and T. Mournet; New York: Continuum, forthcoming).

109. For example, Deut 4:9, 23, 31; 6:12; 8:11, 14, 19; 9:7; 25:19; 1 Sam 1:11; 2 Kgs 17:38; Prov 3:1; 4:5; Sir 37:6.

110. Jocelyn Small quotes Ephorus as recognizing the unlikelihood of people retaining, after a long period of time, a speech that they once heard (*Wax Tablets of the Mind: Cognitive Stud-*

memories of nonhuman primates often deteriorate with age, so this phenomenon cannot be wholly relative to human culture[111]—or that they did not sometimes conflate one event with another like it, or that they were free of the distortion of self-interest and the conventions of narrative and so on?[112]

As for the difference between full-blooded recall and the gist of something, this is nothing new under the sun. Thucydides, when discussing the speeches in his history, admitted the difficulty of recalling "with strict accuracy the words actually spoken," and he defended himself by professing to have adhered "as closely as possible to the general drift of what was actually said."[113] From a much later time, Gaon Sherira, a tenth-century Jewish scholar, argued that although the early sages wrote nothing before the days of Judah the Prince, and although they did not teach in the identical language as their predecessors or with exactly the same words or "expressions" (לשון), they nonetheless were able to understand and hand on the basic "reasonings" or "sense" (טעמיהו) of their tradition.[114] Similarly, Maimonides, when discussing a particular oral tradition, claimed that although the wording was not heard from Moses and so could not have been recalled precisely, the idea was transmitted.[115] Once again, then, the distinction between the general and the particular, so emphasized by modern cognitive psychology, is mirrored in premodern texts.[116]

One might, however, still hesitate to move from contemporary studies of human memory to phenomena in the early churches, on the ground that, in

---

ies of Memory and Literacy in Classical Antiquity [London: Routledge], 199). For a survey of the modern critical literature on the subject, see Aimée M. Surprenant, Tamra J. Bireta, and Lisa A. Farley, "A Brief History of Memory and Aging," in *Foundations of Remembering* (ed. Nairne), 107–23.

111. See Mark B. Moss, Douglas L. Rosene, and Alan Peters, "Effects of Aging on Visual Recognition Memory in the Rhesus Monkey," *Neurobiology of Aging* 9 (1988): 495–502; Peter R. Rapp, "Visual Discrimination and Reversal Learning in the Aged Monkey (*Macca mulatta*)," *Behavioral Neuroscience* 104 (1990): 876–84.

112. Human beings are not alone in being victims of the misinformation effect. Research has shown that misleading information after the fact can alter the memories of other primates and birds. See Bennett L. Schwartz et al., "Event Memory and Misinformation Effects in a Gorilla," *Animal Cognition* 7 (2004): 93–100; William Vaughan and Sharon L. Greene, "Pigeon Visual Memory Capacity," *Journal of Experimental Psychology: Animal Behavior Processes* 10 (1984): 256–71. This, then, is another fact that cannot be reduced to culture.

113. ἐχομένῳ ὅτι ἐγγύτατα τῆς ξυμπάσης γνώμης τῶν ἀληθῶς λεχθέντων (*Hist.* 1.22). For the translation of ξυμπάσης γνώμης as "general drift," see John Wilson, "What Does Thucydides Claim for His Speeches?" *Phoenix* 36 (1982): 99. For the argument that Thucydides may really have achieved his goal on occasion, see John H. Finley Jr., "Euripides and Thucydides," in *Three Essays on Thucydides* (Cambridge, MA: Harvard University Press, 1967), 1–54 (reprinted from *HSCP* 49 [1938]: 23–68).

114. *Iggeret Rav Sherira Ga'on* (ed. B. M. Lewin; Jerusalem: Makor, 1971), 18.

115. Maimonides, *Commentary on the Mishnah* on *m. 'Ed.* 8:7.

116. See also Augustine, *Doctr. chr.* 4.10.24 (one can convey "the substance of thought" with varying, imperfect words); Consultus Fortunatianus, *Ars rhetorica* 3.14 (he distinguishes between memorizing something verbatim and retaining only the substance).

James Dunn's words, it is a mistake "to assume that all remembering is individual and casual in character, or that casual recall typifies all remembering."[117] How can modern studies with modern individuals, and especially with modern individuals in the lab, inform us regarding the collective memory of a first-century religious movement? The traditions about Jesus, before being inscribed in written texts, belonged to an oral society that repeated them publicly, and "the community dimension in the process of remembering Jesus should caution us against too easy inferences that individuals could readily introduce distortions to the tradition. A congregation made up of people whose identity was given in large part by their deposit of Jesus tradition would not take kindly to major divergences in the content of the tradition by individual performers."[118]

One sees the point, and I record some related sentiments at the end of chapter 2. Religious groups can be invested in memories and so motivated to keep them. Augustine tells the story of how, when a new Latin translation for the "gourd" of Jonah 4:6 was read, a translation different from "that which had been of old familiar to the senses and memory of all the worshippers, and had been chanted for so many generations in the church," there arose a "tumult" in a congregation: people—not the priests and teachers but the laity—corrected and denounced what they had heard.[119] Even though the status of the oral Jesus tradition in the first century cannot be equated with the status of Scripture in the fourth century, surely public rehearsals of sayings assigned to Jesus and of stories about him must have bestowed some stability upon the transmission of the tradition. At the least, items that contradicted what Christians already believed and valued about Jesus would not have been welcomed.

Nevertheless, the differences among the Gospels remain eloquent and very concrete testimony to how much freedom Christians could feel about modifying the tradition. Matthew and Luke introduced all sorts of changes into Mark and Q, even though the latter were authorities of some sort for them, as presumably for members of their original audiences. This accords with what anthropologists have found to be the case with tradition in oral cultures: verbatim repetition is not the norm; rather, each performance, even of well-known compositions, is to some extent new. How else could one account for the Fourth Gospel, which so obviously bears the imprint of a late first-century Christian? Tradents are always introducing changes.[120]

---

117. James D. G. Dunn, "Social Memory and the Oral Jesus Tradition," in *Memory in the Bible* (ed. Barton, Stuckenbruck, and Wold), 180. Dunn writes, "The remembering of the disciples was not an individual and isolated affair, and . . . consequently models of how memory works, based on examples of individuals remembering, are less than relevant to the consideration of how Jesus was remembered" (p. 189).

118. Ibid., 193. See also Michael F. Bird, "The Purpose and Preservation of the Jesus Tradition," *BBR* 15 (2005): 179–80.

119. Augustine, *Ep.* 75.21–22 (see also *Ep.* 82.35).

120. See Ian M. L. Hunter, "Lengthy Verbatim Recall: The Role of Text," in *Progress in the Psychology of Language* (ed. Andrew W. Ellis; 2 vols.; London: Lawrence Erlbaum Associates,

But even more to the point: Dunn's protest overlooks that we need to worry not only about those who transmitted the tradition but also about its originators, and here the modern studies of memory in individuals are indisputably relevant. For they teach us that "revising history to accomplish particular objectives" is "a hallmark of the average person's efforts to recall details from his or her life. In comparison to professional writers who derive their historical stories from written records, individuals may be less cognizant of their alterations as they use their present knowledge, beliefs, and goals to construct their pasts."[121]

Even if one grants, for the sake of discussion, that eyewitnesses initiated the tradition and repeated parts of it again and again to multiple audiences,[122] their initial and later tellings cannot have been unsullied by selective recall and distortion. This is because nobody's retrieval is immune to such. Retellings of the past are habitually shaped by (1) the mere prospect that there will be listeners; (2) a speaker's aims; (3) expectations about the interests and attitudes of auditors; and (4) the behavior and reactions of the latter. Context affects what one deems possible, appropriate, or desirable to discuss, and speakers will add, subtract, and distort in order to please and entertain, as well as to forestall negative reactions.[123]

What possible reason could one have for imagining that it was otherwise with the originators of the Jesus tradition? Even if early Christians had tried to memorize vast swaths of the tradition verbatim, which apparently they did not,[124] that tradition originated when recognized leaders or authorities called upon their memories; and those memories must have been subject to all the failures and biases that modern science has so helpfully if disturbingly exposed. The generalization that "a particularly pervasive source of misinformation is one's own repeated retrievals and recountings"[125] cannot have found its exception among the early Christians.

1985), 1:207–36; Walter J. Ong, *Orality and Literacy: The Technologizing of the Word* (London: Methuen, 1982), 57–68. Ong observes, in illustration, that recordings of Yugoslav bard songs, "though metrically regular, . . . were never sung the same way twice. Basically, the same formulas and themes recurred, but they were stitched together or 'rhapsodized' differently in each rendition even by the same poet, depending on audience reaction, the mood of the poet or of the occasion, and other social and psychological factors" (p. 59).

121. Michael Ross and Roger Buehler, "Creative Remembering," in *Remembering Self* (ed. Neisser and Fivush), 230–31.

122. But there must have been various sorts of eyewitnesses. People who heard Jesus only once or occasionally could have won Christian attention by quoting him or telling stories; and I remember Strauss somewhere remarking that such individuals, in the absence of better-informed disciples, might have been tempted to tell more than they really knew firsthand. Would that not be, if I may use the term, human nature?

123. The preceding two sentences borrow heavily from Davis and Loftus, "Misinformation in Adult Witness Memory," 220.

124. "Exact word-for-word parallels are not found in any Synoptic parallel of 32 words or more" (McIver and Carroll, "Existence of Written Sources," 667–87).

125. Davis and Loftus, "Misinformation in Adult Witness Testimony," 218.

2

More Than a Sage

The Eschatology of Jesus

The time scheme, the calendar, for a messianic movement
has but a single date: now.

—Harris Lenowitz

I wish I could believe that Jesus, as one theologian from the nineteenth
century put it, "thrust aside apocalyptic questions, or gave them an ideal
turn, and floated them away on the current of spiritual religion."[1] But I do not.
For many years now, I have thought that, on the controverted issue of Jesus
and eschatology, the evidence compels us to adopt the paradigm that Johannes
Weiss and Albert Schweitzer bequeathed to New Testament scholarship: Jesus
was an apocalyptic prophet.[2] I have revised my theology accordingly.[3]

1. James Martineau, *The Seat of Authority in Religion* (4th ed.; London: Longmans, Green,
1898), 322.
2. Johannes Weiss, *Jesus' Proclamation of the Kingdom of God* (trans. and ed. Richard
Hyde Hiers and David Larrimore Holland; Philadelphia: Fortress, 1971); Albert Schweitzer, *The
Quest of the Historical Jesus* (Minneapolis: Fortress, 2001). For my earlier work on behalf of
this conclusion, see *Jesus of Nazareth: Millenarian Prophet* (Philadelphia: Fortress, 1998) and
my contributions to *The Apocalyptic Jesus: A Debate* (ed. Robert J. Miller; Santa Rosa, CA:
Polebridge, 2001). For a helpful survey of the discussion, see Jörg Frey, "Die Apokalyptik als
Herausforderung der neutestamentlichen Wissenschaft. Zum Problem: Jesus und die Apokalyp-
tik," in *Apokalyptik als Herausforderung neutestamentlicher Theologie* (ed. Michael Becker and
Markus Öhler; WUNT 2/214; Tübingen: Mohr Siebeck, 2006), 23–94. On the ideological factors
usually involved, see Dale C. Allison Jr., *Resurrecting Jesus: The Earliest Christian Tradition and
Its Interpreters* (New York: T & T Clark, 2005), 111–48; also Klaus Koch, *The Rediscovery of
Apocalyptic* (SBT 2/22; London: SCM Press, 1972), esp. 57–97; and the instructive and fascinat-
ing survey of opinion regarding Mark 13 in G. R. Beasley-Murray, *Jesus and the Last Days: The
Interpretation of the Olivet Discourse* (Peabody, MA: Hendrickson, 1993), 1–79.
3. See Dale C. Allison Jr., *The Historical Christ and the Theological Jesus* (Grand Rapids:
Eerdmans, 2009), 90–101.

By "apocalyptic prophet" I do not mean that Jesus belonged to any supposed "apocalyptic movement."[4] Nor do I hold that his teaching featured the defining traits of the extant written apocalypses. If one insists on associating the adjective *apocalyptic* with timetables, numerology, and esoterism, with revelatory ascents, mythological beasts, and maplike forecasts, then *apocalyptic* is the wrong word for Jesus, who, in our sources, is innocent of such interests.[5]

That is not how I use the word in this chapter. My claim, instead, is that Jesus held what we may call, for lack of a better expression, an "apocalyptic eschatology."[6] The words are convenient shorthand for a cluster of themes well attested in postexilic Jewish literature, themes that were prominent in a then-popular account of the world that ran, in brief, as follows. Although God created a good world, evil spirits have filled it with wickedness, so that it is in disarray and full of injustice. A day is coming, however, when God will repair the broken creation and restore scattered Israel. Before that time, the struggle between good and evil will come to a climax, and a period of great tribulation and unmatched woe will descend upon the world. After that period, God will, perhaps through one or more messianic figures, reward the just and requite the unjust, both living and dead, and then establish divine rule forever.

In my view, if Jesus publicly promoted some version of this story, which makes for profound discontinuity between the present and the future, and if that story was integral to his message and self-conception, and if, furthermore, he hoped that its denouement was near, then we may fairly label his eschatology "apocalyptic."[7] The most obvious and sensible reason for drawing this

---

4. On the problems with this term, see John J. Collins, "Genre, Ideology, and Social Movements in Jewish Apocalypticism," in *Mysteries and Revelations: Apocalyptic Studies since the Uppsala Conference* (ed. John J. Collins and James H. Charlesworth; JSPSup 9; Sheffield: JSOT Press, 1991), 23–24. He writes, "It is a gross over-simplification to speak of 'the apocalyptic movement.' At the least, we must allow for several movements, at different times, not necessarily connected with each other genetically."

5. This is what Rudolf Bultmann meant in affirming that although Jesus adopted an apocalyptic picture of the future, he did so "with significant reduction of detail" (*Theology of the New Testament* [2 vols.; New York: Charles Scribner's Sons, 1951–1955], 1:6). Presumably, scribes authored the apocalypses, which accounts for some of their features, such as timetables and numerical patterns; and Jesus was not a scribe. When James H. Charlesworth urges that Jesus was "not one of the apocalyptists," he does this by contrasting him with the authors of the apocalypses (*Jesus within Judaism: New Light from Exciting Archaeological Discoveries* [New York: Doubleday, 1988], 33–42). I do not deny the sorts of contrasts that Charlesworth observes.

6. For me, the term *eschatology* is purely descriptive. I do not attach to it the sort of personal theological freight documented by Dieter Georgi, "The Interest in Life of Jesus Theology as a Paradigm for the Social History of Biblical Criticism," *HTR* 85 (1992): 51–83.

7. I maintain that Jesus was looking not for the literal "end of the world" but instead for the restoration of a world in disrepair (see Allison, *Jesus of Nazareth*, 154–57). For the argument that ancient Jews took their eschatological expectations more or less literally, see Dale C. Allison Jr., "Jesus and the Victory of Apocalyptic," in *Jesus and the Restoration of Israel: A Critical Assessment of N. T. Wright's "Jesus and the Victory of God"* (ed. Carey C. Newman; Downers

inference is simply the mass of relevant sayings in the extant sources.[8] Here is a list:[9]

1. Two logia from Mark and one from Matthew, all three of which may be variants of the same original, openly declare that the sands of ordinary time have just about run out: Mark 9:1; 13:30; Matt 10:23 (cf. Luke 18:8: "he will vindicate them speedily," RSV).[10] The theme of imminence in Isa 40–55 and Daniel is comparable, as are the explicit declarations in Phil 4:5 ("the Lord is at hand," RSV); Rev 22:10 ("the time is near"); 22:12 ("I am coming soon"); *4 Ezra* 4:26 ("the age is hurrying swiftly to its end"); 8:61 ("judgment is now drawing near"); *2 Bar.* 85:10 ("the advent of the times is very short"); 82:20 ("the end which the Most High prepared is near").

2. Matt 23:34–35 // Luke 11:49–51 (Q), which declares that all the blood shed from the foundation of the world will be "required of this generation" (RSV), reflects the same temporal conviction. "This generation" must be, to quote Christopher Tuckett, the last "in the present order of things," which is why it in particular faces "ultimate responsibility for the whole of preceding history."[11] Closely related are *b. Soṭah* 9a, "The Holy One, blessed be He, does not exact punishment of a man until his

Grove, IL: InterVarsity, 1999), 126–41. Edward Adams, *The Stars Will Fall from Heaven: Cosmic Catastrophe in the New Testament and Its World* (LNTS 347; London: T & T Clark, 2007), now offers strong support for my position, as opposed to N. T. Wright, *Jesus and the Victory of God* (Minneapolis: Fortress, 1996).

8. B. B. Scott has argued that my method in *Jesus of Nazareth* begins with a paradigm, whereas "selection of the data should come first" ("How Did We Get Here?" in *Jesus Reconsidered: Scholarship in the Public Eye* [ed. B. B. Scott; Santa Rosa, CA: Polebridge, 2007], 61). Whether or not that is a fair criticism of my earlier work—I do not think that it is—it cannot be lodged against the present chapter.

9. In order to avoid inflating the evidence, I refrain from citing any sentence or pericope more than once, even when it belongs to more than one group or category.

10. The three sayings have the same basic structure:
    (a) "Amen" +
      (b) "I say to you" +
        (c) statement about what will not happen +
          (d) temporal conjunction +
            (e) statement about the consummation
See further Allison, *Jesus of Nazareth*, 148–50. On the closely related John 8:51–52, which appears to be yet another variant of the same saying, see Barnabas Lindars, "Discourse and Tradition: The Use of the Sayings of Jesus in the Discourses of the Fourth Gospel," *JSNT* 13 (1981): 95–96; Wendy E. Sproston North, *The Lazarus Story within Johannine Tradition* (JSNTSup 212; Sheffield: Sheffield Academic Press, 2001), 58–101. In my judgment, no one has demonstrated that Mark 9:1 and Matt 10:23 are post-Easter formulations, although no one has demonstrated the contrary, either.

11. Christopher M. Tuckett, *Q and the History of Early Christianity: Studies on Q* (Edinburgh: T & T Clark, 1996), 145.

measure (of guilt) is filled," and the many Jewish texts that portray the last generation as exceedingly perverse: "the gathering momentum of wickedness just before" eschatological judgment "is a widely attested pattern in apocalyptic literature."[12]

3. "The day of judgment" (ἡμέρα κρίσεως) and its abbreviated stand-ins, "the judgment" and "that day," envisage the eschatological assize: Matt 10:15; Luke 10:12 (Q); Matt 11:22, 24; 12:36; Luke 10:14 (Q); so too the Johannine sayings concerning "the last day": John 6:39–40, 44, 54; 11:24. In Second Temple Judaism, "the day of judgment," which does not occur in the Hebrew Bible or the LXX, had become a synonym for "the day of the Lord," understood as the eschatological trial that will reward the righteous and punish the wicked.[13]

4. Matt 10:28; Luke 12:5 (Q); Mark 9:43–45 (cf. Matt 18:8–9); Matt 5:22; 23:15, 33 refer to "Gehenna" (Γέεννα; rabbinic גיה[י]נם), the antithesis of heaven, the frightful place of postmortem or end-time punishment (see also, e.g., *1 En.* 90:24; *Sib. Or.* 4:186; *2 Bar.* 85:13; P.Oxy. 840 recto; *Gk. Apoc. Ezra* 1:9; *m. Qidd.* 4:14; *y. Pe'ah* 15c [1:1]).

5. That place of punishment, as so often in Jewish apocalyptic texts (e.g., *1 En.* 10:6; 54:1–2; 90:24–25; 100:9; *Sib. Or.* 3:53–54; *4 Ezra* 7:36–38; 13:10–11; *Apoc. Ab.* 31:2–5), is a place of fire according to Matt 7:19; Mark 9:47–48; and perhaps John 15:6. Likely related is Luke 12:49 ("I came to cast fire upon the earth," RSV), which could look back upon the prophecy that Matt 3:11; Luke 3:16 (Q) assigns to John the Baptist: "the one who . . . is to come . . . will baptize you in Spirit and fire."[14]

6. Matt 18:6–7; Luke 17:1–2 (Q); Mark 9:42; *1 Clem.* 46:8 have Jesus warn against harming others, lest one face a fate worse than being thrown into the sea with a millstone around one's neck. As the commentators universally recognize, "the only way it could be better for the offender (συμφέρει αὐτῷ) to have a large millstone fastened around his neck and

---

12. Loren Stuckenbruck, *1 Enoch 91–108* (CEJL; Berlin: de Gruyter, 2007), 174–75, referring to the common link with the cataclysmic evil that preceded the flood. See, for example, *Jub.* 23:11–25; *1 En.* 91:5–7; 93:9; 1QpHab 2:5–10; *Sib. Or.* 3:175–95; 4:152–61; 2 Tim 3:1–5; *m. Soṭah* 9:15; Lactantius, *Epit.* 71(66). See discussion in Evald Lövestam, *Jesus and "This Generation": A New Testament Study* (ConBNT 25; Stockholm: Almqvist & Wiksell, 1995). That wickedness will increase as the golden age approaches is a commonplace in the history of religions; it appears in, for example, the Iranian sources *Jāmāsp Nāmak* 62, 68, 69; *Zand ī Wahman Yašt* 4:21 ("During that most evil time a bird will have more reverence than the religious Iranian").

13. See, for example, *1 En.* 10:12; 100:4; *Jub.* 4:19; Jdt 16:17; *T. Levi* 1:1; *4 Ezra* 12:34; Gk. *L.A.E.* 26:4. Later rabbinic literature uses יום הדין in a similar way—for example, *y. Ber.* 12c (8:6); *y. Ḥag.* 77a (2:1). Variations include "day of great judgment" or "great day of judgment" (*1 En.* 10:6), "day of the wrath of judgment" (*Jub.* 24:30), "day of the Lord's judgment" (*Pss. Sol.* 15:12), "days of judgment" (*1 En.* 27:4), and "hour of his judgment" (Rev 14:7). On how "day" functions in the Synoptics, see Werner Georg Kümmel, *Promise and Fulfilment: The Eschatological Message of Jesus* (SBT 23; London: SCM Press, 1957), 36–43.

14. See further below, pp. 216–18.

drowned in the sea is if he has an even worse eschatological fate in store at the final judgment."[15] Mark's Gospel tellingly follows up 9:42 with sayings about Gehenna (9:43–48).

7. As in Zoroastrian pictures of hell (e.g., *Yasna* 31:20), there are references to "the outer darkness" (Matt 22:13; 25:30; cf. *Gk. Apoc. Ezra* 4:37; *T. Jac.* 5:9) and to "the weeping and gnashing of teeth" (Matt 24:51b; cf. *Sib. Or.* 2:305–6; 8:104–5, 231, 350).

8. The tale of the unfaithful slave in Matt 24:45–51a // Luke 12:42–46 (Q) functions as a warning about the coming judgment. In Luke, the speech introducing the parable concludes with "You also must be ready, for the Son of Man is coming at an unexpected hour" (12:35–40). In Matthew, the parable itself ends with "there will be weeping and gnashing of teeth."

9. The enigmatic Matt 24:40–41; Luke 17:34–35 (Q; cf. *Gos. Thom.* 61), which envisions one person being taken and another left, means either that the wicked will be plucked from the earth (cf. Matt 13:41) or, more likely, that the righteous will be escorted to meet the Son of Man in the air (cf. Mark 13:27; 1 Thess 4:17; *Apoc. El.* 5:4).[16] Whichever option is correct, the saying portends a supernatural sorting at the final judgment.[17]

10. Luke 17:26–30 (Q; cf. Matt 24:37–39)[18] likens the coming assize to Noah's flood and Sodom's demise, both of those primeval calamities being, in Jewish and Christian lore, popular prototypes of the last judgment and end of the present age.[19]

11. Matt 13:36–43 construes the parable of the weeds among the wheat (Matt 13:24–30; *Gos. Thom.* 57) as an allegory of the division, on the final day, of the just and the unjust.

12. The parable of the net, in its Matthean adaptation (13:47–48; contrast *Gos. Thom.* 8), depicts the same division under a different figure: "So it will be at the end of the age. The angels will come out and separate the evil from the righteous and throw them into the furnace of fire, where there will be weeping and gnashing of teeth" (13:49–50).

15. Brian Han Gregg, *The Historical Jesus and the Final Judgment Sayings in Q* (WUNT 2/207; Tübingen: Mohr Siebeck, 2006), 241.

16. John 14:3 ("I will come again and will take you to myself") is likely a revision of this expectation. *Didache* 9:4; 10:5, like Mark 13:27, appear to describe this event in terms of the eschatological return of the Diaspora Jews (see p. 72).

17. See further Christian Riniker, *Die Gerichtsverkündigung Jesu* (EH 23/653; Bern: Peter Lang, 1999), 63–69, 73.

18. On this unit, see below, pp. 382–86.

19. For the flood, see Isa 24:18; *Jub.* 20:5–6; *1 En.* 1–16; 67:10–11; 93:4 (the flood is "the first consummation"); Sir 16:7; 3 Macc 2:4; *L.A.B.* 3:1–3, 9–10; Josephus, *Ant.* 1.72–76; 2 Pet 2:5; 3:6–7; *2 En.* J 70:10; *Apoc. Adam* 3:3; *3 En.* 45:3; *Mek.* on Exod 18:1; *b. Sanh.* 108a. For Sodom, see *Jub.* 16:6, 9; 22:22; 36:10; 2 Pet 2:6; Jude 7; *Gk. Apoc. Ezra* 2:18–19; 7:12.

13. Matt 25:31–46 is a memorable tableau of the great judgment, prefaced by the simile of a shepherd separating sheep from goats.

14. The threat of eschatological retribution has its counterpart in the promise of heavenly or everlasting reward: Matt 5:12 // Luke 6:23 (Q); Matt 6:19–21 // Luke 12:33–34 (Q); Mark 10:29–30; Matt 5:19; John 6:40; 14:2–3; Gos. Thom. 19, 76, 114.

15. This future reward includes "eternal life" (ζωὴ αἰώνιος: Matt 19:16, 29; Mark 10:17; Luke 10:25; 18:18, 30), a set phrase in Jewish literature around the turn of the era.[20] In the Synoptics, the expression consistently adverts to the eschatological future (in contrast to John's Gospel, which stresses "eternal life" as a present possibility [e.g., 3:36; 6:47, 54]).

16. Luke 16:19–31 encourages deeds of loving-kindness by depicting pleasant reward in "Abraham's bosom" and miserable retribution in "Hades."[21] Admittedly, this is only a morality tale; but like the parable of the sower, which does not intend to be a lesson about farming practices yet presupposes such practices, the parable of the rich man and Lazarus, though not intended to offer details about the afterlife, presupposes postmortem rewards and punishments.

17. The paradoxical sayings about dramatic reversal in status—the first will be last, the last first, and so on (Matt 10:39; Luke 17:33 [Q]; Matt 23:12; Luke 14:11 [Q]; Matt 25:29; Luke 19:26 [Q]; Mark 4:25; 8:35; 10:31; Matt 13:12; Luke 18:14; Gos. Thom. 4)—are not naïvely optimistic observations about everyday human experience. Common sense and proverbial wisdom know that the rich get richer, the poor poorer. This is why Jesus' logia instead use the future tense: "will be exalted," "will keep it [life]," "will be first." Like T. Jud. 25:4[22] and b. Pesaḥ. 50a,[23] they envisage God turning the world upside down, which can only be the upshot of the coming judgment.[24]

18. The prayer "your kingdom come" (ἐλθέτω ἡ βασιλεία σου: Matt 6:10; Luke 11:2 [Q]; Did. 8:2) is more likely than not a plea for God to redeem the world once and for all. This follows from (a) the close parallel in the Kaddish ("May he let his kingdom rule in your lifetime and in your days and in the lifetime of the whole house of Israel, speedily and

20. On this idiom, its Semitic equivalents, and its relationship to "the kingdom of God," see below, pp. 186–89.

21. For helpful history-of-religions background and parallels, see Outi Lehtipuu, The Afterlife Imagery in Luke's Story of the Rich Man and Lazarus (NovTSup 123; Leiden: Brill, 2007).

22. "And those who died in sorrow shall be raised in joy; and those who died in poverty for the Lord's sake shall be made rich; those who died on account of the Lord shall be wakened to life."

23. Rabbi Joseph ben Joshua catches a glimpse of the next world and learns that it is "topsy-turvy," for "those who are on top here are at the bottom there, and those who are at the bottom here are on the top there."

24. See further Allison, Jesus of Nazareth, 131–36; Gregg, Historical Jesus, 261–66.

soon");[25] (b) the eschatological associations that the noun "kingdom" (מלכות/βασιλεία) and the verb "to rule" (מלך/βασιλεύω) often have in old Jewish literature;[26] (c) the use of "come" (ἐλθέτω), which recalls the "coming" of God in Jewish expectation;[27] (d) the many Synoptic sayings

25. See b. Ber. 3a; b. Soṭah 49a. Compare also (although their dates are uncertain) the eleventh benediction of the Amidah (Palestinian version: "Restore our judges as at first, and our counselors as at the beginning, and reign over us"); the Aleinu prayer ("We thus hope in you, O Lord our God, that we may soon behold the glory of your might . . . when the world will be perfected under the rule of the Almighty"); and the Musaf prayer for Rosh Hashanah ("You, O Lord our God, speedily rule as king over all your works"). The Kaddish likely originated as a prayer following public sermons, and according to Joseph Heinemann (Prayer in the Talmud: Forms and Patterns [SJ 9; Berlin: de Gruyter, 1977], 24, 256), it existed in Tannaitic times. For the usual reasons for an early dating, see Annette Steudel, "Die Heiligung des Gottesnamens im Vaterunser: Erwägungen zum antik-jüdischen Hintergrund," in Judaistik und neutestamentliche Wissenschaft: Standorte, Grenzen, Beziehungen (ed. Lutz Doering, Hans-Günther Waubke, and Florian Wilk; FRLANT 226; Göttingen: Vandenhoeck & Ruprecht, 2008), 254. Helmut Merkel observes that "your kingdom come" differs from the Kaddish in that it lacks "in your lifetime" and "speedily and soon" ("Die Gottesherrschaft in der Verkündigung Jesu," in Königsherrschaft Gottes und himmlischer Kult im Judentum, Urchristentum und in der hellenistischen Welt [ed. Martin Hengel and Anna Maria Schwemer; WUNT 2/55; Tübingen: Mohr Siebeck, 1991], 138–39). But this hardly matters, as people typically pray in the hope that they will be answered "speedily and soon," and certainly before they are dead and gone.

26. See Isa 24:23; 52:7; Ezek 20:33; Dan 7:14, 18, 27; Mic 4:7; Zech 14:9, 16–17; Pss. Sol. 17:3; 1QM 6:6; 12:7, 16; 4Q246; 4Q521; 1Q28b 3:5; 4:25–26; 5:21; 4Q203 frg. 9; T. Mos. 10:1; Sib. Or. 3:46–48, 767; T. Jud. 22:2–3; 24:4–5; T. Dan 5:13; 2 Bar. 39:7; 73:1; Mek. on Exod 15:18; 17:16; Mek. R. Simeon b. Yohai 36:2 on Exod 15:18; Tg. Isa. on 31:4; 40:9; 52:7; Tg. Mic 4:7; Tg. Zech 14:9; cf. Jub. 1:28. For reviews and discussion, see, in addition to excursus 1 below, pp. 164–204, Odo Camponovo, Königtum, Königsherrschaft und Reich Gottes in den frühjüdischen Schriften (OBO 58; Freiburg: Universitätsverlag; Göttingen: Vandenhoeck & Ruprecht, 1984); Craig A. Evans, "Daniel in the New Testament: Visions of God's Kingdom," in The Book of Daniel: Composition and Reception (ed. John J. Collins and Peter W. Flint; VTSup 83; Leiden: Brill, 2001), 490–527; Christian Grappe, Le royaume de Dieu: Avant, avec et après Jésus (MdB 42; Geneva: Labor et Fides, 2001), 13–135. Those who propose that "kingdom of God" was a sapiential expression for Jesus must appeal to texts from the Diaspora (e.g., Philo and Wisdom of Solomon; cf. Sextus, Sent. 105). Further, the remark by James M. Robinson that "kingdom of God" does not occur in "Jewish apocalypticism" ("Foreword: A Down-to-Earth Jesus," in John J. Rousseau and Rami Arav, Jesus and His World: An Archaeological and Cultural Dictionary [Minneapolis: Fortress, 1995], xvi n. 5) appears to overlook Pss. Sol. 17:3 (ἡ βασιλεία τοῦ θεοῦ ἡμῶν εἰς τὸν αἰῶνα ἐπὶ τὰ ἔθνη ἐν κρίσει). It would, moreover, be beyond pedantic to generalize about ἡ βασιλεία τοῦ θεοῦ without taking notice of the related, more common equivalent expressions, such as "the kingdom," "his kingdom," and "your kingdom" (e.g., Dan 4:31; 6:26; 1 En. 84:2; 103:1; 1QM 6:6; 12:7–8; T. Mos. 10:1; Mek. on Exod 17:16), all of which, as synonyms of ἡ βασιλεία τοῦ θεοῦ, also appear in the Synoptics (Matt 4:23; Matt 6:10 // Luke 11:2 [Q]; Matt 9:35; 13:41; 16:28; Luke 23:42).

27. For example, Isa 35:4; 40:9–10; Zech 14:5; Mal 3:2; 1 En. 1:3–9; 25:3; Jub. 1:22–28; T. Levi 5:2; T. Mos. 10:1–12; Tg. Zech 2:14–15. See discussion in Jacques Schlosser, Le règne de Dieu dans les dits de Jésus (2 vols.; EBib; Paris: Gabalda, 1980), 1:269–84. Compare also the use of "come" in Mic 4:8 ("to you it shall come, the former dominion shall come, the sovereignty of daughter Jerusalem"), in 2 Bar. 44:12 ("that age is coming that will remain forever"), and in the rabbinic העולם הבא (= "the world/age to come"), on which see below, pp. 190–99.

in which the kingdom must be yet future;[28] (e) the close association in
Jewish liturgy between the eschatological arrival of God's kingdom and
the sanctification of God's name (cf. Matt 6:9 // Luke 11:2 [Q]: "hallowed be your name").[29] Theophylact understandably explicated the
petition this way: "This is the second coming . . . the resurrection and
the judgment."[30] The eschatological character of "your kingdom come"
may explain why a scribe altered "your kingdom come" in Luke 11:2
to "your Holy Spirit come (upon us) and cleanse us":[31] as time passed,
a prayer for the Spirit seemed more relevant to some.[32] Were the Lord's
Prayer not about a kingdom yet to come but instead about a kingdom
already present, we might expect something like what appears in another
rewrite of ἐλθέτω ἡ βασιλεία σου, this one in the late Arabic version of
the Lord's Prayer that Shlomo Pines published: "Our Father that art in
heaven, Your name is holy and your dominion precious, your command
is executed in the heavens and earth. Nothing that you demand is beyond
your power and nothing that you wish is withheld from you."[33]

19. In addition to the Lord's Prayer, several additional sentences attach
temporal verbs to βασιλεία: Mark 1:15 (ἤγγικεν); Matt 10:7 // Luke
10:9 (Q) (ἤγγικεν); Matt 12:28 // Luke 11:20 (Q) (ἔφθασεν); Luke 22:18
(ἔλθῃ). These sentences do not refer to a changeless reality or to an
"always available divine kingdom."[34] Here ἤγγικεν means, as the NRSV
translates, "has come near,"[35] and ἔφθασεν scarcely adverts to what has

28. For example, Mark 9:47 (those freed from sins of hand, eye, and foot have not yet entered the kingdom, just as those who have not avoided such sins have not yet been thrown into
Gehenna); 14:25 (Jesus does not yet drink new wine in the kingdom); Matt 8:11–12 // Luke
13:28–29 (Q) (people have not yet come from east and west); Matt 13:41 (the angels have not
yet rounded up the wicked).
29. See Moshe Weinfeld, "The Day of the Lord: Aspirations for the Kingdom of God in
the Bible and Jewish Liturgy," in Studies in Bible 1986 (ScrHier 31; Jerusalem: Magnes, 1986),
366–69; Steudel, "Heiligung des Gottesnamens," 242–56.
30. Theophylact, Comm. Matt. ad loc. (PG 123:203D–205A). Cf. Tertullian, Or. 5; Cyril of
Alexandria, Hom. Luke 73 (CSCO 140 [Scriptores Syri 70], p. 291); and see further the exposition by John P. Meier, A Marginal Jew: Rethinking the Historical Jesus (4 vols.; New York:
Doubleday, 1991–2009), 2:294–301.
31. Luke 11:2 (162 700 Tert GrNy Max); cf. Acts Thom. 27.
32. Note that Tertullian, the earliest witness to the alternative reading (Marc. 4:26), tells us
in his Apology that Christians actually "pray . . . for postponement of the end" (Apol. 39).
33. Shlomo Pines, "'Israel, My Firstborn' and the Sonship of Jesus," in Studies in Mysticism
and Religion, Presented to Gershom G. Scholem on His Seventieth Birthday (ed. E. E. Urbach,
R. J. Zwi Werblowsky, and C. Wirszubski; Jerusalem: Magnes, 1967), 184. The quoted words
are from 'Abd al-Jabbar's Tathbit dala'il al-nubuwwa.
34. The words are those of John Dominic Crossan, The Historical Jesus: The Life of a
Mediterranean Jewish Peasant (San Francisco: HarperCollins, 1991), 292. They do, by contrast,
rightly characterize the sayings in Gos. Thom. 3, 49, 113. See further below, p. 98.
35. Not "has arrived"; see n. 424.

been true all along.[36] Rather, something dramatic and unprecedented has begun to unfold. In these sayings, "the kingdom of God" is, as Gustaf Dalman recognized long ago, nearly synonymous with "the age to come" or "the new creation."[37]

20. The futurity of the kingdom is manifest also in the logia about entering it: Mark 10:15, 23–25; Matt 5:20; 7:21; 23:13. The meaning is plain enough from (a) the future tense in Mark 10:23 (εἰσελεύσονται) and Matt 7:21 (εἰσελεύσεται); (b) the parallelism in Mark 9:43–47 (εἰς τὴν ζωήν . . . εἰς τὴν βασιλείαν); (c) the eschatological orientation of the exhortation to pass through a narrow door or gate in Matt 7:13; Luke 13:24 (Q); and (d) the circumstance that it is not the kingdom that enters people but rather people who enter the kingdom: the saints will, at the end of days, cross the threshold into a redeemed world. As with Paul's statements about the saints "inheriting" the kingdom of God (1 Cor 6:9–10; 15:50; Gal 5:19–21), the background for these sayings is presumably the memory of Israel entering Canaan.[38]

21. Mark 10:30 invokes the disjunction between "this age" and "the age to come" (cf. Matt 12:32; Luke 20:34–35), as do the rabbis when they speak of העולם הזה והעולם הבא.

22. Some logia about the Son of Man allude to the scene of the last judgment in Dan 7: Mark 13:26; 14:62; Matt 10:32–33 // Luke 12:8–9 (Q); John 5:27; P.Oxy. 654.31.[39] Analogous are the texts about the Son of Man in 1 En. 46:3–5; 62:2–16; 69:26–29.

23. The canonical Jesus, like the Pharisaic Paul in Acts 23:6–8 and in accord with orthodox rabbinic opinion in m. Sanh. 10:1, believes in the resurrection of the dead: Mark 12:18–27; Matt 12:41–42 // Luke 11:31–32 (Q);[40]

---

36. Heikki Räisänen remarks, "Q 11:20 does not speak of God's eternal, unchanging kingship, but of something novel, of a change in the situation" ("Exorcisms and the Kingdom: Is Q 11:20 a Saying of the Historical Jesus?" in Symbols and Strata: Essays on the Sayings Gospel Q [ed. Risto Uro; SESJ 45; Helsinki: Finnish Exegetical Society; Göttingen: Vandenhoeck & Ruprecht, 1996], 140).

37. Gustaf Dalman, The Words of Jesus Considered in the Light of Post-biblical Jewish Writings and the Aramaic Language (Edinburgh: T & T Clark, 1902), 135. See further below, pp. 164–204.

38. See further below, pp. 179–81.

39. See also 4 Ezra 13:1–4. On the background of Matt 10:32–33 // Luke 12:8–9 (Q) in Dan 7, see Dale C. Allison Jr., The Intertextual Jesus: Scripture in Q (Valley Forge, PA: Trinity Press International, 2000), 130–31.

40. According to G. B. Caird, Matt 12:41–42 // Luke 11:31–32 (Q) does not refer to the resurrection, for both ἐγείρειν and ἀνιστάναι can mean simply "to appear," and this logion uses these verbs of witnesses appearing in court to give testimony (cf. Mark 14:57) ("Eschatology and Politics: Some Misconceptions," in Biblical Studies: Essays in Honor of William Barclay [ed. Johnston R. McKay and James F. Miller; Philadelphia: Westminster, 1976], 75–77). So too T. Francis Glasson, The Second Advent: The Origin of the New Testament Doctrine (2nd rev. ed.; London: Epworth, 1947), 128. Admittedly, "will not stand/rise in the judgment" occurs in

Luke 14:12–14; John 5:28–29 (cf. P.Oxy. 654.31: "nothing is buried that will not be raised";[41] and the agraphon in Hippolytus, *Haer.* 5.8.23–24: "the dead will spring up from their graves").

24. Mark 13:3–23 features the widespread belief, with roots in Iranian tradition and parallels throughout worldwide millenarian movements, that the kingdom of Satan will not go away without a fight (e.g., 1QM; *T. Dan* 5:10–13), that unprecedented tribulation will herald the advent of the new age, that "there shall be a time of anguish, such as has never occurred since nations first came into existence" (Dan 12:1; cf. Isa 24–27; Ezek 38–39; *4 Ezra* 6:24; Rev 3:10; *m. Sanh.* 9:15), a time when extraordinary trials will afflict the saints. This theologoumenon also probably illuminates Matt 11:12–13 // Luke 16:16 (Q) (the kingdom suffers violence);[42] Matt 10:34–36 // Luke 12:51–53 (Q) (there is not peace but the sword; cf. Mark 13:12; *Gos. Thom.* 16); Mark 9:49 ("everyone will be salted with fire");[43] and perhaps other texts as well.[44]

25. Several times Jesus admonishes people to be on the alert because the eschatological crisis may come at any time: Matt 24:42–44 // Luke 12:39–40 (Q); Mark 13:33–37; Matt 25:1–13; Luke 12:35–38; 21:34–36; *Gos. Thom.* 21 (cf. *1 En.* 94:1, 6–7; 95:6). Justin (*Dial.* 47.5) and Clement

---

Ps 1:5 without eschatological sense, but later the phrase gained such meaning (see *m. Sanh.* 10:3 and Tg. Ps 1:1, which substitutes "in the great day" for "in the judgment"). Further, both Matt 12:41–42 and Luke 11:31–32 have the future tense, and ἐν τῇ κρίσει and γενεὰ ταύτη/αὕτη usually have eschatological content in the Jesus tradition. Note also that the Q saying presupposes a universal judgment, for it involves the Queen of Sheba, the Ninevites, and Jews of Jesus' time.

41. See further Allison, *Jesus of Nazareth*, 136–41. On the reading in P.Oxy. 654.31, see H.-C. Puech, "Un logion de Jésus sur bandelette funéraire," *RHR* 147 (1955): 126–29.

42. In Matt 11:12–13 // Luke 16:16 (Q), John the Baptist marks a division within sacred history. After him, or with his appearance, the kingdom of God suffers violence. Although rudimentary, the schematization reminds one of those Jewish apocalypses that display a periodical understanding of history, separating it into segments (e.g., Dan 7; 9; *Testament of Moses*; the Apocalypse of Weeks [*1 En.* 93 + 91:12–17]).

43. Although this remains in the realm of conjecture, perhaps the best attempt to explain Mark 9:49 is that someone translated כל אנש בנורא יטבל as "Everyone will be salted with fire," a possible rendering of the Aramaic, instead of "Everyone will be baptized with fire" (cf. Matt 3:11 // Luke 3:16 [Q]; Luke 12:49–50), the intended meaning. See T. J. Baarda, "Mark ix.49," *NTS* 5 (1959): 318–21; Daniel Frayer-Griggs, "'Everyone Will Be Baptized in Fire': Mark 9.49, Q 3.16, and the Baptism of the Coming One," *JSHJ* 7 (2009): 254–85.

44. The logion in *Gos. Thom.* 82, "Whoever is near to me is near the fire, and whoever is far from me is far from the kingdom" (cf. Origen, *Hom. Jer.* 50.1[3].3), and the agraphon in Tertullian, "No one can obtain the kingdom of heaven who has not passed through temptation" (*Bapt.* 20 [cf. Acts 14:22]), may at first have related to eschatological distress. On the theme in general and on Mark 13 in particular, see Brant Pitre, *Jesus, the Tribulation, and the End of the Exile: Restoration Eschatology and the Origin of the Atonement* (WUNT 2/204; Tübingen: Mohr Siebeck; Grand Rapids: Baker Academic, 2005). On Matt 11:12–13 // Luke 16:16 (Q), see ibid., 159–77. On Matt 10:34–36 // Luke 12:51–53 (Q) // *Gos. Thom.* 16, see ibid., 198–216; Dale C. Allison Jr., "Q 12.51–53 and Mk 9:11–13 and the Messianic Woes," in *Authenticating the Words of Jesus* (ed. Bruce Chilton and Craig A. Evans; NTTS 28/1; Leiden: Brill, 1998), 289–310.

of Alexandria (*Quis div.* 40.2) transmit an agraphon to similar effect: "In whatever circumstances I overtake you, in them indeed will I judge you."[45] Ben Meyer appropriately comments on this motif: "It does seem almost absurd to conceive of an urgent eschatological appeal based on the motif, not of imminent, but simply of sudden, judgment—leaving open the question whether this or some other generation will be surprised by the actual suddenness of its coming."[46]

26. Mark 14:25 ("drink it new in the kingdom of God"); Luke 14:15 ("eat bread in the kingdom of God"), 24 ("none of those who were invited will taste my dinner"); 22:30 ("eat and drink at my table in my kingdom") envision the eschatological banquet.[47] The prophecy of miraculous agricultural abundance that Papias (*apud* Irenaeus, *Haer.* 5.33.3) attributed to Jesus belongs to the same world of thought.[48]

27. Some texts identify Jesus as "the Messiah," an end-time, royal deliverer: Mark 8:27–30; 9:41; 11:9–10; Matt 23:10; John 1:41; 4:25, 29; 6:14–15; 9:22; 10:24; 11:27 (cf. Mark 15:2, 9, 18, 26, 32).[49]

28. The canonical Jesus, in a way reminiscent of some Dead Sea Scrolls, regards eschatological oracles in the Hebrew Bible as being fulfilled in his own time. Examples include Matt 11:10 // Luke 7:27 (Q), citing Mal

---

45. On this saying, widely attested, see Joachim Jeremias, *Unknown Sayings of Jesus* (2nd ed.; London: SPCK, 1964), 83–88; Aelred Baker, "Justin's Agraphon in the *Dialogue with Trypho*," *JBL* 87 (1968): 277–87.

46. Ben F. Meyer, The Aims of Jesus (London: SCM Press, 1979), 316 n. 40. Similarly, T. W. Manson remarks, "There would be no point in telling men to be on the alert for something which might not happen until centuries after they had died" (The Teaching of Jesus: Studies in Its Form and Content [2nd ed.; Cambridge: Cambridge University Press, 1967], 278). For a different view, see Ben Witherington III, Jesus, Paul, and the End of the World: A Comparative Study in New Testament Eschatology (Downers Grove, IL: InterVarsity, 1992), 15–48. According to Karl Adam, "It was easy enough for the early Christians to interpret his promise, 'The Son of Man will come suddenly,' to mean, 'The Son of Man will come immediately'" (The Christ of Faith: The Christology of the Church [New York: Pantheon, 1957], 281). It was so easy because, for Jesus, "suddenly" and "immediately" amounted to the same thing.

47. Cf. Isa 25:6–8; 55:1–2; 65:13–14; 1Q28a 2:2–22; *1 En.* 62:14; Rev 19:7–9; *2 Bar.* 29:4–6; *2 En.* J 42:5; *3 En.* 48A:10; *m. 'Abot* 3:17; *b. Pesaḥ.* 119b. The eschatological outlook in Mark 14:25 has its parallel in the eucharistic traditions in 1 Cor 11:26 ("For as often as you eat this bread and drink the cup, you proclaim the Lord's death until he comes"); *Did.* 10:6 ("May grace come and may this world pass away . . . Maranatha!"). From this evidence, Helmut Koester argues that the eschatological component of the early Christian community meal "derives directly from Jesus himself" ("The Memory of Jesus' Death and the Worship of the Risen Lord," *HTR* 91 [1998]: 345–46; idem, *From Jesus to the Gospels: Interpreting the New Testament in Its Context* [Minneapolis: Fortress, 2007], 220–21).

48. Cf. Ezek 34:27; 36:21–38; Amos 9:13; *1 En.* 10:18–19; *2 Bar.* 29:5–7. On these two related motifs, see Peter-Ben Smit, *Fellowship and Food in the Kingdom: Eschatological Meals and Scenes of Utopian Abundance in the New Testament* (WUNT 2/234; Tübingen: Mohr Siebeck, 2008).

49. See further below, pp. 279–93.

3:1; Mark 9:13, adverting to Mal 4:5–6; Mark 14:27, quoting Zech 13:7 (cf. P.Vindob. G 2325); and Matt 5:17, asserting in general that Jesus fulfills "the law and the prophets."[50]

29. In Matt 11:2–4 // Luke 7:18–23 (Q), Jesus, responding to a query from John the Baptist, implicitly equates himself with the latter's "coming one," an eschatological judge (see Matt 3:11–12 // Luke 7:16–17 [Q]).[51] He does this, in a way paralleled in 4Q521 (cf. also *Sib. Or.* 8:205–8), by taking up the language of prophetic texts in Isaiah (Isa 26:19; 29:18–19; 35:5–6; 42:18; 61:1), implying his fulfillment of them.[52] The Beatitudes, where Jesus comforts those who mourn (Matt 5:3, 4, 6, 11–12 // Luke 6:20–23 [Q]), similarly echo Isa 61 and so likewise associate his ministry with that eschatological oracle (see p. 265 n. 176); and Luke 4:16–19 has Jesus reading from Isa 61 and declaring its prophecies to be realized in his ministry. Comparable is the repeated borrowing from Isa 61 in 11QMelchizedek, where the central figure, the heavenly Melchizedek, ushers in the eschaton.[53]

30. Matt 19:28 // Luke 22:28–30 (Q) promises the twelve disciples that they will "judge," which means either "rule" or "pass judgment upon,"[54] the twelve tribes of Israel.[55] This presupposes the return of those scattered abroad in the Diaspora, as does Matt 8:11–12 // Luke 13:28–29 (Q), for the "many" who come "from east and west" and are hosted by the patriarchs must be or at least include the lost tribes.[56] Mark 13:27 also

50. See further below, pp. 79–82.

51. See further below, pp. 274–78.

52. On the eschatological interpretation of Isa 61 in Judaism, see James A. Sanders, "From Isaiah 61 to Luke 4," in Craig A. Evans and James A. Sanders, *Luke and Scripture: The Function of Sacred Tradition in Luke-Acts* (Minneapolis: Fortress, 1993), 46–69.

53. On Jesus and Isa 61, see further below, pp. 264–66.

54. For an overview of the discussion on this issue, see J. Verheyden, "The Conclusion of Q: Eschatology in Q 22,28–30," in *The Sayings Source Q and the Historical Jesus* (ed. A. Lindemann; BETL 158; Leuven: Leuven University Press, 2001), 695–718. Perhaps here κρίνω has both meanings.

55. Although Acts 1 tells of finding a replacement for Judas, Acts 12 says nothing about appointing one for the martyred James, son of Zebedee. This probably is because the office of the Twelve was not ecclesiastical but eschatological: James will become a judge when he rises from the dead, whereas Judas has forfeited his position and so needs a replacement. See F. J. Foakes-Jackson and Kirsopp Lake, "The Public Teaching of Jesus and His Choice of the Twelve," in *The Beginnings of Christianity, Part I: The Acts of the Apostles* (ed. F. J. Foakes-Jackson and Kirsopp Lake; 5 vols.; London: Macmillan, 1920), 3:299.

56. See Dale C. Allison Jr., *The Jesus Tradition in Q* (Harrisburg, PA: Trinity Press International, 1997), 176–91; also below, pp. 72–76. Both Gregg ("the many who are coming are principally the Diaspora Jews" [*Historical Jesus*, 229–32]) and Jari Laaksonen (*Jesus und das Land: Das Gelobte Land in der Verkündigung Jesu* [Åbo: Åbo Akademi University Press, 2002], 302–5) endorse my argument to this effect as persuasive. Despite criticism of my view by Pitre (*Jesus*, 279–83) and Michael Bird ("Who Comes from the East and the West? Luke 13.28–29/ Matt 8.11–12 and the Historical Jesus," *NTS* 52 [2006]: 441–57), the two agree that the saying

belongs here, for the gathering of "his elect from the four winds" likely referred at some pre-Markan stage to the ingathering of the Jewish Diaspora (cf. Deut 30:3–4; see also n. 56).

31. Mark 14:58 and John 2:19 have Jesus prophesy that he will build a new temple. The saying posits the destruction of the present sanctuary (cf. Mark 13:2; Luke 19:44; Acts 6:14; *Gos. Thom.* 71), and the scenario of the temple's destruction and renewal is otherwise known from Jewish visions of the latter days: *1 En.* 91:12–13; 11Q19 29:8–10; *Sib. Or.* 5:397–433.[57]

32. *Gos. Thom.* 111 transmits a saying in which Jesus declares, "The heavens and earth will be rolled up in your presence" (cf. Isa 34:4; *Sib. Or.* 3:81–82; 8:233, 413; Heb 1:10–12; Rev 6:14).

Interpretation of the Catalog

Given the abundance of germane materials, we can scarcely scold the author of Mark for including, in his précis of Jesus' proclamation, "The kingdom of God is at hand" (1:15 RSV). Whether or not Jesus uttered some Aramaic equivalent, Mark's words sum up fairly what the evangelist saw when he surveyed his tradition.[58] In fact, more material pertains to eschatology than to exorcism, far more by my reckoning. Should this not give pause to any who

---

includes the ingathering of the Jewish Diaspora. Our disagreement concerns only whether Gentiles are also involved. Note that Matt 8:11–12 // Luke 13:28–29 (Q), taken at face value, possesses a geographical dimension: the people who come from east and west presumably arrive at the eschatological center of the world, Mount Zion.

57. Cf. *Jub.* 1:27; 4Q174 1:1–3; Tob 14:5; *Mek.* on Exod 15:18. For discussion, see Jostein Ådna, *Jesu Stellung zum Tempel: Die Tempelaktion und das Tempelwort als Ausdruck seiner messianischen Sendung* (WUNT 2/119; Tübingen: Mohr Siebeck, 2000), 25–89. See further Allison, *Jesus of Nazareth*, 97–101, and below, pp. 237–38. Although traditionally cited in this connection, *1 En.* 90:28–36 may not be relevant. For the view that it is not, see Patrick A. Tiller, *A Commentary on the Animal Apocalypse of 1 Enoch* (SBLEJL 4; Atlanta: Scholars Press, 1993), 47–51, 376; for the view that it is, see Martha Himmelfarb, "Temple and Priests in the Book of the Watchers, the Animal Apocalpyse, and the Apocalypse of Weeks," in *The Early Enoch Literature* (ed. Gabriele Boccaccini and John J. Collins; JSJSup 121; Leiden: Brill, 2007), 230–31.

58. Scott observes that Mark 1:15 "has often been used as a summary of Jesus' teaching about the kingdom of God, even though it was clearly composed by the gospel's author, not Jesus" ("How Did We Get Here?" 50). For Scott, this is problematic: we cannot identify the Jesus of Mark with the Jesus of history. Compare the position of John Kloppenborg, who maintains that constructions of Jesus should exclude materials belonging to the editorial framing of Q ("Discursive Practices in the Sayings Gospel Q and the Quest of the Historical Jesus," in *Sayings Source Q* [ed. Lindemann], 164–69). Unless, however, we assume that Mark and the tradents of Q always misconstrued the tradition, their readings, which are the earliest we have, should count for something. If we cannot presume continuity as a matter of course, we equally cannot presume discontinuity as a matter of course.

would unearth a Jesus who exorcized demons but did not promote apocalyptic hopes?

On this matter, I differ from Marcus Borg, who maintains that apart from the sayings about the coming Son of Man,[59] "there is very little in the gospels which would lead us to think that Jesus expected the end of the world soon."[60] He specifies these particulars: (1) Mark 9:1 ("Truly I tell you, there are some standing here who will not taste death until they see that the kingdom of God has come with power"); (2) Mark 1:15, if interpreted in the light of Mark 9:1; and (3) "much of the Matthean redaction of Jesus' parables and sayings."[61]

This list is much too short. What about the entirety of Mark 13, the eschatological discourse? Or the admonitions to watch and the theme of suddenness (see p. 40)? What of Luke 19:11, which recalls that the disciples thought the kingdom imminent (cf. Acts 1:6)?[62] Or the various logia that look into the future and see the resurrection of the dead or the eschatological feast or the final judgment or the fires of Gehenna? Unlike Borg, I perceive a global pattern, and it is apocalyptic. Here I can appeal to John Dominic Crossan, who is in many other ways an ally of Borg: "Jesus makes apocalyptic statements at almost every level and in every genre of the tradition."[63]

59. Although I leave these mostly out of account in this chapter, I observe here that they must have entered the tradition very early. Some of the relevant logia appear to be translations from Aramaic (see Maurice Casey, *The Solution to the "Son of Man" Problem* [LNTS 343; London: T & T Clark, 2007]), and Paul may well have known apocalyptic Son of Man sayings, as has been argued by Birger A. Pearson, "A Q Community in Galilee?" *NTS* 50 (2004): 484–86; so too George W. E. Nickelsburg, "Son of Man," *ABD* 6:147. See further below, pp. 293–303.

60. Marcus Borg, "A Temperate Case for a Non-eschatological Jesus," in *Jesus in Contemporary Scholarship* (Valley Forge, PA: Trinity Press International, 1994), 52. See also W. S. Vorster, "Jesus: Eschatological Prophet and/or Wisdom Teacher?" *HvTSt* 47 (1991): 540. Note that Marius Reiser, in building his case that Jesus preached apocalyptic judgment, leaves the Son of Man sayings out of account (*Jesus and Judgment: The Eschatological Proclamation in Its Jewish Context* [trans. Linda M. Maloney; Minneapolis: Fortress, 1997], 203–4). In addition to disagreeing with Borg, I also disagree with Barry S. Crawford: "Over the years those who have found a near expectation in the preaching of Jesus have generally based their case either in whole or in part on" Mark 9:1; 13:30 or Matt 10:23 ("Near Expectation in the Sayings of Jesus," *JBL* 101 [1982]: 226). This was true of neither Bultmann nor Jeremias, nor is it true of either Ed Sanders or John Meier (for the latter, see *Marginal Jew*, 2:350). It also has nothing to do with Reiser's case or with mine. And Schweitzer's famous main point was that near expectation is everywhere in the tradition ("consistent eschatology").

61. Marcus Borg, "Con: Jesus Was Not an Apocalyptic Prophet," in *Apocalyptic Jesus* (ed. Miller), 41.

62. On Luke 19:11, see below, pp. 65–67.

63. John Dominic Crossan, "Assessing the Arguments," in *Apocalyptic Jesus* (ed. Miller), 122. Günther Bornkamm observes, "Certainly, in what has come down to us in the gospels, there is no lack of sayings of an apocalyptic nature" (*Jesus of Nazareth* [New York: Harper & Row, 1975], 93). Crossan, however, does not infer from the data what I do. From his point of view, my collection of materials naïvely ignores source criticism and stratigraphic analysis. For our differences here, see Crossan, "Assessing the Arguments," 123; Allison, *Jesus of Nazareth*, 13–20.

I have no wish to be unfair to Borg, who does not dispute that some or maybe even many eschatological sayings, especially warnings about judgment, go back to Jesus. His case, as he sees it, need only exclude those that are apocalyptic because they state or clearly assume the proximity of the end.[64] Still, one very much doubts that the individual or individuals who composed the sayings about judgment had regular recourse to eschatological subjects and yet did not presume the end to be near. Sober appeal to the latter days is not the customary companion of a *Fernerwartung*. It typically gains its urgency rather from a *Naherwartung*. Was Jesus or anyone among his followers a sort of precursor of Gregory of Tours, who lived in the sixth century but forecast the end for the eighth or ninth century?

Again, that the prophecy of the temple's demise was not, in origin, properly eschatological is quite dubious (see n. 57), no more credible than that its author had two future horizons: an imminent expectation, of the contingent destruction of Israel and its temple, and a long-range expectation, of the universal judgment.[65] Where is the parallel to such an outlook in Jewish texts up to and including the first century? "Neither Testament shows us prophets entertaining a compound, temporally disjoined perspective, both imminent and non-imminent."[66] Rather, in the words of Jonathan Goldstein, "The authors of Israelite prophecy were seldom if ever interested in the remote future, and the audiences who preserved their works were chiefly interested in the present and in a future that included little if any more than their own lifetimes."[67] The rule in the ancient sources is this: if it is coming, it must be close.[68] Here the Jewish prayer tradition is representative. Consider these petitions:

64. See Marcus J. Borg, *Conflict, Holiness and Politics in the Teaching of Jesus* (SBEC 5; Lewiston, NY: Edwin Mellen, 1984), 201–27.

65. Contrast Wright, *Jesus and the Victory of God*, 320–68, who is here indebted to G. B. Caird, *The Language and Imagery of the Bible* (Philadelphia: Westminster, 1980), 243–71. For criticism of Wright, see Allison, "Victory of Apocalyptic."

66. Ben F. Meyer, *Christus Faber: The Master Builder and the House of God* (Allison Park, PA: Pickwick, 1992), 47. He continues a few sentences later: "Another tack has been to subvert the seemingly cogent evidence of imminent judgment by positing a division between 'judgment' and 'judgment': when judgment is imminent it is not final; when it is final it is not imminent. The distinction, however, seems to serve no purpose other than to avoid 'imminent final judgment.' That it contributes to the solution of no other problem and illuminates no other issue or set of texts surely makes the proposal suspect."

67. Jonathan A. Goldstein, "Biblical Promises in 1 and 2 Maccabees," in *Judaisms and Their Messiahs at the Turn of the Christian Era* (ed. Jacob Neusner, William Scott Green, and Ernest S. Frerichs; New York: Cambridge University Press, 1987), 73. Cf. Isa 50:8; 51:5; 56:1; Ezek 7:7; 30:3; Joel 2:1; 3:14; Obad 15; Hab 2:3; Zeph 1:14.

68. Jon Douglas Levenson remarks that in the Hebrew Bible at least, the last things "are always held to be imminent. Israel recognized no distant end to history" (*Theology of the Program of Restoration of Ezekiel 40–48* [HSM 10; Missoula, MT: Scholars Press, 1976], 53 n. 33). One might object that in the Apocalypse of Weeks (1 *En*. 93 + 91:12–17) the eschaton seems to be hundreds of years in the future. But as George W. E. Nickelsburg, observes, "The Apocalypse speaks of three judgments. It is the first of these, which will take place at the end

- "May he let his kingdom rule . . . speedily and soon." (Kaddish prayer)
- "Hasten the year of our redemptive end." (Genizah Amidah, benediction 9)
- "Rebuild it (Jerusalem) soon, in our days." (traditional Amidah, benediction 14)
- "Speedily cause the offspring of your servant David to flourish." (traditional Amidah, benediction 15)
- "We thus hope . . . that we may soon behold the glory of your might." (Aleinu)
- "Speedily rule as king over all your works." (the Musaf prayer for Rosh Hashanah)[69]

The Jesus of the Synoptics is no different. As Wilhelm Bousset put it, "The whole tone of his preaching of the future . . . concentrates the attention of his disciples upon the end as though it were an immediately impending event."[70]

If some judgment texts in the Jesus tradition, like many judgment texts from Qumran, do not make explicit the nearness of the end, this reflects only the mundane circumstance that, because no saying spells out everything, every saying presupposes something. Further, why should one object to construing judgment logia that do not specify imminence in terms of those that do? Declining to interpret the tradition in the light of itself is a peculiar strategy.

As for the question of authenticity, this chapter will nowhere attempt to demonstrate that Jesus formulated any of the sayings in my catalog. Surely some of them are secondary; maybe many or even most of them are secondary. It does not matter. For my argument is this: our choice is not between an apocalyptic Jesus and some other Jesus; it is between an apocalyptic Jesus

---

of the seventh week and, arguably, the beginning of the eighth week, that is most relevant for the author's audience. With deceit and violence overthrown and the wicked judged by the righteous, the immediate problem of the author's time has been solved. If the author is really dependent on theoretical numerical speculation, a date for the final judgment in the distant future seems to be an inevitable conclusion of his method" (*1 Enoch 1: A Commentary on the Book of 1 Enoch, Chapters 1–36; 81–108* [Hermeneia; Minneapolis: Fortress, 2001], 440). I would add that weeks seven and eight include events that are otherwise eschatological in old Jewish texts. So the Apocalypse of Weeks is no more an exception to Goldstein's generalization than is Revelation, where the new heaven and the new earth are at least a thousand years away, while properly eschatological events, including Jesus' parousia, occur long before that. The same remark, mutatis mutandis, covers the apparent schematization of history in *Jubilees*. See James M. Scott, *On Earth as in Heaven: The Restoration of Sacred Time and Sacred Space in the Book of Jubilees* (JSJSup 91; Leiden: Brill, 2005), 119–27.

69. Cf. Tg. Esth 1:1: the kingdom of the Lord "will soon be revealed over the inhabitants of the earth."

70. Wilhelm Bousset, *Jesus* (trans. Janet Penrose Trevelyan; ed. W. D. Morrison; New York: G. P. Putnam's Sons, 1906), 75 n. 1.

and no Jesus at all. This is because the situation regarding apocalyptic eschatology is akin to that regarding combat with Satan (see pp. 17–20). The pertinent material is sufficiently abundant[71] that removing it all should leave one thoroughly skeptical about the mnemonic competence of the tradition.[72] If secondary accretions that seriously misrepresent Jesus attached themselves to the tradition in such abundance from the beginning, then maybe he is gone for good. Sometimes parasites kill the host.

Walter Bundy wrote, many years ago, "The eschatological passages are too numerous and extensive to be eliminated, too deeply set in the bed-rock of our best Gospel tradition to be uprooted without tearing him from his century. If Jesus did not express his faith in eschatological form, if these passages are not genuine, then we can not be sure that any words in the Gospels go back to him."[73] Although I would alter "these passages" to "some of these passages," the point stands. We may doubt that Jesus was an apocalyptic prophet, in which case our sources are miserable witnesses and a robust cynicism should assail us. Or, alternatively, we may surmise that Jesus' version of God's dream was some brand of apocalyptic eschatology, in which case our sources may remember well enough to allow continued questing. Which option imposes itself upon us?

In grappling with this issue, I will, as already intimated, refrain from undertaking the all-but-impossible task of determining which if any of the sayings listed on pp. 33–43 derive from compositions that Jesus himself might

---

71. The list on pp. 33–43 omits much that readily lends itself to being part of an apocalyptic worldview. I have not, for example, cited the many sayings about judgment that, although not explicitly eschatological, are often thought to be so—for example, Matt 7:1–2 // Luke 6:37–38 (Q) (see Reiser, *Jesus and Judgment*, 263–66); Matt 7:22–23 // Luke 13:25, 27 (Q) (cf. *Gos. Naz.* 5); Matt 7:24–27 // Luke 6:47–49 (Q) (on this, see Jacques Schlosser, "Q et la christologie implicite," in *Sayings Source Q* [ed. Lindemann], 307–10); Mark 12:40. Reiser even maintains that "more than a quarter of the traditional discourse material of Jesus is concerned with the theme of the final judgment" (*Jesus and Judgment*, 304). Again, the sayings that refer to Satan's defeat (e.g., Mark 3:23; Luke 10:18; John 12:31–32) are germane because of the then-common Jewish conviction that God will defeat the devil and all evil in the latter days (e.g., Isa 24:21; *1 En.* 10:4–6; 10:13; 54:4–6; *Jub.* 23:29; 1QS 4:17–19; 4Q300 frg. 3; *T. Mos.* 10:1–3; *T. Jud.* 25:3; *T. Levi* 3:3; 18:12; *T. Zeb.* 9:8; *T. Dan* 5:10–11; 6:1–4; *T. Benj.* 3:8; Matt 25:41; 1 Cor 15:24–26; Rev 20:1–15; *Barn.* 21:3). See Simon Gathercole, "Jesus' Eschatological Vision of the Fall of Satan: Luke 10,18 Reconsidered," *ZNW* 94 (2003): 143–63. Jesus' exorcisms advertise the arrival of God's kingdom and the departure of Satan's kingdom: the latter's "end has come" (Mark 3:26). On the relevance of Jesus' healings (cf. 4Q521) and the imagery of harvest (cf. *4 Ezra* 4:30, 39; *2 Bar.* 70:2), see Dale C. Allison Jr., "The Eschatology of Jesus," in *The Origins of Apocalypticism in Judaism and Christianity* (vol. 1 of *The Encyclopedia of Apocalypticism*, ed. John J. Collins; New York: Continuum, 1998), 293–99. On the eschatological aspect of Jesus' celebratory meals, see Koester, "Memory of Jesus' Death," 335–50; idem, *From Jesus to the Gospels*, 285–91.

72. Compare the reasoning of Meier: "If the miracle tradition from Jesus' public ministry were to be rejected *in toto* as unhistorical, so should every other Gospel tradition about him" (*Marginal Jew*, 2:630).

73. Walter E. Bundy, *The Religion of Jesus* (Indianapolis: Bobbs-Merrill, 1928), 123.

have authored. Happily, we can justly decide our question without rendering a verdict on the origin of a single saying. This is because a number of general considerations—I will introduce nine—move us to reckon the apocalyptic figure in the Synoptics a fair representative of the historical Jesus.[74]

Jesus between the Baptist and the First Christians

According to E. P. Sanders, "The most certain fact of all is that early Christianity was an eschatological movement."[75] What is certain to one, however, may be uncertain to another. Stephen Patterson has stated that "Christianity may not have begun as an apocalyptic sect after all," and others share his view.[76] Still, if we prudently eschew Sanders's use of the word "certain" and instead satisfy ourselves with probability, it is not so hard to choose sides on this issue.

The earliest extant Christian writing, 1 Thessalonians, is full of apocalyptic expectation.[77] So, as John A. T. Robinson recognized, this letter is a "challenge" for anyone who denies that Christianity began amid apocalyptic enthusiasm.[78] Equally challenging is the pre-Pauline and Aramaic μαράνα θά/ מרנא תא ("Lord, come!"), known from 1 Cor 16:22; *Did.* 10:6; *Apos. Con.*

74. What follows is an attempt to refine and augment, in view of helpful dissent and criticism as well as the most recent scholarship, arguments that I have forwarded, much more briefly, elsewhere. See Allison, *Jesus of Nazareth*, 39–44; idem, "Pro: Jesus Was an Apocalyptic Prophet," in *Apocalyptic Jesus* (ed. Miller), 20–24.

75. E. P. Sanders, "Jesus: His Religious Type," *Reflections* 87 (1992): 6. Compare this comment by R. J. Zwi Werblowsky: "Original Christianity was a messianic movement from its very beginning" ("Messiah and Messianic Movements," *The New Encyclopedia Britannica* [15th ed.; Chicago: Encyclopedia Britannica, 1983], Macropaedia 11:1019). Although throughout this book I will, for convenience, speak of "Christianity" in the singular, I do not presume the doctrinal or institutional unity of the early churches. I am nonplussed as to why Melanie Johnson-DeBaufre should attribute to me the view, emphatically not mine, that "modern and ancient Christianity is primarily a single, unified movement" (*Jesus among Her Children: Q, Eschatology, and the Construction of Christian Origins* [HTS 55; Cambridge, MA: Harvard University Press, 2005], 32). Not only are the two sentences of mine that she quotes qualified by "perhaps" and "one might wonder," but also they neither say nor intimate anything at all about modern Christianity; and they include the remark that "in the past we have tended to find too much unity in the early church."

76. Stephen J. Patterson, "Q: The Lost Gospel," *BRev* 9, no. 5 (1993): 38. Patterson is now supported by the collection of essays in Ron Cameron and Merrill P. Miller, eds., *Redescribing Christian Origins* (SBLSymS 28; Atlanta: Society of Biblical Literature, 2004). See further below, pp. 157–64.

77. Cf. 1 Thess 1:10; 3:13; 4:13–5:11; 5:23. See David Luckensmeyer, *The Eschatology of First Thessalonians* (NTOA 71; Göttingen: Vandenhoeck & Ruprecht, 2009). There is enough eschatological material in 1–2 Thessalonians that Robert Jewett has been able to interpret the letters in terms of cross-cultural millenarianism (*The Thessalonian Correspondence: Pauline Rhetoric and Millenarian Piety* [Philadelphia: Fortress, 1986]).

78. John A. T. Robinson, *Jesus and His Coming* (2nd ed.; Philadelphia: Westminster, 1979), 104–17.

7.26.5. This imperative is almost certainly "an ancient acclamation, held over from some primitive Palestinian liturgical setting," an acclamation that referred "to Jesus' parousiac coming, understood at least as eschatological and regal, and perhaps also as judicial."[79] And then there are the numerous early Christian texts that exhibit the conviction that God's Spirit has come upon the faithful.[80] The most plausible account of this interpretation of religious experience appeals to the Jewish hope for the end-time giving of the Spirit.[81] Here the author of Acts, quoting Joel 2:28, got it right: "In the last days it will be, God declares, that I will pour out my Spirit upon all flesh" (Acts 2:17).[82]

The apocalyptic religion of Paul, on display throughout his letters, further confirms that we should side with Sanders.[83] The apostle, a Jewish Christian contemporary of Jesus, adopted his faith in the mid 30s, and he claimed to share it with Christian leaders who had personally known Jesus (Gal 1–2). So unless Paul, as Harry Attridge has put it, was "thoroughly deceitful, the fact that he and the Jerusalem leadership agreed in the late forties on the basic 'gospel' that they were preaching (Gal 2:2–10), although certain halakic matters remained disputed, indicates that apocalyptic-kerygmatic Christianity was the form that the movement took among a group that included several of the immediate followers and relatives of Jesus."[84]

79. Joseph A. Fitzmyer, "New Testament *Kyrios* and *Maranatha* and Their Aramaic Background," in *To Advance the Gospel: New Testament Studies* (New York: Crossroad, 1981), 228–29. Cf. ἔρχου κύριε Ἰησοῦ in Rev 22:20, which is a Greek liturgical descendant of מרנא תא (so David E. Aune, *Revelation 17–22* [WBC 52C; Nashville: Thomas Nelson, 1998], 1234–35). See further Martin Hengel, "Abba, Maranatha, Hosanna und die Anfänge der Christologie," in *Studien zur Christologie: Kleine Schriften IV* (WUNT 201; ed. Claus-Jürgen Thornton; Tübingen: Mohr Siebeck, 2006), 496–534. Hengel argues that the imperative was a prayer both for the parousia and for Jesus' spiritual presence in Christian services. My guess is that it was originally a prayer for the parousia but, because of its liturgical setting, very soon came to mean more.

80. For example, Matt 12:28; Mark 1:8; Luke 11:13; John 3:5–8; 7:37–39; 14:16–17, 26; 15:26; 16:13; Acts 1:5, 8; 2:4, 38; Rom 1:4; 5:5; 8:23–24; 1 Cor 12:1–13; 2 Cor 5:5; Gal 4:6; 1 Thess 1:5–6; 4:8; 1 Pet 1:2, 12; 1 John 3:24.

81. Note Isa 32:15; 34:16; 44:3–4; 61:1; Ezek 11:19; 36:25–27; 37:1–14; 39:29; Joel 2:28–29; Zech 12:10; 1QS 4:21–22; 4Q521 frg. 2; *Jub.* 1:23–25; *1 En.* 49:3; 62:2; *Pss. Sol.* 17:37; *T. Jud.* 24:3; *T. Levi* 18:11; Tg. Isa. on 42:1–4; *t. Soṭah* 13:2. Jewish eschatological expectation is also the primary background for the presence of God's Spirit among the Qumran sectarians (e.g., 1QS 4:26; 5:25; 6:25; 1QH[a] 5:25). For discussion, see Johannes Sijko Vos, *Traditionsgeschichtliche Untersuchungen zur paulinischen Pneumatologie* (Assen: Van Gorcum, 1973), 34–73.

82. See Hans Conzelmann, *An Outline of the Theology of the New Testament* (New York: Harper & Row, 1969), 37–38. See also discussion in James D. G. Dunn, *The Theology of Paul the Apostle* (Grand Rapids: Eerdmans, 1998), 416–19; Gordon Fee, *God's Empowering Presence: The Holy Spirit in the Writings of Paul* (Peabody, MA: Hendrickson, 1994), 803–26.

83. On the apocalyptic content of Paul's leading theological ideas, see M. C. de Boer, "Paul and Apocalyptic Theology," in *Origins of Apocalypticism* (ed. Collins), 345–83; J. Louis Martyn, "Apocalyptic Antinomies in Paul's Letter to the Galatians," *NTS* 31 (1985): 410–24.

84. Harold A. Attridge, "Reflections on Research into Q," *Semeia* 55 (1992): 229. Cf. 1 Cor 15:11 ("Whether then it was I or they, so we proclaim and so you have come to believe"); and

The point is fortified by the fact that, to judge from the joint testimony of Paul and Acts, Christianity was, from the beginning, and at least for the first two or three decades, centered in Jerusalem.[85] This surprises on two counts. First, Jesus himself and his family made their home in the north, as evidently did most of the disciples who shared his itinerant ministry (cf. Mark 1:16–20; 14:70; John 1:43). Why, then, did many of these Galileans, such as Peter and the sons of Zebedee, become, at least for a time, residents of Jerusalem? Why did they, after following Jesus from north to south, opt to reside in the capital? Indications are that they did return home after Jesus' crucifixion (Matt 28:16–20; Mark 16:7; John 21:1–25); but their homecoming was short-lived (Acts 1–15; Gal 1:18–2:10). Although Galileans, they soon enough returned to Jerusalem.[86]

The second surprising fact is that Jesus was executed in Jerusalem, which means that Judea must have held some hostility for those associated with him, maybe even danger. So again, why did these people settle in the capital? Why did they not instead go back to their native Galilee, as we might well expect them to have done?

Although the extant sources fail to answer the question directly, the proposition that apocalyptic eschatology was part and parcel of the ideology of the earliest Christians provides the best answer.[87] Many of them, to state the obvious, believed that Jesus would return quickly.[88] If we then ask, Where did they

---

see further Jeffrey Peterson, "The Extent of Christian Theological Diversity: Pauline Evidence," *RestQ* 47 (2005): 1–12.

85. Paul leaves no doubt that Peter and James, the brother of Jesus, resided in Jerusalem when the apostle visited them there three years after his conversion (Gal 1:18–19). Furthermore, Paul reports that after Jesus called him to proclaim the gospel to the Gentiles, he did not "go up to Jerusalem to those who were already apostles before me" (Gal 1:17). This remark implies that Jerusalem was already the ecclesiastical center of the Christian faith when Paul had his experience on the road to Damascus, which means that the city was such very soon after the crucifixion, probably within three years, for Jesus was crucified in the year 30 or 33, and Paul became a Christian in 33, 34, or 35.

86. Despite so much academic opinion to the contrary, it is indeed uncertain that we have any real knowledge of or even evidence for Christianity in pre-70 Galilee. The only explicit statement is the sweeping generalization in Acts 9:31: "Meanwhile the church throughout Judea, Galilee, and Samaria had peace and was built up." Inferences from materials in Q and Mark remain highly speculative. See Marco Frenschkowski, "Galiläa oder Jerusalem? Die topographischen und politischen Hintergründe der Logienquelle," in *Sayings Source Q* (ed. Lindemann), 535–59; Pearson, "Q Community," 476–94.

87. Others in agreement include Paula Fredriksen, *Jesus of Nazareth, King of the Jews: A Jewish Life and the Emergence of Christianity* (New York: Alfred A. Knopf, 2000), 95–96; Ulrich B. Müller, "Auferweckt und erhöht: Zur Genese des Osterglaubens," *NTS* 54 (2008): 220; Heikki Räisänen, "Last Things First: 'Eschatology' as the First Chapter in an Overall Account of Early Christian Ideas," in *Moving beyond New Testament Theology? Essays in Conversation with Heikki Räisänen* (ed. Todd Penner and Caroline Vander Stichele; SESJ 88; Helsinki: Finnish Exegetical Society; Göttingen: Vandenhoeck & Ruprecht, 2005), 462–63.

88. Note especially Acts 3:19–21; Rom 13:11; 1 Cor 7:29–30; 16:22; Heb 10:37; Jas 5:8; 1 Pet 4:17; Rev 1:1, 3; 22:20. The import of these texts is clear, although still occasionally denied. See,

think he was headed? the answer is equally evident: Jerusalem. The religious center of Judea was, in the eschatological imagination, the center of the end-time scenario. The eschatological forecasts in Isa 60–62 and Ezek 40–48 focus upon the place. Jeremiah 17:25 prophesies that the Lord will set David's throne precisely there. Tobit 14:5 looks to the end and sees a new temple in the holy city. Zechariah 8:7–8; Bar 5:5; *Pss. Sol.* 11:1–9, and many liturgical prayers envisage the scattered tribes of the Diaspora returning at the end to Jerusalem. Luke 19:11 has the disciples expecting the kingdom of God just as Jesus approaches the capital. *'Abot de Rabbi Nathan* 35 says that "in the future, Jerusalem will be the gathering place of all the nations and all the kingdoms." In Tg. Zech 14:4–5 the bones of the dead roll through underground tunnels so that they can emerge from the Mount of Olives on the last day and be resurrected.[89] And so it goes. The eschatological events were to transpire above all in the holy city (cf. Rom 11:26), and the kingdom, in the words of Irenaeus, would be "established there" (*Haer.* 5.35). When Matthew and Luke have Jesus foretell the ingathering of people from the east and west (Matt 8:11–12; Luke 13:28–29), the presumed destination of their centripetal movement must be Palestine and its chief city, which Jews imagined to be the *axis mundi.*[90]

It is only natural, then, that some followers of Jesus who were natives of Galilee took up residence in the capital. This is one more sign of their heightened eschatological expectation, of their sincere conviction that they were living in the "last" or "latter days," at "the end of the age."[91] They were like the Montanists in the next century, who encouraged people to gather to the cities of Pepouza and Tymion in Phrygia, where their movement was headquartered and where they expected the new Jerusalem to descend from heaven.[92] One likewise thinks of Melchior Hoffman and his Anabaptist fol-

---

for example, C. E. B. Cranfield, "Thoughts on New Testament Eschatology," in *The Bible and Christian Life: A Collection of Essays* (Edinburgh: T & T Clark, 1985), 105–26; Heinz Giesen, "Naherwartung im Neuen Testament?" *ThG* 30 (1987): 151–64.

89. Cf. *y. Ketub.* 35b (12:4); *y. Kil.* 32b (9:4); *Tanḥ.* Buber Wayehi 12:6; Tg. Cant 8:5; *Gen. Rab.* 96:5; *Pesiq. Rab.* 1:6; 31:10.

90. See Ezek 5:5; 38:12; *1 En.* 26:1; *Jub.* 8:9; *Sib. Or.* 5:250; *b. Sanh.* 37a; discussion in Philip S. Alexander, "Jerusalem as the *Omphalos* of the World: On the History of a Geographical Concept," in *Jerusalem: Its Sanctity and Centrality to Judaism, Christianity, and Islam* (ed. Lee I. Levine; New York: Continuum, 1999), 104–19.

91. For "the last days," see LXX Gen 49:1; Num 24:14; Isa 2:2; Jer 23:20; Dan 10:14; Gk. *L.A.E.* 13:2; *T. Jud.* 18:1; *T. Zeb.* 8:2; 9:5; *T. Dan* 5:4; *T. Jos.* 19:10; Acts 2:17; 2 Tim 3:1; Heb 1:2; Jas 5:3; 2 Pet 3:3; *Did.* 16:3; and *Barn.* 4:9; 12:9; 16:5; 2 *Clem.* 14:2 (cf. 1 Pet 1:20; Jude 18). For "the end of the age(s)," see 1 Cor 10:11; Heb 9:26; 1 Pet 1:20. Compare "the fullness of time" in Gal 4:4. Helpful here is Annette Steudel, "אחרית הימים in the Texts from Qumran," *RevQ* 16 (1993): 225–46. Steudel's conclusion regarding the writings from Qumran holds for the New Testament: the "latter days" or "last days" constitute the final period of ordinary time and include the present as well as recent events in the past and future events soon to come.

92. Eusebius, *Hist. eccl.* 5.18.2; Epiphanius, *Pan.* 48.14.1; 49.1.3. See discussion in William Tabbernee, "Revelation 21 and the Montanist 'New Jerusalem,'" *ABR* 37 (1989): 52–60.

lowers much later on: they all moved to Strasbourg, which was for them the "spiritual Jerusalem" of the end time.[93]

Although there are yet additional reasons for agreeing with Bultmann that "the earliest Church regarded itself as the Congregation of the end of days,"[94] I will mention just one. With the exception of Philemon, 2 John, and 3 John, all three of which are brief and nearly devoid of theology, apocalyptic eschatology or some obvious trace of it appears in all first-century Christian documents.[95] The near ubiquity suggests a common source and so antiquity. Some physicists judge all symmetry—the symmetry in shells, ice crystals, galaxies, and so on—to be a remnant of the original symmetry at the instant of the big bang. Similarly, the presence of some form of apocalyptic eschatology in nearly all early Christian sources must derive from a common, apocalyptic point of origination; and since Jesus was the point of origination for what became Christianity, perhaps he was, one might sensibly infer, an apocalyptic figure.

Helmut Koester once asked, "Were the eschatological schemata of his early followers subsequently assigned to a Jesus whose original ministry and message did not contain any eschatological elements?" He answered, "That seems very unlikely. Within a year or two of Jesus' death, Paul persecuted the followers of Jesus because of their eschatological proclamation. That leaves precious little time in which the followers of a noneschatological Jesus could have developed an entirely new eschatological perspective without a precedent in the preaching and actions of Jesus."[96] Koester's argument is cogent. Eschatology

---

Against John C. Poirier ("Montanist Pepuza-Jerusalem and the Dwelling Place of Wisdom," *JECS* 7 [1999]: 491–507), I see no reason to deny the centrality of eschatological expectation to Montanism, whether or not the movement was properly chiliastic.

93. See Klaus Deppermann, *Melchior Hoffman: Social Unrest and Apocalyptic Visions in the Age of Reformation* (Edinburgh: T & T Clark, 1987), 161, 211, 257–58, 333.

94. Bultmann, *Theology*, 1:37 (italics deleted). Compare Ernst Käsemann's famous dictum that apocalyptic was the mother of Christian theology; see his essay "The Beginnings of Christian Theology," in *New Testament Questions of Today* (London: SCM Press, 1969), 82–107.

95. Ferdinand Hahn observes, "The basic apocalyptic structure is clearly to be recognized in all traditions" of the early Christian preaching. This is why "a comprehensive account of eschatology, which also encompasses its transformation into something else, could easily grow almost to an overall presentation of early Christianity" (*Frühjüdische und urchristliche Apokalyptik: Eine Einführung* [Neukirchen-Vluyn: Neukirchener Verlag, 1998], 96). So rightly Räisänen, "Last Things First," 462–63. For a well-known and fascinating if flawed attempt to do just that, see Martin Warner, *The Formation of Christian Dogma: An Historical Study of Its Problems* (New York: Harper & Row, 1957).

96. Helmut Koester, "Jesus the Victim," *JBL* 111 (1992): 14; idem, *From Jesus to the Gospels*, 209. For similar statements, see W. Sanday, *Outlines of the Life of Christ* (2nd ed.; Edinburgh: T & T Clark, 1906), 154; H. A. Guy, *The New Testament Doctrine of the Last Things: A Study of Eschatology* (London: Oxford University Press, 1948), 84; Cyril W. Emmet, *The Eschatological Question in the Gospels: And Other Studies in Recent New Testament Criticism* (Edinburgh: T & T Clark, 1911), 57 ("The strength of the eschatological belief in the Early Church is probably sufficient proof that He [Jesus] did to some extent countenance it"); Alan F. Segal, "Jesus and First-Century Judaism," in *Jesus at 2000* (ed. Marcus J. Borg; Boulder, CO: Westview, 1997),

was there from the beginning of the Christian movement because it was there before the beginning, with Jesus.

If we find fervent eschatological expectation among some of Jesus' followers immediately after his ministry, we find such expectation right before it too. Jesus associated himself with John the Baptist, whose public speech, if the Synoptics are any guide, featured eschatological judgment, conceived as imminent.[97] Indeed, Jesus seems to have submitted to John's baptism,[98] an action constituting

---

59–65. Even Borg concedes that it seems "natural" to surmise that the church's eschatology was "a continuation of Jesus' proclamation of the imminent end" ("Temperate Case," 58), although he goes on to urge the contrary.

97. See Matt 3:7–10, 11–12 // Luke 3:7–9, 15–18 (Q). Even Origen recognized that John's words in Luke 3 most naturally refer to "the consummation" at "the end of time" (*Hom. Luc.* 23.1). The Jesus Seminar voted that "the historical JB, in all probability, was an apocalyptic preacher." See W. Barnes Tatum, *John the Baptist and Jesus: A Report of the Jesus Seminar* (Sonoma, CA: Polebridge, 1994), 167. Against this, one could counter with not the Gospels but Josephus, whose John is a social reformer, not an apocalyptic prophet (*Ant.* 18.116–119). One might then appeal to William Arnal ("Redactional Fabrication and Group Legitimation: The Baptist's Preaching in Q 3:7–9, 16–17," in *Conflict and Invention: Literary, Rhetorical, and Social Studies on the Sayings Gospel Q* [ed. John S. Kloppenborg; Valley Forge, PA: Trinity Press International, 1995], 165–80) and the few others who assign John's preaching to a later redactional layer of Q and urge that it is only Q's editorial frame that turns John into an apocalyptic prophet. Josephus, however, sought to downplay the eschatological fervor of Judaism, which surely is why his review of the Essenes is silent regarding the restoration of Israel, cosmic dualism, and messianic dreams. Only from the Dead Sea Scrolls, likely composed and copied by Essenes, do we learn these things. A similar revision of John by Josephus would only be expected (and is paralleled in the Fourth Gospel). See Meier, *Marginal Jew*, 2:56–62. As for the redactional nature of John's preaching in Q, the chief argument is that the language and ideas cohere with other Q materials. Yet one might as well contend that the Beatitudes originated with a contributor to Q because they fit so well with Q 7:18–23 (which also alludes to Isa 61) and Matt 23:12 // Luke 14:11 (Q) (which foresees eschatological reversal). Mark 1:1–8, moreover, harmonizes with Q's apocalyptic portrait, for here, in a few scant verses, the Second Gospel makes John out to be Elijah come again (1:6 [cf. 2 Kgs 1:8; Mal 4:5]), the voice prophesied in Isa 40:3 (1:3), and the forerunner of a supernatural baptizer (1:8). See the criticism by James M. Robinson, "Jesus' Theology in the Sayings Source Q," in *Early Christian Voices in Texts, Traditions, and Symbols: Essays in Honor of François Bovon* (ed. David H. Warren, Ann Graham Brock, and David W. Pao; BIS 66; Boston: Brill, 2003), 27 n. 9; idem, "Building Blocks in the Social History of Q," in *Reimagining Christian Origins: A Colloquium Honoring Burton L. Mack* (ed. Elizabeth A. Castelli and Hal Taussig; Valley Forge, PA: Trinity Press International, 1996), 95. I prefer the verdict of C. M. Tuckett: "Q's literary activity in placing the teaching of Jesus in the context of John's preaching may . . . be a *reliable* reflection of the context in which the teaching of Jesus should be placed" ("Q and the Historical Jesus," in *Der historische Jesus: Tendenzen und Perspektiven der gegenwärtigen Forschung* [ed. Jens Schröter and Ralph Brucker; BZNW 114; Berlin: de Gruyter, 2002], 236).

98. This is rarely doubted, although see William Arnal, "Major Episodes in the Biography of Jesus: An Assessment of the Historicity of the Narrative Tradition," *TJT* 13 (1997): 201–26; Leif E. Vaage, "Bird-Watching at the Baptism of Jesus: Early Christian Mythmaking in Mark 1:9–11," in *Reimagining Christian Origins* (ed. Castelli and Taussig), 280–94. Arnal and Vaage do not persuade, in part because, as Mark's account of the crucifixion and Luke's theological use of Jerusalem show, remembered facts may not only serve literary ends but may also be fully clothed in legendary and mythological dress. The snag here is that almost every bit of tradition

his theological stamp of approval. Sanders has put it this way: "John really did baptize Jesus. This, in turn, implies that Jesus agreed with John's message: it was time to repent in view of the coming wrath and redemption."[99]

Beyond having himself baptized, Jesus reportedly endorsed John's ministry in his teaching.[100] Indeed, if the Synoptics remember rightly, "no one engaged the attention of Jesus as thoroughly as did John the Baptist—no one from Israel's past (for example, Abraham, Moses, David, or one of the prophets), no one from among the contemporaries of Jesus."[101] Again, then, one presumes considerable ideological concord between the two men. The upshot is that reconstructing a Jesus without an apocalyptic *Naherwartung* posits a double discontinuity, a major theological break not only between him and people who thought to further his cause but also between him and a man whose message he was remembered as commending.[102] How likely is this? Although "as unlikely as possible"[103] may be overstatement, a Jesus "whose message is

is integrated into the surrounding Synoptic narratives and serves clear editorial ends, so unless we are to find only fiction in the Synoptics, observation of such integration and such ends cannot suffice to determine derivation.

99. E. P. Sanders, *The Historical Figure of Jesus* (London: Penguin, 1993), 94 (italics deleted).

100. Matt 11:7–19 // Luke 7:24–35 (Q); Luke 16:16; Mark 11:27–33; Matt 21:28–32; *Gos. Thom.* 46. The argument is all the stronger if John's Gospel is right in asserting that Jesus himself followed John's precedent and baptized (3:22). On the issue of whether Jesus ever changed his mind, see further below, p. 90 n. 252.

101. Jürgen Becker, *Jesus of Nazareth* (trans. James E. Crouch; New York: de Gruyter, 1998), 34.

102. This argument has a long pedigree. See Heathcote William Garrod, *The Religion of All Good Men* (New York: Macmillan, 1906), 136–39, 212–13; B. Harvie Branscomb, *The Teachings of Jesus* (Nashville: Cokesbury, 1931), 131–33; Klaus Koch, *The Rediscovery of Apocalyptic* (SBT 2/22; London: SCM Press, 1972), 78; James D. G. Dunn, *Jesus and the Spirit* (Philadelphia: Westminster, 1975), 42; Walter Schmithals, "Jesus, Apocalypticism, and the Origins of Christianity," in *The Theology of the First Christians* (Louisville: Westminster John Knox, 1997), 6–7; E. P. Sanders, *Jesus and Judaism* (Philadelphia: Fortress, 1985), 91–95; Meyer, *Christus Faber*, 42; Schweizer, *Jesus*, 14; Ben Wiebe, "The Focus of Jesus' Eschatology," in *Self-Definition and Self-Discovery in Early Christianity: A Study in Changing Horizons* (ed. David J. Hawkin and Tom Robinson; SBEC 26; Lewiston, NY: Edwin Mellen, 1990), 131–33; Adela Yarbro Collins, "The Apocalyptic Son of Man Sayings," in *The Future of Early Christianity: Essays in Honor of Helmut Koester* (ed. Birger A. Pearson; Minneapolis: Fortress, 1991), 227; idem, "Jesus as Son of Man," in Adela Yarbro Collins and John J. Collins, *King and Messiah as Son of God: Divine, Human, and Angelic Messianic Figures in Biblical and Related Literature* (Grand Rapids: Eerdmans, 2008), 170–71; Birger A. Pearson, "The Gospel according to the 'Jesus Seminar,'" in *The Emergence of the Christian Religion: Essays on Early Christianity* (Harrisburg, PA: Trinity Press International, 1997), 37; John J. Collins, *The Apocalyptic Imagination: An Introduction to Jewish Apocalyptic Literature* (2nd ed; Grand Rapids: Eerdmans, 1998), 259–60; Bart Ehrman, *Jesus: Apocalyptic Prophet of the New Millennium* (Oxford: Oxford University Press, 1999); Fredriksen, *Jesus of Nazareth*, 288; Frey, "Apokalyptik als Herausforderung," 58–68, 90; Räisänen, "Last Things First," 458–59.

103. Ulrich B. Müller, "Apocalyptic Currents," in *Christian Beginnings: Word and Community from Jesus to Post-Apostolic Times* (ed. Jürgen Becker; Louisville: Westminster John Knox, 1993), 289.

focused simply on living in this world just does not fit."[104] Right before Jesus is the Baptist, announcing imminent universal judgment. Right after Jesus are Paul and like-minded early Christians, announcing imminent judgment. And in between is Jesus, announcing, at least in many sayings attributed to him, imminent universal judgment. The conclusion is obvious.

John Dominic Crossan, who takes a very different view of Jesus than do I, has nonetheless been candid enough to acknowledge that the argument from presumptive continuity has force. Although not "logically absolute," for "Jesus could have been a non-apocalyptic island in an apocalyptic sea just as Gandhi was a non-violent island in a violent sea," the line of reasoning appears on its face to be "circumstantially compelling."[105]

"God Raised Jesus from the Dead"

According to Paul, who knew Peter, a follower of Jesus, and James, his brother (Gal 1:18–2:14), both sibling and disciple encountered the risen Jesus, who arose "on the third day" (1 Cor 15:3–7). That settles the issue: some people who knew Jesus personally believed, soon after the crucifixion, likely within a few days,[106] that God had raised him from the dead. To this there is no countertestimony: the Synoptics, John, and Acts concur with Paul on this particular.[107]

What occasioned belief that God had brought Jesus back to life? A satisfying answer must account for at least three facts: (a) we know of no comparable claim for any other ancient Jew;[108] (b) whether or not Géza Vermès underestimates when asserting that the Pharisaic notion of bodily resurrection "was on the whole unfamiliar in most layers of Palestinian Jewry,"[109] certainly not all

104. Räisänen, "Last Things First," 459.

105. Crossan, "Assessing the Arguments," 122.

106. See Allison, *Resurrecting Jesus*, 231–32.

107. If one decides that "the notion of Jesus' resurrection was only one among many ways in which early Jesus movements and Christian groups imagined their beginnings" (so Burton Mack, review of *Did Jesus Rise from the Dead? The Resurrection Debate*, by Gary R. Habermas and Antony G. N. Flew, *History and Theory* 28 [1989]: 219) and/or holds that the contributors to Q or to an early stage of the Sayings Source had no belief or interest in the resurrection of Jesus or conceptualized his vindication in other terms (see John S. Kloppenborg, *Excavating Q: The History and Setting of the Sayings Gospel* [Edinburgh: T & T Clark, 2000], 363–79), that would not bear on my argument, which concerns only "some people who knew Jesus personally."

108. This is one good reason for doubting, against Stephen J. Patterson, that "resurrection, as vindication, presupposes only that a righteous person has been killed in faithfulness to a divine cause. In a dissident Jewish context, this is all one needs. The followers of Jesus could have said 'God raised Jesus from the dead' on the day he died, and probably did" ("Why Did Christians Say: 'God Raised Jesus from the Dead'?" *Forum* 10 [1994]: 142). Why, then, is there no record of anyone making a like claim about anybody else? Jesus was far from being the only righteous person killed in faithfulness to a divine cause in a dissident Jewish context.

109. Géza Vermès, *The Resurrection: History and Myth* (New York: Doubleday, 2008), 55. Devorah Dimant, in contrast, maintains that resurrection was "prevalent" and "a central Jew-

first-century Jews embraced the belief;[110] (c) to the extent of our knowledge, those who did believe it tended to envisage the resurrection as a corporate event, with either all people or all righteous people coming back to life.[111]

Given these circumstances, as well as the popularity of anthropological dualism among so many ancient Jews and Christians,[112] we might have expected believers in Jesus to articulate his postmortem vindication in terms of

ish doctrine at the time" ("Resurrection, Restoration, and Time-Curtailing in Qumran, Early Judaism, and Christianity," *RevQ* 19 [2000]: 538).

110. C. D. Elledge contends that near the turn of the era, "hope in the resurrection of the dead was a popular, yet insurgent, and even controversial belief" ("Resurrection of the Dead: Exploring Our Earliest Evidence Today," in James H. Charlesworth et al., *Resurrection: The Origin and Future of a Biblical Doctrine* [New York: T & T Clark, 2006], 41). Émile Puech reviews all possible evidence, although many of his conclusions, especially about the Dead Sea Scrolls, are debatable (*La croyance des Esséniens en la vie future: Immortalité, résurrection, vie éternelle? Histoire d'une croyance dans le judaïsme ancien* [2 vols.; EBib 21, 22; Paris: Gabalda, 1993]).

111. There was, it is true, an exegetical tradition (of what age we know not) that took the resurrection of Ezek 37 to be an event of the past: the bones were those of the Ephraimites who left Egypt prematurely (so Rab in *b. Sanh.* 92b; Tg. Ps.-J. on Exod 13:17; cf. Ezek 37:15, 19), or of those who denied the resurrection (so Samuel in *b. Sanh.* 92b), or of some other group (*b. Sanh.* 92b lists several options). Yet nowhere, to my knowledge, do these resurrected individuals gain eternal life. Indeed, in *b. Sanh.* 92b one rabbi says that they died soon after they came to life, another that they took up their ordinary lives again, marrying and begetting children. One is reminded of the stories in which Jesus raises the dead—those individuals do not enter eschatological existence with God but rather return to earthly life—as well as the peculiar tradition in Mark 6:14–16, about Jesus being the Baptist risen from the dead. Against Joost Holleman (*Resurrection and Parousia: A Traditio-Historical Study of Paul's Eschatology in 1 Corinthians 15* [NovTSup 84; Leiden: Brill, 1996], 144–57) and Ulrich Kellermann (*Auferstehung in den Himmel: 2 Makkabäer 7 und die Auferstehung der Martyrer* [SBS 95; Stuttgart: Katholisches Bibelwerk, 1978]), 2 Macc 7 does not establish the existence of a pre-Christian tradition concerning the noneschatological resurrection of just individuals. For criticism, see Dieter Zeller, "Die Entstehung des Christentums," in *Christentum I: Von den Anfängen bis zur Konstantinischen Wende* (ed. Dieter Zeller; RM 28; Stuttgart: Kohlhammer, 2002), 60 n. 7. Purely literary, and quite possibly under Christian influence, is *T. Job* 39–40, which, although it has an ascension to glory in the middle of history, does not speak of "resurrection." Some have found in Rev 11:3–12 and *Apoc. El.* 4:7–19 (cf. Mark 6:14–16) evidence for Jewish belief in a dying and rising eschatological prophet (so Klaus Berger, *Die Auferstehung des Propheten und die Erhöhung des Menschensohnes: Traditionsgeschichtliche Untersuchungen zur Deutung des Geschickes Jesu in frühchristlichen Texten* [SUNT 13; Göttingen: Vandenhoeck & Ruprecht, 1976]; Rudolf Pesch, "Zur Entstehung des Glaubens an die Auferstehung Jesu," *TQ* 153 [1973]: 222–26). If there was such a belief, it was little known and properly eschatological. See further J. M. Nützel, "Zum Schicksal der eschatologischen Propheten," *BZ* 20 (1976): 59–94; Eduard Schweizer, review of *Die Auferstehung des Propheten und die Erhöhung des Menschensohnes*, by Klaus Berger, *TLZ* 103 (1978): 874–78; Anton Vögtle, "Wie kam es zum Osterglauben?" in Anton Vögtle and Rudolf Pesch, *Wie kam es zum Osterglauben?* (Düsseldorf: Patmos-Verlag, 1975), 80–83. The deficiencies of this theory—among other things, all the relevant sources are Christian or were transmitted by Christian hands—later led Pesch to abandon it.

112. Cf. *1 En.* 22:3–13; *Jub.* 23:31; Bar 2:17; Wis 15:8; 4 Macc 14:6; *T. Ab.* RecLng 20:8–14; Gk. *L.A.E.* 13:6; 31:4; 32:4; Matt 10:28; 14:26; Luke 16:19–31; 23:43; Acts 7:59; 2 Cor 12:3; Phil 1:21–24; 1 Pet 3:18–19; Josephus, *J.W.* 2.154; 3.362; 4 Ezra 7:32; 2 Bar. 30:25; the *Apocryphon of Ezekiel apud* Epiphanius, *Pan.* 64.70.5–17; *b. Sanh.* 91a–b (cf. *Mek.* on Exod 15:1); and many

the triumph of his soul or spirit and to imagine his resurrection, like that of everyone else dead and buried, as still belonging to the future. The followers of Muhammad reportedly thought something like this upon his departure, as did the Lubavitchers when their Rebbe, Menachem Schneerson, died;[113] and the story of Moses' end in *Deut. Rab.* 11:10 adopts this strategy with regard to the lawgiver.[114] Similarly, in 2 Maccabees, eternal life is gained upon death (7:36), although the resurrection remains future (12:43–44); and in old Christian hagiography, when people see the soul of a saint, at the hour of death, ascending on high, they use the language of ascension, not resurrection.[115] So the first Christians could have proclaimed, to borrow from *Jub.* 23:31, that, while his bones rested for now in the earth, Jesus' spirit was exalted in heaven.[116]

Believers might also, like some later so-called heretics, have convinced themselves that Jesus had only seemed to die, that in reality he had ascended to heaven in the manner of Enoch and Elijah.[117] The Dositheans allegedly denied the death of Dositheus, their messianic leader;[118] the Islamic followers of Muhammad b. al-Hanafiyya (d. ca. 700 CE) likewise asserted that he never died;[119] and when Haile Selassie, the Rastafarian messiah, disappeared in 1975,

other Jewish and Christian texts. See Robert H. Gundry, *Sōma in Biblical Theology, with Emphasis upon Pauline Anthropology* (SNTSMS 29; Cambridge: Cambridge University Press, 1976).

113. See Simon Dein, "When Prophecy Fails: Messianism amongst Lubavitcher Hasids," in *The Coming Deliverer: Millennial Themes in World Religions* (ed. Fiona Bowie and Christopher Deacy; Cardiff: University of Wales Press, 1997), 238–60; idem, "Mosiach Is Here Now: Just Open Your Eyes and You Can See Him," *Anthropology and Medicine* 9 (2002): 25–36; idem, "What Really Happens When Prophecy Fails: The Case of Lubavitch," *SocRel* 62 (2001): 383–401; William Shaffir, "When Prophecy Is Not Validated: Explaining the Unexpected in a Messianic Campaign," *JJSoc* 37 (1995): 119–36. Although at first a few of the faithful could not accept their Rebbe's death, the majority did not deny the obvious. The standard response was to regard his physical death as less important than his occult spiritual presence and to hope for his resurrection and return in the future.

114. See Clement of Alexandria, *Strom.* 6.15.132; *Sipre* 305, 339, 357 on Deut 31:14; 32:50; 34:1; *'Abot R. Nat.* A 12; *'Abot R. Nat.* B 25; *Petirat Moshe* (BHM 1:125–28; 6:75–77). The basic story is pre-Christian, for the *Testament of Abraham* rewrites it; see Samuel E. Loewenstamm, "The Testament of Abraham and the Texts concerning the Death of Moses," in *Studies in the Testament of Abraham* (ed. George W. E. Nickelsburg; SBLSCS 6; Missoula, MT: Scholars Press, 1976), 219–25.

115. For example, Athanasius, *Vit. Ant.* 60; Jerome, *Vit. Paul.* 14.

116. Cf. *T. Ab.* RecLng 20:10–11; *L.A.B.* 32:9; Gk. *L.A.E.* 37:1–38:4. See also Gerhard Friedrich, "Die Auferweckung Jesu, eine Tat Gottes oder ein Interpretament der Jünger?" *KD* 17 (1971): 153–87. Friedrich shows how unusual it was, given the religious world in which they lived, that many Christians from the beginning used the language of resurrection for Jesus' vindication. Friedrich justly claims that visions of Jesus after his death would not in themselves have led anyone to think him raised from the dead.

117. Irenaeus (*Haer.* 5.31.1) reports this opinion.

118. Origen, *Comm. Jo.* 13.27.

119. See P. M. Holt, "Islamic Millenarianism and the Fulfilment of Prophecy: A Case Study," in *Prophecy and Millenarianism: Essays in Honour of Marjorie Reeves* (ed. Ann Williams; Essex: Longmans, 1980), 338.

those who believed in him taught that he had gone into hiding, maintaining this even into the 1990s, after his bones were identified.[120] To deny the death of one's hero is not so uncommon.

We do not know whether any of the first followers of Jesus had such thoughts. What we do know is this: several prominent disciples, when conceptualizing his vindication, used a technical term for end-time resurrection, ἀνάστασις νεκρῶν.[121] And their interpretation caught on.[122] These people evidently understood Jesus' resurrection to mark the onset of the general resurrection.[123]

What moved them, in next to no time at all, to clothe the divine vindication of Jesus in properly eschatological dress?[124] Surely a large part of the

120. See Ennis Barrington Edmonds, *Rastafari: From Outcasts to Culture Bearers* (Oxford: Oxford University Press, 2003), 55.

121. Acts 4:2; Rom 1:4; 1 Pet 1:3; cf. Matt 22:31; Acts 23:6; 1 Cor 15:12–13; *Did.* 16:6; Pseudo-Justin, *Quaest. et resp.* (PG 6:1249); and the rabbinic תחיית המתים, as in, for example, *m. Sanh.* 10:1; *t. Ber.* 3:24; *y. Ber.* 9b (5:2).

122. Vögtle lodges a threefold protest: (i) the kerygmatic formulae fail to refer to the general resurrection of the dead; (ii) whereas Jewish sources place the general resurrection on "the earth," the traditions about Jesus' resurrection fail to mention "the earth"; and (iii) in Judaism the resurrection is always general, never about one individual ("Osterglauben," 110–12). But this is unconvincing. The first objection overlooks a popular way of reading Rom 1:3–4: the pre-Pauline confession interprets Jesus' fate in terms of the general resurrection of the dead (cf. Acts 26:8); see Ernst Käsemann, *Commentary on Romans* (Grand Rapids: Eerdmans, 1980), 12; Robert Jewett, *Romans: A Commentary* (Hermeneia; Minneapolis: Fortress, 2006), 105; S. H. Hook, "The Translation of Romans I.4," *NTS* 9 (1963): 370–71. The other two objections neglect the impact that circumstances—in this case, Jesus' bodily absence and the fact that he alone appeared to others—can have upon religious beliefs. As even minimal acquaintance with millenarian movements reveals, theological convictions often morph to fit inescapable facts.

123. Cf. Rom 8:29; 1 Cor 15:20, 23; Col 1:18; Rev 1:5; *1 Clem.* 24:1; and see Ferdinand Hahn, *Die Vielfalt des Neuen Testaments: Theologiegeschichte des Urchristentums* (vol. 1 of *Theologie des Neuen Testaments*; Tübingen: Mohr Siebeck, 2002), 130; Günter Kegel, *Auferstehung Jesu, Auferstehung der Toten: Eine traditionsgeschichtliche Untersuchung zum Neuen Testament* (Gütersloh: Mohn, 1970), 22–25, 31–32. Matthew 27:51b–53 is also relevant (see below, p. 61). The association of Jesus' resurrection with the general resurrection of the dead is more likely to have originated earlier rather than later, for the more time between Jesus' resurrection and history's end, the less natural it would have been to link the two. So also Schmithals: 1 Cor 15:20 "binds imminent expectation and the confession of Jesus' resurrection very closely together and for this reason alone cannot be a late theologoumenon" ("Jesus," 7); James D. G. Dunn: the phrase "firstborn from the dead" in Col 1:18 "encapsulates what appears to have been the earliest Christian understanding, namely, that with Christ's resurrection the end-time resurrection itself had begun" (*The Epistles to the Colossians and to Philemon: A Commentary on the Greek Text* [NIGTC; Grand Rapids: Eerdmans 1996], 98).

124. Against Jürgen Becker (*Die Auferstehung Jesu Christi nach dem Neuen Testament: Ostererfahrung und Osterverständnis im Urchristentum* [Tübingen: Mohr Siebeck, 2007], 90–118), I see no good reason to conjecture that Jesus' vindication was originally conceived as that of an individual martyr instead of as part of the general resurrection. For one thing, the earliest

explanation lies in what they brought to their Easter experiences, namely, their already-existing theological categories and religious expectations. For the foundational proclamation "God raised Jesus from the dead" was scarcely an objective description of events, whatever exactly transpired. It was, rather, a theological interpretation. And it could not have been begotten in an eschatological vacuum. When Borg contends that belief in resurrection stimulated the introduction of apocalyptic eschatology into Christian thought,[125] he begs the question, which should be this: why "resurrection" in the first place? The proclamation "God raised Jesus from the dead" forcefully argues that the disciples looked for the resurrection of the dead before Good Friday; otherwise they would have interpreted their experiences in some other way.[126]

It is not unduly credulous to believe that the theological frame of reference for some early Christian groups was Jesus' preaching, that some or many of their "dreams, ideas, symbols and terms were inherited directly" from him.[127] Most new religions are "initially an extension of the founder's ideas, dreams, and emotional makeup."[128] Easter faith may have been born after the crucifixion, but it was conceived before. Schweitzer saw the truth: the "resurrection experiences" are "intelligible" only if they were "based upon the expectation of the resurrection, and this again as based on references of Jesus to the resurrection."[129] Without antecedent expectation of the imminent resurrection of the dead in general, there would have been no proclamation of the resurrection of Jesus in particular.

Christian formulation, θεὸς (ὁ) ἤγειρεν τὸν Ἰησοῦν ἐκ (τῶν) νεκρῶν, recalls the second benediction of the Shemoneh Esreh, which is properly eschatological: "Blessed are you, O Lord, who raises the dead" (ברוך אתה יי מחיה המתים). Further, the Mishnah more than once refers to this benediction as well known (m. Ber. 5:2; m. Roš. Haš. 4:5; m. Ta'an. 1:1), and 4Q521 frg. 2 col. II 12 (מתים יחיה); frgs. 7 + 5 col. II 6 (המחיה את מתי עמו); Rom 4:17 (ἐπίστευσεν θεοῦ τοῦ ζῳοποιοῦντος τοὺς νεκρούς; 2 Cor 1:9 (τῷ θεῷ τῷ ἐγείροντι τοὺς νεκρούς); and Jos. Asen. 20:7 (τῷ θεῷ τῷ ζῳοποιοῦντι τοὺς νεκρούς) attest to the antiquity of this way of speaking about the resurrection of the dead. Jewett comments that the participial expression in Rom 4:17 "appears to be drawn from the second benediction in the Eighteen Benedictions used by many Jews on a daily basis" (Romans, 333).

125. Borg, "Jesus Was Not an Apocalyptic Prophet," 38.

126. See Paula Fredriksen, "What You See Is What You Get: Context and Content in Current Research on the Historical Jesus," ThTo 52 (1995): 93–94; Gerhard Lohfink, "Der Ablauf der Osterereignisse und die Anfänge der Urgemeinde," ThQ 160 (1980): 168; Müller, "Auferweckt und erhöht," 205; Räisänen, "Last Things First," 458–59.

127. The quoted words are from Charlesworth, Jesus within Judaism, 3.

128. J. Gordon Melton, "When Prophets Die: The Succession Crisis in New Religions," in When Prophets Die: The Postcharismatic Fate of New Religious Movements (ed. Timothy Miller; Albany: State University of New York Press, 1991), 8. Melton also remarks, "The first members [of a new religious movement] are self-selected because of their initial confidence in the leader and/or their agreement with the leader's program" (p. 11).

129. Schweitzer, Quest, 343. Cf. Frey, "Apokalyptik als Herausforderung," 87; Walter Schmithals, "Gibt es Kriterien für die Bestimmung echter Jesusworte?" ZNT 1 (1998): 63–64.

Jesus' End as Eschatological Event

Mark 13, the eschatological discourse, immediately precedes Mark 14–16, the passion narrative. The former foretells events that the latter conspicuously echoes:

Mark 13	Mark 14–16
13:2: the temple will be destroyed	15:38: the temple is symbolically destroyed when its veil is torn
13:9, 11: the disciples will be "delivered up" (παραδίδωμι)	14:10, 11, 18, 21, 41, 42, 44; 15:1, 10, 15: Jesus is "delivered up" (παραδίδωμι)
13:9: the disciples will appear before Jewish councils (συνέδρια)	14:53–15:1: Jesus appears before a council (συνέδριον) of Jewish elders
13:9: the disciples will be beaten	14:65: Jesus is beaten
13:9: the disciples will stand before governors	15:1–15: Jesus appears before Pilate the governor
13:11: the disciples will be "led away" (ἄγω)	14:44, 53; 15:16: Jesus is "led away" (ἀπάγω)
13:12: brother will deliver brother over to death (θανατόω)	14:10, 20, 43: Judas, "one of the Twelve," hands Jesus over to be killed (cf. v. 55: θανατόω)
13:14–16: people will flee (φεύγω)	14:50–52: when Jesus is betrayed, the disciples flee (φεύγω)
13:24: the sun will be darkened (σκοτίζομαι)	15:33: when Jesus is crucified, the sun goes into darkness (σκότος) for three hours
13:35: The master may come in the evening (ὀψέ), at midnight, at cockcrow (ἀλεκτοροφωνία), in the morning (πρωΐ)	14:17: "when it was evening" (ὀψία); 14:72: cockcrow (ἀλέκτωρ φωνέω); 15:1: morning (πρωΐ)
13:35–36: "Watch (γρηγορέω) . . . lest the master come (ἔρχομαι) and find (εὑρίσκω) [them] sleeping" (καθεύδω)	14:34, 37: Jesus tells his disciples to "watch" (γρηγορέω); then he comes (ἔρχομαι) and finds (εὑρίσκω) them sleeping (καθεύδω)

The striking correlations between Mark's eschatological discourse and passion narrative, which cannot credibly be put down to chance, have understandably moved some to affirm that the end of Jesus anticipates or inaugurates the end times.[130] That this is the right inference—that the last days of Jesus belong

130. See further Dale C. Allison Jr., *The End of the Ages Has Come: An Early Interpretation of the Passion and Resurrection of Jesus* (SNTW; Edinburgh: T & T Clark, 1987), esp. 36–38. For related analyses and/or apocalyptic elements in the passion narratives, see Hendrikus Berkhof, *Christ, the Meaning of History* (trans. Lambertus Buurman; London: SCM Press, 1966), 63–64; Peter G. Bolt, "Mark 13: An Apocalyptic Precursor to the Passion Narrative," *RTR* 54 (1995): 10–30; John T. Carroll and Joel B. Green, *The Death of Jesus in Early Christianity* (Peabody, MA: Hendrickson, 1995), 36–37; Dean B. Deppe, "Charting the Future or a Perspective on the Present? The Paraenetic Purpose of Mark 13," *CTJ* 41 (2006): 95–97; Frances Dewar, "Chapter

to or proleptically instantiate the latter days—appears from this, that Mark's passion narrative also puts to good use Zech 9–14, another apocalypse.[131]

The eschatological interpretation of Jesus' passion had some currency in the early churches; it is no peculiarity of Mark. According to Matt 27:51–53, Jesus' death coincided with a strong earthquake and a resurrection of the dead.[132] This tale, which Matthew probably adapted from his tradition, draws upon

13 and the Passion Narrative in Mark," *Theology* 64 (1961): 91–107; Austin Farrer, *A Study in St. Mark* (New York: Oxford University Press, 1952), 135–41; Timothy J. Geddert, *Watchwords: Mark 13 in Markan Eschatology* (JSNTSup 26; Sheffield: JSOT Press, 1989), 89–111; Timothy C. Gray, *The Temple in the Gospel of Mark: A Study in Its Narrative Role* (WUNT 2/42; Tübingen: Mohr Siebeck, 2008), esp. 165–97; R. H. Lightfoot, *The Gospel Message of St. Mark* (Cambridge: Cambridge University Press, 1950), 49–58; Ched Myers, *Binding the Strong Man: A Political Reading of Mark's Story of Jesus* (Maryknoll, NY: Orbis, 1988), 343–48; Wiard Popkes, *Christus Traditus: Eine Untersuchungen zum Begriff der Dahingabe im Neuen Testament* (ATANT 49; Zürich: Zwingli, 1967), 230–32; Timothy Radcliffe, "'The Coming of the Son of Man': Mark's Gospel and the Subversion of 'the Apocalyptic Imagination,'" in *Language, Meaning and God: Essays in Honour of Herbert McCabe* (ed. Brian Davies; London: Geoffrey Chapman, 1987), 183–84; Walter Radl, "Der Tod Jesu in der Darstellung der Evangelien," *ThGl* 72 (1982): 433–36; Johannes Schreiber, *Theologie des Vertrauens: Eine redaktionsgeschichtliche Untersuchung des Markusevangeliums* (Hamburg: Furche, 1967), 33–40. For patristic texts that link Jesus' death with eschatological prophecy, see Dale C. Allison Jr., "Darkness at Noon (Matt. 27:45)," in *Studies in Matthew: Interpretation Past and Present* (Grand Rapids: Baker Academic, 2005), 87–88.

131. C. H. Dodd observes, "The second half of the Book of Zechariah, chs. ix–xiv, has the character of an apocalypse, and while its component visions (like those of many apocalypses) are not easy to bring into a consistent scheme, it can be understood as setting forth a whole eschatological programme" (*According to the Scriptures: The Sub-structure of New Testament Theology* [London: Fontana, 1965], 64). For Zech 9–14 in the passion narratives, see Allison, *End of the Ages*, 33–36; Mark Black, "The Messianic Use of Zechariah 9–14 in Matthew, Mark, and the Pre-Markan Tradition," in *Scripture and Traditions: Essays on Early Judaism and Christianity in Honor of Carl R. Holladay* (ed. Patrick Gray and Gail R. O'Day; NovTSup 129; Leiden: Brill, 2008), 97–114; Charlene McAfee Moss, *The Zechariah Tradition and the Gospel of Matthew* (BZNW 156; Berlin: de Gruyter, 2008), 61–207; Craig A. Evans, "Zechariah in the Markan Passion Narrative," in *The Gospel of Mark* (vol. 1 of *Biblical Interpretation in Early Christian Gospels*, ed. Thomas R. Hatina; LNTS 304; London: T & T Clark, 2006), 64–80; Joel Marcus, *The Way of the Lord: Christological Exegesis of the Old Testament in the Gospel of Mark* (Louisville: Westminster John Knox, 1992), 154–64; Douglas J. Moo, *The Old Testament in the Gospel Passion Narratives* (Sheffield: Almond, 1983), 173–224. According to Paul D. Hanson, the use of Zechariah in the passion narratives implies that "the end-time terrors would have to befall God's son before the final glorious events could be inaugurated (even as the apocalyptic circles of Second Zechariah and elsewhere believed that the apocalyptic woes would have to befall the people before the glorious eschaton could arrive)" (*The Dawn of Apocalyptic: The Historical and Sociological Roots of Jewish Apocalyptic Eschatology* [Philadelphia: Fortress, 1979], 350–51).

132. "After his resurrection" (μετὰ τὴν ἔγερσιν αὐτοῦ) in Matt 27:53 is either a Matthean addition or, more likely, an early gloss; see Dale C. Allison Jr., "Matt 27:51–53 and the Descens ad inferos," in *Neutestamentliche Exegese im Dialog: Hermeneutik–Wirkungsgeschichte–Matthäusevangelium; Festschrift für Ulrich Luz zum 70. Geburtstag* (ed. Peter Lampe, Moisés Mayordomo, and Migaku Sato; Neukirchen-Vluyn: Neukirchener Verlag, 2008), 335–55.

both Ezek 37 (the vision of the valley of dry bones) and Zech 14:4–5 (which foretells the splitting of a mountain, mentions an earthquake, and prophesies the appearance of "the holy ones").[133] Many scholars have understandably felt that the First Gospel here preserves something of the eschatological enthusiasm of the earliest churches.[134]

John's Gospel, different from the Synoptics in so many ways, offers something similar. We find this in 16:21–22: "When a woman is in labor, she has pain, because her hour has come. But when her child is born, she no longer remembers the anguish because of the joy of having brought a human being into the world. So you have pain now; but I will see you again, and your hearts will rejoice, and no one will take your joy from you." These two verses, in the words of C. H. Dodd, reinterpret the traditional expectations of "the messianic woes and the joy attending the final salvation of the people of God . . . in terms of the passion and resurrection of Christ."[135] Elsewhere in the Fourth Gospel, Jesus' crucifixion is "the κρίσις of the world" (12:31).[136] This idea of a global judgment comes directly from Jewish apocalyptic, where it is a stock item in end-time visions.[137] In John, however, this judgment is, astonishingly enough, moved to the crucifixion of Jesus. The κρίσις at the cross somehow calls a halt to the malevolent reign of Satan (12:31–33; 16:8–11; cf. 14:30–31), which is otherwise an eschatological hope for ancient Jews.[138] Jesus' death

133. See Dale C. Allison Jr., "The Scriptural Background of a Matthean Legend: Ezekiel 37, Zechariah 14, and Matthew 27," in *Life beyond Death in Matthew's Gospel* (ed. Wim Weren; Leuven: Peeters, forthcoming).

134. So, for example, Hans-Werner Bartsch, "Zur vorpaulinischen Bekenntnisformel im Eingang der Römerbriefes," *TZ* 23 (1967): 332–35; Joachim Jeremias, *New Testament Theology: The Proclamation of Jesus* (New York: Charles Scribner's Sons, 1971), 309–10; Lohfink, "Ostereereignisse," 169–70.

135. C. H. Dodd, *Historical Tradition in the Fourth Gospel* (Cambridge: Cambridge University Press, 1963), 373. Cf. C. K. Barrett, *The Gospel according to St. John: An Introduction with Commentary and Notes on the Greek Text* (2nd ed.; Philadelphia: Westminster, 1978), 493; Raymond E. Brown, *The Gospel according to John*, vol. 2, *John XIII–XXI* (AB 29A; Garden City, NY: Doubleday, 1970), 732–33.

136. For κρίσις as the eschatological judgment, see, for example, *1 En.* 1:7, 9; 10:12; 100:4; *Pss. Sol.* 15:12; *T. Levi* 1:1; Matt 10:15; 12:36; Matt 11:22 // Luke 10:14 (Q); 2 Thess 1:5; 2 Pet 2:9; 3:7; Jude 6; Rev 14:7; *2 Clem.* 16:3; 17:6; 18:2; Pol. *Phil.* 7:1.

137. For a comprehensive review of the abundant materials, see Reiser, *Jesus and Judgment*, 26–193.

138. For the eschatological end of Satan and/or evil powers, see n. 71; also Josef Blank, *Krisis: Untersuchungen zur johanneischen Christologie und Eschatologie* (Freiburg im Breisgau: Lambertus-Verlag, 1964), 281–94; John Denis, "The 'Lifting Up of the Son of Man' and the Dethroning of the 'Ruler of This World': Jesus' Death as the Defeat of the Devil in John 12:31–32," in *The Death of Jesus in the Fourth Gospel* (ed. G. van Belle; BETL 200; Leuven: Leuven University Press, 2007), 677–91; Judith L. Kovacs, "'Now Shall the Ruler of This World Be Driven Out': Jesus' Death as Cosmic Battle in John 12:20–36," *JBL* 114 (1995): 227–47. It further seems likely that, in John, Judas is a sort of antichrist and plays the traditional role of God's adversary in the latter days; see Barnabas Lindars, *The Gospel of John* (NCB; London:

also, the Fourth Gospel affirms, gathers together "the dispersed children of God" (11:52).[139]

And then there is Paul. According to J. Louis Martyn, the apostle's "perception of Jesus' death is . . . fully as apocalyptic as is his hope for Jesus' parousia."[140] The crucifixion is the rift between the old evil age, over which principalities and powers rule, and the new creation, over which Jesus the messianic Lord reigns.[141] Paul's writings also identify the present with the time of eschatological woe,[142] during which Jesus died.[143] In 1 Cor 15:20, furthermore, Jesus is "the first fruits of those who have died," a conviction that assumes that the eschatological harvest is under way, that the resurrection of Jesus is only the beginning of the general resurrection of the dead (see n. 123). Again, then, the end of Jesus is somehow the end or the beginning of the end.

Oliphants, 1977), 526–27; Wendy E. Sproston, "Satan in the Fourth Gospel," in *Papers on the Gospels* (vol. 2 of *Studia Biblica 1978: Sixth International Congress on Biblical Studies*, ed. E. A. Livingstone; JSNTSup 2; Sheffield: JSOT Press, 1980), 307–11.

139. On this theme and its background in Jewish eschatology, see John Denis, *Jesus' Death and the Gathering of True Israel: The Johannine Appropriation of Restoration Theology in the Light of John 11:47–52* (WUNT 2/217; Tübingen: Mohr Siebeck, 2006).

140. Martyn, "Apocalyptic Antinomies," 421.

141. See 1 Cor 15:25–27, and for this interpretation, Heikki Räisänen, "Did Paul Expect an Earthly Kingdom?" in *Paul, Luke and the Graeco-Roman World: Essays in Honour of Alexander J. M. Wedderburn* (ed. Alf Christophersen et al.; JSNTSup 217; New York: Sheffield Academic Press, 2002), 10–13.

142. See Rom 8:20–22; 1 Cor 7:26–29; Col 1:24; 1 Thess 2:16; 3:3–4; 2 Thess 2:7. So also, among others, Richard J. Bauckham, "Colossians 1:24 Again: The Apocalyptic Motif," *EvQ* 47 (1975): 168–70; J. Christiaan Beker, *Paul the Apostle: The Triumph of God in Life and Thought* (Philadelphia: Fortress, 1980), 145–46; Ernest Best, *One Body in Christ: A Study in the Relationship of the Church to Christ in the Epistles of the Apostle Paul* (London: SPCK, 1955), 136; Franzjosef Froitzheim, *Christologie und Eschatologie bei Paulus* (FB 35; Würzburg: Echter, 1978), 18–28; C. Marvin Pate and Douglas W. Kennard, *Deliverance Now and Not Yet: The New Testament and the Great Tribulation* (New York: Peter Lang, 2003), 119–259; Hans-Heinrich Schade, *Apokalyptische Christologie bei Paulus: Studien zum Zusammenhang von Christologie und Eschatologie in den Paulusbriefen* (GTA 18; Göttingen: Vandenhoeck & Ruprecht, 1981), 130–33; W. Schrage, "Leid, Kreuz und Eschaton: Die Peristasen Katologe als Merkmale paulinischer Theologia Crucis und Eschatologie," *EvT* 34 (1974): 165–66; Ulrich Wilckens, *Röm 6–11* (vol. 2 of *Der Brief an die Römer*; EKKNT 6/2; Zürich: Benzinger; Neukirchen-Vluyn: Neukirchener Verlag, 1978), 290–91.

143. James D. G. Dunn says that "Christ's sufferings and death" belong to "the eschatological tribulation expected as the antecedent to the new age" (*Colossians*, 115 [on Col 1:24]). See further Gerhard Delling, "πλήρης κ.τ.λ.," *TDNT* 6:307; Henry Gustafson, "The Afflictions of Christ: What Is Lacking?" *BR* 7 (1963): 28–42; Franz Zeilinger, *Der Erstegeborene der Schöpfung: Untersuchungen zur Formalstruktur und Theologie des Kolosserbriefes* (Vienna: Herder, 1974), 82–94; Rainer Stuhlmann, *Das eschatologische Maß im Neuen Testament* (FRLANT 132; Göttingen: Vandenhoeck & Ruprecht, 1983), 99–101. This is also how Mark, Revelation, and probably 1 Peter perceive the present; see Allison, *End of the Ages*, 36–38, 70–73; Mark Dubis, *Messianic Woes in First Peter: Suffering and Eschatology in 1 Peter 4:12–19* (New York: Peter Lang, 2002); Ernest Best, *1 Peter* (NCB; London: Oliphants, 1971), 162–64.

Given its appearance in Paul, the Synoptics, and John, the habit of associating the end of Jesus with eschatological motifs must go back to very early times. What explains it? How did it come to pass that some conceptualized a series of past events as belonging to or mirroring the end-time scenario? New Testament scholars, for whatever reason,[144] rarely sense how peculiar this interpretive tradition really is. The end of Jesus, to state the obvious, was neither the end of the present world order nor the beginning of its end. Why, then, did early Christians speak as though it was?[145]

People are, as I have already stressed, inevitably wont to interpret their experiences in terms of previously established categories and prior expectations, even when the fit is poor. Although applicable to almost every sphere of human behavior, religion supplies some of the most striking illustrations of this phenomenon.

Members of messianic movements, for example, have again and again, through creative exegesis, transformed seemingly failed prophecies into fulfillment.[146] The drive to make this hermeneutical move is so strong that eschatological expectations have even created events that, to the eye of history, as opposed to the eye of faith, never happened. When William Miller foretold that Jesus would return on October 2, 1844, and when that date came and went without apparent incident, a handful of Millerites nonetheless maintained that their teacher had not erred. Jesus had come; but, they said, it was a heavenly coming: he had entered the heavenly sanctuary and inaugurated a new phase of salvation history. Seventh-Day Adventists still teach this.[147]

In like manner, the Jehovah's Witnesses believe that Jesus Christ returned to earth in 1874. The reason is that there was, leading up to that year, a prophecy that the second advent would then transpire. When the year came but Jesus did not, the faithful simply reinterpreted the apocalyptic forecast. According to the Jehovah's Witnesses, Christ came, but it was an invisible coming.[148] Something very similar happened again in 1914, when Jesus once more ignored the timetable of the Jehovah's Witnesses, who handled their disappointment not by denying their expectation but rather by affirming

144. One suspects that the explanation has much to do with the theological and existential interpretations of eschatological motifs in the writings of Karl Barth and Rudolf Bultmann (see Allison, *End of the Ages*, 83–84).

145. The answer is not that they knew a good metaphor when they saw one (see Allison, *End of the Ages*, 84–90; idem, "Victory of Apocalyptic").

146. See further below, pp. 149–50.

147. See J. N. Loughborough, *The Great Second Advent Movement: Its Rise and Progress* (Washington, DC: Review & Herald Publishing Association, 1905), 185–97.

148. See James A. Beckford, *The Trumpet of Prophecy: A Sociological Study of Jehovah's Witnesses* (New York: John Wiley & Sons, 1975), 1–21, 108–10; Robert Crompton, *Counting the Days to Armageddon: The Jehovah's Witnesses and the Second Presence of Christ* (Cambridge: James Clarke, 1996).

that Christ "became King of the earth at the time of his second presence, AD 1914."[149]

How do these sorts of *ex eventu* rationalizations bear on Christian origins? If the pattern, fundamental to most Jewish eschatology, of distress presaging victory[150] was already in the minds of Jesus' disciples when they went up to Jerusalem—that is, if they anticipated, before the event, eschatological suffering followed by eschatological vindication, tribulation followed by resurrection, and if Jesus was subsequently crucified and then seen alive again, and especially if there was a story about a vacant grave[151]—then his adherents, instead of discarding their eschatological hopes, would, like other communities longing for the end, have sought to correlate their apocalyptic expectations with what had actually transpired. They would have interpreted his death as eschatological tribulation and his vindication as resurrection from the dead. And this is precisely what we find in our sources. The *Naherwartung* of the historical Jesus and his pre-Easter followers turns what would otherwise be mystifying—the eschatological interpretation of his passion—into something only to be expected.[152]

Explicit Denial in Luke and John

Luke 19:11 purports that when Jesus neared Jerusalem, his disciples "supposed that the kingdom of God was to appear immediately [παραχρῆμα]." Why they should have thought so goes unsaid. Of more concern to the evangelist is the exoneration of their teacher. Jesus did not, according to Luke, share the defective hope of his disciples. We learn this plainly from the accompanying parable about an absentee nobleman, which shows Jesus' clear prescience of the delay of the parousia (Luke 19:12–27).[153] The Son of Man must go away, and for some time, before he comes back.

149. See Christopher Partridge, "The End Is Nigh: Failed Prophecy, Apocalypticism, and the Rationalization of Violence in New Religious Eschatologies," in *The Oxford Handbook of Eschatology* (ed. Jerry L. Walls; Oxford: Oxford University Press, 2008), 196. The secondary exegesis or reinterpretation of prophecy that one finds in millenarian movements lives on, in more sophisticated versions, in the work of some contemporary New Testament exegetes (see Allison, *Jesus of Nazareth*, 167–69).

150. Gershom Scholem remarks, "Jewish Messianism is in its origin and by its nature—this cannot be sufficiently emphasized—a theory of catastrophe"; it involves "the catastrophic and destructive nature of the redemption on the one hand and the utopianism of the content of realized Messianism on the other" (*The Messianic Idea in Judaism and Other Essays on Jewish Spirituality* [New York: Schocken Books, 1971], 7).

151. For this scenario, which I think likely, see Allison, *Resurrecting Jesus*, 299–337.

152. Schmithals observes, "The more one separates the earthly Jesus from apocalypticism, the more incomprehensible becomes the fact that for his disciples Jesus' way ended apocalyptically" ("Jesus," 4).

153. According to Isho'dad of Merv, Jesus wanted "to teach the disciples that the time of his second coming was far distant and not, as was their opinion, near" (*Comm. Luke* ad loc. [HSem 7:73]).

Luke 19:11 betrays the discordant awareness that some sayings attributed to Jesus appear to suggest, or rather had been taken to teach, a *Naherwartung*. The same recognition probably lies behind Acts 1:6, where Jesus' disciples ask him, after he has risen from the dead, if he will forthwith "restore the kingdom to Israel." He does not encourage them to think so but rather prudently counsels, "It is not for you to know the times or periods that the Father has set by his own authority" (Acts 1:7).

We do not, unfortunately, know to what extent tradition lies behind Luke 19:11 and Acts 1:6.[154] We do know, however, that the Third Evangelist, like the author of 2 Pet 3, was aware that ordinary history had moved forward notwithstanding the eschatological expectations of some. We likewise know that, in Luke's mind at least, Jesus' first followers were, even before Easter and Pentecost, looking for the eschatological kingdom of God.

John 21:20–23 is a relative of Luke 19:11. According to the Johannine text, some Christians based their failed eschatological expectations upon the teaching of Jesus himself:

> Peter turned and saw the disciple whom Jesus loved following them; he was the one who had reclined next to Jesus at the supper and had said, "Lord, who is it that is going to betray you?" When Peter saw him, he said to Jesus, "Lord, what about him?" Jesus said to him, "If it is my will that he remain until I come, what is that to you? Follow me!" So the rumor spread in the community that this disciple would not die. Yet Jesus did not say to him that he would not die, but, "If it is my will that he remain until I come, what is that to you?"[155]

Because the Fourth Gospel elsewhere shows knowledge of the prediction preserved in Mark 9:1 ("Truly I tell you, there are some standing here who will not taste death until they see that the kingdom of God has come with power" [see n. 10]), it is more than a good guess that John 21:20–23 reflects antagonistic interpretations of that particular logion. But whether that is so or not, John 21 rejects the belief, which recalls not only Mark 9:1 but also Mark 13:30 ("This generation will not pass away until all these things have taken place," that Jesus promised to return before all of his disciples had died.[156] Tertullian wrote, "Even John underwent death, although concerning him there

154. See Vittorio Vusco, "'Point of View' and 'Implicit Reader' in Two Eschatological Texts: Lk 19,11–28; Acts 1,6–8," in *The Four Gospels, 1992: Festschrift Frans Neirynck* (ed. F. Van Segbroeck et al.; 3 vols.; BETL 100; Leuven: Leuven University Press, 1992), 1677–96.

155. The final "what is that to you?" is missing from $\aleph^*$ C^{vid} f ^{1} 565 a e syr^s arm. Perhaps it is secondary. NA^{27} puts the words in brackets.

156. See further Jörg Frey, *Die eschatologische Verkündigung in den johanneischen Texten* (vol. 3 of *Die johanneische Eschatologie*; WUNT 117; Tübingen: Mohr Siebeck, 2000), 14–22. See further n. 157.

had prevailed an ungrounded expectation that he would remain alive until the coming of the Lord" (*An.* 50, trans. *ANF* 3:228).[157]

How should we account for Luke 19:11 and John 21:20–23? We can tell one of two stories. Here is the first story:

- Jesus did not teach that the end was near.
- Some of his followers nonetheless came to believe that it was near.
- This conviction found its way into logia wrongly assigned to Jesus.
- As time marched on, anxious questions posed themselves.
- Luke and John denied that Jesus thought the end to be near, although they were aware that others believed this.

Nothing renders this account impossible. If, however, not multiplying entities, or in this case historical stages, is a virtue, a simpler sequence commends itself:

- Jesus taught that the end was near.
- As time marched on, anxious questions posed themselves.
- Luke and John denied that Jesus thought the end near, although they were aware that others believed this.

Whichever story one adopts, two things are incontestable. First, Luke affirms that, during Jesus' ministry, the disciples expected the end to come soon. Second, John concedes that some Christians took at least one saying of Jesus to mean that the parousia would occur before all the disciples were dead. Both facts are more than consistent with the thesis that Jesus was an apocalyptic prophet. Indeed, do the evangelists not protest too much?

Jesus and the Twelve

The old creed at the beginning of 1 Cor 15 refers, without explanation, to "the Twelve" (v. 5: οἱ δώδεκα), as though hearers should know who they are. Mark, who supplies a list of names, uses the same designation for a select group of disciples with whom Jesus shared his labors (e.g., Mark 3:14–19; 4:10; 6:7). John's Gospel speaks of this same company (6:67, 70–71; 20:24), as does the story, preserved in Acts, that a replacement was found for Judas after his discreditable exit (1:12–26).[158] Revelation also knows of "the twelve

---

157. The legend about John is an ancestor of the famous tale of the wandering Jew, whom Christ condemned to walk the earth until the end of time.

158. For an overview of recent work on Matthias, see Arie W. Zwiep, *Judas and the Choice of Matthias: A Study on Context and Concern of Acts 1:15–26* (WUNT 2/187; Tübingen: Mohr Siebeck, 2004), 5–31.

apostles" (21:14), and the saying attributed to Jesus in Matt 19:28 // Luke 22:28–30 (Q), which speaks of his followers sitting on thrones and judging the twelve tribes, presupposes the Twelve as its direct addressees.[159] Regarding this logion, John Meier has asserted, "Granted the knowledge of a leadership group called the Twelve in the early church, not only the Matthean and Lukan texts in their redactional contexts but also the traditional logion circulating in the early church could hardly refer to any group of persons except the Twelve."[160] The First Evangelist must have thought so too, for Matt 19:28 mentions "twelve thrones"; and the Third Evangelist was of the same mind, because Luke 22:28–30 addresses itself to "the apostles" (see 22:14), which Luke, according to common opinion, identified with the Twelve.

Several scholars, however, have denied that Jesus selected a group of twelve for a symbolic and/or ministerial end; this is instead a legend.[161] One reason for disputing the New Testament witness comes from 1 Cor 15:5, which mentions a post-Easter appearance to "the Twelve." Walter Schmithals reasoned that since Judas was "one of the Twelve" (Mark 14:10, 43), and since the risen Jesus appeared to that group, the disciple could not have betrayed his Lord before Easter. Schmithals then went on to urge that Judas was a post-Easter apostate, and that when the Twelve, a group constituted only after the resurrection appearance to Peter, was backdated to the time of Jesus, Judas moved with them.[162]

However, instead of this series of conjectures, for which there is no real evidence,[163] discretion counsels reckoning οἱ δώδεκα in 1 Cor 15:5 as the name of a group rather than a meticulous head count. Even with Judas gone, the institution, "the Twelve," remained intact, as the story in Acts 1:12–26, according to which Matthias took Judas's "office" (ἐπισκοπή), illustrates. As Jeremias wrote,

> We can see how stereotyped a term "the twelve" had become . . . from the way in which the term was used even though at the time of the christophany to the

159. Matthew refers to twelve thrones and to twelve tribes, Luke only to the latter. For exhaustive discussion as to what stood in their common source, see Paul Hoffmann et al., *Q 22:28, 30: You Will Judge the Twelve Tribes of Israel* (Documenta Q; Leuven: Peeters, 1998).

160. John P. Meier, "The Circle of the Twelve: Did It Exist during Jesus' Public Ministry?" *JBL* 116 (1997): 653 n. 46. Note that whereas line 7 of 4Q164 frg. 1 refers simply to "the chiefs of the tribes of Israel in the last days," line 4 has the more precise enumeration "twelve chiefs."

161. In addition to Bultmann, *Theology*, 1:37, note especially Andries van Aarde, "The Historicity of the Circle of the Twelve: All Roads Lead to Jerusalem," *HvTSt* 55 (1999): 795–826; Günter Klein, *Die zwölf Apostel: Ursprung und Gehalt einer Idee* (FRLANT 77; Göttingen: Vandenhoeck & Ruprecht, 1961); Philipp Vielhauer, "Gottesreich und Menschensohn in der Verkündigung Jesu," in *Aufsätze zum Neuen Testament* (TB 31; Munich: Kaiser, 1965), 69–71.

162. Walter Schmithals, *The Office of Apostle in the Early Church* (trans. John E. Steely; Nashville: Abingdon, 1969), 68–71.

163. One could just as readily imagine that the Twelve were a pre-Easter group, that Judas was a post-Easter apostate, and that the tradition made him one of the Twelve on the basis of Ps 41:9 ("Even my bosom friend in whom I trusted, who ate of my bread, has lifted the heel against me").

"twelve," Judas was no longer alive. Despite this, it was not said that "he appeared to the eleven," because the term "the twelve" was not a purely numerical designation of twelve individual personalities, but signified the group of the representatives of the twelve tribes in the end time.[164]

This seems reasonable enough. BDAG (s.v. δώδεκα) observes that "X[enophon], *Hell.* 2.4.23, still speaks of οἱ τριάκοντα ['the thirty'], despite the fact that acc[ording] to 2.4.19 Critias and Hippomachus have already been put to death," making for a group of twenty-eight. Similarly, Eduard Meyer noted that Octavian, Mark Antony, and Marcus Aemilius Lepidus were known as "the triumvirate," a title retained by the former two even after the latter was deposed.[165]

Like Schmithals, the Jesus Seminar has also been dubious that Jesus, in the words of Mark 3:14, "appointed twelve to be with him" (RSV). The late Robert Funk, their chief spokesperson, shared the reasons:

> A group called the twelve is not mentioned in the earliest layer of the Sayings Gospel Q nor in the Gospel of Thomas; it appears in the title of the Didache but not in the body of that document (the title "The Teachings of the Twelve Apostles" was undoubtedly added later); the letter of Clement to the church at Corinth written about 96 CE does not mention the twelve, and neither do the letters of Ignatius composed between 110–117 CE. Support for this highly symbolic designation depends on the Gospel of Mark, a reference in the later layer of Q, and a single reference in Paul's letters. However, Paul does not seem to know the twelve as an actual group of leaders with special authority. Instead, he is acquainted with an inner circle of "pillars," to which he refers in his letter to the Galatians (2:1–10).[166]

The absence of the Twelve from the hypothetical Q[1] and the *Gospel of Thomas* is, however, an argument from silence, which is cogent only if the silence is unexpected. But why expect a collection of sayings to name the Twelve? If such a body existed, Jesus for the most part spoke to it, not about it. One recalls that Q also fails to name Peter even once, a circumstance that does not diminish our confidence that a Galilean by that name followed Jesus in his itinerant travels.

As for the absence of the Twelve from the *Didache*, *1 Clement*, and the epistles of Ignatius, not only should it go without saying that much of importance from the pre-Easter period merits no mention in those writings, but the absence of the Twelve in them is more than matched by their presence in other sources:

164. Jeremias, *New Testament Theology*, 233–34.
165. Eduard Meyer, *Die Evangelien* (vol. 1 of *Ursprung und Anfänge des Christentums*; 5th ed.; Stuttgart: J. G. Cotta'sche Buchhandlung, 1924), 297 n. 2.
166. Robert Funk and the Jesus Seminar, *The Acts of Jesus: The Search for the Authentic Deeds of Jesus* (San Francisco: HarperSanFrancisco, 1998), 71.

Matthew, Mark, Luke, John, Acts, the ancient creed in 1 Cor 15, and Revelation. It is an odd line of reasoning that builds upon the failure of only some of our sources to mention this or that. What does it mean that Peter is missing from the *Didache*, that Pilate fails to make an appearance in the *Gospel of Thomas*, or that *1 Clement* takes no notice of James the brother of Jesus? Not much. Crossan has declared, "If the institution of Twelve Apostles, with all its profound symbolic connotations, had been established by Jesus during his lifetime, it would have been more widely known and noted."[167] As Crossan fails to elaborate, I fail to be persuaded. By way of analogy, one thinks of the many stories in the Synoptics and John in which Jesus heals the sick. Despite their manifold and profound symbolic connotations, there is no trace of those stories in Paul's Letters or Hebrews or James or 1 Peter or Revelation or *1 Clement* or the *Didache*. What does this tell us about the historical Jesus? Precisely nothing.

Another argument that, according to Funk's reporting, supposedly swayed the Jesus Seminar was this: "Paul does not seem to know the twelve as an actual group of leaders with special authority. Instead, he is acquainted with an inner circle of 'pillars,' to which he refers in his letter to the Galatians (2:1–10)."[168] It is easy to lay the ax to the root of this argument. Dennis Nineham once used the same observation to draw the opposite conclusion: "The very fact that the twelve did not, as a body, have a very important role in the life of the early Church makes it the less likely that the early Church invented . . . [the] story of their appointment."[169] What good is an argument that one can effortlessly flip to establish its contrary?

I will not further review the cases for and against locating the institution of the Twelve during the ministry of Jesus. In my judgment, Robert Meye's thorough discussion settled the issue long ago: he showed that doubt on this particular is unwarranted.[170] Work since Meye has not dug up any new evidence to offset his major points.[171]

167. John Dominic Crossan, *Jesus: A Revolutionary Biography* (San Francisco: HarperSanFrancisco, 1994), 109.

168. Funk and the Jesus Seminar, *Acts of Jesus*, 71.

169. D. E. Nineham, *Saint Mark* (WPC; Philadelphia: Westminster, 1963). Compare these remarks by Joseph Klausner: "The names, in all four lists, are mostly those of men who were not afterwards remarkable, and there would have been no point in inventing them" (*Jesus of Nazareth: His Life, Times, and Teaching* [New York: Macmillan, 1925], 283); and Vincent Taylor: "The general impression we receive is that, while the existence of the Twelve and the nature of their original appointment were firmly rooted in the tradition, apart from Peter, James, and John, most of them" became early on "a somewhat distant memory" (*The Gospel according to St. Mark: The Greek Text with Introduction, Notes, and Indexes* [2nd ed.; London: Macmillan; New York: St. Martin's Press, 1966], 619–20). This is also the view of Meier, "Circle of the Twelve," 658, 670–71.

170. Robert P. Meye, *Jesus and the Twelve: Discipleship and Revelation in Mark's Gospel* (Grand Rapids: Eerdmans, 1968), 192–209.

171. See, in addition to Meier, "Circle of the Twelve," idem, *Marginal Jew*, 3:128–47; idem, "Jesus, the Twelve, and the Restoration of Israel," in *Restoration: Old Testament, Jewish, and*

What, then, should we infer if we think that Jesus appointed an inner group of twelve disciples? Again and again, and with good reason, the secondary literature says this: he must have been thinking about Israel. Surely, within the context of ancient Judaism, twelve people naturally represented the twelve tribes.[172]

This is not a new insight. The older ecclesiastical commentators often grasped this, despite the far-flung tradition, based upon Matt 28:19, that Jesus chose "twelve apostles to proclaim the news among the nations" (4 Bar. 9:20; cf. Mart. Ascen. Isa. 3:17–18). Theophylact remarked on Matt 10:1 ("Jesus summoned his twelve disciples"): "He chose twelve disciples according to the number of the twelve tribes" (Comm. Matt. ad loc. [PG 123:233D]). The same verse moved Matthew Poole to say much the same thing: Jesus "chooseth out twelve, that as the twelve patriarchs begat the Jewish church, so these twelve men might be the fathers to all the gospel church."[173]

Unlike Poole, however, more recent exegetes tend to think not in ecclesiastical terms but eschatological terms. This is because ancient Jews commonly believed that the ten tribes[174] had not been exiled into oblivion but rather, in the providence of God, had survived.[175] "The number twelve must be related to the twelve tribes of Israel and more precisely to Israel's rebirth in the end time, since the ten and a half tribes of the northern kingdom, overthrown in

Christian Perspectives (ed. James M. Scott; JSJSup 72; Leiden: Brill, 2001), 365–404; Sanders, Jesus and Judaism, 98–106; Wolfgang Trilling, "Zur Entstehung des Zwölferkreises: Eine geschichtskritische Überlegung," in Studien zur Jesusüberlieferung (SBA 1; Stuttgart: Katholisches Bibelwerk, 1988), 185–208.

172. Cf., for example, Gen 49:28 (the twelve sons of Israel are the twelve tribes); Exod 24:4 (twelve pillars represent the twelve tribes); Num 1:44 (twelve leading men of Israel represent the twelve tribes); Deut 1:23 ("twelve of you, one from each tribe"); Josh 3:12 ("twelve men from the tribes of Israel, one from each tribe"); Ezra 6:17 ("twelve male goats, according to the number of the tribes of Israel"); Ezek 48:31 (twelve gates stand for the tribes of Israel); 1QM 2:2–3 (twelve Levites for the twelve tribes); 5:2–3 (twelve commanders of the twelve tribes). Note also the discussion in Pesiq. Rab. 4, where the twelve months of the year, the twelve hours in the night, the twelve signs of the zodiac, and so on are signs of the tribes of Israel. For further examples, see Karen J. Wenell, Jesus and Land: Sacred and Social Space in Second Temple Judaism (LNTS 334; London: T & T Clark, 2007), 105–16.

173. Matthew Poole, Annotations on the Holy Bible (3 vols.; London: Henry G. Bohn, 1846), 3:42. John Wesley comments, "The number seems to have relation to the twelve patriarchs and the twelve tribes of Israel" (Explanatory Notes upon the New Testament [London: Epworth, 1950], 52).

174. Or nine and a half, as in 4 Ezra 13:40 v.l.; 2 Bar. 78:1; or nine, as in T. Benj. 12:2 arm (cf. 1 En. 89:72).

175. Note Josephus's comment that the "ten tribes beyond the Euphrates" constitute "countless myriads whose number cannot be ascertained" (Ant. 11.133); cf. Rev 7:4–8; 2 Bar. 78:1–7; see also the texts in nn. 177, 178. The Letter of Aristeas recounts that the LXX was translated in the postexilic period by seventy-two men, six from each tribe of Israel (Let. Arist. 47–51). The tradition that all twelve tribes still existed lived on in medieval times; see A. Neubauer, "Where Are the Ten Tribes?" JQR 1 (1988–1989): 14–28, 95–114, 185–201, 408–23.

722 BC, were considered lost or at least did not live in Palestine."[176] In fact, the dispersed dwelt, so rumor had it, in a place far away, from whence they would, in the latter days, return to the land: those exported in the past would be imported in the future.

How could it be otherwise, given the biblical oracles that envisage the ingathering of all Israel and the end of *galut*?[177] We are informed by *4 Ezra* 13:40–47 that the lost tribes inhabit a region named "Arzareth" (probably from ארץ אחרת, "another land" [cf. Deut 29:28]), which lies beyond the Euphrates, and that soon, in "the last times," they will "come again," that is, literally return to Palestine.[178] One may compare the tenth benediction of the Amidah: "Sound the great horn for our freedom, and lift up a banner to gather in our exiles. You are praised, O Lord, who gathers in the outcasts of his people Israel."[179] Even Philo, despite his spiritualized definition of Israel and his seeming lack of interest in most matters eschatological, held this hope (see *Rewards* 163–172). In short, many Jews at the turn of the era looked forward to a rebirth of the glory of David and Solomon, to a day when the Israelite dynasty would be again united, when all twelve tribes would be settled in the land, when there would be no more dispersion.

Because this belief in the eschatological homecoming of the lost tribes was, in the words of Sanders, "very common,"[180] and because it appears in two sayings in Q (see p. 42), one naturally associates Jesus' creation of a band of twelve with

176. Christoph Burchard, "Jesus of Nazareth," in *Christian Beginnings* (ed. Becker), 45.

177. For example, Deut 30:1–5; 1 Chr 16:35; Neh 1:8–9; Ps 106:47; 147:2; Isa 11:11–13; 27:12–13; 43:5–6, 14–21; 49:6; 56:8; 60:3–7; 66:18–24; Jer 23:8; 29:10–14; 31:1, 8, 10; 32:37–41; Ezek 11:17–20; 20:33–44; 28:25; 34:11–16; 36:24; 37:11–28; 39:26–27; Hos 11:11; Zeph 3:20; Zech 8:7; 10:6–12; 2 Macc 1:27; 2:7, 18; Sir 36:13; 48:10; Tob 13:5, 13; 14:5; Bar 4:37; 5:5.

178. Note also *Jub.* 1:15; *Pss. Sol.* 8:28; 11:2–3; 17:4, 21, 26–28, 44; *1 En.* 57:1; 90:33; 11Q19 57:5–6; 4Q386 frg. 1 col. II; 4Q504 frgs. 1–2 col. VI 12–14; 4Q509 + 4Q505 3; Philo, *Rewards* 164–165, 168; *4 Ezra* 13:32–50; *2 Bar.* 78:1–7; *Sib. Or.* 2:170–73; *T. Iss.* 6:2–4; *T. Dan* 5:8–9; *T. Naph.* 4:2–5; *T. Ash.* 7:3; *T. Benj.* 9:2; 10:11; *T. Jos.* 19:3–8 (Armenian); *Mek.* on Exod 14:31; *m. Sanh.* 10:3; *t. Sanh.* 13:12; *y. Sanh.* 29c (10:6); *b. Sanh.* 110b; Tg. Neof. I on Num 24:7; Tg. Isa. on 6:13; 53:8; Tg. Hos 2:2; Tg. Mic 5:3; Commodian, *Instr.* 42 (2.1) (CCSL 128:34–36). The inscribing of the names of the twelve tribes on the gates of the new Jerusalem in 4Q554 and Rev 21:12 also belongs here. Despite the silence of many commentators, Luke's Paul, in Acts 26:6–7, may implicitly endorse this expectation. At the very least, he speaks as though "the twelve tribes" (τὸ δωδεκάφυλον) still exist.

179. The content of this line goes back to pre-70 liturgical texts; see Esther G. Chazon, "'Gathering the Dispersed of Judah': Seeking a Return to the Land as a Factor in Jewish Identity of Late Antiquity," in *Heavenly Tablets: Interpretation, Identity and Tradition in Ancient Judaism* (ed. Lynn LiDonnici and Andrea Lieber; JSJSup 119; Leiden: Brill, 2007), 159–75.

180. E. P. Sanders, *Judaism: Practice and Belief, 63 BCE–66 CE* (London: SCM Press; Philadelphia: Trinity Press International, 1992), 290–91. Sanders writes, "The general hope for the restoration of the people of Israel is the most ubiquitous hope of all. The twelve tribes are sometimes explicitly mentioned and often indirectly referred to (e.g., by the name 'Jacob'), but sometimes the hope is stated more vaguely: the children of Israel will be gathered from throughout the world. In such instances we cannot be sure that the lost ten tribes were explicitly

that belief. One also naturally regards that band as a promise or prophetic parable: the twelve tribes will be gathered together once more, and soon.[181] Indeed, the inference is so close to inevitable that Sanders and Fredriksen have found here support for a strongly eschatological Jesus. In the words of the former, "We can see that Jesus fitted his own work into Jewish eschatological expectation if we know only that he thought of there being twelve around him."[182]

I do not know what is wrong with this argument. Marcus Borg has tried to counter it by urging that if Jesus chose twelve disciples, it would indicate only that he "saw his mission as having to do with 'Israel,' but it need not imply the framework of imminent restoration eschatology."[183] This assertion, with its unexplained quotation marks around Israel, will hardly do. We should interpret Jesus within his historical context, which in this case means that we should gauge his apparent intent in terms of what his contemporaries, as best we can judge, believed about the twelve tribes. Beyond that, our sources are quite clear on the link between the Twelve and eschatology. Matthew 19:28 and Luke 22:28–30, as already observed, envisage the Twelve ruling or passing judgment upon the twelve tribes of Israel.[184] Even if Jesus made no such pledge,[185] the saying shows how readily the institution of the Twelve was associated with the regathering of all Israel.[186]

---

in mind, though it seems likely enough; in any case the reassembly of the people of Israel was generally expected" (p. 294).

181. See further Allison, *Jesus of Nazareth*, 101–2; Meier, *Marginal Jew*, 3:148–54; Wenell, *Jesus and Land*, 104–38. I borrow the word *promise* from Heinz Schürmann: "In his twelve disciples Jesus issued to the twelve tribes . . . a great promise: at that time people hoped that the twelve tribes destroyed at the exile would be reestablished at the end—a hope that Jesus makes visible in this symbolic twelve: Israel will obtain salvation, inherit the kingdom and be reinstated as the twelve tribes, if only they turn to him, the sent messianic shepherd" ("Der Jüngerkreis Jesu als Zeichen für Israel [und als Urbild des kirchlichen Rätestandes]," in *Ursprung und Gestalt: Erörterungen und Besinnungen zum Neuen Testament* [KBANT; Düsseldorf: Patmos-Verlag, 1970], 46).

182. Sanders, *Jesus and Judaism*, 104. Cf. Fredriksen, *Jesus of Nazareth*, 98.

183. Marcus Borg, "Jesus and Eschatology: Current Reflections," in *Jesus in Contemporary Scholarship*, 76. In a footnote Borg appeals to the precedent of G. B. Caird and C. H. Dodd, both of whom thought that Jesus had twelve disciples, neither of whom attributed to him apocalyptic eschatology.

184. Parallels include the twenty-four elders of Revelation (they may be the twelve apostles [21:14] and the twelve angels of Israel [21:12]); *T. Ab.* RecLng 13:6: "And in the second parousia, everything that breathes and every person will be judged by the twelve tribes of Israel" (the idea seems to be that Israel judges through its representatives, perhaps the twelve patriarchs or the twelve phylarchs). See further the helpful work of Hanna Roose, *Eschatologische Mitherrschaft: Entwicklungslinien einer urchristlichen Erwartung* (NTOA/SUNT 54; Göttingen: Vandenhoeck & Ruprecht; Fribourg: Academic Press, 2004), 30–95.

185. According to W. D. Davies, he did not (*The Gospel and the Land: Early Christianity and Jewish Territorial Doctrine* [Berkeley: University of California Press, 1974], 363–65); according to Sanders, he did (*Jesus and Judaism*, 98–106).

186. Steven M. Bryan objects that "a framework which allows for a greater degree of realization in Jesus' eschatology would suggest a quite different conclusion" (*Jesus and Israel's Traditions of*

The Jesus Seminar, despite itself, has implicitly confirmed the eschatological conclusion that lies near to hand in Jesus' appointment of twelve disciples. The climax of their argument for denying the pre-Easter origin of the Twelve is, in Funk's report, this: "Most important, the role of the 'twelve' is associated with the eschatological self-consciousness of the Christian community, which thought of itself as the new Israel living at the endtime, just before the judgment. The Seminar doubts that such a notion originated with Jesus."[187]

These words acknowledge that the idea of twelve disciples is eschatological. So one can avoid the inference of Sanders and Fredriksen only by denying that the idea goes back to Jesus, which is what the Seminar does. If, however, its reasons for denial are, as we have seen, inadequate, then its collective wisdom on this topic is not wisdom. Jesus seems rather to have had in mind something like 4Q164 frg. 1, which concerns the twelve chiefs of the tribes of Israel in the last days; or *T. Jud.* 25:1–2, where the twelve risen sons of Jacob will wield the scepter in Israel; or *T. Benj.* 10:7, which has Benjamin predict of himself and his eleven brothers, "Then shall we also be raised, each of us over our tribe."[188] Michael Fuller, moreover, has observed that "several documents from Qumran attest to the belief that Jewish writers understood the reassembly of the twelve tribes to have been inaugurated in the appointment of tribal rules within the group's hierarchy."[189] An analogy with Jesus and his twelve disciples suggests itself.

Two more points are in order regarding the Twelve. First, we are dealing here not with a metaphor but rather with a literal expectation that has been, throughout the centuries, a staple of Jewish messianism.[190] In 1096, German Jews, convinced that the days of the Messiah were upon them, marched for Palestine in the expectation of being met on the way by the ten lost tribes.[191]

Judgement and Restoration [SNTSMS 117; Cambridge: Cambridge University Press, 2002], 123). Although this is true in the abstract, Bryan, in my judgment, finds too much realized eschatology in the tradition. In addition, the two texts that most plainly deal with the restoration of Israel (Matt 8:11–12 // Luke 13:28–29 [Q]; Matt 19:28 // Luke 22:28–30 [Q]) have future tenses ("many will come from east and west," "will sit on thrones"). Clearly, the many have not yet come from east and west, and the disciples are not already seated upon thrones.

187. Funk and the Jesus Seminar, *Acts of Jesus*, 71.

188. H. C. Kee, *OTP* 1:828. My conclusion would be reinforced if David Flusser were right to suppose that Jesus borrowed the idea of twelve disciples from John the Baptist, given John's eschatological orientation ("Qumran und die Zwölf," in *Judaism and the Origins of Christianity* [Jerusalem: Magnes, 1988], 183). But Acts 19:1–7, with its mention of "about twelve" (ὡσεὶ δώδεκα) followers of John, and the Baptist's spiritual affiliation with Qumran, which so emphasized the number *twelve*, do not suffice for Flusser's inference.

189. Michael E. Fuller, *The Restoration of Israel: Israel's Re-gathering and the Fate of the Nations in Early Jewish Literature and Luke-Acts* (BZNW 138; Berlin: de Gruyter, 2006), 255, italics removed.

190. According to Neubauer, "This hope has been connected with every Messianic rising" ("Ten Tribes," 21).

191. See David Kaufmann, "A Hitherto Unknown Messianic Movement among the Jews, Particularly Those of Germany," *JQR* 10 (1897–1898): 139–51.

Amid the messianic excitement of the year 1419, two Roman rabbis went around seeking information about the distant tribes.[192] In the sixteenth century, when David Reuben asked the pope for military equipment for some of the lost tribes, many Jews decided that he must be the Messiah's forerunner.[193] In the next century, Sabbatai Sevi chose twelve rabbinic scholars to represent all Israel, which his followers thought would soon be restored.[194] We have no reason whatsoever to surmise that first-century Jews, including Jesus, conceived the restoration of Israel in an utterly different way than did later Jews. Even Philo, as already remarked, understood this belief literally (*Rewards* 163–168). If, then, Jesus ever spoke of "the twelve tribes of Israel," as Matthew and Luke report, he was not thinking about Galilean or Judean Jews or about a spiritual remnant or a new religious movement but rather about far-off exiles who would someday return to the land that God had long ago promised to Abraham and his descendants.[195]

Second, *m. Sanh.* 10:3 records a debate between Rabbi Akiba and Rabbi Eliezer regarding eschatological expectations, including the fate of the lost ten tribes. Eliezer affirms that those tribes will have a share in the world to come. Akiba, quite unexpectedly, denies this (cf. *t. Sanh.* 13:12). Joseph Heinemann has explained Akiba's position as due to his recognition of Bar Kokhba as the Messiah: if the messianic age has begun and the lost tribes have not yet returned, then clearly they are never going to return. In other words, having identified the present with eschatological time, Akiba was forced to think realistically in terms of contemporary circumstances.[196] This offers a contrast,

---

192. See David Kaufmann, "A Rumour about the Ten Tribes in Pope Martin V's Time," *JQR* 4 (1892): 503–8.

193. On David Reuben, see Harris Lenowitz, *The Jewish Messiahs: From the Galilee to Crown Heights* (Oxford: Oxford University Press, 1998), 103–23; A. Z. Aescoly, "David Reubeni in the Light of History," *JQR* 28 (1937): 1–45.

194. Gershom Scholem, *Sabbatai Sevi: The Mystical Messiah* (Princeton, NJ: Princeton University Press, 1973), 222. Scholem writes, "There was a persistent popular legendary tradition about the lost tribes. In times of eschatological propaganda . . . and millenarist expectation, such reports, combining half-true accounts of Jews in far-away countries with uninhibited imaginings, would naturally proliferate" (p. 337).

195. For this reason, among others, one doubts that Jesus' ideas about the kingdom were free of "nationalistic" concerns (contrast Mary Ann Beavis, *Jesus and Utopia: Looking for the Kingdom of God in the Roman World* [Minneapolis: Fortress, 2006]) or territorial interests (contrast Hans Kvalbein, "The Kingdom of God in the Ethics of Jesus," *CV* 40 [1998]: 210). Rather, Jesus' proclamation had concrete political ramifications involving land and sovereignty. At the very least, the coming of God's kingdom meant the going of Rome's kingdom (cf. *Cant. Rab.* 2:12) and the restoration of a Jewish theocracy. That theocracy might be without boundaries because universal (cf. *Pirqe R. El.* 11; *Yal.* on Isa 46:23), but its capital would be Jerusalem. See p. 51.

196. See Joseph Heinemann, *Aggadah and Its Development* (Jerusalem: Keter, 1974), 108. Consistent with this is the tradition in *Tanḥ.* 'Eqeb 7 and *Midr. Ps.* 90:17 that, according to Akiba, the Messiah would reign for forty years. This relatively short period may have had Bar Kokhba's expected life span in view.

I suggest, with Jesus. If he expected the return of the ten tribes, then he was thinking in more idealistic or utopian terms than was Akiba.

The Popularity of Apocalyptic Eschatology

E. P. Sanders holds that before 66 CE, "common Judaism"—his term—included, among its hopes for the future, the following: the restoration of the tribes of Israel; the conversion, destruction, or subjugation of the Gentiles; the renewal of Jerusalem, including a new or rebuilt temple; and the purification of God's people and their worship.[197]

Whatever one makes of his idea of a common Judaism, surely the beliefs that Sanders highlights were widespread among Jesus' contemporaries, as was apocalyptic eschatology in general.[198] This follows from a number of facts: (a) Daniel was, around the turn of the era, a very popular book, a sort of best seller.[199] (b) Apocalyptic literature, of which only a sample has survived,[200] was then in vogue in at least several quarters.[201] (c) The Qumran sectarians were, in and around Jesus' day, composing, copying, and studying what we today know as the Dead Sea Scrolls, so many of which are charged with apocalyptic expectation.[202] (d) Eschatological expectation appears to have played a significant role in the first revolt against Rome.[203] Josephus reports on the impact, during that time, of a particular biblical oracle, taken to mean that "one from

197. Sanders, *Judaism*, 279–303.

198. Compare S. E. Robinson, "Apocalypticism in the Time of Hillel and Jesus," in *Hillel and Jesus: Comparisons of Two Major Religious Leaders* (ed. James H. Charlesworth and Loren L. Johns; Minneapolis: Fortress, 1997), 21–36; Seth Schwartz, *Imperialism and Jewish Society, 200 B.C.E. to 640 C.E.* (Princeton, NJ: Princeton University Press, 2001), 74–99; contrast Richard A. Horsley, *Sociology and the Jesus Movement* (2nd ed.; New York: Continuum, 1994), 96–99.

199. Note Josephus, *Ant.* 10.268. See further G. K. Beale, *The Use of Daniel in Jewish Apocalyptic Literature and in the Revelation of St. John* (Lanham, MD: University Press of America, 1984), 12–153; John J. Collins, *Daniel: A Commentary on the Book of Daniel* (Hermeneia; Minneapolis: Fortress, 1993), 72–112; Peter W. Flint, "The Daniel Tradition at Qumran," in *Eschatology, Messianism, and the Dead Sea Scrolls* (ed. Craig A. Evans and Peter W. Flint; Grand Rapids: Eerdmans, 1997), 41–60. The Qumran caves contained more manuscripts of Daniel (eight) than of Joshua, Samuel, Kings, Chronicles, and Jeremiah; they also held fragments of three Pseudo-Daniel documents (4Q242; 4Q243 + 4Q244; 4Q245).

200. Although it is badly dated, the old survey by Montague Rhodes James, *The Lost Apocrypha of the Old Testament: Their Titles and Fragments* (London: SPCK, 1920), remains instructive on the matter.

201. For an overview, see Collins, *Apocalyptic Imagination.*

202. See John J. Collins, *Apocalypticism in the Dead Sea Scrolls* (London: Routledge, 1997).

203. But for some caution about the matter, see Martin Goodman, "Messianism and Politics in the Land of Israel, 66–135 C.E.," in *Redemption and Resistance: The Messianic Hopes of Jews and Christians in Antiquity* (ed. Markus Bockmuehl and James Carleton Paget; London: T & T Clark, 2007), 149–57.

their country would become ruler of the world" (*J.W.* 6.312–313).[204] Tacitus likewise has it that the Jewish majority believed that "the ancient scriptures of their priests alluded to the present as the very time when the Orient would triumph and from Judaea would go forth men destined to rule the world" (*Hist.* 5.13). Suetonius (*Vesp.* 4.5) tells the same story, perhaps following the same source as Tacitus, which may not have been Josephus.[205] (e) Rabbinic texts remember Akiba, to his eventual discredit, hailing Simon bar Kokhba as the Messiah. The influential rabbi cannot have been alone in his opinion.[206] (f) Many of the beliefs characteristic of apocalyptic eschatology appear not only in numerous early Christian texts but also in rabbinic sources, which implies that such beliefs were regular religious coin in early Judaism. (g) "The rapid expansion of Christianity," to quote Barnabas Lindars, "would really be inexplicable except against the background of a widespread feeling amongst Jews of the day that they were living in the End Time. For it is . . . only because of the pre-understanding of the Bible in this eschatological sense, attested not only in Qumran and apocalyptic, but also to some extent in rabbinic sources, that the church's application of the whole range of Old Testament to Jesus could be felt to be a plausible undertaking and find acceptance."[207]

Given that many—I do not say all or even most—ancient Jews were, like Luke's Simeon, "looking forward to the consolation of Israel" (2:25), or, like Mark's Joseph of Arimathea, "waiting expectantly for the kingdom of God" (15:43), to categorize Jesus as an apocalyptic prophet is to hold that he believed some things that others in his time and place commonly believed. It would, of course, be fallacious to insist that the currency of particular beliefs in his environment

204. Many have suggested that the mysterious oracle was either Num 24:17 or Dan 9:24–27. For strong arguments for the latter, see Anthony J. Tomasino, "Oracles of Insurrection: The Prophetic Catalyst of the Great Revolt," *JJS* 59 (2008): 86–111. Probably relevant here is the neglected topic of chronological calculations of the end; see Roger T. Beckwith, *Calendar and Chronology, Jewish and Christian: Biblical, Intertestamental and Patristic Studies* (AGJU 33; Leiden: Brill, 1996), 217–75; idem, *Calendar, Chronology and Worship: Studies in Ancient Judaism and Early Christianity* (AGJU 61; Leiden: Brill, 2005), 134–43; L. L. Grabbe, "The End of the World in Early Jewish and Christian Calculations," *RevQ* 11 (1982): 107–8; Steudel, "אחרית הימים in the Texts from Qumran"; Ben Zion Wacholder, *Essays on Jewish Chronology and Chronography* (New York: Ktav, 1976), 240–57; Cana Werman, "Epochs and End-Time: The 490-Year Scheme in Second Temple Literature," *DSD* 13 (2006): 229–55; Michael Owen Wise, "Thunder in Gemini (4Q318)," in *Thunder in Gemini and Other Essays on the History, Language and Literature of Second Temple Palestine* (JSPSup 15; Sheffield: Sheffield Academic Press, 1994), 39–48. Origen probably was right: around the time of Jesus, many had used the Scriptures to calculate the time of the redemption (*Comm. Jo.* 6.16).

205. See Eduard Norden, "Josephus und Tacitus über Jesus Christus und eine messianische Prophetie," *NJahrb* 31 (1913): 636–66.

206. See further below, p. 258 n. 150.

207. Barnabas Lindars, "The Place of the Old Testament in the Formation of New Testament Theology," *NTS* 23 (1976): 62.

is a sure signal that he shared them.[208] Jesus stood out from his contemporaries in several important respects; he was not just like everybody else. Still, it is not otiose to observe that the more common we judge any belief to have been in a particular time and place, the higher the odds that someone from that time and place held it. The corollary is that, in general, the more atypical we judge an idea to have been, the lower the odds that someone held it. The hypothesis that Jesus was a sort of Jewish Cynic has suffered partly for just this reason: the evidence for Cynicism in his Palestinian world is not exactly abundant. It is fair to observe that an apocalyptic Jesus, by contrast, is comfortably at home within what we otherwise know of first-century Judaism.

One more point in this connection. Portions of the Hebrew Bible, which by the first century included all the additions to the prophetic books as well as Daniel, foretell the defeat of Israel's enemies, the influx of the Diaspora, the transformation of the land of promise into a paradise, and the realization of God's perfect will throughout the world. Is it naïve to assume that Jesus, who was a religious Jew if he was anything, heard some of the relevant scriptural oracles and believed them?[209]

The Fulfillment of Biblical Oracles

If Mark 13–16 correlates eschatological prophecies attributed to Jesus with his passion, early Christian literature on the whole does something similar: it lines up eschatological prophecies from the Hebrew Bible with the end of his life as well as with events immediately preceding and following it. Thus Matt 12:18–21 sees in the ministry of Jesus the fulfillment of Isa 42:1–4 ("Behold, my servant whom I have chosen, my beloved with whom my soul is well pleased . . . ," RSV). The pre-Pauline formula in 1 Cor 15:3–7 regards Jesus' death and resurrection as having been "in accordance with the scriptures." The speech attributed to Peter in Acts 2 makes Joel 2:28–32 ("And it shall come to pass afterward, that I will pour out my spirit on all flesh . . . ," RSV) a forecast of Pentecost.

---

208. Against Richard A. Horsley, I have never argued that, because "apocalyptic eschatology permeated Judaism in the late Second Temple times," it "must have been shared by Jesus and his followers" ("Jesus in the New Millennium," *RBL* 10 [2008]: 6, 19, 20). The "must," like the "therefore" on p. 19 and the "hence" on p. 20, is not mine but his. I have simply argued for a snug fit.

209. Adela Yarbro Collins comments, "If Jesus viewed himself as an eschatological prophet, it is likely that he understood the book of Daniel to refer to his own time and to the near future. He need not have been a scribe or a professional interpreter of Scripture to have known the major characters and basic contents of Daniel. He could have acquired this knowledge from the reading of scripture in synagogues or from the teaching of professional scribes that became part of oral tradition in Palestine" ("Jesus as Son of Man," 172–73). I could not be further from the position of James Breech: "Judging from the core sayings and parables, there is absolutely no basis for assuming that Jesus shared the cosmological, mythological, or religious ideas of his contemporaries" (*The Silence of Jesus: The Authentic Voice of the Historical Man* [Philadelphia: Fortress, 1983], 218). These words strike me as incredible.

One can multiply such examples effortlessly because early Christian literature explicitly and implicitly claims, again and again, that biblical oracles have come true in the recent past, and that more will come true in the near future. This is, then, a wide-ranging phenomenon. How should we account for it? One possibility is that at some point a few of Jesus' followers, without his precedent, began to line up biblical prophecies with events, real or imagined, and their work caught on, becoming a popular theological pastime. The other possibility is that, already before his departure, Jesus and his disciples, like the Qumran sectarians, took themselves to be in the latter days, so that they lived within a biblically inspired scenario.[210] Once born, that prophetic scenario survived Jesus' execution and nurtured the apologetic strategy of appealing to Scripture to bolster novel beliefs.[211]

Some modern scholars seemingly lean toward the former alternative: Jesus did not read the signs of his eschatological times through Scripture. Part of the reason for their conviction must be the knowledge that many early Christians assiduously occupied themselves with biblical proof-texting. But that the churches did something is, in and of itself, no cause to suppose that Jesus did something else.[212] On the contrary, given that his followers remembered him as, among other things, a teacher, a presumption of continuity seems as likely or even more likely than its opposite. As Hans Conzelmann wrote, "Continuity is in itself historically more probable than the assertion of a discontinuity that can scarcely explain the origin of the categories of expression for the community's faith."[213]

All this, however, is abstract generalization. What counts is that, on this matter, the sources present us with enough data to establish another global pattern: more than a few times they present Jesus himself quoting from or alluding to prophetic texts of the Jewish Bible. Here is a list, which is representative, not exhaustive:

1. In Paul's version of the words spoken at the Last Supper, Jesus likely refers to the "new covenant" foretold in Jer 31:31 (1 Cor 11:25; cf. Luke 22:20).[214]

---

210. Contrast the rabbis: although they cite Scripture constantly, they do not as a rule see its prophetic texts fulfilled in their own experiences.

211. On the Bible as apologetic in early Christian traditions, see Barnabas Lindars, *New Testament Apologetic: The Doctrinal Significance of the Old Testament Quotations* (London: SCM Press, 1961).

212. Gerd Theissen and Annette Merz note that "the imitated motif does not become less authentic through its imitation" ("The Delay of the Parousia as a Test Case for the Criterion of Coherence," *LS* 32 [2007]: 59).

213. Hans Conzelmann, "Present and Future in the Synoptic Tradition," *JTC* 5 (1968): 29.

214. See Adrian Schenker, *Das Neue am neuen Bund und das Alte am alten: Jer 31 in der hebräischen und griechischen Bibel, von der Textgeschichte zu Theologie, Synagoge und Kirche* (FRLANT 212; Göttingen: Vandenhoeck & Ruprecht, 2006), 73–78.

2. The Beatitudes in Matt 5:3, 4, 6 // Luke 6:20–21 (Q), at least in their Matthean form, and arguably in their Q form, allude to the beginning of Isa 61 ("to bring good news to the oppressed . . . to comfort all who mourn"), which 11Q13 and other Jewish sources draw upon to foretell the latter days.[215]

3. When the disciples of the Baptist, in Matt 11:2–6 // Luke 7:18–23 (Q), ask Jesus whether he is "the coming one" of their master's proclamation, he responds by borrowing the language of several lines from Isaiah, above all 35:5–6 ("Then the eyes of the blind shall be opened, and the ears of the deaf unstopped; then the lame shall leap like a deer") and 61:1–2 ("the LORD . . . has sent me to bring good news to the oppressed").[216]

4. Matt 11:10 // Luke 7:27 (Q) ("This is he of whom it is written, 'Behold, I send my messenger before your face, who will prepare your way before you,'" RSV) apparently conflates Exod 23:20 with Mal 3:1, the latter being part of an eschatological prophecy about judgment and fire (see vv. 2–3).[217]

5. Matt 10:32–33 // Luke 12:8–9 (Q) envisages the Son of Man confessing and denying those who have confessed or denied Jesus; the vision of the last judgment in Dan 7 is in the background.[218]

6. Mic 7:6, which often was taken to presage familial division at the end of days (cf. m. Soṭah 9:15; b. Sanh. 97a), lies behind Jesus' words in Matt 10:34–36 // Luke 12:51–53 (Q): father will be divided against son, and son against father, and so on (see n. 44).

7. The promise that some of his followers will sit on thrones and judge the twelve tribes of Israel, in Matt 19:27–28 // Luke 22:28–30 (Q), depends upon the vision of Dan 7, which also speaks of "thrones."[219]

8. Mark 8:38, like its relative in Matt 10:32–33 // Luke 12:8–9 (Q), also alludes to the depiction of the great assize in Dan 7: the Son of Man will come for judgment with the holy angels.[220]

215. See details in Allison, Intertextual Jesus, 104–7; Martin Hengel, "Zur matthäischen Bergpredigt und ihrem jüdische Hintergrund," TRu 52 (1987): 351–53; C. M. Tuckett, "Isaiah in Q," in Isaiah in the New Testament (ed. Steve Moyise and Maarten J. J. Menken; London: T & T Clark, 2005), 55–57.

216. See Allison, Intertextual Jesus, 109–14.

217. See David S. New, Old Testament Quotations in the Synoptic Gospels, and the Two-Document Hypothesis (SBLSCS 37; Atlanta: Scholars Press, 1993), 59–64.

218. See Allison, Intertextual Jesus, 130–31.

219. See further Jacques Dupont, "Le logion des douze trônes (Mt 19,28; Lc 22,28–30)," Bib 45 (1964): 381–86; Craig A. Evans, "The Twelve Thrones of Israel: Scripture and Politics in Luke 22:24–30," in Bruce Chilton and Craig A. Evans, Jesus in Context: Temple, Purity, and Restoration (AGJU 39; Leiden: Brill, 1997), 455–79. Compare, from an earlier time, John Trapp, A Commentary or Exposition upon All the Books of the New Testament (ed. W. Webster; London: Richard D. Dickinson, 1865), 221.

220. See Maurice Casey, Son of Man: The Interpretation and Influence of Daniel 7 (London: SPCK, 1979), 161–64.

9. The Jesus of Mark 9:12 implicitly identifies John the Baptist as the fulfillment of Mal 3:1: "Elijah does come first to restore all things" (RSV;
cf. Matt 11:10 // Luke 7:27 [Q]).[221]

10. In Mark 9:48, Jesus characterizes Gehenna using language from the
prophetic oracle that concludes the book of Isaiah: "their worm shall
not die, their fire shall not be quenched" (66:24 RSV).

11. It seems more likely than not that the first part of Mark 10:45 ("the
Son of Man came not to be served but to serve") is an ironic reversal
of Dan 7:14, where one like a son of man comes and multitudes serve
him.[222]

12. Mark 13:14 refers to the "desolating sacrilege" of Dan 9:27; 11:31;
12:11.

13. The apocalyptic vision of Dan 7 lies behind the prophecy in Mark
13:26–27, according to which the Son of Man will come on clouds with
great power and glory.[223]

14. In Mark 14:27, Jesus foretells what will happen to his closest followers
by quoting from an obscure prophecy in Zech 13:7 ("I will strike the
shepherd, and the sheep will be scattered").

15. When accused before the Sanhedrin, the Markan Jesus declares that
his hearers will see the Son of Man coming with the clouds of heaven
(14:62), still another clear allusion to Dan 7:13–14.

16. The vision of the final judgment in Matt 25:31–46, in its opening line
("When the Son of Man comes . . . and all the angels with him"), borrows from Zech 14:5 ("Then the LORD my God will come, and all the
holy ones with him").[224]

17. Jesus' forecast of woe, addressed to the daughters of Jerusalem in Luke
23:30, warns, "Then they will begin to say to the mountains, 'Fall on us';
and to the hills, 'Cover us.'" The words are borrowed from a prophecy

221. See Markus Öhler, *Elia im Neuen Testament: Untersuchung zur Bedeutung des alttestamentlichen Propheten im frühen Christentum* (BZNW 88; Berlin: de Gruyter, 1997), 42–43.

222. See Simon Gathercole, "The Son of Man in Mark's Gospel," *ExpTim* 115 (2004): 366–72;
Morna D. Hooker, *The Son of Man in Mark: A Study of the Background of the Term "Son of
Man" and Its Use in St Mark's Gospel* (London: SPCK, 1967), 140–47.

223. Compare the scenario in 1 Thess 4:15–17, which Paul attributes to "the word of the
Lord." Although it has become popular to suppose that here Paul was thinking of a word of the
risen Lord through a Christian prophet, he may equally have taken himself to be interpreting a
word that he thought of (rightly or wrongly) as coming from the earthly Jesus. See Adela Yarbro
Collins, *Mark: A Commentary* (Hermeneia; Minneapolis: Fortress, 2007), 599–600; Traugott
Holtz, *Der erste Brief an die Thessalonicher* (EKKNT 13; Zurich: Benzinger; Neukirchen-
Vluyn: Neukirchener Verlag, 1986), 183–84. For helpful reviews of the inconclusive discussion,
see Luckensmeyer, *Eschatology of First Thessalonians*, 186–90; Michael W. Pahl, *Discerning
the "Word of the Lord": The "Word of the Lord" in 1 Thessalonians 4:15* (LNTS 389; London:
T & T Clark, 2009), 6–34.

224. See Robert H. Gundry, *The Use of the Old Testament in St. Matthew's Gospel, with
Special Reference to the Messianic Hope* (NovTSup 18; Leiden: Brill, 1967), 142.

of lament in Hos 10:8 ("They shall say to the mountains, Cover us, and to the hills, Fall on us").[225]

18. The judgment scene in Dan 7:9–14 (with κριτήριον, υἱὸς ἀνθρώπου, and αὐτῷ ἐδόθη . . . ἐξουσία in the LXX) is the source for Jesus' declaration, in John 5:27, that "he [God] has given him [Jesus] authority [ἐξουσίαν ἔδωκεν αὐτῷ] to execute judgment [κρίσιν], because he is the Son of Man [υἱὸς ἀνθρώπου]."

19. In John 16:22, Jesus uses the language of Isa 66:14 ("You shall see, and your heart shall rejoice") to promise his disciples that they will see him again and then rejoice.[226]

I offer no evidence that any of these verses fairly represent things Jesus said, although I more than suspect that some of them do, just as I more than suspect that some of them do not. Nor do I here contend that the scriptural language must in every case be original; maybe in a few cases it is secondary. All I claim is that these texts constitute a significant pattern in the sources, and that this pattern leaves us with yet one more choice. We may infer either (a) that the early Christian habit of drawing upon eschatological prophecies in Scripture owed something to Jesus' own outlook[227] or (b) that such precedent was lacking. If we opt for (a), we have again reinforced the main thesis of this chapter. If we opt for (b), we find ourselves opposing an early and very well-attested tradition, for Q, Mark, M, L, John, and seemingly Paul all take it for granted that Jesus linked his present ministry and his future fortune to prophetic Scriptures.

Comparison of Jesus to Others

Although Jesus' followers promoted his honor and status far beyond the honor and status of his predecessor John the Baptist, several early Christian texts nevertheless highlight parallels between the two men or record that others observed similarities. In Mark's Gospel, upon learning of Jesus' marvelous activities, Herod Antipas supposes, as do others, that the Nazarene might be John the Baptist risen from the dead: "King Herod heard of it, for

225. Luke 23:30:   λέγειν τοῖς ὄρεσιν πέσετε ἐφ' ἡμᾶς
                    καὶ τοῖς βουνοῖς καλύψατε ἡμᾶς
LXX Hos 10:8:   καὶ ἐροῦσιν τοῖς ὄρεσιν καλύψατε ἡμᾶς
                    καὶ τοῖς βουνοῖς πέσατε ἐφ' ἡμᾶς
226. John 16:22:   ὄψομαι ὑμᾶς καὶ χαρήσεται ὑμῶν ἡ καρδία
LXX Isa 66:14:   καὶ ὄψεσθε καὶ χαρήσεται ὑμῶν ἡ καρδία
227. So James D. Tabor, "Are You the One? The Textual Dynamics of Messianic Self-Identity," in *Knowing the End from the Beginning: The Prophetic, the Apocalyptic and Their Relationships* (ed. Lester L. Grabbe and Robert D. Haak; JSPSup 46; London: T & T Clark International, 2003), 179–89. Tabor calls attention to other historical figures who have understood their own times and activities in terms of Scripture.

Jesus' name had become known. Some were saying, 'John the baptizer has been raised from the dead; and for this reason these powers are at work in him.' But others said, 'It is Elijah.' And others said, 'It is a prophet, like one of the prophets of old.' But when Herod heard of it, he said, 'John, whom I beheaded, has been raised'" (6:14–16). It is the same in Mark 8:27–28. When Jesus asks his disciples, "Who do people say that I am?" they answer that the various opinions include identification with the Baptist. In his editorial work, moreover, Mark himself makes the martyrdoms of John and Jesus parallel. Joel Marcus summarizes: "Each is 'eagerly heard' (see 6:20; 12:37) and becomes the object of the curiosity of a leader (6:12; cf. 15:9–10, 14–15), who tries unsuccessfully to save him (6:20; cf. 15:4, 9–14). Each, however, falls victim to his enemies' murderous intention (6:19; cf. 3:6; 14:1; etc.), is arrested and bound (6:17; cf. 14:46; 15:1), and is ignominiously executed and buried (6:27–29; cf. 15:16–47)."[228]

A tradition common to Matthew and Luke offers something comparable: Matt 11:16–19 // Luke 7:31–35 (Q)—John came not eating and drinking, the Son of Man came eating and drinking—suggests that Jesus and John had similar goals and messages, and even that their differences were more in the delivery than in the substance. The two appealed to the people of "this generation," who responded by slandering them both.

Parallels between John and Jesus appear likewise in Luke's infancy narratives: the stories surrounding the births of both figures are, as is well known, very much alike (cf. 1:5–25, 26–38, 57–80; 2:1–52).[229] Matthew, too, enjoys correlating the two men. In his Gospel, both Jesus and John implore people to repent because the kingdom is at hand (3:2; 4:17), address the Pharisees as "You brood of vipers" (3:7; 12:34), warn about trees that do not bear good fruit and so are cut down and thrown into the fire (3:10; 7:19); and both are seized (κρατέω) and bound (δέω) (14:3; 21:46; 27:2), are feared by authority figures because crowds see them as prophets (14:5; 21:46), and are buried by a disciple or disciples (14:12; 27:57–61).[230]

The habit of making John and Jesus mirror one another is remarkable in view of the Christian tendency to exalt the Messiah over his forerunner. Perhaps the *synkrisis* originated with Jesus, who related himself to John's ministry and expectations in positive ways.[231] But whatever Jesus may have thought, the tradition remembered him as being very much like the Baptist.

Although this fact is suggestive when one takes into account that ecclesiastical tradition also characterized the Baptist as an apocalyptic prophet, it is

228. Joel Marcus, *Mark 1–8* (AB 27; New York: Doubleday, 2000), 404.
229. For a visual presentation, see Charles H. Talbert, *Literary Patterns, Theological Themes, and the Genre of Luke-Acts* (SBLMS 20; Missoula, MT: Scholars Press, 1974), 44–45.
230. See further John P. Meier, "John the Baptist in Matthew's Gospel," *JBL* 99 (1980): 383–405.
231. See further excursus 2, pp. 204–20 below.

more than suggestive when contemplated in conjunction with Acts 5:35–39, where Gamaliel the Pharisee says,

> Fellow Israelites, consider carefully what you propose to do to these men. For some time ago Theudas rose up, claiming to be somebody, and a number of men, about four hundred, joined him; but he was killed, and all who followed him were dispersed and disappeared. After him Judas the Galilean rose up at the time of the census and got people to follow him; he also perished, and all who followed him were scattered. So in the present case, I tell you, keep away from these men and let them alone; because if this plan or this undertaking is of human origin, it will fail; but if it is of God, you will not be able to overthrow them—in that case you may even be found fighting against God!

This text discloses that, in addition to being remembered as akin to the Baptist, some thought that Jesus was also like Judas the Galilean and Theudas. The latter, according to Luke's account, made himself out to be "somebody," and Josephus reports that he persuaded many "to take up their possessions and to follow him to the Jordan River. He stated that he was a prophet and that at his command the river would be parted and would provide them an easy passage" (*Ant.* 20.97–99). Theudas, whom Martin Hengel has labeled a "messianic pretender,"[232] clearly wanted to relive salvation history and liberate his people from foreign domination.[233] As for Judas the Galilean, Origen reports that a few took him to be the Messiah, and some modern historians have judged this likely.[234] Be that as it may, he, like Theudas and John the Baptist, hoped for the liberation of God's people from Roman rule.

Now, Mark 6:14–16 and 8:27–28 attribute the comparison of Jesus with the Baptist to Herod Antipas and unnamed others; and it is yet another outsider, Gamaliel, who in Acts 5:35–39 associates Jesus and his disciples with Theudas, Judas, and their followers. This makes sense. It seems far-fetched to suppose that insiders first thought up these comparisons, which might have been unwelcome. One presumes instead that we have here judgments from people unaligned with Jesus and the churches.[235]

232. Martin Hengel, *The Zealots: Investigations into the Jewish Freedom Movement in the Period from Herod I until 70 A.D.* (Edinburgh: T & T Clark, 1989), 230.

233. Theudas was also a "sign prophet" while Jesus, according to several traditions, had to address the issue of his signs (Matt 12:38–39; 16:1–4; Mark 8:11–13; Luke 11:16; 12:54–56; John 2:18; 4:48; 6:30).

234. Origen, *Hom. Luc.* 25.4. See Hengel, *Zealots*, 293. For Josephus on Judas, see *Ant.* 18.3–10, 23–25; 20.102; *J.W.* 2.118, 433; 7.253. Origen closely associates Theudas and Judas the Galilean with a certain Dositheus, and this last purportedly "wished to persuade the Samaritans that he was the Christ predicted by Moses" (*Cels.* 1.57), a likely reference to Deut 18:15, 18. Many, furthermore, have identified Judas the Galilean with the Judas of *Ant.* 17.271–272 and *J.W.* 2.56 (although this is a disputed issue), and the latter Judas had "an ambition for royal rank."

235. See Jeffrey A. Trumbower, "The Historical Jesus and the Speech of Gamaliel (Acts 5.35–9)," *NTS* 39 (1993): 500–517. Trumbower's inferences from Gamaliel's speech resemble my own.

So we may ask, Why did some judge Jesus to be like John, Theudas, and Judas the Galilean? If popular opinion remembered Jesus as an apocalyptic prophet who proclaimed that the Jewish kingdom would depose the Roman kingdom, a prophet who wanted "to redeem Israel" (Luke 24:21), we have our answer. For people also remembered Judas, Theudas, and John as leaders of movements that hoped for a change of kingdoms. If, however, Jesus was unlike John, Theudas, and Judas in that he did not hope for the imminent and dramatic redemption of Israel, how do we account for the comparisons?

Cross-Cultural Millenarianism

The proposal that Jesus was an apocalyptic prophet enables us not only to give him a plausible context within first-century Palestine but further to fit him into a cross-cultural typology that modern anthropologists have established. Pacific cargo cults, Jewish messianic groups, Amerindian prophetic movements, and Christian sects looking for the immediate end of the present world order display a host of features that reappear in the early traditions about Jesus, as I have documented elsewhere.[236] Such millenarian movements, which are otherwise attested within early Judaism,[237] tend

- to address the disaffected in a period of social change that threatens traditional ways and symbolic universes (they often arise in a time of aspiration for national independence);
- to see the present and near future as times of suffering and/or catastrophe;

236. Here I summarize Allison, *Jesus of Nazareth*, 78–94. For an introduction to the subject, see Hillel Schwartz, "Millenarianism: An Overview," in *Encyclopedia of Religion* (ed. Lindsay Jones; 2nd ed.; Detroit: Macmillan Reference USA, 2005), 9:6028–38. In essential agreement with my earlier work is Gerd Theissen, "Jesus—Prophet einer millenaristischen Bewegung? Sozialgeschichtliche Überlegungen zu einer sozialanthropologischen Deutung der Jesusbewegung," in *Jesus als historische Gestalt: Beiträge zur Jesusforschung* (ed. Annette Merz; FRLANT 202; Göttingen: Vandenhoeck & Ruprecht, 2003), 197–228. My main point has also been endorsed by Jack T. Sanders, *Charisma, Converts, Competitors: Societal and Sociological Factors in the Success of Early Christianity* (London: SCM Press, 2000), 18–20. Others who recognize that at least early Christianity qualifies as a messianic movement include John G. Gager, *Kingdom and Community: The Social World of Early Christianity* (Englewood Cliffs, NJ: Prentice-Hall, 1975); Christopher Rowland, *Christian Origins: An Account of the Setting and Character of the Most Important Messianic Sect of Judaism* (London: SPCK, 1989), 112–13.

237. According to David E. Aune, they were "not uncommon" in the first century ("Understanding Jewish and Christian Apocalyptic," in *Apocalypticism, Prophecy, and Magic in Early Christianity: Collected Essays* [WUNT 199; Tübingen: Mohr Siebeck, 2006], 5). He refers to Theudas, the Qumran community, John the Baptist, and the unnamed Egyptian of Acts 21:38 and Josephus, *Ant.* 20.169–172. See further Sheldon R. Isenberg, "Millenarism in Greco-Roman Palestine," *Religion* 4 (1974): 26–46; Albert I. Baumgarten, *The Flourishing of Jewish Sects in the Maccabean Era: An Interpretation* (JSJSup 55; Leiden: Brill, 1997), 152–87.

- to envision a supernatural agency irrevocably reversing all wrongs and undoing all evil circumstances;
- to depict reversal as imminent and ultimate;
- to be both revivalistic[238] and evangelistic;
- to promote egalitarianism;
- to divide the world into two camps, the saved and the unsaved;
- to break hallowed taboos associated with religious custom;
- to be nativistic and focused upon the salvation of the community;
- to replace traditional familial and social bonds with fictive kin;
- to mediate the sacred through new channels;
- to demand intense commitment and unconditional loyalty;
- to focus upon a charismatic leader;
- to understand their beliefs as the product of special revelation;
- to expect a restored paradise in a transformed world that will return the ancestors;
- to insist on the possibility of experiencing utopia as a present reality;
- to grow out of a precursor movement.

All of these items recur in the early traditions about Jesus, and if the millenarian shoe fits so well, then he probably wore it. To put it otherwise: classifying Jesus as an apocalyptic prophet neatly explains why the traditions about him exhibit so many parallels with worldwide millenarian movements, which typically owe their initial theological profiles to their founding prophets.[239]

238. By this is meant deepening the piety of the faithful and stirring up religious faith among the indifferent. See further Marcus Borg, *Jesus, a New Vision: Spirit, Culture, and the Life of Discipleship* (San Francisco: Harper & Row, 1987), 125–49.

239. Elisabeth Schüssler Fiorenza has objected that my use of a millenarian model in *Jesus of Nazareth* "stands social-scientific method on its head" by seeking to "prove" my "reconstruction of a thoroughly eschatological Jesus by parallelizing and 'proof-texting' it with reference to the cross-cultural model of millennialism" (*Jesus and the Politics of Interpretation* [New York: Continuum, 2000], 106–14). This is not, however, what I took myself to be doing there (or what I take myself to be doing here). I came to a particular understanding of Jesus on the basis of general historical reflections and exegesis of the texts. Only after this (in a section on "Results") did I observe that my findings could be correlated with a cross-cultural model formulated by anthropologists and sociologists. Similarly, in this chapter, as likewise in my own biography of Jesus, the millenarian model comes not at the beginning but at the end. It is the capstone, not the foundation. It is not intended to "prove" anything. It simply shows that my apocalyptic Jesus is all the more credible because he resembles other apocalyptic figures who are even better documented. Schüssler Fiorenza's additional complaints—for example, it is more profitable to compare the traditions about Jesus with present-day social movements of protest, including the civil rights movement and the feminist movement—conflate the historical and theological task in a way that I wish in the present context to avoid. As for the objections of Richard Horsley ("Jesus in the New Millennium," 7–8), regarding my appeal to millenarian movements, the only

Such, then, are some of the reasons for envisaging Jesus as an apocalyptic and millenarian prophet who, as Bultmann put it, "expected a tremendous eschatological drama."[240] To my mind, the arguments are formidable, indeed compelling.[241] The conclusion that they oblige has accordingly become a point of departure for further lines of inquiry. Exactly what role did the prospect of eschatological distress play in Jesus' thinking? Did he prophetically interpret his forebodings in terms of the ordeal of the latter days?[242] Did he apprehend that he must lose his life in the eschatological tribulation in order to gain it at the eschatological renewal? Did he, despite all the doubt in recent decades, allude to Dan 7 when he spoke of "the Son of Man"?[243] Did his moral exhortations sometimes gain force by invoking the prospect of Gehenna?[244] Did his nostalgia for eschatological paradise envisage God's kingdom as this-worldly or otherworldly or something in between?[245]

I have come to believe that even though Jesus was not a cartographer of future states, we can answer some of these questions, as well as kindred others, with a decent measure of conviction, and my endeavors in this connection have gradually verified my working hypothesis. Viewing Jesus as a millenarian figure has proven to be productive. In other words, this take on the tradition has become what Imre Lakatos called a "progressive research programme," which has led to an ever-enlarging series of new questions and useful answers. I have found that once one approaches the early Christian sources with the idea that Jesus was an apocalyptic prophet, much that otherwise has no good explanation falls into place and indeed becomes almost self-evident.[246]

---

one seemingly to the point is this: "Only five or six of the eighteen features he lists are parallel to the themes and motifs he finds in Jesus' sayings." These words unaccountably refer to my discussion of eschatological themes on pp. 131–51 of *Jesus of Nazareth*, whereas it is pp. 61–64 that correlate all, not five or six, of the millenarian features with Jesus and the early churches.

240. Rudolf Bultmann, *Jesus and the Word* (New York: Charles Scribner's Sons, 1934), 38.

241. Kevin J. Madigan and Jon D. Levenson assert, "The evidence for the Schweitzer thesis in its general contours is now extraordinarily strong" (with reference to E. P. Sanders and my earlier work) (*Resurrection: The Power of God for Christians and Jews* [New Haven: Yale University Press, 2008], 10). Although I say "compelling," I recognize that because antecedent opinions vary, estimates of probability will also vary: what seems compelling to one may seem something less to another.

242. I explored this thesis at length in my first book, *The End of the Ages Has Come*. Recent scholars who have agreed, albeit with revisions, include Pitre, *Jesus*; Scot McKnight, *Jesus and His Death: Historiography, the Historical Jesus, and Atonement Theory* (Waco, TX: Baylor University Press, 2005).

243. See further below, pp. 293–303.

244. For my review of this subject, see Allison, *Resurrecting Jesus*, 56–110.

245. For my own judgments, see Allison, *Jesus of Nazareth*, 152–69.

246. Candor, however, moves me to record that I am haunted by this observation by T. C. Chamberlin: once we adopt a theory,

Other scholars, however, have a different view of things. They do not agree that the descendants of Weiss and Schweitzer are on the side of truth. Such dissidents have, in fact, again and again tried to move the mountain of evidence that is the apocalyptic Jesus. In the remainder of this essay, then, I wish to review some of their efforts. My goal is to negate their negation of the apocalyptic Jesus, to show that the mountain has not been lifted up and thrown into the sea.[247]

Too Many Contradictions?

Early attempts to counter Schweitzer's apocalyptic Jesus often confidently forwarded an argument that, when analyzed, looks like this:

a. The Synoptics contain apocalyptic and nonapocalyptic materials.
b. One individual is unlikely to have authored both sorts of materials.
c. Jesus authored some of the nonapocalyptic materials.
d. He thus is unlikely to have authored any of the apocalyptic materials.

---

there is an unconscious selection and magnifying of the phenomena that fall into harmony with the theory and support it, and an unconscious neglect of those that fail of coincidence. The mind lingers with pleasure upon the facts that fall happily into the embrace of the theory, and feels a natural coldness toward those that seem refractory. . . . There springs up, also, an unconscious pressing of the theory to make it fit the facts and the facts to make them fit the theory. . . . The search for facts, the observation of phenomena and their interpretation, are all dominated by affection for the favored theory until it appears to . . . its advocate to have been overwhelmingly established. The theory then rapidly rises to the ruling position, and investigation, observation, and interpretation are controlled and directed by it. ("The Method of Multiple Working Hypotheses," *Science* 148 [1965]: 755)

There is now a large critical literature on "confirmation bias," and much of it is quite unsettling. For an overview, see Raymond S. Nickerson, "Confirmation Bias: A Ubiquitous Phenomenon in Many Guises," *Review of General Psychology* 2 (1998): 175–230. Still, I find comfort in some words of Karl Popper that seem true to my experience:

I do admit that at any moment we are prisoners caught in the framework of our theories; our expectations; our past experiences; our language. But we are prisoners in a Pickwickian sense; if we try, we can break out of our framework at any time. Admittedly, we shall find ourselves again in a framework, but it will be a better and roomier one; and we can at any moment break out of it again. ("Normal Science and Its Dangers," in *Criticism and the Growth of Knowledge* [ed. Imre Lakatos and Alan Musgrave; London: Cambridge University Press, 1970], 56–57)

247. In what follows I pass over the misuse of the criterion of dissimilarity, which in the past contributed appreciably to a nonapocalyptic Jesus (see Dale C. Allison Jr., "A Plea for Thoroughgoing Eschatology," *JBL* 113 [1994]: 664–67). Happily, this criterion seems to be nearing its death throes, so I can ignore it here. I also disregard the vacuous argument from sanity—Jesus was profoundly sane, so he could not have been a half-crazed, apocalyptic visionary—an argument that had some currency in the first half of the twentieth century. See, for example, W. R. Inge, *Christian Ethics and Modern Problems* (London: Hodder & Stoughton, 1930), 19–20.

Many were robustly confident, and clearly relieved, that the ethical teachings of Jesus cannot be those of an apocalyptic prophet, for they appear "to contemplate the indefinite continuance of human life under historical conditions."[248] J. H. Leckie long ago put it this way:

> There are features of His doctrine which imply that He did not feel . . . [a] sense of approaching climax. The sweep and reach of His ethical demands, which call men to be perfect as the Father in heaven is perfect, seem to require a long period of time for their fulfillment. It is remarkable, also, that when He counsels His hearers not to be anxious about the future, He does not enforce the lesson by reminding them that there will be no future to be anxious about—does not say, "Be not anxious about the morrow; for to-morrow the Lord cometh." This would have been a most powerful argument to have used if Jesus had been possessed by the conviction that the end was at hand. Yet He is content to base His appeal on a homely and familiar thought which implies that things will be in the days to come even as they have been in days gone by, and that the old pathetic human experience will go on repeating itself. "The morrow shall take thought for the things of itself: sufficient unto the day is the evil thereof." This is a striking example of a strain in the Gospels which does not suggest a foreshortening of the future.[249]

This line of reasoning is alive and well. Marcus Borg, for one, has reiterated it, urging that Jesus was a teacher of subversive wisdom, that many of his sayings have nothing to do with eschatology, that his words reflect a "mentality deeply aware of the conventions that dominate people's lives, animating, preoccupying, and ensnaring them," and that the combination of imminent eschatology and subversive wisdom is "possible" but "improbable."[250] What shall we say to this?

The implicit assumption that Leckie, Borg, and so many others have made is that the historical Jesus should have been, to our way of thinking, more

248. C. H. Dodd, *The Parables of the Kingdom* (new rev. ed.; New York: Charles Scribner's Sons, 1961), 79. Compare Dodd's remarks in "The Life and Teaching of Jesus Christ," in *A Companion to the Bible* (ed. T. W. Manson; Edinburgh: T & T Clark, 1939), 376.

249. J. H. Leckie, *The World to Come and Final Destiny* (Edinburgh: T & T Clark, 1918), 55–56. The issue is an old one; note Albert Schweitzer, *The Mystery of the Kingdom of God: The Secret of Jesus' Messiahship and Passion* (New York: Macmillan, 1950), 46–47.

250. Borg, "Jesus and Eschatology," 82–83. Cf. idem, "Jesus Was Not an Apocalyptic Prophet," 36; idem, *Jesus: Uncovering the Life, Teachings, and Relevance of a Religious Revolutionary* (San Francisco: HarperSanFrancisco, 2006), 256–58; Martin Ebner, *Jesus—Ein Weisheitslehrer? Synoptische Weisheitslogien im Traditionsprozess* (HBS 15; Freiburg: Herder, 1998), 416–26; Glasson, *Second Advent*, 137–39; Robert Morgan, "From Reimarus to Sanders: The Kingdom of God, Jesus, and the Judaisms of His Day," in *The Kingdom of God and Human Society: Essays by Members of the Scripture, Theology, and Society Group* (ed. Robin Barbour; Edinburgh: T & T Clark, 1993), 108; Francis Greenwood Peabody, *The Christian Life in the Modern World* (New York: Macmillan, 1914), 24–25.

consistent or coherent than the Synoptic Jesus.[251] But is this warranted?[252] The perceived inconcinnities, the supposedly very "different perspectives on life,"[253] belong to the primary sources themselves, and how assured can we be that their authors tolerated tensions that Jesus did not tolerate? Who is to judge how consistent or inconsistent a first-century Galilean prophet must have been?[254]

Why presume that, although the evangelists freely mixed different sorts of materials, Jesus could not equally have done so? Was he, unlike them, clarity itself? Perhaps so. Yet surely "we cannot know, from the start, whether Jesus' teaching was simple or ambiguous and difficult. This is what we are trying to find out, if possible, not what we begin by assuming."[255] Maybe Jesus was like the prophet Isaiah, concerning whom Th. C. Vriezen once wrote that it would be a "misjudgment of the personality of this prophet to demand that his prophecies should always form an airtight system."[256] Or maybe he was like the editors of Proverbs, who created contradictions intentionally, in order to prod critical reflection.[257]

Even particularly reflective individuals sometimes seem to speak against themselves. Students of Paul have often proposed theories of development precisely because what he says in one epistle is not exactly what he says in

251. Interpreters have made this supposition again and again; note, for example, Ernst Käsemann's assertion that Jesus "proclaimed the immediacy of God who was near at hand," and if so, he could not have expected the coming of the Son of Man. "To combine the two would be, for me, to cease to make any sense" ("Beginnings of Christian Theology," 101–2).

252. In addition to what follows, see Stephen J. Patterson, "An Unanswered Question," *JSHJ* (forthcoming). Patterson raises the possibility that Jesus was perhaps divided within himself over John's apocalyptic eschatology, that the ambiguity within the tradition reflects Jesus' own ambiguity, or a failure to be consistent. The article rightly admonishes the guild for too often assuming that Jesus was always decisive and consistent about everything. We are here the unwitting heirs of an ecclesiastical exegetical tradition. Premodern exegetes had little trouble wondering, in view of the tension between Matt 11:2–4 // Luke 7:18–23 (Q) ("Are you the one who is to come, or are we to wait for another?") on the one hand and Matt 3:14 ("I need to be baptized by you, and do you come to me?") and John 1:29 ("Here is the Lamb of God who takes away the sin of the world!") on the other, whether the Baptist wavered in his convictions about Jesus, whether he later came to doubt what he formerly believed. Those same exegetes never, however, asked whether Jesus was ever inconsistent or changed his mind about anything or was uncertain about this or that.

253. Vorster, "Jesus: Eschatological Prophet," 539.

254. Martin Hengel asks, "Who can say what inconsistencies and contradictions an ancient author is to be thought capable of?" ("Tasks of New Testament Scholarship," BBR 6 [1996]: 75).

255. Frederick Houk Borsch, *The Son of Man in Myth and History* (NTL; Philadelphia: Westminster, 1967), 34.

256. Th. C. Vriezen, "Prophecy and Eschatology," in *Congress Volume: Copenhagen 1953* (VTSup 1; Leiden: Brill, 1953), 208.

257. On this topic, see Peter T. H. Hatton, *Contradiction in the Book of Proverbs: The Deep Waters of Counsel* (SOTSMS; Burlington, VT: Ashgate, 2008).

another. The divergence between what the apostle wrote about the law in Galatians and what he had to say about it in Romans is notorious,[258] as are his various and discordant statements about eschatological subjects.[259] Wayne Meeks remarked that Paul's "employment of apocalyptic categories" in 1 Corinthians "seems to be the reverse of that in Galatians," for if in the latter he employs "the present experience of factors traditionally associated with the messianic age to warrant a radical innovation, abandoning the use of the Mosaic law so as to set boundaries between Jew and gentile," in the former he "uses eschatological language in the future tense to restrain innovation and to counsel stability and order: 'In view of the present . . . distress, it is well for a person to remain as he is.'"[260]

That Paul says different and even contradictory things does not mark him out as idiosyncratic. Scholars have also wrestled with striking inconcinnities in Wisdom of Solomon,[261] in Matthew's Gospel,[262] in Luke's Gospel,[263] in Josephus's histories,[264] in Justin's writings,[265] in Origen's thought[266]—in fact, in just about every writing of any length from antiquity.[267] This should come as no revelation. Human beings are bundles of inconsistencies, and we all sometimes appear to disagree with ourselves. Albert Einstein once wrote, "For me the Jewish religion like all others is an incarnation of the

258. For one view, see Heikki Räisänen, *Paul and the Law* (2nd ed.; WUNT 29; Tübingen: Mohr Siebeck, 1987).

259. R. H. Charles found enough variety in the Pauline materials to posit four stages in the apostle's eschatological thinking (*A Critical History of the Doctrine of a Future Life in Israel, in Judaism, and in Christianity* [London: Adam & Charles Black, 1899], 379–417); Henry St. John Thackeray posited three (*The Relation of St. Paul to Contemporary Jewish Thought* [London: Macmillan, 1900], 98–134).

260. Wayne A. Meeks, *The First Urban Christians: The Social World of the Apostle Paul* (New Haven: Yale University Press, 1983), 179.

261. Contrast the statement of universal divine compassion in 11:23–12:1 with the dreadful words about judgment in 4:18–19; 5:17–23.

262. See the overview in Allison, "Deconstructing Matthew," in *Studies in Matthew*, 237–49.

263. On the difficulties in finding a coherent eschatology in Luke-Acts, see Lehtipuu, *Afterlife Imagery*, 250–64.

264. See Steve Mason, "Contradiction or Counterpoint? Josephus and Historical Method," *RRJ* 6 (2003): 145–88. He remarks, "The *Life* . . . contradicts the *War* in almost every place in which their stories overlap" (p. 167).

265. On the conflicting ideas in Justin's eschatology, see Leslie W. Barnard, *Justin Martyr: His Life and Thought* (London: Cambridge University Press, 1967), 157–68.

266. Benjamin Drewery, after observing that the church father says contradictory things about divine impassibility, remarks simply, "But such is Origen's way" (*Origen and the Doctrine of Grace* [London: Epworth, 1960], 106).

267. One recalls here how often older scholarship, because of perceived inconsistencies, denied the unity of several Jewish apocalypses. Representative is G. H. Box, "4 Ezra," in *The Apocrypha and Pseudepigrapha of the Old Testament in English* (ed. R. H. Charles; 2 vols.; Oxford: Clarendon, 1913), 2:542–624.

most childish superstitions." At another time he stated that "science without religion is lame."[268]

Whatever one makes of Einstein's seemingly conflicting statements, we certainly have no evidence that Jesus was as logical as the great scientist, or even as logical as Matthew, Luke, or Paul.[269] Whatever else he may have done, Jesus did not celebrate rationality as a virtue. His tradition was not Greco-Roman philosophy, but popular Galilean Judaism. He was not a scholastic logician, but heir to a religion that at all periods displayed "incongruous and inconsistent elements."[270] His mind, furthermore, was poetic, and his mental universe, filled as it was with invisible spirits and informed by the cosmology of the Hebrew Scriptures, was mythological. He composed parables. He issued warnings. He appealed to religious sentiment. He busied himself neither with defining his terms nor with constructing syllogisms for the intellect. Those were not the vocation of a first-century Jewish prophet.[271]

Here the work of Jack T. Sanders is helpful.[272] Recent sociological study of charismatic leadership in new religious movements has, he observes, established the principle that "randomness increases charisma." That is, the most effective leaders are those who fascinate, and they often achieve this by acting strangely and unexpectedly, by saying things that are unusual and shocking, even contradictory. The charismatic becomes astonishing by doing astonishing things, which includes being inconsistent; and according to Sanders, "given Jesus' effect on his disciples—who did leave all to follow him, as he demanded—we must assume that" he "also understood and employed the principle [that randomness increases charisma]. To assume otherwise is to think that he was not a charismatic leader, that he did not fascinate and astound his audiences, that he was quite predictable, and that he was nevertheless a successful leader."[273]

268. The negative comment on religion is from an unpublished letter that Einstein wrote on January 3, 1954, to the philosopher Eric Gutkind. The positive comment on religion is from Albert Einstein, "Science and Religion," in *Science, Philosophy and Religion: A Symposium* (New York: Conference on Science, Philosophy and Religion in Their Relation to the Democratic Way of Life, 1941), 211.

269. Gerd Theissen and Dagmar Winter observe, "That which we consider coherent is perhaps incoherent for others, and vice versa. The letters of Paul are full of contradictions. Yet when one thinks of the Letter to the Romans, Paul is to be classified among the 'systematic thinkers' among the New Testament authors. Thus figures who think less systematically, including Jesus, probably have at least as many contradictions in their utterances as does Paul, if not more" (*The Quest for the Plausible Jesus: The Question of Criteria* [Louisville: Westminster John Knox, 2002], 236 n. 7).

270. Charles, *Doctrine of a Future Life*, 310.

271. It may be worth noting that the New Testament never labels Jesus a *sophos*, although it does remember that people thought him to be a prophet (Mark 6:4; 8:28; Luke 13:33; John 4:19; 6:14; Acts 3:22–23).

272. Jack T. Sanders, "The Criterion of Coherence and the Randomness of Charisma: Poring through Some Aporias in the Jesus Tradition," *NTS* 44 (1998): 1–25.

273. Ibid., 23.

In line with this, our sources have their hero saying outrageous things, such as "Whoever comes to me and does not hate father and mother, wife and children, brothers and sisters, yes, and even life itself, cannot be my disciple" (Luke 14:26), and doing outrageous things, such as feasting with "toll collectors and sinners." Surely it was in part because he was unpredictable that, as the sources report, he surprised, astounded, and offended people (Matt 7:28; 13:54, 57; 19:25; 22:33; Mark 1:22, 27; 6:3; 11:18; Luke 4:32; John 6:61; 7:46). Presumably, some did think him possessed or out of his mind (Matt 12:24 // Luke 11:15 [Q]; Mark 3:21; John 7:20; 8:48, 52; 10:20).

According to Sanders, if Jesus avoided the routinization of charisma by characteristically doing the unexpected, then we would not be dumbfounded to learn that he uttered apparently clashing sayings. The tradition at least has him doing so. If it remembers him rebuking opponents for not honoring father and mother (Mark 7:9–13; cf. 10:19), it also has him commanding a would-be disciple who wishes to bury a parent, "Let the dead bury their own dead" (Matt 8:22 // Luke 9:60 [Q]). If it has him enjoining people to imitate the deity who overflows with kindness to the just and unjust without distinction (Matt 5:43–48 // Luke 6:32–35 [Q]), it also has him mercilessly castigating opponents (Matt 23; Luke 11:39–52) and dismissing them as destined for destruction (Matt 11:20–24 // Luke 10:13–15 [Q]). If it has him generously declaring that "whoever is not against us is for us" (Mark 9:40), it also has him less generously declaring that "whoever is not with me is against me" (Matt 12:30 // Luke 11:23 [Q]).[274] And if it has him announcing that the kingdom of God has come (Matt 12:28 // Luke 11:20 [Q]; Luke 17:20–21), it also has him teaching others to pray for its coming (Matt 6:10 // Luke 11:2 [Q]). Whether or not Jesus, like Parmenides and Heraclitus, enjoyed constructing paradoxical utterances—"Many that are first will be last, and the last first" (Mark 9:35; 10:31 RSV) suggests that he might have—perhaps we should say of him what Ed Sanders has said of Paul: "As a religious genius, he was free of the academic requirement of systematic consistency."[275]

Our inclination to find a historical Jesus who satisfies our notions of coherence is problematic not only because human beings in general and charismatic leaders in particular are sometimes so unpredictable and inconsistent, but also because apocalyptic eschatology has never incubated pure reason or even practical reason. Rudolf Otto long ago highlighted "the irrationality of

274. Luke, interestingly enough, preserves both sayings: Luke 9:50 // Mark 9:40; Luke 11:23 // Matt 12:30 (Q). The Third Evangelist, at least, found the two contradictory sentences useful in different contexts.

275. E. P. Sanders, "Paul," in *Early Christian Thought in Its Jewish Context* (ed. John Barclay and J. P. Sweet; Cambridge: Cambridge University Press, 1996), 124. Similarly, Burchard notes that Jesus did not "attempt a consistent use of linguistic terms and images; no one did in his time, and it certainly would not have been easy" ("Jesus of Nazareth," 26).

the genuine and typically eschatological attitude."[276] Appealing to Zoroaster and Muhammad, he remarked that "the liveliest feeling of the immediate inbreaking of the supramundane future" does not exclude a message about the current world that "reckons on duration, on continuance in time and in temporal and world affairs."[277] More recently, Marius Reiser has observed that "internal consistency, coherence of ideas, motifs, and conceptions, is foreign to the [ancient] apocalyptic authors."[278] Equally relevant is this judgment by Markus Bockmuehl: "The ability to hold together prophetic urgency with patience and indeed postponement is deeply intrinsic to the biblical and Jewish apocalyptic milieux."[279]

One can adduce dozens and dozens of relevant illustrations. The Gathas record a sense of exigency because "the making wonderful" is near, and yet they concern themselves with life and death in the interim. The Dead Sea Scrolls reveal a people enamored with *1 Enoch* and Daniel and anticipating a dramatic divine intervention in their lifetime, a people who nevertheless copied nonapocalyptic sapiential texts (e.g., 4Q185 and 4Q525) and drew up detailed institutional guidelines for communal living (e.g., 1QS and CD).

Consider in this connection 4QMMT (4Q394–399). This sectarian document concerns itself with a number of halakic issues, among them the calendar, ritual purity, and rules for intermarriage. It discusses all of them without any reference to eschatology. Yet the very same text says explicitly, "This is the end of days" (זה הוא אחרית הימים, 4Q398 frgs. 11–13 4). It also informs its readers that blessings and curses will come upon their generation "at the end of days" (באחרית הימים, 4Q398 frgs. 14–17 col. I 6), and it twice uses the expression אחרית העת ("end of time," 4Q398 frgs. 14–17 col. II 6; cf. 4Q399 col. II 3). Whether or not, as I think, the group responsible for this text took itself to be simultaneously suffering eschatological tribulation and anticipating the blessings of the new age, Albert Baumgarten is right: the Qumran group, which "was devoted to a strict observance of the laws of the Torah, also believed actively in the imminent redemption of the world, and did not find any contradiction between these two aspects of their faith."[280] I am reminded of

276. See Rudolf Otto, *The Kingdom of God and the Son of Man* (trans. Floyd V. Filson and Bertram Lee Woolf; rev. ed.; London: Lutterworth, 1943), 59–63; cf. C. C. McCown, "The Eschatology of Jesus Reconsidered," *JR* 16 (1936): 30–46. Related is a remark by George Foot Moore regarding rabbinic eschatology: "There is in this sphere not merely an indefiniteness of terminology but an indistinctness of conception" (*Judaism in the First Centuries of the Christian Era* [2 vols.; New York: Schocken Books, 1971], 2:378).

277. Otto, *Kingdom of God*, 62.

278. Reiser, *Jesus and Judgment*, 162. Compare, regarding medieval Judaism, Moshe Idel's comment that "intense mystical life does not preclude redemptive or even messianic efforts" (*Messianic Mystics* [New Haven: Yale University Press, 1998], 4).

279. Markus Bockmuehl, "Resistance and Redemption in the Jesus Tradition," in *Redemption and Resistance* (ed. Bockmuehl and Paget), 75.

280. Baumgarten, *Jewish Sects*, 176–77.

the thesis of Ben Zion Wacholder regarding the composition of the Mishnah: Rabbi Judah the Prince and "his fellow redactors were in fact preparing, so to speak, a handbook for Elijah, who as chief courtier of the Messiah would be in charge of the punctilious observance of the Halakah."[281] On this view, halakic discussion *was* messianic expectation.

The book of *2 Baruch* offers more of the same, for it combines the conviction that "the youth of the world has passed away" (15:10) with conventional exhortations to keep the Torah (e.g., 32:1; 46:3).[282] In the words of Matthias Henze,

> In *2 Baruch*, Deuteronomic theology, particularly the call on Israel to live in accordance with the Mosaic Torah and to choose life over death, has become the central aspect of the book's apocalyptic world view. Our author manages to harmonize two distinct strands of early Jewish thought which, by modern literary standards, are not harmonious but appear to be mutually exclusive, to the extent that they are normally kept separate: the *Deuteronomic promise* to those who follow Torah that they will be rewarded with a long and prosperous life, and the *apocalyptic promise* that this life will soon come to an end. The author of *2 Baruch* sees no contradiction here but finds the two to be fully compatible.[283]

One could make not dissimilar comments about Daniel, 1QMysteries, 4QMysteries, 4QInstruction, *Testaments of the Twelve Patriarchs*, James, 1 Peter, and other ancient sources that mingle wisdom materials with apocalyptic motifs and expectation.[284] Even Sirach, although it is a book of traditional Jewish wisdom, offers a prayer for God to hasten and fulfill the prophecies of old, to

---

281. Ben Zion Wacholder, *Messianism and Mishnah: Time and Place in the Early Halakah* (Cincinnati: Hebrew Union College Press, 1979), 10.

282. On how eschatological expectation can reinforce injunctions to keep Torah, see Baumgarten, *Jewish Sects*, 182–87.

283. Matthias Henze, "Torah and Eschatology in the *Syriac Apocalypse of Baruch*," in *The Significance of Sinai: Traditions about Sinai and Divine Revelation in Judaism and Christianity* (ed. George J. Brooke, Hindy Najman, and Loren T. Stuckenbruck; TBN 12; Leiden: Brill, 2008), 204.

284. See further Torleif Elgvin, "Wisdom with and without Apocalyptic," in *Sapiential, Liturgical and Poetical Texts from Qumran: Proceedings of the Third Meeting of the International Organization for Qumran Studies, Oslo, 1998* (ed. Daniel K. Falk, Florentino García Martínez, and Eileen M. Schuller; STDJ 34; Leiden: Brill, 2000), 15–38; Lawrence M. Wills and Benjamin G. Wright III, eds., *Conflicted Boundaries in Wisdom and Apocalypticism* (SBLSymS 35; Atlanta: Society of Biblical Literature, 2005). Philip Sellew speaks of "Q's curious intermingling of both wisdom and apocalyptic form and content" ("The Gospel of Thomas: Prospects for Research," in *The Nag Hammadi Library after Fifty Years: Proceedings of the 1995 Society of Biblical Literature Commemoration* [ed. John D. Turner and Anne McGuire; NHMS 44; Leiden: Brill, 1997], 331), but there is nothing curious about it. See Frey, "Apokalyptik als Herausforderung," 51–53; Rafael Rodríguez, "Structuring Early Christian Memory: Jesus in Tradition, Performance, and Text" (PhD diss., University of Sheffield, 2007), 23–26.

subdue pagan oppressors, and to gather the scattered tribes of Jacob (36:1–17).[285] And Paul, who believed that "salvation is nearer to us now than when we first believed" (Rom 13:11 RSV), could yet regularly argue and exhort in ways unconnected with eschatology.[286] He is "a striking example of the juxtaposition of timeless wisdom and the impetuous expectation of an imminent end."[287] So too is Akiba, who, at least according to rabbinic tradition, concerned himself with both halakah and messianism and also purportedly coined an intentionally paradoxical statement about the judgment: "The world is judged by grace, and all is in accord with the preponderance of [good or evil] deeds" (m. 'Abot 3:16 [this immediately follows the remark "All is foreseen but free will is given"]). Much later, Martin Luther's belief that the world was "old and close to its end did not prompt personal despair or a flight from social responsibility or social ethics."[288] So whereas Borg perceives a disjunction between imminent eschatology and serious attention to everyday lives and conventions, history shows us their incessant union.

So does our own time: things are as they always have been. The Lubavitcher Rebbe, Menachem Schneerson, announced the imminence of the Messiah's coming while simultaneously denouncing Palestinian autonomy because it would eventually lead to a Palestinian state;[289] and one needs only a little knowledge of contemporary American fundamentalism to realize that fervent attention to everyday social questions can go hand in hand with authentic belief in a near end. The late Jerry Falwell believed that Jesus was coming again soon and yet often concerned himself with conventional political and social issues.

Consistency is the hobgoblin of nonapocalyptic minds. If Jesus reworked wisdom materials, that is no reason at all to suppose that he did not also

---

285. Burton Mack opines, without textual warrant, that the prayer was added "by a later hand" (Wisdom and the Hebrew Epic: Ben Sira's Hymn in Praise of the Fathers [Chicago: University of Chicago Press, 1985], 180). His reason is that it represents a "radical displacement of Ben Sira's mythic vision." This judgment says more about the sensibilities of a modern academic than the text of Ben Sira.

286. The failure of Beker, in Paul the Apostle, to explain every aspect of Pauline theology in terms of apocalyptic only establishes my point.

287. Gerd Lüdemann, Jesus after Two Thousand Years: What He Really Said and Did (Amherst, NY: Prometheus Books, 2001), 691. He continues, "In the case of Paul, as with Jesus, expectation of an imminent end, wisdom teaching and ethics stand side by side, contrary to all modern logic."

288. Carter Lindberg, "Eschatology and Fanaticism in the Reformation Era: Luther and the Anabaptists," CTQ 64 (2000): 275. Incidentally, students of Luther, like so many students of Jesus, often have underestimated the importance of his eschatology; see Heiko A. Oberman, The Reformation: Roots and Ramifications (Grand Rapids: Eerdmans, 1994), 23–52.

289. See Joel Marcus, "Modern and Ancient Jewish Apocalypticism," JR 76 (1996): 19 n. 82. On the sharp distinction that the Lubavitchers have often maintained between their messianic consciousness and their practical, everyday life, see further Aviezer Ravitzky, Messianism, Zionism, and Jewish Religious Radicalism (Chicago: University of Chicago, 1996), 202–3.

rework apocalyptic materials, or vice versa.[290] And if he was a social prophet, that does not exclude his having been an apocalyptic prophet. Others have been both. The reason is obvious: as eschatological expectation and instruction cannot cover all of life, no successful apocalyptic prophet can afford to be a monomaniac. So using a criterion of consistency to delete apocalyptic elements from Jesus' speech because they contradict the sapiential elements is no more plausible than arguing that people who pray for God to heal them cannot go to the doctor, or that those who teach that Jesus will come again cannot insist that even now he lives in their hearts.

Otto's observations about the irrationality of eschatology were directed against Schweitzer and his "thoroughgoing eschatology." With his flair for the dramatic, Schweitzer, unlike the more prudent Weiss,[291] wanted to explain nearly everything about Jesus in terms of eschatology, and this extreme view perhaps has allowed some to imagine that since not all of the words of Jesus can be related to apocalyptic expectation, he was not an apocalyptic prophet. In the words of Francis Peabody, "There is nothing apocalyptic in the parable of the good Samaritan, or in the appropriation by Jesus of the two great commandments, or in the prayer for to-day's bread and the forgiveness of trespasses, or in the praise of peace-making and purity of heart."[292]

This is an argument that needs to be put to sleep.[293] It cannot astound that Jesus' "eschatology and ethics" often "stand alongside one another in a relatively disconnected way."[294] The nearness of the end does not in and of itself generate imperatives,[295] for which one rather needs a moral tradition. While some of Jesus' strange instructions to those who followed him were, I believe, motivated by his near expectation, and while his eschatology added urgency to all of his demands, he, like all the other teachers in his time and place, drew most of his moral teaching from the well of traditional Jewish discourse, in large dependence upon the Law, the Prophets, and the Writings.

290. Contrast Schmithals ("Jesus," 4–10), who argues that the wisdom sayings cannot go back to Jesus if he was in fact an apocalyptic prophet (as Schmithals believes he was).

291. See Johannes Weiss, *Die Predigt Jesu vom Reiche Gottes* (Göttingen: Vandenhoeck & Ruprecht, 1900), 134–38, where the author acknowledges that not all of Jesus' teaching is inexorably linked to his eschatology.

292. Francis Greenwood Peabody, "New Testament Eschatology and New Testament Ethics," in *Transactions of the Third International Congress for the History of Religions* (Oxford: Clarendon, 1908), 309.

293. See further Richard H. Hiers, *Jesus and the Future: Unresolved Questions for Eschatology* (Atlanta: John Knox, 1981), 50–61.

294. Hans Conzelmann, *Jesus* (Philadelphia: Fortress, 1973), 51. Although, this fact can be exaggerated; see the helpful discussion in Hermann von Lips, *Weisheitliche Traditionen im Neuen Testament* (WMANT 64; Neukirchen-Vluyn: Neukirchener Verlag, 1990), 241–54.

295. How one responds to the end depends upon one's antecedent theology and ethics. I have a friend who claims that he would sin in new ways if he thought he had little time left, because he would then not have to suffer the consequences.

The Presence of the Kingdom

Luke 17:20–21 reads as follows: "Once Jesus was asked by the Pharisees when the kingdom of God was coming, and he answered, 'The kingdom of God is not coming with things that can be observed; nor will they say, "Look, here it is!" or "There it is!" For, in fact, the kingdom of God is among [or "in"] you.'" *Gospel of Thomas* 113 supplies a variant: "His disciples said to him, 'When will the kingdom come?' Jesus said, 'It will not come by expectation. It will not be a matter of saying "here it is" or "there it is." Rather, the kingdom of the Father is spread out upon the earth, and people do not see it.'"[296]

These two verses from Luke and *Thomas* were, according to Bernard Brandon Scott, foundational for the Jesus Seminar: they "grounded" its "position that Jesus was a preacher of the present kingdom of God."[297] By this Scott means that the Jesus Seminar took Luke 17:20–21 and *Gos. Thom.* 113 to articulate the presence of the kingdom in a way that excludes apocalyptic expectation.[298] John Dominic Crossan, a cofounder of the Jesus Seminar, has rendered the same verdict: the two sayings, which for Crossan faithfully represent Jesus, constitute a rebuttal of "the validity of apocalyptic eschatology."[299] One may also quote to like effect Stephen Patterson, another prominent member of the Jesus Seminar: "Nothing could be more troubling to the apocalyptic hypothesis than Luke 17:20–21."[300]

296. Cf. *Gos. Thom.* 3: "Jesus said: 'If those who lead you say unto you: "Behold, the Kingdom is in heaven," then the birds of the heaven will be before you. If they say unto you: "It is in the sea," then the fish will be before you. But the Kingdom is within you, and it is outside of you. When you know yourselves, then shall you be known, and you shall know that you are the sons of the living Father. But if you do not know yourselves, then you are in poverty, and you are poverty'"; 51: "His disciples said to him, 'On what day will the rest of the dead come into being? And on what day will the new world come?' He said to them: 'That which you await has come, but you know it not.'"

297. Scott, "How Did We Get Here?" 59. His personal judgment is that Luke 17:20–21 "is probably the strongest, most obvious" saying "in support of the non-apocalyptic Jesus."

298. Compare Robert Funk, *Honest to Jesus: Jesus for a New Millennium* (New York: Macmillan, 1996), 166–68.

299. John Dominic Crossan, *The Birth of Christianity: Discovering What Happened in the Years Immediately after the Execution of Jesus* (San Francisco: HarperSanFrancisco, 1998), 316.

300. Stephen Patterson, review of *Jesus of Nazareth: Millenarian Prophet*, by Dale C. Allison Jr., *JBL* 119 (2000): 359. Cf. idem, "Con: Jesus Was Not an Apocalyptic Prophet," in *Apocalyptic Jesus* (ed. Miller), 75. Such is also the view of Dennis C. Duling and Norman Perrin, *The New Testament: Proclamation and Parenesis, Myth and History* (3rd ed.; Fort Worth, TX: Harcourt Brace College Publishers, 1994), 533. I have a letter from Patterson (February 22, 2000) in which he states that "if it weren't for Luke 17:20–21 and Thomas 3 and 113," his attention would not initially have been drawn to other evidence for a nonapocalyptic Jesus. He also politely indicates that my own failure to treat these sayings adequately is a problem for my position. I hope that the following pages remedy this defect.

We have just seen, however, that religious individuals and their texts do not always adhere to our canons of either/or logic.[301] This by itself might make one hesitate regarding the Jesus Seminar's inference. Additional observations lead one not only to hesitate but also respectfully to disagree. Luke 17:20–21; *Gos. Thom.* 113; and related sayings (e.g., Matt 12:28 // Luke 11:20 [Q]; *Gos. Thom.* 3, 51) do not cancel the apocalyptic Jesus.

1. As anyone familiar with the history of interpretation knows, the canonical logia that seem most explicit about the presence of the kingdom are of debatable import,[302] and "although difficult passages cannot be treated as if they did not exist, it is asking for trouble to make them the pillars of a theory."[303] Luke 17:20–21, with its notoriously difficult παρατηρήσεως and ἐντὸς ὑμῶν, "remains a riddle."[304] The verses just might mean that when the kingdom comes, it will come suddenly. This was the view of Bultmann and Jeremias, and we cannot dismiss it as incredible.[305] W. G. Kümmel instead contended that our saying expresses the presence of the inbreaking kingdom not in the world at large but exclusively in the messianic acts of Jesus.[306] Then there is the interpretation of G. R. Beasley-Murray: "Jesus is simply telling the questioners not to concern themselves with trying to determine when . . . the kingdom of God is to appear, but rather to be aware that the kingdom is *within their reach*—which is to say that it lies in their power to enter it and secure its blessings."[307]

The way Bultmann and Jeremias read Luke 17:20–21 does not, to state the obvious, exclude a coming apocalypse. Nor do the interpretations of Kümmel and Beasley-Murray. Even more importantly, the Third Evangelist cannot have understood Luke 17:20 and 17:21 as has the Jesus Seminar, because those verses, in their current literary setting, preface a series of warnings about the

301. In "Unanswered Question," Patterson maintains that Jesus need not have had decisive or consistent opinions on everything. This seems to mark a change in Patterson's view: there now appears to be less reason to jettison apocalyptic eschatology from the teaching of Jesus.

302. See the helpful overview of the linguistic debate in Robert F. Berkey, "ΕΓΓΙΖΕΙΝ, ΦΘΑΝΕΙΝ, and Realized Eschatology," *JBL* 82 (1963): 177–87.

303. H. E. W. Turner, *Jesus, Master and Lord: A Study in the Historical Truth of the Gospels* (London: Mowbray; New York: Morehouse-Gorham, 1953), 245.

304. Gerd Theissen and Annette Merz, *The Historical Jesus: A Comprehensive Guide* (Minneapolis: Fortress, 1998), 261.

305. Rudolf Bultmann, *History of the Synoptic Tradition* (rev. ed.; New York: Harper & Row, 1963), 121–22; Jeremias, *New Testament Theology*, 101.

306. Kümmel, *Promise and Fulfilment*, 33–36.

307. G. R. Beasley-Murray, *Jesus and the Kingdom of God* (Grand Rapids: Eerdmans; Exeter: Paternoster, 1986), 102–3. Cf. Cyril of Alexandria: "It depends upon your wills, and is in your own power, whether or not you receive it" (*Hom. Luke* 117); see also Colin H. Roberts, "The Kingdom of Heaven (Lk. XVII.21)," *HTR* 41 (1948): 1–8. This interpretation reminds one of LXX Deut 30:11–14, where the "commandment" is not "too far away" or "in heaven" or "beyond the sea" but "very near to you" and "in your heart" and "in your hands" (= in your power) to do it. Both *Gos. Thom.* 3 and Tertullian, *Marc.* 4.35, associate the saying in Luke 17:20–21 with Deut 30:11–14.

approaching eschatological catastrophe (17:22–37). In short, Luke and many informed exegetes have not discerned in Luke 17:20–21 an "anti-eschatological intention."[308] This does not entail that such intention is foreign to the saying, only that this is very far from self-evident.

As for Matt 12:28 and Luke 11:20 (Q), which declare that the kingdom of God "has come" (ἔφθασεν), the verb could be, as so many have thought, proleptic, indicating that the kingdom is so near that it can be spoken of as though it were already present.[309] It is incontrovertible that "in confident assertions regarding the future, a vivid, realistic present may be used for the future."[310] This is clearly the case elsewhere in the Jesus tradition,[311] and this may be how the aorist ἔφθασεν functions in 1 Thess 2:16, which seemingly speaks of eschatological punishment (cf. 1:10) as though it were already meted out: "God's wrath has overtaken them at last."[312] Also comparable is *Acts Thom.* 33, where the apostle Thomas says to a wicked serpent: ἔφθασεν . . . σου τὸ τέλος τῆς ἀπωλείας ("your end, destruction, has come upon you"). But the serpent yet lives.

Others have divined in Matt 12:28 // Luke 11:20 (Q) a declaration that the kingdom has in fact entered the present. They could be right.[313] Yet to affirm

308. The words in quotation marks are those of Thomas Zöckler, *Jesu Lehren im Thomasevangelium* (NHMS 47; Leiden: Brill, 1999), 173 ("antieschatologische Absicht").

309. See, for example, Reginald H. Fuller, *The Mission and Achievement of Jesus: An Examination of the Presuppositions of New Testament Theology* (SBT 12; London: SCM Press, 1954), 25–27; Richard H. Hiers, *The Kingdom of God in the Synoptic Tradition* (Gainesville: University of Florida Press, 1970), 22–35; also the useful skepticism of Clayton Sullivan, *Rethinking Realized Eschatology* (Macon, GA: Mercer University Press, 1988), 74–83; and the analysis by Chrys C. Caragounis, "Kingdom of God, Son of Man, and Jesus' Self-Understanding," *TynBul* 40 (1989): 3–23. One might compare LXX Isa 52:7, which turns the present of the MT ("your God reigns") into the future: βασιλεύσει σου ὁ θεός ("your God will reign"). Does the LXX's future tense rightly interpret the Hebrew?

310. BDF §323. In Revelation, ἔρχομαι in the present with future sense occurs often: 1:4, 7, 8; 2:5, 16; 3:11; 4:8; 7:14; 9:12; 11:14; 16:15; 22:7, 12, 20. Many of these verses refer to the parousia.

311. For example, Matt 3:11 // Luke 3:16 (Q) ("the one who comes [ἐρχόμενος] after me"); Matt 24:44 // Luke 12:40 (Q) ("the Son of Man is coming [ἔρχεται] at an hour you do not expect").

312. So James Everett Frame: "ἔφθασεν is proleptic. Instead of speaking of that day as coming upon the sons of disobedience (Eph. 5⁶), he speaks of it as at last arrived. Such a proleptic use of the aorist is natural in a prophetic passage" (*A Critical and Exegetical Commentary on the Epistles of Paul to the Thessalonians* [ICC; New York: Charles Scribner's Sons, 1912], 113–14). Cf. Bruce C. Johanson, "1 Thessalonians 2:15–16: Prophetic Woe Oracle with ἔφθασεν as Proleptic Aorist," in *Texts and Contexts: Biblical Texts in Their Textual and Situational Context; Essays in Honor of Lars Hartman* (ed. Tord Fornberg and David Hellholm; Oslo: Scandinavian University Press, 1995), 519–34; Matthias Konradt, *Gericht und Gemeinde: Eine Studie zur Bedeutung und Funktion von Gerichtsaussagen im Rahmen der paulinischen Ekklesiologie und Ethik im 1 Thess und 1 Kor* (BZNW 117; Berlin: de Gruyter, 2003), 84–87; John Weatherly, "The Authenticity of 1 Thessalonians 2.13–16: Additional Evidence," *JSNT* 42 (1991): 90–91.

313. See Kümmel, *Promise and Fulfilment*, 105–8.

that the kingdom has arrived is not to say that it is already all that it will be.[314]
We should remember that, unlike some modern scholars, neither Matthew
nor Luke understood the saying to disallow a conventional end-time scenario,
because both evangelists, although they reproduced the saying, promoted just
such a scenario. Did the two earliest interpreters whom we know anything
about both get it wrong?

2. At least a few scholars of repute have doubted the authenticity of Luke
17:20–21 and Matt 12:28 // Luke 11:20 (Q). According to Ed Sanders, Luke
wrote 17:20–21 "all by himself, unaided by a transmitted saying of Jesus."[315]
According to Heikki Räisänen, Matt 12:28 // Luke 11:20 is inseparable from
its literary context in Q, and in fact a tradent with that context in view composed it.[316] Others concur.[317]

I cite Sanders and Räisänen not to agree with them but rather to remind
readers of how uncertain is this historical-critical business of ours. It would
indeed be easy enough to regard Luke 17:20–21 and Matt 12:28 // Luke 11:20
(Q) as Christian formulations, responses to the delay of the parousia. The
spiritualization of eschatological language as ordinary time inconveniently
marches on is well known to the history of religions, and it shows up in early
Christianity, in the Gospel of John and the *Gospel of Thomas*.[318] If one were
to judge that Luke's ἐντὸς ὑμῶν means "within you,"[319] would it not be reasonable, given that the Synoptic Jesus nowhere else speaks of the kingdom
being within people, to reckon the verse to which it belongs a post-Easter
composition?

3. Even if Sanders is not wholly right about Luke 17:20–21—I do not pretend
to know one way or the other—he may well be partially right. One surmises
that at least μετὰ παρατηρήσεως ("with things that can be observed") is redactional, for although παρατήρησις is a New Testament *hapax legomenon*, the
related verb (παρατηρέω: Matthew: 0; Mark: 1; Luke: 3) is editorial in Luke

314. See the careful exegesis of Beasley-Murray, *Jesus and the Kingdom*, 75–80.

315. Sanders, *Historical Figure*, 177.

316. Räisänen, "Exorcisms," 119–42.

317. See, for example, Ruthild Geiger, *Die lukanischen Endzeitreden: Studien zur Eschatologie
des Lukas-Evangeliums* (EH 23/16; Bern: Herbert Lang; Frankfurt am Main: Peter Lang, 1973),
45–50; August Strobel, "Die Passa-Erwartung als urchristliches Problem in Lc 17 20f.," *ZNW*
49 (1958): 157–96.

318. See further below, pp. 125–32. Contrast the view of the Jesus Seminar that the "best
explanation" for Luke 11:20; 17:20–21; *Gos. Thom.* 113 "is that they originated with Jesus, who
espoused a view unlike that of his predecessors and successors" (Robert W. Funk, Roy W. Hoover,
and the Jesus Seminar, *The Five Gospels: The Search for the Authentic Words of Jesus* [New
York: Macmillan, 1993], 365, cf. 137). Do these words assume that there were no pre-Christian
Jews or post-Easter followers of Jesus who had a realized eschatology? If so, they are clearly
mistaken; note, for example, John 3:36; Rom 14:17; 2 Tim 2:17–18; *Treat. Res.* 1.43.25–50.18;
see also below, pp. 106–12.

319. See Tom Holmén, "The Alternatives of the Kingdom: Encountering the Semantic Restrictions of Luke 17,20–21 (ἐντὸς ὑμῶν)," *ZNW* 87 (1996): 204–29.

14:1; 20:20; Acts 9:24.[320] If so, if μετὰ παρατηρήσεως is Luke's addition, we have cause to suspect that *Gos. Thom.* 113 depends upon the Third Gospel, for its phrase, "not come by expectation" (or "by looking": ϭⲱϣⲧ ⲉⲃⲟⲗ [cf. *Gos. Thom.* 51]), corresponds to Luke's μετὰ παρατηρήσεως.

There are perhaps additional indications that the *Gospel of Thomas* is not here an independent or wholly independent witness, among them this, that the end of *Gos. Thom.* 113 ("the kingdom of the Father is spread out upon the earth, and people do not see it") may echo Luke 17:22 ("you will long to see one of the days of the Son of Man, and you will not see it"), which presents several Lukan features.[321] Not only, then, is the pre-Lukan shape of Luke 17:20–21 nowhere near certain, but also it is scarcely obvious that the *Gospel of Thomas* is an independent witness to it.[322]

4. Most scholars who have written on the eschatology of Jesus have not denied that he thought and spoke of God's rule as somehow truly present. At the same time, they have not eliminated all the sayings about the future coming of the kingdom. So they have left themselves the task of explaining how the two sorts of sayings can be harmonized. I will make my own attempt below. Before doing that, however, I wish to emphasize that the last hundred years have seen any number of serious and carefully considered proposals as to how the kingdom could have been, for Jesus, both present and coming, and the vast majority of such proposals have allowed for at least some apocalyptic elements in his thought.[323] So to turn the sayings about the presence of the kingdom into a lever with which to pry apocalyptic elements from the historical Jesus cannot be a straightforward task.[324] Those who adopt this strategy need to explain to the rest of us why we must reckon all the earlier attempts to unite realized eschatology with apocalyptic

320. See Joachim Jeremias, *Die Sprache des Lukasevangeliums: Redaktion und Tradition im Nicht-Markusstoff des dritten Evangeliums* (KEK; Göttingen: Vandenhoeck & Ruprecht, 1980), 236, 266.

321. See ibid., 266–67.

322. See further Schlosser, *Règne de Dieu*, 1:197–99. For a different analysis, see Josef Zmijewski, *Die Eschatologiereden des Lukas-Evangeliums: Eine traditions- und redaktionsgeschichtliche Untersuchung zu Lk 21,5–36 und Lk 17,20–37* (BBB 40; Bohn: Peter Hanstein, 1972), 378–87. Although he does not consider μετὰ παρατηρήσεως editorial, Zmijewski does regard "nor will they say, 'Look, here it is!' or 'There it is!'" as Lukan.

323. For a brief overview, see Hahn, *Vielfalt des Neuen Testaments*, 61–62. Still worth knowing is the older survey by Norman Perrin, *The Kingdom of God in the Teaching of Jesus* (NTL; Philadelphia: Westminster, 1963).

324. Especially if one agrees with this century-old verdict by Shailer Mathews: "At the very best the passages which can be quoted in favor of the existing present kingdom are exceedingly few, while those which more naturally must be interpreted to refer to the future kingdom are all but constant" (*The Messianic Hope in the New Testament* [Chicago: University of Chicago Press, 1904], 80). One recalls that Bultmann found no evidence that Jesus saw the presence of the kingdom in his own person: "Such a view cannot be substantiated by a single saying" (*Theology*, 1:22).

expectation as failures beyond exegetical rehabilitation. I am unaware that anyone has done this.

5. Almost half a century ago, C. F. D. Moule urged that early Christians fashioned their eschatological statements according to the different situations in which they found themselves. Formulations were ad hoc and varied according to whether one was envisaging individuals or a collective, addressing insiders or outsiders, pondering the activities of God or of human beings. No one set out to construct a coherent eschatological system, which is why no one achieved such a thing.[325]

The point, which is obvious enough once stated, becomes important for us when we embrace the form-critical axiom that the sayings of Jesus circulated, for the most part, without record of their originating contexts, so that we can only speculate about the circumstance in which Jesus uttered any saying that we might assign to him.

Consider in this light once more Luke 17:20–21: "Once Jesus was asked by the Pharisees when the kingdom of God was coming, and he answered, 'The kingdom of God is not coming with things that can be observed; nor will they say, "Look, here it is!" or "There it is!" For, in fact, the kingdom of God is among you.'" We cannot assume that Luke's introduction ("Once Jesus was asked by the Pharisees when the kingdom of God was coming") preserves the real-life setting of the saying here attributed to Jesus; it may be the evangelist's invention or that of a predecessor. Nor do we know whether the question is supposed to be sincere or to be asked in mockery.[326] In any case, one recalls that *Gos. Thom.* 113 supplies a different setting for the same saying: "His disciples said to him, 'When will the kingdom come?' Jesus said. . . ." If *Thomas* here depends upon Luke, we see how easy it was for a tradent to give a saying a new context. If *Thomas* does not depend upon Luke, it is anyone's guess whether the circumstance in either book is historical memory. Perhaps neither is. In short, we do not know the occasion that first called forth Luke 17:20–21, and given that context determines meaning, how can we be confident about what its author, whether Jesus or not, precisely intended? Without knowing the initial audience, the author's attitude toward that audience, and his rhetorical ends, and without knowing whether he was speaking ironically, polemically, hyperbolically, figuratively, or straightforwardly, we are in the dark.

An analogy from Paul may help. He authored all six of the following sentences:

---

325. C. F. D. Moule, "The Influence of Circumstances on the Use of Eschatological Terms," *JTS* 15 (1964): 1–15.

326. According to Poole, "Whether the Pharisees spake this deriding him, who in his discourses had been often mentioning a kingdom of God to come, or in simple seriousness . . . is very hard to determine; their mean opinion of Christ inclineth some to think the former; their generally received opinion about the kingdom of the Messiah giveth some countenance to the latter" (*Annotations*, 3:234).

- Rom 14:17: "For the kingdom of God is not food and drink but righteousness and peace and joy in the Holy Spirit."
- 1 Cor 4:20: "For the kingdom of God depends not on talk but on power."
- 1 Cor 6:9–10: "Do you not know that wrongdoers will not inherit the kingdom of God? Do not be deceived! Fornicators, idolaters, adulterers, male prostitutes, sodomites, thieves, the greedy, drunkards, revilers, robbers—none of these will inherit the kingdom of God."
- 1 Cor 15:24: "Then comes the end, when he hands over the kingdom to God the Father, after he has destroyed every ruler and every authority and power."
- 1 Cor 15:50: "Flesh and blood cannot inherit the kingdom of God, nor does the perishable inherit the imperishable."
- Gal 5:21: "I am warning you, as I warned you before: those who do such things will not inherit the kingdom of God."

In the first two verses, the kingdom is present; in the last four, it is future. This does not astound. In each case we understand how the different assertions function within Paul's larger discourse. Imagine, however, that instead of Romans, 1 Corinthians, and Galatians, we had a collection of isolated Pauline sentences, excerpts from his letters, lines without their original literary contexts—something like the *Gospel of Thomas*, but for Paul instead of Jesus; and imagine further that this collection included Rom 14:17; 1 Cor 4:20; 6:9–10; 15:24, 50; Gal 5:21 as isolated bits. What would we think then?

Many would no doubt sense some tension between Rom 14:17; 1 Cor 4:20, where the kingdom is already here, and 1 Cor 6:9–10; 15:24, 50; Gal 5:21, where it has yet to come. Not only that, but surely a few scholars, observing that apocalyptic texts sometimes visualize the advent of God's final victory as a great banquet (see p. 41), would contend that Rom 14:17 seems to set this expectation aside: "the kingdom of God is not food and drink." These scholars might then go on to treat 1 Cor 6:9–10; 15:24, 50; Gal 5:21 as deutero-Pauline, on the grounds that the real Paul regarded the kingdom as present (1 Cor 4:20) and did not share apocalyptic expectations (Rom 14:17).

This line of reasoning, however, would miss the mark and so misrepresent Paul. One wonders if some analyses of Luke 17:20–21 and Matt 12:28 // Luke 11:20 (Q) are not similarly off target. Can we really take our bearings from a couple of logia whose originating settings are gone for good, sayings not even (if Jesus spoke them) extant in their original language and so not in their original form?

6. Many today read Luke 17:20–21 as a statement of antithetical exclusion: because the kingdom of God is even now "among you," it cannot, someday down the road, be "coming with things that can be observed; nor

will they say, 'Look, here it is!' or 'There it is!'" Jacques Schlosser, however, has made the intriguing suggestion that this reading fails to see that we have here the common Semitic idiom of relative or dialectical negation, in which all or almost all of the emphasis lies on the second limb of the saying.[327] Although the form of a sentence may be "Not A, but B," nothing is really being said about A; it is negated solely in order to stress B, as in the following sentences:

- Exod 16:8: "Your complaining is not against us but against the LORD."
- 1 Sam 8:7: "And the LORD said to Samuel, 'Listen to the voice of the people in all that they say to you; for they have not rejected you, but they have rejected me from being king over them.'"
- Jer 7:22–23: "For in the day that I brought your ancestors out of the land of Egypt, I did not speak to them or command them concerning burnt offerings and sacrifices. But this command I gave them, 'Obey my voice, and I will be your God, and you shall be my people; and walk only in the way that I command you, so that it may be well with you.'"
- Mark 9:37: "Whoever welcomes me welcomes not me but the one who sent me."
- Acts 5:4: "You [Ananias] did not lie to us but to God!"

In each of these cases the first part of the statement is literally false: the generation in the wilderness did complain against Moses; the Israelites did reject Samuel; God did give commandments regarding sacrifices; those who welcomed Jesus did welcome him; Ananias did lie to the apostles. The denials are not to be taken literally but are instead transparent exaggerations for emphasis, rhetorical ways of setting the stage for and underlining the importance of what follows. They are like Matt 23:3a, where "do whatever they [the scribes and Pharisees] teach you and follow it" cannot, given what Matthew says elsewhere, be taken at face value. The verse is instead just a hyperbolic way of introducing 23:3b: "but do not do as they do, for they do not practice what they teach."[328] It is the same in 1 John 3:18: "Little children,

---

327. Schlosser, *Règne de Dieu*, 1:212–13. See also H. Kruse, "Dialektische Negationen als semitisches Idiom," *VT* 4 (1954): 385–400; cf. BDF §448.1: οὐ . . . ἀλλά can mean "not so much . . . as," so that "the first element is not entirely negated, but only toned down." Comparable are statements that, although they do not use οὐ . . . ἀλλά, nonetheless exaggerate or mislead in the first clause in order to stress a point in the second clause, an example being Rom 6:17 ("I thank God that you were servants of sin, but you have become obedient from the heart to the form of teaching to which you were entrusted"); cf. Chrysostom, *Hom. Matt.* 38.1.

328. One might also compare Luke 16:17: "It is easier for heaven and earth to pass away, than for one stroke of a letter in the law to be dropped"; and this comment by Claude C. Douglas: "Of the two supposedly impossible things one is said to be easier than the other" (*Overstatement in the New Testament* [New York: Henry Holt, 1931], 66).

let us love, not in word or speech, but in truth and action." This is not a call to refrain from speech that is loving. In like manner, Schlosser has suggested that Luke 17:20 does not really deny that the kingdom of God will someday come "with things that can be observed"; rather, Jesus says that solely in order to emphasize the unexpected declaration that follows in 17:21: the kingdom is present among you.[329]

I do not know if Schlosser is correct, in part because, as previously observed, I do not know the particular context in which Jesus might have said something like Luke 17:20–21. Schlosser's proposal is not, however, obviously false, and its truth would mean that Luke 17:20–21, if dominical, is no witness against an apocalyptic Jesus.

7. The antithesis so often presumed between the kingdom as present and the kingdom as future fails, I have long believed, to reflect adequate engagement with Jewish sources. Daniel, which undeniably has influenced portions of the canonical Gospels,[330] announces that "in the days of those kings [of the Greek kingdom] the God of heaven will set up a kingdom that shall never be destroyed" (2:44). Here the kingdom is yet to come (cf. 7:14, 18, 22, 27). In 4:34, however, God's "kingdom endures from generation to generation." Here the kingdom is already a reality (cf. 4:3). Might not ancient Jewish hearers of Daniel, among whom one might plausibly count Jesus,[331] have thought God's kingdom to be both present and coming?[332]

The Hebrew Bible as a whole generates the same thought. In some texts, such as Exod 15:18 ("The LORD will reign [from now on and] forever and ever"); 1 Chr 29:11 ("Yours is the kingdom, O LORD, and you are exalted as head above all"); Ps 103:19 ("The LORD has established his throne in the heavens, and his kingdom rules over all"); 145:13 ("Your kingdom is an everlasting kingdom, and your dominion endures throughout all generations"), God is king even now.[333] In other passages, God will become king in the future. Obadiah 21 declares that "those who have been saved shall go up to Mount Zion to rule

329. More precisely, Schlosser offers this interpretation of what he takes to have been the pre-Lukan saying: οὐκ ἔρχεται ἡ βασιλεία τοῦ θεοῦ. ἰδοὺ (γὰρ) ἡ βασιλεία τοῦ θεοῦ ἐντὸς ὑμῶν ἐστιν ("The kingdom of God does not come. For behold the kingdom of God is among you").

330. See Evans, "Daniel in the New Testament."

331. For an overview of the relevant texts, see James D. G. Dunn, "The Danielic Son of Man in the New Testament," in *Book of Daniel* (ed. Collins and Flint), 528–49. Cf. Craig A. Evans, "Defeating Satan and Liberating Israel: Jesus and Daniel's Vision," *JSHJ* 1 (2003): 161–70.

332. See Klaus Koch, "Jesus apokalyptisch," *ZNT* 3 (1999): 43–44.

333. Cf., for example, Ps 5:2; 10:16; 22:28; 24:7–10; 29:10; 44:4; 47:2–3, 7–8; 48:2; 68:24; 74:12; 84:3; 93:1–2; 95:3; 96:10; 97:1; 99:1; 145:1; 149:2; Isa 6:5; 8:19; 10:7, 10; 33:22; 41:21; 43:15; 44:6; Zeph 3:15; Mal 1:14; *1 En.* 84:2; 2 Macc 1:24; Tob 13:1; *Pss. Sol.* 2:30, 32; 5:19; 15:18–19; 17:1, 3; 4Q400 2; 4Q403 frg. 1 I; 4Q405 frg. 23 II; Wis 6:4; 10:10; *T. Mos.* 4:2; *m. Ber.* 2:2; *m. Yoma* 4:1–2; 6:2; *t. Taʿan.* 1:13. In some of these texts God is king of the world, in others king of heaven, in others king of Israel or Zion or individual Israelites. For discussion of the texts in the Psalms, see Robert D. Rowe, *God's Kingdom and God's Son: The Background to Mark's Christology from Concepts of Kingship in the Psalms* (AGJU 50; Leiden: Brill, 2002), 13–62. On the presence of

Mount Esau; and the kingdom shall be the LORD's," and Zech 14:9 foresees the day when "the LORD will become king over all the earth."[334] So auditors of the Scriptures who pondered the divine kingdom might have thought it to be present and coming, or as being in heaven now[335] and on earth in the future.[336] Is this not the meaning of Tg. Zech 14:9: "The kingdom of the Lord will be revealed upon all the inhabitants of the earth"?[337] Is this not the idea behind Tg. Ps.-J. on Exod 15:18: "He is the king of kings in this world, and his is the kingdom for the world to come"?[338] Is this not the assumption of T. Mos. 10:1–3, where we read that the eschatological kingdom will appear when God, who at present rules from the divine throne in heaven, arises and goes forth to repair the world? It scarcely startles to find in the Jewish liturgy of later times the confession יי מלך יי מלך יי ימלך לעולם ("The Lord was king, the Lord is king, the Lord will be king forever").[339] One guesses that many first-century

God's kingdom in rabbinic literature, see Jacob Neusner, "The Kingdom of Heaven in Kindred Systems, Judaic and Christian," *BBR* 15 (2005): 279–305.

334. See further the texts in n. 26; note also this comment by Paul Joyce: "The Enthronement Psalms are to be seen as affirming Yahweh's eternal sovereignty, which is seen partially in the present and may thus already be celebrated in worship, but whose ultimate fulfilment and vindication awaits the future, a hope to which worship itself bears witness" ("The Kingdom of God and the Psalms," in *Kingdom of God* [ed. Barbour], 44).

335. And yet not beyond reach: ancient Jews could think of themselves as experiencing eschatological realities even now. See David E. Aune, *The Cultic Setting of Realized Eschatology in Early Christianity* (NovTSup 28; Leiden: Brill, 1972), 29–44; Heinz-Wolfgang Kuhn, *Enderwartung und gegenwärtiges Heil: Untersuchungen zu den Gemeindeliedern von Qumran mit einem Anhang über Eschatologie und Gegenwart in der Verkündigung Jesu* (SUNT 4; Göttingen: Vandenhoeck & Ruprecht, 1966); George W. E. Nickelsburg, "The Qumranic Transformation of a Cosmological and Eschatological Tradition (1QH 4:29–40)," in *The Madrid Qumran Congress: Proceedings of the International Congress on the Dead Sea Scrolls, Madrid, 18–21 March, 1991* (ed. Julio Trebolle Barrera and Luis Vegas Montaner; 2 vols.; STDJ 11; Leiden: Editorial Complutense, 1992), 2:649–59. Cf. 1QHª 11:19–36; 19:3–35. For the Sabbath as a foretaste or type of the future age, see Lat. *L.A.E.* 51:2; *'Abot R. Nat.* A 1; *b. Ber.* 57b; *Gen. Rab.* 17:5; also Samuele Bacchiocchi, "Sabbatical Typologies of Messianic Redemption," *JSJ* 17 (1986): 153–76; Theodore Friedman, "The Sabbath: Anticipation of Redemption," *Judaism* 16 (1967): 443–52.

336. See further Martin Hengel and Anna Maria Schwemer, *Jesus und das Judentum* (vol. 1 of *Geschichte des frühen Christentums*; Tübingen: Mohr Siebeck, 2007), 406–11.

337. Dennis Duling remarks, "The fact that YHWH will reign in the future is interpreted to mean that an already present reign of God will be made manifest universally in the future" ("Kingdom of God, Kingdom of Heaven," *ABD* 4:53).

338. מלכותא לעלמא דאתי; cf. Frg. Tgs. P V on the same verse, and see further the discussion of Exod 15:18 in the *Mekilta* ad loc. along with the comments of Beate Ego, "Gottes Weltherrschaft und die Einzigkeit seines Namens," in *Königsherrschaft Gottes* (ed. Hengel and Schwemer), 268–72.

339. *Daily Prayer Book* [= *Ha-Siddur Ha-Shalem*] (trans. Philip Birnbaum; New York: Hebrew Publishing, 1977), 199. The whole context is worth quoting: "Our God who art in heaven, reveal thy Oneness and establish thy kingdom forever; do thou reign over us forever and ever. May our eyes behold, our hearts rejoice, and our souls exult in thy true salvation, when it will be said to Zion: 'Your God is king.' The Lord is king, the Lord was king, the Lord will be king

Jews thought about God's reign in a way not unlike the following formulation of a modern Christian, writing about "Apostolic times": "the kingdom of God was in effect the vindication *de facto* of that sovereignty over the universe which belonged *de jure* to God, but which in the present Age might be regarded as having been more or less successfully challenged by evil powers, who in the world as it now is had, to some extent, succeeded in establishing a temporal control. In the Coming Age God would finally vindicate his sovereignty, and all evil would be brought to an end."[340]

Sipre 313 on Deut 32:10 is here germane: "Until Abraham came into this world, the Holy One, blessed be he, reigned, if one dare say such a thing, only over the heavens, as it is said, 'The Lord, the God of heaven, who took me' (Gen 24:7). But when Abraham came into the world, he made him (God) king over both the heaven and the earth, as it is said, 'And I will make you swear by the Lord, the God of heaven and the God of the earth' (Gen 24:3)."[341] Here God's kingdom was, we are told, once confined to the heavenly realm. When Abraham appeared, it appeared also on earth.[342]

8. Also of likely relevance for understanding Jesus' proclamation is this fact: God's kingdom does not, in Jewish literature, always arrive in a moment, in the twinkling of an eye.[343] *Apocalypse of Abraham* 29:14 says, "Before the age of justice starts to grow, my judgment will come upon the heathen." Here the world to come shows up gradually. The same is true of the Messiah's manifestation in *2 Bar.* 29:3: "the Anointed One will begin to be revealed."[344]

If the eschatological events can take place over a period of time, they can also belong to present experience, as in Deutero-Isaiah. Although Israel has not, in Isa 40–55, left behind the age of trouble and entered the ideal future, that future is nonetheless beginning to unfold, and God's salvific activity is making itself felt in the experience of God's servant, Israel. This is why modern scholars have characterized "Deutero-Isaiah's expectation of salvation . . . as 'realized

---

forever and ever. For the kingdom is thine, and to all eternity thou wilt reign in glory; we have no king except thee. Blessed art thou, O Lord, glorious king, who wilt reign over us and over thy entire creation forever."

340. A. E. J. Rawlinson, "The Kingdom of God in the Apostolic Age," *Theology* 14 (1927): 263. See further the helpful discussion in Clemens Thoma, "Die gegenwärtige und kommende Herrschaft Gottes als fundamentales jüdisches Anliegen im Zeitalter Jesu," in *Zukunft in der Gegenwart: Wegweisungen in Judentum und Christentum* (ed. Clemens Thoma; JC 1; Bern: Herbert Lang, 1976), 57–77.

341. Is this tradition related to *Prayer of Jacob* (= *PGM* 22b:1–26) 5: "He who showed favor to Abraham by giving the kingdom [βασιλεία] to him"?

342. Those who think that in some New Testament passages it is Jesus himself who brings the kingdom might cite this passage from *Sipre* as a parallel.

343. Becker (*Jesus of Nazareth*, 105) has seen the relevance of this for Jesus.

344. That the Messiah was sometimes known as "Branch" (see p. 280 n. 244) might lie in the background: branches grow.

eschatology,' 'present eschatology,' 'actualized eschatology' and 'actualizing eschatology.'"[345]

Similar is *Jubilees*, where the age of blessedness enters history one step at a time.[346] According to 23:26–27, "In those days the children shall begin to study the laws, and to seek the commandments, and to return to the path of righteousness. And the days shall begin to grow many and increase amongst those children of men till their days draw nigh to one thousand years, and to a greater number of years than (before) was the number of days."

This passage is particularly instructive for the study of Jesus because many have concurred with R. H. Charles that, for the author of Jubilees, "the era of the Messianic kingdom had already set in."[347] Whereas the center of *Jub.* 23 is a depiction of the Maccabean revolt, the last few verses, including those just quoted, imagine the final salvation. *Jubilees*, however, draws no clear line between the Hasmonean state and the eschatological redemption. The one era seems to evolve into the other; that is, the kingdom emerges gradually ("And the days will begin to grow"). The consummation is not yet, but it has already begun.[348] To borrow a phrase that Jeremias used to characterize the teaching of Jesus, *Jubilees* displays "an eschatology that is in the process of realization."[349]

The Apocalypse of Weeks (*1 En.* 93 + 91:12–17) also envisages an extended eschatological process already under way. Its schematization of history consists of ten weeks:

First week:	from Adam to Enoch
Second week:	from Enoch to Noah
Third week:	from Noah to Abraham
Fourth week:	from Abraham to Sinai

---

345. Henk Leene, "History and Eschatology in Deutero-Isaiah," in *Studies in the Book of Isaiah: Festschrift Willem A. M. Beuken* (ed. J. van Ruiten and M. Vervenne; BETL 132; Leuven: Leuven University Press, 1997), 234.

346. See discussion in Scott, *On Earth as in Heaven*, 119–27.

347. R. H. Charles, "The Book of Jubilees," in *Apocrypha and Pseudepigrapha* (ed. Charles), 2:9. Cf. Paul Volz, *Die Eschatologie der jüdischen Gemeinde im neutestamentlichen Zeitalter, nach dem Quellen der rabbinischen, apokalyptischen und apokryphen Literatur* (2nd ed.; Tübingen: Mohr Siebeck, 1934), 29; G. L. Davenport, *The Eschatology of the Book of Jubilees* (StPB 20; Leiden: Brill, 1971), 45 (although Davenport finds this true only for one stage in his hypothetical literary history of *Jubilees*).

348. See further Allison, *End of the Ages*, 17–19. We should reject the assertion by David Flusser and R. Steven Notley that Jesus "is the only Jew of ancient times known to us who preached not only that people were on the threshold of the end of time, but that the new age of salvation had already begun" (*The Sage from Galilee: Rediscovering Jesus' Genius* [4th ed.; Grand Rapids: Eerdmans, 2007], 80).

349. Joachim Jeremias, *The Parables of Jesus* (2nd rev. ed.; New York: Charles Scribner's Sons, 1972), 230 ("sich realisierende Eschatologie").

Fifth week:	from Sinai to the first temple
Sixth week:	from the first temple to its destruction
Seventh week:	the elect arise in the midst of an apostate generation
Eighth week:	Israel is judged; a new temple appears
Ninth week:	the world is judged
Tenth week:	angels are judged

After the tenth week, "the first heaven shall depart and pass away; a new heaven shall appear; and all the powers of heaven shall shine forever sevenfold." That the last things span several periods of time is evident from Jacob Licht's diagram of Enoch's numerical scheme:[350]

$$1 \quad 2 \quad 3 \; \blacktriangledown \; 4 \quad 5 \; \blacktriangledown \; 6 \quad 7 \; \blacktriangledown \; 8 \quad 9 \quad 10 \rightarrow$$

Abraham   Temple   Start of eschatological process

When does the kingdom come in the Apocalypse of Weeks? Certainly not at any particular point in time. Already in the seventh week, which is the author's own epoch,[351] "the elect ones of righteousness" are chosen "from the eternal plant of righteousness," and they receive "sevenfold instruction" concerning the flock of Israel (93:10). So God has started the redemptive process. Apocalyptic secrets are being divulged. Blessings associated with the new age are being bestowed. In the words of Michael Stone, we have here the "eschatological reversal" of an "ordinary situation."[352] And yet the new temple will not be built until the end of week eight, and the new heavens and new earth will not appear until after the tenth week. As with *Jub.* 23, the end is in the process of realization; it is already but not yet.

The supporters of Simon bar Kokhba evidently also thought along these lines. Some of them, including reportedly Akiba, hailed Simon as the Messiah,[353]

350. Jacob Licht, "Time and Eschatology in Apocalyptic Literature and in Qumran," *JJS* 16 (1965): 178–79. Licht writes of "several protracted stages of eschatological transition" (p. 179).

351. According to John J. Collins, "If the apocalypse was written in the eighth generation, the sword would presumably be a reference to the Maccabean revolt. It is more likely that it was written in the seventh week, at the time of the emergence of the chosen righteous" ("The Sense of an Ending in Pre-Christian Judaism," in *Fearful Hope: Approaching the Millennium* [ed. Christopher Kleinhenz and Frannie J. LeMoine; Madison: University of Wisconsin Press, 1999], 33). So also Nickelsburg, *1 Enoch 1*, 447; James C. VanderKam, "Studies in the Apocalypse of Weeks," *CBQ* 46 (1984): 522.

352. Michael Stone, "Lists of Revealed Things in Apocalyptic Literature," in *Magnalia Dei: The Mighty Acts of God; Essays on the Bible and Archaeology in Memory of G. Ernest Wright* (ed. Frank Moore Cross, Werner E. Lemke, and Patrick D. Miller Jr.; Garden City, NY: Doubleday, 1976), 415. Cf. Grant Macaskill, *Revealed Wisdom and Inaugurated Eschatology in Ancient Judaism and Early Christianity* (JSJSup 115; Leiden: Brill, 2007), 43–45.

353. Cf. Justin, *1 Apol.* 31.6; *b. Sanh.* 93b; *y. Ta'an.* 68d (4:5). See further below, p. 258 n. 150.

and he called himself "Prince" (נשיא or נסיא), a title with likely messianic associations.[354] Documents show that he considered himself to be the lord of the land of Israel (e.g., Mur 24B),[355] and on a few of his coins grapes could represent the fruitfulness of the messianic era. On other coins a star stands above the Jerusalem temple, which may advert to the popular messianic prophecy in Num 24:17 ("a star shall come out of Jacob").[356] Whatever the truth on that matter, y. Ta'an. 68d (4:5) passes on this tradition: "R. Simeon ben Yohai said, 'My teacher, R. Akiba, used to explain the passage, "A star [כוכב] will come out of Jacob," thus: "Koziba [כוזבה] will come out of Jacob."'"[357]

What counts for us is this: some of the letters written and some of the coins issued during Simon's brief reign contain the words "Year one of the redemption [לגאלת] of Israel" or "Year two of the freedom [לחר]/redemption [לגאלת] of Israel" or "Year three of the freedom [לחרת] of Israel."[358] So for those who thought of Simon as the royal figure foretold in Num 24:17, the Messiah's reign had already begun, even though obviously history had not yet given way to the utopian kingdom.[359] If any of Simon's adherents had expressed their convictions in terms of the kingdom of God, they might well

354. Cf. Ezek 37:25: "My servant David shall be their prince [נשיא] forever." On the messianic import of "Prince," see Peter Schäfer, The History of the Jews in the Greco-Roman World (London: Routledge, 2003), 151–54; also Craig A. Evans, "Was Simon ben Kosiba Recognized as Messiah?" in Jesus and His Contemporaries: Comparative Studies (AGJU 25; Leiden: Brill, 1995), 201–2. There is debate as to whether the Dead Sea Scrolls ever clearly use נשיא with messianic (as opposed to eschatological) sense; for differing opinions, see Martin G. Abegg and Craig A. Evans, "Messianic Passages in the Dead Sea Scrolls," in Qumran-Messianism: Studies on the Messianic Expectations in the Dead Sea Scrolls (ed. James H. Charlesworth, Hermann Lichtenberger, and Gerbern S. Oegema; Tübingen: Mohr Siebeck, 1998), 194–97; C. D. Elledge, "The Prince of the Congregation: Qumran 'Messianism' in the Context of Milḥāmâ," in Qumran Studies: New Approaches, New Questions (ed. Michael Thomas Davis and Brent A. Strawn; Grand Rapids: Eerdmans, 2007), 178–207.

355. See further Hannah M. Cotton, "Ein Gedi between the Two Revolts," SCI 20 (2001): 139–54.

356. So Antti Laato, A Star Is Rising: The Historical Development of the Old Testament Royal Ideology and the Rise of the Jewish Messianic Expectations (ISFCJ 5; Atlanta: Scholars Press, 1997), 371. For messianic interpretations of these words, see LXX Num 24:17; CD-A 7:18–21 ("'A star will come out of Jacob, and a scepter will rise out of Israel.' The scepter is the prince [נשיא] of the whole congregation. . . ."); 4Q175; T. Levi 18:3; T. Jud. 24:1; and the targumim on Num 24:17. But for the argument that the star on the coins is not messianic, see Leo Mildenberg, The Coinage of the Bar Kokhba War (ed. Patricia Erhart Mottahedeh; Typos 6; Aarau: Sauerländer, 1984), 44–45.

357. Cf. Lam. Rab. 2:4; Eusebius, Hist. eccl. 4.6.2.

358. See P. Benoit, J. T. Milik, and R. de Vaux, Les Grottes de Murabba'ât: Texte (DJD 2; Oxford: Clarendon, 1961), 118–37; Ya'akov Meshorer, Ancient Jewish Coinage (2 vols.; Dix Hills, NY: Amphora Books, 1982), 2:135–36, 150–52; Ada Yardeni, "8. XHev/Se papDeed of Sale B ar and heb," in Hannah M. Cotton and Ada Yardeni, Aramaic, Hebrew and Greek Documentary Texts from Nahal Hever and Other Sites (DJD 27; Oxford: Clarendon, 1997), 36.

359. According to Heinemann, Akiba must have thought that the process of redemption had started (Aggadah and Its Development, 108).

have said that it had come and was yet to come. Might not Jesus and his followers have thought analogously?[360]

9. If one wishes to know more precisely how Jesus might have conceptualized, in his own time and place, the arrival or presence of God's kingdom, the Synoptics may hold the answer. Luke 10:18 has him announce, "I saw Satan fall like lightning from heaven" (RSV). It is natural to relate this vision—if that is the right word—to the widespread expectation that the latter days would witness the defeat of Beelzebul and all evil spirits (see n. 71): the kingdom must be here or at hand because the devil is being routed. This was the solution of Johannes Weiss: "If Jesus already speaks of a Kingdom of God which is present, it is not because there is present a community of disciples among whom God's will is done, as if God's rule were realized from the side of men. Rather, Jesus does so because by his own activity the power of Satan, who above all others is the source of evil, is being broken."[361]

This does seem to be the logic in several sayings attributed to Jesus, not just Luke 10:18. In Matt 12:28 // Luke 11:20 (Q) it is put this way: "But if it is by the finger/Spirit of God that I cast out demons, then the kingdom of God has come upon you." Similar is the parable of the strong man: "If a kingdom is divided against itself, that kingdom cannot stand. . . . And if Satan has risen up against himself and is divided, he cannot stand, but his end has come" (Mark 3:24–26; cf. Matt 12:25–26 // Luke 11:17–18 [Q]). Again, the likely sense of Mark 1:15a is "the time of the dominion of Satan has been fulfilled, and the kingdom of God has drawn near."[362] One may compare *T. Mos.* 10:1: "Then his [God's] kingdom will appear throughout his whole creation. Then the devil will have an end" (J. Priest, *OTP* 1:931). When God's kingdom comes, Satan's kingdom goes. So if the historical Jesus, like the Synoptic Jesus, ever thought of his successful ministry of exorcism in eschatological terms, he might well have thought this: since Satan's kingdom is already being ruined, God's kingdom must already be advancing into the world.

360. For additional, later examples of the final redemption being conceptualized as a protracted process, see Elisheva Carlebach, "Two Amens That Delayed the Redemption: Jewish Messianism and Popular Spirituality in the Post-Sabbatian Century," *JQR* 82 (1992): 250–51; Scholem, *Sabbatai Sevi*, 220–21 (Sabbatai Sevi's messianic proclamation was "the beginning of the growth of the kingdom"); Stephen Sharot, *Messianism, Mysticism, and Magic: A Sociological Analysis of Jewish Religious Movements* (Chapel Hill: University of North Carolina Press, 1982), 63–64.

361. Weiss, *Jesus' Proclamation*, 78. Cf. Kümmel, *Promise and Fulfilment*, 105–9.

362. Joel Marcus, "'The Time Has Been Fulfilled!' (Mark 1:15)," in *Apocalyptic in the New Testament: Essays in Honour of J. Louis Martyn* (ed. Joel Marcus and Marion L. Soards; JSNTSup 24; Sheffield: Sheffield Academic Press, 1989), 49–68. Cyril of Alexandria comments, "Of old, before the earthly advent of our savior, Satan ruled over us through sin, and he imposed a tyrannical and perverse yoke on all dwelling upon the earth. But since the King and Lord of all shone upon us, breaking their chains and throwing off the old yoke of the greedy one, we are subject to the royal power of God, and our God and Father has reigned through the Son" (*Comm. Isa.* 52.8).

I do not, regrettably, know how to demonstrate that Luke 10:18; Matt 12:28 // Luke 11:20 (Q); Mark 3:24–26 (cf. Matt 12:25–26 // Luke 11:17–18 [Q]); Mark 1:15a represent sentiments that really go back to Jesus. Perhaps they do; perhaps they do not. In either case, these logia do at least allow us to imagine a plausible scenario in which Jesus could have spoken of God's kingdom as present. And it is an apocalyptic scenario. Beyond that, the kingdom would, on this account, have been only partially realized. As long as there was need for an exorcist, Satan was still in business, and no one could claim that God's kingdom had come without remainder.

10. Another and perhaps complementary, albeit more speculative, explanation of Jesus' realized eschatology begins with the likelihood that he paid heed to the prophetic oracles in Isa 40–66.[363] Some have supposed that he read specifically the opening part of Isa 61 as a sort of biblical script for his ministry and self-understanding. If so, it is worth observing that Isa 61:1 is linked by both theme and catchwords to Isa 52:7–9:[364]

Isa 61:1: "sent me to bring good news [לבשר]"

Isa 52:7: "the messenger [מבשר] who . . . brings good news [מבשר]"[365]

Isa 61:2: "to comfort [לנחם] all who mourn"

Isa 52:9: "the LORD has comforted [נחם] his people"

Isa 61:3: "to provide for those who mourn in Zion [ציון]"

Isa 52:7–8: "who says to Zion [ציון]"; "the return of the LORD to Zion [ציון]"

Given (a) that Christian and Jewish readers of Isaiah often have identified the herald of Isa 61 with the servant in Isa 52,[366] (b) that Jewish exegetes

---

363. For this possibility and discussion of relevant texts, see below, pp. 263–66; also McKnight, *Jesus and His Death*, 207–24.

364. One presumes that this is because the author of Isa 61:1–2 drew upon Isa 40–55, including 52:7. See Walter Zimmerli, "Das 'Gnadenjahr des Herrn,'" in *Archäologie und Altes Testament: Festschrift für Kurt Galling zum 8 Januar 1970* (ed. Arnulf Kuschke and Ernst Kutsch; Tübingen: Mohr Siebeck, 1970), 322–24.

365. LXX Isa 52:7 (εὐαγγελιζόμενος ἀγαθά . . . βασιλεύσει σου ὁ θεός) may well lie behind Matthew's τὸ εὐαγγέλιον τῆς βασιλείας (4:23; 9:35; 24:14) and Luke's εὐαγγελίζομαι τὴν βασιλείαν τοῦ θεοῦ (Luke 4:43; 8:1; Acts 8:12; cf. Luke 16:16). Cf. also Mark 1:14–15: κηρύσσων τὸ εὐαγγέλιον . . . ἤγγικεν ἡ βασιλεία τοῦ θεοῦ . . . πιστεύετε ἐν τῷ εὐαγγελίῳ.

366. See, for example, W. A. M. Beuken, "Servant and Herald of Good Tidings: Isaiah 61 as an Interpretation of Isaiah 40–55," in *The Book of Isaiah, Le livre d'Isaïe: Les oracles et leurs relectures; Unité et complexité de l'ouvrage* (ed. Jacques Vermeylen; BETL 81; Leuven: Leuven University Press, 1989), 411–40. Christians through the centuries typically have read Jesus into both passages.

regularly associated biblical texts sharing the same words,[367] and (c) that
Acts 10:36–38 may allude to both Isa 52:7 and 61:1,[368] one might guess that
ancient, scripturally informed Jews sometimes linked Isa 61:1–2 with Isa
52:7–8. But we do not have to guess, for we find the following in 11Q13
2:15–20:

> This [. . .] is the day of [peace about whi]ch he said [. . . through Isa]iah the
> prophet, who said, ["How] beautiful upon the mountains are the feet [of] the
> messen[ger who] announces peace, the mess[enger of good who announces
> salvati]on, [sa]ying to Zion: your God [reigns"] (*Isa 52:7*). Its interpretation:
> The mountains [are] the prophet[s . . .] . . . [. . .] for all . . . [. . .] And the
> messenger i[s] the anointed of the spir[it] as Dan[iel] said [about him: "Until an
> anointed, a prince, it is seven weeks" (*Dan 9:25*). And the messenger of] good
> who announ[ces salvation] is the one about whom it is written that [. . .] "To
> comfo[rt] the [afflicted" (*Isa 61:2–3*), its interpretation:] to instruct them in all
> the ages of the wo[rld . . .][369]

Although much in this text is obscure, one thing is clear because explicit: the
herald of Isa 52:7 (whether Melchizedek or some other) is the anointed one
of Isa 61:1–3.[370]

These verses from Isaiah also come together in another Dead Sea Scroll, in
1QH[a] 23:12–14 (top): "You [God] have opened a spr[ing] to rebuke the path
of those fashioned from clay, the guilt of the one born of woman according
to his deeds, to open the sp[rin]g of your truth to the creature whom you have
supported with your power, to [be,] according to your truth, a herald [. . .] of
your goodness (מבשר [. . .] טובכה), to proclaim to the poor (לבשר ענוים)
the abundance of your compassion."[371] טובכה [. . .] מבשר borrows from Isa
52:7 (מבשר . . . מבשר טוב), and לבשר ענוים is lifted without alteration from
Isa 61:1. Moreover, whatever 1QH[a] 23:12–14 means precisely, the two phrases
from Isaiah are taken to refer to one individual.

---

367. See Michael L. Klein, "Associative and Complementary Translation in the Targumim,"
ErIsr 16 (1982): 134–40; Jean Koenig, *L'herméneutique analogique du judaïsme antique d'après
les témoins textuels d'Isaïe* (VTSup 33; Leiden: Brill, 1982).

368. Acts 10:36: εὐαγγελιζόμενος εἰρήνην
Isa 52:7: εὐαγγελιζομένου ἀκοὴν εἰρήνης
Acts 10:38: ἔχρισεν αὐτὸν ὁ θεὸς πνεύματι ἁγίῳ
Isa 61:1: πνεῦμα κυρίου ἐπ' ἐμέ, οὗ εἵνεκεν ἔχρισέν με

369. Translation and reconstruction in Florentino García Martínez and Eibert J. C. Tigchelaar,
The Dead Sea Scrolls Study Edition (2 vols.; Leiden: Brill, 1998), 2:1209.

370. See Johannes Zimmermann, *Messianische Texte aus Qumran: Königliche, priesterliche
und prophetische Messiasvorstellung in den Schriftfunden von Qumran* (WUNT 2/104; Tübingen:
Mohr Siebeck, 1998), 410–12.

371. Translation and reconstruction in García Martínez and Tigchelaar, *Dead Sea Scrolls*,
2:197–99.

What does all this have to do with Jesus? Simply this: if he identified himself with the messenger of Isa 61:1–3, the prophet who brings good news to the poor and comforts those who mourn, and if, like the author of 11Q13 and many other readers, he equated that messenger with the herald of Isa 52, then his biblical script would have told him to proclaim, "Your God reigns," because that is the message of the herald in Isa 52:7: "How beautiful upon the mountains are the feet of the messenger who announces peace, who brings good news, who announces salvation, who says to Zion, 'Your God reigns [מלך אלהיך].'"[372] The targum, interestingly enough, turns מלך אלהיך into a sentence with "the kingdom of God" as its subject: אתגליאת מלכותא דאלהיך ("The kingdom of your God is revealed"). In short, a scripturally minded Jesus, who saw himself in Isa 61:1 and so in 52:7, could have found the announcement of realized eschatology dictated to him by a prophetic oracle.[373]

11. One last point about the presence of the kingdom. Millenarian movements often, it should be stressed, follow their own logic when it comes to the tension between fulfillment and expectation. "Messianic excitement can induce a state of mind in which normal ways of thinking are swept aside."[374] Adherents may believe that the "great apocalyptic transformation and the advent of a promised world have dawned."[375] Paul, as we have seen, had no trouble speaking of a present kingdom of God (Rom 14:17; 1 Cor 4:20) and a future kingdom of God (1 Cor 6:9–10; 15:50, 24; Gal 5:21).[376] Menachem Schneerson said, in one sentence, that "the king Messiah . . . will come" and, in the very next sentence, that he "is already present in the world," and his followers have taught that they can even now "taste" the future redemption.[377] The Zionist R. Abraham Kook, who replaced the famous statement in *b. Sanh.* 98a that the Son of David will come in a generation that is entirely innocent or entirely guilty with the irrational proposition that the present generation is

372. The suggestion that Jesus interpreted his ministry in terms of Isa 52:7 has a striking parallel in Paul, who found his own ministry in the very same verse; see Rom 10:14–17 and J. Ross Wagner, *Heralds of the Good News: Isaiah and Paul "In Concert" in the Letter to the Romans* (NovTSup 101; Leiden: Brill, 2002), 170–76.

373. Scholars who have surmised that Jesus himself paid attention to Isa 52:7 include Otto Betz, "Jesus' Gospel of the Kingdom," in *The Gospel and the Gospels* (ed. Peter Stuhlmacher; Grand Rapids: Eerdmans, 1991), 59–60; Rudolf Schnackenburg, *God's Rule and Kingdom* (trans. John Murray; 2nd ed.; London: Burns & Oates; New York: Herder & Herder, 1968), 37. As a speculative aside, one could find in Isa 52:7 a motivation to conduct a ministry in Jerusalem, for the messenger announces salvation and God's reign "to Zion."

374. Marcus, "Jewish Apocalypticism," 19.

375. Richard Landes, "Millennialism," in *The Oxford Handbook of New Religious Movements* (ed. James R. Lewis; Oxford: Oxford University Press, 2004), 335. Landes refers to "the *already/not yet* of apocalyptic time" (p. 340). It is nothing unique to old Jewish and Christian texts.

376. See Karl Paul Donfried, "The Kingdom of God in Paul," in *The Kingdom of God in 20th-Century Interpretation* (ed. Wendell Willis; Peabody, MA: Hendrickson, 1987), 175–90.

377. See Ravitzky, *Messianism*, 185, 195, 197–98.

entirely guilty and entirely innocent, identified the present with both the blessed time of the redemption and the period of the messianic woes.[378] Abraham Abulafia, the thirteenth-century Jewish messiah, announced the imminent apocalypse, the coming fulfillment of Dan 12:2, and the resurrection of the dead. At the very same time, he taught that "the time of salvation and the day of redemption have come" (קץ התשועה ויום הגאולה בא), and that those who had awakened themselves spiritually had already been resurrected from the dead.[379] Before Abulafia, the eighth-century Jewish messianic leader Severus said that the days of the Messiah had begun and simultaneously that the redemption was near and so not yet.[380] Later on, the Jewish philosopher and Bible scholar Isaac Abravanel (1437–1508) argued that although the Messiah had not yet arrived, the messianic age had begun, as evidenced by a conjunction of Jupiter and Saturn and the movement of Jewish populations closer to their homeland.[381]

The upshot of the preceding pages is this: there is no reason to tear asunder what the tradition holds together. If Jesus sometimes, as so many are convinced, proclaimed the presence of God's kingdom, this is insufficient reason to urge that he did not also proclaim its future, apocalyptic revelation.

The Parables and Eschatology

According to Robert Funk, one of the pillars of contemporary scholarship is "the liberation of the non-eschatological Jesus of the aphorisms and parables from Schweitzer's eschatological Jesus."[382] He means that certain influential discussions of the parables and aphorisms over the last four decades have helped to undermine the apocalyptic Jesus. "The evidence of his parables and aphorisms shows that Jesus did not understand the rule of God to be the beginning of a new age, at the end of history, following a cosmic catastrophe."[383]

378. Marcus, "Jewish Apocalypticism," 19, 21–22.
379. See Moshe Idel, "'The Time of the End': Apocalypticism and Its Spiritualization in Abraham Abulafia's Eschatology," in *Apocalyptic Time* (ed. Albert I. Baumgarten; SHR 86; Leiden: Brill, 2000), 155–85; Adolph Jellinek, "Sefer ha-Ôt: Apokalypse des Pseudo-Propheten und Pseudo-Messias Abraham Abulafia," in *Jubelschrift zum siebzigsten Geburtstage des Prof. Dr. H. Graetz* (Breslau: Schottlaender, 1887), part 2, 63–88 (Hebrew citation from p. 79).
380. On Severus, who may or may not have thought himself to be the Messiah, see Joshua Starr, "Le movement messianique au début du VIIIᵉ siècle," *REJ* 102 (1937): 81–92.
381. See Isaac E. Barzilay, *Between Reason and Faith: Anti-Rationalism in Italian Jewish Thought 1250–1650* (PNMES 10; Paris: Mouton, 1967), 112–25.
382. Funk, Hoover, and the Jesus Seminar, *Five Gospels*, 4.
383. Ibid., 40. Compare the comment that "the major parables of Jesus . . . do not reflect an apocalyptic view of history" (p. 137).

Stephen Patterson has made the same point, at least with regard to the parables. The notion that these last are "language events in which the Empire of God becomes a present reality," a notion that now commends itself to many, need have nothing to do with an imminent eschatological judgment; indeed, it seems to stand against it.[384]

I am of another mind. Which parables in and of themselves clearly exclude an apocalyptic worldview? I do not know what others might say, but I cannot think of any. If, however, the argument is that most of the parables do not compel an apocalyptic reading, then I freely grant the point. Jesus' parables, like his aphorisms, are inherently polyvalent and so exceedingly pliable, which is why an exegete's larger frame of reference typically determines interpretation.[385] The fact is on display in Matt 13 and the *Gospel of Thomas*, which construe the very same parables in very different ways.[386]

The subsequent history of the interpretation holds more of the same: exegetes have poured the parables into various interpretive molds. The church fathers and medieval theologians typically read them as allegories.[387] Adolf Jülicher took them to be general religious and moral lessons.[388] C. H. Dodd ingeniously construed them in terms of "realized eschatology,"[389] although Hans Conzelmann could write that in none of the parables is the kingdom "unambiguously . . . present."[390] Joachim Jeremias read most of the parables as expressions of imminent eschatological expectation.[391] That Funk and other fellows of the Jesus Seminar have read them in new ways, and in contradiction to Jeremias, does not astonish, nor does it establish anything about the historical Jesus.

The meanings of parables and their metaphorical possibilities are not inherent properties of the parables as freestanding works of art but rather depend

---

384. Stephen Patterson, *The God of Jesus: The Historical Jesus and the Search for Meaning* (Harrisburg, PA: Trinity Press International, 1998), 177. Compare Charles W. Hedrick's statement that the parables "reflect neither apocalyptic despair nor imminent cosmic destruction" (*Many Things in Parables: Jesus and His Modern Critics* [Louisville: Westminster John Knox, 2004], ix).

385. Patterson seeks a way around this objection by contrasting the "multivalent quality of Jesus' parables" with "the typically closed, fixed quality of apocalyptic" ("Jesus Was Not an Apocalyptic Prophet," 75–76). This reads, I think, a caricature of the literary apocalypses into the unliterary, apocalyptic eschatology of Jesus. See my response in the same volume (Allison, "Jesus Was an Apocalyptic Prophet," 91–93).

386. Useful here is Jacobus Liebenberg, *The Language of the Kingdom and Jesus: Parable, Aphorism, and Metaphor in the Sayings Material Common to the Synoptic Tradition and the Gospel of Thomas* (BZNW 102; Berlin: de Gruyter, 2000).

387. See Stephen L. Wailes, *Medieval Allegories of Jesus' Parables* (Berkeley: University of California Press, 1987).

388. Adolf Jülicher, *Die Gleichnisreden Jesu* (2nd ed.; Tübingen: J. C. B. Mohr, 1910).

389. Dodd, *Parables of the Kingdom*.

390. Conzelmann, "Present and Future," 33.

391. Jeremias, *Parables of Jesus*.

upon the narratives in which they are embedded or upon the nonliterary contexts into which we attempt to place them.[392] Jesus' parables were, after all, "not intended *primarily* as teaching in themselves, but as *instruments* to be used in 'teaching.'"[393] They were auxiliary, elucidatory, as the word παραβολή (cf. מָשָׁל) itself indicates: one of its chief meanings is "illustration" (so BDAG, s.v.). Here, then, I agree with Ben Witherington: "Although the parables may be the characteristic mode of Jesus' teaching, they are certainly an indirect and metaphorical way of speaking on our subject [the kingdom of God], and thus it stands to reason that if there is a more direct and clearer teaching, we should begin with it."[394] It seems to follow that we should elucidate the parables in the light of what we otherwise can learn about Jesus and his proclamation of the kingdom of God, a proclamation that we have every reason to believe was apocalyptic.

The Historical Jesus and the Stages of Q

Dismissal of an apocalyptic Jesus has gained momentum from recent discussion of the compositional history of Q, the lost document widely thought to lie behind both Matthew and Luke.[395] Several scholars recently have endorsed John Kloppenborg's influential analysis[396] and then gone on to argue that the earliest, or at least an early, version of Q (often designated Q[1]) contained no future Son of Man sayings, and that the eschatological pathos present in Q as it was known to Matthew and Luke (Q[3]) entered at a secondary stage (Q[2]).[397]

392. See Thomas Schmeller, "Das Reich Gottes im Gleichnis," *TLZ* 119 (1994): 608; and see further Liebenberg, *Language of the Kingdom*, esp. 495–530 (although I do not share his skepticism about the historical Jesus). Some now seem to assume that if a parable comes with an editorial, apocalyptic frame (e.g., Matt 13:24–30, 36–43), we may remove that frame as secondary and ignore it (see Patterson, "Jesus Was Not an Apocalyptic Prophet," 76). But to show that an interpretation is an interpretation is not to show that it is wrong.

393. Liebenberg, *Language of the Kingdom*, 529. He goes on: "Does the fact that one can so easily identify the eschatological frameworks in which the parables were contextualized in the synoptic Gospels really allow one to dispense with eschatology altogether? Or is it perhaps the case that one is asking of the parables (in questioning them as to whether they are eschatological or not) what they were never intended to answer?"

394. Ben Witherington III, *The Christology of Jesus* (Minneapolis: Fortress, 1990), 198.

395. This generalization is not true of Borg's work, however.

396. John S. Kloppenborg, *The Formation of Q: Trajectories in Ancient Christian Wisdom Collections* (Philadelphia: Fortress, 1987); idem, *Excavating Q*.

397. See Helmut Koester, *Ancient Christian Gospels* (Philadelphia: Trinity Press International, 1990), 133–71 (arguing that the transition from the "apocalyptic" of Q[2] represents a "radical departure" from the "eschatology" of Q[1]); Burton Mack, *The Lost Gospel: The Book of Q and Christian Origins* (San Francisco: HarperSanFrancisco, 1993), 105–47; James M. Robinson, "The Q Trajectory: Between John and Matthew via Jesus," in *Future of Early Christianity* (ed. Pearson), 173–94; idem, "The Critical Edition of Q and the Study of Jesus," in *Sayings Source Q* (ed. Lindemann), 27–52; L. E. Vaage, "The Son of Man Sayings in Q: Stratigraphical Location

If accepted, this result would be consistent with the theory that Christians, without help from Jesus, were responsible for the apocalyptic eschatology in so much of the Gospels.[398] For Burton Mack, "aphoristic wisdom is characteristic of the earliest layer," and "this turns the table on older views of Jesus as an apocalyptic preacher and brings the message of Jesus around to another style of speech altogether."[399] James Robinson, who has spoken of our "new access to Jesus by means of the Sayings Source Q,"[400] has also taken this view of things.[401]

Serious misgivings are in order. While there are, in my judgment, although not in the judgment of all informed scholars, good reasons to posit that Matthew and Luke used a collection of sayings now lost, this remains a hypothesis, and one that continues to be the discussion of reasonable debate. For some of us, it has the appearance of a fact, but we cannot know it to be a fact.[402] Nor, despite the massive deliberations that produced *The Critical Edition of Q*,[403] do we know exactly what was or was not in Q, assuming its existence. Neither Matthew nor Luke reproduced all of Mark. Why, then, should we suppose that either of them reproduced all of the Sayings Source? Some of what we conventionally assign to M or L is almost certainly from Q.

Far more worrisome is the confident faith that so many have placed in Kloppenborg's theory of a three-stage evolutionary history. Whether or not it is the "consensus" of scholarship,[404] not all competent scholars who have sifted the evidence have endorsed his analysis: the source-critical palette offers an array of opinions.[405] The vulnerability of Kloppenborg's analysis is suggested

---

and Significance," *Semeia* 55 (1991): 103–29. For a critical response to Robinson, see Allison, *Resurrecting Jesus*, 47–90. Kloppenborg himself has refrained from privileging Q[1] as a source for the historical Jesus; see especially his article "The Sayings Gospel Q and the Question of the Historical Jesus," *HTR* 89 (1996): 307–44. Kloppenborg has also been careful not to exaggerate the ideological distance between his Q[1] and Q[2].

398. See Stephen J. Patterson, "The End of Apocalypse: Rethinking the Historical Jesus," *ThTo* 52 (1995): 29–58; idem, *God of Jesus*, 171–72.

399. Burton Mack, *A Myth of Innocence: Mark and Christian Origins* (Philadelphia: Fortress, 1988), 59. Cf. Scott, "How Did We Get Here?" 60.

400. Robinson, "Down-to-Earth Jesus," xiii.

401. Robinson, "Critical Edition of Q."

402. Although I still believe that the Q hypothesis is the best explanation of the data, my faith is not free of doubt. This is why I continue to entertain other hypotheses, such as the possibility that Matthew knew and used Luke, or that some or much or all of the material that we conventionally assign to Q came to Matthew and Luke not as a single document but rather as a combination of written sources, oral complexes, and isolated sayings.

403. James M. Robinson, Paul Hoffmann, and John S. Kloppenborg, eds., *The Critical Edition of Q: Synopsis* (Hermeneia; Minneapolis: Fortress; Leuven: Peeters, 2000).

404. So Ron Cameron, "The Sayings Gospel Q and the Quest of the Historical Jesus: A Response to John S. Kloppenborg," *HTR* 4 (1996): 352.

405. For informed criticism of Kloppenborg, see Paul Hoffmann, "Mutmassungen über Q: Zum Problem der literarischen Genese von Q," in *Sayings Source Q* (ed. Lindemann), 255–88; Richard A. Horsley, "The Contours of Q," in Richard A. Horsley and Jonathan A. Draper, *Who-*

not just by the existence of rival accounts and his failure to demonstrate that
Q^1 represents a single coherent document as opposed to several independent
clusters,[406] but also perhaps by the compositional history of another Q scholar,
Siegfried Schulz, who argued almost the opposite of Kloppenborg: the first
layer of Q was apocalyptic, whereas the second stage added Hellenizing ethical teaching.[407] Whatever one makes of Schulz's case, which admittedly has
not held up well in recent years, so much has been written of late about Q^1
and Q^2 that one wonders whether, through the psychological impact of sheer
repetition, their reality has for some become far less theoretical than it is.[408]

All that aside, what would follow if one were to decide that Kloppenborg
has hit the truth? If there were, in fact, two or three different and somewhat
antagonistic editions of Q, what would incline us to suppose that the contributors to the first edition remembered Jesus better than those who contributed

ever Hears You Hears Me: Prophets, Performance, and Tradition in Q (Harrisburg, PA: Trinity
Press International, 1999), 61–83; Christopher M. Tuckett, *Q and the History of Early Chris-
tianity: Studies on Q* (Edinburgh: T & T Clark, 1996), 69–75; Dieter Zeller, "Eine weisheitliche
Grundschrift in der Logienquelle?" in *The Four Gospels, 1992: Festschrift Frans Neirynck* (ed.
F. Van Segbroeck et al.; 3 vols.; BETL 100; Leuven: University Press, 1992), 1:389–401. For my
own hypothesis about the evolution of Q, see Allison, *Jesus Tradition in Q*, 1–66. For criticism
of all stratigraphic analyses, see Harry T. Fleddermann, *Q: A Reconstruction and Commentary*
(BibTS 1; Leuven: Peeters, 2005), 175–80; Alan K. Kirk, *The Composition of the Sayings Source:
Genre, Synchrony, and Wisdom Redaction in Q* (NovTSup 91; Leiden: Brill, 1998). For a recent
survey of theories of Q's compositional history, see Jacques Schlosser, "La composition du
document Q," in *La source des paroles de Jésus (Q): Aux origines du christianisme* (ed. Andreas
Dettwiler and Daniel Marguerat; Paris: Labor et Fides, 2008), 123–48. Helmut Koester has had
the good sense to confess, "I am fully aware of the hypothetical character of reconstructing
an earlier version of a document that is itself the result of a reconstruction" ("The Synoptic
Sayings Gospel Q in the Early Communities of Jesus' Followers," in *Early Christian Voices* [ed.
Warren, Brock, and Pao], 48; idem, *From Jesus to the Gospels*, 75). As Horsley notes, "Much
of the scholarly energy devoted to the form and message of Q during the last generation has
focused on a hypothesis about a hypothesis" ("Contours of Q," 61).

406. See James D. G. Dunn, "'All That Glitters Is Not Gold': In Quest of the Right Key to
Unlock the Way to the Historical Jesus," in *Der historische Jesus: Tendenzen und Perspektiven der
gegenwärtigen Forschung* (ed. Jens Schröter and Ralph Brucker; BZNW 114; Berlin: de Gruyter,
2002), 136–38; Tuckett, *Q and the History of Early Christianity*, 69–74.

407. Siegfried Schulz, *Q: Die Spruchquelle der Evangelisten* (Zürich: Theologischer Verlag,
1972).

408. Maybe Cameron would include me in his complaint against "specious appeals to the
hypothetical nature of the reconstructed text [Q^1]," which "fundamentally misunderstand how
theory works, and thus seek—whether consciously or not—to bypass the results of scholarship
and the actual evidence of the gospel texts" ("Sayings Gospel Q," 352). But the phrase "the results
of scholarship" betrays, I believe, a parochial point of view, being demonstrably spurious with
regard to contemporary work on Q (see n. 405). And whether or not I understand the nature
of "theory," I do understand the mathematics of piling one less-than-certain inference upon
another, which is what some discussions of Q^1 sometimes strike me as doing. If, to illustrate, a
particular conclusion follows from four (statistically independent) propositions, and if, let us
say, the odds of each individually being true is 50 percent, the series as a whole is (all else being
equal) not very likely: $\frac{1}{2} \times \frac{1}{2} \times \frac{1}{2} \times \frac{1}{2} = 1/16$, or 6.25 percent.

to the second edition? If Q^2 were written a century after Q^1, the earlier editors would indeed be privileged. Q, however, was opened and closed within, at most, a period of two or three decades. This allows at least the possibility that an enlarged Q, by virtue of additional material, resulted in a fuller and so more accurate sketch of Jesus' teaching.[409] Kloppenborg himself has said as much: "It is indeed possible, indeed probable, that some of the materials from the secondary compositional phase are dominical or at least very old, and that some of the formative elements are, from the standpoint of authenticity or tradition-history, relatively young. Tradition-history is not convertible with *literary history*."[410]

Matthew and Luke augment Mark with what most of us take to be, on some occasions, genuine memory. It could have been the same with Q^2 and Q^1, the former adding authentic sayings to the latter.[411] When the span between stages is so short, chronological priority is of uncertain import and will not commend one text over the other. This is especially the case as we have no cause to believe that Kloppenborg's Q^1 or Q^2 or Q^3, granted their existence for the sake of discussion, represents an attempt to collect into one place every saying of Jesus known to the contributors.[412] Each phase in Q's evolution must

---

409. See Eckhard Rau, "Wie entstehen unechte Jesusworte?" in *Gemeinschaft am Evangelium: Festschrift für Wiard Popkes zum 60. Geburtstag* (ed. Edwin Brandt, Paul S. Fiddes, and Joachim Molthagen; Leipzig: Evangelische Verlagsanstalt, 1996), 181–82.

410. Kloppenborg, *Formation of Q*, 244–45. Crossan (*Birth of Christianity*, 250) also cites these words and concurs with them (which might lead one to ask why he otherwise so emphasizes stratigraphy). Kloppenborg has reiterated his point on several occasions, presumably because it has so often been ignored; note, for example, "Sayings Gospel Q," 337 ("One must presume a basic continuity in eschatological outlook between Q^1 and Q^2 in spite of the changes in idiom"); *Excavating Q*, 151. Jens Schröter remarks, "Working with different layers of which the supposed oldest one should be the most 'original' in historical respect is definitely unconvincing" ("The Historical Jesus and the Sayings Tradition: Comments on Current Research," *Neot* 30 [1996]: 165).

411. One counter to this might be that the sayings of eschatological judgment in Q^2 cannot come from Jesus because they reflect rather the history of the Q community, which we can reconstruct. According to Mack (*Lost Gospel*, 134–47), among others, experience of rejection led the Q people to formulate their sayings of judgment. But, first, this begs the question of whether such experience might equally have led them to appropriate already existing sayings of judgment that were attributed, perhaps rightly, to Jesus. And second, if it is hard to detect what is going on behind the 433 verses of Romans, with its almost systematic discussions of some subjects, it is even more difficult to divine, by a sort of allegorical reading, the history of the community behind a text that we do not have. One doubts that Q is sufficiently transparent to its social setting in as to let us gaze through it to behold the "entire history of an early 'Christian' community in-the-making" (against Burton Mack, *Who Wrote the New Testament? The Making of the Christian Myth* [San Francisco: HarperSanFrancisco, 1995], 49). How can we say so much about the Q community if the Sayings Source is mute concerning liturgy and ritual and further supplies no narrative history of anyone or anything?

412. See further Pearson, "Q Community," 486–89; Michael Winger, "Word and Deed," *CBQ* 62 (2000): 681–82. But if it did, Paul, Mark, M, and L would be the proof that the compilers' knowledge of the Jesus tradition was quite circumscribed.

rather reflect somebody's selection, for this or that ideological end, from a larger body of material.[413] Why, then, should we imagine that any particular stage of Q mirrors, any more than, let us say, *The Sentences of Sextus* or the mishnaic tractate *'Abot*, the overall ideology of a religious group, including all that it thought about Jesus?[414]

Much that is plausibly historical memory of Jesus is, we should not overlook, missing from Kloppenborg's Q[1], which is a very short text (eighty-four verses or so).[415] If that text had survived and were all we had to go on, we would not know that Jesus was from Nazareth, worked in Galilee, or visited Jerusalem. We would have no reason to associate him with John the Baptist or be informed that he was crucified upon order of Pontius Pilate or know why he was thus executed.[416] We would be unaware that he opposed divorce or was famed as an exorcist. We would not have the names of his parents

413. See Daniel Kosch, "Q und Jesus," *BZ* 36 (1992): 32–40 (generalizing about Q, not Q[1]), and the enlightening article by Marco Frenschkowski, "Welche biographischen Kenntnisse von Jesus setzt die Logienquelle Voraus? Beobachtungen zur Gattung von Q im Kontext antiker Spruchsammlungen," in *From Quest to Q: Festschrift James M. Robinson* (ed. Jon Ma. Asgeirsson, Kristin de Troyer, and Marvin W. Meyer; BETL 146; Leuven: Leuven University Press, 2000), 3–41.

414. See Dunn, "All That Glitters," 152; Kloppenborg, *Excavating Q*, 371 ("Q does not offer a complete catalog of the Q group's beliefs"); Jens Schröter, "The Son of Man as the Representative of God's Kingdom: On the Interpretation of Jesus in Mark and Q," in *Jesus, Mark and Q: The Teaching of Jesus and Its Earliest Records* (JSNTSup 214; ed. Michael Labahn and Andreas Schmidt; Sheffield: Sheffield Academic Press, 2001), 37–39. Contrast Cameron, who asserts that "Q functioned programmatically" ("Sayings Gospel," 352). Dunn rightly rejects the "one document per community" hypothesis that posits behind Q not only a Q community but "a community *defined* by that document in its beliefs and concerns, and not only so, but a community *restricted* in its beliefs and concerns to those evidenced in that document." Useful here are Frenschkowski, "Biographischen Kenntnisse"; Larry W. Hurtado, *Lord Jesus Christ: Devotion to Jesus in Early Christianity* (Grand Rapids: Eerdmans, 2003), 217–57; Jean-Paul Michaud, "Quelle(s) communauté(s) derrière la Source Q?" in *Sayings Source Q* (ed. Lindemann), 577–606; note also Arland J. Hultgren, *The Rise of Normative Christianity* (Minneapolis: Fortress, 1992), 37–38. There is probably something to this complaint by Richard Bauckham: "A Gospel text has to be treated as transparently revelatory of the community for which it was written because the interpretative aim of reconstructing this community would be defeated by any other kind of text" ("For Whom Were the Gospels Written?" in *The Gospels for All Christians: Rethinking the Gospel Audiences* [ed. Richard J. Bauckham; Grand Rapids: Eerdmans, 1998], 26).

415. Although I do not believe that Kloppenborg is guilty of this, others attempting to rewrite the history of Christian beginnings with Q[1] as the key may be victims of what empirical psychologists label "belief in the law of small numbers." This is the mistake of overestimating how much information we have for a conclusion. Sociobiologists have speculated that overestimating the odds was useful to early humans: we learned to run if we only suspected a tiger was nearby; making certain might have proven fatal. Historians, however, are committed to making less hasty judgments, and some of the theories spun out of Q[1] seem to me to arise from a sort of sampling error: too many inferences from too little data.

416. Tuckett has a point: "It may be difficult for some 'Q[1]-based' historical Jesuses that the resulting picture is so unpolemical, and so inoffensive, that it becomes all the harder to envisage why such a Jesus aroused such intense passion and hatred on the part of at least some sectors of

or the names of any of his companions, including Peter, Judas, and Mary Magdalene. Some of this we learn from Kloppenborg's Q^2, some from other sources. The point is that Q^1, just like any other hypothetical stage of Q, and like any other early Christian source, gives us an incomplete view of Jesus, and this may well include an incomplete view of his eschatological expectations. Unimaginatively following the principle *quod non est in actis non est in mundo* ("What is not in the documents does not exist") can lead one astray. Absence from a text need not be absence from life.

To offer an analogy: Mark may not have known the Beatitudes, the Lord's Prayer, and the sayings about anxiety that refer to ravens and lilies. Or he may have known them and decided not to use them. Whatever the truth, Mark's situation is not a statement about Jesus. Put otherwise, the absence of an item from the Gospel of Mark does not imply its absence from the ministry of Jesus. It is no different with Q or its hypothetical stages. "No single source can or should necessarily be privileged in seeking evidence for Jesus,"[417] and "it is illegitimate . . . to argue from silence that what is not in Q was not known to the editors or, still less, that what is not in Q"—much less Q^1—"cannot be ascribed to Jesus."[418] This is all the more so if one acknowledges that in the places where Mark and Q are often thought to overlap, neither source is consistently more primitive than the other.[419]

One more comment on the Sayings Source is in order. The material in Kloppenborg's Q^1 has often, in my view, been mischaracterized. Its Jesus is not untainted by faith in eschatological judgment or devoid of apocalyptic concerns.[420] The Beatitudes (Q 6:20b–23), although they have a moral component—certainly one must take God's side in alleviating the misery of the poor and ill-fed—are at the same time utopian promises of dramatic reversal:

---

the population that he was executed. . . . One needs a real element of polemic and offensiveness in Jesus' teaching to explain his death" ("Q and the Historical Jesus," 237–38).

417. Tuckett, "Q and the Historical Jesus," 215–16. In another article, Tuckett asks why anyone should give preference to Q over pre-Markan tradition ("Sources and Methods," in *The Cambridge Companion to Jesus* [ed. Markus Bockmuehl; Cambridge: Cambridge University Press, 2001], 135).

418. Kloppenborg, "Sayings Gospel Q," 330. Silence often misleads or means little. Although the doctrine of the resurrection was important for Mark (8:31; 9:31; 10:34; 12:18–27; 14:28; 16:1–8), his apocalypse, his summary overview of the latter days, omits it entirely (Mark 13). Likewise, those who drew up the Niceno-Constantinopolitan Creed much valued the sayings and deeds of Jesus in the Gospels, yet their statement of faith moves from his birth to his death without comment.

419. See Rudolf Laufen, *Die Doppelüberlieferungen der Logienquelle und des Markusevangeliums* (BBB 54; Bonn: Peter Hanstein, 1980), along with the review by Charles E. Carlston in *CBQ* 43 (1981): 473–75.

420. See further Helmut Koester, "The Sayings of Q and Their Image of Jesus," in *Sayings of Jesus: Canonical and Non-canonical: Essays in Honor of Tjitze Baarda* (ed. William L. Petersen, Johan S. Vos, and Henk J. de Jonge; NovTSup 89; Leiden: Brill, 1997), 137–54; Koester, *From Jesus to the Gospels*, 251–63; Tuckett, *Q and the History of Early Christianity*, 139–63.

God will, in accord with eschatological expectation, rid the world of poverty, hunger, and mourning.[421] Whoever first uttered Q 6:20b–23 spoke prophetically of unfortunates becoming fortunate, and that in the near future.[422] The imperative "Judge not, lest you be judged" (Q 6:37), likely means "Judge not, lest you be judged [by God at the final judgment]," especially as the following sentence, "And with the measure you measure you will be measured" (Q 6:38), appears sometimes in the targumim with eschatological sense.[423] The proclamation "The kingdom of God has come near [ἤγγικεν] to you" (Q 10:9) means that the denouement is at hand,[424] and the petition "Your kingdom come" (Q 11:2) implores God to hurry it on (cf. p. 36). The warning that God can kill "both body and soul in Gehenna" (Q 12:5) presupposes the resurrec-

421. For poverty, see *Sib. Or.* 8:208; Philo, *Rewards* 98–105; Tg. 2 Sam 22:28; for hunger, Isa 25:6; Ezek 34:27; 36:21–38; Amos 9:13; *1 En.* 10:18–19; *2 Bar.* 29:5–8; Papias *apud* Irenaeus, *Haer.* 5.33.3; *2 En.* J 66:6; for mourning, Isa 25:8; 35:10; 60:20; 65:19; Jer 31:13; *Jub.* 23:29; Rev 7:17; 21:4; *2 Bar.* 73:1–2. See further Tuckett, *Q and the History of Early Christianity*, 142–43. James 2:5 draws upon Matt 5:3 // Luke 6:20b (Q) (see Dean B. Deppe, "The Sayings of Jesus in the Epistle of James" [DTh diss., Free University of Amsterdam, 1989], 89–91) to make an eschatological point: "Has not God chosen the poor in the world to be rich in faith and to be heirs of the kingdom that he has promised to those who love him?"

422. See Gerhard Lohfink, "Die Naherwartung Jesu," in Gisbert Greshake and Gerhard Lohfink, *Naherwartung, Auferstehung, Unsterblichkeit: Untersuchungen zur christlichen Eschatologie* (QD 71: Freiburg: Herder, 1975), 43–44. William E. Arnal remarks on Q's beatitudes, "Any audience might be resistant to simple description of such an outlandish world; it is difficult to imagine how such a description could be or even appear to be, realistic" ("Why Q Failed: From Ideological Project to Group Formation," in *Redescribing Christian Origin* [ed. Cameron and Miller], 82 n. 52). But those living within the fervent hope of apocalyptic reversal, who are expecting a world miraculously made new, would find nothing at all "outlandish" in the Beatitudes. In "millennial time . . . all possibilities seem realistic" (Albert I. Baumgarten, "Four Stages in the Life of a Millennial Movement," in *War in Heaven / Heaven on Earth: Theories of the Apocalyptic* [ed. Stephen D. O'Leary and Glen S. McGhee; London: Equinox, 2005], 64). Robinson objects, "Surely this [Q 6:20b] does not mean that the poor will get into the kingdom of God at the end of time, imminent as it is, but that between now and then the poor should be happy to continue to be hungry and cold beggars. What consolation, blessedness, is there in knowing you will be fed at the eschatological banquet (Q 13:29, 28) even if meanwhile you starve to death!" ("Jesus' Theology," 30–31). This complaint neglects the consolation that the eschatological imagination can bestow upon those unable to find consolation in any other way. See Gager, *Kingdom and Community*, 49–57.

423. See Hans Peter Rüger, "'Mit welchem Maß ihr meßt, wird euch gemessen werden,'" *ZNW* 60 (1969): 174–82. Note, for example, Tg. Neof. I on Gen 38:25; Frg. Tg. on Gen 38:26; Tg. Ps.-J. on Gen 38:27.

424. The meaning of ἤγγικεν is, probably, "on the point of arrival," "at the door," as in Rom 13:12 ("the day ἤγγικεν"); Jas 5:8 ("the coming of the Lord ἤγγικεν"); 1 Pet 4:7 ("the end of all things ἤγγικεν"). The kingdom is imminent but not yet present. See J. Y. Campbell, "'The Kingdom of God Has Come,'" *ExpTim* 48 (1936): 91–94; K. W. Clark, "Realized Eschatology," *JBL* 59 (1940): 367–83; Berkey, "ΕΓΓΙΖΕΙΝ, ΦΘΑΝΕΙΝ, and Realized Eschatology." Note that Matthew, in 3:2, has the Baptist say, just like Jesus (4:17), ἤγγικεν γὰρ ἡ βασιλεία τῶν οὐρανῶν. Clearly, the evangelist did not understand ἤγγικεν to refer to arrival, otherwise the kingdom would have appeared with John, not Jesus.

tion and punishment of the wicked (cf. Dan 12:2; Acts 24:15; John 5:28–29; *Sib. Or.* 4:179–90; *T. Benj.* 10:8; *4 Ezra* 7:32). The counsel not to "store up for yourselves treasures on earth" but rather to "store up for yourselves treasures in heaven" (Q 12:33) acknowledges the overriding importance of a renewed or transcendent world that the faithful will someday inherit (cf. Q 6:23). With regard to eschatology, the Jesus of Kloppenborg's Q[1] is not so different from the Jesus of Kloppenborg's Q[2].

The Gospel of Thomas

Skeptics of an apocalyptic Jesus have tried to score points by appealing to the *Gospel of Thomas*. This collection of sayings, which may be partly independent of the canonical Gospels,[425] perhaps gained its present form between the end of the first century CE and the middle of the second century CE. So it is relatively early. It contains, moreover, not one word about the future coming of the Son of Man.[426] Nor is there any sense that the world is soon to undergo a dramatic transformation.

Several scholars have proposed that *Thomas*, or at least parts of it, reflect a very early stage of the Jesus tradition, one that apocalyptic eschatology had not yet infiltrated.[427] For them, *Thomas* calls "into question the synoptic view of Jesus as necessarily historical" and becomes one more reason to suppose that the Synoptic traditions that advance an apocalyptic eschatology are secondary.[428]

The stumbling block set before this theory is that *Thomas*, whenever it was written and whatever its compositional history might be, shows no fondness

425. My own verdict on *Thomas* is similar to my verdict on John: *Thomas* sometimes depends (directly or indirectly) upon the Synoptics, and sometimes it is independent of them. The issue is complex, and dependence or independence should be decided on a case-by-case basis. See April D. DeConick, *The Original Gospel of Thomas in Translation: With a Commentary and New English Translation of the Complete Gospel* (London: T & T Clark, 2006); J. D. Kaestli, "L'utilisation de l'Évangile selon Thomas dans la recherché actuelle sur les paroles de Jésus," in *Jésus de Nazareth: Nouvelles approches d'une énigme* (ed. D. Marguerat, E. Norelli, and J.-M. Poffet; Geneva: Labor et Fides, 1998), 373–95; Risto Uro, "*Thomas* and the Oral Gospel Tradition," in *Thomas at the Crossroads: Essays on the Gospel of Thomas* (ed. Risto Uro; Edinburgh: T & T Clark, 1998), 8–32. For an overview of recent work on *Thomas* and the historical Jesus, see Nicholas Perrin, "Recent Trends in *Gospel of Thomas* Research (1991–2006): Part I, The Historical Jesus and the Synoptic Gospels," *CBR* 5 (2007): 183–206.

426. The sole Son of Man saying occurs in *Gos. Thom.* 86: "Jesus said, 'The foxes have their holes and the birds have their nests, but the son of man has no place to lay his head.'"

427. For example, Patterson, "End of Apocalypse"; idem, *God of Jesus*, 172–74. Although I cannot here enter into the complexities of Patterson's position regarding *Thomas*, I have raised some questions elsewhere (see Allison, *Jesus of Nazareth*, 123–28).

428. So Stephen J. Patterson, "Understanding the *Gospel of Thomas* Today," in Stephen J. Patterson and James M. Robinson, *The Fifth Gospel: The Gospel of Thomas Comes of Age* (Harrisburg, PA: Trinity Press International, 1998), 75. Cf. Funk, *Honest to Jesus*, 167–68.

for sayings promoting an apocalyptic eschatology (although it still preserves some, as in 57, 111). Indeed, in its current form, *Thomas* "presupposes, and criticizes, a tradition of the eschatological sayings of Jesus."[429]

Consider three of the questions that the disciples ask Jesus in *Thomas*:[430]

- *Gos. Thom.* 18: "The disciples said to Jesus, 'Tell us: How will our end come about?'"
- *Gos. Thom.* 37: "His disciples said, 'When will you be revealed to us and when shall we see you?'"
- *Gos. Thom.* 113: "His disciples said to him, 'When will the kingdom come?'"

These queries, which reflect an editorial hand, betray considerable reflection, and perhaps anxious reflection, on eschatological topics. In each instance, Jesus responds with words that resemble sayings known from other early Christian sources, sayings with apocalyptic content. In *Thomas*, however, that content is gone. The kingdom has become a present reality:

- *Gos. Thom.* 18: "Jesus said, 'Have you discovered, then, the beginning, that you look for the end? For where the beginning is, there will the end be. Blessed is he who will take his place in the beginning; he will know the end and will not taste death.'" The last three words (ⲧⲡⲉ ⲁⲛ ⲙ̅ⲙⲟⲩ) recall Mark 9:1 par. ("Truly I tell you, there are some standing here who will not taste death until they see that the kingdom of God has come with power");[431] and "where the beginning is, there will be the end" is a revision of the traditional equation, *Urzeit = Endzeit* (e.g., *4 Ezra* 7:30–31; *T. Levi* 18:10–11; *Rev* 22:2; *Barn.* 6:13). *Thomas* does not teach that "the end" will restore "the beginning"; rather, "the beginning" is revealed in the present mystical experience of those who have already gained the immortality that others vainly wait for (51) (cf. 19: "For you there are five trees in paradise. . . . Whoever knows them will not die").
- *Gos. Thom.* 37: "Jesus said, 'When you disrobe without being ashamed and take up your garments and place them under your feet like little children and tread on them, then will you see the son of the living one, and you will not be afraid.'" In Mark 10:15 par., becoming like children is a precondition for entering the eschatological kingdom, and in 14:62, as elsewhere in the New Testament, people will see Jesus on the last day

429. So Koester, "Jesus the Victim," 7 n. 17; idem, *From Jesus to the Gospels*, 203 n. 17.

430. For what follows here I am partly indebted to April D. DeConick, *Recovering the Original Gospel of Thomas: A History of the Growth of the Gospel* (London: T & T Clark, 2005).

431. *Gos. Thom.* 1, 19, 85 also hold out the promise of not tasting death.

(cf. Matt 24:30; Rev 1:7). In *Thomas*, those who become like children see Jesus even now.

- *Gos. Thom.* 113: "Jesus said, 'It will not come by waiting for it. It will not be a matter of saying "here it is" or "there it is." Rather, the kingdom of the father is spread out upon the earth, and men do not see it.'" This resembles Luke 17:21: "Nor will they say, 'Look, here it is!' or 'There it is!' For, in fact, the kingdom of God is among you."[432] Luke 17:22–37, however, immediately goes on to prophesy a series of apocalyptic events, which it introduces with the comment "The days are coming when you will long to see one of the days of the Son of Man, and you will not see it." The related logia in Mark 13:21–23 ("And if anyone says to you at that time, 'Look! Here is the Messiah!' or 'Look! There he is!' . . .") and Matt 24:26–27 // Luke 17:23–24 (Q) ("They will say to you, 'Look there!' or 'Look here!' Do not go. . . .") are likewise apocalyptic. *Thomas*, which promotes present fulfillment, offers nothing comparable.

Why does *Thomas* bother to have the disciples ask questions that allow Jesus to dismantle an apocalyptic worldview? According to Arthur Dewey, *Thomas*, having become aware of a "trend towards apocalyptic speculation . . . strenuously speaks in counter-terms. Thomas *knows* of apocalyptic voices and redirects those voices by refining them through other sayings in the tradition or by creating new ones that attempt to uproot any attempt to move the sayings of Jesus away from the present experience of the community."[433]

This sounds as if *Thomas* is defending its nonapocalyptic tradition against the incursion of an apocalyptic ideology. The implied three-stage history seems to be this: nonapocalyptic tradition → apocalyptic influx → reaction against apocalyptic influx. But on this view, it is less than obvious why *Thomas* combats apocalyptic logia through reinterpretation, and more than curious that it preserves the apocalyptic parable in 57 without reinterpretation. Why not just ignore such sayings or deny that Jesus uttered them?

A more attractive view is that *Thomas* seeks to displace the original and dominant apocalyptic tradition by reinterpreting and spiritualizing it.[434] The strategy is well known to the student of millenarian movements.[435] Many

---

432. See above, pp. 99–101.

433. Arthur J. Dewey, "'Keep Speaking Until You Find . . .': Thomas and the School of Oral Mimesis," in *Redescribing Christian Origins* (ed. Cameron and Miller), 128.

434. This is also the conclusion of Enno Edzard Popkes, "Von der Eschatologie zur Protologie: Transformationen apokalyptiker Motive im Thomasevangelium," in Becker and Öhler, *Apokalyptik*, 211–33. Compare this comment by Richard H. Hiers: "Where a tradition appears which seems to have been intended to explain why an earlier expectation was not actualized, it is more plausible that the explanation is secondary than that the expectation was" (*The Historical Jesus and the Kingdom of God: Present and Future in the Message and Ministry of Jesus* [Gainesville: University of Florida Press, 1973], 110).

435. See further below, pp. 149–50.

heirs of an apocalyptic tradition have "ended by spiritualizing themselves into pure interiority."[436] One thinks of the Shakers, who initially believed in the imminent apocalypse but over time came to emphasize instead a realized eschatology. For them, Christ had metaphorically returned on the clouds of heaven in the person of their "Mother," Ann Lee, and the kingdom could be experienced as fully present in the Shaker community.[437] As one of them put it in a poem,

> So stand no longer waiting, ye men of Galilee,
> Into the literal heavens, your Savior there to see;
> But listen to his teaching, and cleanse your souls from sin,
> The everlasting kingdom must be set up within.[438]

In like manner, and in the interest of a "realized eschatology," *Thomas* transforms the future into the present again and again. Here are eight illustrations:

1. *Gos. Thom.* 5: "Recognize what is in your sight, and that which is hidden from you will become plain to you. For there is nothing hidden that will not become manifest." Luke's parallel to this is a prophecy of end-time revelation and reversal (12:2–3: "Nothing is covered up that will not be uncovered, and nothing secret that will not become known. Therefore whatever you have said in the dark will be heard in the light, and what you have whispered behind closed doors will be proclaimed from the housetops"), and the Greek version of *Thomas* in P.Oxy. 654.31 continues with "and buried that will not be raised" (see n. 41). Omission of the clause in the Coptic text permits a noneschatological interpretation.

2. *Gos. Thom.* 11: "Jesus said, 'This heaven will pass away, and the one above it will pass away. The dead are not alive, and the living will not die. In the days when you consumed what is dead, you made it what is alive. When you come to dwell in the light, what will you do? On the day when you were one you became two. But when you become two, what will you do?'" The opening statement resembles a sentence otherwise known from Mark 13:31 par., where, in the midst of an apocalyptic discourse, Jesus refers to the future dissolution of the cosmos: "Heaven and earth will pass away, but my words will not pass

436. R. J. Zwi Werblowsky, "Mysticism and Messianism: The Case of Hasidism," in *Man and His Salvation: Studies in Memory of S. G. F. Brandon* (ed. Eric J. Sharpe and John R. Hinnells; Manchester: Manchester University Press; Totowa, NJ: Rowman & Littlefield, 1973), 306.

437. See Kathleen Deignan, *Christ Spirit: The Eschatology of Shaker Christianity* (ATLAMS 29; Metuchen, NJ: Scarecrow Press, 1992).

438. The Shaker Charles Main, as quoted in Lawrence Foster, "Had Prophecy Failed? Contrasting Perspectives of the Millerites and Shakers," in *The Disappointed: Millerism and Millenarianism in the Nineteenth Century* (ed. Ronald L. Numbers and Jonathan M. Butler; Bloomington: Indiana University Press, 1987), 182.

away."[439] Although the sentence in *Thomas*, taken by itself, would have the same referent, the additional material turns the cosmological forecast into a statement about "personal transformation" and becoming "a 'living being' through a return to the prelapsarian Adam, the primal One."[440]

3. *Gos. Thom.* 16: "Jesus said, 'Men think, perhaps, that it is peace which I have come to cast upon the world. They do not know that it is dissension which I have come to cast upon the earth: fire, sword, and war. For there will be five in a house: three will be against two, and two against three, the father against the son, and the son against the father. And they will stand solitary.'" In Matt 10:34–36 // Luke 12:51–53 (Q), and in accord with the traditional interpretation of the scriptural subtext, Mic 7:6 (cf. *m. Soṭah* 9:15; *b. Sanh.* 97a), this unit concerns the discord of the latter days and is surrounded by eschatological materials. Matthew prefaces the unit with a saying about eschatological judgment (10:32–33). Luke does the same thing (see 12:49–50; cf. 3:16–7). In *Thomas*, which appears to be secondary vis-à-vis Matthew and Luke, we have a recommendation of celibacy.[441]

4. *Gos. Thom.* 21: "Mary said to Jesus, 'Whom are your disciples like?' He said, 'They are like children who have settled in a field which is not theirs. When the owners of the field come, they will say, "Let us have back our field." They (will) undress in their presence in order to let them have back their field and to give it back to them. Therefore I say, if the owner of a house knows that the thief is coming, he will begin his vigil before he comes and will not let him dig through into his house of his domain to carry away his goods. You, then, be on your guard against the world. Arm yourselves with great strength lest the robbers find a way to come to you, for the difficulty which you expect will (surely) materialize.'" The word about the thief is an apocalyptic warning in Matt 24:43 // Luke 12:39 (Q); 1 Thess 5:2; 2 Pet 3:10; Rev 3:3; 16:15. Against all these witnesses, *Thomas* reconfigures the saying into a call to beware of "the world" and to combat "robbers," which are worldly powers, demons, or archons.[442]

439. For this literal interpretation see Adams, *Stars Will Fall*, 161–66.
440. DeConick, *Original Gospel of Thomas*, 77.
441. See Allison, "Q 12.51–53."
442. See Risto Uro, *Thomas: Seeking the Historical Context of the Gospel of Thomas* (London: T & T Clark, 2003), 65–67. Koester ("Sayings of Q," 148–49; idem, *From Jesus to the Gospels*, 259) urges that the application in Q, which involves an unknown future time and watchfulness, is due to the reformulation of a redactor. Does this not improbably imply that 1 Thess 5:2; 2 Pet 3:10; Rev 3:3; 16:15, which likewise give the simile eschatological sense, either depend upon Q or somehow independently managed the same reinterpretation of a traditional saying? See further Christfried Böttrich, "Das Gleichnis vom Dieb in der Nacht: Parusieerwartung und Paränese," in *Eschatologie und Ethik im frühen Christentum: Festschrift für Günter Haufe zum 75. Geburtstag* (ed. Christfried Böttrich; GTF 11; Frankfurt am Main: Peter Lang, 2006), 31–57.

5. *Gos. Thom.* 22: "They said to him, 'Will we enter the kingdom as little babies?' Jesus said to them, 'When . . . you make eyes in place of an eye, and a hand in place of a hand, and a foot in place of a foot, . . . then you will enter [the kingdom].'" Jesus' response, which envisages restoration to the original divine image, seems to be a transformation of Mark 9:43–48, the hyperbolic counsel to cut off hand, sever foot, and pluck out eye (cf. Matt 5:29–30; 18:8–9). Instead of subduing bodily sins in order to avoid Gehenna and gain life—so Mark and Matthew—one even now replaces the old person with a refashioned self or new creation.

6. *Gos. Thom.* 68–69: "Jesus said, 'Blessed are you when you are hated and persecuted. A place will be found where you will not be persecuted.' Jesus said, 'Blessed are they who have been persecuted in their hearts. It is they who have truly known the Father.'" In contrast to Matt 5:10–12 // Luke 6:22–23 (Q), *Thomas* is silent about future "reward in heaven."

7. *Gos. Thom.* 75: "Jesus said, 'Many are standing at the door, but it is the solitary who will enter the bridal chamber.'" Although this seems to be about unmarried disciples spiritually uniting with Jesus (cf. *Acts Thom.* 12; *Dial. Sav.* 50), in Matt 7:13–14 // Luke 13:23–24 (Q) the image of many failing to enter through a door or gate illustrates eschatological ruin, while in Matt 25:10–12 the image of a bridegroom turning some away illustrates lack of preparation for the parousia.

8. *Gos. Thom.* 78: "Jesus said, 'Why have you come out into the desert? To see a reed shaken by the wind? And to see a man clothed in fine garments like your kings and your great ones? Upon them are the fine garments, and they are unable to discern the truth.'" This saying, in Matt 11:7–10 // Luke 7:24–27 (Q), refers to the Baptist, understood as the prophet foretold by the eschatological oracle in Mal 3:1 (cf. also Exod 23:20). In *Thomas*, the logion becomes instead a criticism of the wealthy. The secondary nature of *Thomas* is apparent.[443] (a) "Upon them are the fine garments" is redundant. (b) "And they are unable to discern [ϭⲟⲩⲛ] the truth" sounds editorial (cf. *Gos. Thom.* 3, 12, 16, 18, 31, 56, 67, 69, 91, 103, 105, 109). (c) Unlike the Synoptic parallels, *Thomas* leaves the introductory questions unanswered. (d) *Thomas* otherwise shows no interest in exalting John (see 46), so his exclusion is unsurprising. (e) In its current form, *Thomas* 78 promotes an ascetical praxis, in accord with the rest of the book. (f) *Thomas* tends, on the whole, to generalize, dehistoricize, and decontextualize.[444]

The recurrent reworking of apocalyptic traditions in *Thomas* has recently led April DeConick to posit that the document represents, in large measure, an attempt to come to terms with disillusionment over eschatological hope.

443. See Crossan, *Birth of Christianity*, 306–8.
444. See Eckhard Rau, *Jesus—Freund von Zöllnern und Sündern: Eine methodenkritische Untersuchung* (Stuttgart: Kohlhammer, 2000), 88–90.

Facing the same challenge as the author of 2 Peter ("Where is the promise of his coming?" [3:3–4]), but finding a very different resolution, the contributors to *Thomas* maintained that "their expectations had not actually been disconfirmed, but had been confirmed when the now 'correct' hermeneutic was applied to the old traditions. . . . Thus their interpretative revision shifted the apocalypse from an imminent cosmic event to an immanent personal mystical experience."[445]

DeConick in fact reconstructs an earlier (first-century) version of *Thomas* that proclaimed the impending eschaton, a version that later hands, with a new hermeneutic, emended and supplemented. Whether or not she has that and other details right—there is much to query—her basic understanding of what *Thomas* represents, namely, a spiritualizing reinterpretation of an apocalyptic tradition, is compelling. So, in her words, the view that "this Gospel exemplifies an early Christian, nonapocalyptic Gospel preserving the message of a philosophical Jesus is highly suspect. In fact, the opposite appears to be the case."[446] Put otherwise, and against Ron Cameron, *Thomas* is not "incompatible with the dominant paradigm of Christian origins."[447]

Three final points about *Thomas* are in order. First, the proposal that *Thomas* is partly the product of disenchantment with eschatological expectation gains credibility from what we find in the Fourth Gospel, which perhaps appeared not much before *Thomas*. John explicitly rejects apocalyptic interpretations of traditional logia that probably created anxiety for some (2:19–22; 21:20–23).[448] He reflects discussion over what Jesus meant by coming again μικρόν, "in a little while" (16:16–24).[449] He spiritualizes eschatology by speaking of Jesus' death and resurrection as though they were the second advent (see p. 62). And he rewrites prophecies of the second coming so that they become descriptions

445. April DeConick, "Reading the Gospel of Thomas as a Repository of Early Christian Communal Memory," in *Memory, Tradition, and Text: Uses of the Past in Early Christianity* (ed. Alan Kirk and Tom Thatcher; SBLSymS 52; Boston: Brill, 2005), 213. For a similar view, see Birger A. Pearson, *Ancient Gnosticism: Traditions and Literature* (Minneapolis: Fortress, 2007), 264.

446. DeConick, "Reading the Gospel of Thomas," 213. See further Jean-Marie Sevrin, "Thomas, Q et le Jésus de l'histoire," in *Sayings Source Q* (ed. Lindemann), 461–76.

447. Ron Cameron, "Ancient Myths and Modern Theories of the *Gospel of Thomas* and Christian Origins," in *Redescribing Christian Origins* (ed. Cameron and Miller), 107.

448. See further Alois Stimpfle, *Blinde sehen: Die Eschatologie im traditionsgeschichtlichen Prozess des Johannes-evangeliums* (BZNW 57; Berlin: de Gruyter, 1990).

449. According to John A. T. Robinson, "it looks" as if the church "was wrestling with a remembered 'word of the Lord,' whose interpretation had been subject to debate and misunderstanding" (*The Priority of John* [ed. J. F. Coakley; London: SCM Press, 1985], 341). See further Frey, *Eschatologische Verkündigung*, 41–42, 205–9. For "a little while" as an eschatological motif, see, for example, Isa 10:25 (LXX: μικρόν); 26:20 (LXX: μικρόν); 29:17 (LXX: μικρόν); Hag 2:6; 4Q385 frg. 3 6; Heb 10:37 (μικρόν); 1 Pet 1:6; 5:10; *1 Clem.* 50:4 (μικρόν); *4 Ezra* 16:52; also Dimant, "Resurrection," 539.

of what has already happened.[450] Thus πάλιν ἔρχομαι (14:3; cf. v. 28) does not mean "I will come again (at the parousia)" but "I will come again (when I am raised from the dead)";[451] μέλλεις ἐμφανίζειν σεαυτόν (14:22) does not mean "you are about to reveal yourself (to the world at the parousia)" but "you are about to reveal yourself (to us when you rise from the dead)"; μικρὸν καὶ ὄψεσθέ με (16:17; cf. 14:19) does not mean "shortly and you will see me (at the parousia)" but "shortly you will see me (when I appear to you raised from the dead)."[452] The spiritualization of eschatology in John represents the same sort of secondary hermeneutic that *Thomas* displays. Unlike Stephen Patterson, then, I do not find in John and *Thomas* cause to question "exactly how widespread apocalyptic really was" in early Christianity.[453] On the contrary, those two books betray themselves as later responses to earlier, widespread apocalyptic traditions.

Second, Crossan and Patterson have argued that maybe our best access to Jesus lies in the overlaps between Q and *Thomas*.[454] On their view, Q moves the common tradition in an apocalyptic direction ("apocalyptic eschatology"), whereas *Thomas* moves it in an ascetical direction ("ascetical eschatology"). Both sources represent trajectories away from the pristine tradition and what Crossan calls Jesus' "ethical eschatology." By "ethical eschatology" Crossan means a utopian hope that nonviolently resists structural evils.

Although Crossan is, to my mind, right in regard to much of what he has to say about Jesus and the rejection of transcendent violence,[455] my verdict is that his overall analysis goes astray in privileging at the outset a source that downplays, eliminates, and reinterprets traditional apocalyptic expectations

450. Some time ago, E. C. Hoskyns remarked, "The eschatological sayings of Jesus, which in the earlier Gospels appeared to contemplate the end of the world, are . . . in the Johannine writings, simply and apparently consciously, transformed into prophecies of the coming of the Spirit which was to follow the death and resurrection of the Son of God" ("The Other-Worldly Kingdom of God in the New Testament," *Theology* 14 [1927]: 252). That John knew Mark 13 or traditions related to it is obvious. Compare Mark 13:13 with John 15:19; Mark 13:9 with John 15:20–21; Mark 13:11 with John 15:26–27; 16:7; Mark 13:9–10 with John 15:26–27; 16:7–14; Mark 13:5, 23 with John 16:1, 4; Mark 13:9 with John 16:2; Mark 13:12 with John 16:2; Mark 13:20, 22, 27 with John 15:19; Mark 13:26 with John 16:16–17, 19; Mark 13:8 with John 16:21, 33. See discussion in Brown, *John XIII–XXI*, 693–95; Dodd, *Historical Tradition*, 407–13.

451. See full discussion in Frey, *Eschatologische Verkündigung*, 134–53. Cf. Johannes Beutler, *Habt keine Angst: Die erste johanneische Abschiedsrede (Joh 14)* (SBS 116; Stuttgart: Katholisches Bibelwerk, 1984), 25–50.

452. See further C. H. Dodd, *The Interpretation of the Fourth Gospel* (Cambridge: Cambridge University Press, 1953), 394–96; Frey, *Eschatologische Verkündigung*, 179–222.

453. Patterson, review of Allison, *Jesus of Nazareth*, 360.

454. Crossan, *Birth of Christianity*; Patterson, *The Gospel of Thomas and Jesus* (Sonoma, CA: Polebridge, 1993). On p. 231 of the latter, Patterson states that "the convergence of Thomas and Q¹" makes it difficult to imagine that Jesus "preached an imminent apocalyptic judgment."

455. See Dale C. Allison Jr., "Assessing the Arguments," in *Apocalyptic Jesus* (ed. Miller), 99–105. Crossan's definition of "apocalyptic eschatology" as involving a "violent God" means that he cannot associate "apocalyptic eschatology" with his pacifistic Jesus.

and motifs. If one compares *Thomas* with Mark, or *Thomas* with items only in Matthew, or *Thomas* with material only in Luke, one sees in each case the same pattern: the Synoptic source has apocalyptic features where *Thomas* does not. To illustrate, here are three examples, one from each source:

- Mark 8:27–30 has the disciples offer four opinions regarding Jesus' identity. Some say that he is Elijah, others John the Baptist, others a prophet, still others the Messiah. In the comparable scene in *Gos. Thom.* 13, the eschatological roles and persons fail to appear. Instead, Peter thinks Jesus may be an angel, Matthew that he may be a wise philosopher, Thomas that his identity cannot be named.
- Matthew interprets the parable of the net (13:47–48) as having to do with the eschatological assize (13:49–50). *Thomas* does not (8).[456]
- In Luke 12:35, "Let your loins be girded" (RSV) transforms an exodus motif (cf. Exod 12:11) into an injunction to watch for the parousia (cf. 1 Pet 1:13). In *Gos. Thom.* 21, 103, the same imperative evidently is an exhortation to resist internal evil.

My own take on the matter is not that Q, Mark, M, and L transformed the "ethical eschatology" of Jesus into "apocalyptic eschatology," but rather that the "apocalyptic eschatology" of Q and the Synoptics reflects the earliest stratum of the tradition. The absence of apocalyptic themes from *Thomas* is secondary, not primary.

Third, that the rejection of apocalyptic eschatology by *Thomas* does not mirror Jesus' attitude is consistent with a fact too little remarked upon: *Thomas* has nothing to say about Satan, Beelzebul, the devil, evil spirits, or exorcism. Some have identified the "robbers" of *Gos. Thom.* 21 with demons, but the text itself does not make that identification. Others have suggested that "the enemy" in *Gos. Thom.* 57 might be the devil, but this suggestion derives from Matthew's allegorical interpretation of the parable of the weeds (13:36–43), which has no counterpart in *Thomas*.

The absence of demonological subjects cannot, for reasons introduced on pp. 17–19 above, represent what stood at the beginning of the tradition. Jesus himself undoubtedly was an exorcist who sometimes spoke about demons and Satan. So here we have a clear example of *Thomas* cleansing the tradition

---

456. *Gos. Thom.* 8: "And he said, 'The man is like a wise fisherman who cast his net into the sea and drew it up from the sea full of small fish. Among them the wise fisherman found a fine large fish. He threw all the small fish back into the sea and chose the large fish without difficulty. Whoever has ears to hear, let him hear.'" While one understands a story in which a man gives away all that he has in order to obtain a very valuable pearl or a great treasure (Matt 13:44–45; *Gos. Thom.* 76, 109), why would a fisherman keep only one fish, no matter how large? The little tale seems contrived. Is this not a sign that someone (perhaps influenced by the Aesopian fable in Babrius, *Fab.* 4) rewrote a parable that originally had another point?

of a feature that it considered uncongenial, which is exactly, I submit, what has become of apocalyptic eschatology in *Thomas*. More than this, the two subjects are closely related, for Jesus probably conceptualized his perceived battle with Satan in terms of the latter days (see pp. 112–13 above). It is, accordingly, not unexpected that a book that lays aside demonology also shelves apocalyptic eschatology.

Insufficient Explanatory Scope

Marcus Borg has asked, Did Jesus' gospel for the poor mean, in effect, "'Don't worry, God's going to fix everything soon'? Or was his message to the poor about empowerment and resistance? Was his inclusive meal practice with marginalized people primarily an affirmation that the kingdom, when it comes, will include these? Or was it an affirmation of a different vision of life now?"[457] I judge these tidy antinomies, the reduction of complex issues to bipolarities, to be artificial, and I reject the apparent assumption that "Don't worry" adequately expresses anybody's take on Jesus.[458] I am, however, more interested in where Borg goes next with his argument: "Seeing imminent eschatology as primary excludes much of his [Jesus'] mission and message and risks making it as vapid as the message of many since who have announced, 'The end is at hand—repent.'"[459] Again, "it seems to many of us that the framework of imminent eschatology excludes more of the Gospel data than it accounts for. And the test of a hypothesis is its explanatory power. How much does it explain? How much of the data can it accommodate?"[460] My answer to this last question is "More than enough."

It is ironic, given his nonapocalyptic Jesus, that Borg perpetuates an error of Schweitzer, who tried to make Jesus' eschatology "consistent" or "thoroughgoing" (*Konsequent*). Modern investigation of millenarian movements shows that they are, on the contrary, never reducible to their eschatologies.[461] Religious groups, like human beings, are not simple. They are instead com-

457. Borg, *Jesus: Uncovering the Life*, 257–58.

458. See further Allison, "Assessing the Arguments," 89–90.

459. Borg, *Jesus: Uncovering the Life*, 258. My sense is that those who have sincerely believed the end near have found the idea anything but vapid. But then, "vapid," like everything else, is in the eye of the beholder.

460. Ibid. Stephen Patterson offers a related criticism: to construe Jesus as a millenarian prophet cannot "account for all that we are seeing today as we approach the Jesus tradition with new sources and fresh insights" (review of Allison, *Jesus of Nazareth*, 360). Patterson seems to have in mind primarily studies of Q, *Thomas*, and Paul's opponents in Corinth, whom some believe had a sort of realized eschatology.

461. Further study of the sociological literature on millenarian movements has accordingly led me to repent of my earlier endorsement of Schweitzer's "thoroughgoing eschatology." See further below, pp. 144–46.

pound entities, with all sorts of ingredients. Observing that not all of the tradition can be related to apocalyptic eschatology is not, then, good reason to dissociate Jesus from apocalyptic eschatology.

Whereas, in physical space, solid objects cannot overlap, "in mental space there is no . . . necessary either/or, because many different modes of ideation and discourse can be entertained simultaneously and selectively drawn according to context."[462] To label Jesus an apocalyptic or millenarian prophet is not to say that everything he said or did should or can be explained in these terms, nor does it require that he cannot be characterized in still other, and even seemingly contradictory, ways. Calling a politician a Democrat or Republican may say much, but it scarcely says everything. Similarly, although the Gospel of Matthew contains much that is not directly related to apocalyptic eschatology, the book, taken on the whole, is an apocalyptic document.[463] This circumstance, I submit, mirrors the truth about Jesus. That we cannot subsume everything that he said or did under the rubric of apocalyptic eschatology does not imply that he was no purveyor of apocalyptic eschatology.[464] Nothing in the tradition—besides the person of Jesus himself—coordinates everything, and unless one unaccountably holds that he must have been a Johnny-one-note, granting to him sayings unrelated to apocalyptic eschatology scarcely implies that he had no such eschatology. This no more gets to the point than the defendant who, confronted by a witness who saw him commit murder, responds with the assertion that he could call a hundred people who had not seen him commit the crime.

Having said this, I wonder what Borg would make of the catalog on pp. 85–86 above. Concern for the disaffected, egalitarianism, the breaking of hallowed customs, the replacing of familial bonds with fictive kin, the mediation of the sacred through new channels, the demand for intense commitment and unconditional loyalty, and focus upon a charismatic leader are, for example, characteristic not only of the Jesus tradition but also of millenarian movements.

Furthermore, when Borg gives it as his opinion that "the framework of imminent eschatology excludes more of the gospel data than it accounts for," I believe that he is writing not about "the gospel data" but about his non-apocalyptic interpretation of those data. This is because, on my own reading, imminent eschatological expectation is an integral part of most of the tradition. It animates the many sayings about judgment.[465] It explains why the exor-

462. David Martin, "Does the Advance of Science Mean Secularisation?" *SJT* 61 (2008): 58.

463. See David C. Sim, *Apocalyptic Eschatology in the Gospel of Matthew* (SNTSMS 88; Cambridge: Cambridge University Press, 1996).

464. See further Allison, "A Response," in *Apocalyptic Jesus* (ed. Miller), 101–3; also below, pp. 93–97.

465. See above, pp. 34–36; also Reiser, *Jesus and Judgment*.

cisms are interpreted as the fall of Satan and the advent of God's kingdom.[466] It coheres with Jeremias's interpretation of the parables, an interpretation which, in many respects, remains plausible.[467] It satisfactorily accounts for the recurrent links between Jesus and John the Baptist, who was remembered as a preacher of apocalyptic judgment. It supplies a credible context for some of Jesus' radical injunctions, particularly those about mission and money.[468] It accounts for the numerous eschatological sanctions that recur in the moral imperatives attributed to him.[469] It helps us to understand his purported words

466. See above, pp. 112–13.

467. See pp. 116–18. However, some legitimate criticism is offered by John W. Sider, "Rediscovering the Parables: The Logic of the Jeremias Tradition," *JBL* 102 (1983): 61–83.

468. Moral rigorism often appears in eschatological movements, Montanism being an example. See further Allison, *Jesus of Nazareth*, 188–97. One should remember that if Borg and others find it hard to connect the moral teachings of Jesus with apocalyptic eschatology, others have seen the latter as the best explanation for the former, or at least portions of the former. Garrod remarks, "Only the intense and fierce conviction of the immediate coming of the 'Kingdom of Heaven,' and the end of all things, could have given birth to the ethical system formulated, or adumbrated, by Christ" (*Religion*, 177); cf. Paula Fredriksen, *From Jesus to Christ: The Origins of the New Testament Images* (2nd ed.; New Haven: Yale University Press, 2000), 99–100. Schnackenburg could even write, "The radical moral demands made by Jesus . . . are based primarily on eschatological motives: entry into the kingdom of God, a share in the divine banquet, reign with God, etc." (*God's Rule*, 84). For the argument that the Synoptic teachings on divorce, oaths, and the Sabbath have eschatological content, see Allison, *Resurrecting Jesus*, 149–97.

469. A sampling from Q, Mark, M, and L:

Source	Behavior	Eschatological Sanction
Q		
Matt 7:1 // Luke 6:37	"Judge not"	"you will not be judged"
Matt 10:14–15 // Luke 10:10–12	"Do not welcome"	"for Sodom more bearable"
Matt 10:32–33 // Luke 12:8–9	"Whoever confesses"	"will be confessed"
Matt 6:19–21 // Luke 12:33–34	"Do not lay up"	"treasure in heaven"
Matt 18:4 // Luke 14:11	"All who exalt"	"will be humbled"
Mark		
Mark 8:36	"Gain the whole world"	"forfeit their life"
Mark 9:43–48	"Cut it off"	"thrown into hell [lit., Gehenna]"
Mark 10:17–27	"Sell what you own"	"treasure in heaven"
Mark 12:38–40	"Devour widows' houses"	"the greater condemnation"
Mark 13:13	"Endures to the end"	"will be saved"
M		
Matt 5:19	"Whoever breaks"	"least in the kingdom"
Matt 5:21–22	"If you are angry"	"liable to judgment"
Matt 6:2–4	"Do not let your left hand"	"will reward you"
Matt 10:42	"Gives even a cup"	"their reward"
Matt 25:31–46	"Did it to one of the least"	"eternal life"
L		
Luke 6:35	"Love"	"your reward will be great"
Luke 12:13–21	"Greed"	"your life is being demanded"

about the Jerusalem temple and his actions therein.[470] And it makes sense of why the Roman authorities executed him as a messianic pretender.[471] That "imminent eschatology excludes more of the gospel data than it accounts for" is simply not so. Indeed, the present chapter opens with a very long list of items that, taken together, more than suggest an apocalyptic Jesus. Borg's nonapocalyptic Jesus, to the contrary, requires, to my way of thinking, that many or most of those items be either expunged from the earliest tradition or interpreted tendentiously. In other words, it is not imminent eschatology but rather the denial of it that excludes data.

Differences between Jesus and John the Baptist

Some counter the argument from continuity, which I endorsed on pp. 48–55, by disputing significant concord between Jesus and John on the subject of their eschatological expectations. The two men differed, it is widely thought, in other respects. John was an ascetic; Jesus came eating and drinking. John warned of judgment; Jesus proclaimed salvation. John fretfully kept his eyes on the future; Jesus joyfully celebrated the kingdom's presence.[472] John baptized; Jesus did not.

When one takes full stock of such differences,[473] is it not fallacious to insist on continuity in some other area? In the words of James Robinson, "There is a warning signal in the fact that Jesus' practice did diverge widely from that of John—food and clothing, the locale of his ministry, baptism as a rite of initiation, rituals such as fasting and prayer. Since practice and message tend to be correlated, there is good reason to think that Jesus' message would diverge from that of John just as much as did his practice."[474]

Crossan, staking out a position close to Robinson's, appeals to *Gos. Thom.* 46 ("Whichever one of you comes to be a child will be acquainted with the kingdom and will become superior to John") and Matt 11:11 // Luke 7:28 (Q) ("There has not arisen among those born of woman anyone greater than John the Baptist; yet the least in the kingdom of God is

Source	Behavior	Eschatological Sanction
Luke 14:12–14	"Invite the poor"	"repaid at the resurrection"
Luke 16:19–31	"The rich man"	"tormented"
Luke 21:34–36	"Drunkenness"	"catch you unexpectedly"

470. For details see below, pp. 237–38.

471. See below, pp. 233–40.

472. For the standard disjunctions between Jesus and John, see Theissen and Merz, *Historical Jesus*, 208–11.

473. But for doubts about them, see excursus 2, on the continuity between John and Jesus; also Fernando Bermejo, "Historiografía, exégesis e ideología: La ficción contemporánea de las 'tres búsquedas' del Jesús histórico (y II)," *RCatT* 31 (2006): 86–93.

474. James M. Robinson, *The Gospel of Jesus: In Search of the Original Good News* (San Francisco: HarperSanFrancisco, 2005), 116. Cf. idem, "Jesus' Theology," 27–29.

greater than he"). He discerns behind these two sayings a word of the historical Jesus, who at some juncture must have distanced himself from the Baptist.[475] Although Jesus originally accepted and even defended "John's vision of awaiting the apocalyptic God, the Coming One," later—Crossan refrains from speculating how much later[476]—he found it to be inadequate.[477] Jesus, setting aside his previous expectations, came to propound "an anti-apocalyptic theology."[478]

Although the apostle Paul, who once contested faith in Jesus, reminds us that a committed adult can make a radical about-face, and while the story of Savonarola offers us an instance of a man forsaking belief in imminent doomsday for a more optimistic hope,[479] the argument does not persuade. It is hard to evade the weighty implications of the endorsement implicit in Jesus submitting himself to John's baptism unless there is unambiguous testimony of the former rebutting the latter's eschatological expectations. Are Matt 11:11 // Luke 7:28 (Q) and *Gos. Thom.* 46 really such testimony?

The secondary literature shows us that they are not akin to Augustine's *Retractationes*. Some exegetes take "the least in the kingdom of God" to mean "anyone in the kingdom of God (when it comes)." On this view, the least in the kingdom will be greater than the greatest (John) is now.[480] Others, surmising that John was dead when Jesus spoke the logion, equate "the least" with anyone now in the kingdom: those now alive, who experience the presence of God's reign, are the most blessed and privileged of all, even more blessed and privileged than the revered Baptist, who, like Moses, was unable to obtain the

---

475. Crossan, *Historical Jesus*, 237–38. Compare this comment: "John the Baptist, not Jesus, was the chief advocate of an impending cataclysm, a view that Jesus' first disciples had acquired from the Baptist movement" (Funk, Hoover, and the Jesus Seminar, *Five Gospels*, 4).

476. He has conjectured, however, that it may have been after the execution of the Baptist: Jesus may have been "schooled by John's fate and God's nonintervention" (John Dominic Crossan, *Who Killed Jesus? Exposing the Roots of Anti-Semitism in the Gospel Story of the Death of Jesus* [San Francisco: HarperSanFrancisco, 1996], 47). In any event, the shorter Jesus' public ministry, the less time for him to have made a major change of mind.

477. Crossan, *Historical Jesus*, 238. For similar statements, see John A. T. Robinson, "Elijah, John and Jesus: An Essay in Detection," in *Twelve New Testament Studies* (SBT 34; London: SCM Press, 1962), 28–52; Käsemann, "Beginnings of Christian Theology," 101–2; Ethelbert Stauffer, *Jesus and His Story* (trans. Richard and Clara Wilson; New York: Alfred A. Knopf, 1970), 75–76; Paul W. Hollenbach, "The Conversion of Jesus: From Jesus the Baptizer to Jesus the Healer," *ANRW* 25.1:196–219; Ebner, *Weisheitslehrer*, 421–22.

478. The phrase is from Crossan, *Birth of Christianity*, 311. One is reminded of the old thesis, propounded by Wilfred L. Knox (*St. Paul and the Church of the Gentiles* [Cambridge: Cambridge University Press, 1939]), that Paul, in his encounter with Hellenism, eventually abandoned his apocalyptic worldview—a thesis that has hardly conquered the field.

479. See Donald Weinstein, "Millenarianism in a Civic Setting: The Savonarola Movement in Florence," in *Millennial Dreams in Action: Studies in Revolutionary Religious Movements* (ed. Sylvia L. Thrupp; New York: Schocken Books, 1970), 187–203.

480. See J. C. O'Neill, *Jesus the Messiah: Six Lectures on the Ministry of Jesus* (London: Cochrane, 1980), 10–11.

promise.[481] The first interpretation demotes John not one whit. The second implies nothing about differences between him and Jesus on eschatological topics. In both instances, moreover, it is precisely John's eminence that makes him the appropriate foil for declaring the surpassing greatness of the kingdom.[482] In neither case is the content of John's eschatological proclamation disparaged or even broached.[483]

Even if one were, on the contrary and against most exegetical tradition, to find real disparagement of John in the line about "the least," it would perhaps be sensible to conjecture, as have a few, that someone other than Jesus tacked it on, someone with a desire to mute acclaim for the Baptist, someone like the author of the Fourth Gospel, who, whether or not he was in competition with a Baptist sect, wanted to ensure that people did not think too highly of Jesus' forerunner.[484]

Another difficulty for Crossan is that while criticism of John may or may not lie embedded in Matt 11:11 // Luke 7:28 (Q) and *Gos. Thom.* 46, esteem of him incontrovertibly appears in Matt 11:9 // Luke 7:26 (Q) (John was more than a prophet); in Matt 11:10 // Luke 7:27 (Q) (John fulfilled the prophetic oracle in Mal 3:1; cf. Exod 23:20); in Matt 11:11a // Luke 7:28a (Q) (no one born of women is greater than John—an affirmation that "could scarcely be outdone");[485] and in Matt 11:16–19 // Luke 7:31–35 (Q) ("this generation" foolishly rejected John). What are the odds that followers of Jesus, without significant prodding from him, produced all this high praise? Nothing we know about the early churches leads us to expect such a thing. So Jesus, whatever his differences from John may have been, almost certainly lauded him. Crossan might reply that if these materials faithfully represent Jesus, they come from the time when he still adhered to John's vision. This, however, seems implausible because Matt 11:7–11 // Luke 7:24–28 (Q) sounds like a retrospec-

481. See Schlosser, *Règne de Dieu*, 1:161–67. There is also the possibility that "the least" just might be, as Origen, Hilary, Jerome, and Chrysostom thought, a circumlocution for the speaker, Jesus (so Oscar Cullmann, *The Early Church: Studies in Early Christian History and Theology* [ed. A. J. B. Higgins; Philadelphia: Westminster, 1956], 180).

482. See Joan E. Taylor, *The Immerser: John the Baptist within Second Temple Judaism* (Grand Rapids: Eerdmans, 1997), 302–4.

483. See further Jens Schröter, "Die Frage nach dem historischen Jesus und der Charakter historischer Erkenntnis," in *Sayings Source Q* (ed. Lindemann), 242–44.

484. See John 1:7–8, 20, 30; 3:28, 30; 5:36; 10:41. See also Martin Dibelius, *Die urchristliche Überlieferung von Johannes dem Täufer* (FRLANT 15; Göttingen: Vandenhoeck & Ruprecht, 1911), 12–15. Compare the form of our saying in *Ps.-Clem. Rec.* 1:60 (GCS 42:42): it lacks the qualifying second half. On the other side, contrasting the "least" with the "greatest" is a natural rhetorical move (cf. *'Abot R. Nat.* B 28; *b. B. Bat.* 134a; *b. Sukkah* 28a), and Matt 11:11 // Luke 7:28 (Q) recalls other Synoptic sayings that juxtapose extremes or opposites (e.g., Mark 4:31–32; 9:35; 10:31).

485. David R. Catchpole, *Jesus People: The Historical Jesus and the Beginnings of Community* (London: Darton, Longman & Todd; Grand Rapids: Baker Academic, 2006), 33. Unless we have here hyperbole, John must be greater than Abraham, Moses, and David.

tive on John's ministry, and Matt 11:16–19 // Luke 7:31–35 (Q) sounds like a retrospective on Jesus' ministry.

There is yet one more obstacle to thinking that Jesus and John went in such different directions. How do we account for the old and well-attested tradition that sets the two men in parallel? We have already examined this topic above on pp. 82–85, and, as stated there, the parallelism is unexpected, given the Christian tendency to exalt Jesus over the Baptist and "to prevent people from thinking that Jesus owed the substance of his teaching to John."[486] The tradition presumably originated because the former so much reminded people of the latter, whose message featured repentance in the face of eschatological judgment.[487] In accord with this, Matt 11:16–19 // Luke 7:31–35 (Q), where ἦλθον is used of both John and Jesus and where "this generation" rejects both, suggests that somebody early on took Jesus and John to be allies, their similarities more significant than their differences.[488] Indeed, the comparison might go back to Jesus himself.[489]

Before turning to the next subject, it is perhaps worth remarking that if Jesus was, as Crossan and others have surmised, a onetime proponent of apocalyptic eschatology who later changed his mind, then what justifies attributing every apocalyptic item to the early churches? Why not assign some or many of those items to Jesus in his Baptist stage?[490] Why presuppose instead that the tradition represents exclusively or almost exclusively the last phase of Jesus' ministry, especially if, as Crossan and others suppose, some of Jesus' disciples reverted back to the Baptist's theology? Might they not then have recalled logia from Jesus' early phase? I am unaware of Crossan or like-minded others addressing this issue, which leaves me nonplussed. What prevents them from evaluating the Jesus tradition the way that M.-É. Boismard has evaluated John's Gospel: the apocalyptic passages (e.g., 5:28–29; 6:30–40, 54; 12:48) represent an earlier stage of the evangelist's thought as opposed to his more mature, later thinking, which focused on realized eschatology?[491]

486. Maurice Goguel, *The Life of Jesus* (trans. Olive Wyon; New York: Macmillan, 1933), 271.

487. See further Kosch, "Q und Jesus," 40–44.

488. Risto Uro comments, "The contrast between Jesus and John in Q 7:33–34 has not to do with the preaching of these two prophets, but rather with their lifestyle (similarly Mk 2:18–19). There is no need to doubt that John was more hostile to forms of urban civilization than was Jesus (cf. Mk 1:4–6; Q 7:24–25). But this does not say anything specifically about the content of their preaching" ("John the Baptist and the Jesus Movement: What Does Q Tell Us?" in *The Gospel behind the Gospels: Current Studies in Q* [NovTSup 75; ed. Ronald A. Piper; Leiden: Brill, 1995], 233).

489. Meier (*Marginal Jew*, 2:144–56) thinks so.

490. Crossan seems to do this in one instance. He believes that Matt 11:7–9 // Luke 7:24–27 (Q) preserves Jesus' onetime opinion of John, so this complex seemingly had its origin in an earlier phase of the ministry. See John Dominic Crossan, *God and Empire: Jesus against Rome, Then and Now* (San Francisco: HarperSanFrancisco, 2007), 114–15.

491. M.-É. Boismard, "L'évolution du thème eschatologique dans les traditions johanniques," *RevB* 68 (1961): 507–24. Theissen and Merz ("Delay of the Parousia") have made an interest-

One might also contend for the opposite hypothesis: Jesus, because of disappointment in Galilee, reverted to John's proclamation of the wrath to come. This view and variations upon it have sometimes found advocates,[492] and it does not stretch credulity to suppose that, disappointed by the response to his ministry, Jesus began to brood about judgment.[493] One could then assign nonapocalyptic sayings to the earlier ministry and apocalyptic sayings to the later ministry. One wonders how, in the wake of the form-critical consensus that we cannot determine the chronological order in which Jesus delivered any sayings that we might attribute to him, those who defend a nonapocalyptic Jesus could argue forcibly against this take on things.

The Development of Early Christian Eschatology

Marcus Borg has suggested that events in the 40s and 60s brought an influx of eschatological and even apocalyptic ideas into the churches.[494] This hypothesis has been around in one form or another for a very long time. B. H. Streeter, Ernst von Dobschütz, C. H. Dodd, John A. T. Robinson, and C. L. Mearns contended that the churches borrowed more and more from Jewish apocalyptic as time went on.[495]

There is an initial plausibility in the suggestion that first the Caligula crisis and then the political unrest in the 60s led to increased speculation about

ing case that Jesus himself had to come to terms with the unexpected delay of the Baptist's imminent end-time judgment.

492. See Charles, *Doctrine of a Future Life*, 320–21; E. Rau, "Q-Forschung und Jesusforschung: Versuch eines Brückenschlags," *ETL* 82 (2006): 391–92; Weiss, *Predigt Jesu*, 100–102; Paul Wernle, *The Rise of the Religion* (vol. 1 of *The Beginnings of Christianity*, trans. G. A. Bienemann; ed. W. D. Morrison; London: Williams & Norgate; New York: Putnam, 1903), 60–68. Cf. this comment by F. A. M. Spencer: "While eschatology may not have been entirely absent from the earlier teaching of Jesus, it became far more pronounced and elaborate towards the close" (*The Theory of Christ's Ethics* [London: Allen & Unwin, 1929], 44); and note also the thesis of Joel Marcus that apocalyptic eschatology became more important to Jesus after his baptism ("The Beelzebul Controversy and the Eschatologies of Jesus," in *Authenticating the Activities of Jesus* [ed. Bruce Chilton and Craig A. Evans; NTTS 28/2; Leiden: Brill, 1999], 247–77).

493. Cf. Matt 11:20–24 // Luke 10:13–15 (Q). The old theory of a Galilean crisis during Jesus' ministry has become reincarnated in some recent Q research, which assigns Q's judgment sayings to a secondary stage and takes them to reflect the disappointment and disillusionment of a community whose mission has met with rejection and hostility.

494. Borg, "Jesus Was Not an Apocalyptic Prophet," 39–40.

495. B. H. Streeter, "Professor Burkitt and the Parables of the Kingdom," *The Interpreter* 7 (1910–1911): 241–47; idem, "Synoptic Criticism and the Eschatological Problem," in *Oxford Studies in the Synoptic Problem* (ed. W. Sanday; Oxford: Clarendon, 1911), 425–36; Ernst von Dobschütz, *The Eschatology of the Gospels* (London: Hodder & Stoughton, 1910); C. H. Dodd, *The Apostolic Preaching and Its Developments* (Chicago: Willett, Clark, 1937), 53–64; Robinson, *Jesus and His Coming*; C. L. Mearns, "Early Eschatological Development in Paul: The Evidence of I and II Thessalonians," *NTS* 27 (1981): 137–57.

eschatological subjects. The composition or redaction of Mark 13 has often been associated with one episode or the other,[496] and the commentaries routinely link Caligula's attempt to set up a statue of himself as Jupiter in the Jerusalem temple with the eschatological materials in 2 Thess 2. This makes it easy to imagine that, as time moved on, there was a "momentous influx of apocalyptic ideas,"[497] and that Jesus was, in the words of my teacher W. D. Davies, "increasingly draped in an apocalyptic mantle and specifically Jewish expectations developed in the Church in a form highly enhanced from that which they had assumed in Jesus' own teaching."[498] Does not critical study of the canonical Gospels offer the proof? Whatever one makes of the thesis that Q^2 added apocalyptic materials to Q^1, there is, on the postulate of Markan priority, no doubt that Matthew at least enlarged the number of sayings in which Jesus refers to the final judgment.[499] According to John A. T. Robinson, "the Synoptists witness to a progressive apocalypticization of the message of Jesus . . . as the Gospel of Matthew most forcibly illustrates."[500]

All this, however, makes for a one-sided story. Early Christianity also moved in the opposite direction. Paul's *Naherwartung* is most intense in 1 Thessalonians, his earliest extant letter, less intense in the later Paulines and in the epistles that his circle produced (e.g., Ephesians and Titus). Again, Luke 9:27 drops "with power" from Mark 9:1 ("There are some standing here who will not taste death until they see that the kingdom of God has come with power") and thereby makes it easier to find fulfillment in something this side of the parousia, while Luke 22:69 turns the prophecy of the parousia in Mark 14:62 ("'You will see the Son of Man seated at the right hand of the Power,' and 'coming with the clouds of heaven'") into a statement about Jesus' enthronement ("From now on the Son of Man will be seated at the right hand of the power of God"). And John's Gospel, probably composed after the Synoptics, contains fewer apocalyptic materials than they and uses βασιλεία τοῦ θεοῦ/τῶν οὐρανῶν a scant two times.[501] For reasons such as these, a few have inverted

496. For an attempt to associate the origin of Mark 13 with the Caligula crisis, see Gerd Theissen, *The Gospels in Context: Social and Political History in the Synoptic Tradition* (trans. Linda M. Maloney; Minneapolis: Fortress, 1991), 125–65; N. H. Taylor, "Palestinian Christianity and the Caligula Crisis, Part II: The Markan Eschatological Discourse," *JSNT* 62 (1996): 13–41. On the possible connections with the Jewish War, see Joel Marcus, "The Jewish War and the *Sitz im Leben* of Mark," *JBL* 113 (1992): 441–62.

497. Philipp Vielhauer and Georg Strecker, "Apocalyptic in Early Christianity," in *New Testament Apocrypha* (ed. Edgar Hennecke, Wilhelm Schneemelcher, and R. McL. Wilson; rev. ed.; 2 vols.; Cambridge: James Clarke; Louisville: Westminster John Knox, 1992), 2:571.

498. Davies, *Gospel and the Land*, 365.

499. For details, see Allison, *Resurrecting Jesus*, 63–68.

500. John A. T. Robinson, "The New Look on the Fourth Gospel," in *Twelve New Testament Studies*, 103.

501. John 3:3, 5; contrast the statistics for the Synoptics: Matthew: 37×; Mark: 14×; Luke: 32×.

the conclusion of Streeter, von Dobschütz, and the rest: apocalyptic passion declined over the decades.[502] According to Paula Fredriksen, for instance, "the later the writing, the lower its level of commitment to an imminent Apocalypse; the earlier the writing (i.e., Mark and, before him, Paul) the higher."[503] Bultmann even proposed that Jesus "was probably far more an eschatological prophet than is apparent from the tradition."[504]

Whether there is any justice in this last supposition,[505] a cooling of apocalyptic flames is exactly what we see in *Thomas* as well as in many other texts of the second and third centuries: this-worldly eschatology became Platonic otherworldliness. This is a common pattern in many millenarian movements. When the end does not come, initial eschatological enthusiasm predictably becomes reinterpreted, redirected, spiritualized, internalized.

The truth is that, concerning early Christianity, plotting a one-way eschatological development traverses the facts. A graph would not display a single vector pointing in a single direction. While eschatological enthusiasm was waning in one place, it was waxing in another; there was no unilinear rise or decline. This means that, while Borg's argument is not altogether devoid of substance, because the tradition did gather to itself new apocalyptic elements, he cannot reach his conclusion, because traditional apocalyptic elements were both jettisoned and reinterpreted along the way.[506] Perhaps the two processes effectively canceled each other out, so that what we see now is not far from what was there at the beginning. In any event, on the supposition that the tradition was not an open invitation to the imposition of utterly foreign elements, that accretions tended to stick because of the attraction of like to like,[507] it is perilous to hold that a tradition untainted by apocalyptic expectations was, in so little time, transmuted into a tradition infested by them.

502. So, for example, Willoughby C. Allen, "Mr. Streeter and the Eschatology of the Gospels," *The Interpreter* 7 (1910–1911): 359–64; Paul J. Achtemeier, "An Apocalyptic Shift in Early Christian Tradition: Reflections on Some Canonical Evidence," *CBQ* 45 (1983): 231–48; Fredriksen, *Jesus of Nazareth*, 87–88, 97; Osvaldo D. Vena, *The Parousia and Its Rereadings: The Development of the Eschatological Consciousness in the Writings of the New Testament* (SBL 27; New York: Peter Lang, 2001). Schulz (*Q: Die Spruchquelle*) argued that the second layer of Q dampened apocalyptic eschatology.

503. Fredriksen, *Jesus of Nazareth*, 89.

504. Bultmann, *Jesus and the Word*, 124.

505. Richard Landes observes how apocalyptic movements, when they return to normal time, evolve and retrospectively downplay their enthusiastic beginnings ("On Owls, Roosters, and Apocalyptic Time: A Historical Method for Reading a Refractory Documentation," *USQR* 49 [1995]: 49–69). His observations harmonize with Bultmann's suspicion.

506. According to Funk, Hoover, and the Jesus Seminar, some logia attributed to Jesus do not represent the view that "God was about to bring the age to a close," and it is these, which "contradict the tendencies of the unfolding tradition," that come from Jesus (*Five Gospels*, 40). Because the tradition tended toward realized or spiritualizing eschatology as well as apocalyptic eschatology, the argument is defective.

507. See further below, pp. 159–64.

Prophetic Failure and Ecclesiastical Prosperity

In discussing my earlier work, Crossan wrote the following:

> As the decades of the first hundred years passed without millenarian consum-mation, tiny ripples of surprise appear on the surface of the tradition, but I see no evidence of profound doubt or massive loss of faith. I do not find what I might have expected [on the assumption of an apocalyptic Jesus]: profound defensive strategies, desperate explanatory interpretations, but, despite them, slow and steady attrition in faith. I would have expected, in other words, a steadily decreasing number of converts and communities and I find instead a steadily increasing number of both converts and communities.[508]

In brief, how can we square the success of the churches with the failure of Jesus? If their Lord was an apocalyptic prophet, and if the ever-receding end belied his eschatological hopes, why did Christianity nonetheless flourish?

I do not understand why these questions are more challenging for my posi-tion than for Crossan's. Although denying that Jesus proclaimed a proximate end, Crossan admits that many traditions made him out to have done so, and that from a very early time; and since early Christians, unlike modern schol-ars, did not sort the tradition into two piles, one authentic, one apocryphal, Jesus was for them the author of all the predictions that had found no obvious fulfillment. The issue of how Christians responded to unrealized expectations remains, whatever view modern scholars take of Jesus.

Beyond this, millenarian movements sometimes not only survive but also thrive in the face of disconfirmed expectations. Jehovah's Witnesses, who have suffered prophetic failure after prophetic failure, now number over ten million.[509] Apocalyptic texts can pull off the same trick, as in the case of Daniel, which won a wide readership despite its obvious miscalculations.[510] The explanation is that eschatological expectation is never naked: other aspects of a group's ideology as well as cult and ritual, leadership and organization, and social solidarity and charitable service count toward survival and the prizing of texts. As J. Gordon Melton has written,

---

508. John Dominic Crossan, "Con: Jesus Was Not an Apocalyptic Prophet," in *Apocalyptic Jesus* (ed. Miller), 54.

509. See M. James Penton, *Apocalypse Delayed: The Story of Jehovah's Witnesses* (2nd ed.; Toronto: University of Toronto Press, 1997); Joseph F. Zygmunt, "Prophetic Failure and Chiliastic Identity: The Case of Jehovah's Witnesses," *American Journal of Sociology* 75 (1970): 926–48.

510. See Dan 12:5–12. For other failed forecasts in the canonical prophets, see the illuminat-ing work of Robert P. Carroll, *When Prophecy Failed: Cognitive Dissonance in the Prophetic Traditions of the Old Testament* (New York: Seabury, 1979). On the same phenomenon in early Islam, see Suliman Bashear, "Muslim Apocalypses and the Hour: A Case-Study in Traditional Reinterpretation," *Israel Oriental Studies* 13 (1993): 75–99.

Though one or more prophecies may be important to a group, they will be set within a complex set of beliefs and interpersonal relationships. They may serve as one of several important sources determining group activity, but the prediction is only one support device for the group. . . . If a prediction comes within a context of broad belief and group interaction, then its nonfulfillment provides a test for the system and for the personal ties previously built within the group. Times of testing tend to strengthen, not destroy, religious groups.[511]

Even when eschatological teachings are important, they do not exist in a vacuum; other things matter as well, and often more.

Millenarian movements can find the resources to transform themselves into enduring institutions, especially as what typically counts for adherents is not what others may believe to be true but what the faithful experience as real. Sociologists, moreover, tell us that, to judge by interviews with those who join new religious movements, social networks usually matter far more than doctrine.[512] So it is unsurprising that "if specific prophecies are anchored in a broader and more complex set of beliefs that frame a fairly comprehensive worldview, sense of mission, and collective identity, it is unlikely that specific disconfirmations will have a serious impact on the integrity of the group."[513] This circumstance, to which the Dead Sea Scrolls already bear witness—the community behind them survived despite eschatological disillusionment[514]— is especially true when people have made sacrifices for their faith;[515] and it is clear enough that many of Jesus' pre-Easter disciples gave up much to follow him, as did many early Christians. In other words, "it is not unfulfilled prophecy per se that irrevocably disillusions believers"; rather, "the social conditions in which such disconfirmations are received . . . determine their

511. J. Gordon Melton, "Spiritualization and Reaffirmation: What Really Happens When Prophecy Fails," *American Studies* 26 (1985): 147. See further the still helpful article of David Flusser, "Salvation Present and Future," in *Types of Redemption: Contributions to the Theme of the Study-Conference Held at Jerusalem 14th to 19th July 1968* (ed. R. J. Zwi Werblowsky and C. Jouco Bleeker; SHR 18; Leiden: Brill, 1970), 46–61; also Miguel C. Leatham, "Rethinking Religious Decision-Making in Peasant Millenarianism: The Case of Nueva Jerusalem," *JCR* 12 (1997): 295–309. Leatham documents a case where conversion to a millenarian group was motivated less by eschatological expectations than by "the remedial or reformative social organizational environment—the total institution" that those expectations structured (p. 307).

512. See Rodney Stark and Roger Finke, *Acts of Faith: Explaining the Human Side of Religion* (Berkeley: University of California Press, 2000), 114–38; Rodney Stark and Laurence R. Iannaccone, "Why the Jehovah's Witnesses Grow So Rapidly: A Theoretical Application," *JCR* 12 (1997): 133–57.

513. Lorne L. Dawson, "When Prophecy Fails and Faith Persists: A Theoretical Overview," *Nova Religio* 3 (1999): 72. Helpful here is David A. Snow and Richard Machalek, "On the Presumed Fragility of Unconventional Beliefs," *JSSR* 21 (1982): 15–26.

514. See A. Steudel, "The Development of Essenic Eschatology," in *Apocalyptic Time* (ed. Baumgarten), 79–86.

515. See Laurence R. Iannaccone, "Sacrifice and Stigma: Reducing Free-Riding in Cults, Communes, and Other Collectives," *Journal of Political Economy* 100 (1992): 271–91.

ultimate impact on faith."[516] Religious faith and commitment have manifold sources and objects, and cognitive dissonance often meets its match in "non-cognitive consonance."[517]

In addition to all this, disappointment is always less disturbing for groups that have not set a particular day, month, or year for the end; and Jesus, from what we can tell, was not remembered as having done such.[518] So for the early Christians, as opposed to, let us say, the Millerites, whose eschatological dates arrived without incident, the failure of expectation was never stark.[519] There was (at least after Easter) no one day on which one was forced to confess, "He was wrong; it's over, time to go home." Furthermore, given that Jesus' passion and resurrection were correlated with biblical prophecies as well as with pre-Easter expectations of tribulation and resurrection, eschatological expectations seemed partly confirmed.[520] It was much easier to live with "The end has begun" than with "Nothing has happened."[521]

Crossan sees in our sources "no evidence of profound doubt or massive loss of faith" in response to the delay of the parousia. But why should we expect to run across such evidence even if Jesus was an apocalyptic prophet and even if some or many Christians became disenchanted? The extant texts do not contain objective descriptions of what happened. They are apologetical, pro-Christian witnesses. They seek to instill faith, not to display people's doubts. We know that all sorts of individuals must have become Christians and then left the fold, because this always happens with new religious move-

516. Anson D. Shupe Jr., *Six Perspectives on New Religions: A Case Study Approach* (New York: Edwin Mellen, 1981), 141.

517. I owe this phrase to Susan J. Palmer and Natalie Finn, "Coping with Apocalypse in Canada: Experiences of Endtime in la Mission de l'Esprit Saint and the Institute of Applied Metaphysics," *Sociological Analysis* 53 (1992): 397–415.

518. Although, if Mark 14:25 reflects something that Jesus said during Passover week, we might wonder whether he hoped that the end would come in the next few days (cf. Luke 19:11). For the tradition that the Messiah would come during Passover, see *Mek.* on Exod 12:42 ("In that night were they redeemed [from Egypt] and in that night will they be redeemed in the future—these are the words of R. Joshua"); "The Four Nights," preserved in Frg. Tg. P on Exod 15:18 and in Tg. Neof. I, Tg. Ps.-J., and Frg. Tg. V on Exod 12:42; *Exod. Rab.* 18:12; Jerome, *Comm. Matt.* on 25:6 ("It is a tradition of the Jews that the Messiah will come at midnight according to the manner of the time in Egypt when the Passover was celebrated. Whence I think also the apostolic tradition has persisted that on the day of the paschal vigils it is not permitted to dismiss before midnight the people who are expecting the advent of Christ"). Does Luke 12:35–38 presuppose this exegetical tradition? See p. 228 n. 30.

519. Although some Millerites did not give up the cause after the disillusionment in 1843 and 1844, most did; see the collection of essays in Numbers and Butler, *The Disappointed*. On the difficulties caused for Jehovah's Witnesses by a failed 1975 prophecy, see Stark and Iannaccone, "Jehovah's Witnesses."

520. See Allison, *End of the Ages*, 142–62, on the origins of "realized eschatology."

521. See further Erich Grässer, *Die Naherwartung Jesu* (SBS 61; Stuttgart: Katholisches Bibelwerk, 1973), 28–34, explaining why the delay of the parousia was not a "crisis" for the early churches.

ments.[522] Early Christian literature hardly documents the comings and goings of such people or shares with us their disillusionment (although note John 6:66). If some followers of Jesus gave up the cause because he tarried, we have no reason to think that we would know their stories. (I have sometimes wondered about the canonical lists of the Twelve. We have nothing but names for half of this group. For all we know, some of them did, despite later legends, give up and return to their old lives, for whatever reason. One might indeed in this way account for the genesis of the motif of doubt in stories of Jesus appearing to the Twelve [Matt 28:17; Mark 16:14; Luke 24:36–37].)

Nevertheless, Crossan does acknowledge that "tiny ripples of surprise appear on the surface of the tradition." Although he does not specify, I assume that he has in mind texts such as these:

- Matt 24:45–51 // Luke 12:42–46 (Q); Matt 25:1–13: Jesus uttered parables in which the returning master or the coming bridegroom is delayed (χρονίζω), so he must have known what was coming, known that the end was not really at hand.

- Luke 19:11: As Jesus approached Jerusalem, he, unlike his disciples, did not suppose "that the kingdom of God was to appear immediately" (see pp. 65–67).

- John 2:19–22: Although people heard Jesus say that he would destroy the temple in Jerusalem and raise up another, his followers, after his resurrection, came to understand that he had rather been cryptically referring to his own body.

- John 16:16–24: Jesus says, "A little while, and you will no longer see me, and again a little while, and you will see me." The response of the disciples is odd. They ask, "What does he mean by this 'a little while'?" (v. 18). C. H. Dodd rightly perceived the historical situation behind these verses: "There is sufficient evidence that, in some quarters at least, the interval between Christ's crucifixion and resurrection on the one hand and His second advent on the other was expected to be very short; and it was believed that He said it would be. But by the time this gospel was written the short interval—τὸ μικρόν—was expanding unexpectedly. What had Christ really meant?"[523]

- John 21:20–23: Jesus did not, contrary to rumor, avow that he would return before the last of his disciples passed away (see pp. 66–67).

---

522. There is a growing literature on this subject, although it is necessarily based on the study of modern groups; see the overview of E. Burke Rochford Jr., "The Sociology of New Religious Movements," in *American Sociology of Religion: Histories* (ed. Anthony J. Blasi; RSO 13; Leiden: Brill, 2007), 267–69.

523. Dodd, *Interpretation of the Fourth Gospel*, 396.

- 1 Thess 4–5: Paul's converts are troubled and confused because the end has not yet come and some of their fellow believers have died in the meantime.
- Rev 6:10: The souls of the martyrs cry "with a loud voice, 'Sovereign Lord, holy and true, how long will it be before you judge and avenge our blood on the inhabitants of the earth?'"
- *1 Clem.* 23:3–5: The double-minded doubt and say, "We heard these things even in the days of our fathers, and look, we have grown old, and none of these things have happened to us" (cf. *2 Clem.* 11:1–7).
- 2 Pet 3:1–10: Scoffers may dismiss the promise of Jesus' coming, but with the Lord, a thousand years are as one day.

What do these texts, from various times and places, suggest? As apocalyptic enthusiasm gives way to normal time, believers, in their retrospective accounts, consciously and unconsciously clean up the tradition, so that the uncongenial gets forgotten and goes unrecorded.[524] It is not human nature to parade what embarrasses us. We typically cope with cognitive dissonance not by trumpeting facts that trouble us but rather by setting them aside, or by reconfiguring them so that they suit us.[525] So whereas Crossan counts it as a strike against me that there are only occasional ripples of surprise or discomfort at Jesus failing to return, I think rather that we have enough evidence to posit, below the surface, deeper, larger, stronger currents.

I am confirmed in this judgment because early Christians responded to prophetic delay in ways typical of other deliverance cults:[526]

524. See further Landes, "Owls, Roosters, and Apocalyptic Time."

525. Eric Anderson reviews a fascinating instance of this ("The Millerite Use of Prophecy: A Case Study of a 'Striking Fulfilment,'" in *The Disappointed* [ed. Numbers and Butler], 78–91). He documents how Ellen G. White and others turned a seemingly unfulfilled prophecy of Adventism into stunning evidence for the truth of their movement's understanding of biblical prophecy.

526. There is now a large literature on this subject, with which most New Testament scholars appear to be unfamiliar. An exception is David E. Aune, "Christian Beginnings and Cognitive Dissonance Theory," in *In Other Words: Essays on Social Science Methods and the New Testament in Honor of Jerome H. Neyrey* (ed. Anselm C. Hagedorn, Zeba A. Crook, and Eric Stewart; SWBA 2/1; Sheffield: Sheffield Phoenix Press, 2007), 11–47. Pertinent studies include Chris Bader, "When Prophecy Passes Unnoticed: New Perspectives on Failed Prophecy," *JSSR* 38 (1999): 119–31; Robert W. Balch et al., "Fifteen Years of Failed Prophecy: Coping with Cognitive Dissonance in a Baha'i Sect," in *Millennium, Messiahs, and Mayhem: Contemporary Apocalyptic Movements* (ed. Thomas Robbins and Susan J. Palmer; New York: Routledge, 1997), 73–90; Robert W. Balch, Gwen Farnsworth, and Sue Wilkins, "When the Bombs Drop: Reactions to Disconfirmed Prophecy in a Millennial Sect," *Sociological Perspectives* 26 (1983): 137–58; Dawson, "When Prophecy Fails"; Jane Hardyck and Marcia Braden, "Prophecy Fails Again: A Report of a Failure to Replicate," *Journal of Abnormal Social Psychology* 65 (1962): 136–41; Dein, "When Prophecy Fails"; Ginger Hanks-Harwood, "'Like the Leaves of Autumn:' The Utilization of the Press to Maintain Millennial Expectations in the Wake of Prophetic Failure," *Journal of Millennial Studies* 1, no. 1 (2001), online: www.mille.org/publications/

1. One can cope with the nonoccurrence of predicted events by issuing renewed calls to vigilant watchfulness.[527] The Qumran sectarians, as we know from their commentary on Habakkuk, did this. In 1QpHab 7:5–8, following a quotation of Hab 2:3a ("For there is still a vision for the appointed time; it speaks of the end, and does not lie"), we read "Interpreted, this means that the final age will be prolonged, and will exceed all that the prophets have said, for the mysteries of God are astounding." The subsequent passage, 1QpHab 7:9–14, includes a quote from Hab 2:3b: "If it seems to tarry, wait for it; it will surely come, it will not delay." The interpretation of these words is that "the men of truth" continue to "keep the law" and do not slacken in their endeavors "when the final age is prolonged." In other words, when faced with the delay of the end, the sectarians, with unabated commitment, persist in suspenseful waiting, conscientiously executing their religious duties. One may compare the calls to continued watchfulness that occur in any number of New Testament texts (e.g., Matt 24:42–44 // Luke 12:39–40 [Q]; Mark 13:9, 23, 33–37; Matt 25:13; 1 Thess 5:1–7; Rev 16:15).[528]

2. "Within religious groups, prophecy seldom fails," in part because believers often claim that prophecies have been, whatever the facts might seem to outsiders, partially accomplished.[529] Although the Islamic prophet Muhammad Ahmad died without the anticipated dispensation arriving, his followers, who thought him the Mahdi, could still claim that "he filled the earth with equity and justice after it had been filled with tyranny and oppression by the

---

winter2001/Harwood.html (cited 18 November 2009). Richard Landes, "Rodolfus Glaber and the Dawn of the New Millennium: Eschatology, Historiography, and the Year 1000," *Revue Mabillon* 7 (1996): 57–77; Melton, "Spiritualization and Reaffirmation"; Stephen D. O'Leary, "When Prophecy Fails and When It Succeeds: Apocalyptic Prediction and the Re-entry into Ordinary Time," in *Apocalyptic Time* (ed. Baumgarten), 341–62; Palmer and Finn, "Apocalypse in Canada"; Richard Singelenberg, "The '1975' Prophecy and Its Impact among Dutch Jehovah's Witnesses," *Sociological Analysis* 50 (1989): 23–40; Diana Tumminia, "How Prophecy Never Fails," *SocRel* 59 (1998): 157–70; Neil Weiser, "The Effects of Prophetic Disconfirmation of the Committed," *RRelRes* 16 (1974): 19–30; Zygmunt, "Prophetic Failure"; idem, "When Prophecies Fail: A Theoretical Perspective on the Comparative Evidence," *American Behavioral Scientist* 16 (1972): 245–68. The articles by Melton, Singelenberg, and Zygmunt, along with additional related articles, are collected in Jon R. Stone, ed., *Expecting Armageddon: Essential Readings in Failed Prophecy* (New York: Routledge, 2000).

527. See Zygmunt, "Prophetic Failure," 933–34.

528. All of these texts betray an awareness of eschatological deferral, as Erich Gräßer argued (*Das Problem der Parusieverzögerung in den synoptischen Evangelien und in der Apostelgeschichte* [BZNW 22; Berlin: Töpelmann, 1957]). Cf. LXX Isa 13:22; Hab 1:2; 2:3; Zech 1:12.

529. Melton, "Spiritualization and Reaffirmation," 147. See further Zygmunt, "Prophetic Failure"; Weiser, "Prophetic Disconfirmation." Millenarian movements supply numerous examples of a prophesied event being "reinterpreted in such a way that what was supposed to have been a visible, verifiable occurrence is seen to have been in reality an invisible, spiritual occurrence. The event occurred as predicted, only on a spiritual level" (Melton, "Spiritualization and Reaffirmation," 149, with examples). Cf. Allison, *End of the Ages*, 142–48; idem, *Jesus of Nazareth*, 167–69; Balch et al., "Fifteen Years," 78–79.

Turks. . . . He destroyed oppression and those who caused it, and extirpated falsehood root and branch. The land was good and the people had rest. Islam cast its burdens to the earth, and justice spread far and wide."[530] In analogous fashion, in early Christian literature, the passion and resurrection of Jesus fulfill prophetic oracles, and Jesus is already enthroned as ruler at the right hand of God.[531]

3. Retrospective reinterpretation usually goes hand in hand with the projection of unfulfilled prophecies onto the future.[532] William Miller set a date for the return of Jesus, who failed to show up on time. Miller then recalculated. When this revised prophecy also proved mistaken, those who stuck with his cause decided that Jesus had come, but it had been a spiritual coming, and it took place in heaven, not on earth. This hermeneutical maneuver did not, however, annul the expectation that Jesus will come again and that every eye will see him. It was similar in the early churches. Some prophecies, people thought, had come true; others were yet to materialize. The idea of two messianic fulfillments, of a first advent and a second advent, became orthodox opinion: the one Messiah will come twice.

4. Rather than attributing mistakes to their religious authorities, adherents prefer to think of themselves as having been mistaken.[533] Human error seems possible; divine error does not.[534] The so-called Baha'is Under the Provision of the Covenant, a small contemporary sect based in Montana, responded to failed predictions "by making a sharp distinction between a *prediction* and a *prophecy*. Prophecies come directly from God, whereas the BUPC's predictions were based on research and logic, which are subject to human fallibility."[535] In like fashion, the New Testament preserves Jesus' inerrancy by faulting his hearers, who failed to grasp aright his eschatological teaching (Mark 9:10; Luke 19:11–27; John 2:22; 21:20–24). When Mark 13:32 has Jesus deny knowing when the end will come, we infer that he did not dabble in erroneous calendrical speculation.

---

530. Holt, "Islamic Millenarianism," 345.

531. For example, Luke 22:69; Acts 2:29–36; 1 Cor 15:25. See further Allison, *End of the Ages*, 148–52, and below, pp. 247–51. When scholars routinely remark, with reference to early Christianity, that "the present time of preaching the gospel is really the formerly expected time of the Kingdom of the Messiah" (Rudolf Bultmann, *Jesus Christ and Mythology* [New York: Charles Scribner's Sons, 1958], 33), they often fail to ask what sociological factors could have encouraged such a counterintuitive idea.

532. See Zygmunt, "Prophetic Failure," 934; idem, "When Prophecies Fail," 260.

533. Melton notes that "prophecy does not fail—it is merely misunderstood" ("Spiritualization and Reaffirmation," 151); see also Zygmunt, "When Prophecies Fail," 260.

534. This is why belief in the divinity of Jesus has often stood in the way of acknowledging that he was an apocalyptic prophet with a *Naherwartung*.

535. Balch et al., "Fifteen Years," 79–80. Positing misunderstanding was also a common response of Lubavitchers to the Rebbe's death; see Shaffir, "When Prophecy Is Not Validated," 127–28.

5. In the face of God's seeming procrastination, one can fan the flames of expectation by construing contemporary events and experiences so that they become signs of the approaching end.[536] Jehovah's Witnesses, despite their dismal eschatological track record, have adopted this strategy again and again, continually correlating contemporary disasters with traditional forecasts of apocalyptic woe. In this, the Jehovah's Witnesses imitate the last book of the Bible. Revelation's dramatic eschatological scenario embraces the readers' present. What they see around them now is what the seer saw and recorded earlier. So their days must be the last days, their trials the troubles of the end; and although the saints may be perplexed and cry out, "Sovereign Lord, holy and true, how long will it be before you judge and avenge our blood on the inhabitants of the earth?" (6:10), Jesus must be coming soon (1:1–3; 22:12, 20).

6. Eschatological language can be spiritualized, so that it characterizes the present as opposed to the future. The millennium often "in some sense comes to life in the experience of the community as a whole."[537] Lines between heaven and earth and between the future and the present become blurred. Hope becomes realized, the apocalypse internalized.[538] In the words of Jacob Taubes, with reference to Jewish messianism, when "the hope of redemption crumbles, . . . the Messianic community, because of its inward certainty, does not falter"; rather, "the Messianic experience is bound to turn inward, redemption is bound to be conceived as an event in the spiritual realm, reflected in the human soul."[539] This happened, as already observed, with the Shakers. John's Gospel and the *Gospel of Thomas* serve as the outstanding illustrations of this phenomenon in early Christianity; but, as has been obvious since Dodd's contributions, various forms of "realized eschatology" are all over early Christian literature.[540] Some texts even turn the resurrection of the dead into a present, existential reality.[541]

536. See Zygmunt, "Prophetic Failure," 935; Balch, Farnsworth, and Wilkins, "When the Bombs Drop."

537. Gager, *Kingdom and Community*, 49.

538. For the argument that early Christian mysticism is in part "interiorized apocalypticism," see Alexander Golitzin, "Earthly Angels and Heavenly Men: The Old Testament Pseudepigrapha, Nicetas Stethatos, and the Tradition of Interiorized Apocalyptic in Eastern Christian Ascetical and Mystical Literature," *Dumbarton Oaks Papers* 55 (2001): 125–53; Bogdan G. Bucur, "The Other Clement of Alexandria: Cosmic Hierarchy and Interiorized Apocalypticism," *VC* 60 (2006): 251–67. For a similar argument regarding the origin of early Jewish mysticism, see April D. DeConick, "What Is Early Jewish and Christian Mysticism?" in *Paradise Now: Essays on Early Jewish and Christian Mysticism* (ed. April D. DeConick; SBLSymS 11; Atlanta: Society of Biblical Literature, 2006), 1–24.

539. Jacob Taubes, "The Price of Messianism," *JJS* 33 (1982): 596.

540. See Dodd, *Apostolic Preaching*.

541. See Eph 2:5–6; Col 2:12–13; 2 Tim 2:18; *Gos. Thom.* 51; *Treat. Res.* 1.49; Irenaeus, *Haer.* 1.23.5; 2.31.2.

7. "A group may transfer the responsibility for nonconfirmation to some agency, either internal or external";[542] that is, the faithful can construct a contingent eschatology, thereby placing responsibility upon insiders and/or outsiders for when the end comes. After the eschatological expectations of the Guaraní in South America did not materialize, some rationalized that it was their own fault, because they had eaten European foods.[543] When the Kiowa prophet Paignya set a particular date for the return of the buffalo and the destruction of the white man, and when he saw that date come and go, he explained that disobedience to his ordinances had canceled the destined happiness.[544] After their Rebbe died and he was not revealed as the Messiah, Lubavitchers commonly responded by blaming themselves: if they had been worthy, Moshiach would have come.[545] And in early Christianity, some came to think that the timing of the end depended upon preaching the gospel to all the world (Mark 13:10), or on the repentance of Jerusalem (Acts 3:19–21), or on believers living godly lives (2 Pet 3:11–12; 2 Clem. 12:6).[546]

8. Increased missionary activity can accompany disappointment, although it "is only one of several possible adaptational strategies employed by religions coping with prophetic disconfirmation."[547] The UFO cult famously studied by Leon Festinger, Henry W. Riecken, and Stanley Schachter reacted to a failed prediction by stepping up their missionary efforts;[548] the death of Rebbe led to renewed proselytizing activity among some Lubavitchers;[549] the followers of Joachim of Fiore redoubled their preaching when their initial predictions failed;[550] and the primitive churches were missionizing churches.[551]

542. Tumminia, "How Prophecy Never Fails," 159. Cf. Zygmunt, "When Prophecies Fail," 260–61; and see further Weiser, "Prophetic Disconfirmation," 24–26.

543. Lawrence E. Sullivan, *Icanchu's Drum: An Orientation to Meaning in South American Religions* (New York: Macmillan; London: Collier Macmillan, 1988), 575.

544. James Mooney, *The Ghost-Dance Religion and the Sioux Outbreak of 1890* (abridged ed.; Chicago: University of Chicago Press, 1965), 163–64.

545. Shaffir, "When Prophecy Is Not Validated," 127–28. Yehudah Leib argued that the Messiah was not revealed in 1666 because, despite all the fervor of religious Jews, they had made liturgical errors (see Carlebach, "Two Amens").

546. On contingent eschatology as an apologetical tactic, see Allison, *End of the Ages*, 155–60. For Jewish texts that make the end contingent, see Allison, "The Forsaken House, Q 13:34–35," in *Jesus Tradition in Q*, 192–204.

547. Dawson, "When Prophecy Fails," 64.

548. Leon Festinger, Henry W. Riecken, and Stanley Schachter, *When Prophecy Fails: A Social and Psychological Study of a Modern Group That Predicted the Destruction of the World* (New York: Harper & Row, 1964).

549. Simon Dein, "Lubavitch: A Contemporary Messianic Movement," *JCR* 12 (1997): 191–204; William Shaffir, "Jewish Messianism Lubavitch-Style: An Interim Report," *JJSoc* 35 (1993): 115–28.

550. Emmanuel Wardi, "Cognitive Dissonance and Proselytism: An Application of Festinger's Model to Thirteenth-Century Joachites," in *Apocalyptic Time* (ed. Baumgarten), 269–82.

551. See further Gager, *Kingdom and Community*, 19–49, drawing upon the work of Festinger, Riecken, and Schachter. For a summary of critical responses to Festinger, Riecken, and

In brief: early Christian literature shows all the signs of a millenarian movement gradually outgrowing its enthusiastic origins and liminal status and settling in for the long, institutional haul.[552]

The Method of Subtraction

Liberating Jesus from the sort of eschatology that I attribute to him usually involves arguing, apocalyptic saying after apocalyptic saying, that he uttered none of them. One may contend, for example, that most or all of the material in Mark 13 is secondary, that all of the future Son of Man sayings are from the church, that the précis of Jesus' message in Mark 1:14–15 is redactional, and continue like this until one has excised all the incriminating material. One will then be free to reconfigure what remains.[553]

One problem with this procedure is that our historical-critical instruments are far too blunt for this sort of surgery. We routinely extract materials either because our criteria of authenticity seemingly direct us to do so or because our tradition histories show them to be secondary. Those tradition histories, however, are for the most part notoriously conjectural and highly uncertain,[554] and the deficiencies of our criteria are manifest: they require more knowledge of early Judaism and early Christianity than we possess; they have not brought us consensus on any issue of importance; and they often clash with each other, so that while one criterion points one way for a particular complex, another criterion points another way.[555]

For the sake of argument, however, let us say that I am too cynical about our sleuthing abilities. Let us further say that we have become confident that Jesus contributed little if anything to Mark 13, that he said nothing about the future coming of the Son of Man, that he did not utter an Aramaic version of Mark 1:14–15, and so on. What should we infer? That Jesus was not an apocalyptic prophet?

False testimony establishes nothing. If a witness on the stand avows, "A said B," and then we learn that the witness was lying, we have not discovered anything about A. We certainly do not have reason enough to conclude that A never said anything like B. Why should it be different with Jesus and the

---

Schachter, see Bernard Spilka et al., *The Psychology of Religion: An Empirical Approach* (3rd ed.; New York: Guilford, 2003), 356–60. The issue is complex because multiple variables are involved, and failed prophecy can lead to a decline in proselytizing fervor; see Sanada Takaaki, "A Prophecy Fails: A Reappraisal of a Japanese Case," *JJRS* 6 (1979): 217–37.

552. On millenarianism as a liminal phenomenon, see Victor Turner, *The Ritual Process: Structure and Anti-Structure* (Ithaca, NY: Cornell University Press, 1969), 111–12.

553. For an example of this procedure, see Merkel, "Gottesherrschaft."

554. See Allison, *Jesus of Nazareth*, 27–31.

555. For a lengthy defense of these propositions, see Dale C. Allison Jr., "How to Marginalize the Traditional Criteria of Authenticity," in *The Handbook for the Study of the Historical Jesus* (ed. Tom Holmén and Stanley E. Porter; 4 vols.; Leiden: Brill, 2009), 1:3–30.

Gospels? I have heard several stories about Dale Allison the absent-minded professor. They have all been, if memory serves me, apocryphal. Yet is that any reason to infer that I am not an absent-minded professor?

If one were to conclude, as have I, that every extant story about Jesus' father is legendary—I think this of Matt 1:18–25; 2:13–23; Luke 2:41–51; *Prot. Jas.* 9–18, 21; and *Inf. Gos. Thom.* 2–19—that would be no cause for denying that Jesus' father was named "Joseph." Similarly, even if one were to conclude, against good sense, that Jesus authored none of the apocalyptic sayings attributed to him, that would not be, in and of itself, reason to deny that he was an apocalyptic prophet. Subtraction only subtracts. It puts nothing in place of what it has taken away.

The only counter to this is to claim that once the experts subtract the apocalyptic elements from the tradition, what remains does not cohere with Jesus having been an apocalyptic prophet. This, however, is not the case. As I hope previous pages have shown, neither Jesus' moral teaching nor his wisdom sayings set themselves against apocalyptic eschatology, nor do his parables or the few texts that may speak of the kingdom's presence.

A Misunderstood Jesus

Our sources tell us that people misunderstood the eschatological teaching of Jesus, and some modern scholars have made the same claim. As we have seen, Luke 19:11 reflects the belief that, as they approached Jerusalem, the disciples but not Jesus erroneously expected the kingdom to appear immediately (cf. 24:21; Acts 1:6). Comparable is John 21:23, which denies that Jesus ever said that the end would precede the death of all his disciples (cf. Mark 9:1). One also recalls in this connection the Markan "messianic secret," at least to the extent that it has the disciples not grasping the truth about Jesus before Easter, as well as John 12:16: "His disciples did not understand these things at first" (cf. 2:22).

These ancient verses have their counterparts in more recent writers. Here are two representative quotations:

- Edwin A. Abbott (1910): "Our modern notions of Christ's eschatology are often based on an underrating of the extent to which He used material imagery and of the extent to which He was absorbed—whereas His disciples were by no means similarly absorbed—in Spiritual thought." They failed to fathom apocalyptic language aright because they (unlike Abbott) were "unable to apprehend the intensity with which Jesus gazed into spiritual things—realizing their reality and certainty of fulfillment, apart from any definite details and time."[556]

556. Edwin A. Abbott, *"The Son of Man," or, Contributions to the Study of the Thoughts of Jesus* (Cambridge: Cambridge University Press, 1910), 728.

- Robert Funk (1996): "We can understand the intrusion of the standard apocalyptic hope back into his [Jesus'] gospel at the hands of his disciples, some of whom had formerly been followers of the Baptist: they had not understood the subtleties of Jesus' position, they had not captured the intensity of his vision, and so reverted to the standard, orthodox [?] scenario once Jesus had departed from the scene."[557]

Because both Abbott and Funk are deceased, nothing inhibits me from complaining that their just-so stories are tendentious and self-serving. When these scholars make the disciples obtuse or dull, or turn them into followers of John when the disciples themselves thought they were followers of Jesus, they are mounting an argument from desperation, an argument forwarded only to allow them to discount texts that are at odds with their personal reconstructions of Jesus.[558] One is reminded of the *Gospel of Thomas*, wherein Jesus rejects the apocalyptic outlook of his obtuse disciples (e.g., 51, 52). Abbott and Funk are also a bit like Marcion, who accused the apostles of

557. Funk, *Honest to Jesus*, 168. Note also Matthew Arnold, *God and the Bible* (London: Smith, Elder, 1885), 231–32 (Jesus was "immeasurably" above his disciples, who were "immured . . . in the ideas of their time"); A. B. Bruce, *The Eschatology of Jesus, or, The Kingdom Come and Coming* (New York: A. C. Armstrong & Son, 1904), 35–47; E. C. Dewick, *Primitive Christian Eschatology: The Hulsean Prize Essay for 1908* (Cambridge: Cambridge University Press, 1912), 175–80; H. Erskine Hill, *Apocalyptic Problems* (London: Hodder & Stoughton, 1916), 15–17 (Jesus' "sayings were constantly misinterpreted even by His Apostles, and He knew that they were misunderstood and left them unexplained. . . . He left them as unintelligible as books are to babies, waiting until man should be sufficiently developed to understand them. . . . The popular opinions which prevailed in the primitive Church would seem to be comparatively unimportant as an aid to interpretation"); E. F. Scott, "The Place of Apocalyptical Conceptions in the Mind of Jesus," *JBL* 41 (1922): 138 (the disciples were "very ordinary men, who would interpret in a crude and literal sense much that he [Jesus] may have spoken figuratively"); John Wick Bowman, *The Religion of Maturity* (New York: Abingdon-Cokesbury, 1948), 235–36; Richard Heard, *An Introduction to the New Testament* (London: Adam & Charles Black, 1950), 247, 250; Leroy Waterman, *The Religion of Jesus: Christianity's Unclaimed Heritage of Prophetic Religion* (New York: Harper & Brothers, 1952), 77–79; Stauffer, *Jesus and His Story*, 156–57 (the disciples, unlike Jesus, "were wholly children of their time, furiously tossed upon the waves of Jewish political and apocalyptic messianism"); Georgia Harkness, *Understanding the Kingdom of God* (Nashville: Abingdon, 1974), 84 ("Jesus apparently thought that it was useless to argue with" his closest disciples, who, having failed to "grasp His message," continued to believe in the restoration of the kingdom to Israel [Acts 1:6]); T. Francis Glasson, *Jesus and the End of the World* (Edinburgh: St. Andrews Press, 1980), 109 ("It would be understandable that the first Christians should not at the early stages grasp all that was entailed in his teaching"). This sort of evaluation goes back to the Deists (see, e.g., Thomas Morgan, *The Moral Philosopher* [London: printed for the author, 1737], 354) and has further precedent in the Christian theological tradition (see, e.g., John Calvin, *A Harmony of the Gospels Matthew, Mark, and Luke* [3 vols.; Grand Rapids: Eerdmans, 1972], 3:75). A variant of this strategy is to pin misunderstanding on the evangelists (so, e.g., Lewis A. Muirhead, *The Eschatology of Jesus, or, The Kingdom Come and Coming* [New York: A. C. Armstrong & Son, 1904], 131–34).

558. Cf. Sanders (*Historical Figure*, 183), who speaks of "the triumph of wishful thinking."

mixing falsehoods into the teaching of Jesus,[559] as well as like Eusebius, who, when it served his purposes, castigated Papias as a man of limited intelligence but was otherwise content to quote him as an authority (*Hist. eccl.* 3.39).

How can it be that some of Jesus' immediate followers so badly missed the mark, whereas Abbott and Funk, living in a dissimilar culture and removed by the vast distance of two millennia, have zeroed in on the facts? One has more sympathy for the rhetorical question of that old apologist Tertullian: "What person in complete possession of his mental faculties can believe that they [the apostles] were *ignorant* of anything, whom the Lord ordained to be teachers, keeping them always inseparable from himself . . . and to whom, when they were not in public, he used to clarify all obscure words, saying that to them was given to *know* those *mysteries* which the people were unable to understand?"[560] Condescendingly dismissing the impressions of people who were in every way closer to Jesus than were Abbott and Funk is not obviously prudent.[561]

Final Remarks

"Nobody," Rudolf Bultmann wrote half a century ago, "doubts that Jesus' conception of the Kingdom of God is an eschatological one—at least in European theology and, as far as I can see, also among American New Testament scholars."[562] Whether or not Bultmann was on target for his own time, today's situation is very different. Several years ago, in fact, Marcus Borg gave it as his judgment that "the majority of scholars no longer thinks that Jesus expected the end of the world in his generation."[563] Although I confess to being in the dark as to how one counts the votes in such a matter, I am happily unconcerned about any alleged consensus because opinion is not evidence, and, like

559. Irenaeus, *Haer.* 3.2.1–2; Tertullian, *Marc.* 4.3.

560. Tertullian, *Praescr.* 22.3. Irenaeus likewise asks, "Why did the Lord send the twelve apostles to the lost sheep of the house of Israel, if these men did not know the truth?" (*Haer.* 3.13.2, trans. *ANF* 1:437).

561. The Markan theme of the disciples misunderstanding (4:13; 6:51–52; 8:14–21, 31–33; 9:9–10, 31–32, 38–41; 10:32–34) must be largely retrospective. Some have found here polemic against the Jerusalem church; so, for example, Étienne Trocmé, *The Formation of the Gospel according to Mark* (trans. Pamela Gaughan; Philadelphia: Westminster, 1975), 120–37. My own view is that we have here a didactic device otherwise known to religious history. The literary accounts of founders of religions often depict their disciples as dull or foolish. In this way, those disciples provide a contrast to the wise teacher. They ask questions so that he can answer them. They believe what is false so that he can teach what is true. They get things wrong so that he can make them right. See, for example, the *Analects of Confucius* 3.17, 21, 22, and the *Sutta-Nipāta*, *Cūlavagga* 2. The dialectical method of Plato's Socratic dialogues also belongs here.

562. Bultmann, *Jesus Christ and Mythology*, 13.

563. Borg, *Jesus, a New Vision*, 14. Cf. idem, "Temperate Case," 59–61.

our fashions, it is likely to change soon enough.[564] The ballot box does not recover the past. We should care only for sound arguments, not fret over the abstraction known as "the guild," or worry whether its putative majority has the sense to recognize such arguments. But whether or not others share my disinterest in who is winning at the moment, there is no doubt that, within the contemporary academy, the Jesus who sponsored apocalyptic eschatology has several rivals.

The present chapter has taken sides. I have argued that Weiss and Schweitzer set us on the right path. Like the historical Zoroaster, the historical Jesus foretold a resurrection of the dead, a universal divine judgment, and a new, idyllic world with evil undone, all coming soon. More particularly, he was a proponent of Jewish restoration eschatology: Israel's God would become the world's God. Jesus also, in my judgment, to use the terminology of Richard Landes, appears to have concerned himself more with "chiliastic hope" than "apocalyptic fear." That is, he did not design his message to foster chiefly "numbing terror at the prospect of universal destruction" but rather firstly to instill "an enthusiastic hope at the prospect of heaven on earth."[565] His dream was a millenarian utopia, not an apocalyptic nightmare.

In making my case, I have not found it necessary to argue for the authenticity of any particular logion. I have, however, endorsed and defended, if all too briefly, a number of propositions that some in our discipline now reckon outdated, even naïve. These include the following:

- The Synoptics as they stand, not Q[1] or Q[2] or Q[3] or the *Gospel of Thomas*, are our best sources for the historical Jesus because they contain the most memories of him.
- John the Baptist, who was an apocalyptic prophet, baptized Jesus.
- Christianity began as a Jewish messianic sect that we can profitably classify as a millenarian movement.
- Some people who knew Jesus and regarded themselves as proponents of his cause believed, within a few days of his crucifixion, that God had raised him from the dead.
- Some of those same people believed that his life fulfilled many oracles in Scripture, and they expected him to return soon.

At one time, most of these convictions could have been left undefended. That is true no longer. Members of the Society of Biblical Literature's Seminar on Ancient Myths and Modern Theories of Christian Origins appear to regard all of the statements just made as either controversial or demonstrably false.

---

564. Borg's more recent "impression is that the discipline today is about evenly divided" concerning Jesus and apocalyptic eschatology; see Borg, *Jesus: Uncovering the Life*, 252.
565. Landes, "Rodolfus Glaber," 67.

Their recent collaborative effort, *Redescribing Christian Origins*, is in fact an attempt to hack to bits traditional assumptions and to reconstruct Christian beginnings along altogether different lines.[566]

Herein I cannot enter into detailed discussion of the Seminar's project, only record my doubt about their doubts: their arguments are, on the whole, more clever than cogent. I sympathize with their conviction that "a community's narrative of its origins and (mythic) past cannot serve as the framework for a critical historiography, since the narrative has been constructed to serve as a source of divine legitimation and authorization of that very community."[567] I agree that Paul is no objective witness and that Acts is full of Lukan artistry and theology. And I welcome serious attempts to reexamine presuppositions and to rethink our discipline. As a critical historian, I have no desire to muzzle the facts, whatever they may be. I am, further, sure that I am wrong about much, and I hope that I have sufficient interest in the truth and adequate strength of character to repent of personal error when I run across new and improved arguments.

I am, however, unpersuaded that my more conventional understanding of Christian beginnings should be abandoned. My foundation remains our earliest sources, the Pauline Epistles and the Synoptic Gospels, and I cannot see that any other foundation can really be laid. That foundation may be, or rather is, very imperfect, with gaping crevices and crumbling stones. But what else is there? Overly optimistic evaluations of how much the *Gospel of Thomas* can tell us about pre-70 Christianity or novel reconstructions of pre-Pauline theology on the basis of contentious inferences from Kloppenborg's Q^1 do not move me to forsake the old ways. I remain persuaded that, barring the discovery of important new texts, we must do what most of us have always done, even if this means sometimes reproducing the canonical picture. The Synoptics and the authentic Paulines, although lacunae-riddled and often tendentious, supply our principal data, which we may then extend with whatever we can glean from Acts[568] and other early Christian materials,

---

566. See n. 76; see also Merrill P. Miller, "'Beginning from Jerusalem . . .': Re-examining Canon and Consensus," *Journal of Higher Criticism* 2 (1995), 3–30, an essay that contributed much to the Seminar's ruminations.

567. Ron Cameron and Merrill P. Miller, "Introduction: Ancient Myths and Modern Theories of Christian Origins," in *Redescribing Christian Origins* (ed. Cameron and Miller), 17.

568. First-century Christians must, before Luke wrote, have had memories of their own movement, and he could not have written as though it were otherwise. So Acts cannot be like most novels, which do not have to compete with ostensible memories. For a helpful overview of the issues involved in assessing the historicity of Acts, see Charles H. Talbert, "What Is Meant by the Historicity of Acts?" in *Reading Luke-Acts in Its Mediterranean Milieu* (NovTSup 107; Leiden: Brill, 2003), 197–217. Talbert's own, rather conservative conclusion is this: "Enough corroborating data has been assembled already by scholars to enable one to conclude that Acts is not mere fiction and that its record is reasonably reliable in areas where it can be checked."

almost all of which are in the canon.[569] In other words, much in the conventional accounts of Christian origins remains beyond significant revision, and this alone allows us to construct credible historical-critical edifices. The only judicious alternative is not a radically new history of Christian beginnings but rather an "intellectual blank."[570]

One intractable difference between myself and some members of the Seminar is their apparent conviction that it is not "possible . . . to say very much about the historical Jesus."[571] Heavily influenced by the idea that the past is a social construction determined by contemporary concerns and self-legitimation,[572] they seem persuaded that our sources, if not exactly fairy tales, permit at best only a meager sketch of Jesus. On their view, the past was, in early Christian circles, almost a boundless canvas or a sort of *tabula rasa* for theological imaginations. Academic sleuthhounds may track down some poorly attested early Christian group, but they will never find Jesus, who has forever disappeared behind heavy ideological curtains.[573] Questing for Jesus is no more profitable than questing for the historical Enoch or the historical Thecla.

What should one say to this? It is quite thinkable, in the abstract, that the Jesus tradition never had much integrity of its own, or that it was a markedly plastic resource, so that even at the beginning anybody could add just about anything. The Synoptics, insofar as they seek to persuade people to believe this and to do that, do turn Jesus into a sort of proof text to score theological points. So maybe the earliest tradition was as agreeable to fiction as the Hadith was to legends about Muhammad. Or perhaps Jesus was much like Sabbatai Sevi, who, although historical, quickly became more of "a slogan or image rather than a living personality," so that traditions "unrelated to whatever Sabbatai did or did not do" gained popular credence.[574] Or maybe he was like the Amerindian prophet Wovoka, who started a religion that quickly took

---

569. I am here in essential agreement with Bultmann: "Since Acts offers only an incomplete and legend-tinted picture of the earliest Church, an historical picture of it, so far as one is possible at all, can be won only by the route of reconstruction. The following serve as sources: 1. the tradition utilized by the author of Acts, so far as it can be ascertained by critical analysis; 2. data occurring in the Pauline letters; 3. the synoptic tradition," whose shaping "took place in the earliest Church, and hence the tendencies that were operative in the earliest Church cannot but appear in that tradition" (*Theology*, 1:33).

570. I borrow the expression from Burton Mack, "Backbay Jazz and Blues," in *Redescribing Christian Origins* (ed. Cameron and Miller), 425.

571. Mack, *Who Wrote the New Testament?* 45. See further idem, *The Christian Myth: Origins, Logic, and Legacy* (New York: Continuum, 2001), esp. 25–40.

572. See the works cited on p. 5 n. 30.

573. Robert M. Price, in *The Incredible Shrinking Son of Man: How Reliable Is the Gospel Tradition?* (Amherst, NY: Prometheus Books, 2003), seriously entertains the possibility that Jesus was wholly mythical.

574. Scholem, *Sabbatai Sevi*, 252. Scholem states that while Sabbatai was yet alive, "the realm of imaginative legend . . . dominated the mental climate" of his followers in Palestine (p. 265).

violent forms that he repudiated, and who went into partial seclusion when "he wearied of rumors and falsehoods attributed to him."[575]

On my reading, however, the Synoptics invite us to travel a road less skeptical. Although they are the products of social construction, they are also the products of memory, however partial and distorted. Unlike Sabbatai Sevi, whose words and personality exerted no great force upon his followers, Jesus was more than a feeble memory, more than an amorphous lump of clay waiting for Christian hands to mold him into somebody.

Assuming the existence of Q and Markan priority, it is clear that the Jesus tradition was not, at least for Matthew and Luke, a mere peg upon which to hang their own ideas. They did not just look into the well of tradition and narcissistically see only their own reflections. Instead, they were primarily, if I may so put it, exegetes, and they typically contributed to the sayings of Jesus and stories about him by way of "abbreviation and omission, clarification and explanation, elaboration and extension of motif."[576] In other words, their business was largely that of contextualizing tradition. And since there is no real cause to believe that their handling of the materials was eccentric or radically different from most of the tradents before them, we have some reason to infer that, regarding the tradition behind Matthew, Mark, and Luke, material usually entered because people perceived it as being congruent with beliefs and images of Jesus already valued.[577]

One understands why the tradition—here I mean firstly the Synoptic tradition[578]—was not wholly malleable and why its contributors managed some

575. Michael Hittman, *Wovoka and the Ghost Dance* (ed. Don Lynch; expanded ed.; Lincoln: University of Nebraska Press, 1990), 103.

576. James D. G. Dunn, *Jesus Remembered* (Christianity in the Making 1; Grand Rapids: Eerdmans, 2003), 224. Dunn observes that "developments most likely were along the lines indicated or allowed by the tradition" rather than being "wholly new features or elements which cut across or contradicted the earlier thrust of the tradition" (pp. 333–34). Cf. Nils Dahl, "The Problem of the Historical Jesus," in *Jesus the Christ: The Historical Origins of Christian Doctrine* (ed. Donald H. Juel; Minneapolis: Fortress, 1991), 95: only material was added that "agreed with the total picture as it existed within the circle of the disciples"; Ferdinand Hahn, "Methodological Reflections on the Historical Investigation of Jesus," in *Historical Investigation and New Testament Faith: Two Essays* (Philadelphia: Fortress, 1983), 49: "Completely new creations are an exception, because what was added by the church in its tradition was closely associated with other transmitted materials, and extended them"; Kosch, "Q und Jesus," 37: "In the case of the reception of the proclamation of Jesus through the Q circle, one indeed reckons with a process of transformation and shifts of accent, but not with radical discontinuities"; Graham Stanton, "Matthew as a Creative Interpreter of the Sayings of Jesus," in *The Gospel and the Gospels* (ed. Peter Stuhlmacher; Grand Rapids: Eerdmans, 1991), 257–72. Particularly helpful here is Rau, *Jesus*, 49–74; idem, "Wie entstehen unechte Jesusworte?"

577. Compare Bultmann on our topic: "The certainty with which the Christian community puts the eschatological preaching into the mouth of Jesus is hard to understand if he did not really preach it" (*Jesus and the Word*, 124).

578. The logia in John and *Thomas* are, to my mind, of different character. Although John's discourses often grow out of traditional, Synoptic-like logia, the evangelist is clear that the Spirit

self-abnegation. Not only is invention unpersuasive when it fails to resonate with present perceptions of the past, but also the needs and interests of tradents of the Jesus tradition had to interact with what was already publicly believed (that Jesus was crucified, for instance).[579] A story that had Jesus dying in old age or suffering crucifixion in Rome would never have been accepted. Some things are indeed known.[580] This is why millenarian movements that survive typically reinterpret their traditions; they rarely ignore them altogether.[581] Daniel contains more than one date for the end, its unfulfilled forecasts (8:14; 12:7) remaining despite their falsification and the need for new numbers (12:11–12). Similarly, "there are a large number of dateable apocalyptic predictions still extant in the early Muslim religious literature indicating that the proto-Muslims expected the world to come to an end either during the year 70/689–90 or during the year 100/717. The fact that these predictions are still available in such quantities long after the obvious disconfirmation discrediting the original prediction demonstrates the belief in this date and its power within the community."[582]

There is always an abundance of the past in the present, and the past has its own inertia, its own tendency to self-preservation.[583] This is especially true where, as in early Christianity, there are competing interpretations of the past. Partisans on one side of a debate can help keep the other side honest.

---

will inspire new words and reinterpret old ones (14:26; 15:26; 16:12–13). This amounts to an apology for John's distinct materials. Likewise, *Thomas*, which may implicitly denigrate traditions linked to Peter and Matthew (see 13, 114), justifies its new formulations—approximately half of *Thomas* lacks parallels in the canonical Gospels—by making Thomas into Jesus' "twin," the recipient of "secret sayings" and esoteric teaching (see the prologue and 13). Moreover, 108 ("The one who will drink from my mouth will become like me. I myself shall become that one, and the things that are hidden will be revealed to that one") equates Jesus and his enlightened followers, who can reveal hidden things. See further Rau, *Jesus*, 91–95. I am less skeptical regarding the narrative elements in John; they often strike me as deriving from old tradition.

579. Kloppenborg observes that, given that the Q material was presumably used in oral performance, "it is very unlikely that an author could introduce radically new ideas or recommended behaviors that differed radically from those accepted by the addressees without anticipating considerable resistance or outright rejection. This is especially true in a work such as Q, with its implicit claim to represent the Jesus tradition" ("Sayings Gospel Q," 335). Kloppenborg has helpfully expanded on what he has in mind here in "Discursive Practices," 169–74.

580. Instructive here is Barry Schwartz, *Abraham Lincoln and the Forge of National Memory* (Chicago: University of Chicago Press, 2000), esp. 1–25.

581. Cf. the situation in the *Gospel of Thomas*, and see further Allison, *End of the Ages*, 142–48; idem, *Jesus of Nazareth*, 94, 167–69.

582. David Cook, "The Beginnings of Islam as an Apocalyptic Movement," in *War in Heaven* (ed. O'Leary and McGhee), 85. For details, see Bashear, "Muslim Apocalypses."

583. See Michael Schudson, "The Present in the Past and the Past in the Present," *Communication* 11 (1989): 105–13. Compare this generalization of Yael Zerubavel: "In spite of its dynamic character, collective memory is not an entirely fluid knowledge nor is it totally detached from historical memory" (*Recovered Roots: Collective Memory and the Making of Israeli National Tradition* [Chicago: University of Chicago Press, 1995], 5).

Conflict can inhibit fictions, can prevent people from being wholly untethered to the truth. In a context of antagonism between groups, not all claims are permitted.

With regard to Jesus in particular, he was, whatever else we may think, "a doer of extraordinary deeds" (Josephus, *Ant.* 18.53) and so a truly interesting person; and it is human nature to tell tales about and to quote and misquote interesting people. Memorable things get remembered. Even before Easter, some must have recounted stories—no doubt often exaggerated and sometimes wholly unfounded—regarding Jesus, just as some must have repeated things that he was thought to have said, whether he really said them or not (see above, pp. 24–26). Moreover, early Christians must have had some definite ideas, however derived, about their master. That many wanted to learn about Jesus is strongly suggested by the prestige, in the early churches, of those who had known him[584] as well as by the success of the Gospel genre.

The point to underline here is that soon after images of Jesus, stories about him, and sayings attributed to him entered circulation, and whatever the genesis of those sayings, stories, and images, they must have become, for many committed followers, part and parcel of their religious identity and so objects of allegiance. Once important beliefs generate meaning and become integral to a group's self-conception, a loyalty and a natural conservation develop. People will take pride in a collective past, "imaginarily dwell in it," and resist significant alteration of the shared beliefs that matter to them.[585] This is why so often "the earliest construction of an historical object limits the range of things subsequent generations can say about it."[586] There is a social constraint upon memory.

Religious groups especially can become invested in a series of perceptions of the past, with the result that those perceptions become an intersubjective world that shapes social consensus, becomes authoritative, and endures. This is in fact the definition of tradition—stories and sentiments that express personal and communal identity and so become to some extent stable while being handed down through time. Self-interest and the preservation of tradition go together. This is why religious communities, even if completely uninterested in or incapable of producing critical history, often become custodians of

---

584. James and Peter and John were, according to Paul in Gal 2:9, "pillars," and they had in common a close personal knowledge of Jesus. One recalls the importance of the relatives of Jesus in the early church; on this, see Richard Bauckham, "The Relatives of Jesus in the Early Church," in *Jude and the Relatives of Jesus in the Early Church* (Edinburgh: T & T Clark, 1990), 45–133.

585. Edward Shils, *Tradition* (London: Faber, 1981), 211. Shils writes, "The image of the past is a reservoir of potential objects of attachment" (ibid., 53).

586. Barry Schwartz, "Social Change and Collective Memory: The Democratization of George Washington," *American Sociological Review* 56 (1991): 232. Schudson notes that there is "great power to originating events, the character of 'founding fathers' or constitutional documents" ("Present in the Past," 111).

memory, or create "remembrance environments" in which newcomers undergo "mnemonic socialization."[587] "Familiarizing new members with their collective past is an important part of groups' and communities' general efforts to incorporate them. Business corporations, colleges, and army battalions, for example, often introduce new members to their collective history as part of their general 'orientation.'"[588] It cannot have been so different in the early churches.[589] Collective identity largely depends upon people telling and retelling the same stories.

It is only to be expected that some religions have closed their scriptural canons so that their story cannot be further modified; or that some Lubavitchers memorized their Rebbe's Sabbath addresses so they could recite them to others;[590] or that the Gathas, written many centuries after Zoroaster, nonetheless preserve hymns that he composed: tradents memorized them.[591]

Similarly, 1 Cor 11:23–26 and 1 Cor 15:3–7 are the proof that pre-Pauline Jewish Christians had traditions regarding Jesus, and that their cult and rituals were commemorative of him.[592] The Synoptics, moreover, must descend from those traditions; that is, they must derive in large part from tales told about Jesus and from sayings assigned to him early on. The only alternative, that the earliest communal memories just disappeared, to be replaced by an altogether new set of materials, makes no historical sense. People who recalled events or speeches that nobody else seemed to remember or that did not fit with what everybody already believed would not likely have made much of an impact. Although the tradition in remembrance of Jesus was far from immutable, it

---

587. The quoted terms are from Eviatar Zerubavel, *Social Mindscapes: An Invitation to Cognitive Sociology* (Cambridge, MA: Harvard University Press, 1997), 81, 87.

588. Ibid., 92.

589. According to Rodríguez, "performances of the Jesus tradition accrued to themselves a sense of stability and repetition by way of multiple performances through time" ("Early Christian Memory," 3).

590. Dein, "Mosiach Is Here Now," 28.

591. "They seem to have been memorized word-for-word, or indeed syllable-for-syllable, so that they did not change along with the living language as other parts of the early religious tradition did" (Philip G. Kreyenbroek, "Millennialism and Eschatology in the Zoroastrian Tradition," in *Imagining the End: Visions of Apocalypse from the Ancient Middle East to Modern America* [ed. Abbas Amanat and Magnus Bernhardsson; London: I. B. Tauris, 2002], 40).

592. David Middleton and Derek Edwards observe, "Commemoration silences the contrary interpretations of the past" (introduction to *Collective Remembering* [ed. David Middleton and Derek Edwards; London: Sage, 1990], 8). On the importance of ritual for social memory, see Paul Connerton, *How Societies Remember* (Cambridge: Cambridge University Press, 1989); and see Zerubavel's analysis, in *Recovered Roots*, of the importance of "commemorative narrative." Early Christian texts that refer to memory include Mark 14:9; Luke 22:19; 24:6, 8; John 2:22; 12:16; 14:26; 15:20; 16:4; Acts 11:16; 20:35; 1 Cor 11:24–25; 2 Tim 2:8, 14. Liturgy becomes potentially relevant here, because words associated with actions are better remembered than words alone; see Lars-Göran Nilsson, "Remembering Actions and Words," in *The Oxford Handbook of Memory* (ed. Endel Tulving and Fergus I. M. Craik; Oxford: Oxford University Press, 2000), 137–48.

was nonetheless a tradition.[593] This means that people could not persuasively exnihilate items at will. Some indeed thought of Jesus as their "only teacher" (Matt 23:8–10), or imagined that when they spoke, their audience would hear him: "Whoever listens to you listens to me" (Luke 10:16). Others, as Joachim Wanke has demonstrated, elucidated sayings attributed to Jesus by juxtaposing those sayings with other logia attributed to him, not by inventing their own commentary ad hoc.[594] Thus just as somebody, finding them congenial, managed to collect some of Paul's Epistles, so other early Christians, finding the Jesus tradition congenial, helped preserve memories of him.

I am not here contending for a naïve or robust confidence in the historicity of the Synoptics. Matthew, Mark, and Luke contain legends and embody specifically Christian concerns; and, together with their sources, they must commit all "the sins of memory" cataloged at the beginning of chapter 1. What I do maintain is that the materials gathered into the Synoptics, however stylized and otherwise distorted, descend from narratives and sayings that were in circulation and widely valued from early times, and that we may reasonably hope to find in those Gospels, above all in their repeating patterns, some real impressions or memories that, taken together, produce more than a faint image. Bolstering this hope is the fact that, while the Synoptic Jesus often appears to be an apocalyptic prophet, we can infer his status as such from the foundational beliefs of the earliest churches. In other words, what we otherwise know of primitive Christianity corroborates the general impression that we gather from the Synoptics. Although barnacles cover the rock, we can still see the rock's shape.

Excursus i
The Kingdom of God and the World to Come

Sayings about the Kingdom

The Synoptics attribute to Jesus, by my count, at least fifty-eight different sayings about the kingdom:

593. Helpful here is Tom Holmén, "Knowing about Q and Knowing about Jesus: Mutually Exclusive Undertakings?" (in *Sayings Source Q* [ed. Lindemann], 497–514). He shows that, at least on occasion, "the transmitters of the Jesus tradition were prepared to deal with teachings of Jesus that put forward (theological) points of view that were not favored by them or that made Jesus appear in a dubious light (which was also against their ends)" (p. 512).

594. Joachim Wanke, *"Bezugs- und Kommentarworte" in den synoptischen Evangelien: Beobachtungen zur Interpretationsgeschichte der Herrenworte in der vorevangelischen Überlieferung* (ETS 44; Leipzig: St. Benno-Verlag, 1981).

From Mark

1. Mark 1:15: "The time is fulfilled, and the kingdom of God has come near; repent, and believe in the good news."
2. Mark 4:11: "To you has been given the secret of the kingdom of God, but for those outside, everything comes in parables."
3. Mark 4:26: "The kingdom of God is as if someone would scatter seed on the ground. . . ."
4. Mark 4:30–31: "With what can we compare the kingdom of God, or what parable will we use for it? It is like a mustard seed. . . ."
5. Mark 9:1: "Truly I tell you, there are some standing here who will not taste death until they see that the kingdom of God has come with power."
6. Mark 9:47: "And if your eye causes you to stumble, tear it out; it is better for you to enter the kingdom of God with one eye than to have two eyes and to be thrown into hell."
7. Mark 10:14: "Let the little children come to me; do not stop them; for it is to such as these that the kingdom of God belongs."
8. Mark 10:15: "Truly I tell you, whoever does not receive the kingdom of God as a little child will never enter it."[595]
9. Mark 10:23: "How hard it will be for those who have wealth to enter the kingdom of God!"
10. Mark 10:24: "Children, how hard it is to enter the kingdom of God!"
11. Mark 10:25: "It is easier for a camel to go through the eye of a needle than for someone who is rich to enter the kingdom of God."
12. Mark 12:34: "You are not far from the kingdom of God."
13. Mark 14:25: "Truly I tell you, I will never again drink of the fruit of the vine until that day when I drink it new in the kingdom of God."

Common to Matthew and Luke (Q)[596]

14. Luke 6:20 // Matt 5:3 (Q): "Blessed are you who are poor, for yours is the kingdom of God."
15. Luke 7:28 // Matt 11:11 (Q): "I tell you, among those born of women no one is greater than John; yet the least in the kingdom of God is greater than he."
16. Luke 10:9 // Matt 10:7 (Q): "Say to them, 'The kingdom of God has come near to you.'"
17. Luke 11:2 // Matt 6:10 (Q): "Your kingdom come."

595. Even on the theory of Markan priority, the saying in Matt 18:3 may be independent of Mark; see W. D. Davies and Dale C. Allison Jr., *A Critical and Exegetical Commentary on the Gospel according to Saint Matthew* (3 vols.; ICC; Edinburgh: T & T Clark, 1988–1997), 2:756–57.

596. Except item 23 (Matt 11:12 // Luke 16:16), I cite these in their Lukan versions.

18. Luke 11:20 // Matt 12:28: (Q) "But if it is by the finger of God that I cast out the demons, then the kingdom of God has come to you."

19. Luke 12:31 // Matt 6:33 (Q): "Strive for his kingdom, and these things will be given to you as well."

20. Luke 13:18–19 // Matt 13:31 (Q) (cf. Mark 4:30–31): "What is the kingdom of God like? And to what should I compare it? It is like a mustard seed. . . ."

21. Luke 13:20–21 // Matt 13:33 (Q): "To what shall I compare the kingdom of God? It is like yeast. . . ."

22. Luke 13:28–29 // Matt 8:11–12 (Q): "There will be weeping and gnashing of teeth when you see Abraham and Isaac and Jacob and all the prophets in the kingdom of God, and you yourselves thrown out. Then people will come from east and west, from north and south, and will eat in the kingdom of God."

23. Matt 11:12 // Luke 16:16 (Q): "From the days of John the Baptist until now the kingdom of God has suffered violence, and the violent take it by force."

Unique to Matthew

24. Matt 5:10: "Blessed are those who are persecuted for righteousness' sake, for theirs is the kingdom of heaven."

25. Matt 5:19: "Whoever breaks one of the least of these commandments, and teaches others to do the same, will be called least in the kingdom of heaven; but whoever does them and teaches them will be called great in the kingdom of heaven."

26. Matt 5:20: "For I tell you, unless your righteousness exceeds that of the scribes and Pharisees, you will never enter the kingdom of heaven."

27. Matt 7:21 (the parallel in Luke 6:46 lacks "kingdom"): "Not everyone who says to me, 'Lord, Lord,' will enter the kingdom of heaven, but only the one who does the will of my Father in heaven."

28. Matt 13:19 (the parallel in Mark 4:15 lacks "kingdom"): "When anyone hears the word of the kingdom and does not understand it, the evil one comes and snatches away what is sown in the heart; this is what was sown on the path."

29. Matt 13:24: "The kingdom of heaven may be compared to someone who sowed good seed in his field."

30. Matt 13:38: "The field is the world, and the good seed are the children of the kingdom; the weeds are the children of the evil one."

31. Matt 13:41: "The Son of Man will send his angels, and they will collect out of his kingdom all causes of sin and all evildoers."

32. Matt 13:43: "Then the righteous will shine like the sun in the kingdom of their Father."

33. Matt 13:44: "The kingdom of heaven is like treasure hidden in a field, which someone found and hid."
34. Matt 13:45: "The kingdom of heaven is like a merchant in search of fine pearls."
35. Matt 13:47: "The kingdom of heaven is like a net that was thrown into the sea."
36. Matt 13:52: "Therefore every scribe who has been trained for the kingdom of heaven is like the master of a household who brings out of his treasure what is new and what is old."
37. Matt 16:19: "I will give you the keys of the kingdom of heaven, and whatever you bind on earth will be bound in heaven, and whatever you loose on earth will be loosed in heaven."
38. Matt 18:4: "Whoever becomes humble like this child is the greatest in the kingdom of heaven."
39. Matt 18:23: "For this reason the kingdom of heaven may be compared to a king who wished to settle accounts with his slaves."
40. Matt 19:12: "For there are eunuchs who have been so from birth, and there are eunuchs who have been made eunuchs by others, and there are eunuchs who have made themselves eunuchs for the sake of the kingdom of heaven. Let anyone accept this who can."
41. Matt 20:1: "For the kingdom of heaven is like a landowner who went out early in the morning to hire laborers for his vineyard."
42. Matt 21:31: "Truly I tell you, the tax collectors and the prostitutes are going into the kingdom of God ahead of you."
43. Matt 21:43 (the parallel parable in Mark 12:1–12 lacks this line): "Therefore I tell you, the kingdom of God will be taken away from you and given to a people that produces the fruits of the kingdom."
44. Matt 22:2 (the parallel in Luke 14:16 lacks "kingdom"): "The kingdom of heaven may be compared to a king who gave a wedding banquet for his son."
45. Matt 23:13 (the parallel in Luke 11:52 lacks "kingdom"): "But woe to you, scribes and Pharisees, hypocrites! For you lock people out of the kingdom of heaven. For you do not go in yourselves, and when others are going in, you stop them."
46. Matt 24:14 (the parallel in Mark 13:10 lacks "kingdom"): "And this good news of the kingdom will be proclaimed throughout the world, as a testimony to all the nations; and then the end will come."
47. Matt 25:1: "Then the kingdom of heaven will be like this. Ten bridesmaids took their lamps and went to meet the bridegroom."
48. Matt 25:34: "Then the king will say to those at his right hand, 'Come, you that are blessed by my Father, inherit the kingdom prepared for you from the foundation of the world.'"

Unique to Luke

49. Luke 4:43: "I must proclaim the good news of the kingdom of God to the other cities also; for I was sent for this purpose."
50. Luke 9:60 (without parallel in Matt 8:22): "But as for you, go and proclaim the kingdom of God."
51. Luke 9:62: "No one who puts a hand to the plow and looks back is fit for the kingdom of God."
52. Luke 10:10–11 (the parallel in Matt 10:14 lacks "Yet . . . near"): "Say, 'Even the dust of your town that clings to our feet, we wipe off in protest against you. Yet know this: the kingdom of God has come near.'"
53. Luke 12:32: "Do not be afraid, little flock, for it is your Father's good pleasure to give you the kingdom."
54. Luke 17:20–21: "The kingdom of God is not coming with things that can be observed; nor will they say, 'Look, here it is!' or 'There it is!' For, in fact, the kingdom of God is among [or 'within'] you."
55. Luke 18:29–30 (the parallel in Mark 10:29 lacks "kingdom of God"): "Truly I tell you, there is no one who has left house or wife or brothers or parents or children, for the sake of the kingdom of God, who will not get back very much more in this age, and in the age to come eternal life."
56. Luke 21:31 (the parallel in Mark 13:29 is without "kingdom of God"): "When you see these things taking place, you know that the kingdom of God is near."
57. Luke 22:16: "I will not eat it until it is fulfilled in the kingdom of God."
58. Luke 22:29–30 (the parallel in Matt 19:28 lacks both uses of "kingdom"): "I confer on you, just as my Father has conferred on me, a kingdom, so that you may eat and drink at my table in my kingdom, and you will sit on thrones judging the twelve tribes of Israel."

The Nature of the Kingdom

One often reads that ἡ βασιλεία τοῦ θεοῦ refers not to a royal realm—a territory—but rather to God's dynamic activity as ruler.[597] This judgment ac-

597. Representative of this view are Bruce Chilton, "The Kingdom of God in Recent Discussion," in *Studying the Historical Jesus: Evaluations of the State of Current Research* (ed. Bruce Chilton and Craig A. Evans; NTTS 19; Leiden: Brill, 1994), 265 ("Jesus' preaching of the kingdom is in the first place an announcement of God's dynamic rule"); R. T. France, "The Church and the Kingdom of God," in *Biblical Interpretation and the Church: Text and Context* (ed. D. A. Carson; Exeter: Paternoster, 1984), 33; Jeremias, *New Testament Theology*, 98; Karl Georg Kuhn, "βασιλεία," *TDNT* 1:579–90; T. W. Manson, *The Sayings of Jesus* (London: SCM Press, 1949), 135; Joel Marcus, "Entering into the Kingly Power of God," *JBL* 107 (1988): 663–75;

cords with current lexicography. For instance, BDAG (s.v.) offers, as the first meaning of ἡ βασιλεία in early Christian literature, "kingship, royal power, royal rule." To this it dedicates well over a hundred lines of text plus a long bibliography. The dictionary then lists, as a second meaning, "territory ruled by a king, kingdom," to which it gives a scant ten lines and the briefest of bibliographies. BDAG apparently classifies all the sayings about ἡ βασιλεία τοῦ θεοῦ as exemplars of the first meaning.[598]

Despite the authoritative nature of BDAG and the common opinion that it represents, "kingship" or "royal rule of God" is probably not the exclusive or perhaps even chief meaning of ἡ βασιλεία τοῦ θεοῦ in the Jesus tradition. Although sometimes ἡ βασιλεία τοῦ θεοῦ must be a present or future divine activity, as often as not the expression seems instead to be shorthand for the state of affairs that will come to pass when the divine kingship becomes fully effective over the world and its peoples. In such instances, ἡ βασιλεία τοῦ θεοῦ denotes not God's rule but rather the result or goal of that rule. Or perhaps it denotes both "rule" and "realm" at the same time, for the two meanings are very hard to disentangle. An effective rule entails an established realm, and an established realm entails an effective rule.[599] That Greek dictionaries readily distinguish between "realm" and "reign" does not mean that ancient Greeks always did so. Our categories can be clearer than what we are categorizing.

Nonetheless, sometimes one meaning does seem to come to the fore in Synoptic sayings about ἡ βασιλεία, and my purpose in this excursus is to call attention to how often, despite the modern consensus, the phrase should not be reduced to something like ἡ ἡγεμονία τοῦ θεοῦ, how often it rather refers principally to the future time when and to the future place where the petition "Your kingdom come" will no longer need to be uttered.[600]

Meier, *Marginal Jew*, 2:240; Helmut Merklein, *Jesu Botschaft von der Gottesherrschaft: Eine Skizze* (SBS 111; Stuttgart: Katholisches Bibelwerk, 1983), 37–39. Many who adopt this position appeal to the influential work of Dalman, *Words of Jesus*, 91–147.

598. Cf. Johannes P. Louw and Eugene A. Nida, eds., *Greek-English Lexicon of the New Testament Based on Semantic Domains* (2nd ed.; 2 vols.; New York: United Bible Societies, 1989), 1:480.

599. See Ferdinand Hahn, "Die Worte von Gottes Herrschaft und Reich in Joh 3,3.5," in *Johannes aenigmaticus: Studien zum Johannesevangelium für Herbert Leroy* (ed. Stefan Schreiber and Alois Stimpfle; BU 29; Regensburg: Friedrich Pustet, 2000), 88.

600. Others who have emphasized that the kingdom is often or usually or always a place or like a place include Weiss, *Jesus' Proclamation*; Sverre Aalen, "'Reign' and 'House' in the Kingdom of God in the Gospels," *NTS* 8 (1962): 215–40; George Wesley Buchanan, *The Consequences of the Covenant* (NovTSup 20; Leiden: Brill, 1970), 42–90; idem, *New Testament Eschatology: Historical and Cultural Background* (Lewiston, NY: Mellen Biblical Press, 1993), 90–120; Conzelmann, *Theology*, 108 ("In Judaism, the expression [kingdom of God] means the act of God's rule [*Herrschens*]: with Jesus, it means God's kingdom [*Reich*]"); Kvalbein, "Ethics of Jesus," 197–227; Ernst Lohmeyer, *Lord of the Temple: A Study of the Relation between Cult and Gospel* (Richmond: John Knox, 1962), 62–69; J. C. O'Neill, "The Kingdom of God," *NovT* 34 (1993): 130–41; Otto, *Kingdom of God*, 53–54; Eduard Schweizer, *The Good News according*

1. Gustaf Dalman famously affirmed, "No doubt can be entertained that both in the Old Testament and in Jewish literature מלכות, when applied to God, means always the 'kingly rule' (*Herrschaft*), never the 'kingdom' (*Reich*), as if it were meant to suggest the territory governed."[601] Dalman supported this statement, which much subsequent discussion has almost taken for granted, by appealing to Ps 22:29 (with מלוכה);[602] 103:19; 145:11–13; Obad 21 (with מלוכה); and a number of rabbinic texts.

Is Dalman's proposition really beyond doubt? Obad 19–21 has this:

> Those of the Negeb shall possess Mount Esau, and those of the Shephelah the land of the Philistines; they shall possess the land of Ephraim and the land of Samaria, and Benjamin shall possess Gilead. The exiles of the Israelites who are in Halah shall possess Phoenicia as far as Zarephath; and the exiles of Jerusalem who are in Sepharad shall possess the towns of the Negeb. Those who have been saved shall go up to Mount Zion to rule Mount Esau; and והיתה ליהוה המלוכה (LXX: καὶ ἔσται τῷ κυρίῳ ἡ βασιλεία).[603]

Since these words depict those in one locality subduing those in another— Mount Zion will subjugate Esau[604]—the closing assertion, והיתה ליהוה המלוכה, may well have in view the vast territory that God will govern on or after "the day of the LORD" (v. 15). The context undeniably concerns geography. At the very least, it seems, the Hebrew is ambiguous, and "the realm" or "the kingdom" (so NRSV) may here be the best translation of המלוכה.

Another text that moves one to reconsider Dalman's influential generalization regarding מלכות is 1 Chr 17:14. In this verse, God says of Solomon, "I will confirm him בביתי ובמלכותי forever, and his throne shall be established forever." Here, בביתי ("in my house") is a concrete location, the temple in Jerusalem;[605] and the parallelism—בביתי ובמלכותי—encourages one to give

---

to Mark (trans. Donald H. Madvig; Atlanta: John Knox, 1976), 45–46; Graham Stanton, *The Gospels and Jesus* (2nd ed.; Oxford: Oxford University Press, 2002), 196 (God's "kingly rule" is "the time and place where God's power and will hold sway"); Sullivan, *Rethinking Realized Eschatology*, 48–60; Maren Bohlen, "Die Einlasssprüche in der Reich-Gottes-Verkündigung Jesu," *ZNW* 99 (2008): 167–84.

601. Dalman, *Words of Jesus*, 94 (cf. pp. 134–35, 148).

602. Dalman actually refers to Ps 29:29, which presumably is a misprint for Ps 22:29 (in our English versions, Ps 22:28).

603. The targum reads, "and the kingdom of the Lord [מלכותא דיוי] will be revealed over all the inhabitants of the earth."

604. Cf. vv. 17–18: "But on Mount Zion there shall be those that escape, and it shall be holy; and the house of Jacob shall take possession of those who dispossessed them. The house of Jacob shall be a fire, the house of Joseph a flame, and the house of Esau stubble; they shall burn them and consume them, and there shall be no survivor of the house of Esau."

605. So the targum; see Sara Japhet, *1 Chronik* (HTKAT; Freiburg: Herder, 2002), 317–18; Ralph W. Klein, *1 Chronicles: A Commentary* (Hermeneia; Minneapolis: Fortress, 2006), 382.

local sense also to במלכותי.[606] Is not God's מלכות headquartered in the city that houses the temple and the royal throne?

One can ask the same question of 1 Chr 28:5, where David says, according to the NRSV, "And of all my sons, for the LORD has given me many, he has chosen my son Solomon to sit upon the throne of the kingdom of the LORD [MT: מלכות יהוה; LXX: βασιλείας κυρίου] over Israel." On this George Buchanan understandably remarked, "The throne of the kingdom was the throne on which Solomon sat when he ruled from Jerusalem. This [מלכות] is not any 'reign,' because thrones are not placed in reigns. They are stationed in palaces of kings which are located in kingdoms where kings rule."[607]

Even more problematic for Dalman's generalization are the Dead Sea Scrolls, undiscovered when he wrote. The following words appear in the *Songs of the Sabbath Sacrifice*: "These are the Princes of those marvelously clothed for service, the Princes of the kingdom [מלכות], the kingdom [מלכות] of the holy ones of the king of holiness in all the heights of the sanctuaries of his glorious kingdom" (מלכות, 4Q405 frg. 23 col. II 10–12).[608] This line characterizes the upper world, where God reigns over "his glorious מלכות." This מלכות must be a place, marked out by high sanctuaries and populated by the angelic beings, known as "the princes of the kingdom" and "the holy ones of the king."[609] Column 1 of the same fragment actually refers to God's "territory" (גבול), which is either the equivalent of "his glorious kingdom" or a portion of it, such as the heavenly temple.

4Q400 frg. 1 col. II 1–4 holds more of the same. Although half of the words are missing, one can still make out the following: "[Your] lofty kingdom (מלכותכה) . . . heavens . . . the beauty of your kingdom (מלכותכה) . . . by the gates of the lofty heavens."[610] Enough of this text is extant to establish that "kingdom" must be the right translation. God's מלכות is high. It is in

---

The possessive pronoun "my" makes it all but impossible to identify "house" with the house of David.

606. For which the LXX has ἐν βασιλείᾳ αὐτοῦ ("in his [Solomon's] kingdom").

607. George Wesley Buchanan, "Meyer's Support for Weiss' Eschatology," *Journal of the Radical Reformation* 2 (1993): 48.

608. Translation by Géza Vermès, *The Complete Dead Sea Scrolls in English* (New York: Penguin, 1997), 329.

609. See Anna Maria Schwemer, "Gott als König und seine Königsherrschaft in den Sabbatliedern aus Qumran," in *Königsherrschaft Gottes* (ed. Hengel and Schwemer), 114; she finds here "räumlichen Sinn."

610. So Carol Newsom, *Songs of the Sabbath Sacrifice: A Critical Edition* (HSS; Atlanta: Scholars Press, 1985), 94. The Hebrew is as follows:

1 [. . . רום מלכות]כה
2 [. . . מרומים וחנ]
3 [. . . תפארת מלכותכה]
4 [. . . בשערי מרומי רום]

the heavens. It is beautiful. And there are entrance gates. All these are features of a place.

Unfortunately less clear is the fragmentary 4Q286 frg. 7 col. I: "and your kingdom (מלכותכה) is elevated in the midst of [. . . the coun]cil of the pure divine beings with all those who know eternal things" (lines 5–6). In this doxology, מלכות may mean what it does in 4Q400 and 4Q405: the heavenly realm that God rules.[611]

Whether that is so or not, βασιλεία, the Greek synonym of מלכות, unquestionably designates the place where God's sovereignty is fully effective—the upper world—in several Jewish texts: Wis 10:10 (Jacob was shown the βασιλεία θεοῦ);[612] *T. Job* 33:9 (ἐμοῦ [= Job's] βασιλείαν, "the holy land," "the unchangeable world" above [see v. 5]); *T. Ab.* RecLng 7:7 (τὴν βασιλείαν ἄνω, "the upper kingdom"); *3 Bar.* 11:2 (ὁ κλειδοῦχος τῆς βασιλείας τῶν οὐρανῶν, "the holder of the keys of the kingdom of heaven").[613] That Jews could think of the highest heaven as God's realm or kingdom makes perfect sense, for God was known as "the king of/over heaven(s)" (e.g., Dan 4:37; Tob 1:18 S; 13:13, 17 v.l.; 1 Esd 4:46, 58; 3 Macc 2:2; *Pss. Sol.* 2:30), and his throne was there (e.g., Ps 11:4; 103:19; Isa 66:1; Wis 18:15; *1 En.* 14:18–24; *Apoc. Ab.* 18:3; *2 En.* 20:3).

Another germane Greek text appears at the end of the second of the *Sibylline Oracles*. Here the sibyl cries out, "But you, savior, rescue me, a brazen one, from my scourges, though I have done shameless deeds. I beseech you to give me a little rest from the refrain, holy giver of manna, βασιλεῦ μεγάλης βασιλείης" (2:344–47).[614] John Collins takes the last three Greek words to mean

611. Cf. also probably 4Q287 frg. 2 11 (. . . קוד[ש בהיכלי מ[לכותיכה . . .)—"holy in the palaces of your kingdom"—and perhaps 4Q381 frg. 19 1, "in your heavens . . . your kingdom (מלכותך)."

612. Crossan remarks on this verse, "The kingdom of God is the kingdom of Wisdom eternally present, available, on the one hand, to anyone who heeds her call and, on the other, punitively transcendent to all the evil rulers of the world" (*Historical Jesus*, 290). It is much more likely that Wis 10:10—unlike 6:20, which is indeed about a sapiential kingdom (cf. 4 Macc 2:23; Philo, *Abraham* 261)—has in view the heavenly temple; see Camponovo, *Königtum*, 373–75; John J. Collins, "The Kingdom of God in the Apocrypha and Pseudepigrapha," in *Kingdom of God* (ed. Willis), 87; Otto, *Kingdom of God*, 36–37; David Winston, *The Wisdom of Solomon* (AB 43; Garden City, NY: Doubleday, 1979), 217.

613. Cf. 2 Tim 4:18 (τὴν βασιλείαν αὐτοῦ τὴν ἐπουράνιον); *Mart. Pol.* 22:3 (τὴν οὐράνιον βασιλείαν); *Diogn.* 10:2 (τὴν ἐν οὐρανῷ βασιλείαν); also Tertullian, *Bapt.* 20 (*regna caelestia*); *Gen. Rab.* 9:13 ("'Behold, it is very good' refers to the kingdom of heaven. 'And behold, it is very good' encompasses the kingdom here on earth"). It is understandable that in Christian sources "the kingdom (of God)" sometimes means "heaven"; see, for example, Justin, *Dial.* 117.3; Irenaeus, *Haer.* 3.16.4; *Apoc. Sedr.* 5:5; Chrysostom, *Hom. Matt.* 26:5; Calvin, *Institutes* 3.25.6. In like fashion, "the world to come" can, in Jewish sources, mean "the other world," as in Tg. Neof. I on Gen 4:8; see Volz, *Eschatologie*, 120–21.

614. Given that there are Christian insertions elsewhere in this oracle, we cannot exclude the possibility that these words are Christian; but the language neither demands this nor even suggests it (cf. *Sib. Or.* 3:1–7).

"king of a great kingdom."[615] This seems to be how the author of *Sib. Or.* 12:289–99 also understood them, for in rewriting 2:344–47 for his own oracle, he designated God as the "king of every kingdom" (βασιλεῦ πάσης βασιλείας).[616] Admittedly, the *Sibylline Oracles* were written in Greek, so we cannot, without qualification, draw conclusions from them about the Hebrew מלכות. Nonetheless, *Sib. Or.* 2:344–47 is yet another witness to the notion that God does not just rule, but rules over a realm, a kingdom.

The same holds for a sentence in the Song of the Three Young Men, part of the Greek additions to Daniel: "Blessed are you ἐπὶ θρόνου τῆς βασιλείας σου" (LXX Θ Dan 3:54). One might take this makarism to mean something like "Blessed are you on the throne of your royal rule, and to be extolled and highly exalted forever." The problem with this is the context. "Blessed are you in the temple of your holy glory, and to be extolled and highly glorified forever" (3:53) precedes the line about God's βασιλεία, and following the latter is this: "Blessed are you in the firmament (of heaven) (Θ: ἐν τῷ στερεώματι τοῦ οὐρανοῦ; LXX: ἐν τῷ στερεώματι), and to be sung and glorified forever" (3:56).[617] So the sentences before and after 3:54 concern God's heavenly abode, with its firmament, temple, and throne. Given this, βασιλείας σου most naturally means "your kingdom," that is, the heavenly realm. "The throne of your kingdom" is the equivalent of what we find in Ps 103:19: God's "throne in the heavens."[618]

2. None of this should surprise. Both βασιλεία and מלכות, as the dictionaries indicate, often mean "kingdom,"[619] and it takes only rudimentary acquaintance with Jewish texts to realize that God is the ruler of the realm known as "heaven," and further that, in both this age and the age to come, God's kingship cannot be separated from the people of Israel, who in turn are inextricably bound up with the fate of their land and its capital, Jerusalem.[620] It is almost inescapable, then, that many passages about God's eschatological rule, even some in which מלכות could mean "royal rule," have a territorial dimension:

615. John J. Collins, "Sibylline Oracles," *OTP* 1:353.

616. Cf. also *Sib. Or.* 3:47–48: βασιλεία μεγίστη ἀθανάτου βασιλῆος. Collins translates this as "the most great kingdom of the immortal king."

617. Dan 3:55 ("Blessed are you who look into the depths from your throne on the cherubim, and to be praised and highly exalted forever") follows v. 54 in the LXX and precedes it in Theodotion.

618. Cf. Ps 11:4; Heb 8:1; Rev 4:2. Because it would be tedious to make the argument, I simply note that in my judgment, the phrase "the throne of X's מלכות/βασιλεία" must typically refer to X's kingdom, not X's reign. See Deut 17:18; 2 Sam 7:13; 1 Chr 28:5 (see above, p. 171); 1 Macc 7:4; 10:53, 55; 11:52; 11Q19 59:17–18. One sits in a realm, not in a reign (cf. Matt 20:21).

619. Cf., for example, 2 Chr 20:30; *1 En.* 93:7; Matt 4:8; *T. Sol.* 26:4. LSJ (s.v.) lists "kingdom, dominion" as the first meaning of βασιλεία, "reign" as the third.

620. See Davies, *Gospel and the Land.*

- Isa 24:23: "The LORD of hosts will reign on Mount Zion and in Jerusalem."
- Mic 4:7: "The LORD will reign over them in Mount Zion now and for-evermore" (cf. the targum: "The kingdom [מלכותא] of the Lord will be revealed upon them on Mount Zion now and forever").
- Zech 14:9: "And the LORD will become king over all the earth" (or "the land" [הארץ]).
- Tob 13:15–16: "My soul blesses the Lord, the great king. For Jerusalem will be built as his house for all ages. How happy I will be if a remnant of my descendants should survive to see your glory and acknowledge the King of heaven."
- 1Q28b 4:25–26: "May you attend upon the service in the temple of the kingdom [מלכות]."
- *Sib. Or.* 3:767–73: God "will raise up a βασιλήιον for all ages among people. . . . From every land they will bring incense and gifts to the house of the great God."
- *2 Bar.* 40:2–4: "And after these things, he [the Messiah] will . . . protect the rest of my people who will be found in the place that I have chosen. And his dominion [רשיתה] will last forever until the world of corruption has ended and until the times which have been mentioned before have been fulfilled."
- *2 Bar.* 73:1: "After he has brought down everything which is in the world, and has sat down in eternal peace on the throne of the kingdom [מלכותא], then joy will be revealed and rest will appear."
- Tg. Isa. on 31:4: "The kingdom [מלכותא] of the Lord of hosts will be revealed to settle upon the Mount of Zion and upon its hill."[621]

In the light of texts such as these, we should hold no antecedent prejudice against the possibility that some of the Synoptic sayings about the βασιλεία have or include a local sense, so that "kingdom" is a perfectly correct render-ing. Indeed, since God typically, in the Hebrew Bible, reigns from Jerusalem or Zion,[622] would it not be exceedingly odd to learn of a Jewish prophet who, although he proclaimed God's kingdom, altogether ignored this theologou-menon or rejected it?

621. Cf. Tg. Mic 4:7–8. For the argument that in the targumim God's מלכותא typically means "kingdom" (*Reich*) rather than "royal rule" (*Königsherrschaft*), see Klaus Koch, "Offenbaren wird sich das Reich Gottes," *NTS* 25 (1979): 158–65. For the opposite view, see Bruce D. Chilton, "Regnum dei deus est," *SJT* 31 (1978): 261–70.

622. Cf. Helmut Merklein, *Die Gottesherrschaft als Handlungsprinzip: Untersuchung zur Ethik Jesu* (FB 34; Würzburg: Echter-Verlag, 1981), 111, citing Isa 24:23; Obad 21; Zech 14:9, 16.

3. Christian exegetical tradition has, however, habitually sought to separate the kingdom of God from Jewish territorial expectations.[623] The old commentators on Luke 19:11 habitually remark that the disciples not only got the time of the kingdom's coming wrong but also misconstrued that kingdom. Johann Albrecht Bengel is representative: the disciples, being Jews, thought that the Messiah would gather "the brethren scattered in the world" and lead "them to the city of Jerusalem, as the center of his kingdom," where he would "commence his reign." Jesus, however, forsook Jewish eschatology and displaced his followers' faulty opinion with "a correct view of the subject."[624] In other words, he rejected the idea of an earthly, messianic kingdom centered in Jerusalem.

This is ecclesiastical eisegesis. Luke's Jesus does not, in chapter 19, revise his disciples' conception of the kingdom but only their misconception of its imminence. The same is true in Acts 1, where the question "Lord, is this the time when you will restore the kingdom to Israel?" (v. 6) fetches this reply: "It is not for you to know the times or periods that the Father has set by his own authority" (v. 7). Jesus does not dispute that he will restore the kingdom to Israel; he says only that he will not necessarily do so immediately.[625]

The notion of an earthly reign, sometimes imagined (in accord with Rev 20) as lasting a thousand years, was popular in Christian circles until Hippolytus's *Chronicon* and Origen's exegetical writings.[626] After those two theologians, the allegorical reading of biblical prophecy became more and more the fashion, until finally belief in a temporal, millennial kingdom turned into a heresy.

After the fourth century, conceptualizing the kingdom of God as an earthly, territorial kingdom ceased to be an option for the vast majority of exegetes. Thereafter orthodox theologians and commentators usually agreed with Augustine, who closely associated the kingdom with the church invisible, that is, the elect on earth and in heaven.[627] A millennium and a half later, however,

623. For a conveniently concise treatment of the kingdom in Christian thought, see Benedict T. Viviano, *The Kingdom of God in History* (GNS 27; Wilmington, DE: Michael Glazier, 1988).

624. Johann Albrecht Bengel, *Gnomon Novi Testamenti* (2 vols.; Tübingen: Ludov. Frid. Fues, 1850), 1:327. For similar comments, see Theophylact, *Comm. Luke* ad loc. (PG 123:1024C–D) (the disciples, when approaching Jerusalem, wrongly expected the liberation of the Jewish people); Bede, *Comm. Acts* at 1:6 (CCSL 121:7–8); Trapp, *Books of the New Testament*, 335 (Jesus confutes the "misconceit" of the disciples, who expected a "temporal, earthly kingdom").

625. See further Jacob Jervell, *Luke and the People of God: A New Look at Luke-Acts* (Minneapolis: Augsburg, 1979), 75–112.

626. Note, for example, Justin, *Dial.* 80.4; Irenaeus, *Haer.* 5.32.1. See additional references and discussion in Hans Bietenhard, "The Millennial Hope in the Early Church," *SJT* 5 (1953): 12–30; Jean Daniélou, *The Theology of Jewish Christianity* (trans. and ed. John A. Baker; London: Darton, Longman & Todd; Chicago: H. Regnery, 1964), 377–404.

627. Augustine, *Civ.* 20.9. Calvin's commentary on the Synoptics makes this identification several times (see, e.g., *Harmony of the Gospels*, 2:74–78, 83–84). He also, however, can equate the kingdom with the perfected future (*Institutes* 3.20.42–43) as well as heaven (see n. 613).

when this ecclesiastical construal rightly began to suffer decline,[628] those in the shadows of Kant, Schleiermacher, and Hegel, faced with a choice between "realm" (*Reich*) and "reign" (*Herrschaft*), found the latter more pliable and so more congenial, the former less congenial because less readily translated into ethical, existential, and Christian theological categories. It also has not helped that, in recent times, we tend to favor things that are "dynamic" over things that are "static," and on that score "realm" once more loses to "reign."

That theological preferences have influenced and continue to influence discussions of ἡ βασιλεία τοῦ θεοῦ should be obvious. Dalman wrote, "There was already in existence, prior to the time of Jesus, a tendency which laid little stress on the Jewish national element in the hope for the future. This aspect of the future hope Jesus thrust still further into the background, placing the purely religious element decisively in the foreground."[629] It takes little reading between the lines to recognize that a "purely religious element" is a good thing, a "Jewish national element" not so good. One finds the same sentiment in Adolf Harnack. Although conceding that Jesus adopted the eschatological expectations of his first-century Jewish world, Harnack urged that he was at the same time highly original, for he taught that God's kingdom is "the rule of the holy God in the hearts of individuals," that is, "God himself in his power," and that "from this point of view everything that is dramatic in the external and historical sense has vanished. . . . It is not a question of angels and devils, thrones and principalities, but of God and the soul, the soul and its God."[630] No doubt many have operated and continue to operate with the unhistorical and prejudicial antithesis that Harnack here formulates so clearly. Historical criticism, however, should attempt, as far as possible, to eschew this sort of theological partiality.

4. βασιλεία τοῦ θεοῦ is an instance of a standard expression: βασιλεία + name of king. The corresponding Hebrew is מלכות/מלוכה/ממלכה/מלכות + name of king. Most frequently this construction means "the reign of so-and-so," in which case it serves to date something. So it is typically qualified by "during"

---

628. The identification remained common through the nineteenth century (e.g., Charles Hodge, *Systematic Theology* [3 vols.; New York: Charles Scribner's Sons, 1883], 2:596–97; E. C. Blackman, "The Church and the Kingdom of God: Need for Discrimination," *ExpTim* 47 [1936]: 369–73), and it still lives on in some quarters (e.g., Jean Carmignac, *Le mirage de l'eschatologie: Royauté, règne et royaume de Dieu sans eschatologie* [Paris: Letouzey et Ané, 1979]; Glasson, *Jesus and the End*).

629. Dalman, *Words of Jesus*, 137.

630. Adolf Harnack, *What Is Christianity?* (trans. Thomas Bailey Saunders; LRC; New York: Harper, 1957), 56 (italics deleted). Compare this famous statement by Friedrich Nietzsche: "The 'kingdom of heaven' is a state of the heart—not something to come 'beyond the world' or 'after death.' . . . The 'kingdom of God' is not something that men wait for: it had no yesterday and no day after tomorrow, it is not going to come at a 'millennium'—it is an expression of the heart, it is everywhere and it is nowhere" (*The Antichrist* [trans. H. L. Mencken; New York: Alfred A. Knopf, 1920], 105).

(בְּ/ἐν [e.g., Ezra 4:6; Dan 6:28]) or "until" (עַד/ἕως [e.g., Ezra 4:5; 1 Esd 5:73]) or "in year X of" (e.g., 2 Chr 15:10; Ezra 4:24; Jdt 1:1) or some other indicator of time (e.g., Jer 26:1; 27:1; 28:1). When such indicators are absent, however, the idiom usually refers to a ruler's realm, as in the following:

- Num 32:33a: "the kingdom of King Sihon of the Amorites"
- Num 32:33b: "the kingdom of King Og of Bashan, the land and its towns, with the territories of the surrounding towns"
- Deut 3:4: "sixty towns, the whole region of Argob, the kingdom of Og in Bashan"
- Deut 3:10: "all the towns of the tableland, the whole of Gilead, and all of Bashan, as far as Salecah and Edrei, towns of Og's kingdom in Bashan"
- Deut 3:13: "the rest of Gilead and all of Bashan, Og's kingdom. (The whole region of Argob: all that portion of Bashan used to be called a land of Rephaim)"
- Josh 13:12: "all the kingdom of Og in Bashan, who reigned in Ashtaroth and in Edrei"
- Josh 13:21: "all the towns of the tableland, and all the kingdom of King Sihon of the Amorites, who reigned in Heshbon"
- Josh 13:27: "the rest of the kingdom of King Sihon of Heshbon, the Jordan and its banks, as far as the lower end of the Sea of Chinnereth, eastward beyond the Jordan"
- Josh 13:30: "their territory extended from Mahanaim, through all Bashan, the whole kingdom of King Og of Bashan, and all the settlements of Jair, which are in Bashan, sixty towns"
- Josh 13:31: "the towns of the kingdom of Og in Bashan"
- 1 Chr 12:23: "these are the numbers of the divisions of the armed troops who came to David in Hebron to turn the kingdom of Saul over to him"
- Esth 3:6: "Haman plotted to destroy all the Jews, the people of Mordecai, throughout the whole kingdom of Ahasuerus"
- Esth 9:30: "the one hundred twenty-seven provinces of the kingdom of Ahasuerus"

Even a cursory reading of these passages reveals that in most of them the primary denotation is territory. So when we find Synoptic sayings in which the idiom "βασιλεία + name of king (God)" does not serve to date events, should we not at least ask whether some of them may not have local sense?

5. The Synoptics sometimes use βασιλεία without reference to God's kingdom:

- Mark 3:24: "If a kingdom is divided against itself, that kingdom cannot stand."
- Mark 6:23: "Whatever you ask me, I will give you, even half of my kingdom."
- Mark 13:8 (par. Matt 24:7; Luke 21:10): "For nation will rise against nation, and kingdom against kingdom."
- Matt 4:8 // Luke 4:5 (Q): "The devil took him to a very high mountain and showed him all the kingdoms of the world."
- Matt 12:25–26 // Luke 11:17–18 (Q, RSV): "Every kingdom divided against itself is laid waste. . . . If Satan . . . is divided against himself, how will his kingdom stand?"
- Luke 19:12 (RSV): "A nobleman went into a far country to receive a kingdom."
- Luke 19:15 (RSV): "When he returned, having received the kingdom . . ."

BDAG (s.v.) lists all but the last two under the definition "territory ruled by a king, kingdom." Those two verses, however, have uncertain connotations. In both cases, thinking in terms of territory would make just as much sense.[631] The upshot is this: if we set aside for a moment the sayings about ἡ βασιλεία τοῦ θεοῦ, the dominant meaning of βασιλεία in the Synoptics is "territory ruled by a king, kingdom." Is this not further impetus for asking whether a local or territorial dimension is likely to be absent from all the other texts?

6. A close review of the Synoptics reveals that, in at least several verses, ἡ βασιλεία τοῦ θεοῦ sounds very much like a place. In Matt 13:41–42, angels remove evildoers from the Son of Man's βασιλεία (συλλέξουσιν ἐκ τῆς βασιλείας αὐτοῦ) and deposit them in "the furnace of fire, where there will be weeping and gnashing of teeth." Can the βασιλεία here be anything other than a locale? In Mark 14:25, Jesus foretells drinking new wine in the future βασιλεία. His prophetic promise almost inevitably conjures up the image of people reclining at a table, which is an object located somewhere in space (cf. Luke 22:16). The related Luke 22:29–30 offers more of the same: "I confer on you . . . a βασιλεία, so that you may eat and drink at my table in my βασιλεία." Surely these words advert to a time and place not yet arrived,[632] as do the words of an anonymous dinner guest in Luke 14:15: "Blessed is anyone who will eat bread in the kingdom of God!" And then there is Matt 8:11–12 // Luke 13:28–29, where crowds come from afar while Abraham, Isaac, Jacob, and their guests feast in the βασιλεία. The mind's eye envisages that βασιλεία as a place with a central location. In the Lukan (Q?) context, moreover, 13:28–29 follows vv.

631. In these two verses, "reign" and "realm" cannot, I suspect, be usefully distinguished.
632. Cf. 'Abot R. Nat. B 27: "eat and drink in the world to come."

22–27, which liken salvation to entering through a narrow door and losing salvation to facing a door firmly shut. Here the βασιλεία is like a house (cf. Matt 25:1–13) or a city.

Matthew 16:19, where Matthew's Jesus gives Peter "the keys of the βασιλεία of heaven," conjures a similar picture. Is not the apostle a gatekeeper before the entrance to a kingdom, just as in traditional images of him standing before the doorway to heaven?[633] Again, what of Mark 9:47, where εἰσελθεῖν εἰς τὴν βασιλείαν ("to enter the kingdom") stands over against βληθῆναι εἰς τὴν γέενναν ("to be thrown into hell [lit., Gehenna]") (cf. Matt 8:11–12 // Luke 13:28–29 [Q])? The miserable fate of the condemned, which is that they are to be flung into Gehenna, the name of a valley beside Jerusalem, moves one to conceptualize its antithesis in like fashion: one goes to a good place instead of a bad place.

In Matt 25:34, the βασιλεία has been "prepared . . . from the foundation of the world" (ἡτοιμασμένην . . . ἀπὸ καταβολῆς κόσμου). This is a divine passive, so the meaning is "prepared (by God) from the foundation of the world." Now, it makes perfect sense to say that God has prepared a place.[634] What, however, would be the sense of saying that God prepared the divine royal rule from the foundation of the world? Similarly, what are we to make of Matt 23:13, "you lock people out of τὴν βασιλείαν τῶν οὐρανῶν," if τὴν βασιλείαν means heaven's "rule" or "reign" as opposed to "realm"? Is not the latter, which matches the spatial imagery, the much more credible translation? And what of those sayings in which possessive personal pronouns modify ἡ βασιλεία: Mark 10:14 (τῶν γὰρ τοιούτων ἐστὶν ἡ βασιλεία τοῦ θεοῦ, "for it is to such as these that the kingdom of God belongs"); Luke 6:20 // Matt 5:3 (Q) (ὑμετέρα ἐστὶν ἡ βασιλεία τοῦ θεοῦ, "for yours is the kingdom of God"); Matt 5:10 (αὐτῶν ἐστιν ἡ βασιλεία τῶν οὐρανῶν, "for theirs is the kingdom of heaven")? "How can one really speak of persons 'possessing' or 'owning' the Kingdom of heaven . . . if the Kingdom of heaven is taken in the sense of the rule of God?"[635]

7. Mark 9:47 is not the only Synoptic text about entering the kingdom. Synoptic sayings 8, 9, 10, 11, 26, 27, 45 listed at the beginning of this excursus employ the idiom εἰσελθεῖν εἰς τὴν βασιλείαν.[636] As a group, these logia appear

---

633. Cf. 3 Bar. 11:2; Rev 21:12–13, 15, 21, 25.

634. Cf. John 14:3: ἐὰν . . . ἑτοιμάσω τόπον ὑμῖν ("if I . . . prepare a place for you"); Did. 10:5: "From the four winds gather the sanctified church into your kingdom, which you have prepared for it [εἰς τὴν σὴν βασιλείαν ἣν ἡτοίμασας αὐτῇ]."

635. Barclay M. Newman Jr., "Translating 'the Kingdom of God' and 'the Kingdom of Heaven' in the New Testament," BT 25 (1974): 403.

636. Cf. John 3:5; Acts 14:22; Matt 21:31 (with προάγω); also Gos. Thom. 22, 114; Hermas, Sim. 9.12.8; 9.15.2; 9.16.2; 9.20.2–3; Justin, 1 Apol. 61.4–5; 2 Clem. 6:9; as well as the related expressions "enter life" (Matt 19:17; Mark 9:43, 45 RSV), "enter into . . . joy" (Matt 25:21, 23 RSV), "enter by the narrow gate/door" (Matt 7:13 // Luke 13:24 [Q] RSV), "[enter] into the wedding banquet" (Matt 25:10), "entry into the eternal kingdom" (2 Pet 1:11), and "enter

to be modeled upon the traditional idiom "to enter the land (of Canaan)," as in, for example, LXX Exod 12:25 (εἰσέλθητε εἰς τὴν γῆν); Lev 19:23 (εἰσέλθητε εἰς τὴν γῆν); Num 15:2 (εἰσέλθητε εἰς τὴν γῆν); Deut 1:8 (εἰσπορευθέντες κληρονομήσατε τὴν γῆν); 4:1 (εἰσελθόντες κληρονομήσητε τὴν τῆν); 6:18 (εἰσέλθῃς καὶ κληρονομήσῃς τὴν γῆν); 16:20 (εἰσελθόντες κληρονομήσητε τὴν γῆν); 27:3 (εἰσέλθητε εἰς τὴν γῆν); Judg 18:9 (ἐλθεῖν τοῦ κληρονομῆσαι τὴν γῆν); and T. Mos. 2:1 (*intrabunt . . . in terram*); T. Levi 12:5 (εἰσῆλθον εἰς γῆν).[637]

Particularly interesting are those passages that, like Synoptic sayings 8, 26, 27, 45, warn of someone not entering the land as a consequence of moral failure: Num 20:24 ("For he [Aaron] shall not enter the land [LXX: οὐ μὴ εἰσέλθητε εἰς τὴν γῆν; cf. Matt 5:20] that I have given to the Israelites, because you rebelled against my command at the waters of Meribah"); Deut 4:21 ("The LORD was angry with me [Moses] because of you, and he vowed that I should . . . not enter the good land [LXX: μὴ εἰσέλθω εἰς τὴν γῆν] that the LORD your God is giving for your possession"); Ezek 13:9 ("My hand will be against the prophets who see false visions and utter lying divinations; they shall not be in the council of my people, nor be enrolled

the city" (Rev 22:14). In my view, some sayings that do not use ἔρχομαι are nonetheless about entering the kingdom—for example, Mark 12:34 ("You are not far from [entering] the kingdom of God"); Luke 12:31 // Matt 6:33 (Q) ("Strive for [i.e., strive to enter] his kingdom, and these things will be given to you as well"); Luke 9:62 ("No one who puts a hand to the plow and looks back is fit for [i.e., fit to enter] the kingdom of God"). This sort of implicit abbreviation is common in the sayings about the kingdom of God (and not only, as long recognized, in the βασιλεία sayings that introduce some of the parables). Thus "The kingdom of God has come near" (Mark 1:15) means "(The time of) the kingdom of God has come near." "Whoever does not receive the kingdom of God as a little child will never enter it" (Mark 10:15) means "Whoever does not receive (the good news of) the kingdom of God as a little child will never enter it." "From the days of John the Baptist until now the kingdom of God has suffered violence" (Matt 11:12 // Luke 16:16 [Q]) means "From the days of John the Baptist until now the (sons of the) kingdom of God have suffered violence." "I will give you the keys of the kingdom of heaven" (Matt 16:19) means "I will give you the keys of (the gate or door of) the kingdom of heaven." "Then the kingdom of heaven will be like this. Ten bridesmaids . . ." (Matt 25:1) means "Then (the last judgment that will inaugurate) the kingdom of heaven will be like this. Ten bridesmaids. . . ." Compare how the rabbis abbreviate "take up the yoke of the kingdom" (as in *m. Ber.* 2:2; *Tanḥ.* Buber Lekh-Lekha 1; *y. Ber.* 4b [2:1]; *b. Ber.* 13a–b; 14b; 61b) with "take up the kingdom" (as in *Tanḥ.* Buber Lekh-Lekha 1; *y. Ber.* 4a [2:1]; *b. Ber.* 10b). I leave to the side here the debate as to whether any of the sayings about entering the kingdom go back to Jesus. This is denied by Friedrich W. Horn ("Die synoptischen Einlaßsprüche," ZNW 87 [1996]: 187–203), whereas Bohlen ("Einlasssprüche," 167–84) and Laaksonen (*Jesus und das Land*, 305–16) argue otherwise.

637. This insight goes back to Hans Windisch, "Die Sprüche vom Eingehen in das Reich Gottes," ZNW 27 (1928): 163–92. Windisch also observed parallels—to my mind, less significant and probably parasitic upon the idiom of entering the land—with traditions about entering the temple (e.g., Ps 24) and the city of Jerusalem (e.g., Isa 26:2–3). Also of lesser or even no significance is the idea of entering the assembly in Deut 23:2–3, although this parallel is emphasized by Klaus Berger, *Formgeschichte des Neuen Testaments* (Heidelberg: Quelle & Meyer, 1984), 183–84.

in the register of the house of Israel, nor shall they enter the land of Israel" [LXX: εἰς τὴν γῆν τοῦ Ἰσραηλ οὐκ εἰσελεύσονται; cf. Mark 10:23]); 20:38 ("I will purge out the rebels among you, and those who transgress against me; I will bring them out of the land where they reside as aliens, but they shall not enter the land of Israel" [LXX: εἰς τὴν γῆν τοῦ Ἰσραηλ οὐκ εἰσελεύσονται; cf. Mark 10:23]).[638]

That some of Jesus' followers understood God's מלכות or βασιλεία to be analogous to the promised land and so imagined it as a place or like a place also follows from the phrase "to inherit the kingdom" (κληρονομεῖν τὴν βασιλείαν), which appears in Matt 25:34; 1 Cor 6:9–10; 15:50; Gal 5:19–21 (cf. Jas 2:5: κληρονόμους τῆς βασιλείας; Ign. Eph. 16:1: βασιλείαν θεοῦ οὐ κληρονομήσουσιν; Acts Thom. 136: κληρονόμον τῆς αὐτοῦ βασιλείας).[639] This expression almost certainly was formulated on analogy with the phrase "to inherit the land" (e.g., Num 33:54; Deut 1:8; 6:18; 16:20; Josh 1:6; Ps 37:11; Tob 4:12). Inheriting the kingdom is like taking possession of the land.

If, incidentally, the sayings about entering and inheriting the kingdom are modeled upon biblical sentences about entering and inheriting the land of Canaan, they promote a new exodus typology.[640] That is, they presuppose, as LXX Isa 61:7 has it, that the redeemed "will inherit the land a second time" (ἐκ δευτέρας κληρονομήσουσιν τὴν γῆν), and that there will be, in the words of b. Sanh. 98b, "a second entry" (שניה ביאה).[641]

8. Jonathan Pennington, in an important recent study, has reopened the question of why Matthew, unlike the other evangelists, or the authors of the rest of the New Testament for that matter, prefers the expression "kingdom of heaven" (ἡ βασιλεία τῶν οὐρανῶν [32×]) over "kingdom of God" (ἡ βασιλεία

638. Marcus ("Kingly Power of God") demonstrates that εἰσελθεῖν εἰς τὴν βασιλείαν need not require a spatial reading: one can enter into an action. Nonetheless, he begins with Dalman's equation of מלכות/βασιλεία with "rule," which I have disputed; and I prefer a different analysis partly because of the comparisons in Mark 9:47; 10:25; Matt 7:21. In Mark 9:47, being thrown into Gehenna is the opposite of εἰσελθεῖν κ.τ.λ. In Mark 10:25, εἰσελθεῖν κ.τ.λ. is compared to a camel going through the eye of a needle. In Matt 7:21, those who do not enter εἰς τὴν βασιλείαν are told to "depart" (ἀποχωρεῖτε). In each case, εἰσελθεῖν κ.τ.λ. is set over against movement into or from a place.

639. Compare also the phrase "inherit (eternal) life," as in Pss. Sol. 14:10; 1 En. 40:9; Matt 19:29; Mark 10:17; Luke 10:25; 18:18; Sib. Or. frg. 3 47.

640. The βασιλεία saying in Luke 11:20 // Matt 12:28 (Q) ("But if it is by the finger of God that I cast out the demons, then the kingdom of God has come to you") indisputably has its background in Mosaic and exodus traditions; see Allison, Intertextual Jesus, 53–57; Martin Hengel, "Der Finger und die Herrschaft Gottes in Lk 11,20," in La Main de Dieu. Die Hand Gottes (ed. René Kieffer and Jan Bergman; WUNT 94; Tübingen: Mohr Siebeck, 1997), 87–106.

641. Cf. also Isa 60:21; 1 En. 5:6–8; Matt 5:5; m. Sanh. 10:1; and perhaps m. Qidd. 1:10. Is it worth noting that just as there are texts in which one sees the kingdom (Mark 9:1; John 3:3; Gos. Thom. 113) and in which the kingdom is paired with "life" (see pp. 186–87), so too are there texts in which one sees the land (e.g., Gen 13:15; Num 13:18; 14:23; Deut 1:35) and in which the land is paired with life (e.g., Deut 30:20; 32:47)?

τοῦ θεοῦ [4×]).[642] The standard explanation, which goes back to Dalman,[643] is that Matthew was here indebted to Jewish tradition, in which "heaven" had already become for the scrupulous a reverential periphrasis for "God." Pennington, however, convincingly argues, among other things, (a) that there is little evidence from the first century CE or before for avoiding the generic "God" (אלוהים or θεός [Matthew himself uses θεός over fifty times]); (b) that Dalman failed to distinguish between a circumlocution motivated by pious avoidance of the divine name and the rhetorical use of epithets (e.g., Rock, Father, Shepherd, the Ancient of Days, the First and the Last, the Power); (c) that while "kingdom of God" and "kingdom of heaven" in Matthew denote the same reality, they have different connotations, the latter serving the Matthean theme of the contrast between heaven and earth;[644] and (d) that, apart from the sayings about the "kingdom of heaven," "heaven" in Matthew always has spatial sense (as in "Our Father in heaven" [6:9]); so "to deny a spatial sense to ἡ βασιλεία τῶν οὐρανῶν would require interpreting οὐρανός in this phrase as bearing no relation to the rest of the spatial uses of οὐρανός throughout Matthew—especially the spatial sense of the many references to the Father in heaven."[645] Pennington elaborates:

> Both the source genitive and attributive genitive understandings of ἡ βασιλεία τοῦ οὐρανοῦ retain some sense of territory and space. As a source genitive, the kingdom is one which comes *from heaven* and whose origin is *in heaven*. As an attributive genitive, the kingdom is one that is characterized as having a heavenly nature, referring to the realm of heaven in distinction to the earth. . . . The addition of τῶν οὐρανῶν to βασιλεία in Matthew makes it inevitable that some sense of a spatial understanding of the kingdom is communicated: understanding ἡ βασιλεία τῶν οὐρανῶν as meaning only the rule or reign of God in a non-spatial sense fails to account for the importance of Matthew's ascription of the kingdom as τῶν οὐρανῶν.[646]

If one concurs, as I do, with Pennington's main conclusions, then one of the earliest Jewish-Christian interpreters of the Jesus tradition understood most of its references to God's βασιλεία to connote a spatial or local sense.

9. The beatitudes in the Sermon on the Mount confirm Pennington's work. Matthew's Jesus says in 5:3, "Blessed are the poor [πτωχοί] in spirit, for theirs is the kingdom of heaven." Then, in 5:5, borrowing from Ps 37:11, he says,

---

642. Jonathan T. Pennington, *Heaven and Earth in the Gospel of Matthew* (NovTSup 126; Leiden: Brill, 2007; repr. Grand Rapids: Baker Academic, 2009).

643. Dalman, *Words of Jesus*, 91–95.

644. Pennington writes, "Matthew's choice to regularly depict the kingdom as τῶν οὐρανῶν is designed to emphasize that God's kingdom is not like earthly kingdoms, stands over against them, and will eschatologically replace them (on earth)" (*Heaven and Earth*, 321 [italics deleted]).

645. Ibid., 297.

646. Ibid., 296.

"Blessed are the meek [πραεῖς], for they will inherit the earth [or 'the land'] [τὴν γῆν]."[647] The parallelism between these two verses is obvious. In the LXX, πραΰς as well as πτωχός translate עָנָו and עָנִי; and commentators have often taken "the poor in spirit" and "the meek" to be nearly synonymous, both denoting humility.[648] It is noteworthy that v. 5 immediately follows v. 3 in parts of the textual tradition (D 33 lat syᶜ boᵐˢˢ Or Eus), an order that, if original, suggests that v. 5 was formulated precisely in order to explicate v. 3. If, instead, the original order matched the conventional versification (v. 3 → v. 4 → v. 5), then presumably a scribe, observing the correlations between v. 3 and v. 5, put them side by side, displacing v. 4. In either event, it is natural to regard "theirs is the kingdom of heaven" and "they will inherit the earth [or 'the land']" as saying much the same thing, or at least to suppose that "the promise of the earth makes clear that the kingdom of heaven includes a this-worldly earth."[649] So whether αὐτοὶ κληρονομήσουσιν τὴν γῆν means that the meek will inherit "the earth" in general or "the land (of Israel)" in particular, 5:3 and 5:5 show us that Matthew or a contributor to his tradition thought of possessing the kingdom of God as inheriting a place.[650]

10. In Luke's account of the passion, a repentant criminal crucified with Jesus entreats him, "Remember me when you come into your kingdom [ὅταν ἔλθῃς εἰς τὴν βασιλείαν σου]" (23:42).[651] "Your kingdom" is presumably the same as God's kingdom.[652] Jesus responds, in the next verse, with the comforting promise "Today you will be with me in Paradise" (παράδεισος). Now, given that Jesus does not correct or reject the criminal's request,[653] given that "paradise" seems to be Jesus' substitute for "your kingdom," and given that "paradise" is always, in Jewish literature, a place—the garden Adam and Eve lived in, the garden the just enter at death, the garden that the redeemed will

647. The Latin parallel to *Did.* 3:7 in *Doctrina XII Apostolorum* (ed. Schlecht, p. 102) has the meek possessing the *sanctam terram*, "holy land," and this accords with the intertext behind Matt 5:5, which is Ps 37:11.

648. See Ulrich Luz, *Matthew: A Commentary* (trans. James E. Crouch; ed. Helmut Koester; 3 vols.; Hermeneia; Minneapolis: Fortress, 2001–2007), 1:190–94.

649. Ibid., 1:195.

650. See further Joel Willitts, *Matthew's Messianic Shepherd-King: In Search of "The Lost Sheep of the House of Israel"* (BZNW 147; Berlin: de Gruyter, 2007), who finds in Matthew a concrete, territorial expectation. Note also that whereas Luke 22:28–30 speaks of the disciples sitting on thrones in the kingdom, Matt 19:28 speaks of them sitting on thrones in the παλιγγενεσία, "the renewal of all things," a likely synonym of the rabbinic "the world to come," which is a time and place; see Jonathan T. Pennington, "Heaven, Earth, and a New Genesis: Theological Cosmology in Matthew," in *Cosmology and the New Testament* (ed. Jonathan T. Pennington and Sean M. McDonough; London: T & T Clark, 2008), 40–43.

651. So 𝔓⁷⁵ B L saᵐˢˢ boᵖᵗ Chr Hil Or, which NA²⁷ prints. The variant, ἔλθῃς ἐν τῇ βασιλείᾳ σου, seems to envisage the parousia.

652. Cf. Luke 1:33; also Matt 13:41; 16:28; 20:21; John 18:36; Eph 5:5; Rev 11:15.

653. Jesus' words—"Today you will be with me in paradise"—do not gainsay the criminal's expectation, only specify what the latter leaves open (ὅταν).

enjoy in the world to come—we have here evidence that Luke, like Matthew, could think of the kingdom as a locale, indeed as something akin to what later Christians meant by "heaven."[654]

11. The *Gospel of Thomas* contains nineteen sayings about "the kingdom" (ⲦⲘⲚⲦⲉⲣⲟ) or "the kingdom of the/my Father" or "the kingdom of heaven."[655] Not a single one puts the kingdom in the future. Moreover, when the disciples inquire when the kingdom will come, Jesus rejects their question as uninformed (see 113). All of this reflects the redactional theology of the editor, who eliminates an apocalyptic conception of the kingdom.

In three other respects, however, *Thomas* preserves traditional discourse about the kingdom of God. (a) Like the Synoptics, it introduces several parables with "The kingdom (of heaven/the Father) is like . . ." (20, 57, 76, 96, 97, 98, 107, 109). (b) The Jesus of *Thomas* speaks of entering the kingdom (22, 99, 114). (c) In accord with this last fact, and of importance for this excursus, *Thomas*, like the Synoptic tradition, conceptualizes the kingdom as a place. Not only can one enter it, but also one can come from and return to it (49; cf. 50) as well as be far from it (82). Further, "the place [ⲠⲦⲟⲠⲟⲥ] of life" (4) and "a place [ⲦⲟⲠⲟⲥ] for yourselves in rest" (60; cf. 51) seem to be synonyms for "kingdom," while "enter the places [ⲉⲚⲦⲟⲠⲟⲥ] of my Father" (64) is the equivalent of "enter the kingdom."[656]

12. Although much Christian theology eventually made the exegetical mistake of more or less identifying the kingdom with the church, sources up until the fourth century often envision the kingdom as a future time and place. In many of these, moreover, ἡ βασιλεία and *regnum* seem to mean above all "realm" or "kingdom."[657] In this respect, these later, extracanonical texts preserve, in my judgment, an original feature of the Jesus tradition. Consider the following:[658]

654. See Lehtipuu, *Afterlife Imagery*, 254–55, 280–84; Witherington, *Jesus, Paul, and the End*, 60–61; for another view of Luke 23:42, see Marcus, "Kingly Power of God," 670–71.

655. *Gos. Thom.* 3 (cf. Luke 17:20–21), 20 (cf. Mark 4:30–31), 22 (*bis*; cf. Mark 9:47; 10:14, 15), 27, 46 (cf. Mark 10:14, 15; Matt 11:11 // Luke 7:28 [Q]), 49 (cf. Matt 19:12?), 54 (cf. Matt 5:3 // Luke 6:20 [Q]), 57 (cf. Matt 13:24), 76 (cf. Matt 13:45), 82, 96 (cf. Matt 13:33 // Luke 13:20–21 [Q]), 97, 98, 99 (the parallel in Mark 3:35 does not have "kingdom"), 107 (the parallel in Matt 18:10–14 // Luke 15:3–7 [Q] does not have "kingdom"), 109 (cf. Matt 13:44), 113 (cf. Luke 17:20–21), 114. Only five of these do not seem to be variants of sayings known from the Synoptics: 27, 82, 97, 98, 114. Unlike the Coptic, the fragmentary Greek version of *Thomas* attested in P.Oxy. 1, 654, 655 employs the expression "the kingdom of God" (ἡ βασιλεία τοῦ θεοῦ in sayings 3, 27).

656. See further Hans Kvalbein, "The Kingdom of the Father in the Gospel of Thomas," in *The New Testament and Early Christian Literature in Greco-Roman Context: Studies in Honor of David E. Aune* (ed. John Fotopoulos; NovTSup 122; Leiden: Brill, 2006), 203–28.

657. According to Everett Ferguson ("The Kingdom of God in Early Patristic Literature," in *Kingdom of God* [ed. Willis], 192), in early patristic literature, "realm" as opposed to "reign" is the prevailing meaning of βασιλεία.

658. For additional references and discussion, see Ferguson, "Kingdom of God," 191–208; Robert Frick, *Die Geschichte des Reich-Gottes-Gedankens in der alten Kirche bis zu Origenes*

- *Did.* 9:4: "May your church be gathered together from the ends of the earth into your kingdom" (cf. 10:5).
- Papias *apud* Eusebius, *Hist. eccl.* 3.39.12: "There will be a period of some thousand years after the resurrection of the dead, and the kingdom of Christ will be set up in material form on this very earth."
- Cerinthus *apud* Gaius *apud* Eusebius, *Hist. eccl.* 3.28.2: "After the resurrection, there will be a kingdom of Christ . . . in Jerusalem."
- Pol. *Phil.* 5:3: "Neither fornicators nor effeminate persons nor those who defile themselves with men will inherit the kingdom of God, nor those who do perverse things."[659]
- *4 Ezra* 2:10: "Tell my people that I will give them the kingdom of Jerusalem, which I was going to give to Israel."
- Hegesippus *apud* Eusebius, *Hist. eccl.* 3.19–20.5: the grandsons of Jude told Domitian that Christ's kingdom "was neither of the world nor earthly, but heavenly and angelic, and that it would be at the end of the world, when he would come in glory to judge the living and the dead and to reward all according to their deeds."
- Irenaeus, *Haer.* 5.33.3: "The predicted blessing belongs unquestionably to the times of the kingdom, when the righteous, upon rising from the dead, will rule, and when the creation, having been renovated and set free, will become fruitful with an abundance of all kinds of food, from the dew of heaven, and from the fertility of the earth" (cf. 5.34.2).
- Tertullian, *Marc.* 5.10: "The resurrection is one thing, and the kingdom is another. The resurrection is first and the kingdom after. So we say that the flesh rises again and that when it is changed it obtains the kingdom."
- Pseudo-Justin, *Quaest. et resp.* 120: according to the Scriptures, the kingdom of God is "not simply the resurrection, but the renewal [ἀπο-κατάστασιν] after the resurrection" (PG 6:1369C).
- *T. Isaac* 8:5: "Blessed is everyone who manifests mercy on the memorial day of the father of fathers, our father Abraham and our father Isaac, for each of them will have a dwelling in the kingdom of heaven. . . . Whatever person has manifested mercy in the name of my beloved Isaac, behold I will give him to you in the kingdom of heaven and he will be present with them at the first moment of the millennial banquet to celebrate with them in the everlasting light of the kingdom of our Master and our God and our King and our Savior, Jesus the Messiah" (cf. 6:13).

---

und Augustin (BZNW 6; Gießen: Töpelmann, 1928); G. W. H. Lampe, "Some Notes on the Significance of ΒΑΣΙΛΕΙΑ ΤΟΥ ΘΕΟΥ, ΒΑΣΙΛΕΙΑ ΧΡΙΣΤΟΥ, in the Greek Fathers," *JTS* 49 (1948): 58–73.

659. Cf. 1 Cor 6:9; and on inheriting the kingdom, see above, pp. 179–81.

13. Two Synoptic sayings usually assigned to Q take up traditional eschatological beliefs involving the land of Israel. In the first Q text, Matt 8:11–12 //
Luke 13:28–29, crowds come from east and west and, in Luke at least, from
north and south, whereupon they eat in the kingdom of God. Whether these
multitudes were, for whoever first composed the prophetic warning, Jews from
the Diaspora (as I think) or Gentiles (as most exegetes suppose), the saying
assumes that the eschatological scenario will involve throngs streaming to a
central location. Within a Jewish context, that location can only be the land
of Israel and its capital, Jerusalem.

The second Q text is Matt 19:28 // Luke 22:29–30, where Jesus avows that
some of his followers will sit on thrones and judge or rule the twelve tribes of
Israel. The prediction assumes the end of exile and the return of those tribes
to the land of Israel.

Other sayings in which the kingdom has a local sense probably presuppose the sort of territorial eschatology that these two Q sayings exhibit.
Many or most ancient Jews would not have distinguished clearly between
God's kingdom and David's kingdom,[660] and the latter was inevitably a
political and territorial reality. If Jesus ever spoke of the kingdom of God
as a place, as the Synoptics more than suggest he did, we can be sure that
his Jewish hearers would have thought in terms of the land of Israel, its
capital, and the temple, which together "were the sacred centre of the earth"
that "would one day attract all peoples."[661] Once his sayings became the
property of Gentile churches, alternative, nonterritorial readings could
and did come into being. That, however, tells us next to nothing about the
historical Jesus.

14. The Synoptics sometimes associate the kingdom of God with "eternal
life" (ζωὴ αἰώνιος) or, more simply, "life" (ζωή). A glance at the synonymous
parallelism in Mark 9:43–47 reveals that "to enter life" (εἰσελθεῖν εἰς τὴν ζωήν
[vv. 43, 45]) is, for Mark's Jesus, the rough equivalent of "to enter the kingdom
of God" (εἰσελθεῖν εἰς τὴν βασιλείαν τοῦ θεοῦ [v. 47]):

> (v. 43) If your hand causes you to stumble,
>   cut it off;
>   it is better for you to enter life maimed

---

660. Cf. 1 Chr 17:14; 28:5; 29:23; 2 Chr 13:8; *Pss. Sol.* 17:3–21; Mark 11:10. It is worth remembering that "with the accession of David to the throne, . . . the king was understood to reign as
Yahweh's representative and be under Yahweh's suzerainty. In other words, the monarchy was
looked upon as the concrete manifestation of Yahweh's rule" (C. C. Caragounis, "Kingdom of
God/Heaven," *DJG* 418). See further Rowe, *God's Kingdom*, 59–62. In Chronicles, Solomon
sits on the Lord's throne. As for the rabbis, Solomon Schechter wrote, "The two ideas of the
kingdom of heaven, over which God reigns, and the kingdom of Israel, in which the Messiah
holds the scepter," became for the rabbis "almost identical" (*Aspects of Rabbinic Theology*
[New York: Schocken Books, 1961], 103).
    661. Lohmeyer, *Lord of the Temple*, 64.

> than to have two hands
>> and to go to hell. . . .
> (v. 45) And if your foot causes you to stumble,
>> cut it off;
>>> it is better for you to enter life lame
>>>> than to have two feet
>>>>> and to be thrown into hell.
> (v. 47) And if your eye causes you to stumble,
>> tear it out;
>>> it is better for you to enter the kingdom of God with one eye
>>>> than to have two eyes
>>>>> and to be thrown into hell.

Mark 10:17–25 holds the same lesson. After a rich man asks what he must do in order to gain eternal life and then fails to comply with the answer, Jesus mourns that it is easier for a camel to go through the eye of a needle than for one with great possessions to enter the kingdom. So to enter the kingdom is to have eternal life, and to fail to enter the kingdom is to lose eternal life (cf. Mark 10:30; Matt 19:17). Similarly, in the account of the last judgment in Matt 25:31–46, the happy future of the just is, in v. 34, to inherit the kingdom prepared for them from the foundation of the world, whereas, in v. 46, it is to enter eternal life.

The alternation between "kingdom" and "life" also shows itself when one places Mark 9:47 beside its Matthean equivalent:

Matthew 18:9	Mark 9:47
And if your eye causes you to stumble,	And if your eye causes you to stumble,
tear it out	tear it out;
and throw it away;	
it is better for you	it is better for you
to enter life	to enter the kingdom of God
with one eye	with one eye
than to have two eyes	than to have two eyes
and to be thrown into the hell of fire.	and to be thrown into hell.

On the theory of Markan priority, Matthew replaced Mark's εἰσελθεῖν εἰς τὴν βασιλείαν τοῦ θεοῦ with εἰς τὴν ζωὴν εἰσελθεῖν.

The intersection of meaning between kingdom and eschatological life, also apparent in the *Gospel of Thomas*,[662] helps account for one of the leading features of the Fourth Gospel. According to John 20:31, the Gospel's very purpose is that people find ζωή in Jesus' name, and ζωή is John's favorite

---

662. In response to Peter's assertion that "women are not worthy of life," Jesus says that "every woman who will make herself male will enter the kingdom of heaven" (*Gos. Thom.* 114).

comprehensive term for salvation (35×; contrast Matt: 7×; Mark: 4×; Luke: 5×). So ζωή (αἰώνιος)[663] in John, like ἡ βασιλεία τοῦ θεοῦ in the Synoptics, sums up the telos of Jesus' advent.

John was familiar with sayings about the kingdom of God.[664] He presumably also knew the tradition that ἡ βασιλεία τοῦ θεοῦ was the central theme of Jesus' preaching (cf. Mark 1:14–15; Matt 10:7–8 // Luke 10:9 [Q]). If so, then the Fourth Evangelist deliberately displaced ἡ βασιλεία τοῦ θεοῦ with ἡ ζωή (αἰώνιος). Put otherwise, he did systematically what Matthew did once: he turned "kingdom of God" into "(eternal) life."[665] So when John's Jesus, in 3:3–16, unfolds the meaning of his own statements about "the kingdom of God" (vv. 3, 5), it does not startle us that his subject becomes "eternal life" (vv. 15–16). Nor is one surprised that what is true of the kingdom in the Synoptics is true of "(eternal) life" in the Fourth Gospel: it is both a promise for the future as well as a present reality (5:24, 29; 6:40; 11:25); it is like a possession (3:15, 16; 5:40; 6:47; 10:10); it is a gift of God (5:21; 6:27, 33, 63; 10:28); it is something that one can "see" (3:36); and it is the antithesis of eschatological death (3:16, 36; 5:24).

How does this bear on one's understanding of ἡ βασιλεία τοῦ θεοῦ in the Jesus tradition? Ζωή (αἰώνιος)/(עולם) חיי was a standard Jewish expression for the future lot of the righteous, for the state that the redeemed will enjoy after death or in the eschatological future.[666] So if, in parts of the Jesus tradition,

663. "Life" and "eternal life" are usually synonyms in John; see J. G. Van der Watt, "The Use of αἰώνιος in the Concept ζωὴ αἰώνιος in John's Gospel," *NovT* 31 (1989): 217–28. The same is true of the Synoptics.

664. See John 3:3, 5; 18:36. The first two are variants of the saying also found in Matt 18:3; Mark 10:15; *Gos. Thom.* 22, 46. For discussion, see Hans Kvalbein, "The Kingdom of God and the Kingship of Christ in the Fourth Gospel," in *Neotestamentica et Philonica: Studies in Honor of Peter Borgen* (ed. David E. Aune, Torrey Seland, and Jarl Henning Ulrichsen; NovTSup 106; Leiden: Brill, 2003), 215–32.

665. So also, among others, John Ashton, *Understanding the Fourth Gospel* (Oxford: Clarendon, 1991), 218 (John replaced "the kingdom of God" with "a term more suggestive of the benefits that follow upon the acceptance of the gospel"); Frey, *Eschatologische Verkündigung*, 254–70; E. F. Scott, "Life," in *A Dictionary of Christ and the Gospels* (ed. James Hastings; 2 vols.; Edinburgh: T & T Clark, 1908), 2:31 (in John, "the future 'kingdom' becomes simply 'life'").

666. See, for example, Dan 12:2 (MT: חיי עולם; LXX: ζωὴν αἰώνιον); 1QS 4:7 (חיי נצח [cf. CD-A 3:20]); 4Q181 frg. 1 col. II 4 (חיי עולם); *Pss. Sol.* 3:12 (ζωὴν αἰώνιον [cf. 13:11]); *1 En.* 15:4, 6; 37:4; 40:9; 58:3; 2 Macc 7:9 (αἰώνιον ἀναβίωσιν ζωῆς); 7:36 (ἀενάου ζωῆς); *T. Ash.* 5:2 (ἡ αἰώνιος ζωή); 6:6 v.l. (ζωὴν αἰώνιον); *L.A.B.* 23:13 (*vita eterna*); 4 Macc 15:3 (αἰώνιον ζωήν); *Jos. Asen.* 8:11 (τῇ αἰωνίᾳ ζωῇ); *2 En.* J 42:10; *m. Tamid* 7:4 (חיי העלמים); *Tanḥ.* Buber Shelah 28 (חיי עולם); *y. Ber.* 6a (3:1) (חיי עולם); *b. Ber.* 21a (חיי עולם). The popularity of the hope for "eternal life" is indicated not only by the texts just cited but also by the frequency with which לחיי עולם appears on Jewish epitaphs (*JIGRE* 133; *JIWE* 1.81, 82, 118, 129a, 183; cf. *BS* 2.129 [εἰς τὸν [βίον] αἰόνιο{ν}]; 2.130 [ἀθανάτου βίου]), by how often the targumim use the Aramaic equivalent, חיי עלמא (e.g., Tg. Ps.-J. and Tg. Onq. on Lev 18:5; Tg. Onq. on Deut 33:6; Tg. 1 Sam 2:6; 25:29; Tg. Ezek 13:9; 20:11, 13, 21; Tg. Hos 14:10), and by the rabbinic fondness for the synonymous חיי העולם הבא, "life of the world to come" (e.g., *m. 'Abot* 4:16; *Mek.* on Exod

ἡ βασιλεία τοῦ θεοῦ is the near synonym of ζωή (αἰώνιος), is this not cause, on at least some occasions, for identifying the kingdom less with God's rule than with the result of that rule, with the future state that the redeemed will enjoy?

Another reason for this identification is that the interchange between ἡ βασιλεία τοῦ θεοῦ and ζωή (αἰώνιος) in the sayings attributed to Jesus has its counterpart in rabbinic phrases that refer to the utopian future God's rule will bring: חיי עולם הבא ("the life of the world to come") and העולם הבא ("the world to come") are practically synonymous. For example, in 'Abot R. Nat. B 22, the phrase "he has laid up merit for himself to enjoy in the world to come" (לאכול לעולם הבא) comes shortly before "he has laid up merit for himself to enjoy in the life of the world to come" (לאכול לחיי לעולם הבא). Here "the life of the world to come" substitutes for "the world to come." Again, while any number of rabbinic texts speak of inheriting the world to come (בעולם הבא + נחל [see below, p. 191]), others speak, with identical import, of inheriting the life of the world to come (חיי העולם הבא + נחל; e.g., Tanḥ. Buber Shelah 28; b. Soṭah 7b; Num. Rab. 9:17); and if "to enter the world to come" (לעולם הבא + בוא) is a common rabbinic expression (see below, p. 191), the synonymous "to enter the life of the world to come" (בוא + להיי העולם הבא) also occurs (e.g., m. B. Meṣi'a 2:11; t. Sanh. 12:11; b. Giṭ. 57b; Gen. Rab. 9:8). Perhaps most telling of all, the unqualified "to live" (חיה) is sometimes an abbreviation for "to live (in the world to come)" (e.g., t. Sanh. 13:2; 'Abot R. Nat. A 36; Gen. Rab. 14:3). In short, "the world to come" is a way of referring to eschatological life. If, then, as we have seen, the same is true of ἡ βασιλεία τοῦ θεοῦ in the Jesus tradition, then maybe the real rabbinic correlate of the latter is not מלכות שמים but העולם הבא.

15. מלכות, in the familiar rabbinic phrase מלכות שמים, means "authority" or "reign"; and when one takes up, in the idiom of the rabbis, "the yoke of the kingdom of heaven," one is submitting to the law, doing Torah, living under heaven's rule. This fact has no doubt encouraged scholars to equate the corresponding Greek, ἡ βασιλεία τοῦ θεοῦ, with "the reign of God." Dalman himself, however, did not follow this line of reasoning, for his comparison of Jewish literature with the canonical Gospels led him to judge that "the true affinity of the idea of the sovereignty of God, as taught by Jesus, is to be found, not so much in the Jewish conception of מלכות שמים as in the idea of the 'future age' (העולם הבא), or that of the 'life of the future age' (חיי העולם הבא)."[667]

How this intriguing verdict comports with Dalman's equation of מלכות with "Königsregiment" is a mystery to me. If ἡ βασιλεία τοῦ θεοῦ is, like "the

---

20:20; 'Abot R. Nat. A 2; 19; 'Abot R. Nat. B 29; 45; Tanḥ. Buber Ki-Tavo 4; y. Kelim 32b [9:4]; b. 'Abod. Zar. 17a; Gen. Rab. 11:10).

667. Dalman, Words of Jesus, 135.

world to come," a "comprehensive term for salvation,"[668] how can it denote God's kingly rule over against what that rule achieves? If ἡ βασιλεία τοῦ θεοῦ corresponds closely to העולם הבא, and if the latter is a future place and time, how can ἡ βασιλεία τοῦ θεοῦ not also be a future place and time? Whatever the resolution of these perplexing questions, Dalman has not been alone in proposing that the kingdom of God was "Jesus' way of speaking about the age to come."[669]

The World to Come and the Kingdom

The previous pages carry me likewise to the same conclusion; and, as further justification, I offer the following catalog. It reviews some of the many ways in which ἡ βασιλεία τοῦ θεοῦ in the Jesus tradition is like העולם הבא in Jewish sources.[670]

a. ἡ βασιλεία τοῦ θεοῦ is the subject of the verb ἔρχομαι ("to come") in Mark 9:1; Matt 6:10 // Luke 11:2 (Q); Luke 17:20 as well as in Luke 22:18 (ἕως οὗ ἡ βασιλεία τοῦ θεοῦ ἔλθῃ) diff. Mark 14:25.[671] Related are the uses of ἐγγίζω ("come near") in Mark 1:15; Matt 10:7 // Luke 10:9 (Q); Luke 10:11 and of φθάνω ("arrive") in Matt 12:28 // Luke 11:20 (Q). Corresponding to all this, the rabbinic העולם הבא (Aramaic עלמא דאתי) is, literally, "the world/age that is coming" (cf. also the regular use of לעתיד לבוא to mean "for the age to come," as in, e.g., 'Abot R. Nat. A 21; Tanḥ. Buber Lekh-Lekha 12; y. Mo'ed Qaṭ. 83b [3:7] v.l.; y. Ḥag. 77a [2:1]; b. 'Abod. Zar. 3b). Furthermore, העולם הבא is itself the subject

668. Ibid.

669. The quoted words are from James D. G. Dunn, *Unity and Diversity in the New Testament: An Inquiry Into the Character of Earliest Christianity* (Philadelphia: Westminster, 1977), 318. Cf. Ernst Baasland, "Jesu Verkündigung vom Reich Gottes," in *Reich Gottes und Kirche* (Veröffentlichungen der Luther-Akademie e.V. Ratzenburg 12; Erlangen: Martin-Luther-Verlag, 1988), 25; Eberhard Jüngel, *Paulus und Jesus: Eine Untersuchung zur Präzisierung der Frage nach dem Ursprung der Christologie* (HUT 2; Tübingen: Mohr Siebeck, 1964), 179–80; Ulrich Luz, "βασιλεία," *EDNT* 1:203; I. Howard Marshall, "The Hope of a New Age: The Kingdom of God in the New Testament," *Themelios* 11 (1985): 7; Merklein, *Gottesherrschaft als Handlungsprinzip*, 118; Neusner, "Kingdom of Heaven," 294 n. 5; Georg Strecker, *Theology of the New Testament* (trans. M. Eugene Boring; New York: de Gruyter; Louisville: Westminster John Knox, 2000), 257; Vielhauer, "Gottesreich und Menschensohn," 87–88; Volz, *Eschatologie*, 167; Windisch, "Sprüche vom Eingehen," 172 ("the real synonym for the NT's β. τ. θ. is the עולם הבא, the Garden of Eden or life").

670. Dalman (*Words of Jesus*, 101–39) already observed many of the parallels. Unfortunately, subsequent scholarship, when it has addressed this issue, seems to have been largely content with appealing to his sketch plus a few entries from the first volume of Strack-Billerbeck. I have found a fresh examination of the rabbinic evidence to be instructive.

671. Cf. also Mark 11:10: ἡ ἐρχομένη βασιλεία τοῦ πατρὸς ἡμῶν Δαυίδ, "the coming kingdom of our ancestor David."

of בוא ("come") in *Tanḥ*. Buber Shelah 25 (יבא העולם הבא) and *Num. Rab*. 16:23 (יבא העולם הבא). The precise Greek parallel to העולם הבא in Mark 10:30 (τῷ αἰῶνι τῷ ἐρχομένῳ) as well as the wording of Eph 2:7 (τοῖς αἰῶσιν τοῖς ἐπερχομένοις, "in the ages to come") and *2 Bar*. 44:12 ("the time that is coming [אתא]" [cf. 15:8]) guarantee the premishnaic origin of the Hebrew expression.[672]

b. If, as already observed, several sayings attributed to Jesus associate the kingdom of God with "life," rabbinic texts also associate "life" (חיי) with the world to come (e.g., *m. Sanh*. 10:2; *m. ʾAbot* 2:7; 6:7; *t. Sanh*. 13:2, 6–8, 10, 12; *Sipra* 193 on Lev 18:5; *ʾAbot R. Nat*. B 27; 43; *Tanḥ*. Buber Shelah 28; *y. Šabb*. 3c [1:3]; *Gen. Rab*. 90:6; *Lev. Rab*. 34:4; *Cant. Rab*. 1.1.9; *Pirqe R. El*. 19 [18]). Indeed, the texts cited on p. 189 establish that just as "life" and "the kingdom of God" are interchangeable in the Jesus tradition, so too are "the world to come" and "the life of the world to come" interchangeable in the rabbinic corpus.

c. The Synoptics use the expression εἰσελθεῖν εἰς τὴν βασιλείαν τοῦ θεοῦ/ τῶν οὐρανῶν, "to enter into the kingdom of God/heaven" (see p. 179). This has its parallel in the Hebrew בוא לעולם הבא, Aramaic אתא לעלמא דאתי ("enter the world to come"), as in *t. Sanh*. 13:1; *ʾAbot R. Nat*. A 14; *b. Ḥag*. 15b; *b. Sanh*. 101b; 102b; 104b; 105a; 110b; *b. Soṭah* 35a; *Lev. Rab*. 3:2; *Midr. Ps*. 49:3; *Pirqe R. El*. 19 (18). One may also compare *2 Bar*. 44:12, which speaks of those who "enter into" the beginning of "the new world," and *2 En*. 61:2–3, which blesses those who enter into the blessed dwellings prepared for "the great age."

d. In Matt 25:34, the saints inherit the kingdom, as they also do in 1 Cor 6:9–10; 15:50; Gal 5:19–21 (all with κληρονομέω). The rabbis speak similarly of inheriting the world to come. The expression נחל ("inherit") + בעולם הבא appears in *m. ʾAbot* 5:19; *ʾAbot R. Nat*. A 40; *ʾAbot R. Nat*. B 10; 29; 45; *y. Ned*. 38a (3:8); *b. Ber*. 51a; *b. Soṭah* 7b; *Num. Rab*. 9:17, and ירש ("possess, inherit") + העולם הבא in *Mek*. on Exod 14:31; *y. Ber*. 11d (7:3); *y. Pesaḥ*. 33a (6:1); *b. Qidd*. 40b. Additional parallels include Tg. Ruth 2:13 (למיחסן עלמא דאתי, "to take possession of the world to come"); *2 Bar*. 44:13 ("those are the ones who will inherit this time of which it is spoken"); *2 En*. 50:2 ("inherit the endless age that is coming").

e. Logia about entering and inheriting the kingdom are, in the Jesus tradition, modeled on locutions about entering and inheriting the land—we have here a new exodus typology (see p. 181). The same holds for rabbinic sayings pertaining to entering and possessing the world to come.

672. Compare also this phrase in *2 Clem*. 5:5: τῆς μελλούσης βασιλείας. Given that, in the Jesus tradition, the kingdom will come soon, worth noting is *ʾAbot R. Nat*. A 21, where Isa 60:22 ("in its time I will accomplish it quickly") is applied to the age to come (לעתיד לבא).

The rabbis, as just observed, use both נחל and ירש when speaking of possessing or inheriting the world to come, and the Bible employs those two verbs again and again in lines about Israel gaining the land (נחל in, e.g., Exod 23:30; Num 18:20; 34:17; Deut 4:38; 26:1; ירש in, e.g., Gen 15:7; Lev 20:24; Deut 1:8, 21). Similarly, בוא repeatedly appears in biblical sentences about entering the land (e.g., Exod 12:25; Lev 19:23; Num 15:2; Deut 1:8; 27:3), while, as noted above, בוא לעולם הבא ("enter the world to come") is a common rabbinic expression. Even more common is חלק לעולם/עתיד הבא ("portion in the world/future to come"), as in, for example, m. Sanh. 10:1–4; m. 'Abot 3:12; t. Sanh. 12:9–13:12; Tanḥ. Buber Metsora' 1; y. Pe'ah 16b (1:1); b. B. Meṣi'a 59a; b. Sanh. 99a (cf. 1 En. 71:15–16).[673] This matters because in the Tanak, חלק often appears in verses having to do with the allotments of the land to the tribes (e.g., Deut 10:9; 14:27; Josh 14:4; 15:13; 19:9; Ezek 45:7). The correlation between entering the land and entering the world to come becomes undeniable when m. Sanh. 10:1 appeals to Isa 60:21 ("they shall possess [lit., inherit] the land forever") as the proof text for "all Israel has a share in the world to come"; or when b. Sanh. 98b looks forward to "a second entry" (ביאה שניה); or when m. Sanh. 10:3 moves from Num 14:25–35, a divine speech explaining why the generation in the wilderness will not enter the land of Canaan, to discuss whether that generation will enter the world to come.[674]

f. Synoptic sayings 3, 4, 20, 21, 29, 30, 33, 34, 35, 36, 39, 41, 44, 47 listed at the beginning of this excursus introduce parables with variations on the phrase "The kingdom of God is/will be like" (cf. Gos. Thom. 20, 57, 76, 96–98, 107, 109). Rabbinic sources also contain parables about the world or time to come, parables that come moreover with open-

---

673. Pieter W. van der Horst suggests that the popularity of εὐμοίρει (= "have a good share or portion") on the grave inscriptions at Beth She'arim may be due to its resonance, for Jews, with the formula חלק לעולם הבא (Ancient Jewish Epigraphs: An Introductory Survey of a Millennium of Jewish Funerary Epigraphy [300 BCE – 700 CE] [Kampen: Kok Pharos, 1991], 120).

674. Cf. t. Sanh. 13:10; 'Abot R. Nat. A 36; b. Sanh. 110b; Num. Rab. 19:13. Note also the developed typology in Pesiq. Rab. 15:22, where R. Eliezer ben Jose and R. Aha comment on Exod 12:2 as follows:

Here you are to have a completely new experience which you will have again only in the time to come [לעתיד לבוא]. As in the time to come [לעתיד לבוא], "The eyes of the blind shall be opened, and the ears of the deaf shall be unstopped" (Isa. 35:5) [so that all will see and all will hear], so here, too, for Scripture says, "All the people . . . said, 'All that the Lord has spoken we will do'" (Exod. 19:8), and "all the people saw the thunderings" (Exod. 20:18). As in the time to come [לעתיד לבוא], "Then will the lame leap as a hart" (Isa. 35:6), so here, too, for Scripture says, "Moses brought forth [all of] the people out of the camp to meet God; and they [including the lame] stood at the nether part of the Mount" (Exod. 19:17). As in the time to come [לעתיד לבוא], "The tongue of the dumb will sing" (Isa. 35:6), so here, too, for Scripture says, "All the people sang out together" (Exod. 19:8). The arrival of the world to come will replay the ancient experiences in the wilderness.

ings that remind one of the Jesus tradition. The word מָשָׁל ("fable, example, parable, allegory") prefaces the parables in *Sipre* 356 on Deut 33:29; *Gen. Rab.* 62:2; *Lev. Rab.* 4:5 (מֹשֶׁל מֶלֶךְ, "A parable. It is like to a king . . ."); 27:1. The words לָמֶה הֵם ("To what are they like?") come before the illustration in *'Abot R. Nat.* A 28. The words מָשְׁלוֹ מָשָׁל לָמָה הַדָּבָר דּוֹמֶה ("They parabled a parable. To what is the matter like?") are the lead-in to parables in *'Abot R. Nat.* A 28; *Sipra* 263 on Lev 26:12; 26:13. And the words דּוּגְמָא שֶׁל לָעוֹלָם הַבָּא ("an illustration/token of the world to come") introduce similes about the world to come in *Tanḥ.* Yelammedenu Tsaw 13; *Gen. Rab.* 51:8; 73:11; *Pesiq. Rab Kah.* 7:10 (cf. 12:19; *Midr. Ps.* 14:6). That these texts, to which one may add the similes concerning the world to come in *m. 'Abot* 3:17; 4:16; *b. Qidd.* 40b, preserve an old rhetorical strategy is guaranteed by a late first-century text, *4 Ezra* 8:1–3: "The Most High made this world [*hoc saeculum*] for the sake of many, but the world to come [*futurum*] for the sake of only a few. But I tell you a parable [*similitudinem*], Ezra. Just as, when you ask the earth, it will tell you that it provides a large amount of clay from which earthenware is made, but only a little dust from which gold comes, so is the course of the present world. Many have been created, but only a few shall be saved."

g. Mark 14:25; Matt 8:11–12 // Luke 13:28–29 (Q); Matt 22:2; Luke 22:29–30 envisage the kingdom of God or its advent as a banquet. Likewise, *m. 'Abot* 3:17; 4:16; *'Abot R. Nat.* B 27; *t. Ber.* 7:21; *b. B. Bat.* 75a; *b. Pesaḥ.* 119b; *Lev. Rab.* 13:3; *Pesiq. Rab.* 41:5 envision the world to come or its advent as a banquet.

h. In Matt 5:3 // Luke 6:20 (Q); Matt 6:33 // Luke 12:31 (Q); Matt 5:10, 19, 20; 7:21; 25:1, 34; Luke 18:29–30, the kingdom of God is a reward for the righteous and compensation for deprivations experienced in this life. The same is true of the world to come in Mark 10:28–30 and repeatedly in rabbinic tradition (e.g., *m. 'Abot* 2:16; 5:19; *m. Qidd.* 4:14 [the last two are remarkable parallels to Mark 10:28–30]; *Tanḥ.* Buber Pequde 7; *'Abot R. Nat.* A 25; *'Abot R. Nat.* B 10; 44; *y. Pe'ah* 16b [1:1]; *b. Qidd.* 39b; *b. Menaḥ.* 44a; *Gen. Rab.* 33:1; 44:4; *Exod. Rab.* 30:24; 31:5; 52:3; *Deut. Rab.* 7:9; *Cant. Rab.* 2.5.3; *Midr. Ps.* 37:3; Tg. Neof. I on Gen 4:8; Tg. Ps.-J. on Gen 15:1; *Tan. d. El.* 18). The idiom הַקֶּרֶן קַיֶּמֶת לָעוֹלָם הַבָּא means "capital laid up for the world to come" (e.g., *m. Pe'ah* 1:1; *y. Pe'ah* 15d [1:1]; *b. Šabb.* 127a), and a Dura-Europos synagogue inscription from 244/5 CE (CIJ 828b) appears to have עָלְמָה הַהַבָּא shortly following אַגְרְהוֹן ("their reward").[675]

---

675. See Charles C. Torrey, "The Aramaic Texts," in Carl H. Kraeling, *The Excavations at Dura-Europos: Final Report VIII, Part 1: The Synagogue* (New Haven: Yale University Press, 1956), 263; David Noy and Hanswulf Bloedhorn, *Syria and Cyprus* (vol. 3 of *Inscriptiones*

i. Suffering is the prelude to gaining the kingdom in Matt 11:12 // Luke 16:16 (Q); Matt 5:10.[676] One may compare the rabbinic texts in which those who suffer and deny themselves in this world thereby gain life in the world to come (e.g., *Sipre* 32 on Deut 6:5; 53 on Deut 11:26; *'Abot R. Nat.* A 28; 39; *'Abot R. Nat.* B 44; *b. Qidd.* 40b; *Gen. Rab.* 9:8; *Exod. Rab.* 31:3; *Midr. Prov.* 13). This is already a theme in *2 Baruch* (15:8: "This world is to them [the righteous] a struggle and an effort with much trouble. Accordingly that [world] which will come [will be] a crown with great glory"; 48:50: "As you endured much labor in the short time in which you live in this passing world, so you will receive great light in that world which has no end" [cf. *2 En.* J 66:6]).

j. ἡ βασιλεία τοῦ θεοῦ stands over against Gehenna in Mark 9:47 and over against Hades in Matt 16:18. In like fashion, those who have no share in the world to come suffer in Sheol or Gehenna in, for example, *m. Qidd.* 4:14; *m. 'Abot* 5:19; *t. Sanh.* 13:1–5; *t. Yoma* 4:10–11; *Tanḥ.* Buber Metsora' 1; *'Abot R. Nat.* A 25; 40; *y. Qidd.* 61d (1:9); *y. Sanh.* 29b (10:3); *b. Sanh.* 105a; *Gen. Rab.* 28:8; *Exod. Rab.* 50:5; *Num. Rab.* 18:13; *Midr. Ps.* 31:3; *Pirqe R. El.* 19 (18) (cf. *2 Bar.* 44:15: those who do not gain the world to come will inhabit "the fire").

k. *Sipre* 356, in explicating Deut 33:29 ("Happy are you, O Israel! Who is like you, a people saved by the LORD?"), has the Israelites ask Moses, "Tell us what good things the Holy One, blessed be he, has in store for us in the world to come [לעולם הבא]." Moses responds with a parable that he introduces and concludes with this beatitude: "Blessed are you [אשריכם] because of that which is prepared for you."[677] The form and sentiment resemble the beatitudes in Luke 6:20–23 and their Matthean counterparts, where Jesus blesses those who will possess the kingdom of God.

l. "Sons of the kingdom" (οἱ υἱοὶ τῆς βασιλείας), which appears in Matt 8:12 (diff. Luke 13:28); 13:38, has its counterpart in the Hebrew בן/בני and the Aramaic בר/בני עלמא דאתי, "son/s of the world to come" (e.g., *y. Ber.* 13d [9:2]; *y. Šeqal.* 47c [3:3]; *b. Ber.* 4b; 9b; 57a;

Judaicae Orientis; TSAJ 102; Tübingen: Mohr Siebeck, 2004), 139–46. Note also that the world to come can be a reward for love in particular. In *Tan. d. El.* 26 (28), Israel enjoys the world to come because of its love for God, and *'Abot R. Nat.* B 10 v.l. has this: "The one who acts out of love inherits the life of this world and the life of the world to come" (cf. *2 En.* J 66:6; *b. Ber.* 28b). This recalls Mark 12:28–34, where a scribe who agrees with Jesus that the two chief commandments are to love God and to love neighbor is said to be "not far from the kingdom of God."

676. Cf. Luke 22:28–30; Acts 14:22. The meaning of Matt 11:12 // Luke 16:16 (Q) is especially controversial. The most likely interpretation is that it has to do with the suffering of the saints in the eschatological tribulation; see most recently Pitre, *Jesus*, 159–77.

677. That the world to come has been "prepared" (מתוקן) for Israel has a parallel in Matt 25:34; see also *Did.* 10:5; *4 Ezra* 8:52; *Tanḥ.* Buber Pequde 7; *b. Ḥag.* 14b.

b. *Meg.* 28b; b. *Šabb.* 153a; b. *Taʿan.* 22a; b. *Yoma* 88a; b. *Ketub.* 111a; *Midr. Prov.* 17; *Pirqe R. El.* 45 [44]; "Daughter [בת] of the world to come" occurs in b. *Ketub.* 111a.)

m. Matt 11:11 // Luke 7:28 (Q) ("the least in the kingdom of God"); Matt 5:19 ("called least in the kingdom of heaven," "called great in the kingdom of heaven"); Matt 18:4 ("the greatest in the kingdom of heaven") speak as though there is and/or will be rank or hierarchy in the kingdom of God. The same idea appears with reference to paradise or the world to come in *Sipre* 10 on Deut 1:10 ("seven groups of the righteous in paradise" [cf. *Midr. Ps.* 11:6]); 47 on Deut 11:21 ("just as the brightness of one star is not like that of another, so will this be true of the righteous"); y. *Ḥag.* 77a (2:1) ("there are seven classes of the righteous in the time to come"); b. *Pesaḥ.* 50a (martyrs are above everyone else in the world to come [cf. b. *B. Bat.* 10b]); b. *Qidd.* 40b ("the lowest rank"); b. *B. Meṣiʿa* 85b ("great in the world to come"); b. *Sanh.* 99a (repentant sinners are above the righteous [cf. b. *Ber.* 34a]); b. *Ḥag.* 14b (a reference to "the third class"); *Pesiq. Rab.* 50:3 (in the world to come it will be evident who is great and who is small).

n. Jesus says, in Luke 9:62, "No one who puts a hand to the plow and looks back is worthy [εὔθετος] of the kingdom of God" (cf. 2 Thess 1:5: "to make you worthy [καταξιωθῆναι] of the kingdom of God"). With this one may compare a series of examples from rabbinic texts: *ʾAbot R. Nat.* A 19 (תזכו לחיי העולם הבא, "you will be worthy of the life of the world to come"); *ʾAbot R. Nat.* B 29 (זכה לי לנחול . . . חיי העולם הבא, "for me to be worthy to inherit . . . the life of the world to come"); *Tanḥ.* Yelammedenu Tsaw 14 (זוכה לחיי העולם הבא, "worthy of the life of the world to come"); y. *Ber.* 11d (7:3) (זוכה לירש העולם הזה והעולם הבא, "to be worthy of inheriting this world and the world to come"); b. *ʿErub.* 54b (דתיזכו את ודרך לעלמא דאתי, "that you and your generation might be worthy of the world to come"); b. *Giṭ.* 68b (זכי לעלמא דאתי, "will be worthy of the world to come"); b. *B. Bat.* 10b (אזכה לעולם הבא, "that I may be worthy of the world to come"); *Midr. Ps.* 78:12 (זכי לעלמא דאתי, "will be worthy of the world to come"). Luke 20:34–35 establishes that these rabbinic texts preserve an old way of speaking: "Those who belong to this age [τοῦ αἰῶνος τούτου] marry and are given in marriage; but those who are considered worthy of a place in that age [καταξιωθέντες τοῦ αἰῶνος ἐκείνου] and in the resurrection from the dead neither marry nor are given in marriage."

o. In Mark 10:17–27, a rich man who does not distribute all that he has to the poor fails to enter the kingdom of God. In a story preserved in t. *Peʾah* 4:18–19; y. *Peʾah* 15b (1:1); b. *B. Bat.* 11a, a king who distributes all his possessions to the poor saves himself and stores up treasures for the world to come.[678]

p. In Matt 8:11–12 // Luke 13:28–29 (Q), the faithless are "thrown out" (Matthew: ἐκβληθήσονται; Luke: ἐκβαλλομένους) of the kingdom (cf. Matt 13:41: συλλέξουσιν ἐκ τῆς βασιλείας αὐτοῦ, "will collect out of his kingdom"). Similar to this is the use of טרד with the meaning "expel" in *b. Ḥag.* 15a ("I have been expelled [איטריד] from the other world"); *b. B. Bat.* 15b ("to expel him [לטרדו] from the world to come"); *b. Qidd.* 40b ("in order to expel them [לטורדן] [from the world to come] and to consign them to the lowest rank"); and *Midr. Ps.* 18:30 ("Doeg was expelled [נטרד] from the world to come"). Also comparable are עקר ("uproot, remove") in *Sipre* 48 on Deut 11:22 ("removed from this world and the world to come") and טרף ("to tear out, to throw away") in *'Abot R. Nat.* B 29 ("to remove my soul from . . . the life of the world to come" [cf. 33; 34]).

q. *2 Bar.* 44:15, which speaks of the world to come (עלמא דאתא) being "given" (מתיהב) to those prepared for the treasures of wisdom is similar to Luke 12:32, where Jesus says that it is God's good pleasure to "give" (δοῦναι) his followers the kingdom (cf. Matt 21:43; Luke 22:29; also *Sipre* 310 on Deut 32:7: "the good things and consolations that he [God] will give to you [ליתן] in the world to come").

r. Possessive personal pronouns modify "the kingdom of God" in Mark 10:14 (τῶν τοιούτων ἐστὶν ἡ βασιλεία τοῦ θεοῦ, "to such as these is the kingdom of God"); Luke 6:20 // Matt 5:3 (Q) (ὑμετέρα ἐστὶν ἡ βασιλεία τοῦ θεοῦ, "yours is the kingdom of God"); Matt 5:10 (αὐτῶν ἐστιν ἡ βασιλεία τῶν οὐρανῶν, "theirs is the kingdom of heaven"). Reminiscent of these texts are the expressions העולם הבא שלהם ("the world to come is theirs") in *Midr. Prov.* 13:4 and העולם הבא שלכם ("the world to come is yours") in *Num. Rab.* 21:20; *Pesiq. Rab.* 16:6; *Pesiq. Rab Kah.* 6:2. One may also cite, from a much earlier time, *2 Bar.* 44:13: "theirs is the heritage of the age (to come) that has been promised."

s. The Synoptics, probably influenced by Isa 52:7, link εὐαγγελίζομαι and εὐαγγέλιον to the noun βασιλεία: Jesus and the disciples preach the good news of the kingdom (Mark 1:14–15; Matt 9:35; 24:14; Luke 4:43; 8:1; 16:16; cf. Acts 8:12; see above, pp. 113–15). Remarkable parallels occur in *y. Ketub.* 35a (12:3); *y. Kil.* 32b (9:4) (both with מבושר לחיי העולם הבא, "let there be announced [to him] the good news of the life of the world to come"); *y. Šeqal.* 47c (3:3) (מבושר שבן העולם הבא הוא, "announcing the good news that he is an inhabitant of the world to come"); and the so-called *Mekilta* on Deut 32:43 (מבושר הוא שיש

---

678. Cf. also *2 En.* J 50:5; *Lev. Rab.* 34:4, both of which teach that giving alms to the needy will bring eschatological reward.

לו הלק לעולם הבא, "announcing that there is for him a portion in the world to come").

t. According to Mark 9:1, some of Jesus' hearers will not die before they see (ἴδωσιν) the kingdom of God come with power. The world to come is similarly the object of sight in 2 Bar. 51:8 ("they will see that world which is now invisible to them, and they will see a time which is now hidden to them"); y. Sanh. 29b–c (10:3) ("they will not see the future to come"); Tg. Ps.-J. on Gen 49:15 ("he saw the resting place of the world to come"); a marginal note to Tg. Neof. I on Exod 2:12 (Moses saw this world and the world to come); Gen. Rab. 9:3 (God "looked at this world and at the world to come").

u. Taken together, Matt 16:19 ("the keys of the kingdom of heaven") and 23:13 ("lock people out of the kingdom of heaven") encourage us to envisage the kingdom as surrounded by a wall with entrances or gates. We find the same image of the world to come in 4 Ezra 7:13 ("the entrances of the greater world"); Lev. Rab. 30:2 ("by which gate one is led to the life of the world to come").

v. Luke 22:29–30, where Jesus imagines the Twelve eating and drinking "in my kingdom" and sitting on thrones to judge the twelve tribes of Israel, has a substantial parallel in Tanḥ. Buber Qedoshim 1: "In the age to come, the holy one, blessed be he, will sit down, and the angels will place thrones for the great ones of Israel for them to sit down, so that the holy one will be sitting with them like the president of the court. Then they will judge the peoples of the world."

w. The parables of the buried treasure (Matt 13:44; Gos. Thom. 109) and of the pearl of great price (Matt 13:45–46) present the kingdom as being of inestimable value; and texts that enjoin great personal sacrifice for the sake of the kingdom presuppose this idea (Mark 9:47; 10:23–25; Matt 19:12; Luke 9:62; 18:29–30). In like manner, m. 'Abot 4:17; 'Abot R. Nat. B 33; Lev. Rab. 3:1; Eccl. Rab. 4:5 declare the world to come to be of incomparable worth: "Better is one hour of bliss in the world to come than the whole life of this world." Related sentiments appear in 'Abot R. Nat. B 32 ("it is better for you to die in this world . . . than to die in the age to come"); Eccl. Rab. 2:1 ("all the prosperity that one enjoys in this world is vanity compared to the prosperity of the world to come"); 11:8 ("the Torah that one learns in this world is vanity compared with the Torah of the Messiah"), and are regularly presumed elsewhere.

x. Matt 13:43 teaches that after the final judgment, "the righteous will shine like the sun in the kingdom of their Father." Rabbinic literature says the same thing again and again with reference to the world to come (e.g., Sipre 9 on Deut 1:10; 47 on 11:21; Midr. Ps. 11:6; Pesiq. Rab. 18:1; Pesiq. Rab Kah. 8:1).

y. In Luke 23:42–43, Jesus answers the thief's request, "Remember me when you come into your kingdom," with a promise about "paradise" (παράδεισος), as though the two refer to the same eschatological reality, one that can be experienced even before the end, upon death. Rabbinic texts sometimes conceive of the world to come as a "garden" (גן, גנה), as "(the garden of) Eden" ([גן] עדן), or as "paradise" (פרדס, παράδεισος), which one can enter upon death (e.g., *Sipre* 10 on Deut 1:10; *'Abot R. Nat.* A 25; *y. Pe'ah* 15c [1:1]; *y. Qidd.* 61b [1:7]; *b. Ber.* 16b; *b. Tem.* 16a; *Exod. Rab.* 7:4; *Pesiq. Rab.* 50:1). Nonrabbinic examples include *T. Levi* 18:10–11; *1 En.* 61:12; *4 Ezra* 7:36, 123; *T. Ab.* RecLng 11:10; 14:8; 20:14; *Apoc. Ab.* 21:6; *2 En.* 42:3. Moreover, *y. Sanh.* 27c (10:1) moves from speaking of the world to come to speaking about the garden of Eden, and already *4 Ezra* 8:52 has this: "It is for you that paradise is opened, the tree of life is planted, the age to come is prepared." In this last text, paradise is the world to come or a portion of it, just as paradise is the kingdom or a portion of it in Luke 23:42–43 (cf. *Midr. Ps.* 31:6).

z. Many of the logia about ἡ βασιλεία τοῦ θεοῦ envisage moving into it (εἰς) or being within it (ἐν) or being removed from it (ἐκ). Visually:[679]

εἰς: sayings 6, 9, 10, 11, 26, 27, 42
ἐν: sayings 13, 15, 22, 25, 32, 57, 58
ἐκ: sayings 22, 31

In like fashion, the rabbis often speak of people going into the world to come (ל) or being in it (ב) or being removed from it (מן). So one may offer an analogous diagram:

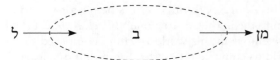

ל: *t. Sanh.* 13:1; *'Abot R. Nat.* A 14; *b. Ḥag.* 15b; *b. Sanh.* 101b; *Lev. Rab.* 3:2; et al.

ב: *m. 'Abot* 5:19; *'Abot R. Nat.* B 10; *y. Ma'aś.* 51a (3:10); *b. Šabb.* 30b; et al.

679. I borrow this image from Baasland, "Jesu Verkündigung," 23.

מן: *Sipre* 48; *'Abot R. Nat.* A 12; *'Abot R. Nat.* B 29; 33; 34; *b. Ḥag.* 15a; *b. B. Bat.* 15b; et al.

Both the world to come and the kingdom of God are conceptualized as future destinations from which some will be expelled.

Jesus, the World to Come, and the Kingdom

How should we interpret this catalog of parallels, and what might it tell us about Jesus? Caution is in order. Not only are the rabbinic texts later than those in the Jesus tradition, sometimes much later, but also the sayings about ἡ βασιλεία τοῦ θεοῦ do not all derive from Jesus and so have more than one origin, as do their rabbinic counterparts. Furthermore, ἡ βασιλεία τοῦ θεοῦ and העולם הבא are not perfect synonyms. For instance, the rabbis sometimes define העולם הבא over against the messianic age, a distinction that probably plays no role in the Jesus tradition;[680] and whereas "the kingdom of God" is always positive on the lips of Jesus, "the world to come" can be, for the rabbis, a place of punishment, as though Gehenna were a part of it.[681]

Observations such as these do not, however, annul the import of the extensive and sometimes quite striking parallels. (i) Even late texts can preserve early tradition.[682] (ii) As the preceding pages reveal, rabbinic sources show

680. My guess is that, for Jesus—if he ever gave the issue thought, which perhaps he did not—the immediate future was the ultimate future. To use rabbinic terminology, the messianic kingdom and the world to come amounted to the same thing, as also seemingly in *Sib. Or.* 3:49, 50, 766; *Pss. Sol.* 17:4; *1 En.* 62:14; John 12:34; *m. Ber.* 1:5 (?); Tg. 2 Sam 23:5; *Gen. Rab.* 12:10.

681. Cf. *Mek.* on Exod 14:24; *Tanḥ.* Buber Wayyera 11; *'Abot R. Nat.* A 21; 40; *'Abot R. Nat.* B 44; *y. Pe'ah* 16b (1:1); Tg. Neof. I on Deut 32:35; *Gen. Rab.* 20:1; 87:6; also *4 Ezra* 7:47.

682. Two instructive examples: (a) To my knowledge, the only Jewish sources to teach that Cain was literally the devil's offspring are Tg. Ps.-J. on Gen 4:1 (of uncertain date and origin; revisions were made up to the seventh century CE) and *Pirqe R. El.* 21 (eighth or ninth century CE). But Christian sources demonstrate that this legend was in circulation by the turn of the era; see 1 John 3:10–12; Tertullian, *Pat.* 5:15; *Carn. Chr.* 17.5–6; *Gos. Phil.* 61:5–10; Epiphanius, *Pan.* 40.5.3. See discussion in Israel Knohl, "Cain: Son of God or Son of Satan?" in *Jewish Biblical Interpretation and Cultural Exchange: Comparative Exegesis in Context* (ed. Natalie B. Dohrmann and David Stern; Philadelphia: University of Pennsylvania Press, 2008), 37–50. (b) According to *Exod. Rab.* 15:15 and *Yalqut Shimoni* on 1 Kgs 18:26, the prophets of Baal, in order to rig their contest with Elijah, hollowed out the altar and concealed therein a man, instructing him to ignite a fire when signaled to do so. God, however, sent a snake to bite the hidden conspirator. *Exodus Rabbah* is the earliest literary witness to this legend, of which the Bible holds no hint. But it is already depicted in one of the paintings at the Dura-Europos synagogue, from the middle of the third century; its representation of the contest between Elijah and the prophets of Baal features a miniature man standing inside the altar. See Joseph Gutmann, "The Illustrated Midrash in the Dura Synagogue Paintings: A New Dimension for the Study of Judaism," *AAJRP* 50 (1983): 91–104. In the rabbinic tradition, the man who conspires with the prophets of Baal is named "Hiel," and the Elijah panel has an Aramaic graffito which

much stability over the centuries with regard to locutions employing הָעוֹלָם הבא. (iii) *1 En.* 71:15 ("peace to you in the name of the world to come"), the canonical Gospels (Matt 12:32; Mark 10:30; Luke 16:8; 20:34–35; John 12:25),[683] Ephesians (1:21; 2:7), *4 Ezra* (4:2, 27; 6:9; 7:12–13, 47, 50, 112–13; 8:1–2, 52), and *2 Baruch* (14:13; 15:8; 44:11–15; 48:50; 59:9) establish that the Tannaim were not the first to speak about two ages or worlds, this one and the next.[684] (iv) The same Jewish and Christian sources establish that many of the idioms recurrently linked with הָעוֹלָם הבא in the rabbinic corpus were known in premishnaic times. Clearly, they were beginning to establish themselves by the first century.[685]

That certain expressions associated with the eschatological redemption were already traditional before publication of the Mishnah explains why they show up in the sayings of Jesus. He and his followers no more invented them than did the Tannaim; they were rather common religious coin. Further, as Christian sources link those ways of speaking with the kingdom of God, and the rabbinic corpus with the world to come, it appears that, in many respects, ἡ βασιλεία τοῦ θεοῦ = הָעוֹלָם הבא.

The Jesus tradition itself implies that "the kingdom of God" and "the world to come" are homologous. In Mark 10:17, a man with many possessions asks Jesus what he can do "to inherit eternal life." When the man cannot bring himself to do what Jesus asks—sell all and give it to the poor—the topic becomes failure to enter "the kingdom of God" (10:23–27), which in context means the failure to inherit eternal life. After Peter then observes that, unlike the rich man, he and others have left behind everything, Jesus avows that

---

appears to read חיאעל; see Carl H. Kraeling, "The Wall Decorations," in *Preliminary Report on the Synagogue at Dura* (New Haven: Yale University Press, 1936), 56. Gutmann ("Illustrated Midrash") and Kraeling (*Excavations: Synagogue*, 140–41, 351–54) offer additional examples of Dura images with their literary counterparts in later midrash. The lesson is that the extant literary remains are scarcely reliable reflections of what was known when.

683. C. H. Dodd plausibly argued, regarding John 12:25 ("Those who love their life lose it, and those who hate their life in this world will keep it for eternal life"), that "the Fourth Evangelist . . . has given it a form which obviously alludes to the Jewish antithesis of the two ages: he who hates his soul בָּעוֹלָם הזה will keep it לָעוֹלָם הבא, and consequently will possess חיי הָעוֹלָם הבא" (*Interpretation of the Fourth Gospel*, 146).

684. Note also LXX Isa 9:5 v.l. (μέλλοντος αἰῶνος); Paul's use of ὁ αἰὼν οὗτος (Rom 12:2; 1 Cor 1:20; 2:6–8; 3:18; 2 Cor 4:4); ὁ νῦν αἰών in the Pastoral Epistles (1 Tim 6:17; 2 Tim 4:10; Titus 2:12); Heb 6:5 (μέλλοντος αἰῶνος); Pol. *Phil.* 5:2 (ἐν τῷ νῦν αἰῶνι . . . τὸν μέλλοντα); *Liv. Pro.* 3:13 (ὧδε καὶ ἐπὶ τοῦ μέλλοντος; v.l.: ὧδε καὶ ἐν τῷ μέλλοντι αἰῶνι). Dalman asserted that although the expressions "this age" and "the age to come" were current by the end of the first Christian century, they probably "characterized the language of the learned rather than that of the people" (*Words of Jesus*, 151). This, however, scarcely accounts for the New Testament evidence. See further Martin McNamara, *Targum and Testament: Aramaic Paraphrases of the Hebrew Bible; A Light on the New Testament* (Grand Rapids: Eerdmans, 1972), 134–35.

685. But not much before then, since עוֹלָם הזה and עוֹלָם הבא appear nowhere in the Dead Sea Scrolls.

they will have eternal life in the coming aeon (ἐν τῷ αἰῶνι τῷ ἐρχομένῳ ζωὴν αἰώνιον; cf. the rabbinic חיי העולם הבא). To have life in the world to come is to have life in the kingdom; not to have life in the kingdom is not to have life in the world to come.[686]

What follows? If one can pass from speaking about "the kingdom of God" to "the world to come" without changing the subject, then the two terms must overlap significantly. That this is indeed the case appears if one substitutes "the world to come" for "the kingdom of God" in the logia attributed to Jesus, for the result almost always makes perfect sense—for example, "Let the little children come to me; do not stop them; for it is to such as these that the world to come belongs" (Mark 10:14); "Blessed are you who are poor, for yours is the world to come" (Luke 6:20 // Matt 5:3 [Q]); "Do not be afraid, little flock, for it is your Father's good pleasure to give you the world to come" (Luke 12:32).

My judgment, then, is that ἡ βασιλεία τοῦ θεοῦ is, in the Synoptics, a realm as well as a reign; it is a place and a time yet to come in which God will reign supreme. The term designates, in many or perhaps most cases, the "große Heilszustand am Ende der Tage,"[687] "the future which God will bring about."[688] The formulation of Johannes Weiss remains valid: ἡ βασιλεία τοῦ θεοῦ is "the objective messianic Kingdom, which usually is pictured as a territory into which one enters, or as a land in which one has a share."[689] So the NRSV has not erred by keeping the old translation "the kingdom of God," and *Die Gute Nachricht* is justified in sometimes rendering ἡ βασιλεία τοῦ θεοῦ as "die neue Welt Gottes."[690]

16. In order to make my position clear, I wish to reaffirm emphatically that מלכות and βασιλεία often do, in Jewish and Christian sources, refer to kingly authority or royal reign.[691] I also wish to stress that βασιλεία probably

686. How much of Mark 10:17–31 goes back to Jesus is of no concern here. It is also irrelevant whether he used the terminology of the two ages (the evidence is meager); see Anton Vögtle, *Das Neue Testament und die Zukunft des Kosmos* (KBANT; Düsseldorf: Patmos-Verlag, 1970), 147–48. All that matters here is that someone who contributed to the Jesus tradition thought of the kingdom as being the same as the world to come.

687. Windisch, "Sprüche vom Eingehen," 164.

688. Rudolf Bultmann, *This World and the Beyond: Marburg Sermons* (trans. Harold Knight; New York: Charles Scribner's Sons, 1960), 204.

689. Weiss, *Jesus' Proclamation*, 133. Compare these remarks by Hans Windisch: "The kingdom of God is the holy habitation of the messianic salvation era. It is a fusion of the holy land, the holy city, and the holy temple" (*The Meaning of the Sermon on the Mount* [trans. S. MacLean Gilmour; Philadelphia: Westminster, 1951], 28); and Géza Vermès: the kingdom is "in general terms the transformation of the conditions of existence from those that prevail in the present era to the state of affairs in the world to come" (*Resurrection*, 70).

690. *Die Gute Nachricht: Das Neue Testament in heutigem Deutsch* (Stuttgart: Bibelanstalt Stuttgart, 1972), on, for example, Mark 4:26; 9:47.

691. For example, 1 Chr 29:30; 2 Chr 13:8; Dan 2:44; Tob 13:1; Luke 1:33; Rev 17:12, 17, 18. This is the meaning of מלכות in the rabbinic phrase מלכות שמים.

does, in several sayings attributed to Jesus, mean "regal rule" or "reign." An excellent candidate is Luke 11:20 // Matt 12:28 (Q): "But if it is by the finger of God that I cast out the demons, then the kingdom of God has come to you."[692] Other logia in which βασιλεία τοῦ θεοῦ plausibly means "kingly rule of God" either first of all or exclusively include Luke 13:18 // Matt 13:31 (Q) ("What is the kingdom of God like? And to what should I compare it? It is like a mustard seed . . ."); Luke 13:20–21 // Matt 13:33 (Q) ("To what shall I compare the kingdom of God? It is like yeast . . ."); Luke 17:20–21 ("The kingdom of God is not coming with things that can be observed; nor will they say, 'Look, here it is!' or 'There it is!' For, in fact, the kingdom of God is among you" [cf. *Gos. Thom.* 113]).

We should not, however, make these texts the key to the rest, especially those in which a territorial dimension is likely present. We should avoid the temptation to flatten the data, to make every saying about ἡ βασιλεία τοῦ θεοῦ refer to the same thing.[693] We should also beware of choosing "reign" over "realm" or vice versa when both meanings make good sense. A word need not confine itself to one dictionary meaning at a time.

So even though I have come to the conclusion that ἡ βασιλεία τοῦ θεοῦ is more often than not, in the Jesus tradition, God's new world, that does not exclude other meanings. The term in fact is polysemous, so that in some verses we can scarcely decide whether βασιλεία means "realm" or "reign" or both or perhaps even something else. Ulrich Luz recognizes this when he writes that the kingdom of God "is not only the sovereignty of God in a functional sense; it is also a particular place, in which one can be . . . or into which one can enter."[694] Although I would prefer to turn this around—the kingdom "is not only a particular place . . . it is also the sovereignty of God"—the inclusive formulation "not only . . . also" is right. Like ἡ συναγωγή, which can refer alternately to a building, to an institution, or to its people, or sometimes to all three at once, ἡ βασιλεία τοῦ θεοῦ can specify one or more things, depending upon the context.[695]

17. With this in mind, I want to suggest that, in addition to the meanings given in the dictionaries, ἡ βασιλεία τοῦ θεοῦ may on occasion mean neither God's "rule" nor "reign" but refer rather, by metonymy, to God's people.[696] One recalls Ps 102:22, where "peoples" and "kingdoms" (MT: ממלכות; LXX:

---

692. O'Neill ("Kingdom of God") can avoid the notion of "reign" here only by arguing for textual corruption.

693. Stanton (*Gospels and Jesus*, 203–17) rightly insisted on this point.

694. Luz, "βασιλεία," *TDNT* 1:203.

695. The occasional argument that, if Jesus spoke of the kingdom as coming, he probably did not also speak about it as a place (see Merklein, *Jesu Botschaft*, 23–24; M. Wolter, "Was heisset nu Gottes reich?" *ZNW* 86 [1995]: 5–19) is unimaginative and unrealistic; it is to put Jesus in a linguistic and theological straitjacket.

696. For a similar suggestion, see Stanton, *Gospels and Jesus*, 208, regarding Mark 10:23–25. On metonymy in sayings about the kingdom, see n. 636.

βασιλείας) are in synonymous parallelism: "when peoples gather together, and kingdoms, to worship the LORD" (cf. Ps 105:13; 1 Esd 1:24).

A kingdom is empty and so nothing without its subjects, and Exod 19:6 famously declares, "You [Israel] will be to me a kingdom [MT: ממלכת; Aquila, Symmachus, Theodotion: βασιλεία] of priests and a holy nation." That this pentateuchal line was well known is obvious from 1Q28b 5:21 ("to establish the kingdom of his people"); 4Q504 frg. 4 10 (a quotation of Exod 19:6); *Jub.* 16:18 (a paraphrase of Exod 19:6); 33:20 ("Israel is a holy people, . . . a priestly kingdom"); Rev 1:6 ("made us to be a kingdom, priests serving his God and Father"); 5:10 ("made them to be a kingdom").[697]

Perhaps, then, the notion of a royal people is the key to Synoptic sayings 3 (the parable of the seed growing secretly), 20 (the parable of the mustard seed), 21 (the parable of the leaven), 23 ("the kingdom of God has suffered violence"), 29 (the parable of the weeds and wheat), 35 (the parable of the net), 44 (the parable of the wedding banquet), 47 (the parable of the ten bridesmaids). That is, maybe these logia and parables originally were lessons not about God's reign but those under God's reign, lessons not about God's kingdom but its future inhabitants. Some of these texts involve growth, and the growth in view might be the expected increase in the number of what Matt 13:38 calls "the children of the kingdom."

18. A final note is needed. When speaking of the eschatological future, the rabbis preferred to use the phrase "the world to come." Some modern scholars, observing that Jesus, if the Synoptics have it right, preferred instead to employ "the kingdom of God," have found here verbal innovation, maybe even a deliberate theological decision.[698]

One wonders. While Jesus may have been a linguistic innovator in certain respects—his prefatory "amen" comes to mind—the terminology of the two ages, while attested for the first century, may not by then have been widespread. We have no idea how common it was in pre-70 Galilee. So how can we surmise that he deliberately displaced that terminology in favor of another?

We also do not know whence Jesus derived his preference for "the kingdom of God." Perhaps he was inspired by the book of Daniel, where God's kingdom

697. On the early history of interpretation of Exod 19:6, see James L. Kugel, *Traditions of the Bible: A Guide to the Bible As It Was at the Start of the Common Era* (Cambridge, MA: Harvard University Press, 1998), 671–74; R. B. Y. Scott, "A Kingdom of Priests (Exodus xix 6)," *OtSt* 8 (1950): 213–19.

698. So, for example, Hengel, "Zur matthäischen Bergpredigt," 386; Vielhauer, "Gottesreich und Menschensohn," 88; Vögtle, *Zukunft des Kosmos*, 146; cf. Jeremias, *New Testament Theology*, 32–35. Incidentally, the latter's well-known list of unparalleled expressions employing "the kingdom of God" in the sayings attributed to Jesus shrinks considerably when one takes into account Jewish sentences regarding "the world to come."

is a major theme,[699] or by prayer traditions learned as a youth.[700] Or, since the extant targumim use the phrase מלכותא דיוי, maybe targumic scriptures influenced him. He might also have borrowed his manner of speaking from a teacher unknown to us or even from the Baptist, about whom we know so little; certainly the few lines attributed to him are no index of his entire vocabulary. In all of these scenarios, Jesus would be an imitator, not an innovator. But the truth is that, given the breadth of our ignorance, determining the degree to which Jesus' repetitive use of "the kingdom of God" might have struck his contemporaries as novel or unusual is beyond our ability.[701]

Excursus 2
The Continuity between John the Baptist and Jesus

In his *New Testament Theology*, Joachim Jeremias wrote that John the Baptist and Jesus were alike in several respects: both taught out-of-doors, gave their disciples a special prayer (Luke 11:1–4), called hearers to repentance, announced the imminent divine judgment, and were open to "people who had been written off by the synagogue, the Pharisaic coventicles and Qumran."[702] In brief, Jesus "followed the Baptist in many ways."[703] For Jeremias, however, such parallels were little more than prolegomena to his recovery of Jesus, for a "fundamental" difference overshadows them. Whereas John demanded repentance in the face of the judgment, Jesus instead announced the dawning of the kingdom. Jeremias put it this way: "John the Baptist remains within the framework of expectation; Jesus claims to bring fulfillment. John still belongs in the realm of the law; with Jesus, the gospel begins."[704]

The strategy of elucidating Jesus by contrasting him with John, a tactic that early Christian texts already use to Jesus' advantage, remains a commonplace of critical scholarship. According to John Dominic Crossan, Jesus' submission to John's baptism tells us that the former initially believed much as the latter did, an inference supported by Matt 11:7–9 // Luke 7:24–26 (Q), which

---

699. So Dalman, *Words of Jesus*, 136; Evans, "Daniel in the New Testament"; Jeremias, *New Testament Theology*, 102; David Wenham, "The Kingdom of God and Daniel," *ExpTim* 98 (1987): 132–34.

700. See above, p. 46.

701. For what it is worth, the tradition saw no need to confine "the kingdom (of God)" to Jesus' speech; see Matt 3:2 (John the Baptist); 18:1 (the disciples); 20:21 (the mother of the sons of Zebedee); Mark 15:43 (the evangelist, Mark); Luke 1:33 (an angel); 14:15 (a dinner guest); 17:20 (the Pharisees); 19:11 (the evangelist, Luke); 23:42 (the so-called good thief).

702. Jeremias, *New Testament Theology*, 48.

703. Ibid., 47.

704. Ibid., 49.

Crossan thinks "reads like an attempt to maintain faith in John's apocalyptic vision."[705] But things changed. Matthew 11:11 // Luke 7:28 (Q), which makes the Baptist less than the least in the kingdom, contradicts Matt 11:7–9 // Luke 7:24–26 (Q) and so reflects a significant modification of opinion.[706] What that modification involved appears from Mark 2:18–20 and Matt 11:18–19 // Luke 7:33–34 (Q), both of which draw a "contrast between a *fasting John* and a *feasting Jesus*."[707] John "lived in apocalyptic asceticism," which Jesus at some time abandoned.[708] Indeed, Jesus became "almost the exact opposite of John the Baptist."[709]

Whether one agrees with Crossan's assessment or thinks, as I do, that it is overdone, at least two difficulties beset attempts to understand Jesus by using the Baptist as a rhetorical foil. The first is simply that in our eagerness to stress the undoubted and important differences, we may run the risk of not heeding the significant continuities; that is, we may underestimate the extent of Jesus' debt to his predecessor. We have here potentially the same bias that has commonly afflicted application of the criterion of dissimilarity: we may be so keen to find what was distinctive about Jesus that we ignore or downplay what he shared with others or learned from them.

The other difficulty, which derives not from ourselves but rather from our sources, is that we know far less about John the Baptist than we are wont to imagine. It is ironic that we expect John to shed light on Jesus, for the forerunner is the darker figure.[710] Apart from a passing summary by Josephus (*Ant.* 18.116–119) and a handful of pertinent passages in the Jesus tradition, we just do not have much to go on. Perhaps the very paucity of the relevant texts sometimes fosters the illusion that finding John is easier than finding Jesus. But when did having fewer sources ever help us to recover more history?

Despite the problems indicated, it would be foolish to eschew the utility of contrasting John and Jesus, and I wish to do no such thing. It remains useful, however, to remind ourselves of how difficult it can be to make broad generalizations about the differences between the two figures, and this is my goal in the first part of this excursus. In the second part, I will call attention to some crucial continuities that the secondary literature has sometimes neglected.

705. Crossan, *Jesus*, 47.
706. For my criticism of this analysis, see above, pp. 137–40.
707. Crossan, *Jesus*, 48.
708. Ibid.
709. Ibid.
710. Robert L. Webb comments, "Our data concerning John is much more limited than is our data concerning Jesus, so that it is impossible to make actual comparisons in areas where we have no information concerning John" ("John the Baptist and His Relationship to Jesus," in *Studying the Historical Jesus* [ed. Chilton and Evans], 226).

The Standard Disjunctions

In *The Historical Jesus: A Comprehensive Guide*, Gerd Theissen and Annette Merz conveniently set forth what are, in their judgment, five "of the most important differences" between Jesus and John.[711] Because their analysis is typical of much modern scholarship, a critical review is instructive.

1. The first difference that Theissen and Merz espy concerns eschatology. John threatened people with the coming wrath. Jesus did the same, except that he, in the words of Theissen and Merz, "seems to have put more emphasis on the offer of salvation (even to sinners) bound up with the preaching of the βασιλεία."[712] This sentiment appears in dozens of recent books and articles on Jesus,[713] and one can scarcely disprove it. And yet, does it not presuppose that we have a far better idea of John's proclamation than we do? Are not the sources too constricted for such a large generalization? Josephus, who transforms John "into a popular moral philosopher of Stoic hue, with a somewhat neo-Pythagorean rite of lustration,"[714] sums up the Baptist's message in two short sentences (*Ant.* 18.117). Q contains no narrative material about the Baptist aside from Matt 11:2–3 // Luke 7:18–19, and it attributes to him words that, in both Matthew and Luke, span only six verses (Matt 3:7–10, 11–12 // Luke 3:7–9, 16–18). Q also has Jesus speak about John a few times, but the relevant sayings are scarcely rich with helpful detail (Matt 11:7–11, 16–19; 11:12–13 // Luke 7:24–28, 31–35; 16:16). In Mark, we find a scant three-verse synopsis of John's ministry (1:4–6), an account of his martyrdom that has "something of the character of the fairy tale"[715] (6:14–29), and a couple of words of Jesus that add next to nothing to our modest store of knowledge (9:13; 11:27–33). And John's own speech occupies just two verses (1:7–8)—verses that fail to expand our knowledge because they more or less duplicate sentences from Q. Matthew for his part adds two further utterances, "Repent, for the kingdom of heaven is at hand" (3:2 RSV) and "I need to be baptized by you, and do you come to me?" (3:14), but these are widely and rightly suspected of being Matthean redaction and are probably without substantial basis in his tradition. As for Luke, he contributes to our sparse store merely three short sentences that, even if they represent things John said, do little more than show him to have been a sponsor of generosity and fairness (Luke 3:10–14). Finally, John's Gospel has an intriguing notice in 3:23 that may well be historical—John baptized at Aenon near Salim—and it gives the Baptist a bit more to say. Yet most of the

711. Theissen and Merz, *Historical Jesus*, 208–11.
712. Ibid., 208.
713. For example, Meier, *Marginal Jew*, 2:124 (Jesus' "message becomes much more a joyful announcement of the offer and experience of salvation"); Helmut Merklein, "Die Umkehrpredigt bei Johannes dem Täufer und Jesus von Nazaret," *BZ* 25 (1981): 37.
714. Meier, *Marginal Jew*, 2:21.
715. Nineham, *Saint Mark*, 173.

lines in the Fourth Gospel so well serve apologetical interests that one hardly feels comfortable using them to reconstruct the authentic Baptist.[716] Many would assign to late Christian reflection all but the variant of Matt 3:11 // Luke 3:16 (Q) // Mark 1:7–8 in John 1:26–27 (cf. 1:15, 30).

Given the dearth of data, when Theissen and Merz affirm that Jesus put more emphasis upon the offer of salvation than did John, and then add, in implicit contrast, that for Jesus that offer was bound up with the βασιλεία, is this not a leap of faith? The brief summary descriptions of the Baptist are just that, brief summary descriptions,[717] and we have beyond them at best only a handful of sentences with a claim to reflect things that John really said (Matt 3:7–10, 11–12 // Luke 3:7–9, 16–17 [Q] are usually thought to be the best candidates); and how do we know to what extent those sentences fairly represent the whole of what he had to say? Unless he was exceedingly boring or was akin to Jesus son of Ananias, who, according to Josephus (J.W. 6.301–302), uttered the same refrain over and over again, the Baptist must have said much more than the few utterances preserved by our sources.

Neither Josephus nor anyone who contributed to the Jesus tradition was interested in passing on an objective, dispassionate summary of John's proclamation. Beyond that, much, even much of importance, must be missing. This follows simply from the few words that Josephus and the evangelists give to the Baptist. Selection inevitably distorts. Maybe the little bits that we do have are not unlike those annoying synopses of television shows that appear in the daily papers: even when they are strictly true, they leave so much out of account as to be practically useless. Or, to choose an ancient analogy, what do we make of the fact that not one of the traditions about Hillel explicitly refers to God? Does not good sense warn that this may be an artificial upshot of happenstance and/or the narrow focus of the relevant rabbinic traditions, not a sure indicator of something important about Hillel or his teachings?

Now, with regard to the Baptist and Theissen and Merz's comment about the βασιλεία, if John sometimes or even often spoke of "the kingdom of God," we have no reason to think that our small number of abbreviating sources would have taken note. Should not sober historical judgment, then, reluctantly concede that we simply do not know whether John ever proclaimed the kingdom of God, or what exactly he might have meant if he had? It is, in the end, possible that Jesus' focus upon the kingdom was inherited from John (although for this there is no evidence, if we leave aside the redactional Matt 3:2). It is equally possible that John never once spoke of the kingdom (again, there simply is no evidence). Should we not, then, prudently eschew an opinion on the matter? How can we justify equating John's textual silence

716. See John 1:20–23, 26–27, 29–34; 3:27–30.
717. For a review of all the materials, see Edmondo F. Lupieri, "John the Baptist in New Testament Traditions and History," ANRW 26.1:430–61.

with a historical silence and then go on to highlight Jesus' originality? One might as well observe that whereas John nowhere mentions Adam or Moses or David or Solomon or any other biblical person, Jesus sometimes does, and then infer that the latter but not the former cared about the scriptural story. Would that not be ridiculous reasoning?

Theissen and Merz's assertion that Jesus laid more stress upon salvation than did John also comes up against our ignorance. Unless, by some miracle, our sources accurately summarize everything that the Baptist taught, what do we really know about him and this subject? How much can we infer from the tiny bits or abridgements that we do have? Is there not, to repeat yet again what should be obvious, a danger of generalizing from too few instances? While we may have the impression that John was primarily a preacher of judgment, this impression comes from Q, not Josephus, Mark, or John; and while it would probably be unwise to doubt that John proclaimed the imminent eschatological judgment, is it not Q's interest in such judgment that explains why Matthew and Luke, in dependence upon the Sayings Source, highlight this aspect of his proclamation?

But Q's main interests need not exhaust what was front and center in John's ministry. Maybe the Baptist was, as Josephus and Luke 3:10–14 have it, also much interested in social reform, even though this dimension is altogether missing from Q. Proclamation of a near and retributive end does not, to judge from the record of worldwide millenarian movements, preclude social concern. Again, perhaps, like Jesus, John not only preached judgment but also had much to say or at least something to say about salvation and its experience in the here and now. Here we are in the dark, for while the absence of something from the traditions about John may reflect its absence from his ministry, it may equally reflect a lack of potential Christian utility. When Jürgen Becker says of John that "nothing even approaching a promise of salvation crosses his lips,"[718] has he not forsaken good sense and forgotten the nature of our sources?

Theissen and Merz conjecture that Jesus experienced eschatological delay when John's imminent expectation went unfulfilled.[719] This may well be. But perhaps John already had the same experience. We have no idea how long his ministry lasted. Was it weeks or months or years? Maybe he also at some point had to grapple with the problem of receding fulfillment.[720] One can believe that the night is far spent only so long before pangs of doubt make themselves felt. But again, how would we ever know?[721]

718. Becker, *Jesus of Nazareth*, 38.

719. See Theissen and Merz, "Delay of the Parousia."

720. See Meier, *Marginal Jew*, 2:132–33.

721. W. Barnes Tatum ("The Jewish Jesus: Apocalyptic Prophet or Subversive Sage?" *The Fourth R* 14, no. 1 [2001]: 8) exploits another alleged contrast in order to characterize Jesus' eschatology—a contrast that, like Theissen's, also oversteps the boundaries of what we know. Many have surmised, from Jesus' submission to John's baptism, which amounts to an endorse-

2. The second contrast made by Theissen and Merz concerns what they call "messianic preaching." John, they assert, expected the ἰσχυρότερος ("stronger one"), which, before Christian interpretation, may have been either God or "a judge figure (like the Son of Man)."[722] Jesus, to the contrary, spoke about the coming Son of Man, which he may have identified with himself or his circle. The assumption here seems to be that the Baptist spoke about a "stronger one" but not about the "Son of Man," a term that Jesus by contrast used. Yet where is the evidence? We have no knowledge of whether John used one messianic title or many, or even whether he expected one figure or two or three. Nothing demonstrates or even hints that he could not have spoken of the "Messiah" or of the "Son of David" or of the "Son of Man" or of the coming Elijah. One certainly doubts that John used "the stronger one" exclusively. The term in and of itself, as the secondary literature makes clear, is ambiguous. Scholars debate whether the Baptist was speaking of God, an angelic deliverer, or an exalted human being. So unless John was riddler as much as baptizer, he must have clarified "the stronger one" for his hearers, and perhaps he did so by speaking of the coming of God or the Son of Man or the Davidic Messiah or the high-priestly Messiah or some other stock figure from prophecy.[723] Our sources, however, do not preserve whatever clarification he may have offered.

---

ment, and from Paul's eschatological orientation, which tells us so much about the early church, that Jesus must have been a millenarian or apocalyptic prophet (for my own version of this argument, see above, pp. 48–55). In countering this line of reasoning, Tatum contends, following the Jesus Seminar, that "Jesus' parables . . . represent a critique of an apocalyptic world-view," and further that "neither John the Jew nor Paul taught in parables." This generalization about Paul, from whom we have several letters, some of them very long, seems fair enough. But what is the basis for making the assertion about John? How does Tatum, who makes his observation as though it were obvious to all, know that John did not use parables? Is it because the four or five sentences that Q attributes to John feature no parable? This seems a large supposition from so small a starting point. What would Tatum infer if Q did, on the contrary, contain a parable from the Baptist? Would he guess that John used parables often, only sometimes, or only once? Obviously, none of these conclusions would be safe, and it is the same with Tatum's inference from there being no parable at all. One remembers that Mark's two-verse summary of what Jesus proclaimed (1:14–15) omits that Jesus spoke in parables, even though the evangelist knew the fact well enough. The failure of the canonical Baptist to employ parables should not be equated with the historical John's failure to use parables, from which therefore nothing follows about Jesus' eschatology.

722. Theissen and Merz, *Historical Jesus*, 209. They also say, "this mediator figure bore none of the usual messianic titles" (p. 211).

723. Contrast Meier (*Marginal Jew*, 2:35), who conjectures that John intended to be vague. Against this, see Robert L. Webb, *John the Baptizer and Prophet: A Socio-Historical Study* (Eugene, OR: Wipf & Stock, 2006), 288–89. Webb himself suggests instead that maybe "John did not wish to identify himself with any one particular form of Jewish expectation, but wished to emphasize the divine nature of the imminent judgment and restoration. To have engaged in eschatological speculation as to the type of agent may have sidetracked his audience from the prime issue at hand: repentance in the face of imminent judgment."

What we do know is that "the stronger one," which shows up in the summaries in Q and Mark, is the one title (if that is the right word) that in and of itself makes a comparison. While John may have used other honorifics for the eschatological figure or figures he expected, it is precisely "the stronger one" that clearly demotes the speaker even as it promotes another, and what could have better served Christian interests? The reason for the appearance of this title as opposed to some other is manifest. And certainly, if John (like some of the authors of the Dead Sea Scrolls) expected more than one eschatological figure, we need not wonder why the Christian tradition kept a discreet silence about it and remembered him speaking of a single individual.

3. "Imminent futurist eschatology" is the subject of Theissen and Merz's third distinction. John believed the eschatological consummation to be close to hand: the ax was laid at the root of the tree.[724] Jesus shared the same conviction. Yet he also looked back on John as "a decisive turning point" (cf. Q 7:28; Luke 16:16; Gos. Thom. 46), and he had "a present eschatology" as well as a "future eschatology."[725] This dissimilarity, like those already considered, holds only if our records preserve all of the major themes in John's repertoire. But Josephus (who purges John's proclamation of eschatology) is defective on this subject; and, to belabor the obvious again because it needs belaboring, our Christian sources, even if one imagines them to be reasonably accurate, are not likely in their brief recaps to introduce us to John in his entirety. They are, first and foremost, testimonies to Jesus, not reports about the Baptist as he was in and of himself. So one wonders how Theissen and Merz know that John, unlike Jesus, other Jews, and many early Christians, did not believe in a present or partially realized eschatology as well as in imminent judgment. Followers of Jesus had a keen interest in keeping John's vision focused on the future, so that they could locate the realization of all expectations in Jesus, who came after John. It follows that if the Baptist had laid any emphasis upon fulfillment, or if he had thought of his own ministry as the beginning of the era of redemption, one would not expect Christian sources to inform us on the matter. Once again, then, we are left with a silence that we should respect, not a silence from which we may draw far-reaching inferences.

4. The fourth antithesis Theissen and Merz propose concerns baptism. John administered an eschatological sacrament associated with the confession of sins, a sacrament that brought salvation if accompanied by fruits of repentance. Jesus, on the other hand, although he recognized John's baptism, did not, Theissen and Merz think, baptize (cf. John 4:2). Jesus, rather, detached "the notion of repentance from baptism." Theissen and Merz explain that Jesus' notion of purity (cf. Mark 7:15) stood "in tension with the sacrament of baptism."[726]

724. Even Origen (Hom. Luc. 23) recognized that John's words in Luke 3 most naturally refer to "the end of time."
725. Theissen and Merz, Historical Jesus, 209.
726. Ibid.

The appeal here to John 4:2 ("it was not Jesus himself but his disciples who baptized") is odd, for it is likely an apologetic qualification of the truth preserved in 3:22: "Jesus and his disciples went into the Judean countryside and he spent some time there with them and baptized." Maybe Jesus baptized for a while, or maybe longer than a while.[727] Indeed, maybe he baptized throughout his ministry, and maybe the Synoptic tradition, like John 4:2, found this fact less than edifying.[728] The Synoptic silence cannot be the last word, because it is no word at all. Once more, then, we have no guidance.

Nor can any supposed tension with Jesus' notion of purity prove that he did not baptize. Such a contradiction is not spelled out in the sources, and it may exist nowhere but in the mind of a modern scholar. Jesus was no systematic theologian or analytic philosopher, nor can we expect that things ill-fitting for us did not go together for him. We have, as an illustration of this, some pretty good evidence that he believed in both a good, loving God and some sort of fiery hell, two things that many of us find all but impossible to reconcile. But our difficulty in this matter is no criterion for figuring out what an ancient Jew believed or did not believe.[729] Similarly, with regard to purity and baptism, a better guide than Theissen and Merz may be the evangelist Matthew, who passed on the command to baptize (28:16–20) as well as a version of Mark 7:15 ("there is nothing outside a person that by going in can defile, but the things that come out are what defile" [see Matt 15:17–18]). Matthew evidently could hold the two things together. So maybe Jesus uttered Mark 7:15 and at the same time baptized. Or, if he ceased to baptize, maybe this had nothing at all to do with his ideas about purity. Who knows?

5. The final distinction that Theissen and Merz draw between John and Jesus is that whereas the former was an ascetic, as evidenced by his food, clothing, and dwelling in the desert, the latter was not. Jesus lived in such a way as to be called a "glutton and drunkard" (Q 7:34), and he carried on his ministry in populated areas. John's asceticism was self-stigmatization intended as a criticism of society. With Jesus, asceticism appears only in the missionary discourse, where it is "a means of mission."[730]

The main problem here is not our ignorance of John, whose ascetic credentials admit of little question.[731] It is rather that the missionary discourse is not, as I read the facts, anomalous; that is, it is not the only ascetic feature

727. Meier (*Marginal Jew*, 2:116–30) offers a helpful overview of the issue.

728. See ibid., 2:126–29.

729. Although scholars have again and again made the attempt. The most egregious example of this is the instructive—because so insistent—work of Lily Dougall and Cyril W. Emmet, *The Lord of Thought: A Study of the Problems Which Confronted Jesus Christ and the Solution He Offered* (London: SCM Press, 1922).

730. Theissen and Merz, *Historical Jesus*, 209.

731. Although whether he ever challenged others to take up his ascetical lifestyle we do not know.

of the pre-Easter tradition.[732] Jesus himself almost certainly was unmarried,[733] and our sources attribute to him several demanding sayings about guarding sexual desire.[734] He also issued strident warnings about money and property, and he and his followers lived, at least part of the time, as itinerants.[735] Some of them abandoned families and business.[736] Jesus himself, in the language of Matt 8:20 // Luke 9:58 (Q), from time to time had nowhere to lay his head. Tradents, furthermore, found no difficulty depicting him fasting and seeking to be alone[737]—all of which harmonizes nicely with the ascetic demands of the missionary discourse. It is hard to avoid thinking that religious self-discipline and rigorous self-denial were characteristic of the historical Jesus.[738]

Contemporary exegetes, living in an age nonplussed by or antagonistic to even mild asceticism, have read far too much into Matt 11:18–19 // Luke 7:33–34 (Q) and its rhetorical differentiation between a caricatured Jesus and a caricatured John, as though that passage were a dispassionate depiction rather than a piece of clever, hyperbolic rhetoric occasioned by slander ("and you say").[739] Nothing contradicts the canonical picture of a Jesus who sometimes feasts and sometimes fasts, of a Jesus who is sometimes put up for the night and sometimes without a place to lay his head, of a Jesus who is sometimes joyful and sometimes stern.

732. In addition to what follows, see Allison, *Jesus of Nazareth*, 172–216.

733. Matthew 19:12, which may well go back to Jesus, is readily explained as his own retort to those who mocked his single state; see J. Blinzler, "Εὐνοῦχοι," *ZNW* 48 (1957): 254–70. That the saying uses the plural, "eunuchs," probably indicates that some of his followers were also unmarried.

734. See especially Matt 5:27–28; Mark 9:43–48. On the original application of the latter to sexual sins, see Will Deming, "Mark 9.42–10.12, Matthew 5.27–32, and *b. Nid.* 13b: A First Century Discussion of Male Sexuality," *NTS* 36 (1990): 130–41; Kurt Niederwimmer, *Askese und Mysterium: Über Ehe, Ehescheidung und Eheverzicht in den Anfängen des christlichen Glaubens* (FRLANT 113; Göttingen: Vandenhoeck & Ruprecht, 1975), 29–33. On Mark 12:18–27, which envisages the possibility of human nature without the sexual impulse, see Davies and Allison, *Matthew*, 3:221–34.

735. See Peter Nagel, *Die Motivierung der Askese in der alten Kirche und der Ursprung des Mönchtums* (TU 95; Berlin: Akademie-Verlag, 1966), 6–7. Relevant texts include Matt 10:9–11; 6:24–33 // Luke 10:4, 7–8; 12:22–31, 33–34; 16:13 (Q); Mark 1:16–20; 2:13–14; 10:17–27; *Gos. Thom.* 42. Luke 8:1–3 purports that certain women provided for Jesus and his disciples out of their resources.

736. See Matt 8:21–22; 10:34–37 // Luke 9:59–60; 12:51–53; 14:26 (Q); Mark 1:16–20; 2:14; 10:28–31; Luke 9:61–62.

737. Texts that place Jesus in the wilderness and/or depict him seeking solitude include Matt 4:1 // Luke 4:1 (Q); Mark 1:35, 45; 6:31–44; 8:1–10; John 3:22.

738. See Matt 23:12; 10:38–39 // Luke 14:11, 27; 17:33 (Q); Mark 8:34; 9:43–48; *Gos. Thom.* 55.

739. On its stereotypical character, and indeed scriptural background in Deut 21:20, see David Daube, *Appeasement or Resistance and Other Essays on New Testament Judaism* (Berkeley: University of California Press, 1987), 23–26. Also helpful is James M. Robinson, "Galilean Upstarts: A Sot's Cynical Disciples?" in *Sayings of Jesus* (ed. Petersen, Vos, and de Jonge), 223–49. Certainly nothing in the tradition contradicts the claim of Clement of Alexandria (*Paed.* 2.2.32.2–3) that Jesus ate and drank in moderation.

At this juncture I wish to state clearly that all of the antitheses proposed by Theissen and Merz need not be false. Nor, with the exception of the last disjunction, have I tried to refute them. My point is not that Theissen and Merz must be wrong but rather that they are not clearly right, and that the cause of their failing is typical. Again and again discussions of the Baptist and Jesus manifest a superfluity of inference; they fail to persuade not because they go against the evidence but because they go beyond it. Our unfortunate ignorance, which so inconveniences us, sets large question marks over several of the conventional contrasts so often drawn between the two men. More caution is called for. Extrapolating from what our all-too-brief sources fail to say about the Baptist is a risky business.[740]

Elements of Continuity

But what, then, of the continuity between John and Jesus? Needless to say, the want of evidence hampers us here also. Christians, furthermore, may have been inclined to attribute sentiments to Jesus alone that John also expressed. It is, for instance, possible in theory to imagine that the Baptist composed some of the sayings in the Sermon on the Plain and that Jesus learned them from John, and that Christians, for understandable reasons, preferred to forget this fact.[741] In such a case, however, the truth would be beyond our ability to discover it; the historical continuity would have left no trace in the records. One can likewise imagine that John and Jesus were indeed, as Luke has it, relatives, and that they talked about theology off and on over the years, so that they influenced each other in manifold ways no longer recoverable. Such a suggestion, while baseless and fanciful, does serve to remind us how little we know.

The only historical continuity that we can recover is, to state the obvious, limited to what the extant sources, imperfect as they are, actually say, both about John and about Jesus. Given this, and given how little those sources tell us about the Baptist, we might anticipate that the outcome of a comparison would yield little. Yet what in fact emerges is, as I will now seek to show, unexpectedly suggestive. Jesus appears to have been fundamentally indebted to John throughout his ministry.[742]

1. *Descent from Abraham and Judgment.* Mishnah *Sanh.* 10:1 declares that all Israel has a place in the world to come. The text goes on to list exceptions,

---

740. For another skeptical review of the differences between John and Jesus that scholars parade so often, see Bermejo, "Historiografía," 89–93.

741. Joan Taylor has raised the possibility that John composed the Lord's Prayer, or something close to it (*The Immerser*, 151–53), and Clare K. Rothschild has urged that much in Q came originally from the Baptist (*Baptist Traditions and Q* [WUNT 190; Tübingen: Mohr Siebeck, 2005]). Although I disagree with both authors, their suggestions are not impossible, just without sufficient warrant.

742. In addition to what follows, see Bermejo, "Historiografía," 86–89.

these being various apostates, heretics, and so on. Now whether or not, as Ed Sanders has argued, this view characterized what he calls "common Judaism," we can scarcely doubt that more than a few Palestinian Jews near the turn of the era held something close to what Sanders has dubbed "covenantal nomism."[743] Such people hoped that descent from Abraham would, as long as they did not abandon the Torah, gain them entry into the world to come.

John appears to have rejected this hope. The chief evidence is Matt 3:9 // Luke 3:8 (Q), on the assumption that it fairly represents the sort of thing the Baptist said: "Do not presume to tell yourselves: We have Abraham as our father! For I tell you: God can produce children for Abraham right out of these stones."[744] This line, which appears to set aside Isa 51:1–2,[745] seems to oppose precisely what Sanders has called "covenantal nomism." Indeed, one could scarcely hope to find a more straightforward rejection of the notion that to be born into the covenant with Abraham is to be saved. As David Daube remarked, John the Baptist's words mean that "you must acquire him [Abraham] just like strangers."[746] Daube, to be sure, assumed that the Baptist's water rite was a transmutation of Jewish proselyte ritual, so that in calling for baptism John was asking Jews to think of themselves as Gentiles, as people outside the covenant community. This may or may not be correct. Recent discussion has come to no certain conclusion as to whether such baptism appeared already in pre-Christian Judaism, although seemingly most experts currently guess that it had not.[747]

Yet even if we are to look elsewhere for an explanation of John's baptism, Daube's exegesis of Matt 3:8–9 // Luke 3:8 (Q) stands. It is not enough to be descended from Abraham; one must, according to the saying attributed to the Baptist, be "born again." Deliverance comes not by belonging to the Jewish people but only by a radical turning around, by repentance that produces good fruit. One cannot inherit the merit of the patriarchs; rather, such "has to be earned individually in the present time by each person in his or her own life; only then can s/he truly continue the spirit of Abraham."[748]

743. Sanders, *Judaism*, 262–78. For critical discussion, see D. A. Carson, Peter T. O'Brien, and Mark A. Seifrid, eds., *The Complexities of Second Temple Judaism* (vol. 1 of *Justification and Variegated Nomism*; Tübingen: Mohr Siebeck; Grand Rapids: Baker Academic, 2001).

744. All quotations from Q are from Robinson, Hoffmann, and Kloppenborg, eds., *Critical Edition of Q*.

745. "Look to the rock from whence you were hewn and to the quarry whence you were dug. Look to Abraham your father and to Sarah who bore you. For when he was but one I called him and blessed him and I caused him to increase." See Allison, *Intertextual Jesus*, 101–4.

746. David Daube, *Ancient Jewish Law: Three Inaugural Lectures* (Leiden: Brill, 1981), 10.

747. For an overview of the issues, see Scot McKnight, *A Light among the Gentiles: Jewish Missionary Activity in the Second Temple Period* (Minneapolis: Fortress, 1991), 82–85.

748. Taylor, *The Immerser*, 130. See further R. Menahem, "A Jewish Commentary on the New Testament: A Sample Verse," *Immanuel* 21 (1987): 43–54. There are Hebrew Bible parallels to this sort of warning; see, for example, Jer 9:24–25; also the exposition of Richard C. Steiner, "Incomplete Circumcision in Egypt and Edom: Jeremiah (9:24–25) in the Light of Josephus and Jonckheere," *JBL* 118 (1999): 497–505.

John's warning about confidence in Abrahamic descent is the context for the warnings about judgment in Matt 3:10, 12 // Luke 3:9, 17 (Q): "And the ax already lies at the root of the trees. So every tree not bearing healthy fruit is to be chopped down and thrown on the fire"; "His pitchfork is in his hand, and he will clear his threshing floor and gather the wheat into his granary, but the chaff he will burn on a fire that can never be put out." If we can trust these texts, the Baptist evidently did not believe that, except for heretics who had put themselves outside the covenant, all Israelites would enter the world to come. He appears instead to have uttered his sweeping, earnest warnings about damnation precisely because he denied the belief, held by some, that those born of Abraham could for that reason alone hope to pass the final judgment.

What does all this have to do with Jesus? He almost certainly shared John's rejection of what Sanders takes to have been a common idea.[749] Sanders has, of course, denied this, but as far as I can see, the tradition nowhere leaves the impression that good Jews are saved by virtue of being good Jews—that is, because they are descended from the patriarchs. From beginning to end it presupposes, rather, that the question of salvation is open and that Jesus' audience, above all his Jewish opponents, should, notwithstanding their heritage, fret about their fate in the world to come. They should not presume to be safely in and okay as opposed to out and still in danger. When Mark 1:15 summarizes Jesus' proclamation with words that include "repent," surely this catches the spirit of his message.

Mark 10:15 remembers Jesus as saying, "Truly I tell you, whoever does not receive the kingdom of God as a little child will never enter it." Although some have thought this saying calls for trust or humility, or for the ability to say "Abba," it is far more likely that, if Jesus urged people to become children, he was, like the Baptist in Matt 3:8–10 // Luke 3:8–9 (Q), telling them to start their religious lives over, telling them to go back to the beginning. In later Judaism, the convert is "like a newborn child" (*b. Yebam.* 22a),[750] and the Fourth Gospel clearly takes our saying to mean that one must be born again, or from above (3:3).[751] The saying about becoming children is akin to John's call for repentance and baptism: one has to start from scratch.

The theological premise of Jesus' call to begin one's religious life anew was the same as that of the Baptist, namely, eschatological judgment. Both prophets looked to the future and saw judgment. Both believed its arrival time to be sooner rather than later. And both believed that some or many of their Jewish contemporaries might flunk the coming assize. The evidence with

749. In addition to what follows, see Dale C. Allison Jr., "Jesus and the Covenant: A Response to E. P. Sanders," in *The Historical Jesus* (ed. Craig A. Evans and Stanley E. Porter; BibSem 33; Sheffield: Sheffield Academic Press, 1996), 61–82 (reprinted from *JSNT* 29 [1987]: 57–78).

750. See also, for example, *b. Yebam.* 48b; 62a; 97b; *b. Ber.* 47a.

751. See Barnabas Lindars, "John and the Synoptic Gospels: A Test Case," *NTS* 27 (1981): 287–94. Cf. 2 Cor 5:17.

regard to John is in Q, on the common assumption that it rightly preserves the spirit of John's message. With regard to Jesus, the evidence for these assertions is considerable, and I have introduced it elsewhere.[752] More importantly, three recent monographs have concluded that a strong and recurring sense of imminent eschatological judgment cannot be eliminated from the original tradition.[753] Jesus was, as the Synoptics depict him, an eschatological prophet who urgently warned hearers to prepare for the coming judgments. For him the judgment was, as it was for John, looming, and it threatened precisely because Abrahamic descent guaranteed nothing. In this respect at least, Jesus' ministry continued John's mission, and on this fundamental point there is no hint that Jesus ever departed from the Baptist.

2. *Common Images.* Several sayings attributed to John share images with sayings attributed to Jesus:

- In Matt 3:8–9 // Luke 3:8 (Q), the Baptist commands his hearers to "bear fruit worthy of repentance," and in Matt 3:10 // Luke 3:9 (Q) he warns of the peril of not bearing "healthy fruit." In Matt 7:16–21; 12:33–35 // Luke 6:43–45 (Q), Jesus also calls upon human beings to bear fruit: "No healthy tree bears rotten fruit, nor does a decayed tree bear healthy fruit. For from the fruit the tree is known. Are figs picked from thorns, or grapes from thistles? The good person from one's good treasure casts up good things. . . ."

- John, according to Matt 3:10 // Luke 3:9 (Q), declared that "the ax already lies at the root of the trees. So every tree not bearing healthy fruit is to be chopped down. . . ." In Luke 13:6–9, Jesus tells a parable about a fruit-bearing tree that does not bear fruit. The owner orders it to be cut down. The vinedresser then pleads for the tree, that it be given a little more time before it is destroyed.

- At the end of Matt 3:10 // Luke 3:9 (Q), the tree that is cut down is then "thrown on the fire." The image of being "thrown" into eschatological fire appears several times in the Jesus tradition: Matt 7:19 (redactional); 13:40 (M); Mark 9:47–50; John 15:1–16.

- Matt 3:11 // Luke 3:16 (Q) contains the striking image of baptizing not with water but with fire. The same image reappears in Luke 12:49–50, where lines about fire and baptism stand in nearly synonymous parallelism: "I came to cast fire upon the earth; and would that it were already kindled! I have a baptism to be baptized with; and how I am constrained until it is accomplished!" (RSV).

752. See Dale C. Allison Jr., "The Problem of Gehenna," in *Resurrecting Jesus*, 56–100.
753. Reiser, *Jesus and Judgment*; Riniker, *Gerichtsverkündigung Jesu*; Werner Zager, *Gottesherrschaft und Endgericht in der Verkündigung Jesu: Eine Untersuchung zur markinischen Jesusüberlieferung einschließlich der Q-Parallelen* (BZNW 82; Berlin: de Gruyter, 1996).

• John speaks, in Matt 3:12 // Luke 3:17 (Q), of the eschatological judgment as a harvest: "His pitchfork is in his hand, and he will clear his
  threshing floor and gather the wheat into his granary, but the chaff he
  will burn on a fire that can never be put out." The comparison of eschatological judgment to harvesting appears in the Jesus tradition in Matt
  9:37–38 // Luke 10:2 (Q) (the plentiful harvest [cf. John 4:35–38]); Matt
  13:24–30 // *Gos. Thom.* 57 (the parable of the weeds and wheat); Mark
  4:1–9 (the parable of the sower); 4:26–29 (the parable of the growing
  seed).

What should we make of these parallels? Likening good deeds to fruit and
the last judgment to a harvest are fairly common rhetorical moves in Jewish
sources, so much so that we cannot justifiably hold that Jesus, if he composed
sayings with those topoi, must have been borrowing from John.[754]
The other parallels have a different character. The picture of people being
"thrown" into a fire does occur in Dan 3, in the story of the three young men
and the fiery furnace, but that story is not about eschatological judgment. The
closest Jewish parallels seemingly are confined to the Enoch traditions: *1 En.*
54:2–6; 90:25; 91:9; 98:3 v.l.; *2 En.* J 63:4.[755] In other words, this evidently was
not a far-flung way of speaking. Given, then, that Jesus heard John preach,
does not the rarity of the violent image common to Matt 3:10 // Luke 3:9 (Q)
and several logia attributed to Jesus (e.g., Mark 9:47–50) raise the possibility
that one teacher borrowed from the other?
It is the same with Matt 3:10 // Luke 3:9 (Q) and Luke 13:6–9. Cutting
down a fruitless tree to represent the last judgment occurs, to my knowledge,
in Matt 3:10 // Luke 3:9 (Q), in Luke 13:6–9, in literature influenced by the
canonical Gospels, and nowhere else. There are, to be sure, Jewish texts in
which chopping a tree down illustrates divine judgment,[756] but these do not
attribute that judgment to a failure to bear fruit, as do our two sentences; and
the interesting parallel in *Ahiqar* Syriac 8:35 (Arabic 8:30),[757] which might in

754. For the figurative use of "fruit" in ethico-religious speech, see, for example, Ps 1:3; Prov
1:31; Isa 3:10; Hos 10:1; Sir 23:25; Rom 6:22; Jas 3:18; Josephus, *Ant.* 20.48; *2 Bar.* 32:1; *Apoc.
Adam* 6:1; *b. Qidd.* 40a. For imagery of the harvest in connection with judgment, see, for example, Isa 41:14–16; Jer 15:7; 51:33; Hos 6:11; Mic 4:12–13; Joel 3:13; Rev 14:14–20; *4 Ezra* 4:30,
38–39; Tg. Ps.-J. on Isa 28:28; 33:11.
755. The latter two may be Christian. For Christian texts, see, in addition to Matt 7:19; 13:40
(M); Mark 9:47–50; John 15:1–16, also Rev 19:20; 20:10, 14–15; and John of Damascus, *Sacred
Parallels* (PG 96:344C).
756. See, for example, Isa 6:13; 10:33–34; Dan 4:11, 19–23.
757. "My son, you have been to me like that palm-tree that stood by a river, and cast all its
fruit into the river, and when its lord came to cut it down, it said to him, 'Let me alone this year,
and I will bring you forth carobs.' And its lord said to it, 'You have not been industrious in what
is your own, and how will you be industrious in what is not you own?'" The parallel in *CMC*
94 presumably depends upon Luke.

any case be Christian, does not concern eschatological judgment. So if Luke 13:6–9 comes from Jesus himself,[758] he may have had John's words in mind.

It is a fact of exegetical history that Luke 13:6–9 has evoked John's warning in Matt 3:10 and Luke 3:9. Codex Bezae (D), for example, adds φέρε τὴν ἀξίνην to Luke 13:7, surely in recollection of John's prophecy. Matthew Henry thought that Jesus' parable "enlarges upon" the Baptist's saying, while Alfred Nevin spoke of Jesus' "personal application" of the same utterance.[759] Others have simply assimilated the two texts without comment; thus Peter of Alexandria, *Epistula canonica* 3.23, in interpreting the parable of the barren fig tree, uses the phrase ἐνδειξάμενοι καρπὸν ἄξιον τῆς μετανοίας, which is from Matt 3:8 // Luke 3:8 (Q).

As for Matt 3:11 // Luke 3:16 (Q), Luke 12:49–50 and being baptized in fire, certainly many texts, perhaps under Zoroastrian influence, envisage the eschatological fire as a flood that comes upon the world. Yet the juxtaposition of this molten stream with the language of baptism does not seem to have any close pre-Christian parallels. So if we knew that Jesus really did say something like Luke 12:49–50, we would have to suspect that John's proclamation of a coming torrent of fire inspired him.[760] Commentators through the centuries have repeatedly linked the two passages.[761]

I submit that these results, meager as they might appear upon initial scrutiny, are on the contrary not so meager. If we keep in mind how little we have from the Baptist, then to find two or three instances in which teaching attributed

758. There do not seem to be strong arguments for or against the dominical origin of Luke 13:6–9. A few observations: (i) There are linguistic signs of a pre-Lukan origin; see Jeremias, *Sprache*, 227–28. (ii) The parallel in *Gos. Pet.* E 2 may be independent of Luke; so Richard Bauckham, "The Two Fig Tree Parables in the Apocalypse of Peter," *JBL* 104 (1985): 269–87. I am unsure. (iii) Jesus surely was fond of agricultural parables. (iv) The theme of unexpected grace is at home in Jesus' proclamation, as is the concern with judgment. (v) Luke 13:6–9 is not likely to derive from either the story of the withered fig tree in Mark 11:13–14, 20–21 or the parable in Mark 13:28–29. Indeed, the opposite sometimes has been alleged, that the story of the withered fig tree derives from the parable.

759. Matthew Henry, *Matthew to John* (vol. 5 of *Commentary on the Whole Bible*; Old Tappan, NJ: Fleming H. Revell, n.d.), 721; Alfred Nevin, *Popular Expositor of the Gospels and Acts* (Philadelphia: Ziegler & McCurdy, 1872), 856. See also Origen, *Hom. Jer.* 18.5; Cyril of Alexandria, *Comm. Luke* 96 (PG 72:764A–B); Albertus Magnus, *Enarrationes in primam partem Evangelii Lucae (I–IX)* (vol. 22 of *Opera Omnia*, ed. A. Borgnet; Paris: Ludovicus Vivès, 1894), 282; Robert C. Tannehill, *Luke* (ANTC; Nashville: Abingdon, 1996), 275; Theissen and Merz, *Historical Jesus*, 210; Peter Böhlemann, *Jesus und der Täufer: Schlüssel zur Theologie und Ethik des Lukas* (SNTSMS 99; Cambridge: Cambridge University Press, 1997), 163–64.

760. See further below, pp. 276–77.

761. For example, Origen, *Selecta in Psalmos* (PG 12:1236C); *Hom. Luc.* 26.1; Jerome, *Comm. Matt.* 3:11; Theodore of Heraclea, *Comm. Matt.* frg. 18 (J. Reuss, ed., *Matthäus-Kommentare aus der griechischen Kirche* [TU 61; Berlin: Akademie-Verlag, 1957], 62); Albertus Magnus, *Enarrationes in primam partem Evangelii Lucae (I–IX)*, 153; Henry, *Matthew to John*, 27; I. Howard Marshall, *The Gospel of Luke: A Commentary on the Greek Text* (NIGTC; Grand Rapids: Eerdmans, 1978), 547; Böhlemann, *Jesus und der Täufer*, 168–70.

to Jesus mirrors teaching attributed to John is noteworthy. We can reasonably presume that if more of John's teaching had been preserved, Jesus' debt to him would appear even larger. We would then see all the more that "Jesus' vision, message, and tactics were shaped by John."[762]

3. *The Coming One.* According to Matt 3:11–12 // Luke 3:16–17 (Q), the Baptist, when he looked into the future, saw a coming judge: "I baptize you in water; but the one to come after me is more powerful than I, whose sandals I am not fit to take off. He will baptize you in holy Spirit and fire. His pitchfork is in his hand, and he will clear his threshing floor and gather the wheat into his granary, but the chaff he will burn on a fire that can never be put out." According to Matt 11:2–6 // Luke 7:18–23 (Q), Jesus took himself to be that judge: "Go and tell John what you have seen and heard: the blind receive their sight. . . . And blessed is anyone who takes no offense at me." The identification implicit in these words lines up well with Luke 12:49–50, where Jesus claims he will cast fire upon the earth (cf. *Gos. Thom.* 10). One might also entertain a connection with the parable of the strong man in Mark 3:27; Matt 12:29 // Luke 11:21–22 (Q); *Gos. Thom.* 35, for this makes Jesus stronger than the strong man, or as Luke 11:22 puts it, ὁ ἰσχυρότερος.

I will discuss all of these texts and their relationship to each other in the following chapter, urging that they may preserve the memory that, at some point in time, Jesus decided that he was the coming one of John's proclamation.[763] If this is the right conclusion, it is not enough to say that Jesus' eschatological expectations were congruent with those of the Baptist. Rather, and much more than this, Jesus' very self-conception was informed by his predecessor's vision of a judge baptizing with fire.

Final Remarks

Paul Hollenbach has stated that the differences between Jesus and John were "so deep that it was not so much a matter of Jesus disagreeing with John as it was a matter of John's actions and message becoming irrelevant to Jesus."[764] This seems altogether unlikely. Even in Christian texts, which promote Jesus far beyond John, the two are made out to be similar, as we have seen in the present chapter. There was a tradition of linking and comparing John and Jesus, and surely it originated because Jesus so much reminded people of John and because the historical Jesus related himself to John's ministry and expectations in positive ways. One should always come back to the nearly

762. Scot McKnight, *A New Vision for Israel: The Teachings of Jesus in National Context* (Grand Rapids: Eerdmans, 1999), 4.

763. See below, pp. 274–78.

764. Hollenbach, "Conversion of Jesus," 217.

incontrovertible fact that Jesus underwent John's baptism, an act that constitutes theological endorsement.

All of this is definitely not to say, as stressed earlier, that there were no important differences between Jesus and John. These last, however, are less obvious and less easy to establish than often imagined. Further, they should not eclipse the many important similarities, which bespeak Jesus' large indebtedness to his predecessor.

3

More Than a Prophet

The Christology of Jesus

The Jesus of the parables, of the healings, the preacher of the
good tidings of the Kingdom of God, is no Messiah traveling
about incognito. If anything is certain, it is that Jesus had no
wish, either then or ever, to be the king of Israel.

—Frederick C. Grant

Jesus knew himself to be the Messiah chosen by God, especially when he made his entrance into Jerusalem and appeared
in the Temple as Lord.

—Martin Dibelius

One can scarcely gain a stronger impression of the uncertainty of our knowledge concerning the person of Jesus than
by putting together what the various investigators of the Messianic consciousness of Jesus have thought.

—Rudolf Bultmann

Christological doctrine was not the growth of a day. It rather developed,
amid much passionate reflection and debate, over several centuries.
Major developments had, moreover, already transpired during the period
that produced our earliest Christian texts, as a comparison of John with
the Synoptics or of Matthew with Mark reveals. Even our earliest texts, we
now know, mix pre-Easter memories with post-Easter reflections. So Jesus'
self-conception, for those of us interested in it, becomes problematic. What

represents fairly what he said or thought of himself? What represents chiefly the ideas of others?[1]

The questions gain urgency because religions are adept at turning people into what they never were. In antiquity, Enoch, who was nothing but a legend (Gen 4:17–18; 5:18–24), eventually morphed into Metatron, occupant of God's throne (3 En. 4). In our own time, the Rastafarians transformed Haile Selassie, while he was yet alive, and without any help from him, into "the lion of the tribe of Judah," their messiah, an incarnation of God. The religious imagination has again and again piled layer upon layer of legend upon heroes and saints—Buddha and Moses, Muhammad and Bahaullah, and on it goes—effectively giving them new identities. The eighth-century Jew, Yudghan of Hamadan, made himself out to be only the Messiah's forerunner. To his disciples, he was the Messiah.[2] Similarly, although the famous Paiute prophet Wovoka, founder of the Ghost Dance, did not claim to be Christ, his followers so acclaimed him.[3] The facts are sobering.

One cannot but wonder to what extent early Christians did something similar with Jesus. Indeed, many modern scholars, despite the general impression that our sources instill, have decided that Jesus did not, if I may so put it, have much of a Christology. According to Robert Funk, he "had nothing to say about himself, other than that he had no permanent address, no bed to sleep in, no respect on his home turf."[4] Jesus, this generality implies, never imagined himself to be the Davidic Messiah, never envisaged himself as the eschatological Son of Man, never thought himself to be God's Son in a singular sense.[5] At most, it seems, from Funk's echo of Mark 6:4 ("Prophets are not without honor, except in their hometown"), Jesus might have fancied himself some sort of prophet.

Although there are purely historical reasons for this judgment, theological convictions have sometimes, one more than suspects, played their role or even

---

1. In what follows I am looking less for the private thoughts of Jesus, more for how he represented himself to those who embraced his cause. We should in any case be wary of imagining Jesus as though he were our contemporary, whose inner secrets we can inspect. See Richard L. Rohrbaugh, The New Testament in Cross-Cultural Perspective (Eugene, OR: Cascade Books, 2007), 61–76.

2. Abba Hillel Silver, A History of Messianic Speculation in Israel from the First through the Seventeenth Centuries (New York: Macmillan, 1927), 56.

3. L. G. Moses, "'The Father Tells Me So!' Wovoka: The Ghost Dance Prophet," American Indian Quarterly 9 (1985): 340–41.

4. Robert Funk, Honest to Jesus: Jesus for a New Millennium (New York: Macmillan, 1996), 320. For a similar statement, see James M. Robinson, "Theological Autobiography," in The Craft of Religious Studies (ed. Jon R. Stone; New York: Palgrave, 2000), 144–45.

5. According to John Dominic Crossan, Jesus "was neither broker nor mediator but, somewhat paradoxically, the announcer that neither should exist between humanity and divinity or between humanity and itself" (The Historical Jesus: The Life of a Mediterranean Jewish Peasant [San Francisco: HarperCollins, 1991], 422).

taken the lead.[6] John Knox was unable to "imagine a sane human being, of any historical period or culture, entertaining the thoughts about himself which the Gospels, as they stand, often attribute to" their main character;[7] and Knox, an ordained Episcopalian, did not, unsurprisingly, attribute such thoughts to Jesus. Knox thereby skirted what would have been for him an awkward religious predicament.

In like fashion, and more recently, Marcus Borg has urged that

> if you think you are the light of the world, you're not. That is, perceiving oneself in such grand terms is a fairly good indicator that you're off base. The parallel statement, of course, is: if you think you are the messiah, you're not. . . . Though saints and Spirit persons are a bit crazy, when judged by conventional standards, they typically do not think of themselves in grandiose terms. I don't think people like Jesus have an exalted perception of themselves.[8]

It does not startle to learn that Borg, for whom Jesus is a profound religious teacher, finds that he did not egoistically imagine himself to be the Messiah.[9]

If ideological factors have encouraged some to doubt or deny that Jesus thought too highly of himself, such factors have also prodded others to do just the opposite, to attribute to him as high a Christology as possible. The orthodox church fathers, in their ardent crusades against the Arians, again and again construed and misconstrued texts so as to make Jesus champion their own orthodoxy;[10] and "it has always been a vital question in Christology to discover how far the impact made by the earthly life of Jesus and his own understanding of his person can sustain the weight of the Christological construction put upon them by the early church."[11]

A seminary student once sat in my office and told me that if Jesus did not think he was God, then he could not have been so; but since he was God, he must have known it, and we should read the New Testament texts accord-

6. For the evidence of this among German scholars, see the enlightening review of Martin Hengel, "Jesus, the Messiah of Israel," in *Studies in Early Christology* (Edinburgh: T & T Clark, 1995), 15–32.

7. John Knox, *The Death of Christ: The Cross in New Testament History and Faith* (New York/Nashville: Abingdon, 1958), 58, 71.

8. Marcus Borg, "Was Jesus God?" in *The Meaning of Jesus: Two Visions* (by Marcus Borg and N. T. Wright; San Francisco: HarperSanFrancisco, 1999), 146–47.

9. Compare these melodramatic words of Frederick C. Grant: Jesus "was certainly no mad fanatic, no deluded pretender to a celestial and really mythical title, no claimant to a throne which did not exist, no prophet of a coming judgment to be carried out by a heavenly figure seated on the clouds with whom he identified himself—which judgment never took place, never could take place" (*The Gospel of the Kingdom* [New York: Macmillan, 1940], 67).

10. See examples in Dale C. Allison Jr., *The Historical Christ and the Theological Jesus* (Grand Rapids: Eerdmans, 2009), 82–85.

11. I. Howard Marshall, *The Origins of New Testament Christology* (Downers Grove, IL: InterVarsity, 1976), 13.

ingly. If this means disregarding the historical-critical conclusions of one's teacher, then so be it. While unsophisticated, and from my point of view sincerely regrettable, this line of reasoning derives from a desire, shared by many biblical scholars of my acquaintance, to discern substantial continuity between the historical Jesus and subsequent doctrinal formulations. R. H. Fuller once confessed that, in writing *The Mission and Achievement of Jesus*, his goal was "to rescue a basis for the kerygma in the historical Jesus, which appeared to have been denied by Bultmann."[12] Fuller was anxious to establish "a direct line of continuity between Jesus' self-understanding and the church's christological interpretation of him."[13]

Fuller's desire has not been his alone. Others have likewise shunned the prospect that New Testament Christology might be historically untrue to Jesus himself. For would this not, in the words of Hendrikus Boers, undercut "the basic assumption on which the Christology of the NT depends, namely, that it is an expression of the truth about the historical Jesus"?[14] Surely most Christians think that "some degree of continuity between what Jesus thought of himself and what early Christians claimed about him is at least desirable and perhaps necessary."[15] In accord with this, C. F. D. Moule insisted that early Christology was "developmental." For Moule, the canonical estimates of Jesus are

in essence, only attempts to describe what was already there from the beginning. They are not successive additions of something new, but only the drawing out and articulating of what is there. They represent various stages in the development of perception, but they do not represent the accretion of any alien factors that were not inherent from the beginning: they are analogous not so much to the emergence of a new species, as to the unfolding (if you like) of flower from bud and the growth of fruit from flower.[16]

One understands both sides of this issue, which matters so much to so many. On the one hand, bona fide doubt is, for a critical scholar, assuredly in order. The

---

12. R. H. Fuller, *The Foundations of New Testament Christology* (London: Collins, 1969), 108, referring to idem, *The Mission and Achievement of Jesus: An Examination of the Presuppositions of New Testament Theology* (SBT 12; London: SCM Press, 1954).

13. Fuller, *Foundations*, 15.

14. Hendrikus Boers, "Jesus and the Christian Faith: New Testament Christology Since Bousset's Kyrios Christos," *JBL* 89 (1970): 452. According to Boers, "NT Christology is confronted by an irresolvable dilemma." For "to recognize that Christology is a composite product of the early Christian communities and not the truth about the historical Jesus is the historical dissolution of Christology itself," and "to justify a Christology by attempting to confirm that its claims about Jesus are somehow valid is possible only at the expense of not recognizing the early Christian communities as its true authors."

15. Larry Hurtado, *Lord Jesus Christ: Devotion to Jesus in Earliest Christianity* (Grand Rapids: Eerdmans, 2003), 9.

16. C. F. D. Moule, *The Origin of Christology* (Cambridge: University of Cambridge Press, 1977), 3.

christological evolution—or, if one prefers, development—between the second and fourth centuries was only the continuation of the story, not its beginning. Assuming (as I do) Markan priority, it says much that in Matthew people address Jesus with the vocative "Lord" (κύριε) far more often than they do in Mark, and that the First Evangelist redactionally introduces προσκυνέω ("worship, do obeisance") about a dozen times into his narrative. The word occurs only twice in Mark.[17] But Mark itself is the product of a process of Christianizing Jesus.

To pass, moreover, from redaction criticism to contemporary faith, it is manifest why some Christians, wishing to pursue interreligious dialogue, might be less than thrilled with a founder who claimed too much for himself exclusively, or why people interested in Jesus as a moral or spiritual model might prefer him to be more like the rest of us.

On the other hand, and as we will soon see, all the primary sources repeatedly purport that Jesus had astounding things to say about himself. One can dissociate him from an exalted self-conception only through multiple radical surgeries on our texts. Further, and to revert to the theological issue, I sympathize with those whose religion seems inextricably bound up with traditional creeds and confessions, and who believe that if Jesus thought of himself too differently than did his later followers, then Christian faith is in dire straits. For such individuals, the choice between Funk and Moule will not be a purely historical matter but instead and inescapably a theological decision, existentially vital, a decision having the potential to alter their religious faith, a faith that may be the most important thing in their lives.

Having said all this, I will, in what follows, deliberately lay all theological musings to the side. The little that I wish to say about Christology from a theological point of view I have said elsewhere, and I need not write the same things again.[18] My ambition in this chapter is instead to relate the methodological reflections developed in chapter 1 to the genesis of Christology. The limited goal is to think as a historian and to let the facts, as best I can make them out, mean what they may. I am neither setting out to confirm my own religious convictions nor to disparage anyone else's theological tradition or program. I seek, in the following pages, only to give my best historical judgment as to what Jesus of Nazareth encouraged others to think about him.

The Wealth of Material

I begin with the obvious: the Jesus tradition is about Jesus, and not about him first or foremost but about him utterly. He is the perpetual center of attention.

17. For these facts as well as a collection and analysis of closely related phenomena, see Peter M. Head, *Christology and the Synoptic Problem: An Argument for Markan Priority* (SNTSMS 94; Cambridge: Cambridge University Press, 1997).
    18. See Allison, *Historical Christ*.

All the other characters come and go, entering and exiting entirely for his sake. He is the "only teacher" (Matt 23:10), so when anyone else speaks, it is in response to him, or to set him up for a word, or to say something regarding him. It is much the same with the stories, all of which concern him, either directly or indirectly. Even the report of John the Baptist's martyrdom (Mark 6:14–29; Matt 14:1–12) has to do with Jesus: by illustrating the fate of a true prophet, that tale becomes a christological parable foreshadowing Jesus' martyrdom.

If our earliest sources for the Jesus tradition are thoroughly christocentric, they also conspicuously emphasize Jesus' uniqueness and unprecedented eminence. The thanksgiving preserved in Matt 11:25–27 // Luke 10:21–22 (Q) presents him as the unique recipient and dispenser of divine revelation, as indeed greater than Moses.[19] And the divine voice at the baptism, like that at the transfiguration, declares that Jesus is "my beloved Son" (Mark 1:11; 9:7).

These exalted estimations have parallels outside the Gospels, most importantly in the earliest Christian document, 1 Thessalonians. In this letter, written around 50 CE, Paul designates Jesus as "Lord" (κύριος) and associates him closely with God, so much so that "God the Father and the/our Lord Jesus Christ" appears to be a fixed phrase (1:1, 3; 3:11). The apostle affirms that Jesus is now active in the lives of the Thessalonians (3:11–13), that resurrection and salvation will occur "through" (διά) him (4:14; 5:9), and that he will return from heaven and rescue the saints from the coming wrath (1:10; 3:13; 4:13–18; 5:23).

It is this last point to which I wish to call special attention: Jesus is the focus of Paul's eschatological scenario. When the apostle thinks of the last things, he sees Jesus returning on the clouds of heaven. He may also envision an archangel blowing a trumpet, or resurrected and raptured saints descending to the earth; but, as in later Christian art, Jesus is the center of the picture. Everything revolves around him, and everything gains its meaning from its relationship to him.[20]

This christocentric eschatology was not Paul's alone, for the expectations of 1 Thessalonians are no anomaly. They belong rather to a much larger pattern: Jesus is the axis of all things eschatological also in Acts and the non-Pauline Epistles as well as in the Jesus tradition itself. On this matter, the extant sources are at one: Jesus does not just announce the events of the end time; he also directs them. Above all, he conducts the final judgment.

The maxim, familiar to critical scholars, that Jesus proclaimed not himself but the kingdom[21] corresponds not to the Jesus tradition as we know it but

19. On the Mosaic background of the saying, see Dale C. Allison Jr., *The Intertextual Jesus: Scripture in Q* (Valley Forge, PA: Trinity Press International, 2000), 43–51.

20. See details in L. Joseph Kreitzer, *Jesus and God in Paul's Eschatology* (JSNTSup 19; Sheffield: JSOT Press, 1987). For Paul's "high" Christology, see David B. Capes, *Old Testament Yahweh Texts in Paul's Christology* (WUNT 2/47; Tübingen: Mohr Siebeck, 1992).

21. Hartmut Stegemann's view represents many: while the churches considered Jesus "to be a mediator of the kingdom of God, a royal messiah, 'the son of God,' . . . to Jesus himself such

only to that tradition after scholars have excised large portions of it. As proof, consider the following texts, all from the Synoptics:[22]

1. According to Mark 13:26–27 (which resembles 1 Thess 4:13–18),[23] Jesus the Son of Man will return on the clouds of heaven, sending angels to gather the elect from throughout the world.[24]

2. Several logia conventionally assigned to Q also envision Jesus' dramatic future descent from heaven: Matt 23:37–39 // Luke 13:34–35 ("You will not see me again until you say . . .");[25] Matt 24:27 // Luke 17:24 ("For as the lightning comes . . ."); Matt 24:37 // Luke 17:26 ("As it was in the days of Noah . . ."); Matt 24:39 // Luke 17:30 ("So will it be on the day when the Son of man is revealed," RSV).

3. A prophecy from M anticipates the same event: "You will not have gone through all the towns of Israel before the Son of Man comes" (Matt 10:23).[26]

4. So too Luke 18:8, a logion from L: "When the Son of Man comes, will he find faith on the earth?"[27]

5. As usually reconstructed, Q contained two parables enjoining preparation for the coming of the Son of Man, who must be the Lord Jesus: the unexpected thief (Matt 24:43–44 // Luke 12:39–40)[28] and the faithful and wise servant (Matt 24:45–51 // Luke 12:41–46).

---

views were quite strange; he was witness to and involved in God's actions, but he did not feel that he had the leading role or function in this cosmic drama" ("The 'Teacher of Righteousness' and Jesus: Two Types of Religious Leadership in Judaism at the Turn of the Era," in *Jewish Civilization in the Hellenistic-Roman Period* [ed. Shemaryahu Talmon; Philadelphia: Trinity Press International, 1991], 205).

22. My list for the most part fails to include non-Synoptic sources, for although they are far from irrelevant, Matthew, Mark, and Luke supply more than enough material to carry my argument. Also, for convenience I have, as with the catalog on pp. 31–43 above, grouped certain sayings together. The list would be longer and even more impressive were one to enter each saying separately.

23. Like others before them, E. P. Sanders and Margaret Davies discern behind Paul's text and its Synoptic parallels an old saying about "the appearance of a heavenly being accompanied by angels and the end of the present age" (*Studying the Synoptic Gospels* [London: SCM Press; Philadelphia: Trinity Press International, 1989], 329–30). See further p. 81 n. 223. Some sort of relationship is obvious, whatever the explanation.

24. Even if one suspects that the Son of Man was originally someone other than Jesus (see below, pp. 293–303), the larger Markan context demands the equation, the Son of Man–Jesus.

25. For the interpretation of this saying within its Q context, see Daniel A. Smith, *The Post-Mortem Vindication of Jesus in the Sayings Gospel Q* (LNTS 338; London: T & T Clark, 2006).

26. On the relationship of this saying to Mark 9:1; 13:30; John 8:51–52, see p. 33 n. 10.

27. On the pre-Lukan character of this saying, see David R. Catchpole, "The Son of Man's Search for Faith (Luke XVIII 8b)," *NovT* 19 (1977): 81–104. According to Catchpole, Luke 18:8 belonged from the beginning with 18:2–5 and 18:7.

28. The parallels in 1 Thess 5:2; 2 Pet 3:10; Rev 3:3; 16:15 speak against attempts to detach the simile from eschatology; see p. 129 n. 442.

6. Matthew's special material contains another such parable, that of the ten virgins (Matt 25:1–13).[29]

7. The tradition unique to Luke 12:35–38 also belongs here: "Let your loins be girded and have your lamps lit; be like those who are waiting for their master to return from the wedding banquet."[30]

8. Both Q and Mark pass on a saying in which the fate of at least some individuals at the final assize depends upon whether they have acknowledged or denied Jesus: the Son of Man will confess those who have confessed Jesus and will deny those who have denied Jesus (Mark 8:38; Matt 10:32–33 // Luke 12:8–9).[31] On this, James Robinson has rightly remarked that Jesus is "the decisive character witness; that is, in substance he determines one's fate. Whoever he is, technically speaking, the judge has no choice but to follow Jesus' recommendation! So Jesus is in effect the judge."[32]

9. Matters are similar in Q's discourse on mission. Here those who do not embrace the proclamation of Jesus' disciples will fare worse than Sodom (Matt 10:15 // Luke 10:12). Not receiving Jesus' disciples, which is the same as not receiving him (cf. Matt 10:40 // Luke 10:16), seals one's eschatological fate.

10. In the closely related Matt 11:21–24 // Luke 10:13–15 (Q), cities that have rejected Jesus, not John the Baptist or someone else, will pay the price at the end.

11. Q's Jesus, in Matt 7:21, 24–27 // Luke 6:46–49, dubs himself "Lord" (κύριος)—"Why do you call me 'Lord, Lord'"—and warns that those who do not do what he commands will call down destruction upon themselves: "the fall of that house was great." The last judgment is presumably in view.[33]

---

29. Although some have ascribed this parable, with its partial parallels in Luke 12:35–38; 13:25, to Matthean redaction, the evangelist likely took it from oral tradition; see W. D. Davies and Dale C. Allison Jr., *A Critical and Exegetical Commentary on the Gospel according to Saint Matthew* (3 vols.; ICC; Edinburgh: T & T Clark, 1988–97), 3:375–76; Ulrich Luz, *Matthew: A Commentary* (trans. James E. Crouch; ed. Helmut Koester; 3 vols.; Hermeneia; Minneapolis: Fortress, 2001–7), 3:227–28.

30. Despite only a distant parallel in Matt 25:1–13, some assign Luke's text to Q; see Bernd Kollmann, "Lk 12.35–38—ein Gleichnis der Logienquelle," *ZNW* 81 (1990): 254–61; Claus-Peter März, ". . . *lasst eure Lampen brennen!" Studien zur Q-Vorlage von Lk 12,35–14,24* (ETS 20; Leipzig: St. Benno-Verlag, 1991), 58–71. Whatever the origin, the verses borrow language about the exodus from Egypt and presuppose the old belief that the last redemption will be reminiscent of the first, and probably even the belief that the Messiah will return on Passover night (see Allison, *Intertextual Jesus*, 59–62).

31. Other citations of or allusions to this saying include 2 Tim 2:12; Rev 3:5; Ign. *Smyrn.* 10:2; *2 Clem.* 3:2. For the likely background in the vision of the last judgment in Dan 7, see Allison, *Intertextual Jesus*, 130–31.

32. James M. Robinson, *The Gospel of Jesus: In Search of the Original Good News* (San Francisco: HarperSanFrancisco, 2005), 188.

33. See Luz, *Matthew*, 1:385–87. For the forceful argument that Matt 7:21 // Luke 6:46 (Q) implies a "Kyrioskult," see Marco Frenschkowski, "Welche biographischen Kenntnisse von Jesus

12. In another Q text, Matt 11:2–4 // Luke 7:18–23, Jesus, in response to a query from John the Baptist, tacitly equates himself with the latter's "coming one." Jesus' answer draws upon Isa 35:5–6; 61:1–2 and lays implicit claim to fulfill those eschatological oracles.[34]

13. The Jesus of Luke 11:20 (Q) (cf. Matt 12:28) casts out demons "by the finger of God," an allusion to Exod 8:19 that makes him Mosaic; the upshot is that God's kingdom has arrived: ἔφθασεν ἐφ' ὑμᾶς ἡ βασιλεία τοῦ θεοῦ. Jesus thereby appears to be the chief means or manifestation of its arrival.

14. According to Matt 10:34–36 // Luke 12:51–53 (Q), the oracle in Mic 7:6, which foresees in the latter days the sundering of families, comes to fulfillment when Jesus brings a sword that divides parents from children.[35]

15. Matt 19:28 // Luke 22:28–30 (Q) pledges that Jesus' followers will "judge," which means either "rule" or "pass judgment upon," restored Israel. As the one who appoints them to that office, he cannot be less than they: the disciple is not above the master. He must, then, also be a judge or ruler, perhaps even more.

16. Mark 8:29 has Peter confessing Jesus to be "the Messiah," and "it is clear from the context that the Davidic Messiah or royal Messiah is meant here, because the acclamation is offered as an alternative to the opinion of some that Jesus is 'one of the prophets.'"[36]

17. The sons of Zebedee, in Mark 10:35–40, ask to sit at the right and the left hand of Jesus in his glory. Their petition presupposes his enthronement.

18. When, in Mark 11:9–10, Jesus enters Jerusalem, crowds hail him as a messianic deliverer: "Hosanna! Blessed is the one who comes in the name of the Lord! Blessed is the coming kingdom of our ancestor David." Immediately before this, a blind man addresses his pleas to "Jesus, Son of David" (10:46–52).

---

setzt die Logienquelle Voraus? Beobachtungen zur Gattung von Q im Kontext antiker Spruch-sammlungen," in *From Quest to Q: Festschrift James M. Robinson* (ed. Jon Ma. Asgeirsson, Kristin de Troyer, and Marvin W. Meyer; BETL 146; Leuven: Leuven University Press, 2000), 23–24.

34. See p. 275; cf. also the allusions to Isa 61:1–3 in the Beatitudes (p. 80 n. 215). I agree with Christopher Tuckett: "Jesus' words here imply a claim not only to be inaugurating the new age predicted by Isaiah; they also imply a claim that he himself has the role of being the agent who brings about the hoped-for events (the references to the blind seeing, the deaf hearing, etc., are echoing Isaianic texts and also referring to the activities of Jesus himself), but in addition interpret that role as that of the eschatological prophet of Isaiah 61. Thus implicit here is a powerful claim to an (implicit) *prophetic* Christology" ("Isaiah in Q," in *Isaiah in the New Testament* [ed. Steve Moyise and Maarten J. J. Menken; London: T & T Clark International, 2005], 54–55).

35. For the interpretation of this passage, see p. 40 n. 44.

36. Adela Yarbro Collins, "The Messiah as Son of God in the Synoptic Gospels," in *The Messiah in Early Judaism and Christianity* (ed. Magnus Zetterholm; Minneapolis: Fortress, 2007), 24.

19. According to the witnesses in Mark 14:58, Jesus prophesied that he would destroy and rebuild the temple (cf. Mark 13:2).[37]

20. Upon being asked by the chief priest whether he is "the Messiah," Mark's Jesus, in 14:61–62, appropriates for himself the royal language of Ps 110:1 ("The LORD says to my lord, 'Sit at my right hand'") and the eschatological language of Dan 7:13 ("I saw one like a human being [lit., son of man] coming with the clouds of heaven").[38]

21. In Mark's version of the hearing before Pilate, the governor asks Jesus whether he is "king of the Jews." Jesus does not say, "No," but rather evasively responds, "You say so," after which he becomes uncommunicative (15:2–5), offering in effect a plea of *nolo contendere*. Pilate then orders the undefended defendant to be crucified on the original charge (15:26).

22. In Mark's account of the crucifixion, the Roman soldiers in charge engage in a mock coronation ceremony (15:16–20). They dress Jesus in a purple cloak, place a crown of thorns on his brow, and salute him with "Hail, King of the Jews!" All of this assumes that he has made himself out to be a sovereign.

23. The interpretation of the parable of the wheat and the tares in Matthew envisions Jesus the Son of Man sending his angels to collect evildoers from out of the kingdom (13:41).

24. The depiction of the last judgment in Matt 25:31–46 has Jesus coming in glory with his angels and sitting on a throne, with all the nations gathered before him. People's treatment of "the least," of the hungry and thirsty, of the unclothed and strangers, of the sick and prisoners, with all of whom the Son of Man somehow identifies himself, determines their fate.

25. Luke's Jesus, at the beginning of his ministry, reads from the first section of Isa 61 and declares that its prophecies have come to pass in his ministry (Luke 4:16–19). He thereby claims to be the anointed prophet of Isaiah's eschatological vision.[39]

26. Jesus declares, in Luke 12:49–50, that he has come to cast fire on the earth (cf. *Gos. Thom.* 10, 16, 82). This identifies him with the stronger one of the Baptist's proclamation, the eschatological figure who will baptize with fire (cf. Luke 3:17).[40]

What should we make of these many and varied texts and traditions, which purport, in each instance, to recount words of Jesus or to relate an event from his life? They include apophthegmata, prophetic sayings, and parables, and

37. For the eschatological content of this tradition, see below, pp. 237–38.
38. On whether the compound citation followed "I am" or "You say that I am," see p. 287.
39. See further below, pp. 263–66.
40. See further below, pp. 276–78.

they derive from Q, Mark, M, and L. At the least, their very number renders Funk's remark that Jesus "had nothing to say about himself" less than transparently obvious. The ostensible evidence to the contrary is copious.

The collective force of the traditions just listed has often, one guesses, not been fully appreciated. Scholars have inherited the habit of pondering individual items or isolating subgroups of sayings. There are, for example, books and articles on the Son of Man, which can become a topic unto itself; and there are books and articles on the Messiah, which also can become a topic unto itself; and on it goes. From my point of view, however, all the texts that I have cited are closely related; they constitute a family of traditions that requires explanation. All of them, whether they use a formal title or not, are united in one particular: when they look into the future, they see Jesus, and indeed Jesus front and center.

How should we account for this? One could engage the question by constructing tradition histories of the various units and then applying criteria of authenticity to the materials judged preredactional and ancient. We have, however, good reasons to be skeptical of and so disillusioned with such a procedure. At least I no longer have much faith that our tradition histories and authenticating criteria can show us that Peter did or did not confess Jesus to be the Messiah, or that they will ever tell us whether or not the sons of Zebedee really aspired to sit on either side of a regnant Jesus. The same holds for most of the other traditions in my list; and as for the few that I am firmly persuaded preserve memory, debate remains: informed disagreement we will always have with us.

How, then, should we proceed? As with my earlier argument that Jesus conducted a campaign against evil spirits and my case that he promoted an apocalyptic eschatology, so here too: I will forgo trying to establish that he formulated any of the relevant sayings. And of the stories and events on my list, I will likewise, with one exception—Pilate sentencing Jesus for the crime of being "king of the Jews"—not endeavor to show that any happened as told. And yet, despite this, we can draw some large and interesting conclusions.

Jesus' starring role in the eschatological drama appears in all the Synoptic strata, in logia attributed to him and in words assigned to others, and in stories as well as in sayings; and in this matter the Synoptics are at one with John, Acts, Paul, and other early Christian sources—a fact that needs no documentation. The pattern, I submit, is sufficiently early and prevalent to intimate a pre-Easter genesis, and indeed to establish such a genesis if, as we will see is the case soon enough, additional facts fall in line.

This, however, is not the only option on the table. We could also shrug our shoulders and confess ignorance: because we cannot gauge the reliability of the sources, we cannot know what Jesus thought of himself. Yet a third option would be to argue against all the extant witnesses and, like Funk, assert that Jesus never made himself out to be somebody special.

Of these three positions, I can muster some sympathy for the second—agnosticism—although it is not my own. I will instead advocate the first option. The third, by contrast, strikes me as woefully implausible. Although not without important sponsors, it entails that, despite our primary sources being consistently wrong, we can nonetheless get it right. We can divine all the post-Easter contributions, toss them into the discard bucket, and discover that Jesus did not have an exalted self-conception. In other words, we can, through subtraction, prove a negative. Yet if the sources—all of them, and in abundance—mislead on this central subject, if the larger pattern is a false memory, how can anyone credibly exhume the truth beneath all the obfuscating additions?

"And He Appointed Twelve"

These, however, are very general reflections. In attempting to pass beyond them, I should like at this juncture to revert to the likely fact that Jesus selected a group of men, twelve in number, to represent the anticipated restoration of the twelve tribes of Israel. I have already, in the previous chapter, argued for the historicity of this circumstance and found in it evidence that Jesus had a particular brand of eschatology.[41] Here I wish to draw another inference.

If there are twelve disciples, and if Jesus, who appointed them, stands outside the group, it is hard to avoid the following logic:

- The twelve disciples represent the dispersed but soon-to-be gathered tribes.[42]
- Jesus is the undisputed leader of this symbolic group of twelve.
- He is probably the destined leader of the twelve tribes.[43]

One recalls, in this connection, the first chapter of Numbers, where God directs Moses and Aaron to appoint the twelve phylarchs, one for each tribe (see 1:4, 44),[44] as well as Deut 1:23, where the lawgiver sends out "twelve

---

41. See above, pp. 67–76.

42. On the return of the twelve tribes, see p. 72. In 4 Ezra 13:12–13, 39–50, it is the Messiah who returns the scattered to their land; cf. Gen. Rab. 98:9; Frg. Tg. on Num 24:7; Tg. Cant 1:1. The idea probably stems from Isa 11:10–12: "On that day the root of Jesse shall stand as a signal to the peoples. . . . On that day the LORD will extend his hand yet a second time to recover the remnant that is left of his people."

43. E. P. Sanders offers a similar argument: "Jesus thought that the twelve disciples represented the tribes of Israel, but also that they would judge them. Jesus was clearly above the disciples; a person who is above the judges of Israel is very high indeed" (The Historical Figure of Jesus [London: Penguin, 1993], 248).

44. On the importance of this group for first-century readers of the Bible, see William Horbury, "The Twelve and the Phylarchs," NTS 32 (1986): 503–27.

men . . . , one man for each tribe," in order to spy out the land. Similarly, in Josh 3:12; 4:8, Joshua selects another group of twelve to fulfill certain functions, and again the number stands for the twelve tribes. The point is that in each instance it is the leaders of Israel—Moses, Aaron, Joshua—who create a symbolic group of twelve. If Jesus behaved similarly, he was acting like Israel's leader, and he must have "had a very lofty idea of the role with which God had entrusted him for the establishment of his kingdom."[45]

Ecclesiastical history supplies an instructive parallel, in the person of Jan van Leiden, a.k.a. Jan Bokelson (1510–1536). Becoming king of Münster after the death of Jan Matthys, Bokelson set up a theocracy. In order to institute his rule, he appointed "twelve elders of the race of Israel." Their task was to oversee the daily affairs of Münster, which he thought of as the new Jerusalem. Bokelson was not one of the twelve. He instead bestowed upon himself the title "King of Zion."[46] Knowing the Bible well, he was acting according to precedent: the leader of God's people selects, to assist him in governing, a symbolic body of twelve men. My suggestion is that, long before Bokelson, Jesus did something similar.

Later Jewish history also offers an analogous episode. Once, in a synagogue, Sabbatai Sevi, who knew not only the Hebrew Bible but also something of Jesus, "chose twelve of the rabbinic scholars of Gaza to represent the twelve tribes," a fact that elicited this remark from Gershom Scholem: "The analogy with the Gospel account of the choice of the apostles comes to mind, though, of course, the idea of a symbolic representation of Israel by twelve disciples or adherents may well have struck Sabbatai spontaneously and without outside influence, much as it did in the case of Jesus."[47] Whatever the inspiration for his deed, Sabbatai, a self-declared messiah, chose twelve men to represent the tribes of Israel. His act, I suggest, was like that of Jesus.[48]

Execution as "King of the Jews"

My contention about Jesus' self-conception can appeal to a second likely fact: he was crucified as "king of the Jews." The circumstance, according to John Collins, suggests that Jesus "was viewed as a messianic pretender and that the kingdom he proclaimed was understood, at least by some of his followers, as

45. Étienne Trocmé, *The Childhood of Christianity* (trans. John Bowden; London: SCM Press, 1997), 10.

46. See further George Huntston Williams, *The Radical Reformation* (Kirksville, MO: Sixteenth Century Journal Publishers, 1992), 553–88; James M. Stayer, *Anabaptists and the Sword* (2nd ed.; Lawrence, KS: Coronado, 1876), 211–80.

47. Gershom Scholem, *Sabbatai Sevi: The Mystical Messiah* (Princeton, NJ: University Press, 1973), 222.

48. Mani also appears to have appointed twelve disciples, but since I have been unable to learn much more than the fact itself, I leave it to the side here, except to note that Mani also had an exalted conception of his own person (see below, pp. 257–58).

a messianic kingdom."[49] This makes sense. If Rome executed Jesus for making himself out to be a king, then in all probability some people, including presumably some sympathizers, or maybe even Jesus himself, hoped him to be such. There is no problem with the logic. The only hitch is the premise. Did Pilate, when sentencing Jesus, and/or did Pilate's soldiers, when carrying out that sentence, mock Jesus as "king of the Jews"?

Aside from Matt 2:2, the title ὁ βασιλεὺς τῶν Ἰουδαίων is confined to Mark's passion narrative (15:2, 9, 12, 18, 26), to the parallels to these verses in Matthew and Luke, and to John 18:33, 39; 19:3, 19, 21. The expression appears in three connections: Pilate's interrogation of Jesus (Mark 15:2, 9, 12 par.; John 18:33, 39), Roman mockery of Jesus (Mark 15:18 par.; John 19:3), and the inscription on the cross (Mark 15:26 par.; John 19:19, 21).

It is, unfortunately, impossible to decide, with any degree of assurance, who first formulated these materials. Further, the extent of John's dependence upon the Synoptics, if any, remains controverted. There will, then, be no agreement on whether the title entered the tradition at one point or several.

Many have nonetheless judged at least the content of the sardonic inscription to preserve reliable memory.[50] Nils Dahl succinctly put the case this way: "The formulation 'King of the Jews' stems neither from proof from prophecy[51] nor

49. John J. Collins, *The Apocalyptic Imagination: An Introduction to Jewish Apocalyptic Literature* (2nd ed.; Grand Rapids: Eerdmans, 1998), 257.

50. So, for example, Ernst Bammel, "The Titulus," in *Jesus and the Politics of His Day* (ed. Ernst Bammel and C. F. D. Moule; Cambridge: Cambridge University Press, 1984), 353–64; Jürgen Becker, *Jesus of Nazareth* (trans. James E. Crouch; New York: de Gruyter, 1998), 352–54; Peter Egger, *"Crucifixus sub Pontio Pilato": Das "Crimen" Jesu von Nazareth im Spannungsfeld römischer und jüdischer Verwaltungs- und Rechtsstrukturen* (NTAbh 32; Münster: Aschendorff, 1997), 195–200; Jack Finegan, *Die Überlieferung der Leidens- und Auferstehungsgeschichte Jesu* (BZNW 15; Gießen: Töpelmann, 1934), 78; Joachim Gnilka, *Jesus of Nazareth: Message and History* (trans. Siegfried S. Schatzmann; Peabody, MA: Hendrickson, 1997), 304; Ferdinand Hahn, *Christologische Hoheitstitel: Ihre Geschichte im frühen Christentum* (5th ed.; Göttingen: Vandenhoeck & Ruprecht, 1995), 178; Hengel, "Messiah of Israel," 41–58; Rudolf Pesch, *Das Markusevangelium: Teil 2, Einleitung und Kommentar zu Kap. 8,27–16,20* (HTKNT 2/2; Freiburg: Herder, 1977), 484; Gerd Theissen and Annette Merz, *The Historical Jesus: A Comprehensive Guide* (Minneapolis: Fortress, 1998), 458; Paul Winter, *On the Trial of Jesus* (2nd rev. ed.; SJ 1; Berlin: de Gruyter, 1974), 153–56. For another view, see Wolfgang Reinbold, *Der Prozess Jesu* (BTSc 28; Göttingen: Vandenhoeck & Ruprecht, 2006), 91–95 ("It is uncertain whether the *titulus* on the cross is an historical fact. In my view, more speaks against this than for it"). Also skeptical are David Catchpole, "The 'Triumphal' Entry," in *Jesus and the Politics of His Day* (ed. Bammel and Moule), 328–30; Adela Yarbro Collins, *Mark: A Commentary* (Hermeneia; Minneapolis: Fortress, 2007), 747–48. According to Robert Funk and the Jesus Seminar, "The Seminar was dubious . . . that proclaiming himself 'king of the Judeans' was actually Jesus' crime. A gray vote [Jesus probably did not say it] was the result" (*The Acts of Jesus: The Search for the Authentic Deeds of Jesus* [San Francisco: HarperSanFrancisco, 1998], 156). No justification is offered.

51. That is, the title is not taken from the Jewish Bible. The famous variant to LXX Ps 95:10 ("the Lord reigned [ἐβασίλευσεν] from the tree"), much employed in early Christian apologetics (e.g., Justin, *Dial.* 73.1; *Barn.* 8:5; Tertullian, *Marc.* 19.1), is a Christian emendation.

from the Christology of the community. In general early Christians hesitated to use the title 'King' for Jesus. Would the formulation of the inscription, with its decidedly political ring, really rest on a historicization of a dogmatic motif? This is not very plausible."[52]

To this line of argument, which has some force, one can add the following: (a) the Romans did sometimes write criminal charges on placards;[53] (b) the succinct indictment against Jesus resembles other succinct indictments purportedly displayed;[54] (c) although "king of the Jews"—the words betray a derisive, non-Jewish perspective[55]—was not, as Dahl observed, a religious title among Christians, it was a political term in the first century;[56] (d) the irony of "king of the Jews" matches the parodic character of Roman crucifixion;[57] (e) the Roman authority, interested in deterrence, did not hide executions in a corner, so the *causa mortis* in Jesus' case presumably would have become public knowledge.[58] As Martin Dibelius observed, "Doubtless the crucifixion of Jesus, like all executions at that time, took place with the fullest publicity, and everybody knew what the crime was that was to be atoned for by such an execution."[59]

Yet perhaps the strongest argument for Jesus having been in fact crucified as "king of the Jews" is the lack of a better suggestion regarding his alleged crime.

52. Nils Alstrup Dahl, "The Crucified Messiah," in *Jesus the Christ: The Historical Origins of Christology Doctrine* (ed. Donald H. Juel; Minneapolis: Fortress, 1991), 36–37.

53. See Suetonius, *Cal.* 32.2 ("displaying a placard in explanation of his punishment"); *Dom.* 10.1 ("a placard tied around his neck"); Dio Cassius, *Hist.* 54.3.7 ("through the center of the forum with the inscription"); Eusebius, *Hist. eccl.* 5.1.43–44 ("a tablet being carried before him"). Cf. also Tertullian, *Apol.* 2.20: the Romans read from their "tablet-lists" (*tabella*) the crime of being a Christian. One might guess, for lack of direct evidence, that the tablets hung around criminals' necks or paraded in front of them were sometimes subsequently displayed near or on their crosses; so at least Otto Zöckler, *The Cross of Christ: Studies in the History of Religion and the Inner Life of the Church* (trans. Maurice J. Evans; London: Hodder & Stoughton, 1877), 405–6.

54. Mark 15:26: "King of the Jews"; Suetonius, *Dom.* 10.1: "A Thracian supporter who spoke evil of his emperor"; Eusebius, *Hist. eccl.* 5.1.44: "This is Attalus the Christian." Note in each case the ethnic or religious identity of the convicted.

55. According to Jorg Frey, the titulus is a "cynical, anti-Jewish assertion, a defaming of the Jewish people through the Roman occupying power" ("Der historische Jesus und der Christus der Evangelien," in *Der historische Jesus: Tendenzen und Perspektiven der gegenwärtigen Forschung* [ed. Jens Schröter and Ralph Brucker; BZNW 114; Berlin: de Gruyter, 2002], 305). Contrast *Gos. Pet.* 4:11: "this is the king of Israel" (cf., e.g., 1 Sam 24:14; Prov 1:1; John 1:49).

56. See Josephus, *Ant.* 14.36; 15.373; 16.311; *J.W.* 6.104; 7.171; Plutarch, *Pomp.* 45.5. It is unattested as a Jewish messianic title.

57. On this, see Joel Marcus, "Crucifixion as Parodic Exaltation," *JBL* 125 (2006): 73–87. "Crucifixion was," Marcus urges, "widely understood as parodic enthronement in the ancient world."

58. Cf. Mark 15:16; John 19:13. According to Philo, *Embassy* 302, Pilate repeatedly executed people without trial. Even though this remark appears in a passage full of polemic, we should perhaps give it some weight. Nonetheless, crucifixions were public displays, and unless the reason for an execution were known, it would not have fully served its purpose.

59. Martin Dibelius, *Jesus* (Philadelphia: Westminster, 1949), 94.

Roman officials did not try people for perceived infractions of the Sabbath or for any other halakic controversy. The occupying forces were, rather, guardians of the public order, and typically they crucified people for theft, murder, and insurrection. Now nobody, to our knowledge, ever accused Jesus of being a thief or a murderer; and that no large Roman force arrayed itself against him seems evidence enough that a militant revolt was not afoot.[60] Why, then, did the government put him away? Somebody must have represented Jesus, despite his lack of an army, to be a potential threat to the political order; and coming forward as a royal liberator, or being put forward as such by others, would account for this[61]—all the more since, to the extent of our knowledge, the Romans, beginning with their occupation of Palestine in 63 BCE and continuing until shortly before the Jewish War, crucified "only insurrectionists or those reckoned to be such or in sympathy with such."[62]

This argument, one might retort, overlooks the commotion in the temple (Mark 11:15–17; John 2:14–16). In Mark, this episode prompts Jewish authorities to want Jesus out of the way, or rather gives them a pretense for doing so, and the Sanhedrin's verdict against him immediately follows testimony that he foretold the temple's undoing.[63] So maybe Pilate, upon being informed of Jesus' prophetic word or deed, regarded him, for that reason alone, as a threat

60. On why Jesus alone was arrested, see Justin J. Meggitt, "The Madness of King Jesus: Why Was Jesus Put to Death, but His Followers Were Not?" *JSNT* 29 (2007): 379–413, and the responses by Paula Fredriksen (pp. 415–19) and Joel Marcus (pp. 421–24). Even if, as Meggitt proposes, the Romans ignored the disciples and executed Jesus alone because they deemed him mad, that scarcely excludes their having mocked and crucified him as "king of the Jews." Moreover, maybe the Romans did attempt to arrest others besides Jesus. If the disciples indeed ran away, as Mark 14:50 purports, was it not because they sensed danger for themselves? Maybe Jesus alone was arrested because he alone did not flee.

61. Cf. Paula Fredriksen, *Jesus of Nazareth, King of the Jews: A Jewish Life and the Emergence of Christianity* (New York: Alfred A. Knopf, 2000), 232–59—although, I am skeptical that Jesus "lost control of his audience" (p. 247), by which she means that people in Jerusalem hailed him as king even though he probably thought otherwise.

62. Heinz-Wolfgang Kuhn, "Die Kreuzesstrafe während der frühen Kaiserzeit: Ihre Wirklichkeit und Wertung in der Umwelt des Urchristentums," *ANRW* 25.1:724. Cf. Josephus, *Ant.* 2.102, 129; *J.W.* 2.253, 305–306. Kuhn goes on to argue that the Romans must have perceived Jesus as a "political rebel" (p. 733).

63. Mark 14:58; cf. 13:2; Luke 19:44; Acts 6:14; John 2:19; *Gos. Thom.* 71. If, incidentally, Jesus really did prophesy, four decades before the arrival of Vespasian and Titus, the temple's destruction or its destruction and renewal, this is additional evidence for the major thesis of chapter 2, for then he was not reading the political signs of the times but rather taking up a scenario from Jewish apocalyptic eschatology. See further Jostein Ådna, *Jesu Stellung zum Tempel: Die Tempelaktion und das Tempelwort als Ausdruck seiner messianischen Sendung* (WUNT 2/119; Tübingen: Mohr Siebeck, 2000), 97–101; E. P. Sanders, *Jesus and Judaism* (Philadelphia: Fortress, 1985), 61–90. *Jubilees* 1:27; 4Q174 1:1–3; Tob 14:5; and *Mek.* on Exod 15:18 foretell the rebuilding of the temple in the latter days (cf. Tob 13:16–18); further, 11Q19 29:8–10; *Sib. Or.* 5:397–433; and perhaps 1 En. 90:28–29 (see p. 43 n. 57) prophesy both the end of the temple and the advent of a new temple.

against the civil order.[64] In this case, perhaps pretending to be "king of the Jews" was not Jesus' crime.[65]

Does this do away with Collins's argument? I think not, for three reasons. First, even if a violent act in the temple and a verbal threat against it were, as is quite possible, the proximate cause of Jesus' arrest,[66] Pilate's decision to crucify him must have reckoned with additional facts. Josephus tells of another Jesus who, in the 60s, warned of the temple's coming destruction. This Jesus received a flogging and was released, not executed (*J.W.* 6.300–309). Evidently, verbal and/or symbolic prophecies against the temple were not, in and of themselves, sufficient to bring one before the executioners.[67]

Second, Jesus' purported activities on the temple mount did not instigate a riot, otherwise he presumably would have been arrested on the spot.[68] This in turn suggests that any action he undertook there must have been more symbolic than anything else. In line with this, "no one—neither Jesus, nor those who heard and saw him, nor the high priest, nor Pilate—thought that he could actually tear the Temple walls down. If, however, he only said what God was going to do, why arrest him? Since God would do whatever he willed, why could not the high priest and others simply have disagreed that Jesus knew?"[69] Again, something more must have been involved.

Third, we can directly link the allegation of royal pretension with what Jesus said about the temple. Jewish tradition was familiar with the prospect of a royal

---

64. This view is today associated especially with Sanders (*Jesus and Judaism*, 309–18). One may compare the opposition to Jeremiah for prophesying the temple's ruin (see Jer 26).

65. This point of view is upheld by Crossan (*Historical Jesus*, 359–60).

66. But for doubt concerning the historicity of the incident in the temple, see Robert J. Miller, "The (A)historicity of Jesus' Temple Demonstration: A Test Case in Methodology," in *Society of Biblical Literature 1991 Seminar Papers* (ed. Eugene H. Lovering Jr.; Atlanta: Scholars Press, 1991), 235–52; David Seeley, "Jesus' Temple Act," *CBQ* 55 (1993): 263–83; for the opposing opinion, see Ådna, *Jesu Stellung zum Tempel*, 300–333. One can also dissociate Jesus' purported action from his fate by accepting the Johannine chronology, which puts it earlier in the ministry (John 2:13–22), or by regarding the tradition as having once circulated without a context; cf. Fredriksen, *Jesus of Nazareth*, 220–59, 290–92; against Fredriksen, see Stephen Hultgren, "The Incident at the Temple as the Occasion for Jesus' Death: Meeting Some Objections," in *Redefining First-Century Jewish and Christian Identities: Essays in Honor of Ed Parish Sanders* (ed. Fabian E. Udoh; Notre Dame, IN: University of Notre Dame Press, 2008), 283–96.

67. According to Theodore J. Weeden ("Two Jesuses, Jesus of Jerusalem and Jesus of Nazareth: Provocative Parallels and Imagination Imitation," *Forum* 6 [2003]: 137–341), the Christian accounts of Jesus' passion depend upon Josephus's account in *J.W.* 6.300–309. I am inclined to think that Weeden's case underestimates the reach of chance: sometimes history does hand us strikingly similar but unrelated events (see Dale C. Allison Jr., "Peter and Cephas: One and the Same," *JBL* 111 [1992]: 489–95).

68. Lynn H. Cohick credibly opines, "The crowd size was large enough to be noticed, but not small enough to warrant a wait-and-see attitude" ("Jesus as King of the Jews," in *Who Do My Opponents Say That I Am? An Investigation of the Accusations against Jesus* [ed. Scot McKnight and Joseph B. Modica; LNTS 327; London: T & T Clark, 2008], 122).

69. Sanders, *Historical Figure*, 259–60.

figure building or rebuilding the temple. Illustrations include 2 Sam 7:10–14 (David's son [cf. 4Q174]); Zech 6:12 (the man whose name is "Branch"); *Sib. Or.* 5:422 ("a blessed man" who comes "from the expanses of heaven"); Tg. Isa. on 53:5 (the Messiah "will rebuild the sanctuary which has been profaned"); Tg. Zech 6:12–13 ("the Messiah will build the temple of the Lord"). So if—I leave the issue open—Jesus ever said, as Mark 14:58 and John 2:19 have him say, that he himself would raise or build a new temple, the implication would have been patent. Opponents could readily have moved from "He claims he will destroy and rebuild the temple" to "He claims to be king."[70]

The odds remain high, then, that Jesus was mocked with the title "king of the Jews." What, then, does this say about him? The Romans, one doubts, executed Jesus for a crime for which the evidence was nil. At the very least, someone must have put the charge of royal ambition before the governor. This is in fact what the extant sources report. In both the Synoptics and John, some Jewish authorities, having interrogated Jesus about his claims, conduct him to Pilate.[71] The latter then asks Jesus if he claims to be a king. Whether or not that sequence of events matches what happened, word must have reached Pilate that Jesus aspired to kingship.

How would the governor have responded? The Gospels have him looking into the matter by confronting Jesus himself. This seems likely enough. In Josephus, *J.W.* 6.300–309, Jesus son of Ananias appears before Albinus; and in *Ant.* 20.102, James and Simon the sons of Judas the Galilean stand before Tiberius Alexander. Similarly, Acts 24–26 has Paul defend himself before Festus and Felix. Investigating alleged crimes against the state was the business of Roman procurators. Further, the evidence for Pilate's involvement with Jesus' death extends well beyond the canonical Gospels. There are passing references to his role in Josephus, *Ant.* 18.64 ("Pilate . . . condemned him to the cross"); 1 Tim 6:13 ("Christ Jesus . . . in his testimony before Pontius Pilate made the good confession"); Tacitus, *Ann.* 15.44 ("Christ . . . was executed by sentence of the procurator Pontius Pilate").[72]

Whether Jesus met his end in 30 or 33 CE, it was not a time of war or rebellion, and since Jesus was not the commander of troops, presumably there was time to look into the matter. If, further, Pilate knew that some Jews admired or supported Jesus, executing him without any sort of hearing or on obviously

70. Nils A. Dahl comments, "If Jesus was also supposed to have said that he would, by a miracle, destroy the temple and build it up again, that would . . . be proof that he claimed something appropriate only to a king" ("Messianic Ideas and the Crucifixion of Jesus," in *The Messiah: Developments in Earliest Judaism and Christianity* [ed. James H. Charlesworth; Minneapolis: Fortress, 1992], 403).

71. Cf. Josephus, *Ant.* 18.63: "Pilate, at the suggestion of the principal men among us, . . . condemned him to the cross."

72. Note also Acts 3:13; 4:27; 13:28–29; Ign. *Magn.* 11:1; Ign. *Trall.* 9:1; Ign. *Smyrn.* 1:2; Justin, *1 Apol.* 13.3; *Gos. Pet.* 1:1; 2:3–5; 8:29, 31; 11:43–49.

trumped-up charges would likely have been politically imprudent, especially after earlier failures to take into account Jewish sensibilities (see Josephus, *Ant.* 18.56, 60–62; *J.W.* 2.169, 175–176). In such a context, it would have been expedient to learn something about Jesus; and if Jesus and Pilate were in Jerusalem at the same time, an occasion to judge the affair was at hand.

So the Gospels surely are correct in having Pilate encounter Jesus, if only briefly.[73] Of the few but dramatic details that they supply, one may harbor doubts. Of the outcome, however, there is no doubt at all: Pilate sent Jesus to a cross.

Now, courts do not always come to fair and impartial verdicts. Justice can miscarry, so that punishment falls upon the innocent. Yet if Jesus had repudiated the accusation of kingship, Pilate presumably would have spared his life, or at least crucified him for some other crime. In order for the ironic title "king of the Jews" to be intelligible and to carry some semblance of justice, it had to correspond to something generally known or believed about Jesus, which he did not, in Pilate's presence, effectively rebut. The Synoptics, for what it is worth, do not have him protesting. Rather, he courts death by uttering the enigmatic phrase "You have said so," after which he retreats into silence (Mark 15:1–5 par.).[74]

Nothing in the previous paragraphs approaches proof of anything. I contend only that the least convoluted explanation for the political charge against Jesus is that it corresponded in some way to his self-perception, as opposed to being conjured against everything he stood for. As Dibelius rightly remarked, there must have been something in Jesus' "way of speaking and acting that gave" Pilate's "charge a certain amount of justification."[75]

One might, playing the skeptic, retort that the Gospels have Pilate knowing better. Indeed, the governor is, in the Synoptics and John, so reluctant to execute Jesus that he offers the crowd Barabbas in his stead.[76] How could this have happened if the governor truly believed that Jesus hoped to rule Israel?

To this there are two adequate responses. First, many scholars have suspected that Pilate's vacillation and protest as well as the proposed exchange for Barabbas reflect, in part or in whole, Christian apologetics.[77] Although a

---

73. Funk reports "that Jesus was executed on the authority of Pilate" is a "completely reliable piece of information . . . the vote [of the Jesus Seminar to that effect] was virtually unanimous" (Funk and the Jesus Seminar, *Acts of Jesus*, 152).

74. Theissen and Merz remark, "If Jesus was executed as a royal pretender, one thing is certain: he did not distance himself from the messianic expectations of his followers (and the corresponding fears of his opponents) before his accusers and judges" (*Historical Jesus*, 540).

75. Dibelius, *Jesus*, 95. Cf. Andrew Chester, "The Nature and Scope of Messianism," in *Messiah and Exaltation: Jewish Messianic and Visionary Traditions and New Testament Christology* (WUNT 207; Tübingen: Mohr Siebeck, 2007), 311–12.

76. See Matt 27:15–26; Mark 15:6–15; Luke 23:17–25; John 18:38–40.

77. See John Dominic Crossan, *Who Killed Jesus? Exposing the Roots of Anti-Semitism in the Gospel Story of the Death of Jesus* (San Francisco: HarperSanFrancisco, 1996), 150–52.

Roman governor could release a prisoner in order to curry favor, we have no certain evidence from Palestine of an annual custom of release during Passover or any other festival.[78] So one might judge Mark 15:6–15 to be no more historical than Matthew's legend about Pilate's fretful wife (Matt 27:19).

Second, even if one thinks otherwise—that is, even if one finds more history than fiction in the story[79]—the implication would be only that Pilate judged Jesus, despite his claim to be a king, to be no authentic threat. If someone aspires to be king and has an army in the wings, it is one thing; but if someone claims to be a king and has nothing to show for it but words, it is something else altogether: there will be less cause for alarm. Again one thinks of Jesus the son of Ananias. The Roman governor Albinus "pronounced him a maniac and let him go" (Josephus, J.W. 6.305). What matters for us, then, is that whether Pilate himself formulated the derisive indictment in the Gospels or borrowed it from others, and whether he judged Jesus to be truly dangerous or would have been just as happy to let him go, he let the charge against Jesus stand. Which is to say: Pilate must, after looking into the matter, have had cause for sending Jesus to death under the sentence "king of the Jews."

The upshot of the previous pages is this: the Romans probably crucified Jesus as "king of the Jews" because he did not distance himself from that derisive epithet.

The Function of the Resurrection

Let us say, however, that one rejects this conclusion, holding instead that Jesus did not see himself as the lead performer in the eschatological spectacle. Is there some other story that credibly explains the rapidity with which, after his death, he moved to center stage? If, for instance, he envisioned someone else as the Son of Man and so taught his followers to look for another, what

---

Note how the Roman authorities in Acts repeatedly observe—this amounts to a refrain—that Christianity is not a crime: 16:39; 17:6–9; 18:12–17; 19:37–41; 23:29; 25:25; 26:31–32.

78. For full discussion, see Raymond E. Brown, *The Death of the Messiah: From Gethsemane to the Grave; A Commentary on the Passion Narratives of the Four Gospels* (2 vols.; New York: Doubleday, 1994), 1:814–20. Analogies lend historical verisimilitude to the scene, so maybe the Synoptics preserve the memory of a short-lived local custom, perhaps one of Pilate's invention; or, alternately, they wrongly present an occasional affair as an annual ritual. Josephus (*Ant.* 20.208–209) tells of Ananias imploring Albinus to release ten sicarii; and Albinus brings "out those prisoners who clearly deserved to be put to death and sentenced them to execution, but released for a personal consideration those who had been cast into prison for a trifling and commonplace offence" (*Ant.* 20.215). Note also Josephus, *Ant.* 17.204; Livy, *Hist.* 5.13.5–8; Pliny the Younger, *Ep.* 10.31; P.Flor. 61; *m. Pesaḥ.* 8:6.

79. For a less skeptical judgment, see William Horbury, "The Passion Narratives and Historical Criticism," *Theology* 75 (1972): 66–69; Ellis Rivkin, *What Crucified Jesus?* (Nashville: Abingdon, 1984), 104–5.

might have moved them, on the contrary, to identify the coming one with their teacher?

Many have affirmed that, with Easter, the proclaimer became the proclaimed. This notion, incessantly repeated in the secondary literature and so now an empty mantra, begs the question. Consider these words of R. H. Fuller, which typify so much scholarship:

> Jesus had declared that his own eschatological word and deed would be vindicated by the Son of man at the end. Now his word and deed had received preliminary yet certain vindication by the act of God in the resurrection. The earliest church expressed this new-born conviction by identifying Jesus with the Son of man who was to come. He would come as his own rubber stamp, vindicating his own word and deed, as he had already done in a preliminary way in the resurrection appearances. In preserving those sayings in which Jesus speaks of the coming Son of man, the church identifies Jesus with the coming Son of man. So sayings such as Mark 8:38, Luke 12:8f. are now repeated, but on the assumption that it is Jesus who is the coming Son of man, and who will appear at the End to vindicate his word and work openly as he had already appeared in his resurrection appearances to his disciples.[80]

That the disciples understood the resurrection as the vindication of Jesus goes without saying. But why or how the resurrection turned Jesus into the Son of Man does not go without saying. It is very far from self-evident. Yet on that score, Fuller sayings nothing. Why did God's vindication of Jesus erase somebody else's eschatological role? Why, we might ask, did believers not envision Jesus and the Son of Man returning together, or one serving as the forerunner of the other? If Christians were able to identify John the Baptist with Elijah, why were they unable to identify someone else with the Son of Man? Fuller's story cannot be the whole story.

The decades since the publication of Fuller's once-standard work on early Christology (1965) have seen immense progress in our study of its subject. We have learned much about how Jewish mysticism, speculation about angels, and devotional practices influenced perceptions of and confessions about Jesus.[81] Too often, however, at least from the point of view of this chapter, the

---

80. Fuller, *Foundations*, 143–44.

81. Important works include Richard Bauckham, *Jesus and the God of Israel: God Crucified and Other Studies on the New Testament's Christology of Divine Identity* (Grand Rapids: Eerdmans, 2008); Timo Eskola, *Messiah and the Throne: Jewish Merkabah Mysticism and Early Christian Exaltation Discourse* (WUNT 2/142; Tübingen: Mohr Siebeck, 2001); J. E. Fossum, *The Name of God and the Angel of the Lord: Samaritan and Jewish Concepts of Intermediation and the Origin of Gnosticism* (WUNT 36; Tübingen: Mohr Siebeck, 1985); Hurtado, *Lord Jesus Christ*; Carey C. Newman, James R. Davila, and Gladys S. Lewis, eds., *The Jewish Roots of Christological Monotheism: Papers from the St. Andrews Conference on the Historical Origins of the Worship of Jesus* (JSJSup 63; Leiden: Brill, 1999).

literature has failed to begin at the beginning.[82] It is one thing, for instance, to explicate the angelic terms in which some thought about Jesus, quite another to explain why anybody found those terms appropriate in the first place. And so it is with other christological conceptions and titles. Why did Jesus draw them all to himself?

Bultmann (following William Wrede) thought it "possible" that "belief in the messiahship of Jesus arose with and out of belief in his resurrection."[83] This opinion, which he supported solely by arguing that Jesus did not think that he was the Messiah,[84] is akin to Fuller's remark that the resurrection led to identifying Jesus and the Son of Man: elucidation is lacking. Bultmann simply asserted that the resurrection could have turned Jesus into the Messiah. It is as though the resurrection wins by default. Since Jesus did not, according to Bultmann, claim to be the Messiah, the resurrection must have done the trick. One gets the impression that Easter is a magic wand that, being waved, somehow explains things.

Only a little reflection, however, discloses that belief in Jesus' resurrection alone cannot have led people to deem him Messiah or Son of Man. The two witnesses in Rev 11 rise from the dead and ascend without garnering further attention, and *T. Job* 39–40 tells of the disappearance of the bodies of Job's

---

82. James R. Davila suggests that "the historical Jesus may be more or less irrelevant" for understanding how Jesus came to be worshiped as a "divine being" ("Of Methodology, Monotheism and Metatron: Introductory Reflections on Divine Mediators and the Origins of the Worship of Jesus," in *Christological Monotheism* [ed. Newman, Davila, and Lewis], 3).

83. Rudolf Bultmann, *Theology of the New Testament* (2 vols.; New York: Charles Scribner's Sons, 1951–1955), 1:26.

84. Bultmann's case (ibid.) has five parts: (a) The baptismal story, Peter's confession, and the entry into Jerusalem are, at least as we now have them, legends, as is Mark's passion narrative (pp. 26–27). (b) If "measured by traditional messianic ideas," Jesus' life "was not messianic," and there is "nothing of might and glory" in his life (p. 27). (c) Jesus did not spiritualize or reinterpret the traditional messianic ideas, which Bultmann establishes by denying the historicity of Mark 12:35–37 (p. 28). (d) Jesus did not think of himself as destined to be the future Messiah because the oldest sayings about the Son of Man are in the third person, as though they refer to someone else (pp. 28–30). (e) Jesus could not have thought of himself as the coming Son of Man without imagining first being removed from the earth; yet there is no trace anywhere that he expected a "miraculous translation," and the passion predictions are all *vaticinia ex eventu*. Those predictions, moreover, and the prophecies of the coming Son of Man have nothing to do with each other; and since Jesus was not conscious of being the servant of Deutero-Isaiah, we should not think that he expected first to die and return (pp. 29–31). Little of this is persuasive. Point (a) grossly underestimates the materials that need to be utterly legendary, and in any case a negative does not establish a positive. Points (b) and (c) presuppose outdated ideas about Jewish messianism. I address point (d) below on pp. 293–303 and find it wanting. As for (e), aside from whether or not Jesus understood his death in terms of Deutero-Isaiah and whether or not the passion predictions preserve anything of his speech, we have sufficient reason to believe that he envisaged an untimely death; see below, pp. 387–433; also Heinz Schürmann, "Wie hat Jesus seinen Tod bestanden und verstanden? Eine methodenkritische Besinnung," in *Orientierung an Jesus: Zur Theologie der Synoptiker; Für Josef Schmid* (ed. Paul Hoffmann with Norbert Brox and Wilhelm Pesch; Freiburg: Herder, 1973), 325–63.

dead children and their glorification in heaven without turning them into messianic figures.[85] Indeed, in some Jewish texts everybody rises from the dead, including the wicked; but not everybody, it goes without saying, is the Messiah.

Suppose, to conjure a hypothetical, Simon Peter, before getting the chance to forsake his nets and follow Jesus, met a premature death at the hands of bandits. Suppose also that, after Simon Peter's burial, a necromancer rifled his tomb, taking the body; and suppose, beyond all this, that some of his friends, as so often happens with the bereaved, occasionally felt his continuing presence and even, on a couple of occasions, had visions of him. Would all of this have turned him into the Messiah? Or would his friends have decided that Simon bar Jonah must be the Son of Man, destined to return on the clouds of heaven? Or would anyone have read about him in Ps 110, seating him, in their imaginations, on a throne in the heavens?

The answer to all three questions is the same: surely not. The reason is that context determines meaning, that already-held convictions construe experience. But this means that if, on the contrary, a few of Simon Peter's friends, who knew of his empty tomb and felt his postmortem presence, had antecedently expected the dead to rise in the near future and had also hoped for Simon's eschatological reign as the Davidic Messiah, then they might very well have honored him as the subject of Ps 110.

The first Christians did not preach—as they might, had Jesus not already been the focus of their messianic hopes and dreams—that God had raised somebody from the dead, so the end must be near. Instead, from what we can gather, they proclaimed that God had raised Jesus from the dead, installing him as both Lord and Christ (cf. Acts 2:32–36; Rom 1:2–3). Their gospel presupposed not only that Jesus was a known individual but also that he was a certain sort of individual, of whom it made sense to say, despite the scandal of crucifixion, that he was king Messiah.

The resurrection alone cannot account for Christology, and Easter did not turn Jesus into someone or something altogether different than he was before. The resurrection, rather, sanctioned and so reactivated beliefs previously held about him.[86] That is, post-Easter convictions confirmed pre-Easter expecta-

---

85. There are serious questions about the date of the *Testament of Job* and the extent to which Christian hands have contributed to its current form. See James R. Davila, *The Provenance of the Pseudepigrapha: Jewish, Christian, or Other?* (JSJSup 105; Leiden: Brill, 2005), 195–99.

86. So already Johannes Weiss, "Das Problem der Entstehung des Christentums," *AR* 16 (1913): 468–71; Albert Schweitzer, *The Quest of the Historical Jesus* (Minneapolis: Fortress, 2001 [German original, 1906]), 343. Cf., more recently, Chester, "Messianism," 308–9; Collins, *Apocalyptic Imagination*, 263; Dahl, "Messianic Ideas," 390–91; David Flusser, "Salvation Present and Future," in *Types of Redemption: Contributions to the Theme of the Study-Conference Held at Jerusalem 14th to 19th July 1968* (ed. R. J. Zwi Werblowsky and C. Jouco Bleeker; SHR 18; Leiden: Brill, 1970), 52; Hengel, "Messiah of Israel," 12–15; Joachim Jeremias, *New Testament Theology: The Proclamation of Jesus* (New York: Charles Scribner's Sons, 1971), 255; Gerd

tions. The vindication of Jesus in the resurrection meant the vindication of hopes his followers had before the resurrection. As A. E. J. Rawlinson wrote many years ago,

> The belief in our Lord's Messiahship could not . . . have arisen simply as a conviction formed with regard to Him after His death by His disciples. Not even the Resurrection, regarded as an objective historical event, could have given rise by itself to such a remarkable belief. The disciples might have concluded, from the fact that their Master was believed to have been seen again after His Passion, that He was in some sense alive. They might have inferred from the fact that His tomb was believed to be empty that He had been raised from the dead. From the fact that He was believed to have been seen ascending into heaven they might have inferred that He had been caught up to God, and in virtue of such an "assumption" they might have been led to rank Him with Moses and Enoch and Elijah and Isaiah, about whom Hebrew tradition told similar stories. The conviction that He was the Messiah could not possibly have arisen in this way, but must have existed already. Regarded as the vindication of a Messiahship *already* ascribed to Jesus, the Resurrection falls into line.[87]

That so many scholars since Rawlinson have failed to see the point, while others of us find it close to obvious, remains perplexing.

The King of the Kingdom of God

Let me approach this issue from another angle. The major theme of Jesus' preaching was the kingdom of God. We might, then, expect the tradition about him to depict God as a king, and with some frequency. Yet, if one leaves aside the sentences with ἡ βασιλεία τοῦ θεοῦ/τῶν οὐρανῶν, it does so rarely, and in fact only in the First Gospel. Matthew 5:35 characterizes Jerusalem as "the city of the great king," which means "God's city" (cf. Ps 48:2). There is no Synoptic parallel, and the closely related passage in Jas 5:12 lacks the relevant phrase. Matthew 18:23–35, the parable of the unmerciful servant,

---

Theissen, "Jesus—Prophet einer millenaristischen Bewegung? Sozialgeschichtliche Überlegungen zu einer sozialanthropologischen Deutung der Jesusbewegung," in *Jesus als historische Gestalt: Beiträge zur Jesusforschung* (ed. Annette Merz; FRLANT 202; Göttingen: Vandenhoeck & Ruprecht, 2003), 223 (since messianic expectations do not suit a crucified figure, they must have existed before Easter).

87. A. E. J. Rawlinson, *The New Testament Doctrine of the Christ* (London: Green, 1926), 11–12. Compare this observation of Joseph Klausner: "It would never have occurred to his disciples . . . that one who had suffered crucifixion ('a curse of God is he that is hanged') could be the Messiah. . . . *Ex nihilo nihil fit*: when we see that Jesus' messianic claims became a fundamental principle of Christianity soon after his crucifixion, this is a standing proof that even in his lifetime Jesus regarded himself as the Messiah" (*Jesus of Nazareth: His Life, Times and Teaching* [New York: Macmillan, 1926], 255–56).

likens God to "a king who wished to settle accounts with his slaves." Again, there is no Synoptic equivalent. Nor is there one for Matt 17:24–27, where Jesus' pronouncement regarding the temple tax presupposes that, in one important respect, God relates to the disciples just as earthly kings relate to their children: "'From whom do kings of the earth take toll or tribute? From their children or from others?' When Peter said, 'From others,' Jesus said to him, 'Then the children are free.'" Matthew 22:1–14, the parable of the wedding banquet, also likens God to a king: "The kingdom of heaven may be compared to a king who gave a wedding banquet for his son." The Lukan counterpart is instead about a "master" (κύριος), the "owner of a house" (οἰκοδεσπότης), who is nowhere dubbed a βασιλεύς (Luke 14:16–24).

The contrast between the ubiquity of the phrase "kingdom of God" and the failure of the Synoptic tradition, with the exception of four texts from M and/ or Matthew's editorial hand, to depict God as a king, is wholly unexpected. The disproportion is all the more perplexing when one recalls that Jewish texts, including the Hebrew Bible, recurrently speak of God as a monarch and regularly envision the divinity seated on a throne. Indeed, the metaphor of God as king is "the predominant relational metaphor used of God in the Bible."[88] Why is it otherwise in the Synoptics?

Surely part of the answer must be Jesus' habit of speaking of the deity as father.[89] It may also matter that Jesus and his hearers had no access to a royal court, so that, unlike weddings and fathers, lilies and the birds of the air, their firsthand knowledge of kings was nil.

But there is another reason, utterly obvious, why, aside from the phrase ἡ βασιλεία τοῦ θεοῦ, the Synoptics so rarely portray God as a king. It is this: Jesus himself is, in the canonical Gospels, the eschatological king, or destined to be such. The mainspring of Matthew's infancy narrative is that the Davidic Messiah (χριστός) has been born, and he will rule "my people Israel" (2:6). As "king of the Jews" (2:2), he is Herod's rival, which is why the tyrant decrees death for Bethlehem's children. Luke's infancy narrative is similar, for it too records the birth of royalty. The angel Gabriel announces to Mary, regarding her child, that "the Lord God will give to him the throne of his ancestor David," and that he "will reign over the house of Jacob forever, and of his kingdom there will be no end" (1:32–33).

Mark's passion narrative prominently features the same theme. Jesus enters Jerusalem on a donkey, implicitly fulfilling Zech 9:9 ("your king comes to you . . . humble and riding on a donkey" [cf. Matt 21:5; John 12:15]).[90] The crowd

88. Marc Zvi Brettler, *God Is King: Understanding an Israelite Metaphor* (JSOTSup 76; Sheffield: JSOT Press, 1989), 160.

89. See Richard Bauckham, "Kingdom and Church according to Jesus and Paul," *HBT* 18 (1996): 1–27.

90. That the colt is "tied up" (11:2, 4) is also a royal motif; see J. Blenkinsopp, "The Oracle of Judah and the Messianic Entry," *JBL* 80 (1961): 55–64.

cries, "Blessed is the coming kingdom of our ancestor David." Later, before
the Sanhedrin, Jesus asserts that people will see him "seated at the right hand
of the Power" (Mark 14:62); and when he is crucified, it is as "king of the
Jews" (15:2, 9, 12, 18, 26, 32). Earlier in Mark, in 10:35–40, James and John
recognize Jesus' royal rank when they ask to sit on either side of him; and the
same status is implicit throughout the Synoptics, whenever Jesus is the "Son
of David" (Matt 12:23; 15:22; Mark 10:47–48; 12:35), or when events in his
life are modeled upon events in the life of David.[91]

Luke 19:11–27 (the parable of the ten pounds, in which a nobleman, representing Jesus, goes away to receive a kingdom) and several Q texts belong here too.[92]
Regarding the latter, Q's account of the temptation has the devil, in exchange
for worship, offering Jesus rule over all the kingdoms of the world (Matt 4:1–11;
Luke 4:1–13). The legend clearly assumes that Jesus will eventually come to reign
through other means.[93] In agreement with this, although the original wording
of the saying behind Matt 19:28 and Luke 22:28–30 is beyond recovery, both the
Matthean and Lukan versions present Jesus as a king. In Matthew, Jesus is the
Son of Man seated "on the throne of his glory." In Luke, the Father confers upon
him a kingdom (cf. Matt 13:41). Furthermore, Jesus' royal role probably is present
in his authority to pass eschatological judgment (Matt 10:32–33 // Luke 12:8–9
[Q]; Matt 25:10–12 + 7:22–23 // Luke 13:24–27 [Q]), for kings were judges (cf.
Matt 25:31–46, where Jesus "the king" conducts the eschatological assize).

One may well be undecided or skeptical as to how much of this material
closely reflects circumstances from Jesus' lifetime; and, once again, I will
disappoint by not endeavoring to establish that he uttered one or more of the
pertinent logia. I can, however, observe the following. If, in agreement with
previous pages, one recognizes the likelihood (i) that Jesus was executed as
"king of the Jews," (ii) that this circumstance was related to his self-perception,
and (iii) that pre-Easter eschatological expectations must have contributed to
post-Easter belief in his status as the Messiah, then we have at hand a straight-

91. The parallels are particularly impressive for the night of Jesus' arrest; see Crossan, *Who
Killed Jesus?* 76–78. Some have suggested that when people hail Jesus as "the Son of David,"
we might in some cases think not of the Davidic Messiah but rather of David or Solomon as
miracle-worker or exorcist; cf. 1 Sam 16:14–23; Josephus, *Ant.* 6.166–168; 11Q5; *L.A.B.* 59–60;
and see Klaus Berger, "Die königlichen Messiastraditionen des Neuen Testaments," *NTS* 20
(1973): 1–44; idem, "Zur Problem der Messianität Jesu," *ZTK* 71 (1974): 1–30; Dennis C. Duling,
"Solomon, Exorcism, and the Son of David," *HTR* 68 (1975): 235–52. The categories, however,
are not antithetical but go together; see Anthony Le Donne, *The Historiographical Jesus: Memory,
Typology and the Son of David* (Waco, TX: Baylor University Press, 2009).

92. John's Gospel also supplies quite a bit of material: 1:49; 6:15; 12:13, 15; 18:33, 36–39;
19:3, 12–21. See Ekkehard Stegemann and Wolfgang Stegemann, "König Israels, nicht König
der Juden? Jesus als König im Johannesevangelium," in *Messias-Vorstellungen bei Juden und
Christen* (ed. Ekkehard Stegemann; Stuttgart: Kohlhammer, 1993), 41–56.

93. Cf. Matt 28:16–20. See C. Michael Robbins, *The Testing of Jesus in Q* (SBL 108; New
York: Peter Lang, 2007).

forward explanation of why the Synoptics, despite repeated reference to the kingdom of God, otherwise say next to nothing about God as king: Jesus, when he imagined the future, saw himself ruling on God's behalf, saw himself being like the worthy Israelite and Jewish kings in the Bible. God's kingdom was his kingdom (cf. Matt 13:41; 16:28; Luke 22:30).

"Christ Jesus, Who Died . . . Is at the Right Hand of God"

So far I have urged that several considerations shore up the inference that one is otherwise inclined to draw from the catalog on pp. 227–30: even before Easter, Jesus was destined, in his mind and in the minds of his followers, to play a royal role in the end-time drama. At this point I should like to add that this finding helps us to understand a familiar refrain in early Christian literature, including Paul's Epistles: Jesus is even now seated at God's right hand.[94]

Perhaps most scholars writing on this confession, which must go back to very early times,[95] have chiefly interested themselves in its background in the Tanak or in the larger history of religions.[96] Fewer have asked the more basic question, What led anyone to believe that Jesus was already enthroned in the heavens? Was this an inference from some other conviction, or did it arise through religious experience?

Several possibilities come to mind. Believers, one may imagine, inferred the session at the right hand from Scripture, above all Ps 110.[97] Certainly that biblical text explains why the words, "the right hand of God," appear regularly in confessions of Jesus' exaltation. Or, alternatively, maybe someone saw Jesus enthroned in a *merkabah*-like vision.[98] Stephen, Acts purports, beheld Jesus

94. For example, Mark 14:62; Ps.-Mark 16:19; Acts 2:30–35; 5:31; 7:55–56; Rom 8:34; Eph 1:20; 4:10; Phil 2:9–11; Col 3:1; 1 Tim 6:15; Heb 1:3; 8:1; 10:12; 12:2; 1 Pet 3:22; Rev 3:21; 7:17; 12:5; 22:1, 3; *1 Clem.* 36:5; *Apoc. Pet.* 6:1; *Barn.* 12:10; Pol. *Phil.* 2:1; *Ep. Apost.* 3; *Mart. Ascen. Isa.* 10:14; 11:32–33; *Sib. Or.* 2:243.

95. See the convincing argument of Hengel, "'Sit at My Right Hand!' The Enthronement of Christ at the Right Hand of God and Psalm 110:1," in *Early Christology*, 172–75. Later in the essay, he affirms that Jesus' session at the right hand of God was "already central for earliest Christianity" (p. 133). According to Michel Gourgues, the belief appeared "très tôt" (*A la droite de Dieu: Résurrection de Jésus et actualisation du Psaume 110,1 dans le Nouveau Testament* [EBib; Paris: Gabalda, 1978], 210).

96. See, for example, Eskola, *Messiah and the Throne*; David M. Hay, *Glory at the Right Hand: Psalm 110 in Early Christianity* (SBLMS 18; Nashville: Abingdon, 1973); Hengel, "'Sit at My Right Hand!'" 119–226.

97. See John H. Hayes, "The Resurrection as Enthronement and the Earliest Church Christology," *Int* 22 (1968): 333–45.

98. For this argument, see David E. Aune, "Christian Prophecy and the Messianic Status of Jesus," in *Apocalypticism, Prophecy, and Magic in Early Christianity: Collected Essays* (WUNT 199; Tübingen: Mohr Siebeck, 2006), 300–319. For *merkabah* elements in early Christology, see Eskola, *Messiah and the Throne*.

"standing at the right hand of God" (7:55).[99] One could also speculate that the original resurrection experiences, whatever their precise nature, somehow instilled the conviction that the risen Jesus was exalted above the earth. The story in Matt 28:16–20 has him declare, in his risen state, "All authority in heaven and on earth has been given to me";[100] and, in Luke 24:26, the resurrected Lord asks two people on the road to Emmaus, "Was it not necessary that the Messiah should suffer these things and then enter into his glory?"

All of these suggestions fall short. Matthew 28:18 and Luke 24:26, being late first-century texts and without earlier precedent, are no firm foundation on which to build.[101] Moreover, resurrection in and of itself did not entail enthronement. Those raised from the dead do not, in Jewish sources, automatically sit on thrones, in heaven or anywhere else.[102] Resurrection seemingly meant enthronement only if one had antecedently been an exalted leader or was otherwise destined to rule, as in *T. Jud.* 25:1–3 (the twelve patriarchs are given scepters, so thrones may be implied) and *T. Benj.* 10:6 (Enoch, Seth, Abraham, Isaac, and Jacob are "raised up at the right hand").[103] Indeed, according to Timo Eskola, "in Jewish writings resurrection was never actually identified with any heavenly enthronement," so when early Christians fused Jesus' enthronement with his resurrection (as in Acts 2:22–36), they were combining two eschatological themes that had "no immediately causal relationship to each other."[104] Given this, it seems dubious that faith in Jesus' resurrection, all by itself, led to his *sessio ad dexteram Dei.*

Perhaps, then, Christians inferred Jesus' enthronement not from his resurrection but from their belief, encouraged by his bodily absence, that he was

99. Cf. Rev 1:13; 14:14. As to why Jesus, in Acts, stands instead of sits remains unexplained to my satisfaction. (I note that Moses stands and serves on high in *Sipre* 357 on Deut 34:5, and also that angels, who in Jewish folklore have no knees, often stand in heaven—e.g., 4Q225 frg. 2 col. II 5; 4Q405 frg. 20 col. II 21–22 2; Tob 12:15; *1 En.* 40:1–2; Luke 1:19; Rev 8:2; *T. Ab.* RecLng 1:4; 4:5; 8:1; 9:7; 15:11; *y. Ber.* 2c [1:1]; *b. Ḥag.* 15a.)

100. For enthronement themes in this passage, see Otto Michel, "Der Abschluss des Matthäus-Evangeliums," *EvT* 10 (1950): 16–26. An allusion to Dan 7:13–14 seems likely: "to him [the one like a son of man] was given dominion [LXX: ἐξουσία, 'authority'] and glory and kingship. . . . His dominion is an everlasting dominion."

101. Mark 16:19 ("Then the Lord Jesus . . . was taken up into heaven and sat down at the right hand of God"), from the second century, is even later.

102. See, for example, LXX Job 19:26; 42:17; Isa 26:19; Ezek 37:1–14; *Pss. Sol.* 3:12; 2 Macc 7:9–23; 12:44; *1 En.* 62:15–16; *Sib. Or.* 4:181–92; *L.A.B.* 3:10; 19:12–13; Gk. *L.A.E.* 28:4; *4 Ezra* 7:32–44; *2 Bar.* 30:1–2; 50:2–51:5.

103. Some, however, consider both of these texts to be Christian. For discussion, see Hengel, "'Sit at My Right Hand!'" 206–12. Whether or not the *Testament of Job* is Christian, Job's heavenly throne corresponds to his earthly throne. It is his appropriate compensation in the afterlife, because in this book he is, before Satan destroys his life, enthroned as the glorious king of Egypt (20:4–5; 28:7; 32:2–12; 33:2–5, 7; 41:4; 43:7). For traditions about the exalted patriarchs, see Eskola, *Messiah and the Throne*, 65–123.

104. Eskola, *Messiah and the Throne*, 248.

in heaven. According to some texts, the righteous will have thrones there.[105] This proposal, however, cannot account for the place of honor that Jesus receives: he is not just enthroned in heaven but is enthroned precisely "at the right hand of God." Why this special, unique position of honor (which, to the extent of my recall, is not bestowed upon anyone else in ancient Jewish sources except "David"—does this mean the Davidic Messiah?—in b. Ḥag. 14a; b. Sanh. 38b)? The very circumstance that, in Mark 14:62, Jesus' words about taking a heavenly seat provoke a charge of "blasphemy" (βλασφημία) shows that he is not adverting to the usual fate of righteous individuals.

Beyond that, enthronement typically was an eschatological idea. With very few exceptions—among them Moses' enthronement in Ezekiel the Tragedian[106] and Abel's enthronement in the *Testament of Abraham*[107]—the righteous gain their thrones only at the end of days. Eskola has summed up the evidence in these words:

> Visions that speak of the enthronement of prominent figures are usually eschatological. The enthronement will take place in the eschatological future, in the end of days. This is true also as regards the enthronement of the patriarchs. The stories of their exaltation usually mention their death and the departure of the soul from the body. A throne is promised to these significant persons, but the enthronement itself will be an eschatological event.[108]

Why, then, did early Christians not think of Jesus' enthronement as an impending event, to take place at his parousia? The Son of Man in *1 En.* 51:3 and the Son of David in Tg. Isa. on 16:5 sit on their thrones at the end. It is the same in Dan 7:9–11: thrones are set for the last judgment. So how did it come to pass that the future tense of Mark 14:62—"'You will see the Son of Man seated at the right hand of the Power,' and 'coming with the clouds of

---

105. For example, 4Q521; *1 En.* 108:12–15; Gk. *L.A.E.* 39:2–3; Rev 3:21; 20:4; *Mart. Ascen. Isa.* 9:24–26; 11:40; *Apoc. El.* 4:27–29.

106. Frg. 6 *apud* Eusebius, *Praep. ev.* 9.29.4–5. There is doubt, however, as to how we should understand this enthronement, given that it appears to be part of an allegorical dream; see Richard J. Bauckham, "The Throne of God and the Worship of Jesus," in *The Jewish Roots of Christological Monotheism: Papers from the St. Andrews Conference on the Historical Origins of the Worship of Jesus* (ed. Carey C. Newman, James R. Davila, and Gladys S. Lewis; JSJSup 63; Leiden: Brill, 1999), 55–57.

107. Yet here Abel is not the typical righteous individual but rather the judge of souls. See Dale C. Allison Jr., *The Testament of Abraham* (CEJL; Berlin: de Gruyter, 2003), 280–83.

108. Eskola, *Messiah and the Throne*, 134. See the texts in n. 105; see also John J. Collins, "Teacher, Priest, and Prophet," in *The Scepter and the Star: The Messiahs of the Dead Sea Scrolls and Other Ancient Literature* (New York: Doubleday, 1995), 143–44; and note the summary by Darrell D. Hannah, "The Throne of His Glory: The Divine Throne and Heavenly Mediators in Revelation and the Similitudes of Enoch," *ZNW* 94 (2003): 89: "Those denizens of heaven who are granted the privilege, in the present pre-eschatological period, of sitting on a heavenly throne other than God's are extremely rare."

heaven'"—became the present tense of Acts 2:33: "Being therefore exalted at the right hand of God . . ."?

As for attributing belief in Jesus' session to religious experience, such as a vision, the truth is that prior beliefs and expectations interpret and shape experience. Visions that do not conform to and confirm what is already given usually do not gain credence. Disbelief would greet any Roman Catholic visionary who heard Mother Mary spouting heresy. Likewise, had an early Christian declared, "I have seen Jesus seated at God's right hand," and if the religious context were not already favorable to such a belief, it would have gone nowhere.

The same principle holds for exegesis. To refer Ps 110 to the risen Jesus presupposes already well-developed beliefs about him. One would hardly have inferred from Scripture that Jesus now sits on a heavenly throne unless one antecedently believed him to be a king in waiting. Merrill Miller is right: "It is hardly likely that Ps 110:1 could be used at the outset to establish Jesus' messianic status; rather, it presupposes that status and provides royal imagery with which to interpret the resurrection."[109]

So is there a better story? My own proposal takes seriously the elemental fact that events do not dictate their religious interpretations; rather, adherents of a faith come to events with religious categories and expectations at hand, and they interpret accordingly.[110] This is why, as the previous chapter has documented, prophecy seldom fails. Believers regularly interpret their experiences so that expectations become, whatever has transpired, fulfilled or partially fulfilled.[111] It was so, I submit, with the enthronement of Jesus. Soon after Easter, some of his followers envisaged him as enthroned because, already before Easter, they had expected his enthronement.[112] In other words, they had hoped that God would install him as king, so when they became persuaded of his divine vindication, they naturally came to believe that God had seated him upon a heavenly throne—a conviction that, once born, could find support in Scripture, above all in Ps 110.

The virtue of this account is twofold. First, it can appeal to parallel after parallel in the history of millenarian movements, where, as the sociologists know, promise has regularly begotten fulfillment. Second, it does not contradict the

109. Merrill P. Miller, "The Problem of the Origins of a Messianic Conception of Jesus," in *Redescribing Christian Origins* (ed. Ron Cameron and Merrill P. Miller; SBLSymS 28; Atlanta: Society of Biblical Literature, 2004), 308.

110. Helpful in this connection, even if his radical contextualism goes too far, is Steven T. Katz, "The 'Conservative' Character of Mystical Experience," in *Mysticism and Religious Traditions* (ed. Steven T. Katz; Oxford: Oxford University Press, 1983), 3–60.

111. See above, pp. 127–28, 149–50.

112. Hengel explains, "Because Jewish hopes about the future nowhere include the enthronement in messianic-eschatological honour through resurrection from the dead, the origin of christology appears unthinkable without the assumption of a messianic claim of Jesus" ("'Sit at My Right Hand!'" 217). This explanation requires disagreement with Hahn (*Christologische Hoheitstitel*, 112–25), for whom the idea of exaltation and enthronement was not known to "the oldest tradition of the Palestinian church."

primary sources but rather fully accords with them. The Jesus tradition itself purports that Jesus and his followers, before Easter, expected his enthronement in the near future. In Mark 10:35–40, James and John ask of their leader, "Grant us to sit, one at your right hand and one at your left, in your glory." In Mark 14:62, Jesus prophesies that his audience will "see the Son of Man seated at the right hand of the Power." In Matt 19:28 // Luke 22:28–30 (Q), Jesus promises disciples that they will sit on thrones, and it is unthinkable that he who grants them this privilege will have anything less—as Matthew's version ("when the Son of Man is seated on the throne of his glory") makes explicit (see also 25:31).

In making this last point, I do not maintain that the sons of Zebedee really requested to sit at his right and left, although, for all I know, they did. Nor do I insist that Jesus spoke something close to Mark 14:62 or Matt 19:28 // Luke 22:28–30 (Q), although, for all I know, he did. I observe only that, in the Synoptics, Jesus' enthronement is a pre-Easter hope, whereas in the rest of the New Testament, his enthronement has become a postmortem reality, and that the former is a straightforward, credible explanation of the latter.

The Jewish Context

For some, one stumbling block laid before the view that I have endorsed is the difficulty of understanding the psychology that must have been involved. I have already quoted John Knox, to the effect that no sane person from any time or place could entertain the thoughts that Jesus entertains in the Gospels. This, however, is a gratuitous assumption.[113] It fails to reckon seriously with Jesus' Jewish context, and it neglects certain facts of religious psychology.[114] I begin with the former subject.

Scholars have, over the past few decades, become accustomed to recognizing the diversity of Jewish eschatologies and messianic expectations at the turn of the era, as well as the fact that, for some groups and documents, all such ideas were seemingly marginal.[115] Large simplifications are, accordingly, harder to come by now than they were before. Yet some generalizations still stand, among them this: an exalted human being is, in a significant number of Second Temple writings, the pivot of the eschatological turning point;[116] and

113. And one that is oddly reminiscent of the old apologetical argument, associated with C. S. Lewis, that Jesus must have been a liar or a lunatic or the Son of God. See C. S. Lewis, *Mere Christianity* (New York: Macmillan, 1960), 56.

114. On the latter subject one can still learn from Walter E. Bundy, *The Psychic Health of Jesus* (New York: Macmillan, 1922); Albert Schweitzer, *The Psychiatric Study of Jesus: Exposition and Criticism* (Boston: Beacon, 1948).

115. For example, *Jub.* 23 and the *Testament of Moses* imagine the end without speaking of messianic figures.

116. Barnabas Lindars, in "Re-enter the Apocalyptic Son of Man" (*NTS* 22 [1975]: 52–72), emphasized this and its importance for the study of Jesus. Later, his work on the "Son of Man"

those texts often assign to that human intermediary two key roles—king and judge—that the Jesus tradition again and again bestows upon its hero.

Regarding the office of judge, 1Q28b 5:20–22 (according to the usual reconstruction—the text is fragmentary) pledges that "the prince of the congregation" will "judge the poor with righteousness and reproach the humble of the earth."[117] 11Q13 2:13 prophesies that Melchizedek will, in the future, "exact the vengeance of El's judgments."[118] According to *Pss. Sol.* 17, the messianic Son of David will judge the tribes of Israel as well as the nations (cf. Isa 11:3–4). The current ending of the Similitudes of *1 Enoch* seems to identify Enoch with the Son of Man, who sits on the eschatological throne of judgment.[119] According to *4 Ezra* 12:31–32, the Messiah, "whom the Most High has kept until the end of days, who will arise from the offspring of David," will speak to wicked Roman emperors and "denounce them for their ungodliness and for their wickedness, and will display before them their contemptuous dealings" (cf. 13:37–38). In *2 Bar.* 72:2–6, God's Messiah "will summon all the nations, and some of them he will spare, and some of them he will slay" (cf. 40:1; 70:9).[120] Also relevant, although they are Christian, are 1 Cor 6:2 ("the saints will judge the world") and Rev 20:4, which assumes that certain followers of Jesus, presumably martyrs (cf. vv. 4–6), will conduct the eschatological assize.[121]

As for Second Temple Jewish texts in which a divinely appointed human being rules as the eschatological king, they are just as numerous. Indeed, we

title took him in another direction. Other biblical scholars, however, have focused upon the subject of God's chief agent or the issue of divine agency; see especially P. G. Davis, "Divine Agents, Mediators, and New Testament Christology," *JTS* 45 (1992): 470–503; Larry W. Hurtado, *One God, One Lord: Early Christian Devotion and Ancient Jewish Monotheism* (Philadelphia: Fortress, 1988).

117. Cf. 4Q246 2:5–6, where "he will judge the earth" likely refers to the messianic king. See Karl A. Kuhn, "The 'One Like a Son of Man' Becomes the 'Son of God,'" *CBQ* 69 (2007): 22–42; for another view, see Émile Puech, "Some Remarks on 4Q246 and 4Q521 and Qumran Messianism," in *The Provo International Conference on the Dead Sea Scrolls: Technological Innovations, New Texts, and Reformulated Issues* (ed. Donald W. Parry and Eugene Ulrich; STDJ 30; Leiden: Brill, 1999), 545–65.

118. Unlike Gareth Lee Cockerill ("Melchizedek or 'King of Righteousness,'" *EvQ* 63 [1991]: 305–12), most scholars identify the Melchizedek of this document with the individual of Gen 14, as in Heb 7; see the argument to this effect in Eric F. Mason, *"You Are a Priest Forever": Second Temple Jewish Messianism and the Priestly Christology of the Epistle to the Hebrews* (STDJ 74; Leiden: Brill, 2008), 187–88. Among other things, the man in Genesis is a priest, and the figure in 11Q13 is associated with the Day of Atonement.

119. *1 En.* 46:4–6; 49:4; 55:4; 61:8; 62:3–5; 69:26–29. In *1 En.* 92:1, Enoch appears as "judge of all the earth." See also *Jub.* 4:23; 10:17; *T. Ab.* RecShrt 11:3–4; in the latter, Enoch the heavenly scribe records the deeds of human beings.

120. For additional texts and discussion, see Johannes Theisohn, *Der auserwählte Richter: Untersuchungen zum traditionsgeschichtlichem Ort der Menschensohngestalt der Bilderreden des Äthiopischen Henoch* (SUNT 12; Göttingen: Vandenhoeck & Ruprecht, 1974), 100–113.

121. See David E. Aune, *Revelation 17–22* (WBC 52C; Nashville: Thomas Nelson, 1998), 1084–85.

have here an embarrassment of riches, for every passage that awaits a Davidic Messiah is expecting the eschatological advent of a royal human figure.[122] 4Q174 1:11–13 cites 2 Sam 7:11–14, which is about King David's heir, and applies it to the "Shoot of David," who will arrive "at the end of days." CD-A 7:15–21 interprets Num 24:17 ("A star shall come out of Jacob, and a scepter shall rise out of Israel") with reference to "the prince of the congregation," an eschatological figure for the Qumran sectarians.[123] 4Q252 5:1–4, in interpreting Gen 49:10 ("The scepter shall not depart from Judah, nor the ruler's staff from between his feet, until tribute comes to him; and the obedience of the peoples is his"), looks forward to the "Messiah of righteousness, the Shoot of David," who has "the covenant of kingship." *Psalms of Solomon* 17:32 foretells the coming of "the Lord Messiah," who will be "a righteous king." And so it goes. Jesus' Jewish world was quite familiar with the idea of a human being serving as eschatological king and/or judge.[124]

Real-Life Analogies

It is, however, one thing to recognize that some Jews hoped, at least in their writings, for this or that eschatological figure, and quite another to imagine that a particular Jew identified himself with such a one. Here we run up against Marcus Borg's protest: "Though saints and Spirit persons are a bit crazy, when judged by conventional standards, they typically do not think of themselves in grandiose terms. I don't think people like Jesus have an exalted perception of themselves."[125]

Everything hinges upon what Borg means by "people like Jesus." If Borg has in mind individuals whom he has judged, in his firsthand experience, to be "like Jesus," then I partly sympathize. The few people whom I have known and deemed to be saintly have been uniformly humble. They have not uttered grandiose thoughts about themselves.

I have not, however, met everybody, and the historical Jesus belongs neither to my immediate experience nor to Borg's. Jesus was from another place and

---

122. The Davidic Messiah, to state the obvious, is a king (e.g., 4Q252 5:1–4; 1Q28b 5:21; 4Q161 frgs. 8–10 col. III 20–21; *Pss. Sol.* 17:21, 32). In rabbinic literature, he is indeed sometimes named "King Messiah," as in *y. Ber.* 5a (2:3); *y. Ta'an.* 68d (4:5); and often in the targumim: Ps.-J. on Gen 3:15; Frg. Tg. on Exod 12:42; Tg. Ps 45:3; 80:16.

123. See p. 111 n. 356.

124. See further below, p. 280 n. 244; also Jer 23:5–6; 33:14–16; Amos 9:11; Mic 5:2; Zech 9:9. Much of Jewish theological history has displayed a "dualistic pattern," according to which, in addition to the supreme creator God, there is also "his vizier or prime minister, or some other spiritual agency, who really 'runs the show,' or at least provides the point of contact between God and humanity" (Peter Hayman, "Monotheism—A Misused Word in Jewish Studies?" *JJS* 42 [1991]: 2).

125. Borg, "Was Jesus God?" 147.

an altogether different time, and it is perilous to look back at the receding past and to decide, on the basis of our limited personal experience, what a premodern Jew might or might not have thought about himself. What would Borg make of Abraham Abulafia (b. 1240)? This man took himself to be the Messiah and destined to alter the nature of reality itself, yet he displayed "personal humility in his relations with colleagues and pupils," wrote in an elegant style, and reasoned on occasion as a rationalist.[126]

To judge that someone "like Jesus" could not have thought himself called to be a divine agent is surely an ahistorical prejudice, no more plausible than urging that, as a general rule, new religious "cults are invented by individuals suffering from certain forms of mental illness."[127] Apart from the fact that people can be reluctant about a divine call and accept it anyway (Jeremiah is an illustration), or that they can enter a high office and yet remain genuinely humble (Gregory I comes to mind),[128] history is full of human beings who have aspired to greatness, who have sought to lead others, and who have imagined themselves to be at the center of what they believed the gods or God were doing. How do we know that all such people were not "like Jesus" in the pertinent respects? Do we really have reason to suppose that they were all, to our way of thinking, either narcissistic or mentally ill whereas, happily and to the contrary, the historical Jesus was mentally fit and spiritually healthy and so cannot have been much like any of them?[129] Human beings often explode our expectations. Who would, after reading the massively learned, brilliant works of Gershom Scholem, the great twentieth-century Jewish historian, dream that he once seriously entertained the idea that he himself might be the Messiah? But he did.[130]

126. See Abraham Berger, "The Messianic Self-Consciousness of Abraham Abulafia: A Tentative Evaluation," in *Essential Papers on Messianic Movements and Personalities in Jewish History* (ed. Marc Saperstein; New York: New York University Press, 1992), 250–55.

127. Robert W. Balch, "Bo and Peep: A Case Study of the Origins of Messianic Leadership," in *Millennialism and Charisma* (ed. Roy Wallis; Belfast: Queen's University, 1982), 65 (italics deleted).

128. Gregory is instructive for an additional reason. Some have found the popular religion of miracles in the final book of the *Dialogues* to be so at odds with the rest of Gregory's theological works that they have denied he wrote it. This, however, is a mistake: Gregory's mental universe was more expansive and varied than that of some of his modern readers. See Paul Meyvaert, "The Enigma of Gregory the Great's *Dialogues*: A Response to Francis Clark," *JEH* 39 (1988): 335–81.

129. Bruce Chilton asks, "Can we understand Jesus at all, if we make the liberal assumption that he was rational by our standards of rationality?" ("[The] Son of [the] Man, and Jesus," in *Authenticating the Words of Jesus* [ed. Bruce Chilton and Craig A. Evans; NTTS 28/1; Leiden: Brill, 1998], 283). Some of Jesus' contemporaries, we should not forget, according to our sources, thought him to be mad (Mark 3:21) and/or possessed (Mark 3:22; John 8:48).

130. See Michael Brenner, "From Self-Declared Messiah to Scholar of Messianism: The Recently Published Diaries Present Young Gerhard Scholem in a New Light," *Jewish Social Studies* 3 (1996): 177–82.

I sometimes have confided to others my belief that anyone who aspires to be president of the United States in this day and age must be crazy. I suppose that I half believe that. Yet it would be folly for me to move from my generalization to conclusions about any particular individual running for that office. Our simplifications about people in general are no sure guide to any one man or woman in particular, and surely this is all the more true if we are looking across cultures and back in time.

The Tanak, the center of Jesus' religious culture, is full of individuals who were, by the purported will of God, judges and kings, and much Jewish tradition, going back to Isaiah and Micah, plainly taught that God would send a mighty king in the ideal future. Psalm 110:1, moreover, evidently speaks of an Israelite monarch who reigns "with the power and authority of Yahweh himself."[131] Outside the Bible, it is no different. A number of extracanonical texts know of divine agents who, although human, "represent God in a unique capacity and stand in a role second only to God himself, thus being distinct from all the other servants and agents of God."[132] For the critical historian, what matters is not what any of us make of these ideas but what first-century Jews such as Jesus might have made of them if they took them seriously, which their religion seemingly compelled them to do.[133]

Far weightier, moreover, than Borg's sweeping generalization regarding what someone "like Jesus" probably thought or did not think about himself is the fact that history is full of people, not all of whom one can dismiss as ill or foolish, who have had extravagant religious aspirations of one sort or another.[134] Just as many have sought to be, in the world of practical politics, kings, prime ministers, and presidents, so others have aspired to be, in the world of religious hope, messianic leaders or mediators of the divine. The difference, I submit, lies not in mental health or intelligence but in social context.[135] Plausibility structures vary. Perceptions are relative. Our sober

131. Hay, *Glory at the Right Hand*, 20.

132. Hurtado, *One God*, 18.

133. This is one of the main points of Schweitzer's *Psychiatric Study of Jesus*. See also the brief but prudent remarks of John G. Gager, "Messiahs and Their Followers," in *Toward the Third Millennium: Messianic Expectations from the Bible to Waco* (ed. Peter Schäfer and Mark Cohen; SHR 77; Leiden: Brill, 1998), 45–46.

134. In his cross-cultural study of several millenarian prophets, each with an exalted self-conception, Michael Adas observes that they were all "well educated by the standards of their societies" (*Prophets of Rebellion: Millenarian Protest Movements against the European Colonial Order* [Chapel Hill: University of North Carolina Press, 1979], 119).

135. Scholem probably was right to diagnose Sabbatai Sevi as manic depressive, or what we now call bipolar; and Jen Yu-wen (*The Taiping Revolutionary Movement* [New Haven: Yale University Press, 1973], 15–19) may well have reason to assert that the Chinese messiah Hong Xiuquan was psychotic and suffered from "twilight state." All such judgments, however, require a great deal of evidence, more than we have for most religious figures from antiquity, including Jesus; and they must be sensitive to and respect the different norms of different societies.

Western standards are not universal. What makes sense in one context might not make sense in another.[136]

Let me offer some examples.

Simon Kimbangu, the twentieth-century charismatic miracle-worker in the Lower Congo, believed that God had, in a vision, called him to teach and heal.[137] He thought of himself as a sort of Christ figure and imitated the New Testament Jesus. On one occasion, for instance, he spat on the ground, made a paste, and anointed the eyes of a blind man. He also appointed "twelve apostles" to assist him in his ministry. He carried a staff in his hand, symbolizing his prophetic and regal authority. When the Belgian authorities arrested him for promoting anti-European sentiments, he again emulated Christ, refusing to resist his captors. Subsequently, as a prisoner, he behaved in exemplary fashion. His sincere self-conception, which was that God was at work through him to change the face of Africa, seems to have existed beside earnest efforts to be pious and holy.[138]

Hong Xiuquan was the leader of the Taiping rebellion in the middle of the nineteenth century.[139] A Christian convert, he came to believe, through dreams and visions, that apocalyptic catastrophe was on the horizon, and that God had appointed him, as the "younger brother of Jesus Christ," to liberate China from the Qing or Manchu Dynasty. Through military campaigns, he successfully subdued large portions of southern China, setting up his capital

136. Hengel remarks, "In my judgment, the real Jesus was more enthusiastic, more ecstatic, more passionate, and that means also, *more alien to us*, than we enlightened Central Europeans care to admit today. We all tend to interpret and adapt him in ways appropriate to ourselves. . . . The enthusiastic, messianic Jesus is further from us than the 'rabbi and prophet' who has become dear to us" ("Messiah of Israel," 67). Pieter F. Craffert, in *The Life of a Galilean Shaman: Jesus of Nazareth in Anthropological-Historical Perspective* (Eugene, OR: Cascade Books, 2008), provides much to ponder in this connection. Also very helpful here is Michele Stephen, "Cargo Cults, Cultural Creativity, and Autonomous Imagination," *Ethos* 25 (1997): 333–58. For Stephen, a strong tendency to think in terms of madness and hysteria when dealing with cultures that understand dreams, trances, and possession differently than do Western academics has crippled our understanding.

137. See Marie-Louise Martin, *Kimbangu: An African Prophet and His Church* (Oxford: Basil Blackwell, 1975), esp. 38–64. For other African messianic prophets, see Bengt G. M. Sundkler, *Bantu Prophets in South Africa* (London: Oxford University Press, 1961), 323–30.

138. It is fascinating to learn what religious tradition has done with another recent African charismatic, Isaiah Shembe. Sermons of his grandson, for instance, refer to his preexistence ("When Moses saw the burning bush, I was there") and seem to assume that "extra Shembe, nulla salus." See J. A. Loubser, "The Oral Christ of Shembe: Believing in Jesus in Oral and Literate Societies," *Scriptura* 12 (1993): 70–80. According to one observer, Shembe, for his followers, "has usurped the position of God" (G. C. Oosthuizen, "Isaiah Shembe and the Zulu World View," *HR* 8 [1968]: 9). For a fascinating collection of oral traditions about him that again and again reminds one of New Testament materials, see *History and Traditions Centered on Ekuphakameni and Mount Nhlangakazi* (vol. 1 of *The Story of Isaiah Shembe*, ed. Irving Hexham and G. C. Oosthuizen; Lewiston, NY: Edwin Mellen, 1996).

139. I have consulted Yu-wen, *Taiping Revolutionary Movement*; Jonathan D. Spence, *God's Chinese Son: The Taiping Heavenly Kingdom of Hong Xiuquan* (New York: W. W. Norton, 1996).

in Nanjing, renamed Taiping Tianguo, "the heavenly kingdom of peace," from which city he ruled over his territories as absolute monarch. Some writings from him are extant, among which is the following poem:

> God is vexed most by idols and images,
> So human beings are not allowed to see the Father's likeness.
> But Christ and myself were begotten by the Father,
> And because we were in the Father's bosom, therefore we saw God.
> The Father created Adam and Pangu in his own image—
> If you acknowledge the truth of this, you can still be pardoned.
> The Elder Brother and I have personally seen the Father's heavenly face;
> Father and Sons, Elder and Younger Brother, nothing is indistinct.
> The Father and the Elder Brother have brought me to sit in the Heavenly Court;
> Those who believe this truth will enjoy eternal bliss.[140]

Whatever one makes of such words, they are the words of Hong himself, not his followers.

The founder of Manichaeism, Mani, evidently declared, "I teach mankind wisdom and knowledge and save them from Az and Ahrmen."[141] He had, or so he believed, the ability to overcome witchcraft, cure illnesses, free people from demons, and revive those at the point of death. He was further persuaded that although he was in the same revelatory line as Zoroaster, Buddha, and Jesus, the religion that he had founded was superior to theirs, and indeed to all previous faiths; in his own mind, Mani was the last and most important of God's emissaries.[142] He "regarded himself," in other words, "as the fulfillment of the great world religions."[143] He reportedly called himself the "Paraclete" (promised by Jesus in John's Gospel)[144] and the "seal of the prophets."[145] He

140. As quoted by Spence, *God's Chinese Son*, 289.

141. L. J. R. Ort, *Mani: A Religio-Historical Description of His Personality* (DHRP 1; Leiden: Brill, 1967), 49.

142. See Samuel N. C. Lieu, "'My Church Is Superior . . .': Mani's Missionary Statement in Coptic and Middle Persian," in *Coptica, Gnostica, Manichaica: Mélanges offerts à Wolf-Peter Funk* (ed. Louis Painchaud and Paul-Hubert Poirier; BCNH 7; Quebec: University Press of Laval; Leuven: Peeters, 2006), 519–27.

143. Alexander Böhlig, "Zum Selbstverständnis des Manichäismus," in *Gnosis und Synkretismus: Gesammelte Aufsätze zur spätantiken Religionsgeschichte*, vol. 2 (WUNT 48; Tübingen: Mohr Siebeck, 1989), 532.

144. See *Keph.* 14:3–7. For scholarly discussion of this issue, see Majella Franzmann, "Jesus in the Manichaean Writings—Work in Progress," in *Studia Manichaica IV: Internationaler Kongreß zum Manichäismus, Berlin, 14.–18. Juli 1997* (ed. Ronald E. Emmerick, Werner Sundermann, and Peter Zieme; Berlin: Akademie-Verlag, 2000), 226–27; Werner Sundermann, "Der Paraklet in der ostmanichäischen Überlieferung," in *Manichaean Studies: Proceedings of the First International Conference on Manichaeism, August 5–9, 1987, Department of History of Religions, Lund University, Sweden* (ed. P. Bryder; LSAAR 1; Lund: Lund Plus Ultra, 1988), 201–12.

145. See Ort, *Mani*, 53, 71, 108, 123–25.

claimed, "Everything that has happened and that will happen was unveiled to me. . . . I have understood . . . everything. I have seen the totality."[146]

By referring, in an investigation of the historical Jesus, to Simon Kimbangu, Hong Xiuquan, and Mani, my intent is not to suggest that all three belong to some sort of cross-cultural religious type. They do not. Instead, I intend solely to make two points. First, some religious figures have had exalted self-conceptions and given themselves very large roles to play in the divine economy.[147] Second, this fact does not dictate what they otherwise might have believed or taught. Simon Kimbangu considered himself a follower of Jesus, and he promoted many traditional Christian virtues; and Mani was, from everything we can determine, sensitive, highly intelligent, and sincere about his religious convictions, including his stupendous self-claims.[148] It follows, I submit, that one who judges Jesus to have been a profound moral teacher and free of mental pathology can hardly decide, on the basis of those two attributes, what he must have or could have thought about himself in the grand scheme of things.[149]

Because Jesus was a Jew, even more pertinent perhaps than Simon Kimbangu, Hong Xiuquan, and Mani are the many Jewish messianic claimants throughout history, among them Simon bar Kokhba,[150] Abu Isa of Pispahan (eighth century),

146. *Keph.* 15:19–23; cf. *CMC* 66:4–69:8. Böhlig ("Selbstverständnis des Manichäismus," 531) attributes *Keph.* 258:26–259:23 to Mani, and in this the prophet declares,

People who love me are called by my name. Also, by the apostolate of my father, who sent me to the world, they who are mine accept me for themselves. Behold, they swear by my fortune in every place and every city. Who is as great as I in the universe? Or who was active in this creation the way I myself have been active, other than my brothers the apostles who were before me? . . . Every one who will believe in me and also be persuaded to my word can become with me inheritors in the new aeon.

147. For numerous additional examples, see Vittorio Lanternari, *The Religions of the Oppressed: A Study of Modern Messianic Cults* (trans. Lisa Sergio; London: MacGibbon & Kee, 1963); for figures from Chinese history, see Anna K. Seidel, "The Image of the Perfect Ruler in Early Taoist Messianism: Lao-Tzu and Li Hung," *HR* 9 (1969–1970): 216–47. Of special interest are the many Islamic figures who have claimed to be the Mahdi.

148. Compare this characterization of Mani in a famous article of A. V. Williams Jackson: Mani had "a peculiar idealism and refinement, combined with rare vision"; he "had a poetic imagination"; he had "a highly ideal and creative mind"; he had a "sensitive and spiritual nature" ("The Personality of Mānī, the Founder of Manichaeism," *JAOS* 58 [1938]: 240).

149. One might say the same of Bahaullah, the central figure of the Baha'i movement. The claims that he made for himself were astounding, notwithstanding the conventional nature of much of his religious and moral teaching; see Christopher Buck, "The Eschatology of Globalization: The Multiple-Messiahship of Bahā'u'llāh Revisited," in *Studies in Modern Religions, Religious Movements and the Bābī-Bahā'ī Faiths* (ed. Moshe Sharon; SHR 104; Leiden: Brill, 2004), 148–78.

150. Against G. S. Aleksandrov ("The Role of 'Aqiba in the Bar-Kokhba Rebellion," *REJ* 132 [1974]: 65–77) and others, it seems likely that, even if only late in his career, Bar Kokhba accepted the messianic office. (1) "The denunciation of Bar Kosiba as a false Messiah . . . is irrefutable proof of the popularity of the identification of Bar Kosiba as the true Messiah" (Adele Reinhartz, "Rabbinic Perceptions of Simeon Bar Kosiba," *JSJ* 20 [1989]: 177). (2) The association of Bar Kokhba's name with Num 24:17 ("a star [כוכב] goes forth from Jacob" [cf. *y. Ta'an.* 68d (4:5); *Lam. Rab.* 2.2.4]) can only have occurred before defeat and disgrace, not after (so too Reinhartz,

Serene of Shirin (eighth century), Menahem of Chazaria (twelfth century), David
Alroy (twelfth century), Abraham Abulafia (thirteenth century), Moses Botarel
of Spain (fourteenth century), Solomon Molko (1500–1532), and Sabbatai Sevi.[151]
Consider one in particular: the man who, on the Island of Crete in the second half
of the fifth century, took for himself the name of Moses. Perhaps prompted by
belief that the Son of David would come in the eighty-fifth Jubilee (cf. *b. 'Abod.
Zar.* 9a–b), as well as by deteriorating conditions for Jews throughout the empire,

---

"Bar Kosiba," 175–76). Peter Schäfer, although doubting the attribution of this tradition to
Akiba, recognizes that "it must have originated during the Bar Kokhba revolt" ("Bar Kokhba
and the Rabbis," in *The Bar Kokhba War Reconsidered: New Perspectives on the Second Jewish
Revolt against Rome* [ed. Peter Schäfer; TSAJ 100; Tübingen: Mohr Siebeck, 2003], 4). Justin
(*1 Apol.* 31.6), writing perhaps only two decades after the revolt, gives the name as Βαρχωχέβας
("Bar Kokhba," "son of the star"), presupposing the pun on Numbers. (3) Both Christian and
Jewish sources have him claiming to be the Messiah: Eusebius, *Hist. eccl.* 4.6.2 (Bar Kokhba
"pretended that he was a star that had come down to them out of heaven to bring them light in
the midst of their misfortunes"); *b. Sanh.* 93b ("Bar Kosiba was king for two and a half years,
and then said to the rabbis, 'I am Messiah'"). The two and a half years in this latter text is hard
to explain. Do we have here a memory (see Reinhartz, "Bar Kosiba," 188)? (4) Bar Kokhba's
use of "Prince" (נשיא) in letters and on coins could bear messianic sense (see p. 111 n. 354; and
Schäfer, "Bar Kokhba," 15–20). Further, is it just coincidence that the militant Bar Kokhba called
himself נשיא, that some enthusiasts linked his name to Num 24:17, and that CD-A 7:18–21 finds
in Num 24:17 a prophecy of the נשיא who will fight the final battle? (5) According to Justin
(*1 Apol.* 31.6), Bar Kokhba persecuted only Christians, and "so far as we know, Christians were
the only sect among second-century Jews to hold fiercely to a particular person as Israel's 'Messiah'"; it is natural to infer that "Christians' refusal to support the revolt was probably due . . .
to their refusal to recognize neither Bar Kokhba's messianic identification nor the goals of the
revolt itself," for which reason they encountered oppression (Craig A. Evans, "Was Simon ben
Kosiba Recognized as Messiah?" in *Jesus and His Contemporaries: Comparative Studies* [AGJU
25; Leiden: Brill, 1995], 193). (6) The *Apocalypse of Peter* not only shows a special interest in
the bogus claim "I am the Messiah," but also it prophesies that those who reject the claims of
the false messiah will, as a consequence, suffer martyrdom. This apocalypse likely reflects the
perceptions of Christians in Palestine during Bar Kokhba's revolt (see Richard J. Bauckham,
"The Apocalypse of Peter: A Jewish-Christian Apocalypse from the Time of Bar Kokhba," in
The Fate of the Dead: Studies on the Jewish and Christian Apocalypses [NovTSup 93; Leiden:
Brill, 1998], 160–258, esp. 176–94). See further above, pp. 110–12.

    151. Helpful works include Harris Lenowitz, *The Jewish Messiahs: From the Galilee to Crown
Heights* (Oxford: Oxford University Press, 1998); Scholem, *Sabbatai Sevi*; Silver, *Messianic
Speculation*. The Jewish king Loukuas-Andreas, who led the Jewish revolt in 115–117 CE, in
circumstances that are, unfortunately, poorly documented, was also probably a messianic figure;
see Alexander Fuks, "Aspects of the Jewish Revolt in A.D. 115–117," *JRS* 51 (1961): 98–104; Martin
Hengel, "Messianische Hoffnung und politischer 'Radikalismus' in der 'jüdisch-hellenistischen
Diaspora': Zur Frage der Voraussetzungen des jüdischen Aufstandes unter Trajan 115–117
n. Chr.," in *Judaica et Hellenistica: Kleine Schriften I* (WUNT 90; Tübingen: Mohr Siebeck,
1996), 314–43; James Carleton Paget, "Egypt," in *Redemption and Resistance: The Messianic
Hopes of Jews and Christians in Antiquity* (ed. Markus Bockmuehl and James Carleton Paget;
London: T & T Clark, 2007), 189–91. Compare Shim'on Applebaum's observation that "the
spirit of the movement [in 115–117 CE] was messianic," its task "to inaugurate the messianic
era" (*Jews and Greek in Ancient Cyrene* [SJLA 28; Leiden: Brill, 1979], 260). Eusebius (*Hist.
eccl.* 4.2.5) refers to Loukuas as a "king" (Λουκούα τῷ βασιλεῖ αὐτῶν).

Moses, over the course of a year of itinerant ministry, persuaded large numbers that he was the long-awaited Messiah, who would lead the faithful, via a dry sea, to the land of Israel. Those who believed in him abandoned their businesses and possessions. On the appointed day of redemption, he promised followers that they would, following their second Moses, see the miracle of the Red Sea duplicated. Some of the faithful, having ventured to a promontory overlooking the sea, flung themselves from the precipice, expecting the waves to part before them. The sea, indifferent as always, took no notice, with predictable and disastrous consequences.[152] That Moses let events go to the bitter end is near proof that he really did expect God's intervention.

Moses had a first-century predecessor. According to Josephus (*J.W.* 2.261–263 [cf. *Ant.* 20.169–172]), a prophet hailing from Egypt won many followers within Judea. These he led "by a circuitous route from the desert to the mount called the Mount of Olives. From there he proposed to force an entrance into Jerusalem and, after overpowering the Roman garrison, to set himself up as tyrant of the people, employing those who poured in with him as his bodyguard." Josephus adds (*Ant.* 20.170) that at the command of this Egyptian prophet, Jerusalem's walls were supposed to fall down. Tragically for him and his followers, the procurator Felix (CE 52–60) fell upon the expectant group with heavy infantry, which ended the affair, the leader escaping with his life and earning no further notice from the history books.

If Josephus is close to the facts, this unnamed leader hoped to emulate the achievements of the great Joshua, who, in conquering the Holy Land, saw the walls of a city come tumbling down (Josh 6). But the Egyptian clearly saw himself as more than a new Joshua. For the latter was himself a second Moses,[153] and the unnamed prophet, as we meet him in Josephus, is full of Mosaic traits. His title is "the Egyptian" (ὁ Αἰγύπτιος [cf. Acts 21:38]). He reckons himself a "prophet" (cf. Deut 18:15, 18; 34:10). He leads a crowd into "the desert" (τῆς ἐρημίας [cf. Acts 21:38]). And he conducts the people by a circuitous route (περιαγαγών [cf. Exod 13:18; and esp. LXX Amos 2:10: περιήγαγον ὑμᾶς ἐν τῇ ἐρήμῳ, "I led you around in the desert").[154] Regrettably, we know little more. The Egyptian did, however, wish to set himself up as a king.[155] Surely he thought of himself as the Mosaic viceroy of the latter days.[156]

152. See Socrates Scholasticus, *Hist. eccl.* 7.38 (SC 506:136–38).
153. See Dale C. Allison Jr., *The New Moses: A Matthean Typology* (Minneapolis: Fortress, 1993), 23–28.
154. Cf. Tg. Onq. on Gen 49:11, where the Messiah leads his people *around* (יסחר) Jerusalem.
155. Josephus says that he sought to be a "tyrant" (τυραννεῖν), and kingship is another Mosaic trait; cf. Ezekiel the Tragedian, in Eusebius, *Praep. ev.* 9.28–29; Philo, *Moses* 1.148–149, 158; *Sib. Or.* 1:435; *Mek.* on Exod 18:14; *b. Zebaḥ.* 102a; *Exod. Rab.* 15:13; *Midr. Ps.* 1:2; Tg. Ps.-J. on Deut 33:5.
156. This is all the more evident given the eschatological associations of the Mount of Olives, on which, see John Briggs Curtis, "The Mount of Olives in Tradition," *HUCA* 28 (1957): 137–80. That Josephus refers to this mountain and to the walls of Jerusalem falling down puts

The Egyptian was not alone. We know of a number of other sign prophets[157] as well as a few contemporaries or near contemporaries of Jesus who sought to set themselves up as kings.[158] Because they all ultimately came to naught, our knowledge of them, including their eschatological convictions and the religious claims that they might have made for themselves, is minimal. With the Egyptian, however, we find somebody very near Jesus' time and place with, it appears, a remarkable self-conception—a second Moses, wonder-worker, and would-be ruler of Israel. This takes us a considerable way, I suggest, toward the figure we find in the Gospels and thereby makes the latter more historically plausible.

Also relevant for evaluating the exalted figure in the Gospels is 4Q491 frg. 11, the so-called *Self-Glorification Hymn* preserved at Qumran. Although Maurice Baillet, the original editor, assigned this text to the *War Scroll*,[159] this now seems doubtful. Instead, further work has shown that the fragment is somehow related to 4Q427 frg. 7; 4Q471b; 1QH[a] 25–26.[160] Baillet was also likely mistaken in identifying the speaker with the archangel Michael. Morton Smith persuaded many that he is, rather, a human being.[161]

---

one in mind of Zech 14:4–5, which prophesies an earthquake associated with Jerusalem and the Mount of Olives.

157. See Josephus, *Ant.* 18.85–87 (the Samaritan who claimed that he would recover the sacred vessels that Moses had deposited); 20.97–99 (Theudas, who tried to part the Jordan in imitation of Moses' successor, Joshua), 167–168 (unnamed "impostors and deceivers" who called upon people to follow them into the desert and who promised to show "unmistakable marvels and signs that would be wrought in harmony with God's design" [cf. *J.W.* 2.258–260]), 188 (an unnamed "impostor" "who had promised" people "salvation and rest from troubles if they chose to follow him into the wilderness"). For the general argument that the sign prophets in Josephus had eschatological expectations, see Robert L. Webb, *John the Baptizer and Prophet: A Socio-Historical Study* (Eugene, OR: Wipf & Stock, 2006), 336.

158. See Josephus, *J.W.* 2.56; *Ant.* 17.271–272 (Judas son of Hezekiah); *J.W.* 2.57–59; *Ant.* 17.273 (Simon the slave); *J.W.* 2.60–65; *Ant.* 17.278–285 (Anthronges); *J.W.* 2.433–448 (Menahem); 4.389–393, 564–566 (John of Gischala), 503–584 (Simon bar Giora). For helpful discussion of these figures, see Richard A. Horsley, "Menahem in Jerusalem: A Brief Episode among the Sicarii—Not 'Zealot Messianism,'" *NovT* 27 (1985): 334–48; idem, "'Messianic' Figures and Movements in First-Century Palestine," in *Messiah* (ed. Charlesworth), 285–93; idem, "Popular Messianic Movements around the Time of Jesus," *CBQ* 46 (1984): 471–95.

159. Maurice Baillet, *Qumrân Grotte 4. III (4Q482–4Q520)* (DJD 7; Oxford: Clarendon, 1982), 26–30.

160. See Martin G. Abegg Jr., "Who Ascended to Heaven? 4Q491, 4Q427, and the Teacher of Righteousness," in *Eschatology, Messianism, and the Dead Sea Scrolls* (ed. Craig A. Evans and Peter W. Flint; Grand Rapids: Eerdmans, 1997), 61–73; Esther Eshel, "The Identification of the 'Speaker' of the Self-Glorification Hymn," in *Provo International Conference* (ed. Parry and Ulrich), 619–35. According to Eshel, 4Q427 frg. 7; 4Q471b; and 1QH[a] 25–26 belong to the same recension, 4Q491 frg. 11 to another recension. See further idem, "4Q471B: A Self-Glorification Hymn," *RevQ* 17 (1996): 175–203; also John J. Collins and Devorah Dimant, "A Thrice-Told Hymn: A Response to Eileen Schuller," *JQR* 85 (1994): 151–55. But all this remains open to debate; see F. García Martínez, "The 'I' of Two Qumran Hymns," *ETL* 78 (2002): 321–39.

161. Morton Smith, "Ascent to the Heavens and Deification in 4QM[a]," in *Archaeology and History in the Dead Sea Scrolls: The New York University Conference in Memory of Yigael*

Discussion since Smith has not determined whether we should identify the speaker with the Teacher of Righteousness or the priestly Messiah or some other figure.[162] It has also failed to resolve whether or not frg. 11 is autobiographical or rather records someone speaking on behalf of a revered figure. Whatever the case may be, the relevant words are these:

> . . . a mighty throne in the divine (אלים) council. No king of yore will sit therein, neith[er] will their nobles. [Who can be compared to me?] None can compare [to] my glory, and none has been exalted save myself, and none can accompany me. I sit [. . .] in heaven (ה בשמים [ ]ישבתי ב), and none [. . .] I shall be reckoned with the gods (אלים), my dwelling is in the holy council. . . . [W]ho has been accounted despicable like me, yet who is like me in my glory? . . . I am reckoned with the gods (אלים), and my glory with the sons of the King.[163]

This passage recounts the exaltation to heaven and enthronement there of a human being who is "reckoned with the gods." This goes beyond anything else we find in the *Hodayot*. It is not a statement about a representative member of the community but instead a declaration about a very special figure.

As already indicated, the identity of this individual, unfortunately, remains unclear. Yet no one, to my knowledge, has argued that the hymn cannot be autobiographical because no ancient Jew would have made such grandiose claims for himself. Put otherwise, interpreters of the Dead Sea Scrolls have recognized the possibility that someone could have claimed a mighty throne in the divine counsel. Likewise, although we do not know whether the Teacher of Righteousness authored the *Self-Glorification Hymn*, no one has insisted that this is impossible because other hymns often assigned to the Teacher of Righteousness reflect profound humility and religiosity.[164] I submit that the

---

Yadin (ed. Lawrence H. Schiffman; JSPSup 8; Sheffield: JSOT Press, 1990), 181–88. Cf. Devorah Dimant, "A Synoptic Comparison of Parallel Sections in 4Q427 7, 4Q491 11 and 4Q471B," *JQR* 85 (1994): 161. García Martínez ("Two Qumran Hymns") offers a dissenting opinion: Baillet was correct.

162. For Abegg ("Who Ascended to Heaven?") the speaker is likely the Teacher of Righteousness. John J. Collins ("A Throne in the Heavens," in *Scepter*, 136–53) thinks of the eschatological high priest (although more recently he has emphasized that the implied author remains enigmatic; see idem, *Apocalypticism in the Dead Sea Scrolls* [London: Routledge, 1997], 147). Cf. Eshel, "Identification of the 'Speaker,'" 631, 634. Hartmut Stegemann ("Some Remarks to 1QSa, to 1QSb, and to Qumran Messianism," *RevQ* 17 [1996]: 502) and Annette Steudel ("The Eternal Reign of the People of God—Collective Expectations in Qumran Texts [4Q246 and 1QM]," *RevQ* 17 [1996]: 525) offer a collective interpretation: the first person of the hymn is Israel. For Israel Knohl (*The Messiah before Jesus: The Suffering Servant of the Dead Sea Scrolls* [Berkeley: University of California Press, 2000], 75–86), the speaker is the royal Messiah.

163. This is the translation (with minor changes) by Eshel, "Identification of the 'Speaker,'" 622.

164. Although Morton Smith derisively labels the author of 4Q491 an "egomaniac" ("Two Ascended to Heaven—Jesus and the Author of 4Q491," in *Jesus and the Dead Sea Scrolls* [ed.

situation regarding Jesus is similar. Nothing we know about him excludes the possibility that he made stupendous claims for himself.[165]

The Herald of Isaiah 61:1–3?

I have not, to this point, insisted that Jesus' speech must have featured any particular title, whether "Messiah" or "Son of Man" or some other. Nor have I maintained that he claimed descent from David or related his ministry to this or that scriptural text. I have deliberately sidestepped those issues because of my conviction that the traditional fixation upon titles and upon Jesus' relationship to particular messianic ideas has tended to isolate data that we should rather contemplate in the aggregate. As throughout most of this book, I am interested more in the general than in the particular. From this point of view, the logia and stories in which Jesus is the Messiah are at one with those in which he is the Son of Man; and these in turn are at one with those in which he is the eschatological advocate, and in which he is the eschatological judge, and so on. Although the titles and functions vary, as may the origins of the various traditions, all of them, when they envisage the end, envisage Jesus, which is precisely what, I have argued, he himself did.

So far I have claimed that Jesus took himself to be, like John the Baptist, "more than a prophet" (Matt 11:9 // Luke 7:26 [Q]), indeed much more: he believed himself destined to judge and rule as the chief human figure of the latter days. This way of putting things, however, is a large, abstract generalization. Is it possible to hazard more about how Jesus, in the religious idiom of his Jewish world, conceived his own role?

Several possibilities suggest themselves. Each demands the sort of lengthy discussion that I eschew here. I wish simply, in an attempt to situate Jesus more concretely within his first-century context, to introduce a few options.

According to John's Gospel, some of Jesus' contemporaries regarded him as a prophet (4:19; 6:14; 7:40; 9:17). Mark 6:15 and 8:27–28 report the same thing, as do Matt 21:11, 46; Luke 7:39; 24:19 (cf. Acts 3:22–23; 7:37). I can think of no scholar who has rejected this combined testimony, and no reason to become the exception. Jesus, we may confidently believe, was, in his lifetime, reputed to be a prophet.[166]

James H. Charlesworth; New York: Doubleday, 1992], 295), at least he recognizes that the text could be authentically autobiographical.

165. Contrast Matthias Kreplin (*Das Selbstverständnis Jesu: Hermeneutische und christologische Reflexion; Historisch-kritische Analyse* [WUNT 2/141; Tübingen: Mohr Siebeck, 2001]), who urges that although Jesus took himself to be God's eschatological representative, his moral teaching required him to renounce titles, decline honors, and say as little about himself as possible.

166. Reviews of the topic include David E. Aune, *Prophecy in Early Christianity and the Ancient Mediterranean World* (Grand Rapids: Eerdmans, 1983), 153–88; C. H. Dodd, "Jesus

Did he share this assessment? "Prophet" appears as an implicit self-designation in a few sayings credited to him (Mark 6:4; Luke 13:33; *Gos. Thom.* 31); also, several of the actions ascribed to him, such as cursing a fig tree (Mark 11:12–14) and turning over tables in the temple (Mark 11:15–16), put one in mind of the strange symbolic actions of certain prophets in the Tanak.[167] What is more, recurrent features in the logia evidence a prophetic consciousness. Jesus regularly proclaims judgment and promises salvation, and instead of saying, "I give my opinion" (cf. 1 Cor 7:25), he authoritatively declares, "But I say to you" or "Amen, I say to you."[168] The tradition also contains the polemical accusations of detractors who deride Jesus as a false prophet.[169] One naturally supposes that he held the contrary position, that he took himself to be a true prophet. In coming to this conclusion, it may help to recall that even the relatively sober Josephus considered himself some sort of prophet.[170]

If Jesus made himself out to be a prophet, and if, in accord with chapter 2, he thought mundane history almost defunct, he may well have associated his ministry with particular eschatological prophecies, reckoning himself to be something other than yet one more in a series. According to several modern scholars, he did just this, finding himself in Isa 61:1–3, which reads, "The Spirit of the Lord GOD is upon me, because the LORD has anointed me; he has sent me to bring good news to the oppressed, to bind up the brokenhearted, to proclaim liberty to the captives, and release to the prisoners; to proclaim the year of the LORD's favor, and the day of vengeance of our God; to comfort all who mourn; to provide for those who mourn in Zion—to give them a garland instead of ashes, the oil of gladness instead of mourning. . . ."[171]

---

as Teacher and Prophet," in *Mysterium Christi: Christological Studies by British and German Theologians* (ed. G. K. A. Bell and D. Adolf Deissmann; London: Longmans, Green, 1930), 53–66; Franz Schnider, *Jesus der Prophet* (OBO 2; Fribourg: Universitätsverlag; Göttingen: Vandenhoeck & Ruprecht, 1973). On the various meanings of "prophet" then and now, see Markus Öhler, "Jesus as Prophet: Remarks on Terminology," in *Jesus, Mark and Q: The Teaching of Jesus and Its Earliest Records* (ed. Michael Labahn and Andreas Schmidt; JSNTSup 214; Sheffield: Sheffield Academic Press, 2001), 125–42.

167. See Morna D. Hooker, *The Signs of a Prophet: The Prophetic Actions of Jesus* (Harrisburg, PA: Trinity Press International, 1997).

168. See, for example, Mark 3:28; 9:1; 10:15; Matt 24:47 // Luke 12:44 (Q); Matt 5:21–48; 10:23. On the formal prophetic features of Jesus' speech, see Aune, *Prophecy*, 163–69.

169. For example, Mark 14:65 ("Some began to spit on him, to blindfold him, and to strike him, saying to him, 'Prophesy!'"); Luke 7:39 ("If this man were a prophet, he would have known who and what kind of woman this is"). For extracanonical sources, see Graham N. Stanton, "Jesus of Nazareth: A Magician and a False Prophet Who Deceived God's People," in *Jesus of Nazareth: Lord and Christ; Essays on the Historical Jesus and New Testament Christology* (ed. Joel B. Green and Max Turner; Grand Rapids: Eerdmans, 1994), 164–80.

170. See Webb, *John the Baptizer*, 318–20. According to David Daube ("Typology in Josephus," *JJS* 31 [1980]: 26–27), Josephus thought that he was like Jeremiah in particular.

171. For example, Otto Betz, "Jesus' Gospel of the Kingdom," in *The Gospel and the Gospels* (ed. Peter Stuhlmacher; Grand Rapids: Eerdmans, 1991), 53–74; Michael F. Bird, *Are You the One Who Is to Come? The Historical Jesus and the Messianic Question* (Grand Rapids: Baker Academic,

One presumes that, in Jesus' time and place, these words would have been received as something like a blueprint for the latter days. 11Q13 and 4Q521 use Isa 61 to portray the final liberation of Israel's captives,[172] and the targum on Isaiah offers an eschatological interpretation of the opening verses.[173]

That Jesus associated his ministry with Isa 61:1–3 is an attractive possibility. Not only does Luke 4:16–30, whatever its tradition history,[174] deem a sermon on this text fitting introduction to his ministry, but also Mark's introductory summation of Jesus' message (1:14–15) is indebted to Deutero-Isaiah,[175] while Matthew's Beatitudes depend upon Isa 61:1–3, as did probably their Q precursor (Matt 5:3–12 // Luke 6:20–23).[176] Another Q text, Matt 11:2–4 // Luke 7:22–23, likewise draws upon Isa 61:1–3: "The blind receive their sight [τυφλοὶ ἀναβλέπουσιν; cf. LXX Isa 61:1], the lame walk, the lepers are cleansed, the deaf hear, the dead are raised, the poor have good news brought to them [πτωχοὶ εὐαγγελίζονται; cf. Isa 61:1]. And blessed is anyone who takes no offense at me."[177]

2009), 98–104; James D. G. Dunn, *Jesus and the Spirit* (Philadelphia: Westminster, 1975), 53–62; Michael Goulder, "The Anointed," in *The Old Testament in the New: Essays in Honour of J. J. North* (ed. Steve Moyise; JSNTSup 189; Sheffield: Sheffield Academic Press, 2000), 66–74; Christian Grappe, "Jésus: Messie prétendu ou messie prétendant?" in *Jésus de Nazareth: Nouvelles approches d'une énigme* (ed. D. Marguerat, E. Norelli, and J.-M. Poffet; Geneva: Labor et Fides, 1998), 269–91; Werner Grimm, *Weil ich dich liebe: Die Verkündigung Jesu und Deuterojesaja* (ANTJ 1; Bern: Herbert Lang, 1976), 128–30; A. E. Harvey, *Jesus and the Constraints of History* (Philadelphia: Westminster, 1982), 120–53; Hengel, "Messiah of Israel," 38; J. Schmitt, "L'oracle d'Is., LXI, 1 SS. et sa relecture par Jésus," *RSR* 54 (1980): 97–108. Contrast Becker, *Jesus of Nazareth*, 214. The latter, while acknowledging that Jesus drew upon Isa 61:1–3, denies that he considered himself to be the Spirit-bearer of that oracle. Compare the skeptical position of Hubert Frankemölle, "Jesus als deuterojesajanischer Freudenbote? Zur Rezeption von Jes 52,7 und 61,1 im Neuen Testament, durch Jesus und in den Targumim," in *Vom Urchristentum zu Jesus: Für Joachim Gnilka* (ed. Hubert Frankemölle and Karl Kertelge; Freiburg: Herder, 1989), 34–67.

172. For the former, see Merrill P. Miller, "The Function of Isa 61:1–2 in 11Q Melchizedek," *JBL* 88 (1969): 467–69; for the latter, see Johannes Zimmermann, *Messianische Texte aus Qumran: Königliche, priesterliche und prophetische Messiasvorstellungen in den Schriftfunden von Qumran* (WUNT 2/104; Tübingen: Mohr Siebeck, 1998), 377–78.

173. For the eschatological interpretation of Isa 61 in Judaism in general, see James A. Sanders, "From Isaiah 61 to Luke 4," in Craig A. Evans and James A. Sanders, *Luke and Scripture: The Function of Sacred Tradition in Luke-Acts* (Minneapolis: Fortress, 1993), 46–69.

174. Although many now attribute it to Lukan redaction, C. M. Tuckett ("Luke 4:16–30 and Q," in *Logia: Les Paroles de Jésus—The Sayings of Jesus* [ed. Joël Delobel; BETL 59; Leuven: Leuven University Press, 1982], 343–54) posits derivation from Q. John C. Poirier ("Jesus as an Elijanic Figure in Luke 4:16–30," *CBQ* 71 [2009]: 349–63), although he rejects the Q hypothesis, sees signs of a pre-Lukan source.

175. See Bruce David Chilton, *God in Strength: Jesus' Announcement of the Kingdom* (SNTSU 1; Freistadt: Plöchl, 1979), 75–95; Rikki E. Watts, *Isaiah's New Exodus and Mark* (WUNT 2/88; Tübingen: Mohr Siebeck, 1997), 96–102. For additional ways in which Isa 61 may have influenced the opening sections of Mark, see Goulder, "Anointed," 67–68.

176. See Allison, *Intertextual Jesus*, 104–7; Martin Hengel, "Zur matthäischen Bergpredigt und ihrem jüdische Hintergrund," *TRu* 52 (1987): 351–53; Tuckett, "Isaiah in Q," 55–57. Contrast Frankemölle, "Freudenbote," 49–50.

177. See further Allison, *Intertextual Jesus*, 109–14.

If Jesus found himself and his ministry in Isa 61:1–3, we are perhaps some way to understanding why early Christians came to regard him as ὁ χριστός, "the anointed one." For if, before Easter, some acknowledged him to be the divinely anointed prophet of Isa 61:1 (MT: משח; LXX: ἔχρισεν), then confession of him as "the anointed one" after Easter would not have come out of the blue. To the contrary, "it is a short step from 'the Lord anointed me' to 'I am the Lord's Anointed.'"[178]

Particularly suggestive in this connection is 4Q521, Qumran's so-called *Messianic Apocalypse*. After foretelling that "[the hea]vens and the earth will listen to his [God's] Messiah" (משיחו), frg. 2 goes on to list miraculous healings very reminiscent of Matt 11:2–4 // Luke 7:22–23 (Q), and it ends up citing Isa 61:1: "He will heal the wounded, and revive the dead, and bring good news to the poor."[179] John Collins has made the intriguing case that in the Qumran text, משיחו not only preaches good news to the poor but also performs the miracles listed.[180] If he is right—I remain unsure—then not only is the figure in 4Q521 remarkably like the Synoptic Jesus, but also we additionally have here an example of how the prophet in Isa 61:1 could gain the title משיח.[181]

178. So Goulder ("Anointed," 70), who urges that Jesus himself took this step. He observes, among other things, the potential link between Isa 11:1–10, where the Spirit of God rests upon "the shoot of Jesse," and Isa 61:1–3. See further Randall Heskett, *Messianism within the Scriptural Scroll of Isaiah* (LHB/OTS 46; New York: T & T Clark, 2007), 128, 225–63. For prophets as "anointed," see 1 Kgs 19:16; Ps 105:15; CD-A 2:12; 6:1; 1QM 11:7; 11Q13 18; 4Q377; also Heinz-Josef Fabry, "Mose, der 'Gesalbte JHWHs': Messianische Aspekte der Mose-Interpretation in Qumran," in *Moses in Biblical and Extra-Biblical Traditions* (ed. Axel Gaupner and Michael Wolter; BZNW 372; Berlin: de Gruyter, 2007), 129–42. Stefan Schreiber (*Gesalbter und König: Titel und Konzeptionen der königlichen Gesalbtenerwartung in frühjüdischen und urchristlichen Schriften* [BZAW 105; Berlin: de Gruyter, 2000], 275–317) documents from Josephus the large overlap between royal and prophetic figures in first-century Judaism.

179. There has been much discussion of the relationship between 4Q521 and the Q text; see especially Karl-Wilhelm Niebuhr, "4Q521, 2 II—Ein eschatologischer Psalm," in *Mogilany 1995: Papers on the Dead Sea Scrolls Offered in Memory of Aleksy Klawek* (ed. Z. J. Kapera; Qumranica Mogilanensia 15; Kraków: Enigma, 1998), 151–68.

180. John J. Collins, "A Herald of Good Tidings: Isaiah 61:1–3 and Its Actualization in the Dead Sea Scrolls," in *The Quest for Context and Meaning: Studies in Biblical Intertextuality in Honor of James A. Sanders* (ed. Craig A. Evans and Shemaryahu Talmon; BIS 28; Leiden: Brill, 1997), 225–40; idem, "Teacher, Priest, and Prophet," 118–20; idem, "The Works of the Messiah," *DSD* 1 (1994): 98–112.

181. Note also 1QH[a] 23:10–15, where the author, who may be the Teacher of Righteousness, borrows language from Isa 61:1–3: "You have opened a [spr]ing in the mouth of your servant. . . . You have opened a spr[ing] to rebuke the path of the one fashioned from clay, the guilt of the one born of woman according to his deeds, to open the sp[rin]g of your truth to the creature whom you have supported with your power, to [be,] according to your truth, a herald [. . .] of your goodness, to proclaim to the poor the abundance of your compassion [. . .] . . . from the spring [. . . the bro]ken of spirit, and the mourning to everlasting joy." These lines raise the "intriguing possibility . . . that the Teacher may have claimed to be the 'anointed of the spirit' who is identified as the one who preaches good news in 11QMelchizedek" (Collins, "Herald of Good Tidings," 231). Collins, however, goes on to suggest that, perhaps, "when the Teacher

A Prophet Like Elijah?

Jesus, in John Meier's judgment, "consciously took upon himself the role of the prophet Elijah, who was expected to return to restore Israel and prepare it for the coming of its God."[182] Meier gives four reasons for his view. First, Jesus had an itinerant prophetic ministry in northern Israel, which is where Elijah worked. Second, in calling disciples to follow him, Jesus imitated Elijah's calling of Elisha.[183] Third, by appointing a group of twelve, Jesus showed himself to be about the same task as the Tishbite, namely, stirring up all Israel to religious renewal. One recalls Sir 48:10: the returning Elijah will turn the hearts of parents to their children and restore the tribes of Jacob.[184] Fourth, as a reputed miracle-worker, Jesus must have reminded his contemporaries of the wonder-working Elijah, who in Scripture raises the dead.[185] Meier sums up: "If the historical record had contained only one of these elements, one might question Jesus' intention of evoking the image of Elijah. But the convergence of so many carefully chosen, programmatic actions inevitably bespeaks the intention of Jesus to present himself to his fellow Jews as the Elijah-like prophet of the end time."[186]

The argument intrigues, especially when one takes into account the well-attested expectation of *Elias redivivus*,[187] which might have captured the at-

---

plays the role of the herald of Isaiah 61 in preaching good news to the poor, he is not necessarily claiming to be the eschatological prophet, only to be filling a similar role" (p. 232).

182. John P. Meier, *A Marginal Jew: Rethinking the Historical Jesus* (4 vols.; New York: Doubleday, 1991–2009), 3:623.

183. The call stories in Mark 1:16–20; Matt 8:18–22 // Luke 9:57–60 (Q); Luke 9:61–62 (Q?) are intertextually linked to 1 Kgs 19:19–21, as the commentators, both ancient and modern, have recognized. See Allison, *Intertextual Jesus*, 142–45.

184. This line, which probably combines Mal 4:5–6 with Isa 49:6, may refer to the return of the Diaspora to the land (cf. Tg. Ps.-J. on Deut 30:4), a task that other texts give to the Messiah (see n. 42).

185. See 1 Kgs 17:8–24, to which Luke 7:11–17 clearly alludes; cf. François Bovon, *Luke 1: A Commentary on the Gospel of Luke 1:1–9:50* (trans. Christine M. Thomas; Hermeneia; Minneapolis: Fortress, 2002), 268.

186. Meier, *Marginal Jew*, 3:624–25. Likewise, John J. Collins ("Jesus and the Messiahs of Israel," in *Encounters with Biblical Theology* [Minneapolis: Fortress, 2005], 176) understands Jesus as a messianic prophet who played the role of Elijah.

187. For the expectation of the returning Elijah, see Mal 4:5; Sir 48:10; 4Q558 frg. 1 col. II 4; 1 Macc 4:46 (?); 14:41; *1 En.* 90:31; *L.A.B.* 48:1; *Sib. Or.* 2:187–89; Mark 9:12; Luke 1:16–17; 4 Ezra 6:25–26; Justin, *Dial.* 8.4; *Liv. Pro.* 21 (Ep2); *Apoc. El.* 4:7–20; *m. 'Ed.* 8:7; *m. Soṭah* 9:15; *m. Šeqal.* 2:5; *Tanḥ.* Buber Mishpatim 12; *b. 'Erub.* 43a–b; *b. Sanh.* 96b–99a; *Deut. Rab.* 3:17; *Pesiq. Rab.* 35:3; *Pirqe R. El.* 43; Tg. Ps.-J. on Exod 4:13; 6:18; 40:10; Deut 30:4. Discussion in Markus Öhler, *Elia im Neuen Testament: Untersuchungen zur Bedeutung des alttestamentlichen Propheten im frühen Christentum* (BZNW 88; Berlin: de Gruyter, 1997), 1–30. This expectation appears to have been well known, the only question being whether, as Mark 9:11 has so often been taken to imply, pre-Christian Jews ever thought of Elijah as the forerunner of the Messiah. Current opinion seems for the most part to run against this, although see Chaim Milikowsky, "Trajectories of Return, Restoration and Redemption in Rabbinic Judaism: Elijah, the Messiah,

tention of an apocalyptic prophet such as Jesus, as well as the Synoptic notices that some did indeed identify him as Elijah come again.[188] Meier's position, moreover, harmonizes with the solid possibility, introduced above, that Jesus found his ministry in Isa 61:1–3, for the figure in 4Q521 who, like the anointed prophet of Isa 61:1, preaches good news to the poor sounds very much like Elijah.[189] In other words, there may have been precedent for associating Isa 61:1–3 with the returning Elijah.[190]

Yet I remain conflicted on the matter. Parallels between Jesus and Elisha, whose story is told in 1 Kgs 19:16–21 and 2 Kgs 2–13, are perhaps as numerous as those between Jesus and Elijah.[191] The latter's successor, according to 2 Kings, began his career at the Jordan by receiving a double portion of Elijah's spirit (2:6–12). He worked in the northern kingdom, as Jesus worked in Galilee. He purportedly raised the dead (4:18–37; cf. 13:20–21), healed lepers (5:1–19), and multiplied loaves (4:42–44).[192] Elisha also sought to help the poor and needy (2 Kgs 4:1–7). Beyond all that, Luke 4:27 compares Jesus' situation with that of Elisha; and, in Luke 10:4, Jesus commands his missionaries not to greet anyone on the way, which has often reminded exegetes of 2 Kgs 4:29, where Elisha says to his servant, "If you meet anyone, give no greeting, and if anyone greets you, do not answer."[193] So did Jesus or some of his first follow-

---

the War of Gog and the World to Come," in *Restoration: Old Testament, Jewish, and Christian Perspectives* (ed. James M. Scott; JSJSup 72; Leiden: Brill, 2002), 265–77. Mark's text may allude instead to Elijah appearing before the resurrection, an event with which the prophet is associated in rabbinic literature (e.g., *m. Soṭah* 9:15; *y. Šeqal.* 47c [3:3]) and perhaps already LXX Sir 48:11. See Ulrich Kellermann, "Elia Redivivus und die heilszeitliche Auferweckung der Toten: Erwägungen zur ältesten Bezeugung einer Erwartung," in *Was suchst du hier, Elia? Ein hermeneutisches Arbeitsbuch* (ed. Klaus Grüwaldt and Harald Schroeter; Hermeneutica 4; Rheinbach-Merzbach: CMZ-Verlag, 1995), 72–84.

188. Mark 6:15; 8:28. Later Christian tradition did not hesitate to draw parallels between Jesus and the Tishbite; see Daniel Wanke, "Vorläufer, Typus und Asket: Bemerkungen zur Gestalt des Elia in der altchristlichen Literatur," in *Was suchst du hier, Elia?* (ed. Grüwaldt and Schroeter), 102–14.

189. For details, see Collins, "Teacher, Priest, and Prophet," 119–21; David M. Miller, "The Messenger, the Lord, and the Coming Judgement in the Reception History of Malachi 3," *NTS* 53 (2007): 8–10; Géza G. Xeravits, *King, Priest, Prophet: Positive Eschatological Protagonists of the Qumran Library* (STDJ 47; Leiden: Brill, 2003), 98–110.

190. *Pesiqta Rabbati* 35:4 can identify Elijah as the herald of Isa 52:7, and exegetical tradition often associated the latter with Isa 61:1–3. See above, pp. 113–15; also Poirier, "Elijanic Figure," 349–63.

191. See further Raymond E. Brown, "Jesus and Elisha," *Perspectives* 12 (1971): 85–99.

192. The feeding of the five thousand in the Synoptics and in John clearly is modeled upon this last. Note that the bread that Jesus multiplies in John 6 is barley bread (ἄρτους κριθίνους [v. 9]), obviously because it is barley bread that Elisha feeds his crowd (LXX: ἄρτους κριθίνους). So C. H. Dodd, *Historical Tradition in the Fourth Gospel* (Cambridge: Cambridge University Press, 1963), 206; Ernst Haenchen, *John: A Commentary on the Gospel of John* (trans. Robert W. Funk; 2 vols.; Hermeneia; Philadelphia: Fortress, 1984), 1:271–72. Cf. Chrysostom, *Hom. Jo.* 42: Andrew remarked upon the young lad with five barley loaves and two fishes because he knew the story about Elisha in 2 Kgs 4:42–44.

193. See Allison, *Intertextual Jesus*, 145–47.

ers understand his relationship to John to be analogous to the relationship between Elisha and Elijah, Jesus being the successor with a double portion of his predecessor's spirit?[194] Or is this to sort things too neatly? Could Jesus have thought of himself as being like both Elijah and Elisha? The latter is, in the Hebrew Bible, much like the former.[195] Or did Jesus believe that both he and John were like Elijah?

Not only are these open questions, but anyone adopting Meier's assessment must concede that not one word attributed to Jesus plainly implies his identification with Elijah. On the contrary: three logia may cast doubt upon that equation, the first being Mark 9:12–13, where Jesus says, "Elijah is indeed coming first to restore all things. How then is it written about the Son of Man, that he is to go through many sufferings and be treated with contempt? But I tell you that Elijah has come, and they did to him whatever they pleased, as it is written about him." Although much about these verses remains obscure, they do clearly if implicitly equate John the Baptist with the eschatological Elijah of Mal 4:5–6. This eliminates that role for Jesus.[196] One is moved to ask, Would Christians have turned John into Elijah if Jesus had claimed that role for himself?

The second relevant text is Luke 9:52–56, where James and John desire to act as Elijah once did and call down fire from heaven (2 Kgs 1:9–12). Jesus rebuffs them: "He sent messengers ahead of him. On their way they entered a village of the Samaritans to make ready for him; but they did not receive him, because his face was set toward Jerusalem. When his disciples James and John saw it, they said, 'Lord, do you want us to command fire to come down from heaven and consume them?' But he turned and rebuked them. Then they went on to another village." The lesson seems to be that those who follow Jesus will not follow the example of the vengeful Elijah.[197]

194. For the case that this idea actually goes back to the Baptist, see Joel Marcus, "John the Baptist and Jesus," in *Christianity in the Beginning* (vol. 1 of *When Judaism and Christianity Began: Essays in Memory of Anthony J. Saldarini*, ed. Daniel Harrington, Alan J. Avery-Peck, and Jacob Neusner; JSJSup 85; Leiden: Brill, 2003), 179–97.

195. For example, 2 Kgs 4:1–7, where Elisha provides oil for a poor widow, resembles 1 Kgs 17:8–16, where Elijah provides oil and flour for a poor widow; and 2 Kgs 4:8–37, where Elisha brings the Shunammite's son back to life, is much like 1 Kgs 17:17–24, where Elijah brings a widow's son back to life.

196. Cf. Matt 11:14; Luke 1:17. Matt 11:10 // Luke 7:27 (Q) equates John with the messenger of Mal 3:1, and Tg. Ps.-J. on Num 25:12, like many modern exegetes, identifies that messenger with the coming Elijah of Mal 4:4–5 (see p. 274 n. 218), so the equation of Mark 9:12–13 may be implicit in Q. However that may be, some have thought that the evidence suffices to infer that the Baptist himself thought he was Elijah; for example, in addition to Marcus, "John the Baptist and Jesus," see Markus Öhler, "The Expectation of Elijah and the Presence of the Kingdom of God," *JBL* 118 (1999): 461–76; Jeffrey A. Trumbower, "The Role of Malachi in the Career of John the Baptist," in *The Gospels and the Scriptures of Israel* (ed. Craig A. Evans and W. Richard Stegner; JSNTSup 104; Sheffield: Sheffield Academic Press, 1994), 28–41.

197. A C D W Θ Ψ *f* [1.13] Maj it sy[p.h] bo[pt] Marcion add, at the end of the disciples' question in 9:54, "as also Elijah did." See further Dale C. Allison Jr., "Rejecting Violent Judgment: Luke

The third text is Matt 10:34–36 // Luke 12:51–53 (Q): "Do not think that I have come to bring peace to the earth; I have not come to bring peace, but a sword. For I have come to set a man against his father, and a daughter against her mother, and a daughter-in-law against her mother-in-law; and one's foes will be members of one's own household." Commentators have now and again sensed a conflict with Mal 4:6.[198] The latter foresees the prophet Elijah coming before the great and terrible day of the Lord, his goal being to turn "the hearts of parents to their children and the hearts of children to their parents." The Synoptic text has Jesus doing exactly the opposite, turning parents and children against each other. Once more, then, Jesus is not like Elijah but unlike him.

So the truth is harder to make out than a reader of Meier might presume. Although we have some cause to infer that Jesus identified with Elijah, evidence exists to the contrary too. One could, in theory, account for the conflicting indicators by positing that Jesus thought of himself as Elijah only for a time, later laying that self-conception to rest. Another possibility is that while he partly modeled his ministry upon Elijah, this was at the periphery of his self-understanding and so less significant than Meier supposes. One is unsure what to think.

The Prophet Like Moses?

The expectation of an eschatological prophet like Moses, derived from Deut 18:15–18, had some currency in Second Temple Judaism.[199] Since several New Testament writings identify this figure with Jesus,[200] our question becomes, Did somebody first make this equation after Jesus was gone, or did he make it before he left?[201] The latter alternative would put him in the company of

---

9:52–56 and Its Relatives," *JBL* 121 (2002): 459–78; also Bonaventure, *Commentary on Luke* ad loc. (in *Opera omnia* [ed. A. C. Peltier; 15 vols.; Paris: Ludovicus Vivès, 1864–1871], 10:483); Matthew Tindal, *Christianity as Old as the Creation; or, The Gospel, a Republication of the Religion of Nature* (London: 1730), 268–69.

198. For example, A. H. McNeile, *The Gospel according to St. Matthew* (London: Macmillan, 1915), 147; T. W. Manson, *The Sayings of Jesus* (London: SCM Press, 1949), 121; John A. T. Robinson, "Elijah, John and Jesus: An Essay in Detection," in *Twelve New Testament Studies* (SBT 34; London: SCM Press, 1962), 43–44; Richard A. Horsley, *Jesus and the Spiral of Violence: Popular Jewish Resistance in Roman Palestine* (San Francisco: Harper & Row, 1987), 234.

199. See especially 1QS 9:11; 4Q175; see also A. S. van der Woude, *Die messianischen Vorstellungen der Gemeinde von Qumrân* (SSN 3; Assen: Van Gorcum, 1957), 78–89; for a collection of the evidence, see Allison, *New Moses*, 73–84.

200. Note especially the voice at the transfiguration (Mark 9:7 par.); Acts 3:22; 7:37. For a dated but still helpful overview of the evidence, see Howard M. Teeple, *The Mosaic Eschatological Prophet* (SBLMS 10; Philadelphia: Society of Biblical Literature, 1957).

201. For an affirmative response, see Allison, *Intertextual Jesus*, 216–20; idem, "The Allusive Jesus," in *The Historical Jesus in Recent Research* (ed. James D. G. Dunn and Scot McKnight; Winona Lake, IN: Eisenbrauns, 2005), 238–48; Scot McKnight, "Jesus and Prophetic Actions,"

other ancient Jews. Not only did the historical Jeremiah, it appears, interpret his prophetic calling in terms of Deut 18:15–18,[202] but, more importantly, some of the sign prophets about whom Josephus imperfectly informs us must have consciously imitated saving acts of Moses.[203] What, then, does the Jesus tradition tell us about its hero?

If Luke 11:20 preserves something Jesus said, then he claimed to cast out demons by "the finger of God," which would make him resemble the lawgiver, who similarly worked marvels by "the finger of God" (Exod 8:19).[204] And if Jesus instructed hearers to pray for bread for the coming day (Matt 6:11 // Luke 11:3 [Q]) by alluding to the miracle of the manna (Exod 16; Num 11), he may well have perceived his time as that of a new exodus.[205] Again, if he composed any of the misnamed "antitheses" in Matt 5 (vv. 21–26, 27–30, 31–32, 33–36, 37–42, 43–48), then he provocatively set some of his imperatives above imperatives of the lawgiver.

For reasons outlined earlier in this book, I cannot dissolve the conditional nature of these sentences. Nor does anyone else, in my judgment, have the

---

BBR 10 (2000): 197–232; Ben F. Meyer, "Appointed Deed, Appointed Doer: Jesus and the Scriptures," in *Authenticating the Activities of Jesus* (ed. Bruce Chilton and Craig A. Evans; NTTS 28/2; Leiden: Brill, 1999), 171. Richard A. Horsley writes, "If we can combine the new Moses as reconstituting the covenantal people (as leader of the new exodus) evident in the Righteous Teacher of the Qumran Movement with the new Moses as leader of the new exodus evident in the popular prophetic movements, then we have a more complete sense of the popular prophetic script that may have been followed by the historical Jesus" ("The Dead Sea Scrolls and the Historical Jesus," in *The Scrolls and Christian Origins* [vol. 3 of *The Bible and the Dead Sea Scrolls*, ed. James H. Charlesworth; Waco, TX: Baylor University Press, 2006], 59). Teeple (*Mosaic Eschatological Prophet*, 115–18), was of another mind; and according to Hengel, "a prophet 'like Moses' is just what Jesus is not; rather, he stands at concrete points in antithesis to him who formerly had yielded to Israel's hard-heartedness (Mark 10:5 = Matt. 19:8)" ("Messiah of Israel," 27). Yet surely one can be like Moses and transcend him at the same time. Would anyone insist that if Jesus declared the advent of someone/something greater than Jonah (Matt 12:41 // Luke 11:32 [Q]), he could not also have likened himself to that prophet (Matt 12:38–40 // Luke 11:29–32 [Q])?

202. See Sebastian Grätz, "'Einen Propheten wie mich wird dir der Herr, dein Gott, erwecken': Der Berufungsbericht Jeremias und seine Rückbindung an das Amt des Mose," in *Moses in Biblical and Extra-Biblical Traditions* (ed. Axel Gaupner and Michael Wolter; BZNW 372; Berlin: de Gruyter, 2007), 61–77; William L. Holladay, "The Background of Jeremiah's Self-Understanding: Moses, Samuel, and Psalm 22," *JBL* 83 (1964): 153–64; idem, "Jeremiah and Moses: Further Observations," *JBL* 85 (1966): 17–27.

203. See Allison, *New Moses*, 78–83; McKnight, "Jesus and Prophetic Actions." There are also later parallels of a sort. Martin Luther King Jr., for instance, sometimes likened himself to Moses, as in the closing words of his famed 1968 speech at the Mason Temple in Memphis.

204. See Allison, *Intertextual Jesus*, 53–57; Martin Hengel, "Der Finger und die Herrschaft Gottes in Lk 11,20," in *La Main de Dieu* [= *Die Hand Gottes*] (ed. René Kieffer and Jan Bergman; WUNT 94; Tübingen: Mohr Siebeck, 1997), 87–106. In Matt 12:29, however, Jesus casts out demons by "the Spirit of God," which some have thought original.

205. Commentators throughout exegetical history have moved from the Lord's Prayer to Exod 16 and Num 11; see Allison, *Intertextual Jesus*, 51–53.

ability to turn "if" into "as was the case." I can, however, observe that we have here another pattern, and it extends beyond the several texts just cited. Matthew 12:39–40 // Luke 11:29–30 (Q) characterizes the generation of Jesus with language descriptive of the generation of Moses ("This generation is an evil generation" [cf. Deut 1:35]).[206] Matthew 10:37 // Luke 14:26 (Q) daringly inverts the commandment to honor father and mother, seemingly raising a question mark over a Mosaic commandment, or at least its applicability to those literally following Jesus.[207] And, as I will urge in the next chapter, the central portion of Q's inaugural sermon, preserved more or less faithfully in Luke 6:27–42, rewrites Lev 19, sometimes in the process turning the sacred text upside down. In thus reiterating, revising, and revealing new Torah, the speaker takes up the mantle of Moses.

The Last Supper also belongs here. In Mark 14:24, Jesus hosts a Passover meal and speaks of "my blood of the covenant" (τὸ αἷμά μου τῆς διαθήκης [cf. Matt 26:28]). Similarly, in Luke 22:20 and 1 Cor 11:25, he uses the expression "the new covenant in my blood" (Luke: ἡ καινὴ διαθήκη ἐν τῷ αἵματί μου; Paul: ἡ καινὴ διαθήκη ἐστὶν ἐν τῷ ἐμῷ αἵματι). Both phrases, as is widely recognized, function partly as allusions to Exod 24:8: "Moses took the blood and dashed it on the people and said, 'See the blood of the covenant [MT: דם־הברית; LXX: τὸ αἷμα τῆς διαθήκης] that the LORD has made with you in accordance with all these words.'"[208] Matthew clearly divined the allusion and enlarged it,[209] and the perception that the Lord's Supper should be connected with the exodus appears in John 6, where allusions to the Last Supper (see esp. 6:52–58) belong to a discourse that associates the miracle of the manna with the feeding of the five thousand (see esp. 6:30–34).[210] There is also 1 Cor 10:1–5, where the Eucharist is likened to the supernatural food that Israel ate in the wilderness. From a very early time, then, Christian tradition consistently linked the Last Supper to exodus themes.[211] Maybe it did this in part because Jesus himself had already done so.

206. See discussion in Allison, *Intertextual Jesus*, 57–59; Evald Lövestam, *Jesus and "This Generation": A New Testament Study* (ConBNT 25; Stockholm: Almqvist & Wiksell, 1995).

207. See Allison, *Intertextual Jesus*, 62–64.

208. Although Zech 9:11 also has "blood of my covenant," (a) the Greek of Mark 14:24 // Matt 26:28 (τὸ αἷμά μου τῆς διαθήκης) is closer to LXX Exod 24:8 (τὸ αἷμα τῆς διαθήκης) than to LXX Zech 9:11 (ἐν αἵματι διαθήκης); (b) the Peshitta as well as Tg. Ps.-J. and Tg. Onq. on Exod 24:8 use a demonstrative (הא דין), which agrees with the New Testament's τοῦτο; (c) Exod 24:8 is connected with a meal (cf. 24:11) whereas Zech 9:11 is not; (d) the latter may itself be an allusion to Exod 24:8 (cf. Tg. Zech 9:11: "You also, for whom a covenant was made by blood, I have delivered you from bondage to the Egyptians").

209. See details in Allison, *New Moses*, 256–61.

210. See Peder Borgen, *Bread from Heaven: An Exegetical Study of the Concept of Manna in the Gospel of John and the Writings of Philo* (NovTSup 10; Leiden: Brill, 1965).

211. I cannot here discuss the tradition history of the Lord's Supper or the question of a Semitic equivalent for "my blood of the covenant." For the argument that the allusion to Exod 24:8 is secondary, see Scot McKnight, *Jesus and His Death: Historiography, the Historical Jesus,*

One more tradition is relevant. The Gospels report that Jesus, on at least one occasion, fed a large crowd in the wilderness (Matt 14:13–21; 15:32–39; Mark 6:30–44; 8:1–10; Luke 9:10–17; John 6:1–15). One can hardly demonstrate that these texts preserve memory, just as one can hardly establish the opposite. All we can say is this: given what we know of the so-called sign prophets of Jesus' day,[212] it is not implausible that he too once retreated into the wilderness in order to stir up memories of the exodus. Beginning with the church fathers, commentators on the feeding stories have certainly recalled the tale of the manna.[213] John's account, moreover, not only has the crowd hail Jesus as "the prophet" (6:14), by which they must mean the prophet like Moses of Deut 18:15–18,[214] but John 6:25–34 further draws explicit comparisons between Jesus and the lawgiver.

The signs that Jesus reckoned himself the subject of Deut 18:15–18 are, to my mind, as substantial as the indications that he thought himself to be the herald of Isa 61, and more substantial than the evidence that he thought himself to be Elijah come again.[215] Did he, then, make himself out to be more than one of these figures?

We can hardly object that, if he identified himself with one, he could not have identified himself with another. In Judaism, important persons could hold more than one office or fulfill more than one function. Solomon was sage as well as king. Elijah acted as a priest as well as a prophet. The author of the Tg. Ps 45:3 could envisage king Messiah having "the spirit of prophecy."[216] *Ecclesiastes Rabbah* 1:8 assumes that the Messiah and the prophet like Moses

---

and Atonement Theory (Waco, TX: Baylor University Press, 2005), 293–321; for the case to the contrary, see Rudolf Pesch, *Das Abendmahl und Jesu Todesverständnis* (QD 80; Freiburg: Herder, 1978).

212. See n. 157; see also P. W. Barnett, "The Jewish Sign Prophets—A.D. 40–70: Their Intentions and Origin," *NTS* 27 (1981): 679–97. Recall also Dositheus, of whom, sadly, we know little. He appears to have been "an early first century AD eschatological figure among the Samaritans, who applied the 'Prophet like Moses' passage of Dt. 18 to himself. As the Prophet, he was, in all likelihood a miracle-worker and the author of new texts and/or interpretations of biblical law" (Stanley Jerome Isser, *The Dositheans: A Samaritan Sect in Late Antiquity* [SJLA 17; Leiden: Brill, 1976], 163).

213. For example, Cyril of Alexandria, *Comm. Luke* 48 (CSCO 140 [Scriptores Syri 70], p. 159) (citing Ps 78:24); Eusebius, *Dem. ev.* 3.2 (92b–c).

214. See T. Francis Glasson, *Moses in the Fourth Gospel* (SBT 40; London: SCM Press, 1963), 27–32; van der Woude, *Messianischen Vorstellungen*, 82–83.

215. After an analysis of relevant actions attributed to Jesus, McKnight concludes, "Jesus' actions are more like the Prophet par excellence, Moses, than any other sort of prophet" ("Jesus and Prophetic Actions," 228). I agree. Contrast this injudicious pronouncement of Becker as to whether Jesus regarded himself as the returning Moses or Elijah: "The answer in both cases is a firm no. Not only is there not the slightest evidence that he did so; neither figure has anything in common with Jesus' activity" (*Jesus of Nazareth*, 214).

216. Cf. Tg. Isa. on 11:1–2 v.l. On King David as a prophet, see Craig A. Evans, "From Anointed Prophet to Anointed King: Probing Aspects of Jesus' Self-Understanding," in *Jesus and His Contemporaries*, 447–48.

are one and the same. Beyond all this, Moses was remembered as both a king and a prophet;[217] and if some ancient readers of the Tanak may have identified the returning Elijah with the prophet like Moses,[218] some modern scholars have identified that prophet with the figure who, in 11Q13, fulfills Isa 52:7 and 61:1–2.[219] Jesus, for all we know, made analogous equations.

The Coming One?

John the Baptist, according to Matt 3:11–12 // Luke 3:16–17 (Q), spoke in these terms of an eschatological figure yet to come: "I baptize you in water; but the one to come after me is more powerful than I, whose sandals I am not fit to take off. He will baptize you in holy Spirit and fire. His pitchfork is in his hand, and he will clear his threshing floor and gather the wheat into his granary, but the chaff he will burn on a fire that can never be put out." Critical scholars, although generally agreed that these words probably preserve themes

217. For Moses as a king, see p. 260 n. 155. For Moses as a prophet, see, for example, Deut 18:15, 18; 34:10; Hos 12:13; Sir 46:1; Wis 11:1; Aristobulus, frg. 2 *apud* Eusebius, *Praep. ev.* 8:10:4; Justus of Tiberius, frg. 2 *apud* Eusebius, *Chronicon apud* George Syncellus, *Chronographia* (CSHB 1:122); Philo, *QG* 1.86; 4.29; *Virtues* 5.1; *T. Mos.* 1:5; 3:11; 11:16; 12:7; Josephus, *Ant.* 2.327; 4.165, 329; *As. Mos.* 3:11; 11:16; 2 *Bar.* 59:4–11; *Mart. Ascen. Isa.* 3:8; *m. Soṭah* 1:9; *Deut. Rab.* 1:10; Tg. Cant 1:8.

218. According to Joseph Blenkinsopp (*Prophecy and Canon: A Contribution to the Study of Jewish Origins* [Notre Dame, IN: Notre Dame University Press, 1977]), Mal 4:4–5 ("Remember the teaching of my servant Moses, the statutes and ordinances that I commanded him at Horeb for all Israel. Lo, I will send you the prophet Elijah before the great and terrible day of the LORD comes" [RSV]) may take up the prophecy of Deut 18:15–18. Malachi mentions Elijah and Moses in close connection (4:4–5); and if, as is widely assumed, the author of 4:4–5 (like the author of Tg. Ps.-J. on Num 25:12) identified the "messenger of the covenant" in 3:1 with Elijah—a common interpretation; the former closely parallels the latter, and Matt 11:10 and Mark 1:2 apply Mal. 3:1 to John the Baptist, who in Matthew and Mark is the eschatological Elijah of Mal 4:5—then Elijah would be (as he is in the Hebrew Bible [see Allison, *New Moses*, 39–45]) like Moses, for presumably the messenger is to renew the Mosaic covenant. On the links between 3:1 and 4:4–5, see further Beth Glazier-McDonald, *Malachi: The Divine Messenger* (SBLDS 98; Atlanta: Scholars Press, 1987), 263–64. Note also that Peter's speech in Acts 3, which contains pre-Lukan elements, presents Jesus as being like both Moses and Elijah; see Richard F. Zehnle, *Peter's Pentecost Discourse: Tradition and Lukan Reinterpretation in Peter's Speeches of Acts 2 and 3* (SBLMS 15; Nashville: Abingdon, 1971), 71–94. Some have found the equation of Elijah with the prophet like Moses implicit in some Dead Sea Scrolls.

219. For example, Paul J. Kobelski, *Melchizedek and Melchireša'* (CBQMS 10; Washington, DC: Catholic Biblical Association, 1981), 61; A. S. van der Woude and M. de Jonge, "11QMelchizedek and the New Testament," *NTS* 12 (1966): 306–7; G. G. Xeravits, "Wisdom Traits in the Qumranic Presentation of the Eschatological Prophet," in *Wisdom and Apocalypticism in the Dead Sea Scrolls and in the Biblical Tradition* (ed. F. García Martínez; BETL 148; Leuven: Leuven University Press, 2003), 189. Note that 4Q377 frg. 1 recto col. II 5 characterizes Moses as משיחו, "his [God's] anointed one." That Isa 52:7 belongs to a section of Isaiah rich in new exodus themes—see Carroll Stuhlmueller, *Creative Redemption in Deutero-Isaiah* (AnBib 43; Rome: Biblical Institute Press, 1970), 66–94—is also relevant.

from John's preaching,[220] cannot agree upon what figure John had in mind—Yahweh, Elijah, the Messiah, the Son of Man, or some other. A few have even imagined that the Baptist was deliberately vague. The Gospel writers, however, had no second thoughts on the matter. For them, John obviously was thinking of Jesus. But if Jesus was a hearer of John, what did he think?

I suggest that the Christian interpretation—"the coming one" is Jesus—may accord, not with the interpretation of the Baptist, but with the interpretation of Jesus.[221] That is, whomever John had in mind, Jesus believed himself to be the object of John's expectation, believed himself to be the stronger one who would baptize with fire.

The first piece of evidence for this claim comes from the little episode in Matt 11:2–6 // Luke 7:18–23 (Q). Notwithstanding the difficulties of reconstructing the narrative setting in Q—Matthew and Luke differ on the details—the drift of the story is clear. John sends disciples to ask Jesus if he is the coming one of John's prophetic scenario. Jesus answers indirectly yet affirmatively with a list of items from his ministry,[222] a list that clearly alludes to prophecies from Isaiah: the blind see (cf. Isa 29:18; 35:5; 42:7, 18; 61:1), the lame walk (cf. Isa 35:6), the deaf hear (cf. Isa 29:18; 35:5; 42:18), the dead are raised (cf. Isa 26:19), and the poor have good news preached to them (cf. Isa 29:19; 61:1). The dramatic statement ends with "and blessed is anyone who takes no offense at me."

I will not here rehearse the arguments over the origin of this pericope, to which I can add nothing new, except to observe that since it unexpectedly depicts a doubting Baptist and contains no record of the latter's positive response, it is not obviously a free fabrication.[223] In any case, if the passage rightly remembers the gist of some exchange between John and Jesus, a couple of things would follow. One is that John's apocalyptic warning about "the one to come after me" envisaged not God or an angel but instead a human agent, for otherwise asking Jesus whether he might be "the coming one" would be senseless.[224] The other inference is that Jesus saw himself as

220. For dissenters, see p. 53 n. 97.

221. So too Theissen and Merz: "Jesus identified himself with the mediator figure announced by John" (*Historical Jesus*, 211).

222. On how the implicit yes is qualified, see Thomas Hieke, "Q 7,22—A Compendium of Isaian Eschatology," *ETL* 82 (2006): 175–87. Clare K. Rothschild (*Luke-Acts and the Rhetoric of History: An Investigation of Early Christian Historiography* [WUNT 2/175; Tübingen: Mohr Siebeck, 2004], 194), however, urges that Jesus' answer amounts to a no.

223. According to Meier, the "most probable origin" of Q 7:18–23 "is in the life of Jesus" (*Marginal Jew*, 2:136 [full discussion of the issue, pp. 131–37]). Others in essential agreement include Webb, *John the Baptizer*, 278–82; Walter Wink, "Jesus' Reply to John: Matt 11:2–67/Luke 7:18–23," *Forum* 5, no. 1 (1989): 121–28. For a more skeptical view, see Joseph Ernst, *Johannes der Täufer: Interpretation, Geschichte, Wirkungsgeschichte* (BZNW 53; Berlin: de Gruyter, 1989), 315–19.

224. Moreover, John's question in Q, if historical, implies that he "at the very least entertained the possibility that the answer might be 'Yes'" (T. W. Manson, "John the Baptist," *BJRL* 36 [1954]: 399).

that agent. Not only is he the one through whom the miracles of healing are being worked and through whom the good news is being announced, but also the declaration, "Blessed is anyone who takes no offense at me," puts him at the center of things. In other words, if Matt 11:2–6 // Luke 7:18–23 (Q) is not misleading, Jesus' self-conception incorporated John's eschatological expectation.

At least a couple of other texts may offer support for this inference. One is Luke 12:49–50: "I came to bring fire to the earth, and how I wish that it were already kindled! I have a baptism with which to be baptized, and what stress I am under until it is completed!" Although found only in the Third Gospel, these two sentences, which should not be dissolved into two separate sayings with separate tradition histories,[225] were not Luke's invention. Clear signs of Lukan redaction are missing,[226] and the difficult τί θέλω εἰ is best explained as a non-Lukan Semitism.[227] Moreover, the metaphorical characterization of martyrdom as a baptism has its analogy in Mark 10:38–39, and there are even closer parallels in *Gos. Thom.* 10 ("I have cast fire upon the world, and see, I guard it until it is afire" [cf. v. 16]) and in another extracanonical saying attributed to Jesus: "Whoever is near to me is near to the fire; whoever is far from me is far from the kingdom."[228] A tradition, whatever its origin, remembered Jesus saying that he would dispense fire.

As for the meaning of Luke 12:49–50, the line originally must have concerned the final judgment.[229] Not only does the Tanak link fire with God's wrath, eschatological destruction, and the day of the Lord,[230] but the same is

---

225. Synonymous parallelism—from Origen (*Mart.* 37) onward, commentators often have understood v. 49 and v. 50 to be roughly synonymous—is a feature of the Synoptic tradition (see Joachim Jeremias, *New Testament Theology: The Proclamation of Jesus* [New York: Charles Scribner's Sons, 1971], 14–20); and in Luke 17:26–30, the threat of fire is paired with the threat of a flood. Fire and water are, further, traditionally associated with judgment (e.g., Ps 66:10–12; Isa 30:27–28, 30; 43:2; *Sib. Or.* 3:689–91; Josephus, *Ant.* 1.70; Lat. *L.A.E.* 49:3). They indeed are sometimes joined to become one—a stream or lake of fire (e.g., Dan 7:10; 1QH^a 3:29–36; *1 En.* 14:19; 17:5; 67:13; *Sib. Or.* 3:54, 84; Rev 19:20; 20:10, 14–15; 21:8; *4 Ezra* 13:10–11; *2 En.* 10:2; *Mek.* on Exod 18:1; *b. Zebaḥ.* 116a).

226. See Joachim Jeremias, *Die Sprache des Lukasevangeliums: Redaktion und Tradition im Nicht-Markusstoff des dritten Evangeliums* (KEK; Göttingen: Vandenhoeck & Ruprecht, 1980), 223.

227. See F. H. Seper, "ΚΑΙ ΤΙ ΘΕΛΩ ΕΙ ΗΔΗ ΑΝΗΦΘΗ (Lc 12,49b)," *VD* 36 (1958): 147–53.

228. Known from *Gos. Thom.* 82; *Gos. Sav.* 107:43–48; Origen, *Hom. Jer.* 50.1(3).3; Didymus of Alexandria, *Fr. Ps.* frg. 883.

229. In addition to what follows, see G. R. Beasley-Murray, *Jesus and the Kingdom of God* (Grand Rapids: Eerdmans; London: Paternoster, 1986), 247–52; François Bovon, *Das Evangelium nach Lukas (Lk 9,51–14,35)* (EKKNT 3/2; Zürich: Benziger; Neukirchen-Vluyn: Neukirchener Verlag, 1996), 350.

230. See, for example, Isa 66:24; Mal 3:19 (Eng. 4:1); Jdt 16:17; for additional texts and discussion, see Vinzenz Hamp, "אֵשׁ," *TDOT* 1:424–28; Friedrich Lang, "πῦρ κ.τ.λ.," *TDNT* 6:934–37.

true of later literature.[231] More importantly, everywhere else in the Synoptics, with the exception of Mark 9:22 (the possessed boy who throws himself into the fire) and Luke 22:55 (Peter warming himself in the courtyard), πῦρ has to do with the great assize.

How, then, is Luke 12:49–50 related to the message of the Baptist? Among the handful of logia that Q puts into the mouth of John, three refer to fire: Matt 3:10 // Luke 3:9 ("thrown into the fire"); Matt 3:11 // Luke 3:16 ("baptize in fire"); Matt 3:12 // Luke 3:17 ("burn with unquenchable fire"). If these sentences are anything to go by, John imagined that the last judgment would, as in Zoroastrian eschatology, fall upon the world as a fiery stream; and he drew a contrast between that future ordeal, baptism in fire, and his own ritual, baptism in water. Presumably, the one immersion would protect people during the other immersion.[232]

Now if—I have not abandoned the conditional—Jesus ever similarly spoke of baptism and of fire in the same utterance, as Luke 12:49–50 purports, it is altogether likely that conceptions similar to those of the Baptist were on his mind.[233] Jesus, that is, would have anticipated going through the eschatological baptism himself, as his submission to John's prophylactic baptism independently attests. He would have expected to "be salted with fire" (Mark 9:49), to suffer eschatological trial, to enter the fire that "will test what sort of work each has done" (1 Cor 3:13).[234]

But Luke 12:49–50 says more than this. It, like *Gos. Thom.* 10 and the related agraphon in Origen and Didymus, makes Jesus himself the dispenser of that baptizing fire: "I came to bring fire to the earth." On the natural assumption

---

231. For example, *Jub.* 9:15; *1 En.* 10:6; 54:1–2, 6; 90:24–25; 91:9; 100:9; 102:1; *Pss. Sol.* 15:4–5; *Sib. Or.* 3:53–54; 4:159–60; *4 Macc* 9:9; 12:12; *T. Zeb.* 10:3; *T. Jud.* 25:3; *4 Ezra* 7:36–38; 13:10–11; *2 Bar.* 37:1; 44:15; 59:2; *3 Bar.* 4:16.

232. Matt 3:7 // Luke 3:7 (Q) ("Who warned you to flee from the wrath to come?") assumes that people went to John's baptism in order to escape judgment. Cf. *Sib. Or.* 4:165–70: "Wash your bodies in perennial rivers. . . . He will stop his wrath again if you all practice honorable piety in your hearts."

233. As the commentators often recognize: Origen, *Selecta in Psalmos* (PG 12:1236C); *Hom. Luc.* 26.1; Theodore of Heraclea, *Comm. Matt.* frg. 18 (J. Reuss, ed., *Matthäus-Kommentare aus der griechischen Kirche* [TU 61; Berlin: Akademie-Verlag, 1957], 62); Albertus Magnus, *Enarrationes in primam partem Evangelii Lucae (I–IX)* (vol. 22 of *Opera omnia*, ed. A. Borgnet; Paris: Ludovicus Vivès, 1894), 153; Matthew Henry, *Matthew to John* (vol. 5 of *Commentary on the Whole Bible*; Old Tappan, NJ: Fleming H. Revell, n.d.), 27; Robinson, "Elijah, John and Jesus," 43–44; I. Howard Marshall, *The Gospel of Luke: A Commentary on the Greek Text* (NIGTC; Grand Rapids: Eerdmans, 1978), 547; Peter Böhlemann, *Jesus und der Täufer: Schlüssel zur Theologie und Ethik des Lukas* (SNTSMS 99; Cambridge: Cambridge University Press, 1997), 168–70; James D. G. Dunn, "The Birth of a Metaphor—Baptized in Spirit," in *Pneumatology* (vol. 2 of *The Christ and the Spirit: Collected Essays of James D. G. Dunn*; Grand Rapids: Eerdmans, 1998), 103–17.

234. See further Dale C. Allison Jr., *The End of the Ages Has Come: An Early Interpretation of the Passion and Resurrection of Jesus* (SNTW; Edinburgh: T & T Clark, 1987), 124–28; Daniel Frayer-Griggs, "'Everyone Will Be Baptized in Fire': Mark 9.49, Q 3.16, and the Baptism of the Coming One," *JSHJ* 7 (2009): 254–85.

that some of his hearers had been John's hearers and so were familiar with the latter's proclamation of a coming one who would baptize with fire, would Jesus not be making a stupendous albeit implicit claim? If one believed that Jesus had come to cast fire upon the earth, then must he not be the eschatological figure of judgment prophesied by John?[235] "I came to bring fire to the earth" seems, as Jerome saw, to answer to John's "He will baptize you with fire."[236] Luke 12:49–50 is L's analogue to the Q text, Matt 11:2–6 // Luke 7:18–23. The coming one (ὁ ἐρχόμενος) has come (ἦλθον).

There is yet one more text that may—I do not say does, but only may—link Jesus with the figure of John's expectation. The parable of the binding of the strong man, preserved in Mark 3:27; Matt 12:29 // Luke 11:21–22 (Q); *Gos. Thom.* 35, runs as follows in its Markan form: "But no one can enter a strong man's house and plunder his property without first tying up the strong man; then indeed the house can be plundered." As most commentators from patristic times to the present have seen, ὁ ἰσχυρός is the devil, Satan. The designation is unusual, because whether or not Isa 49:24–25 and 53:12 lie behind the parable, no extant pre-Christian text calls Satan "the strong one."[237]

Within its parabolic context, ἰσχυρός emphasizes the power of the house-holder, which in turn becomes a statement about the strength of the other figure in the parable, the one who can bind the strong man and plunder his goods. Now, there can be no doubt as to who this second character is. Jesus, in his successful ministry of exorcism, has overcome the power of the devil. He is the one who is stronger than the strong man. He is, one could say, and as Luke does say in 11:22 (perhaps reproducing Q's wording), ὁ ἰσχυρότερος. Although the strong man may overcome human beings, he himself is overcome by the stronger Jesus. So the parable of the binding of the strong man is christological. It is a statement about Jesus the exorcist, about his strength, about his being stronger than the strong one.

What would follow if we knew both that Jesus composed the parable of the strong man, and that, before him, John the Baptist had publicly proclaimed a stronger one to come? We might then decide that Mark 3:27 was intended not just to make a statement about exorcistic powers but to provoke thought about Jesus' eschatological role: can this be the stronger one who is to come? Some exegetes, for what it is worth, have read Mark 3:27 or one of its Synoptic parallels just this way.[238]

235. So also Ulrich Luz, "Warum zog Jesus nach Jerusalem?" in *Historische Jesus* (ed. Schröter and Brucker), 422–23.

236. Jerome, *Comm. Matt.* 3:11. See further those cited in n. 233.

237. The closest parallels are in the late magical papyri, in which demons are occasionally strong; see BDAG, s.v. ἰσχυρός, 1a.

238. See, for example, Albertus Magnus, *Enarrationes in primam partem Evangelii Lucae (I–IX)*, 282; Henry Alford, *The Four Gospels* (vol. 1 of *The Greek Testament*; 2nd ed.; London: Rivingtons, 1854), 553; William Lane, *The Gospel according to Mark* (NICNT; Grand Rapids:

Davidic Messiah?

The title "Christ" (χριστός) appears neither in Q nor in the *Gospel of Thomas*.[239] This fact does not require or imply that the equation "Jesus = Messiah" was a "later development."[240] Romans 1:3–4 and 1 Cor 15:3 establish that, from a very early time, some followers of Jesus confessed him to be "Messiah,"[241] as does the repeated use of Ps 2, understood as messianic, in so many first-century Christian texts.[242] Our best bet is that, like the Peter of Acts 2–3, some who first announced Jesus' resurrection also called him משיח;[243] that is, they crowned him Israel's eschatological king, just as Akiba reportedly hailed Simon bar Kokhba as Messiah.[244] Indeed, the double name, "Jesus Christ," probably goes back to

Eerdmans, 1974), 143 n. 92; Hugh Anderson, *The Gospel of Mark* (NCB; London: Oliphants, 1976), 72; Leopold Sabourin, *The Gospel according to St. Matthew* (2 vols. in 1; Bombay: St. Paul Publications, 1982), 263–64; Beasley-Murray, *Jesus and the Kingdom*, 110; Joel Marcus, *Mark 1–8* (AB 27; New York: Doubleday, 2000), 283; Luz, *Matthew*, 2:200, 205 n. 72.

239. Yet *Gos. Thom.* 13 obviously has omitted "Christ" from its tradition (see p. 133), and the application to Jesus of Isa 61 in Q 6:20–23; 7:18–23 implicitly makes him an anointed herald (cf. LXX Isa 61:1: ἔχρισεν); see above, pp. 263–66; also Allison, *Intertextual Jesus*, 104–14.

240. Against Burton Mack, as quoted by Ron Cameron, "Proposal for the Second Year of the Seminar," in *Redescribing Christian Origins* (ed. Cameron and Miller), 290. I also disagree with Hahn (*Christologische Hoheitstitel*, 179–80), for whom the step of confessing Jesus as the Messiah was taken early but not "in the very earliest times." Our sources are too thin for such a fine distinction.

241. Cf. Mark 8:27–30; and see Detlef Häusser, *Christusbekenntnis und Jesusüberlieferung bei Paulus* (WUNT 2/210; Tübingen: Mohr Siebeck, 2006), 106–9; Werner Kramer, *Christ, Lord, Son of God* (trans. Brian Hardy; SBT 50; London: SCM Press, 1966), 19–64. On Rom 1:3–4 in particular, see Robert Jewett, *Romans: A Commentary* (Hermeneia; Minneapolis: Fortress, 2006), 97–99, 103–5. Acts 2:36 ("God has [at the resurrection] made him both Lord and Messiah") also presumably preserves a very old way of speaking; see C. K. Barrett, *A Critical and Exegetical Commentary on the Acts of the Apostles* (2 vols.; ICC; Edinburgh: T & T Clark, 1994–1998), 1:133, 151–52. Furthermore, the formulas with "Christ" dying "for us" or "for sins" must be pre-Pauline (cf. Rom 5:6, 8; 14:15; 1 Cor 8:11; 2 Cor 5:14; 1 Thess 5:9–10).

242. See especially Mark 1:11; Acts 4:25–26; 13:33; Heb 1:5; 5:5; Rev 2:26–27; 19:15; *1 Clem.* 36:4. For additional texts and discussion, see Aquila H. I. Lee, *From Messiah to Preexistent Son: Jesus' Self-Consciousness and Early Christian Exegesis of Messianic Psalms* (WUNT 2/192; Tübingen: Mohr Siebeck, 2005), 240–83.

243. *Pace* Barry S. Crawford, "Christos as Nickname," in *Redescribing Christian Origins* (ed. Cameron and Miller), 347; also, Miller ("Messianic Conception"), who thinks that the title might have originated as a "relatively innocuous nickname." Crawford admits that nicknames were, from what we can gather, bestowed during life, not after death, and he offers no example of χριστός as a nickname; and Miller ends up arguing that "prior to the writing of the Gospel of Mark, those who cultivated and transmitted Jesus traditions had not thought of Jesus in messianic terms" (p. 313). To my mind, this assigns far too much creativity to Mark and comes up against, among other things, the high probability that an old, pre-Markan passion narrative featured a David typology and Jesus' crucifixion as "king of the Jews" (see below, pp. 392–423).

244. See p. 258 n. 150. For "Messiah" in Judaism, see Charlesworth, ed., *Messiah*; Joseph A. Fitzmyer, *The One Who Is To Come* (Grand Rapids: Eerdmans, 2007); Jacob Neusner, William Scott Green, and Ernest S. Frerichs, eds., *Judaisms and Their Messiahs at the Turn of the Christian Era* (New York: Cambridge University Press, 1987). Despite all the diversity in ancient

the Aramaic confession יֵשׁוּעַ מְשִׁיחָא, "Jesus [is] the Messiah," which became, in Greek, the compound designation, Ἰησοῦς Χριστός.[245]

The identification of Jesus as ὁ χριστός and so as a royal deliverer indicates that some early Christians hoped for the redemption of Israel and an end to Roman rule; and if, as we have no reason to doubt, some of those who thus hoped had listened to Jesus himself—several New Testament texts assume that at least Peter regarded his teacher as "Messiah" (Mark 8:27–30; Acts 2:36; 3:18, 20; 1 Pet 1:1–3)—this certainly ups the odds that Jesus moved in a world of messianic expectations, for presumably his followers followed him "precisely because they agreed with him."[246]

Does the evidence allow us to go any further? Countering a far-flung conviction among New Testament scholars,[247] John Meier recently has contended that Jesus took himself to be the Davidic Messiah.[248] Meier's argument unfolds through a number of steps. They are worth examining.

Judaism—a point that the collections edited by Charlesworth and by Neusner, Green, and Frerichs repeatedly emphasize—many Jews shared hope for a future Davidic king, as in, for example, Isa 11:1–5; Jer 23:5; 33:17–22; Ezek 34:23; 37:24. In this connection, Chester, "Messianism"; Collins, *Scepter*; and William Horbury, *Jewish Messianism and the Cult of Christ* (London: SCM Press, 1998) serve as useful responses to recent attempts that may unduly marginalize messianic expectation and overstate its diversity. As the New Testament itself proves, הַמָּשִׁיחַ/χριστός, just like צֶמַח/"branch" (cf., e.g., Jer 23:5–6; 33:15; Dan 9:25–26; LXX Amos 4:13; Zech 3:8; 6:12; 4Q161 3:11–25 [?]; 4Q174 1:10–13; 4Q252 5:1–7; 4Q285 frg. 5), could, in the appropriate context, refer to the future Davidic king; see, for example, LXX Amos 4:13; CD-A 12:23–13:1; 14:18–19; CD-B 19:10–11; 20:1; 1QS 9:9–11; 1Q28a 2:11–15; 4Q252 5:3; 4Q521 frg. 2 col. II 1; 11Q13 2:18; *Pss. Sol.* 17–18; *1 En.* 48:10; 52:4; *2 Bar.* 29:3; 30:1; 39:7; 40:1; 70:9; 72:2; *4 Ezra* 7:28–29; 12:32; *m. Ber.* 1:5; *m. Soṭah* 9:15; Tg. Isa. on 9:5; 10:27; 11:1.

245. See Frey, "Historische Jesus," 302–3.

246. Bart Ehrman, *Jesus: Apocalyptic Prophet of the New Millennium* (Oxford: Oxford University Press, 1999), 135.

247. For Bultmann, who represents much scholarship on this issue, see n. 84. Cf. Otfried Hofius, "Ist Jesus der Messias? Thesen," in *Der Messias* (ed. Ingo Baldermann et al.; JBT 8; Neukirchen-Vluyn: Neukirchener Verlag, 1993), 119–22. James D. G. Dunn ("Messianic Ideas and Their Influence on the Jesus of History," in *Messiah* [ed. Charlesworth], 375) speaks for many when he surmises that Jesus seemingly displayed an unwillingness to be associated with the title "Messiah." The nuanced view of Sanders (*Historical Figure*, 239–48) is that although Jesus thought himself as "in some sense 'king,'" he is unlikely to have dubbed himself "Messiah." Even stronger is Hahn's view that "it is extremely probable in fact that Jesus Himself repudiated the messianic title" (*Christologische Hoheitstitel*, 179). Although I do not share Hahn's view, I am reminded of Krishnamurti, who deliberately declined the honorifics that others tried to bestow upon him. When he "was only a boy, his famous sponsors in the Theosophical Society proclaimed him the next World-Teacher, the successor to Krishna, Buddha, and Jesus Christ, and they presented him with a ready-made organization over which to preside. . . . But Krishnamurti rejected all efforts to turn him into the charismatic hero he could have become" (P. Benton Johnson, "On Founders and Followers: Some Factors in the Development of New Religious Movements," *Sociological Analysis* 53 [supplement, 1992]: 2).

248. John P. Meier, "From Elijah-Like Prophet to Royal Davidic Messiah," in *Jesus: A Colloquium in the Holy Land* (ed. Doris Donnelly; New York: Continuum, 2001), 45–83.

a. The infancy narratives in Matthew and Luke reveal that, independently of Mark, sources for Matthew and Luke depicted Jesus as the messianic Son of David.

b. Paul's use of a traditional formula in Rom 1:3–4—"the gospel concerning his Son, who was descended from David according to the flesh and was declared to be Son of God with power according to the spirit of holiness by resurrection from the dead, Jesus Christ our Lord"—assumes that Christians whom the apostle has never met will take its contents for granted. This implies the antiquity of belief in Jesus' descent from David as well as its popularity in the churches. Paul himself, notably, nowhere else evinces interest in this theme.

c. 2 Tim 2:8 reinforces what we learn from Rom 1:3–4, for the verse incorporates a variant of the tradition in Romans and may even be, from the tradition-historical perspective, older.[249]

d. Although the Fourth Gospel names David only once, that single occurrence suffices to show John's familiarity with the tradition that Jesus was a Davidide: "Has not the scripture said that the Messiah is descended from David and comes from Bethlehem, the village where David lived?" (7:42).

e. Mark 10:47–48 (blind Bartimaeus imploringly addresses Jesus as "Son of David"); 11:1–10 (a crowd hails Jesus' entry into Jerusalem with the words "Blessed is the coming kingdom of our ancestor David"); and 12:35–37 (Jesus poses the enigmatic query about David's "son" and "lord") establish, for Meier, that Jesus' identification as the Son of David belonged to Mark's tradition as well.

f. Insofar as we can distinguish Matthean redaction from M material, the latter does not appear to have been much concerned to promote a Son-of-David Christology.

g. On Meier's reading, Luke's Gospel, aside from its infancy story and its version of the genealogy of Jesus, which lists David as an ancestor of Jesus without stressing the fact (3:23–38), also fails to develop Davidic themes; and the few places in Acts that feature or presuppose a Son-of-David Christology echo, in all probability, early Jewish-Christian proclamation.

h. Hebrews acknowledges Jesus' Davidic status only in passing (1:5; 7:14).

i. Although neither "Son of David" nor "seed of David" appears in Revelation, the book identifies Jesus as the Davidic Messiah in 3:7; 5:5; 22:16.

---

249. But for the argument that Rom 1:3–4 is older, see Hanna Stettler, *Die Christologie der Pastoralbriefe* (WUNT 2/105; Tübingen: Mohr Siebeck, 1998), 165–70.

The upshot of Meier's survey of the New Testament is this: belief in Jesus' Davidic descent was tradition for John the seer, the author of Hebrews, the four evangelists, and Paul; and it "reaches back in many forms to the earliest days of the church and continues to be referred to throughout the first and second Christian generations down to the relatively late books of Acts and Revelation. Yet no New Testament author makes Davidic descent the main focus of his redactional Christology."[250]

With all this as prologue, Meier finally addresses the key issue: when did belief in Jesus' Davidic messiahship first surface? Meier answers with three further propositions.

> j. Given the variety of first-century eschatological figures to choose from, nothing necessitated that Christians remake Jesus into a descendant of David after Easter if he had not already been one before Easter. There were other ways of promoting the significance of one's religious savior.[251]
>
> k. Second Temple Judaism knew nothing of the death and resurrection of the royal Davidic Messiah, at least before the end of the age.[252]
>
> l. One could become "king of the Jews" and not be a Davidide, as the Hasmonean dynasty shows.

All of this, according to Meier, makes it less than obvious that Christian theology fabricated, against the facts, Jesus' descent from David. Given, then,

---

250. Meier, "Royal Davidic Messiah," 61.

251. For the variety of messianic ideas in Judaism, see Andrew Chester, "Jewish Messianic Expectations and Mediatorial Figures and Pauline Christology," in *Paulus und das antike Judentum* (ed. Martin Hengel and Ulrich Heckel; WUNT 58; Tübingen: Mohr Siebeck, 1991), 17–89. For texts that seemingly minimize the role of a Davidic Messiah, see Reuven Kimelman, "The Messiah of the Amidah: A Study in Comparative Messianism," *JBL* 116 (1997): 313–30. Already Deutero-Isaiah and Trito-Isaiah appear to reserve no role for a future Davidic king—God is the only king they name—and neither Ezra nor Nehemiah says anything about a reinstated monarchy.

252. However, *4 Ezra* 7:29 does have the Messiah die after a reign of four hundred years. Israel Knohl ("'By Three Days, Live': Messiahs, Resurrection, and Ascent to Heaven in *Hazon Gabriel*," *JR* 88 [2008]: 147–58) finds, in the so-called Vision of Gabriel, a suffering and rising Messiah. The text, however, remains exceedingly obscure and full of lacunae. Its general drift remains highly uncertain. For details, see David Hamidović, "La vision de Gabriel," *RHPR* 89 (2009): 147–68. As for the rabbinic tradition of the death of the Messiah of Ephraim—the figure himself is quite possibly pre-Christian (see David C. Mitchell, "The Fourth Deliverer: A Josephite Messiah in 4QTestimonia," *Bib* 86 [2005]: 545–53; idem, "Rabbi Dosa and the Rabbis Differ: Messiah ben Joseph in the Babylonian Talmud," *RRJ* 8 [2005]: 77–90)—this was perhaps born of the Bar Kokhba disaster (so Joseph Heinemann, "The Messiah of Ephraim and the Premature Exodus of the Tribe of Ephraim," *HTR* 68 [1975]: 1–15; but for criticism of Heinemann's proposal, see David Berger, "Three Typological Themes in Early Jewish Messianism: Messiah Son of Joseph, Rabbinic Calculations, and the Figure of Armilus," *AJSR* 10 [1985]: 141–64).

the antiquity of the Son-of-David Christology, it plausibly, for lack of a better story, reaches back to the time of the historical Jesus himself.[253]

So far Meier. Does he compel? He is right to urge that Christians could have exalted Jesus without insisting on his Davidic descent, and he is right to insist that Christians, from very early times, thought Jesus to be a Davidide. Beyond that, one might add, some first-century Jews did, rightly or wrongly, think themselves to be David's descendants.[254] Maybe Jesus' immediate family was among them.[255]

And yet Meier has not exorcised all my doubt. For one thing, he has overlooked some of the pertinent evidence—for example, the Davidic typology in Mark 14—and so probably underestimated the interest of the Synoptic evangelists and John in Jesus' Davidic status.[256] For another, while one acknowledges that turning Jesus into the Son of David was not theologically incumbent—the extant sources, or at least the early ones, fail to remark on Simon bar Kokhba's Davidic ancestry[257]—several biblical oracles as well as dissatisfaction with the non-Davidic Hasmoneans could have strongly suggested that Israel's chief redeemer be from David's house.[258] The Messiah's

253. Meier goes on to speculate that early in his ministry Jesus deliberately took up the mantel of Elijah in order to counter hope that he might be the royal Messiah. Later, however, as the stories of the entry into Jerusalem and the protest in the temple suggest, he embraced the messianic office.

254. See David Flusser, "'The House of David' on an Ossuary," *IMJ* 5 (1986): 37–49.

255. For traditions about Jesus' family, see Richard Bauckham, "The Relatives of Jesus in the Early Church," in *Jude and the Relatives of Jesus* (Edinburgh: T & T Clark, 1990), 45–133. According to Eusebius (*Hist. eccl.* 3.20), the grandchildren of Jude claimed to belong to the family of David. Raymond E. Brown (*The Birth of the Messiah: A Commentary on the Infancy Narratives in the Gospels of Matthew and Luke* [new updated ed.; New York: Doubleday, 1993], 505–12) surveys the issues involved in deciding whether Jesus was really of the house of David. His own verdict is positive. Contrast Pieter F. Craffert, "How Historiography Creates (Some)Body: Jesus, the Son of David—Royal Stock or Social Construct?" *Scriptura* 90 (2005): 608–20. The issue, of course, is whether Jesus' family believed that it was Davidic, not whether it in fact was. (Given that most people in an ethnic group are ultimately related, "not only Jesus of Nazareth but also most of his first Israelite followers would probably have connections to David" [Craffert].)

256. On Mark 14, see below, p. 387; for the Gospels in general, see Brian M. Nolan, *The Royal Son of God: The Christology of Matthew 1–2 in the Setting of the Gospel* (OBO 23; Fribourg: Éditions Universitaires; Göttingen: Vandenhoeck & Ruprecht, 1979); Lidija Novakovic, *Messiah, the Healer of the Sick: A Study of Jesus as the Son of David in the Gospel of Matthew* (WUNT 2/170; Tübingen: Mohr Siebeck, 2003); Mark L. Strauss, *The Davidic Messiah in Luke-Acts: The Promise and Its Fulfillment in Lukan Christology* (JSNTSup 110; Sheffield: Sheffield Academic Press, 1995); Margaret Daly-Denton, *David in the Fourth Gospel: The Johannine Reception of the Psalms* (AGJU 47; Leiden: Brill, 2000); Joel Willitts, *Matthew's Messianic Shepherd-King: In Search of "The Lost Sheep of the House of Israel"* (BZNW 147; Berlin: de Gruyter, 2007).

257. On this issue, see Dan Jaffé, "La figure messianique de Bar-Kokhba: Nouvelles perspectives," *Henoch* 28 (2006): 106–10.

258. Horsley comments, "The Roman conquest must . . . have served to intensify the feeling among Pharisees and others already suffering under the Hasmonean usurpers that they needed

Davidic lineage clearly mattered to some Jews, such as the authors of 4Q252 5:1–4; 4Q174; *Pss. Sol.* 17.[259]

Such lineage might equally have mattered to some early Christians, whatever pre-Easter memories did or did not call to mind. This is all the more true because many Christian texts that concern themselves with the promises to David borrow the language of 2 Sam 7:12: "I will raise up [MT: הקימתי; LXX: ἀναστήσω] your offspring after you." One has no difficulty imagining early Christians divining in this oracle a testimony to Jesus' resurrection, which would in turn imply that he was David's son.[260] The manipulation of pedigrees in the ancient world was no doubt common.[261] Rabbinic legend, one recalls, seemingly created a Davidic ancestry for Hillel in order to enhance his status.[262]

Another issue for Meier, one that has in the past proven decisive for many, is the "gap between the nonmilitant, nonroyal career of Jesus as reported in the Gospels and his death and subsequent veneration as king-messiah, and it may not be possible to bridge it."[263] This is because, even though there was no "standard concept of the Messiah,"[264] we may nonetheless "speak of a common Jewish hope for a royal messiah from the Davidic line";[265] and much Jewish imagination, it seems fair to generalize, associated that Messiah with warfare.[266] As John Collins observes, forecasts of the Davidic king to come often cite or allude to Isa 11:4 and Num 24:17–19, which are texts of militant

---

not only legitimate but righteous royal leadership—i.e., the new David, anointed by God and empowered to liberate the Jews" ("Messianic Movements," 482).

259. Cf., for example, Isa 9:7; 11:1–2; 16:5; Jer 23:5–6; 30:9; 33:15–17; Ezek 34:24; 37:24–25; Amos 9:11; Zech 3:8; 6:12; 12:7–8; 4Q161 frgs. 8–10; *4 Ezra* 12:32.

260. See Dennis C. Duling, "The Promises to David and Their Entrance into Christianity— Nailing Down a Likely Hypothesis," *NTS* 19 (1973): 55–77. The confession behind Rom 1:3–4 clearly borrows from 2 Sam 7:12–14.

261. For this phenomenon in recent times, see Laura Bohannan, "A Genealogical Charter," *Africa* 22 (1952): 301–15.

262. Menahem Stern, "A. Schalit's Herod," *JJS* 11 (1960): 55–56.

263. So Collins, "Jesus and the Messiahs of Israel," 176–77.

264. The phrase is from Hahn, *Christologische Hoheitstitel*, 159 ("das maßgebende Messiasvorstellung").

265. John J. Collins, "What Was Distinctive about Messianic Expectation at Qumran?" in *The Dead Sea Scrolls and the Qumran Community* (vol. 2 of *The Bible and the Dead Sea Scrolls*, ed. James H. Charlesworth; Waco, TX: Baylor University Press, 2006), 73.

266. See, for example, CD-A 7:15–21; CD-B 19:10–11; 1Q28b 5:24–29; 4Q161 3:18–25; 4Q285 5:4; *2 Bar.* 39:7; 70:9; 72:2, 6; *b. Sanh.* 94a–b; *b. 'Abod. Zar.* 3b; *Lev. Rab.* 9:6; Tg. Ps.-J. and Frg. Tg. on Gen 49:10–12; Tg. Ps.-J. on Exod 40:11; Frg. Tg. on Num 11:26; Tg. Onq., Frg. Tg., and Tg. Ps.-J. on Num 24:17–19. Note also Hippolytus's summary of Jewish messianic expectation in *Haer.* 9.30. According to Collins, "the expectation of a Davidic messiah was not a peculiarly sectarian idea, but was grounded in an exegetical tradition that was widely known across sectarian lines. Equally, the role of the Davidic messiah is consistently understood as that of militant liberator, from Qumran to Alexandria, and from the *Psalms of Solomon* to the latter apocalypses of *4 Ezra* and *2 Baruch*" ("Messianic Expectation," 83).

conquest.[267] The former foresees a figure who "shall strike the earth with the rod of his mouth, and with the breath of his lips . . . shall kill the wicked." The latter prophesies that "a star shall come out of Jacob, and a scepter shall rise out of Israel; it shall crush the borderlands of Moab, and the territory of all the Shethites. . . . One out of Jacob shall rule, and destroy the survivors of Ir." One also recalls Philo, *Rewards* 95: "For there will come forth a man, says the oracle, and commanding his troops and fighting war he will subdue great and populous nations."[268] Even *Pss. Sol.* 17:21–44, where "the Son of David" relies not on horse and rider or bow, collects neither gold nor silver for war, and strikes the earth not with a sword but with "the word of his mouth," is full of the imagery of combat. The "Lord Messiah" will "destroy the unrighteous rulers," will "purge Jerusalem from Gentiles," will "drive out sinners from the inheritance," will "smash the arrogance of sinners like a potter's jar," and will "shatter all their substance with an iron rod" (vv. 22–24). He is, in short, a "violent warrior."[269] Could Jesus, remembered as the author of "love your enemies" (Matt 5:44 // Luke 6:27 [Q]), have thought of himself in such terms?[270]

Although this objection carries weight, it probably should not carry the day. Not only did Jesus believe in divine judgment,[271] but also, as we have seen, some scholars think that he took himself to be Elijah come again; and yet the Tishbite's memory was thoroughly implicated in violence. He commanded the prophets of Baal to be slaughtered (1 Kgs 18:40); he twice called down fire from heaven to incinerate perceived enemies (2 Kgs 1:9–12); and tradition identified him with Phinehas, the priest famed for his zeal, which manifested itself in spearing an Israelite and the Midianite woman whom he had brought into his family.[272] One understands why *Apoc. El.* 4:7–13, when recounting events of the end time, has the prophet fighting the antichrist.

267. Collins, "Jesus and the Messiahs of Israel," 170–71. Compare this remark by Goulder: "Even if the Davidic Messiah is not always thought of as leading an army, he is generally associated with the expulsion of occupying powers and collaborators, and the enforcing of righteousness" ("Anointed," 69).

268. For the interpretation of this passage, see Peder Borgen, *Philo of Alexandria: An Exegete for His Time* (NovTSup 86; Leiden: Brill, 1997), 269–76; Schreiber, *Gesalbter und König*, 269–74.

269. Kenneth Atkinson, *An Intertextual Study of the Psalms of Solomon: Pseudepigrapha* (SBEC 49; Lewiston, NY: Edwin Mellen, 2001), 349. See further idem, *I Cried to the Lord: A Study of the Psalms of Solomon's Historical Background and Social Setting* (JSJSup 84; Leiden: Brill, 2004), 128–79. But for qualification of this characterization, see Le Donne, *Historiographical Jesus*, 122–32.

270. On Jesus' apparent rejection of militarism, see John Riches, *Jesus and the Transformation of Judaism* (New York: Seabury, 1982), 87–111.

271. See Dale C. Allison Jr., "The Problem of Gehenna," in *Resurrecting Jesus: The Earliest Christian Tradition and Its Interpreters* (New York: T & T Clark, 2005), 56–110.

272. See Num 25:6–16; cf. 1 Macc 2:26; Sir 45:23; and for the identification of Phinehas with Elijah, see *L.A.B.* 48:1–2; Tg. Ps.-J. on Exod 6:18; see discussion in Robert Hayward,

Similarly, although Jesus may well have thought of himself as the prophet like Moses—I believe that he probably did—Moses too failed to turn the other cheek. He murdered an Egyptian who smote a Hebrew (Exod 2:11–12). He repeatedly called down plagues upon the Egyptians, the last of which took their firstborn (Exod 7–12). He stretched forth his hand so that the waters of the Red Sea turned back upon Pharaoh's army and swept it all away (Exod 14:26–29). And he quashed Korah's rebellion by calling the earth to open up and swallow his opponents (Num 16).

If, notwithstanding all the violent associations, Jesus identified with Moses and/or Elijah, then maybe he also, notwithstanding the militant associations, identified with the Davidic Messiah.

Early Christians were fond of referring Ps 110 to him, despite its battlefield rhetoric—"your enemies your footstool," "you lead your forces," "shatter kings," "shatter heads." If they could adopt and transform this brief psalm, emphasizing some of its elements and ignoring others, then could Jesus not have adopted and transformed Davidic messianism, emphasizing some of its elements and ignoring others?

Meier, however, faces yet another objection: the Jesus tradition has its protagonist saying next to nothing about the messianic Son of David. Direct statements appear only in Mark 9:41 ("whoever gives you a cup of water to drink because you bear the name of Christ will by no means lose the reward"); Matt 23:10 ("have one instructor, the Messiah"); Luke 24:26, 46 (the risen Jesus speaks of himself as "the Christ"); John 4:25–26 ("The woman said to him, 'I know that Messiah is coming. . . .' Jesus said to her, 'I who speak to you am he,'" RSV); 17:3 ("this is eternal life, that they may know you, the only true God, and Jesus Christ whom you have sent"). All these verses are, by common consent, late and secondary.[273]

One might counter by appealing to Mark 12:35–37, holding that here Jesus assumes his own messianic status: "While Jesus was teaching in the temple, he said, 'How can the scribes say that the Messiah is the son of David?'" Yet the import of this text is notoriously obscure.[274] It has always left me nonplussed.

Equally frustrating, at least for our immediate purposes, is Mark's story of Jesus' entry into Jerusalem, where crowds hail the coming of David's kingdom

---

"Phinehas—the Same Is Elijah: The Origins of a Rabbinic Tradition," *JJS* 29 (1978): 22–34, and Öhler, *Elia*, 24–27.

273. Perhaps one should include here also the prophecy of "false messiahs" in Mark 13:21–22; Matt 24:23–24, for the implication is that the speaker is the true Messiah.

274. Joel Marcus can hold that the passage distances Jesus from Davidic expectation; see "Identity and Ambiguity in Markan Christology," in *Seeking the Identity of Jesus: A Pilgrimage* (ed. Beverly Roberts Gaventa and Richard B. Hays; Grand Rapids: Eerdmans, 2008), 136–40. Compare this remark by Doron Mendels: "According to this tradition Jesus divorced himself publicly from David, who was viewed as a political and nationalistic king" ("Jesus and the Politics of His Day," in *Identity, Religion and Historiography: Studies in Hellenistic History* [JSPSup 24; Sheffield Academic Press, 1998], 447).

and where Zech 9:9 may be in the background (cf. Matt 21:4–5; John 12:15). Since it is nearly impossible to determine what details are theological and literary expansion, it is perilous to conjecture exactly what Jesus had in mind.[275] The same doubt hangs over Matthew's version of events at Caesarea Philippi, which might at first glance seem to be of help. For although the evangelist has Jesus respond to Peter's confession ("You are the Messiah, the Son of the living God") with a beatitude ("Blessed are you, Simon son of Jonah!") (16:13–20), in Mark's parallel, which most scholars suppose more primitive, the response is equivocal: "He sternly ordered them not to tell anyone about him" (8:30).[276]

More promising is the scene before the Sanhedrin, because Otto Betz was right: the subtext is 2 Sam 7:12–16, Nathan's oracle about David's son.[277] When the high priest, reacting to the charge that Jesus will destroy the present temple and raise up a new one, inquires if he thinks himself to be Messiah and Son of God, the reason must lie in Nathan's oracle, which prophesies that a Davidic descendant will be God's "son" and will build the temple (2 Sam 7:12–16). In addition, Jesus responds with "I am" (ἐγώ εἰμι).

Even here, however, there are problems, aside from the knotty issue of historicity.[278] The words ἐγώ εἰμι are the majority reading; Θ *f*[13] 565 700 2542ˢ *pc* Or have, instead, εἶπας ὅτι ἐγώ εἰμι, "you say that I am." Although the latter might be assimilation to the Matthean and Lukan parallels (σὺ εἶπας and ὑμεῖς λέγετε ὅτι ἐγώ εἰμι, Matt 26:64 and Luke 22:70, respectively), the minor agreement against Mark is readily explained by positing, as the Markan original, εἶπας ὅτι ἐγώ εἰμι.[279]

Looking over the previous pages, I find it very hard to know what to think. The data are not harmonious. If, however, Jesus did read himself into Isa 61:1–3, where the prophet says, "The LORD has anointed me," it would have been natural for others to think of him as "anointed," as a "messiah."

275. But see Chester, "Messianism," 312–13; Le Donne, *Historiographical Jesus: Memory, Typology and the Son of David*, 191–220; they defend the basic historicity of the story and the implication that Jesus presented himself as a royal Davidide, or at least that witnesses to the event thought in such terms.

276. In Davies and Allison, *Matthew*, 2:605–15, I maintained that Matthew might preserve the original conclusion. I ended the discussion, however, with this: "The judicious course is to be undogmatic. Mt 16.17–19 *may* preserve the original conclusion to the incident at Caesarea Philippi, and the text *may* give us an important glimpse into the life of Jesus." My goal was not to establish the integrity and antiquity of Matthew's text but to counter the dogmatism of so many who assume that the issue is closed. The point remains valid: I am unsure what to think.

277. Otto Betz, *What Do We Know about Jesus?* (Philadelphia: Westminster, 1968), 83–93.

278. All I need to say here is this: attempts to confirm the essential historicity of the dialogue between Jesus and the high priest are no more persuasive than attempts to establish a purely fictional origin.

279. The longer reading is preferred by Joel Marcus, *Mark 8–16* (AB 27A; New Haven: Yale University Press, 2009), 1005–6.

Furthermore, the less central that one supposes the title "(the) Messiah" to have been among Jews in general—much recent scholarship has tended to downplay its significance—the less obvious it is why the early Christians alighted on that particular designation, all the more if Jesus drew no attention to it.[280] This is, for me, a weighty consideration, especially in view of what I have maintained throughout this chapter, that Jesus thought of himself as a king, destined to take center stage in God's eschatological drama. So maybe he encouraged or at least did not counter belief in his status as a royal Davidide.[281]

Still, if that is the right inference, the evidence remains frustratingly meager. The Gospel of Matthew itself may indirectly attest to this circumstance. It has Jesus, in response to Peter's confession of his messiahship, categorize the apostle's declaration as a revelation of God: "Flesh and blood has not revealed this to you, but my Father in heaven" (16:17). The words seemingly assume that the apostle is not just repeating what he has learned from anyone else, including Jesus, who before Matt 16 has been wholly mum about "the Messiah."[282]

I am left with questions. Was Jesus like the author of the Similitudes of *1 Enoch*, for whom eschatological subjects were central but the expectation of a Davidic Messiah seemingly marginal?[283] Or did Jesus deliberately, for practical reasons, distance himself from messianic expectations, perhaps because he wanted, at least for a time, to avoid controversy or arrest?[284] Or was his motivation, as one who taught love of enemies and perhaps deliberately rode into Jerusalem on a donkey instead of a warhorse, more ideological? Was he uneasy with some of the violence of his tradition? Or was he perhaps uncer-

---

280. Chester comments, "If Jesus made no messianic claim, or at least if no claim was made about Jesus or on his behalf during his lifetime, it would be very difficult to account for the prominence of this title in the rest of the New Testament; this is above all the case since it is used without any special pleading, but with a simple assumption that it does and should apply to Jesus" ("Messianism," 311).

281. This would also be consistent with his having thought himself to be like Moses, for at some point in time some Jews came to identify the Messiah with the prophet like Moses; see *Tanḥ.* 'Eqeb 7b; *Exod. Rab.* 1:26; *Ruth Rab.* 5:6; *Eccl. Rab.* 1:28; *Pesiq. Rab.* 15:10; Tg. Cant 4:4; 7:4; Tg. Lam 2:22. The equation already seems at hand in John 1:43–51; 6:14–15; Acts 3:17–26; see Allison, *New Moses*, 85–90.

282. See J. C. O'Neill, *The Point of It All: Essays on Jesus Christ* (TSS 1; Leiden: Deo Publications, 2000), 78.

283. On *1 En.* 36–71, see Davila, "Methodology," 10. "Messiah" appears only in 48:10; 52:4.

284. Cf. John 6:15: "When Jesus realized that they were about to come and take him by force to make him king, he withdrew again to the mountain by himself." This view was a staple in the older literature; see, for example, Oscar Holtzmann, *The Life of Jesus* (trans. J. T. Bealby and M. A. Canney; London: Adam & Charles Black, 1904), 399–401. Perhaps Paul's restraint in using βασιλεύς of God or Jesus similarly reflects political caution; see Chester, "Messianic Expectations," 66.

tain, less than fully persuaded in his own mind about his own role?[285] Or did his convictions change over time?[286]

Or, to add one more possibility, did he think himself not yet the Messiah but destined to be such in the future?[287] Jewish kings were not born but made. They ascended the throne only when they received anointing.[288] During his

---

285. Even authoritative religious teachers might entertain doubts about this or that, or change their mind about this or that; see Stephen J. Patterson, "An Unanswered Question," *JSHJ* (forthcoming). Perhaps Jesus was to some degree undecided about his relationship to certain traditional messianic ideas. Frederick Houk Borsch (*The Son of Man in Myth and History* [NTL; Philadelphia: Westminster, 1967], 355–60) suggested that Jesus experienced "uncertainty both with regard to this role and his own person," not knowing, for instance, whether he would become the heavenly Son of Man. Sabbatai Sevi sometimes suffered from "hard misgivings" (so Yehuda Liebes, *Studies in Jewish Myth and Jewish Messianism* [trans. Batya Stein; Albany: State University of New York Press, 1993], 99); he was for some time plagued by indecision about his messianic role. It was Nathan of Gaza who dissolved his doubts; see Gershom Scholem, *The Messianic Idea in Judaism and Other Essays on Jewish Spirituality* (New York: Schocken Books, 1971), 60.

286. Henri Desroch makes two relevant generalizations about messianic figures: (1) the claim to be such is "most often progressive: one is first of all a messenger, a representative, a prophet of the god, and the consciousness of the mission only changes gradually into the consciousness of messiahship"; (ii) "the collective consciousness . . . precedes and catalyses the claim of the individual consciousness to messiahship. The individual is at first a claimed messiah before being a claiming messiah. In the end the messianic claim is shared, the collective attribution being individually confirmed by the person" (*The Sociology of Hope* [London: Routledge & Kegan Paul, 1979], 88–89). One recalls the view held by David Friedrich Strauss (*The Life of Jesus Critically Examined* [trans. George Eliot; ed. Peter C. Hodgson; Philadelphia: Fortress, 1972], 281–88): Jesus originally thought of the Messiah/Son of Man as another; only gradually did he come to believe he might be that figure.

287. So Ragnar Leivestad, *Jesus in His Own Perspective: An Examination of His Sayings, Actions, and Eschatological Titles* (Minneapolis: Augsburg, 1987), 99. This thesis, in one form or another, was once quite common; note, for example, Gustaf Dalman, *The Words of Jesus Considered in the Light of Post-biblical Jewish Writings and the Aramaic Language* (Edinburgh: T & T Clark, 1902), 315–16; Maurice Goguel, *The Life of Jesus* (trans. Olive Wyon; New York: Macmillan, 1933), 366. Compare this observation of Schweitzer: "Jesus did not permit the conviction that he was destined to be the coming Messiah to play a part in his message. . . . He holds out the prospect of the immediate coming of the Son of Man but always speaks of him in the third person so that none of his listeners could get the thought that he himself expected to be clad with this honor. Until the last day he remained for the people the prophet from Nazareth. . . . One is aware that the High Priest is not able to summon a single witness at the trial to testify to the Messianic claims of Jesus. Only the disciples know something of his secret" (*Psychiatric Study of Jesus*, 51). Since William Wrede's *Das Messiasgeheimnis in den Evangelien*, first published in 1901, this way of sorting the data has often been dismissed out of hand. Wrede famously urged that Mark's "messianic secret" reflects the post-Easter awareness that Jesus' ministry was not messianic (see p. 291).

288. "The idiom מָשַׁח לְמֶלֶךְ, 'to anoint as king,' indicates that the anointing was the performative action" marking royal accession (Brettler, *God Is King*, 129). He further writes, "In some complexes or coronation rituals the anointing is the main or only ritual (1 Sam. 16:13; 2 Sam. 2:4; 2 Kgs 23:30), suggesting that it was (one of) the main performative rite(s) of the coronation" (p. 133). In the judgment of Tryggve N. D. Mettinger, "the anointing of the king was the

lifetime, Jesus of Nazareth, it is obvious, never sat on a throne; and even if a historical episode lies behind the anointing story in Mark 14:3–9, where an unnamed woman pours ointment on his head, it can hardly have served to make him a sovereign.[289] Jesus was no king. At best, he could have hoped to become such.[290]

I would, if forced, place my bet on this last option, Jesus as *messias designatus*: he saw kingship as a hope or a destiny, not an accomplishment. This hypothesis elucidates three intriguing texts:

- Acts 2:36: "Let the entire house of Israel know with certainty that God has made him both Lord and Messiah, this Jesus whom you crucified."

- Acts 13:32–33: "We bring you the good news that what God promised to our ancestors he has fulfilled for us, their children, by raising Jesus; as also it is written in the second psalm, 'You are my Son; today I have begotten you.'"

---

essential element of the royal ritual" (*King and Messiah: The Civil and Sacral Legitimation of the Israelite Kings* [ConBOT 8; Lund: Gleerup, 1976], 185).

289. However one interprets the story within the context of Mark or Matthew, and whatever one makes of the parallels in Luke 7:36–50; John 12:1–8, the story, in and of itself, fails to remark on the possible messianic meaning of the woman's act of anointing. See further Kathleen E. Corley, "The Anointing of Jesus in the Synoptic Tradition: An Argument for Authenticity," *JSHJ* 1 (2003): 61–72.

290. There is another related issue. Given the collective messianism in some ancient Jewish texts, to what extent did Jesus identify with his followers and to what extent did he differentiate himself as their leader? For a whole people or collectivity reigning, see the targumim on Exod 19:6 (which replace "kingdom" with "kings"); Dan 7:27 ("The kingship and dominion and the greatness of the kingdoms under the whole heaven shall be given to the people of the holy ones of the Most High; their kingdom shall be an everlasting kingdom, and all dominions shall serve and obey them"); *Sib. Or.* 2:288–90 ("There is a certain royal tribe whose race will never stumble. This too . . . will reign, as it will begin to raise up a new temple of God"); 4Q521 ("he will honor the saints upon the throne of eternal kingship"); *T. Levi* 13:9 ("whoever teaches good things and does them will be enthroned with kings"); 2 Tim 2:12 ("we will also reign with him"); Rev 3:21 ("to the one who conquers I will give a place with me on my throne"); 20:4 ("reigned with Christ a thousand years"); 22:5 ("they will reign forever and ever"); Pol. *Phil.* 5:2 ("we will also reign with him"). Important recent discussions of collective messianism in Judaism and/or the Jesus tradition include Suzanne Watts Henderson, "Jesus' Messianic Self-Consciousness Revisited: Christology and Community in Context," *JSHJ* 7 (2009): 168–97; Thomas Kazen, "The Coming Son of Man Revisited," *JSHJ* 5 (2007): 157–76; idem, "Son of Man and Early Christian Identity Formation," in *Identity Formation in the New Testament* (ed. Bengt Holmberg and Mikael Winninge; WUNT 227; Tübingen: Mohr Siebeck, 2008), 97–122; idem, "Son of Man as Kingdom Imagery: Jesus between Corporate Symbol and Individual Redeemer Figure," in *Jesus from Judaism to Christianity: Continuum Approaches to the Historical Jesus* (ed. Tom Holmén; London: T & T Clark, 2007), 87–108; Adrian M. Leske, "Context and Meaning of Zechariah 9:9," *CBQ* 62 (2000): 663–78; Hanna Roose, *Eschatologische Mitherrschaft: Entwicklungslinien einer urchristlichen Erwartung* (NTOA/SUNT 54; Göttingen: Vandenhoeck & Ruprecht; Fribourg: Academic Press, 2004); Steudel, "Eternal Reign," 507–25.

- Rom 1:3–4: ". . . the gospel concerning his Son, who was descended from David according to the flesh and was declared to be Son of God with power according to the spirit of holiness by resurrection from the dead."

William Wrede famously found in these passages awareness on the part of early Christians that Jesus received his messianic status only at the resurrection, from which fact Wrede inferred that Jesus had no messianic awareness.[291] The conclusion, however, is not obligatory. Is it not more likely, given what we have learned throughout this chapter, that Jesus thought of himself as a king in waiting, and that his followers, after his departure, declared that he was waiting no longer: he had come into his kingdom?[292]

Although our uncertainty on the subject frustrates, we should perhaps not be so surprised at the outcome. As observed in the previous chapter, charismatic leaders are often deliberately enigmatic. Being inscrutable, failing to meet expectations, and keeping others guessing are effective ways of gaining and retaining people's attention, ways of producing fascination. As illustration, it appears nearly certain that Rabbi Menachem Schneerson, the late leader of the Lubavitchers, believed that he was the Messiah. He assured his followers that their generation was the generation of Messiah, that Messiah had already been revealed, and that Messiah's first name was "Menachem." And yet he remained equivocal:

> The Rebbe refrained from any open, explicit proclamation of his own messianic identity . . . and continued to encourage leadership roles for people who were known to oppose the messianists. A long-time aide has reported that the Rebbe once told him, "The man who is the Messiah has to have this revealed to him from above, and at present this has not been revealed to me." Though in his last years the Rebbe tolerated and even appears to have encouraged the singing of the formula declaring his messiahship—"May our Master, Teacher, and Rabbi the King Messiah live forever"—he also remarked that he should really leave the room when the slogan was sung and remained only because leaving would do no good. In the 80's he expressed strong criticisms of people who published messianist material, and he made a similar remark as late as 1991. On one occasion,

291. William Wrede, *The Messianic Secret* (trans. J. C. G. Greig; LTT; Cambridge: James Clarke, 1971), 216–30; cf. more recently Becker, *Jesus of Nazareth*, 197. Wrede later changed his mind, however; see H. Rollmann and W. Zager, "Unveröffentlichte Briefe William Wredes zur Problematisierung des messianischen Selbstbewußtseins Jesu," *ZNTh/JHMT* 8 (2001): 274–322. For a different view of the passages cited, see Marinus de Jonge, "Jesus, Son of David and Son of God," in *Intertextuality in Biblical Writings: Essays in Honour of Bas van Iersel* (ed. Sipke Draisma; Kampen: J. H. Kok, 1989), 102–3; Hengel, "Messiah of Israel," 11–12. For a helpful review of the discussion, see C. Kavin Rowe, "Acts 2:36 and the Continuity of Lukan Christology," *NTS* 53 (2007): 37–56.

292. Cf. Luke 23:42–43. This might help explain why traditions about Jesus' status as Son of David are so often linked to his resurrection; see Duling, "Promises to David."

he is reported to have responded to a petition addressed to him in his capacity as the messiah by saying, "When he comes I will give it to him."[293]

The Rebbe's enigmatic conduct is not anomalous but rather typical. It illustrates the general circumstance that, although some Jewish messiahs "may call themselves messiahs," on the whole "they prefer to have others call them that."[294] This brings to mind Mark 8:27–30, where Jesus' response to Peter's confession of his messianic status is summed up in the words "And he sternly ordered them not to tell anyone about him" (v. 30). Even if, as so many often presume, v. 30 is editorial, one might speculate that Mark's pericope nonetheless remembers Jesus' strategy of neither denying nor affirming messianic claims made on his behalf,[295] or of keeping his eschatological identity mostly to himself. We might even wonder whether Jesus was familiar with a tradition that the Messiah will be hidden,[296] to be revealed only by God.[297] Could he have thought something akin to what Justin attributed to Trypho, that the Messiah, "if he has indeed been born and exists anywhere, is unrecognized and does not even know himself, nor does he have any power, until Elijah comes and anoints him and reveals him to all"?[298] This would have been consistent with

293. David Berger, "The Rebbe, the Jews, and the Messiah," *Commentary* 112, no. 2 (2001): 26. See further Simon Dien, "When Prophecy Fails: Messianism amongst Lubavitcher Hasids," in *The Coming Deliverer: Millennial Themes in World Religions* (ed. Fiona Bowie and Christopher Deacy; Cardiff: University of Wales Press, 1997), 238–60; Joel Marcus, "The Once and Future Messiah in Early Christianity and Chabad," *NTS* 47 (2001): 392–94. Marcus cautiously suggests a parallel with the messianic secret in the Gospels.

294. So Lenowitz, *Jewish Messiahs*, 20.

295. The famous attempt by Eric Dinkler ("Peter's Confession and the 'Satan' Saying: The Problem of Jesus' Messiahship," in *The Future of Our Religious Past: Essays in Honor of Rudolf Bultmann* [ed. James M. Robinson; New York: Harper & Row, 1971], 169–203) to establish that Jesus responded to Peter's confession (Mark 8:29) with a rebuke (Mark 8:33) (cf. Theissen and Merz, *Historical Jesus*, 539) is less plausible than the conjecture by Rudolf Bultmann (*History of the Synoptic Tradition* [rev. ed.; New York: Harper & Row, 1963], 258–59) that Matt 16:17–19 contains the original response to Peter's confession, although Bultmann thought in terms of a resurrection appearance. See further n. 276.

296. Cf. LXX Isa 32:1–2; *1 En.* 62:7; John 7:27; *4 Ezra* 12:32 (?); Justin, *Dial.* 8.4; Tg. Mic 4:8. For discussion and rabbinic texts, see Sigmund Mowinckel, *He That Cometh: The Messiah Concept in the Old Testament and Later Judaism* (Grand Rapids: Eerdmans, 2005), 304–8. The older work of Erik Sjöberg, *Die Menschensohn im äthiopischen Henochbuch* (Lund: Gleerup, 1946), 102–15, remains informative on this topic.

297. In the Hebrew Bible, kings do not anoint themselves but are anointed by others (e.g., 1 Sam 9:27–10:8; 16:1–13; 2 Kgs 9:1–10), and that the Messiah will be "announced" or "revealed" is a common theme (e.g., LXX Amos 4:13; *4 Ezra* 7:28; 13:32; *2 Bar.* 29:3; 39:7; Tg. Zech 3:8; 4:7; 6:12). In Ps 2:7, God, using what is probably an adoption formula, declares to the king, "Today I have begotten you" (cf. 1Q28a 2:11–14). Here the heavenly king appoints the earthly king.

298. Justin, *Dial.* 8.4. Cf. Ps 110:1 and see J. C. O'Neill, *Who Did Jesus Think He Was?* (BIS 11; Leiden: Brill, 1995), 42–54. According to Gerd Theissen, Jesus may have shared the belief that "only God can grant the status of a Messiah, and only through him can he be made known" ("Vom historischen Jesus zum kerygmatischen Gottessohn," *EvT* 68 [2008]: 298).

Jesus' conviction that the kingdom of God would come not through human effort, but entirely through God's miraculous intervention[299]—a conviction at home in Jewish messianism, which has often regarded the redemption as worked by "God and God alone, independently of human behaviour or religious achievements."[300]

Son of Man?

At this juncture an objection presents itself. My list illustrating christocentric eschatology (pp. 227–30) contains sayings in which Jesus speaks of "the Son of Man" in the third person, and one can ask, Might it not be, as Bultmann and others have surmised, that these sayings originally adverted to someone besides Jesus?[301] And if so, does this not mean that he gave someone else star billing?

In response, I wish to make six points, which together seem to me to nullify this possible protest.[302]

1. The large number of logia that feature the expression ὁ υἱὸς τοῦ ἀνθρώπου, so odd in Greek, as well as its appearance across the sources—Mark, Q, M, L, John, *Thomas*[303]—more than incline me to assume that an Aramaic equivalent (presumably [א]שׁנ[א]־בר) goes back to Jesus.[304] In

299. See further E. P. Sanders, "Jesus: His Religious Type," *Reflections* 87 (1992): 4–12. That the Jesus tradition nowhere describes how the transition from this age to the next will come about but instead presents it as a brute fact strongly hints that it is no human achievement. One might compare here the messianic reticence of Rabbi Schneerson, who, being critical of Zionism, taught that only God could end the exile and bring the redemption; see Aviezer Ravitzky, *Messianism, Zionism, and Jewish Religious Radicalism* (CSHR; Chicago: University of Chicago Press, 1996), 10–39.

300. Joseph Dan, "Scholem's View of Jewish Messianism," *Modern Judaism* 12 (1992): 123.

301. Bultmann, *Theology*, 1:29; idem, *Synoptic Tradition*, 122; cf. Becker, *Jesus of Nazareth*, 200; Adela Yarbro Collins, "The Origins of the Designation of Jesus as 'Son of Man,'" *HTR* 80 (1987): 391–408; Barnabas Lindars, *Jesus Son of Man: A Fresh Examination of the Son of Man Sayings in the Gospels in the Light of Recent Research* (London: SPCK, 1983); H. E. Tödt, *The Son of Man in the Synoptic Tradition* (NTL; London: SCM Press, 1965); and many others.

302. As the books and articles on this subject are now as the sands of the sea, I can offer only a few absurdly brief remarks. For the history of the discussion, see Delbert Burkett, *The Son of Man Debate: A History and Evaluation* (SNTSMS 107; Cambridge: Cambridge University Press, 1999); Mogens Müller, *The Expression "Son of Man" and the Development of Christology: A History of Interpretation* (London: Equinox, 2008).

303. Mark: 2:10, 28; 8:31, 38; 9:9, 12, 31; 10:33, 45; 13:26; 14:21 (*bis*), 41, 62
Q: 6:22; 7:34; 9:58; 11:30; 12:8, 10, 40; 17:24, 26
Unique to Matthew: 10:23; 13:37, 41; 16:13, 27, 28; 19:28; 24:30, 39; 25:31; 26:2
Unique to Luke: 17:22, 24, 30; 18:8; 19:10; 21:36; 22:48; 24:7
John: 1:51; 3:13, 14; 5:27; 6:27, 53, 62; 8:28; 9:35; 12:23, 34 (*bis*); 13:31
Gospel of Thomas: 86

304. Paul also probably knew Son-of-Man sayings; see Birger A. Pearson, "A Q Community in Galilee?" *NTS* 50 (2004): 484–86; George W. E. Nickelsburg, "Son of Man," *ABD* 6:147.

addition, given my understanding of his eschatology, I have no difficulty believing that he used the phrase of an eschatological figure. I reject the hypothesis that he always employed "the son of man" as a mundane idiom, to refer to his present circumstances, and that it was only later Christians who, with an eye on Dan 7, bestowed eschatological content on (א)נש(א)־בר and ὁ υἱὸς τοῦ ἀνθρώπου.[305] I am rather persuaded that Jesus probably used the Aramaic idiom, at least on occasion, to refer to Daniel's vision of the final judgment.[306]

2. In the sources as we have them, Jesus is the Son of Man, and this must also have been true for Q as Matthew and Luke knew it.[307] Even if, then, Jesus did have in view another yet to come, some tradents found it appropriate to suppose that he spoke of himself instead. This in itself would be significant: his memory was such that equating Jesus with a heavenly redeemer made sense to some.

Compare the situation with the *Didache*: although the final redactor was acquainted with logia about the Son of Man, he never used the title; see Frederick Houk Borsch, *The Christian and Gnostic Son of Man* (SBT 14; London: SCM Press, 1970), 38–42.

305. This thesis is fairly old; see, for example, James Martineau, *The Seat of Authority in Religion* (4th ed.; London: Longmans, Green, 1898), 581; Nathaniel Schmidt, *The Prophet of Nazareth* (New York: Macmillan, 1905), 94–134. Schmidt claimed to be "the first to suggest that Jesus never used this term [the Son of Man] concerning himself, either to claim Messiahship in any sense, or to hint that he was a 'mere man,' or 'the true man,' but in some pregnant utterances used it in reference to 'man' in general" (p. vii). But Johann Adrian Bolten, *Der Bericht des Matthäus von Jesu dem Messia* (Leipzig: Altona, 1792; online: www.archive.org/stream/MN40365ucmf_2#page/n0/mode/1up [cited 18 November 2009]), had already forwarded the same judgment. More recent advocates include Maurice Casey, *The Solution to the "Son of Man" Problem* (LNTS 343; London: T & T Clark, 2007); Kreplin, *Selbstverständnis Jesu*, 102–97; Ulrich B. Müller, "Jesus als 'der Menschensohn,'" in *Gottessohn und Menschensohn: Exegetische Studien zu zwei Paradigmen biblischer Intertextualität* (ed. Dieter Sänger; BTSt 67; Neukirchen-Vluyn: Neukirchener Verlag, 2004), 91–129. Despite intensive research on the question, I remain uncertain about the precise status of (א)נש(א)־בר in first-century Galilean Aramaic and wonder about the view that the emphatic expression was an idiom for self-reference; see Paul Owen and David Shepherd, "Speaking Up for Qumran, Dalman and the Son of Man: Was *Bar Enasha* a Common Term for 'Man' in the Time of Jesus?" *JSNT* 81 (2001): 81–122.

306. Here I find myself agreeing with Christopher Tuckett, "The Son of Man and Daniel 7: Q and Jesus," in *The Sayings Source Q and the Historical Jesus* (ed. A. Lindemann; BETL 158; Leuven: Leuven University Press, 2001), 371–94; idem, "The Son of Man and Daniel 7: Inclusive Aspects of Early Christologies," in *Christian Origins: Worship, Belief and Society; The Milltown Institute and the Irish Biblical Association Millennium Conference* (ed. Kieran J. O'Mahony; JSNTSup 241; Sheffield: Sheffield Academic Press, 2003), 164–90. Even in John, the Danielic background of the sayings about the Son of Man is obvious; see Benjamin E. Reynolds, *The Apocalyptic Son of Man in the Gospel of John* (WUNT 2/249; Tübingen: Mohr Siebeck, 2008).

307. This is self-evident in the Synoptics, which contain sayings about Jesus the Son of Man in the present. The same holds for Q, as Matt 11:19 // Luke 7:34 ("the Son of Man has come eating and drinking") and Matt 8:20 // Luke 9:58 ("the Son of Man has nowhere to lay his head") attest. In other words, if Jesus is ὁ υἱὸς τοῦ ἀνθρώπου in Q 7:34; 9:58, this is sufficient cause to make that identification elsewhere in Q, at least for any stage that included those two sayings.

3. Whether Jesus envisaged himself or another coming as "the Son of Man" is a contested issue because the repeated use of the third person is so striking. It is, however, far from determinative. Autobiographical statements need not be, for any number of reasons, in the first person.[308] Paul opens his reminiscence in 2 Cor 12:1–4 with "I know a person in Christ,"[309] and Solomon declares in *T. Sol.* 3:5, "Blessed are you, O Lord God almighty, who gave to your servant Solomon the wisdom that attends to your thrones and who subjected to me all the power of the demons."[310]

Often in biblical texts, "self-reference by title is used where the speaker's public aspect, which is thus presented, is significant in the situation, while his personal aspect, which is thus obscured, is not."[311] Did Jesus then perhaps employ "the Son of Man" as a sort of title, in allusions to Dan 7:13–14?

Consider a parallel. Mark's Jesus says, in 13:32, that the angels do not know the time of the end, and neither does "the Son." The unqualified "the Son" (ὁ υἱός), although in itself a mundane Greek expression, is, for Mark, a title. It shows up again in Q, in the saying about the Father knowing "the Son" (e.g., Matt 11:25–27 // Luke 10:21–22; cf. John 3:17, 35–36; 5:19–27). To my knowledge, no one has ever suggested that the logia about "the Son," whoever first composed them, ever envisioned anybody besides Jesus, despite use of the third person. The same is true of Mark 9:41; Matt 23:10; John 17:3, in which Jesus speaks of "the Messiah," as also of the following sentences, in which generic third-person nouns carry autobiographical sense:

308. Müller ("Menschensohn," 107) offers that in Luke 12:8–9 (Q), the move from first person to third person ("everyone who acknowledges me before others, the Son of Man also will acknowledge") is a function of synonymous Semitic parallelism: one repeats the same thought with different words.

309. That Paul was not speaking of himself here is a distinctly minority opinion; but see Michael D. Goulder, "Visions and Revelations of the Lord (2 Corinthians 12:1–10)," in *Paul and the Corinthians: Studies on a Community in Conflict; Essays in Honour of Margaret Thrall* (ed. Trevor J. Burke and J. Keith Elliott; NovTSup 109; Leiden: Brill, 2003), 303–12.

310. Additional examples include Gen 4:23–24; 18:3; 19:2, 19; 47:3; 1 Sam 17:32; 20:8, 13; 22:15; 25:8, 22; 27:5; 29:8; 2 Sam 3:9; 7:19–29; 19:12, 20; 20:6; 24:23; 1 Kgs 1:33; 2:45; 2 Kgs 10:18; 1QH^a 4:11, 21–24; 6:8–12; 8:16–26; 19:27–33; 4Q264 1–4; Luke 1:48; 2:29–30; *T. Levi* e 2:17. See discussion in E. J. Revell, *The Designation of the Individual: Expression Usage in Biblical Narrative* (CBET 14; Kampen: Kok Pharos, 1996), 350–55. Extrabiblical examples of the autobiographical third person are also common, especially for the sake of humility; see, for example, Palladius, *Historica Lausiaca* 71 (TS 6, 2:167–68), along with the comments of Martin Hinterberger, "Autobiography and Hagiography in Byzantium," *SO* 75 (2000): 154–55; idem, *Autobiographische Traditionen in Byzanz* (WBS 22; Vienna: Verlag des Österreichischen Akademie der Wissenschaften, 1999), 164–65. Hinterberger supplies additional examples from Sophronius, Leontius, and Symeon the New Theologian. Rudolf Otto (*The Kingdom of God and the Son of Man* [trans. Floyd V. Filson and Bertram Lee Woolf; rev. ed.; London: Lutterworth, 1943], 232) observed how often, in Buddhist sources, Siddhārtha Gautama uses the third person to speak of himself.

311. Revell, *Designation of the Individual*, 352.

- Matt 10:24–25: "A disciple is not above the teacher."
- Mark 6:4: "Prophets are not without honor."
- Luke 13:33: "I must be on my way, because it is impossible for a prophet to be killed outside of Jerusalem."[312]

One can, then, if so inclined, sensibly hold that Jesus was a bit like the Lubavitcher Rebbe, who almost certainly thought himself to be the Messiah and yet consistently spoke of that figure in the third person.[313]

4. Even if, and despite the observations just made, Jesus did have in view someone other than himself, that need not remove him from center stage. The eschatological spotlight could be on more than one individual at a time, as 1QS 9:9–11 ("the prophet and the anointed ones of Aaron and Israel") and 4Q175 (citing Deut 18:18–20; Num 24:15–17; Deut 33:8–11) attest. These texts anticipate two messiahs as well as a prophet like Moses.[314]

5. Jesus' words about the coming of the Son of Man were, one might conjecture, deliberately open-ended because their realization had to be left to the Deity. Riding clouds and assembling the quick and the dead for judgment are beyond human ability.[315] If Jesus were ever to do such things, divine intervention would have to make them possible.[316]

6. A final point of potential relevance: some ancient texts attest to the idea of celestial doubles or heavenly alter egos.[317] In Manichaean sources, Mani has

312. According to Michael Cahill, "It is surely significant that Jesus is never presented as talking about himself in the third person in any other way"—that is, except with reference to the Son of Man ("Did Jesus Refer to Himself in the Third Person? A Contribution to the Son of Man Debate," *PIBA* 25 [2002]: 63). Cahill has overlooked the texts I have cited.

313. For an instance, see William Shaffir, "Interpreting Adversity: Dynamics of a Commitment in a Messianic Redemption Campaign," *JJSoc* 36 (1994): 44; see also above, p. 291.

314. On pairs of eschatological redeemers, see Rimon Kasher, "On the Portrayal of Messiahs in Light of an Unknown Targum to Lam 4:21–22," *JSQ* 7 (2000): 22–41.

315. Notwithstanding contemporary exegetes who view cloud-riding as a metaphor, many ancients understood the idea literally; see *1 En.* 14:8; Acts 1:9; Rev 11:12; 14:14; *T. Ab.* RecShrt 10:2; *Ep. Apost.* 51; Ps.-Chrysostom, *Leg.* (PG 56:407); *Acts Andr. Mth.* 21; *Transitus Mariae* B 17; *Adam, Eve, and the Incarnation* 48 v.l.; Ps.-Bartholomew, *Book of the Resurrection of Jesus Christ* fol. 20b; Serapion, *A New Life of John the Baptist* (trans. A. Mingana [Manchester: University of Manchester Press, 1927], 447); *Syr. Apoc. Dan.* 30; *b. Sanh.* 98a; *b. Yoma* 4a (Moses ascending to heaven on a cloud, as also in *Pesiq. Rab.* 20:4); and the liturgical and iconographic tradition that the apostles were miraculously brought on clouds to gather for the Dormition of Mary; see John of Thessalonica, *Dormition of the Blessed Virgin Mary* A 7–8 (PO 19.3:386, 388–89); *Transitus Mariae* (StSin 11:49).

316. Theissen states, "God alone can define and bestow the role of the future Son of man" ("Vom historischen Jesus zum kerygmatischen Gottessohn," 301).

317. For the possibility of this idea in *Jubilees*, Ezekiel the Tragedian, *2 Enoch*, and the *Ladder of Jacob*, see Andrei A. Orlov, *The Enoch-Metatron Tradition* (TSAJ 107; Tübingen: Mohr Siebeck, 2005), 165–76; idem, "The Face as the Heavenly Counterpart of the Visionary in the Slavonic *Ladder of Jacob*," in *From Apocalypticism to Merkabah Mysticism: Studies in the Slavonic Pseudepigrapha* (JSJSup 114; Leiden: Brill, 2007), 399–419; idem, "God's Face

a twin who brings him revelation. This twin in the upper world, his "mirror image" (*CMC* 17:15–16), is the Paraclete, but then so is Mani.[318] As Mani says

in the Enochic Tradition," in *Paradise Now: Essays on Early Jewish and Christian Mysticism* (ed. April D. DeConick; SBLSymS 11; Atlanta: Scholars Press, 2006), 179–93; idem, "In the Mirror of the Divine Face: The Enochic Features of the *Exagoge* of Ezekiel the Tragedian," in *The Significance of Sinai: Traditions about Sinai and Divine Revelation in Judaism and Christianity* (ed. George J. Brooke, Hindy Najman, and Loren T. Stuckenbruck; TBN 12; Leiden: Brill, 2008), 183–99; idem, "Moses' Heavenly Counterpart in the Book of Jubilees and the *Exagoge* of Ezekiel the Tragedian," *Bib* 88 (2007): 326–50. For the Shepherd of Hermas, see Peter Dronke, "Arbor Caritatis," in *Medieval Studies for J. A. W. Bennett: Aetatis Suae LXX* (ed. P. L. Heyworth; Oxford: Clarendon, 1981), 221–22. The Zoroastrian idea of the Fravashi, the heavenly component and transcendent double of the human being, seems to be related; so Wilhelm Bousset and Hugo Gressmann, *Die Religion des Judentums im späthellenistischen Zeitalter* (3rd ed.; HNT 21; Tübingen: Mohr Siebeck, 1926), 324; James Hope Moulton, "'It Is His Angel,'" *JTS* 3 (1902): 514–27. Compare the personification of the *daēnā* or conscience (another component of the self in Zoroastrianism) as a beautiful woman who greets and then unites with the righteous after death, as well as the Egyptian notion of the *ka*, the external soul that Egyptian sources often refer to as a "spiritual twin"; see Ursula Schweitzer, *Das Wesen des Ka im Diesseits und Jenseits der alten Ägypter* (Glückstadt: J. J. Augustin, 1956). It may also be relevant that in Greco-Roman mythology, one twin alone can be a heavenly being. Castor, son of Tyndareus, and Pollux, son of Zeus, were star twins. Likewise, Heracles, son of Zeus, was the twin of Iphicles, son of Amphitryon (at least in some sources). On the whole topic, see the fascinating work of J. Rendell Harris, *The Cult of the Heavenly Twins* (Cambridge: Cambridge University Press, 1906); idem, *The Dioscuri in the Christian Legends* (London: C. J. Clay & Sons, 1903). Whatever the history-of-religions background, real human experience surely contributed to the idea, for although rare, the phenomenon of autoscopy, or seeing one's look-alike (*Doppelgänger*), is well attested; see Olaf Blanke and Christine Mohr, "Out-of-Body Experience, Heautoscopy, and Autoscopic Hallucination of Neurological Origin: Implications for Neurocognitive Mechanisms of Corporeal Awareness and Self Consciousness," *Brain Research Reviews* 50 (2005): 184–99. Both Goethe and the poet Shelley had this experience, and Aristotle already reported on it; so Graham Reed, *The Psychology of Anomalous Experience: A Cognitive Approach* (rev. ed.; Buffalo, NY: Prometheus Books, 1988), 52–55. As a curiosity, I note that the idea of a heavenly double has not become extinct; it lives on in some modern quarters. For example, Kenneth Ring proposes that "the individual personality is but a split-off fragment of the total self with which it is reunited at the point of death. During ordinary life, the individual personality functions in a seemingly autonomous way, as though it were a separate entity. In fact, however, it is invisibly tied to the larger self structure of which it is a part" (*Life at Death: A Scientific Investigation of the Near-Death Experience* [New York: Coward, McCann & Geoghegan, 1980], 240).

318. See Michel Tardieu, *Manichaeism* (Urbana: University of Illinois Press, 2008), 9–10, 20, citing *CMC* 17–20; *Keph.* 1; Ibn al-Nadim, *Fihrist*. Note also *CMC* 23:5 ("my inseparable twin"); 32:8; 69:15; 72:21; *Keph.* 7 36:6–7. For discussion, see Franzmann, "Jesus in the Manichaean Writings"; A. Heinrichs and L. Koenen, "Ein griechischer Mani-Codex (P. Colon. Inv. Nr. 4780; vgl. Tafeln IV–VI)," *ZPE* 5 (1970): 161–90; Ludwig Koenen, "Augustine and Manichaeism in Light of the Cologne Mani Codex," *Illinois Classical Studies* 3 (1978): 167–74; Ort, *Mani*, 77–95; Gilles Quispel, "Das ewige Ebenbild des Menschen zur Begegnung mit dem Selbst in der Gnosis," in *Gnostic Studies 1* (Istanbul: Nederlands Historisch-Archaeologisch Instituut, 1974), 140–57; Sundermann, "Paraklet." According to Koenen, "When Mani, i.e., the Νοῦς of Mani, was sent into the world, a mirror image of the Νοῦς, i.e., his *alter ego*, remained in heaven. The one ego, the Νοῦς, was imprisoned in the body and, consequently, forgot his mission. Then the

in *CMC* 24:12–15, "I am that one from whom I was separated. . . . I myself am that one who is unshakable."[319] In Acts 12:12–15, Peter, miraculously freed from prison, is mistaken for "his angel": Peter "went to the house of Mary, the mother of John whose other name was Mark, where many had gathered and were praying. When he knocked at the outer gate, a maid named Rhoda came to answer. On recognizing Peter's voice, she was so overjoyed that, instead of opening the gate, she ran in and announced that Peter was standing at the gate. They said to her, 'You are out of your mind!' But she insisted that it was so. They said, 'It is his angel.'" Although not all exegetes agree, the reasoning of the skeptics seems to be this: if Peter is in jail yet someone at the gate resembles him, it must be his guardian angel, who is his twin.[320]

In some gnostic circles, Judas was evidently the human alter ego of the astral king of demons, Ialdabaoth, who resides in the thirteenth level above earth.[321] And among Valentinians, to judge from a fragment of Heracleon, the

---

Twin, the *alter ego*, was sent to him from heaven. He brought Mani the revelation by reminding him of his divine nature and mission and, like an angel, protected him. The Νοῦς of Mani and his Twin are the two complementary aspects of Mani's identity. The first represents him as incorporated in the body; the second represents his being as it is outside the body. Together they are the one complete Mani" ("Augustine and Manichaeism," 173).

319. For Manichaean texts that speak of the heavenly counterparts of the elect in general, see Carsten Colpe, "Daēnā, Lichtjungfrau, Zweite Gestalt: Verbindungen und Unterschiede zwischen zarathustrischer und manichäischer Selbst-Anschauung," in *Studies in Gnosticism and Hellenistic Religions Presented to Gilles Quispel on the Occasion of His 65th Birthday* (ed. R. van den Broek and M. J. Vermaseren; EPRO 91; Leiden: Brill, 1981), 56–77.

320. Matthew Poole comments, "They did probably mean some angel that had assumed Peter's shape, and imitated his voice; and the Jews having had a constant opinion, that at least every good man hath a guardian angel which God appoints to him for a means of his preservation, might be apt to imagine that this was that angel whose charge St. Peter was" (*Annotations on the Holy Bible* [3 vols.; London: Henry G. Bohn, 1846], 3:424). This is the dominant interpretation in exegetical history; cf. Origen, *Princ.* 1.8.1; Bede, *Comm. Acts* ad loc. (CCSL 121:59); also Moulton, "Angel"; Otto, *Kingdom of God*, 181. For guardian angels, which in so many ways remind one of the personal gods of Mesopotamia, see, for example, Gen 48:16; Ps 34:7; 91:11–12; Dan 11:1 (?); 1QHᵃ 5:20; *1 En.* 100:5; *Jub.* 35:16–17; Tobit (passim); *T. Levi* 5:3; *T. Jos.* 6:7; Philo, *Giants* 12; *QG* 1.23; *T. Job* 43:10; *L.A.B.* 11:12; 15:5; 33:1; 59:4; Matt 18:10; Heb 1:14; *3 Bar.* 12–13; *T. Adam* 4:1; *T. Jac.* 2:5; *Apoc. Paul* 7–10; *b. Taʿan.* 11a; *Midr. Ps.* 55:3; *Pirqe R. El.* 15; Tg. Ps.-J. on Gen 48:16. These personal angels are akin to the heavenly patrons of the nations, as in LXX Deut 32:8; Dan 10:13, 20–21; Sir 17:17; *1 En.* 20:5; and it may be that "the angels of the seven churches" in Rev 2–3 are the guardian angels of those churches and/or their heavenly or spiritual counterparts; see David E. Aune, *Revelation 1–5* (WBC 52A; Nashville: Thomas Nelson, 1997), 109–11. That guardian angels look like their charges is implicit not only in Acts 12; *Gen. Rab.* 78:3, but also Tg. Ps.-J. on Gen 33:10. Note also *Testament of Our Lord* 40 (ed. J. Cooper and A. J. Maclean [Edinburgh: T & T Clark, 1902], 96): "Before the foundation of the world there stands the image or type of every soul." On the whole subject of guardian angels, see Darrell D. Hannah, "Guardian Angels and Angelic National Patrons in Second Temple Judaism and Early Christianity," in *Angels: The Concept of Celestial Beings—Origins, Development and Reception* (ed. Friedrich V. Reiterer, Tobias Nicklas, and Karin Schöpflin; DCLY; Berlin: de Gruyter, 2007), 413–35.

321. See April D. DeConick, *The Thirteenth Apostle: What the Gospel of Judas Really Says* (New York/London: Continuum: 2007), 109–24. DeConick has more recently announced the

elect individual has an angelic σύζυγος or partner in the Pleroma, with whom he or she will eventually be united.[322]

In *Joseph and Aseneth*, the archangel Michael seems to be the "angelic double"[323] of the patriarch Joseph. Each character is in charge of his master's kingdom (4:7; 14:8; 15:12; 21:21). Each bears the title ἄρχων (1:3; 4:7; 14:8; 15:12; 20:9; 21:21). Each appears as a great heavenly light (6:2; 14:2). Each rides a chariot and initially arrives from the east (5:4; 6:1; 17:7). Each, when he appears, causes Aseneth to tremble with fear (6:1; 14:11). Above all, the two look alike: "And Aseneth raised her head and looked, and behold, a man [Michael the archangel] in every respect like Joseph [κατὰ πάντα ὅμοιος τῷ Ἰωσήφ], with stole and crown and the royal staff [cf. 5:5], except that his face was like lightning and his eyes as light from the sun and the hairs of his head like a flame of fire from a burning torch and hands and feet like iron shining forth from a fire" (14:8–9).

In the *Prayer of Joseph*, frg. A, the patriarch Jacob utters these arresting words: "I, Jacob, who speak with you, am also Israel, an angel of God and a ruling spirit. Abraham and Isaac were created before any work. But I, Jacob, whom men call Jacob but whose name is Israel, am he whom God called Israel which means, a man seeing God, because I am the firstborn of every living thing to whom God gives life."[324] Although this obscure fragment probably equates Jacob with the angel Israel, who has come to earth and somehow forgotten his true identity, it must be related to the well-known tradition that the features of the patriarch Jacob/Israel have a heavenly correlative on or near God's throne.[325] It seems likely enough, reading between the lines, and as James Kugel has suggested, that some Jews held the earthly Jacob to have a heavenly counterpart. Such a belief could have arisen from the Hebrew of Gen 32:29 (שרית עם־אלהים), taken to mean, "you [Jacob] have been exalted with God," and/or from the popular etymology of Israel's name, "the man who sees God" (ישראל being supposed to derive from איש ראה אל).[326] Since Jacob was on earth, not in heaven, he was neither exalted in that place nor privileged with the constant vision of God; so it must have

discovery of an antique gem (from perhaps the second century) that has a lion-headed god on one side, a god sometimes identified with Ialdabaoth, and the name "Judas" is on the other side.

322. See Origen, *Comm. Jo.* 13.11(67).

323. So Ross Shepard Kraemer, *When Aseneth Met Joseph: A Late Antique Tale of the Biblical Patriarch and His Egyptian Wife, Reconsidered* (New York: Oxford University Press, 1998), 164.

324. Preserved in Origen, *Comm. Jo.* 2.31. For discussion, see Jonathan Z. Smith, "The Prayer of Joseph," in *Religions in Antiquity: Essays in Memory of Erwin Randsell Goodenough* (ed. Jacob Neusner; SHR 14; Leiden: Brill, 1968), 253–94.

325. See Tg. Ps.-J. on Gen 28:13–17; Tg. Onq. on Gen 28:13–16; *Gen. Rab.* 68:12; *Pirqe R. El.* 35. For a related refrain in later Jewish thought, "the patriarchs themselves are the Merkabah," see, for example, *Gen. Rab.* 47:6; 69:3; 82:6.

326. Cf. Philo, *Flight* 208; *Dreams* 1.171; *Pr. Jos.* 3; Origen, *Princ.* 4.3.12.

seemed incumbent to posit a supercelestial twin. Surmising such an idea helps account for the unnamed Nag Hammadi text that turns the figure in Exod 4:22 ("Israel is my firstborn son") into a heavenly being,[327] as well as *Pirqe R. El.* 37, which recounts that the angel who wrestled with Jacob gave him his own name, for he too was called "Israel"[328]—a legend known already to Justin.[329]

A related idea probably appears in the Similitudes of *1 Enoch*, at least as we now have them. Throughout this text, Enoch sees and writes about the Son of Man in the third person. In (the probably secondary) chapter 71, however, we learn (although this is subject to dispute) that the seer and heavenly Son of Man are somehow one and the same: "you are the son of man who was born to righteousness" (v. 14).[330]

Is it possible, then, that some of Jesus' words about the Son of Man were about his heavenly twin or counterpart, with whom he was one or would become one?[331] I leave the question open,[332] recognizing its speculative nature, yet adding that an affirmative response would be consistent with several facts:

327. See *Die Koptisch-gnostische Schrift ohne Titel aus Codex II von Nag Hammadi* (ed. Alexander Böhlig and Pahor Labib; Berlin: Akademie-Verlag, 1962), 52, 54 (153 lines 20–25).

328. For traditions about the angel "Israel," see Smith, "Prayer of Joseph," 262–65.

329. According to Justin (*Dial.* 125.3), Jesus bore the name "Israel," with which he christened Jacob after wrestling with him.

330. Cf. *3 Enoch*, where Enoch is the enthroned Metatron. The issue is complex and involves both text-critical and literary-critical judgments. Relevant literature includes Christfried Böttrich, "Konturen des 'Menschensohnes' in äthHen 37–71," in *Gottessohn und Menschensohn* (ed. Sänger), 53–90; John J. Collins, "Enoch and the Son of Man: A Response to Sabino Chialà and Helge Kvanvig," in *Enoch and the Messiah Son of Man: Revisiting the Book of Parables* (ed. Gabriele Boccaccini; Grand Rapids: Eerdmans, 2007), 216–27; Michael A. Knibb, "Messianism in the Pseudepigrapha in the Light of the Scrolls," *DSD* 2 (1995): 170–80; Helge S. Kvanvig, "The Son of Man in the Parables of Enoch," in *Enoch* (ed. Boccaccini), 179–215; Daniel C. Olson, "Enoch and the Son of Man in the Epilogue of the Parables," *JSP* 18 (1998): 27–38; Stefan Schreiber, "Henoch als Menschensohn: Zur problematischen Schlußidentifikation in den Bilderreden des äthiopischen Henochbuches (äthHen 71,14)," *ZNW* 91 (2000): 1–17; James C. VanderKam, "Righteous One, Messiah, Chosen One, and Son of Man in 1 Enoch 37–71," in *Messiah* (ed. Charlesworth), 182–83.

331. Only after asking this question did I learn that Klaus Koch also has asked it; see his article "Questions Regarding the So-Called Son of Man in the Parables of Enoch: A Response to Sabino Chialà and Helge Kvanvig," in *Enoch* (ed. Boccaccini), 237 n. 24. Already David R. Catchpole ("The Angelic Son of Man in Luke 12:8," *NovT* 24 [1982]: 255–65) had suggested, with reference to Matt 18:10, that in Luke 12:8–9, the Son of Man is Jesus' guardian angel. Catchpole did not, however, explore the background of this idea in the wider history of religions. There is perhaps a remote parallel in the thought of Abraham Abulafia, who used the word *Messiah* both of himself and of a transcendent reality; see Moshe Idel, *Messianic Mystics* (New Haven: Yale University Press, 1998), 58–100.

332. Elsewhere I have argued for a collective interpretation (Allison, *Jesus of Nazareth*, 65–66).

a. If Jesus and the heavenly Son of Man were two yet one, this would neatly explain why in some sayings the Son of Man is Jesus on earth, while in others he is a heavenly figure who for now remains in heaven.

b. Whatever the original intention of the author of Dan 7, it is easy enough to construe "the one like a son of man" in 7:14 as an angel, maybe Michael.[333] On this reading, the people of God have a heavenly representative, for their future triumph is his future triumph, as is made plain by a comparison of 7:14 ("To him was given dominion and glory and kingship, that all peoples, nations, and languages should serve him. His dominion is an everlasting dominion that shall not pass away, and his kingship is one that shall never be destroyed") with the strikingly similar 7:27 ("The kingship and dominion and the greatness of the kingdoms under the whole heaven shall be given to the people of the holy ones of the Most High; their kingdom shall be an everlasting kingdom, and all dominions shall serve and obey them").[334] When one further reckons with the Similitudes of *1 Enoch*, which depend upon Daniel's vision of the last judgment[335] and seemingly identify Enoch the seer with the Son of Man, it appears that Dan 7 might very well have prompted hearers to think in terms of correlations between the heavenly and the earthly and indeed of otherworldly representatives or counterparts.

c. The hope that humanity's eschatological destiny will be angelic is well attested,[336] and this also could have encouraged Jesus to imagine his future identification with an angelic savior, which in turn might help explain why Christians often characterized Jesus in angelic terms.[337] (Alternately, Jesus could have drawn the same inference if he thought of

---

333. See John J. Collins, *Daniel: A Commentary on the Book of Daniel* (Hermeneia; Minneapolis: Fortress, 1993), 304–10; Catchpole, "Angelic Son of Man."

334. On the Danielic "one like a son of man" as the heavenly counterpart of the faithful community, see John J. Collins, "The Heavenly Representative: The 'Son of Man' in the Similitudes of Enoch," in *Ideal Figures in Ancient Judaism* (ed. George W. E. Nickelsburg and John J. Collins; SBLSCS 12; Chico, CA: Scholars Press, 1980), 111–33.

335. See Collins, *Daniel*, 79–82.

336. See, for example, Wis 5:5 (assuming that "sons of God" are angels); 1QSb 4:25; 4Q511 frg. 35; *1 En.* 104:1–6; *2 Bar.* 51:5, 10; Acts 6:15; *T. Isaac* 4:43–8. Also relevant are those texts that promise the saints that they will become stars or like stars (e.g., Dan 12:2–3; *1 En.* 104:2–7; 4 Macc 17:5; *2 Bar.* 51:10; *L.A.B.* 33:5; *As. Mos.* 10:9; CIJ 2:43–44, no. 788), for stars typically were thought of as angels; see Dale C. Allison Jr., "The Magi's Angel (Matt. 2:2, 9–10)," in *Studies in Matthew: Interpretation Past and Present* (Grand Rapids: Baker Academic, 2005), 17–41.

337. See details in Joseph Barbel, *Christos Angelos: Die Anschauung von Christus als Bote und Engel in der gelehrten und volkstümlichen Literatur des christlichen Altertums* (Theophania 3; Bonn: Peter Hanstein, 1941); Crispin H. T. Fletcher-Louis, *Luke-Acts: Angels, Christology and Soteriology* (WUNT 2/94; Tübingen: Mohr Siebeck, 1997); Charles A. Gieschen, *Angelmorphic Christology: Antecedents and Early Evidence* (AGJU 42; Leiden: Boston, 1998); Darrell D. Hannah, *Michael and Christ: Michael Traditions and Angel Christology in Early Christianity* (WUNT 2/109; Tübingen: Mohr Siebeck, 1999).

himself as the Davidic Messiah, because both *1 En*. 37–71 and *4 Ezra*
identify Daniel's "one like a son of man" with the Messiah,[338] as may
also 4Q246.[339] We have here an old exegetical tradition, which the New
Testament [e.g., Matt 16:13–20; Mark 14:61–62] and the rabbis [e.g.,
b. Sanh. 98a; *Num. Rab*. 13:14] also attest.)[340]

d. Bultmann observed that, had Jesus imagined himself coming on clouds
of heaven as the Son of Man, he would "have had to count upon being
removed from the earth and raised to heaven before the final End . . .
in order to come from there on the clouds of heaven to perform his real
office." Bultmann then asked, "But how would he have conceived his
removal from the earth? As a miraculous translation?" He answered,
"Among his sayings there is no trace of any such fantastic idea."[341] The
problem, however, would dissolve if Jesus had been speaking of his
heavenly counterpart.

e. Although I cannot see that they anywhere relate themselves to traditions
about the Son of Man, some ancient texts do indeed teach that Jesus
had a twin.[342] Could this curious idea descend ultimately from belief

338. See John J. Collins, "The Danielic Son of Man," in *Scepter*, 173–94; note also *Sib. Or.*
5:414 (the "blessed man [a militant eschatological ruler and savior] came from the expanses of
heaven" may allude to Dan 7:13–14); Justin, *Dial.* 32 (Trypho refers Dan 7:13–14 to the Messiah); *b. Ḥag.* 14a (Akiba spoke of two thrones in heaven, one for God, one for the Messiah [cf.
the plural in Dan 7:9]). For the argument that the Old Greek already presupposes a messianic
interpretation, see Benjamin E. Reynolds, "The 'One Like a Son of Man' according to the Old
Greek of Daniel 7,13–14," *Bib* 89 (2008): 70–80.

339. See John J. Collins, "The Messiah as the Son of God," in *Scepter*, 154–72; Johannes
Zimmermann, "Observations on 4Q246—The 'Son of God,'" in *Qumran-Messianism: Studies
on the Messianic Expectations in the Dead Sea Scrolls* (ed. James H. Charlesworth, Hermann
Lichtenberger, and Gerbern S. Oegema; Tübingen: Mohr Siebeck, 1998), 185–88. For an examination of all the evidence bearing on when Jews began to see the Messiah in Daniel's vision
of "one like a son of man," see William Horbury, "The Messianic Associations of 'The Son
of Man,'" in *Messianism among Jews and Christians: Twelve Biblical and Historical Studies*
(London: T & T Clark, 2003), 125–55.

340. On the correlations between Davidic traditions and Dan 7, see Wolfgang Bittner, "Gott—
Menschensohn—Davidssohn: Eine Untersuchung zur Traditionsgeschichte von Daniel 7,13f.,"
FZPhTh 32 (1985): 343–72.

341. Bultmann, *Theology*, 1:29.

342. For example, *Acts Thom*. 1, 11, 31, 34–35, 39, 45, 57, 147–53; *Thom. Cont*. 138. Some
readers of the New Testament identified the Judas of Mark 6:3 (one of Jesus' brothers) with
the Thomas of John 11:16 ("Thomas, who was called the Twin": Θωμᾶς [Aramaic תאומא] ὁ
λεγόμενος Δίδυμος [cf. 20:24; 21:2]); see, for example, *Gos. Thom*. 1; John 14:22 sy[s(c)]; Eusebius,
Hist. eccl. 1.13.11; *The Doctrine of Addai, the Apostle* (ed. G. Philips; London: Trübner, 1876),
p. ד. See discussion in Lloyd R. Bailey, "The Cult of Twins at Edessa," *JAOS* 88 (1968): 342–44;
Marco Frenschkowski, "The Enigma of the Three Words of Jesus in Gospel of Thomas Logion
13," *Journal of Higher Criticism* 1 (1994): 73–84; John J. Gunther, "The Meaning and Origin of
the Name 'Judas Thomas,'" *Mus* 93 (1980): 113–48; Harris, *Cult*, 105–25; idem, *Dioscuri*, 20–41;
Martina Janssen, "'Evangelium des Zwillings?' Das *Thomasevangelium* als Thomas-Schrift," in
Das Thomasevangelium: Entstehung, Rezeption, Theologie (ed. Jörg Frey, Enno Edzard Popkes,

in his heavenly *Doppelgänger*? Oddly enough, Jesus himself seems to become a heavenly twin in some Manichaean sources.[343]

So, then, did Jesus think of the Son of Man as his celestial twin, his heavenly alter ego or true self? I do not pretend to know. The previous pages, which contain much speculation, do not move from possibility to probability. They do, however, suffice to show that if Jesus did use the third person to speak of the future coming of the Son of Man, that is no good reason to reject the main thesis of this chapter, which is that he was the center of his own eschatological scenario.

Final Remarks

Barnabas Lindars wrote,

> The apocalyptic notion of the agent of the divine intervention is the foundation of New Testament Christology. . . . The most primitive Christology can thus be formulated as follows: Jesus is the man whom God has designated to perform the judgement and to usher in the everlasting kingdom of God's righteousness; as such he has been exalted to the throne at the right hand of God and declared to be the Messiah; he will soon be revealed, wickedness will be extirpated, and the righteous . . . will enter the joy of the kingdom.[344]

The main thesis of the present chapter offers an explanation for both the great age of this Christology and its prevalence in our sources: Jesus himself already promoted a version of it, so it was there from the beginning.

Jesus did not envisage a "brokerless kingdom."[345] Nor did he proclaim a "kingless kingdom."[346] Rather, when he looked into the future, he saw thrones, including one for himself.[347] What caused him to hold such a conviction is not subject to analysis. We can know only the fact, not the why.

---

and Jens Schröter; BZNW 157; Berlin: de Gruyter, 2008), 222–48. The earthly Jesus also has a heavenly look-alike in *Pist. Soph.* 21; here the twin descends to earth, takes the young Jesus in his arms and kisses him, and the two become one.

343. For example, *Psalms of the Bema* (C. R. C. Allberry, ed., *A Manichaean Psalm-Book* [Stuttgart: W. Kohlhammer, 1938], 2:42, lines 22–23); Ψαλμοὶ Σαρακωτῶν (ibid., 1:166, lines 33–34). For discussion, see Majella Franzmann, *Jesus in the Manichaean Writings* (London: Continuum, 2003), 21–23.

344. Lindars, "Apocalyptic Son of Man," 61–62.

345. The phrase is from Crossan, *Historical Jesus*, 225.

346. Against Richard A. Horsley and Neil Asher Silberman, *The Message and the Kingdom: How Jesus and Paul Ignited a Revolution and Transformed the Ancient World* (New York: Grossett/Putnam, 1997), 73.

347. This is also the conclusion reached by Lindars: "Jesus did think of himself as destined to perform the functions of God's agent" ("Apocalyptic Son of Man," 65). Cf. Paul A. Rainbow,

For my major conclusion, I claim exactly what Thucydides did for his history: "We have used only the plainest evidence and reached conclusions which are reasonably accurate, considering that we have been dealing with ancient history" (*Hist.* 1.20). I have not, I concede, constructed a proof, because my arguments will not convince those firmly persuaded already to the contrary. But I do contend that I have made a compelling argument, because it should persuade those not antecedently committed to its falsehood.

No follower of Jesus, to our knowledge, ever called Paul divine or reckoned him a god.[348] Christians did, however, say astounding things about Jesus, and that from the very beginning. The differing evaluations, I submit, had something to do with who those two people actually were.[349] We should hold a funeral for the view that Jesus entertained no exalted thoughts about himself.[350]

"Jewish Monotheism as a Matrix for New Testament Christology: A Review Article," *NovT* 33 (1991): 78–91.

348. The appraisals in Acts 14:12 ("Paul they called Hermes"); 28:6 ("they . . . began to say that he was a god") do not come from informed Christians.

349. According to John J. Collins, "there is good evidence that the Davidic messiah was regarded as divine in a qualified sense (which certainly did not imply equality with the Almighty) not only in the Dead Sea Scrolls but also in Jewish tradition more generally" ("Powers in Heaven: God, Gods, and Angels in the Dead Sea Scrolls," in *Religion in the Dead Sea Scrolls* [ed. John J. Collins and Robert A. Kugler; Grand Rapids: Eerdmans, 2000], 22). Since this is true of additional mediating figures, one can all the more easily see how a very high Christology could take root early on in Christian history.

350. A remaining issue is to what extent Jesus may have presented himself one way to outsiders, another way to insiders. Unfortunately, we cannot know because, in the wake of form criticism, we cannot confidently identify the audience with whom Jesus may originally have shared this or that statement. One suspects, however, that he was much more reticent in public than in private. Such a circumstance would clarify some of the texts conventionally lumped together under the rubric "the messianic secret," and for what it is worth, most of the texts listed on pp. 227–30 do, in the Gospels as they stand, in fact address insiders. I doubt that the proclaimer became the proclaimed in his own public proclamation, but I am sure that Jesus' followers heard more. As a parallel, I recall that the Bab, the central figure of the Baha'i faith, was often equivocal about his true office, and he instructed his disciples not to reveal all of his claims to outsiders. This not only kept the general populace wondering about him and anticipating the future but also served a political purpose: had he openly declared himself to be the Mahdi, he would have risked arrest and execution. See Sepehr Manuchehri, "The Practice of Taqiyyah (Dissimulation) in the Babi and Baha'i Religions," *Research Notes in Shaykhi, Babi and Baha'i Studies* 3, no. 3 (September 1999), online: www.h-net.org/~bahai/notes/vol3/taqiya. htm (cited 18 November 2009); Nader Saiedi, *Gate of the Heart: Understanding the Writings of the Báb* (Waterloo, ON: Wilfrid Laurier University Press, 2008), esp. 83–110. The history of the Unification Church may supply yet another parallel: Sun Myung Moon's messianic identity was a truth only for insiders until a public announcement in July of 1992; see Sarah M. Lewis, "The Lord of the Second Advent—the Deliverer Is Here!" in *The Coming Deliverer: Millennial Themes in World Religions* (ed. Fiona Bowie and Christopher Deacy; Cardiff: University of Wales Press, 1997), 202–23.

4

More Than an Aphorist

The Discourses of Jesus

Aphorisms and parables do not lend themselves to long
speeches. By definition the sage is a person of few words.
Accordingly, Jesus probably did not collect his sayings into
extended discourses such as we find in the Sermon on the
Mount (Matthew 5–7) or in the Gospel of John.

—Robert W. Funk

It is hardly to be supposed that Jesus went round peppering
his auditors with pellets of disconnected apophthegms.

—John A. T. Robinson

Jesus of Nazareth was an aphorist, a rhetorically gifted teacher adept at
constructing brief parables and delivering memorable one-liners. After his
departure, however, his followers remembered his pithy formulations by combining them into collections, much as the book of Proverbs gathers wisdom
sayings that were originally independent. Isolated logia gained interpretive
company, so that the one came to circulate with the many. To give an example:
surely Matt 11:2–19 // Luke 7:18–35 (Q) is an anthology of varied traditions
brought together, perhaps gradually, because of their common topic, which
is John the Baptist.

That the discourses attributed to Jesus are secondary constructions is no
recent discovery. John Calvin already perceived the true character of Matt
5–7, the Sermon on the Mount, and of Matt 10, the speech on mission: the

305

First Evangelist, for thematic reasons, gathered into his discourses words that before him were scattered, words of diverse origins.[1]

Modern historical criticism has reinforced and extended Calvin's inference from common sense, which has now become a commonplace. The successes of source criticism, form criticism, and redaction criticism have together revealed that tradents and editors typically annexed saying to saying to fashion the discourses as we now have them. Many would add that the *Gospel of Thomas*, which strings together largely unrelated sayings, shows us that, in the beginning, the tradition consisted not of unified speeches but of solitary logia.

The conviction that Jesus was an aphorist is so much a part of our consciousness, and the secondary character of the Synoptic speeches so taken for granted, that many of us may no longer even wonder whether Jesus ever said more than one thing at a time, or whether his hearers could remember more than one thing at a time. Likewise, and for the same reasons, we may never seriously entertain the possibility that a Synoptic discourse might partly reflect a speech that Jesus himself spoke.

Maybe, however, we should contemplate these possibilities. For the canonical Gospels remember Jesus as uttering connected discourses. In fact, they portray him doing this on multiple occasions. Mark has Jesus utter two extended speeches:

- Mark 4:1–34, parables and commentary
- Mark 13:1–37, eschatological prophecies

Matthew, who enlarges both of these Markan chapters (see Matt 13:1–52; 24:1–25:46), adds several more connected discourses:

- Matt 5:1–7:28, the Sermon on the Mount
- Matt 10:1–42, the missionary discourse
- Matt 11:7–19, commentary on John the Baptist
- Matt 18:1–35, guidance for ecclesiastical relations
- Matt 23:1–39, polemic against Jewish leaders

Luke preserves parallels to all but one of the speeches in Mark and Matthew (he has only scattered parallels to Matt 18:1–35):

- Luke 6:17–49, the Sermon on the Plain (cf. Matt 5:1–7:28)
- Luke 7:24–35, commentary on John the Baptist (cf. Matt 11:7–19)

1. John Calvin, *A Harmony of the Gospels Matthew, Mark and Luke* (3 vols.; Grand Rapids: Eerdmans, 1972), 1:168, 297. Compare Juan Maldonatus's view that the discourses of Jesus "neither report all that he said, nor quote him in the order in which he spoke" (*Commentarii in Quatuor Evangelistas* [ed. J. M. Raich; 2 vols.; London: Moguntiae, 1853–1854], 1:59).

- Luke 8:4–18, parables and commentary (cf. Mark 4:1–34; Matt 13:10–52)
- Luke 10:1–16, the missionary discourse (cf. Matt 10:1–42)
- Luke 11:37–54, polemic against Jewish leaders (cf. Matt 23:1–39)
- Luke 21:5–38, eschatological prophecies (cf. Mark 13:1–37; Matt 24:1–25:46)

Luke further contains three speeches found neither in Mark nor Matthew:

- Luke 15:3–32, parables about the lost (cf. Matt 18:12–14)
- Luke 16:1–31, instruction on mammon (cf. Matt 5:18, 31–32; 6:24; 11:12–13)
- Luke 17:22–37, warnings about the latter days (cf. Matt 25:26–28, 37–41)

Beyond the testimony of the Synoptics, the Gospel of John also presents Jesus as composing thematically related discourses, three of the longer instances being the following:

- John 5:19–47, the Father and the authority of Jesus
- John 14:1–16:33, the farewell discourse at the final supper
- John 17:1–26, the high-priestly prayer

Moreover, for those of us who accept the Q hypothesis, that source appears to have had several coherent speeches:

- Q 6:17–49 (cf. Matt 5:1–7:28), the Sermon on the Plain[2]
- Q 10:1–16 (cf. Matt 10:1–42), the missionary discourse
- Q 7:24–35 (cf. Matt 11:7–19), commentary on John the Baptist
- Q 11:37–54 (cf. Matt 23:1–39), polemic against Jewish leaders
- Q 17:22–37 (cf. Matt 25:26–28, 37–41), the day of the Son of Man

In addition to the discourses in Q and the canonical Gospels, the authors of the latter have it that, on several occasions, Jesus taught in a synagogue, which implies that he composed short homilies.[3] There are also the various editorial commentaries that envisage him addressing crowds in the open; and

2. Throughout this chapter I adopt the convention of referring to a Q text by its Lukan numbering. Thus Q 6:17–49 signifies the Q material found in Luke 6:17–49.
3. Matt 4:23; 9:35; 13:54; Mark 1:21, 39; 6:2; Luke 4:15–16, 44; 6:6; 13:10; John 6:59; 18:20. For other references to teaching in synagogues, see Acts 13:14–15; Philo, *Hypothetica* (*apud* Eusebius, *Praep. ev.* 8.7.12–13); *Spec. Laws* 2.62; *Good Person* 81–82; *Dreams* 2.123–28.

surely readers are left with the impression that people did not come together only to be accosted by a cryptic sentence or two, followed by Jesus' immediate departure. Must we not rather think that he was a little less enigmatic than that and so went on for at least a little while? As John A. T. Robinson once put it, "It is hardly to be supposed that Jesus went round peppering his auditors with pellets of disconnected apophthegms."[4]

What, then, should we make of the fact that Matthew, Mark, Luke, and John depict Jesus delivering not just one-liners but also speeches? Is this entirely an artifact of the oral tradition and the literary work of the evangelists? Or do we have here a pattern in the sources that retains memory? If Plato's dialogues, despite their largely fictional character, accurately remember the circumstance that Socrates' preferred method of instruction was the dialectic of question and answer, do the Synoptics and John rightly recall that Jesus sometimes spoke for more than a minute or two and so strung together more than a sentence or two? And if they do rightly remember on this score, might any Synoptic discourse give us some sense for an oral composition of Jesus? Or were all of his discourses wholly dissolved as the fluid oral tradition carried memories away from their source?

I am not so bold as to return robustly confident answers to these questions. Over the years I have, in general, found the form critics persuasive.[5] Time and again, it has seemed to me, as to so many others, that the speeches are, in truth, secondary elaborations, artificial composites made up of what were once much smaller pieces.

Nonetheless, I have not been fully persuaded of this in every single instance. If Jesus was more than an aphorist, then maybe we should expect to have more than just aphorisms, more than just isolated fragments of his speech. As it turns out, I have come to believe that at least one Synoptic speech does indeed enshrine the remnants of a discourse from Jesus himself. In other words, it—or at least its central portion—cannot be convincingly disintegrated; it rather preserves a group of sayings that were joined from the beginning.

Rudolf Bultmann wrote the following:

> In the written collections the principles on which larger units are formed are at first no different from what they were in the oral tradition, i.e., it is simply a quite primitive process of adding one small unit to another, and in this similarity of content or some outward likeness (the use of some catchword) is the guiding

---

4. John A. T. Robinson, *The Priority of John* (ed. J. F. Coakley; London: SCM Press, 1985), 304. Robinson urges that Jesus "engaged in connected conversation and sustained argument, like Paul after him."

5. Note, however, that Martin Dibelius, one of the most famous and influential of form critics, appears to have thought that Matt 5:21–37 (the sayings about murder, divorce, and oaths) and 6:2–6, 16–18 (on almsgiving, prayer, and fasting) preserve "interconnected utterances" of Jesus; see his *Jesus* (Philadelphia: Westminster, 1949), 26.

principle, though now and then pure chance takes a hand. In some such manner as this we can account for comparatively extensive "speeches" i.e., collections of particular units, and in such collections some sort of conceptual development in the "speech" could give some sort of guidance. But we cannot in this way account for organic composition, speeches that are a real unity, dominated by a specific theme and systematically arranged, unless the peculiar character of the ancient traditional material has been completely altered. Happily that did not take place in the Synoptic Gospels. Where it has to a certain extent taken place, as in the Fourth Gospel, it is no longer simply a question of a development of the older tradition, but something quite new comes to light as well.[6]

Although Bultmann did not, to judge from these words, deny that Synoptic speeches could exhibit "some sort of conceptual development," he thought that only in John do we find "organic composition," or speeches that have "real unity" and are dominated by a "specific theme." I should now like to argue that this view of things, which is for the most part accurate, may not hold up for all the Synoptic speeches. There appears to be an exception, a longer unit that preserves logia that kept close company with each other from the beginning.

The Sermon on the Plain

Apart from the woes (Luke 6:24–26) and two short proverbs (Luke 6:39–40), all of the units in Luke's Sermon on the Plain (Luke 6:20–49) have parallels in the Sermon on the Mount (Matt 5–7). Further, all of the shared materials, with the sole exception of the golden rule, are in nearly identical order:

Luke 6:20a	cf. Matt 5:1–2
Luke 6:20b–23	cf. Matt 5:3–12
Luke 6:24–26	——
Luke 6:27–36	cf. Matt 5:38–48; 7:12
Luke 6:37–38	cf. Matt 7:1
Luke 6:39	(cf. Matt 15:14)
Luke 6:40	(cf. Matt 10:24–25)
Luke 6:41–42	cf. Matt 7:3–5
Luke 6:43–45	cf. Matt 7:16–18
Luke 6:46	cf. Matt 7:21
Luke 6:47–49	cf. Matt 7:24–27
Luke 7:1	cf. Matt 7:28–8:1

6. Rudolf Bultmann, *History of the Synoptic Tradition* (rev. ed.; New York: Harper & Row, 1963), 322.

On the thesis that Matthew did not know Luke and that Luke did not know Matthew, these ordered parallels require that Matt 5–7 and Luke 6 go back to the same pre-Synoptic discourse.[7] Many modern scholars have assigned that discourse to the so-called Q source, a lost collection of sayings attributed to Jesus. I belong to their company.

As to the shape of that discourse, we have sound reasons, even if we do not accept the Q hypothesis, for believing that Luke's shorter Sermon on the Plain, not Matthew's Sermon on the Mount, is, on the whole, closer to what lies behind both. This is largely because Matt 5–7 exhibits so many redactional features that are absent from Luke 6:

- The triad is the structural key to the Sermon on the Mount, and Luke 6 contains none of Matthew's triads.[8]
- Much of the obviously redactional vocabulary in Matt 5–7 is missing from Luke 6, including βασιλεία τῶν οὐρανῶν (5:3, 10, 19, 20; 7:21); δικαιοσύνη (5:6, 10, 20; 6:1, 33); διώκω (5:10, 11, 12, 44); πατὴρ ὁ ἐν (τοῖς) οὐρανοῖς (5:16, 45; 6:1, 9; 7:11); ἀποδίδωμι (5:26, 33; 6:4, 6, 18); and πατήρ + οὐράνιος (5:48; 6:14, 26, 32).
- The Beatitudes in Matt 5:7, 8, 9 are, unlike the surrounding makarisms, conventional, not paradoxical, which suggests that they are secondary additions, and they have no parallel in Luke 6.
- The present placement of Matt 5:17–20—it is the editorial introduction to the following supertheses—as well as much of its language is Matthew's own work. Luke has only a partial parallel, and it occurs outside the Sermon on the Plain, in 16:17: "But it is easier for heaven and earth to pass away, than for one stroke of a letter in the law to be dropped."
- Two or more instances of the formula of contrast, "You have heard that it was said, . . . but I say to you" (5:21, 27, 31, 33, 38, 43), are widely reckoned to be Matthean,[9] and the corresponding Lukan material lacks the phrase (Luke 6:27 being an imperfect parallel).
- Matt 6:1–18 appears to preserve a onetime independent piece whose present location is due to Matthean redaction.[10] Luke's only parallel is

7. For a detailed argument, see Dale C. Allison Jr., "The Sermon on the Plain, Q 6:20–49: Its Plan and Its Sources," in *The Jesus Tradition in Q* (Valley Forge, PA: Trinity Press International, 1997), 67–79.

8. See Dale C. Allison Jr., "The Configuration of the Sermon on the Mount and Its Meaning," in *Studies in Matthew: Interpretation Past and Present* (Grand Rapids: Baker Academic, 2005), 172–215.

9. Ulrich Luz (*Matthew: A Commentary* [3 vols.; Hermeneia; Minneapolis: Fortress, 2007], 1:227–28) regards at least three of them as redactional.

10. See Hans Dieter Betz, "A Jewish-Christian Cultic *Didache* in Matt. 6:1–18: Reflections and Questions on the Problem of the Historical Jesus," in *Essays on the Sermon on the Mount* (Philadelphia: Fortress, 1985), 55–69.

his version of the Lord's Prayer, which appears outside the Sermon on the Plain, in 11:2–4.

In short, the more we subtract from the Sermon on the Mount the elements that we have excellent reason to assign to Matthew, the closer we come to the Sermon on the Plain.[11]

The International Q Project (IQP), which assigned itself the task of reconstructing, insofar as possible, the contents of the Sayings Source, determined that Q's inaugural discourse contained these materials:

- Q 6:20–23, a collection of beatitudes
- Q 6:27–28, 35c–d, "Love your enemies"
- Q 6:29–30, renunciation of rights
- Q 6:31, the golden rule
- Q 6:32, 34, impartial love
- Q 6:36, the merciful imitation of God
- Q 6:37–38, not judging
- Q 6:39, blind leading the blind
- Q 6:40, disciple and teacher
- Q 6:41–42, speck and beam
- Q 6:43–45, the tree known by its fruit
- Q 6:46, not just saying, "Master, Master"
- Q 6:47–49, the two builders[12]

One may query several of the judgments that led to this reconstruction. For instance, that Luke 6:33 ("If you do good to those who do good to you, what credit is that to you? For even sinners do the same") is entirely or even mostly Lukan redaction is not at all clear.[13] Nor do I see sufficient reason to suppose that Luke 6:35 ("But love your enemies, do good, and lend, expecting nothing in return. Your reward will be great") is Luke's expansion rather than a line from his tradition.[14] The same holds for Luke 6:38, or at least its opening injunction ("Give and it will be given to you").[15] Since these matters

11. See further n. 7. For another view, revealed by the title, note *Beyond the Q Impasse—Luke's Use of Matthew: A Demonstration by the Research Team of the International Institute for Gospel Studies* (ed. Allan J. McNicol, with David L. Dungan and David B. Peabody; Valley Forge, PA: Trinity Press International, 1996), 103–7.

12. James M. Robinson, Paul Hoffmann, and John S. Kloppenborg, eds., *The Critical Edition of Q: Synopsis* (Hermeneia; Minneapolis: Fortress; Leuven: Peeters, 2000).

13. See further below, pp. 319–21.

14. For a survey of the differing judgments on this question, see John S. Kloppenborg, *Q Parallels: Synopsis, Critical Notes, and Concordance* (Sonoma, CA: Polebridge, 1988), 30.

15. See further below, n. 51.

do not, however, substantially affect the main contours of my argument, I will pay them scant heed in the following pages. What matters most is that the IQP's reconstruction probably gives us a fair sense of the defunct source that lies beneath Luke 6:20–49 and its Matthean parallels.[16]

What might we conjecture about the prehistory of that discourse? To use Bultmann's words, it does not appear to be, in its entirety, an "organic composition." Understandably, scholars have insisted, for instance, that the inaugural blessings (Q 6:20–23) probably once circulated by themselves,[17] that 6:39 (the blind leading the blind [cf. Gos. Thom. 34]) and 6:40 (the disciple being like the master [cf. John 13:16; 15:20]) were secondary insertions,[18] and further that the saying about trees and fruit (6:43–45 [cf. Gos. Thom. 45]) was a wandering logion.[19] I am inclined to agree with each of these judgments.

The heart of the discourse, 6:27–42, is another matter, or so I should now like to argue. Several considerations suggest, notwithstanding the judgment of so many to the contrary, that most of this material circulated together from the start.[20] In other words, the central part of the Sermon on the Plain is not an anthology made up of smaller anthologies, nor was its history as

16. The vexed problem of the possible differences between Matthew's Q and Luke's Q is beyond the scope of this essay.

17. The blessings at the beginning of the discourse (6:20–23), with their allusions to Isa 61, their mention of the "poor," and their implicit Christology, prepare for Jesus' answer to John the Baptist's query about the coming one in Q 7:18–23, which also alludes to Isa 61, refers to the poor, and implicitly addresses Jesus' identity.

18. See Joachim Wanke, *"Bezugs- und Kommentarworte" in den synoptischen Evangelien: Beobachtungen zur Interpretationsgeschichte der Herrenworte in der vorevangelischen Überlieferung* (ETS 44; Leipzig: St. Benno-Verlag, 1981), 21–25. That Matthew moved these verses to other locales (10:24–25; 15:14) may reflect his sense of their intrusive character. Note also the new introduction in Luke 6:39: "He also told them a parable." Whether or not this is Lukan redaction, it marks a formal break in the discourse.

19. See idem, 26–31. The logion does not demand a specific context, as Matthew's ability to insert a variant of it into 12:33–34 shows.

20. The consensus is represented by Bultmann, *Synoptic Tradition*, 96; François Bovon, *Luke 1: A Commentary on the Gospel of Luke 1:1–9:50* (Hermeneia; Minneapolis: Fortress, 2002), 232; Dieter Lührmann, "Liebet eure Feinde (Lk 6,27–36/Mt 5,39–48)," *ZNW* 69 (1972): 412–38. An exception is David Wenham, "The Rock on Which to Build: Some Mainly Pauline Observations about the Sermon on the Mount," in *Built upon the Rock: Studies in the Gospel of Matthew* (ed. Daniel M. Gurtner and John Nolland; Grand Rapids: Eerdmans, 2008), 187–206. Wenham, however, argues that "the Matthean form of the Sermon may well go back to Jesus," whereas I regard Matt 5–7 as a secondary expansion of a discourse more faithfully preserved in Luke 6:27–42. Long before Wenham, David Friedrich Strauss, despite his skepticism about much, held that "a real harangue of Jesus, more than ordinarily solemn and public, was the foundation of the evangelical accounts" in Matt 5–7 and Luke 6 (*The Life of Jesus Critically Examined* [trans. George Eliot; ed. Peter C. Hodgson; Philadelphia: Fortress, 1972], 336). One finds similar comments still in Vincent Taylor, *The Life and Ministry of Jesus* (Nashville: Abingdon, n.d.), 100–101; Joseph A. Fitzmyer, *The Gospel according to Luke*, vol. 1, *Luke I–IX* (AB 28; Garden City, NY: Doubleday, 1981), 627. For the state of the question in Germany during Strauss's day, see A. Tholuck, *Commentary on the Sermon on the Mount* (Edinburgh: T & T Clark, 1874), 17–33.

protracted and complex as often imagined; rather, it represents, by and large, the work of a single individual. Before making my case, however, some other views fall to be considered.

Some Current Views

According to Heinz Schürmann, Q 6:27–38 and 39–45 once circulated as separate units.[21] The latter anthology united six independent logia (Q 6:39, 40, 41–42, 43–44a, 44b, 45). It was initially anti-Pharisaic and probably originated in Palestine. The other collection, Q 6:27–38, grew out of yet-smaller compilations. First there was Q 6:27–28, 32–33, 35a, 35c. Into this someone inserted Q 6:29, 30, 31. The next stage was the addition of Q 6:36, 37, 38, and Matt 7:6. After that, 6:34 and perhaps 6:35b were tacked on. An editor then supplied, as an introduction, the Beatitudes, Q 6:20–23. These were later balanced by the woes in Q 6:24–26. Finally, someone added, as the conclusion to the whole, the parable of the two builders, Q 6:46–49.

This complex evolutionary history, Schürmann contends, commenced and ended in a relatively short time, indeed within two decades of the crucifixion. He holds this partly because he believes that Paul probably knew the whole discourse. The evidence for this is a series of links between the Sermon on the Plain and 1 Cor 4.[22] These include the following:

- 1 Cor 4:5: "Therefore do not pronounce judgment [μή . . . κρίνετε] before the time, before the Lord comes, who will bring to light the things now hidden in darkness and will disclose the purposes of the heart. Then each one will receive commendation from God." Comparable is Q 6:37: "Do not judge [μὴ κρίνετε], lest you be judged. [[For with the judgment you judge, you will be judged.]]"[23]

- 1 Cor 4:8: "Already you have all you want! Already you have become rich [ἐπλουτήσατε]! Quite apart from us you have become kings [ἐβασιλεύσατε]! Indeed, I wish that you had become kings [ἐβασιλεύσατε], so that we might be kings with you [συμβασιλεύσωμεν]!" This recalls Q 6:20 ("Blessed are the poor, because yours is the kingdom [βασιλεία] of God"); 6:24–25 ("But woe to you who are rich [πλουσίοις], for you

---

21. For this and what follows, see Heinz Schürmann, *Das Lukasevangelium: Erster Teil: Kommentar zu Kap. 1,1–9,50* (HTKNT 3/1; Freiburg: Herder, 1969), 385–86. For a survey of recent critical analyses of Q 6:27–42, see Alan Kirk, *The Composition of the Sayings Source: Genre, Synchrony, and Wisdom Redaction in Q* (NovTSup 91; Leiden: Brill, 1998), 152–76.

22. Here Schürmann is indebted to James M. Robinson, "Kerygma and History in the New Testament," in James M. Robinson and Helmut Koester, *Trajectories through Early Christianity* (Philadelphia: Fortress, 1971), 43–45.

23. Double square brackets—[[ ]]—indicate the IQP's uncertainty as to whether the relevant lines stood in Q.

have received your consolation. Woe to you who are full now, for you will be hungry").[24]

- 1 Cor 4:11–12a: "To the present hour we are hungry [πεινῶμεν] and thirsty, we are poorly clothed and beaten and homeless, and we grow weary from the work of our own hands." Q 6:21–23 is similar: "Blessed are you who hunger [πεινῶντες], for you will eat your fill. Blessed are you who mourn, for you will be comforted. Blessed are you when people insult and persecute you, and utter every kind of evil against you because of the Son of Man. Rejoice and be glad, because great is your reward in heaven. For this is how they persecuted the prophets who were before you."

- 1 Cor 4:12b–13a: "When reviled, we bless [εὐλογοῦμεν]; when persecuted [διωκόμενοι], we endure; when slandered, we speak kindly." This reminds one of Q 6:27–28: "Do good to those who hate you. Bless [εὐλογεῖτε] those who revile you. Pray for those who persecute [διωκόντων] you."

Whatever we make of these intriguing resemblances between Paul and Q's inaugural sermon, Schürmann's general approach typifies much modern scholarship. He regards Q 6:27–42 as the end result of a complex, aggregate growth, an amalgamation gradually produced through the addition of initially disparate items.[25]

Not all have gone along. Leif Vaage has insisted that although Q 6:27–42 incorporates once-separate units, nothing compels us to suppose that the collection grew up gradually:

> The composite nature of the saying-complex in 6:27–35 does not require that we imagine a "rather complex process" [Kloppenborg] of antecedent material aggregation, gradually forming what we now know as the discourse in Q on love of enemies, as though the text were a piece of sedimentary rock, laid down in successive waves of application. The development of the discourse in 6:27–35 need reflect nothing more than the progressive elaboration of an argument for which a series of imperatives (6:27–28, 29–30), a well-known proverb (6:31), a couple of comparisons (6:32–33), and a corresponding pair of promises (6:35b)

24. Whether Luke's woes belonged to Q is difficult to decide. The IQP text excludes them. Others have assigned them to Q; see Kloppenborg, *Q Parallels*, 26.

25. See John S. Kloppenborg, *The Formation of Q: Trajectories in Ancient Christian Wisdom Collections* (Philadelphia: Fortress, 1986), 171–90; Ulrich Wilckens, *Geschichte des Wirkens Jesu in Galiläa* (part 1 of *Geschichte der urchristlichen Theologie*; vol. 1 of *Theologie des Neuen Testaments*; Neukirchen-Vluyn: Neukirchener Verlag, 2002), 136. Both Kloppenborg and Wilckens refer favorably to Schürmann, and Kloppenborg says that the composite nature of 6:27–35 is "obvious" (p. 176). Similar theories abound in biblical scholarship in general. For example, Arndt Meinhold (*Die Sprüche* [2 vols.; ZBK 16; Zürich: Theologischer Verlag, 1991]) reconstructs the evolution of the biblical book of Proverbs in terms of very small units gradually being expanded into larger and larger groups.

are employed. Again, some textual unevenness is evident. The role of reasoning in this regard is not seamless. What is not apparent, however, is why such unevenness would necessarily signal a compositional history antecedent to the production of the "sermon" itself in Q (6:20b–49).[26]

These words take for granted the composite nature of the central part of Q's sermon; I will forward another judgment below. Still, Vaage's main point is cogent. Nothing requires us to posit multiple hands or a lengthy compositional process.

A similar argument comes from Richard Horsley. His conclusion is that the sayings in Q 6:29–49 constitute "an overall unity," and that there is "considerable coherence" within the various subsections, with "clear links among them."[27] Horsley's contribution is of note for at least two emphases, one being his contention that Q 6:20–49 features parallelism and rhythm. In this he is correct, as we will see below.

Horsley's other notable claim is that Q's sermon is not a collection of sapiential sayings. It is instead reminiscent of the covenantal teaching in Exodus, Leviticus, and Deuteronomy. More particularly, Q 6:20–49 is a text of covenant renewal, much like Deuteronomy and Josh 24. Appealing to 1QS and the *Damascus Document*, Horsley contends that the language of covenant renewal was alive in the first century CE and that awareness of this clarifies Q 6:20–49, which he divides into five parts:

1. the reversal of the present political order (6:20–26)
2. admonitions on economic relations in the local community (6:27–36)
3. admonitions on social relations in the local community (6:37–42)
4. reflections on the motivation for good economic and social relations (6:43–45)
5. closing sanction for the admonitions in parts 2 and 3 (6:46–49)

The proposal that Q reflects a religious movement concerned for covenant renewal is worth pondering, and Horsley certainly is correct about some of the literary features of Q's first discourse. From my point of view, however, his work needs to be supplemented in at least three respects. First, although he has perceived a couple of the contacts between the Sermon on the Plain and Leviticus, especially Lev 19, Horsley has overlooked others, and the extent of

---

26. See Leif E. Vaage, "Composite Texts and Oral Mythology: The Case of the 'Sermon' in Q (6:20–49)," in *Conflict and Invention: Literary, Rhetorical, and Social Studies on the Sayings Gospel Q* (ed. John S. Kloppenborg; Valley Forge, PA: Trinity Press International, 1995), 75–97 (quotation, p. 83).

27. See Richard A. Horsley, "The Covenant Renewal Discourse: Q 6:20–49," in Richard A. Horsley and Jonathan A. Draper, *Whoever Hears You Hears Me: Prophets, Performance, and Tradition in Q* (Harrisburg, PA: Trinity Press International, 1999), 195–227 (quotations, pp. 195, 196).

Q's intertextual dialogue with Lev 19 has far-reaching implications. Second, although Horsley refers to the relevant parallels in *1 Clem*. 13:2; Pol. *Phil*. 2:3; *Did*. 1:2–5, he moves through these much-discussed extracanonical texts all too quickly, glossing over a number of pertinent and very vexing issues. Much more needs to be said. Third, Horsley nowhere explicitly entertains the question that I ultimately wish to address: Is it credible that Q 6:27–42 preserves not only some of the distinctive themes of Jesus' teaching but, more than that, reflects to some extent a discourse that he himself delivered?[28]

Thematic Unity

As best we can tell, Q 6:27–42 fell into three closely related sections: 6:27–30 (loving enemies), 31–36 (abounding in mercy), 37–42 (refraining from judgment). The first section commenced with "love your enemies" (6:27). This striking, memorable imperative was then elaborated with "pray for those who persecute you" (6:28) and probably additional injunctions (cf. Luke 6:27b–28: "do good to them who hate you; bless those who curse you").[29]

These introductory exhortations were then illustrated by a series of imagined scenarios, each designed to display the extraordinary, self-sacrificing spirit needed to fulfill the initial injunctions:[30]

- what to do when struck on the cheek (Luke 6:29; Matt 5:39)
- what to do when a garment is taken (Luke 6:29; Matt 5:40)
[[• what to do when conscripted for a mile's labor (Matt 5:41)]][31]
- what to do when asked to give (Luke 6:30; Matt 5:42)
[[• what to do when asked to lend (Matt 5:42)]]
[[• what to do when goods are taken away (Luke 6:30)]]

The illustrations in Q 6:29–30 exhibit extensive parallelism of form as well as content:

28. Since I consider the material before and after Q 6:27–42 to be secondary, in the following pages I will focus not upon the entirety of the Sermon on the Plain but rather upon its central portion.

29. The IQP regards Luke 6:27b–28a as secondary, despite the close parallel between 6:28a (εὐλογεῖτε τοὺς καταρωμένους ὑμᾶς) and Rom 12:14 (εὐλογεῖτε καὶ μὴ καταρᾶσθε). If Paul's formulation is indebted to the Jesus tradition, as many have thought, this counts as evidence against the redactional origin of Luke 6:27b–28a. See Lührmann, "Liebet eure Feinde," 416.

30. Many have regarded 6:29–30 as secondary because of the switch from the second-person plural in vv. 27–28 to the second-person singular in vv. 29–30. I reject this argument; see below, pp. 378–79.

31. On whether Matt 5:41 was in Q, see below, p. 344.

- Action of other:
    When someone strikes you on the cheek,
  Action of self:
    offer the other as well.
- Action of other:
    When someone takes your garment,
  Action of self:
    hand over your other garment as well.

[[• Action of other:
    When someone conscripts you for one mile,
  Action of self:
    go a second as well.]]

- Action of other:
    When someone begs from you,
  Action of self:
    give.

[[• Action of other:
    When someone wants to borrow from you,
  Action of self:
    lend.]]

[[• Action of other:
    When someone takes away your goods,
  Action of self:
    do not ask for them back.]]

In brief, all six couplets display the same simple pattern:

- Action of other:
    When you are mistreated or asked for something difficult or incon-
      venient,
  Action of self:
    suffer the wrong or meet the demand or do even more.

This pattern is already implicit in the preceding verses, 6:27–28:

- Action of other:
    Some behave as your enemies;
  Action of self:
    love them.

- Action of other:
    Some persecute you;
  Action of self:
    pray for them.
- Action of other:
    Some hate you;
  Action of self:
    do good to them.
- Action of other:
    Some curse you;
  Action of self:
    bless them.

Q 6:27–28 and 6:29–30 are more than literary neighbors; they are, thematically and structurally, close relations.

According to the text of the IQP, and in agreement with Luke's order, the several illustrations in Q 6:29–30 were followed directly by the so-called golden rule, 6:31, a brief, effective summary of moral responsibility, well known from Jewish and non-Jewish sources.[32] Modern scholars have often regarded 6:31 as secondary, reckoning it much less radical than the surrounding verses, even platitudinous.[33] To my knowledge, however, no ancient Christian commentator felt, or at least expressed, any ideological tension; and the common modern reading overlooks the obvious fact that the import of a general maxim derives from its context. As Alan Kirk has written, "The Golden Rule was invoked in a wide variety of paraenetic settings dealing with reciprocity and accordingly

32. Jewish examples: Tob 4:15 (perhaps dependent upon *Ahiqar*; see 8:88 of the Armenian version); Sir 31:15; *Let. Arist.* 207; Philo, *Hypothetica apud* Eusebius, *Praep. ev.* 8.7.6; *L.A.B.* 11:10 (on this, see Howard Jacobsen, *A Commentary on Pseudo-Philo's Liber Antiquitatum Biblicarum* [2 vols.; AGJU 31; Leiden: Brill, 1996], 1:473–75); *2 En.* 61:1–2; *T. Naph.* 1:6 (Hebrew); *m. 'Abot* 2:10; *'Abot R. Nat.* A 15; 16; *'Abot R. Nat.* B 26; *b. Šabb.* 31a (here the rule is "the whole Torah, while the rest is commentary"); Tg. Ps.-J. on Lev 19:18. *Syr. Men.* 250–51 is also probably Jewish. Greco-Roman examples: Herodotus, *Hist.* 3.142; 7.136; Isocrates, *Aeginet.* 51; *Ad Nic.* 49; 61; *Demon.* 14; Diogenes Laertius, *Vit.* 1.9; 5.21; Seneca, *Ep.* 47.11; *Ben.* 2.1.1; Sextus, *Sent.* 87–90.

33. Typical is this comment of R. G. Hamerton-Kelly: "The very attitude of reciprocity which the rule seems to advocate in vs. 31 is condemned by the vss. immediately following (32–34)" ("Golden Rule, The," *IDBSup* 369). Compare John Nolland: "A return to the second person plural marks a break between vv 28–30 and v 31. The denial of any reciprocity ethic in vv 32–35 makes it difficult . . . to connect v 31 with what follows" (*Luke 1–9:20* [WBC 35A; Dallas: Word, 1989], 297). Albrecht Dihle doubts that Jesus spoke the golden rule because it does not, he judges, harmonize with the demand to love one's enemies (*Die goldene Regel: Eine Einführung in die Geschichte der antiken und frühchristlichen Vulgärethik* [StA 7; Göttingen: Vandenhoeck & Ruprecht, 1962], 112–14).

was made to display various shades of interpretation. In a similar manner the Love Enemies cluster, every syllable of which is bound up in issues relating either to reciprocity or its flip side, retaliation, expropriates the Golden Rule and infuses it with meaning from the unconventional Jesus ethic advocated by the encompassing materials."[34]

In its Q setting, the golden rule was not pedestrian. It rather effectively continued the theme of living outside of oneself. Moreover, the logic of the injunction to altruism is similar to the logic of the materials in 6:29–30; that is, it is another couplet relating what others might do to what hearers should do:

> Action of other:
> 	As you wish that people would treat you,
> Action of self:
> 	that is how you should treat them.

Although Q 6:31 carried forward both the teaching and logic of 6:27–30, it also enlarged the subject matter. For the golden rule enjoins not "response to an action"—as do vv. 28–30—but instead encourages "appropriate *first* action."[35] To do unto others as one wishes to be done to oneself means not reacting but initiating action; it means to imagine, on analogy with what one wants, what others might want, and then acting accordingly.

Beyond that, the rhetorical questions that followed 6:31 made it perfectly clear that the golden rule should be practiced without discrimination, that it should be, if I may borrow from Kant, a universal law: "And as you wish that (all) people [οἱ ἄνθρωποι] do to you, that is how you should (always) treat (all of) them." One must do more than the tax collectors, who love only those who love them (6:32). And one must do more than the sinners, who lend only to those from whom they expect to receive (6:34). Mutuality should embrace those unlike oneself. The widespread conviction that the "golden rule" must be a secondary insertion is ill founded.[36]

Q's golden rule marked the transition from the subsection on loving enemies (vv. 27–30) to the subsection on reciprocity and mercy (vv. 32–36). The latter

34. Kirk, *Composition*, 163. See further idem, "'Love Your Enemies,' the Golden Rule, and Ancient Reciprocity (Luke 6:27–35)," *JBL* 122 (2003): 667–86.

35. The quoted words are from John Topel, "The Tarnished Golden Rule (Luke 6:31): The Inescapable Radicalness of Christian Ethics," *TS* 59 (1998): 477. He continues: "The fact that one ponders what he or she would want others to do to him or her does not make his or her actions a response to the other's act; there is no other's act." Ronald A. Piper says that the golden rule introduces the idea of "active love" (*Wisdom in the Q-Tradition: The Aphoristic Teaching of Jesus* [SNTSMS 61; Cambridge: Cambridge University Press, 1989], 83).

36. This marks a change from my earlier opinion: Allison, *Jesus Tradition in Q*, 83. For further discussion see below, p. 358.

opened with a series of rhetorical questions that, like Q 6:29–30, exhibited strong parallelism:

Luke 6:32 = Matt 5:46	If you love those who love you, what reward do you have? Do not even tax collectors do the same?
[[Luke 6:33	If you do good to those who do good to you, what credit is that to you? For even sinners do the same.]]
Luke 6:34	If you lend to those from whom you hope to receive, what credit is that to you? Even sinners lend to sinners to receive the same back.
[[Matt 5:47	If you salute only your brothers, what more are you doing than others? Do not even the Gentiles do the same?]][37]

That these lines ever circulated by themselves seems altogether unlikely.[38] They not only elucidate how one should enact the golden rule[39] but also comment on and support the difficult imperatives in vv. 27–30. "If you lend (δανίσητε) to those from whom you hope to receive" (6:34) harks back to the probable Q text of 6:30: "and from the one borrowing (δανιζομένου) do not ask back what is yours." And "if you love those who love you" (6:32) returns to the opening command of Q 6:27 ("love your enemies"): benefiting those from whom one benefits is nothing special; Jesus demands doing good to all, including enemies.

At some point, Q rooted Jesus' radical instruction in the *imitatio Dei*. In Matthew, "love your enemies and pray for those who persecute you" comes immediately before "so that you may be sons of your Father who is in heaven; for he makes his sun rise on the evil and on the good, and he sends rain on the just and on the unjust" (5:45 RSV). In Luke, the proper theological justification of Jesus' moral teaching occurs in 6:35, after the rhetorical questions in

37. Menahem Kister ("Words and Formulae in the Gospels in the Light of Hebrew and Aramaic Sources," in *The Sermon on the Mount and Its Jewish Setting* [ed. Hans-Jürgen Becker and Serge Ruzer; CahRB 60; Paris: Gabalda, 2005], 133–34) has called attention to a close parallel, heretofore missed, in the *Midrash ha-Gadol*: "R. Shim'on used to say: money-lovers love each other, robbers love each other and usurers love each other. Who is the appropriate one to give reward to all of these? It is I [God], for none of these traits can be found in me" (Ya'akov Naḥum Epstein and Ezra Tsiyon Melamed, eds., *Mekhilta de-Rabi Shim'on ben Yoḥai: 'Al pi kitve yad min ha-Genizah umi-Midrash ha-gadol* [מכילתא דרבי שמעון בן יוחאי, עפ״י כתבי יד מן הגניזה וממדרש הגדול; Schriften des Vereins Mekize Nirdamim; Jerusalem: Meḳitse Nirdamim, 1955], 212–13). According to Kister, this text derives from the tannaitic *Mekilta* of R. Shim'on ben Yohai.

38. See David R. Catchpole, *The Quest for Q* (Edinburgh: T & T Clark, 1993), 101–3.

39. See further Hans Dieter Betz, *The Sermon on the Mount: A Commentary on the Sermon on the Mount, Including the Sermon on the Plain (Matthew 5:3–7:27 and Luke 6:20–49)* (Hermeneia; Minneapolis: Fortress, 1995), 599–604.

6:32–34: "Love your enemies, and do good, and lend, expecting nothing in return; and your reward will be great, and you will be sons of the Most High; for he is kind to the ungrateful and to the selfish" (RSV). Wherever exactly the call to emulate God appeared in the Sayings Source, it was needed, because Jesus' demands, which counter common practice and common sense, cried out for a compelling rationale, and the golden rule, being a conventional maxim, would probably not in and of itself have amounted to such.

Q's section on reciprocity wound up by further specifying the call to imitate the Deity: "Be merciful, just as your Father is merciful" (Luke 6:36 [cf. Matt 5:48: "Be perfect, therefore, as your heavenly Father is perfect"]). This sentence underlined Q 6:32–35 by calling to mind God's universal benignity, a traditional Jewish theme.[40] It also reinforced Q 6:27–31 + 35b: if there is an imperative to imitate the divine mercy, and if the divine mercy knows no bounds, then human mercy should know no bounds.

What, then, of Q 6:37–38, the imperatives not to judge or to condemn others, and vv. 41, 42, which warn against removing the speck from a brother's eye when one has a log in one's own eye? Although many have sensed a caesura between 6:36 and 6:37, the formal pattern of 6:37–38 + 41–42 is similar to that in 6:27–30. Difficult imperatives (vv. 27–28, 37a), with the generalizing second-person plural, are followed by concrete illustration (vv. 29–30, 41–42), with the second-person singular:

Q 6:27–30
    a. General imperatives in second-person plural, vv. 27–28
        love, do good, bless, pray[41]
    b. Illustrations in second-person singular, vv. 29–30
        garment taken, begged to give, and so on
Q 6:37–38 + 41–42
    a. General imperatives in second-person plural, vv. 37–38
        do not judge, do not condemn, forgive, give[42]
    b. Illustration in second-person singular, vv. 41–42
        speck in another's eye, beam in one's own

Both sections, moreover, feature rhetorical questions: "What reward do you have?" and "Do not even tax collectors do the same?" in vv. 32–34, "Why do you see . . . ?" and "How can you say . . . ?" in vv. 41–42.

The focus shifts somewhat with the note of warning in 6:37–38, yet the thematic continuity with 6:27–36 is manifest. The fundamental issue of how

40. See Dale C. Allison Jr., "Rejecting Violent Judgment: Luke 9:52–56 and Its Relatives," *JBL* 121 (2002): 459–78.

41. For the argument that 6:27–28 originally contained four imperatives, see below, pp. 342–43.

42. On the possibility that this entire fourfold series stood in Q, see below, pp. 344–46.

one should treat others continues, as does the insistence on abandoning animosity and demonstrating unexpected generosity. Indeed, in its present context, 6:37–38 "develops the preceding speech on love of enemies and, more specifically, explicates the programmatic injunction to imitate divine mercy (6:36)."[43] To forgo judging or condemning others (6:37, 41–42) is to show them mercy (6:36), to practice the golden rule (6:31), and to extend kindness to the undeserving (6:29–30, 32–35). Beyond that, the subject of eschatological reward (6:37–38: "you will be judged," "it will be measured to you") sends one back to 6:32 ("what reward have you?"), while "judge not" (μὴ κρίνετε) makes for a nice antithesis with the IQP's reconstruction of 6:29: "and to the one wanting to judge" (κριθῆναι). Furthermore, the correlation between condemning others and being condemned can be expressed along the lines of the golden rule in 6:31: As you do not wish to be condemned, so you should not condemn others.[44]

The upshot of the previous pages is this: Q 6:27–42 (minus 39–40) is a coherent piece. The question of how Jesus' followers should treat others is the topic throughout, the injunctive mood is consistently maintained—the IQP text has eleven imperatives in this section: Q 6:27, 28, 29 (bis); Matt 5:41; Q 6:30 (bis), 31, 36, 37, 38e—and almost every saying builds upon or reverts to what has come before. In other words, each group of imperatives naturally leads to the next. So the whole hangs together nicely. This is not what one expects from an anthology of aphorisms manufactured independently for multiple occasions.

Added support for this view of the matter comes from *Let. Arist.* 207, which offers this advice for a king: "As you wish that no evil should befall you, but to share in every good thing, so you should act on the same principle towards your subjects, including the wrongdoers, and admonish the good and upright also mercifully [ἐπιεικέστερον]. For God guides all in mercy [ἐπιεικείᾳ]." The similarities between these words and Q 6:27–42 are remarkable. Both passages offer a version of the golden rule: "As you wish that no evil should befall you, but to share in every good thing, so you should act on the same principle towards your subjects" in the *Letter of Aristeas*, "As you wish that people would do to you, do so to them" in Q. Both speak against restricting mercy or kindness. *Aristeas* enjoins, "Act on the same principle towards your subjects, including the wrongdoers." Q 6:27–28 demands,

43. Kloppenborg, *Formation of Q*, 181. He continues: "The effect of the juxtaposition of 6:37–38 and 6:36 is twofold: to interpret the ethic of noncondemnation as an act of mercy, and to see this mercy as imitation of divine action. This motif binds 6:36, 37–38 closely with 6:27–35." See also ibid., 172; Catchpole, *Quest for Q*, 125.

44. Cf. the formulation in *Ps.-Clem. Hom.* 18:16: "In order that it might happen to them as they did to others, and that with what measure they measured, it will be measured equally to them."

"Love your enemies and pray for those who persecute you," and 6:32–34 asks, "If you love (only) those who love you . . . ?" *Aristeas* encourages reproof: "Admonish the good and upright also mercifully"; Q permits the same if it is not hypocritical: "Remove first from your eye the log, and then you will see clearly to cast out the speck from the eye of your brother" (6:42). Both texts commend mercy: "Admonish the good and upright also mercifully" is the direction in *Aristeas*; the succinct "Be merciful" is the demand in Q 6:36. And in both texts, God is the model of universal mercy or kindness. *Aristeas* teaches that "God guides all in kindness." For his part, Q's Jesus affirms that God "makes his sun rise on the evil and on the good" (6:35), and then he backs up his demand to "be merciful" by observing that "your Father is merciful" (6:36).

We have no reason to posit Q's dependence upon the *Letter of Aristeas*. Nor do we have cause to think of *Let. Arist.* 207 as an artificial compilation of originally isolated sayings. So the similar deployment of the same themes in Q 6:27–42 moves us once more to wonder whether this last can really be the result of something like Schürmann's complex tradition history, according to which several hands, over the span of several years, cobbled together a dozen or more originally isolated sayings. I hope to show that there is a better explanation for the thematic coherence of Q 6:27–42 and for its resemblance to *Let. Arist.* 207.

Parallels outside Matthew and Luke

I begin by considering several extracanonical texts that contain close parallels to Q 6:27–42.[45]

1. 1 Clement

The following appears in *1 Clem.* 13:1–2:

> Let us then be humble, brothers, laying aside all arrogance and conceit and foolishness and anger. . . . Most of all, let us remember the words of the Lord Jesus, which he spoke as he taught gentleness and patience. For in this way he

45. In the following pages I leave to the side *2 Clem.* 13:4, which resembles both Luke 6:27 and 6:32. I suspect that it draws upon Luke. If, however, as Karl P. Donfried (*The Setting of Second Clement in Early Christianity* [NovTSup 38; Leiden: Brill, 1974], 78) has claimed, it is free of Lukan influence, that would offer further support for my main conclusions. I also ignore Irenaeus, *Haer.* 4.13.3; Tertullian, *Marc.* 4.16; *Liber Graduum* 2:2–3 (PS 3:28–29); Aphraates, *Demonstrationes* 2.12 (PS 1:72–73). These later texts cannot be free of Synoptic influence. See discussion in Michael Mees, *Ausserkanonische Parallelstellen zu den Herrenworten und ihre Bedeutung* (Quaderni di "Vetera Christianorum" 10; Bari: Istituto di Letteratura Cristiana Antica, 1975), 119–27.

spoke: "Be merciful, so that you will receive mercy; forgive, so that you may be forgiven. As you do, so will it be done to you. As you give, so will it be given to you. As you judge, so will you be judged. As you show kindness, so will kindness be shown to you. With the measurement that you measure, according to that will it be measured to you."

Those who have carefully scrutinized this text have often, maybe more often than not, decided that it is independent of Matthew and Luke,[46] a prudent generalization that we can extend to their common source: 1 Clement probably does not borrow directly from the Sayings Source either.[47] With this in mind, the following parallels to Q 6:27–42 become instructive:

• "Be merciful" (ἐλεᾶτε) (1 Clem. 13:2) has the same import as Q 6:36, "Be merciful" (γίνεσθε οἰκτίρμονες), even though the Greek verbs are different.[48]

• "As you do [ποιεῖτε], so will it be done [ποιηθήσεται] to you" (1 Clem. 13:2) sounds like a conflation of Q's golden rule—"And as you wish that people would treat [ποιῶσιν] you, that is how you should treat [ποιεῖτε] them" (6:31)—with the eschatological principle in Q 6:37–38: "[[with the judgment that you judge, you will be judged.]] And with the measure that you measure, it will be measured to you."[49]

• "As you give, so will it be given to you" (1 Clem. 13:2) matches the logic of Q 6:37–38: "[[with the judgment you judge, you will be

46. See Andrew F. Gregory, "1 Clement and the Writings That Later Formed the New Testament," in The Reception of the New Testament in the Apostolic Fathers (ed. Andrew F. Gregory and Christopher M. Tuckett; Oxford: Oxford University Press, 2005), 131–34; Donald A. Hagner, The Use of the Old and New Testaments in Clement of Rome (NovTSup 34; Leiden: Brill, 1973), 135–51; Helmut Koester, Ancient Christian Gospels: Their History and Development (Philadelphia: Trinity Press International, 1990), 66–69. For the contrasting view that 1 Clement drew upon a catechism much influenced by Matthew, see Édouard Massaux, The Influence of the Gospel of Saint Matthew on Christian Literature before Saint Irenaeus (trans. Norman J. Belval and Suzanne Hechted; ed. Arthur J. Bellinzoni; 3 vols.; NGS 5; Leuven: Peeters; Macon, GA: Mercer University Press, 1990), 1:7–12. The parallel in Clement of Alexandria, Strom. 2.91.2, depends directly upon 1 Clement.

47. So too Koester, Ancient Christian Gospels, 68.

48. But compare the Greek of Matt 5:7: "Blessed are the merciful [οἱ ἐλεήμονες], for they will receive mercy [ἐλεηθήσονται]." On the premise that Clement is free of Matthean influence, perhaps the Matthean beatitude rewrites the agraphon preserved in 1 Clem. 13:2 (cf. Pol. Phil. 2:3).

49. Horacio E. Lona (Der erste Clemensbrief [KAV 2; Göttingen: Vandenhoeck & Ruprecht, 1998], 215) cites Matt 7:12 and Luke 6:31 as the Synoptic parallels to Clement's "as you do, so will it be done to you." Hagner appears uncertain whether 1 Clem. 13:2 offers a rewritten golden rule, but he observes that if it does, Clement's version is "a stylized form nowhere else encountered," the explanation being this: it has "been patterned after the four sayings which it introduces and may well have been devised as an introductory epitome for just such a collection of maxims" (Old and New Testaments, 139).

judged.]][50] And with the measure that you measure, it will be measured to you."[51]

- "As you judge [κρίνετε], so will you be judged [κριθήσεσθε]" (*1 Clem*. 13:2) is a close relative of Q 6:37: "Do not judge [κρίνετε] lest you be judged [κριθῆτε], [[for with the judgment you judge you will be judged]]."

- "As you show kindness [χρηστεύεσθε], so will kindness be shown [χρηστευθήσεται] you" (*1 Clem*. 13:2) summarizes the spirit of Q 6:27–42 in its entirety and calls to mind Luke 6:35, which is at least partly from Q, and where the *imitatio Dei* includes being "kind": "love your enemies . . . because he [God] is kind [χρηστός] to the ungrateful and the wicked."[52]

- "With the measurement that you measure, by that will it be measured to you" (ᾧ μέτρῳ μετρεῖτε ἐν αὐτῷ μετρηθήσεται ὑμῖν) (*1 Clem*. 13:2) is a variant of the saying that also occurs in Q 6:38: "with the measure that you measure, it will be measured to you" (ἐν ᾧ μέτρῳ μετρεῖτε μετρηθήσεται ὑμῖν).[53]

- *1 Clement* 13 begins with a call to adopt humility (ταπεινοφρονήσωμεν) and to abandon anger, and it interprets the quoted words of Jesus as promoting "gentleness" (ἐπιείκειαν) and "patience" (μακροθυμίαν) (*1 Clem*. 13:1). Following the quotation in 13:2, moreover, Clement expresses his hope that his hearers will respond by behaving with humble minds (ταπεινοφρονοῦντες). All of this resonates with the spirit of self-abnegation in Q 6:27–42.[54]

Given this series of resemblances, it appears that Clement was familiar not only with a version of the logion in Q 6:37–38 but also probably knew that logion in connection with materials closely related to other portions of 6:27–42. Unfortunately, the data do not allow us to say much more than that. The parallels listed do, however, bolster the proposal that the imperative not

50. The bracketed words appear in Matt 7:2 (ἐν ᾧ γὰρ κρίματι κρίνετε κριθήσεσθε) and may or may not have stood in Matthew's source.

51. It also resembles Luke 6:38, which the IQP does not assign to Q. Luke has δίδοτε καὶ δοθήσεται; Clement has ὡς δίδοτε οὕτως δοθήσεται ὑμῖν. This can scarcely be coincidence, and it supplies some reason for wondering about the IQP's verdict here. I see no connection with Acts 20:35 ("It is more blessed to give than to receive"), a saying known from several ancient sources (e.g., Thucydides, *Hist*. 2.97.4).

52. Luke 6:36 may supply the closest verbal parallel: γίνεσθε οἰκτίρμονες, "be merciful"; see Hagner, *Old and New Testaments*, 139–40.

53. Cf. also Mark 4:24, which is the only verbatim overlap between the Sermon on the Plain and Mark: ἐν ᾧ μέτρῳ μετρεῖτε μετρηθήσεται ὑμῖν.

54. Although the IQP excludes "forgive and you will be forgiven" (ἀπολύετε καὶ ἀπολυθήσεσθε [Luke 6:37]) from Q, this is an uncertain judgment; see below, pp. 344–45. If one includes the line in Q, it becomes relevant that *1 Clem*. 13:2 supplies a parallel: ἀφίετε ἵνα ἀφεθῇ ("forgive so that you may be forgiven").

to condemn or judge others (Q 6:37–38) was, independently of the Synoptics and Q, associated with sayings and sentiments akin to those that surrounded it in Q, including the golden rule.

2. Polycarp

The one surviving epistle of Polycarp also contains a cluster of injunctions that recalls the central portion of Q's Sermon on the Plain:

> The one who raised him [Jesus] from the dead will also raise us, if we do his will and walk in his commandments and love what he loved, refraining from all unrighteousness, greed, love of money, slander and false witness, not returning evil for evil or insult for insult or blow for blow or curse for curse, but rather remembering what the Lord said when he taught: "Do not judge so that you will not be judged. Forgive, and it will be forgiven you. Be merciful, so that mercy will be shown to you. With the measurement that you measure, it will be measured back to you. And blessed are the poor and those persecuted for righteousness' sake, because theirs is the kingdom of God." (Pol. *Phil.* 2:2–3)

The compound, closing beatitude, tacked onto the anthology with καί ("and"), likely betrays a knowledge of the First Gospel, for Matt 5:10 ("Blessed are those who are persecuted for righteousness' sake, for theirs is the kingdom of heaven") is often, and rightly in my judgment, assigned to Matthean redaction.[55] For the rest, however, it is debatable whether or to what extent Polycarp is under Synoptic influence.[56]

One reason many have detected an independent tradition in Polycarp is that the closest parallels to the first part of the quotation appear neither in Matthew nor in Luke but rather in *1 Clem.* 13:2:

1 Clem. 13:2	Pol. *Phil.* 2:3
ἐλεᾶτε ἵνα ἐλεηθῆτε	μὴ κρίνετε ἵνα μὴ κριθῆτε
ἀφίετε ἵνα ἀφεθῇ ὑμῖν . . .	ἀφίετε καὶ ἀφεθήσεται ὑμῖν
ὡς κρίνετε οὕτως κριθήσεσθε . . .	ἐλεᾶτε ἵνα ἐλεηθῆτε
ᾧ μέτρῳ μετρεῖτε	ᾧ μέτρῳ μετρεῖτε
ἐν αὐτῷ μετρηθήσεται ὑμῖν	ἀντιμετρηθήσεται ὑμῖν

55. See W. D. Davies and Dale C. Allison Jr., *A Critical and Exegetical Commentary on the Gospel according to Saint Matthew* (3 vols.; ICC; Edinburgh: T & T Clark, 1988–1997), 1:459–60. Yet while Polycarp agrees with Matthew against Luke in having the third person and a participial form of διώκω + ἕνεκεν δικαιοσύνης, the unqualified "the poor" matches Luke (as against Matthew's "the poor in spirit"), as does "the kingdom of God" (instead of the characteristically Matthean "the kingdom of heaven"). This complicates analysis and prevents full assurance on the matter.

56. For a survey of differing opinions, see Michael W. Holmes, "Polycarp's *Letter to the Philippians* and the Writings That Later Formed the New Testament," in *Reception of the New Testament* (ed. Gregory and Tuckett), 191–93.

What is the relationship between these two passages? One might posit that Polycarp borrowed from the earlier epistle, which undoubtedly he knew.[57] Nonetheless, certain observations may be thought to throw doubt upon this verdict, which some have disputed. (a) The order of the injunctions in the two works is different. If Clement's order is a, b, c, d, Polycarp's is c, b, a, d. (b) Some of the material in *1 Clem.* 13:2 is not in Polycarp despite being germane (e.g., "As you show kindness, so shall kindness be shown to you"). (c) Clement's distinctive ὡς . . . οὕτως, repeated four times, fails to turn up even once in Pol. *Phil.* 2:3. (d) The saying about judgment has a negative form in Polycarp (μὴ κρίνετε ἵνα μὴ κριθῆτε [so too Matthew and Luke]), a positive form in *1 Clement* (ὡς κρίνετε οὕτως κριθήσεσθε). (e) Polycarp's "not repaying evil for evil or insult for insult or blow for blow or curse for curse" is clearly independent of *1 Clement*, which supplies no parallel. Instead, the sentence, which nicely summarizes the spirit of the central section of the Sermon on the Plain, likely derives from 1 Pet 3:9, with which it agrees exactly:

Polycarp: μὴ ἀποδιδόντες κακὸν ἀντὶ κακοῦ ἢ λοιδορίαν ἀντὶ λοιδορίας

1 Peter: μὴ ἀποδιδόντες κακὸν ἀντὶ κακοῦ ἢ λοιδορίαν ἀντὶ λοιδορίας[58]

Note, however, that the continuation in Polycarp—"or blow for blow or curse for curse"—has no counterpart in 1 Peter. (f) Polycarp agrees with Matt 7:1 against Luke 6:37 and Clement in having μὴ κρίνετε ἵνα μὴ κριθῆτε and with Luke 6:38 against Matt 7:2 and Clement (and Mark 4:24) in having μέτρῳ μετρεῖτε ἀντιμετρηθήσεται. (g) Although a list of vices introduces the similar material in *1 Clem.* 13:1–2 and Pol. *Phil.* 2:3, the lists have nothing in common. The former exhorts readers to lay aside "all arrogance and conceit and foolishness and anger," whereas the latter enjoins avoidance of "unrighteousness, greed, love of money, slander, and false testimony."

These considerations scarcely entail that Pol. *Phil.* 2:3 is independent of *1 Clem.* 13:2, for ancient writers often took it upon themselves creatively to rewrite their sources.[59] Surmising that Polycarp rewrote *1 Clem.* 13:2 by bor-

57. See J. B. Lightfoot, *The Apostolic Fathers: Part I, S. Clement of Rome* (2nd ed.; 2 vols.; London: Macmillan, 1890), 1:149–52; Daniel B. Völter, *Polykarp und Ignatius und die ihnen zugeschriebenen Briefe* (Leiden: Brill, 1910), 31, 40–43.

58. Cf. also *Jos. Asen.* 23:9; 28:5, 10, 14; 29:3; Rom 12:17; 1 Thess 5:15; *Acts John* 81; *Apoc. Sedr.* 7:10, 12. See discussion in William Dettwiller Stroker, "The Formation of Secondary Sayings of Jesus" (PhD diss., Yale University, 1970), 179–237. For Polycarp's knowledge of 1 Peter—a fact that Eusebius (*Hist. eccl.* 4.14.9) already remarked upon—see Holmes, "Polycarp's Letter," 220–23. As for the parallel in *Joseph and Aseneth*, the origin of that book remains unclear. Christian authorship or revision is possible.

59. Helpful here is John S. Kloppenborg, "Variation in the Reproduction of the Double Tradition and an Oral Q?" *ETL* 83 (2007): 53–80.

rowing from Matthew, Luke, and 1 Peter will explain the facts.[60] Yet then it is perhaps unexpected that the result is a rhyming quatrain.[61] In any event, the hypothesis that Polycarp and Clement had access to a common, non-Synoptic source or to closely related non-Synoptic sources, oral or written, has appealed to some,[62] and we cannot rule it out.[63]

We come, then, to no conclusion. The facts are messy; the data do not point in one direction. So we do not know what sources Polycarp had at hand. For our purposes, the one useful observation that we can make without fear of contradiction is that Polycarp's parallels to Q 6:37–38 are prefaced by material closely related to 6:27–30:

- "Not returning evil for evil" (cf. Q 6:27–30)
- "or insult for insult" (cf. Q 6:29)
- "or blow for blow" (cf. Q 6:29)
- "or curse for curse" (cf. Q 6:28)[64]

On the theory of independent tradition, Polycarp supplies additional evidence for the circulation of something like Q 6:37–38 along with something related to Q 6:27–36, for his résumé of Jesus' teaching repeats the basic pattern of Q's inaugural sermon: first there are injunctions to nonretaliation, then a list of correlations between what one gives and what one gets. On the theory that Polycarp is not independent but rather borrows from Matthew, Luke, 1 Peter, and *1 Clement*, we can at least say that the future martyr recognized the thematic coherence of the sayings now found in Luke 6:27–42, for Pol. *Phil.* 2:3 has parallels to or fitting summaries of most of them.

60. According to Helmut Koester (*Synoptische Überlieferung bei den apostolischen Vätern* [TU 65; Berlin: Akademie-Verlag, 1957], 114–20), Polycarp revised *1 Clem.* 13:2 with Matthew and Luke in mind. Cf. Kenneth Berding, *Polycarp and Paul: An Analysis of Their Literary and Theological Relationship in Light of Polycarp's Use of Biblical and Extra-biblical Literature* (VCSup 62; Leiden: Brill, 2002), 53–59; P. N. Harrison, *Polycarp's Two Epistles to the Philippians* (London: Cambridge University Press, 1936), 286.

61. First clause: ἵνα . . . -θῆτε
    Second clause: -ίετε . . . -θήσεται ὑμῖν
    Third clause: ἵνα . . . -θῆτε
    Fourth clause: -εῖτε . . . -θήσεται ὑμῖν

62. For example, Richard Glover, "Patristic Quotations and Gospel Sources," *NTS* 31 (1985): 240–43; Hagner, *1 Clement*, 141–43, 279; Wolf-Dietrich Köhler, *Die Rezeption des Matthäusevangeliums in der Zeit vor Irenäus* (WUNT 2/24; Tübingen: Mohr Siebeck, 1987), 105–9. According to Massaux (*Influence*, 2:28–30), Polycarp was influenced by the source behind *1 Clem.* 13:2.

63. On this view, one could also argue that Pol. *Phil.* 12:3 ("Pray . . . for those who persecute and hate you") borrows from the same source. Again, however, one might find dependence upon both Matt 5:44 and Luke 6:28.

64. κατάραν ἀντὶ κατάρας. Luke 6:28 (against Matt 5:44) has καταρωμένους, which may or may not represent Q.

3. The Didache

The first chapter of the *Didache* contains a number of close parallels to the end of Matt 5 and the middle of Luke 6:

Didache 1:2–6	Matthew 5:38–48 + 7:12	Luke 6:27–36
1:2: "whatever you do not wish to happen to you, do not do to another"	7:12: "in everything do to others as you would have them do to you"	6:31: "do to others as you would have them do to you"
1:3: "bless those who curse you"	—	6:28: "bless those who curse you"
1:3: "pray for your enemies"	5:44: "love your enemies and pray for those who persecute you"	6:27–28: "love your enemies . . . pray for those who abuse you"
1:3: "fast for those who persecute you"	5:44: "pray for those who persecute you"	—
1:3: "what credit [ποία χάρις] is it?"	5:46, 47: "what reward do you have?"; "what more are you doing?"	6:32, 33, 34: "what credit [ποία χάρις] is that to you?"
1:3: "if you love those who love you"	5:46: "if you love those who love you"	6:32: "if you love those who love you"
1:3: "do not also the Gentiles do the same?"	5:46, 47: "do not even the tax collectors do the same?"; "do not even the Gentiles do the same?"	6:32, 33, 34: "even sinners love those who love them"; "even sinners do the same"; "even sinners lend to sinners"
1:3: "you must love those who hate you"	—	6:27: "love your enemies, do good to those who hate you"
1:3: "and you will have no enemy"	—	—
1:4: "abstain from fleshly and bodily cravings"	—	—
1:4: "if anyone strikes you on the right cheek, turn to him also the other [στρέψον αὐτῷ καὶ τὴν ἄλλην]"	5:39: "if anyone strikes you on the right cheek, turn the other also [στρέψον αὐτῷ καὶ τὴν ἄλλην]"	6:29: "if anyone strikes you on the cheek, offer the other also [πάρεχε καὶ τὴν ἄλλην]"
1:4: "and you will be perfect"	5:48: "be perfect . . . as your heavenly Father is perfect"	—
1:4: "if someone forces you to go one mile, go with him two miles"	5:41: "if anyone forces you to go one mile, go also the second mile"	—
1:4: "if someone takes [ἄρῃ] your cloak [ἱμάτιον], give him your tunic [χιτῶνα] as well"	5:40: "if anyone wants to sue you and take your tunic [χιτῶνα], give your cloak [ἱμάτιον] as well"	6:29: "from anyone who takes away [αἴροντος] your cloak [ἱμάτιον] do not withhold even your tunic [χιτῶνα]"

Didache 1:2–6	Matthew 5:38–48 + 7:12	Luke 6:27–36
1:4: "if someone takes from you what is yours, do not ask for it back [μὴ ἀπαίτει]"	——	6:30: "if anyone takes away your goods, do not ask for them again [μὴ ἀπαίτει]"
1:5: "to everyone who begs from you, give [παντὶ τῷ αἰτοῦντι σε δίδου] and do not demand it back"	5:42: "give to those who beg from you" (τῷ αἰτοῦντι σε δός)	6:30: "give to everyone who begs from you" (παντὶ αἰτοῦντι σε δίδου)
1:5: "the Father wants something from his own gifts to be given to everyone"	5:45: "he makes his sun rise on the evil and on the good, and sends rain on the righteous and on the unrighteous"	6:35–36: "he is kind to the ungrateful and the wicked . . . your Father is merciful"
1:5: "blessed is the one who gives according to the command . . . woe to the one who receives . . ."	——	——
1:6: "let your gift sweat in your hands"	——	——

Matthew and Luke agree against the *Didache* in almost a dozen particulars:

- *Didache* 1:2 has the more-common, negative form of the golden rule; both Matt 7:12 and Luke 6:31 have the rarer positive form.
- The imperative to pray for enemies (*Did.* 1:3) has no precise parallel in the Synoptics, although one could urge that it is a conflation of "love your enemies" and "pray for those who persecute/abuse you" (Matt 5:44; Luke 6:27–28). Extracanonical parallels include P.Oxy. 10.1224 (from an apocryphal Gospel?); Justin, *1 Apol.* 15.9; *Dial.* 96.3; 133.6; *Didascalia* 5:14:22; *Ps.-Clem. Hom.* 12:32.
- Unlike *Did.* 1:3 ("fast for those who persecute you," νηστεύετε ὑπὲρ τῶν διωκόντων ὑμᾶς), neither Matthew nor Luke has anything about fasting for others, although Matt 5:44 has a similar sentiment: "pray for those who persecute you" (προεύχεσθε ὑπὲρ τῶν διωκόντων ὑμᾶς).
- "If you love those who love you" (*Did.* 1:3) ends rather than opens its sentence; Matt 5:46–47 and Luke 6:32–34 put things the other way around.
- Although "if you love those who love you" is common to Matthew, Luke, and the *Didache*, the latter originally is likely to have read φιλῆτε . . . φιλοῦντας (so P.Oxy. 15 1782; cf. perhaps Ign. *Pol.* 2:1).[65] The Synoptics say the same thing with ἀγαπᾶτε/ἀγαπήσητε . . . ἀγαπῶντας.

65. But for caution here, see Christopher M. Tuckett, "Synoptic Tradition in the Didache," in *The New Testament in Early Christianity* (ed. Jean-Marie Sevrin; BETL 86; Leuven: Leuven University Press, 1989), 221–22.

- The original text of *Did.* 1:3 probably had "Do not even the Gentiles do this [τοῦτο ποιοῦσιν]?" (so P.Oxy. 15 1782 and the *Apostolic Constitutions*). In Matthew and Luke, the corresponding phrase is "do the same," with τὸ αὐτὸ ποιοῦσιν (to which scribes assimilated some later texts of the *Didache*).

- The optimistic assurance "And you will have no enemy" (*Did.* 1:3) has no equivalent in Matthew or Luke; those Gospels make eschatological promises, not pragmatic pledges.

- "Abstain from fleshly and bodily cravings" (*Did.* 1:4) is unique to the *Didache*.

- In the saying about the Father giving good gifts, *Did.* 1:5 fails to mention "the evil and the good" (so Matt 5:45) or "the ungrateful and the wicked" (so Luke 6:35–36).

- Neither Matt 5:38–48 nor Luke 6:27–38 has anything corresponding to the makarism or to the woe in *Did.* 1:5, nor do they feature the *Didache*'s concluding proverb: "It has also been said concerning this: 'Let your gift sweat in your hands until you know to whom to give it'" (1:6).[66]

Yet the *Didache* and Matthew concur against Luke in a number of particulars:

- Luke nowhere speaks of persecution, in contrast to *Did.* 1:3 and Matt 5:44, both of which have διωκόντων ὑμᾶς.

- In Matt 5:47 and *Did.* 1:3, the faithful are unlike "Gentiles" (Matthew: οἱ ἐθνικοί; *Didache*: τὰ ἔθνη); in Luke, they are unlike "sinners" (6:32, 33, 34).

- Luke 6:29 depicts someone being slapped on "the cheek," while *Did.* 1:4 and Matt 5:39 specify "the right cheek" (εἰς τὴν δεξιὰν σιαγόνα).

- στρέψον αὐτῷ καὶ τὴν ἄλλην ("turn to him also the other") is common to Matt 5:39 and *Did.* 1:4; πάρεχε καὶ τὴν ἄλλην ("offer also the other") is the parallel in Luke 6:29.

- Although Luke says nothing about being "perfect," the promise in *Did.* 1:4, "you will be perfect" (ἔσῃ τέλειος), has a parallel in Matthew's closing imperative (5:48): "Be perfect [ἔσεσθε οὖν ὑμεῖς τέλειοι], therefore, as your heavenly Father is perfect [τέλειος]."

- The imperative to go the second mile after being compelled to go one appears only in *Did.* 1:4 and Matt 5:41, in nearly identical form:

66. But the *Didache*'s "upon being imprisoned will be interrogated about what he has done and will not be released from there until he has repaid every last cent" (1:5) resembles Matt 5:25–26 // Luke 12:58–59 (Q).

Did. 1:4:   ἐὰν   ἀγγαρεύσῃ σέ τις μίλιον ἕν ὕπαγε μετ' αὐτοῦ δύο
Matt 5:41: καὶ ὅστις σε ἀγγαρεύσει   μίλιον ἕν ὕπαγε μετ' αὐτοῦ δύο

Likewise, sometimes Luke and the *Didache* are in accord against Matthew:

- Matthew has nothing corresponding to εὐλογεῖτε τοὺς καταρωμένους ("bless those who curse you"), which appears in both *Did.* 1:3 and Luke 6:28 (cf. also Rom 12:14).

- Only *Did.* 1:3 and Luke 6:32–34 use ποία χάρις ("what credit is it?"); slightly different rhetorical questions appear in Matt 5:46 ("what reward [μισθόν] do you have?") and 5:47 ("what more do you do?").

- In contrast to Matthew, *Did.* 1:3 (τοὺς μισοῦντας ὑμᾶς) and Luke 6:27 (τοῖς μισοῦσιν ὑμᾶς) refer to "those who hate you" (cf. Justin, *1 Apol.* 15.9; *Dial.* 133.6; *Ps.-Clem. Hom.* 3:19).

- In the saying about garments, Luke 6:29 (ἀπὸ τοῦ αἴροντος) and the *Did.* 1:4 (ἐὰν ἄρῃ τις) use the verb αἴρω and envision the outer cloak (τὸ ἱμάτιον) being forcibly taken first, the inner tunic (τὸν χιτῶνα) being offered next; Matthew, which is not about robbery but Jewish judicial procedure (cf. Exod 22:25–27; Deut 24:12–13), has it the other way around and employs λαμβάνω.

- The command in *Did.* 1:4 and Luke 6:30 not to demand one's property back (μὴ ἀπαίτει) has no match in Matthew.

- "Give to everyone who begs from you" (παντὶ [τῷ] αἰτοῦντί σε δίδου) appears in *Did.* 1:5 and Luke 6:30; "give to everyone who begs from you" (τῷ αἰτοῦντί σε δός) is the corresponding command in Matthew (5:42).

What story best accounts for the perplexing data, which have generated so many conflicting hypotheses?[67] *Didache* 1:3b–2:1 appears to be a block of Christian tradition that a redactor inserted into a traditional Jewish text on the "two ways" (which explains the form of the golden rule in *Did.* 1:2: it is from that non-Christian text, not from the Jesus tradition).[68] So even if one judges, as I have, that the Didachist knew Matthew, that does not entail the dependence of the introductory *sectio evangelica* upon the First Gospel. For we cannot identify the author of the section following 1:1–3a with the redactor

67. Although not the most recent, a helpful survey of the data and various opinions is that of Kurt Niederwimmer, *The Didache: A Commentary* (trans. Linda M. Maloney; Hermeneia; Minneapolis: Fortress, 1998), 68–72.

68. *Didache* 1:3b–2:1 is without parallel in *Barn.* 18–20 and the *Doctrina XII Apostolorum*, texts that are otherwise close to *Did.* 1–6 (see Niederwimmer, *Didache*, 68). The section is also unlike the surrounding material in having such clear Christian features: it looks like a Christianizing addition.

of the *Didache* as a whole. In other words, we must evaluate 1:3b–2:1 as an isolated or independent unit, one that could just as well have been inserted into the "two ways" tradition before the Didachist as by him or even after him.

Determining whether that introductory unit presupposes Matthew or Luke demands a judgment as to whether the Christian source taken up into *Did.* 1–2 contains redactional features of either or both of those Gospels.[69] Here the experts quarrel. Some see use of neither canonical text.[70] Others find evidence for dependence upon both or only one.[71] My own view is that *Did.* 1:3b–2:1 incorporates an oral composition influenced by but not wholly dependent upon Matthew. Whereas I see no clear traces of Lukan influence,[72] I find it hard not to detect the influence of Matt 5:48 (ἔσεσθε . . . ὑμεῖς τέλειοι, "be perfect") upon the ἔσῃ τέλειος ("you will be perfect") of *Did.* 1:4.[73]

69. One can also, if one dates the *Didache* or the *sectio evangelica* early enough, ask whether Matthew or Luke might have drawn upon the one or the other. For the argument that Matthew depends upon an early form of the *Didache*, see Alan J. P. Garrow, *The Gospel of Matthew's Dependence on the Didache* (JSNTSup 254; London: T & T Clark International, 2004).

70. For the theory that the Didachist and Matthew knew the same sayings collection, see Clayton N. Jefford, *The Sayings of Jesus in the Teaching of the Twelve Apostles* (VCSup 11; Leiden: Brill, 1989). According to Jonathan Draper ("The Jesus Tradition in the Didache," in *The Jesus Tradition outside the Gospels* [vol. 5 of *Gospel Perspectives*, ed. David Wenham; Sheffield: JSOT, 1985], 273–79), the *Didache* relies upon oral or written Q material, not Matthew or Luke. Huub van de Sandt and David Flusser (*The Didache: Its Jewish Sources and Its Place in Early Judaism and Christianity* [CRINT 3/5; Assen: Royal Van Gorcum; Minneapolis: Fortress, 2002], 40–48) also argue for independence from the Synoptic tradition, as do Glover, "Patristic Quotations," 234–51; Aaron Milavec, "Synoptic Tradition in the *Didache* Revisited," *JECS* 11 (2003): 443–80; Willy Rordorf, "Does the Didache Contain Jesus Tradition Independently of the Synoptic Gospels?" in *Jesus and the Oral Gospel Tradition* (ed. Henry Wansbrough; JSNTSup 64; Sheffield: JSOT Press, 1991), 394–423.

71. Christopher M. Tuckett ("The *Didache* and the Writings That Later Formed the New Testament," in *Reception of the New Testament* [ed. Gregory and Tuckett], 119–25) and Bentley Layton ("The Sources, Date and Transmission of *Didache* 1.3b–2.1," *HTR* 61 [1968]: 343–83) see dependence upon Matthew and Luke; so too Koester, *Synoptische Überlieferung*, 217–38; Massaux, *Influence*, 1:148–50. John S. Kloppenborg ("The Use of the Synoptics or Q in *Did.* 1:3b–2:1," in *Matthew and the Didache: Two Documents from the Same Jewish-Christian Milieu?* [ed. Huub van de Sandt; Assen: Royal Van Gorcum; Minneapolis: Fortress, 2005], 105–29) argues for a knowledge of Luke.

72. For Kloppenborg ("Use of the Synoptics"), the strongest sign of Lukan influence is the agreement between *Did.* 1:4 and Luke 6:29 (these two texts concern robbery) against Matt 5:40 (which is about a courtroom scene). But Tuckett remains correct: "The argument about originality can go (and has gone) either way. Luke could be generalizing Matthew's more technical language for a non-Jewish audience; or it could have been Matthew who has introduced the legal ideas here (cf. Mt 5,38)" ("Synoptic Tradition in the Didache," 227). See further Catchpole (*Quest for Q*, 110–11), who argues that Luke represents Q, and that the order in Matthew is redactional.

73. Contrast Tuckett's view: "Whilst this feature looks at first sight to be a clear example of an agreement between the Didache and MattR, its value should probably not be over-estimated" ("Synoptic Tradition in the Didache," 226). Tuckett appeals to *Did.* 6:2 ("If you are able to bear the whole yoke of the Lord, you will be perfect"), which indicates an independent interest by the Didachist in "perfection." Another plausible point of contact is the "right cheek" of *Did.*

Regarding the precise shape of that oral composition before or aside from Matthean influence, it is impossible to say much. Certainly we cannot reconstruct it by mechanically subtracting from the *Didache* items with parallels in Matthew alone, for sometimes Matt 5, not Luke 6, preserves the earlier tradition. In any case, this is not the place to pursue further the labyrinthine issues arising from source criticism of the *Didache*, especially since no single set of conclusions has garnered anything approaching a general consensus. What counts instead is that *Did.* 1:3b–2:1 displays parallels to every single line that the IQP assigns to Q 6:27–36. It thus offers additional support for my claim that the central section of the Sermon on the Plain is a coherent and thematically unified piece. The Didachist found it appropriate to gather into one place the golden rule (cf. Q 6:31), injunctions to benefit opponents (cf. Q 6:27–30), and teaching about reciprocity extending beyond group boundaries (cf. Q 6:32–36).

4. Quadripartite Structures

One of the prominent features of Luke 6:27–42 is that it contains three quatrains with extensive parallelism.[74] Two of them open the section:

Luke 6:27–28
"love your enemies" (27a) ἀγαπᾶτε τοὺς ἐχθροὺς ὑμῶν
"do good to those who hate you" (27b) καλῶς ποιεῖτε τοῖς μισοῦσιν ὑμᾶς
"bless those who curse you" (28a) εὐλογεῖτε τοὺς καταρωμένους ὑμᾶς
"pray for those who abuse you" (28b) προσεύχεσθε περὶ τῶν ἐπηρεαζόντων ὑμᾶς

Luke 6:29–30
"to the one striking you on the cheek, offer the other also" (29a) τῷ τύπτοντί σε ἐπὶ τὴν σιαγόνα πάρεχε καὶ τὴν ἄλλην
"and from the one taking your coat do not withhold even your shirt" (29b) καὶ ἀπὸ τοῦ αἴροντός σου τὸ ἱμάτιον καὶ τὸν χιτῶνα μὴ κωλύσῃς
"to everyone who begs from you, give" (30a) παντὶ αἰτοῦντί σε δίδου
"and from the one taking away your goods, do not ask for them again" (30b) καὶ ἀπὸ τοῦ αἴροντος τὰ σὰ μὴ ἀπαίτει

1:4 and Matt 5:39; Luke has the unqualified "cheek." According to Fitzmyer, "Luke's fondness for the 'right' hand/ear . . . makes it difficult to think that he would have suppressed the adjective here, if it were in his source" (*Luke I–IX*, 638).

74. Although some have recognized one or more of these quatrains—for example, Bovon, *Luke 1*, 231; M. D. Goulder, *Midrash and Lection in Matthew* (London: SPCK, 1974), 91; Robert C. Tannehill, *Luke* (ANTC; Nashville: Abingdon, 1996), 116–17; Richard B. Vinson, *Luke* (SHBC; Macon, GA: Smyth & Helwys, 2008), 186—I do not recall ever coming across the observation that this makes for resemblance with the extracanonical parallels to Luke 6:27–42.

The first four imperatives display the same pattern: second-person plural present imperative + noun or verbal substantive characterizing opponents + ὑμῶν/ᾶς. We also, however, have here two pairs. Both the first and third imperatives have four words, the second and fourth five; and while the first and third commands consist of imperative + τούς + -ους + ὑμῶν/ᾶς, the second and third commands exhibit a slightly different arrangement. Visually:

imperative + τούς + object ending in -ους + ὑμῶν (27a: four words)
   imperative (with adverb) + τοῖς + participle + ὑμᾶς (27b: five words)
imperative + τούς + object ending in -ους + ὑμᾶς[75] (28a: four words)
   imperative + περί + τῶν + participle + ὑμᾶς (28b: five words)

Matters are, as one can see at a glance, similar with the second set of hyperbolic imperatives; that is, here too we find pairs created by alternating formulas:

dative + σε + imperative (29a)
   καὶ ἀπὸ τοῦ + imperative with μή (29b)
dative + σε + imperative (30a)
   καὶ ἀπὸ τοῦ + imperative with μή (30b)[76]

Yet another quartet resides in the middle of Luke's sermon. Four times in 6:37–38a Jesus makes a demand and explains the consequence:

"and do not judge, and you will not be judged" (v. 37a)
   καὶ μὴ κρίνετε καὶ οὐ μὴ κριθῆτε
"and do not condemn, and you will not be condemned" (v. 37b)
   καὶ μὴ καταδικάζετε καὶ οὐ μὴ καταδικασθῆτε
"forgive, and you will be forgiven" (v. 37c)
   ἀπολύετε καὶ ἀπολυθήσεσθε
"give, and it will be given to you" (v. 38a)
   δίδοτε καὶ δοθήσεται ὑμῖν

The underlying pattern here seems to be this:

First pair:
καὶ μή + imperative beginning with κ- and ending in -ετε + καὶ οὐ μή + aorist subjunctive passive ending in -θητε

75. The parallelism would increase slightly if in 6:28a we were to read ὑμῖν (so 𝔓⁷⁵ L Δ Θ Ψ *pm*) instead of ὑμᾶς: the -ν ending of ὑμῖν would match the -ν ending of ὑμῶν.
76. In v. 29, the subjunctive serves as the imperative; v. 30 uses the simple imperative.

καὶ μή + imperative beginning with κ- ending in -ετε + καὶ οὐ μή +
  aorist subjunctive passive ending in -θητε[77]

Second pair:

positive imperative ending in -τε + καί + future passive with -θησε

positive imperative ending in -τε + καί + future passive with -θησε

How does it stand with Matthew? In general, the First Evangelist preferred triads and two-membered parallelism, which largely explains what we discover in his fifth chapter.[78] Nonetheless, even Matthew has two series of four in his parallels to Luke 6:27–42, the first being in 5:38–42. This opens with a summary contrast between what Moses taught and what Jesus teaches: "You have heard that it was said, 'An eye for an eye and a tooth for a tooth.' But I say to you, Do not resist an evildoer." These words serve as the heading for four double-membered injunctions that envisage four brief scenes: the disciple is (a) personally insulted, then (b) taken to court, then (c) impressed to do a soldier's bidding, then (d) asked to help people in need of funds:[79]

"but if anyone strikes you on the right cheek, turn the other also"
> ὅστις σε ῥαπίζει εἰς τὴν δεξιὰν σιαγόνα σου, στρέψον αὐτῷ καὶ τὴν ἄλλην

"and if anyone wants to sue you and take your coat, give your cloak as well"
> καὶ τῷ θέλοντί σοι κριθῆναι καὶ τὸν χιτῶνά σου λαβεῖν, ἄφες αὐτῷ καὶ τὸ ἱμάτιον

"and if anyone forces you to go one mile, go also the second mile"
> καὶ ὅστις σε ἀγγαρεύσει μίλιον ἕν, ὕπαγε μετ' αὐτοῦ δύο

"give to everyone who begs from you, and do not refuse anyone who wants to borrow from you"
> τῷ αἰτοῦντί σε δός, καὶ τὸν θέλοντα ἀπὸ σοῦ δανίσασθαι μὴ ἀποστραφῇς

Alternating correlations appear in these lines, just as in the Lukan parallel:

77. The textual tradition betrays an awareness that the two lines go together, for several witnesses that have ἵνα instead of καὶ οὐ in 6:37a also have ἵνα instead of καὶ οὐ in 6:37b (D W* a c e f sy^s sa Marcion).

78. See Allison, "Configuration of the Sermon on the Mount."

79. This is the analysis in Davies and Allison, *Matthew*, 1:538: the two halves of v. 42 are a single imperative. Compare Luz's view: "Following the actual antithesis in vv. 38–39a there is . . . a transition to the second person singular with four admonitions as concrete examples, introduced alternatively with 'whoever' (ὅστις) and a participle . . . only v. 42 leaves the symmetry of the concrete examples. The double imperative concluding the two clauses gives it a special accent" (*Matthew*, 1:270).

ὅστις σε + verb ending in -ζ(σ)ει: ὅστις σε ῥαπίζει

τῷ + participle ending in -ο(υ)ντι + σοι/σε, with θελοντ-:
τῷ θέλοντί σοι

ὅστις σε + verb ending in -ζ(σ)ει: ὅστις σε ἀγγαρεύσει

τῷ + participle ending in -ο(υ)ντι + σοι/σε, with θελοντ-:
τῷ αἰτοῦντί σε δός . . . θέλοντα

Matthew 5:46–47 features another alternating pattern:

"For if you love those who love you, what reward do you have?"

ἐὰν γὰρ ἀγαπήσητε τοὺς ἀγαπῶντας ὑμᾶς, τίνα μισθὸν ἔχετε;

"Do not even the tax collectors do the same?"

οὐχὶ καὶ οἱ τελῶναι τὸ αὐτὸ ποιοῦσιν;

"And if you greet only your brothers and sisters, what more are you doing than others?"

καὶ ἐὰν ἀσπάσησθε τοὺς ἀδελφοὺς ὑμῶν μόνον, τί περισσὸν ποιεῖτε;

Do not even the Gentiles do the same?"

οὐχὶ καὶ οἱ ἐθνικοὶ τὸ αὐτὸ ποιοῦσιν;

As with Matt 5:39–42 and Luke 6:27–28, 29–30, the first line resembles the third, the second line resembles the fourth:

question with ἐὰν + verb in second person beginning with ἀ- + τοὺς + ὑμᾶς + τίνα + concluding verb ending in -ετε

οὐχὶ καὶ οἱ τελῶναι τὸ αὐτὸ ποιοῦσιν;

question with ἐὰν + verb in second person beginning with ἀ- + τοὺς + ὑμῶν + τί + concluding verb ending in -ειτε

οὐχὶ καὶ οἱ ἐθνικοὶ τὸ αὐτὸ ποιοῦσιν;

The quadripartite structures that appear in Luke 6 and at the end of Matt 5 intrigue so much because similar structures appear in their extracanonical parallels. Consider, for instance, the four eschatological correlatives in Pol. *Phil.* 2:3:

"do not judge, so that you will not be judged"

μὴ κρίνετε ἵνα μὴ κριθῆτε

"forgive, and it will be forgiven you"

ἀφίετε καὶ ἀφεθήσεται ὑμῖν

"be merciful, so that mercy will be shown to you"

ἐλεᾶτε ἵνα ἐλεηθῆτε

"with the measurement that you measure, it will be measured back to
   you"
      ᾧ μέτρῳ μετρεῖτε ἀντιμετρηθήσεται ὑμῖν

As in Luke 6:27–28 and 6:29–30 and Matt 5:39–42 and 5:46–47, the first and
third lines are similar while the second and fourth lines mirror each other:[80]

imperative + ἵνα + passive verb ending in -θητε
   verb + passive verb ending in -θησεται + ὑμῖν
imperative + ἵνα + passive verb ending in -θητε
   verb + passive verb ending in -θησεται + ὑμῖν

The paragraph is, moreover, introduced by yet another series of four with
manifest parallelism:

"not returning evil for evil"
      μὴ ἀποδιδόντες κακὸν ἀντὶ κακοῦ
"or insult for insult"
      ἢ λοιδορίαν ἀντὶ λοιδορίας
"or blow for blow"
      ἢ γρόνθον ἀντὶ γρόνθου
"or curse for curse"
      ἢ κατάραν ἀντὶ κατάρας

Here, too, the first and third entries seem to match each other as do the second
and fourth:

accusative ending in -ον + ἀντί + genitive ending in -ου
   accusative ending in -ριαν + ἀντί + genitive ending in -ριας
accusative ending in -ον + ἀντί + genitive ending in -ου
   accusative ending in -ραν + ἀντί + genitive ending in -ρας

An obvious fourfold series featuring parallelism also marks *1 Clem.* 13:2.
Although the first two imperatives in v. 2 constitute a pair, "Be merciful, so
that you will receive mercy; forgive, so that you may be forgiven,"[81] and while
the last saying stands on its own, "With the measurement that you measure,

---

80. See the analysis in Massaux, *Influence*, 1:29.
81. In each case the structure consists of an imperative ending in -τε + ἵνα + aorist passive
with -θη.

according to that will it be measured to you," the declarations in the middle
are, by contrast, formally very similar and create a series:

"as you do, so will it be done to you"
  ὡς ποιεῖτε οὕτω ποιηθήσεται ὑμῖν
"as you give, so will it be given to you"
  ὡς δίδοτε οὕτως δοθήσεται ὑμῖν
"as you judge, so will you be judged"
  ὡς κρίνετε οὕτως κριθήσεσθε
"as you show kindness, so will kindness be shown to you"
  ὡς χρηστεύεσθε οὕτως χρηστευθήσεται ὑμῖν

Each of these sentences has the form ὡς + second-person plural present in-
dicative ending in -τ(θ)ε + οὕτω(ς) + future passive.
  We also find a quartet in the *Didache*'s *sectio evangelica*, in 1:4:[82]

"if someone gives you a blow on your right cheek, turn to him the other
  also"
  ἐάν τις σοι δῷ ῥάπισμα εἰς τὴν δεξιὰν σιαγόνα, στρέψον αὐτῷ καὶ τὴν
  ἄλλην
"if someone forces you to go one mile, go with him two miles"
  ἐὰν ἀγγαρεύσῃ σέ τις μίλιον ἕν, ὕπαγε μετ' αὐτοῦ δύο
"if someone takes your cloak, give him your tunic also"
  ἐὰν ἄρῃ τις τὸ ἱμάτιόν σου, δὸς αὐτῷ καὶ τὸν χιτῶνα
"if someone takes from you what belongs to you, do not demand it back"
  ἐὰν λάβῃ τις ἀπὸ σοῦ τὸ σόν, μὴ ἀπαίτει

One can see the parallelism at a glance:

ἐάν + τις + σοι + aorist subjunctive + imperative + αὐτῷ καὶ + definite
  article + substantive/noun
  ἐάν + aorist subjunctive + σε + τις + imperative
ἐάν + aorist subjunctive + τις + σου + imperative + αὐτῷ καὶ + definite
  article + substantive/noun
  ἐάν + aorist subjunctive + τις + σου + imperative

The first and third lines mirror each other.

82. Niederwimmer observes, "The first four logia [in 1:4] belong together, both formally
and in content (cf. the fourfold ἐὰν . . . στρέψον, ὕπαγε, δός, μὴ ἀπαίτει)" (*Didache*, 78).

Yet another series of four imperatives occurs in *Did.* 1:3, although in this instance a clarifying rhetorical question intrudes itself between the third and fourth members:

"bless those who curse you"
εὐλογεῖτε τοὺς καταρωμένους ὑμῖν
"pray for your enemies"
καὶ προσεύχεσθε ὑπὲρ τῶν ἐχθρῶν ὑμῶν
"fast for those who persecute you"
νηστεύετε δὲ ὑπὲρ τῶν διωκόντων ὑμᾶς
[["for what credit if you love those who love you?" etc.]]
"but you must love those who hate you, and you will not have an enemy"
ὑμεῖς δὲ ἀγαπᾶτε τοὺς μισοῦντας ὑμᾶς καὶ οὐχ ἕξετε ἐχθρόν

In this connection, one can also refer to the fourfold imperative in Justin, *1 Apol.* 15.9. This text probably comes from an early harmony of Matthew and Luke:[83]

"pray for your enemies"
εὔχεσθε ὑπὲρ τῶν ἐχθρῶν ὑμῶν
"and love those who hate you"
καὶ ἀγαπᾶτε τοὺς μισοῦντας ὑμᾶς
"and bless those who curse you"
καὶ εὐλογεῖτε τοὺς καταρωμένους ὑμῖν
"and pray for those who despitefully use you"
καὶ εὔχεσθε ὑπὲρ τῶν ἐπηρεαζόντων ὑμᾶς

So the material in Luke 6:27–42 and its extracanonical relatives again and again employ not only extensive parallelism but also fourfold repetition. An appeal to coincidence passes credulity. What, then, is the explanation?

Ancient Jews and Christians, for poetic and mnemonic reasons, often arranged material into two parallel lines or two antithetical lines. They were also fond of triadic structures. All of this is well known. But quadripartite arrangements are also attested.[84] They appear, for instance, in Psalms,[85]

---

83. See Arthur J. Bellinzoni, *The Sayings of Jesus in the Writings of Justin Martyr* (NovTSup 17; Leiden: Brill, 1967), 77–80.

84. For useful material and discussion, see T. A. Perry, *Wisdom Literature and the Structure of Proverbs* (University Park: Pennsylvania State University Press, 1993).

85. Two examples: Ps 136:4–7 ("who alone does great wonders, for his steadfast love endures forever // who by understanding made the heavens, for his steadfast love endures forever // who spread out the earth on the waters, for his steadfast love endures forever // who made the great

Proverbs,[86] Lamentations,[87] the Prophets,[88] and rabbinic literature.[89] They further show up in the Jesus tradition—in Q's four beatitudes (Q 6:20–23), for example, and Luke's four woes (Luke 6:24–26), and in the four yields in the parable of the sower (Mark 4:3–9).

My suggestion, then, is that Luke 6:27–42; Matt 5:38–48; *1 Clem.* 13:2; Pol. *Phil.* 2:3; *Did.* 1:3–5; Justin, *1 Apol.* 15.9 not only reflect a widespread sense that several injunctions of Jesus naturally belong together but also show us that early Christian tradents associated those sayings with a particular format: the series of four with parallel members, often with the first member formally related to the third, the second to the fourth. The various texts may execute the plan in different ways, but it is the same plan:

Doing Good to Enemies

Luke 6:27–28	*Did.* 1:3	Justin, *1 Apol.* 15.9
love	bless	pray
do good	pray	love
bless	fast	bless
pray	love	pray

Not Responding in Kind

Luke 6:29–30	Matt 5:39–42	*Did.* 1:4	Pol. *Phil.* 2:3
to the one striking	to the one striking	if struck a blow	not returning evil for evil
from the one taking	to the one wanting to sue	if forced to go	insult for insult

---

lights, for his steadfast love endures forever"); 148:9–12 ("Mountains and all hills // fruit trees and all cedars! // Wild animals and all cattle // creeping things and flying birds!").

86. Above all in Prov 30: vv. 11–14 ("There are those" introduces four consecutive sentences), vv. 15–16 ("Three things are never satisfied; four never say, 'Enough'"), vv. 18–19 ("Three things are too wonderful for me; four I do not understand"), vv. 21–23 ("Under three things the earth trembles; under four it cannot bear up"), vv. 24–28 ("Four things on earth are small, yet they are exceedingly wise"), vv. 29–31 ("Three things are stately in their stride; four are stately in their gait").

87. Lamentations 4 consists exclusively of couplets featuring bicolas, which means that each stanza has four lines. See the visual presentation in Johan Renkema, *Lamentations* (trans. Brian Doyle; HCOT; Leuven: Peeters, 1998), 479–82.

88. For example, the oracles in Amos 1–2 are built around the structure "For three transgressions of X, and for four, I will not revoke the punishment."

89. For example, *m. 'Abot* 5:10 ("There are four types among men . . ."), 11 ("There are four types of character . . ."), 12 ("There are four types of disciple . . ."), 13 ("There are four types of almsgivers . . ."), 14 ("There are four types among them that frequent the house of study . . ."), 15 ("There are four types among them that sit in the presence of the sages . . ."). For a long list of additional examples, see August Wünsch, "Die Zahlensprüche in Talmud und Midrasch," *ZDMG* 65 (1911): 395–412.

Luke 6:29–30	Matt 5:39–42	*Did.* 1:4	Pol. *Phil.* 2:3
to everyone who begs	to the one compelling	if cloak taken	blow for blow
from the one taking	give to all who beg	if property taken	curse for curse

Refraining from Judgment

Luke 6:37–38	Pol. *Phil.* 2:3	*1 Clem.* 13:2
do not judge	do not judge	as you do
do not condemn	forgive	give
forgive	be merciful	do not judge
give	with the measure you use . . .	show kindness

Reciprocity

Matt 5:46–47 (four questions)
If you love . . . ?
Do not even . . . ?
If you greet . . . ?
Do not even . . . ?

Surely this formal similarity strengthens the conviction that the sayings in Q 6:27–42 were not passed on in isolation from each other but rather were perceived of as a group, one linked with a very specific formal configuration.[90]

Quadripartite Structures and Q 6. Before the next topic is approached, a few comments on the Sayings Source are in order. We have good reason to believe that it too featured one or more quadripartite structures.

In his parallel to Luke 6:27–28—"love your enemies" (v. 27a) // "do good to those who hate you" (v. 27b) // "bless those who curse you" (v. 28a) // "pray for those who abuse you" (v. 28b)—Matthew has only the first and final imperatives: "Love your enemies, and pray for those who persecute you" (5:44). That the First Evangelist has here abbreviated is, however, highly likely. (a) Luke does not favor asyndetic strings of imperatives.[91] (b) He also shows no tendency to enhance the sort of close verbal parallelism that 6:27–28 displays.[92]

90. John Dominic Crossan (*In Fragments: The Aphorisms of Jesus* [San Francisco: Harper & Row, 1983]) does a first-rate job of showing how the tradition often retains structures even as it makes all sorts of revisions. The phenomenon is hardly unique to Luke 6:27–42 and its parallels.

91. See Joachim Jeremias, *Die Sprache des Lukasevangeliums: Redaktion und Tradition im Nicht-Markusstoff des dritten Evangeliums* (KEK; Göttingen: Vandenhoeck & Ruprecht, 1980), 141–42.

92. See Eduard Norden, *Agnostos Theos: Untersuchungen zur Formengeschichte religiöser Rede* (Leipzig: B. G. Teubner, 1913), 355–64.

(c) While Luke does not typically expand sayings, Matthew often abbreviates them.[93] (d) Since Luke prefers ἀγαθοποιέω over καλῶς ποιέω ("do good"), the occurrence of the latter in 6:27b is unlikely to be redactional.[94] (e) Lastly, the redactional Matt 5:43 ("hate your enemy") can be understood as a reminiscence of the Sayings Source if Luke 6:27b ("do good to those who hate you") represents Q. One understands why Harry Fleddermann's reconstruction of Q 6:27–28 is very close to Luke's quatrain.[95]

Incidentally, if Fleddermann is right, and if, in accord with the IQP, one prefers Matthew's διωκόντων ("persecuting") over Luke's ἐπηρεαζόντων ("abusing"), the resulting text reminds one of LXX Deut 30:7: "The LORD your God will put these curses upon your enemies, and upon those who hate you, who have persecuted you."[96]

LXX Deut 30:7	Q 6:27–28
τὰς ἀρὰς ταύτας	τοὺς καταρωμένους ὑμᾶς
τοὺς ἐχθρούς σου	τοὺς ἐχθροὺς ὑμῶν
τοὺς μισοῦντάς σε	τοῖς μισοῦσιν ὑμᾶς
οἳ ἐδίωξάν σε	τῶν διωκόντων ὑμᾶς

I am inclined to see here antithetical, ironic intertextuality,[97] especially since three of the four imperatives in Q 6:27–28 also have verbal counterparts in the immediate context of LXX Deut 30:7:

LXX Deut 30:7	Q 6:27–28
ἀγαπᾶν (v. 6)	ἀγαπᾶτε (v. 27)
εὖ ποιήσει (v. 5)	καλῶς ποιεῖτε (v. 27)
εὐλογήσει (v. 9)	εὐλογεῖτε (v. 28)

In Deuteronomy, Israelites are to love God, who will bless them and do them good; in turn, God will curse their enemies, who hate and persecute them. In Q, Jesus' followers are, to the contrary, to love their enemies, do good to those who hate them, bless those who curse them, and pray for those who persecute them.

Whatever one makes of this intertextual proposal, the next two verses, Luke 6:29–30, could also represent a fourfold series from Q,[98] especially since

93. So Catchpole, *Quest for Q*, 103, appealing to Jacques Dupont, *Les Béatitudes*, vol. 1, *Le problème littéraire* (EB; Paris: Gabalda, 1969), 155. Cf. Matt 18:8–9 diff. Mark 9:43–48.

94. ἀγαθοποιέω: Matt: 0; Mark: 1; Luke: 3. Cf. Luke 6:33 diff. Matt 5:46.

95. Harry T. Fleddermann, *Q: A Reconstruction and Commentary* (BibTS 1; Leuven: Peeters, 2005), 289–91. Cf. Catchpole, *Quest for Q*, 103–5.

96. That there might be a link between Q 6:27–28 and Deut 30:7 is an observation that I owe to O. J. F. Seitz, "Love Your Enemies: The Historical Setting of Matthew v.43f.; Luke vi.27f.," *NTS* 16 (1969): 44–45. His suggestion seems to have gone unnoticed.

97. On this phenomenon elsewhere in Q, see Allison, *Intertextual Jesus*, 192–97.

98. So also Fleddermann, *Q: A Reconstruction*, 284–89.

the Matthean parallel, Matt 5:39–42, features a quartet. But the matter is complex. Matthew's series is constructed differently from Luke's. In the First Gospel, the commands to "give" and "not refuse" are combined into a single injunction ("Give to everyone who begs from you, and do not refuse anyone who wants to borrow from you"), and 5:41 ("If anyone forces you to go one mile, go also the second mile") lacks a Lukan counterpart:

Luke 6:29–30	Matthew 5:39–42
If anyone strikes you on the cheek, offer the other also;	If anyone strikes you on the right cheek, turn the other also;
and from anyone who takes away your coat do not withhold even your shirt.	and if anyone wants to sue you and take your coat, give your cloak as well;
	and if anyone forces you to go one mile, go also the second mile.
Give to everyone who begs from you;	Give to everyone who begs from you, and do not refuse anyone who wants to borrow from you.
and if anyone takes away your goods, do not ask for them again.	

This raises the possibility that Q had a series of five—turn the other cheek, let go of one's garment, go the extra mile, give to beggars, lend to borrowers—and that Matthew and Luke in their different ways reduced five to four.

One can, however, hardly verify this conjecture. We do not know the source of Matt 5:41.[99] Some have thought it redactional,[100] others that it stood in Q, Luke having dropped it either because of his general tendency to exonerate the Romans or because there were no Roman troops in his area. But then it is also possible that 5:41 stood only in Matthew's version of Q, a copyist or scribe having inserted it along the way.[101] Unfortunately, we lack enough clues to adjudicate the matter. So the question as to whether Q 6:29–30 had four parallel sentences must remain open.[102]

What, then, of Luke's third quartet: "do not judge, and you will not be judged" // "do not condemn, and you will not be condemned" // "forgive, and you will be forgiven" // "give, and it will be given to you. A good measure . . ."

99. For a survey of opinion, see Kloppenborg, *Q Parallels*, 30. The IQP includes Matt 5:41 in Q but surrounds it with double brackets.

100. For example, Fleddermann, *Q: A Reconstruction*, 286–87; Robert H. Gundry, *Matthew: A Commentary on His Handbook for a Mixed Church under Persecution* (2nd ed.; Grand Rapids: Eerdmans, 1994), 93–94.

101. According to Luz, Matt 5:41 is "usually regarded as a preredactional addition in Q^Mt" (*Matthew*, 1:271).

102. It is worth observing, however, that if Q did have four lines, and if Matthew added 5:41, then perhaps he turned the commands to "give" and "not refuse" into a single unit precisely because he wanted to preserve a quadripartite arrangement.

(6:37–38)? The IQP excludes most of this material from Q, implicitly assigning the fourfold structure to Luke.[103] David Catchpole, to the contrary, has argued that the whole comes from Q, and this is no less plausible.[104] I am inclined to follow his lead. (a) As already remarked, it was not Luke's wont to extend and enhance close parallelism. (b) The continuation of the fourth member, itself containing a quartet—"a good measure, pressed down, shaken together, running over, will be put into your lap"—probably refers to "the Palestinian custom of using the fold of a garment as a container for grain, . . . something which is unlikely to have been introduced into the tradition by Luke."[105] (c) Luke nowhere else uses καταδικάζω ("condemn"), and he often drops οὐ μή, which appears here twice, both times in v. 37.[106] (d) Most significantly of all, *1 Clem.* 13:2 has a series of four imperatives that is a close relative of Luke 6:37–38—"as you do, so will it be done to you" // "as you give, so will it be given to you" // "as you judge, so will you be judged" // "as you show kindness, so will kindness be shown to you"—and the independence of the former from the latter has been apparent to many.[107] We can, then, hardly exclude the possibility that Q 6:37–38 had a series of four imperatives. Indeed, this seems to be a probability rather than a possibility.

What, finally, of the quartet of questions in Matt 5:46–47? Here is the text with its Lukan parallel:

Matthew 5:46–47	Luke 6:32–34
For if you love those who love you, what reward do you have?	If you love those who love you, what credit is that to you?
Do not even the tax collectors do the same?	For even sinners love those who love them.
And if you greet only your brothers and sisters, what more are you doing than others?	If you do good to those who do good to you, what credit is that to you?
Do not even the Gentiles do the same?	For even sinners do the same.
	If you lend to those from whom you hope to receive, what credit is that to you?
	Even sinners lend to sinners, to receive as much again.

Instead of Matthew's four questions, Luke has a triad with an alternating sequence: question + comment; question + comment; question + comment.

103. See Fleddermann, *Q: A Reconstruction*, 294–95; Piper, *Wisdom in the Q-Tradition*, 37–38.
104. Catchpole, *Quest for Q*, 121–22. For a review of opinion, see Kloppenborg, *Q Parallels*, 34.
105. Catchpole, *Quest for Q*, 121–22.
106. See Jeremias, *Sprache*, 36.
107. The point would be reinforced if one were to view Pol. *Phil.* 2:3 as also independent; but this is, as became clear above, quite uncertain.

The IQP, although it does not simply reproduce Matthew, prints a text with four questions.[108] This implies that Luke turned two questions into statements (Luke 6:32b diff. Matt 5:46b; Luke 6:33b diff. Matt 5:47b) and then inserted 6:34.[109] Perhaps that is the correct judgment. I have, however, failed to discover in the secondary literature arguments to persuade me of this, or to satisfy me of the contrary; and there would be little point in rehearsing unconvincing arguments. So I must leave it at this: Q 6:32–33 may or may not have consisted of four rhetorical questions.

Despite failure to resolve that issue, we have found evidence that Q 6:27–47 contained at least one quartet. Indeed, the very fact that Luke has three quadripartite structures, Matthew two, suggests that the section probably had more than one.

5. Paul

Several verses in Rom 12–14 have reminded commentators of logia assigned to Q 6:27–42. The two most prominent are the following:

- Rom 12:14: "Bless [εὐλογεῖτε] those who persecute [διώκοντας] you; bless [εὐλογεῖτε] and do not curse [καταρᾶσθε] them." This shows significant conceptual and verbal overlap with what likely stood in Q 6:27–28: "Love your enemies, do good to those who hate you, bless [εὐλογεῖτε] those who curse [καταρωμένους] you, pray for those who persecute [διωκόντων] you." Both Rom 12:14 and Q, moreover, have a present imperative + present participle, and Paul goes on to refer explicitly to one's "enemy" (12:17–21: ἐχθρός, from LXX Prov 25:21). This recalls Q's opening injunction to "love your enemies [ἐχθρούς]." Throughout exegetical history, commentators on Rom 12:14 have called to mind Luke 6:27–38 or its Matthean twin and Jesus' teaching on nonresistance.[110]

108. See Robinson, Hoffmann, and Kloppenborg, eds., *Critical Edition of Q*, 68, 72: "If you love those loving you, what reward do you have? Do not even the tax collectors do the same? And if you lend to those from whom you hope to receive, what reward do you have? Do not even the Gentiles do the same?"

109. See Catchpole, *Quest for Q*, 109; Fleddermann, *Q: A Reconstruction*, 291–93.

110. So recently, for example, Eduard Lohse, "Herrenworte im Römerbrief," in *Rechenschaft vom Evangelium: Exegetische Studien zum Römerbrief* (BZNW 150; Berlin: de Gruyter, 2007), 82–84; Ulrich Wilckens, *Röm 12–16* (vol. 3 of *Der Brief an die Römer*; EKKNT 6/3; Zürich: Benziger; Neukirchen Vluyn: Neukirchener-Verlag, 1982), 22–23. Earlier commentators include Theodoret of Cyrus, *Comm. Rom.* ad loc. (PG 82:192A); Hugo Grotius, *Opera omnia theologica* (3 vols.; Amsterdam: Joannis Blaeu, 1679), 2:748; Matthew Poole, *Annotations on the Holy Bible* (3 vols.; London: Henry G. Bohn, 1846), 3:523; F. Godet, *Commentary on St. Paul's Epistle to the Romans* (New York: Funk & Wagnalls, 1885), 436; Charles Hodge, *Commentary on the Epistle to the Romans* (new ed.; Philadelphia: James S. Clayton, 1864), 627; H. P. Liddon, *Explanatory Analysis of St. Paul's Epistle to the Romans* (2nd ed.; London: Longmans, Green,

- Rom 14:10–13: "Why do you pass judgment [κρίνεις] on your brother [τὸν ἀδελφόν σου] . . . ? Or you, why do you despise your brother . . . ? For we will all stand before the judgment seat of God. . . . So then, each of us will be accountable to God. Let us therefore no longer pass judgment [μηκέτι . . . κρίνωμεν] on one another" (cf. Rom 14:3: μὴ κρινέτω). This is remarkably close to Q 6:37–42, which is dominated by the κριν-root, contains the unqualified, present-tense imperative not to condemn others (6:37: μὴ κρίνετε), refers several times to a "brother" (6:41–42: τοῦ ἀδελφοῦ σου), and discourages judging others by referring to the eschatological judgment (6:37–38: "[[With the judgment that you judge, you will be judged.]] And with the measure that you measure, it will be measured to you").[111]

Some have doubted that these verses from Paul really depend upon the Jesus tradition.[112] To rehearse the arguments pro and con would transgress the bounds of this chapter. I can, however, record my conviction that the reviews of Michael Thompson and James Dunn have settled the issue: that Paul, when writing Rom 12–14, was at several points, including 12:14 and 14:10–13, drawing upon and indeed recalling sayings of Jesus is overwhelmingly likely.[113]

1893), 242. Also worth noting, given the discussion of Lev 19 below, is that Tertullian (*Marc.* 5.14) links Rom 12:14 with Lev 19:17–18.

111. See further Michael Thompson, *Clothed with Christ: The Example and Teaching of Jesus in Romans 12.1–15.13* (JSNTSup 59; Sheffield: JSOT Press, 1991), 161–73. Thompson (pp. 91–94) suggests that Paul's reference to ἀνυπόκριτος ἀγάπη might have a background in the Jesus tradition, above all in Matt 7:5 // Luke 6:42 (Q). Commentators have sometimes moved from Rom 14:10–13 to Matt 7:1–2 or Luke 6:37; so, for example, Apollinaris of Laodicea, *Fragmenta in Rom* ad loc. (NTAbh 15:79); Grotius, *Opera omnia theologica*, 2:756; Thomas Chalmers, *Lectures on the Epistle of Paul to the Romans* (New York: Robert Carter, 1843), 488; Anders Nygren, *Commentary on Romans* (Philadelphia: Muhlenberg, 1949), 445; Robert Jewett, *Romans: A Commentary* (Hermeneia; Minneapolis: Fortress, 2006), 850.

112. For example, Franz Neirynck, "Paul and the Sayings of Jesus," in *Evangelica II, 1982–1991: Collected Essays* (ed. F. Van Segbroeck; BETL 99; Leuven: Leuven University Press, 1991), 541–46; Walter T. Wilson, *Love without Pretense: Romans 12.9–21 and Hellenistic-Jewish Wisdom Literature* (WUNT 2/46; Tübingen: Mohr Siebeck, 1991), 165–71; Dieter Zeller, *Der Brief an die Römer* (RNT; Regensburg: Friedrich Pustet, 1985), 210.

113. James D. G. Dunn, "Jesus Tradition in Paul," in *Studying the Historical Jesus: Evaluations of the State of Current Research* (ed. Bruce Chilton and Craig A. Evans; NTTS 19; Leiden: Brill, 1994), 155–78; idem, "Paul's Knowledge of the Jesus Tradition," in *Christus Bezeugen: Festschrift für Wolfgang Trilling* (ed. Karl Kertelge, Traugott Holts, and Claus-Peter März; ETS 19; Leipzig: St. Benno-Verlag, 1989), 193–207; Thompson, *Clothed with Christ*, 90–110, 161–73. Michael Goulder cites these parallels in making his case that Matthew knew Romans (*The Evangelists' Calendar: A Lectionary Explanation of the Development of Scripture* [London: SPCK, 1978], 228–29). Additional verses in Rom 12–14 often thought to echo the central part of the Sermon on the Plain include Rom 12:17 ("Do not repay anyone evil for evil, but take thought for what is noble in the sight of all"), 19 ("Beloved, never avenge yourselves"), 21 ("Be not overcome by evil, but overcome evil with good").

Perhaps the apostle implies as much when, in 13:14, he exhorts the Romans to "put on the Lord Jesus Christ."[114]

What follows from all of this, especially when one adds that a few Pauline texts outside of Rom 12–14 also recall portions of Q 6:27–42?[115] Certainly the apostle had not read Matthew or Luke, and few have taken his writings to disclose an acquaintance with Q in its entirety, as opposed to various traditions taken up into Q.[116] This leaves us to surmise that whatever Jesus tradition the apostle had at hand, most of it was probably in the form of isolated sayings and/or small collections.[117] It is, then, reasonable to posit, as have Heinz Schürmann and Helmut Koester,[118] that Paul may have known something like Q's Sermon on the Plain or a relative of the anthology in *1 Clem.* 13:2.

6. Ephesians

I wish tentatively to propose one last possible witness to the cluster of sayings now found in Luke 6:27–42. Ephesians 4:31–5:1 reads as follows: "Put away from you all bitterness and wrath and anger and wrangling and slander, together with all malice, and be kind to one another, tenderhearted, forgiving one another, as God in Christ has forgiven you. Therefore be imitators of God, as beloved children, and live in love, as Christ loved us and gave himself up for us, a fragrant offering and sacrifice to God."

Our best guess is that someone wrote these words in Paul's name during the last quarter of the first century.[119] We have no evidence that the author,

114. For the argument that Paul's general exhortation presumes knowledge of traditions about Jesus, see Thompson, *Clothed with Christ*, 149–58.

115. For example, Rom 2:1 ("for in passing judgment on another you condemn yourself," ἐν ᾧ γὰρ κρίνεις τὸν ἕτερον σεαυτὸν κατακρίνεις [cf. the IQP for Q 6:37: ἐν ᾧ γὰρ κρίματι κρίνετε κριθήσεσθε]); 1 Cor 4:5, 12 ("When reviled, we bless; when persecuted, we endure," λοιδορούμενοι εὐλογοῦμεν, διωκόμενοι ἀνεχόμεθα [cf. Q 6:28–30, with διώκω; also 1 Pet 3:9]); 1 Thess 5:15 ("See that none of you repays evil for evil, but always seek to do good to one another and to all," ὁρᾶτε μή τις κακὸν ἀντὶ κακοῦ τινι ἀποδῷ ἀλλὰ πάντοτε τὸ ἀγαθὸν διώκετε καὶ εἰς ἀλλήλους καὶ εἰς πάντας [cf. Q 6:27–30 and Luke 6:35 (= Q?), with ἀγαθοποιεῖτε]). Although not returning evil for evil was a traditional injunction, the extension of doing good always and to "all" in 1 Thess 5:15 (cf. Rom 12:17) recalls the Jesus tradition specifically.

116. Although I once fashioned an argument for Paul's knowledge of Q as a whole, it involved a bit of conjecture and has not influenced subsequent discussion; see Allison, *Jesus Tradition*, 54–60.

117. I once made the case for this in Dale C. Allison Jr., "The Pauline Epistles and the Synoptic Gospels: The Pattern of the Parallels," *NTS* 28 (1982): 1–32. Despite my changes of mind on several matters as well as some significant criticism from others, I remain convinced that this article was moving in the right direction.

118. Schürmann, *Lukasevangelium: Erster Teil*, 385–86; Koester, *Ancient Christian Gospels*, 54.

119. Ernest Best (*A Critical and Exegetical Commentary on Ephesians* [ICC; Edinburgh: T & T Clark, 1998], 44–46) dates the letter between 80 and 90 CE.

whoever he may have been, knew either Luke or Matthew. With this in mind, the links between Eph 4:31–5:1 and Luke 6:27–42 are intriguing.

Modern commentators on Ephesians regularly assert that 5:1 is the only passage in the New Testament to use the language of imitation (μιμητής, μιμέομαι) with reference to God. They then typically observe that the notion of the imitation of the divinity is prominent in Plato and Philo but rare in the New Testament, although there is a substantive parallel (without μιμητής or μιμέομαι) in Matt 5:44–45, 48 ("But I say to you, Love your enemies and pray for those who persecute you, so that you may be children of your Father in heaven; for he makes his sun rise on the evil and on the good, and sends rain on the righteous and on the unrighteous. . . . Be perfect, therefore, as your heavenly Father is perfect") and Luke 6:35–36 ("Love your enemies, do good, and lend, expecting nothing in return. Your reward will be great, and you will be children of the Most High; for he is kind to the ungrateful and the wicked. Be merciful, just as your father is merciful").[120] Observation of the parallel with the Synoptics usually remains unelaborated; it issues in no further discussion.[121]

This strikes me as an oversight, because Eph 4:32–5:2 and the central section of the Sermon on the Plain share a series of parallels:

120. Cf. T. K. Abbott, *A Critical and Exegetical Commentary on the Epistles to the Ephesians and to the Colossians* (ICC; Edinburgh: T & T Clark, 1902), 146 ("The idea is a grand and ennobling one; and our Lord Himself sets it before us, and in the same aspect, when He says, 'Ye therefore shall be perfect, as your heavenly Father is perfect,' namely, in that 'He maketh His sun to rise on the evil and on the good . . .' [Matt. v. 45, 48]"); John Muddiman, *A Commentary on the Epistle of the Ephesians* (BNTC; London: Continuum, 2001), 230 ("the thought" of Eph 5:1 "is similar to the antithesis on love of enemies in the Sermon on the Mount"); Rudolf Schnackenburg, *Der Brief an die Epheser* (EKKNT 10; Zurich: Benzinger; Neukirchen-Vluyn: Neukirchener Verlag, 1982), 216 (the closest substantial parallel to Eph 5:1 is Jesus' imperative to be merciful because God is merciful [Luke 6:36]); Gerhard Sellin, *Der Brief an die Epheser* (KEK 8; Göttingen: Vandenhoeck & Ruprecht, 2008), 381 n. 12 ("the nearest parallel to it [Eph 5:1] is Lk 6,36"); B. F. Westcott, *Saint Paul's Epistle to the Ephesians* (London: Macmillan, 1906), 75. Earlier writers associating Eph 5:1 with Matt 5:44–48 or Luke 6:35–36 include Origen, *Cels.* 6.63; Ps.-Clem. *Hom.* 12:26; Jerome, *Comm. Eph.* ad loc.; Basil of Caesarea, *Reg. br.* 276 (PG 31:1276A); Chrysostom, *Hom. Eph.* ad loc.; Pelagius, *Comm. Eph.* ad loc. (TS 9:372); Grotius, *Opera omnia theologica*, 2:899; Johann Albrecht Bengel, *Gnomon Novi Testamenti* (2 vols.; Tübingen: Ludov. Frid. Fues, 1850), 2:275–76. Some commentaries, however, overlook the parallel entirely—for example, Markus Barth, *Ephesians: Translation and Commentary on Chapters 4–6* (AB 34A; Garden City, NY: Doubleday, 1974), 555–56, 588–92; Petr Pokorný, *Der Brief des Paulus an die Epheser* (THKNT 10/2; Leipzig: Evangelische Verlagsanstalt, 1992), 196–97.

121. But M.-É Boismard (*L'Énigme de la lettre aux Éphésiens* [EB 39; Paris: Gabalda, 1999], 124) speculates that Ephesians, as we know it, is a rewritten letter of Paul, and that the redactor's version of Eph 5:1–2 was "probably inspired" by Matt 5:45–48. Long before Boismard, Alfred Resch (*Agrapha: Aussercanonische Evangelienfragmente* [TU 5/4; Leipzig: J. C. Hinrichs, 1989], 217) observed the parallel, which he attributed to common dependence upon a precanonical source.

	Ephesians 4:32–5:2	Luke 6:27–37
Imperative to imitate God	"be [γίνεσθε] imitators of God" (5:1)	"be [γίνεσθε] merciful, just as your Father is merciful" (6:36)
To imitate God is to be a child of God	"be imitators of God, as beloved children [τέκνα]" (5:1)	"you will be children [υἱοί] of the Most High; for he is kind to the ungrateful and the wicked" (6:35)
Imitating God manifests itself above all in loving others	"live in love [ἀγάπῃ], as Christ loved [ἠγάπησεν] us" (5:2)	"love [ἀγαπᾶτε] your enemies" (6:27, 35); "if you love [ἀγαπᾶτε] those who love you" (6:32)
Model for imitation introduced with καθὼς καί following γίνεσθε	"be . . . as also God [γίνεσθε . . . καθὼς καὶ ὁ θεός]" (4:32); cf. "be . . . as also Christ [γίνεσθε . . . καθὼς καὶ ὁ Χριστός]" (5:1–2)	"be . . . as also your Father is merciful [γίνεσθε . . . καθὼς καὶ ὁ πατὴρ ὑμῶν]" (6:36)
One should be kind because God is kind	"be kind [χρηστοί] to one another, tenderhearted, forgiving one another, as God in Christ has forgiven you" (4:32)[122]	"Love your enemies, do good, and lend, expecting nothing in return. . . . You will be children of the Most High; for he is kind [χρηστός] to the ungrateful and the wicked" (6:35)[123]
Correlation between forgiving and being forgiven	"forgiving [χαριζόμενοι] one another, as God in Christ has forgiven [ἐχαρίσατο] you" (4:32)	"forgive [ἀπολύετε], and you will be forgiven [ἀπολυθήσεσθε]" (6:37)[124]
Call to be benevolent	"be tenderhearted [γίνεσθε . . . εὔσπλαγχνοι]" (4:32)	"be merciful [γίνεσθε οἰκτίρμονες]" (6:36)

What should one make of these parallels? I am uncertain that they suffice to establish that Eph 4:32–5:2 alludes to a well-known anthology of sayings of Jesus. That is, I am not so bold as to affirm that the author of the epistle wanted readers to recall the logia preserved as a family in Luke 6:27–42 and elsewhere. The connections may be too fleeting for that. Given, however, that those logia enjoyed wide circulation in the early church, the similarities just observed do raise the realistic possibility that a relative of the central section of the Sermon on the Plain influenced Eph 4:32–5:2. The latter may not function

122. Is it only a coincidence that Ephesians' γίνεσθε . . . χρηστοί, εὔσπλαγχνοι resembles the form of Matt 5:48 // Luke 6:36 (Q) that Justin gives in both *1 Apol.* 15.13 and *Dial.* 96.3: γίνεσθε (δὲ) χρηστοὶ καὶ οἰτίρμονες?

123. Poole observed this parallel and the next: "Be ye therefore followers of God: particularly in being kind, and forgiving injuries, Matt. v. 45, 48; so that this relates to the last verse of the former chapter" (*Annotations*, 3:675). Thomas Aquinas (*Comm. Eph.* ad loc.) rather connects Eph 4:32 and Luke 6:36, no doubt because the Vulgate has "estote . . . misericordes" in both places.

124. Theophylact, *Exp. Eph.* ad loc. (PG 124:1101B), quotes Luke 6:37 when expounding Eph 4:32.

as an allusion, as a deliberate prod to readers to recall another text, but the verses may nonetheless be indebted to something like Luke 6:27–42 or *Did*. 1:3–5 or *1 Clem*. 13:2 or Pol. *Phil*. 2:3.

So far I have urged that literary considerations are more than consistent with supposing that most of Q 6:27–42 is a coherent whole, not an anthology of originally independent logia, and further that the parallels in Paul and extracanonical sources establish that close relatives of that text were known to several writers apart from Q and the Synoptics. My next step is to argue that Q 6:27–42 in its entirety is in dialogue with a particular text from the Torah, a fact wholly unexpected if we have here logia that grew together only gradually. Consistent interaction with a single intertext seems rather to suggest one principal author.

The Levitical Subtext

The major topics of Q 6:27–42 are love, retaliation, and judging others: "Love your enemies. . . . If anyone strikes you on the cheek, offer the other also. . . . Do not judge." In Jewish tradition, the classical locus for these three topics is Lev 19, which is "a compendium of sorts illustrating the requirements of a holy life."[125] This part of the Holiness Code teaches that "vindictiveness is diametrically opposed to holy living within the covenant community,"[126] and its central portion calls for love over against hate: "You shall not hate in your heart anyone of your kin. . . . But you shall love your neighbor as yourself" (vv. 17–18).[127] Leviticus 19 further contains instruction for judging one's neighbor: "With justice you shall judge your neighbor. . . . You shall reprove your neighbor, or you will incur guilt yourself" (vv. 15, 17).

The overlap in subject matter with Q 6:27–42 is patent. David Catchpole, like a few before him, has in fact argued that Lev 19:17–18 is a tacit influence throughout the Sermon on the Plain.[128] His view is persuasive, except

125. Christophe Nihan, *From Priestly Torah to Pentateuch: A Study in the Composition of the Book of Leviticus* (FAT 2/25; Tübingen: Mohr Siebeck, 2007), 466.

126. So H. G. L. Peels, *The Vengeance of God: The Meaning of the Root NQM and the Function of the NQM-Texts in the Context of Divine Revelation in the Old Testament* (OtSt 31; Leiden: Brill, 1995), 51.

127. Erhard S. Gerstenberger sees vv. 17–18 as the "crowning conclusion to everything that has been said about the welfare of one's fellow human beings within the community" (*Leviticus: A Commentary* [OTL; Louisville: Westminster John Knox, 1966], 270).

128. Catchpole, *Quest for Q*, 101–34. Others who have observed links to Lev 19 include J. Duncan M. Derrett, "Christ and Reproof (Matthew 7.1–5/Luke 6.37–42)," *NTS* 34 (1988): 271–81; J. W. Doeve, *Jewish Hermeneutics in the Synoptic Gospels and Acts* (Assen: Van Gorcum, 1954), 191–98; Goulder, *Midrash and Lection*, 462–63; Richard A. Horsley, *Jesus and the*

that the links between Q's sermon and Lev 19 are more wide-ranging than Catchpole or anyone else has recognized, a fact that I should now like to demonstrate.[129]

1. The Status of Leviticus 19

I begin by stressing that Lev 19, which "occupies the central position in Leviticus and therefore in the Pentateuch,"[130] was much pondered in antiquity, its importance often stressed. *Sipra* 195 on Lev 19:1 affirms that "this chapter was spoken in the assembly of all Israel" because "most of the essential principles of the Torah depend upon its contents." Rabbi Hiyya, in *Lev. Rab.* 24:5, says the same thing, after which R. Levi adds that "the ten commandments are included in it." That the New Testament cites the pivotal verse of Lev 19, the famous 19:18, more than any other line from the Torah, surely suggests the chapter's popularity.[131] Jewish sources likewise favor this encapsulating commandment.[132] Akiba, according to tradition, identified it as the great principle in the Torah.[133]

The notion attributed to R. Levi, that Lev 19 contains the Decalogue, probably was an old one. The overlaps between those two patches of Scripture are both extensive and obvious,[134] and according to Pieter van der Horst, the

---

Spiral of Violence: Popular Jewish Resistance in Roman Palestine (San Francisco: Harper & Row, 1987), 271; idem, "Covenant Renewal Discourse," 198, 200, 222; idem, "Moral Economy and Renewal Movement in Q," in *Oral Performance, Popular Tradition, and Hidden Transcript in Q* (ed. Richard A. Horsley; SemeiaSt 60; Atlanta: Society of Biblical Literature, 2006), 67; Siegfried Schulz, *Q: Die Spruchquelle der Evangelisten* (Zürich: Theologischer Verlag, 1972), 137; Seitz, "Love Your Enemies," 39–54; C. M. Tuckett, "Scripture in Q," in *The Scriptures in the Gospels* (ed. C. M. Tuckett; BETL 131; Leuven: Leuven University Press, 1997), 25; idem, *Q and the History of Early Christianity* (Edinburgh: T & T Clark, 1996), 431–34.

129. I first explored the correlations between the Sermon on the Plain and Lev 19 in Allison, *Intertextual Jesus*, 29–38. The following pages both repeat and significantly expand, add to, and correct the observations made there.

130. J. H. Hertz, *The Pentateuch and Haftorahs* (London: Soncino, 1950), 497. For the claim that Leviticus is the central book of the Pentateuch, that chapter 19 is the culminating point of the Holiness Code, and that Lev 19:18 is at the center of its chapter, so that the verse is implicitly "the summit of the entire Torah," see Yehuda T. Radday, "Chiastic Patterns in Biblical Hebrew Poetry," in *Chiasmus in Antiquity: Structures, Analyses, Exegesis* (ed. John W. Welch; Provo, UT: Research Press, 1999), 88–89.

131. Matt 5:43; 19:19; Mark 12:31, 33; Rom 12:9; 13:9; Gal 5:14; Jas 2:8. Cf. *Gos. Thom.* 25; *Did.* 1:2; *Gos. Naz.* frg. 16; *Sib. Or.* 8:481.

132. See Sir 13:15; *Jub.* 7:20; 20:2; 36:4, 8; CD-A 6:20; 1QS 5:25; *T. Reub.* 6:9; *T. Iss.* 5:2; *T. Gad* 4:2; *T. Benj.* 3:3–4. According to E. P. Sanders (*Judaism: Practice and Belief, 63 BCE–66 CE* [London: SCM Press; Philadelphia: Trinity Press International, 1992], 257), Lev 19:18 is intended to incorporate the imperatives preceding it.

133. *Sipra* 200 on Lev 19:18; *y. Ned.* 41c (9:4); *Gen. Rab.* 24:7.

134. See Hertz, *Pentateuch and Haftorahs*, 495. Cf. Lev 19:3 with the fourth and fifth commandments, 19:4 with the second commandment, 19:11 with the eighth commandment, 19:12 with the third commandment, 19:16 with the ninth commandment. These are only the more

author of *Pseudo-Phocylides* saw Lev 19 as "a kind of summary of the Torah or a counterpart of the Decalogue."[135] Tradition, moreover, took Lev 19:18 to be a summary of the second table of the law.[136] The main point for us, however, is simply this: Lev 19 was a popular and important text. It follows that scripturally literate Jews, by which I mean auditors of Torah as well as readers,[137] would not have missed clear allusions to it.

2. Loving Neighbor and Enemy

Jesus' counterintuitive exhortation to "love your enemies" (Q 6:27) is an interpretation or revision of "love your neighbor" (Lev 19:18).[138] The former is the structural twin of the latter:

Q 6:27:	ἀγαπᾶτε τοὺς ἐχθροὺς ὑμῶν
LXX Lev 19:18:	ἀγαπήσεις τὸν πλησίον σου
MT Lev 19:18:	אהבת לרעך

Q and the LXX agree in having a second-person imperative of ἀγαπάω + definite article + object + second-person pronoun. Further, Matthew indisputably thought of Lev 19:18 when editing Q's saying about the enemy, for he redactionally introduced Jesus' command to love one's enemy with these words: "You have heard that it was said, 'Love your neighbor and hate your

---

obvious connections. Others have found allusions to all of the Ten Commandments in Lev 19. This was in fact a rabbinic tradition; see *Tanḥ.* Buber Qedoshim 7:3; *Lev. Rab.* 24:5. The latter correlates Exod 20:2 with Lev 19:3, Exod 20:3 with Lev 19:4, Exod 20:7 with Lev 19:12, Exod 20:8 with Lev 19:3, Exod 20:12 with Lev 19:3, Exod 20:13 with Lev 19:16, Exod 20:13 with Lev 20:10, Exod 20:13 with Lev 19:11, Exod 20:13 with Lev 19:16, and Exod 20:14 with Lev 19:18. Note also *Mek.* on Exod 13:18, which remembers Joseph as having fulfilled the Ten Commandments as well as the injunctions in Lev 19:17, 18; 25:36. For the modern discussion, see Jacob Milgrom, *Leviticus 17–22* (AB 3A; New York: Doubleday, 2000), 1600–1602.

135. P. W. van der Horst, *The Sentences of Pseudo-Phocylides* (SVTP 4; Leiden: Brill, 1978), 66. *Pseudo-Phocylides* 3–8 first summarizes the decalogue, then 9–41 rewrites much of Lev 19.

136. See Dale C. Allison Jr., "Torah, Urzeit, Endzeit," in *Resurrecting Jesus: The Earliest Christian Tradition and Its Interpreters* (New York: T & T Clark, 2005), 153–60.

137. On the scriptural literacy that Q presupposes, see Allison, *Intertextual Jesus*, 1–24.

138. See, in addition to the authors named in n. 128, Philip Carrington, *The Primitive Christian Catechism: A Study in the Epistles* (Cambridge: Cambridge University Press, 1940), 95; Patrick J. Hartin, "James and the Q Sermon on the Mount/Plain," in *Society of Biblical Literature 1989 Seminar Papers* (ed. David J. Lull; Atlanta: Scholars Press, 1989), 452; Lührmann, "Liebet eure Feinde," 426; C. G. Montefiore, *The Synoptic Gospels* (2nd rev. ed.; 2 vols; London: Macmillan, 1927), 1:80, 85; Gerbern S. Oegema, "The Historical Jesus and Judaism," in *Jüdische Schriften in ihrem antik-jüdischen und urchristlichen Kontext* (ed. Hermann Lichtenberger and Gerbern S. Oegema; SJSHRZ 1; Gütersloh: Gütersloher Verlagshaus, 2002), 462 ("Jesus' command to love your enemies is . . . an interpretation of the Holiness Code, Leviticus 17–26, especially of Lev 19:2, 18, 33"). So already Tertullian, *Marc.* 4.16; *Scap.* 1. Contrast Kloppenborg, *Formation of Q*, 179.

enemy, but I say to you . . .'" (5:43). Ecclesiastical history naturally followed Matthew's lead. Irenaeus observed that Jesus taught "us not only to love our neighbors [Lev 19:18] but also our enemies" (*Haer.* 4.13.3); and Tertullian, after remarking that "we are ordered to love our enemies," moved immediately to a discussion of Lev 19:18: "The rule about loving the stranger or the enemy comes later in time than the command [in Lev 19:18] to love your neighbor as yourself, which command, although from the Creator's law, you will need to adopt also, since Christ did not overthrow it [the law] but established it all the more firmly. You are told to love the enemy and the stranger so that you love your neighbor all the more [cf. Lev 19:18]. To require a kindness not owed is to emphasize what is due" (*Marc.* 1.23).[139]

That "love your enemies" rewrites "love your neighbor" is all the more assured from three further considerations:

a. In Leviticus, "you will not take vengeance" immediately precedes "love your neighbor"; in Q, "love your enemies" immediately precedes imperatives that oppose vengeance: "turn the other cheek," etc.

b. Lev 19 itself offers precedent for rewriting Lev 19:18, as one can see by comparing that verse with Lev 19:34:

19:18	
	"You shall love your neighbor as yourself."
MT	ואהבת לרעך כמוך
LXX	καὶ ἀγαπήσεις τὸν πλησίον σου ὡς σεαυτόν
19:34	
	"You shall love him [the stranger who sojourns among you] as yourself."
MT	ואהבת לו כמוך
LXX	καὶ ἀγαπήσεις αὐτὸν ὡς σεαυτόν

c. The subject of Q 6:27–29, which is how to deal with enemies, arises more than once in postbiblical discussions of Lev 19:17–18. Consider the following three texts:

• CD-A 9:2–8: "And concerning that which says, 'You will not take vengeance or bear a grudge against any of your people' [Lev 19:18], everyone brought into the covenant who brings an accusation against his fellow (unless it is with reproach before witnesses) or who brings it when he is angry or who tells it to his elders so that they might despise him, he is the one who takes vengeance and bears a grudge. Is it not perhaps written [in Nah 1:2] that only 'he [God] takes vengeance on his adversaries and rages against his enemies [אויביו]'? If he kept silent about him from one

---

139. Cf. Basil of Caesarea, *Comm. Isa.* 51 (PG 20:212C).

day to the other, and then, when he was angry, accused him of a capital offense, he has witnessed against himself, for he did not fulfill the commandment of God, who said to him, 'You will reprove your neighbor and you will not incur sin because of him' [Lev 19:17]."

- *'Abot R. Nat.* A 16: "David said: 'Do I not hate them, O Lord, who hate you? And do I not strive with those who rise up against you? I hate them with utmost hatred; I count them my enemies [אויבים]' [Ps 139:21–22]. But does it not say, 'You will love your neighbor as yourself. I am the Lord'? [Lev 19:18]."

- *Gen. Rab.* 55:3: "Israel said to God: 'Master of the world, you wrote in the Torah, "You will not take revenge" [Lev 19:18], yet you yourself are "avenging and wrathful; [you] the Lord take vengeance on his enemies [אויביו] . . ."' (Nah 1:2). God said to them, 'I wrote in the Torah, "You will not take revenge and you will not hold a grudge against Israel." But as regards the nations, "Avenge the children of Israel"' (Num 31:2)."[140]

Although "love your enemies" appears to have no precise verbal equivalent in old Jewish sources,[141] the transformation of "love your neighbor" into that imperative likely reflects an exegetical tradition that brought Lev 19:17–18 to bear on how one should treat adversaries.

3. Imitating God

Q 6:36 exhorts disciples to "be merciful" just as "your Father is merciful." This imperative and its Matthean parallel (5:48: "Be perfect, therefore, as your heavenly Father is perfect") have understandably reminded many commentators of Lev 19:2, where God declares, "You shall be holy, for I the LORD your God am holy."[142] In both places, the quality demanded of human beings is

140. Cf. *Eccl. Rab.* 8.4.1. Note also the common application of Lev 19:18 to people convicted and sentenced to death in *t. Sanh.* 9:11; *y. Sanh.* 23c (6:4); *y. Soṭah* 17a (1:5); *b. Pesaḥ.* 75a; *b. Soṭah* 8b; *b. B. Qam.* 51a; *b. Sanh.* 45a, 52a–b; *b. Ketub.* 37b: "love your neighbor as yourself" means that such people should have "an easy death."

141. The closest parallel that I have found, *Tanḥ.* Buber Qedoshim 2, appears to have been overlooked: "Isaac came and they [the angels] said to him [God], 'Is this the one [who will be named Israel]?' He said to them: '[No, because] this one loves my enemy [זה אוהב את שונאי], as it says, "And Isaac loved Esau"'" (Gen 35:10). Although this is of interest, especially as it belongs to an interpretation of Lev 19:2, loving the enemy is here not a virtue but rather a vice.

142. See, for example, Origen, *Cels.* 6.63; Grotius, *Opera omnia theologica*, 2:74; Poole, *Commentary*, 3:26; Marcus J. Borg, *Conflict, Holiness and Politics in the Teaching of Jesus* (SBEC 5; Lewiston, NY: Edwin Mellen, 1984), 128; Bovon, *Luke 1*, 241; Richard A. Burridge, *Imitating Jesus: An Inclusive Approach to New Testament Ethics* (Grand Rapids: Eerdmans, 2007), 75; Millar Burrows, "Old Testament Ethics and the Ethics of Jesus," in *Essays in Old Testament Ethics (J. Philip Hyatt, In Memoriam)* (ed. James L. Crenshaw and John T. Willis; New York: Ktav, 1974), 240–41; Catchpole, *Quest for Q*, 117; Fitzmyer, *Luke I–IX*, 641; R. T. France, *The Gospel of Matthew* (NICNT; Grand Rapids: Eerdmans, 2007), 228; Goulder,

one that God demonstrates, and in both, a second-person imperative precedes appeal to the *imitatio Dei*:

MT	תהיו	+ ethical attribute	+ כי	+ יהוה אלהיכם
LXX	ἔσεσθε	+ ethical attribute	+ ὅτι	+ θεὸς ὑμῶν
Q	ἔσεσθε or γίνεσθε	+ ethical attribute	+ καθώς/ὡς	+ ὁ πατὴρ ὑμῶν

Q 6:36 seems to be an adaptation or reinterpretation of Lev 19:2, a verse that gains prominence by being repeated in Lev 20:26: "You shall be holy to me, for I the LORD am holy" (LXX: ἔσεσθέ μοι ἅγιοι ὅτι ἐγὼ ἅγιος κύριος ὁ θεὸς ὑμῶν; MT: והייתם לי קדשים כי קדוש אני יהוה).[143] Jesus, retaining the form of the pentateuchal imperative, replaces holiness with mercy. *Sipra* 121 on Lev 11:44, which turns "Be holy for I am holy" into "Be separate for I am separate" (cf. *Lev. Rab.* 24:4), makes a similar rhetorical move.[144]

Midrash and Lection, 462; Robert H. Gundry, *The Use of the Old Testament in St. Matthew's Gospel, with Special Reference to the Messianic Hope* (NovTSup 18; Leiden: Brill, 1967), 73; Kloppenborg, *Q Parallels*, 33; John Nolland, *The Gospel of Matthew: A Commentary on the Greek Text* (NIGTC; Grand Rapids: Eerdmans, 2005), 270; Gerhard Schneider, "Imitatio Dei als Motiv der 'Ethik Jesu,'" in *Jesusüberlieferung und Christologie: Neutestamentliche Aufsätze, 1970–1990* (NovTSup 67; Leiden: Brill, 1992), 163; Hans Joachim Schoeps, "Von der imitation dei zur Nachfolge Christi," in *Aus frühchristlicher Zeit: Religionsgeschichtliche Untersuchungen* (Tübingen: Mohr Siebeck, 1950), 290; Schürmann, *Lukasevangelium: Erster Teil*, 360; David L. Turner, *Matthew* (BECNT; Grand Rapids: Baker Academic, 2008), 177; Dieter Zeller, *Die weisheitlichen Mahnsprüche bei den Synoptikern* (FB 17; Würzburg: Echter, 1977), 111.

143. Cf. also Lev 11:45–46. Observe further that if the imitation of God is explicit in Lev 19:2; 20:26, it probably is implicit at the end of chapter 19, in vv. 33–34: "When an alien resides with you in your land, you shall not oppress the alien. The alien who resides with you shall be to you as the citizen among you; you shall love the alien as yourself, for you were aliens in the land of Egypt: I am the LORD your God." According to Milgrom, the meaning of this is as follows: "Since YHWH redeemed you from oppression when you were aliens in the land of Egypt, so you should not oppress him [the alien] but 'redeem' him by granting him equivalent civil rights" (*Leviticus 17–22*, 1605).

144. It seems also likely that *Sipre* 49 on Deut 11:22 rewrites Lev 19:2: "As God is called merciful, so should you be merciful. . . . As God is called righteous, . . . so you too should be called righteous." It is possible that Q associates "love your enemy" with the imitation of God not only because of Lev 19:2 but also because Lev 19:18 ends with "I am the LORD your God." Did the juxtaposition suggest grounding the imperative in the divine nature? So Menahem Kister, "The Sayings of Jesus and the Midrash," *Immanuel* 15 (1982): 46–47. Cf. *'Abot R. Nat.* A 16, which discusses why "I am the LORD" follows "love your neighbor," and how Abrabanel moved from "I am the LORD" in Lev 19:18 to 19:2: "It says, 'I am the Lord' [Lev 19:18] which means: 'Have I not told you to act in accordance with my deeds and to walk in my ways, and to be holy, for I am holy?' [Lev 19:2]." According to John Piper, "The repeated phrase 'I am the LORD' (15 times) which follows the individual commands of Lev 19 shows that the intention of the chapter is to give specific instances of how to be holy as God is holy" (*"Love Your Enemies": Jesus' Love Command in the Synoptic Gospels and in the Early Christian Paraenesis; A History of the Tradition and Interpretation of Its Uses* [SNTSMS 38; Cambridge: Cambridge University Press, 1979], 31).

4. Judging

Q's "Do not judge" (μὴ κρίνετε, 6:37) stands in provocative, antithetical relationship to Lev 19:15–17.[145] This last, which also lies behind Q 17:3–4 ("If your brother sins, rebuke him"),[146] commands one to judge and, if necessary, reprove a neighbor:

Lev 19:15	
LXX	κρινεῖς τὸν πλησίον σου
	"you shall judge your neighbor"
MT	תשפט עמיתך
	"you shall judge your neighbor"
Lev 19:17	
LXX	ἐλεγμῷ ἐλέγξεις τὸν πλησίον σου
	"with reproof you will reprove your neighbor"
MT	הוכח תוכיח את־עמיתך
	"you will surely reprove your neighbor"

We might paraphrase the intent of the Q text, understood over against Leviticus, this way: "You have heard that it was said to those of old, 'You will judge your neighbor.' But I say to you, 'Do not judge.'" We have here the same phenomenon as in Q 14:26, where "Hate your father and mother" sets itself against Exod 20:12 // Deut 5:16, "Honor your father and mother."[147]

That Q 6:37–38 is related to Lev 19:15–17 gains indirect support from the interesting circumstance that, while many commentators have found in Jas 4:11–12—"Do not speak evil against one another, brothers and sisters. Whoever speaks evil against another or judges [κρίνων] another, speaks evil against the law and judges the law. . . . So who, then, are you to judge [κρίνων] your neighbor"—an adaptation of the dominical tradition preserved in Q 6:37–38,[148] others have found in the very same verse an allusion to Lev 19:15–18, which includes the imperative "You shall not go around as a slanderer among your people."[149] If, as I am arguing, the logion Q 6:37–38 rewrites Lev 19:15–18,

---

145. Cf. Carrington, *Catechism*, 95; Catchpole, *Quest for Q*, 144; Doeve, *Jewish Hermeneutics*, 197.

146. See Allison, *Intertextual Jesus*, 65–68.

147. See ibid., 62–63.

148. See Hartin, "James and the Q Sermon," 453–54. John S. Kloppenborg ("The Reception of the Jesus Tradition in James," in *The Catholic Epistles and the Tradition* [ed. Jacques Schlosser; BETL 176; Leuven: Leuven University Press, 2004], 111) regards Jas 4:11 as among the "likely contacts" between James and Q. Note further the verbal links between Jas 5:6 (κατεδικάσατε) and Luke 6:37 (μὴ καταδικάζετε καὶ οὐ μὴ καταδικασθῆτε) and between Jas 5:9 and Luke 6:37 (both of which have μή . . . μὴ κριθῆτε).

149. So, for example, Hubert Frankemölle, *Der Brief des Jakobus* (2 vols.; ÖTKNT 17; Gütersloh: Gütersloher Verlagshaus; Würzburg: Echter, 1994), 2:620–25. According to Luke

this would neatly explain why the commentators have espied two different intertexts for Jas 4:11: the immediate source, that being the saying preserved in Q 6:37–38, as well as the subtext of that source, Lev 19:15–18.

5. The Golden Rule

The so-called golden rule, which appears in Q 6:31, was traditionally linked with Lev 19, as a host of witnesses attests.[150] Tobit 4:14–15 juxtaposes the golden rule with a rewriting of Lev 19:13.[151] *Jubilees* 36:4 appears to conflate the golden rule with Lev 19:18: "And among yourselves, my sons, be loving of your brothers as a man loves himself, with each man seeking for his brother what is good for him and acting together on the earth, and loving each other as themselves."[152] *Letter of Aristeas* 207 attaches the golden rule both to the *imitatio Dei* (cf. Lev 19:2) and to instruction to rebuke mildly, which depends upon Lev 19:15–18.[153] The Hebrew of Sir 31:15 seems to offer a rewording of Lev 19:18 whereas the Greek version recalls the golden rule.[154] Again, if Matthew's Gospel designates the golden rule as the sum of the Law and the Prophets (7:12), it says the same of Lev 19:18 (Matt 22:39). In like manner,

---

Timothy Johnson, "Four points converge to support the probability of an allusion here: a) the negative command; b) its content; c) the reference to 'the neighbor' [cf. Lev 19:18]; d) its attachment to observance of the law" ("The Use of Leviticus 19 in the Letter of James," *JBL* 101 [1982]: 395–96).

150. Indeed, for the argument that, in Judaism, the golden rule was based upon exegesis of Lev 19:18, see George Brockwell King, "The 'Negative' Golden Rule," *JR* 8 (1928): 274–75, following Wilhelm Bacher, *Die Agada der Tannaiten* (2 vols.; Berlin: de Gruyter, 1965–1966), 1:4. According to the latter, Hillel's negative golden rule "is nothing other than a negative expression of the biblical 'love your neighbor as yourself.'" Cf. Maimonides, *Sefer Ha-Mitzvoh* 206; Isaac Abravanel, *Mikraot Ketanot 613 Mitsvot Ha-Torah* (Cincinnati: Bloch, 1892), 19; Hertz, *Pentateuch and Haftorahs*, 502. Gerald Friedlander states that "the Golden Rule is an interpretation or paraphrase (Targum) of the Old Testament Law of Love, found in Leviticus (xix.18): 'love thy neighbor as thyself'" (*The Jewish Sources of the Sermon on the Mount* [New York: Ktav, 1969], 230–31). The "as yourself" of Lev 19:18 might well imply the golden rule.

151. Tobit 4:14–15: "Do not keep over until the next day the wages of those who work for you, but pay them at once. . . . And what you hate, do not do to anyone." Cf. Lev 19:13 (RSV): "You shall not oppress your neighbor or rob him. The wages of a hired servant shall not remain with you all night until the morning."

152. Jacob Milgrom thinks that *Jub*. 36:4 (which he mistakenly references as 30:24) rightly understands "as yourself" in Lev 19:18 as adverbial, so the meaning is "Love (the good) for your fellow as you (love the good for) yourself" (*Leviticus: A Book of Ritual Ethics* [Minneapolis: Fortress, 2004], 234).

153. The parallels between *Let. Arist.* 207 and the Sermon on the Plain, introduced above on p. 322, derive from common dependence upon traditions tied to Lev 19.

154. Cf. Dihle, *Goldene Regel*, 83–84; see further Martin Hengel, "Zur matthäischen Bergpredigt und ihrem jüdischen Hintergrund," *TRu* 52 (1987): 392. The Hebrew reads, רעה [דעה] .v.l.[רעך כנפשך . . . דע שרעך כמוך], "Honor [or 'Think of'] your neighbor as yourself. . . . Know that your neighbor is as yourself." The Greek reads, νόει τὰ τοῦ πλησίον ἐκ σεαυτοῦ, "Consider the things of your neighbor by your own (things)."

Akiba reportedly christened Lev 19:18 as "the great general principle in the Torah" (כלל גדול בתורה; *Sipra* 200 on Lev 19:18; *t. Soṭah* 9:11; *y. Ned.* 41c [9:4]; *Gen. Rab.* 24:7), whereas *'Abot R. Nat.* B 26, where the subject is love of neighbor, has him bestow this honor upon the golden rule: "What is hateful to you, do not do to your fellow man" is "the general principle of the Torah" (כלל של בתורה).[155]

Targum Pseudo-Jonathan places the rule of reciprocity near the end of Lev 19 (v. 34: "The stranger who sojourns with you will be to you as the native among you; you will love him as yourself, so that what you hate for yourself you will not do to him") and further combines it with the command to love one's neighbor in v. 18: "You will not take revenge nor harbor enmity against your kinsmen. You will love your neighbor, so that what is hateful to you, you will not do to him." With this one may compare *Did.* 1:2, where the golden rule and Lev 19:18 once more appear side by side. The same combination of the golden rule and Lev 19:18 also shows up in *Ps.-Clem. Hom.* 12:32: "The one who loves his neighbor as himself, knowing that when he has sinned he does not want to be punished, does not punish others who sin. And as he wishes to be praised and blessed and honored and to have all of his sins forgiven, in this way he acts with his neighbor, loving him as himself. In a word, what he wishes for himself, he wishes also for his neighbor." And all this hardly exhausts the evidence.[156]

155. Note also that *'Abot R. Nat.* B 26 goes on to use the phrase "love your neighbor," so here too the golden rule and Lev 19:18 go together.

156. See further Justin, *Dial.* 93.2–3; *Ep. Apost.* 18; *Ps.-Clem. Hom.* 7:4 (ἅπερ ἕκαστος ἑαυτῷ βούλεται καλά, τὰ αὐτὰ βουλευέσθω καὶ τῷ πλησίον [this form of the golden rule borrows πλησίον from Lev 19:18]); Aristides, *Apol.* 15 (TU 4:36–37); Clement of Alexandria, *Paed.* 3.12; Cyprian, *Dom. or.* 28; *Apos. Con.* 7.2; Augustine, *Serm. Dom.* 2.22.75; Ephraem, *Comm. Exod.* 20.2 (CSCO 152 [Scriptores Syri 71], p. 149). Does Philo (*Hypothetica apud* Eusebius, *Praep. ev.* 8.7.6) assign "The things that someone hates to suffer, let him not do to another" to "the laws" (τοῖς νόμοις)? If so, Lev 19:18 must be in mind. For the substitution of the golden rule for Lev 19:18 in Aphraates and Philoxenus, see R. H. Connolly, "A Negative Form of the Golden Rule in the Diatessaron?" *JTS* 35 (1934): 351–57. One can still see the equation in Maimonides, *Mishneh Torah* Hilkot Ebel 14.1. Compare, from a later time still, Poole, *Commentary*, 3:31; John Trapp, *A Commentary or Exposition upon All the Books of the New Testament* (ed. W. Webster; London: Richard D. Dickinson, 1865), 125; Thomas Scott, *The Holy Bible: Containing the Old and New Testaments, according to the Authorized Version, with Explanatory Notes, Practical Observations, and Copious Marginal References* (6 vols.; Boston: Crocker & Brewster, 1844), vol. 1, *ad* Lev 19:18. It may also be relevant that some textual authorities add a form of the golden rule to Acts 15:20, which otherwise seems to summarize legislation in Lev 17–18 (see Jürgen Wehnert, *Die Reinheit des "christlichen Gottesvolkes" aus Juden und Heiden: Studien zum historischen und theologischen Hintergrund des sogenannten Aposteldekrets* [FRLANT 173; Göttingen: Vandenhoeck & Ruprecht, 1997], 213–38), and that if Lev 19:18 was often associated with the second part of the Decalogue (see n. 136), the same was true for the golden rule, which in its negative form parallels the "do nots" of the Decalogue; see *L.A.B.* 11:10; *Did.* 1:2–2:2 (on the common assumption that 1:3–2:1 is a secondary insertion, whether by the author of the *Didache* or a later editor); *Ps.-Clem. Hom.*

Perhaps it is not out of line here to appeal to *Midrash Petirat Moshe*, the *Midrash on the Death of Moses*. In this Jewish text, which may date from the seventh century or before, the lawgiver, about to die, addresses Joshua with these words: "With the measure with which you have measured to me, so I now measure to you. Because you have served me with a friendly countenance, I also now serve you. Have I not taught you, 'You will love your neighbor as yourself'? Have I not also taught you, 'Let the honor of your student be to you as your own honor'?"[157] This farewell address not only puts Lev 19:18 beside a rabbinic variant of the golden rule ("Let the honor of your student be to you as your own honor") but also contains a version of the "measure for measure" maxim, which also shows up in Q 6:38. While the small midrash is too late to supply background for a first-century text, it does suggest how natural it is to bring together the golden rule, the command to love others, and the "measure for measure" proverb, which in turn reinforces the case for the thematic unity of the central section of Q's inaugural discourse.

6. Vengeance

Q 6:27–30 prohibits vengeance. Instead of hating enemies, one is to love them, which means not returning evil for evil (cf. Matt 5:38–39). It is the same with the demands to turn the other cheek when struck and to hand over a second garment after the first has been taken: Jesus leaves no place for revenge.

All this makes for thematic continuity with Lev 19:18: "You shall not take vengeance or bear a grudge against any of your people." It does not surprise that Albertus Magnus, when commenting on Luke 6:27, cited Lev 19:18,[158] nor that Michael Goulder takes Luke 6:29 to "recall" the same verse.[159] Perhaps one should add that the LXX translates the MT's לא־תקם ("you shall not take vengeance") with the phrase οὐκ ἐκδικᾶταί σου ἡ χείρ ("your hand shall not exact vengeance"). This, if taken literally, perhaps presents to the mind's eye the same image as does Luke 6:29, where turning the other cheek when struck means not raising one's hand to strike back.

7:4; 11:4–5; *Ps.-Clem. Rec.* 8:56; *Didascalia* 1. Some have conjectured that the negative form of the golden rule was born of reflection on the Decalogue (e.g., C. Taylor, *The Teaching of the Twelve Apostles* [Cambridge: Deighton, Bell, 1886], 10). According to James D. G. Dunn (*Romans 9–16* [WBC 38B; Nashville: Thomas Nelson, 1988], 780), in Rom 13:9–10, Paul follows his citation of Lev 19:18 with a paraphrase of "a negative form of the golden rule" (ἡ ἀγάπη τῷ πλησίον κακὸν οὐκ ἐργάζεται); cf. D. M. Beck, "Golden Rule," *IDB* 2:438. But "love works no evil against a neighbor" is rather from Ps 15:3 (LXX: οὐδὲ ἐποίησεν τῷ πλησίον αὐτοῦ κακόν). Cf. Irenaeus, *Haer.* 4.16.3 ("do no injury to their neighbor"); *Epid.* 87 ("the love of neighbor adds no evil to a neighbor").

157. Adolph Jellinek, *Bet ha-Midrasch: Sammlung kleiner Midraschim und vermischter Abhandlungen aus der ältern jüdischen Literatur* (3rd ed.; Jerusalem: Wahrman, 1967), part 1, 124.

158. Albertus Magnus, *Enarrationes in primam partem Evangelii Lucae (I–IX)* (vol. 22 of *Opera omnia* [ed. A. Borgnet; Paris: Ludovicus Vivès, 1894], 429.

159. Goulder, *Midrash and Lection*, 462. Cf. Doeve, *Jewish Hermeneutics*, 197.

7. Who Is My Neighbor?

The prohibition against vengeance in Lev 19:18 concerns actions directed against and feelings felt for "any of your people" (MT: בְּנֵי עַמֶּךְ; LXX: τοῖς υἱοῖς τοῦ λαοῦ σου). The Sermon on the Plain implicitly enlarges the application when it declares that one must not take vengeance against anybody, even one's enemies, whom one must rather love. Leviticus 19:18, by contrast, commands love of neighbor, leaving the identity of one's neighbor unspecified.[160]

Jesus' stance on these matters seems to be a deliberate counter to some Jewish exegesis of Lev 19. It is true that Lev 19:34 already includes the foreigner or resident alien within the purview of the command to love one's neighbor ("You shall love the alien as yourself") and so takes a step beyond a familial or national ethic;[161] and it is further true that *Let. Arist.* 207, which includes "wrongdoers" within the purview of the golden rule, and *T. Iss.* 7:6, where a patriarch retrospectively declares, "I loved every human being as I love my children," seem to reflect expansive interpretations of Lev 19:18.[162] But *Sipra* 205 on Lev 19:33–34 turns the alien into a proselyte, as does the LXX before it.[163] Moreover, *Sipra* 200 takes Lev 19:18 to mean that "you may take vengeance and bear a grudge against others," that is, non-Jews, and *Sipre* 89 on Deut 13:9 teaches that the love commanded in Lev 19:18 should not embrace those who entice the people to idolatry.[164]

These restrictions are perfectly understandable in view of biblical texts such as 2 Chr 19:2 ("Should you help the wicked and love those who hate the LORD?") and Ps 139:21 ("Do I not hate those who hate you, O LORD?"). 'Abot de Rabbi Nathan A 16 cites Lev 19:18 and then adds, "If he acts as your people do, you will love him; but if not, you will not love him." This reminds one of Matt 5:43, where "You have heard that it was said, 'You shall love your neighbor and hate your enemy'" probably represents a point of view known to the evangelist.[165] A marginal gloss to Tg. Neof. I on Lev 19:18 interprets the

160. According to Milgrom (*Leviticus 17–22*, 1654), the original application was to fellow Israelites. Typically in the Holiness Code, "neighbor" seems to be a fellow Israelite; see Klaus Berger, *Die Gesetzesauslegung Jesu: Ihr historischer Hintergrund im Judentum und im Alten Testament* (WMANT 40; Neukirchen-Vluyn: Neukirchener Verlag, 1972), 81–91.

161. Nachmonides (*Commentary on the Torah* [5 vols.; New York: Shiloh, 1971–1976], 3:293) associates 19:34 with 19:18, thereby enlarging the scope of the latter.

162. Cf. *T. Zeb.* 6:6; 8:3. See, however, Michael Ebersohn, *Das Nächstenliebegebot in der synoptischen Tradition* (MTS 37; Marburg: Elwert, 1993), 46–152.

163. See the discussion in ibid., 49–51; and in addition to what follows, the collection of texts in Str-B 1:353–64.

164. Restrictive interpretations of Lev 19:18 dominate Jewish exegetical tradition; see Ernst Simon, "The Neighbor (*Re'a*) Whom We Shall Love," in *Modern Jewish Ethics: Theory and Practice* (ed. Marvin Fox; Columbus: Ohio State University Press, 1975), 29–56.

165. See James L. Kugel, *In Potiphar's House: The Interpretive Life of Biblical Texts* (San Francisco: Harper & Row, 1990), 231–40; and cf. 1QS 1:10 (the sectarians are to "hate all the sons of darkness"); Sir 12:5–7 ("Do good to the humble, but do not give to the ungodly. . . . Give

text in this manner: "And you will love your friend who is like to yourselves" (לרחמכון דכוותכון ותרחמון [cf. 'Abot R. Nat. B 26]). This, as opposed to Q's Jesus, does not require that one love people outside one's own group.[166]

So the question, probably often posed in connection with Lev 19:18, "Who is my neighbor?" (Luke 10:29),[167] received different answers, and Q 6:27–42 represents one exegetical option: everybody.[168] Perhaps comparable is the famous tradition found in *Sipra* 200 on Lev 19:18; *t. Soṭah* 9:11; *y. Ned.* 41c (9:4); *Gen. Rab.* 24:7: "'And you shall love your neighbor as yourself.' Rabbi Akiba said: 'This is the great principle in the Torah.' Ben Azzari said: 'This is the book of the generation of Adam, when God created man he made him in the likeness of God' [Gen 5:1] is an even greater principle." The point of Ben Azzari's comment may be this: whereas Akiba's great principle, Lev 19:18, fails to specify the scope of "neighbor," the proof text from Genesis goes one better and envisages all of humanity.[169] Jesus' command to love enemies does something similar, because the practical implication of loving enemies is that one will love all people (cf. Q 6:32–36). Tertullian, recognizing "Love your enemies" as an interpretive expansion of Lev 19:18, got it right:

> For Christ has prescribed the same action towards all people, as the Creator did toward the brethren [*fratres*, cf. Lev 19:17]. For although the sort of kindness shown to strangers [which is what Jesus demands] is the greater, it does not eclipse that (love) which was previously owed to the neighbor [*quae . . . in proximos*, cf. Lev 19:18]. For who is able to love [*diligere*, cf. Lev 19:18] strangers? But if the second step in kindness is that towards strangers while the first step is that towards one's neighbors [*in proximos*], that second step will belong to the individual to whom the first step also belongs—much more easily than that the second step should belong to one without the first step. . . . The Creator first taught kindness towards neighbors [*in proximos*], intending afterwards to extend it towards strangers, and, according to the method of his dispensation, at first towards Jews, and later also towards all peoples. (*Marc.* 4.16 [cf. *Scap.* 1])

---

to the one who is good, but do not help the sinner"); *Ps.-Phoc.* 152 ("Do no good to a bad man; it is like sowing in the sea"); Josephus, *J.W.* 2.139 (the Essenes take an oath to "hate the unjust forever"); and *b. Ta'an.* 7b (it is permitted to hate the insolent).

166. Compare Rashbam's later interpretation, which confined love of neighbor to love of those who are good—that is, Torah-observant Jews. See Samuel ben Meir, *Rashbam's Commentary on Leviticus and Numbers: An Annotated Translation* (ed. Martin I. Lockshin; BJS 330; Providence: Brown Judaic Studies, 2001), 106–7.

167. According to Kugel (*Potiphar's House*, 239), the question in Luke 10:29, "Who is my neighbor?" really means "How restrictively should Lev. 19:17–18 be interpreted?"

168. The Bible itself offers some precedent; see, for example, Exod 23:4–5 (helping the ox or ass of one's enemy); Prov 24:17–18 ("Do not rejoice when your enemy falls").

169. Compare the interpretations in *'Abot R. Nat.* A 16; *Gen. Rab.* 24:7. For a different view, however, see Louis Finkelstein, "The Underlying Concepts of Conservative Judaism," *Conservative Judaism* 26 (1972): 8–9.

8. Speck and Log

Jesus' parable about the speck and the log (Q 6:41–42) explicates the earlier prohibition of judgment: "Do not judge, lest you be judged" (6:37). Now, as already observed, the subject of correcting others in and of itself takes one to Lev 19:15–18, Judaism's classic passage for reflection on that subject, and a portion of Scripture much expounded in antiquity.[170] *Barnabas* 19:4–5 naturally enough moves from the subject of reproof—"You shall not show partiality (οὐ λήμψῃ πρόσωπον [cf. LXX Lev 19:15: οὐ λήμψῃ πρόσωπον]) when you reprove (ἐλέγξαι [cf. Lev 19:17: ἐλέγξεις]) someone," "you shall not hold a grudge against your brother" (cf. MT Lev 19:18a)—to a paraphrase of Lev 19:18b: "You shall love your neighbor more than your own life."

But more needs to be said. The saying about speck and log turns up twice in the Babylonian Talmud. When it appears in *b. B. Bat.* 15b, it is in connection with the subject of judges being judged: "R. Joshua said, 'What is the importance of the words, "And it came to pass in the days of judging the judges" [Ruth 1:1]? It was a generation that judged its judges. If the judge said to a man, "Take the splinter from between your teeth," he would retort, "Take the beam from between your eyes." If the judge said, "Your silver is dross," he would retort, "Your liquor is mixed with water."'" This recalls Q 6:37, which is also about judges being judged: "with the judgment you judge, you will be judged."

When the speck and log appear in *b. ʿArak.* 16b, they serve to expound Lev 19:17, "You shall reprove your neighbor":

Our Rabbis taught: You will not hate your brother in your heart [Lev 19:17]. One might have believed one may only not smite him, slap him, curse him, therefore the text states, "In your heart." Scripture speaks of "hatred in the heart." Whence do we know that if a man sees something unseemly in his neighbor, he is obliged to reprove him? Because it is said, "You will surely rebuke" [Lev 19:17]. If he rebuked him and he did not accept it, whence do we know that he must rebuke him again? The text states, "surely rebuke" all ways. One might assume [this to be obligatory] even though his face blanched, therefore the text states, "You will not bear sin because of him" [Lev 19:17]. It was taught [in a baraitha]: R. Tarfon said, "I wonder whether there is any one in this generation who accepts reproof, for if one says to him, 'Remove the speck from between your eyes,' he would answer, 'Remove the beam from between your eyes.'"

---

170. See James L. Kugel, "On Hidden Hatred and Open Reproach: Early Exegesis of Leviticus 19:17," *HTR* 80 (1987): 43–62; Bilhah Nitzan, "The Laws of Reproof in 4QBerakhot (4Q286–290) in Light of Their Parallels in the Damascus Covenant and Other Texts from Qumran," in *Legal Texts and Issues: Proceedings of the Second Meeting of the International Organization for Qumran Studies, Cambridge 1995* (ed. Moshe Bernstein, Florentino García Martínez, and John Kampen; STDJ 23; Leiden: Brill, 1997), 149–65.

That *b. 'Arak*. 16b and *b. B. Bat*. 15b represent old tradition we cannot prove. The attribution of the latter to Tarfon (early second century CE) need not be reliable, especially since parallel discussions in *Sipra* 200 on Lev 19:17–18 and *Sipre* 1 on Deut 1:1 lack the saying about speck and beam.[171] Should we then posit that our two talmudic tractates owe a debt to Christianity? Although some have suggested this,[172] I am doubtful. It was not rabbinic routine to adopt sayings attributed to Jesus. Beyond that generalization, if the beam and speck in *b. 'Arak*. 16b help explicate Lev 19:17, in Q they belong to a speech that, as I have already established, interacts with Lev 19, especially vv. 19:15–18. So we have not only the same figure of speech but also the same intertextual setting. The odds of this being a coincidence are long. Either, it appears, a word of Jesus entered rabbinic tradition with knowledge of its implicit Levitical engagement retained or, much more likely, Q 6:41–42 was not Jesus' invention but rather a traditional Jewish parable associated with a particular portion of Scripture.

9. Hypocrisy

Jesus' plea to be conscious of one's failings when contemplating the failings of another (Q 6:41–42) and so not to fall into hypocrisy lines up with pre-Christian reflection upon Lev 19:15–18. Leviticus itself joins the command to reprove others with the imperatives to be impartial, to do justice, to hate not, to drop grudges, and to love neighbor. Such generosity, which serves as the context for the awkward yet necessary job of correcting others, was not lost on Jewish tradition, as these passages show:

- Sirach 19:13–17, in taking up Leviticus's law of reproach,[173] includes the following: "A person may slip without intending it. Who has not sinned with his tongue?" The question implicitly recommends mercy, on the ground that one may be guilty of the same sin that one finds in someone else.

- Similar is *4QBerakhot*, which explicitly counsels mercy (ירחם) when following the command to reprove in Lev 19:15, 17–18.[174] One recalls

---

171. The R. Joseph of *b. B. Bat*. 15b presumably is a third-century Amoraic.

172. For example, Adolf Schlatter, *Der Evangelist Matthäus: Seine Sprache, seine Ziel, seine Selbständigkeit* (Stuttgart: Calwer, 1948), 243; T. W. Manson, *The Sayings of Jesus* (London: SCM Press, 1948), 58.

173. That Ben Sira has Lev 19 in view is, according to Kugel, "announced both by his insistent use of the word 'reproach' at the beginning of successive lines, along with the coupling of this verb with 'neighbor' (as in Lev. 19:17) and the equivalent terms 'friend' and 'fellow,' as well as by his final invocation of the 'Law of the Most High,' that is, the Pentateuch in which this law appears" (*Potiphar's House*, 219).

174. Text and translation in Bilhah Nitzan, "4QBerakhot*a-e* (4Q286–290): A Covenantal Ceremony in the Light of Related Texts," *RevQ* 16 (1995): 498–99. Cf. 1QS 5:24–25: "Each should reprove his fellow in truth, in meekness, and in compassionate love."

that, in Q 6:36–42, Jesus' words about judging others directly follow the imperative to be merciful as God is merciful.

- Equally relevant is 4Q417 frg. 1 col. I 1–4, which counsels one to reprove another "quickly" and then adds, "Do not overlook your own sin."

- From a later time, Targum Pseudo-Jonathan, when translating Lev 19:17 into Aramaic, introduces the subject of hypocrisy: "You shall not speak flattering words with your mouth while hating your brother in your heart."[175]

All of which is to say: when Q's Jesus turns to the subject of judging or reproving others, for which Lev 19:15–18 was Judaism's *locus classicus*, his demand for mercy and his disdain of hypocrisy can be paralleled in Jewish elaborations of that particular passage.

10. *"Your Brother"*

The word ἀδελφός occurs four times in the official IQP text of Q, all four times with the possessive pronoun σου. Three occurrences belong to Q 6:41–42: τοῦ ἀδελφοῦ σου, τῷ ἀδελφῷ σου, τοῦ ἀδελφοῦ σου. The explanation for the repeated expression is that the discussion of reproof in Lev 19:15–18 refers to "your brother": "You shall not hate your brother [MT: אחיך; LXX: τὸν ἀδελφόν σου] in your heart" (19:17). The other instance of ἀδελφός + σου in the Sayings Source is in 17:3, where, as the history of interpretation confirms, Lev 19:15–18 is obviously the subtext.[176] One may compare the paraphrase of Lev 19:15–17 in *Barn.* 19:4: "You shall not show partiality when reproving someone for transgression. . . . You shall not keep a grudge against your brother [τῷ ἀδελφῷ σου]."

11. *Lending without Profit or Return*

Regarding the patriarch Joseph, *Mek.* on Exod 13:18 reports the following:

It is written, "You will not hate in your heart any of your kin" [Lev 19:17], and of Joseph it says, "In this way he reassured them, speaking kindly to them" [Gen 50:21]. It is written, "You will not take vengeance or bear a grudge" [Lev 19:18], and (of Joseph) it is written, "Even though you intended to do harm to me, God intended it for good" [Gen 50:20]. It is written, "That your brother may live with you" [Lev 25:36], and of Joseph it is written, "And Joseph provided for his father and his brothers" [Gen 47:12].

175. Cf. *b. 'Arak.* 16b, which considers those who reprove with "honest purpose" and those who reprove with "false modesty."
176. See Allison, *Intertextual Jesus*, 65–68.

For the *Mekilta*, the life of Joseph, as told in Genesis, illustrates three verses from the Pentateuch: Lev 19:17, 18; 25:36. These three verses were traditionally associated, for they appear again together, in another connection, in *m. Ned.* 9:4:

> R. Meier said: "They may open the way (of repentance) by reason of what is written in the law and say to him, 'Had you known that you would transgress the command "You will not take vengeance or bear a grudge" [Lev 19:18] or "You will not hate you brother in your heart" [Lev 19:17] or "You will love your neighbor as yourself" [Lev 19:18] or "That your brother may live with you" [Lev 25:36] (would you have made that vow?)'. . . . If he said, 'Had I known that this was so I would not have made my vow,' then he may be released from his vow."

Although the application in the Mishnah is different from that in the *Mekilta*, we have here the same collocation of Levitical imperatives, with "Love your neighbor as yourself" added.

The several commandments that are joined in *m. Ned.* 9:4 also stand side by side in *t. Soṭah* 5:11; *Sipre* 186/7 on Deut 19:10–11; 235 on 22:13; *'Abot R. Nat.* A 26. In these, the subject is the sins that a man commits by entering into a bad marriage. According to *'Abot R. Nat.* A 26, "Rabbi Akiba says: If one weds a woman who is unfit for him, he transgresses five negative commandments: 'You will not take vengeance' [Lev 19:18], 'Nor bear a grudge' [Lev 19:18], 'You will not hate your brother in your heart' [Lev 19:17], 'You will love your neighbor as yourself' [Lev 19:18], 'That your brother will live with you' [Lev 25:36]."

Clearly, we are dealing here with a rabbinic tradition. It reckoned injunctions from Lev 19:17–18 and 25:36 as a sort of unit, which one could draw upon to make varied points:

- Lev 19:17: do not hate your brother
- Lev 19:18: do not take vengeance or bear a grudge
- Lev 19:18: love your neighbor
- Lev 25:36: let your brother live with you

One guesses that a verbal connection largely explains the association. "Your brother" (אחיך), which appears five times in Lev 25, twice in vv. 35–36 in particular, also occurs in Lev 19:17–18.

The first three exhortations—love, do not hate, do not take vengeance—are clear enough. But what meaning attached itself to "Let your brother live with you"? The biblical context of Lev 25:36 gives us the answer:

> If your brother falls into difficulty and becomes dependent on you, you will support him; he will live with you as though a resident alien. Do not take interest in

advance or otherwise make a profit from him, but fear your God; let him live with you. You will not lend him your money at interest taken in advance, or provide him food at a profit. I am the LORD your God, who brought you out of the land of Egypt, to give you the land of Canaan, to be your God. (Lev 25:35–38)

To let your brother "live with you" is to assist him when he is impoverished, to let him live on the land and not lend him money at interest. In other words, Lev 25:36 requires offering financial support to those in need. This explains why *Mek.* on Exod 13:19 finds in Joseph the fulfillment of this commandment: he provided for his father and his brothers when they sojourned in Egypt for food.

How does all this relate to the Sermon on the Plain? Q 6:34, if the IQP has it right, contained this: "And if you lend to those from whom you hope to receive, what reward do you have? Do not even the Gentiles do the same?" The IQP's text for 6:30 also concerns lending and borrowing: "To the one who asks of you, give; and from the one who borrows, do not ask back what is yours." Both lines are thematically akin to Lev 25:35–38, which encourages charity, enjoins giving without fee, and prohibits lending at interest. That the commentaries on Matt 5:42 // Luke 6:30 (Q) and Matt 5:47 // Luke 6:34 (Q) occasionally cite Lev 25:35–38 is understandable.[177]

Given what we find in the rabbis, it is altogether natural that the Sermon on the Plain touches upon the lending of money. Jewish tradition linked the Levitical commands to love one's neighbor, to not take vengeance, and to let go of a grudge with Lev 25:35–38 and its mandate to share with those in need. The Sermon on the Plain, in addressing the same issues in one place, follows suit.

Sipra 200 on Lev 19:17–18, although it does not cite Lev 25:36 in expounding 19:17–18, offers further evidence that the latter was conventionally coupled with the subject of lending. For *Sipra* takes up precisely that topic when discussing the imperatives in Lev 19:17–18:

"You will not take vengeance" [Lev 19:18]. To what extent is the force of vengeance? If one says to him, "Lend me your sickle," and the other did not do so. On the next day, the other says to him, "Lend me your spade." The one then replies, "I am not going to lend it, because you did not lend me your sickle." In that context, it is said, "You will not take vengeance or bear a grudge" [Lev 19:18]. To what extent is the force of a grudge? If one says to him, "Lend me your spade," but he did not do so. The next day the other one says to him, "Lend me your sickle," and the other replies, "I am not like you, for you did not lend me your spade [but here, take the sickle]!" In that context, it is said, "or bear any grudge" [cf. *b. Yoma* 23a].

177. For example, Bovon, *Luke 1*, 237 n. 45; Davies and Allison, *Matthew*, 1:547; I. Howard Marshall, *The Gospel of Luke: A Commentary on the Greek Text* (NIGTC; Grand Rapids: Eerdmans, 1978), 263.

Sipra, in its exposition of Lev 19:17–18, attends to the same subject as do Q 6:30 and 34, and like the Jesus tradition, it envisions the possibility of someone breaking the cycle of tit for tat.

12. The Sun Rises on the Good and the Bad

In prohibiting retaliation, Q's Jesus appeals directly to the goodness of God: disciples should become sons of their divine father, who makes the sun rise on the good and the bad (6:35). To my knowledge, *b. Yoma* 23a supplies the closest ancient parallel to this: "Has it not been taught, Concerning those who are insulted but do not (on account of revenge) insult others and who hear themselves reproached without replying and who (do good) work out of love of the Lord and rejoice in their sufferings, the Scripture says this: 'But they that love him are as the sun when he goes forth in his might' [Judg 5:31]?" This teaching, which recurs in *b. Šabb.* 88b and *b. Giṭ.* 36b and bears such a striking resemblance to Q 6:35, belongs to an exposition of Lev 19:18, "You shall not take vengeance or bear a grudge against any of your people." Once more, then, a rabbinic parallel to an item in Q 6:27–42 is associated with Lev 19.

To this one might respond that *b. Yoma* 23a is not a first-century text. Perhaps, then, the parallel is a coincidence. Or perhaps the Talmud here owes something to Christian influence. Yet in view of the many other links between Jewish commentary on Lev 19 and Q 6:27–42, surely we are entitled at least to wonder whether *b. Yoma* 23a does not instead preserve an exegetical tradition that the Sermon on the Plain already puts to use.

13. More Than Gentiles

The gist of Q 6:32–34 is that Jesus' obedient hearers are to be unlike others, including the Gentiles (οἱ ἐθνικοί). This is yet one more motif at home in Lev 19.[178] The chapter opens with the call to be holy because God is holy. In *Midr. Ps.* 10:1 this is taken to mean that Israel's behavior should be different from the behavior of the nations because Israel's God is different. Jacob Milgrom thinks that this rightly catches the intention of Leviticus itself.[179] His verdict seems confirmed by Lev 20:26, which repeats 19:2 and then elaborates: "You shall be holy to me, for I the LORD am holy, and I have separated you from the other peoples [MT: העמים; LXX: οἱ ἐθνοί] to be mine." Just as Lev 19 calls Israel to be different from other peoples, so too does Q's Jesus call his listeners to behave differently from everybody else, including οἱ ἐθνοί.

---

178. Burrows remarks, "The conception of holiness was associated in the Old Testament with the separation of Israel from the nations and their defilements. A few echoes of such an idea are heard in Jesus' sayings (Mt. 5:47; 6:7, 32; 20:25 par.)" ("Old Testament Ethics," 241).

179. Milgrom notes, "The *imitatio dei* implied by this verse [19:2] is that just as God differs from human beings, so Israel should differ from the nations (20:26), a meaning corroborated by the generalization that encloses this chapter (v. 37)" (*Leviticus 17–22*, 1604).

14. Divine and Human Mercy

The command to be merciful even as God is merciful (Q 6:36) reproduces a traditional Jewish sentiment more than once attributed to Abba Saul of the first or second century CE:

Mek. on Exod 15:2: "Abba Saul says: 'O be like him. Just as he is gracious and merciful so you be gracious and merciful.'"

y. Pe'ah 15b (1:1): "Abba Saul says: '("I will glorify him" [Exod 15:2] means) "I will be like him."' Just as God is gracious and merciful, so you also must be gracious and merciful."

b. Šabb. 133b: "Abba Saul interpreted, 'and I will praise him' [Exod 15:2]: be like him; just as he is gracious and merciful so you be gracious and merciful" (cf. *Sop.* 3:13).

These parallels to Q 6:36 all have to do with the interpretation of Exod 15:2. It is otherwise, however, with three other texts, which instead belong to commentary on the Levitical Holiness Code:

Tg. Ps.-J. on Lev 22:28: "My people, sons of Israel, just as I am merciful in heaven, so will you be merciful on earth. Cow or ewe, itself and its young, you will not kill in one day."[180]

y. Ber. 9c (5:3): "R. Yose b. R. Bun said, 'It is not good to imply that God's traits [are derived from his attribute of] mercy. Those who translate [Lev 22:28 as follows], "My people, sons of Israel, just as I am merciful in heaven, so will you be merciful on earth: Cow or ewe, itself and its young, you will not kill in one day"—that is not good, for it implies that God's traits [are derived from the attribute of] mercy.'"

y. Meg. 75c (4:10): "R. Yose b. R. Bun said, 'They do not do well, for they treat the measure of the Holy One, blessed be he, as acts only of mercy. Those who translate [Lev 22:28 as follows], "My people, sons of Israel, just as we are merciful in heaven, so you must be merciful on earth; whether the mother is a cow or a ewe, you will not kill both her and her young in one day," do not do well, for they treat the decrees of the Holy One, blessed be He, as acts of mercy.'"

These last three texts are very close to Q's "Be merciful just as your Father is merciful" (6:36 [cf. 6:35: "so that you may become sons of your Father, for he makes his sun rise on the good and on the bad"]). Again, then, Jewish paral-

---

180. So the London manuscript. The Polyglot text reads, "My people, sons of Israel, just as our Father [Moses is speaking] is merciful in heaven, so will you be merciful on earth. Cow or ewe, itself and its young, you will not kill in one day."

lels to the Sermon on the Plain take us back to the Holiness Code, although in this instance we are dealing with Lev 22, not Lev 19.

Unless we take the Synoptics to be sufficient evidence, we cannot, unfortunately, demonstrate that the rejected exegesis of Lev 22:28 goes back to the time of Q, to pre-70 Judaism. Yet the occurrence of Abba Saul's sentence in the *Mekilta* and the likelihood that the Mishnah criticizes his sentiment in a couple of places[181] push the date back at least to the second century;[182] and if our choice is between holding that the rabbinic texts depend ultimately upon Christian tradition or that the Synoptics draw upon an exegetical tradition that Pseudo-Jonathan and the Jerusalem Talmud attest, it is unclear to me why we should prefer the former alternative over the latter.

15. Measuring

Q 6:38 had Jesus say, "And with the measure that you measure, it will be measured to you" (ἐν ᾧ μέτρῳ μετρεῖτε μετρηθήσεται ὑμῖν). The sentence has close parallels in Jewish texts, particularly the targumim, and in fact it qualifies as a proverb.[183] For our purposes, however, the interesting observation is this: Lev 19 concerns itself with measuring. Leviticus 19:35 enjoins, "You shall do no wrong in judgment, in measures of length or weight or quantity" (RSV). One might dismiss the coincidence of topic as just that, coincidence. Yet we have already seen sufficient evidence that Q 6:37 otherwise interacts with Lev 19; and if Q's saying about measuring is joined to the imperative not to judge (μὴ κρίνετε), the commandment in Leviticus is also about judging: "You shall do no wrong in judgment [LXX: οὐ ποιήσετε ἄδικον ἐν κρίσει (cf. 19:15)], in measures of length. . . ." When one adds that ἐν ᾧ μέτρῳ appears in Q, ἐν μέτροις in Leviticus, it becomes possible—I claim no more—to see this as one more intertextual link between the Sermon on the Plain and Lev 19.[184]

16. Leviticus 19 as a Popular Intertext

To this point, I have urged that Q 6:27–42 consistently interacts with portions of Lev 19. The case gains credence when one discovers that other

181. Cf. *m. Ber.* 5:3; *m. Meg.* 4:9; and see the discussion by Ephraim E. Urbach, *The Sages: Their Concepts and Beliefs* (2 vols.; Jerusalem: Magnes, 1975), 1:384–85.

182. See further Martin McNamara, *The New Testament and the Palestinian Targum to the Pentateuch* (AnBib 27; Rome: Pontifical Biblical Institute, 1964), 133–38. He shows that the relevant words found in Tg. Ps.-J. on Lev 22:28 were cut out of the other Palestinian targumim, and he thinks that the New Testament shows knowledge of them.

183. See Hans Peter Rüger, "Mit welchem Maß ihr meßt, wird euch gemessen warden," *ZNW* 60 (1969): 174–82.

184. Christopher N. Chandler, in a lecture at the Society of Biblical Literature annual meeting in Boston, November 2008 ("Jesus and James on Justice in the Courts: A Reconsideration of the Ward/Allison Thesis"), argued for a link between Lev 19:35 and Matt 7:1–2.

passages from antiquity do the same. One may even speak of a convention here. CD-A 6:14–7:5 is based upon a series of imperatives from Lev 18–20.[185] *Testament of Gad* 4–6 is a partial reworking of LXX Lev 19.[186] *Pseudo-Phocylides* 3–41 is largely a creative transformation of the Decalogue and Lev 19.[187] The book of James returns repeatedly to Lev 19.[188] And the first four chapters of the *Didache* consistently interact with Lev 19.[189] So the

185. Cf. CD-A 6:16 with Lev 19:11 (do not steal); CD-A 6:16, 21 with Lev 19:9–10 (care for the poor); CD-A 6:18, 20; 7:5 with Lev 19:2, 5–8 (on the holy and the profane); CD-A 6:18 with Lev 19:3 (keep the Sabbath); CD-A 6:20 with Lev 19:18 (love your neighbor); CD-A 6:21 with Lev 19:13–14 (care for the needy); CD-A 6:21 with Lev 19:33–34 (care for the foreigner); CD-A 7:1 with Lev 18:6 (do not sin with a blood relation); CD-A 7:2–3 with Lev 19:17–18 (reprove a neighbor); CD-A 7:2–3 with Lev 19:18 (do not keep a grudge); CD-A 7:4 with Lev 20:25 (do not be defiled by what God has set apart as unclean). Also, CD-A 8:5–6 returns to Lev 19:15–18.

186. There is an overlap of main themes—avoiding vengeance, loving others, speaking to those who have offended—and some crystal clear allusions. Both *T. Gad* 4:2 ("Hatred does not want to hear repeated his commands concerning love of neighbor") and 6:1 ("Each of you love his brother. Drive hatred out of your hearts") plainly recall Lev 19:17–18 ("You shall not hate in your heart anyone of your kin. . . . But you shall love your neighbor as yourself"). See further Kugel, "Hidden Hatred," 49–52. The large overlap in vocabulary includes the key words "love" (ἀγαπάω [*T. Gad* 6:1, 3; Lev 19:18, 34]), "brother" (ἀδελφός [*T. Gad* 4:3; 6:1; Lev 19:17]), "sin" (ἁμαρτία [*T. Gad* 6:5; Lev 19:8, 17, 22]), "mind" (διάνοια [*T. Gad* 6:1; Lev 19:17]), "(take) revenge" (ἐκδίκησις/ἐκδικάζω [*T. Gad* 6:7; Lev 19:18]), "hate" (μισέω [*T. Gad* 6:5; Lev 19:17]), and "neighbor" (πλησίον [*T. Gad* 4:2; Lev 19:11, 13, 15, 16, 17, 18]).

187. Cf. *Ps.-Phoc.* 8 with Lev 19:3 (honor parents); *Ps.-Phoc.* 9–10 with Lev 19:15 (care for the poor, do justice, do not show partiality); *Ps.-Phoc.* 11, 14–15 with Lev 19:35–36 (make a just measure); *Ps.-Phoc.* 16–17 with Lev 19:12 (do not commit perjury); *Ps.-Phoc.* 19 with Lev 19:13 (give laborers their pay); *Ps.-Phoc.* 39 with Lev 19:33–34 (honor strangers as native citizens); *Ps.-Phoc.* 40 with Lev 19:34 (be kind to those in a position you once were in). See further Karl-Wilhelm Niebuhr, *Gesetz und Paränese: Katechismusartige Weisungsreihen in der frühjüdischen Literatur* (WUNT 2/28; Tübingen: Mohr Siebeck, 1987), 7–31; Johannes Thomas, *Der jüdische Phokylides: Formgeschicthliche Zugänge zu Pseudo-Phokylides und Vergleich mit der neu-testamentlichen Paränese* (NTOA 23; Freiburg: Universitätsverlag; Göttingen: Vandenhoeck & Ruprecht, 1992), 162–70.

188. See Johnson, "Leviticus 19," 391–401. Johnson correlates Lev 19:12 with Jas 5:12 (do not swear falsely); Lev 19:13 with Jas 5:4 (pay laborers their wages); Lev 19:15 with Jas 2:1, 9 (do not show partiality in judgment); Lev 19:16 with Jas 4:11 (do not slander others); Lev 19:17b with Jas 5:20 (correct a sinner); Lev 19:18a with Jas 5:9 (do not keep a grudge); Lev 19:18b with Jas 2:8 (love your neighbor as yourself). To these parallels we should add Jas 2:2–4, which takes up a tradition attested in *t. Sanh.* 6:2; *Sipra Lev.* 200 on Lev 19:15–16; *b. Šeb.* 30a; 31a; *Deut. Rab.* 5:6, and others; see R. B. Ward, "Partiality in the Assembly: James 2:2–4," *HTR* 62 (1969): 87–97. This tradition was firmly associated with Lev 19:15 (thus *t. Sanh.* 6:2 cites the verse, and the passage from *Sipra* is commentary on it).

189. Note *Did.* 1:2 (part of the programmatic opening), "love your neighbor as yourself" (cf. Lev 19:18); 1:2, the golden rule (see above, p. 358); 2:2, "you shall not steal" (οὐ κλέψεις [cf. Lev 19:11: οὐ κλέψετε]); 2:2, "you shall not practice magic" (cf. Lev 19:26, 31, with prohibitions of augury, witchcraft, mediums, and wizards); 2:3, "you shall not commit perjury, you shall not bear false witness" (cf. Lev. 19:12: "you shall not swear falsely"); 2:5, "your speech shall not be vain or false" (ψευδής [cf. Lev 19:11: "you shall not deal falsely (ψεύσεσθε); and you shall not

proposal that Q 6:27–42 rewrites Lev 19 puts the evangelical text firmly within a tradition.

17. The Didache

As just observed, the first part of the *Didache* repeatedly reworks Lev 19. The fact is of special interest because the *Didache* opens with lines that in many ways recall Q 6:27–42. Now, the relationship between these lines and the Synoptics is, as we have seen, notoriously difficult to unravel. But whatever the truth of that murky matter, the crucial point for us is that the *Didache*, in the form we have it, places sayings closely related to Q 6:27–42 within a section that is not only introduced by a quotation from Lev 19 (v. 18: "love your neighbor as yourself") but also permeated by allusions to that chapter. The *Didache*, then, at least in its final form, may show some awareness of the close relationship between Lev 19 and the materials in Q 6:27–42.[190]

---

lie to one another"; 19:12: "you shall not swear falsely"]); 2:7, "you shall not hate [μισήσεις] any one but some you shall reprove [ἐλέγξεις] and for some you shall pray, and some you shall love [ἀγαπήσεις] more than your own life" (cf. Lev 19:17, 18, with οὐ μισήσεις, ἐλέγξεις, ἀγαπήσεις); 3:4, "regard not omens" (μὴ γίνου οἰωνοσκόπος [cf. Lev 19:26: οὐκ οἰωνιεῖσθε, "you shall not heed omens"]); 3:4, warning against idolatry (εἰδωλολατρίαν, εἰδωλολατρία [cf. Lev 19:4: οὐκ ἐπακολουθήσετε εἰδώλοις, "you shall not follow idols"]); 3:4: "be not an enchanter" (ἐπαοιδός [cf. Lev 19:31: τοῖς ἐπαοιδοῖς οὐ προσκολληθήσεσθε, "you shall not attach yourselves to enchanters"]); 3:5, "be not a liar" (μὴ γίνου ψεύστης [cf. Lev 19:11: οὐ ψεύσεσθε, "you shall not lie"]); 4:4, "You shall give righteous judgment" (κρινεῖς δικαίως [cf. Lev 19:15: ἐν δικαιοσύνῃ κρίνεις, "in justice you shall judge"]); 4:3, "you shall favor no one's person [οὐ λήψῃ πρόσωπον] in reproving [ἐλέγξαι] transgression" (cf. Lev 19:15, 17, the two classic texts on impartiality and reproof; both οὐ λήψῃ πρόσωπον and ἐλέγξεις appear); 4:8, "you shall not turn away the needy but shall share everything with your brother" (cf. Lev 19:9–10: instruction on leaving the gleanings for the poor and aliens). Most of the relevant verses from the *Didache* do not have counterparts in the "two ways" section of *Barnabas*. They may, then, come from the Didachist himself. But see John S. Kloppenborg, "Did. 1.1–6.1, James, Matthew, and Torah," in *Trajectories through the New Testament and the Apostolic Fathers* (ed. Andrew F. Gregory and Christopher M. Tuckett; Oxford: Oxford University Press, 2005), 193–221. Kloppenborg observes that at least the promotion of Lev 19:18 to a prominent position at the head of the "two ways" document was part of the *Vorlage* common to the *Didache* and the *Doctrina XII Apostolorum*.

190. Paul may also show this awareness. In the very chapters, Rom 12–14, where he composes sentences related to Q 6:27–42 (see pp. 346–48), the apostle also turns his thoughts to Lev 19. Not only does he enjoin hospitality (Rom 12:13: φιλοξενία), for which Lev 19:33–34 was a well-known proof text, but also he focuses on the problem of vengeance (Rom 12:17–21: μὴ ἑαυτοὺς ἐκδικοῦντες), which Lev 19:18 famously prohibits (LXX: οὐκ ἐκδικᾶταί σου ἡ χείρ); and in Rom 13:9 he expressly quotes the command to love one's neighbor (Lev 19:18). He also, in Rom 14:13 (μὴ τιθέναι πρόσκομμα τῷ ἀδελφῷ ἢ σκάνδαλον), may recall Lev 19:14 (οὐ προσθήσεις σκάνδαλον); see Thompson, *Clothed with Christ*, 174–84. In other words, Paul's thoughts seemingly move to Lev 19 at the same time that he rewrites dominical traditions related to Q 6:27–42. The circumstance is more than consistent with the argument of this chapter.

The chief points of continuity and contrast between Q 6:27–42 and Lev 19, introduced over the previous pages, may be set forth briefly as follows:

The Sermon on the Plain	Leviticus 19
Love your enemies (6:27)	Love your neighbor (19:18)
Do not take vengeance (6:27–30)	Do not take vengeance (19:18)
Lend without demanding return (6:30)	*Sipra*, in its commentary on 19:17–18, discusses those who refuse to lend and counsels meeting stinginess with generosity
Do unto others as you would have them do unto you (6:31)	Jewish tradition regularly associates 19:18 with the golden rule
Jesus' followers are to behave differently than Gentiles (6:32–34)	Lev 20:26 and other Jewish texts understand Lev 19:2 (cf. 11:44; 20:26) to mean that Israel must behave differently than Gentiles
Be merciful because God is merciful (6:36)	Be holy because God is holy (19:2)
Do not judge (6:37)	Judge your neighbor (19:15, 17)
Take the log out of your own eye before removing the splinter from the eye of "your brother" (6:41–42)	Jewish exegesis of 19:17 requires one to reflect upon one's own faults before reproving "your brother," and *b. 'Arak.* 16b associates the saying in Q 6:41–42 with Lev 19:17

When one reads Q 6:27–42 with Lev 19 as the chief intertext, the section as a whole functions as does Matt 5:21–48 (which is partly based on Q 6:27–42): it reinterprets Moses. While Q's Jesus follows Lev 19 in countering vengeance, encouraging love, and prohibiting usury, he otherwise modifies or adds to the Mosaic demands. He substitutes mercy for holiness, enjoins his hearers not to judge, speaks of love of enemy rather than love of neighbor, and says that it is not enough to have right fraternal relations (the subject of Lev 19:17), for even Gentiles do that. It is also possible that the positive form of the golden rule is intended to transcend the well-known negative form of the golden rule, although on this issue it is all but impossible to make up one's mind.[191]

Every part of Q 6:27–42 relates itself, directly or indirectly, to Lev 19 or to Jewish traditions parasitic upon that chapter.[192] What follows? It seems al-

191. For the argument that the two forms are significantly different, see Gerd Theissen, "Die Goldene Regel (Matthäus 7:12//Lukas 6:31): Über den Sitz im Leben ihrer positiven und negativen Form," *BibInt* 11 (2003): 386–99; Topel, "Golden Rule"; Zeller, *Mahnsprüche*, 119. For the argument that the ancients at least did not distinguish the two forms, see King, "Golden Rule." Note that *Gos. Thom.* 6 attributes the negative form to Jesus ("do not do what you hate"), as did some church fathers, and that rabbinic sources can put positive and negative variations of the golden rule side by side (e.g., *'Abot R. Nat.* A 15). The tendency of most contemporary scholarship is to see little if any difference between the two forms.

192. Although my analysis has confined itself to the central portion of the Sermon on the Plain, it may be worth noting that the end of Q's discourse roughly corresponds to Lev 19:37, which concludes its chapter with this: "You shall keep all my statutes and all my ordinances,

together implausible that a consistent, subtle interplay with a single section of the Pentateuch chapter was the product either of happenstance or of multiple hands over time inserting now this and then adding that, especially since the intertextual links are not detachable ornamentation but rather integral parts of the relevant logia. That a single author was responsible for the intertextual coherence is a far more credible proposal.[193]

The Reach of Memory

If Q 6:27–42 does indeed preserve portions of a pre-Synoptic speech, those portions must have been transmitted together. What are the chances of that, especially if we take into account the possibility that, before incorporation into Q, the speech was not written down?

The IQP's reconstruction of Q 6:27–42 (minus vv. 39–40) runs to just over two hundred words. Because the committee often was unable to establish or conjecture the original text, its critical edition is regularly peppered with dots indicating where material is missing or may be missing. This means that its version of Q 6:27–42 must be shorter than the original Q text. Nonetheless, if the IQP has come anywhere near the mark, Q 6:27–42 was not much longer than the Nicene Creed, which in Greek contains 175 words, a creed that so many Christians have been able to repeat by rote. Countless Jews over the centuries, moreover, have been able to recite, without the aid of a prayer book, the Amidah, which is far longer than the IQP's text for Q 6:27–42.[194] So to suggest that someone properly motivated could have recalled, with some accuracy, a much shorter oral text is not to envision anything extraordinary.[195]

With this in mind, we can turn to an observation made by Walter Ong:

and observe them: I am the Lord [LXX: κύριος]"; see Doeve, *Jewish Hermeneutics*, 199. Here the speaker's identity as "Lord"—a chief theme of Lev 19—grounds the requirement to do what is said. It is the same in Q 6:46–49, which calls for obedience by stressing the lordship of the speaker. Q's Jesus asks, "Why do you call me 'Lord, Lord' and not do what I say?" The parable of the two builders follows.

193. Although I have, in the previous pages, assumed the truth of the Q hypothesis, or at least that Matthew's Sermon on the Mount is largely secondary vis-à-vis Luke's Sermon on the Plain, the assumption seems confirmed by the consistent use of Lev 19 and related traditions in Luke 6:27–42. How likely is it that Luke managed to move into one section only those items related to Leviticus, either by accident (surely a far-fetched proposal) or by design, in the latter case eliminating Matthew's most explicit pointer to Lev 19 (5:43: "You have heard that it was said, 'Love your neighbor'")?

194. On the oral nature of ancient Jewish liturgy, see Stefan C. Reif, "Codicological Aspects of Jewish Liturgical History," *BJRL* 75 (1993): 117–31.

195. I agree with Alan Millard: there is no reason to imagine that Christian oral tradition was "incapable of handling anything longer than one- or two-line sayings or very short stories" (*Reading and Writing in the Time of Jesus* [Washington Square: New York University Press, 2000], 197).

In a primary oral culture, to solve effectively the problem of retaining and retrieving carefully articulated thought, you have to do your thinking in mnemonic patterns, shaped for ready oral recurrence. Your thought must come into being in heavily rhythmic, balanced patterns, in repetitions or antitheses, in alliterations and assonances, in epithetic or other formulary expressions . . . in proverbs which are constantly heard by everyone so that they come to mind readily and which themselves are patterned for retention and ready recall, or in other mnemonic form.[196]

Q 6:27–42 lines up remarkably well with Ong's sketch of what people in an oral world need in order to remember a text. The passage includes traditional Jewish proverbs—the golden rule and the "measure for measure" logion— and conventional Jewish motifs: the good and the bad/wicked,[197] the just and unjust,[198] God as the cause of sun and rain,[199] the righteous as sons of God,[200] and the imitation of divine attributes.[201] The central part of the Sermon on the Plain also features striking images: someone turning the other cheek, a person going the extra mile, a log jutting from an eye;[202] as well as provocative imperatives: love your enemy, pray for those persecuting you, give away your remaining garment.[203] It further exhibits parallelism, balance, alliteration, and repetition, as one can see from the following:[204]

- imperative + definite article + plural noun + ὑμ-

  27 ἀγαπᾶτε τοὺς ἐχθροὺς ὑμῶν
  28 προσεύχεσθε ὑπὲρ τῶν διωκόντων ὑμᾶς

196. Walter J. Ong, *Orality and Literacy: The Technologizing of the Word* (London: Methuen, 1982), 34. Ong's generalizations find detailed empirical support in David C. Rubin, *Memory in Oral Traditions: The Cognitive Psychology of Epic, Ballads, and Counting-Out Rhymes* (New York: Oxford University Press, 1995).

197. For example, Prov 14:9; 15:3; Matt 13:38; Josephus, *Ant.* 6.307; 8.314; *Mek.* on Exod 18:12; *b. Taʿan.* 7a.

198. For example, *1 En.* 100:7; *Pss. Sol.* 15:3–6; *T. Jud.* 21:6; Acts 24:15; 1 Pet 3:18; *Mek.* on Exod 18:12.

199. For example, Gen 7:4; Lev 26:4; Deut 11:14; 1 Sam 12:17–18; Ps 104:13; Amos 4:7; Jdt 8:31; *b. Roš. Haš.* 17b.

200. For example, Prov 3:12; Jer 3:19; Hos 11:1; Sir 4:10; Wis 2:18; *b. B. Bat.* 17b; *b. Ber.* 7a; *b. Ḥul.* 86a; *b. Taʿan.* 24b–25a.

201. For example, Lev 11:44; 19:2; 20:26; *Let. Arist.* 188, 210, 281; *T. Ash.* 4:3, 5; *Sipra* 121 on Lev 11:44; *Sipre* 49 on Deut 11:22; Tg. Ps.-J. on Lev 22:28.

202. Cf. perhaps Num 33:55; Josh 23:13: "barbs in your eyes." On the importance of imagery for memory, see Quintilian, *Rhet. Her.* 3.30–40; Cicero, *De or.* 2.353–54; see also Rubin, *Memory in Oral Traditions*, 39–64.

203. Cf. Quintilian, *Rhet. Her.* 3.35: "Ordinary things easily slip from the memory while the striking and novel stay longer in the mind."

204. In addition to what follows, see above, pp. 316–23, 342–46; also Horsley, "Covenant Renewal Discourse," 213–16. I have again used the IQP's reconstructed text.

- verb ending in -ει + ἐπί + pair of nouns with three syllables and ending with -ους

    35c   ἀνατέλλει ἐπὶ πονηροὺς καὶ ἀγαθούς

    35c   βρέχει ἐπὶ δικαίους καὶ ἀδίκους

- ὅστις + σε + verb ending in -ζει/-σει + imperative + αὐτ-

    29   ὅστις σε ῥαπίζει . . . στρέψον αὐτῷ

    Matt 5:41   ὅστις σε ἀγγαρεύσει . . . ὕπαγε μετ᾽ αὐτοῦ

- τῷ + participle ending in -οντι/-οῦντί + σοι/σε + imperative ending in -ς

    29   τῷ θέλοντί σοι . . . ἄφες

    30   τῷ αἰτοῦντί σε δός

- adverb ending in -ως + form of ποιέω + noun in dative case

    31   καθὼς . . . ποιῶσιν ὑμῖν

    31   οὕτως ποιεῖτε αὐτοῖς

- εἰ/ἐάν + verb ending in -τε + τίνα μισθὸν ἔχετε;

    32   εἰ ἀγαπᾶτε . . . τίνα μισθὸν ἔχετε;

    34   ἐὰν δανίσητε . . . τίνα μισθὸν ἔχετε;

- οὐχὶ καὶ οἱ + noun ending in -αι/οι + τὸ αὐτὸ ποιοῦσιν;

    32   οὐχὶ καὶ οἱ τελῶναι τὸ αὐτὸ ποιοῦσιν;

    34   οὐχὶ καὶ οἱ ἐθνικοὶ τὸ αὐτὸ ποιοῦσιν;

- repetition of οἰκτίρμ-

    36   οἰκτίρμονες

    36   οἰκτίρμων

- repetition of κρίνετε + passive of κρίνω

    37a   κρίνετε . . . κριθῆτε

    37b   κρίνετε . . . κριθήσεσθε

- ἐν ᾧ + singular dative noun + verb ending in -ετε/-εῖτε + future passive

    37   ἐν ᾧ γὰρ κρίματι κρίνετε κριθήσεσθε

    38   ἐν ᾧ μέτρῳ μετρεῖτε μετρηθήσεται

- definite article + ἐν τῷ + ὀφθαλμῷ

    41   τὸ κάρφος τὸ ἐν τῷ ὀφθαλμῷ

    41   τὴν δὲ ἐν τῷ ἰδίῳ ὀφθαλμῷ

- definite article + -ος + preposition + definitive article + ὀφθαλμ- σοῦ

    42   τὸ κάρφος ἐκ τοῦ ὀφθαλμοῦ σου

    42   ἡ δοκὸς ἐν τῷ ὀφθαλμῷ σοῦ

- repetition of βλέπω and ἐκβάλλω
  41 βλέπεις . . . ἐκβάλω
  42 ἔκβαλε . . . διαβλέψεις ἐκβαλεῖν
- repetition of τὸ κάρφος + definite article + ὀφθαλμ- + σου
  41 τὸ κάρφος τὸ ἐν τῷ ὀφθαλμῷ τοῦ ἀδελφοῦ σου
  41 τὸ κάρφος ἐκ τοῦ ὀφθαλμοῦ σου
  42 τὸ κάρφος τοῦ ὀφθαλμοῦ τοῦ ἀδελφοῦ σου
- repetition of definite article + ἀδελφ- + σου
  41 τοῦ ἀδελφοῦ σου
  41 τῷ ἀδελφῷ σου
  42 τοῦ ἀδελφοῦ σου

Such repetition, alliteration, balance, and parallelism would have been aids to memory. As Quintilian observed, "It is easier to learn prose when it is artistically constructed than when it has no such organization" (*Inst.* 11.2.39).[205]

I neither believe nor contend, however, that somebody committed to memory, word for word, a speech thought to derive from Jesus. Early Christian literature leaves the definite impression that his followers were uninterested in parrot-like, verbatim memorization. The different versions of the Lord's Prayer (Matt 6:9–13; Luke 11:2–4; *Did.* 8:2) and of the words of institution at the Last Supper (Matt 26:26–29; Mark 14:22–25; Luke 22:15–20; 1 Cor 11:23–25) settle the matter: even important communal or liturgical texts were fluid. I suggest, rather, that we can believe, without undue credulity, that the tradition kept more or less intact, from a very early time, some memorable imperatives, illustrations, and well-turned phrases, and further that it often structured those materials in fourfold forms (see pp. 334–46) and may also have remembered a general topical pattern:

- benefaction (cf. Q 6:27–30)
- reciprocity (cf. Q 6:31–34)
- judgment (cf. Q 6:37–42)

My contention is not that Q 6:27–42 is a word-perfect transcript of somebody's oral performance but rather that it is a version or adaptation of a more or less stable composition.[206]

205. See further Rubin, *Memory in Oral Traditions*, 65–89.

206. Although I will put no weight on the argument here, I can note that some have seen in Luke 6:27–36 signs of an Aramaic substratum; so, for example, Matthew Black, *An Aramaic Approach to the Gospels and Acts* (3rd ed.; Oxford: Clarendon, 1967), 179–81; Raymond A. Martin, *Syntax Criticism of the Synoptic Gospels* (SBEC 10; Lewiston, NY: Edwin Mellen, 1987), 89–103.

Objections

Before contemplating the origin of that discourse, I need to return, if only briefly, to the issue of literary unity. In mustering evidence for the common view that Q 6:27–35 is composite, Kloppenborg has observed that "the first four imperatives are formulated in the second-person plural and all agree in placing the imperative in first position. Verses 29, 30, on the other hand, are in the second-person singular and follow the form τῷ + participle + imperative (or prohibitive)."[207] Others have denied the unity of Q 6:27–42 and its parts because they have supposed that the various sayings exhibit thematic tension—for instance, they have imagined the golden rule to be disharmonious with "Love your enemies"—or because smaller portions could stand on their own. I hope that, in the previous pages, I have introduced evidence against these last two objections. The section holds together well—in my judgment, better than does the noncomposite Jas 1—and its consistent use of Lev 19 makes it unlikely that it is the textual equivalent of a patchwork quilt. For myself, attempts to argue, on the basis of thematic dissonance, that Q 6:27–42 is a catena of one-time independent logia are no more persuasive than endeavors to impeach the integrity of the Lord's Prayer and regard it as an assembly of diverse traditions because of an alleged lack of internal theological harmony.[208]

What, then, of the switch from the second-person plural (Q 6:27–28) to the second-person singular (Q 6:29–30) and back again (Q 6:31–34)? This is less than an impressive argument. We know of any number of ancient Jewish and Christian texts that move from one person to another, and the explanation cannot in every case be that we are looking at an amalgam. In Isa 63:10–14, the prophet first speaks of God in the third person, then in the second person. The same phenomenon (presumably with some sort of liturgical explanation) appears in, for example, Ps 3; 4; 6; 7; 9; 10: God is alternately "you" and "he." Sirach 47:12–23, which tells the story of Solomon, begins and ends with a third-person narrative—"Solomon reigned . . . God made all his borders tranquil"; "Solomon rested with his ancestors" (vv. 12–13, 23)—but in the middle, Sirach addresses Solomon directly: "How wise you were . . ." (vv. 14–22). Similarly, Sir 48:1–12 frames a second-person address to Elijah ("How glorious you were . . ." [vv. 4–11]) with a third-person account of the prophet's career (vv. 1–3, 12). In 4Q286 frg. 7 col. II 2–13, a series of curses opens with lines in the third person ("Cursed be Belial . . .") and then becomes more intense as it moves on to address evil spirits directly ("Damned be you . . ."). The exhortations in Jas 1:2–5a use the second-person plural, those in 1:5b–15 the third-person singular, and there

207. Kloppenborg, *Formation of Q*, 176. Cf. Lührmann, "Liebet eure Feinde," 417; Manson, *Sayings of Jesus*, 51; Piper, *Wisdom in the Q-Tradition*, 79.
208. Contrast Douglas E. Oakman, "The Lord's Prayer in Social Perspective," in *Authenticating the Words of Jesus* (ed. Bruce Chilton and Craig A. Evans; NTTS 28/1; Leiden: Brill, 1998), 137–86.

is more alternation in the rest of the chapter. *Acts of Thomas* 94 consists of eleven beatitudes, the first three of which are in the third person, the remainder of which are in the second. Perhaps it is worth adding that, although modern scholarship considers it composite, Lev 19, the subtext of Q 6:27–42, goes back and forth between the second-person singular and the second-person plural.[209] Ancient readers presumably would not have sensed anything amiss.

Some modern scholars have inferred that in ancient literature in general, "the switch from plural to singular second-person address is a rhetorical technique aimed at arresting attention, not a redaction-history indicator."[210] This seems to be an informed verdict.

But there is more to be said on this subject with regard to Q 6:27–42 in particular. The move from the second-person plural in 6:27–28 to the second-person singular in 6:29–30 reflects the nature of the materials. Q 6:27–28 contains all-encompassing injunctions, demands that hold for everyone in every time and place. The command to love one's enemy, for example, is incumbent upon everybody, because everybody has enemies. So the second-person plural is appropriate. The illustrations that follow, in vv. 29–30, are different. These put before the imagination particular scenes that instantiate the general injunctions, scenes that may or may not come to pass in everyone's life, scenes—such as being conscripted for labor or having one's garment taken—that, if they do become real, happen to individuals one at a time. So the second-person singular is appropriate. In other words, the generalizing imperatives applicable to all are naturally couched in the plural (vv. 27–28), whereas the concrete illustrations of how an individual might act in this or that hypothetical situation understandably use the singular (vv. 29–30).[211]

That this is the right take on Q 6:27–30 is confirmed by what follows. Verses 31–38, which again offer large, general imperatives—"Do good," "Be merciful," "Do not judge," "Do to others as you would have them do to you," for example—appropriately revert to the second-person plural. And when the second-person singular shows up again, it is in vv. 41–42, where we again pass from general statements to a concrete illustration: "Why do you see the speck that is in your brother's eye . . . ?" So in Q 6:31–42, as in 6:27–30, the general imperatives come with the plural, the particular illustrations with the singular. A source-critical explanation for the alternation is beside the point.

209. The singular appears in vv. 9–10, 13–14, 15–16, 17–18, 29, 32, the plural in vv. 11–12, 19, 26–28, 31, 35–36; both appear in vv. 33–34. If one includes pronominal suffixes, first- and second-person-plural forms vary all the more.

210. Kirk, *Composition*, 160. Cf. Leif Vaage, *Galilean Upstarts: Jesus' First Followers according to Q* (Valley Forge, PA: Trinity Press International, 1994), 122–24. The latter cites Longinus, *Subl.* 26.3, as well as an unpublished paper by Shawn Carruth.

211. Note the slightly different explanation by Michael Wolter (*Das Lukasevangelium* [HNT 5; Tübingen: Mohr Siebeck, 2008], 255): vv. 27–28 use the plural because they concern relations between groups; vv. 29–30 use the singular because they are directed to individuals.

With that objection out of the way, it remains to consider the origin of Q 6:27–42.

The Historical Jesus

Various observations on the preceding pages, above all the thematic coherence of the discourse and its consistent interaction with Lev 19 and associated exegetical tradition, point in the same direction, or rather to the same person. As to that person's identity, my reasoning, which I freely concede falls short of demonstration, is this: (i) Matthew and Luke attribute the words in Q 6:27–42 to Jesus; (ii) Clement and Polycarp also assign closely related logia to him; (iii) the parallels in Paul show that at least some of the sayings in Q 6:27–42 were already tradition for our earliest Christian writer; (iv) the apostle's characterization of Jesus as unselfish, humble, and gentle (Rom 15:1–3; 2 Cor 10:1; Phil 2:7–8) accords with Jesus' having uttered sentences like those in Q 6:27–42; (v) the pre-Markan passion narrative, which I will argue in chapter 5 is not bereft of memory, depicts Jesus as someone who behaved much as Q 6:27–42 enjoins; (vi) Mark 12:28–34 entails, if it remembers rightly, that Jesus paid heed to Lev 19, for in this pericope he dubs "You shall love your neighbor as yourself" (Lev 19:18) the "second" commandment; and (vii) we gain no explanatory advantage by assigning Q 6:27–42 to a contemporary of Jesus rather than to Jesus himself—so we may, if we wish, surmise that he was its primary author.[212]

This does not mean that we have here the memory of a single oral performance. Who among Jesus' followers could have recalled so much of an unwritten speech delivered on one occasion only?[213] And have we cause to imagine that any of Jesus' disciples, like a few of the students of Socrates, jotted notes after hearing their teacher?[214] To the extent of our knowledge, Jesus had no Boswell, nor were any of his followers memorists.

It seems much more likely that Q 6:27–42 incorporates recollection of a series of sentences that Jesus uttered on more than one occasion, or even uttered regularly, perhaps something like a stock sermon. In such a case, Luke 6 would incorporate the memory of multiple oral performances in which Jesus, in dialogue with Lev 19 and its history of interpretation, encouraged unrestricted benefaction and reciprocity and discouraged revenge and judging

212. For another view, see J. Sauer, "Traditionsgeschichtliche Erwägungen zu den synoptischen und paulinischen Aussagen über Feindesliebe und Wiedervergeltungsverzicht," *ZNW* 76 (1985): 1–28. Against Sauer, see Jacques Schlosser, *Le Dieu de Jésus: Étude exégétique* (LD 129; Paris: Cerf, 1987), 239–47.

213. Lengthy verbatim recall seems in many times and places to require writing; see Ian M. L. Hunter, "Lengthy Verbatim Recall: The Role of Text," in *Progress in the Psychology of Language* (ed. Andrew W. Ellis; 2 vols.; London: Lawrence Erlbaum Associates, 1985), 1:207–35.

214. Cf. Plato, *Theaet.* 142d; contrast Millard, *Reading and Writing*, 185–209.

others. The middle of Luke 6 would then rest upon what Ulric Neisser has called "repisodic" memory, this being "the repeated characteristics of an entire series of events" that can be "faithful to invariant themes across episodes" without necessarily being "faithful to the details of any one episode."[215] In other words, the text does not record anybody's personal memory of a single occasion; rather, it descends from somebody's generic memory, which was the product of multiple episodes. Such generic memory later took the form of Christian discourses, which is what enabled others who had never heard Jesus to quote him. At some point, tradents were recalling not a performance of Jesus himself but someone else's performance in the name of Jesus.

Of course, we have no idea who these tradents were, nor can we count or even estimate the number of links in the chain of tradition between Jesus and the written source behind Matthew and Luke. We also cannot determine what changes, large and small, found their way into the tradition as it moved from one performer to another and from Aramaic to Greek and from the spoken word to the written word. What we are justified in surmising is that Q 6:27–42 probably preserves the general import of some important and characteristic themes in Jesus' teaching, themes that he linked in his discourses.

Other Speeches?

If the central portion of the Sermon on the Plain may give us some sense for a connected discourse of Jesus, can we say the same of any other Synoptic speeches? I am uncertain what the answer should be, although for the most part I remain skeptical.

Some modern scholars have thought that the eschatological discourse in Mark 13, either in whole or in part, reflects an address of Jesus, perhaps one based largely on Daniel.[216] My undogmatic judgment is instead that analysis of its intertextuality does not require a unitary midrash.[217] The passage may

215. Darryl Bruce, "Functional Explanations of Memory," in *Everyday Cognition in Adulthood and Late Life* (ed. Leonard W. Poon, David C. Rubin, and Barbara A. Wilson; Cambridge: Cambridge University Press, 1989), 50. The term "repisodic memory" comes originally from Ulric Neisser, "John Dean's Memory: A Case Study," *Cognition* 9 (1981): 1–22.

216. So, for example, Lars Hartman, *Prophecy Interpreted: The Formation of Some Jewish Apocalyptic Texts and of the Eschatological Discourse Mark 13* (ConBNT 1; Uppsala: Gleerup, 1966); David Wenham, *The Rediscovery of Jesus' Eschatological Discourse* (GP 4; Sheffield: JSOT Press, 1984). Hartman tentatively proposes that Mark 13:5b–8, 12–16, 19–22, 24–27 are a "midrash" on Dan (2:31–45); 7:7–27; 8:9–26; 9:24–27; 11:21–12:4(13), and that it could go back to Jesus. Wenham reconstructs a pre-Synoptic discourse that Mark 13 reproduces only in part, a discourse that accurately preserves the teaching of Jesus.

217. See further Keith D. Dyer, *The Prophecy on the Mount: Mark 13 and the Gathering of the New Community* (ITS 2; Bern: Peter Lang, 1998), 93–122; note also Klaus Koch, "Spätisraelitisch-jüdische und urchristliche Danielrezeption vor und nach der Zerstörung des zweiten Tempels," in *Rezeption und Auslegung im Altem Testament und in seinem Umfeld: Ein Symposion aus*

be not the growth of a day but a compilation of several oracles, or of a small oracle that attracted sayings as it moved forward in time. If so, a complex tradition history seems in order.

I am also disinclined to nominate, as a candidate for a speech of Jesus, the instructions on mission in Matt 10:5–42; Mark 6:7–10; Luke 9:3–5; 10:2–16. These related texts presumably do descend from someone's summary of what Jesus required of his immediate disciples. Yet the Synoptics leave the impression that he sent out missionaries on only one or two occasions, in which case we would have here sentences that, unlike those in Q 6:27–42, cannot have been repeated on multiple occasions. Even if that is not a decisive objection, the elements common to Mark and Q hardly constitute a real speech. They amount to a couple of prohibitions: do not take money and do not carry a bag; and a couple of commandments: stay in whatever place you find yourselves and shake off the dust of your feet when not welcomed. For the rest, there are many notorious contradictions.[218]

A better candidate for a Synoptic sequence that might in part go back to Jesus is the harangue against the Jewish leaders in Matt 23 and Luke 11 (Q). Unfortunately, the many differences between Matthew and Luke, which perhaps are due to the evangelists' heavy redactional work in these two chapters, make the reconstruction of Q all but impossible; and without that, a plausible tracing of the discourse's development can be nothing save speculation, from which it is prudent to refrain.

This leaves, to my mind, only one other decent possibility. The small eschatological discourse in Luke 17:22–37, which is mostly Q material, "displays obvious topical cohesion."[219] Verse 22 ("Then he said to the disciples, 'The days are coming when you will long to see one of the days of the Son of Man, and you will not see it'") is presumably Luke's work,[220] v. 25 ("But first he must endure much suffering and be rejected by this generation") probably his insertion, adopted from Mark.[221] By contrast, vv. 26–27, which speak about Noah and the flood, and vv. 28–29(30), which speak about Lot and Sodom, likely belonged together from the beginning,[222] and there is no reason why they might

---

Anlass des 60. Geburtstags von Odil Hannes Steck (ed. Reinhard G. Kratz and Thomas Krüger; OBO 153; Freiburg: Universitätsverlag; Vandenhoeck & Ruprecht, 1997), 110.

218. For analysis, see Ferdinand Hahn, *Mission in the New Testament* (trans. Frank Clarke; SBT 47; London: SCM Press, 1965), 41–46; Risto Uro, *Sheep among the Wolves: A Study of the Mission Instructions in Q* (AASF 47; Helsinki: Suomalainen Tiedeakatemia, 1987).

219. Kirk, *Composition*, 255.

220. See Ruthild Geiger, *Die lukanischen Endzeitreden: Studien zur Eschatologie des Lukas-Evangeliums* (EH 23/16; Bern: Herbert Lang; Frankfurt am Main: Peter Lang, 1973), 53–58.

221. Cf. Mark 8:31, 35; 9:31; 10:33–34. So Rudolf Schnackenburg, "Der eschatologische Abschnitt Lk 17,20–37," in *Mélanges bibliques: En homage au R. P. Béda Rigaux* (ed. Albert Descamps and André de Halleux; Gembloux: Duculot, 1970), 222–23.

222. For relevant observations, see A. J. B. Higgins, *The Son of Man in the Teaching of Jesus* (SNTSMS 39; Cambridge: Cambridge University Press, 1980), 62–63. The IQP lists the verses

not always have followed something resembling Luke 17:23–24 (Q): "They will say to you, 'Look there!' or 'Look here!' Do not go, do not set off in pursuit. For as the lightning flashes and lights up the sky from one side to the other, so will the Son of Man be in his day."[223] Furthermore, vv. 31–32 ("On that day, anyone on the housetop who has belongings in the house must not come down to take them away; and likewise anyone in the field must not turn back. Remember Lot's wife"), which I tentatively assign to Q, are intimately related to vv. 28–29(30) because they take readers back to Gen 19, to the story of Lot and Sodom. They constitute, then, a natural continuation. The same is true of v. 33, which could serve as a moral to the story in Gen 19: "Those who try to secure their life [ψυχή] will lose it, but those who lose their life [ψυχή] will keep it."[224] The legend in Genesis is about saving "life":

---

about Lot and Sodom as "?17:28–29?" indicating uncertainty about their place in Q. But see Kloppenborg, *Q Parallels*, 192–94; and compare the twin illustrations in Q 11:31–32.

223. The IQP assigns Luke 17:23–24 to Q. Cf. Matt 24:26–27 and see the detailed argument in Ulrich Bauer, "Der Anfang der Endzeitrede in der Logienquelle (Q 17): Probleme der Rekonstruktion und Interpretation des Q-Texts," in *Wenn drei das Gleiche sagen: Studien zu den ersten drei Evangelien* (ed. Stefan H. Brandenburger and Thomas Hieke; Theologie 14; Münster: Lit Verlag, 1998), 79–101. The source behind Mark 13 probably began with v. 6 ("Many will come in my name and say, 'I am he!' and they will lead many astray"), which is a variant of Mark 13:21 ("And if anyone says to you at that time, 'Look! Here is the Messiah!' or 'Look! There he is!'—do not believe it"), and it is precisely the Q parallel to Mark 13:21 that opened Q's eschatological discourse. Is this just a coincidence?

224. My view that all of Luke 17:31–33 derives from Q is a minority position; see Kloppenborg, *Q Parallels*, 195. Regarding v. 31, many have supposed that Luke took it from Mark 13:15–16. Several observations tend to counter this opinion. (i) It is unexpected, were Luke here revising Mark 13:15–16, that he would introduce anacoluthon; see Jeremias, *Sprache*, 269. (ii) It was not Luke's habit to insert Markan sentences into stretches of Q material. (iii) The minor agreements of Matt 24:17–18 and Luke 17:31 against Mark 13:16 might hint at an origin in Q; see Jan Lambrecht, *Die Redaktion der Markus-apokalypse: Literarische Analyse und Strukturuntersuchung* (AnBib 28; Rome: Pontifical Institute, 1967), 157–58. (iv) Both Mark 13:16 and Luke 17:31 warn against turning εἰς τὰ ὀπίσω. This evokes Gen 19, where Lot's wife is warned not to look εἰς τὰ ὀπίσω (LXX 19:17) but then does look εἰς τὰ ὀπίσω, thereby becoming a pillar of salt (19:26). One suspects that the saying of Jesus originally had this legend in mind, which well suits the Q context, with its mentions of Lot and Sodom. Mark 13, by contrast, does not otherwise allude to the tale. On formal grounds, moreover, Mark 13:15–16 seems to be an insertion into its Markan context; so Joachim Gnilka, *Das Evangelium nach Markus (Mk 8,27–16,20)* (EKKNT 2/2; Zurich: Benziger; Neukirchen-Vluyn: Neukirchener Verlag, 1979), 195. My suggestion is that the Q setting is original. The saying then acquired its current place in Mark because a saying alluding to Lot's flight from Sodom seemed an appropriate addendum to the imperative to "flee to the mountains" (Mark 13:14; cf. Gen 19:17, 19). (v) εἰς τὰ ὀπίσω appears only one other time in Luke, in 9:62, where it is likely to be from Q; see Karl Löning, "Die Füchse, die Vögel und der Menschensohn (Mt 8,19f par Lk 9,57f)," in *Vom Urchristentum zu Jesus: Für Joachim Gnilka* (ed. Hubert Frankemölle and Karl Kertelge; Freiburg: Herder, 1989), 83–84; Heinz Schürmann, *Das Lukasevangelium: Zweiter Teil, Erste Folge: Kommentar zu Kap. 9,51–11,54* (HTKNT 3/2; Freiburg: Herder, 1994), 44–47. According to Kloppenborg, "Of all the Lukan *Sondergut*," Luke 9:61–62 "has the strongest probability of deriving from Q since it is found in a Q context, the saying coheres with the preceding sayings formally, and it evinces the same theology

- LXX Gen 19:17: "save your life" (σῷζε τὴν σεαυτοῦ ψυχήν)
- LXX Gen 19:19: "to make my soul live" (τοῦ ζῆν τὴν ψυχήν μου)
- LXX Gen 19:20: "my life will be saved" (ζήσεται ἡ ψυχή μου)

In addition, Lot's wife, according to a common reading, became a pillar of salt because she was too attached to her life in Sodom, as signified by her looking back,[225] whereas Lot kept his life by leaving his old world behind.

As for the remaining material, 17:34–35 ("I tell you, on that night there will be two in one bed; one will be taken and the other left. There will be two women grinding meal together; one will be taken and the other left") and the enigmatic v. 37 ("Then they asked him, 'Where, Lord?' He said to them, 'Where the corpse is, there the vultures will gather'"),[226] one is disposed to think them secondary additions from a contributor to Q. Either v. 32 or v. 33 would have served well as a conclusion of the sentences before them.

The result of this analysis is a small speech with a tight, straightforward argument:

---

of discipleship typical of other Q sayings" (*Q Parallels*, 64). (vi) Many have urged that there is an awkward break between Luke 17:31–33, where escape from the judgment is possible, and what comes before it, where the parousia comes suddenly upon all; so, for example, Manson, *Sayings of Jesus*, 145. Against this, see Steven L. Bridge, *"Where the Eagles Are Gathered": The Deliverance of the Elect in Lukan Eschatology* (JSNTSup 240; London: Sheffield Academic Press, 2003), 40–41, 44–45. Although the coming of the Son of Man is sudden and unexpected for those unprepared (vv. 26–30), the righteous, like Noah and Lot, can prepare themselves and so escape the destruction (vv. 31–33). (vii) It is easy to explain Matthew's omission of Q 17:31–32. Having moved Q 17:26–30 to the end of chapter 24 (see Matt 24:37–39), a chapter that earlier reproduces Mark 13:15–16 (see Matt 24:17–18), the variant in Q 17:31 had to be omitted to avoid redundancy. And with the saying about Lot and Sodom in Q 17:28–29 having been dropped (an omission for which there are several explanations [see Davies and Allison, *Matthew*, 3:381]), 17:32 ("Remember Lot's wife") had no antecedent and so fell away.

As for the source of v. 32, it could never have stood on its own and so must either have come into being with Q 17:28–29(30) or as subsequent commentary on the latter. Verse 33 is a Lukan doublet; see Luke 9:23–24 // Mark 8:34–35. Franz Neirynck ("Saving/Losing One's Life: Luke 17,33 [Q?] and Mark 8,35," in *Evangelica III, 1992–2000: Collected Essays* [BETL 150; Leuven: Leuven University Press, 2001], 480–503) denies that the verse comes from Q. But the IQP thinks that it does (cf. Matt 10:39), placing it, however, between Q 14:26–27 and 14:34–35, following Matthew's order (Matt 10:37–38 // Luke 14:26–27, and Matt 10:39 // Luke 17:33). Yet (i) Matthew otherwise skips around Q in the last half of chapter 10; see Davies and Allison, *Matthew*, 2:213. (ii) Matthew's order probably has been influenced by Mark 8:34, where the saying about losing one's life (cf. Matt 10:39) is joined to the saying about taking up one's cross (cf. Matt 10:38). (iii) Luke 17:33 fits its Q context perfectly; see the discussion above and also Christoph Heil, *Lukas und Q: Studien zur lukanischen Redaktion des Spruchevangeliums Q* (BZNW 111; Berlin: de Gruyter, 2003), 103–6. (iv) Luke, in general, adheres closer to Q's order than does Matthew.

225. Philo, *Drunkenness* 164; *Alleg. Interp.* 3.213; *QG* 4.52; *1 Clem.* 11:1–2; Clement of Alexandria, *Prot.* 10(103); Athanasius, *Vit. Ant.* 20.1; Augustine, *Civ.* 10.8; 16.30; Tg. Ps.-J. on Gen 19:26; Tg. Neof. I on Gen 19:26.

226. The IQP prints Q 17:37 after 17:24, following the order of Matt 24:27–28.

- Exhortation, 17:23
  "Do not go, do not set off in pursuit . . ."
- Justification, 17:24
  "For as the lightning flashes . . ."
- First illustration, 17:26–27
  "Just as it was in the days of Noah . . ."
- Second illustration, 17:28–30
  "Just as it was in the days of Lot . . ."
- Elaboration of second illustration, 17:31–32(33)
  "Anyone . . . must not come down. Remember Lot's wife."
  ("Those who try to make their life secure . . .")

Such a brief oration would also have featured a remarkable degree of parallelism:

- ἰδού + adverb (so Luke) or ἰδοὺ ἐν + dative (so Matthew)[227]
  - 23a ἰδοὺ ἐκεῖ (so Luke) or ἰδοὺ ἐν τῇ ἐρήμῳ (so Matthew)
  - 23a ἰδοὺ ὧδε (so Luke) or ἰδοὺ ἐν τοῖς ταμείοις (so Matthew)
- μή + second-person plural aorist subjunctive ending in -ητε
  - 23b μὴ ἀπέλθητε (so Luke) or μὴ εξέλθητε (so Matthew)[228]
  - 23b μὴ . . . διώξητε
- "in his/that day"
  - 24b ἐν τῇ ἡμέρᾳ αὐτοῦ
  - 31a ἐν ἐκείνῃ τῇ ἡμέρᾳ
- "as it was in the days of X"
  - 26a καθὼς ἐγένετο ἐν ταῖς ἡμέραις Νῶε
  - 28a καθὼς ἐγένετο ἐν ταῖς ἡμέραις Λώτ
- ἔσται + dative form of ἡμέρα + "the Son of Man"
  - 26b ἔσται . . . ἐν ταῖς ἡμέραις τοῦ υἱοῦ τοῦ ἀνθρώπου
  - 30a ἔσται ᾗ ἡμέρᾳ ὁ υἱὸς τοῦ ἀνθρώπου
- "they ate, they drank"
  - 27a ἤσθιον, ἔπινον[229]
  - 28b ἤσθιον, ἔπινον

227. The IQP prints Matt 24:26 as the Q text.
228. The IQP prints Matt 24:26 as the Q text.
229. This is Luke's text. The IQP prefers Matt 24:38 here: τρώγοντες καὶ πίνοντες. Although τρώγω is a Matthean *hapax legomenon* and so for that reason might be attributed to Q, Matthew's balanced καίs and participial forms are likely redactional.

- form of ἡμέρα + -ῆλθεν + proper name + preposition + place
  27b   ἡμέρας εἰσῆλθεν Νῶε εἰς τὴν κιβωτόν
  29a   ἡμέρᾳ ἐξῆλθεν Λῶτ ἀπὸ Σοδόμων
- aorist ending in -εν + subject + καί + aorist ending in -εν + (ἀ)πάντας
  27c   ἦλθεν ὁ κατακλυσμὸς καὶ ἦρεν (ἀ)πάντας[230]
  29c   ἔβρεξεν πῦρ καὶ θεῖον ἀπ' οὐρανοῦ καὶ ἀπώλεσεν πάντας
- ἐν + dative + μή + aorist imperative ending in -άτω
  31a   ἐν τῇ οἰκίᾳ . . . μὴ καταβάτω
  31b   ἐν ἀγρῷ . . . μὴ ἐπιστρεψάτω
- ὅς + (ἐ)άν + aorist subjunctive ending in -ση + future ending in -σει + αὐτήν
  33a   ὃς ἐὰν ζητήσῃ . . . ἀπολέσει αὐτήν
  33b   ὃς δ' ἂν ἀπολέσῃ ζωογονήσει αὐτήν

Even granting the validity of my reconstruction of Q 17:23–33, some would no doubt protest that the sort of eschatology promoted by this passage is not what Jesus himself proclaimed, so he could not have composed anything like it. Given my own view of Jesus' eschatology, as set forth in chapter 2, I can make no such objection. So I am left to wonder whether—not to claim that—Luke 17:23–33, with its extensive parallelism and its focus on Noah's flood and Sodom's fate, connects some sentences or sentiments that Jesus himself connected.

---

230. So the IQP, following Matt 24:39. Luke has καὶ ἀπώλεσεν πάντας.

5

Death and Memory

The Passion of Jesus

Often we cleave to things because they possess a heavy negative charge. Pain has strong arms.

—Patricia Hampl

For John Dominic Crossan, the canonical accounts of Jesus' passion are less "history remembered" than they are "prophecy historicized."[1] Jesus did not climb the Mount of Olives and there, in his distress, pray for deliverance. Someone, in order to make a theological point, fabricated this poignant episode by borrowing from 2 Sam 15, where King David flees to the Mount of Olives after learning that he has been betrayed. Nor did the sky go dark at noon when Jesus hung from his cross. A Christian concocted this marvel on the basis of Amos 8:9–10: "On that day, says the Lord GOD, I will make the sun go down at noon, and darken the earth in broad daylight. I will turn your feasts into mourning, and all your songs into lamentation; I will bring sackcloth on all loins, and baldness on every head; I will make it like the mourning for an only son, and the end of it like a bitter day." Mark's darkness is not memory but myth, not prophecy come to pass but prophecy turned into story.

1. John Dominic Crossan, *Who Killed Jesus? Exposing the Roots of Anti-Semitism in the Gospel Story of the Death of Jesus* (San Francisco: HarperSanFrancisco, 1996).

387

Jesus did, on Crossan's view, create a disturbance in Jerusalem's temple, and a sympathizer did betray him; and he did come to grief on a Roman cross. Yet the individual paragraphs that make up the passion narratives "are so linked to prophetic fulfillment" that subtracting the latter "leaves nothing but the barest facts."[2] Prophetic proof texts, not veridical recollections, were the chief inspiration for Mark 14–16 and its canonical and extracanonical counterparts.

Crossan's position is familiar music to those acquainted with the history of critical scholarship. Rudolf Bultmann was, regarding the historicity of the episodes in Mark 14–16 and its parallels, almost as reserved as is Crossan;[3] and long before both of them, David Friedrich Strauss gave the passion narratives a very critical going-over.[4]

Those who have read the secondary literature will also know of scholars who have been less skeptical.[5] Crossan's *Who Killed Jesus?* is largely a response to Raymond Brown's *The Death of the Messiah*, a massive and massively informed two-volume work that represents a scholarship much more sanguine about finding history in the passion narratives.[6] Crossan put the difference between himself and Brown this way: "Ray Brown is 80 percent in the direction of history remembered. I'm 80 percent in the opposite direction."[7]

If Crossan has rejected what is, to his mind, Brown's excessive confidence, Mark Goodacre has in turn criticized what he regards as Crossan's undue skepticism.[8] Goodacre contends that Crossan cannot plausibly explain why so many items in the passion narratives—Golgotha, Simon of Cyrene, and the inscription over the cross, for instance—were not manufactured from the Tanak. Beyond that, "history remembered" and "prophecy historicized" are not, according to Goodacre, mutually exclusive categories, as though we must dub each episode one or the other. Such a contrast is too stark. The untidy

2. Ibid., 11.

3. Rudolf Bultmann, *History of the Synoptic Tradition* (rev. ed.; New York: Harper & Row, 1963), 261–84.

4. David Friedrich Strauss, *The Life of Jesus Critically Examined* (trans. George Eliot; ed. Peter C. Hodgson; Philadelphia: Fortress, 1972 [German original, 1836]), 563–690.

5. They will also experience déjà vu, because so much of the contemporary discussion reruns, to a surprising measure, debates of the past; see, for example, Maurice Goguel, *Jesus the Nazarene: Myth or History?* (trans. Frederick Stephens; New York: D. Appleton, 1926), 198–228, on "The Theory of the Prophetic Origin of the Gospel Tradition."

6. Raymond E. Brown, *The Death of the Messiah: From Gethsemane to the Grave; A Commentary on the Passion Narratives of the Four Gospels* (2 vols.; New York: Doubleday, 1994).

7. Crossan, *Who Killed Jesus?* 1.

8. Mark Goodacre, "Scripturalization in Mark's Crucifixion Narrative," in *The Trial and Death of Jesus: Essays on the Passion Narrative in Mark* (ed. Geert Van Oyen and Tom Shepherd; CBET 45; Leuven: Peeters, 2006), 33–47; idem, "Prophecy Historicized or History Scripturized? Reflections on the Origin of the Crucifixion Narrative" (paper presented at the annual meeting of the Society of Biblical Literature, Denver, November 2001).

truth is that "traditions generated scriptural reflection, which in turn influenced the way the traditions were recast."[9]

To illustrate: Goodacre believes (as does Crossan) that some female followers of Jesus witnessed his crucifixion. Yet the account of this in Mark 15:40— "There were also women looking on from a distance [ἀπὸ μακρόθεν]; among them were Mary Magdalene, and Mary the mother of James the younger and of Joses, and Salome"—seems to take up the language of LXX Ps 37:12: "My friends and my neighbors drew near before me and stood, and those closest to me from a distance [ἀπὸ μακρόθεν]." Here, then, we cannot say that the Second Gospel gives us nothing but "history remembered" or nothing but "prophecy historicized." Mark 15:40 is rather, to use Goodacre's apt term, "history scripturalized"—that is, memory written up in the language of the Jewish Bible. As Goodacre finds this to be the case elsewhere and indeed often in the passion narratives, he sees things differently than does Crossan. Memories and biblical phrasing need not be indirectly proportional, as though when one increases, the other must decrease.

Who has the better of the argument? Although Crossan's analysis of the wide-ranging intertextuality of the passion traditions is largely persuasive, those traditions likely contain more memory than he supposes. The Qumran pesharim show us that ancient Jews could move from history to Scripture as well as from Scripture to history; and it requires no imagination but only knowledge of Matthew's use of Mark to grasp how almost effortlessly a scripturally learned mind can infuse inherited materials with biblical idioms and phrases.[10]

To biblicize is not necessarily to invent.[11] Eusebius, when recounting Constantine's victory over Maxentius at the battle of the Milvian bridge, cast the latter in the role of Pharaoh, the former in the role of Moses, which does not mean that they fought no such battle;[12] and John Bunyan, writing of his own conversion, drew heavily upon the New Testament accounts of Paul's becoming a Christian, which scarcely entails that Bunyan's recollections are free of facts.[13] So Goodacre is correct on one crucial point: that a story is scripturally indebted or lays implicit or explicit claim to fulfill prophecy does not, in and of itself, tell us whether it has an anchor in history. A memory can be told in many languages, including the language of Scripture.[14]

---

9. Goodacre, "Scripturalization," 40.

10. For an example, see below, p. 407, on Matt 27:34 diff. Mark 15:23.

11. On this point, some very valuable observations are made by Anthony Le Donne, *The Historiographical Jesus: Memory, Typology and the Son of David* (Waco, TX: Baylor University Press, 2009); see, for example, pp. 52–59, 115–36.

12. See texts and discussion in Dale C. Allison Jr., *The New Moses: A Matthean Typology* (Philadelphia: Fortress, 1993), 118–21.

13. See William York Tindall, *John Bunyan: Mechanick Preacher* (New York: Columbia University Press, 1934), 23–24.

14. See further Anthony Le Donne, "Theological Memory Distortion in the Jesus Tradition: A Study in Social Memory Theory," in *Memory in the Bible and Antiquity: The Fifth Durham-*

Additional difficulties beset Crossan's approach. One is his confidence that the Fourth Gospel depends upon the Second Gospel. I cannot justify my dissent here;[15] I can only observe that those of us who often find independent testimony in John will not always see eye to eye with those holding a different opinion.[16]

Yet another issue is that Crossan almost certainly underestimates general public knowledge about Jesus' end. Consider the following three texts, each of which has to do with female followers of Jesus:

- Mark 15:40–41, the crucifixion: "There were also women looking on from a distance; among them were Mary Magdalene, and Mary the mother of James the younger and of Joses, and Salome. These used to follow him and provided for him when he was in Galilee; and there were many other women who had come up with him to Jerusalem."

- Mark 15:47, the burial: "Mary Magdalene and Mary the mother of Joses saw where the body was laid."

- Mark 16:1, the resurrection: "When the sabbath was over, Mary Magdalene, and Mary the mother of James, and Salome bought spices, so that they might go and anoint him."

Crossan judges the assertions in 15:47 and 16:1 to be redactional, the notice in 15:40–41 to preserve memory. His argument concerning the latter passage is as follows: "The male disciples had fled" (cf. Mark 14:50), and "if the women had not been watching, we would not know even the brute fact of crucifixion (as distinct, for example, from Jesus being summarily speared or beheaded in prison)."[17]

Tübingen Research Symposium (ed. Stephen C. Barton, Loren T. Stuckenbruck, and Benjamin G. Wold; WUNT 212; Tübingen: Mohr Siebeck, 2007), 163–78.

15. For an informed review of opinion, see D. Moody Smith, *John among the Gospels* (2nd ed.; Columbia: University of South Carolina Press, 2001). My own verdict is this: even if the primary author of John had heard or read one or more of the Synoptics, his Gospel typically draws upon independent tradition.

16. If John is largely independent of Mark, this allows us to reconstruct with some plausibility the general contours of a pre-Markan passion narrative; see Wolfgang Reinbold, *Der älteste Bericht über den Tod Jesu: Literarische Analyse und historische Kritik der Passionsdarstellungen der Evangelien* (BZNW 69; Berlin: de Gruyter, 1994), 73–177. For an overview of what modern scholars have had to say about the relationship of John's passion narrative to the Synoptics, see Frank Schleritt, *Der vorjohanneische Passionsbericht: Eine historisch-kritische und theologische Untersuchung zu Joh 2,13–22; 11,47–14,31 und 18,1–20,29* (BZNW 154; Berlin: de Gruyter, 2007), 3–63. Schleritt (pp. 93–106) gives his own reasons for inferring the independence of the Johannine passion narrative. He is persuasive.

17. John Dominic Crossan, *The Birth of Christianity: Discovering What Happened in the Years Immediately after the Execution of Jesus* (San Francisco: HarperSanFrancisco, 1998), 559.

This line of reasoning fails to gain my assent. Mark presents the flight of the disciples (14:50) as the fulfillment of a prophetic oracle (see 14:27, quoting Zech 13:7). Why, then, does Crossan not postulate, given his method, that this episode is "prophecy historicized" rather than "history remembered"?[18]

Much more importantly, how plausible is it that "if the women had not been watching, we would not know even the brute fact of crucifixion"? One has trouble imagining such a curtain of ignorance falling upon the end of Jesus. During Passover, Jerusalem was crowded with people, and the city was scarcely a modern metropolis. It was rather, by our standards, a very small place: the Herodian walls enclosed less than one square mile. Jesus was, furthermore, of sufficient public interest and conversation to come to the governor's attention; and if Jesus did not have sympathizers beyond the Twelve, indeed quite a few sympathizers beyond the Twelve, it is unlikely that Pilate would have had him nailed to a cross.[19] When one adds that crucifixions were intended to deter and so were typically public events, how likely is it that Jesus' execution took place in a corner, sans passersby?[20] Or that those who knew or thought they knew what happened did not regale others with some of the details? Or that the churches of Jerusalem were devoid of individuals who had heard the rumors and intrigues that must have flown over the cobblestones even as events were unfolding? It makes far more historical sense to believe that some people—some sympathetic, some hostile, some undecided—shared with others what they had seen or heard. Stories both accurate and inaccurate must have made the rounds from the beginning, and surely some of those stories found their way into Christian tradition, just as they found their way into the writings of Josephus: "Pilate, upon hearing him accused by men of the highest standing among us, condemned him to be crucified" (*Ant.* 18.64).[21]

There is one more reason for deeming Crossan's doubt needlessly generous. It arises from the epistles of Paul. Those epistles, when closely considered, have much to say about the end of Jesus. The implications for reconstructing

---

18. See Goodacre, "Scripturalization," 42.

19. For what it is worth, the sources at hand imply that Jesus had any number of supporters. As Helen Bond notes, "It is clear from . . . Mark's account that there were other followers of Jesus in Jerusalem: the owner of the colt, the owner of the upper room, Simon the Pharisee, Simon of Cyrene, and his sons Alexander and Rufus (whose very presence in the narrative suggests they were known to Mark's church), the women at the cross, and Joseph of Arimathea" (*Caiaphas: Friend of Rome and Judge of Jesus?* [Louisville: Westminster John Knox, 2004], 59).

20. Mark assumes that there were passersby (15:29–32, 35), as does John 19:20 ("Many of the Jews read this inscription, because the place where Jesus was crucified was near the city"). Hebrews 13:12 states that Jesus "suffered outside the city gate" (cf. John 19:20), where there would have been much traffic. Hebrews 6:6 asserts that he was a "public disgrace" (παραδειγματίζοντας).

21. Does Crossan's view, that only some female followers of Jesus reported what happened, require that the information in Josephus and all other non-Christian references to Jesus' crucifixion ultimately descend from the women's testimony?

the prehistory of our passion narratives and, ultimately, for understanding Jesus himself, are, I hope to show, considerable.[22]

An Experiment: The Death of Jesus Based on Paul Alone

At this point, I wish to set aside the canonical and noncanonical Gospels, pretend that we never knew them, and ask, What might we think and what might we conjecture about the end of Jesus on the basis of Paul's Letters alone, among which I include Colossians?[23]

1. To begin with the indubitable: on four occasions Paul writes of "the cross [σταυρός] of Christ" (1 Cor 1:17; Gal 6:12, 14; Phil 3:18). He elsewhere refers more succinctly to "the cross" (1 Cor 1:18; Gal 5:11; Col 2:14) or "his cross" (Col 1:20), and in Phil 2:8, Paul speaks of Jesus' "death on a cross." Eight times the apostle uses the verb σταυρόω ("to crucify"), all but one with reference to "Christ (Jesus)" (1 Cor 1:23; 2:2, 8; 2 Cor 13:4; Gal 3:1; 5:24; 6:14), the exception being the ironic 1 Cor 1:13, "Was Paul crucified for you?" The related compound verb, συσταυρόω ("crucified with"), appears twice (Rom 6:6; Gal 2:19).

To state the obvious, then, our first finding would be that Jesus was crucified. We would, furthermore, confidently infer that this was a piece of public knowledge, not Paul's invention or surmise. Not only do his letters repeatedly take Jesus' crucifixion for granted—it is always a premise, never the conclusion of an argument—but also the apostle assumed that Christians in Rome, a place he had never visited, at least as a Christian, believed this too (Rom 6:6).

2. There was no one way of crucifying people.[24] Sometimes nails fastened victims. Other times, they were lashed with ropes to a stake or tree.[25] What, to judge by Paul, happened to Jesus?

22. The following pages enter into the long-running debate over the relationship between Paul and the historical Jesus. On this fascinating subject we now have the excellent survey and analysis by Frank Holzbrecher, *Paulus und der historische Jesus: Darstellung und Analyse der bisherigen Forschungsgeschichte* (TANZ 48; Tübingen: Francke, 2007).

23. For a sagacious review of the authorship of Colossians, see John M. G. Barclay, *Colossians and Philemon* (NTG; Sheffield: Sheffield Academic Press, 1997), 18–36.

24. The standard reviews of crucifixion in the ancient world are Heinz-Wolfgang Kuhn, "Die Kreuzesstrafe während der frühen Kaiserzeit: Ihre Wirklichkeit und Wertung in der Umwelt des Urchristentums," *ANRW* 25.1:648–793; Martin Hengel, *Crucifixion in the Ancient World and the Folly of the Message of the Cross* (Philadelphia: Fortress, 1977). See also now David W. Chapman, *Ancient Jewish and Christian Perceptions of Crucifixion* (WUNT 2/244; Tübingen: Mohr Siebeck, 2008; repr. Grand Rapids: Baker Academic, 2010).

25. See Joseph William Hewitt, "The Use of Nails in the Crucifixion," *HTR* 25 (1932): 29–45; Joe Zias, "Crucifixion in Antiquity: The Evidence" (online: www.centuryone.org/crucifixion2 .html [cited 18 November 2009]). The latter observes that "in Christian art, the Good and the Bad thieves are depicted as being tied to the cross despite the fact that the Gospels do not go into detail as to how they were affixed to the cross."

The apostle's letters mention the blood (αἷμα) of Jesus half a dozen times (Rom 3:25; 5:9; 1 Cor 10:16; 11:25, 27; Col 1:20). Although these texts make theological points, not historical observations, they do assume that Jesus' execution was not bloodless, which it might have been were ropes alone employed. Evidently, the apostle believed that Jesus was nailed to a cross, and/or that, in accord with common custom, he was flogged or otherwise tortured before and/or after being hung up.[26]

Colossians 2:13–14 may take us a bit further. Some have thought that these verses advert to Jesus being nailed to a cross. God, we here read, "forgave us all our trespasses, erasing the record that stood against us with its legal demands. He set this aside, nailing it to the cross." In the second century, the author of the *Gospel of Truth*, in obvious dependence upon Col 2:13–14, wrote, "For this reason Jesus appeared; he put on that book; he was nailed to a tree; he published the edict of the Father on the cross" (20:23–27). In our own time, Eduard Lohse remarked, "God canceled the certificate by nailing it onto the cross. Because Christ was nailed to the cross in our stead, the debt is forgiven once and for all."[27] Other commentators, ancient and modern, have tendered similar statements.[28] Perhaps they have unfolded what is implicit in Col 2:13–14. Maybe those two verses do assume that Jesus was pinned to his cross with nails.[29]

In this connection, Gal 6:17 also intrigues. According to this, Paul had "stigmata": "I carry the marks [τὰ στίγματα] of Jesus in my body." Exegetes through the ages have regularly presumed that these arresting words refer to the scars that physically marred the apostle, who had been beaten and flogged, as he relates in 2 Cor 6:5; 11:23–24.[30] In the words of James Dunn, "There is a strong consensus that by 'the marks of Jesus' . . . Paul means the scars and

---

26. Cf. John 19:34, where a soldier puts a spear into Jesus' side. It is possible that 1 Thess 1:6, which indirectly refers to Jesus' "tribulation" or "affliction" ("You became imitators of us and of the Lord, having received the word in much affliction [θλίψει] with joy inspired by the Holy Spirit"), includes torture; but Paul's language remains too general for assurance on the matter.

27. Eduard Lohse, *Colossians and Philemon: A Commentary on the Epistles to the Colossians and to Philemon* (Hermeneia; Philadelphia: Fortress, 1971), 111.

28. For example, Theodoret of Cyrus, *Comm. Col.* ad loc. (PG 82:612B); John Gill, *Gill's Commentary* (6 vols.; Grand Rapids: Baker Books, 1980), 6:522 (Gill also sees a reference to the inscription on Jesus' cross); Henry Alford, *The Greek Testament* (4 vols. in 2; Chicago: Moody, 1958), 3:223; Douglas J. Moo, *The Letters of the Colossians and to Philemon* (PilNTC; Grand Rapids: Eerdmans, 2008), 211–12 ("The imagery probably . . . arises from the actual nature of Christ's crucifixion. In causing him to be nailed to the cross, God . . . has provided the full cancellation of the debt of obedience that we had incurred"); Roy Yates, *The Epistle to the Colossians* (EC; London: Epworth, 1993), 49.

29. But for another reading and possible inference, see below, pp. 413–14.

30. Cf. Acts 16:23; 21:32. For an array of exegetical options on Gal 6:17, see Erhardt Güttgemanns, *Der leidende Apostel und sein Herr: Studien zur paulinischen Christologie* (FRLANT 90; Göttingen: Vandenhoeck & Ruprecht, 1966), 126–35.

physical effects of the various beatings and severe hardship (including being stoned) which Paul had already experienced in the course of his missionary work."[31] Modern exegetes in addition often suspect that Paul was thinking of the circumstance that masters branded their slaves with a mark of ownership[32] or of the fact that tattoos might signify allegiance to a particular god and that god's protection.[33] Yet then perhaps it is a bit unexpected that the apostle speaks not of "Jesus Christ" or "the Lord Jesus," but instead, without any exalted title, of "Jesus." Scribes apparently saw something not quite right here, for a large number of manuscripts replace "Jesus" with "the Christ" or expand "Jesus" into "the Lord Jesus" or "our Lord Jesus Christ."

Some have understood τὰ στίγματα τοῦ Ἰησοῦ to signify not only Paul's scars but also and at the same time the wounds that torture left upon Jesus himself.[34] The context suggests this, for Paul has just written about "the cross of Christ" in Gal 6:12 and of "the cross of our Lord Jesus Christ" in 6:14. In the latter verse, moreover, he declares that "the world has been crucified to me, and I to the world." So in some way Paul identifies his own afflictions with the afflictions that Jesus suffered during crucifixion.[35] It would be but a small step for him and his readers to associate his wounds with Jesus' wounds. Was Paul not an imitator of the afflicted Christ and a participant in his sufferings?[36]

31. James D. G. Dunn, *The Epistle to the Galatians* (BNTC 9; London: A & C Black, 1993), 347. Cf. Jerome, *Comm. Gal.* ad loc.; Augustine, *Exp. Gal.* 64; Theodoret of Cyrus, *Comm. Gal.* ad loc. (PG 82:504C).

32. See Hans Dieter Betz, *Galatians: A Commentary on Paul's Letter to the Churches in Galatia* (Hermeneia; Philadelphia: Fortress, 1979), 324–25; C. P. Jones, "Stigma: Tattooing and Branding in Graeco-Roman Antiquity," *JRS* 77 (1987): 150–51. Compare, much earlier, Marius Victorinus, *Comm. Gal.* ad loc. (CSEL 81/3:68); Photius, *Frag. Gal.* on 6:17 (NTAbh 15:610); Thomas Aquinas, *Comm. Gal.* ad loc.

33. See Gen 4:15; Ezek 9:4; Rev 7:2–4. See further Otto Betz, "στίγμα," *TDNT* 7:659–63.

34. So Udo Borse, "Die Wundermale und der Todesbescheid," *BZ* 14 (1970): 88–111; Martin Hengel, "Das Mahl in der Nacht, 'in der Jesus ausgeliefert wurde' (1 Kor 11,23)," in *Studie zur Christologie: Kleine Schriften IV* (ed. Claus-Jürgen Thornton; WUNT 201; Tübingen: Mohr Siebeck, 2006), 467; Hans Lietzmann, *An die Galater* (HNT 10; Tübingen: Mohr Siebeck, 1923), 46; James Hope Moulton, "The Marks of Jesus," *ExpTim* 21 (1910): 284; Johannes Schneider, *Die Passionsmystik des Paulus: Ihr Wesen, ihr Hintergrund und ihre Nachwirkungen* (UNT 15; Leipzig: J. C. Hinrichs, 1929), 51; Werner Straub, *Die Bildersprache des Apostels Paulus* (Tübingen: Mohr Siebeck, 1937), 59–60; David Wenham, *Paul: Follower of Jesus or Founder of Christianity?* (Grand Rapids: Eerdmans, 1995), 364; Friedrich Heinrich Hugo Windischmann, *Erklärung des Briefes an die Galater* (Mainz: Kirchheim, Schott & Thielmann, 1843), 170–71; Christian Wolff, "Humility and Self-Denial in Jesus' Life and Message and in the Apostolic Existence of Paul," in *Paul and Jesus: Collected Essays* (ed. A. J. M. Wedderburn; JSNTSup 37; Sheffield: Sheffield Academic Press, 1989), 156. Compare, much earlier, Tertullian, *Marc.* 5.4, and Adamantius: "the marks of Christ, through which is our salvation" (*Dial.* 5.22 [GCS 4:222]).

35. J. Louis Martyn comments, "The painful wounds he has endured and continues to endure in his preaching are like those endured by Jesus, in the sense that Paul's own injuries are inflicted by the same powers that crucified Jesus (1 Cor 2:8; Gal 4:19)" (*Galatians: A New Translation with Introduction and Commentary* [AB 33A; New York: Doubleday, 1997], 568–69).

36. See 1 Cor 11:1; cf. Rom 8:17; 2 Cor 1:5; Phil 3:10; Col 1:24.

Supporting this appraisal is 2 Cor 4:8–10: "We are afflicted in every way, but not crushed; perplexed, but not driven to despair; persecuted, but not forsaken; struck down, but not destroyed; always carrying in the body the death of Jesus, so that the life of Jesus may also be made visible in our bodies." The phrase "always carrying in the body the death of Jesus" is strikingly similar to the end of Gal 6:17:

2 Cor 4:10   τὴν νέκρωσιν τοῦ Ἰησοῦ ἐν τῷ σώματι περιφέροντες

Gal 6:17   τὰ στίγματα τοῦ Ἰησοῦ ἐν τῷ σώματί μου βαστάζω

In both lines, Paul is like his Lord; and if in 2 Cor 4:10 the phrase τὴν νέκρωσιν τοῦ Ἰησοῦ presupposes that Jesus died, is it not natural to hold that in Gal 6:17, the phrase τὰ στίγματα τοῦ Ἰησοῦ presupposes that he had wounds on his body?

All this is not to suggest that Paul imagined his own scars to match the lesions on Jesus' tortured body, as though the apostle were a stigmatist like Francis of Assisi.[37] Nonetheless, Gal 6:17 seems to presuppose Paul's physical identification with the wounds of Jesus' crucifixion.[38] Once again, then, one infers that Jesus was not just hung up with ropes and left to die. His executioners rather tortured him, drawing blood and marring his body.

3. Whereas 1 Tim 6:13 characterizes Jesus Christ as having "made the good confession" before Pontius Pilate, the genuine letters of Paul fail to mention the Roman prefect. His writings do, however, imply that Jesus ran afoul of the imperial authorities. This is because in Palestine in the first half of the first century CE, the Romans, with few exceptions, reserved for themselves the political authority to impose capital punishment. Some scholars, to be sure, have disputed this; but John 18:31 ("The Jews said to him [Pilate], 'It is not lawful for us to put any man to death,'" RSV) seems by and large to be correct: the Romans

37. Yet Catholic theologians sometimes have thought otherwise. Bonaventure, *Legenda maior Sancti Francisci* 13:9 (*Bonaventure: The Soul's Journey into God; The Tree of Life; The Life of St. Francis* [trans. Ewert Cousins; New York: Paulist Press, 1978], 312), applies Gal 6:17 to the wounds of Francis.

38. Protestant commentators, one suspects, have often rejected or neglected this possibility because of a residual prejudice against Roman Catholic devotion to the five sacred wounds and the honor paid to stigmatists, whose bloody sores supposedly correspond to those of the crucified Christ. Martin Luther opens his commentary on Gal 6:17 with polemic against Francis and his stigmata, calling them "a vain imagination and idle sport" and unjustly charging that the saint "printed them on himself through some foolish devotion, or rather vainglory, whereby he could flatter himself that he was so dear to Christ" (*A Commentary on St. Paul's Epistle to the Galatians* [Westwood, NJ: Fleming H. Revell, n.d.], 566). Alford is only a little less shrill: any "allusion whatever to any similarity between [Paul] himself and our Lord . . . would be quite irrelevant; and with its irrelevancy falls a whole fabric of Romanist superstition which has been raised on this verse" (*Greek Testament*, 3:67).

retained the right to decide cases of life and death.[39] So when Paul reiterates that Jesus was crucified, his words implicitly implicate the Romans.

The same inference is at hand in 1 Cor 2:8, according to which "the rulers of this age [τῶν ἀρχόντων τοῦ αἰῶνος τούτου] . . . crucified the Lord of glory." It has been popular, over the past one hundred years or so, to identify these rulers with hostile spirits.[40] Paul can characterize Satan as "the god of this world" (ὁ θεὸς τοῦ αἰῶνος τούτου [2 Cor 4:4]), whom the Fourth Evangelist in turn calls "the ruler [ὁ ἄρχων] of this world" (John 12:31; 14:30; 16:11); and "the rulers and authorities" (αἱ ἀρχαὶ καὶ αἱ ἐξουσίαι) of Col 2:15 generally are held to be demonic beings (cf. Eph 6:12).

Yet this interpretation has increasingly met opposition, and for good reasons.[41] The main points to be made against it are, in brief, these: (a) Apart from 1 Cor 2:6–8, the only other time Paul uses ἄρχων is in Rom 13:3, where the substantive undeniably refers to the Roman authorities: "For rulers [οἱ ἄρχοντες] are not a terror to good conduct, but to bad."[42] (b) The plural οἱ ἄρχοντες is the normal Greek expression for governing authorities, and the New Testament otherwise reserves οἱ ἄρχοντες for human rulers.[43] (c) The use

---

39. Cf. *b. Sanh.* 41a; *y. Sanh.* 18a (1:1). See Ernst Bammel, "Die Blutgerichtsbarkeit in der römischen Provinz Judäa vor dem ersten jüdischen Aufstand," in *Judaica: Kleine Schriften 1* (WUNT 37; Tübingen: Mohr Siebeck, 1986), 59–72; Brown, *Death of the Messiah*, 1:363–72; Christopher Bryan, *Render to Caesar: Jesus, the Early Church, and the Roman Superpower* (Oxford: Oxford University Press, 2005), 71–75; Gerd Theissen, *The Gospels in Context: Social and Political History in the Synoptic Tradition* (trans. Linda M. Maloney; Minneapolis: Fortress, 1991), 191–92.

40. Representative of this view, which goes back to Marcion and Origen, are M. E. Adeyemi, "The Rulers of This Age in First Corinthians 2:6–8: An Exegetical Exposition," *DBM* 28 (1999): 38–45; Johannes Weiss, *Der erste Korintherbrief* (9th ed.; KEK 5; Göttingen: Vandenhoeck & Ruprecht, 1910), 53–54.

41. Detractors include Wesley Carr, "The Rulers of This Age—1 Corinthians II.6–8," *NTS* 23 (1976): 20–35; Andrew D. Clarke, *Secular and Christian Leadership in Corinth: A Socio-Historical and Exegetical Study of 1 Corinthians 1–6* (AGJU 18; Leiden: Brill, 1993), 114–17; Gordon Fee, *The First Epistle to the Corinthians* (NICNT; Grand Rapids: Eerdmans, 1987), 103–4; Joseph A. Fitzmyer, *First Corinthians: A New Translation with Introduction and Commentary* (AYB 32; New Haven: Yale University Press, 2008), 175–76; Hermann von Lips, *Weisheitliche Traditionen im Neuen Testament* (WMANT 64; Neukirchen-Vluyn: Neukirchener Verlag, 1990), 337–38; Gene Miller, "ΑΡΧΟΝΤΩΝ ΤΟΥ ΑΙΩΝΟΣ ΤΟΥΤΟΥ—A New Look at 1 Corinthians 2:6–8," *JBL* 91 (1972): 522–28; Mauro Pesce, *Paolo e gli arconti a Corinto: Storia della ricerca (1888–1975) ed esegesi di 1 Cor. 2,6.8* (TRSR 13; Brescia: Paideia Editrice, 1977), the first half of which contains a thorough review of modern scholarship up through 1975; Karl Olav Sandnes, *Paul—One of the Prophets? A Contribution to the Apostle's Self-Understanding* (WUNT 2/43; Tübingen: Mohr Siebeck, 1991), 81–82; Julius Schniewind, "Die Archonten dieses Äons, 1 Kor. 2,6–8," in *Nachgelassene Reden und Aufsätze* (ThBT 1; Berlin: Töpelmann, 1952), 104–9; and Ben Witherington III, *Jesus the Sage: The Pilgrimage of Wisdom* (Minneapolis: Fortress, 1994), 313.

42. See Robert Jewett, *Romans: A Commentary* (Hermeneia; Minneapolis: Fortress, 2006), 792.

43. For example, John 3:1; Acts 3:17; Rev 1:5. When the New Testament employs the word ἄρχων of Satan, it is in the singular, and the context makes the meaning evident (Matt 9:34;

of the plural οἱ ἄρχοντες to refer to invisible spirits does not demonstrably predate Paul. It appears to be a later Christian development.[44] (d) The apostle nowhere else holds invisible powers responsible for the death of Jesus. He says only, assuming his authorship of Col 2:14–15, that Christ's death defeated them. (e) Most of the church fathers identified "the rulers of this age" with earthly political rulers.[45] (f) The broader literary context of τοῦ αἰῶνος τούτου suggests that the phrase refers to the world of human beings, for ὁ αἰών is, in 1 Cor 1:20 ("the debater of this αἰών"), 2:6 ("a wisdom of this αἰών"), and 3:18 ("wise in this αἰών"), the human world, not the world of spirits.[46] (g) In 1 Cor 2:6, "the rulers of this age" are "being reduced to nothing" (καταργουμένων). The verb translated as "being reduced to nothing" appears just a few verses before, in 1:28, where Paul declares that God has "reduced to nothing" (καταργήσῃ) the "things that are not [low and despised]," which in context refers to the wise, the powerful, the noble, the strong (see vv. 26–27). The verbal link prods readers to associate "the rulers of this world" with the human classes mentioned earlier.[47] (h) 1 Cor 2:6 has close parallels in Acts 3:17 ("I know that you acted in ignorance, as did also your rulers [οἱ ἄρχοντες ὑμῶν]"); 13:27 ("Because the residents of Jerusalem and their rulers [οἱ ἄρχοντες αὐτῶν] did not recognize him or understand the words of the prophets that are read every sabbath, they fulfilled those words by condemning him").[48] In all three places we read of οἱ ἄρχοντες who killed or crucified Jesus out of ignorance, and in Acts they are clearly human authorities. Perhaps 1 Cor 2:8 takes up traditional Christian apologetic with its roots in the much-mined Ps 2, where οἱ ἄρχοντες "take counsel together against the LORD and his anointed" (cf. Acts 4:25–26).

12:24; Mark 3:22; Luke 11:15; John 12:31; 14:30; 16:11). L. L. Welborn remarks, "Decisive for the resolution of the debate would seem to be the fact that the plural form of ἄρχων is never used in the New Testament to designate demonic powers" (*Paul, the Fool of Christ: A Study of 1 Corinthians 1–4 in the Comic-Philosophic Tradition* [JSNTSup 293; London: T & T Clark International, 2005], 126 n. 62).

44. Carr ("Rulers of This Age," 27–30) reviews the evidence and comes to this conclusion.

45. So Anthony C. Thiselton, *The First Epistle of the Corinthians: A Commentary on the Greek Text* (NIGTC; Grand Rapids: Eerdmans, 2000), 236–37. Cf. Chrysostom, *Hom. 1 Cor.* ad loc.; Pelagius, *Comm. 1 Cor.* ad loc. (TS 9:138); Theodoret of Cyrus, *1 Cor.* ad loc. (PG 82:241B–C); Haymo of Halberstadt, *Exp. Rom.* ad loc. (PL 117:520C); Theophylact, *Exp. 1 Cor.* ad loc. (PG 124:589A); Severian of Gabala, *Frag. 1 Cor.* ad loc. (NTAbh 15:232); Oecumenius of Trikka, *Frag. 1 Cor.* ad loc. (NTAbh 15:432). This remained the dominant interpretation until recent times; cf. John Calvin, *Commentary on the Epistles of Paul the Apostle to the Corinthians*, vol. 1 (Grand Rapids: Eerdmans, 1958), 105; Hugo Grotius, *Opera omnia theologica* (3 vols.; Amsterdam: Joannis Blaeu, 1679), 2:771.

46. See further Schniewind, "Archonten," 105–6.

47. So too J. B. Lightfoot: the rulers of 1 Cor 2:6 are "the great men of the world, as the whole context seems imperatively to demand; the princes whether in intellect or in power or in rank, so that οἱ ἄρχοντες κ.τ.λ. would include the σοφοί, δυνατοί, εὐγενεῖς of i. 26" (*Notes on the Epistles of St Paul from Unpublished Commentaries* [London: Macmillan, 1895], 174).

48. See further Schniewind, "Archonten," 107–8; also Luke 23:34.

(i) Because it is hard to fathom evil spirits, on their own, crucifying Jesus, some have identified "the rulers of this age" with both the governing authorities and the invisible demonic powers that stand behind them and carry out their will through them.[49] Against this, "the angels, when they are concerned with the world of men, may relate to the fate of nations as a whole, but never to the individual king, ruler or government."[50]

Given these observations, it seems likely enough that, in 1 Cor 2:8, "the rulers of this age" are this world's ruling authorities, which for Paul and his Corinthian readers must include the Romans. Again, then, the empire appears to be implicated in Jesus' execution.

4. Paul nowhere says why Jesus found himself on a cross. Yet we would, without any of the Gospel materials, not be wholly in the dark. Paul reports three relevant items about Jesus: (a) he was said to be descended from David (Rom 1:3), progenitor of the Israelite kings;[51] (b) he was known as "(the) Christ" (e.g., Rom 1:4; 9:5; 1 Cor 15:3), a title with royal associations in Jewish literature;[52] (c) he was thought of as reigning and having a kingdom, which means that some reckoned him a king (Rom 15:12; 1 Cor 15:24–25; Col 1:13; 2:10). All this matters because crucifixion was standard punishment for political rebels. Indeed, all the other crucifixions in Palestine between the turn of the era and 70 CE were, to the extent of our knowledge, of insurrectionists or their sympathizers.[53] So would we not, even without Mark or any of its relatives, hazard the guess that the Romans dispatched Jesus because they perceived him to be a royal pretender?

We would be emboldened all the more to suspect this because Josephus recounts stories of the Romans responding with military force to would-be Jewish kings and their followers, including the so-called Egyptian prophet (*Ant.* 20.169–172; *J.W.* 2.261–263), Simon the slave (*Ant.* 17.273–277; *J.W.* 2.57–59), Athrongaeus the Shepherd (*Ant.* 17.278–284; *J.W.* 2.60–65), Menachem son of Judas (*J.W.* 2.433–448), and Simon son of Giora (*J.W.* 4.503–544; 7:21–36, 153–157). Josephus also tells of individuals who, although their royal aspirations are uncertain because of his laconic and unsympathetic characterizations,

---

49. Most famously Oscar Cullmann, *The State in the New Testament* (New York: Charles Scribner's Sons, 1956), 62–66. Cf. Gerd Theissen, *Psychological Aspects of Pauline Theology* (trans. John P. Galvin; Philadelphia: Fortress, 1987), 374–78; Walter Wink, *Naming the Powers: The Language of Power in the New Testament* (Philadelphia: Fortress, 1984), 40–45.

50. So Carr, "Rulers of This Age," 22. Carr's article contains additional criticisms of this position.

51. Modern scholarship tends to regard Rom 1:3 as coming from a pre-Pauline tradition; see Jewett, *Romans*, 97–98, 103–8.

52. For example, 2 Chr 1:1; Prov 1:1; Eccl 1:1; *Pss. Sol.* 17:21; *4 Ezra* 12:32; *b. Sanh.* 97a–98a. For the relevant first-century evidence, see Brian M. Nolan, *The Royal Son of God: The Christology of Matthew 1–2 in the Setting of the Gospel* (OBO 23; Fribourg: Éditions Universitaires; Göttingen: Vandenhoeck & Ruprecht, 1979), 158–69; also above, p. 279 n. 244.

53. See Kuhn, "Kreuzesstrafe," 724.

led religious movements that the Romans understood as threats to political stability and so sought to execute: Theudas (*Ant.* 20.97–99), a Samaritan prophet like Moses (*Ant.* 18.85–87), and certain unnamed "impostors" (*Ant.* 20.167–168, 188; *J.W.* 2.258–260).

If we did offer the tentative hypothesis that the Romans executed Jesus because they perceived him to be an insurrectionist with regal pretensions, we might also suppose that he was a militant of some sort. Maybe, we might even imagine, he was captured on the battlefield. But then we would have a problem. Paul summarily characterizes Jesus as humble (Phil 2:8); he calls him meek and gentle (2 Cor 10:1); and he asserts that he did not please himself (Rom 15:2–3). All this is very much the antithesis of a military leader. Paul's Letters, moreover, regularly designate Jesus as a source of εἰρήνη, "peace" (e.g., Rom 1:7; 5:1; Gal 1:3; Col 3:15), and they hold no hint that Christians are insurrectionists in any conventional sense; and the striking phrase in Phil 2:8—"became obedient to the point of death, even death on a cross"—is unexpected if the Romans had captured Jesus during battle. It sounds rather, as we will see, as though he died like Socrates, willingly. So without knowing the Gospels, we would be left with questions that we could not answer. Did Paul mischaracterize as meek and mild a Jesus who was otherwise? Did a movement that began in a militant fashion quickly become something else? Or did the Romans execute Jesus as an insurrectionist even though he was not a militant figure?

5. Our conclusion about Roman involvement would lead to puzzlement over 1 Thess 2:14–16: "For you, brothers and sisters, became imitators of the churches of God in Christ Jesus that are in Judea, for you suffered the same things from your own compatriots as they did from the Jews [or, 'Judeans'],[54] who killed both the Lord Jesus and the prophets, and drove us out; they displease God and oppose everyone by hindering us from speaking to the Gentiles so that they may be saved. Thus they have constantly been filling up the measure of their sins; but God's wrath has overtaken them at last." How would we reconcile these words with our conviction, already established, that the Romans crucified Jesus?

One option would be to argue that the seeming contradiction dissolves because Paul did not write 1 Thess 2:14–16: it is an ill-informed, post-Pauline interpolation. The thesis has appealed to many over the past forty years.[55] We should, however, reject it.[56] The Greek texts and versions offer it no support.

54. The Greek is τῶν Ἰουδαίων. On this, see below, p. 401.

55. See Hendrikus Boers, "The Form-Critical Study of Paul's Letters: 1 Thessalonians as a Case Study," *NTS* 22 (1976): 140–58; Birger A. Pearson, "1 Thessalonians 2:14–16: A Deutero-Pauline Interpolation," *HTR* 64 (1971): 79–94; Daryl Schmidt, "1 Thess 2:13–16: Linguistic Evidence for an Interpolation," *JBL* 102 (1993): 269–79; William O. Walker, *Interpolations in the Pauline Letters* (JSNTSup 213; London: Sheffield Academic Press, 2001), 210–20.

56. This appears to be the trend of recent scholarship; see Markus Bockmuehl, "1 Thessalonians 2:14–16 and the Church in Jerusalem," *TynBul* 52 (2001): 1–31; Ingo Broer, "'Der ganze Zorn ist

The linguistic and structural reasons for excision are far from forceful.[57] And, as Carol Schlueter has persuasively argued at length, we can credibly comprehend the apparent tensions with what Paul says elsewhere as arising from Pauline rhetoric. The text of 1 Thess 2:14–16, with its intense antinomies—wrath over against salvation, Judeans over against Judean churches, Thessalonians over against Thessalonian Christians—is an instance of polemical hyperbole.[58] Exaggeration or caricature for argumentative ends has always been a well-known rhetorical strategy (cf. Quintilian, *Inst.* 8.6.67–76), and it was not foreign to Paul, as 2 Cor 11 so memorably illustrates.

What would follow, were we to reckon Paul the author of 1 Thess 2:14–16 or at least the editor of the tradition behind those verses?[59] We would, given the apostle's sweeping statement—"the Jews (or, 'Judeans') who killed Jesus"— infer that he did not hold the Romans solely responsible for Jesus' execution.[60] How this could be, that is, how both Romans and Jews could be to blame in Paul's eyes, we could only guess. Yet we might recall that, according to Josephus, the Jewish authorities arrested another Jesus, son of Ananias, a Jewish

schon über sie gekommen': Bemerkungen zur Interpolationshypothese und zur Interpretation von 1 Thess 2,14–16," in *The Thessalonian Correspondence* (ed. Raymond F. Collins; BETL 87; Leuven: Leuven University Press, 1990), 137–59; Raymond F. Collins, "Apropos the Integrity of 1 Thess," in *Studies on the First Letter to the Thessalonians* (BETL 66; Leuven: Leuven University Press, 1984), 96–135; Karl Paul Donfried, "Paul and Judaism: 1 Thessalonians 2:13–16 as a Test Case," *Int* 38 (1984): 242–53; Jonas Holmstrand, *Markers and Meaning in Paul: An Analysis of 1 Thessalonians, Philippians and Galatians* (ConBNT 28; Stockholm: Almqvist & Wiksell, 1997), 42–46; Traugott Holtz, *Der erste Brief an die Thessalonicher* (EKKNT 13; Zurich: Benzinger; Neukirchen-Vluyn: Neukirchener Verlag, 1986), 110–12; John C. Hurd, "Paul ahead of His Time: 1 Thess 2:13–16," in *Paul and the Gospels* (ed. Peter Richardson and David Granskou; vol. 1 of *Anti-Judaism in Early Christianity*; SCJ 2; Waterloo, ON: Wilfrid Laurier University Press, 1986), 21–36; David Luckensmeyer, *The Eschatology of First Thessalonians* (NTOA 71; Göttingen: Vandenhoeck & Ruprecht, 2009), 161–67; Robert Jewett, *The Thessalonian Correspondence: Pauline Rhetoric and Millenarian Piety* (Philadelphia: Fortress, 1986), 36–41; Gerd Lüdemann, *Paulus und das Judentum* (TEH 215; Munich: Chr. Kaiser, 1983), 25–27; Abraham J. Malherbe, *The Letters to the Thessalonians* (AB 32B; New York: Doubleday, 2000), 164–79; Hans-Heinrich Schade, *Apokalyptische Christologie bei Paulus: Studien zum Zusammenhang von Christologie und Eschatologie in den Paulusbriefen* (GTA 18; Göttingen: Vandenhoeck & Ruprecht, 1981), 263–64; Carol J. Schlueter, *Filling Up the Measure: Polemical Hyperbole in 1 Thessalonians 2.14–16* (JSNTSup 98; Sheffield: JSOT Press, 1994); John Weatherly, "The Authenticity of 1 Thessalonians 2.13–16: Additional Evidence," *JSNT* 42 (1991): 79–98. Wolfgang Reinbold remarks, "For myself, I wish it [1 Thess 2:14–16] were not in the New Testament (many affirm that it was later inserted into the manuscripts, but unfortunately the wish is the father of the thought)" (*Der Prozess Jesu* [BTSc 28; Göttingen: Vandenhoeck & Ruprecht, 2006], 129).

57. See Hurd, "Paul," and Weatherly, "Authenticity."

58. Schlueter, *Filling Up the Measure.*

59. Some have thought 1 Thess 2:14–16 to be largely pre-Pauline tradition; see, for example, Odil Hannes Steck, *Israel und das gewaltsame Geschick der Propheten: Untersuchungen zur Überlieferung des deuteronomistischen Geschichtsbildes im Alten Testament* (WMANT 23; Neukirchen-Vluyn: Neukirchener Verlag, 1967), 274–78.

60. See further Reinbold, *Bericht,* 291–93.

prophet, for his opposition to the temple, and that eventually "they brought him before the Roman governor" (*J.W.* 6.309). Did Jewish magistrates, we might ask, similarly hand over Jesus of Nazareth to the Roman government?[61] We could think this consistent with Rom 15:8, where the apostle to the Gentiles says that Jesus was "a servant to the circumcised." This characterization implies a thoroughly Jewish context for Jesus' ministry.

6. We might perhaps mine even more from 1 Thess 2:14–16. Paul writes that the churches in Judea suffered "ὑπὸ τῶν Ἰουδαίων who killed Jesus." Exegetical tradition has, without much thought, typically identified these people as "the Jews," and the modern translations, such as the NRSV, have gone along. One can, however, urge that "the Judeans" fits the context better, because Paul has just referred to the churches ἐν Ἰουδαίᾳ, "in Judea."[62] Even if one prefers to translate τῶν Ἰουδαίων as "the Jews," Paul's remark cannot be all-encompassing, for the members of the Judean churches, Jews themselves, do not belong to the polemical generalization. Furthermore, the parallelism established between the Judean churches and the Thessalonian Christians—"you suffered the same things from your own compatriots as they did"—requires that the Judean disciples were oppressed by their fellow citizens, which means Judeans. If so, and if those citizens are, as it appears, the same people responsible for Jesus' demise (τῶν Ἰουδαίων τῶν καὶ τὸν κύριον ἀποκτεινάντων Ἰησοῦν),[63] Paul seemingly presupposes that Jesus died in the south, in Judea.

7. Paul has it from tradition, he says in 1 Cor 11:23, that Jesus was handed over during the night: ἐν τῇ νυκτὶ ᾗ παρεδίδετο. Whatever event the apostle has in view must have happened late, because it followed the blessing over the cup, which itself took place after the evening meal (cf. 11:25: μετὰ τὸ δειπνῆσαι).

61. Cf. Josephus, *Ant.* 19.64: "When Pilate, upon hearing him [Jesus] accused by men of the highest standing among us, had condemned him to be crucified." According to Bond, these words and most of their immediate context do "not seem to be a secondhand reworking of the Gospels but in all probability [come] from Jewish circles" (*Caiaphas*, 61). On the issue of Jewish and Roman involvement in the death of Jesus, see the helpful essay by Ingo Broer, "The Death of Jesus from a Historical Perspective," in *Jesus from Judaism to Christianity: Continuum Approaches to the Historical Jesus* (ed. Tom Holmén; London: T & T Clark, 2007), 145–68.

62. See further Weatherly, "Authenticity," 85–88; also Malcolm Lowe, "Who Were the Ἰουδαῖοι?" *NovT* 18 (1976): 130 n. 89. On the more general discussion of what Ἰουδαῖος/Ἰουδαῖοι means in early Christian and ancient Jewish texts, see John H. Elliott, "Jesus the Israelite Was Neither a 'Jew' nor a 'Christian': On Correcting Misleading Nomenclature," *JSHJ* 5 (2007): 119–54; Philip F. Esler, *Conflict and Identity in Romans: The Social Setting of Paul's Letter* (Minneapolis: Fortress, 2003), 40–76; Daniel R. Schwartz, "'Judean' or 'Jew'? How Should We Translate *Ioudaios* in Josephus?" in *Jewish Identity in the Greco-Roman World = Jüdische Identität in der griechisch-römischen Welt* (ed. Jörg Frey, Daniel R. Schwartz, and Stephanie Gripentrog; AJEC/AGJU 71; Leiden: Brill, 2007), 3–28; Margaret H. Williams, "The Meaning and Function of *Ioudaios* in Graeco-Roman Inscriptions," *ZPE* 116 (1997): 249–62.

63. I take τῶν καὶ τὸν κύριον ἀποκτεινάντων Ἰησοῦν to be restrictive: it specifies which Jews or Judeans (τῶν Ἰουδαίων) are in view; see Frank D. Gilliard, "The Problem of the Antisemitic Comma between 1 Thessalonians 2.14 and 15," *NTS* 35 (1989): 481–502.

While the chronological circumstance is clear enough, the meaning of παρεδίδετο is not. Although the NRSV, like the KJV long before it, takes the verb to mean "betrayed," knowledge of the story of Judas has obviously dictated this choice. If, however, we did not know that episode, about which Paul is otherwise mute, we would be left with only conjecture concerning the precise import of the verb παραδίδωμι in 1 Cor 11:23. Romans 4:25—Jesus was "handed over [παρεδόθη] to death for our trespasses"—would offer no help, because it is a theological statement (based upon Isa 53:5, 12) without historical elaboration. Romans 8:32, where it is God who hands Jesus over, raises the possibility of finding similar meaning in 1 Cor 11:23.[64] Yet even if such a thought is in the background, the content and context of 1 Cor 11:23 indicate that a concrete event must also be in mind: something happened ἐν τῇ νυκτί. So all that we could safely infer is that Paul's tradition held that Jesus was captured or arrested late at night. Whether παρεδίδετο adverts to Jewish authorities handing Jesus over to the Romans, or to some individual or group assisting those authorities in capturing Jesus, or to something else again would not appear.

8. Although it seems unlikely that we should construe the παρεδίδετο of 1 Cor 11:23 as being in the middle voice—"he handed himself over"—a few Pauline sentences leave the distinct impression that Jesus did not resist his fate but rather embraced it:

- Gal 1:4: Jesus Christ "gave [δόντος] himself for our sins"
- Gal 2:20: he "loved me and gave [παραδόντος] himself for me"
- Phil 2:8: "He humbled himself and became obedient to the point of death—even death on a cross"

This cannot surprise given that, for Paul, the crucifixion was God's intention or even, somehow, God's doing (e.g., Rom 5:8; 8:32). Since Jesus "did not please himself" (Rom 15:3), he must have acquiesced to the divine will.[65]

Even though the texts cited are theological statements devoid of historical detail, Paul could not have written them, or at least not have written them

64. See Beverly Roberts Gaventa, "Interpreting the Death of Jesus Apocalyptically: Reconsidering Romans 8:32," in *Jesus and Paul Reconnected: Fresh Pathways into an Old Debate* (ed. Todd D. Still; Grand Rapids: Eerdmans, 2007), 125–45.

65. See below, pp. 427–33, for further relevant passages, to which some might wish to add Rom 8:32. This last verse affirms that God "did not withhold his own Son, but gave him up for all of us." If these words, as many presume, allude to the sacrifice of Isaac—I have no fixed opinion on the question (for doubt, see Sigrid Brandt, *Opfer als Gedächtnis: Auf dem Weg zu einer befreienden theologischen Rede von Opfer* [ATM 2; Münster: Lit Verlag, 2001], 162–67; Jewett, *Romans*, 536–38)—it is worth observing that by Paul's day, Isaac was widely thought of as having offered himself willingly (see, e.g., 4 Macc 13:12; 16:20; *L.A.B.* 32:2–3; Josephus, *Ant.* 1.232; *1 Clem.* 31:2–4; Tg. Ps.-J. on Gen 11:1, 10).

with a clear conscience, if he had known or believed that Jesus resisted arrest or capture, or had tried to flee, or had put up a fight. Although the apostle's assertions do not require that Jesus actively courted death, they do more than suggest that Jesus did not oppose his fate when it finally caught up with him. Perhaps indeed the apostle imagined Jesus to have faced death much like Socrates, who was famed for remaining in Athens and accepting his death sentence so nobly.[66] However that may be, Paul clearly believed that Jesus died willingly. Indeed, this belief was for the apostle a foundational conviction.

9. 1 Cor 11:23–25 attributes to Jesus the following: "This is my body that is for you. Do this in remembrance of me. . . . This cup is the new covenant in my blood. Do this, as often as you drink it, in remembrance of me." These words purport that Jesus foresaw his death, for they interpret it ahead of time. They also indicate that he interpreted his demise as being somehow "for" others, as conferring a benefit.

10. Another pre-Pauline tradition about Jesus' death appears in 1 Cor 15:4, which asserts that Jesus was "buried" (ἐτάφη). The assertion is bare. Who buried him? Where? When? The text holds no hints. It does, nonetheless, clearly assume that Jesus' body did not suffer the fate of so many victims of Roman crucifixion: his corpse was neither left upon its cross to rot in the sun nor unceremoniously dumped into an unmarked trench or pile to become food for scavengers.[67] Rather, somebody—the passive verb ἐτάφη leaves us in the dark—laid Jesus in the ground or in a cave.

Two additional texts require the same conclusion. In Rom 6:4, Paul speaks of being buried with Christ (συνετάφημεν οὖν αὐτῷ) in baptism in death. Colossians 2:12 contains a similar statement (συνταφέντες αὐτῷ). Just as Paul's provocative conviction that he has been "crucified with Christ" (Rom 6:6; Gal 2:19—both with συσταυρόω) presupposes that Jesus was crucified, so too the notion of being buried with Christ presupposes the ritual of burial.

Return to Mark (and John)

Having seen what Paul's Letters both say and imply about the circumstances of Jesus' death, I should like to correlate the results with passion traditions in Mark and, because I take it to be largely independent of the latter, John:

66. The Socratic model influenced accounts of the Maccabean martyrs as well as Luke's portrait of Jesus; see Jan Willem van Henten, *The Maccabean Martyrs as Saviours of the Jewish People: A Study of 2 and 4 Maccabees* (JSJSup 57; Leiden: Brill, 1997), 272–78; Greg Sterling, "*Mors philosophi*: The Death of Jesus in Luke," *HTR* 94 (2001): 383–402.

67. Contrast Suetonius, *Aug.* 13.1–2; Tacitus, *Ann.* 6.29; Petronius, *Satyr.* 111; Horace, *Ep.* 1.16.48; Artemidorus, *Onir.* 2.53; 4.49; Eusebius, *Hist. eccl.* 5.1.57–63; *Mart. Pal.* 9:9–10. See discussion in Brown, *Death of the Messiah*, 2:1207–9.

Paul	Mark and John
Jesus spoke in advance of his own death: 1 Cor 11:23–25	Jesus spoke in advance of his own death: Mark 14:7–8, 18–21, 27; John 13:21–26; 14:19; 16:16; et al.
Jesus was "handed over" (παραδίδωμι) at night: 1 Cor 11:23	Jesus was "handed over" (παραδίδωμι) at night: Mark 14:10, 27, 43–49; John 13:30; 18:1–11, 30, 35–36; 19:11 (cf. also Luke 22:47–48)
On the evening when he was handed over, Jesus recited words over bread and a cup and interpreted his death as "for" others: 1 Cor 11:23–25	On the evening when he was handed over, Jesus recited words over bread and a cup and interpreted his death as "for" others: Mark 14:22–25; cf. John 6:53
Jesus went to his death willingly: 1 Cor 11:23–25; Gal 1:4; 2:20; Phil 2:8	Jesus did not resist his arrest or capture or defend himself when on trial: Mark 14:48–49, 61; 15:1–5; John 18:6–11
Jewish individuals, perhaps specifically Judeans, were implicated in Jesus' death: 1 Thess 2:14–16	Jewish authorities in Jerusalem arrested Jesus, interrogated him, and delivered him to the Roman governor: Mark 14:53–65; 15:1; John 18:12–14, 19–24
Roman authorities were also involved in Jesus' execution: 1 Cor 2:8; cf. Paul's repeated avowal that Jesus was crucified (the Romans generally reserved the right to capital punishment)	Pilate ordered Jesus' execution: Mark 15:1–39; John 18:28–19:30
Jesus was crucified: 1 Cor 1:17–18; Gal 6:12, 14; Phil 3:18; Col 1:20; et al.	Jesus was crucified: Mark 15:25; John 19:18
Jesus bled: Rom 3:25; 5:9; 1 Cor 10:16; 11:25, 27; Col 1:20; also, Gal 6:17 probably presupposes that Jesus' body was disfigured by torture	Jesus was flogged (so Mark and John) and bled (so John): Mark 15:15; John 19:1, 34; cf. the references to nail prints in John 20:25, 27; also *Gos. Pet.* 6:21
Jesus may have been executed as an insurrectionist or royal claimant—an inference from his being a Davidide (Rom 1:3), being called "(the) Christ" (e.g., Rom 1:4; 9:5; 1 Cor 15:3), and being thought of as a king (1 Cor 15:24–25; Col 1:13; 2:10)	Jesus was crucified as "king of the Jews": Mark 15:26; John 19:19
Jesus was buried: 1 Cor 15:4; cf. Rom 6:4; Col 2:12	Jesus was buried: Mark 15:42–47; John 19:38–42

What should we make of these parallels? The answer depends partly on whether one finds the evidence for a pre-Markan passion narrative persuasive. Because I do—one reason being that I judge John to be mostly independent of the Synoptics—it becomes possible to entertain the notion that Paul, writing a decade or more before Mark, knew an early passion narrative, a relative or ancestor of what we find in Mark 14–16.[68]

68. So too Rudolf Pesch, *Das Markusevangelium: Teil 2, Einleitung und Kommentar zu Kap. 8,27–16,20* (HTKNT 2/2; Freiburg: Herder, 1977), 21; Peter Stuhlmacher, "Eighteen Theses on

I not only entertain this possibility but think it much more likely than not. Beyond the common elements just listed, which surely are suggestive, the most important evidence for supposing Paul's knowledge of a connected passion story is 1 Cor 11:23–25: "For I received from the Lord what I also handed on to you, that the Lord Jesus on the night when he was handed over took a loaf of bread. . . . 'Do this in remembrance of me.'" Whatever the historical Jesus may or may not have said or intended, these sentences, with their injunction to remember, add up to a threefold conviction: (i) Paul heard one or more persons recite words attributed to Jesus at his last meal ("I received");[69] (ii) those words became for Paul a tradition that he handed on to churches that he founded, which means that he publicly recited them on multiple occasions ("I also handed on" [cf. 1 Cor 11:2]); (iii) he not only repeated words attributed to Jesus but also knew them in a narrative context. This is clear from the phrase "on the night when he was handed over," concerning which Helmut Koester has remarked, "Paul's reference to 'the night in which he was handed over' . . . reveals that both the apostle and the Corinthian community knew an entire story about Jesus' death and suffering—otherwise, the mention of a specific time would not make sense."[70]

Paul's Theology of the Cross," in *Reconciliation, Law, and Righteousness: Essays in Biblical Theology* (Philadelphia: Fortress, 1986), 164; Wenham, *Paul*, 363–66.

69. Francis Watson ("'I Received from the Lord . . .': Paul, Jesus, and the Last Supper," in *Jesus and Paul Reconnected* [ed. Still], 102–24), urges, as have others, that 1 Cor 11:23–25 is not pre-Pauline tradition but a revelation from Jesus to Paul. This view requires, as Watson himself acknowledges, that Mark 14:22–24 and Luke 22:17–20 (and I would add, John 6:53) ultimately derive from that revelation, which in turn implies significant Pauline influence upon the Jesus tradition, concerning which I have reservations (although see p. 412 n. 91). Further, Paul attributes the sayings of Jesus in 1 Cor 7:10–11 (cf. Matt 5:31–32; 19:3–9; Mark 10:2–12; Luke 16:18) and 9:14 (cf. Matt 10:10; Luke 10:7) to "the Lord"; and the one other place where the apostle employs λαμβάνω . . . παραδίδωμι—words that correspond to the rabbinic ל מסר—מן קבל, as in, for example, *m. 'Abot* 1:1, 3 (a point quite relevant for a onetime Pharisee [Phil 3:5])—is 1 Cor 15:3, where clearly we are dealing with tradition, as evidenced by the number of expressions not used elsewhere in the Pauline Epistles: "sins" in the plural (ἁμαρτιῶν), "according to the scriptures" (κατὰ τὰς γραφάς), ἐγείρω ("was raised") in the perfect (ἐγήγερται) instead of the aorist, "he was seen/appeared" (ὤφθη), and "the Twelve" (τοῖς δώδεκα). Watson's response to this, that 1 Cor 15:3 lacks "from the Lord" and so is different from 1 Cor 11:23, seems to me inadequate. Moreover, 1 Cor 11:23–25 includes some un-Pauline idioms; see Joachim Jeremias, *The Eucharistic Words of Jesus* (trans. Norman Perrin; London: SCM Press, 1966), 103–4. The right conclusion regarding the formula in 1 Cor 11:23 appears to be that of Günther Bornkamm: "The alternative: either a tradition mediated through men, going back to the historical Jesus, or a revelation through the Exalted One, is a false one. Both belong together: the mediated word is the word of the Living One" ("Lord's Supper and Church in Paul," in *Early Christian Experience* [London: SCM Press, 1969], 131). Compare the formulation in *Did.* 4:1: "My child, remember night and day the one who preaches God's word to you, and honor him as though he were the Lord. For wherever the Lord's nature is preached, there the Lord is."

70. Helmut Koester, "The Memory of Jesus' Death and the Worship of the Risen Lord," *HTR* 91 (1998): 348; cf. idem, *From Jesus to the Gospels: Interpreting the New Testament in Its Context* (Minneapolis: Fortress, 2007), 222. Ellen Bradshaw Aitken likewise maintains that "on the night

More Correlations

As further support for the inference that Paul knew a passion narrative, I wish to consider some additional links between his letters and the narrative accounts of Jesus' end. These show themselves only when we read Paul with the Gospels in hand.

1. The apostle had a definite impression of Jesus' character, as appears from several sentences, one of them being Rom 15:1–3: "We who are strong ought to put up with the failings of the weak, and not to please ourselves. Each of us must please our neighbor for the good purpose of building up the neighbor. For Christ did not please himself; but, as it is written, 'The insults of those who insult you have fallen on me.'" Similar are 1 Cor 10:33–11:1 ("I try to please everyone in everything I do, not seeking my own advantage, but that of many, so that they may be saved. Be imitators of me, as I am of Christ") and 2 Cor 10:1 ("I myself, Paul, appeal to you by the meekness and gentleness of Christ—I who am humble when face to face with you, but bold toward you when I am away!"). Closely related is Phil 2:7–8, which emphasizes Jesus' humility: he "emptied himself, taking the form of a slave, being born in human likeness. And being found in human form, he humbled himself and became obedient to the point of death—even death on a cross."[71] The same virtue is implicit in 2 Cor 8:9: "You know the generous act of our Lord Jesus Christ, that though he was rich, yet for your sakes he became poor."

Paul believed that Jesus was unselfish, meek, humble. How did he gain this impression? He can hardly, to state the obvious, have gathered it from the so-called controversy stories, nor can he have developed his image of Jesus while reflecting on his miracles. In these, as in most of the stories of the public ministry, while Jesus is often kind and forgiving, he is also much else besides: forceful, antagonistic, combative. The Jesus of the logia is the same—often argumentative, demanding, polemical.

The one stretch of the Jesus tradition as we have it where the hero is consistently humble and self-effacing is the passion narratives, where he willingly goes to his death for the sake of others (Mark 14:22–25, 43–49), where he is reviled and does not revile (Mark 14:65; 15:16–32), where he forgoes almost all defense of himself, even verbal defense (Mark 14:43–49, 60–61; 15:1–5). In view of this, it occurs that behind Rom 15:2–3; 1 Cor 10:33–11:1; 2 Cor 10:1; and Phil 2:7–8 lies not an impression of Jesus in general but much more specifi-

---

when he was handed over" connects the account of the institution "to an existing narrative of Jesus' passion" (*Jesus' Death in Early Christian Memory: The Poetics of the Passion* [NTOA/SUNT 53; Göttingen: Vandenhoeck & Ruprecht; Fribourg: Academic Press, 2004], 50).

71. Also relevant is 2 Cor 13:4 ("he was crucified in weakness") if it means, as Thomas Stegman has argued, that "Jesus' death was the climactic consummation of a life lived in love and service of others in obedience to God and God's will" (*The Character of Jesus: The Linchpin to Paul's Argument in 2 Corinthians* [AnBib 158; Rome: Pontifical Biblical Institute, 2005], 205–11).

cally an impression fostered by stories of his final days or hours.[72] Philippians 2:7–8, which specifies that Jesus humbled himself precisely in his obedience unto death, is more than consistent with this suggestion.

2. So too is Rom 15:3: "For Christ did not please himself; but, as it is written, 'The insults of those who insult you have fallen on me.'" The proof text for Paul's generalization that "Christ did not please himself" is v. 10 of Ps 69. This psalm was popular in the early churches. John 2:17 ("His disciples remembered that it was written, 'Zeal for your house will consume me'" [cf. Ps 69:9]), Acts 1:20 ("For it is written in the book of Psalms, 'Let his homestead become desolate, and let there be no one to live in it'" [cf. Ps 69:25]), and Rom 11:9–10 ("And David says, 'Let their table become a snare and a trap, a stumbling block and a retribution for them; let their eyes be darkened so that they cannot see, and keep their backs forever bent'" [cf. Ps 69:22–23]) all put it to use.[73]

It is of particular interest that Ps 69 (LXX Ps 68), which includes lamentation (vv. 2–5, 7–12, 19–21, 29), pleas for deliverance (vv. 1, 6, 13–18, 22–28), and the vindication of the speaker (vv. 30–36), informed extant passion traditions:

- Matt 27:34 (ἔδωκαν αὐτῷ πιεῖν οἶνον μετὰ χολῆς μεμιγμένον, "they offered him wine to drink, mixed with gall") diff. Mark 15:23 (ἐδίδουν αὐτῷ ἐσμυρνισμένον οἶνον, "they gave him wine mixed with myrrh") creates an allusion to the righteous sufferer of LXX Ps 68:22: ἔδωκαν εἰς τὸ βρῶμά μου χολήν . . . ἐπότισάν με ("they gave me gall for my food . . . gave me to drink").[74]
- Mark 15:36 (γεμίσας σπόγγον ὄξους περιθεὶς καλάμῳ ἐπότιζεν αὐτόν, "filled a sponge with sour wine, put it on a stick, and gave it to him to drink") alludes to the same verse, as do the close parallels in Matt 27:48; Luke 23:36; Gos. Pet. 5:16.[75]

72. Thompson (Clothed with Christ, 213) argues this with regard to 2 Cor 10:1 in particular and notes that "not seeking my own advantage, but that of many, so that they may be saved" might echo Mark 10:45, a logion that the Pauline school certainly knew (cf. 1 Tim 2:6; Titus 2:14). For further discussion, see Hanna Stettler, Die Christologie der Pastoralbriefe (WUNT 2/105; Tübingen: Mohr Siebeck, 1998), 67–74; Rainer Riesner, "Back to the Historical Jesus through Paul and His School (The Ransom Logion—Mark 10.45; Matthew 20.28)," JSHJ 1 (2003): 171–99.

73. Note also 1 Clem. 52:2. See Barnabas Lindars, New Testament Apologetic: The Doctrinal Significance of the Old Testament Quotations (London: SCM Press, 1961), 99–108.

74. This is the consensus of the modern critical commentaries, and it is not a new insight; cf. Ambrose, Exp. Luc. (SC 52:196–97); Jerome, Comm. Matt. ad loc.; Albertus Magnus, Super Matthaeum Capitula XV–XXVIII ad loc. (vol. 21/2 of Opera omnia [ed. B. Schmidt; Aschendorff: Monasterii Westfalorum, 1987], 644); Sedulius Scottus, Comm. Matt. ad loc. (Kommentar zum Evangelium nach Matthäus, vol. 2 [ed. Bengt Löfstedt; Freiburg: Herder, 1991], 608). ὄξος ("sour wine") replaces οἶνος ("wine") in A W 0250 Maj c f h q sy^{p, h} mae bo^{mss}, which is further assimilation to LXX Ps 68:22: "for my thirst they made me drink ὄξος."

75. See also Sib. Or. 1:367–68; 6:24; 8:303. Here too the critical and precritical commentators agree; cf. Chrysostom, Hom. Matt. 87.1; Paschasius Radbertus, Exp. Matt. Libri XII ad

- Given the previous two allusions, one wonders whether the use of ὀνειδίζω ("to reproach") in Mark 15:32 ("Those who were crucified with him also taunted him") and in its Matthean parallel (27:44) might echo Ps 69, where (in the LXX) ὀνειδίζω occurs (68:10) and the related noun ὀνειδισμός ("reproach") appears repeatedly (vv. 8, 10, 11, 20, 21 [it appears no more than once in any other psalm]).[76]

- The Jesus of John 15:25, in explicating the hatred that will culminate in his crucifixion, declares, "It was to fulfill the word that is written in their law, 'They hated me without a cause' [ἐμίσησάν με δωρεάν]." The last words are from LXX Ps 68:5: οἱ μισοῦντές με δωρεάν.[77]

- John 19:28–29 is explicit that the sour wine offered to Jesus on the cross fulfills the Scripture: "After this, when Jesus knew that all was now finished, he said (in order to fulfill the scripture), 'I am thirsty.' A jar full of sour wine [ὄξους] was standing there. So they put a sponge full of the wine on a branch of hyssop and held it to his mouth." These words allude to the same lines as do Matt 27:34, 48; Mark 15:36; Luke 23:36; Gos. Pet. 5:16, namely, LXX Ps 68:22.[78]

In the light of the early Christian habit of associating Ps 69 with the end of Jesus, what should we make of Rom 15:3, where Paul assumes that Jesus did not please himself, that he was reviled, and that he was the righteous sufferer of Ps 69? These same convictions are plainly on display in the canonical passion narratives as well as in the *Gospel of Peter*; and if Paul uses ὀνειδισμός and ὀνειδίζω, the latter appears likewise in Mark 15:32, of the thieves reproaching Jesus (cf. Matt 27:44). Maybe, then, when Paul penned Rom 15:3, he had in mind what most of his subsequent readers have had in mind, namely, something like the tableau in Mark 15 and parallels.[79]

---

loc. (CCCM 56b:1388); Sedulius Scottus, *Comm. Matt.* ad loc. (*Kommentar* [ed. Bengt], 616); Stephen P. Ahearne-Kroll, *The Psalms of Lament in Mark's Passion: Jesus' Davidic Suffering* (SNTSMS 142; Cambridge: Cambridge University Press, 2007), 74–77; Joachim Gnilka, *Das Evangelium nach Markus (Mk 8,27–16,20)* (EKKNT 2/2; Zurich: Benziger; Neukirchen-Vluyn: Neukirchener Verlag, 1979), 323; Joel Marcus, *Mark 8–16* (AB 27A; New Haven: Yale University Press, 2009), 1065.

76. Cf. Cassiodorus, *Exp. Ps.* at 68:10 (CCSL 97:609–10); C. E. B. Cranfield, *The Gospel according to Saint Mark* (rev. ed.; CGTC; Cambridge: Cambridge University Press, 1977), 457; J. C. Fenton, *Matthew* (PNTC; Baltimore: Penguin, 1963), 441; D. E. Nineham, *Saint Mark* (WPC; Philadelphia: Westminster, 1977), 425.

77. See Margaret Daly-Denton, *David in the Fourth Gospel: The Johannine Reception of the Psalms* (AGJU 47; Leiden: Brill, 2000), 201–8. Cf. Augustine, *Trin.* 15.17.30.

78. Full discussion in Daly-Denton, *David in the Fourth Gospel*, 219–29. Cf. Albertus Magnus, *Enarrationes in Joannem* ad loc. (vol. 24 of *Opera omnia* [ed. A. Borgnet; Paris: Ludovicus Vivès, 1890], 661).

79. Chrysostom (*Hom. Rom.* 27.2) cites Matt 27:40, 42 when commenting on Rom 15:3. Cf. Pelagius, *Comm. Rom.* ad loc. (TS 9:112); Theodoret of Cyrus, *Comm. Rom.* ad loc. (PG 82:214A); Theophylact, *Exp. Rom.* ad loc. (PG 124:536B); Grotius, *Opera omnia theologica,*

3. This is all the more likely because, in Rom 15:3, it is Jesus himself who recites Ps 69: "For Christ did not please himself; but, as it is written, 'The insults of those who insult you have fallen on me.'" In an important article, Richard Hays has called attention to the fact that although Paul typically applies lines from Psalms to the church, here he has Jesus himself reciting the Psalter with reference to his own person.[80] Just a few verses later, moreover, in Rom 15:8–9, 11, Hays argues that the first-person singular in the scriptural citations is again Jesus, who presents himself "as standing in the midst of an eschatological congregation composed of both Gentiles and Jews (see especially v. 10, quoting Deut 32:43), offering praise to God."[81] The relevant words are these: "For I tell you that Christ has become a servant of the circumcised on behalf of the truth of God in order that he might confirm the promises given to the patriarchs, and in order that the Gentiles might glorify God for his mercy. As it is written, 'Therefore I will confess you among the Gentiles, and sing praises to your name' [Ps 18:49]. . . . And again, 'Praise the Lord, all you Gentiles, and let all the peoples praise him' [Ps 117:1]."

Hays goes on to observe that Rom 15 features an early Christian convention. A number of non-Pauline texts identify Jesus as the "I" or "me" of a psalm. He is correct, as the following list makes clear:[82]

- Matt 13:34–35: "Jesus told the crowds all these things in parables; without a parable he told them nothing. This was to fulfill what had been spoken through the prophet: 'I will open my mouth to speak in parables; I will proclaim what has been hidden from the foundation of the world' [ἀνοίξω ἐν παραβολαῖς τὸ στόμα μου, ἐρεύξομαι κεκρυμμένα ἀπὸ καταβολῆς κόσμου]" (cf. LXX Ps 77:2: ἀνοίξω ἐν παραβολαῖς τὸ στόμα μου, φθέγξομαι προβλήματα ἀπ' ἀρχῆς).

2:757. According to Douglas Moo, "the reference to Christ 'not pleasing himself' is almost certainly to the crucifixion. . . . Paul probably thinks of the 'reproaches' born by Christ as those tauntings Jesus endured at the time of his crucifixion (see [Matt] 27:27–31, 39–41 and pars.)" (*The Epistle to the Romans* [NICNT; Grand Rapids: Eerdmans, 1996], 868–69). Cf. Ernst Käsemann, *Commentary on Romans* (Grand Rapids: Eerdmans, 1980), 382. Perhaps one should note Paul's introduction to his citation of Ps 69: "ὁ χριστός did not please himself." In Mark 15:32, Jesus is mockingly reproached as "ὁ χριστός, the king of Israel." Is this a coincidence? Perhaps one should also note that, in Rom 15:1, Paul employs βαστάζω ("bear the failings of the weak"), and that Luke 14:27 and John 19:17 use this of carrying a cross (cf. Chariton, *Chaereas and Callirhoë* 4.2.7; 3.10; Artemidorus, *Onir.* 2.56). In Aquila Isa 53:11, moreover, the suffering servant is the subject of this verb (cf. Matt 8:17). So some early Christians might have divined in βαστάζω an echo of Jesus' passion. The same verb reappears in Gal 6:17, where Paul "bears" the "stigmata" of Jesus. See above, pp. 393–95.

80. Richard B. Hays, "Christ Prays the Psalms: Israel's Psalter as Matrix of Early Christology," in *The Conversion of the Imagination: Paul as Interpreter of Israel's Scripture* (Grand Rapids: Eerdmans, 2005), 101–18.

81. Ibid., 103.

82. Hays fails to cite John 12:27; 13:18; 15:25, for reasons that remain unclear to me.

- Mark 14:34 (cf. Matt 26:38): "And he said to them, 'I am deeply grieved, even to death [περίλυπός ἐστιν ἡ ψυχή μου ἕως θανάτου]'" (cf. LXX Ps 41:6, 12; 42:5: ἵνα τί περίλυπος εἶ, ψυχή).

- Mark 15:34 (cf. Matt 27:46; Gos. Pet. 5:19): "Jesus cried out with a loud voice, 'Eloi, Eloi, lema sabachthani?' which means, 'My God, my God, why have you forsaken me?' [ὁ θεός μου ὁ θεός μου, εἰς τί ἐγκατέλιπές με;]" (cf. LXX Ps 21:2: ὁ θεός ὁ θεός μου . . . ἵνα τί ἐγκατέλιπές με;).[83]

- Luke 23:46: "Then Jesus, crying with a loud voice, said, 'Father, into your hands I commend my spirit' [εἰς χεῖράς σου παρατίθεμαι τὸ πνεῦμά μου]" (cf. LXX Ps 30:6: εἰς χεῖράς σου παραθήσομαι τὸ πνεῦμά μου).[84]

- John 2:17: "His disciples remembered that it was written, 'Zeal for your house will consume me' [ὁ ζῆλος τοῦ οἴκου σου καταφάγεταί με]" (cf. LXX Ps 68:10: ὁ ζῆλος τοῦ οἴκου σου κατέφαγέν με).[85]

- John 12:27: "Now my soul is troubled [ἡ ψυχή μου τετάρακται]" (cf. LXX Ps 6:4: ἡ ψυχή μου ἐταράχθη).

- John 13:18: "I am not speaking of all of you; I know whom I have chosen. But it is to fulfill the scripture, 'The one who ate my bread has lifted his heel against me' [ὁ τρώγων μου τὸν ἄρτον ἐπῆρεν ἐπ' ἐμὲ τὴν πτέρναν αὐτοῦ]" (cf. LXX Ps 40:10: ὁ ἐσθίων ἄρτους μου, ἐμεγάλυνεν ἐπ' ἐμὲ πτερνισμόν).

- John 15:25: "It was to fulfill the word that is written in their law, 'They hated me without a cause' [ἐμίσησάν με δωρεάν]" (cf. LXX Ps 68:5: οἱ μισοῦντές με δωρεάν [see n. 77]).

- John 19:28–29: "After this, when Jesus knew that all was now finished, he said (in order to fulfill the scripture), 'I am thirsty' [διψῶ]" (cf. LXX Ps 68:22: τὴν δίψαν μου [see above, p. 408]).

- Heb 2:10–11: "It was fitting that God, for whom and through whom all things exist, in bringing many children to glory, should make the pioneer of their salvation perfect through sufferings. For the one who sanctifies and those who are sanctified all have one Father. For this reason Jesus is not ashamed to call them brothers and sisters, saying, 'I will proclaim your name to my brothers and sisters, in the midst of the congregation I will praise you' [ἀπαγγελῶ τὸ ὄνομά σου τοῖς ἀδελφοῖς μου, ἐν μέσῳ ἐκκλησίας ὑμνήσω σε]" (cf. LXX Ps 21:23: διηγήσομαι τὸ ὄνομά σου τοῖς ἀδελφοῖς μου, ἐν μέσῳ ἐκκλησίας ὑμνήσω σε).

83. See discussion in J. Samuel Subramanian, The Synoptic Gospels and the Psalms as Prophecy (LNTS 351; London: T & T Clark, 2007), 64–69, 118–21.
84. For the critical issues involved in this citation, see ibid., 85–89.
85. Hays remarks that "although Jesus is not represented in John's Gospel as having spoken these words at the time of his temple action, the quotation makes sense here only if the disciples understand the 'me' of the Psalm to be Jesus himself" ("Christ Prays the Psalms," 105). Cf. Origen, Comm. Jo. 10.222.

- Heb 10:5–7: "When Christ came into the world, he said, 'Sacrifices and offerings you have not desired, but a body you have prepared for me; in burnt offerings and sin offerings you have taken no pleasure. Then I said, 'See, God, I have come to do your will, O God' (in the scroll of the book it is written of me)" (cf. Ps 40:6–7: "Sacrifice and offering you do not desire, but you have given me an open ear. Burnt offering and sin offering you have not required. Then I said, 'Here I am; in the scroll of the book it is written of me'").[86]

For our immediate purposes, the striking fact is this: with the single exception of Matt 13:34–35 (quoting Ps 78), all of the non-Pauline texts apply the quoted verses from Psalms to the passion of Jesus,[87] or they borrow from a psalm that early Christians otherwise associated with his death.[88] This cannot be coincidence. It rather appears that, from a very early time, Christians identified Jesus as the speaker of several psalms of suffering that are attributed to David, psalms that begin with the enigmatic εἰς τὸ τέλος ("unto the end" [LXX Ps 17; 21; 30; 39; 41; 68]).

It is the passion narratives above all that have Jesus utter lines and phrases from these psalms. So when Paul, in Rom 15:3, has Jesus recite Ps 69:10 (9) and, in Rom 15:9, has Jesus quote Ps 18:50 (49), he makes, and assumes that his readers will make,[89] the same hermeneutical move that is on display over half a dozen times in the extant passion narratives. One cannot, of course, demonstrate that Paul became acquainted with this way of reading certain psalms through hearing stories about the end of Jesus; yet given what we find in the Synoptics and John, and given that Paul, as already argued, knew some sort of passion narrative, the possibility naturally offers itself for our consideration.

4. Paul sometimes speaks of suffering and dying with Christ as well as of being baptized into his death (e.g., Rom 6:3–11; 8:17; Phil 3:10; Col 2:12, 20; 3:3). Scholars have much debated the history-of-religions background for this conception, which does not concern us here. What is of interest is that twice Paul employs the arresting image of being crucified with Christ (Rom 6:6; Gal 2:19), for which he uses the very rare verb συσταυρόω ("to crucify with"). BDAG (s.v.) lists only three occurrences of this word in addition to Paul's two verses: Matt 27:44; Mark 15:32; John 19:32. All three of these concern Jesus

86. Hays ("Christ Prays the Psalms," 108–9) would add 2 Cor 4:13–14 to this list because he finds here the voice of Jesus praying Ps 116:10. I am unsure and thus leave it out of account.

87. Mark 14:34; 15:34; Luke 23:46; John 12:27; 13:18; 15:25; 19:28–29; Heb 10:5–7. The subject, in Heb 10:5–7, is Christ's sacrifice: it is to that end that he came into the world (cf. vv. 1–4, 8–18).

88. John 2:17, quoting Ps 69; Heb 2:12, quoting Ps 22.

89. Unless one identifies Jesus as the speaker of Ps 69, which Paul assumes but does not state, the argument of Rom 15:1–3 becomes opaque.

and the two men crucified along with him. LSJ (s.v.) adds nothing beyond this. Nor has my own *TLG* search, save for patristic writers familiar with the New Testament.[90] What does this imply?

It is not inconceivable that Mark and John, or contributors to their traditions, and Paul independently manufactured the same word. Coincidences do happen. Nor is it impossible that Paul first coined the word, which then entered a pre-Markan passion narrative and so found its way into Mark and John as well as Matthew.[91] If, however, we are looking for what is likely as opposed to what is conceivable, a better guess is that συσταυρόω appeared first in an early account of the passion, coined for the occasion. From there it entered the Synoptic tradition and the Johannine tradition; and from such an account Paul picked it up and then redeployed it for his own purposes.

If this is the right inference, the apostle knew the tradition that Jesus was crucified with others (Mark 15:27, 32; John 19:18, 32). The possibility intrigues all the more because that particular tradition has people insult Jesus (Mark 15:32: ὠνείδιζον), and we have just seen that Paul, in Rom 15:3, refers to the insults (ὀνειδισμοί) of those who insulted (ὀνειδιζόντων) Jesus (see p. 407).

5. Paul, in 1 Cor 5:7, implores the Corinthians, "Cleanse out the old leaven that you may be a new lump, as you really are unleavened. For Christ, our paschal lamb, has been sacrificed" (RSV). The association of Jesus' death with Passover, although it probably lies behind the image of the slaughtered lamb in Rev 5:6–14,[92] is rare in early Christian literature—rare, that is, aside from the passion narratives, where it is to the fore. In the Synoptics, Jesus' last meal with his disciples is a Passover seder, a circumstance that Matthew, Mark, and Luke reiterate (Mark 14:1–2, 12–16 par.). In John's Gospel, Jesus also goes to Jerusalem during Passover (11:55; 12:1; 13:1; 18:28, 39) and indeed dies at the very moment when the Passover lamb is being slaughtered (19:36; cf. 1:29, 36).

How Jesus can celebrate the Passover meal before the lambs have been prepared has always been a question. Modern scholars, unlike earlier ecclesiastical exegetes, by and large have decided that the contradiction is ineradicable. There nonetheless remains disagreement as to whether or not Jesus' last meal was a seder service and whether or not John's chronology is pre-Johannine or

90. Cf. *PGL* (s.v.). According to Heinz-Wolfgang Kuhn, "the vb. is attested only in Christian writings" ("συσταυρόω," *EDNT* 3:313).

91. For the possibility of Paul's influence upon at least Mark, see Joel Marcus, "Mark—Interpreter of Paul," *NTS* 46 (2000): 473–87; Wolfgang Schenk, "Sekundäre jesuanisierungen von primären Paulus-Aussagen bei Markus," in *The Four Gospels, 1992: Festschrift Frans Neirynck* (ed. F. Van Segbroeck et al.; 3 vols.; BETL 100; Leuven: University Press, 1992), 2:877–904.

92. See David E. Aune, *Revelation 1–5* (WBC 52A; Nashville: Thomas Nelson, 1997), 353, 367–73. By contrast, 1 Pet 1:19 ("the precious blood of Christ, like that of a lamb without defect or blemish") probably does not allude to Passover; see Paul J. Achtemeier, *1 Peter: A Commentary on 1 Peter* (Hermeneia; Minneapolis: Fortress, 1996), 28–29.

redactional. Within the confines of this chapter we need not, fortunately, review those convoluted and ultimately irresolvable issues. What matters alone is this: in all four canonical Gospels, Jesus goes up to Jerusalem and suffers and dies during the season of Passover. So if Paul was familiar with an early passion narrative, it also presumably placed Jesus' demise during Passover week, which in turn would explain why it was natural for the apostle to associate his Lord's death with the paschal lamb. In other words, Paul's tradition that Jesus was betrayed at night may well have been a tradition that had him crucified at the time of the Passover, just as the canonical Gospels have it.[93]

6. Col 2:13–14 reads, "And when you were dead in trespasses and the un-circumcision of your flesh, God made you alive together with him, when he forgave us all our trespasses, erasing the record that stood against us with its legal demands. He set this aside, nailing it to the cross." As already observed, the final clause, "nailing it to the cross" (προσηλώσας αὐτὸ τῷ σταυρῷ), has moved many to think of what happened to Jesus himself. Others, however, have found in the same words an allusion to the tradition that the charges against Jesus were displayed on or above his cross.[94]

I do not know which reading to endorse. Colossians 2:13–14 is, as the fanci-ful history of interpretation reveals,[95] obscure, the logic convoluted. Yet what-ever else may be said, the image of a legal statement affixed to Jesus' cross for

93. See Fritz Chenderlin, *"Do This as My Memorial": The Semantic and Conceptual Back-ground and Value of Ἀνάμνησις in 1 Corinthians 11:24–25* (AnBib 99; Rome: Biblical Institute Press, 1982), 184; Hengel, "Das Mahl in der Nacht," 462–65; Jeffrey Peterson, "Christ Our Pasch: Shaping Christian Identity in Corinth," in *Renewing Tradition: Studies in Honor of James W. Thompson* (ed. Mark W. Hamilton, Thomas H. Olbricht, and Jeffrey Peterson; PTMS 65; Eugene, OR: Pickwick, 2007), 133–44. Paul's language also, according to Hengel, implies that Jesus, like the Passover lamb, was sacrificed in Jerusalem. Whether that is so or not, 1 Cor 5:7 has often moved commentators to remark upon the chronology of Jesus' last days; see, for example, G. G. Findlay, "St. Paul's First Epistle to the Corinthians," in *The Expositor's Greek Testament*, vol. 2 (ed. W. Robertson Nicoll; New York: George Doran, n.d.), 810; Fitzmyer, *First Corinthians*, 241; Archibald Robertson and Alfred Plummer, *A Critical and Exegetical Commentary on the First Epistle of St Paul to the Corinthians* (ICC; Edinburgh: T & T Clark, 1914), 103.

94. So, for example, Gill, *Commentary*, 6:522 (Gill also sees a reference to Jesus himself being nailed to the cross); Martin Dibelius, *An die Kolosser, Epheser, an Philemon* (HNT 12; Tübingen: Mohr Siebeck, 1953), 13; Peter T. O'Brien, *Colossians, Philemon* (WBC 33; Waco, TX: Word, 1982), 126; Michael Wolter, *Der Brief an die Kolosser; Die Brief an Philemon* (ÖTKNT 12; Gü-tersloh: Gütersloher Verlagshaus; Würzburg: Echter, 1993), 137. The relevant texts are these:

Matt 27:37:   "Over his head they put the charge against him. . . ."
Mark 15:26:   "The inscription of the charge against him read. . . ."
Luke 23:38:   "There was also an inscription over him. . . ."
John 19:19:   "Pilate . . . had an inscription written and put on the cross. . . ."
Gos. Pet. 4:11: "Having raised the cross, they wrote the title. . . ."

95. See Michael E. Stone, *Adam's Contract with Satan: The Legend of the Cheirograph of Adam* (Bloomington: Indiana University Press, 2002). For recent views, see Roy Yates, "Colos-sians 2,14: Metaphor of Forgiveness," *Bib* 71 (1990): 248–59; and see above, p. 393.

public display is common to both the Gospel accounts and the epistle attributed to Paul. Indeed, to my knowledge, nowhere else in ancient literature—apart from Paul, the canonical Gospels, and later writings familiar with them—do we read of a declaration or document being displayed on a cross. This is reason enough for at least asking whether we should connect Col 2:13–14 with what we find in the Gospels.

7. Paul uses (παρα)δίδωμι in connection with the death of Jesus on five occasions: Rom 4:25 ("who was handed over [παρεδόθη] to death for our trespasses and was raised for our justification"); Rom 8:32 ("he who did not withhold his own Son, but gave him up [παρέδωκεν] for all of us"); 1 Cor 11:23 ("the Lord Jesus on the night when he was betrayed [παρεδίδετο]"); Gal 1:3–4 ("the Lord Jesus Christ, who gave [δόντος] himself for our sins"); Gal 2:20 ("the Son of God, who loved me and gave himself [παραδόντος] for me").

This is of interest because, in Mark 14–15, phrases with παραδίδωμι constitute a refrain, the verb appearing a full ten times;[96] and some of those texts, just like Rom 4:25,[97] no doubt allude to Isa 53.[98] If, moreover, the subject of the verb varies in Paul—it is alternately God (Rom 4:25; 8:32; cf. *1 Clem.* 16:7), Jesus (Gal 1:3–4, 20; cf. Eph 5:2, 25; 1 Tim 2:6; Titus 2:14), and perhaps Jesus' betrayer (1 Cor 11:23)—Mark offers something comparable, for commentators often see God as a sort of joint subject of παραδίδωμι beside or behind Judas and the ruling authorities.[99] Beyond all this, Paul sets the scene for the words of institution with παραδίδωμι and in this immediate connection speaks of it having been evening (1 Cor 11:23: νύξ); Mark introduces his account of Jesus' final meal with a pericope whose topic is Jesus' betrayal, a pericope in which παραδίδωμι appears twice (Mark 14:17–21) and in which the setting is evening (καὶ ὀψίας γενομένης [v. 17]); further, Mark immediately follows up the story of the Last Supper with

96. Mark 14:10, 11, 18, 21, 41, 42, 44; 15:1, 10, 15. The verb παραδίδωμι is also a prominent feature of John's passion narrative (12:4; 13:2, 11, 21; 18:2, 5, 30, 35, 36; 19:11, 16).

97. According to Morna D. Hooker, Rom 4:25 supplies the "one clear echo of Isaiah 53 in Paul" ("Did the Use of Isaiah 53 to Interpret His Mission Begin with Jesus?" in *Jesus and the Suffering Servant: Isaiah 53 and Christian Origins* [ed. William H. Bellinger Jr. and William R. Farmer; Harrisburg, PA: Trinity Press International, 1998], 101).

98. Cf. LXX Isa 53:6, 12; and see Joel Marcus, *The Way of the Lord: Christological Exegesis of the Old Testament in the Gospel of Mark* (Louisville: Westminster John Knox, 1992), 188. The Synoptic passion narratives otherwise implicitly equate Jesus with Isaiah's suffering servant; see Mark 14:24 (blood poured out for many [cf. Isa 53:12]); 14:61; 15:5 (silence before accusers [cf. Isa 53:7]); 14:65; 15:19 (slapping, spitting [cf. LXX Isa 50:6]); 15:5, 39 (amazement of Gentile ruler [cf. Isa 52:15]); 15:6–15 (criminal saved/innocent killed [cf. Isa 53:6, 12]); 15:27 (association with criminals in death [cf. Isa 53:12]); Matt 27:57 (burial by a rich man [cf. LXX Isa 53:9]); Luke 22:37 (fate shared with transgressors [cf. LXX Isa 53:12]); John 19:1 (scourging [cf. LXX Isa 50:6]). See further Marcus, *Way of the Lord*, 186–96; Douglas J. Moo, *The Old Testament in the Gospel Passion Narratives* (Sheffield: Almond, 1983), 79–182.

99. So, for example, Marcus, *Mark 8–16*, 952. Cf., early on, Origen, *Comm. Matt.* 13.8.

a paragraph, 14:26–31, in which Jesus foretells what will happen "in this night" (ταύτῃ τῇ νυκτί):

Mark 14:17–31	1 Cor 11:23–25
ὀψίας γενομένης (v. 17)	ἐν τῇ νυκτί (v. 23)
ταύτῃ τῇ νυκτί (v. 30)	
παραδώσει (v. 18)	παρεδίδετο (v. 23)
παραδίδοται (v. 21)	
the Last Supper (vv. 22–25)	the Last Supper (vv. 24–25)

In other words, the Markan setting for the Last Supper lines up perfectly with what Paul has to say. Clearly, the apostle's tradition and Mark's repeated use of παραδίδωμι are somehow related.

8. 2 Cor 12:7–9 reads, "To keep me from being too elated, a thorn was given to me in the flesh, a messenger of Satan to torment me, to keep me from being too elated. Three times I appealed to the Lord about this, that it would leave me, but he said to me, 'My grace is sufficient for you, for power is made perfect in weakness.' So, I will boast all the more gladly of my weaknesses, so that the power of Christ may dwell in me."

What is the background of this threefold appeal that goes unanswered? Although Jews and Christians sometimes prayed three times daily (Dan 6:10; t. Ber. 3:6; y. Ber. 7a [4:1]; cf. Ps 55:17; Did. 8:3), this does not illuminate Paul's remark.[100] Neither does b. Yoma 87a, which teaches that "one who asks pardon of his neighbor need do no more than three times." Perhaps more relevant are the magical texts that pledge that asking or doing something three times will be efficacious.[101]

The one parallel that the commentators mention again and again is the story of Jesus in Gethsemane.[102] This is understandable because the resem-

100. Ulrich Heckel (Kraft in Schwachheit: Untersuchungen zu 2.Kor 10–13 [WUNT 2/56; Tübingen: Mohr Siebeck, 1993], 85) observes that the exceptional situation and the intensity of Paul's request make an allusion to daily prayer unlikely.

101. Cf. the prayers in Sefer ha-Razim 1:102, 183; 2:96; and the spells in PGM 4:3172–3208; 36:102–33; also 1 Kgs 17:21; Aristophanes, Ran. 1177 ("who cannot hear us though we call them thrice").

102. For example, Grotius, Opera omnia theologica, 2:858; Johann Albrecht Bengel, Gnomon Novi Testamenti (2 vols.; Tübingen: Ludov. Frid. Fues, 1850), 1:256; James Denney, "The Second Epistle to the Corinthians," in St. Luke–Galatians (vol. 5 of The Expositor's Bible, ed. W. Robertson Nicoll; Rahway, NJ: Expositor Bible Company, n.d.), 802; Heckel, Kraft in Schwachheit, 84–85; Jacob Kremer, 2. Korintherbrief (2nd ed.; SKKNT 8; Stuttgart: Katholisches Bibelwerk, 1998), 107, 109; Jerry W. McCant, "Paul's Thorn of Rejected Apostleship," NTS 34 (1988): 571; Ralph P. Martin, 2 Corinthians (WBC 40; Waco, TX: Word, 1986), 416; Hans Windisch, Der zweite Korintherbrief (9th ed.; KEK 6; Göttingen: Vandenhoeck & Ruprecht, 1924), 386; Christian Wolff, Der zweite Brief des Paulus an die Korinther (THKNT 8; Berlin: Evangelische Verlagsanstalt, 1989), 248.

blances are so strong.[103] In both passages, someone faces great distress and physical pain.[104] In both, that individual thrice (τὸ τρίτον [Mark 14:41]; τρίς [2 Cor 12:8]) asks God to take his burden from him (ἀπ' ἐμοῦ [Mark 14:36; 2 Cor 12:8]).[105] In both, the "flesh" (σάρξ [Mark 14:38; 2 Cor 12:7]) and "weakness" (ἀσθενής [Mark 14:38]; ἀσθένεια, ἀσθενέω [2 Cor 12:5, 9, 10]) are prominent themes. And in both instances, God's will is otherwise; that is, the prayer for relief is not granted, so the petitioner must continue in his ordeal. Moreover, if Jesus, even though he must drink his cup, is ultimately vindicated (Mark 16:1–8), Paul, although not freed from his distress, says of himself and others, "We will live with him [Christ] by the power of God" (2 Cor 13:4).

A few exegetes, even when not observing these parallels, have suggested that "the crucifixion of Jesus Christ" may lie "at the heart of Paul's statement" about his σκόλοψ τῇ σαρκί.[106] By the second century at least, σκόλοψ (usually translated "thorn" [cf. LXX Num 33:55]) could refer to the wood of crucifixion (Origen, Cels. 2.55, 68); and long before that, the related verb ἀνασκολοπίζω was used with the sense "to crucify."[107] The fact is all the more interesting when one remembers that, if "weakness" (ἀσθένεια) is the condition that the σκόλοψ τῇ σαρκί produces in Paul (2 Cor 12:5, 9, 10), he says elsewhere that this was the condition of the crucified Jesus (ἐξ ἀσθενείας [2 Cor 13:4]). The fate of the apostle matches that of his Lord.

Although such considerations hardly establish beyond reasonable doubt that 2 Cor 12:7–9 betrays acquaintance with the episode of Jesus in Gethsemane, they do move one to wonder.[108] Six further observations move one to wonder all the more.

a. The story of Jesus in Gethsemane probably enjoyed wide circulation in the early churches. It appears in Mark 14; the parallel in Luke 22:39–46 may

103. Gerhard Delling remarks, "One can hardly miss the fact that the incidents are in some sense parallel, though not intentionally so" ("τρεῖς κ.τ.λ.," *TDNT* 8:222).

104. Although some commentators on Paul identify his thorn in the flesh with opponents (e.g., Terence Y. Mullins, "Paul's Thorn in the Flesh," *JBL* 76 [1957]: 299–303), exegetical history has more often thought of a physical and/or mental impediment. See the survey in Margaret Thrall, *The Second Epistle to the Corinthians* (2 vols.; ICC; Edinburgh: T & T Clark, 1994–2000), 2:809–818. Thrall concludes, "Paul may have suffered from some recurrent malady."

105. Thrall argues that "the apostle's prayer was a repeated petition made at one particular time" (*Second Epistle*, 2:819).

106. The quoted words are from Larry Kreitzer, *2 Corinthians* (NTG; Sheffield: Sheffield Academic Press, 1996), 125.

107. For example, Herodotus, *Hist.* 1.128; Philo, *Posterity* 61. For additional texts, including several from Christian writers, and discussion, see David M. Park, "Paul's σκόλοψ τῇ σαρκί: Thorn or Stake?" *NovT* 22 (1980): 179–83; also Kuhn, "Kreuzesstrafe," 680 n. 170; *PGL* (s.v.).

108. Heckel (*Kraft in Schwachheit*, 85 n. 154) thinks it possible that Paul had Jesus' prayer in Gethsemane in mind, but one cannot prove it. Particularly interesting on this matter are remarks by Wenham (*Paul*, 276–80), to which I am indebted.

incorporate tradition independent of Mark;[109] Hebrews 5:7–8 probably refers to this episode;[110] and John's Gospel seemingly reacts against it.[111]

b. Twice Paul uses the word ἀββά ("Abba"), once in Rom 8:15 ("For you did not receive a spirit of slavery to fall back into fear, but you have received a spirit of adoption. When we cry, 'Abba! Father!' it is that very Spirit bearing witness with our spirit that we are children of God"), once in Gal 4:6 ("And because you are children, God has sent the Spirit of his Son into our hearts, crying, 'Abba! Father!'"). In neither verse do Christians "pray" ἀββά; rather, they "cry" ἀββά (κράζομεν ἀββὰ ὁ πατήρ in Romans; κρᾶζον ἀββὰ ὁ πατήρ in Galatians).

109. See C. H. Dodd, *Historical Tradition in the Fourth Gospel* (Cambridge: Cambridge University Press, 1963), 65–66; Joel B. Green, "Jesus on the Mount of Olives (Luke 22.39–46)," *JSNT* 26 (1986): 29–48; Karl Georg Kuhn, "Jesus in Gethsemane," *EvT* 12 (1952): 260–85; J. Warren Hollerna, *The Synoptic Gethsemane: A Critical Study* (AnGreg 191; Rome: Università Gregoriana, 1973), 181–93.

110. This is the traditional interpretation; see Theodoret of Cyrus, *Comm. Heb.* ad loc. (PG 82:712D–714A); Grotius, *Opera omnia theologica*, 2:1025; Bengel, *Gnomon Novi Testamenti*, 2:420–21. Some, however, have thought of both Gethsemane and the cross, or of the passion as a whole; see Matthew Poole, *Annotations on the Holy Bible* (3 vols.; London: Henry G. Bohn, 1846), 3:828; David G. Peterson, *Hebrews and Perfection: An Examination of the Concept of Perfection in the Epistle to the Hebrews* (SNTSMS 47; Cambridge: Cambridge University Press, 1982), 86–94. It is much less common to think only of the cross, although see Christopher Richardson, "The Passion: Reconsidering Hebrews 5.7–8," in *A Cloud of Witnesses: The Theology of Hebrews in Its Ancient Contexts* (ed. Richard Bauckham et al.; London: T & T Clark, 2008), 51–67; James Swetnam, "The Crux at Hebrews 5,7–8," *Bib* 81 (2000): 347–61. According to Harold Attridge, "It is impossible to know what reminiscence of Jesus, if any, inspired this verse"; he does add, however, that "it is certainly unlikely that the description refers to some specific episode of Jesus at prayer unconnected with his passion," and that it "may derive from some divergent Gethsemane tradition" (*The Epistle to the Hebrews* [ed. Helmut Koester; Hermeneia; Philadelphia: Fortress, 1989], 148). Others who see in Heb 5:7–8 an interpretation of some version of the Gethsemane story include Claire Clivaz, "Hebrews 5.7, Jesus' Prayer on the Mount of Olives and Jewish Christianity: Hearing Early Christian Voices in Canonical and Apocryphal Texts," in *Cloud of Witnesses* (ed. Bauckham et al.), 187–209; Peterson, *Hebrews and Perfection*, 86–96. I remain attracted to the proposal that Heb 5:7, where Jesus apparently (although this is disputed) asks to be saved from death and is heard (at the resurrection?) because of his submission, stands midway between Mark 14:32–42, where Jesus balks at his fate and is not answered, and John 12:23, 27–28; 14:30–31, where Jesus declines to ask to be spared from death and a voice from heaven responds. This is the view held by Joachim Jeremias, "Hebräer 5,7–10," in *Abba: Studien zur neutestamentlichen Theologie und Zeitgeschichte* (Göttingen: Vandenhoeck & Ruprecht, 1966), 319–23.

111. See John 12:27 ("Now my soul is troubled. And what should I say—'Father, save me from this hour'? No, it is for this reason that I have come to this hour"); 13:21 ("Jesus was troubled in spirit"); 18:11 ("Jesus said to Peter, 'Put your sword back into its sheath. Am I not to drink the cup that the Father has given me?'"). See discussion in Raymond E. Brown, "John and the Synoptic Gospels: A Comparison," in *New Testament Essays* (Garden City, NY: Doubleday, 1968), 246–53; Richard Feldmeier, *Die Krisis des Gottessohnes: Die Gethsemaneerzählung als Schlüssel der Markuspassion* (WUNT 2/21; Tübingen: Mohr Siebeck, 1987), 39–49; Schleritt, *Passionsbericht*, 332–33. The sentences in John may derive from an interpretation of Gethsemane that put all the emphasis upon "not what I want, but what you want."

The verb κράζω is not a Pauline favorite. Only one other time does the apostle use it, in Rom 9:27, where it has nothing to do with prayer. This, plus the fact that κράζω twice introduces the same phrase, ἀββὰ ὁ πατήρ, a phrase that contains an Aramaic word (אבא), suggests debt to tradition.[112] This is all the more so as the designation for God is neither ἀββά alone nor ὁ πατήρ alone nor ὁ πατὴρ ἀββά but instead ἀββὰ ὁ πατήρ. This last is precisely what we find in Mark 14:36, which is the only verse in the extant Jesus tradition to preserve the Aramaic אבא, transliterated as ἀββά. Maybe, then, Rom 8:15 and Gal 4:6 betray Paul's knowledge of the story in Gethsemane, especially since several of the prominent themes of Mark 14:32–42—suffering (14:33–34), death (θάνατος [14:34]), weakness (ἀσθενής [14:38]), flesh versus spirit (σάρξ and πνεῦμα [14:38])—reappear in the immediate context of Rom 8:15: suffering in 8:17, 18, 35; death (θάνατος, θανατόω, νεκρός) in 8:2, 6, 10–11, 13, 36, 38; weakness (ἀσθενέω, ἀσθένεια) in 8:3, 26; flesh versus spirit (σάρξ versus πνεῦμα) in 8:1–5, 8–16.

Matthew Henry asked why Paul, in Rom 8:15, has both "Abba" and "Father." Henry returned this answer: "Because Christ said so in prayer (Mark xiv.36), Abba, Father: and we have received the Spirit of the Son."[113] One suspects that modern scholars often fail to discern in Paul's ἀββά an echo of Gethsemane because, rightly or wrongly, they think of ἀββά as characteristic of Jesus' speech as a whole. Yet the fact remains that the Jesus tradition, as we have it in Greek, retains this Aramaic word only once, in Mark 14:36. Perhaps this was already true in Paul's day.

One might object that κράζω is absent from Mark 14:32–42 and its parallels. But the urgency of Paul's κράζω—it "implies an intensity of feeling or fervor of expression"[114]—well suits the description of Jesus in Mark 14:32–42: he does not pray serenely but rather is "distressed," "agitated," and "deeply grieved," so much so that he throws himself upon the ground (Mark 14:33–35). Hebrews 5:7–8, moreover, in its apparent précis of Jesus' experience in Gethsemane, employs κραυγή, from the same root as κραυγάζω/κράζω: "In the days of his flesh, Jesus offered up prayers and supplications, with loud cries [κραυγῆς] and tears, to the one who was able to save him from death, and he was heard because of his reverent submission."[115]

112. James D. G. Dunn (*Romans 1–8* [WBC 38A; Nashville: Thomas Nelson, 1988], 453) speaks of a "distinctive formula" and puts the verses side by side:
πνεῦμα υἱοθεσίας ἐν ᾧ κράζομεν, Ἀββὰ ὁ πατήρ (Rom 8:15)
τὸ πνεῦμα τοῦ υἱοῦ αὐτοῦ . . . κρᾶζον, Ἀββὰ ὁ πατήρ (Gal 4:6)

113. Matthew Henry, *Acts to Revelation* (vol. 6 of *Commentary on the Whole Bible*; Old Tappan, NJ: Fleming H. Revell, n.d.), at Rom 8:15. Cf. Haymo of Halberstadt, *Exp. Rom.* ad loc. (PL 117:430B-C); Grotius, *Opera omnia theologica*, 2:858; Poole, *Annotations*, 3:304.

114. So Dunn, *Romans 1–8*, 461. Compare its use in, for example, LXX Ps 4:3; 16:6; 17:6; 31:3.

115. Hebrews also uses the word σάρξ ("flesh") and speaks of Jesus being a υἱός ("son"), whereas Paul, in his possible allusions to the story of Gethsemane, speaks of his own σάρξ

c. Col 4:2 contains a dual imperative: τῇ προσευχῇ προσκαρτερεῖτε, γρηγο-
ροῦντες ("in prayer continue, watching"). Paul does not often use γρηγορέω;
in fact, it turns up elsewhere in his letters only in 1 Cor 16:3; 1 Thess 5:6, 10.
The verb is, however, prominent in Mark's story of Gethsemane, where it
occurs three times, twice as an imperative: 14:34, 37, 38. The other verb that
dominates Mark's story of Jesus in prayerful distress is προσεύχομαι, which
appears four times, once as an imperative (14:32, 35, 38, 39). In fact, it is
joined with γρηγορέω in 14:38: γρηγορεῖτε καὶ προσεύχεσθε, "watch and pray"
(cf. Matt 26:41). This twofold exhortation is quite close to the compound
injunction in Col 4:2.

Is this simply coincidence? Perhaps not. A *TLG* search reveals that γρηγορέω is juxtaposed to προσεύχομαι or προσευχή only in Mark 14:38 (= Matt
26:41); Col 4:2; and Christian texts familiar with Paul and the Gospels. For a
second time, then, we find in Paul's writings a rare phrase or idiom that has
its counterpart in the story of Jesus in Gethsemane.

d. In Rom 15:2–3, which has in view the passion, the apostle says that
Christ did not please himself (see above, p. 406). The same idea reappears
in 1 Cor 10:33–11:1: "I try to please everyone in everything I do, not seeking
my own advantage, but that of many, so that they may be saved. Be imitators of me, as I am of Christ." In not pleasing himself, Paul is imitating
Jesus.

The understanding of Jesus in these two Pauline texts agrees with what
we read in Mark 14:32–42. In the latter, Jesus is divided within himself.
There are two wills at play, his will and God's will, and they do not initially
coincide: "He . . . prayed that, if it were possible, the hour might pass from
him" (v. 35). The whole point of the story is that although Jesus for a time
shrank before his impending crucifixion—he was "distressed and agitated"
and confessed, "I am deeply grieved, even to death" (vv. 33–34)—he decided,
in the end, to embrace his wretched fate: "not what I want, but what you
want" (v. 36). In short, Mark depicts a Jesus who, facing death, did not please
himself, which is what Paul says that his Lord did. One is not surprised to
find N. T. Wright claiming that Paul, in Rom 15:2–3, "assumes . . . that his
hearers are familiar with the basic story of Jesus, perhaps with oral traditions of such scenes as Gethsemane in which the Messiah shrank from his
fate."[116] Nor is it surprising that many centuries before Wright, Theodoret
of Cyrus, when considering Rom 15:2–3, also thought of Gethsemane: "The
Master himself did not seek his own but gave himself over to death for our
salvation. For from the passion we hear of his praying and saying, 'Father,

---

("flesh" [Rom 8:1–5, 8–16; 2 Cor 12:7]) and of Christians being God's υἱοί ("sons" [Rom 8:14;
Gal 4:6]).

116. N. T. Wright, "Romans," in *The New Interpreter's Bible*, vol. 10 (ed. Leander E. Keck;
Nashville: Abingdon, 2002), 745.

if it is possible, let this cup pass from me; yet not what I want but what you want.'"[117]

e. The apostle, who more than once presents himself as the imitator of his Lord (1 Cor 11:1; 1 Thess 1:6), thinks of his life as "a recapitulation of the life-pattern shown forth in Christ."[118] We have seen how this is the case especially with regard to the passion. Paul is "always carrying in the body the death of Jesus" (2 Cor 4:10), and he aspires to share in "his sufferings by becoming like him in his death" (Phil 3:10).[119] Like Christ, the apostle has been persecuted (1 Thess 1:6; cf. Rom 8:17), crucified (Rom 6:5–6; Gal 2:19; 5:24; 6:14), inflicted with scars (Gal 6:17), and buried (Rom 6:4; Col 2:12). To suggest, then, as I have in the previous pages, that he may also think of himself as being like Jesus in Gethsemane is just to add one more member to the series. In other words, to propose that 2 Cor 12:7–9 resonates with the story of Jesus praying before his arrest is to set the passage within a larger Pauline pattern.[120]

f. According to 2 Cor 12:7–9, Paul's passionate, threefold prayer was occasioned by something that, he says, was given "to torment me" (ἵνα με κολαφίζῃ). The verb κολαφίζω is not common in the New Testament. Paul uses it elsewhere only in 1 Cor 4:11, where it retains its literal sense, which is "strike sharply" or "beat": "To the present hour we are hungry and thirsty, we are poorly clothed and beaten [κολαφιζόμενοι] and homeless." In 1 Pet 2:20, the verb describes the suffering of Christian slaves, whose behavioral paradigm is the suffering and crucified Jesus:

If you endure when you are beaten [κολαφιζόμενοι] for doing wrong, what credit is that? But if you endure when you do right and suffer for it, you have God's

---

117. Theodoret of Cyrus, *Comm. Rom.* ad loc. (PG 82:809). See also Ambrosiaster, *Comm. Rom.* ad loc. (CSEL 81/1:455–56).

118. Richard B. Hays, "Christology and Ethics in Galatians," *CBQ* 49 (1987): 280.

119. See further Richard B. Hays, *The Moral Vision of the New Testament: Community, Cross, New Creation; A Contemporary Introduction to New Testament Ethics* (San Francisco: HarperSanFrancisco, 1996), 27–32.

120. One should also not neglect that other early Christians draw parallels between Jesus' passion and the suffering and martyrdom of others. Acts 7:54–60 has Stephen utter a dying prayer that recalls Jesus' last words (Luke 23:34, 46). In Ign. *Rom.* 6.3, the author expresses the desire "to be an imitator of the suffering of my God." In Pol. *Phil.* 8:2, Christians are enjoined to "become imitators" of Christ's "patient endurance," and are further urged, "if we should suffer for the sake of his name, let us glorify him." In *Mart. Pol.* 1:1–2 the author speaks of "a martyrdom in accord with the gospel," specifying that Polycarp, when "handed over," behaved "as the Lord did"; and the stabbing of Polycarp at his execution, after which a dove and blood come from his side, may be intended as an echo of John 19:34 (*Mart. Pol.* 16:1). See Michael W. Holmes, "The Martyrdom of Polycarp and the New Testament Passion Narratives," in *Trajectories through the New Testament and the Apostolic Fathers* (ed. Andrew F. Gregory and Christopher M. Tuckett; Oxford: Oxford University Press, 2005), 407–32. The Christian redaction of *T. Ab.* 20, in narrating the death of the patriarch, borrows motifs from the passion stories of Luke and John; see Dale C. Allison Jr., *The Testament of Abraham* (CEJL; Berlin: de Gruyter, 2003), 386.

approval. For to this you have been called, because Christ also suffered for you, leaving you an example, so that you should follow in his steps. . . . When he was abused, he did not return abuse; when he suffered, he did not threaten; but he entrusted himself to the one who judges justly. He himself bore our sins in his body on the cross. (1 Pet 2:20–24)

Whether or not 1 Peter implies that Jesus himself was beaten, Mark 14:65 and Matt 26:67 say it plainly. The former reads, "Some began to spit on him, to blindfold him, and to strike [κολαφίζειν] him." If Paul's pre-Markan passion narrative already used this verb of Jesus, the parallels between apostle and Lord already cataloged would have one more member: both disciple and Lord were "tormented."

So much, then, for the evidence that Paul knew a pre-Markan passion narrative.

Some of it is imperfect, and sometimes in making my case I have not refrained from conjecture. So I do not claim to have come within sight of the shore of certainty. Still, we have seen enough to make the bet much better than fifty-fifty. We should not lose sight of the occasional nature of Paul's correspondence, nor of the fact that he often presupposed much that he either briefly recapitulated or just alluded to, as in 1 Cor 11:23 ("on the night when he was betrayed").[121] We know far less about Paul, his churches, and their traditions than modern scholars often presume. We can be sure that not everything the apostle knew or believed about Jesus is on display in his letters. Indeed, I would hazard that most of what he believed about Jesus cannot be evidenced in a small collection of occasional, ad hoc correspondence.[122]

I am inclined to think that my major conclusion, that Paul knew some sort of passion narrative, so far from being surprising, is only what common historical sense should advocate. Could Paul have retained anyone's attention by incessantly repeating bare kerygmatic statements or story-shorn assertions? Would he, if unable to tell stories about Jesus and elucidate the circumstances of his scandalous death by crucifixion, have succeeded as an evangelist and

121. See Margaret M. Mitchell, "Rhetorical Shorthand in Pauline Argumentation: The Functions of 'the Gospel' in the Corinthian Correspondence," in *Gospel in Paul: Studies on Corinthians, Galatians and Romans for Richard N. Longenecker* (ed. L. Ann Jervis and Peter Richardson; JSNTSup 108; Sheffield: Sheffield Academic Press, 1994), 63–88.

122. Worth pondering is this observation made by Michael W. Pahl: "If it were not for the evidence of 1 Corinthians, one could easily conclude that Paul was simply ignorant or apathetic regarding the Jesus tradition. If 1 Corinthians were all we had from Paul's hand, one could conversely conclude that the Jesus tradition was relatively important in Paul's theological and ethical thinking and discourse" (*Discerning the "Word of the Lord": The "Word of the Lord" in 1 Thessalonians 4:15* [LNTS 389; London: T & T Clark, 2009], 67–68).

church leader?[123] Were Paul and the first Christians inexplicably incurious regarding what took place before and after the meal at which Jesus reportedly spoke the words of institution? Certainly all the ingredients for good stories were at hand—a hero, a conflict, a dramatic ending. So if believers ever lacked such stories, would they not swiftly have invented some? Do we know of any religious communities around the ancient Mediterranean that did not love to tell and listen to tales about their gods and heroes?[124] As these questions almost answer themselves, I agree with Calvin Roetzel: "We must assume that when Paul preached he told the story of Jesus, and when he wrote occasional letters to the churches there was no need to retell the story."[125]

To all this I wish to add three brief, final points regarding Paul and traditions of Jesus' passion. First, the apostle spent time in Jerusalem not long after the crucifixion, and he knew some people who were there when Jesus was (Gal 1:18–19; 2:9). So if Paul desired to learn anything of the purported circumstances of Jesus' demise, he would have been in a position to hear others who were around at the time tell their stories.[126] We cannot, of course, say whether he took advantage of the opportunity, but we do know that he had it.

Second, several modern scholars have contended that a pre-Markan passion narrative circulated already in the 30s or 40s.[127] Although I find most of their arguments more intriguing than probative, certainly nothing requires a date after the middle of the first century, so the proposition that Paul knew such a narrative, presumably from oral cultic performance,[128] is not problematic on chronological grounds.[129] In fact, Paul himself supplies evidence, in my view, that a passion narrative of some sort was extant at least by the 40s.[130]

123. See Hengel, "Das Mahl in der Nacht," 454–55; Koester, "Memory of Jesus' Death," 347; idem, *From Jesus to the Gospels*, 221.

124. One might wish to broaden the generalization: the human being in general is *homo narrans*. As Alisdair MacIntyre observes, "Man is in his actions and practice, as well as in his fictions, essentially a story-telling animal" (*After Virtue: A Study in Moral Theory* [Notre Dame, IN: University of Notre Dame Press, 1981], 201). The implication is that we are also story-listening animals.

125. Calvin J. Roetzel, *Paul: The Man and the Myth* (Minneapolis: Fortress, 1999), 95.

126. Gal 1:18 may reflect this fact; see James D. G. Dunn, "The Relationship between Paul and Jerusalem according to Galatians 1 and 2," *NTS* 28 (1982): 463–66; idem, "Once More—Gal 1:18: ἱστορῆσαι Κηφᾶν," *ZNW* 76 (1985): 138–39.

127. For example, Pesch, *Markusevangelium*, 2:1–27; Gerd Theissen, "A Major Narrative Unit (the Passion Story) and the Jerusalem Community in the Years 40–50 C.E.," in *Gospels in Context*, 166–99.

128. Useful here is Aitken, *Jesus' Death*.

129. For the interesting argument that certain chronological notes in Mark's passion narrative preserve the idiom of Jews in the environs of pre-70 Jerusalem, see Troy W. Martin, "Watch during the Watches (Mark 13:35)," *JBL* 120 (2001): 685–701.

130. For the psychological need for stories about Jesus' crucifixion soon after the fact, see Dale C. Allison Jr., *Resurrecting Jesus: The Earliest Christian Traditions and Its Interpreters* (New York: T & T Clark, 2005), 364–75; Chris Keith and Tom Thatcher, "The Scar of the Cross: The Violence Ratio and the Earliest Christian Memories of Jesus," in *Jesus, the Voice,*

Third, as far as I can see, Paul says nothing that contradicts Mark's account. A few have supposed that 1 Cor 5:7 ("Our paschal lamb, Christ, has been sacrificed") supports John's chronology of the passion, not Mark's. This, however, probably reads too much into Paul's words. In any case, since Mark sets Jesus' crucifixion during the week of Passover, one could hardly make much of the difference.

Death and Memory

It is one thing to decide that Paul probably knew a passion narrative, another to determine what traditions, if any, whether attested by Paul or Mark or some other writer, might reflect real events. What should we make of that issue?

It is hard to return an evenhanded answer. In trying to do so, I cannot circumvent chapter 1, which catalogs the typical transgressions of human memory. We now know that "recollection of the personal past is (1) essentially a reconstruction . . . (2) prompted by a person's affective states and ongoing beliefs and goals, and (3) constituted by the sociocultural world of the rememberer. . . . Attention to the features of experience is selective. Furthermore, a process of revision in light of one's beliefs and expectations is almost immediate, if not simultaneous. From the first, memories are shaped . . . fitted, constructed."[131] Fully absorbing all this cannot but tame our historical ambitions.

At the same time, this should not be the end of the matter. Not only have I, throughout the course of this book, urged—I hope with some success—that the Synoptic Gospels are not bereft of recollection of the historical Jesus, but people in all cultures typically respond to death by seeking out and telling stories about a deceased friend or relative. Further, memories and imaginations, shortly after a death, often converge upon a life's end, upon "the events leading up to the loss."[132] The newly bereaved commonly focus upon "the actions taken by them or by the dead person in the days and hours before the death."[133] This is especially true when death has been unexpected, premature, or violent.[134] A tragic and cruel death draws attention to itself in powerfully

---

and the Text: Beyond the Oral and the Written Gospel (ed. Tom Thatcher; Waco, TX: Baylor University Press, 2008), 197–214.

131. Robert W. Schrauf, "¡Costalero Quiero Ser! Autobiographical Memory and the Oral Life Story of a Holy Week Brother in Southern Spain," *Ethos* 25 (1997): 429.

132. Murray Parkes, *Bereavement: Studies of Grief in Adult Life* (New York: International Universities Press, 1972), 40.

133. Marion Gibson, *Order from Chaos: Responding to Traumatic Events* (Birmingham, UK: Venture, 1998), 63.

134. See Jane Littlewood, *Aspects of Grief: Bereavement in Adult Life* (London: Tavistock/Routledge, 1992), 46 ("Events leading up to the death may be obsessively reviewed in an increasingly desperate attempt to understand what has happened"); Edward K. Rynearson, *Retelling*

emotional ways. Indeed, after a violent death "the story of the dying may become preoccupying," so that it "eclipses the retelling of their living—the way
they died takes precedence over the way they lived."[135] If it was not otherwise
with Jesus and those who knew him, then doubtless some of the traditions
behind the passion narratives had their genesis very early on, which surely ups
the odds of their containing some true-to-life memory.[136]

Violent Death (Philadelphia: Brunner-Routledge, 2001), xiv ("The continued retelling of a violent
death is fundamental to anyone who loved the deceased").

135. See Rynearson, *Violent Death*, ix, x.

136. Four additional factors are perhaps—I do not say probably—relevant. (1) On the assumption that some of the events at the end of Jesus' life took his immediate followers by surprise,
it may matter that incidents incongruent with prior expectations are better remembered than
other events, probably either because they demand explanation and so rehearsal, or because
encoding requires additional time; see Reid Hastie, "Memory for Behavioral Information that
Confirms or Contradicts a Personality Impression," in *Person Memory: The Cognitive Basis of
Social Perception* (ed. Reid Hastie et al.; Hillsdale, NJ: Lawrence Erlbaum Associates, 1980),
155–78; idem, "Schematic Principles in Human Memory," in *Social Cognition* (ed. E. Tory
Higgins, C. Peter Herman, and Mark P. Zanna; Ontario Symposium 1; Hillsdale, NJ: Lawrence
Erlbaum Associates, 1981), 39–88; Pascale Michelon et al., "Neural Correlates of Incongruous
Visual Information: An Event-Related fMRI Study," *NeuroImage* 19 (2003): 1612–26. (2) The passion narrative runs together a series of closely connected, causally related stories, and "the
memorability of an event increases when that event is related to other events at the time of the
encoding" (John F. Kihlstrom, "Memory Research: The Convergence of Theory and Practice,"
in *Theory in Context* [vol. 1 of *Basic and Applied Memory Research*; ed Douglas J. Herrmann
et al.; Mahwah, NJ: Lawrence Erlbaum Associates, 1996], 8). (3) Memory often does better
with emotion-laden events, including traumatic or violent events; see David C. Rubin and Marc
Kozin, "Vivid Memories," *Cognition* 16 (1984): 81–95. Presumably, this facilitates avoidance of
trauma-inducing situations in the future; see Stephen Porter and Kristine A. Peace, "The Scars
of Memory: A Prospective, Longitudinal Investigation of the Consistency of Traumatic and
Positive Memories in Adulthood," *Psychological Science* 18 (2007): 435–41; Anne E. van Giezen
et al., "Consistency of Memory for Emotionally Arousing Events: A Review of Prospective and
Experimental Studies," *Clinical Psychology Review* 25 (2005): 935–53. Yet at the same time and
so paradoxically, trauma sometimes (although far less often than Freud presumed) inhibits recall;
see Sven-Åke Christianson and Elizabeth F. Loftus, "Memory for Traumatic Events," *Applied
Cognitive Psychology* 1 (1987): 225–39. (4) At least among modern individuals, a "reminiscence
bump" exists on either side of the age of twenty: if we are over the age of forty, we remember best,
beyond recent items, knowledge acquired between the ages of ten and thirty; see Martin Conway
and Christopher W. Pleydell-Pearce, "The Construction of Autobiographical Memories in the
Self-Memory System," *Psychological Review* 107 (2000): 277–80; David C. Rubin, Tamara A.
Rahhal, and Leonard W. Poon, "Things Learned in Early Adulthood Are Remembered Best,"
Memory and Cognition 26 (1998): 3–19. This appears to be a cross-cultural fact (see Martin A.
Conway et al., "A Cross-Cultural Investigation of Autobiographical Memory: On the Universality
and Cultural Variation of the Reminiscence Bump," *Journal of Cross-Cultural Psychology* 36
[2005]: 739–49), so it might have some relevance for the Jesus tradition. The call stories (Mark
1:16–20; Matt 8:18–22 // Luke 9:57–60 [Q]; Luke 9:61–62) and the sayings about familial conflict
(Matt 10:34–36 // Luke 12:51–53 [Q]; Matt 10:37 // Luke 14:26 [Q]) imply that the average age
of Jesus' itinerant followers presumably was somewhere around twenty or even less. So if they
ever recalled events from the ministry, those events would either have been from the relatively
recent past or from the period of their "reminiscence bump."

This, however, is only a very large and conditional generalization. Does the evidence allow us to say anything more specific?

Some have urged that at least a few of the stories are likely to mirror real events because they cannot be derived from the Jewish Bible and because there is no obvious motivation for Christian invention:[137] conscription of a passerby, Simon of Cyrene, to carry Jesus' cross;[138] crucifixion by order of Pontius Pilate;[139] execution at a place known as Golgotha;[140] the presence of female followers at the cross;[141] burial by a Jewish official, Joseph of Arimathea.[142] To my mind, the argument is substantive; and since I have not, with regard to the items just listed, run across effective counterarguments, I accept them as likely historical.

137. Compare the common argument of Buddhist scholars that some of the traditions about Gautama's life are likely to be authentic because they seem to be unmotivated by Buddhist ideology—for example, his birth in the Sakya clan (not the most distinguished), his conflict with a cousin regarding leadership of his movement, and his death from a tainted meal.

138. Mark 15:21. Additional considerations concerning this story: (i) John's assertion that Jesus carried his own cross (19:17) is probably a denial, for theological reasons, of the Simon tradition. If so, John indirectly attests the story. (ii) Mark's note that Simon was "the father of Alexander and Rufus," which Matthew and Luke dropped, is often viewed as evidence that Simon was not a fictional character: presumably, his sons were known to Mark's audience. (iii) On a first-century CE ossuary discovered by E. L. Sukenik in the Kidron Valley in 1941 and published by N. Avigad ("A Depository of Inscribed Ossuaries," *IEJ* 12 [1962]: 9–11), "Alexander son of Simon" appears in Greek on the front and back, and on the lid in Hebrew is "of Alexander" in Greek as well as אלכסנדרוס קרנית. The Hebrew may mean "Alexander the Cyrenian," and this ossuary may have held the bones of Simon of Cyrene. See Craig A. Evans, *Jesus and the Ossuaries* (Waco, TX: Baylor University Press, 2003), 94–96. (iv) Invention on the basis of Jesus' saying about taking up one's cross and following him (Matt 10:38 // Luke 14:27 [Q]; Mark 8:34; *Gos. Thom.* 55) is far-fetched. Not only is Simon's task involuntary, but the evangelists do not appear to exploit the possible link. For further discussion, see William John Lyons, "The Hermeneutics of Fictional Black and Factual Red: The Markan Simon of Cyrene and the Quest for the Historical Jesus," *JSHJ* 4 (2006): 139–54.

139. See above, pp. 233–40; also Reinbold, *Prozess*, 73–78.

140. Mark 15:22; John 19:17. The place is otherwise unknown. Eusebius says that "it is shown in Jerusalem north of Mount Zion" (*Onom.* 365/74:19). The Greek Γολγοθᾶ represents the Aramaic גלגלתא or Hebrew גלגלת ("skull") (cf. Judg 9:53; 2 Kgs 9:35; Matt 27:33; Mark 15:22; Luke 23:33; John 19:17; *T. Sol.* 12:3). The legend identifying Golgotha with the site of Adam's skull does not go back to New Testament times.

141. Mark 15:40–41; John 19:25. See above, pp. 390–91. The Jesus Seminar voted this "pink," indicating probable historicity; for their reasons, see Robert W. Funk and The Jesus Seminar, *The Acts of Jesus: The Search for the Authentic Deeds of Jesus* (San Francisco: HarperSan-Francisco, 1998), 158.

142. Mark 15:42–46; John 19:38–42; *Gos. Pet.* 2:3; 6:23–24. On this see Allison, *Resurrecting Jesus*, 352–63; Reinbold, *Bericht*, 277–80. According to Jodi Magness, "the Gospel accounts of Jesus' burial are largely consistent with the archaeological evidence. Although archaeology does not prove there was a follower of Jesus named Joseph of Arimathea or that Pontius Pilate granted his request for Jesus' body, the Gospel accounts describing Jesus' removal from the cross and burial are consistent with archaeological evidence and with Jewish law" ("Jesus' Tomb—What Did It Look Like?" in *Where Christianity Was Born: A Collection from the Biblical Archaeology Society* [ed. Hershel Shanks; Washington, DC: Biblical Archaeology Society, 2006], 224).

Others would go further than this. Persuaded, as George Orwell famously put it, that "a man who gives a good account of himself is probably lying,"[143] some historians have also inferred that certain traditions remember rightly because they fail to flatter either Jesus or the disciples: Judas's betrayal of Jesus;[144] Jesus' vacillation in Gethsemane;[145] Peter's denial;[146] Jesus' cry from the cross.[147] Although it seems imprudent to write off the reported actions

143. George Orwell, "Benefit of Clergy: Some Notes on Salvador Dali," in *Dickens, Dali and Others: Studies in Popular Culture* (ed. George Orwell; Cornwall, NY: Cornwall Press, 1946), 170.

144. Mark 14:10–11, 43–46; John 18:2–3. For E. P. Sanders (*Jesus and Judaism* [Philadelphia: Fortress, 1985], 99–101), the historicity of Judas's betrayal of Jesus commends itself because, among other things, it was an "embarrassment" to early Christians. Perhaps he is right. In any case, the motif that Jesus foresaw his betrayal and foreknew his betrayer (Mark 14:17–21; John 13:21–30) confirms that the story of Judas distressed some from an early time; and as Origen (*Cels.* 2.11) reveals, it did so later, too. See further Reinbold, *Bericht*, 234–36.

145. Mark 14:32–42. For a review of the arguments pro and con and a verdict pro, see Feldmeier, *Krisis*, 133–40. For reasons for rejecting historicity, see Martin Dibelius, "Gethsemane," in *Botschaft und Geschichte: Gesammelte Aufsätze* (ed. Günther Bornkamm; 2 vols.; Tübingen: Mohr Siebeck, 1953–1956), 1:258–71. That the story was at least well known is clear (see p. 416), and that it has troubled some Christians is without dispute. John 12:27; 18:11 revise the tradition to make Jesus look better (see n. 111); and in one place Origen raises the possibility—a possibility for him, not us—that "my soul is deeply grieved, even to death" means "my apostles are deeply grieved, even to death" (*Princ.* 2.8.5). In another place, Origen (*Hom. Jer.* 14.6) suggests that Jesus' soul was troubled but that the Logos was untroubled, an idea that many later theologians, including the Cappadocians, adopted. Justin (*Dial.* 99) tries to dispel the notion that Jesus' prayer reveals ignorance of his upcoming suffering and death. In the *Acts Pil.* 4(20):1, Pilate says that Jesus "is a man, and I heard him saying, 'My soul is very sorrowful, even to death.'" Compare the polemic of Celsus reported in Origen, *Cels.* 2.24: Gethsemane shows that Jesus was afraid of death. But we must be careful with argument from Christian discomfiture: because doctrine developed, what bothered later believers may not have bothered earlier believers. See further n. 150.

146. Mark 14:54, 66–72; John 18:15–18, 25–27. Dieter Sänger ("'Auf Betreiben der Vornehmsten unseres Volkes' (Iosephus ant. Iud. XVIII 64): Zur Frage einer jüdische Beteiligung an der Kreuzigung Jesu," in *Das Urchristentum in seiner literarischen Geschichte: Festschrift für Jürgen Becker zum 65. Geburtstag* [ed. Ulrich Mell and Ulrich B. Müller; BZNW 100; Berlin: de Gruyter, 1999], 17–18) argues for historicity on these grounds. The argument goes all the way back to Origen: if the disciples "had not been lovers of truth but rather, as Celsus has it, creators of fictions, they would not have represented Peter as denying nor the disciples of Jesus as being scandalized" (*Cels.* 2.15). Many, however, have had doubts. Maurice Goguel (*The Life of Jesus* [trans. Olive Wyon; New York: Macmillan, 1933], 483–92) argued that Peter could not have held high office in the church if he had denied his Lord, that Paul in Gal 2 would have mentioned the denial if he had known of it, and that although no one could have created the story out of nothing, the prediction in Mark 14:26–31 sufficed for this. Compare the skepticism of Crossan: "I do not consider Peter's explicit denials to be historical and conclude that Mark created them as part of his own theological program for Christians who had to see an *ideal* model in Jesus and a *hopeful* model in Peter. Loss of nerve is not irrevocable, and even denial under persecution is not unforgivable. Markan Christians who had denied Jesus under duress could still be forgiven just as Peter had been before them" (*Who Killed Jesus?* 105).

147. Mark 15:34; *Gos. Pet.* 5:19. The words of Ps 22:1 are conspicuously absent from Luke and John, who preferred to give Jesus different last words—"Father, into your hands I commend

of Judas and Peter as nothing save fiction,[148] I am less comfortable with this sort of reasoning. If anything were too embarrassing, one might expect the tradition to have dropped it. Further, Christians drew heavily upon the Psalter when writing up the passion, and the cry of dereliction in Mark 15:34 is from Ps 22:1, while the words of distress in Gethsemane (Mark 14:34) echo other psalms (Ps 42:5–6, 11; 43:5).[149] It is also the case that both Mark 14:32–42 and 15:34 contribute to the stark pathos of Mark's moving passion narrative and are part and parcel of the drama.[150] So while "Let this cup pass" and "My God, my God, why have you forsaken me?" may have eventually become problems for christological dogma, it is far from obvious that they troubled Mark or his tradition.[151] For these reasons, I find it difficult to summon much conviction about the words attributed to Jesus in Mark 14:32–42; 15:34. Maybe he said something like them.[152] Maybe he did not.

Assent to Death

At this juncture, I do not want to discuss further whether this or that word or deed might mirror a historical event. I wish instead to return to the opening

---

my spirit" (Luke 23:46); "It is finished" (John 19:30)—and the potential embarrassment of the citation is visible in the ecclesiastical commentators, who offer such implausible interpretations as that the Father forsook Jesus only in that he gave his human substance up to death (so Tertullian, *Prax.* 30), or that "forsaken me" really meant (because Jesus was a Jew) "forsaken my people" (so Theophylact, *Comm. Matt.* ad loc. [PG 123:472]). Bultmann (*Synoptic Tradition*, 313), however, held that the tradition filled out the memory of an inarticulate cry (cf. Matt 27:50) with a verse from the Psalms.

148. On Judas, see above, pp. 68–69.

149. On this, see Ahearne-Kroll, *Psalms of Lament*, 66–69.

150. They also contribute to a David typology; see ibid., passim. Still instructive are the observations of Dibelius ("Gethsemane") on how well the story of Gethsemane fits its Markan context and the extent to which 14:32–42 reflects and would have been serviceable to early Christian piety.

151. On later ecclesiastical anxiety, see notes 145, 147. The cry of dereliction was also evidently not embarrassing to the author of P.Heid. inv. G 1359. That papyrus fragment, presumably an amulet, contains a list of comforting names along with Jesus' words from the cross as found in Matthew and Mark; see Adolf Deissmann, *Light from the Ancient East: The New Testament Illustrated by Recently Discovered Texts of the Graeco-Roman World* (trans. Lionel R. M. Strachan; rev. ed.; New York: George H. Doran, 1927), 405.

152. The standard argument against finding memory in Mark 14:32–42, that the disciples could not have heard or observed anything because they were asleep, has always struck me as less than decisive, even lame. (i) The exhortation to stay awake and watch is stylized, of obvious hortatory interest, and perhaps even redactional (there are strong links to Mark 13:33–37). (ii) If Jesus and a few disciples really went to Gethsemane, did all but Jesus irresistibly fall into slumber the second they entered the place? (iii) The ancients typically prayed not silently but rather out loud; see Pieter W. van der Horst, "Silent Prayer in Antiquity," *Numen* 41 (1994): 1–25. (iv) Mark 14:32–42 attributes to Jesus not a discourse but a scant few words.

chapter of this book, to the method there outlined, and show how it helps here.

A pattern runs throughout the early Christian texts regarding the death of Jesus, a pattern that I take to enshrine authentic memory. Before making my case, however, I first wish to quote, as a foil, some well-known words of Bultmann:

> The greatest embarrassment to the attempt to reconstruct a portrait of Jesus is the fact that we cannot know how Jesus understood his end, his death. It is symptomatic that it is practically universally assumed that he understood this as the organic or necessary conclusion to his activity. But how do we know this, when prophecies of the passion must be understood by critical research as *vaticinia ex eventu*? That Jesus, after learning of the Baptist's death, had to reckon with his own equally violent death is an improbable psychological construction, because Jesus clearly conceived his life in an entirely different fashion than did the Baptist from whom he distinguished himself (Matt. 11:16–19). . . . What is certain is that he was merely crucified by the Romans, and thus suffered the death of a political criminal. This death can scarcely be understood as an inherent and necessary consequence of his activity; rather it took place because his activity was misunderstood as a political activity. In that case it would have been—historically speaking—a meaningless fate. We cannot tell whether or how Jesus found meaning in it. We may not veil from ourselves the possibility that he suffered a collapse.[153]

These sentences, which no doubt speak for many, are too skeptical. We can know more about how Jesus approached his end than Bultmann allowed. Consider the following family of texts, which come from early Christian epistles and several Gospels:

1. Matt 10:38 // Luke 14:27 (Q); Mark 8:34; *Gos. Thom.* 55. Jesus purportedly enjoined his hearers to prepare for the possibility of martyrdom: "Whoever does not carry the cross and follow me cannot be my disciple."
2. Matt 10:39 // Luke 17:33 (Q); Mark 8:35; John 12:25. These verses also call for accepting martyrdom if or when it comes: "Those who try to make their life secure will lose it, but those who lose their life will keep it."
3. Mark 8:31–33; 9:31; 10:33–34. Jesus purportedly foresaw his fate, spoke of it, and acquiesced to it: "The Son of Man is to be betrayed into human hands, and they will kill him" (cf. 2:20; 9:12; 12:6–8; 14:8, 27).
4. Mark 10:45. "The Son of Man came not to be served but to serve, and to give his life a ransom for many."

153. Rudolf Bultmann, "The Primitive Christian Kerygma and the Historical Jesus," in *The Historical Jesus and the Kerygmatic Christ: Essays on the New Quest of the Historical Jesus* (ed. Carl E. Braaten and Roy A. Harrisville; New York: Abingdon, 1964), 22–23.

5. Mark 14:17–21. Jesus anticipated that one of his own followers would betray him: "Truly I tell you, one of you will betray me, one who is eating with me" (cf. John 13:21–30).

6. Mark 14:32–42. Shortly before his arrest, Jesus resigned himself to death: "Abba, Father, for you all things are possible; remove this cup from me; yet, not what I want, but what you want."

7. Mark 14:43–50. Jesus did not resist arrest: "Have you come out with swords and clubs to arrest me as though I were a bandit? Day after day I was with you in the temple teaching, and you did not arrest me. But let the scriptures be fulfilled" (cf. John 18:1–9).

8. Mark 14:53–65. Jesus did not defend himself before the Jewish authorities: "Then the high priest stood up before them and asked Jesus, 'Have you no answer? What is it that they testify against you?' But he was silent and did not answer" (cf. John 18:13–24).

9. Mark 15:1–15. Jesus did not defend himself before Pilate: "Pilate asked him, 'Are you the King of the Jews?' He answered him, 'You say so.' Then the chief priests accused him of many things. Pilate asked him again, 'Have you no answer? See how many charges they bring against you.' But Jesus made no further reply, so that Pilate was amazed" (cf. John 18:28–19:16).

10. Matt 26:51–54. A disciple, drawing a sword to protect Jesus from those come to arrest him, was rebuked: "Put your sword back into its place; for all who take the sword will perish by the sword."

11. Luke 13:31–33. "At that very hour some Pharisees came and said to him, 'Get away from here, for Herod wants to kill you.' He said to them, 'Go and tell that fox for me, "Listen, I am casting out demons and performing cures today and tomorrow, and on the third day I finish my work. Yet today, tomorrow, and the next day I must be on my way, because it is impossible for a prophet to be killed outside of Jerusalem."'"

12. Luke 23:6–12. Jesus did not defend himself before Herod: "He questioned him at some length, but Jesus gave him no answer."

13. John 10:11–18. "The good shepherd lays down his life for the sheep. . . . I lay down my life for the sheep. . . . For this reason the Father loves me, because I lay down my life in order to take it up again. No one takes it from me, but I lay it down of my own accord. I have power to lay it down, and I have power to take it up again. I have received this command from my Father."

14. John 12:23–27. Jesus speaks about his death: "The hour has come for the Son of Man to be glorified. Very truly, I tell you, unless a grain of wheat falls into the earth and dies, it remains just a single grain; but if it dies, it bears much fruit. Those who love their life lose it, and those who hate their life in this world will keep it for eternal life. . . . Now

my soul is troubled. And what should I say—'Father, save me from this hour'? No, it is for this reason that I have come to this hour."

15. John 15:12–13. "This is my commandment, that you love one another as I have loved you. No one has greater love than this, to lay down one's life for one's friends."

16. John 16:5–10. "Now I am going to him who sent me; yet none of you asks me, 'Where are you going?' But because I have said these things to you, sorrow has filled your hearts. Nevertheless, I tell you the truth: it is to your advantage that I go away, for if I do not go away, the Advocate will not come to you; but if I go, I will send him to you. . . . I am going to the Father and you will see me no longer."

17. John 18:10–12. When Peter draws a sword and cuts off the ear of the slave Malchus, Jesus commands him: "Put your sword back into its sheath. Am I not to drink the cup that the Father has given me?"

18. Rom 5:18–19. "Therefore just as one man's trespass led to condemnation for all, so one man's act of righteousness leads to justification and life for all. For just as by the one man's disobedience the many were made sinners, so by the one man's obedience the many will be made righteous."[154]

19. Rom 15:1–3. "We who are strong ought to put up with the failings of the weak, and not to please ourselves. Each of us must please our neighbor for the good purpose of building up the neighbor. For Christ did not please himself; but, as it is written, 'The insults of those who insult you have fallen on me.'"

20. 1 Cor 11:23–26. "For I received from the Lord what I also handed on to you, that the Lord Jesus on the night when he was betrayed took a loaf of bread, and when he had given thanks, he broke it and said, 'This is my body that is for you. Do this in remembrance of me.' In the same way he took the cup also, after supper, saying, 'This cup is the new covenant in my blood. Do this, as often as you drink it, in remembrance of me'" (cf. Mark 14:22–25).

21. Gal 1:3–4. "The Lord Jesus Christ . . . gave himself for our sins."

22. Gal 2:20. "The Son of God . . . loved me and gave himself for me."

23. Eph 5:2. "Live in love, as Christ loved us and gave himself up for us, a fragrant offering and sacrifice to God."

24. Phil 2:7–8. Jesus "emptied himself, taking the form of a slave, being born in human likeness. And being found in human form, he humbled himself and became obedient to the point of death—even death on a cross" (cf. Rom 5:18–21).

25. Several passages in Paul, according to some modern scholarship, refer to the faith or faithfulness of Jesus (πίστις Ἰησοῦ), among them Rom 3:22,

154. See Jewett, *Romans*, 385–86.

26; Gal 2:16; 2:20; 3:22; Phil 3:9.[155] If they are right, then it is relevant that the context of most of these verses has to do with the saving death of Jesus (Rom 3:21–26; Gal 2:15–21; Phil 3:7–11). In other words, Jesus' faithfulness is in large measure his obedient death on a cross.[156]

26. 1 Tim 2:5–6. "Christ Jesus . . . gave himself a ransom for all."

27. 1 Tim 6:12–13. This line probably takes up liturgical language that made Jesus a model of faithfulness in the face of death: "Fight the good fight of the faith; take hold of the eternal life, to which you were called and for which you made the good confession in the presence of many witnesses. In the presence of God, who gives life to all things, and of Christ Jesus, who in his testimony before Pontius Pilate made the good confession, I charge you. . . ."[157]

28. Titus 2:14. "He it is who gave himself for us that he might redeem us from all iniquity."

29. Heb 5:7–10. "In the days of his flesh, Jesus offered up prayers and supplications, with loud cries and tears, to the one who was able to save him from death, and he was heard because of his reverent submission. Although he was a Son, he learned obedience through what he suffered; and having been made perfect, he became the source of eternal salvation for all who obey him, having been designated by God a high priest according to the order of Melchizedek."[158]

30. Heb 12:1–2. "Therefore, since we are surrounded by so great a cloud of witnesses, let us also lay aside every weight and the sin that clings so closely, and let us run with perseverance the race that is set before us, looking to Jesus the pioneer and perfecter of our faith, who for the sake of the joy that was set before him endured the cross, disregarding its shame, and has taken his seat at the right hand of the throne of God."

31. 1 Pet 2:20–24. "If you endure when you are beaten for doing wrong, what credit is that? But if you endure when you do right and suffer for

155. For a review of the discussion, see Ian G. Wallis, *The Faith of Jesus Christ in Early Christian Traditions* (SNTSMS 84; Cambridge: Cambridge University Press, 1984), 65–127; also the exchange between James D. G. Dunn and Richard Hays in Hays, *The Faith of Jesus Christ: The Narrative Substructure of Galatians 3:1–4:11* (2nd ed.; Grand Rapids: Eerdmans; Dearborn, MI: Dove Booksellers, 2002), 249–97.

156. Cf. Phil 2:8; Heb 12:2; Rev 1:5; 3:14. See further Luke Timothy Johnson, "Rom 3:21–26 and the Faith of Jesus," *CBQ* 44 (1982): 87–90; Sam K. Williams, *Jesus' Death as Saving Event: The Background and Origin of a Concept* (HDR 2; Missoula, MT: Scholars Press, 1975), 49–50.

157. According to William Mounce, the author is "referring to Jesus' perseverance in his mission, not only in his life . . . but especially in his death" (*Pastoral Epistles* [WBC 46; Nashville: Thomas Nelson, 2000], 358). See further I. Howard Marshall and Philip H. Towner, *A Critical and Exegetical Commentary on the Pastoral Epistles* (ICC; Edinburgh: T & T Clark, 1999), 662–63.

158. On this text see above, p. 417 n. 110.

it, you have God's approval. For to this you have been called, because Christ also suffered for you, leaving you an example, so that you should follow in his steps. 'He committed no sin, and no deceit was found in his mouth.' When he was abused, he did not return abuse; when he suffered, he did not threaten; but he entrusted himself to the one who judges justly. He himself bore our sins in his body on the cross."

These texts come from Q, Mark, M, L, John, *Thomas*, the authentic Paulines, 1 Timothy, Hebrews, and 1 Peter. They obviously reflect a very widespread belief: Jesus did not run from his death or otherwise resist it. On the contrary, anticipating his cruel end, he submitted to it, trusting that his unhappy fate was somehow for the good.

How should we evaluate this conviction, diffused throughout so many different traditions and so many different sources, including our earliest source, Paul?[159] We might dismiss it as so much theological wish fulfillment, observing that the catalog includes (i) logia of debated provenance (e.g., the passion predictions) and of presumably redactional origin (e.g., most or all of the sentences from John); (ii) stories of doubtful historicity (e.g., the interview with Herod); (iii) scenes indebted to prophetic proof-texting (e.g., Jesus' silence before the high priest and Pilate); and (iv) properly theological statements formulated for rhetorical ends (all the assertions in Paul's Epistles belong here). One might also appeal to the hesitation of Jesus in Gethsemane (Mark 14:32–42) and to the cry from the cross (Mark 15:34). Do these not, if authentic, reveal that Jesus was less than wholeheartedly committed to martyrdom?[160]

Against such a wholesale dismissal, the cry from the cross proves nothing. For even if Jesus experienced despair and voiced it in the words of Ps 22:1, that would tell us only about his disoriented state of mind following torture, nothing about his convictions before being arrested. As for Gethsemane, the passage as we have it depicts Jesus retaining his resolve, not losing it. "Remove this cup from me"

159. Jerome Murphy-O'Connor ("The Origins of Paul's Christology: From Thessalonians to Galatians," in *Christian Origins: Worship, Belief and Society. The Milltown Institute and the Irish Biblical Association Millennium Conference* [ed. Kieran J. O'Mahony; JSNTSup 241; Sheffield: Sheffield Academic Press, 2003], 113–42) contends that "Paul was the first to understand the death of Christ as a matter of choice" (p. 131). In my judgment, this view grossly underestimates the large number of non-Pauline texts involved, not all of which can be under Pauline influence.

160. This was the view of Hermann Samuel Reimarus: Jesus "began to quiver and to shake when he saw that his adventure might cost him his life. . . . He ended his life with the words, '*Eli, Eli, lama sabachthani*? My God, my God, why hast thou forsaken me?' [Matt. 27:46]—a confession which can hardly be otherwise interpreted than that God had not helped him to carry out his intention and attain his object as he had hoped he would have done. It was then clearly not the intention or the object of Jesus to suffer and to die, but to build up a worldly kingdom, and to deliver the Israelites from bondage. It was in this that God had forsaken him, it was in this that his hopes had been frustrated" (*Reimarus: Fragments* [ed. Charles Talbert; Philadelphia: Fortress, 1970], 150).

immediately precedes "yet not what I want, but what you want." Mark 14:32–42, if it holds memory, is testimony to anguish, not to a failure of nerve.

Similarly, that some of the relevant stories are fiction and that doubt hangs over the various logia assigned to Jesus is of little consequence for my purposes.[161] Maybe Jesus never appeared before Herod (Luke is the only witness to this), and surely he never said, "The good shepherd lays down his life for the sheep" (I take those to be the words of the Fourth Evangelist). But the author of that story and the composer of that saying went about their creative work with a definite image of Jesus in mind, an image that they did not invent, an image they inherited from tradition. And what matters for my case is not the historicity of this or that item on my list but rather the list as a whole and the genesis of the traditional image, so widely attested.

Why did Paul, the tradents of the Jesus tradition, and other early Christians believe that Jesus did not shun execution but rather, when it came, accepted it? My answer is this: they believed it because that is what he did, and people remembered. Like other martyrs such as Socrates, Justin, Martin Luther King Jr., and Oscar Romero, his eyes appear to have been wide open.[162] He saw death coming, and he did not run away. If he had instead refused to consent to his unhappy lot, one wonders how it has come to pass that we have so much confident testimony to the contrary. There is less evidence for the proposition that Jesus cast out demons, yet who disputes that he was an exorcist? I agree with Justin Meggitt:

> The personality of Jesus left a clear impression on the earliest believers. . . . In particular, the virtues that Jesus exhibited in the face of death, of both forbearance and submission to God, and his refusal to return violence with violence, seem to have been recurring motifs in the pictures of Jesus that emerge from these traditions and tell us something about the enduring impression his personality made on his followers.[163]

To entertain the suggestion that Jesus did not go to his death willingly requires positing either a widespread conscious cover-up or a catastrophic memory failure in the early Christian sources. Perhaps some will find one of those options plausible. I consider it much more likely that, in this particular, our sources are not bereft of memory. Jesus' decision to die, whenever made and whatever the motivation and whatever his precise interpretation, left a vivid impression. Indeed, next to the fact that Jesus was crucified by order of Pontius Pilate, his acquiescence to his fate is probably the best-attested fact about his last days. At some point, he determined to assent to his miserable end, accepting it as the will of God.

161. For the methodological issues here, see above, pp. 15–20.
162. For Justin, see 2 *Apol.* 3.1.
163. Justin J. Meggitt, "Psychology and the Historical Jesus," in *Jesus and Psychology* (ed. Fraser Watts; Philadelphia: Templeton Foundation Press, 2007), 24.

6

Memory and Invention

How Much History?

One must know when it is right to doubt. Some . . . affirm
that everything can be proved, because they know nothing
about proof.

—Pascal

The previous chapters have mined the Jesus tradition for memory and
not come up empty. I have urged that we are able, with a clear critical
conscience, to establish a number of significant claims about Jesus. The discussion, however, has moved forward with an unexamined assumption: the
Synoptic evangelists were, for the most part, not writing creative fiction but
rather reconfiguring traditions informed by the past. In this final chapter, then,
I should like to inquire to what extent this assumption is justified. Having done
that, I will offer some final thoughts on this book as a whole.

Did the Evangelists Believe Their Own Stories?

When I undertook critical study of the canonical Gospels, so many years ago,
my chief aim was to unearth the history behind the texts.[1] My assumption
was this: if an evangelist told a story about Jesus, we should be able to deter-

---

1. Although the following discussion focuses on Matthew, Mark, and Luke, I believe that most
of my observations also hold for John. Ideally, of course, I should treat each of these writings
separately and consider as well a few extracanonical Gospels. Given, however, the boundaries
of the present volume, my remarks focus on the Synoptics.

mine whether or not it happened, and if an evangelist quoted Jesus as saying something, we should be able to determine whether or not he said it.

I was, in retrospect, both vain and naïve. It was as though I were the master sleuth in a detective novel, imagining that I could, in each and every case, figure out what had actually transpired. In real life, however, many crimes go unsolved. Likewise, when it comes to the traditions about Jesus and their historicity, experience teaches that our questions often will go unanswered. My current judgment is this: notwithstanding all the efforts of modern scholarship, the majority of sayings—maybe the vast majority of sayings—the Synoptics attribute to Jesus are neither demonstrably of pre-Easter origin nor manifestly post-Easter inventions; they are instead best classified as "possibly authentic" or, if one prefers, "possibly not authentic." The same holds, I believe, for most of the stories that the Synoptics tell about Jesus.[2] I have lost my former confidence in anyone's ability, including my own, to trace with assurance the history of most of the traditions. I no longer presume that removing the literary wrapper to behold a historical event or saying of Jesus is a straightforward affair. Even when reminiscence lies within a text, that text is likely to have been consciously and unconsciously reworked before being written down. Our sources are complex artifacts, the collaboration of, among other things, fallible perceptions, imperfect memories, linguistic conventions, cultural assumptions, and personal and communal agendas. Differentiating an original event or saying from all that has mingled with it and been superimposed upon is often perhaps a bit like trying to separate streams after they have flowed into a river.

There was a second way in which, looking back, I was naïve. I worked with the unexamined assumption that the Gospel writers intended, from first to last, to record past events. When, for example, Matthew wrote that Peter walked on the water, or that Jesus was born of a virgin, or that some dead people woke up, exited their graves, and walked into Jerusalem, he really meant it: the evangelist expected readers to believe that those things really happened.

I cannot be too harsh on myself for making this assumption. It was understandable, given the Christian tradition in which I had grown up as well as the academic tradition in which I was then being trained. Everybody seemed to assume that the evangelists, notwithstanding their manifest theological and literary interests, took themselves to be writing of the past. It was only a question of whether or not we could believe them. I knew, for example, that most Christians through the ages had believed in the virginal conception, and that theologians, at least until recent times, had deemed its literal truth a very important tenet of the faith, so much so that it found its way into the standard creeds: *natus ex Maria Virgine*. I also, on a lighter note, remember running across a story about Francis of Assisi in which he comments upon a

2. See further above, p. 22.

large rock in the Italian countryside, accounting for its huge fissure by appeal to the earthquake at Jesus' crucifixion, as Matthew's Gospel relates.[3] The saint, or at least somebody writing about him, obviously read Matt 27:51b–53 as a record of real events.

When I passed from studying theological and ecclesiastical texts to historical-critical books and articles, the notion that the evangelists intended uniformly to write of things that really happened seemed close to the rule there, too. When, for instance, I read through Vincent Taylor's then-standard commentary on Mark's Gospel and came to Mark 15:33, which states that during the crucifixion, the sun went dark for three hours, I discovered that the modern exegete leaned toward seeing legend here. As justification, he cited other ancient texts in which darkness accompanies the death of great individuals. Taylor also dismissed the possibility of an eclipse—it was, after all, the time of the full moon—although he did not reckon altogether incredible the possibility of a "black sirocco." But what interests me today is this comment: "Probably Mark thought of the darkness as supernatural."[4] In other words, although this miracle likely never happened, Mark thought that it did. Taylor nowhere entertains the possibility that the author of Mark might have understood the darkness in a poetical or symbolic or less-than-literal manner.

The Possibility of "Purely Metaphorical Narratives"

This, however, is an option that is now before us, as it should have been all along.[5] Marcus Borg recently has proposed that some of the narratives in the canonical Gospels should be classified as "metaphorical" or "purely metaphorical narratives." These, he affirms, "are not based on the memory of particular events, but are symbolic narratives created for their metaphorical meaning. As such, they are not meant to be historical reports. Rather, the stories use symbolic language that points beyond a factual meaning."[6]

Borg, who is not alone in his point of view—scholars as far apart on the ideological spectrum as Robert Gundry and John Dominic Crossan share it[7]—illustrates by examining the wedding at Cana (John 2:1–11), Peter walk-

---

3. See Candide Chalippe, *The Life of Saint Francis of Assisi* (New York: D. & J. Sadlier, 1889), 129–30. I have no idea whether the story reports something that Francis actually said.

4. Vincent Taylor, *The Gospel according to St. Mark: The Greek Text with Introduction, Notes, and Indexes* (2nd ed.; London: Macmillan; New York: St. Martin's Press, 1966), 593.

5. David Friedrich Strauss (*A New Life of Jesus* [2 vols.; London: Williams & Norgate, 1865], 1:208–10) offered some rudimentary reflections on this topic, but no one seems to have pursued them further.

6. Marcus Borg, *Jesus: Uncovering the Life, Teachings, and Relevance of a Religious Revolutionary* (San Francisco: HarperSanFrancisco, 2006), 57.

7. See Robert H. Gundry, *Matthew: A Commentary on His Handbook for a Mixed Church under Persecution* (Grand Rapids: Eerdmans, 1994), 627–40; John Dominic Crossan, *A Long*

ing on the water (Matt 14:28–31), and the infancy narratives in Matthew and Luke. These are all, in his mind, parables. Their authors intended to make theological statements, not record history.[8]

From one point of view, Borg is saying nothing new. Christians have always allegorized Scripture, and post-Enlightenment interpreters have long accustomed themselves to finding meaning in texts that they, unlike their theological predecessors, no longer view as historical. But Borg and like-minded others are saying something more. They are not claiming that we must, because of modern knowledge, reinterpret the old texts in new ways, against their authors' original intentions. They are instead contending that the texts were not intended to be understood literally in the first place. John Dominic Crossan, in a retrospect on his career, has written,

> When I looked at the so-called nature miracles of Jesus, . . . those stories screamed parable at me, not history, not miracle, but parable. They shouted at me: "It's a parable, dummy." They were never intended to be about a miraculous walking on the water, a miraculous stilling of the storm, or a miraculous catch of fishes. They were not historical stories about Jesus' power over natural forces, but parabolic stories about Jesus' power over community leaders. With him they could do anything and get anywhere; without him they could do nothing and get nowhere. . . . When Jesus wanted to say something very important about God he went into parable; when the early church wanted to say something very important about Jesus they too went into parable. It seemed to me terribly obvious: the more important the subject, the more necessary the parable.[9]

Roger David Aus, urging that the Gospels contain large tracts of haggadah, which their Jewish-Christian authors knew to be true only in a less-than-literal sense, has written to similar effect:

Way from Tipperary: A Memoir (San Francisco: HarperSanFrancisco, 2000), 133–41, 164–70. Cf. Robert J. Miller, *Born Divine: The Births of Jesus and Other Sons of God* (Santa Rosa, CA: Polebridge, 2003), 175–79; Jerome Murphy O'Connor, *The Holy Land: An Oxford Archaeological Guide from Earliest Times to 1700* (4th ed.; Oxford: Oxford University Press, 1998), 124. According to the latter, Luke's two accounts of the ascension differ because "he was aware that he was not recounting an historical event." John Shelby Spong has also promoted the same view in several books, including *Born of a Woman: A Bishop Rethinks the Birth of Jesus* (San Francisco: HarperSanFrancisco, 1992), 15–22; *Liberating the Gospels: Reading the Bible with Jewish Eyes; Freeing Jesus from 2,000 Years of Misunderstanding* (San Francisco: HarperSanFrancisco, 1996), 23–55; *Resurrection: Myth or Reality? A Bishop's Search for the Origins of Christianity* (San Francisco: HarperSanFrancisco, 1994), 3–22. For Spong, the Gospels have been held in "gentile captivity" (*Liberating the Gospels*, 53). The transition from Jewish to Gentile Christianity led to the literalization of stories that were initially intended to be midrashic or purely metaphorical. Gundry (*Matthew*, 634) made the same argument. For a helpful, critical response to Spong's thesis, see Mark Allan Powell, "Authorial Intention and Historical Reporting: Putting Spong's Literalization Thesis to the Test," *JSHJ* 1 (2003): 225–49.

8. Borg, *Jesus: Uncovering the Life*, 57–69.

9. Crossan, *Long Way from Tipperary*, 167–68.

It is one of the tragedies of the Christian church that the number of its Palestinian Jewish members dwindled so rapidly after the very successful missionizing of the Gentiles. The latter soon made the former into small sects such as the Palestinian Ebionites. Early Palestinian and later even Hellenistic Jewish Christians, however, could have conveyed to Gentile Christians the nature of Jewish haggadah, and the centuries-old Gentile Christian debate about the "historicity" or "facticity" of haggadic sayings or narratives [in the canonical Gospels] would have been basically unnecessary.[10]

This is clearly a claim about the authors of the Gospels and/or about their predecessors.

How does one determine which narratives are wholly metaphorical and which are not? Consider this passage from the Jerusalem Talmud:

> When R. Aha died, a star appeared at noon. When R. Hanan died, the statues bowed low. When R. Yohanan died, the icons bowed down. . . . When R. Hanina of Bet Hauran died, the Sea of Tiberias split open. . . . When R. Hoshaiah died, the palm of Tiberias fell down. When R. Isaac b. Eliasheb died, seventy [infirm] thresholds of houses in Galilee were shaken down. . . . When R. Samuel bar R. Isaac died, cedars of the land of Israel were uprooted . . . [and] a flame came forth from heaven and intervened between his bier and the congregation. For three hours there were voices and thunderings in the world: "Come and see what a sprig of cedar has done for this old man!" And a voice came forth and said, "Woe that R. Samuel b. R. Isaac has died, the doer of merciful deeds." When R. Yasa bar Halputa died, the gutters ran with blood in Laodicea. . . . When R. Abbahu died, the pillars of Caesarea wept. . . . When R. Yasa died, the castle of Tiberias collapsed, and members of the patriarchate were rejoicing. (y. ʿAbod. Zar. 3:1)

Although my guess is that students of the Talmud understood all or most of this passage to preserve something other than a list of facts—I certainly am full of doubt—one is hard pressed for compelling justification. We can scarcely urge that the rabbis were skeptical of miracles in general or of supernatural portents in particular. After all, they had read the Bible.

Borg suggests two criteria by which we can detect "purely metaphorical narratives," at least in the canonical Gospels.[11] The first is this: we may deem a

---

10. Roger David Aus, *The Death, Burial, and Resurrection of Jesus, and the Death, Burial, and Translation of Moses in Judaic Tradition* (Lanham, MD: University Press of America, 2008), 291. Note Aus's view that the question of the historicity of Jewish-Christian haggadic stories "was simply not asked by the first Palestinian Jewish Christian hearers of the incidents before they entered the Gospels. Instead, they greatly appreciated the respective narrator's creative abilities in reshaping traditions already known to them in order to express a religious truth (or truths) about Jesus, their Lord, the Messiah of Israel" (pp. 297–98).

11. In *Reading the Bible Again for the First Time: Taking the Bible Seriously but Not Literally* (San Francisco: HarperSanFrancisco, 2002), 46–47, Borg offers yet another aid: "the limits of the spectacular," by which he means that a story is "purely metaphorical" if it narrates a type of event,

story such when so-called mainstream scholars no longer find a historical event behind it. The second criterion is that a narrative may "look like" it "belongs to the literary genre of metaphorical or symbolic narrative." His comment on the infancy narratives shows us what he has in mind here:

> Angels abound. In Matthew, they speak frequently to Joseph in dreams. In Luke, the angel Gabriel speaks to Zechariah, the father of John the Baptizer, and then goes to Nazareth to speak to Mary. Another angel speaks to the shepherds and is then joined by a host of angels singing in the night sky. Characters burst into memorable hymns. A special star moves through the sky leading wise men from the East to the place of Jesus's birth. In both, there is a divine conception. When we find features like these in a story, we commonly conclude that its literary genre is not a literal-factual report, but a metaphorical or symbolic narrative.[12]

Before I pose questions, let me emphasize that from a theological point of view, I sympathize with Borg's larger aim. He is urging that if we take modern scholarship seriously, we can no longer be literalists about certain stories that people used to be literalists about, and further, that the meaning of those stories need not depend upon their historicity. Most of us within church or synagogue are by now used to finding meaning in Genesis while dispensing with it as a historical document. Should we not, Borg is asking, be able to do something similar with portions of the canonical Gospels?

As just indicated, I agree. My problem with Borg and those expressing a like opinion is not so much theological as historical. They affirm that the canonical evangelists or their predecessors never intended certain narratives to be read as anything other than parabolic. I am not so sure. This turns out to be a very tricky question. One may, as I do, believe that some stories in the Gospels are the products of popular and theological imagination, in which the history is of homeopathic proportions, and that other stories, even if they derive from things that happened, are now draped with secondary, supernatural overlay, such as the dove and the voice at Jesus' baptism. What, however, did the evangelists think?

Borg, as already indicated, employs two criteria by which to decide whether a narrative was designed to be metaphorical instead of historical. In my judgment, neither criterion is of use. What modern scholars think about a story need not, it goes without saying, correspond to what the ancients thought.[13]

---

such as changing water into wine, that goes "beyond what we commonly think to be possible." This, however, is a rule for contemporary readers; it says nothing about ancient audiences.

12. Borg, *Jesus: Uncovering the Life*, 62. These words echo, whether intentionally or not, the similar remarks of David Friedrich Strauss, *The Life of Jesus Critically Examined* (trans. George Eliot; ed. Peter C. Hodgson; Philadelphia: Fortress, 1972), 87–92, on "criteria by which to distinguish the unhistorical in the gospel narrative." Unlike Borg, however, Strauss held that the evangelists believed their own stories (see pp. 75–87).

13. On this matter I have found helpful Clare Stancliffe, *St. Martin and His Hagiographer: History and Miracle in Sulpicius Severus* (Oxford: Clarendon, 1983), 249–61.

Although Diodorus Siculus included a lot in his history that we cannot deem true, he evidently did not regard his own prose as extravagant fiction; and it would be futile to urge that since modern scholars no longer believe in a worldwide flood a few millennia ago, the authors of Gen 6–9 intended their narrative to be fictional. Again, although we must classify *Joseph and Aseneth* as some sort of romance, we cannot exclude the possibility that its author intended it to be received as history.[14]

Borg's second criterion, that a narrative may "look like" it "belongs to the literary genre of metaphorical or symbolic narrative," is also problematic, because what looks like blatant fiction to us may not have appeared so to our predecessors. If we set aside our modern convictions and try to think ourselves back into the first century, what evidence do we have that the evangelists or their audiences would have understood a narrative that included angels, supernatural celestial phenomena, and a divine conception to be, on the ground of content alone, something other than "a literal-factual report, but a metaphorical or symbolic narrative"? I can name no ancient Christian who doubted the existence of angelic beings, or who argued that supernatural celestial phenomena never occur, or who denied that a woman could become pregnant without help from a man.

So even though I concur with Borg that there are unhistorical stories in the Gospels, he has not, in my judgment, established that the evangelists were, on this matter, of the same mind. I am still left asking, What reasons might one have for supposing that, on this or that occasion, the authors of the canonical Gospels knew themselves to be writing a sort of edifying fiction, to be recounting things that never really happened?

Fiction and Genre

One answer, with a nod toward Borg, immediately suggests itself: genre. If we know what sort of a book we have at hand, we should have some idea of what to expect from it. And maybe the Gospels belong to a genre with room for haggadic fiction.

Sometime in the middle of the 1970s, when I was still in college, I purchased a book entitled *Mark of the Taw*.[15] Its author, Jack Finegan, was a well-known and respected biblical scholar. As I started to read, I became more and more puzzled. The book, which was full of Greek and discussed Eusebius and the Muratorian canon, detailed the author's discovery of an old manuscript in the Church of St. Mark in Alexandria. That manuscript, although copied in the eleventh century, went back to a fourth-century exemplar entitled the "Mar-

---

14. As C. Burchard remarks, "We can only speculate whether the author intended to write a piece of fiction or a work of history" ("Joseph and Aseneth," *OTP* 2:186).

15. Jack Finegan, *Mark of the Taw* (Richmond: John Knox, 1972).

tyrdom of the Holy Apostle and Evangelist Mark of Alexandria." It contained all sorts of fascinating tidbits that illumined both the Gospel of Mark and early Christianity. Of all this I had heard nothing. I was deeply puzzled, until I finally figured out that *Mark of the Taw* was a work of historical fiction. I had been reading fiction as though it were fact, which is possible because both genres can take the form of narrative.[16] The result was bewilderment.

Have we made an analogous mistake with the Gospels, failing to get their genre right? Have we taken them to be history of a sort or biography of a sort when they were never intended to be either? The question has force because the evangelists were, it appears, far more interested in the practical and theological meanings of their stories than in literal facticity. Moreover, some have recently decided that the guild has long misconstrued the genre of Acts, and that the book contains features more typical of light fiction than ancient historiography.[17] Perhaps they are right,[18] and perhaps light fiction is also the category into which we should place the Gospels. In recent years, several scholars have called attention to possible affiliations between the canonical Gospels and Hellenistic romance, or between the Gospels and Homer.[19]

It is perhaps too early to know whether this recent take on the Gospels will lead to a dead end or to a new world of profitable discourse. In the latter case,

16. Ernst Axel Knauf observes that "what is no longer real because it is past is told in the same mode as that which is not real because it is imagined" ("From History to Interpretation," in *The Fabric of History: Text, Artifact and Israel's Past* [ed. Diana Vikander Edelman; JSOTSup 127; Sheffield: JSOT Press, 1992], 48).

17. See Richard I. Pervo, *Profit with Delight: The Literary Genre of the Acts of the Apostles* (Philadelphia: Fortress, 1987). Pervo maintains that if Luke "composed what we should call a historical novel, he was engaged in activity at least partly frivolous and he did not always tell the truth" (p. 138). Dennis R. MacDonald suggests that the purpose of Acts was not to preserve memories but rather to supply a Christian alternative to Homer and Virgil (*Does the New Testament Imitate Homer? Four Cases from the Acts of the Apostles* [New Haven: Yale University Press, 2003]).

18. But I am doubtful; see Clare K. Rothschild, *Luke-Acts and the Rhetoric of History: An Investigation of Early Christian Historiography* (WUNT 2/175; Tübingen: Mohr Siebeck, 2004). For a survey of recent scholarship, see Thomas E. Phillips, "The Genre of Acts: Moving toward a Consensus?" *CBR* 4 (2006): 365–96. His conclusion is this: "In the eyes of most scholars, it [Acts] is history—but not of the kind that precludes fiction" (385).

19. According to Richard Pervo, Matthew, Mark, Luke, and John "can be understood as fictional biographies roughly analogous to the *Alexander-Romance*, the *Life of Aesop*, or Philostratus's novel about Apollonius of Tyana. The activity of shaping various independent stories about Jesus into a coherent narrative plot required compositional strategies very much like those of fiction" ("The Ancient Novel Becomes Christian," in *The Novel in the Ancient World* [ed. Gareth Schmeling; Leiden: Brill, 1996], 689). See further Dennis R. MacDonald, *The Homeric Epics and the Gospel of Mark* (New Haven: Yale University Press, 2000). Yet from the point of view of an early Christian audience, surely the canonical Gospels did not feature ancient times, fictional characters, exotic customs, or mythical locations—all common topoi in Greek novels. For questions about MacDonald's approach, see Karl Olav Sandnes, "*Imitatio Homeri*? An Appraisal of Dennis R. MacDonald's 'Mimesis Criticism,'" *JBL* 124 (2005): 715–32.

we will have to rethink much, and perhaps the proposition that the Gospels contain in part or in whole "purely metaphorical narratives" will become not just credible but blindingly obvious.

In the meantime, many scholars remain persuaded that the Gospels are a subspecies of Greco-Roman biography.[20] What would acceptance of that classification imply for the thesis about "purely metaphorical narratives"?

Greek and Roman biographers and historians were quite capable of handing on stories that they did not consider factual or about which they had doubts. Often, however, they made this clear. Plutarch told one version of the conception of Alexander the Great, after which he added: "There is another version of this story." Having then related that second account, he added that Alexander's mother, Olympia, repudiated it (*Alex.* 2–3). In this way, Plutarch signaled to his readers that they were not on firm historical ground. The Gospels, however, offer nothing remotely similar. No evangelist confronts us with differing versions of the same story that push us to ask which is true. Instead, they present everything from a single point of view—there are no competing narrators—and they never drop a hint that they have doubts about any of their stories. Nor, unlike Herodotus, do they ever measure the plausibility of a story against "what usually happens" or concede that they have no firsthand knowledge of something (see Herodotus, *Hist.* 2.27–28, 68–72).

One can also ask what might follow if we think of the Gospels not as instances of Greco-Roman biography but rather as being modeled after the so-called historical books of the Hebrew Bible. Maybe Matthew and the other evangelists wanted to set forth the foundational stories of the Christians and, to accomplish this end, deliberately imitated the Pentateuch, Samuel, Kings, and Chronicles, which preserve the foundational stories of Israel.[21] In such a case, our authors would have been modeling their books after writings that, from our point of view, contain large tracts of fiction. As already indicated, however, our own point of view cannot be decisive in this matter. We must ask instead how the ancients understood Genesis and the collection that it introduces.

We know that some Jews did not find history everywhere in the Bible. According to the Talmud, Rabbi Samuel b. Na'hmeni asserted that "Job never was; he never existed. He is only a parable" (*b. B. Bat.* 15a).[22] Philo, moreover, occasionally dispensed with the literal reading of a text altogether, as did Origen and Gregory of Nyssa later;[23] and Philo (*Confusion* 2–3) knew

20. See Richard A. Burridge, *What Are the Gospels? A Comparison with Graeco-Roman Biography* (2nd ed.; Grand Rapids: Eerdmans; Dearborn, MI: Dove Booksellers, 2004).

21. See Ulrich Luz, *Matthew 1–7: A Commentary* (Hermeneia; Minneapolis: Fortress, 2007), 15.

22. Cf. Theodore of Mopsuestia, *Job* (PG 66:6978B).

23. Philo, *Worse* 95; *God* 21; *Posterity* 7; Origen, *Hom. Jos.* 8.7; *Princ.* 4.2.5, 9; 4.3.1, 5; Gregory of Nyssa, *Vit. Mos.* 2.91–93 (SC 1:158–60).

of apostate Jews who found myths in Genesis, which raises the possibility that some who thought of themselves as faithful Jews did likewise. And yet, the Talmud has another rabbi refute Samuel's opinion that Job is a fiction; and the sophisticated Josephus regards the Pentateuch as an unimpeachable source for history.[24] There is little evidence of Jews reading stories in the so-called historical books of the Hebrew Scriptures the way Borg wants to read portions of the Gospels.[25] Indeed, the sorts of interpretive moves and harmonizing explanations that one sees everywhere on display in James Kugel's masterpiece, *Traditions of the Bible: A Guide to the Bible as It Was at the Start of the Common Era*, leave the forceful impression that, whatever else they thought it was, ancient Jewish readers found their past in the so-called historical books of the Hebrew Bible.[26] Chaim Milikowsky probably is right: no one "in the Jewish world . . . questioned the facticity of the events described in the Bible. . . . They were a given."[27] From this it follows that, if the evangelists thought of themselves as imitating the Hebrew Bible, then they presumably believed that they, like it, were relating what really happened.

Early Reader Response

If considerations about genre do little to establish that the evangelists thought some of their stories to be less than historical, other factors remain to be considered. We can ask, for instance, whether any ancient Christians understood the Gospels in a less-than-literal manner, to which the answer is that at least

24. See Josephus, *Ant.* 1–9; and especially *Ag. Ap.* 1.15–52, where the Greek historians come off as less reliable than the Hebrew Bible. Although Josephus, when retelling the Bible, adds and subtracts items, inserts new speeches, and otherwise revises for his own ends, he takes the narrative details of even Genesis at face value, which is why he can use them to calculate the date of the flood (*Ant.* 1.80–88). Compare the use of the Hebrew Bible in 4Q559 (on this, see Michael Owen Wise, "To Know the Times and the Seasons: A Study of the Aramaic Chronograph 4Q599," *JSP* 15 [1997]: 3–51) and in the later *Seder Olam*, which may well preserve much early material; see Chaim Milikowsky, "Josephus between Rabbinic Culture and Hellenistic Historiography," in *Shem in the Tents of Japhet: Essays on the Encounter of Judaism and Hellenism* (ed. James L. Kugel; JSJSup 74; Leiden: Brill, 2002), 159–90.

25. As far as I can determine, until recent times Jewish and Christian expositors have read even the fable of Baalam's donkey (Num 22) as history (note, e.g., Josephus, *Ant.* 4.108–109).

26. James Kugel, *Traditions of the Bible: A Guide to the Bible as It Was at the Start of the Common Era* (Cambridge, MA: Harvard University Press, 1998).

27. Chaim Milikowsky, "Midrash as Fiction and Midrash as History: What Did the Rabbis Mean?" in *Ancient Fiction: The Matrix of Early Christian and Jewish Narrative* (ed. Jo-Ann A. Brant, Charles W. Hedrick, and Chris Shea; SBLSymS 32; Atlanta: Society of Biblical Literature, 2006), 121. Milikowsky remarks, "Never in rabbinic literature is the facticity of the events described in the Bible questioned. The rabbis, like most other social groupings in Judaism of the ancient world, postulated a direct one-to-one correspondence between the biblical narrative and the past" (p. 126).

one did so: Origen. He was able to observe that at "many points" the four Gospels "do not agree." Persuaded that their truth does not reside in "the material letter," he famously argued that the evangelists "sometimes altered things which, from the eye of history, occurred otherwise." They could "speak of something that happened in one place as if it had happened in another, or of what happened at a certain time as if it had happened at another time," and they introduced "into what was spoken in a certain way some changes of their own." "The spiritual truth was often preserved, one might say, in the material falsehood."[28]

Origen is the proof that a purely metaphorical reading of certain segments of the Gospels was not utterly foreign to the ancient world. One cannot, however, credibly move from Origen's sophisticated hermeneutical reflections to the evangelists, whose intellectual universe was much different from his. From what we can tell, they had studied neither Philo nor the writings of other Hellenistic allegorists. No less importantly, Origen did not balk at the same stories as do modern scholars such as Borg. This ancient writer defended the historicity of the virgin birth, believed in the star of Bethlehem, and argued at length for the credibility of the dove and the voice at Jesus' baptism. He thought that there was a local darkness when Jesus died.[29] And although he allegorized the story of Peter walking on the water, he nowhere said that it did not happen.[30] Origen did not end up where Borg does.

If all this is true for the great allegorizer, it is all the more true for the rest of the early Christians whom we know anything about.[31] Julius Africanus vainly endeavored to harmonize the genealogies of Jesus in Matthew and Luke.[32] Justin evidently thought of Mark's Gospel as preserving "the memoirs [ἀπομνημονεύμασιν] of Peter" (*Dial.* 106), a tag less than obvious for a partly haggadic narrative.[33] Papias apparently felt a need to apologize for Mark because its "order" (σύνταξις) was not the order of one or more of the other Gospels (see Eusebius, *Hist. eccl.* 3.39.14–16). I know of no evidence that these individuals, or anyone else for that matter before Origen, found any

28. Origen, *Comm. Jo.* 10.2, 4.

29. See Origen, *Cels.* 1.40–48, 58–60; 2.69; 3.25; *Hom. Num.* 18.3(4); *Comm. Matt.* frg. 134.

30. Origen, *Comm. Matt.* 11.5–6.

31. See Powell, "Authorial Intention," 237–42. Although some so-called gnostic Christians rejected a literal view of the resurrection, this involved not allegorical interpretation of stories about the empty tomb but rather rejection of their truth. See Elaine Pagels, *The Gnostic Gospels* (New York: Random House, 1979), 3–27.

32. For the many attempts to harmonize the Gospels in the early church, see Helmut Merkel, *Die Widersprüche zwischen den Evangelien: Ihre polemische und apologetische Behandlung in der Alten Kirche bis zu Augustin* (WUNT 2/13; Tübingen: Mohr Siebeck, 1971).

33. For the background of Justin's language, see Samuel Byrskog, "From Memory to Memoirs: Tracing the Background of a Literary Genre," in *Remembering Jesus: Essays in Honor of James D. G. Dunn* (ed. Scot McKnight and T. Mournet; New York: Continuum, forthcoming).

"purely metaphorical narratives" in the Gospels.[34] And he did not find many.[35] So again we have been unable to establish the claim that some of the Gospel stories were never intended to be understood as historical.

Humor and Absurdity

There has been some discussion as to how the rabbis understood midrash and their own haggadic tales.[36] When they reported on what Elijah had said to this or that rabbi, or when they quoted a *bat qol* to end a story, or when they said that the manna piled up to sixty cubits or was so high as to be seen around the world,[37] what did they think they were doing? Without addressing those fascinating questions here, I wish to underline that sometimes the rabbis appear to signal the fictional nature of an anecdote by employing humor or absurdity. The Jerusalem Talmud *Sanh.* 25d (7:13) tells a tale about Rabbis Eleazar, Joshua, and Akiba. When in Tiberias, they met a heretic who spoke to the Sea of Galilee, split it asunder, and then mockingly asked, "Is this not what Moses, your rabbi, did at the sea?" The rabbis answered the question with one of their own: "Do you not concede to us that Moses, our rabbi, walked through it?" When the heretic nodded assent, the rabbis challenged him: "Walk through it then." He began to do so, whereupon Rabbi Joshua spoke, and the sea fell back in on itself, swallowing the heretic, who got his comeuppance. One has trouble imagining that those who heard this outrageous story did anything other than laugh.

It is the same in the famous *b. B. Meṣiʿa* 59b.[38] Rabbi Eliezer, in debate with his fellows, says, "If the halakah agrees with me, let this carob-tree prove it." Immediately the tree moves from its place. Eliezer's partners in debate are unimpressed: "No proof can be brought from a carob-tree." The rabbi next

---

34. As far as I know, Gundry is alone in urging that Papias's comments on Matthew "may show an early awareness of midrashic and haggadic characteristics in the first gospel" (*Matthew*, 634).

35. See Origen, *Princ.* 4.3.4: "Those (passages) that are true according to history are much more numerous than (those passages) interwoven with purely spiritual meanings." It is typical of Origen, when berating those who interpret the Gospels literally, not to deny the literal meaning but to regard it as of lesser importance and to insist on additional spiritual or allegorical meaning; see, for example, *Comm. Jo.* 10.17–18.

36. See, for example, Milikowsky, "Midrash," 117–27; idem, "Rabbinic Interpretation of the Bible in the Light of Ancient Hermeneutical Practice: The Question of Literal Meaning," in *"The Words of a Wise Man's Mouth Are Gracious" (Qoh 10,12): Festschrift for Günther Stemberger on the Occasion of His 65th Birthday* (ed. Mauro Perani; SJ 32; Berlin: de Gruyter, 2005), 7–28.

37. For this last idea, see *Mek.* on Exod 16:14; *b. Yoma* 76a; *Midr. Ps.* 23:5. The latter comments that whoever does not believe this will not have sweetness in the world to come. But in the *Mekilta*, "the elders" are incredulous, calling the statement "astonishing."

38. There is a variant in *y. Moʿed Qaṭ.* 81c–d (3:1).

says, "If I am right, the stream will prove it." At his word, a nearby stream flows backward. Again, his opponents are unmoved. Exasperated, Eliezer tries again: "If the halakah agrees with me, let the walls of the yeshiva prove it." The walls then start to fall, but Rabbi Joshua rebukes them, and they stop, having fallen only halfway to the ground. Finally, Eliezer cries out, "If I'm right, let Heaven prove it!" A voice from heaven then endorses his ruling. Joshua, however, appealing to Deuteronomy—"The Torah is not in Heaven"—declares that "since the day Torah was given at Mount Sinai, we pay no attention to heavenly voices."[39] What counts is the ruling of the majority. Later, Rabbi Nathan meets Elijah, who tells him that God reacted to the whole affair with laughter and exclaimed, "My sons have defeated me."

If we do not misconstrue this flight of fancy as history, it must be partly because the text makes us laugh along with God. The story is winking at us, which is not what historical narratives typically do. I assume that it was intended as fiction.[40] And yet, one must concede, even in a seemingly obvious case such as this, that it is possible to name learned Jews who have thought otherwise. Nissim Gaon (990–1062) fretted over how God could permit Eliezer to do miracles if his compatriots were right to hold that the Torah is not in heaven. God, suggested Gaon, was only testing the rabbis![41] A contemporary of Gaon, Rabbi Hananeel (d. 1055/56), rationalized the story by turning it into a dream of one of those listening to the debate.[42]

Whatever one makes of the Talmuds, some old Christian stories appear to communicate their fictional nature by way of hilarity. One of my favorites appears in *The Acts of Peter and Andrew*. This tells the delightful tale of a certain rich man, Onesiphorus. When Peter tells him that it is easier for a camel to go through the eye of a needle than for a rich person to enter into the kingdom of heaven, Onesiphorus becomes furious. Still, he says, he will believe if Peter can demonstrate that a camel can go through the eye of a needle. Peter then asks for God's help, whereupon Jesus appears and instructs him to get a camel and a needle. When others learn what Peter wants, a sympathetic merchant, thinking to do Peter a favor, looks for the biggest needle he can find. Peter tells him instead to get a tiny needle, which he does. The apostle then sticks the needle in the ground and as the camel approaches it, the eye opens like a gate and the camel goes through, not once, but twice. Yet Onesiphorus is

39. One guesses that the reference to Deut 30:12 carries with it an allusion to 30:11: "This commandment that I am commanding you today is not too wondrous [נפלאת] for you." The literal meaning of נפלא is "miracle" (Jastrow, s.v.).

40. For the explicit recognition of haggadah as the product of the imagination, see the rabbinic authorities cited by Judah Goldin, "Freedom and Restraint of Haggadah," in *Midrash and Literature* (ed. Geoffrey H. Hartman and Sanford Budick; New Haven: Yale University Press, 1986), 57–76.

41. See A. I. Baumgarten, "Miracles and Halakah in Rabbinic Judaism," *JQR* 73 (1983): 241–42.

42. Ibid., 241.

not won over. He demands that the trick be done with a camel and needle of his own choosing. He also seats a prostitute upon the camel and further puts a pig's carcass in front of the needle. (Camels, presumably, do not like dead pigs.) It makes no difference. The camel goes through and turns around and comes back again. Onesiphorus converts on the spot.

The author of this vivid and outlandish fantasy must have known, while he was making it all up, that he was indeed making it all up. So too, one imagines, did the audience that he entertained, because they were chuckling. It probably was the same with those who heard the *Infancy Gospel of Thomas*. Were its auditors not amused by a five-year-old Jesus making clay sparrows, clapping his hands, and watching them fly away chirping? Or by the bizarre tale of a rude lad who, having bumped into Jesus decades before the Sermon on the Mount took shape, is cursed and dies on the spot?[43]

So we may ask, Do the Gospels ever make us laugh, and by so doing intimate that they are not representing the historical past? The question has hardly been raised. One reason must be that modern academics have done a very poor job of espying humor in ancient religious texts; and there has been, on the whole, very little study of mirth in early Christian writings. One guesses that there is more humor in at least some of the sayings of Jesus than we have usually imagined.[44] Is the same true of the narratives?

One of the lessons I learned from writing a commentary on the *Testament of Abraham* is that scholars of religion can be very slow at getting a joke. Although this pseudepigraphon is full of levity,[45] the secondary literature is not.[46] The scholars have been like some of the pedantic scribes who wrote in the Greek manuscripts of the *Testament of Abraham*: their carping marginalia reveal that, again and again, the jests went over their all-too-pious heads.

Having said that, I am doubtful that the Gospels offer us much on this score. Maybe Matthew intended Peter sinking into the waves to be funny, but this is far from obvious. The same goes for the rest of his Gospel. If we find fiction in his infancy narrative, it cannot be because we find it humorous.[47] We may regard Matt 2 as mostly haggadah, but the main event is the slaughter of infants in Bethlehem. Rachel weeps. We do not laugh. Nor is

---

43. One may compare the parodic humor of *The Alphabet of Ben Sira*. See David Stern, "The Alphabet of Ben Sira and the Early History of Parody in Jewish Literature," in *The Idea of Biblical Interpretation: Essays in Honor of James L. Kugel* (ed. Hindy Najman and Judith H. Newman; JSJSup 83; Leiden: Brill, 2004), 423–48.

44. See Jakob Jónsson, *Humor and Irony in the New Testament Illuminated by Parallels in Talmud and Midrash* (BZRG 28; Leiden: Brill, 1985).

45. Dale C. Allison Jr., *The Testament of Abraham* (CEJL; Berlin: de Gruyter, 2003), 51–52.

46. Pervo (*Profit with Delight*, 58–66) finds a similar deficiency in critical readings of Acts.

47. Although it is true that the magi trick Herod in Matt 2, I doubt that ancient audiences would have found humor in this. Jónsson (*Humor and Irony*, 160–61) thinks otherwise.

Luke 1–2 full of mirth. The powerful hymns, in which the hungry are filled with good things and the rich sent away empty, are dead serious. So too are the chapters that follow them. Once more, then, we have not found evidence that a "purely metaphorical" reading was what our authors expected.

Textual Guidance?

Although general considerations about genre, ancient readers, and humor have not established that the evangelists intended some of their tales to be received as fiction-with-a-message, it still remains to look more closely at the texts themselves. Have they left any clear clues as to their intentions?

The *Testament of Abraham* opens with these words: "Abraham lived the measure of his life, nine hundred and ninety-five years, and all the years of his life he passed in quietness, meekness, and righteousness." This jolts because it drastically disagrees with Gen 25:7, which says that Abraham lived to be a more modest, albeit still unbelievable, 175. By greatly inflating Abraham's life span to an incredible 995, the *Testament of Abraham* makes the patriarch live longer than anyone else, including Methuselah. The latter, according to Gen 5:27, made it to 969. The author of the *Testament of Abraham* wants us to feel the absurdity when, later in the story, the patriarch tells God that he wants more time. Even the longest-lived human being balked at death when it came. So the number 995 is part of the setup for the fictional narrative that follows. The reader knows, in the very first verse, that the text is not going to adhere to the biblical history. In other words, the *Testament of Abraham* is declaring its nature up front: this cannot be the way that it really was, because this is not how it is in the Bible.

The book of Judith does something similar. Its opening verses assert that Nebuchadnezzar was ruler of the Assyrians, that Nineveh was his capital city, that he made war on Media, that he was "lord of all the earth," and that Arphaxad was king of the Medes, all of which are manifestly against the facts. C. C. Torrey commented, "It is just as though a modern story-teller should say: It happened at the time when Napoleon Bonaparte was king of England, and Otto von Bismarck was on the throne in Mexico. The Jewish novelist shows his humor, as well as his care for the right appreciation of his work. He knew that the readers and hearers of his own day, the young and the old alike, would see his meaning."[48] In other words, the absurdities and

---

48. Charles C. Torrey, *The Apocryphal Literature: A Brief Introduction* (New Haven: Yale University Press, 1945), 89–90. He continues in a footnote: "The humor and its purpose are quite lost on our modern commentators, who, without exception, believe the author of the narrative to be aiming to give it a real historical setting, and are astonished at his ignorance." See further Toni Craven, *Artistry and Faith in the Book of Judith* (SBLDS 70; Chico, CA: Scholars Press, 1983), 71–74.

contradictions of established knowledge, which continue to add up as the story moves forward,[49] advertise fiction.[50]

I cannot see that the canonical Gospels ever do this sort of thing. Indeed, they appear to do just the opposite. Consider Mark's baptismal narrative. We may infer, for any number of higher-critical or philosophical reasons, that the voice and the dove are theological interpretation. But the text itself does nothing to encourage one to think this, as the history of interpretation proves. Christians before the Enlightenment uniformly understood Mark 1:9–11 to be, among other things, the record of a genuine event—dove, voice, and all. The miraculous motifs are completely intertwined with the notice, surely historical, that John baptized Jesus. What in the text itself would prod a Christian reader to suppose the baptism to be historical but the dove unhistorical?[51]

It is the same with the darkness at noon in Mark 15:33. Notwithstanding the symbolic meaning(s) that all readers have found, to my knowledge no one, until recent times, thought the darkness to be "purely metaphorical."[52] This is understandable. The sun's failure is precisely dated: "When it was noon, darkness came over the whole land until three in the afternoon."[53] Beyond that, what premodern Christian did not believe in supernatural portents? Even Josephus believed in them, as did Philo, who observed that

49. See further Carey A. Moore, *Judith: A New Translation and Commentary* (AB 40; Garden City, NY: Doubleday, 1985), 47–48.

50. Perhaps something similar takes place in the *Life of Adam and Eve* and the *Liber antiquitatum biblicarum*. Even when these books do not contradict the Bible, they go far beyond it. Perhaps the numerous, substantial expansions would have encouraged ancient hearers to think in terms of edifying fiction rather than the real past.

51. See Powell, "Authorial Intent," 233–37. He observes that "the frequent intra-narrative shift from 'historical reporting' to 'parable' in the Gospels is marked . . . by a change in narration (i.e., by introduction of discourse): the character Jesus tells parables; the narrator does not. Even then, the narrator sometimes instructs the reader explicitly by stating outright, 'And he told them a parable' (or some such similar language)." One could compare haggadic midrash, which takes the form of commentary upon a biblical text and in this way distinguishes itself from Scripture. The evangelists offer no analogous guide. But against Powell, note this statement by Gundry: "It might be argued that biblical clarity demands that Matthew identify the unhistorical elements in his gospel. But the argument presumes it was always important for a biblical writer to distinguish between history and nonhistory. This presumption betrays a modern preoccupation with historical-critical concerns. Whether the distinction was always important to make is one of the points in question" (*Matthew*, 632).

52. See Dale C. Allison Jr., "Darkness at Noon (Matt 27:45)," in *Studies in Matthew: Interpretation Past and Present* (Grand Rapids: Baker Academic, 2005), 79–106.

53. Raymond E. Brown observes, "There is no way to know whether the individual evangelists, Mark and Matt, thought that there was physical darkness at midday on Golgotha—more likely they did, for they attach to it an 'hour' specification similar to those they attach to events they posit as real" (*The Death of the Messiah: From Gethsemane to the Grave; A Commentary on the Passion Narratives of the Four Gospels* [2 vols.; New York: Doubleday, 1994], 2:1034). That Luke thought of a real event is a near certainty (see ibid., 2:1038–43).

eclipses "are indications either of the death of kings or of the destruction of cities."[54]

Consider next Luke's infancy narrative. What does the text itself intimate? The colorful miracle stories about John and Jesus are prefaced by the dedication to Theophilus, in which Luke stresses that he has investigated everything carefully and is going to present an orderly account that stems ultimately from eyewitnesses (Luke 1:1–4). Loveday Alexander has commented that Luke's preface "breathes a measured air of moderate rationalism which the ancient reader must have found deeply reassuring."[55] If such comes before the infancy narrative, immediately following is not "Once upon a time" but this: "In the fifteenth year of the reign of Emperor Tiberius, when Pontius Pilate was governor of Judea, and Herod was ruler of Galilee, and his brother Philip ruler of the region of Ituraea and Trachonitis, and Lysanias ruler of Abilene, during the high priesthood of Annas and Caiaphas, the word of God came to John son of Zechariah in the wilderness" (Luke 3:1–2). If Luke thought of his stories about the conception, birth, and youth of John and Jesus as being more haggadic than historical, is it not odd that he sandwiched them between a preface that makes him sound like a would-be historian and a sentence full of bona fide chronological data?[56]

Matthew leaves me with a similar question. If he thought of his infancy narrative as haggadic fiction, why does he adorn it with several so-called formula quotations? Do these not leave the strong impression of literal promise and fulfillment? After the angel of the Lord appears to Joseph in a dream, telling him to take Mary as his wife and name her child "Jesus," Matthew appends these words: "All this took place to fulfill what had been spoken by the Lord through the prophet: 'Look, the virgin shall conceive and bear a son. . . .'" (1:18–23). I am struck by the phrase "all this took place" (τοῦτο . . . ὅλον γέγονεν). Does this not prod readers to think in terms of a real past event that brought an ancient prophecy to realization?

---

54. Josephus, *J.W.* 6.288–300. For Philo, see Eusebius, *Praep. ev.* 8.14.50. Note that Thucydides, despite his rationalistic tendencies, records natural events that people took to presage human events (*Hist.* 1.23.3; 2.8.3; 3.89.2–4).

55. Loveday C. A. Alexander, "Fact, Fiction and the Genre of Acts," in *Acts in Its Ancient Literary Context: A Classicist Looks at the Acts of the Apostles* (LNTS 298; London: T & T Clark, 2005), 161.

56. Yet ancient novels, such as Chariton's *Chaereas and Callirhoë*, can incorporate accurate historical details or sound in part like serious historical works (see the remarks in G. P. Goold's LCL edition, pp. 10–12). The book of 3 Maccabees supplies a Jewish example: "The author adopts all of the outward mannerisms of a serious historian and, yet, seems unconcerned by the fact that the fictional character of his work would be apparent to any reader who was historically sophisticated enough to appreciate his use of the conventions of Hellenistic historiography" (Sara R. Johnson, "Third Maccabees: Historical Fictions and the Shaping of Jewish Identity in the Hellenistic Period," in *Ancient Fiction: The Matrix of Early Christian and Jewish Narrative* [ed. Jo-Ann Brant, Charles W. Hedrick, and Chris Shea; SBLSymS 32; Atlanta: Society of Biblical Literature, 2005], 188).

Again, and to move from the beginning of the Gospel to its end: according to Matt 27:51–53, when Jesus died, "the earth shook, and the rocks were
split. The tombs also were opened, and many bodies of the saints who had
fallen asleep were raised. After his resurrection they came out of the tombs
and entered the holy city and appeared to many." My guess is that if we could
somehow poll contemporary New Testament scholars, we would find more
doubt about the historicity of this story than any other in the Synoptics.[57] I, for
one, would bet my soul that this is theological fiction, a "purely metaphorical
narrative." But look at the text closely. Although the passage begins as though
it is narrating events that took place when Jesus died, we soon enough run
into the phrase, "after his resurrection." This postdates some or all of the
events recounted until Easter Sunday or later. The notice is very confusing.
Why narrate in chapter 27 events that occur only later, after the beginning of
chapter 28? And what exactly takes place only "after his resurrection"—all of
the events recounted, including the earthquake and the opening of tombs, or
only some of them? The commentators display more than ordinary confusion
on the matter. Some of us have even found "after his resurrection" so awkward
that we have inferred it to be a secondary addition, either tacked on by Matthew to a tradition he inherited or (despite the near unanimity of the textual
tradition) by someone after him.[58] Whether or not such surgery is justified,
somebody seemingly wanted to make sure that Jesus was, in fact, really the
firstborn from the dead (Col 1:18; cf. Acts 26:23; Rom 8:29; Rev 1:5) or, perhaps
at the same time, wished to give him enough time to get to Hades to rescue
the saints from death, because who else could "the holy ones" have been?[59] In

57. I have formed the impression that of all the passages in the Gospels, it is Matt 27:51–53
that has most often prodded commentators to see it as fiction; note Floyd V. Filson, *The Gospel
according to St Matthew* (2nd ed.; BNTC; London: Adam & Charles Black, 1971), 297 (Matt
27:51–53 "may originally have been a figurative teaching, but 'Matthew' takes it as a real event");
Donald A. Hagner, *Matthew 14–28* (WBC 33B; Dallas: Word, 1995), 851 ("there is a strong possibility that Matthew in these verses is making a theological point rather than simply relating
history"); John Nolland, *The Gospel of Matthew: A Commentary on the Greek Text* (NIGTC;
Grand Rapids: Eerdmans, 2005), 1203–4; Rudolf Schnackenburg, *The Gospel of Matthew* (trans.
Robert R. Barr; Grand Rapids: Eerdmans, 2002), 290 ("the entire passage belongs to a stylistic
genre peculiar to Matthew and is not to be analyzed historically"); Donald Senior, *The Passion
according to Matthew: A Redactional Study* (BETL 29; Leuven: Leuven University Press, 1975),
321 (Matthew intended 27:51–53 to be "theological," not historical). Even the theologically
conservative Frederick Dale Bruner concedes, "I think the probabilities are that the historical
critics are right and that Matthew writes pictorially here" (*The Churchbook, Matthew 13–28*
[vol. 2 of *Matthew: A Commentary*; rev. ed.; Grand Rapids: Eerdmans, 2004], 761).

58. See Dale C. Allison Jr., "Matt 27:51–53 and the *Descens ad inferos*," in *Neutestamentliche
Exegese im Dialog: Hermeneutik–Wirkungsgeschichte–Matthäusevangelium; Festschrift für
Ulrich Luz zum 70. Geburtstag* (ed. Peter Lampe, Moisés Mayordomo, and Migaku Sato; Neu-
kirchen-Vluyn: Neukirchener Verlag, 2008), 335–55.

59. Cf. *Gos. Nic.* Latin B 10(26):1: "Then we all went forth with the Lord, leaving Satan
and Hades in Tartarus. And to us and many others it was commanded that we should rise in

either case, the notice betrays an attempt to resolve a perceived chronological quandary. How could B have taken place before A? Despite our modern incredulity, the evangelist or a very early copyist was thinking about Matt 27:51–53 as though it really happened. But perhaps this should not surprise so much. If one believed that God had literally raised Jesus from the dead and will, in the end, also literally raise the faithful, surely it would be no problem to credit God with literally raising a few saints in between. From what I have been able to gather, all Christians until the eighteenth century understood Matthew's amazing tale to be a historical event.[60]

Redaction Criticism

Despite the uncertain results so far, there is one last criterion by which we might decide that a Synoptic author did not take himself to be writing about real past events: redaction criticism. On the supposition that one evangelist used and rewrote another, we might be able to uncover what an evangelist changed or added and infer that he must, at points, have known that he was not adhering to the real past.[61] If, for instance, Matthew turned Mark's lone Gerasene demoniac into two, or if he had Jesus deliver a long sermon on a mountain when his tradition did no such thing (Matt 5:1–7:28; contrast Luke 6), or if he made up the story of Peter walking on the water, which has no Markan counterpart, surely he must have known that he was writing fiction. Again, if we could credit the view that Matt 1–2 is a free rewriting of Luke 1–2 or of its traditions (Gundry has argued this),[62] or that Luke 1–2 is a free rewriting of Matt 1–2 (such is the view of Michael Goulder),[63] then we might draw the same inference.

If I could persuade myself that Goulder or Gundry were right, it would be hard not to surmise that at least Matthew or Luke, for a significant stretch of text, was consciously doing something other than narrating past events.

---

the body to testify in the world of the resurrection of our Lord Jesus Christ and of those things which had been done in the underworld."

60. Jerome (*Comm. Matt.* ad loc.) speaks of "the literal sense" of the "great prodigies" of the earthquake and the splitting of rocks. I know of no justification for the generalization, made by Pierre Benoit, that "this passage of Matthew is a piece of theology rather than historical in substance, as many of the Fathers realised" (*The Passion and Resurrection of Jesus Christ* [trans. Benet Weatherhead; New York: Herder & Herder; London: Darton, Longman & Todd, 1969], 204).

61. This appears to be the logic that led Gundry to his conclusion that parts of Matthew were intended to be haggadic or midrashic. In addition, he argues that "early Christians may well have been able to compare his gospel with the tradition, may actually have done so, and thus may have distinguished clearly between history and embroidery" (*Matthew*, 635).

62. Ibid., 13–41.

63. Michael D. Goulder, *Luke: A New Paradigm* (2 vols.; JSNTSup 20; Sheffield: Sheffield Academic Press, 1989), 1:205–69.

Gundry and Goulder have not, however, persuaded me or many others that Matt 1–2 is the basis for Luke 1–2 or vice versa. So I am left to ponder a host of lesser changes, and I am uncertain what they establish. Matthew may have copied much of Mark, and Mark may not have Peter walking on the water, but that scarcely establishes that Matthew wholly concocted the episode, which occurs only in his Gospel. Some version of it may already have circulated in his Christian community. How could one ever know otherwise? Again, Matthew narrates events at the empty tomb that Mark does not—the posting of guards and an earthquake, for example—yet one fails to see how we could ever demonstrate a purely redactional origin for any of this material. We have no reason to believe that Matthew's community had no stories of Jesus besides those known from Mark and Q. Indeed, as soon as that community began to use Mark, elaborations upon and expansions of it would have come into being. The First Gospel must be as much a repository of popular traditions as it is the creative work of its author.[64]

A psychological issue also presents itself here. Even if we could somehow decide that a story had no traditional basis, one would be uncertain what to infer. It is, to illustrate, possible that the story of the virgin birth derived from a reading of Isa 7:14, and that its inventor nonetheless thought it happened. If Scripture prophesied it, must it not have come to pass? Early Christians were otherwise capable of moving from should have happened to did happen.[65] John 19:17 says that Jesus carried his "cross by himself." Many modern commentators have understandably inferred that the Fourth Evangelist knew the tradition about Simon of Cyrene (see Mark 15:21) and rejected it. My guess is that he corrected the story not on the basis of historical information but from theological conviction. And yet, just like the author of *Jubilees*, who made Mastema instead of God the instigator of Abraham's undertaking to sacrifice Isaac, he no doubt thought that his version of events must have been true, because he thought his theological convictions to be true. Similarly, when Matthew ran across Mark's Jesus asking, "Why do you call me good?" (Mark 10:18) and turned it into "Why do you ask me about what is good?" (Matt 19:17), he may not have thought that he was being tendentious, because how

64. Ulrich Luz ("Fictionality and Loyalty to Tradition in Matthew's Gospel in the Light of Greek Literature," in *Studies in Matthew* [Grand Rapids: Eerdmans, 2005], 54–79) predicates his comments about Matthew and fiction upon the argument that Matthew consciously composed several fictional episodes, such as Peter walking on the water (14:28–31) and Pilate washing his hands (27:24–25). As indicated, I am uncertain that Luz is right about those episodes; there may be more debt to tradition than he recognizes. I simply do not know. Luz's own conclusion, however, is this: "Matthew is a tradition-oriented author who resorts to bold fictions when it suits his purpose. These are not mythical fictions but operate on the level of real history. Matthew was well aware of them. He must have realized too that in some cases he verges on the historically grotesque" (p. 63).

65. This was the famous (and convincing) argument made by Strauss (*Life of Jesus Critically Examined*, 55–87, and passim).

could his Jesus have asked what he appears to ask in Mark? In other words, Matthew may have been, in his own mind, correcting the record, just as perhaps the Chronicler thought that he was improving upon Samuel and Kings, without any sense that he was falsifying the facts. All of which is to say: even when, from our point of view, the evangelists were departing from their traditions, they may not have thought that they were moving away from history.[66] It is perhaps like the speeches in Acts. Although Luke probably did not have sources for most of them, he need not have understood himself to be writing fiction. He may instead have believed that he could reproduce the gist of what Peter or Stephen or Paul must have said or thought: "this or something like this" had to have been true.[67]

Summing Up

I have not, I am sure, canvassed all the ways an evangelist might have signified that a particular passage is fiction or has haggadic features. I also have not explored the possibility, forwarded by anti-Christian polemicists from time to time, that the authors of our Gospels knew that what they were writing was mere fiction yet wanted everyone to regard their products as fact,[68] or the related possibility that the evangelists, like perhaps the author of the *Epistle of Aristeas* or the authors of some of the apocryphal books of acts,[69] were doing something akin to Plato when he constructed, as a

66. Note this observation by Milikowsky: "A medieval historian who invented events or documents was neither necessarily intent on deceiving his audience, nor had he failed to understand the difference between history and nonhistory. Rather, his basic presuppositions concerning God's working in history caused him to be the first to believe the 'history' he was presenting" ("Midrash," 120). Perhaps relevant here is the psychology of producing pseudonymous texts. Sometimes, no doubt, the intention was to deceive. Other times, however, authors must have sincerely believed that they were, with divine assistance, faithfully representing those in whose names they wrote. See Kurt Aland, "The Problem of Anonymity and Pseudonymity in Christian Literature of the First Two Centuries," in *The Authorship and Integrity of the New Testament* (London: SPCK, 1965), 1–13.

67. Cf. Plato, *Phaed.* 114d. The discourses in John's Gospel seem to me to offer a different phenomenon: the author can expound and expand traditional sayings because he believes that his own words are inspired (see 14:25–26; 15:26–27; 16:12–15).

68. See the polemical take of Hermann Samuel Reimarus, *Reimarus: Fragments* (ed. Charles Talbert; Philadelphia: Fortress, 1970); also the opponents in Matt 28:11–15.

69. Josephus (*Ant.* 12.100) took the *Letter of Aristeas* to be history. Hippolytus evidently read the apocryphal acts of the apostles as though they were intended to be something more than theological entertainment; note *Comm. Dan.* 3.29—"when Paul was condemned to the beasts, the lion loosed against him fell at his feet and licked him"—which depends upon *Acts Paul* 7. On the nature of the apocryphal acts, see Christine M. Thomas, *The Acts of Peter, Gospel Literature, and the Ancient Novel: Rewriting the Past* (Oxford: Oxford University Press, 2003). Along with Thomas, I doubt that the authors of the apocryphal acts thought that they were simply composing fiction.

"noble lie," his myth of Atlantis.[70] And I have said nothing about how legends arise in the first place or how they can so quickly become received as history—fascinating, if murky, topics.[71] Furthermore, I have failed to discuss the exceedingly complex issue of how our categories of history and fiction correlate with the perceptions of early Christians. Our predecessors cannot have perceived things as we do.[72]

This last issue is particularly important. All I can say about it here is this: although the evangelists, compared to Greco-Roman historians or Celsus or Origen, must have had woefully undeveloped notions of myth and history, they did at least know about competing narratives and of the difference between telling truth and telling lies. Not only is the fundamental distinction between truth and falsehood probably inherent in the descriptive function of language—ordinary descriptive claims present themselves as correct, not incorrect, which means true, not false—but Matthew was acquainted with a story, circulating outside the churches, about the guards at Jesus' tomb, a story that he deemed false (Matt 28:11–15); and Luke and his audience were—as we know from Luke 24:11, where the apostles disbelieve the women who have been to the empty tomb—familiar with the category of "idle tale" (λῆρος).

At this point, however, I do not wish to explore any of those issues, interesting and important as they are. Instead, I wish to stress, here near the end, that we should not underestimate how literal minded people have been about stories that so many of us in the academy routinely think of as fictional or purely metaphorical. This matters because the stories that some within the guild now reckon to be "purely metaphorical" in intention involve, in almost every case, a miracle.

I once heard an Eastern Orthodox priest give a sermon in which he recounted how Saint Thekla (or Thecla), being pursued by her enemies, ran straight into the side of a mountain—not into a cave in the mountain, but into the solid side of the mountain. He told it as unsullied fact. I have read that, in 1890,

70. Strauss (*New Life of Jesus*, 2:208–10) argued this for John's Gospel. For Plato's ability to write a "likely story," see Elizabeth Belfiore, "'Lies Unlike the Truth': Plato on Hesiod, *Theogony* 27," *TAPA* 115 (1985): 47–57. Belfiore believes that Hesiod may already have understood his own work to be true and false at the same time.

71. Strauss (*New Life of Jesus*, 2:206–8) offers some plausible conjectures on this matter. According to Northrop Frye, it is generally true that "accepted myths soon cease to function as myths: they are asserted to be historical facts or descriptive accounts of what 'really happened'" (*Words with Power: Being a Second Study of "The Bible and Literature"* [San Diego: Harcourt, Brace, Jovanovich, 1990], 34).

72. Strauss observed that "the line of distinction between history and fiction, prose and poetry, was not drawn so clearly as with us" (*Life of Jesus Critically Examined*, 85). Compare Alexander's observation that "historical writing in the first centuries of our era suffered from a fundamental failure to distinguish 'fact' from 'fiction'" ("Genre of Acts," 142). Luz ("Fictionality and Loyalty") offers some helpful reflections on this issue.

some Shoshones and Arapahos sincerely testified that "while traveling along on the prairie they had met with a party of Indians who had been dead thirty or forty years, and who had been resurrected by the Messiah."[73] I am further familiar with the *Shivhei ha-Besht*, which collects astounding tales about the Hasidic wonder-worker, the Baal Shem Tov.[74] Many of those tales go back to eyewitnesses and friends of the Besht. They sincerely believed in his miracles.[75] And, to cite an example much closer to the world and time of Jesus, there are the comments of Aristobulus on Exod 19:16–18, on the thunder, lightning, trumpet blast, smoke, fire, and earthquake that accompanied the giving of the law on Sinai: the allegorist saw none of this as metaphor but accepted it all as sober fact.[76]

One could go on and on. The point is that our critical sensibilities are deficient guides for figuring out whether an ancient author intended a text to be read as faithful to the past or as something else. Despite our modern judgments, it is quite possible that the Synoptic evangelists, who knew nothing of modern critical history and little or nothing about Greek historiography,[77] believed most or even all of the spectacular stories that they narrated—just as Augustine, Gregory of Tours, Gregory the Great, and Bede, who did not distinguish between historiography and hagiography, believed the miracle stories that they recounted.[78]

Early Christians took for granted that miracles enveloped the life of their Savior. Indeed, their foundational communal narrative consisted of the scriptural accounts of Israel, stories regarding Jesus' ministry, and traditions about the beginnings of the churches; in other words, it was one long string of miracles. Further, they believed that "with God all things are possible" (Mark 10:27). In short, they may have had no social context for thinking of certain stories in the Jesus tradition what Augustine says somewhere of the tales of Apuleius, that they are either falsehoods or so anomalous that they are deserv-

---

73. George Bird Grinnell, "Account of the Northern Cheyennes concerning the Messiah Superstition," *Journal of American Folklore* 4 (1891): 61.

74. Dan Ben-Amos and Jerome R. Mintz, trans. and eds., *In Praise of the Baal Shem Tov [Shivhei ha-Besht]: The Earliest Collection of Legends about the Founder of Hasidism* (Bloomington: Indiana University Press, 1970).

75. See Immanuel Etkes, *The Besht: Magician, Mystic, and Leader* (trans. Saadya Sternberg; Waltham, MA: Brandeis University Press; Hanover, NH: University Press of New England, 2005), 237–44.

76. See Eusebius, *Praep. ev.* 10.8.

77. According to Emilio Gabba, "classical Greek historiography did have some influence in antiquity, but in very restricted circles" ("True History and False History in Classical Antiquity," *JRS* 71 [1981]: 52).

78. On Gregory of Tours, see Giselle de Nie, "History and Miracle: Gregory's Use of Metaphor," in *The World of Gregory of Tours* (ed. Kathleen Mitchell and Ian Wood; CBT 8; Leiden: Brill, 2002), 261–79; on Gregory the Great, Paul Meyvaert, "The Enigma of Gregory the Great's *Dialogues*: A Response to Francis Clark," *JEH* 39 (1988): 335–81; on Bede, Joel T. Rosenthal, "Bede's Use of Miracles in 'The Ecclesiastical History,'" *Traditio* 31 (1975): 328–35.

edly disbelieved. To have doubted miracles associated with Jesus would, for them, have been the same thing as having no Christian faith at all.[79]

Since reality is socially constructed, plausibility and the line between credulity and incredulity are relative.[80] The worldview of those who first heard the canonical Gospels was necessarily shaped not only by the slew of spectacular miracle stories in the Jewish Bible, which they reverenced as Scripture, but also by the conviction that Jesus had, not long ago, risen from the dead, and that many who believed in him had received miraculous healings. Had the first followers of Jesus known anything about skeptical historiography, they would have rejected it, just as some modern fundamentalists dismiss out of hand all higher-critical conclusions about the Bible. The earliest Christians of whom we have record lived in a world of miraculous possibilities. Finding "purely metaphorical narratives" in their stories about Jesus may be no more plausible than finding "purely metaphorical stories" in the miracle tales about Sabbatai Sevi. That we differentiate metaphorical narratives from historical narratives is a fact about us, not necessarily a fact about first-century Christians.

Outcome

The upshot of my discussion, which has been mostly negative, is twofold. First, it is not at all clear that the stories that many of us now regard as "purely metaphorical" were so intended by the canonical evangelists. In my own religious context, this is unfortunate. It would be to my advantage, when sharing with my seminary students or other adult learners my belief that a particular biblical text is unhistorical, to be able to say, with a clear conscience, that its author thought so too. Alas, it is not so. As far as I can determine, from beginning to end, "the authors of the Gospels believed that they were reporting a true story."[81]

Second, however, there is no room for certainty here. Although I have not sided with those who insist that we should attribute "purely metaphorical" readings to the evangelists and their early audiences, they could nonetheless be right, however scanty the evidence for their position. The Gospels, written

79. Serious critical discussion of miracles within a Christian context did not get much under way until the twelfth-century scholastic philosophers; see Benedicta Ward, *Miracles and the Medieval Mind: Theory, Record, and Event, 1000–1215* (Philadelphia: University of Pennsylvania Press, 1982), esp. 3–19.

80. Helpful here are de Nie, "History and Miracle"; Paul Veyne, *Did the Greeks Believe in Their Myths? An Essay on the Constitutive Imagination* (Chicago: University of Chicago Press, 1988).

81. So Doron Mendels, *The Rise and Fall of Jewish Nationalism* (ABRL; New York: Doubleday, 1992), 48. According to Mendels, the "various techniques found in Hellenistic historiography" have influenced the canonical Gospels.

to be recited aloud, were interpreted not by individuals silently reading alone in their rooms but rather by groups hearing words together in social settings; and those settings surely offered clues as to how texts or episodes within them should be understood. "Textual characteristics are only the final influence on reception, conditioned by and moderating in turn the influences which precede them."[82] Maybe the prefatory or interpretive comments that accompanied a reading of Matthew's infancy narrative would have made it plain enough to an audience that "not everything that is remembered happened."[83] And maybe the ecclesiastical setting for a reading of Mark's passion narrative would have made it evident that the darkness at noon was true only theologically. We can never know otherwise.[84] The original settings are gone for good, so we can say next to nothing about them. It stands to reason, however, that if a respected religious authority, while introducing or reciting an amazing tale, clearly indicated that it was a fable instead of history, the audience would happily have gone along—this must have been the situation when Jesus told his parables—just as that same audience would have gone along had its trusted leader instead claimed to be relating what really happened. "The problem of belief is inextricably involved with the problem of authority."[85]

Meta-Analysis

Despite the required hesitation, my inference, after taking everything into account, remains conventional: our Synoptic writers thought that they were reconfiguring memories of Jesus, not inventing theological tales. Such a supposition, however, does nothing to clarify whether or not the evangelists were right about the mnemonic nature of their traditions. This is where chapters 1–5 have sought to make a contribution.

82. M. J. Wheeldon, "'True Stories': The Reception of 'Historiography' in Antiquity," in *History as Text: The Writing of Ancient History* (ed. Averil Cameron; Chapel Hill: University of North Carolina Press, 1989), 44. Werner Kelber writes, "Oral and orally dependent texts, as many of our classical texts are, were tradition bound, variously interfacing with orality, continuously reinventing themselves in variant versions, and deriving meaning from extratextual signals no less (or even more) than from internal signification" ("Orality and Biblical Studies: A Review Essay" [online: www.bookreviews.org/pdf/2107_6748.pdf (cited 18 November 2009)]).

83. Thomas M. Bolin, "History, Historiography, and the Use of the Past in the Hebrew Bible," in *The Limits of Historiography: Genre and Narrative in Ancient Historical Texts* (ed. Christina Shuttleworth Kraus; MBCBSup 191; Leiden: Brill, 1999), 123.

84. Christopher Gill remarks, "It is the presumptions of author and audience that distinguish fictional from factual accounts. For a fictional narrative in the past tense is not formally distinguishable from a narrative of past factual events" ("Plato's Atlantis Story and the Birth of Fiction," *Philosophy and Literature* 3 [1979]: 64).

85. D. C. Feeney, "Towards an Account of the Ancient World's Concepts of Fictive Belief," in *Lies and Fiction in the Ancient World* (ed. Christopher Gill and T. P. Wiseman; Austin: University of Texas Press, 1993), 242.

The problem that those chapters confront—How much history can we show the Gospels to have preserved?[86]—has long called to mind a famous analogy that Albert Einstein and Leopold Infeld employed to clarify the mystifying nature of physics:

> In our endeavor to understand reality we are somewhat like a man trying to understand the mechanism of a closed watch. He sees the face and the moving hands, even hears its ticking, but he has no way of opening the case. If he is ingenious he may form some picture of a mechanism which could be responsible for all the things he observes, but he may never be quite sure his picture is the only one which could explain his observations. He will never be able to compare his picture with the real mechanism.[87]

It is similar with our sources for Jesus. We see the faces of our texts, but the history of Jesus himself and the history of the traditions about him remain eternally out of sight. So we must conjure them in our informed imaginations. Further, since we are not looking at things that can be explained in only one way, critical reconstructions compete with each other. We cannot, so to speak, open the case, check the facts, and quit telling falsehoods.

We can, nonetheless, make numerous informed judgments—for instance, that the Romans crucified Jesus as "king of the Jews"—and we can, happily, judge many propositions more probable than others. It is, for example, much more credible that Jesus was a millenarian prophet than that the eschatological enthusiasm reflected in so many early Christian texts appeared independently of his influence. Still, a vast ignorance remains, and our reach often exceeds our grasp. Time after time, if we are honest, arguments concocted to demonstrate that Jesus really did say this or really did do that fall flat. Historians of Jesus, including myself, have too often assumed that we should be able, with sufficient ingenuity, to reconstruct the genealogy of almost every individual tradition. But it is not so. Some things just cannot be done, and desire does not beget ability.

My response to this situation is not to throw in the towel but to play the game differently. Instead of attempting to authenticate individual item after individual item, I have preferred, for the most part, to identify larger patterns across the sources and then to seek for the best explanation. This strategy has been born of two circumstances, the first being my disillusionment with much of the critical scholarship that I imbibed and practiced in my younger days, the second being my education into modern cognitive studies of memory, which

86. "How much history do the Gospels preserve?" is a different question with a different answer. My concern is with the abilities of less-than-omniscient historians, who must leave many questions unanswered.

87. Albert Einstein and Leopold Infeld, *The Evolution of Physics: From Early Concepts to Relativity and Quanta* (New York: Simon & Schuster, 1966), 31.

on the whole have made me much more cautious about making historical claims than in the past.

Some will surely consider me excessively skeptical, although others will no doubt deem me, on the contrary, unduly credulous. I view myself as simply heeding common historical sense, a course that I cannot but commend to others. Yet I must add that I do not presume to have stumbled upon the one true method for conducting the quest. I do not invite others to follow my lead, much less insist that they do so. There is more than one profitable way to puzzle out the figure of Jesus. This book defends and deploys just one. It is simply the record of where one scholar, after pondering much of the critical literature on Jesus and some of the critical literature on memory, has ended up.

Coda

A friendly reviewer of an earlier book of mine judged that it marks the end of the third quest for the historical Jesus.[88] Apart from the inordinate importance that this verdict assigns to my work, two circumstances prevent me from going along. One is that the typology to which the appellation "third quest" belongs—old quest, new quest, third quest—is a mistake best forgotten.[89] I can hardly flatter myself with having closed out a period or endeavor that never existed.

The other, and more important, fact is this: Although I usually move from one book to the next without concern for how they relate to each other—each is its own beginning and end—I cannot recall writing anything that makes the preceding pages unexpected. Yet whether or not I have unwittingly deconstructed my own endeavors, the present volume, in which I continue to pursue the historical Jesus, finds me still toiling at the old tasks. While I may have abandoned some of the traditional means, I have not abandoned the traditional end, which is knowledge of a historical figure.

Perhaps, nonetheless, my reviewer's point of view is not so far from my own. If he construes the quest as a positive theological enterprise, and of my work as persuasively expressing some cynicism on that score, we are kindred spirits. It is not that the historical Jesus is theologically neither here nor there. The quest has, as a matter of modern theological history, had far-reaching consequences. Still, my take is that it is, by nature, primarily negative. Its chief

88. See Scot McKnight, "Historical Jesus Studies: A Dead End?" (online: http://blog.beliefnet.com/jesuscreed/2009/05/historical-jesus-studies-a-dea.html [cited 18 November 2009]). McKnight's words are these: "Allison's book brings the quest for the historical Jesus to a new dead-end. We can't do what we thought we were going to do. The Third Quest is, at least for me, officially over."

89. See Dale C. Allison Jr., *Resurrecting Jesus: The Earliest Christian Tradition and Its Interpreters* (New York: T & T Clark, 2005), 1–26.

function has been to discourage many of us from believing some of the things that we were taught in our youth or have heard in the churches.

We should be grateful, then, that the so-called historical Jesus is only one of numerous theological resources, and far from the most important. Consider the present volume, which, if its author is any good at introspection, is much more the product of historical curiosity and professional habits of mind than of theological aspirations. Even if, let us say, a Christian reader is cheered by my case that Jesus had an exalted self-conception, christological reflection is much more than what the first-century Jesus is likely to have thought or said about himself. Would that it were so easy. Christology must wrestle with Paul, study the Cappadocians, engage modern philosophy, and do much else besides. Similarly, while Christians may deem it necessary that Jesus did not run from death, a historian's conclusion to that effect hardly constitutes a theory of the atonement. And so it goes. To do history is not to do theology.

Although I have no desire to contract the circle of my readers, it seems to me both vain and inane to imagine that a book such as this can contribute to our knowledge of God, or that it should draw much attention from the theologians. Even though the quest has served many of us as a wake-up call from our dogmatic slumbers, it is no substitute for constructive theology. It can be, at best, only prologue.

While it may be an "emotional necessity to exalt the problem to which one wants to devote a lifetime,"[90] and while I am proudly a historian, I must confess that history is not what matters most. If my deathbed finds me alert and not overly racked with pain, I will then be preoccupied with how I have witnessed and embodied faith, hope, and charity. I will not be fretting over the historicity of this or that part of the Bible.

---

90. So Eugene P. Wigner, "Remarks on the Mind-Body Question," in *Quantum Theory and Measurement* (ed. John Archibald Wheeler and Wojciech Hubert Zurek; Princeton: Princeton University Press, 1983), 174.

Bibliography

Aalen, Sverre. "'Reign' and 'House' in the Kingdom of God in the Gospels." *NTS* 8 (1962): 215–40.

Aarde, Andries van. "The Historicity of the Circle of the Twelve: All Roads Lead to Jerusalem." *HvTSt* 55 (1999): 795–826.

Abbott, Edwin A. *"The Son of Man," or, Contributions to the Study of the Thoughts of Jesus.* Cambridge: Cambridge University Press, 1910.

Abbott, T. K. *A Critical and Exegetical Commentary on the Epistles to the Ephesians and to the Colossians.* ICC. Edinburgh: T & T Clark, 1902.

Abegg, Martin G., Jr. "Who Ascended to Heaven? 4Q491, 4Q427, and the Teacher of Righteousness." Pages 61–73 in *Eschatology, Messianism, and the Dead Sea Scrolls.* Edited by Craig A. Evans and Peter W. Flint. Grand Rapids: Eerdmans, 1997.

Abegg, Martin G., Jr., and Craig A. Evans. "Messianic Passages in the Dead Sea Scrolls." Pages 191–203 in *Qumran-Messianism: Studies on the Messianic Expectations in the Dead Sea Scrolls.* Edited by James H. Charlesworth, Hermann Lichtenberger, and Gerbern S. Oegema. Tübingen: Mohr Siebeck, 1998.

Abravanel, Isaac. *Mikraot Ketanot 613 Mitsvot Ha-Torah.* Cincinnati: Bloch, 1892.

Achtemeier, Paul J. "An Apocalyptic Shift in Early Christian Tradition: Reflections on Some Canonical Evidence." *CBQ* 45 (1983): 231–48.

———. *1 Peter: A Commentary on 1 Peter.* Hermeneia. Minneapolis: Fortress, 1996.

Adam, Karl. *The Christ of Faith: The Christology of the Church.* New York: Pantheon, 1957.

Adams, Edward. *The Stars Will Fall from Heaven: Cosmic Catastrophe in the New Testament and Its World.* LNTS 347. London: T & T Clark, 2007.

Adas, Michael. *Prophets of Rebellion: Millenarian Protest Movements against the European Colonial Order.* Chapel Hill: University of North Carolina Press, 1979.

Adeyemi, M. E. "The Rulers of This Age in First Corinthians 2:6–8: An Exegetical Exposition." *DBM* 18 (1992): 38–45.

Adler, Alfred. "Early Recollections and Dreams." Pages 350–65 in *The Individual Psychology of Alfred Adler.* Edited by Heinz L. Ansbacher and Rowena R. Ansbacher. New York: Harper & Row, 1956.

Ådna, Jostein. *Jesu Stellung zum Tempel: Die Tempelaktion und das Tempelwort als Ausdruck seiner messianischen Sendung.* WUNT 2/119. Tübingen: Mohr Siebeck, 2000.

Aešcoly, A. Z. "David Reubeni in the Light of History." *JQR* 28 (1937): 1–45.

Ahearne-Kroll, Stephen P. *The Psalms of La-ment in Mark's Passion: Jesus' Davidic Suf-fering*. SNTSMS 142. Cambridge: Cam-bridge University Press, 2007.

Aichele, George, Peter Miscall, and Richard Walsh. "An Elephant in the Room: Histor-ical-Critical and Postmodern Interpretation of the Bible." *JBL* 128 (2009): 383–404.

Aitken, Ellen Bradshaw. *Jesus' Death in Early Christian Memory: The Poetics of the Pas-sion*. NTOA/SUNT 53. Göttingen: Van-denhoeck & Ruprecht; Fribourg: Academic Press, 2004.

Aland, Kurt. "The Problem of Anonymity and Pseudonymity in Christian Literature of the First Two Centuries." Pages 1–13 in *The Authorship and Integrity of the New Testament*. London: SPCK, 1965.

Albertus Magnus. *Enarrationes in Joannem*. Vol. 24 of *Opera omnia*. Edited by A. Bor-gnet. Paris: Ludovicus Vivès, 1890.

———. *Enarrationes in primam partem Evan-gelii Lucae (I–IX)*. Vol. 22 of *Opera omnia*. Edited by A. Borgnet. Paris: Ludovicus Vivès, 1894.

———. *Super Matthaeum capitula XV–XXVIII*. Vol. 21/2 of *Opera omnia*. Edited by B. Schmidt. Aschendorff: Monasterii Westfalorum, 1987.

Aleksandrov, G. S. "The Role of 'Aqiba in the Bar-Kokhba Rebellion." *REJ* 132 (1974): 65–77.

Alexander, Loveday C. A. "Fact, Fiction and the Genre of Acts." Pages 133–64 in *Acts in Its Ancient Literary Context: A Classicist Looks at the Acts of the Apostles*. LNTS 298. London: T & T Clark, 2005.

Alexander, Philip S. "Jerusalem as the *Ompha-los* of the World: On the History of a Geographical Concept." Pages 104–19 in *Jerusalem: Its Sanctity and Centrality to Judaism, Christianity, and Islam*. Edited by Lee I. Levine. New York: Continuum, 1999.

Alford, Henry. *The Four Gospels*. Vol. 1 of *The Greek Testament*. 2nd ed. London: Riving-tons, 1854.

———. *The Greek Testament*. 4 vols in 2. Chicago: Moody, 1958.

Allberry, C. R. C., ed. *A Manichaean Psalm-Book*. With a contribution by Hugo Ibscher. 2 vols. Stuttgart: W. Kohlhammer, 1938.

Allen, Willoughby C. "Mr. Streeter and the Es-chatology of the Gospels." *The Interpreter* 7 (1910–11): 359–64.

Allison, Dale C., Jr. "The Allusive Jesus." Pages 238–48 in *The Historical Jesus in Recent Research*. Edited by James D. G. Dunn and Scot McKnight. Winona Lake, IN: Eisen-brauns, 2005.

———. "Assessing the Arguments." Pages 99–105 in *The Apocalyptic Jesus: A Debate*. Edited by Robert J. Miller. Santa Rosa, CA: Polebridge, 2001.

———. "Behind the Temptations of Jesus: Q 4:1–13 and Mark 1:12–13." Pages 195–214 in *Authenticating the Activities of Jesus*. Edited by Bruce Chilton and Craig A. Evans. NTTS 28/2. Leiden: Brill, 1999.

———. "The Configuration of the Sermon on the Mount and Its Meaning." Pages 172–215 in *Studies in Matthew: Interpretation Past and Present*. Grand Rapids: Baker Aca-demic, 2005.

———. "Darkness at Noon (Matt. 27:45)." Pages 79–105 in *Studies in Matthew: Inter-pretation Past and Present*. Grand Rapids: Baker Academic, 2005.

———. "Deconstructing Matthew." Pages 237–49 in *Studies in Matthew: Interpreta-tion Past and Present*. Grand Rapids: Baker Academic, 2005.

———. *The End of the Ages Has Come: An Early Interpretation of the Passion and Resurrection of Jesus*. SNTW. Edinburgh: T & T Clark, 1987.

———. "The Eschatology of Jesus." Pages 293–99 in *The Origins of Apocalypticism in Judaism and Christianity*. Vol. 1 of *The Encyclopedia of Apocalypticism*. Edited by John J. Collins. New York: Continuum, 1998.

———. "The Forsaken House, Q 13:34–35." Pages 192–204 in *The Jesus Tradition in Q*. Harrisburg, PA: Trinity Press International, 1997.

———. *The Historical Christ and the Theological Jesus*. Grand Rapids: Eerdmans, 2009.

———. "How to Marginalize the Traditional Criteria of Authenticity." Pages 3–30 in vol. 1 of *The Handbook for the Study of the Historical Jesus*. Edited by Tom Holmén and Stanley E. Porter. 4 vols. Leiden: Brill, 2009.

———. *The Intertextual Jesus: Scripture in Q*. Valley Forge, PA: Trinity Press International, 2000.

———. "Jesus and the Covenant: A Response to E. P. Sanders." Pages 61–82 in *The Historical Jesus*. Edited by Craig A. Evans and Stanley E. Porter. BibSem 33. Sheffield: Sheffield Academic Press, 1996. Repr. from *JSNT* 29 (1987): 57–78.

———. "Jesus and the Victory of Apocalyptic." Pages 126–41 in *Jesus and the Restoration of Israel: A Critical Assessment of N. T. Wright's "Jesus and the Victory of God."* Edited by Carey C. Newman. Downers Grove, IL: InterVarsity, 1999.

———. *Jesus of Nazareth: Millenarian Prophet*. Philadelphia: Fortress, 1998.

———. *The Jesus Tradition in Q*. Harrisburg, PA: Trinity Press International, 1997.

———. "The Magi's Angel (Matt. 2:2, 9–10)." Pages 17–41 in *Studies in Matthew: Interpretation Past and Present*. Grand Rapids: Baker Academic, 2005.

———. "Matt 27:51–53 and the *Descens ad inferos*." Pages 335–55 in *Neutestamentliche Exegese im Dialog: Hermeneutik–Wirkungsgeschichte–Matthäusevangelium; Festschrift für Ulrich Luz zum 70. Geburtstag*. Edited by Peter Lampe, Moisés Mayordomo, and Migaku Sato. Neukirchen-Vluyn: Neukirchener Verlag, 2008.

———. "The Missionary Discourse, Q 10:2–16: Its Use by Paul." Pages 104–19 in *The Jesus Tradition in Q*. Harrisburg, PA: Trinity Press International, 1997.

———. *The New Moses: A Matthean Typology*. Minneapolis: Fortress, 1993.

———. "The Pauline Epistles and the Synoptic Gospels: The Pattern of the Parallels." *NTS* 28 (1982): 1–32.

———. "Peter and Cephas: One and the Same." *JBL* 111 (1992): 489–95.

———. "A Plea for Thoroughgoing Eschatology." *JBL* 113 (1994): 651–68.

———. "The Problem of Gehenna." Pages 56–100 in *Resurrecting Jesus: The Earliest Christian Tradition and Its Interpreters*. New York: T & T Clark, 2005.

———. "Pro: Jesus Was an Apocalyptic Prophet." Pages 17–29 in *The Apocalyptic Jesus: A Debate*. Edited by Robert J. Miller. Santa Rosa, CA: Polebridge, 2001.

———. "Q 12:51–53 and Mk 9:11–13 and the Messianic Woes." Pages 289–310 in *Authenticating the Words of Jesus*. Edited by Bruce Chilton and Craig A. Evans. NTTS 28/1. Leiden: Brill, 1998.

———. "Rejecting Violent Judgment: Luke 9:52–56 and Its Relatives." *JBL* 121 (2002): 459–78.

———. "A Response." Pages 83–105 in *The Apocalyptic Jesus: A Debate*. Edited by Robert J. Miller. Santa Rosa, CA: Polebridge, 2001.

———. *Resurrecting Jesus: The Earliest Christian Tradition and Its Interpreters*. New York: T & T Clark, 2005.

———. "The Scriptural Background of a Matthean Legend: Ezekiel 37, Zechariah 14, and Matthew 27." In *Life beyond Death in Matthew's Gospel: Religious Metaphor of Bodily Reality?* Edited by Wim Weren. Leuven: Peeters, forthcoming.

———. "The Sermon on the Plain, Q 6:20–49: Its Plan and Its Sources." Pages 67–79 in *The Jesus Tradition in Q*. Valley Forge, PA: Trinity Press International, 1997.

———. *Studies in Matthew: Interpretation Past and Present*. Grand Rapids: Baker Academic, 2005.

———. *The Testament of Abraham*. CEJL. Berlin: de Gruyter, 2003.

———. "Torah, Urzeit, Endzeit." Pages 149–97 in *Resurrecting Jesus: The Earliest Christian Tradition and Its Interpreters*. New York: T & T Clark, 2005.

Anderson, Eric. "The Millerite Use of Prophecy: A Case Study of a 'Striking Fulfilment.'" Pages 78–91 in *The Disappointed: Miller-*

ism and Millenarianism in the Nineteenth Century. Edited by Ronald L. Numbers and Jonathan M. Butler. Bloomington: Indiana University Press, 1987.

Anderson, Hugh. The Gospel of Mark. NCB. London: Oliphants, 1976.

Applebaum, Shim'on. Jews and Greek in Ancient Cyrene. SJLA 28. Leiden: Brill, 1979.

Arnal, William. "Major Episodes in the Biography of Jesus: An Assessment of the Historicity of the Narrative Tradition." TJT 13 (1997): 201–26.

———. "Redactional Fabrication and Group Legitimation: The Baptist's Preaching in Q 3:7–9, 16–17." Pages 165–80 in Conflict and Invention: Literary, Rhetorical, and Social Studies on the Sayings Gospel Q. Edited by John S. Kloppenborg. Valley Forge, PA: Trinity Press International, 1995.

———. "Why Q Failed: From Ideological Project to Group Formation." Pages 67–87 in Redescribing Christian Origins. Edited by Ron Cameron and Merrill P. Miller. SBLSymS 28. Atlanta: Society of Biblical Literature, 2004.

Arnold, Matthew. God and the Bible. London: Smith, Elder, 1885.

Ashton, John. Understanding the Fourth Gospel. Oxford: Clarendon, 1991.

Assmann, Jan. "Ancient Egyptian Antijudaism: A Case of Distorted Memory." Pages 365–76 in Memory Distortion: How Minds, Brains, and Societies Reconstruct the Past. Edited by Daniel L. Schacter. Cambridge, MA: Harvard University Press, 1995.

———. Religion and Cultural Memory: Ten Studies. Translated by Rodney Livingstone. Stanford: Stanford University Press, 2006.

Atkinson, Kenneth. I Cried to the Lord: A Study of the Psalms of Solomon's Historical Background and Social Setting. JSJSup 84. Leiden: Brill, 2004.

———. An Intertextual Study of the Psalms of Solomon: Pseudepigrapha. SBEC 49. Lewiston, NY: Edwin Mellen, 2001.

Attridge, Harold A. The Epistle to the Hebrews. Edited by Helmut Koester. Hermeneia. Philadelphia: Fortress, 1989.

———. "Reflections on Research into Q." Semeia 55 (1992): 223–34.

Aune, David E. "Christian Beginnings and Cognitive Dissonance Theory." Pages 11–47 in In Other Words: Essays on Social Science Methods and the New Testament in Honor of Jerome H. Neyrey. Edited by Anselm C. Hagedorn, Zeba A. Crook, and Eric Stewart. SWBA 2/1. Sheffield: Sheffield Phoenix Press, 2007.

———. "Christian Prophecy and the Messianic Status of Jesus." Pages 300–319 in Apocalypticism, Prophecy, and Magic in Early Christianity: Collected Essays. WUNT 199. Tübingen: Mohr Siebeck, 2006.

———. The Cultic Setting of Realized Eschatology in Early Christianity. NovTSup 28. Leiden: Brill, 1972.

———. "Oral Tradition and the Aphorisms of Jesus." Pages 211–65 in Jesus and the Oral Gospel Tradition. Edited by Henry Wansbrough. JSNTSup 64. Sheffield: JSOT Press, 1991.

———. Prophecy in Early Christianity and the Ancient Mediterranean World. Grand Rapids: Eerdmans, 1983.

———. Revelation 1–5. WBC 52A. Nashville: Thomas Nelson, 1997.

———. Revelation 17–22. WBC 52C. Nashville: Thomas Nelson, 1998.

———. "Understanding Jewish and Christian Apocalyptic." Pages 1–12 in Apocalypticism, Prophecy, and Magic in Early Christianity: Collected Essays. WUNT 199. Tübingen: Mohr Siebeck, 2006.

Aus, Roger David. The Death, Burial, and Resurrection of Jesus, and the Death, Burial, and Translation of Moses in Judaic Tradition. Lanham, MD: University Press of America, 2008.

Avigad, N. "A Depository of Inscribed Ossuaries." IEJ 12 (1962): 9–11.

Baarda, T. J. "Mark ix.49." NTS 5 (1959): 318–21.

Baasland, Ernst. "Jesu Verkündigung vom Reich Gottes." Pages 15–35 in Reich Gottes und Kirche. Veröffentlichungen der Luther-Akademie e.V. Ratzenburg 12. Erlangen: Martin-Luther-Verlag, 1988.

Bacchiocchi, Samuele. "Sabbatical Typologies of Messianic Redemption." *JSJ* 17 (1986): 153–76.

Bacher, Wilhelm. *Die Agada der Tannaiten.* 2 vols. Berlin: de Gruyter, 1965–1966.

Baddeley, Alan. *Human Memory: Theory and Practice.* Boston: Allyn & Bacon, 1990.

Baddeley, Alan, Michael W. Eysenck, and Michael C. Anderson. *Memory.* New York: Psychology Press, 2009.

Bader, Chris. "When Prophecy Passes Unnoticed: New Perspectives on Failed Prophecy." *JSSR* 38 (1999): 119–31.

Bailey, Lloyd R. "The Cult of Twins at Edessa." *JAOS* 88 (1968): 342–44.

Baillet, Maurice. *Qumrân Grotte 4. III (4Q482–4Q520).* DJD 7. Oxford: Clarendon, 1982.

Baker, Aelred. "Justin's Agraphon in the *Dialogue with Trypho.*" *JBL* 87 (1968): 277–87.

Balch, Robert W. "Bo and Peep: A Case Study of the Origins of Messianic Leadership." Pages 13–72 in *Millennialism and Charisma.* Edited by Roy Wallis. Belfast: Queen's University, 1982.

Balch, Robert W., et al. "Fifteen Years of Failed Prophecy: Coping with Cognitive Dissonance in a Baha'i Sect." Pages 73–90 in *Millennium, Messiahs, and Mayhem: Contemporary Apocalyptic Movements.* Edited by Thomas Robbins and Susan J. Palmer. New York: Routledge, 1997.

Balch, Robert W., Gwen Farnsworth, and Sue Wilkins. "When the Bombs Drop: Reactions to Disconfirmed Prophecy in a Millennial Sect." *Sociological Perspectives* 26 (1983): 137–58.

Balota, David A., Janet M. Duchek, and Jessica M. Logan. "Is Expanded Retrieval Practice a Superior Form of Spaced Retrieval? A Critical Review of the Extant Literature." Pages 83–105 in *The Foundations of Remembering: Essays in Honor of Henry L. Roediger III.* Edited by James S. Nairne. New York: Psychology Press, 2007.

Bammel, Ernst. "Die Blutgerichtsbarkeit in der römischen Provinz Judäa vor dem ersten jüdischen Aufstand." Pages 59–72 in *Judaica: Kleine Schriften 1.* WUNT 37. Tübingen: Mohr Siebeck, 1986.

———. "Erwägungen zur Eschatologie Jesu." Pages 3–32 in *The New Testament Message.* Part 2 of *Studia Evangelica II–III: Papers Presented to the Second International Congress on New Testament Studies Held at Christ Church, Oxford, 1961.* Edited by F. L. Cross. TU 88. Berlin: Akademie-Verlag, 1964.

———. "The Titulus." Pages 353–64 in *Jesus and the Politics of His Day.* Edited by Ernst Bammel and C. F. D. Moule. Cambridge: Cambridge University Press, 1984.

Barbel, Joseph. *Christos Angelos: Die Anschauung von Christus als Bote und Engel in der gelehrten und volkstümlichen Literatur des christlichen Altertums.* Theophania 3. Bonn: Peter Hanstein, 1941.

Barclay, Craig R. "Schematization of Autobiographical Memory." Pages 82–99 in *Autobiographical Memory.* Edited by David C. Rubin. Cambridge: Cambridge University Press, 1986.

Barclay, John M. G. *Colossians and Philemon.* NTG. Sheffield: Sheffield Academic Press, 1997.

Barnard, Leslie W. *Justin Martyr: His Life and Thought.* London: Cambridge University Press, 1967.

Barnett, P. W. "The Jewish Sign Prophets—A.D. 40–70: Their Intentions and Origin." *NTS* 27 (1981): 679–97.

Barrett, C. K. *A Critical and Exegetical Commentary on the Acts of the Apostles.* 2 vols. ICC. Edinburgh: T & T Clark, 1994–1998.

———. *The Gospel according to St. John: An Introduction with Commentary and Notes on the Greek Text.* 2nd ed. Philadelphia: Westminster, 1978.

Barth, Markus. *Ephesians: Translation and Commentary on Chapters 4–6.* AB 34A. Garden City, NY: Doubleday, 1974.

Bartlett, F. C. *Remembering: A Study in Experiment and Social Psychology.* Cambridge: Cambridge University Press, 1932.

Bartsch, Hans-Werner. "Zur vorpaulinischen Bekenntnisformel im Eingang der Römerbriefes." *TZ* 23 (1967): 329–39.

Barzilay, Isaac E. *Between Reason and Faith: Anti-Rationalism in Italian Jewish Thought 1250–1650.* PNMES 10. Paris: Mouton, 1967.

Bashear, Suliman. "Muslim Apocalypses and the Hour: A Case-Study in Traditional Reinterpretation." *Israel Oriental Studies* 13 (1993): 75–99.

Bauckham, Richard J. "The Apocalypse of Peter: A Jewish-Christian Apocalypse from the Time of Bar Kokhba." Pages 160–258 in *The Fate of the Dead: Studies on the Jewish and Christian Apocalypses.* NovTSup 93. Leiden: Brill, 1998.

———. "Colossians 1:24 Again: The Apocalyptic Motif." *EvQ* 47 (1975): 168–70.

———. "Eyewitness and Critical History: A Response to Jens Schröter and Craig Evans." *JSNT* 31 (2008): 221–35.

———. "For Whom Were the Gospels Written?" Pages 9–48 in *The Gospels for All Christians: Rethinking the Gospel Audiences.* Edited by Richard J. Bauckham. Grand Rapids: Eerdmans, 1998.

———, ed. *The Gospels for All Christians: Rethinking the Gospel Audiences.* Grand Rapids: Eerdmans, 1998.

———. *Jesus and the Eyewitnesses: The Gospels as Eyewitness Testimony.* Grand Rapids: Eerdmans, 2006.

———. *Jesus and the God of Israel: God Crucified and Other Studies on the New Testament's Christology of Divine Identity.* Grand Rapids: Eerdmans, 2008.

———. "Kingdom and Church according to Jesus and Paul." *HBT* 18 (1996): 1–27.

———. "The Relatives of Jesus in the Early Church." Pages 45–133 in *Jude and the Relatives of Jesus in the Early Church.* Edinburgh: T & T Clark, 1990.

———. "The Throne of God and the Worship of Jesus." Pages 43–69 in *The Jewish Roots of Christological Monotheism: Papers from the St. Andrews Conference on the Historical Origins of the Worship of Jesus.* Edited by Carey C. Newman, James R. Davila, and Gladys S. Lewis. JSJSup 63. Leiden: Brill, 1999.

———. "The Two Fig Tree Parables in the Apocalypse of Peter." *JBL* 104 (1985): 269–87.

Bauer, Patricia J. *Remembering the Times of Our Lives: Memory in Infancy and Beyond.* Mahwah, NJ: Lawrence Erlbaum Associates, 2007.

Bauer, Ulrich. "Der Anfang der Endzeitrede in der Logienquelle (Q 17): Probleme der Rekonstruktion und Interpretation des Q-Texts." Pages 79–101 in *Wenn drei das Gleiche sagen: Studien zu den ersten drei Evangelien.* Edited by Stefan H. Brandenburger and Thomas Hieke. Theologie 14. Münster: Lit Verlag, 1998.

Baum, Armin Daniel. "Experimentalpsychologische Erwägungen zur synoptische Frage." *BZ* 44 (2000): 37–55.

Baumeister, Roy F. "Lying to Oneself: The Enigma of Self-Deception." Pages 166–83 in *Lying and Deception in Everyday Life.* Edited by Michael Lewis and Carolyn Saarni. New York: Guilford, 1993.

Baumgarten, Albert I. *The Flourishing of Jewish Sects in the Maccabean Era: An Interpretation.* JSJSup 55. Leiden: Brill, 1997.

———. "Four Stages in the Life of a Millennial Movement." Pages 61–75 in *War in Heaven / Heaven on Earth: Theories of the Apocalyptic.* Edited by Stephen D. O'Leary and Glen S. McGhee. London: Equinox, 2005.

———. "Miracles and Halakah in Rabbinic Judaism." *JQR* 73 (1983): 238–53.

Beale, G. K. *The Use of Daniel in Jewish Apocalyptic Literature and in the Revelation of St. John.* Lanham, MD: University Press of America, 1984.

Beasley-Murray, G. R. *Jesus and the Kingdom of God.* Grand Rapids: Eerdmans; Exeter: Paternoster, 1986.

———. *Jesus and the Last Days: The Interpretation of the Olivet Discourse.* Peabody, MA: Hendrickson, 1993.

Beavis, Mary Ann. *Jesus and Utopia: Looking for the Kingdom of God in the Roman World.* Minneapolis: Fortress, 2006.

Beck, D. M. "Golden Rule." *IDB* 2:438–39.

Becker, Jürgen. *Die Auferstehung Jesu Christi nach dem Neuen Testament: Ostererfahrung und Osterverständnis im Urchristentum.* Tübingen: Mohr Siebeck, 2007.

———. *Jesus of Nazareth.* Translated by James E. Crouch. New York: de Gruyter, 1998.

Beckford, James A. *The Trumpet of Prophecy: A Sociological Study of Jehovah's Witnesses.* New York: John Wiley & Sons, 1975.

Beckwith, Roger T. *Calendar and Chronology, Jewish and Christian: Biblical, Intertestamental, and Patristic Studies.* AGJU 33. Leiden: Brill, 1996.

———. *Calendar, Chronology and Worship: Studies in Ancient Judaism and Early Christianity.* AGJU 61. Leiden: Brill, 2005.

Beker, J. Christiaan. *Paul the Apostle: The Triumph of God in Life and Thought.* Philadelphia: Fortress, 1980.

Belfiore, Elizabeth. "'Lies Unlike the Truth': Plato on Hesiod, *Theogony* 27." *TAPA* 115 (1985): 47–57.

Bellinzoni, Arthur J. *The Sayings of Jesus in the Writings of Justin Martyr.* NovTSup 17. Leiden: Brill, 1967.

Ben-Amos, Dan, and Jerome R. Mintz, trans. and eds. *In Praise of the Baal Shem Tov [Shivhei ha-Besht]: The Earliest Collection of Legends about the Founder of Hasidism.* Bloomington: Indiana University Press, 1970.

Bengel, Johann Albrecht. *Gnomon Novi Testamenti.* 2 vols. Tübingen: Ludov. Frid. Fues, 1850.

Benoit, Pierre. *The Passion and Resurrection of Jesus Christ.* Translated by Benet Weatherhead. New York: Herder & Herder; London: Darton, Longman & Todd, 1969.

Benoit, P., J. T. Milik, and R. de Vaux. *Les Grottes de Murabba'ât: Texte.* DJD 2. Oxford: Clarendon, 1961.

Berding, Kenneth. *Polycarp and Paul: An Analysis of Their Literary and Theological Relationship in Light of Polycarp's Use of Biblical and Extra-biblical Literature.* VCSup 62. Leiden: Brill, 2002.

Berger, Abraham. "The Messianic Self-Consciousness of Abraham Abulafia: A Tentative Evaluation." Pages 250–55 in *Essential Papers on Messianic Movements and Personalities in Jewish History.* Edited by Marc Saperstein. New York: New York University Press, 1992.

Berger, David. "The Rebbe, the Jews, and the Messiah." *Commentary* 112, no. 2 (2001): 23–30.

———. "Three Typological Themes in Early Jewish Messianism: Messiah Son of Joseph, Rabbinic Calculations, and the Figure of Armilus." *AJSR* 10 (1985): 141–64.

Berger, Klaus. *Die Auferstehung des Propheten und die Erhöhung des Menschensohnes: Traditionsgeschichtliche Untersuchungen zur Deutung des Geschickes Jesu in frühchristlichen Texten.* SUNT 13. Göttingen: Vandenhoeck & Ruprecht, 1976.

———. *Die Gesetzesauslegung Jesu: Ihr historischer Hintergrund im Judentum und im Alten Testament.* WMANT 40. Neukirchen-Vluyn: Neukirchener Verlag, 1972.

———. "Die königlichen Messiastraditionen des Neuen Testaments." *NTS* 20 (1973): 1–44.

———. *Formgeschichte des Neuen Testaments.* Heidelberg: Quelle & Meyer, 1984.

———. "Kriterien für echte Jesusworte?" *ZNT* 1 (1998): 52–58.

———. "Zur Problem der Messianität Jesu." *ZTK* 71 (1974): 1–30.

Berkey, Robert F. "ΕΓΓΙΖΕΙΝ, ΦΘΑΝΕΙΝ, and Realized Eschatology." *JBL* 82 (1963): 177–87.

Berkhof, Hendrikus. *Christ, the Meaning of History.* Translated by Lambertus Buurman. London: SCM Press, 1966.

Bermejo, Fernando. "Historiografía, exégesis e ideología: La ficción contemporánea de las 'tres búsquedas' del Jesús histórico (y II)." *RCatT* 31 (2006): 53–114.

Best, Ernest. *A Critical and Exegetical Commentary on Ephesians.* ICC. Edinburgh: T & T Clark, 1998.

———. *One Body in Christ: A Study in the Relationship of the Church to Christ in the Epistles of the Apostle Paul.* London: SPCK, 1955.

———. *1 Peter.* NCB. London: Oliphants, 1971.

Betz, Hans Dieter. *Galatians: A Commentary on Paul's Letter to the Churches in Galatia.* Hermeneia. Philadelphia: Fortress, 1979.

———. "A Jewish-Christian Cultic *Didache* in Matt. 6:1–18: Reflections and Questions on the Problem of the Historical Jesus." Pages 55–69 in *Essays on the Sermon on the Mount.* Philadelphia: Fortress, 1985.

———. *The Sermon on the Mount: A Commentary on the Sermon on the Mount, Including the Sermon on the Plain (Matthew 5:3–7:27 and Luke 6:20–49).* Hermeneia. Minneapolis: Fortress, 1995.

Betz, Otto. "Jesus' Gospel of the Kingdom." Pages 53–74 in *The Gospel and the Gospels.* Edited by Peter Stuhlmacher. Grand Rapids: Eerdmans, 1991.

———. "στίγμα." *TDNT* 7:657–64.

———. *What Do We Know about Jesus?* Philadelphia: Westminster, 1968.

Beuken, W. A. M. "Servant and Herald of Good Tidings: Isaiah 61 as an Interpretation of Isaiah 40–55." Pages 411–40 in *The Book of Isaiah, Le livre d'Isaïe: Les oracles et leurs relectures; Unité et complexité de l'ouvrage.* Edited by Jacques Vermeylen. BETL 81. Leuven: Leuven University Press, 1989.

Beutler, Johannes. *Habt keine Angst: Die erste johanneische Abschiedsrede (Joh 14).* SBS 116. Stuttgart: Katholisches Bibelwerk, 1984.

Bietenhard, Hans. "The Millennial Hope in the Early Church." *SJT* 5 (1953): 12–30.

Bird, Michael F. *Are You the One Who Is to Come? The Historical Jesus and the Messianic Question.* Grand Rapids: Baker Academic, 2009.

———. "The Purpose and Preservation of the Jesus Tradition." *BBR* 15 (2005): 161–85.

———. "Who Comes from the East and the West? Luke 13.28–29/Matt 8.11–12 and the Historical Jesus." *NTS* 52 (2006): 441–57.

Birnbaum, Philip, trans. *Daily Prayer Book* [= *Ha-Siddur Ha-Shalem*]. New York: Hebrew Publishing, 1977.

Bittner, Wolfgang. "Gott—Menschensohn—Davidssohn: Eine Untersuchung zur Traditionsgeschichte von Daniel 7,13f." *FZPhTh* 32 (1985): 343–72.

Black, Mark. "The Messianic Use of Zechariah 9–14 in Matthew, Mark, and the Pre-Markan Tradition." Pages 97–114 in *Scripture and Traditions: Essays on Early Judaism and Christianity in Honor of Carl R. Holladay.* Edited by Patrick Gray and Gail R. O'Day. NovTSup 129. Leiden: Brill, 2008.

Black, Matthew. *An Aramaic Approach to the Gospels and Acts.* 3rd ed. Oxford: Clarendon, 1967.

Blackman, E. C. "The Church and the Kingdom of God: Need for Discrimination." *ExpTim* 47 (1936): 369–73.

Blank, Josef. *Krisis: Untersuchungen zur johanneischen Christologie und Eschatologie.* Freiburg im Breisgau: Lambertus-Verlag, 1964.

Blanke, Olaf, and Christine Mohr. "Out-of-Body Experience, Heautoscopy, and Autoscopic Hallucination of Neurological Origin: Implications for Neurocognitive Mechanisms of Corporeal Awareness and Self Consciousness." *Brain Research Reviews* 50 (2005): 184–99.

Blasi, Anthony J., ed. *American Sociology of Religion: Histories.* Religion and the Social Order 13. Leiden: Brill, 2007.

Blenkinsopp, Joseph. "The Oracle of Judah and the Messianic Entry." *JBL* 80 (1961): 55–64.

Bockmuehl, Markus. *Prophecy and Canon: A Contribution to the Study of Jewish Origins.* Notre Dame, IN: Notre Dame University Press, 1977.

Blinzler, J. "Εὐνοῦχοι." *ZNW* 48 (1957): 254–70.

Bockmuehl, Markus. "Resistance and Redemption in the Jesus Tradition." Pages 65–77 in *Redemption and Resistance: The Messianic Hopes of Jews and Christians in Antiquity.* Edited by Markus Bockmuehl and James Carleton Paget. London: T & T Clark, 2007.

———. *Seeing the Word: Refocusing New Testament Study.* Grand Rapids: Baker Academic, 2006.

———. "1 Thessalonians 2:14–16 and the Church in Jerusalem." *TynBul* 52 (2001): 1–31.

Boer, M. C., de. "Paul and Apocalyptic The-ology." Pages 345–83 in *The Origins of Apocalypticism in Judaism and Christianity.* Vol. 1 of *The Encyclopedia of Apocalypti-cism.* Edited by John J. Collins. New York: Continuum, 1998.

Boers, Hendrikus. "The Form-Critical Study of Paul's Letters: 1 Thessalonians as a Case Study." *NTS* 22 (1976): 140–58.

———. "Jesus and the Christian Faith: New Testament Christology Since Bousset's Kyrios Christos." *JBL* 89 (1970): 450–56.

Bohannan, Laura. "A Genealogical Charter." *Africa* 22 (1952): 301–15.

Böhlemann, Peter. *Jesus und der Täufer: Schlüs-sel zur Theologie und Ethik des Lukas.* SNTSMS 99. Cambridge: Cambridge Uni-versity Press, 1997.

Bohlen, Maren. "Die Einlasssprüche in der Reich-Gottes-Verkündigung Jesu." *ZNW* 99 (2008): 167–84.

Böhlig, Alexander. "Zum Selbstverständnis des Manichäismus." Pages 520–50 in vol. 2 of *Gnosis und Synkretismus: Gesam-melte Aufsätze zur spätantike Religions-geschichte.* WUNT 48. Tübingen: Mohr Siebeck, 1989.

Boismard, M.-É. *L'Énigme de la lettre aux Éphésiens.* EB 39. Paris: Gabalda, 1999.

———. "L'evolution du thème eschatologique dans les traditions johanniques." *RevB* 68 (1961): 507–24.

Bolin, Thomas M. "History, Historiography, and the Use of the Past in the Hebrew Bible." Pages 113–40 in *The Limits of His-toriography: Genre and Narrative in An-cient Historical Texts.* Edited by Christina Shuttleworth Kraus. MBCBSup 191. Leiden: Brill, 1999.

Bolt, Peter G. "Mark 13: An Apocalyptic Pre-cursor to the Passion Narrative." *RTR* 54 (1995): 10–30.

Bolten, Johann Adrian. *Der Bericht des Mat-thäus von Jesu dem Messia.* Leipzig: Altona, 1792. Online: www.archive.org/stream/MN40365ucmf_2page/n0/mode/1up. Cited 18 November 2009.

Bonanno, George A. "Remembering and Psychotherapy." *Psychotherapy* 27 (1990): 175–86.

Bonaventure. *Opera omnia.* Edited by A. C. Peltier. 15 vols. Paris: Ludovicus Vivès, 1864–1871.

Bond, Helen. *Caiaphas: Friend of Rome and Judge of Jesus?* Louisville: Westminster John Knox, 2004.

Borg, Marcus J. *Conflict, Holiness, and Politics in the Teaching of Jesus.* SBEC 5. Lewiston, NY: Edwin Mellen, 1984.

———. "Con: Jesus Was Not an Apocalyptic Prophet." Pages 31–48 in *The Apocalyptic Jesus: A Debate.* Edited by Robert J. Miller. Santa Rosa, CA: Polebridge, 2001.

———. "Jesus and Eschatology: Current Re-flections." Pages 69–96 in *Jesus in Contem-porary Scholarship.* Valley Forge, PA: Trinity Press International, 1994.

———. *Jesus, a New Vision: Spirit, Culture, and the Life of Discipleship.* San Francisco: Harper & Row, 1987.

———. *Jesus: Uncovering the Life, Teachings, and Relevance of a Religious Revolutionary.* San Francisco: HarperSanFrancisco, 2006.

———. *Reading the Bible Again for the First Time: Taking the Bible Seriously but Not Literally.* San Francisco: HarperSanFran-cisco, 2002.

———. "A Temperate Case for a Non-escha-tological Jesus." Pages 47–68 in *Jesus in Contemporary Scholarship.* Valley Forge, PA: Trinity Press International, 1994.

———. "Was Jesus God?" Pages 145–56 in *The Meaning of Jesus: Two Visions.* By Marcus Borg and N. T. Wright. San Francisco: Harp-erSanFrancisco, 1999.

Borgen, Peder. *Bread from Heaven: An Exegeti-cal Study of the Concept of Manna in the Gospel of John and the Writings of Philo.* NovTSup 10. Leiden: Brill, 1965.

———. *Philo of Alexandria: An Exegete for His Time.* NovTSup 86. Leiden: Brill, 1997.

Borges, Jorge Luis. "Funes, the Memorious." Pages 107–15 in *Ficciones.* Translated and edited by Anthony Kerrigan. New York: Grove, 1962.

Bornkamm, Günther. *Jesus of Nazareth*. New York: Harper & Row, 1975.

———. "Lord's Supper and Church in Paul." Pages 123–60 in *Early Christian Experience*. London: SCM Press, 1969.

Borsch, Frederick Houk. *The Christian and Gnostic Son of Man*. SBT 14. London: SCM Press, 1970.

———. *The Son of Man in Myth and History*. NTL. Philadelphia: Westminster, 1967.

Borse, Udo. "Die Wundermale und der Todesbescheid." *BZ* 14 (1970): 88–111.

Böttrich, Christfried. "Das Gleichnis vom Dieb in der Nacht: Parusieerwartung und Paränese." Pages 31–57 in *Eschatologie und Ethik im frühen Christentum: Festschrift für Günter Haufe zum 75. Geburtstag*. Edited by Christfried Böttrich. GTF 11. Frankfurt am Main: Peter Lang, 2006.

———. "Konturen des 'Menschensohnes' in äthHen 37–71." Pages 53–90 in *Gottessohn und Menschensohn: Exegetische Studien zu zwei Paradigmen biblischer Intertextualität*. Edited by Dieter Sänger. BTSt 67. Neukirchen-Vluyn: Neukirchener Verlag, 2004.

Bousset, Wilhelm. *Jesus*. Translated by Janet Penrose Trevelyan. Edited by W. D. Morrison. New York: G. P. Putnam's Sons, 1906.

Bousset, Wilhelm, and Hugo Gressmann. *Die Religion des Judentums im späthellenistischen Zeitalter*. 3rd ed. HNT 21. Tübingen: Mohr Siebeck, 1926.

Bovon, François. *Das Evangelium nach Lukas (Lk 9,51–14,35)*. EKKNT 3/2. Zürich: Benziger; Neukirchen-Vluyn: Neukirchener Verlag, 1996.

———. *Luke 1: A Commentary on the Gospel of Luke 1:1–9:50*. Translated by Christine M. Thomas. Hermeneia. Minneapolis: Fortress, 2002.

Bowman, John Wick. *The Religion of Maturity*. New York: Abingdon-Cokesbury, 1948.

Box, G. H. "4 Ezra." Pages 542–624 in vol. 2 of *The Apocrypha and Pseudepigrapha of the Old Testament*. Edited by R. H. Charles. Oxford: Clarendon, 1913.

Bradshaw, John. "Oral Transmission and Human Memory." *ExpTim* 92 (1981): 303–7.

Brainerd, C. J., and V. F. Reyna. *The Science of False Memory*. Oxford: Oxford University Press, 2005.

Brandt, Sigrid. *Opfer als Gedächtnis: Auf dem Weg zu einer befreienden theologischen Rede von Opfer*. ATM 2. Münster: Lit Verlag, 2001.

Branscomb, B. Harvie. *The Teachings of Jesus*. Nashville: Cokesbury, 1931.

Bransford, John D., and Jeffery J. Franks. "The Abstraction of Linguistic Ideas." *Cognitive Psychology* 2 (1971): 331–50.

Breech, James. *The Silence of Jesus: The Authentic Voice of the Historical Man*. Philadelphia: Fortress, 1983.

Brenner, Michael. "From Self-Declared Messiah to Scholar of Messianism: The Recently Published Diaries Present Young Gerhard Scholem in a New Light." *Jewish Social Studies* 3 (1996): 177–82.

Brettler, Marc Zvi. *God Is King: Understanding an Israelite Metaphor*. JSOTSup 76. Sheffield: JSOT Press, 1989.

Brewer, William F. "What Is Recollective Memory?" Pages 19–66 in *Remembering Our Past: Studies in Autobiographical Memory*. Edited by David C. Rubin. Cambridge: Cambridge University Press, 1996.

Brewin, C. R., B. Andrews, and I. H. Gotlib. "Psychopathology and Early Experience: A Reappraisal of Retrospective Reports." *Psychological Bulletin* 113 (1993): 82–98.

Bridge, Steven L. *"Where the Eagles Are Gathered": The Deliverance of the Elect in Lukan Eschatology*. JSNTSup 240. London: Sheffield Academic Press, 2003.

Broad, C. D. *The Mind and Its Place in Nature*. London: Kegan Paul, Trench, Trübner, 1925.

Broer, Ingo. "The Death of Jesus from a Historical Perspective." Pages 145–68 in *Jesus from Judaism to Christianity: Continuum Approaches to the Historical Jesus*. Edited by Tom Holmén. London: T & T Clark, 2007.

———. "'Der ganze Zorn ist schon über sie gekommen': Bemerkungen zur Interpolationshypothese und zur Interpretation von 1 Thess 2,14–16." Pages 137–59 in *The Thessalonian Correspondence*. Edited by Raymond F. Collins. BETL 87. Leuven: Leuven University Press, 1990.

Brown, Norman R., Lance J. Rips, and Steven K. Shevell. "Subjective Dates of Natural Events in Very Long Term Memory." *Cognitive Psychology* 17 (1985): 139–77.

Brown, Raymond E. *The Birth of the Messiah: A Commentary on the Infancy Narratives in the Gospels of Matthew and Luke*. New updated ed. New York: Doubleday, 1993.

———. *The Death of the Messiah: From Gethsemane to the Grave; A Commentary on the Passion Narratives of the Four Gospels*. 2 vols. New York: Doubleday, 1994.

———. *The Gospel according to John*, vol. 2, *John XIII–XXI*. AB 29A. Garden City, NY: Doubleday, 1970.

———. "Jesus and Elisha." *Perspectives* 12 (1971): 85–99.

———. "John and the Synoptic Gospels: A Comparison." Pages 246–71 in *New Testament Essays*. Garden City, NY: Doubleday, 1968.

Brown, R., and J. Kulik. "Flashbulb Memories." *Cognition* 5 (1977): 73–99.

Bruce, A. B. *The Eschatology of Jesus, or, The Kingdom Come and Coming*. New York: A. C. Armstrong & Son, 1904.

Bruce, Darryl. "Functional Explanations of Memory." Pages 44–58 in *Everyday Cognition in Adulthood and Late Life*. Edited by Leonard W. Poon, David C. Rubin, and Barbara A. Wilson. Cambridge: Cambridge University Press, 1989.

Bruner, Frederick Dale. *The Churchbook, Matthew 13–28*. Vol. 2 of *Matthew: A Commentary*. Rev. ed. Grand Rapids: Eerdmans, 2004.

Bryan, Christopher. *Render to Caesar: Jesus, the Early Church, and the Roman Superpower*. Oxford: Oxford University Press, 2005.

Bryan, Steven M. *Jesus and Israel's Traditions of Judgement and Restoration*. SNTSMS 117. Cambridge: Cambridge University Press, 2002.

Buchanan, George Wesley. *The Consequences of the Covenant*. NovTSup 20. Leiden: Brill, 1970.

———. "Meyer's Support for Weiss' Eschatology." *Journal of the Radical Reformation* 2 (1993): 45–57.

———. *New Testament Eschatology: Historical and Cultural Background*. Lewiston, NY: Mellen Biblical Press, 1993.

Buck, Christopher. "The Eschatology of Globalization: The Multiple-Messiahship of Bahā'u'llāh Revisited." Pages 148–78 in *Studies in Modern Religions, Religious Movements, and the Bābī-Bahā'ī Faiths*. Edited by Moshe Sharon. SHR 104. Leiden: Brill, 2004.

Bucur, Bogdan G. "The Other Clement of Alexandria: Cosmic Hierarchy and Interiorized Apocalypticism." *VC* 60 (2006): 251–67.

Bultmann, Rudolf. *History of the Synoptic Tradition*. Rev. ed. New York: Harper & Row, 1963.

———. *Jesus and the Word*. New York: Charles Scribner's Sons, 1934.

———. *Jesus Christ and Mythology*. New York: Charles Scribner's Sons, 1958.

———. "The Primitive Christian Kerygma and the Historical Jesus." Pages 15–42 in *The Historical Jesus and the Kerygmatic Christ: Essays on the New Quest of the Historical Jesus*. Edited by Carl E. Braaten and Roy A. Harrisville. New York: Abingdon, 1964.

———. *Theology of the New Testament*. 2 vols. New York: Charles Scribner's Sons, 1951–1955.

———. *This World and the Beyond: Marburg Sermons*. Translated by Harold Knight. New York: Charles Scribner's Sons, 1960.

Bundy, Walter E. *The Psychic Health of Jesus*. New York: Macmillan, 1922.

———. *The Religion of Jesus*. Indianapolis: Bobb-Merrill, 1928.

Burchard, Christoph. "Jesus of Nazareth." Pages 15–72 in *Christian Beginnings: Word and Community from Jesus to Post-Apos-*

tolic Times. Edited by Jürgen Becker. Louisville: Westminster John Knox, 1993.

———. "Joseph and Aseneth." *OTP* 2:147–247.

Burkett, Delbert. *The Son of Man Debate: A History and Evaluation.* SNTSMS 107. Cambridge: Cambridge University Press, 1999.

Burridge, Richard A. *Imitating Jesus: An Inclusive Approach to New Testament Ethics.* Grand Rapids: Eerdmans, 2007.

———. *What Are the Gospels? A Comparison with Graeco-Roman Biography.* 2nd ed. Grand Rapids: Eerdmans; Dearborn, MI: Dove Booksellers, 2004.

Burrows, Millar. "Old Testament Ethics and the Ethics of Jesus." Pages 225–43 in *Essays in Old Testament Ethics (J. Philip Hyatt, In Memoriam).* Edited by James L. Crenshaw and John T. Willis. New York: Ktav, 1974.

Byrskog, Samuel. "From Memory to Memoirs: Tracing the Background of a Literary Genre." In *Remembering Jesus: Essays in Honor of James D. G. Dunn.* Edited by Scot McKnight and T. Mournet. New York: Continuum, forthcoming.

Cahill, Michael. "Did Jesus Refer to Himself in the Third Person? A Contribution to the Son of Man Debate." *PIBA* 25 (2002): 58–68.

Caird, G. B. "Eschatology and Politics: Some Misconceptions." Pages 72–86 in *Biblical Studies: Essays in Honor of William Barclay.* Edited by Johnston R. McKay and James F. Miller. Philadelphia: Westminster, 1976.

———. *The Language and Imagery of the Bible.* Philadelphia: Westminster, 1980.

Calvin, John. *Commentary on the Epistles of Paul the Apostle to the Corinthians.* Vol. 1. Grand Rapids: Eerdmans, 1958.

———. *A Harmony of the Gospels Matthew, Mark, and Luke.* 3 vols. Grand Rapids: Eerdmans, 1972.

Cameron, Ron. "Ancient Myths and Modern Theories of the *Gospel of Thomas* and Christian Origins." Pages 89–108 in *Redescribing Christian Origins.* Edited by Ron Cameron and Merrill P. Miller. SBLSymS

28. Atlanta: Society of Biblical Literature, 2004.

———. "Proposal for the Second Year of the Seminar." Pages 285–92 in *Redescribing Christian Origins.* Edited by Ron Cameron and Merrill P. Miller. SBLSymS 28. Atlanta: Society of Biblical Literature, 2004.

———. "The Sayings Gospel Q and the Quest of the Historical Jesus: A Response to John S. Kloppenborg." *HTR* 4 (1996): 351–54.

Cameron, Ron, and Merrill P. Miller. "Introduction: Ancient Myths and Modern Theories of Christian Origins." Pages 1–30 in *Redescribing Christian Origins.* Edited by Ron Cameron and Merrill P. Miller. SBLSymS 28. Atlanta: Society of Biblical Literature, 2004.

———, eds. *Redescribing Christian Origins.* SBLSymS 28. Atlanta: Society of Biblical Literature, 2004.

Campbell, J. Y. "'The Kingdom of God Has Come.'" *ExpTim* 48 (1936): 91–94.

Camponovo, Odo. *Königtum, Königsherrschaft, und Reich Gottes in den frühjüdischen Schriften.* OBO 58. Freiburg: Universitätsverlag; Göttingen: Vandenhoeck & Ruprecht, 1984.

Capes, David B. *Old Testament Yahweh Texts in Paul's Christology.* WUNT 2/47. Tübingen: Mohr Siebeck, 1992.

Caragounis, Chrys C. "Kingdom of God/Heaven." *DJG* 417–30.

———. "Kingdom of God, Son of Man, and Jesus' Self-Understanding." *TynBul* 40 (1989): 3–23.

Carlebach, Elisheva. "Two Amens That Delayed the Redemption: Jewish Messianism and Popular Spirituality in the Post-Sabbatian Century." *JQR* 82 (1992): 241–61.

Carlston, Charles E. Review of Rudolf Laufen, *Die Doppelüberlieferungen der Logienquelle und des Markusevangeliums. CBQ* 43 (1981): 473–75.

Carmignac, Jean. *Le mirage de l'eschatologie: Royauté, règne, et royaume de Dieu sans eschatologie.* Paris: Letouzey et Ané, 1979.

Carr, Wesley. "The Rulers of This Age—1 Corinthians II.6–8." *NTS* 23 (1976): 20–35.

Carrington, Philip. *The Primitive Christian Catechism: A Study in the Epistles.* Cambridge: Cambridge University Press, 1940.

Carroll, John T., and Joel B. Green. *The Death of Jesus in Early Christianity.* Peabody, MA: Hendrickson, 1995.

Carroll, Robert P. *When Prophecy Failed: Cognitive Dissonance in the Prophetic Traditions of the Old Testament.* New York: Seabury, 1979.

Carson, D. A., Peter T. O'Brien, and Mark A. Seifrid, eds. *The Complexities of Second Temple Judaism.* Vol. 1 of *Justification and Variegated Nomism.* Tübingen: Mohr Siebeck; Grand Rapids: Baker Academic, 2001.

Casey, Maurice. *The Solution to the "Son of Man" Problem.* LNTS 343. London: T & T Clark, 2007.

———. *Son of Man: The Interpretation and Influence of Daniel 7.* London: SPCK, 1979.

Catchpole, David R. "The Angelic Son of Man in Luke 12:8." *NovT* 24 (1982): 255–65.

———. *Jesus People: The Historical Jesus and the Beginnings of Community.* London: Darton, Longman & Todd; Grand Rapids: Baker Academic, 2006.

———. *The Quest for Q.* Edinburgh: T & T Clark, 1993.

———. "The Son of Man's Search for Faith (Luke XVIII 8b)." *NovT* 19 (1977): 81–104.

———. "The 'Triumphal' Entry." Pages 319–334 in *Jesus and the Politics of His Day.* Edited by Ernst Bammel and C. F. D. Moule. Cambridge: Cambridge University Press, 1984.

Ceci, Stephen J. "False Beliefs: Some Developmental and Clinical Considerations." Pages 91–127 in *Memory Distortion: How Minds, Brains, and Societies Reconstruct the Past.* Edited by Daniel L. Schacter. Cambridge, MA: Harvard University Press, 1995.

Ceci, Stephen J., et al. "Repeatedly Thinking about a Non-event: Source Misattributions among Preschoolers." *Consciousness and Cognition* 3 (1994): 388–407.

Chalippe, Candide. *The Life of Saint Francis of Assisi.* New York: D. & J. Sadlier, 1889.

Chalmers, Thomas. *Lectures on the Epistle of Paul to the Romans.* New York: Robert Carter, 1843.

Chamberlin, T. C. "The Method of Multiple Working Hypotheses." *Science* 148 (1965): 754–59.

Chandler, Christopher N. "Jesus and James on Justice in the Courts: A Reconsideration of the Ward/Allison Thesis." Lecture presented at the annual meeting of the Society of Biblical Literature, Boston, November 2008.

Charles, R. H. "The Book of Jubilees." Pages 1–82 in vol. 2 of *The Apocrypha and Pseudepigrapha of the Old Testament in English.* Edited by R. H. Charles. 2 vols. Oxford: Clarendon, 1913.

———. *A Critical History of the Doctrine of a Future Life in Israel, in Judaism, and in Christianity.* London: Adam & Charles Black, 1899.

Charlesworth, James H. *Jesus within Judaism: New Light from Exciting Archaeological Discoveries.* New York: Doubleday, 1988.

———. *Resurrection: The Origin and Future of a Biblical Doctrine.* New York: T & T Clark, 2006.

Chazon, Esther G. "'Gathering the Dispersed of Judah': Seeking a Return to the Land as a Factor in Jewish Identity of Late Antiquity." Pages 159–75 in *Heavenly Tablets: Interpretation, Identity, and Tradition in Ancient Judaism.* Edited by Lynn LiDonnici and Andrea Lieber. JSJSup 119. Leiden: Brill, 2007.

Chenderlin, Fritz. *"Do This as My Memorial": The Semantic and Conceptual Background and Value of Ἀνάμνησις in 1 Corinthians 11:24–25.* AnBib 99. Rome: Biblical Institute Press, 1982.

Chester, Andrew. "Jewish Messianic Expectations and Mediatorial Figures and Pauline Christology." Pages 17–89 in *Paulus und das antike Judentum.* Edited by Martin Hengel and Ulrich Heckel. WUNT 2/58. Tübingen: Mohr Siebeck, 1991.

———. "The Nature and Scope of Messianism." Pages 191–327 in *Messiah and Ex-*

altation: Jewish Messianic and Visionary Traditions and New Testament Christology. WUNT 2/207. Tübingen: Mohr Siebeck, 2007.

Chilton, Bruce David. God in Strength: Jesus' Announcement of the Kingdom. SNTSU 1. Freistadt: Plöchl, 1979.

———. "The Kingdom of God in Recent Discussion." Pages 255–80 in Studying the Historical Jesus: Evaluations of the State of Current Research. Edited by Bruce Chilton and Craig A. Evans. NTTS 19. Leiden: Brill, 1994.

———. "Regnum dei deus est." SJT 31 (1978): 261–70.

———. "(The) Son of (the) Man, and Jesus." Pages 259–88 in Authenticating the Words of Jesus. Edited by Bruce Chilton and Craig A. Evans. NTTS 28/1. Leiden: Brill, 1998.

Chilton, Bruce, and Craig A. Evans. Jesus in Context: Temple, Purity, and Restoration. AGJU 39. Leiden: Brill, 1997.

Christianson, Sven-Åke, and Elizabeth F. Loftus. "Memory for Traumatic Events." Applied Cognitive Psychology 1 (1987): 225–39.

Clark, K. W. "Realized Eschatology." JBL 59 (1940): 367–83.

Clarke, Andrew D. Secular and Christian Leadership in Corinth: A Socio-Historical and Exegetical Study of 1 Corinthians 1–6. AGJU 18. Leiden: Brill, 1993.

Clivaz, Claire. "Hebrews 5.7, Jesus' Prayer on the Mount of Olives and Jewish Christianity: Hearing Early Christian Voices in Canonical and Apocryphal Texts." Pages 187–209 in A Cloud of Witnesses: The Theology of Hebrews in Its Ancient Contexts. Edited by Richard Bauckham et al. London: T & T Clark, 2008.

Cockerill, Gareth Lee. "Melchizedek or 'King of Righteousness.'" EvQ 63 (1991): 305–12.

Cohen, Gillian. "Overview: Conclusions and Speculations." Pages 381–92 in Memory in the Real World. Edited by Gillian Cohen and Martin Conway. 3rd ed. New York: Psychology Press, 2008.

Cohick, Lynn H. "Jesus as King of the Jews." Pages 111–32 in Who Do My Opponents Say That I Am? An Investigation of the Accusations against Jesus. Edited by Scot McKnight and Joseph B. Modica. LNTS 327. London: T & T Clark, 2008.

Collins, Adela Yarbro. "The Apocalyptic Son of Man Sayings." Pages 220–28 in The Future of Early Christianity: Essays in Honor of Helmut Koester. Edited by Birger A. Pearson. Minneapolis: Fortress, 1991.

——— "Jesus as Son of Man." Pages 149–74 in King and Messiah as Son of God: Divine, Human, and Angelic Messianic Figures in Biblical and Related Literature. By Adela Yarbro Collins and John J. Collins. Grand Rapids: Eerdmans, 2008.

———. Mark: A Commentary. Hermeneia. Minneapolis: Fortress, 2007.

———. "The Messiah as Son of God in the Synoptic Gospels." Pages 21–32 in The Messiah in Early Judaism and Christianity. Edited by Magnus Zetterholm. Minneapolis: Fortress, 2007.

———. "The Origins of the Designation of Jesus as 'Son of Man.'" HTR 80 (1987): 391–408.

Collins, John J. The Apocalyptic Imagination: An Introduction to Jewish Apocalyptic Literature. 2nd ed. Grand Rapids: Eerdmans, 1998.

———. Apocalypticism in the Dead Sea Scrolls. London: Routledge, 1997.

———. Daniel: A Commentary on the Book of Daniel. Hermeneia. Minneapolis: Fortress, 1993.

———. "The Danielic Son of Man." Pages 173–94 in The Scepter and the Star: The Messiahs of the Dead Sea Scrolls and Other Ancient Literature. New York: Doubleday, 1995.

———. "Enoch and the Son of Man: A Response to Sabino Chialà and Helge Kvanvig." Pages 216–27 in Enoch and the Messiah Son of Man: Revisiting the Book of Parables. Edited by Gabriele Boccaccini. Grand Rapids: Eerdmans, 2007.

———. "Genre, Ideology, and Social Movements in Jewish Apocalypticism." Pages

11–32 in *Mysteries and Revelations: Apocalyptic Studies Since the Uppsala Conference.* Edited by John J. Collins and James H. Charlesworth. JSPSup 9. Sheffield: JSOT Press, 1991.

———. "The Heavenly Representative: The 'Son of Man' in the Similitudes of Enoch." Pages 111–33 in *Ideal Figures in Ancient Judaism.* Edited by George W. E. Nickelsburg and John J. Collins. SBLSCS 12. Chico, CA: Scholars Press, 1980.

———. "A Herald of Good Tidings: Isaiah 61:1–3 and Its Actualization in the Dead Sea Scrolls." Pages 225–40 in *The Quest for Context and Meaning: Studies in Biblical Intertextuality in Honor of James A. Sanders.* Edited by Craig A. Evans and Shemaryahu Talmon. BIS 28. Leiden: Brill, 1997.

———. "Jesus and the Messiahs of Israel." Pages 169–78 in *Encounters with Biblical Theology.* Minneapolis: Fortress, 2005.

———. "The Kingdom of God in the Apocrypha and Pseudepigrapha." Pages 81–95 in *The Kingdom of God in 20th-Century Interpretation.* Edited by Wendell Willis. Peabody, MA: Hendrickson, 1987.

———. "The Messiah as the Son of God." Pages 154–72 in *The Scepter and the Star: The Messiahs of the Dead Sea Scrolls and Other Ancient Literature.* New York: Doubleday, 1995.

———. "Powers in Heaven: God, Gods, and Angels in the Dead Sea Scrolls." Pages 9–28 in *Religion in the Dead Sea Scrolls.* Edited by John J. Collins and Robert A. Kugler. Grand Rapids: Eerdmans, 2000.

———. "The Sense of an Ending in Pre-Christian Judaism." Pages 25–43 in *Fearful Hope: Approaching the Millennium.* Edited by Christopher Kleinhenz and Frannie J. LeMoine. Madison: University of Wisconsin Press, 1999.

———. "Sibylline Oracles." *OTP* 1:317–472.

———. "Teacher, Priest, and Prophet." Pages 102–35 in *The Scepter and the Star: The Messiahs of the Dead Sea Scrolls and Other Ancient Literature.* New York: Doubleday, 1995.

———. "A Throne in the Heavens." Pages 136–53 in *The Scepter and the Star: The Messiahs of the Dead Sea Scrolls and Other Ancient Literature.* New York: Doubleday, 1995.

———. "What Was Distinctive about Messianic Expectation at Qumran?" Pages 71–92 in *The Dead Sea Scrolls and the Qumran Community.* Vol. 2 of *The Bible and the Dead Sea Scrolls.* Edited by James H. Charlesworth. Waco, TX: Baylor University Press, 2006.

———. "The Works of the Messiah." *DSD* 1 (1994): 98–112.

Collins, John J., and Devorah Dimant. "A Thrice-Told Hymn: A Response to Eileen Schuller." *JQR* 85 (1994): 151–55.

Collins, Raymond F. "Apropos the Integrity of 1 Thess." Pages 96–135 in *Studies on the First Letter to the Thessalonians.* BETL 66. Leuven: Leuven University Press, 1984.

Colpe, Carsten. "Daēnā, Lichtjungfrau, Zweite Gestalt: Verbindungen und Unterschiede zwischen zarathustrischer und manichäischer Selbst-Anschauung." Pages 56–77 in *Studies in Gnosticism and Hellenistic Religions Presented to Gilles Quispel on the Occasion of His 65th Birthday.* Edited by R. van den Broek and M. J. Vermaseren. EPRO 91. Leiden: Brill, 1981.

Connerton, Paul. *How Societies Remember.* Cambridge: Cambridge University Press, 1989.

Connolly, R. H. "A Negative Form of the Golden Rule in the Diatessaron?" *JTS* 35 (1934): 351–57.

Conway, Martin A., and Christopher W. Pleydell-Pearce. "The Construction of Autobiographical Memories in the Self-Memory System." *Psychological Review* 107 (2000): 261–88.

Conway, Martin A., Qi Wang, Kazunori Hanyu, and Shamsul Haque. "A Cross-Cultural Investigation of Autobiographical Memory: On the Universality and Cultural Variation of the Reminiscence Bump." *Journal of Cross-Cultural Psychology* 36 (2005): 739–49.

Conzelmann, Hans. *Jesus.* Philadelphia: Fortress, 1973.

———. *An Outline of the Theology of the New Testament*. New York: Harper & Row, 1969.

———. "Present and Future in the Synoptic Tradition." *JTC* 5 (1968): 26–44.

Cook, David. "The Beginnings of Islam as an Apocalyptic Movement." Pages 79–93 in *War in Heaven / Heaven on Earth: Theories of the Apocalyptic*. Edited by Stephen D. O'Leary and Glen S. McGhee. London: Equinox, 2005.

Corley, Kathleen E. "The Anointing of Jesus in the Synoptic Tradition: An Argument for Authenticity." *JSHJ* 1 (2003): 61–72.

Cotton, Hannah M. "Ein Gedi between the Two Revolts." *SCI* 20 (2001): 139–54.

Craffert, Pieter F. "How Historiography Creates (Some)Body: Jesus, the Son of David— Royal Stock or Social Construct?" *Scriptura* 90 (2005): 608–20.

———. *The Life of a Galilean Shaman: Jesus of Nazareth in Anthropological-Historical Perspective*. Eugene, OR: Cascade Books, 2008.

Cranfield, C. E. B. *The Gospel according to Saint Mark*. Rev. ed. CGTC. Cambridge: Cambridge University Press, 1977.

———. "Thoughts on New Testament Eschatology." Pages 105–26 in *The Bible and Christian Life: A Collection of Essays*. Edinburgh: T & T Clark, 1985.

Craven, Toni. *Artistry and Faith in the Book of Judith*. SBLDS 70. Chico, CA: Scholars Press, 1983.

Crawford, Barry S. "Christos as Nickname." Pages 337–48 in *Redescribing Christian Origins*. Edited by Ron Cameron and Merrill P. Miller. SBLSymS 28. Atlanta: Society of Biblical Literature, 2004.

———. "Near Expectation in the Sayings of Jesus." *JBL* 101 (1982): 225–44.

Crompton, Robert. *Counting the Days to Armageddon: The Jehovah's Witnesses and the Second Presence of Christ*. Cambridge: James Clarke, 1996.

Crossan, John Dominic. "Assessing the Arguments." Pages 119–23 in *The Apocalyptic Jesus: A Debate*. Edited by Robert J. Miller. Santa Rosa, CA: Polebridge, 2001.

———. *The Birth of Christianity: Discovering What Happened in the Years Immediately after the Execution of Jesus*. San Francisco: HarperSanFrancisco, 1998.

———. "Con: Jesus Was Not an Apocalyptic Prophet." Pages 49–68 in *The Apocalyptic Jesus: A Debate*. Edited by Robert J. Miller. Santa Rosa, CA: Polebridge, 2001.

———. *God and Empire: Jesus against Rome, Then and Now*. San Francisco: HarperSanFrancisco, 2007.

———. *The Historical Jesus: The Life of a Mediterranean Jewish Peasant*. San Francisco: HarperCollins, 1991.

———. *In Fragments: The Aphorisms of Jesus*. San Francisco: Harper & Row, 1983.

———. *Jesus: A Revolutionary Biography*. San Francisco: HarperSanFrancisco, 1994.

———. *A Long Way from Tipperary: A Memoir*. San Francisco: HarperSanFrancisco, 2000.

———. *Who Killed Jesus? Exposing the Roots of Anti-Semitism in the Gospel Story of the Death of Jesus*. San Francisco: HarperSanFrancisco, 1996.

Cullmann, Oscar. *The Early Church: Studies in Early Christian History and Theology*. Edited by A. J. B. Higgins. Philadelphia: Westminster, 1956.

———. *The State in the New Testament*. New York: Charles Scribner's Sons, 1956.

Curci, Antonietta. "Measurement Issues in the Study of Flashbulb Memory." Pages 13–32 in *Flashbulb Memories: New Issues and New Perspectives*. Edited by Olivier Luminet and Antonietta Curci. New York: Psychology Press, 2009.

Curtis, John Briggs. "The Mount of Olives in Tradition." *HUCA* 28 (1957): 137–80.

Dahl, Nils Alstrup. "The Crucified Messiah." Pages 27–47 in *Jesus the Christ: The Historical Origins of Christian Doctrine*. Edited by Donald H. Juel. Minneapolis: Fortress, 1991.

———. "Messianic Ideas and the Crucifixion of Jesus." Pages 382–403 in *The Messiah: Developments in Earliest Judaism and Christianity*. Edited by James H. Charlesworth. Minneapolis: Fortress, 1992.

———. "The Problem of the Historical Jesus." Pages 81–111 in *Jesus the Christ: The Historical Origins of Christian Doctrine.* Edited by Donald H. Juel. Minneapolis: Fortress, 1991.

Dalman, Gustaf. *The Words of Jesus Considered in the Light of Post-biblical Jewish Writings and the Aramaic Language.* Edinburgh: T & T Clark, 1902.

Daly-Denton, Margaret. *David in the Fourth Gospel: The Johannine Reception of the Psalms.* AGJU 47. Leiden: Brill, 2000.

Dan, Joseph. "Scholem's View of Jewish Messianism." *Modern Judaism* 12 (1992): 117–28.

Daniélou, Jean. *The Theology of Jewish Christianity.* Translated and edited by John A. Baker. London: Darton, Longman & Todd; Chicago: H. Regnery, 1964.

Daube, David. *Ancient Jewish Law: Three Inaugural Lectures.* Leiden: Brill, 1981.

———. *Appeasement or Resistance and Other Essays on New Testament Judaism.* Berkeley: University of California Press, 1987.

———. "Typology in Josephus." *JJS* 31 (1980): 18–36.

Davenport, G. L. *The Eschatology of the Book of Jubilees.* StPB 20. Leiden: Brill, 1971.

Davies, W. D. *The Gospel and the Land: Early Christianity and Jewish Territorial Doctrine.* Berkeley: University of California Press, 1974.

Davies, W. D., and Dale C. Allison Jr. *A Critical and Exegetical Commentary on the Gospel according to Saint Matthew.* 3 vols. ICC. Edinburgh: T & T Clark, 1988–1997.

Davila, James R. "Of Methodology, Monotheism and Metatron: Introductory Reflections on Divine Mediators and the Origins of the Worship of Jesus." Pages 3–18 in *The Jewish Roots of Christological Monotheism: Papers from the St. Andrews Conference on the Historical Origins of the Worship of Jesus.* Edited by Carey C. Newman, James R. Davila, and Gladys S. Lewis. JSJSup 63. Leiden: Brill, 1999.

———. *The Provenance of the Pseudepigrapha: Jewish, Christian, or Other?* JSJSup 105. Leiden: Brill, 2005.

Davis, Deborah, and Elizabeth F. Loftus. "Internal and External Sources of Misinformation in Adult Witness Memory." Pages 195–238 in *Memory for Events.* Vol. 1 of *Handbook of Eyewitness Psychology.* Edited by Michael P. Toglia et al. Mahwah, NJ: Lawrence Erlbaum Associates, 2007.

Davis, P. G. "Divine Agents, Mediators, and New Testament Christology." *JTS* 45 (1992): 470–503.

Dawes, R. M. "Biases of Retrospection." *Issues in Child Abuse Accusations* 1 (1991): 25–28.

Dawson, Lorne L. "When Prophecy Fails and Faith Persists: A Theoretical Overview." *Nova Religio* 3 (1999): 60–82.

DeConick, April D. "Human Memory and the Sayings of Jesus: Contemporary Experimental Exercises in the Transmission of Jesus Traditions." Pages 135–79 in *Jesus, the Voice, and the Text: Beyond the Oral and the Written Gospel.* Edited by Tom Thatcher. Waco, TX: Baylor University Press, 2008.

———. *The Original Gospel of Thomas in Translation: With a Commentary and New English Translation of the Complete Gospel.* London: T & T Clark, 2006.

———. "Reading the Gospel of Thomas as a Repository of Early Christian Communal Memory." Pages 207–20 in *Memory, Tradition, and Text: Uses of the Past in Early Christianity.* Edited by Alan Kirk and Tom Thatcher. SBLSymS 52. Leiden: Brill, 2005.

———. *Recovering the Original Gospel of Thomas: A History of the Growth of the Gospel.* London: T & T Clark, 2005.

———. *The Thirteenth Apostle: What the Gospel of Judas Really Says.* New York: Continuum, 2007.

———. "What Is Early Jewish and Christian Mysticism?" Pages 1–24 in *Paradise Now: Essays on Early Jewish and Christian Mysticism.* Edited by April D. DeConick. SBLSymS 11. Atlanta: Society of Biblical Literature, 2006.

Deignan, Kathleen. *Christ Spirit: The Eschatology of Shaker Christianity.* ATLAMS 29. Metuchen, NJ: Scarecrow Press, 1992.

Dein, Simon. "Lubavitch: A Contemporary Messianic Movement." *JCR* 12 (1997): 191–204.

———. "Mosiach Is Here Now: Just Open Your Eyes and You Can See Him." *Anthropology and Medicine* 9 (2002): 25–36.

———. "What Really Happens When Prophecy Fails: The Case of Lubavitch." *SocRel* 62 (2001): 383–401.

———. "When Prophecy Fails: Messianism amongst Lubavitcher Hasids." Pages 238–60 in *The Coming Deliverer: Millennial Themes in World Religions*. Edited by Fiona Bowie and Christopher Deacy. Cardiff: University of Wales Press, 1997.

Deissmann, Adolf. *Light from the Ancient East: The New Testament Illustrated by Recently Discovered Texts of the Graeco-Roman World*. Translated by Lionel R. M. Strachan. Rev. ed. New York: George H. Doran, 1927.

Delling, Gerhard. "πλήρης κ.τ.λ." *TDNT* 6:283–311.

———. "τρεῖς κ.τ.λ." *TDNT* 8:216–25.

Deming, Will. "Mark 9.42–10.12, Matthew 5.27–32, and *b. Nid.* 13b: A First Century Discussion of Male Sexuality." *NTS* 36 (1990): 130–41.

Denis, John A. *Jesus' Death and the Gathering of True Israel: The Johannine Appropriation of Restoration Theology in the Light of John 11:47–52*. WUNT 2/217. Tübingen: Mohr Siebeck, 2006.

———. "The 'Lifting Up of the Son of Man' and the Dethroning of the 'Ruler of this World': Jesus' Death as the Defeat of the Devil in John 12:31–32." Pages 677–91 in *The Death of Jesus in the Fourth Gospel*. Edited by G. van Belle. BETL 200. Leuven: Leuven University Press, 2007.

Denney, James. "The Second Epistle to the Corinthians." Pages 718–809 in *St. Luke–Galatians*. Vol. 5 of *The Expositor's Bible*. Edited by W. Robertson Nicoll. Rahway, NJ: Expositor Bible Company, n.d.

Deppe, Dean B. "Charting the Future or a Perspective on the Present? The Paraenetic Purpose of Mark 13." *CTJ* 41 (2006): 89–101.

———. "The Sayings of Jesus in the Epistle of James." DTh diss., Free University of Amsterdam, 1989.

Deppermann, Klaus. *Melchior Hoffman: Social Unrest and Apocalyptic Visions in the Age of Reformation*. Edinburgh: T & T Clark, 1987.

Derrett, J. Duncan M. "Christ and Reproof (Matthew 7.1–5/Luke 6.37–42)." *NTS* 34 (1988): 271–81.

Desroch, Henri. *The Sociology of Hope*. London: Routledge & Kegan Paul, 1979.

Dewar, Frances. "Chapter 13 and the Passion Narrative in Mark." *Theology* 64 (1961): 91–107.

Dewey, Arthur J. "'Keep Speaking Until You Find . . .': Thomas and the School of Oral Mimesis." Pages 109–32 in *Redescribing Christian Origins*. Edited by Ron Cameron and Merrill P. Miller. SBLSymS 28. Atlanta: Society of Biblical Literature, 2004.

Dewick, E. C. *Primitive Christian Eschatology: The Hulsean Prize Essay for 1908*. Cambridge: Cambridge University Press, 1912.

Dibelius, Martin. *An die Kolosser, Epheser, an Philemon*. HNT 12. Tübingen: Mohr Siebeck, 1953.

———. *Die urchristliche Überlieferung von Johannes dem Täufer*. FRLANT 15. Göttingen: Vandenhoeck & Ruprecht, 1911.

———. *From Tradition to Gospel*. New York: Charles Scribner's Sons, n.d.

———. "Gethsemane." Pages 258–71 in vol. 1 of *Botschaft und Geschichte: Gesammelte Aufsätze*. 2 vols. Edited by Günther Bornkamm. Tübingen: Mohr Siebeck, 1953–56.

———. *Jesus*. Philadelphia: Westminster, 1949.

Dihle, Albrecht. *Die goldene Regel: Eine Einführung in die Geschichte der antiken und frühchristlichen Vulgärethik*. StA 7. Göttingen: Vandenhoeck & Ruprecht, 1962.

Dimant, Devorah. "Resurrection, Restoration, and Time-Curtailing in Qumran, Early Judaism, and Christianity." *RevQ* 19 (2000): 527–48.

———. "A Synoptic Comparison of Parallel Sections in 4Q427 7, 4Q491 11 and 4Q471B." *JQR* 85 (1994): 157–61.

Dinkler, Eric. "Peter's Confession and the 'Satan' Saying: The Problem of Jesus' Messiahship." Pages 169–203 in *The Future of Our Religious Past: Essays in Honor of Rudolf Bultmann.* Edited by James M. Robinson. New York: Harper & Row, 1971.

Dobschütz, Ernst von. *The Eschatology of the Gospels.* London: Hodder & Stoughton, 1910.

Dodd, C. H. *According to the Scriptures: The Sub-structure of New Testament Theology.* London: Fontana, 1965.

———. *The Apostolic Preaching and Its Developments.* Chicago: Willett, Clark, 1937.

———. *The Founder of Christianity.* London: Fontana, 1973.

———. *Historical Tradition in the Fourth Gospel.* Cambridge: Cambridge University Press, 1963.

———. *History and the Gospel.* New York: Charles Scribner's Sons, 1938.

———. *The Interpretation of the Fourth Gospel.* Cambridge: Cambridge University Press, 1953.

———. "Jesus as Teacher and Prophet." Pages 53–66 in *Mysterium Christi: Christological Studies by British and German Theologians.* Edited by G. K. A. Bell and D. Adolf Deissmann. London: Longmans, Green, 1930.

———. "The Life and Teaching of Jesus Christ." Pages 367–89 in *A Companion to the Bible.* Edited by T. W. Manson. Edinburgh: T & T Clark, 1939.

———. *The Parables of the Kingdom.* New rev. ed. New York: Charles Scribner's Sons, 1961.

Doeve, J. W. *Jewish Hermeneutics in the Synoptic Gospels and Acts.* Assen: Van Gorcum, 1954.

Donfried, Karl P. "The Kingdom of God in Paul." Pages 175–90 in *The Kingdom of God in 20th-Century Interpretation.* Edited by Wendell Willis. Peabody, MA: Hendrickson, 1987.

———. "Paul and Judaism: 1 Thessalonians 2:13–16 as a Test Case." *Int* 38 (1984): 242–53.

———. *The Setting of Second Clement in Early Christianity.* NovTSup 38. Leiden: Brill, 1974.

Dougall, Lily, and Cyril W. Emmet. *The Lord of Thought: A Study of the Problems Which Confronted Jesus Christ and the Solution He Offered.* London: SCM Press, 1922.

Douglas, Claude C. *Overstatement in the New Testament.* New York: Henry Holt, 1931.

Draper, Jonathan. "The Jesus Tradition in the Didache." Pages 269–87 in *The Jesus Tradition outside the Gospels.* Vol. 5 of *Gospel Perspectives.* Edited by David Wenham. Sheffield: JSOT Press, 1985.

Drewery, Benjamin. *Origen and the Doctrine of Grace.* London: Epworth, 1960.

Dronke, Peter. "Arbor Caritatis." Pages 207–54 in *Medieval Studies for J. A. W. Bennett: Aetatis Suae LXX.* Edited by P. L. Heyworth. Oxford: Clarendon, 1981.

Dubis, Mark. *Messianic Woes in First Peter: Suffering and Eschatology in 1 Peter 4:12–19.* New York: Peter Lang, 2002.

Duling, Dennis. "Kingdom of God, Kingdom of Heaven." *ABD* 4:49–69.

———. "The Promises to David and Their Entrance into Christianity—Nailing Down a Likely Hypothesis." *NTS* 19 (1973): 55–77.

———. "Solomon, Exorcism, and the Son of David." *HTR* 68 (1975): 235–52.

Duling, Dennis C., and Norman Perrin. *The New Testament: Proclamation and Parenesis, Myth and History.* 3rd ed. Fort Worth, TX: Harcourt Brace College Publishers, 1994.

Dunn, James D. G. "'All That Glitters Is Not Gold': In Quest of the Right Key to Unlock the Way to the Historical Jesus." Pages 131–61 in *Der historische Jesus: Tendenzen und Perspektiven der gegenwärtigen Forschung.* Edited by Jens Schröter and Ralph Brucker. BZNW 114. Berlin: de Gruyter, 2002.

———. "The Birth of a Metaphor—Baptized in Spirit." Pages 103–17 in *Pneumatology.* Vol. 2 of *The Christ and the Spirit: Collected*

Essays of James D. G. Dunn. Grand Rapids: Eerdmans, 1998.

———. "The Danielic Son of Man in the New Testament." Pages 528–49 in *The Book of Daniel: Composition and Reception.* Edited by John J. Collins and Peter W. Flint. VTSup 83. Leiden: Brill, 2001.

———. *The Epistles to the Colossians and to Philemon: A Commentary on the Greek Text.* NIGTC. Grand Rapids: Eerdmans, 1996.

———. *The Epistle to the Galatians.* BNTC 9. London: A & C Black, 1993.

———. *Jesus and the Spirit.* Philadelphia: Westminster, 1975.

———. *Jesus Remembered.* Christianity in the Making 1. Grand Rapids: Eerdmans, 2003.

———. "Jesus Tradition in Paul." Pages 155–78 in *Studying the Historical Jesus: Evaluations of the State of Current Research.* Edited by Bruce Chilton and Craig Evans. NTTS 19. Leiden: Brill, 1994.

———. "Messianic Ideas and Their Influence on the Jesus of History." Pages 365–81 in *The Messiah: Developments in Earliest Judaism and Christianity.* Edited by James H. Charlesworth. Minneapolis: Fortress, 1992.

———. "Once More—Gal 1:18: ἱστορῆσαι Κηφᾶν." *ZNW* 76 (1985): 138–39.

———. "Paul's Knowledge of the Jesus Tradition." Pages 193–207 in *Christus Bezeugen: Festschrift für Wolfgang Trilling.* Edited by Karl Kertelge, Traugott Holts, and Claus-Peter März. ETS. Leipzig: St. Benno-Verlag, 1989.

———. "The Relationship between Paul and Jerusalem according to Galatians 1 and 2." *NTS* 28 (1982): 461–78.

———. *Romans 1–8.* WBC 38A. Nashville: Thomas Nelson, 1988.

———. *Romans 9–16.* WBC 38B. Nashville: Thomas Nelson, 1988.

———. "Social Memory and the Oral Jesus Tradition." Pages 179–94 in *Memory in the Bible and Antiquity: The Fifth Durham-Tübingen Research Symposium.* Edited by Stephen C. Barton, Loren T. Stuckenbruck,

and Benjamin G. Wold. WUNT 212. Tübingen: Mohr Siebeck, 2007.

———. *The Theology of Paul the Apostle.* Grand Rapids: Eerdmans, 1998.

———. *Unity and Diversity in the New Testament: An Inquiry into the Character of Earliest Christianity.* Philadelphia: Westminster, 1977.

Dupont, Jacques. "Le logion des douze trônes (Mt 19,28; Lc 22,28–30)." *Bib* 45 (1964): 355–92.

———. *Les Béatitudes*, vol. 1, *Le problème littéraire.* EB. Paris: Gabalda, 1969.

Dyer, Keith D. *The Prophecy on the Mount: Mark 13 and the Gathering of the New Community.* ITS 2. Bern: Peter Lang, 1998.

Easton, Burton Scott. "The First Evangelic Tradition." *JBL* 50 (1931): 148–55.

Ebersohn, Michael. *Das Nächstenliebegebot in der synoptischen Tradition.* MTS 37. Marburg: Elwert, 1993.

Ebner, Martin. *Jesus—Ein Weisheitslehrer? Synoptische Weisheitslogien im Traditionsprozess.* HBS 15. Freiburg: Herder, 1998.

Eddy, Paul Rhodes, and Gregory A. Boyd. *The Jesus Legend: A Case for the Historical Reliability of the Synoptic Jesus Tradition.* Grand Rapids: Baker Academic, 2007.

Edmonds, Ennis Barrington. *Rastafari: From Outcasts to Culture Bearers.* Oxford: Oxford University Press, 2003.

Egger, Peter. *"Crucifixus sub Pontio Pilato": Das "Crimen" Jesu von Nazareth im Spannungsfeld römischer und jüdischer Verwaltungs- und Rechtsstrukturen.* NTAbh 32. Münster: Aschendorff, 1997.

Ego, Beate. "Gottes Weltherrschaft und die Einzigkeit seines Namens." Pages 257–83 in *Königsherrschaft Gottes und himmlischer Kult im Judentum, Urchristentum und in der hellenistischen Welt.* Edited by Martin Hengel and Anna Maria Schwemer. WUNT 2/55. Tübingen: Mohr Siebeck, 1991.

Ehrman, Bart. *Jesus: Apocalyptic Prophet of the New Millennium.* Oxford: Oxford University Press, 1999.

Einstein, Albert. "Science and Religion." Pages 209–14 in *Science, Philosophy and Religion: A Symposium.* New York: Conference on

Science, Philosophy and Religion in Their Relation to the Democratic Way of Life, 1941.

Einstein, Albert, and Leopold Infeld. *The Evolution of Physics: From Early Concepts to Relativity and Quanta.* New York: Simon & Schuster, 1966.

Elgvin, Torleif. "Wisdom with and without Apocalyptic." Pages 15–38 in *Sapiential, Liturgical, and Poetical Texts from Qumran: Proceedings of the Third Meeting of the International Organization for Qumran Studies, Oslo, 1998.* Edited by Daniel K. Falk, Florentino García Martínez, and Eileen M. Schuller. STDJ 34. Leiden: Brill, 2000.

Elledge, C. D. "The Prince of the Congregation: Qumran 'Messianism' in the Context of *Milḥāmâ*." Pages 178–207 in *Qumran Studies: New Approaches, New Questions.* Edited by Michael Thomas David and Brent A. Strawn. Grand Rapids: Eerdmans, 2007.

———. "Resurrection of the Dead: Exploring Our Earliest Evidence Today." Pages 22–52 in *Resurrection: The Origin and Future of a Biblical Doctrine.* By James H. Charlesworth et al. New York: T & T Clark, 2006.

Elliott, John H. "Jesus the Israelite Was Neither a 'Jew' nor a 'Christian': On Correcting Misleading Nomenclature." *JSHJ* 5 (2007): 119–54.

Emmet, Cyril W. *The Eschatological Question in the Gospels: And Other Studies in Recent New Testament Criticism.* Edinburgh: T & T Clark, 1911.

Engel, Susan. *Context Is Everything: The Nature of Memory.* New York: W. H. Freeman, 1999.

Epstein, Yaʿakov Naḥum, and Ezra Tsiyon Melamed, eds. *Mekhilta de-Rabi Shimʿon ben Yoḥai: ʿAl pi kitve yad min ha-Genizah umi-Midrash ha-gadol.* [מכילתא דרבי שמעון בן יוחאי, עפ "י כתבי יד מן הגניזה וממדרש הגדול]. Schriften des Vereins Mekize Nirdamim. Jerusalem: Meḳiṭse Nirdamim, 1955.

Ernst, Joseph. *Johannes der Täufer: Interpretation, Geschichte, Wirkungsgeschichte.* BZNW 53. Berlin: de Gruyter, 1989.

Eshel, Esther. "The Identification of the 'Speaker' of the Self-Glorification Hymn." Pages 619–35 in *The Provo International Conference on the Dead Sea Scrolls: Technological Innovations, New Texts, and Reformulated Issues.* Edited by Donald W. Parry and Eugene Ulrich. STDJ 30. Leiden: Brill, 1999.

———. "4Q471B: A Self-Glorification Hymn." *RevQ* 17 (1996): 175–203.

Eskola, Timo. *Messiah and the Throne: Jewish Merkabah Mysticism and Early Christian Exaltation Discourse.* WUNT 2/142. Tübingen: Mohr Siebeck, 2001.

Esler, Philip F. *Conflict and Identity in Romans: The Social Setting of Paul's Letter.* Minneapolis: Fortress, 2003.

Etkes, Immanuel. *The Besht: Magician, Mystic, and Leader.* Translated by Saadya Sternberg. Waltham, MA: Brandeis University Press; Hanover, NH: University Press of New England, 2005.

Evans, Craig A. "Daniel in the New Testament: Visions of God's Kingdom." Pages 490–527 in *The Book of Daniel: Composition and Reception.* Edited by John J. Collins and Peter W. Flint. VTSup 83. Leiden: Brill, 2001.

———. "Defeating Satan and Liberating Israel: Jesus and Daniel's Vision." *JSHJ* 1 (2003): 161–70.

———. "From Anointed Prophet to Anointed King: Probing Aspects of Jesus' Self-Understanding." Pages 437–56 in *Jesus and His Contemporaries: Comparative Studies.* AGJU 25. Leiden: Brill, 1995.

———. *Jesus and the Ossuaries.* Waco, TX: Baylor University Press, 2003.

———. "The Twelve Thrones of Israel: Scripture and Politics in Luke 22:24–30." Pages 455–79 in *Jesus in Context: Temple, Purity, and Restoration.* By Bruce Chilton and Craig A. Evans. AGJU 39. Leiden: Brill, 1997.

———. "Was Simon ben Kosiba Recognized as Messiah?" Pages 183–212 in *Jesus and His Contemporaries: Comparative Studies.* AGJU 25. Leiden: Brill, 1995.

————. "Zechariah in the Markan Passion Narrative." Pages 64–80 in *The Gospel of Mark*. Vol. 1 of *Biblical Interpretation in Early Christian Gospels*. Edited by Thomas R. Hatina. LNTS 304. London: T & T Clark, 2006.

Evans, Craig A., and James A. Sanders. *Luke and Scripture: The Function of Sacred Tradition in Luke-Acts*. Minneapolis: Fortress, 1993.

Eve, Eric. "Meier, Miracle, and Multiple Attestation." *JSHJ* 3 (2005): 23–45.

Fabry, Heinz-Josef. "Mose, der 'Gesalbte JHWHs': Messianische Aspekte der Mose-Interpretation in Qumran." Pages 129–42 in *Moses in Biblical and Extra-Biblical Traditions*. Edited by Axel Gaupner and Michael Wolter. BZNW 372. Berlin: de Gruyter, 2007.

Farrer, Austin. *A Study in St. Mark*. New York: Oxford University Press, 1952.

Fee, Gordon. *The First Epistle to the Corinthians*. NICNT. Grand Rapids: Eerdmans, 1987.

————. *God's Empowering Presence: The Holy Spirit in the Writings of Paul*. Peabody, MA: Hendrickson, 1994.

Feeney, D. C. "Towards an Account of the Ancient World's Concepts of Fictive Belief." Pages 230–44 in *Lies and Fiction in the Ancient World*. Edited by Christopher Gill and T. P. Wiseman. Austin: University of Texas Press, 1993.

Feldmeier, Richard. *Die Krisis des Gottessohnes: Die Gethsemaneerzählung als Schlüssel der Markuspassion*. WUNT 2/21. Tübingen: Mohr Siebeck, 1987.

Fenton, J. C. *Matthew*. PNTC. Baltimore: Penguin, 1963.

Fentress, James, and Chris Wickham. *Social Memory*. Oxford: Blackwell, 1992.

Ferguson, Everett. "The Kingdom of God in Early Patristic Literature." Pages 191–208 in *The Kingdom of God in 20th-Century Interpretation*. Edited by Wendell Willis. Peabody, MA: Hendrickson, 1987.

Festinger, Leon, Henry W. Riecken, and Stanley Schachter. *When Prophecy Fails: A Social and Psychological Study of a Modern Group That Predicted the Destruction of the World*. New York: Harper & Row, 1964.

Filson, Floyd V. *The Gospel according to St Matthew*. 2nd ed. BNTC. London: Adam & Charles Black, 1971.

Findlay, G. G. "St. Paul's First Epistle to the Corinthians." Pages 729–953 in vol. 2 of *The Expositor's Greek Testament*. Edited by W. Robertson Nicoll. New York: George H. Doran, n.d.

Finegan, Jack. *Die Überlieferung der Leidens- und Auferstehungsgeschichte Jesu*. BZNW 15. Gießen: Töpelmann, 1934.

————. *Mark of the Taw*. Richmond: John Knox, 1972.

Finkelstein, Louis. "The Underlying Concepts of Conservative Judaism." *Conservative Judaism* 26 (1972): 2–12.

Finley, John H., Jr. "Euripides and Thucydides." Pages 1–54 in *Three Essays on Thucydides*. Cambridge, MA: Harvard University Press, 1967. Repr. from *HSCP* 49 (1938): 23–68.

Fitzmyer, Joseph A. *First Corinthians: A New Translation with Introduction and Commentary*. AYB 32. New Haven: Yale University Press, 2008.

————. *The Gospel according to Luke*, vol. 1, *Luke I–IX*. AB 28A. Garden City, NY: Doubleday, 1981.

————. "New Testament *Kyrios* and *Maranatha* and Their Aramaic Background." Pages 218–35 in *To Advance the Gospel: New Testament Studies*. New York: Crossroad, 1981.

————. *The One Who Is to Come*. Grand Rapids: Eerdmans, 2007.

Fleddermann, Harry T. *Q: A Reconstruction and Commentary*. BibTS 1. Leuven: Peeters, 2005.

Fletcher-Louis, Crispin H. T. *Luke-Acts: Angels, Christology, and Soteriology*. WUNT 2/94. Tübingen: Mohr Siebeck, 1997.

Flint, Peter W. "The Daniel Tradition at Qumran." Pages 41–60 in *Eschatology, Messianism, and the Dead Sea Scrolls*. Edited by Craig A. Evans and Peter W. Flint. Grand Rapids: Eerdmans, 1997.

Flusser, David. "'The House of David' on an Ossuary." *IMJ* 5 (1986): 37–49.

———. "Qumran und die Zwölf." Pages 173–85 in *Judaism and the Origins of Christianity*. Jerusalem: Magnes, 1988.

———. "Salvation Present and Future." Pages 46–61 in *Types of Redemption: Contributions to the Theme of the Study-Conference Held at Jerusalem 14th to 19th July 1968*. Edited by R. J. Zwi Werblowsky and C. Jouco Bleeker. SHR 18. Leiden: Brill, 1970.

Flusser, David, and R. Steven Notley. *The Sage from Galilee: Rediscovering Jesus' Genius*. 4th ed. Grand Rapids: Eerdmans, 2007.

Foakes-Jackson, F. J., and Kirsopp Lake. "The Public Teaching of Jesus and His Choice of the Twelve." Pages 267–99 in vol. 3 of *The Beginnings of Christianity, Part I: The Acts of the Apostles*. Edited by F. J. Foakes-Jackson and Kirsopp Lake. London: Macmillan, 1920.

Fossum, J. E. *The Name of God and the Angel of the Lord: Samaritan and Jewish Concepts of Intermediation and the Origin of Gnosticism*. WUNT 36. Tübingen: Mohr Siebeck, 1985.

Foster, Lawrence. "Had Prophecy Failed? Contrasting Perspectives of the Millerites and Shakers." Pages 173–88 in *The Disappointed: Millerism and Millenarianism in the Nineteenth Century*. Edited by Ronald L. Numbers and Jonathan M. Butler. Bloomington: Indiana University Press, 1987.

Frame, James Everett. *A Critical and Exegetical Commentary on the Epistles of Paul to the Thessalonians*. ICC. New York: Charles Scribner's Sons, 1912.

France, R. T. "The Church and the Kingdom of God." Pages 30–44 in *Biblical Interpretation and the Church: Text and Context*. Edited by D. A. Carson. Exeter: Paternoster, 1984.

———. *The Gospel of Matthew*. NICNT. Grand Rapids: Eerdmans, 2007.

Frankemölle, Hubert. *Der Brief des Jakobus*. 2 vols. ÖTKNT 17. Gütersloh: Gütersloher Verlagshaus; Würzburg: Echter, 1994.

———. "Jesus als deuterojesajanischer Freudenbote? Zur Rezeption von Jes 52,7 und 61,1 im Neuen Testament, durch Jesus und in den Targumim." Pages 34–67 in *Vom Urchristentum zu Jesus: Für Joachim Gnilka*. Edited by Hubert Frankemölle and Karl Kertelge. Freiburg: Herder, 1989.

Franzmann, Majella. *Jesus in the Manichaean Writings*. London: Continuum, 2003.

———. "Jesus in the Manichaean Writings—Work in Progress." Pages 226–27 in *Studia Manichaica IV: Internationaler Kongreß zum Manichäismus, Berlin, 14.–18. Juli 1997*. Edited by Ronald E. Emmerick, Werner Sundermann, and Peter Zieme. BA 4. Berlin: Akademie-Verlag, 2000.

Frayer-Griggs, Daniel. "'Everyone Will Be Baptized in Fire': Mark 9.49, Q 3.16, and the Baptism of the Coming One." *JSHJ* 7 (2009): 254–85.

Fredriksen, Paula. *From Jesus to Christ: The Origins of the New Testament Images*. 2nd ed. New Haven: Yale University Press, 2000.

———. *Jesus of Nazareth, King of the Jews: A Jewish Life and the Emergence of Christianity*. New York: Alfred A. Knopf, 2000.

———. "What You See Is What You Get: Context and Content in Current Research on the Historical Jesus." *ThTo* 52 (1995): 75–97.

———. "Why Was Jesus Put to Death, but His Followers Were Not?" *JSNT* 29 (2007): 415–19.

Frenschkowski, Marco. "The Enigma of the Three Words of Jesus in Gospel of Thomas Logion 13." *Journal of Higher Criticism* 1 (1994): 73–84.

———. "Galiläa oder Jerusalem? Die topographischen und politischen Hintergründe der Logienquelle." Pages 476–94 in *The Sayings Source Q and the Historical Jesus*. Edited by A. Lindemann. BETL 158. Leuven: Leuven University Press, 2001.

———. "Welche biographischen Kenntnisse von Jesus setzt die Logienquelle Voraus? Beobachtungen zur Gattung von Q im Kontext antiker Spruchsammlungen." Pages 3–41 in *From Quest to Q: Festschrift James M. Rob-*

inson. Edited by Jon Ma. Asgeirsson, Kristin de Troyer, and Marvin W. Meyer. BETL 146. Leuven: Leuven University Press, 2000.

Frey, Jörg. "Der historische Jesus und der Christus der Evangelien." Pages 273–336 in *Der historische Jesus: Tendenzen und Perspektiven der gegenwärtigen Forschung.* Edited by Jens Schröter and Ralph Brucker. BZNW 114. Berlin: de Gruyter, 2002.

———. "Die Apokalyptik als Herausforderung der neutestamentlichen Wissenschaft. Zum Problem: Jesus und die Apokalyptik." Pages 23–94 in *Apokalyptik als Herausforderung neutestamentlicher Theologie.* Edited by Michael Becker and Markus Öhler. WUNT 2/214. Tübingen: Mohr Siebeck, 2006.

———. *Die eschatologische Verkündigung in den johanneischen Texten.* Vol. 3 of *Die johanneische Eschatologie.* WUNT 117. Tübingen: Mohr Siebeck, 2000.

Frick, Robert. *Die Geschichte des Reich-Gottes-Gedankens in der alten Kirche bis zu Origenes und Augustin.* BZNW 6. Gießen: Töpelmann, 1928.

Friedlander, Gerald. *The Jewish Sources of the Sermon on the Mount.* New York: Ktav, 1969.

Friedman, Theodore. "The Sabbath: Anticipation of Redemption." *Judaism* 16 (1967): 443–52.

Friedrich, G. "Die Auferweckung Jesu, eine Tat Gottes oder ein Interpretament der Jünger?" *KD* 17 (1971): 153–87.

Froitzheim, Franzjosef. *Christologie und Eschatologie bei Paulus.* FB 35. Würzburg: Echter, 1978.

Frye, Northrop. *Words with Power: Being a Second Study of "The Bible and Literature."* San Diego: Harcourt, Brace, Jovanovich, 1990.

Fuks, Alexander. "Aspects of the Jewish Revolt in A.D. 115–117." *JRS* 51 (1961): 98–104.

Fuller, Michael E. *The Restoration of Israel: Israel's Re-gathering and the Fate of the Nations in Early Jewish Literature and Luke-Acts.* BZNW 138. Berlin: de Gruyter, 2006.

Fuller, Reginald H. *The Foundations of New Testament Christology.* London: Collins, 1969.

———. *The Mission and Achievement of Jesus: An Examination of the Presuppositions of New Testament Theology.* SBT 12. London: SCM Press, 1954.

Funk, Robert. *Honest to Jesus: Jesus for a New Millennium.* New York: Macmillan, 1996.

Funk, Robert W., Roy W. Hoover, and the Jesus Seminar. *The Five Gospels: The Search for the Authentic Words of Jesus.* New York: Macmillan, 1993.

Funk, Robert, and the Jesus Seminar. *The Acts of Jesus: The Search for the Authentic Deeds of Jesus.* San Francisco: HarperSanFrancisco, 1998.

Gabba, Emilio. "True History and False History in Classical Antiquity." *JRS* 71 (1981): 50–62.

Gager, John G. *Kingdom and Community: The Social World of Early Christianity.* Englewood Cliffs, NJ: Prentice-Hall, 1975.

———. "Messiahs and Their Followers." Pages 37–46 in *Toward the Third Millennium: Messianic Expectations from the Bible to Waco.* Edited by Peter Schäfer and Mark Cohen. SHR 77. Leiden: Brill, 1998.

García Martínez, F. "The 'I' of Two Qumran Hymns." *ETL* 78 (2002): 321–39.

García Martínez, Florentino, and Eibert J. C. Tigchelaar. *The Dead Sea Scrolls Study Edition.* 2 vols. Leiden: Brill, 1998.

Garrod, Heathcote William. *The Religion of All Good Men.* New York: Macmillan, 1906.

Garrow, Alan J. P. *The Gospel of Matthew's Dependence on the Didache.* JSNTSup 254. London: T & T Clark, 2004.

Garry, Maryanne, and Devon Polaschek. "Reinventing Yourself." *Psychology Today* 32, no. 6 (November/December 1999): 64–68.

Gaskell, George D., Daniel B. Wright, and Colm A. O'Muircheartaigh. "Telescoping of Landmark Events: Implications for Survey Research." *Public Opinion Quarterly Review* 64 (2000): 77–89.

Gathercole, Simon. "Jesus' Eschatological Vision of the Fall of Satan: Luke 10,18 Reconsidered." *ZNW* 94 (2003): 143–63.

———. "The Son of Man in Mark's Gospel." *ExpTim* 115 (2004): 366–72.

Gaventa, Beverly Roberts. "Interpreting the Death of Jesus Apocalyptically: Reconsidering Romans 8:32." Pages 125–45 in *Jesus and Paul Reconnected: Fresh Pathways into an Old Debate*. Edited by Todd D. Still. Grand Rapids: Eerdmans, 2007.

Geddert, Timothy J. *Watchwords: Mark 13 in Markan Eschatology*. JSNTSup 26. Sheffield: JSOT Press, 1989.

Gedi, Noa, and Yigal Elam. "Collective Memory—What Is It?" *History and Memory* 8 (1996): 30–50.

Geiger, Ruthild. *Die lukanischen Endzeitreden: Studien zur Eschatologie des Lukas-Evangeliums*. EH 23/16. Bern: Herbert Lang; Frankfurt am Main: Peter Lang, 1973.

Georgi, Dieter. "The Interest in Life of Jesus Theology as a Paradigm for the Social History of Biblical Criticism." *HTR* 85 (1992): 51–83.

Gerhardsson, Birger. *Memory and Manuscript: Oral Tradition and Written Transmission in Rabbinic Judaism and Early Christianity*. Translated by Eric J. Sharpe. ASNU 22. Lund: Gleerup, 1961.

———. *The Origins of the Gospel Traditions*. Philadelphia: Fortress, 1979.

———. *The Reliability of the Gospel Tradition*. Peabody, MA: Hendrickson, 2001.

———. *Tradition and Transmission in Early Christianity*. ConBNT 20. Lund: Gleerup, 1964.

Gerstenberger, Erhard S. *Leviticus*. OTL. Louisville: Westminster John Knox, 1966.

Gibson, Marion. *Order from Chaos: Responding to Traumatic Events*. Birmingham, UK: Venture, 1998.

Gieschen, Charles A. *Angelmorphic Christology: Antecedents and Early Evidence*. AGJU 42. Leiden: Boston, 1998.

Giesen, H. "Naherwartung im Neuen Testament?" *ThG* 30 (1987): 151–64.

Giezen, Anne E. van, et al. "Consistency of Memory for Emotionally Arousing Events: A Review of Prospective and Experimental Studies." *Clinical Psychology Review* 25 (2005): 935–53.

Gill, Christopher. "Plato's Atlantis Story and the Birth of Fiction." *Philosophy and Literature* 3 (1979): 64–78.

Gill, John. *Gill's Commentary*. 6 vols. Grand Rapids: Baker Books, 1980.

Gilliard, Frank D. "The Problem of the Antisemitic Comma between 1 Thessalonians 2.14 and 15." *NTS* 35 (1989): 481–502.

Glasson, T. Francis. *Jesus and the End of the World*. Edinburgh: St. Andrews Press, 1980.

———. *Moses in the Fourth Gospel*. SBT 40. London: SCM Press, 1963.

———. *The Second Advent: The Origin of the New Testament Doctrine*. 2nd rev. ed. London: Epworth, 1947.

Glazier-McDonald, Beth. *Malachi: The Divine Messenger*. SBLDS 98. Atlanta: Scholars Press, 1987.

Glover, Richard. "Patristic Quotations and Gospel Sources." *NTS* 31 (1985): 234–51.

Gnilka, Joachim. *Das Evangelium nach Markus (Mk 8,27–16,20)*. EKKNT 2/2. Zurich: Benzinger; Neukirchen-Vluyn: Neukirchener Verlag, 1979.

———. *Jesus of Nazareth: Message and History*. Translated by Siegfried S. Schatzmann. Peabody, MA: Hendrickson, 1997.

Godet, F. *Commentary on St. Paul's Epistle to the Romans*. New York: Funk & Wagnalls, 1885.

Goethals, George R., and Richard F. Reckman. "Recalling Previously Held Attitudes." *Journal of Experimental Social Psychology* 9 (1973): 491–501.

Goff, Lynn M., and Henry L. Roediger III. "Imagination Inflation for Action Events: Repeated Imaginings Lead to Illusory Recollections." *Memory and Cognition* 26 (1998): 20–33.

Goffman, Erving. *The Presentation of the Self in Everyday Life*. New York: Doubleday, 1959.

Goguel, Maurice. *Jesus the Nazarene: Myth or History?* Translated by Frederick Stephens. New York: D. Appleton, 1926.

———. *The Life of Jesus.* Translated by Olive Wyon. New York: Macmillan, 1933.

Goldin, Judah. "Freedom and Restraint of Haggadah." Pages 57–76 in *Midrash and Literature.* Edited by Geoffrey H. Hartman and Sanford Budick. New Haven: Yale University Press, 1986.

Goldstein, Jonathan A. "Biblical Promises in 1 and 2 Maccabees." Pages 69–96 in *Judaisms and Their Messiahs at the Turn of the Christian Era.* Edited by Jacob Neusner, William Scott Green, and Ernest S. Frerichs. New York: Cambridge University Press, 1987.

Golitzin, Alexander. "Earthly Angels and Heavenly Men: The Old Testament Pseudepigrapha, Nicetas Stethatos, and the Tradition of Interiorized Apocalyptic in Eastern Christian Ascetical and Mystical Literature." *Dumbarton Oaks Papers* 55 (2001): 125–53.

Gomulicki, B. R. "Recall as an Abstractive Process." *Acta Psychologica* 12 (1956): 77–94.

Goodacre, Mark. "Prophecy Historicized or History Scripturized? Reflections on the Origin of the Crucifixion Narrative." Paper presented at the annual meeting of the Society of Biblical Literature, Denver, November 2001.

———. "Scripturalization in Mark's Crucifixion Narrative." Pages 33–47 in *The Trial and Death of Jesus: Essays on the Passion Narrative in Mark.* Edited by Geert Van Oyen and Tom Shepherd. CBET 45. Leuven: Peeters, 2006.

Goodman, Martin. "Messianism and Politics in the Land of Israel, 66–135 C.E." Pages 149–57 in *Redemption and Resistance: The Messianic Hopes of Jews and Christians in Antiquity.* Edited by Markus Bockmuehl and James Carleton Paget. London: T & T Clark, 2007.

Goulder, Michael. "The Anointed." Pages 66–74 in *The Old Testament in the New: Essays in Honour of J. J. North.* Edited by Steve Moyise. JSNTSup 189. Sheffield: Sheffield Academic Press, 2000.

———. *The Evangelists' Calendar: A Lectionary Explanation of the Development of Scripture.* London: SPCK, 1978.

———. *Luke: A New Paradigm.* 2 vols. JSNTSup 20. Sheffield: Sheffield Academic Press, 1989.

———. *Midrash and Lection in Matthew.* London: SPCK, 1974.

———. "Visions and Revelations of the Lord (2 Corinthians 12:1–10)." Pages 303–12 in *Paul and the Corinthians: Studies on a Community in Conflict; Essays in Honour of Margaret Thrall.* Edited by Trevor J. Burke and J. Keith Elliott. NovTSup 109. Leiden: Brill, 2003.

Gourgues, Michel. *A la droite de Dieu: Résurrection de Jésus et actualisation du Psaume 110,1 dans le Nouveau Testament.* EBib. Paris: Gabalda, 1978.

Grabbe, L. L. "The End of the World in Early Jewish and Christian Calculations." *RevQ* 11 (1982): 107–8.

Grant, Frederick C. *The Gospel of the Kingdom.* New York: Macmillan, 1940.

Grappe, Christian. "Jésus: Messie prétendu ou messie prétendant?" Pages 269–91 in *Jésus de Nazareth: Nouvelles approches d'une enigma.* Edited by D. Marguerat, E. Norelli, and J.-M. Poffet. Geneva: Labor et Fides, 1998.

———. *Le royaume de Dieu: Avant, avec et après Jésus.* MdB 42. Geneva: Labor et Fides, 2001.

Gräßer, Eric. *Das Problem der Parusieverzögerung in den synoptischen Evangelien und in der Apostelgeschichte.* BZNW 22. Berlin: Töpelmann, 1957.

———. *Die Naherwartung Jesu.* SBS 61. Stuttgart: Katholisches Bibelwerk, 1973.

Grätz, Sebastian. "'Einen Propheten wie mich wird dir der Herr, dein Gott, erwecken': Der Berufungsbericht Jeremias und seine Rückbindung an das Amt des Mose." Pages 61–77 in *Moses in Biblical and Extra-Biblical Traditions.* Edited by Axel Gaupner and Michael Wolter. BZNW 372. Berlin: de Gruyter, 2007.

Gray, Timothy C. *The Temple in the Gospel of Mark: A Study in Its Narrative Role.* WUNT 2/42. Tübingen: Mohr Siebeck, 2008.

Green, Joel B. "Jesus on the Mount of Olives (Luke 22.39–46)." *JSNT* 26 (1986): 29–48.

Greene, Gayle. "Feminist Fiction and the Uses of Memory." *Signs: Journal of Women in Culture and Society* 16 (1991): 290–321.

Gregg, Brian Han. *The Historical Jesus and the Final Judgment Sayings in Q.* WUNT 2/207. Tübingen: Mohr Siebeck, 2006.

Gregory, Andrew F. "*1 Clement* and the Writings That Later Formed the New Testament." Pages 129–58 in *The Reception of the New Testament in the Apostolic Fathers.* Edited by Andrew F. Gregory and Christopher M. Tuckett. Oxford: Oxford University Press, 2005.

Greshake, Gisbert, and Gerhard Lohfink. *Naherwartung, Auferstehung, Unsterblichkeit: Untersuchungen zur christlichen Eschatologie.* QD 71. Freiburg: Herder, 1975.

Grimm, Werner. *Weil ich dich liebe: Die Verkündigung Jesu und Deuterojesaja.* ANTJ. Bern: Herbert Lang, 1976.

Grinnell, George Bird. "Account of the Northern Cheyennes concerning the Messiah Superstition." *Journal of American Folklore* 4 (1891): 61–69.

Grotius, Hugo. *Opera omnia theologica.* 3 vols. Amsterdam: Joannis Blaeu, 1679.

Gundry, Robert H. *Matthew: A Commentary on His Handbook for a Mixed Church under Persecution.* 2nd ed. Grand Rapids: Eerdmans, 1994.

———. *Sōma in Biblical Theology, with Emphasis upon Pauline Anthropology.* SNTSMS 29. Cambridge: Cambridge University Press, 1976.

———. *The Use of the Old Testament in St. Matthew's Gospel with Special Reference to the Messianic Hope.* NovTSup 18. Leiden: Brill, 1967.

Gunther, John J. "The Meaning and Origin of the Name, 'Judas Thomas.'" *Mus* 93 (1980): 113–48.

Gustafson, Henry. "The Afflictions of Christ: What Is Lacking?" *BR* 7 (1963): 28–42.

Guthrie, W. K. C. *Socrates.* Cambridge: Cambridge University Press, 1971.

Gutmann, Joseph. "The Illustrated Midrash in the Dura Synagogue Paintings: A New Dimension for the Study of Judaism." *AAJRP* 50 (1983): 91–104.

Güttgemanns, Erhardt. *Der leidende Apostel und sein Herr: Studien zur paulinischen Christologie.* FRLANT 90. Göttingen: Vandenhoeck & Ruprecht, 1966.

Guy, H. A. *The New Testament Doctrine of the Last Things: A Study of Eschatology.* London: Oxford University Press, 1948.

Haenchen, Ernst. *John: A Commentary on the Gospel of John.* Translated by Robert W. Funk. 2 vols. Hermeneia. Philadelphia: Fortress, 1984.

Häfner, Gerd. "Das Ende der Kriterien? Jesusforschung angesichts der geschichtstheoretischen Diskussion." Pages 97–130 in *Historiographie und fiktionales Erzählen: Zur Konstruktivität in Geschichtstheorie und Exegese.* By Knut Backhaus and Gerd Häfner. Neukirchen-Vluyn: Neukirchener Verlag, 2007.

Hagner, Donald. "How Well Was Jesus Remembered? What Model of Oral Transmission Is Most Persuasive?" In *Remembering Jesus: Essays in Honor of James D. G. Dunn.* Edited by Scot McKnight and T. Mournet. New York: Continuum, forthcoming.

———. *Matthew 14–28.* WBC 33B. Dallas: Word, 1995.

———. *The Use of the Old and New Testaments in Clement of Rome.* NovTSup 34. Leiden: Brill, 1973.

Hahn, Ferdinand. *Christologische Hoheitstitel: Ihre Geschichte im frühen Christentum.* 5th ed. Göttingen: Vandenhoeck & Ruprecht, 1995.

———. "Die Verkündigung Jesu und das Osterzeugnis der Jünger." Pages 19–27 *Bekenntnisbildung und Theologie in urchristlicher Zeit.* Vol. 2 of *Studien zum Neuen Testament.* Edited by Jörg Frey and Unliane Schlegel. WUNT 192. Tübingen: Mohr Siebeck, 2006.

———. *Die Vielfalt des Neuen Testaments: Theologiegeschichte des Urchristentums.*

Vol. 1 of *Theologie des Neuen Testaments*. Tübingen: Mohr Siebeck, 2002.

———. "Die Worte von Gottes Herrschaft und Reich in Joh 3,3.5." Pages 87–89 in *Johannes aenigmaticus: Studien zum Johannesevangelium für Herbert Leroy*. Edited by Stefan Schreiber and Alois Stimpfle. BU 29. Regensburg: Friedrich Pustet, 2000.

———. *Frühjüdische und urchristliche Apokalyptik: Eine Einführung*. Neukirchen-Vluyn: Neukirchener Verlag, 1998.

———. "Methodological Reflections on the Historical Investigation of Jesus." Pages 36–50 in *Historical Investigation and New Testament Faith: Two Essays*. Philadelphia: Fortress, 1983.

———. *Mission in the New Testament*. Translated by Frank Clarke. SBT 47. London: SCM Press, 1965.

Halbwachs, Maurice. *The Collective Memory*. Translated by Francis J. Ditter Jr. and Vida Yazdi Ditter. New York: Harper & Row, 1980.

Halpern, Sue. *Can't Remember What I Forgot: The Good News from the Front Lines of Memory Research*. New York: Harmony Books, 2008.

Hamerton-Kelly, R. G. "Golden Rule, The." *IDBSup* 369.

Hamidović, David. "La vision de Gabriel." *RHPR* 89 (2009): 147–68.

Hamp, Vinzenz. "אֵשׁ." *TDOT* 1:423–28.

Hanks-Harwood, Ginger. "'Like the Leaves of Autumn': The Utilization of the Press to Maintain Millennial Expectations in the Wake of Prophetic Failure." *Journal of Millennial Studies* 1, no. 1 (2001). Online: www.mille.org/publications/winter2001/Harwood.html. Cited 18 November 2009.

Hannah, Darrell D. "Guardian Angels and Angelic National Patrons in Second Temple Judaism and Early Christianity." Pages 413–35 in *Angels: The Concept of Celestial Beings—Origins, Development, and Reception*. Edited by Friedrich V. Reiterer, Tobias Nicklas, and Karin Schöpflin. DCLY. Berlin: de Gruyter, 2007.

———. *Michael and Christ: Michael Traditions and Angel Christology in Early Chris-*

tianity. WUNT 2/109. Tübingen: Mohr Siebeck, 1999.

———. "The Throne of His Glory: The Divine Throne and Heavenly Mediators in Revelation and the Similitudes of Enoch." *ZNW* 94 (2003): 68–96.

Hanson, Paul D. *The Dawn of Apocalyptic: The Historical and Sociological Roots of Jewish Apocalyptic Eschatology*. Philadelphia: Fortress, 1979.

Hardyck, Jane, and Marcia Braden. "Prophecy Fails Again: A Report of a Failure to Replicate." *Journal of Abnormal Social Psychology* 65 (1962): 136–41.

Harkness, Georgia. *Understanding the Kingdom of God*. Nashville: Abingdon, 1974.

Harnack, Adolf. *What Is Christianity?* Translated by Thomas Bailey Saunders. LRC. New York: Harper, 1957.

Harris, J. Rendell. *The Cult of the Heavenly Twins*. Cambridge: Cambridge University Press, 1906.

———. *The Dioscuri in the Christian Legends*. London: C. J. Clay & Sons, 1903.

Harrison, P. N. *Polycarp's Two Epistles to the Philippians*. London: Cambridge University Press, 1936.

Hartin, Patrick J. "James and the Q Sermon on the Mount/Plain." Pages 440–57 in *Society of Biblical Literature 1989 Seminar Papers*. Edited by David J. Lull. Atlanta: Scholars Press, 1989.

Hartman, Lars. *Prophecy Interpreted: The Formation of Some Jewish Apocalyptic Texts and of the Eschatological Discourse Mark 13*. ConBNT 1. Uppsala: Gleerup, 1966.

Harvey, A. E. *Jesus and the Constraints of History*. Philadelphia: Westminster, 1982.

Hastie, Reid. "Memory for Behavioral Information That Confirms or Contradicts a Personality Impression." Pages 155–78 in *Person Memory: The Cognitive Basis of Social Perception*. Edited by Reid Hastie et al. Hillsdale, NJ: Lawrence Erlbaum Associates, 1980.

———. "Schematic Principles in Human Memory." Pages 39–88 in *Social Cognition*. Edited by E. Tory Higgins, C. Peter

Herman, and Mark P. Zanna. *Ontario Symposium 1.* Hillsdale, NJ: Lawrence Erlbaum Associates, 1981.

Hatton, Peter T. H. *Contradiction in the Book of Proverbs: The Deep Waters of Counsel.* SOTSMS. Burlington, VT: Ashgate, 2008.

Häusser, Detlef. *Christusbekenntnis und Jesusüberlieferung bei Paulus.* WUNT 2/210. Tübingen: Mohr Siebeck, 2006.

Hawkins, Scott A., and Reid Hastie. "Hindsight: Biased Judgments of Past Events after the Outcomes Are Known." *Psychological Bulletin* 107 (1990): 311–27.

Hay, David M. *Glory at the Right Hand: Psalm 110 in Early Christianity.* SBLMS 18. Nashville: Abingdon, 1973.

Hayes, John H. "The Resurrection as Enthronement and the Earliest Church Christology." *Int* 22 (1968): 333–45.

Hayman, Peter. "Monotheism—A Misused Word in Jewish Studies?" *JJS* 42 (1991): 1–15.

Hays, Richard B. "Christology and Ethics in Galatians." *CBQ* 49 (1987): 268–90.

———. "Christ Prays the Psalms: Israel's Psalter as Matrix of Early Christology." Pages 101–18 in *The Conversion of the Imagination: Paul as Interpreter of Israel's Scripture.* Grand Rapids: Eerdmans, 2005.

———. *The Faith of Jesus Christ: The Narrative Substructure of Galatians 3:1–4:11.* 2nd ed. Grand Rapids: Eerdmans; Dearborn, MI: Dove Booksellers, 2002.

———. *The Moral Vision of the New Testament: Community, Cross, New Creation; A Contemporary Introduction to New Testament Ethics.* San Francisco: HarperSanFrancisco, 1996.

Hayward, Robert. "Phinehas—the Same Is Elijah: The Origins of a Rabbinic Tradition." *JJS* 29 (1978): 22–34.

Head, Peter M. *Christology and the Synoptic Problem: An Argument for Markan Priority.* SNTSMS 94. Cambridge: Cambridge University Press, 1997.

Heard, Richard. *An Introduction to the New Testament.* London: Adam & Charles Black, 1950.

Heckel, Ulrich. *Kraft in Schwachheit: Untersuchungen zu 2.Kor 10–13.* WUNT 2/56. Tübingen: Mohr Siebeck, 1993.

Hedrick, Charles W. *Many Things in Parables: Jesus and His Modern Critics.* Louisville: Westminster John Knox, 2004.

———. "Parable and Kingdom: A Survey of the Evidence in Mark." *PRSt* 27 (2000): 179–99.

Heil, Christoph. *Lukas und Q: Studien zur lukanischen Redaktion des Spruchevangeliums Q.* BZNW 111. Berlin: de Gruyter, 2003.

Heinemann, Joseph. *Aggadah and Its Development.* Jerusalem: Keter, 1974.

———. "The Messiah of Ephraim and the Premature Exodus of the Tribe of Ephraim." *HTR* 68 (1975): 1–15.

———. *Prayer in the Talmud: Forms and Patterns.* SJ 9. Berlin: de Gruyter, 1977.

Heinrichs, A., and L. Koenen. "Ein griechischer Mani-Codex (P. Colon. Inv. Nr. 4780; vgl. Tafeln IV–VI)." *ZPE* 5 (1970): 161–90.

Henderson, John. *Memory and Forgetting.* London: Routledge, 1999.

Henderson, Suzanne Watts. "Jesus' Messianic Self-Consciousness Revisited: Christology and Community in Context." *JSHJ* 7 (2009): 168–97.

Hengel, Martin. "Abba, Maranatha, Hosanna und die Anfänge der Christologie." Pages 496–534 in *Studien zur Christologie: Kleine Schriften IV.* Edited by Claus-Jürgen Thornton. WUNT 201. Tübingen: Mohr Siebeck, 2006.

———. *Crucifixion in the Ancient World and the Folly of the Message of the Cross.* Philadelphia: Fortress, 1977.

———. "Das Mahl in der Nacht, 'in der Jesus ausgeliefert wurde' (1 Kor 11,23)." Pages 451–95 in *Studien zur Christologie: Kleine Schriften IV.* Edited by Claus-Jürgen Thornton. WUNT 201. Tübingen: Mohr Siebeck, 2006.

———. "Der Finger und die Herrschaft Gottes in Lk 11,20." Pages 87–106 in *La Main de Dieu* [= *Die Hand Gottes*]. Edited by René Kieffer and Jan Bergman. WUNT 94. Tübingen: Mohr Siebeck, 1997.

———. "Eye-Witness Memory and the Writing of the Gospels." Pages 70–96 in *The Written Gospel*. Edited by Markus Bockmuehl and Donald Hagner. Cambridge: Cambridge University Press, 2005.

———. "Jesus, the Messiah of Israel." Pages 1–72 in *Studies in Early Christology*. Edinburgh: T & T Clark, 1995.

———. "Messianische Hoffnung und politischer 'Radikalismus' in der 'jüdisch-hellenistischen Diaspora': Zur Frage der Voraussetzungen des jüdischen Aufstandes unter Trajan 115–117 n. Chr." Pages 314–43 in *Judaica et Hellenistica: Kleine Schriften I*. WUNT 90. Tübingen: Mohr Siebeck, 1996.

———. "'Sit at My Right Hand!' The Enthronement of Christ at the Right Hand of God and Psalm 110:1." Pages 119–226 in *Studies in Early Christology*. Edinburgh: T & T Clark, 1995.

———. "Tasks of New Testament Scholarship." *BBR* 6 (1996): 67–86.

———. *The Zealots: Investigations into the Jewish Freedom Movement in the Period from Herod I until 70 A.D.* Edinburgh: T & T Clark, 1989.

———. "Zur matthäischen Bergpredigt und ihrem jüdische Hintergrund." *TRu* 52 (1987): 327–400.

Hengel, Martin, and Anna Maria Schwemer. *Jesus und das Judentum*. Vol. 1 of *Geschichte des frühen Christentums*. Tübingen: Mohr Siebeck, 2007.

Henry, Matthew. *Acts to Revelation*. Vol. 6 of *Commentary on the Whole Bible*. Old Tappan, NJ: Fleming H. Revell, n.d.

———. *Matthew to John*. Vol. 5 of *Commentary on the Whole Bible*. Old Tappan, NJ: Fleming H. Revell, n.d.

Henten, Jan Willem van. *The Maccabean Martyrs as Saviours of the Jewish People: A Study of 2 and 4 Maccabees*. JSJSup 57. Leiden: Brill, 1997.

Henze, Matthias. "Torah and Eschatology in the *Syriac Apocalypse of Baruch*." Pages 201–15 in *The Significance of Sinai: Traditions about Sinai and Divine Revelation in Judaism and Christianity*. Edited by

George J. Brooke, Hindy Najman, and Loren T. Stuckenbruck. TBN 12. Leiden: Brill, 2008.

Hertz, J. H. *The Pentateuch and Haftorahs*. London: Soncino, 1950.

Heskett, Randall. *Messianism within the Scriptural Scroll of Isaiah*. LHB/OTS 46. New York: T & T Clark, 2007.

Hewitt, Joseph William. "The Use of Nails in the Crucifixion." *HTR* 25 (1932): 29–45.

Hexham, Irving, and G. C. Oosthuizen, eds. *History and Traditions Centered on Ekuphakameni and Mount Nhlangakazi*. Vol. 1 of *The Story of Isaiah Shembe*. Lewiston, NY: Edwin Mellen, 1996.

Hieke, Thomas. "Q 7,22—A Compendium of Isaian Eschatology." *ETL* 82 (2006): 175–87.

Hiers, Richard H. *The Historical Jesus and the Kingdom of God: Present and Future in the Message and Ministry of Jesus*. Gainesville: University of Florida Press, 1973.

———. *Jesus and the Future: Unresolved Questions for Eschatology*. Atlanta: John Knox, 1981.

———. *The Kingdom of God in the Synoptic Tradition*. Gainesville: University of Florida Press, 1970.

Higgins, A. J. B. *The Son of Man in the Teaching of Jesus*. SNTSMS 39. Cambridge: Cambridge University Press, 1980.

Hill, H. Erskine. *Apocalyptic Problems*. London: Hodder & Stoughton, 1916.

Himmelfarb, Martha. "Temple and Priests in the Book of the Watchers, the Animal Apocalypse, and the Apocalypse of Weeks." Pages 219–35 in *The Early Enoch Literature*. Edited by Gabriele Boccaccini and John J. Collins. JSJSup 121. Leiden: Brill, 2007.

Hinterberger, Martin. *Autobiographische Traditionen in Byzanz*. WBS 22. Vienna: Verlag des Österreichischen Akademie der Wissenschaften, 1999.

———. "Autobiography and Hagiography in Byzantium." *SO* 75 (2000): 139–64.

Hirstein, William. *Brain Fiction: Self-Deception and the Riddle of Confabulation*. Cambridge, MA: MIT Press, 2005.

Hittman, Michael. *Wovoka and the Ghost Dance*. Edited by Don Lynch. Expanded ed. Lincoln: University of Nebraska Press, 1990.

Hobsbawm, Eric, and Terence Ranger. *The Invention of Tradition*. Cambridge: Cambridge University Press, 1983.

Hodge, Charles. *Commentary on the Epistle to the Romans*. New ed. Philadelphia: James S. Clayton, 1864.

―――. *Systematic Theology*. 3 vols. New York: Charles Scribner's Sons, 1883.

Hoffmann, Paul. "Mutmassungen über Q: Zum Problem der literarischen Genese von Q." Pages 255–88 in *The Sayings Source Q and the Historical Jesus*. Edited by A. Lindemann. BETL 158. Leuven: Leuven University Press, 2001.

Hoffmann, Paul, et al. *Q 22:28, 30: You Will Judge the Twelve Tribes of Israel*. Documenta Q. Leuven: Peeters, 1998.

Hofius, Otfried. "Ist Jesus der Messias? Thesen." Pages 103–29 in *Der Messias*. Edited by Ingo Baldermann et al. JBT 8. Neukirchen-Vluyn: Neukirchener Verlag, 1993.

Holladay, William L. "The Background of Jeremiah's Self-Understanding: Moses, Samuel, and Psalm 22." *JBL* 83 (1964): 153–64.

―――. "Jeremiah and Moses: Further Observations." *JBL* 85 (1966): 17–27.

Holleman, Joost. *Resurrection and Parousia: A Traditio-Historical Study of Paul's Eschatology in 1 Corinthians 15*. NovTSup 84. Leiden: Brill, 1996.

Hollenbach, Paul W. "The Conversion of Jesus: From Jesus the Baptizer to Jesus the Healer." *ANRW* 25.1:196–219. Part 2, *Principat*, 25.1. Edited by H. Temporini and W. Haase. New York: de Gruyter, 1982.

Hollerna, J. Warren. *The Synoptic Gethsemane: A Critical Study*. AnGreg 191. Rome: Università Gregoriana, 1973.

Holmén, Tom. "The Alternatives of the Kingdom: Encountering the Semantic Restrictions of Luke 17,20–21 (ἐντὸς ὑμῶν)." *ZNW* 87 (1996): 204–29.

―――. "Authenticity Criteria." Pages 43–54 in *Encyclopedia of the Historical Jesus*. Edited

by Craig A. Evans. New York: Routledge, 2008.

―――. "Knowing about Q and Knowing about Jesus: Mutually Exclusive Undertakings?" Pages 497–514 in *The Sayings Source Q and the Historical Jesus*. Edited by A. Lindemann. BETL 158. Leuven: Leuven University Press, 2001.

Holmes, Michael W. "The Martyrdom of Polycarp and the New Testament Passion Narratives." Pages 407–32 in *Trajectories through the New Testament and the Apostolic Fathers*. Edited by Andrew F. Gregory and Christopher M. Tuckett. Oxford: Oxford University Press, 2005.

―――. "Polycarp's *Letter to the Philippians* and the Writings That Later Formed the New Testament." Pages 187–228 in *The Reception of the New Testament in the Apostolic Fathers*. Edited by Andrew F. Gregory and Christopher M. Tuckett. Oxford: Oxford University Press, 2005.

Holmstrand, Jonas. *Markers and Meaning in Paul: An Analysis of 1 Thessalonians, Philippians, and Galatians*. ConBNT 28. Stockholm: Almqvist & Wiksell, 1997.

Holt, P. M. "Islamic Millenarianism and the Fulfilment of Prophecy: A Case Study." Pages 335–48 in *Prophecy and Millenarianism: Essays in Honour of Marjorie Reeves*. Edited by Ann Williams. Essex: Longmans, 1980.

Holtz, Traugott. *Der erste Brief an die Thessalonicher*. EKKNT 13. Zurich: Benzinger; Neukirchen-Vluyn: Neukirchener Verlag, 1986.

Holtzmann, Oscar. *The Life of Jesus*. Translated by J. T. Bealby and M. A. Canney. London: Adam & Charles Black, 1904.

Holzbrecher, Frank. *Paulus und der historische Jesus: Darstellung und Analyse der bisherigen Forschungsgeschichte*. TANZ 48. Tübingen: Francke, 2007.

Hook, S. H. "The Translation of Romans I.4." *NTS* 9 (1963): 370–71.

Hooker, Morna D. "Did the Use of Isaiah 53 to Interpret His Mission Begin with Jesus?" Pages 88–103 in *Jesus and the Suffering Servant: Isaiah 53 and Christian Origins*.

Edited by William H. Bellinger Jr. and William R. Farmer. Harrisburg, PA: Trinity Press International, 1998.

————. *The Signs of a Prophet: The Prophetic Actions of Jesus.* Harrisburg, PA: Trinity Press International, 1997.

————. *The Son of Man in Mark: A Study of the Background of the Term "Son of Man" and Its Use in St Mark's Gospel.* London: SPCK, 1967.

Horbury, William. *Jewish Messianism and the Cult of Christ.* London: SCM Press, 1998.

————. "The Messianic Associations of 'The Son of Man.'" Pages 125–55 in *Messianism among Jews and Christians: Twelve Biblical and Historical Studies.* London: T & T Clark, 2003.

————. "The Passion Narratives and Historical Criticism." *Theology* 75 (1972): 58–71.

————. "The Twelve and the Phylarchs." *NTS* 32 (1986): 503–27.

Horn, Friedrich W. "Die synoptischen Einlaßsprüche." *ZNW* 87 (1996): 187–203.

Horsley, Richard A. "The Contours of Q." Pages 61–83 in *Whoever Hears You Hears Me: Prophets, Performance, and Tradition in Q.* By Richard A. Horsley and Jonathan A. Draper. Harrisburg, PA: Trinity Press International, 1999.

————. "The Covenant Renewal Discourse: Q 6:20–49." Pages 195–227 in *Whoever Hears You Hears Me: Prophets, Performance, and Tradition in Q.* By Richard A. Horsley and Jonathan A. Draper. Harrisburg, PA: Trinity Press International, 1999.

————. "The Dead Sea Scrolls and the Historical Jesus." Pages 37–60 in *The Scrolls and Christian Origins.* Vol. 3 of *The Bible and the Dead Sea Scrolls.* Edited by James H. Charlesworth. Waco, TX: Baylor University Press, 2006.

————. *Jesus and the Spiral of Violence: Popular Jewish Resistance in Roman Palestine.* San Francisco: Harper & Row, 1987.

————. "Jesus in the New Millennium." *RBL* 10 (2008): 1–28.

————. "Menahem in Jerusalem: A Brief Episode among the Sicarii—Not 'Zealot Messianism.'" *NovT* 27 (1985): 334–48.

————. "'Messianic' Figures and Movements in First-Century Palestine." Pages 285–93 in *The Messiah: Developments in Earliest Judaism and Christianity.* Edited by James H. Charlesworth. Minneapolis: Fortress, 1992.

————. "Moral Economy and Renewal Movement in Q." Pages 143–57 in *Oral Performance, Popular Tradition, and Hidden Transcript in Q.* Edited by Richard A. Horsley. SemeiaSt 60. Atlanta: Society of Biblical Literature, 2006.

————. "Popular Messianic Movements around the Time of Jesus." *CBQ* 46 (1984): 471–95.

————. "Prominent Patterns in the Social Memory of Jesus and Friends." Pages 57–78 in *Memory, Tradition, and Text: Uses of the Past in Early Christianity.* Edited by Alan Kirk and Tom Thatcher. SBLSymS 52. Leiden: Brill, 2005.

————. *Sociology and the Jesus Movement.* 2nd ed. New York: Continuum, 1994.

Horsley, Richard A., and Neil Asher Silberman. *The Message and the Kingdom: How Jesus and Paul Ignited a Revolution and Transformed the Ancient World.* New York: Grossett/Putnam, 1997.

Horst, Pieter W. van der. *Ancient Jewish Epigraphs: An Introductory Survey of a Millennium of Jewish Funerary Epigraphy (300 BCE–700 CE).* Kampen: Kok Pharos, 1991.

————. *The Sentences of Pseudo-Phocylides.* SVTP 4. Leiden: Brill, 1978.

————. "Silent Prayer in Antiquity." *Numen* 41 (1994): 1–25.

Hoskyns, E. C. "The Other-Worldly Kingdom of God in the New Testament." *Theology* 14 (1927): 249–55.

Hultgren, Arland J. *The Rise of Normative Christianity.* Minneapolis: Fortress, 1992.

Hultgren, Stephen. "The Incident at the Temple as the Occasion for Jesus' Death: Meeting Some Objections." Pages 283–96 in *Redefining First-Century Jewish and Christian Identities: Essays in Honor of Ed Parish Sanders.* Edited by Fabian E. Udoh. Notre Dame, IN: University of Notre Dame Press, 2008.

Hunt, Earl, and Tom Love. "How Good Can Memory Be?" Pages 237–60 in *Coding Processes in Human Memory.* Edited by Arthur W. Melton and Edwin Martin. Washington, DC: V. H. Winston, 1972.

Hunter, Ian M. L. "Lengthy Verbatim Recall: The Role of Text." Pages 207–36 in vol. 1 of *Progress in the Psychology of Language.* Edited by Andrew W. Ellis. 2 vols. London: Lawrence Erlbaum Associates, 1985.

Hurd, John C. "Paul ahead of His Time: 1 Thess 2:13–16." Pages 21–36 in *Paul and the Gospels.* Edited by Peter Richardson and David Granskou. Vol. 1 of *Anti-Judaism in Early Christianity.* SCJ 2. Waterloo, ON: Wilfrid Laurier University Press, 1986.

Hurtado, Larry W. *Lord Jesus Christ: Devotion to Jesus in Early Christianity.* Grand Rapids: Eerdmans, 2003.

———. *One God, One Lord: Early Christian Devotion and Ancient Jewish Monotheism.* Philadelphia: Fortress, 1988.

Iannaccone, Laurence R. "Sacrifice and Stigma: Reducing Free-Riding in Cults, Communes, and Other Collectives." *Journal of Political Economy* 100 (1992): 271–91.

Idel, Moshe. *Messianic Mystics.* New Haven: Yale University Press, 1998.

———. "'The Time of the End': Apocalypticism and Its Spiritualization in Abraham Abulafia's Eschatology." Pages 155–85 in *Apocalyptic Time.* Edited by Albert I. Baumgarten. SHR 86. Leiden: Brill, 2000.

Inge, W. R. *Christian Ethics and Modern Problems.* London: Hodder & Stoughton, 1930.

Isenberg, Sheldon R. "Millenarism in Greco-Roman Palestine." *Religion* 4 (1974): 26–46.

Isser, Stanley Jerome. *The Dositheans: A Samaritan Sect in Late Antiquity.* SJLA 17. Leiden: Brill, 1976.

Jackson, A. V. Williams. "The Personality of Mānī, the Founder of Manichaeism." *JAOS* 58 (1938): 235–40.

Jacobsen, Howard. *A Commentary on Pseudo-Philo's Liber Antiquitatum Biblicarum.* 2 vols. AGJU 31. Leiden: Brill, 1996.

Jaffé, Dan. "La figure messianique de Bar-Kokhba: Nouvelles perspectives." *Henoch* 28 (2006): 106–10.

James, Montague Rhodes. *The Lost Apocrypha of the Old Testament: Their Titles and Fragments.* London: SPCK, 1920.

Janssen, Martina. "'Evangelium des Zwillings?' Das *Thomasevangelium* als Thomas-Schrift." Pages 222–48 in *Das Thomasevangelium: Entstehung, Rezeption, Theologie.* Edited by Jörg Frey, Enno Edzard Popkes, and Jens Schröter. BZNW 157. Berlin: de Gruyter, 2008.

Japhet, Sara. *1 Chronik.* HTKAT. Freiburg: Herder, 2002.

Jefford, Clayton N. *The Sayings of Jesus in the Teaching of the Twelve Apostles.* VCSup 11. Leiden: Brill, 1989.

Jellinek, Adolph. *Bet ha-Midrasch: Sammlung kleiner Midraschim und vermischter Abhandlungen aus der ältern jüdischen Literatur.* 3rd ed. 6 vols. in 2. Jerusalem: Wahrmann, 1967.

———. "Sefer ha-Ôt: Apokalypse des Pseudo-Propheten und Pseudo-Messias Abraham Abulafia." Pages 63–88 in *Jubelschrift zum siebzigsten Geburtstage des Prof. Dr. H. Graetz.* Breslau: Schottlaender, 1887.

Jeremias, Joachim. *Die Sprache des Lukasevangeliums: Redaktion und Tradition im Nicht-Markusstoff des dritten Evangeliums.* KEK. Göttingen: Vandenhoeck & Ruprecht, 1980.

———. *The Eucharistic Words of Jesus.* Translated by Norman Perrin. London: SCM Press, 1966.

———. "Hebräer 5,7–10." Pages 319–23 in *Abba: Studien zur neutestamentlichen Theologie und Zeitgeschichte.* Göttingen: Vandenhoeck & Ruprecht, 1966.

———. *New Testament Theology: The Proclamation of Jesus.* New York: Charles Scribner's Sons, 1971.

———. *The Parables of Jesus.* 2nd rev. ed. New York: Charles Scribner's Sons, 1972.

———. *Unknown Sayings of Jesus.* 2nd ed. London: SPCK, 1964.

Jervell, Jacob. *Luke and the People of God: A New Look at Luke-Acts.* Minneapolis: Augsburg, 1979.

Jewett, Robert. *Romans: A Commentary.* Hermeneia. Minneapolis: Fortress, 2006.

————. *The Thessalonian Correspondence: Pauline Rhetoric and Millenarian Piety.* Philadelphia: Fortress, 1986.

Johanson, Bruce C. "1 Thessalonians 2:15–16: Prophetic Woe Oracle with ἔφθασεν as Proleptic Aorist." Pages 519–34 in *Texts and Contexts: Biblical Texts in Their Textual and Situational Contexts; Essays in Honor of Lars Hartman.* Edited by Tord Fornberg and David Hellholm. Oslo: Scandinavian University Press, 1995.

Johnson, Luke Timothy. "Rom 3:21–26 and the Faith of Jesus." *CBQ* 44 (1982): 77–90.

————. "The Use of Leviticus 19 in the Letter of James." *JBL* 101 (1982): 391–401.

Johnson, P. Benton. "On Founders and Followers: Some Factors in the Development of New Religious Movements." *Sociological Analysis* 53 (supplement, 1992): 1–13.

Johnson, Sara R. "Third Maccabees: Historical Fictions and the Shaping of Jewish Identity in the Hellenistic Period." Pages 185–98 in *Ancient Fiction: The Matrix of Early Christian and Jewish Narrative.* Edited by Jo-Ann Brant, Charles W. Hedrick, and Chris Shea. SBLSymS 32. Atlanta: Society of Biblical Literature, 2005.

Johnson-DeBaufre, Melanie. *Jesus among Her Children: Q, Eschatology, and the Construction of Christian Origins.* HTS 55. Cambridge, MA: Harvard University Press, 2005.

Jones, C. P. "Stigma: Tattooing and Branding in Graeco-Roman Antiquity." *JRS* 77 (1987): 139–55.

Jonge, Marinus de. *God's Final Envoy: Early Christology and Jesus' Own View of His Mission.* Grand Rapids: Eerdmans, 1998.

————. "Jesus, Son of David and Son of God." Pages 95–104 in *Intertextuality in Biblical Writings: Essays in Honour of Bas van Iersel.* Edited by Sipke Draisma. Kampen: J. H. Kok, 1989.

Jónsson, Jakob. *Humor and Irony in the New Testament Illuminated by Parallels in Talmud and Midrash.* BZRG 28. Leiden: Brill, 1985.

Joyce, Paul. "The Kingdom of God and the Psalms." Pages 42–59 in *The Kingdom of God and Human Society: Essays by Members of the Scripture, Theology, and Society Group.* Edited by Robin Barbour. Edinburgh: T & T Clark, 1993.

Jülicher, Adolf. *Die Gleichnisreden Jesu.* 2nd ed. Tübingen: J. C. B. Mohr, 1910.

Jüngel, Eberhard. *Paulus und Jesus: Eine Untersuchung zur Präzisierung der Frage nach dem Ursprung der Christologie.* HUT 2. Tübingen: Mohr Siebeck, 1964.

Kaestli, J. D. "L'utilisation de l'Évangile selon Thomas dans la recherché actuelle sur les paroles de Jésus." Pages 373–95 in *Jésus de Nazareth: Nouvelles approches d'une enigma.* Edited by D. Marguerat, E. Norelli, and J.-M. Poffet. Geneva: Labor et Fides, 1998.

Kammen, Michael. *Mystic Chords of Memory: The Transformation of Tradition in American Culture.* New York: Alfred A. Knopf, 1991.

Kansteiner, Wulf. "Finding Meaning in Memory: A Methodological Critique of Collective Memory Studies." *History and Theory* 41 (2002): 179–97.

Käsemann, Ernst. "The Beginnings of Christian Theology." Pages 82–107 in *New Testament Questions of Today.* London: SCM Press, 1969.

————. *Commentary on Romans.* Grand Rapids: Eerdmans, 1980.

Kasher, Rimon. "On the Portrayal of Messiahs in Light of an Unknown Targum to Lam 4:21–22." *JSQ* 7 (2000): 22–41.

Kassin, Saul M., and Katherine L. Kiechel. "The Social Psychology of False Confessions: Compliance, Internalization, and Confabulation." *Psychological Science* 7 (1996): 125–28.

Katz, Steven T. "The 'Conservative' Character of Mystical Experience." Pages 3–60 in *Mysticism and Religious Traditions.* Edited by Steven T. Katz. Oxford: Oxford University Press, 1983.

Kaufmann, David. "A Hitherto Unknown Messianic Movement among the Jews, Particularly Those of Germany." *JQR* 10 (1897–1898): 139–51.

———. "A Rumour about the Ten Tribes in Pope Martin V's Time." *JQR* 4 (1892): 503–8.

Kazen, Thomas. "The Coming Son of Man Revisited." *JSHJ* 5 (2007): 157–76.

———. "Son of Man and Early Christian Identity Formation." Pages 97–122 in *Identity Formation in the New Testament*. Edited by Bengt Holmberg and Mikael Winninge. WUNT 227. Tübingen: Mohr Siebeck, 2008.

———. "Son of Man as Kingdom Imagery: Jesus between Corporate Symbol and Individual Redeemer Figure." Pages 87–108 in *Jesus from Judaism to Christianity: Continuum Approaches to the Historical Jesus*. Edited by Tom Holmén. London: T & T Clark, 2007.

Kegel, Günter. *Auferstehung Jesu, Auferstehung der Toten: Eine traditionsgeschichtliche Untersuchung zum Neuen Testament*. Gütersloh: Mohn, 1970.

Keith, Chris, and Tom Thatcher. "The Scar of the Cross: The Violence Ratio and the Earliest Christian Memories of Jesus." Pages 197–214 in *Jesus, the Voice, and the Text: Beyond the Oral and the Written Gospel*. Edited by Tom Thatcher. Waco, TX: Baylor University Press, 2008.

Kelber, Werner H. "The Case of the Gospels: Memory's Desire and the Limits of Historical Criticism." *Oral Tradition* 17 (2002): 55–86.

———. "Orality and Biblical Studies: A Review Essay." Online: www.bookreviews.org/pdf/2107_6748.pdf. Cited 18 November 2009.

Kellermann, Ulrich. *Auferstehung in den Himmel: 2 Makkabäer 7 und die Auferstehung der Martyrer*. SBS 95. Stuttgart: Katholisches Bibelwerk, 1978.

———. "Elia Redivivus und die heilszeitliche Auferweckung der Toten: Erwägungen zur ältesten Bezeugung einer Erwartung." Pages 72–84 in *Was suchst du hier, Elia? Ein hermeneutisches Arbeitsbuch*. Edited by Klaus Grüwaldt and Harald Schroeter. Hermeneutica 4. Rheinbach-Merzbach: CMZ-Verlag, 1995.

Kihlstrom, John F. "Memory, Autobiography, History." Online: http://socrates.berkeley.edu/~kihlstrm/rmpa00.htm. Cited 18 November 2009.

———. "Memory Research: The Convergence of Theory and Practice." Pages 5–26 in *Theory in Context*. Vol. 1 of *Basic and Applied Memory Research*. Edited by Douglas J. Herrmann et al. Mahwah, NJ: Lawrence Erlbaum Associates, 1996.

Kimelman, Reuven. "The Messiah of the Amidah: A Study in Comparative Messianism." *JBL* 116 (1997): 313–30.

King, George Brockwell. "The 'Negative' Golden Rule." *JR* 8 (1928): 268–79.

Kirk, Alan K. *The Composition of the Sayings Source: Genre, Synchrony, and Wisdom Redaction in Q*. NovTSup 91. Leiden: Brill, 1998.

———. "'Love Your Enemies,' the Golden Rule, and Ancient Reciprocity (Luke 6:27–35)." *JBL* 122 (2003): 667–86.

Kirk, Alan, and Tom Thatcher. "Jesus Tradition as Social Memory." Pages 25–42 in *Memory, Tradition, and Text: Uses of the Past in Early Christianity*. Edited by Alan Kirk and Tom Thatcher. SBLSymS 52. Leiden: Brill, 2005.

———, eds. *Memory, Tradition, and Text: Uses of the Past in Early Christianity*. SBLSymS 52. Leiden: Brill, 2005.

Kister, Menahem. "The Sayings of Jesus and the Midrash." *Immanuel* 15 (1982): 38–50.

———. "Words and Formulae in the Gospels in the Light of Hebrew and Aramaic Sources." Pages 117–47 in *The Sermon on the Mount and Its Jewish Setting*. Edited by Hans-Jürgen Becker and Serge Ruzer. CahRB 60. Paris: Gabalda, 2005.

Klausner, Joseph. *Jesus of Nazareth: His Life, Times, and Teaching*. New York: Macmillan, 1925.

Klein, Günter. *Die zwölf Apostel: Ursprung und Gehalt einer Idee*. FRLANT 77. Göttingen: Vandenhoeck & Ruprecht, 1961.

Klein, Kerwin Lee. "On the Emergence of Memory in Historical Discourse." *Representations* 69 (2000): 127–50.

Klein, Michael L. "Associative and Complementary Translation in the Targumim." *ErIsr* 16 (1982): 134–40.

Klein, Ralph W. *1 Chronicles: A Commentary.* Hermeneia. Minneapolis: Fortress, 2006.

Kloppenborg, John S. "Did. 1.1–6.1, James, Matthew, and Torah." Pages 193–221 in *Trajectories through the New Testament and the Apostolic Fathers.* Edited by Andrew F. Gregory and Christopher M. Tuckett. Oxford: Oxford University Press, 2005.

———. "Discursive Practices in the Sayings Gospel Q and the Quest of the Historical Jesus." Pages 149–90 in *The Sayings Source Q and the Historical Jesus.* Edited by A. Lindemann. BETL 158. Leuven: Leuven University Press, 2001.

———. *Excavating Q: The History and Setting of the Sayings Gospel.* Edinburgh: T & T Clark, 2000.

———. *The Formation of Q: Trajectories in Ancient Christian Wisdom Collections.* Philadelphia: Fortress, 1987.

———. *Q Parallels: Synopsis, Critical Notes, and Concordance.* Sonoma, CA: Polebridge, 1988.

———. "The Reception of the Jesus Tradition in James." Pages 93–141 in *The Catholic Epistles and the Tradition.* Edited by Jacques Schlosser. BETL 176. Leuven: Leuven University Press, 2004.

———. "The Sayings Gospel Q and the Question of the Historical Jesus." *HTR* 89 (1996): 307–44.

———. "The Use of the Synoptics or Q in *Did.* 1:3b–2:1." Pages 105–29 in *Matthew and the Didache: Two Documents from the Same Jewish-Christian Milieu?* Edited by Huub van de Sandt. Assen: Royal Van Gorcum; Minneapolis: Fortress, 2005.

———. "Variation in the Reproduction of the Double Tradition and an Oral Q?" *ETL* 83 (2007): 53–80.

Knauf, Ernst Axel. "From History to Interpretation." Pages 26–64 in *The Fabric of History: Text, Artifact, and Israel's Past.* Edited by Diana Vikander Edelman. JSOTSup 127. Sheffield: JSOT Press, 1992.

Knibb, Michael A. "Messianism in the Pseudepigrapha in the Light of the Scrolls." *DSD* 2 (1995): 170–80.

Knohl, Israel. "'By Three Days, Live': Messiahs, Resurrection, and Ascent to Heaven in *Hazon Gabriel.*" *JR* 88 (2008): 147–58.

———. "Cain: Son of God or Son of Satan?" Pages 37–50 in *Jewish Biblical Interpretation and Cultural Exchange: Comparative Exegesis in Context.* Edited by Natalie B. Dohrmann and David Stern. Philadelphia: University of Pennsylvania Press, 2008.

———. *The Messiah before Jesus: The Suffering Servant of the Dead Sea Scrolls.* Berkeley: University of California Press, 2000.

Knox, John. *The Death of Christ: The Cross in New Testament History and Faith.* New York: Abingdon, 1958.

———. *Jesus Lord and Christ.* New York: Harper, 1958.

Knox, Wilfred L. *St. Paul and the Church of the Gentiles.* Cambridge: Cambridge University Press, 1939.

Kobelski, Paul J. *Melchizedek and Melchireša'.* CBQMS 10. Washington, DC: Catholic Biblical Association, 1981.

Koch, Klaus. "Jesus apokalyptisch." *ZNT* 3 (1999): 41–49.

———. "Offenbaren wird sich das Reich Gottes." *NTS* 25 (1979): 158–65.

———. "Questions Regarding the So-Called Son of Man in the Parables of Enoch: A Response to Sabino Chialà and Helge Kvanvig." Pages 228–37 in *Enoch and the Messiah Son of Man: Revisiting the Book of Parables.* Edited by Gabriele Boccaccini. Grand Rapids: Eerdmans, 2007.

———. *The Rediscovery of Apocalyptic.* SBT 2/22. London: SCM Press, 1972.

———. "Spätisraelitisch-jüdische und urchristliche Danielrezeption vor und nach der Zerstörung des zweiten Tempels." Pages 93–123 in *Rezeption und Auslegung im Altem Testament und in seinem Umfeld: Ein Symposion aus Anlass des 60. Geburtstags von Odil Hannes Steck.* Edited by Reinhard G. Kratz and Thomas Krüger. OBO 153. Freiburg: Universitätsverlag; Vandenhoeck & Ruprecht, 1997.

Koenen, Ludwig. "Augustine and Manichaeism in Light of the Cologne Mani Codex." *Illinois Classical Studies* 3 (1978): 167–74.

Koenig, Jean. *L'herméneutique analogique du judaïsme antique d'après les témoins textuels d'Isaïe.* VTSup 33. Leiden: Brill, 1982.

Koester, Helmut. *Ancient Christian Gospels.* Philadelphia: Trinity Press International, 1990.

———. *From Jesus to the Gospels: Interpreting the New Testament in Its Context.* Minneapolis: Fortress, 2007.

———. "Jesus the Victim." *JBL* 111 (1992): 3–15.

———. "The Memory of Jesus' Death and the Worship of the Risen Lord." *HTR* 91 (1998): 345–46.

———. "The Sayings of Q and Their Image of Jesus." Pages 137–54 in *Sayings of Jesus: Canonical and Non-canonical: Essays in Honor of Tjitze Baarda.* Edited by William L. Petersen, Johan S. Vos, and Henk J. de Jonge. NovTSup 89. Leiden: Brill, 1997.

———. "The Synoptic Sayings Gospel Q in the Early Communities of Jesus' Followers." Pages 45–58 in *Early Christian Voices in Texts, Traditions, and Symbols: Essays in Honor of François Bovon.* Edited by David H. Warren, Ann Graham Brock, and David W. Pao. BIS 66. Boston: Brill, 2003.

———. *Synoptische Überlieferung bei den apostolischen Vätern.* TU 65. Berlin: Akademie-Verlag, 1957.

Köhler, Wolf-Dietrich. *Die Rezeption des Matthäusevangeliums in der Zeit vor Irenäus.* WUNT 2/24. Tübingen: Mohr Siebeck, 1987.

Kollmann, Bernd. "Lk 12.35–38—ein Gleichnis der Logienquelle." *ZNW* 81 (1990): 254–61.

Konradt, Matthias. *Gericht und Gemeinde: Eine Studie zur Bedeutung und Funktion von Gerichtsaussagen im Rahmen der paulinischen Ekklesiologie und Ethik im 1 Thess und 1 Kor.* BZNW 117. Berlin: de Gruyter, 2003.

Kosch, Daniel. "Q und Jesus." *BZ* 36 (1992): 32–40.

Kovacs, Judith L. "'Now Shall the Ruler of This World Be Driven Out': Jesus' Death as Cosmic Battle in John 12:20–36." *JBL* 114 (1995): 227–47.

Kraeling, Carl H. *The Excavations at Dura-Europos: Final Report VIII, Part 1: The Synagogue.* New Haven: Yale University Press, 1956.

———. "The Wall Decorations." Pages 29–75 in *Preliminary Report on the Synagogue at Dura.* New Haven: Yale University Press, 1936.

Kraemer, Ross Shepard. *When Aseneth Met Joseph: A Late Antique Tale of the Biblical Patriarch and His Egyptian Wife, Reconsidered.* New York: Oxford University Press, 1998.

Kramer, Werner. *Christ, Lord, Son of God.* Translated by Brian Hardy. SBT 50. London: SCM Press, 1966.

Kreitzer, Larry Joseph. *2 Corinthians.* NTG. Sheffield: Sheffield Academic Press, 1996.

———. *Jesus and God in Paul's Eschatology.* JSNTSup 19. Sheffield: JSOT Press, 1987.

Kremer, Jacob. *2. Korintherbrief.* 2nd ed. SKKNT 8. Stuttgart: Katholisches Bibelwerk, 1998.

Kreplin, Matthias. *Das Selbstverständnis Jesu: Hermeneutische und christologische Reflexion; Historisch-kritische Analyse.* WUNT 2/141. Tübingen: Mohr Siebeck, 2001.

Kreyenbroek, Philip G. "Millennialism and Eschatology in the Zoroastrian Tradition." Pages 33–55 in *Imagining the End: Visions of Apocalypse from the Ancient Middle East to Modern America.* Edited by Abbas Amanat and Magnus Bernhardsson. London: I. B. Tauris, 2002.

Kruse, H. "Dialektische Negationen als semitisches Idiom." *VT* 4 (1954): 385–400.

Kugel, James L. *In Potiphar's House: The Interpretive Life of Biblical Texts.* San Francisco: Harper & Row, 1990.

———. "On Hidden Hatred and Open Reproach: Early Exegesis of Leviticus 19:17." *HTR* 80 (1987): 43–62.

———. *Traditions of the Bible: A Guide to the Bible as It Was at the Start of the Common*

Era. Cambridge, MA: Harvard University Press, 1998.

Kuhn, Heinz-Wolfgang. "Die Kreuzesstrafe während der frühen Kaiserzeit: Ihre Wirklichkeit und Wertung in der Umwelt des Urchristentums." *ANRW* 25.1:648–793. Part 2, *Principat*, 25.1. Edited by H. Temporini and W. Haase. New York: de Gruyter, 1982.

———. *Enderwartung und gegenwärtiges Heil: Untersuchungen zu den Gemeindeliedern von Qumran mit einem Anhang über Eschatologie und Gegenwart in der Verkündigung Jesu*. SUNT 4. Göttingen: Vandenhoeck & Ruprecht, 1966.

———. "συσταυρόω." *EDNT* 3:313.

Kuhn, Karl A. "The 'One Like a Son of Man' Becomes the 'Son of God.'" *CBQ* 69 (2007): 22–42.

Kuhn, Karl Georg. "βασιλεία." *TDNT* 1:579–90.

———. "Jesus in Gethsemane." *EvT* 12 (1952): 260–85.

Kümmel, Werner Georg. *Promise and Fulfilment: The Eschatological Message of Jesus*. SBT 23. London: SCM Press, 1957.

Kvalbein, Hans. "The Kingdom of the Father in the Gospel of Thomas." Pages 203–28 in *The New Testament and Early Christian Literature in Greco-Roman Context: Studies in Honor of David E. Aune*. Edited by John Fotopoulos. NovTSup 122. Leiden: Brill, 2006.

———. "The Kingdom of God and the Kingship of Christ in the Fourth Gospel." Pages 215–32 in *Neotestamentica et Philonica: Studies in Honor of Peter Borgen*. Edited by David E. Aune, Torrey Seland, and Jarl Henning Ulrichsen. NovTSup 106. Leiden: Brill, 2003.

———. "The Kingdom of God in the Ethics of Jesus." *CV* 40 (1998): 197–227.

———. "The Son of Man in the Parables of Enoch." Pages 179–215 in *Enoch and the Messiah Son of Man: Revisiting the Book of Parables*. Edited by Gabriele Boccaccini. Grand Rapids: Eerdmans, 2007.

Laaksonen, Jari. *Jesus und das Land: Das Gelobte Land in der Verkündigung Jesu*. Åbo: Åbo Akademi University Press, 2002.

Laato, Antti. *A Star Is Rising: The Historical Development of the Old Testament Royal Ideology and the Rise of the Jewish Messianic Expectations*. ISFCJ 5. Atlanta: Scholars Press, 1997.

Lambrecht, Jan. *Die Redaktion der Markus-apokalypse: Literarische Analyse und Struckturuntersuchung*. AnBib 28. Rome: Pontifical Institute, 1967.

Lampe, G. W. H. "Some Notes on the Significance of ΒΑΣΙΛΕΙΑ ΤΟΥ ΘΕΟΥ, ΒΑΣΙΛΕΙΑ ΧΡΙΣΤΟΥ, in the Greek Fathers." *JTS* 49 (1948): 58–73.

Landes, Richard. "Millennialism." Pages 333–58 in *The Oxford Handbook of New Religious Movements*. Edited by James R. Lewis. Oxford: Oxford University Press, 2004.

———. "On Owls, Roosters, and Apocalyptic Time: A Historical Method for Reading a Refractory Documentation." *USQR* 49 (1995): 49–69.

———. "Rodolfus Glaber and the Dawn of the New Millennium: Eschatology, Historiography, and the Year 1000." *Revue Mabillon* 7 (1996): 57–77.

Lane, William. *The Gospel according to Mark*. NICNT. Grand Rapids: Eerdmans, 1974.

Lang, Friedrich. "πῦρ κ.τ.λ." *TDNT* 6:928–52.

Lanternari, Vittorio. *The Religions of the Oppressed: A Study of Modern Messianic Cults*. Translated by Lisa Sergio. London: MacGibbon & Kee, 1963.

Larsen, Steen F. "Remembering without Experiencing: Memory for Reported Events." Pages 326–55 in *Remembering Reconsidered: Ecological and Traditional Approaches to the Study of Memory*. Edited by Ulric Neisser and Eugene Winograd. Cambridge: Cambridge University Press, 1988.

Laufen, Rudolf. *Die Doppelüberlieferungen der Logienquelle und des Markusevangeliums*. BBB 54. Bonn: Peter Hanstein, 1980.

Layton, Bentley. "The Sources, Date, and Transmission of *Didache* 1.3b–2.1." *HTR* 61 (1968): 343–83.

Leatham, Miguel C. "Rethinking Religious Decision-Making in Peasant Millenarianism: The Case of Nueva Jerusalem." *JCR* 12 (1997): 295–309.

Leckie, J. H. *The World to Come and Final Destiny*. Edinburgh: T & T Clark, 1918.

Le Donne, Anthony. *The Historiographical Jesus: Memory, Typology, and the Son of David*. Waco, TX: Baylor University Press, 2009.

———. "Theological Memory Distortion in the Jesus Tradition: A Study in Social Memory Theory." Pages 163–78 in *Memory in the Bible and Antiquity: The Fifth Durham-Tübingen Research Symposium*. Edited by Stephen C. Barton, Loren T. Stuckenbruck, and Benjamin G. Wold. WUNT 212. Tübingen: Mohr Siebeck, 2007.

Lee, Aquila H. I. *From Messiah to Preexistent Son: Jesus' Self-Consciousness and Early Christian Exegesis of Messianic Psalms*. WUNT 2/192. Tübingen: Mohr Siebeck, 2005.

Leene, Henk. "History and Eschatology in Deutero-Isaiah." Pages 223–49 in *Studies in the Book of Isaiah: Festschrift Willem A. M. Beuken*. Edited by J. van Ruiten and M. Vervenne. BETL 132. Leuven: Leuven University Press, 1997.

Le Goff, Jacques. *History and Memory*. New York: Columbia University Press, 1992.

Lehtipuu, Outi. *The Afterlife Imagery in Luke's Story of the Rich Man and Lazarus*. NovTSup 123. Leiden: Brill, 2007.

Leivestad, Ragnar. *Jesus in His Own Perspective: An Examination of His Sayings, Actions, and Eschatological Titles*. Minneapolis: Augsburg, 1987.

Lenowitz, Harris. *The Jewish Messiahs: From the Galilee to Crown Heights*. Oxford: Oxford University Press, 1998.

Leske, Adrian M. "Context and Meaning of Zechariah 9:9." *CBQ* 62 (2000): 663–78.

Levenson, Jon Douglas. *Theology of the Program of Restoration of Ezekiel 40–48*. HSM 10. Missoula, MT: Scholars Press, 1976.

Levine, Linda J. "Reconstructing Memory for Emotions." *Journal of Experimental Psychology: General* 126 (1997): 165–77.

Levy, Becca, and Ellen Langer. "Aging Free from Negative Stereotypes: Successful Memory in China and among the American Deaf." *Journal of Personality and Social Psychology* 66 (1994): 989–97.

Lewin, B. M., ed. *Iggeret Rav Sherira Ga'on*. Jerusalem: Makor, 1971.

Lewis, Sarah M. "The Lord of the Second Advent—the Deliverer Is Here!" Pages 202–23 in *The Coming Deliverer: Millennial Themes in World Religions*. Edited by Fiona Bowie and Christopher Deacy. Cardiff: University of Wales Press, 1997.

Licht, Jacob. "Time and Eschatology in Apocalyptic Literature and in Qumran." *JJS* 16 (1965): 177–82.

Liddon, H. P. *Explanatory Analysis of St. Paul's Epistle to the Romans*. 2nd ed. London: Longmans, Green, 1893.

Liebenberg, Jacobus. *The Language of the Kingdom and Jesus: Parable, Aphorism, and Metaphor in the Sayings Material Common to the Synoptic Tradition and the Gospel of Thomas*. BZNW 102. Berlin: de Gruyter, 2000.

Liebes, Yehuda. *Studies in Jewish Myth and Jewish Messianism*. Translated by Batya Stein. Albany: State University of New York Press, 1993.

Lietzmann, Hans. *An die Galater*. HNT 10. Tübingen: Mohr Siebeck, 1923.

Lieu, Samuel N. C. "'My Church Is Superior . . .': Mani's Missionary Statement in Coptic and Middle Persian." Pages 519–27 in *Coptica, Gnostica, Manichaica: Mélanges offerts à Wolf-Peter Funk*. Edited by Louis Painchaud and Paul-Hubert Poirier. BCNH 7. Quebec: University Press of Laval; Leuven: Peeters, 2006.

Lightfoot, J. B. *The Apostolic Fathers: Part I, S. Clement of Rome*. 2nd ed. 2 vols. London: Macmillan, 1890.

———. *Notes on the Epistles of St Paul from Unpublished Commentaries*. London: Macmillan, 1895.

Lightfoot, R. H. *The Gospel Message of St. Mark*. Cambridge: Cambridge University Press, 1950.

Lindars, Barnabas. "Discourse and Tradition: The Use of the Sayings of Jesus in the Discourses of the Fourth Gospel." *JSNT* 13 (1981): 83–101.

———. *The Gospel of John*. NCB. London: Oliphants, 1977.

———. *Jesus Son of Man: A Fresh Examination of the Son of Man Sayings in the Gospels in the Light of Recent Research*. London: SPCK, 1983.

———. "John and the Synoptic Gospels: A Test Case." *NTS* 27 (1981): 287–94.

———. *New Testament Apologetic: The Doctrinal Significance of the Old Testament Quotations*. London: SCM Press, 1961.

———. "The Place of the Old Testament in the Formation of New Testament Theology." *NTS* 23 (1976): 59–66.

———. "Re-enter the Apocalyptic Son of Man." *NTS* 22 (1975): 52–72.

Lindberg, Carter. "Eschatology and Fanaticism in the Reformation Era: Luther and the Anabaptists." *CTQ* 64 (2000): 259–78.

Linton, Marigold. "Transformations of Memory in Everyday Life." Pages 77–91 in *Memory Observed: Remembering in Natural Contexts*. Edited by Ulric Neisser. New York: W. H. Freeman, 1982.

Lips, Hermann von. *Weisheitliche Traditionen im Neuen Testament*. WMANT 64. Neukirchen-Vluyn: Neukirchener Verlag, 1990.

Littlewood, Jane. *Aspects of Grief: Bereavement in Adult Life*. London: Tavistock/Routledge, 1992.

Llewellyn, Russ. "Religious and Spiritual Miracle Events in Real-Life Experience." Pages 241–63 in *Religious and Spiritual Events*. Vol. 1 of *Miracles: God, Science, and Psychology in the Paranormal*. Edited by J. Harold Ellens. Westport, CT: Praeger, 2008.

Loewenstamm, Samuel E. "The Testament of Abraham and the Texts concerning the Death of Moses." Pages 219–25 in *Studies in the Testament of Abraham*. Edited by George W. E. Nickelsburg. SBLSCS 6. Missoula, MT: Scholars Press, 1976.

Loftus, Elizabeth F. "Illusions of Memory." *PAPS* 142, no. 1 (1998): 60–73.

———. "Make-Believe Memories." *American Psychologist* 58 (2003): 867–73.

———. "Memory Faults and Fixes." Pages 127–44 in *The Best American Science and Nature Writing 2003*. Edited by Richard Dawkins and Tim Folger. New York: Houghton Mifflin, 2003.

———. "Our Changeable Memories: Legal and Practical Implications." *Nature Reviews: Neuroscience* 4 (2003): 231–34.

———. "Planting Misinformation in the Human Mind: A 30-Year Investigation of the Malleability of Memory." *Learning and Memory* 12 (2005): 361–66.

Loftus, Elizabeth F., and Daniel M. Bernstein. "Rich False Memories: The Royal Road to Success." Pages 101–13 in *Experimental Cognitive Psychology and Its Applications*. Edited by Alice F. Healy. Washington, DC: American Psychological Association, 2005.

Loftus, Elizabeth F., James A. Coan, and Jacqueline E. Pickrell. "Manufacturing False Memories Using Bits of Reality." Pages 195–220 in *Implicit Memory and Metacognition*. Edited by Lynne M. Reder. Mahwah, NJ: Lawrence Erlbaum Associates, 1996.

Loftus, Elizabeth, and J. E. Pickrell. "The Formation of False Memories." *Psychiatric Annals* 25 (1995): 720–25.

Lohfink, Gerhard. "Der Ablauf der Osterereignisse und die Anfänge der Urgemeinde." *ThQ* 160 (1980): 162–76.

———. "Die Naherwartung Jesu." Pages 38–51 in *Naherwartung, Auferstehung, Unsterblichkeit: Untersuchungen zur christlichen Eschatologie*. By Gisbert Greshake and Gerhard Lohfink. QD 71. Freiburg: Herder, 1975.

Lohmeyer, Ernst. *Lord of the Temple: A Study of the Relation between Cult and Gospel*. Richmond: John Knox, 1962.

Lohse, Eduard. *Colossians and Philemon: A Commentary on the Epistles to the Colossians and to Philemon*. Hermeneia. Philadelphia: Fortress, 1971.

———. "Herrenworte im Römerbrief." Pages 80–87 in *Rechenschaft vom Evangelium: Exegetische Studien zum Römerbrief*. BZNW 150. Berlin: de Gruyter, 2007.

Lona, Horacio E. *Der erste Clemensbrief.* KAV 2. Göttingen: Vandenhoeck & Ruprecht, 1998.

Löning, Karl. "Die Füchse, die Vögel und der Menschensohn (Mt 8,19f par Lk 9,57f)." Pages 82–102 in *Vom Urchristentum zu Jesus: Für Joachim Gnilka.* Edited by Hubert Frankemölle and Karl Kertelge. Freiburg: Herder, 1989.

Loofs, Friedrich. *What Is the Truth about Jesus Christ? Problems of Christology.* New York: Charles Scribner's Sons, 1913.

Loubser, J. A. "The Oral Christ of Shembe: Believing in Jesus in Oral and Literature Societies." *Scriptura* 12 (1993): 70–80.

Loughborough, J. N. *The Great Second Advent Movement: Its Rise and Progress.* Washington, DC: Review & Herald Publishing Association, 1905.

Louw, Johannes P., and Eugene A. Nida, eds. *Greek-English Lexicon of the New Testament Based on Semantic Domains.* 2nd ed. 2 vols. New York: United Bible Societies, 1989.

Lövestam, Evald. *Jesus and "This Generation": A New Testament Study.* ConBNT 25. Stockholm: Almqvist & Wiksell, 1995.

Lowe, Malcolm. "Who Were the Ἰουδαῖοι?" *NovT* 18 (1976): 101–30.

Luckensmeyer, David. *The Eschatology of First Thessalonians.* NTOA 71. Göttingen: Vandenhoeck & Ruprecht, 2009.

Lüdemann, Gerd. *Jesus after Two Thousand Years: What He Really Said and Did.* Amherst, NY: Prometheus Books, 2001.

———. *Paulus und das Judentum.* TEH 215. Munich: Chr. Kaiser, 1983.

Luftig, Richard. "Abstractive Memory, the Central-Incidental Hypothesis, and the Use of Structure Importance in Text: Control Processes or Structural Features?" *Reading Research Quarterly* 19 (1983): 28–37.

Lührmann, Dieter. "Liebet eure Feinde (Lk 6,27–36/Mt 5,39–48)." *ZNW* 69 (1972): 412–38.

Luminet, Olivier, and Antonietta Curci, eds. *Flashbulb Memories: New Issues and New Perspectives.* New York: Psychology Press, 2009.

Lupieri, Edmondo F. "John the Baptist in New Testament Traditions and History." *ANRW* 26.1:430–61. Part 2, *Principat,* 26.1. Edited by H. Temporini and W. Haase. New York: de Gruyter, 1992.

Luther, Martin. *A Commentary on St. Paul's Epistle to the Galatians.* Westwood, NJ: Fleming H. Revell, n.d.

Luz, Ulrich. "βασιλεία." *EDNT* 1:201–5.

———. "Fictionality and Loyalty to Tradition in Matthew's Gospel in the Light of Greek Literature." Pages 54–79 in *Studies in Matthew.* Translated by Rosemary Selle. Grand Rapids: Eerdmans, 2005.

———. *Matthew: A Commentary.* Translated by James E. Crouch. Edited by Helmut Koester. 3 vols. Hermeneia. Minneapolis: Fortress, 2001–2007.

———. "Warum zog Jesus nach Jerusalem?" Pages 409–27 in *Der historische Jesus: Tendenzen und Perspektiven der gegenwärtigen Forschung.* Edited by Jens Schröter and Ralph Brucker. BZNW 114. Berlin: de Gruyter, 2002.

Lyons, William John. "The Hermeneutics of Fictional Black and Factual Red: The Markan Simon of Cyrene and the Quest for the Historical Jesus." *JSHJ* 4 (2006): 139–54.

Macaskill, Grant. *Revealed Wisdom and Inaugurated Eschatology in Ancient Judaism and Early Christianity.* JSJSup 115. Leiden: Brill, 2007.

MacDonald, Dennis R. *Does the New Testament Imitate Homer? Four Cases from the Acts of the Apostles.* New Haven: Yale University Press, 2003.

———. *The Homeric Epics and the Gospel of Mark.* New Haven: Yale University Press, 2000.

MacIntyre, Alisdair. *After Virtue: A Study in Moral Theory.* Notre Dame, IN: University of Notre Dame Press, 1981.

Mack, Burton. "Backbay Jazz and Blues." Pages 421–31 in *Redescribing Christian Origins.* Edited by Ron Cameron and Merrill P. Miller. SBLSymS 28. Atlanta: Society of Biblical Literature, 2004.

———. *The Christian Myth: Origins, Logic, and Legacy.* New York: Continuum, 2001.

———. *The Lost Gospel: The Book of Q and Christian Origins*. San Francisco: HarperSanFrancisco, 1993.

———. *A Myth of Innocence: Mark and Christian Origins*. Philadelphia: Fortress, 1988.

———. Review of Gary R. Habermas and Antony G. N. Flew, *Did Jesus Rise from the Dead? The Resurrection Debate*. *History and Theory* 28 (1989): 215–24.

———. *Who Wrote the New Testament? The Making of the Christian Myth*. San Francisco: HarperSanFrancisco, 1995.

———. *Wisdom and the Hebrew Epic: Ben Sira's Hymn in Praise of the Fathers*. Chicago: University of Chicago Press, 1985.

Madigan, Kevin J., and Jon D. Levenson. *Resurrection: The Power of God for Christians and Jews*. New Haven: Yale University Press, 2008.

Magness, Jodi. "Jesus' Tomb—What Did It Look Like?" Pages 212–26 in *Where Christianity Was Born: A Collection from the Biblical Archaeology Society*. Edited by Hershel Shanks. Washington, DC: Biblical Archaeological Society, 2006.

Maldonatus, Juan. *Comentarii in Quatuor Evangelistas*. Edited by J. M. Raich. 2 vols. London: Moguntiae, 1853–1854.

Malherbe, Abraham J. *The Letters to the Thessalonians*. AB 32B. New York: Doubleday, 2000.

Mandel, Barrett J. "Full of Life Now." Pages 49–72 in *Autobiography: Essays Theoretical and Critical*. Edited by James Olney. Princeton, NJ: Princeton University Press, 1980.

Mandler, Jean M., and Nancy S. Johnson. "Remembrance of Things Parsed: Story Structure and Recall." *Cognitive Psychology* 9 (1977): 111–51.

Manson, T. W. "John the Baptist." *BJRL* 36 (1954): 395–412.

———. *The Sayings of Jesus*. London: SCM Press, 1949.

———. *The Teaching of Jesus: Studies in Its Form and Content*. 2nd ed. Cambridge: Cambridge University Press, 1967.

Manuchehri, Sepehr. "The Practice of Taqiyyah (Dissimulation) in the Babi and Bahai Religions." *Research Notes in Shaykhi, Babi and Baha'i Studies* 3, no. 3 (1999). Online: www.h-net.org/~bahai/notes/vol3/taqiya.htm. Cited 18 November 2009.

Marcus, Joel. "The Beelzebul Controversy and the Eschatologies of Jesus." Pages 247–77 in *Authenticating the Activities of Jesus*. Edited by Bruce Chilton and Craig A. Evans. NTTS 28/2. Leiden: Brill, 1999.

———. "Crucifixion as Parodic Exaltation." *JBL* 125 (2006): 73–87.

———. "Entering into the Kingly Power of God." *JBL* 107 (1988): 663–75.

———. "Identity and Ambiguity in Markan Christology." Pages 133–47 in *Seeking the Identity of Jesus: A Pilgrimage*. Edited by Beverly Roberts Gaventa and Richard B. Hays. Grand Rapids: Eerdmans, 2008.

———. "The Jewish War and the *Sitz im Leben* of Mark." *JBL* 113 (1992): 441–62.

———. "John the Baptist and Jesus." Pages 179–97 in *Christianity in the Beginning*. Vol. 1 of *When Judaism and Christianity Began: Essays in Memory of Anthony J. Saldarini*. Edited by Daniel Harrington, Alan J. Avery-Peck, and Jacob Neusner. JSJSup 85. Leiden: Brill, 2003.

———. *Mark 1–8: A New Translation with Introduction and Commentary*. AB 27. New York: Doubleday, 1999.

———. *Mark 8–16: A New Translation with Introduction and Commentary*. AB 27A. New Haven: Yale University Press, 2009.

———. "Mark—Interpreter of Paul." *NTS* 46 (2000): 473–87.

———. "Meggitt on the Madness and Kingship of Jesus." *JSNT* 29 (2007): 421–24.

———. "Modern and Ancient Jewish Apocalypticism." *JR* 76 (1996): 1–27.

———. "The Once and Future Messiah in Early Christianity and Chabad." *NTS* 47 (2001): 381–401.

———. "'The Time Has Been Fulfilled!' (Mark 1:15)." Pages 49–68 in *Apocalyptic in the New Testament: Essays in Honour of J. Louis Martyn*. Edited by Joel Marcus and

Marion L. Soards. JSNTSup 24. Sheffield: Sheffield Academic Press, 1989.

―――. *The Way of the Lord: Christological Exegesis of the Old Testament in the Gospel of Mark*. Louisville: Westminster John Knox, 1992.

Markus, Gregory B. "Stability and Change in Political Attitudes: Observed, Recalled, and 'Explained.'" *Political Behavior* 8 (1986): 21–44.

Marshall, I. Howard. *The Gospel of Luke: A Commentary on the Greek Text*. NIGTC. Grand Rapids: Eerdmans, 1978.

―――. "The Hope of a New Age: The Kingdom of God in the New Testament." *Themelios* 11 (1985): 5–15.

―――. *The Origins of New Testament Christology*. Downers Grove, IL: InterVarsity, 1976.

Marshall, I. Howard, and Philip H. Towner. *A Critical and Exegetical Commentary on the Pastoral Epistles*. ICC. Edinburgh: T & T Clark, 1999.

Martin, David. "Does the Advance of Science Mean Secularisation?" *SJT* 61 (2008): 3–14.

Martin, Marie-Louise. *Kimbangu: An African Prophet and His Church*. Oxford: Basil Blackwell, 1975.

Martin, Ralph P. *2 Corinthians*. WBC 40. Waco, TX: Word, 1986.

Martin, Raymond A. *Syntax Criticism of the Synoptic Gospels*. SBEC 10. Lewiston, NY: Edwin Mellen, 1987.

Martin, Troy W. "Watch during the Watches (Mark 13:35)." *JBL* 120 (2001): 685–701.

Martineau, James. *The Seat of Authority in Religion*. 4th ed. London: Longmans, Green, 1898.

Martyn, J. Louis. "Apocalyptic Antinomies in Paul's Letter to the Galatians." *NTS* 31 (1985): 410–24.

―――. *Galatians: A New Translation with Introduction and Commentary*. AB 33A. New York: Doubleday, 1997.

März, Claus-Peter. ". . . *lasst eure Lampen brennen!" Studien zur Q-Vorlage von Lk 12,35–14,24*. ETS 20. Leipzig: St. Benno-Verlag, 1991.

Mason, Eric F. *"You Are a Priest Forever": Second Temple Jewish Messianism and the Priestly Christology of the Epistle to the Hebrews*. STDJ 74. Leiden: Brill, 2008.

Mason, Steve. "Contradiction or Counterpoint? Josephus and Historical Method." *RRJ* 6 (2003): 145–88.

Massaux, Édouard. *The Influence of the Gospel of Saint Matthew on Christian Literature before Saint Irenaeus*. Translated by Norman J. Belval and Suzanne Hechted. Edited by Arthur J. Bellinzoni. 3 vols. NGS 5. Leuven: Peeters; Macon, GA: Mercer University Press, 1990.

Mathews, Shailer. *The Messianic Hope in the New Testament*. Chicago: University of Chicago Press, 1904.

Mazzoni, Giuliana A. L., Elizabeth F. Loftus, and Irving Kirsch. "Changing Beliefs about Implausible Autobiographical Events: A Little Plausibility Goes a Long Way." *Journal of Experimental Psychology: Applied* 7 (2001): 51–59.

McAfee Moss, Charlene. *The Zechariah Tradition and the Gospel of Matthew*. BZNW 156. Berlin: de Gruyter, 2008.

McCant, Jerry W. "Paul's Thorn of Rejected Apostleship." *NTS* 34 (1988): 550–72.

McCown, C. C. "The Eschatology of Jesus Reconsidered." *JR* 16 (1936): 30–46.

McIver, Robert K., and Marie Carroll. "Experiments to Develop Criteria for Determining the Existence of Written Sources, and Their Potential Implications for the Synoptic Problem." *JBL* 121 (2002): 667–87.

McKnight, Scot. "Historical Jesus Studies: A Dead End?" Online: http://blog.beliefnet.com/jesuscreed/2009/05/historical-jesus-studies-a-dea.html. Cited 18 November 2009.

―――. *Jesus and His Death: Historiography, the Historical Jesus, and Atonement Theory*. Waco, TX: Baylor University Press, 2005.

―――. "Jesus and Prophetic Actions." *BBR* 10 (2000): 197–232.

―――. *A Light among the Gentiles: Jewish Missionary Activity in the Second Temple Period*. Minneapolis: Fortress, 1991.

————. *A New Vision for Israel: The Teachings of Jesus in National Context*. Grand Rapids: Eerdmans, 1999.

McNamara, Martin. *The New Testament and the Palestinian Targum to the Pentateuch*. AnBib 27. Rome: Pontifical Biblical Institute, 1964.

————. *Targum and Testament: Aramaic Paraphrases of the Hebrew Bible; A Light on the New Testament*. Grand Rapids: Eerdmans, 1972.

McNeile, A. H. *The Gospel according to St. Matthew*. London: Macmillan, 1915.

McNicol, Allan J., ed., with David L. Dungan and David B. Peabody. *Beyond the Q Impasse—Luke's Use of Matthew: A Demonstration by the Research Team of the International Institute for Gospel Studies*. Valley Forge, PA: Trinity Press International, 1996.

Mearns, C. L. "Early Eschatological Development in Paul: The Evidence of I and II Thessalonians." *NTS* 27 (1981): 137–57.

Meeks, Wayne A. *The First Urban Christians: The Social World of the Apostle Paul*. New Haven: Yale University Press, 1983.

Mees, Michael. *Ausserkanonische Parallelstellen zu den Herrenworten und ihre Bedeutung*. Quaderni di "Vetera Christianorum" 10. Bari: Istituto di Letteratura Cristiana Antica, 1975.

Meggitt, Justin J. "The Madness of King Jesus: Why Was Jesus Put to Death, but His Followers Were Not?" *JSNT* 29 (2007): 379–413.

————. "Psychology and the Historical Jesus." Pages 16–26 in *Jesus and Psychology*. Edited by Fraser Watts. Philadelphia: Templeton Foundation Press, 2007.

Meier, John P. "The Circle of the Twelve: Did It Exist during Jesus' Public Ministry?" *JBL* 116 (1997): 635–72.

————. "From Elijah-Like Prophet to Royal Davidic Messiah." Pages 45–83 in *Jesus: A Colloquium in the Holy Land*. Edited by Doris Donnelly. New York: Continuum, 2001.

————. "Jesus, the Twelve, and the Restoration of Israel." Pages 365–404 in *Restoration: Old Testament, Jewish, and Christian Perspectives*. Edited by James M. Scott. JSJSup 72. Leiden: Brill, 2001.

————. "John the Baptist in Matthew's Gospel." *JBL* 99 (1980): 383–405.

————. *A Marginal Jew: Rethinking the Historical Jesus*. 4 vols. New York: Doubleday, 1991–2009.

Meinhold, Arndt. *Die Sprüche*. 2 vols. ZBK 16. Zürich: Theologischer Verlag, 1991.

Meir, Samuel ben. *Rashbam's Commentary on Leviticus and Numbers: An Annotated Translation*. Edited by Martin I. Lockshin. BJS 330. Providence: Brown Judaic Studies, 2001.

Melton, J. Gordon. "Spiritualization and Reaffirmation: What Really Happens When Prophecy Fails." *American Studies* 26 (1985): 145–57.

————. "When Prophets Die: The Succession Crisis in New Religions." Pages 1–12 in *When Prophets Die: The Postcharismatic Fate of New Religious Movements*. Edited by Timothy Miller. Albany: State University of New York Press, 1991.

Menahem, R. "A Jewish Commentary on the New Testament: A Sample Verse." *Immanuel* 21 (1987): 43–54.

Mendels, Doron. "Jesus and the Politics of His Day." Pages 440–51 in *Identity, Religion, and Historiography: Studies in Hellenistic History*. JSPSup 24. Sheffield: Sheffield Academic Press, 1998.

————. *The Rise and Fall of Jewish Nationalism*. ABRL. New York: Doubleday, 1992.

Merkel, Helmut. "Die Gottesherrschaft in der Verkündigung Jesu." Pages 119–61 in *Königsherrschaft Gottes und himmlischer Kult im Judentum, Urchristentum und in der hellenistischen Welt*. Edited by Martin Hengel and Anna Maria Schwemer. WUNT 2/55. Tübingen: Mohr Siebeck, 1991.

————. *Die Widersprüche zwischen den Evangelien: Ihre polemische und apologetische Behandlung in der Alten Kirche bis zu Augustin*. WUNT 2/13. Tübingen: Mohr Siebeck, 1971.

Merklein, Helmut. *Die Gottesherrschaft als Handlungsprinzip: Untersuchung zur Ethik*

Jesu. FB 34. Würzburg: Echter-Verlag, 1981.

———. "Die Umkehrpredigt bei Johannes dem Täufer und Jesus von Nazaret." *BZ* 25 (1981): 29–46.

———. *Jesu Botschaft von der Gottesherrschaft: Eine Skizze*. SBS 111. Stuttgart: Katholisches Bibelwerk, 1983.

Meshorer, Ya'akov. *Ancient Jewish Coinage*. 2 vols. Dix Hills, NY: Amphora Books, 1982.

Mettinger, Tryggve N. D. *King and Messiah: The Civil and Sacral Legitimation of the Israelite Kings*. ConBOT 8. Lund: Gleerup, 1976.

Meye, Robert P. *Jesus and the Twelve: Discipleship and Revelation in Mark's Gospel*. Grand Rapids: Eerdmans, 1968.

Meyer, Ben F. *The Aims of Jesus*. London: SCM, 1979.

———. "Appointed Deed, Appointed Doer: Jesus and the Scriptures." Pages 155–76 in *Authenticating the Activities of Jesus*. Edited by Bruce D. Chilton and Craig A. Evans. NTTS 28/2. Leiden: Brill, 1999.

———. *Christus Faber: The Master Builder and the House of God*. Allison Park, PA: Pickwick, 1992.

Meyer, Eduard. *Die Evangelien*. Vol. 1 of *Ursprung und Anfänge des Christentum*. 5th ed. Stuttgart: J. G. Cotta'sche Buchhandlung, 1924.

Meyvaert, Paul. "The Enigma of Gregory the Great's *Dialogues*: A Response to Francis Clark." *JEH* 39 (1988): 335–81.

Michaud, Jean-Paul. "Quelle(s) communauté(s) derrière la Source Q?" Pages 577–606 in *The Sayings Source Q and the Historical Jesus*. Edited by A. Lindemann. BETL 158. Leuven: Leuven University Press, 2001.

Michel, Otto. "Der Abschluss des Matthäus-Evangeliums." *EvT* 10 (1950): 16–26.

Michelon, Pascale, et al. "Neural Correlates of Incongruous Visual Information: An Event-Related fMRI Study." *NeuroImage* 19 (2003): 1612–26.

Middleton, David, and Derek Edwards, eds. *Collective Remembering*. London: Sage, 1990.

Milavec, Aaron. "Synoptic Tradition in the *Didache* Revisited." *JECS* 11 (2003): 443–80.

Mildenberg, Leo. *The Coinage of the Bar Kokhba War*. Edited by Patricia Erhart Mottahedeh. Typos 6. Aarau: Sauerländer, 1984.

Milgrom, Jacob. *Leviticus 17–22*. AB 3A. New York: Doubleday, 2000.

———. *Leviticus: A Book of Ritual Ethics*. Minneapolis: Fortress, 2004.

Milikowsky, Chaim. "Josephus between Rabbinic Culture and Hellenistic Historiography." Pages 159–90 in *Shem in the Tents of Japhet: Essays on the Encounter of Judaism and Hellenism*. Edited by James L. Kugel. JSJSup 74. Leiden: Brill, 2002.

———. "Midrash as Fiction and Midrash as History: What Did the Rabbis Mean?" Pages 117–27 in *Ancient Fiction: The Matrix of Early Christian and Jewish Narrative*. Edited by Jo-Ann A. Brant, Charles W. Hedrick, and Chris Shea. SBLSymS 32. Atlanta: Society of Biblical Literature, 2006.

———. "Rabbinic Interpretation of the Bible in the Light of Ancient Hermeneutical Practice: The Question of Literal Meaning." Pages 7–28 in *"The Words of a Wise Man's Mouth Are Gracious" (Qoh 10,12): Festschrift for Günther Stemberger on the Occasion of His 65th Birthday*. Edited by Mauro Perani. SJ 32. Berlin: de Gruyter, 2005.

———. "Trajectories of Return, Restoration and Redemption in Rabbinic Judaism: Elijah, the Messiah, the War of Gog and the World to Come." Pages 265–77 in *Restoration: Old Testament, Jewish, and Christian Perspectives*. Edited by James M. Scott. JSJSup 72. Leiden: Brill, 2001.

Millard, Alan. *Reading and Writing in the Time of Jesus*. Washington Square: New York University Press, 2000.

Miller, David M. "The Messenger, the Lord, and the Coming Judgement in the Reception History of Malachi 3." *NTS* 53 (2007): 1–16.

Miller, Gene. "ΑΡΧΟΝΤΩΝ ΤΟΥ ΑΙΩΝΟΣ ΤΟΥΤΟΥ—A New Look at 1 Corinthians 2:6–8." *JBL* 91 (1972): 522–28.

Miller, Merrill P. "'Beginning from Jerusalem . . .': Re-examining Canon and Consensus." *Journal of Higher Criticism* 2 (1995): 3–30.

———. "The Function of Isa 61:1–2 in 11Q Melchizedek." *JBL* 88 (1969): 467–69.

———. "The Problem of the Origins of a Messianic Conception of Jesus." Pages 301–35 in *Redescribing Christian Origins*. Edited by Ron Cameron and Merrill P. Miller. SBLSymS 28. Atlanta: Society of Biblical Literature, 2004.

Miller, Robert J. "The (A)historicity of Jesus' Temple Demonstration: A Test Case in Methodology." Pages 235–52 in *Society of Biblical Literature 1991 Seminar Papers*. Edited by Eugene H. Lovering Jr. Atlanta: Scholars Press, 1991.

———. *Born Divine: The Births of Jesus and Other Sons of God*. Santa Rosa, CA: Polebridge, 2003.

Mitchell, David C. "The Fourth Deliverer: A Josephite Messiah in 4QTestimonia." *Bib* 86 (2005): 545–53.

———. "Rabbi Dosa and the Rabbis Differ: Messiah ben Joseph in the Babylonian Talmud." *RRJ* 8 (2005): 77–90.

Mitchell, Margaret M. "Rhetorical Shorthand in Pauline Argumentation: The Functions of 'the Gospel' in the Corinthian Correspondence." Pages 63–88 in *Gospel in Paul: Studies on Corinthians, Galatians, and Romans for Richard N. Longenecker*. Edited by L. Ann Jervis and Peter Richardson. JSNTSup 108. Sheffield: Sheffield Academic Press, 1994.

Mitton, C. Leslie. "Threefoldness in the Teaching of Jesus." *ExpTim* 75 (1964): 228–30.

Montefiore, C. G. *The Synoptic Gospels*. 2nd rev. ed. 2 vols. London: Macmillan, 1927.

Moo, Douglas J. *The Epistle to the Romans*. NICNT. Grand Rapids: Eerdmans, 1996.

———. *The Letters of the Colossians and to Philemon*. PilNTC. Grand Rapids: Eerdmans, 2008.

———. *The Old Testament in the Gospel Passion Narratives*. Sheffield: Almond, 1983.

Mooney, James. *The Ghost-Dance Religion and the Sioux Outbreak of 1890*. Abridged ed. Chicago: University of Chicago Press, 1965.

Moore, Carey A. *Judith: A New Translation and Commentary*. AB 40. Garden City, NY: Doubleday, 1985.

Moore, George Foot. *Judaism in the First Centuries of the Christian Era*. 2 vols. New York: Schocken Books, 1971.

Morgan, Robert. "From Reimarus to Sanders: The Kingdom of God, Jesus, and the Judaisms of His Day." Pages 80–139 in *The Kingdom of God and Human Society: Essays by Members of the Scripture, Theology, and Society Group*. Edited by Robin Barbour. Edinburgh: T & T Clark, 1993.

Morgan, Thomas. *The Moral Philosopher*. London: printed for the author, 1737.

Moscovitch, Morris. "Confabulation." Pages 226–53 in *Memory Distortion: How Minds, Brains, and Societies Reconstruct the Past*. Edited by Daniel L. Schacter. Cambridge, MA: Harvard University Press, 1995.

Moses, L. G. "'The Father Tells Me So!' Wovoka: The Ghost Dance Prophet." *American Indian Quarterly* 9 (1985): 335–51.

Moss, Mark B., Douglas L. Rosene, and Alan Peters. "Effects of Aging on Visual Recognition Memory in the Rhesus Monkey." *Neurobiology of Aging* 9 (1988): 495–502.

Moule, C. F. D. "The Influence of Circumstances on the Use of Eschatological Terms." *JTS* 15 (1964): 1–15.

———. *The Origin of Christology*. Cambridge: University of Cambridge Press, 1977.

Moulton, James Hope. "'It Is His Angel.'" *JTS* 3 (1902): 514–27.

———. "The Marks of Jesus." *ExpTim* 21 (1910): 284.

Mounce, William. *Pastoral Epistles*. WBC 46. Nashville: Thomas Nelson, 2000.

Mowinckel, Sigmund. *He That Cometh: The Messiah Concept in the Old Testament and Later Judaism*. Grand Rapids: Eerdmans, 2005.

Muddiman, John. *A Commentary on the Epistle of the Ephesians*. BNTC. London: Continuum, 2001.

Muggeridge, Malcolm. "The Eye-Witness Fallacy." *Encounter* (May 1961): 86–89.

Muirhead, Lewis A. *The Eschatology of Jesus, or, The Kingdom Come and Coming.* New York: A. C. Armstrong & Son, 1904.

Mullen, Mary K. "Earliest Recollections of Childhood: A Demographic Analysis." *Cognition* 52 (1994): 55–79.

Müller, Mogens. *The Expression "Son of Man" and the Development of Christology: A History of Interpretation.* London: Equinox, 2008.

Müller, Ulrich B. "Apocalyptic Currents." Pages 281–329 in *Christian Beginnings: Word and Community from Jesus to Post-Apostolic Times.* Edited by Jürgen Becker. Louisville: Westminster John Knox, 1993.

———. "Auferweckt und erhöht: Zur Genese des Osterglaubens." *NTS* 54 (2008): 201–20.

———. "Jesus als 'der Menschensohn.'" Pages 91–129 in *Gottessohn und Menschensohn: Exegetische Studien zu zwei Paradigmen biblischer Intertextualität.* Edited by Dieter Sänger. BTSt 67. Neukirchen-Vluyn: Neukirchener Verlag, 2004.

Mullins, Terence Y. "Paul's Thorn in the Flesh." *JBL* 76 (1957): 299–303.

Münsterberg, Hugo. *On the Witness Stand: Essays on Psychology and Crime.* New York: Doubleday, Page, 1909. Online: http://psych classics.yorku.ca/Munster/Witness/. Cited 18 November 2009.

Murphy-O'Connor, Jerome. *The Holy Land: An Oxford Archaeological Guide from Earliest Times to 1700.* 4th ed. Oxford: Oxford University Press, 1998.

———. "The Origins of Paul's Christology: From Thessalonians to Galatians." Pages 113–42 in *Christian Origins: Worship, Belief and Society; The Milltown Institute and the Irish Biblical Association Millennium Conference.* Edited by Kieran J. O'Mahony. JSNTSup 241. Sheffield: Sheffield Academic Press, 2003.

Myers, Ched. *Binding the Strong Man: Political Reading of Mark's Story of Jesus.* Maryknoll, NY: Orbis, 1988.

Nachmonides. *Commentary on the Torah.* 5 vols. New York: Shiloh, 1971–1976.

Nagel, Peter. *Die Motivierung der Askese in der alten Kirche und der Ursprung des Mönchtums.* TU 95. Berlin: Akademie-Verlag, 1966.

Neimeyer, Greg J., and April E. Metzler. "Personal Identity and Autobiographical Recall." Pages 105–35 in *The Remembering Self: Construction and Accuracy in the Self-Narrative.* Edited by Ulric Neisser and Robyn Fivush. Cambridge: Cambridge University Press, 1994.

Neirynck, Franz. "Paul and the Sayings of Jesus." Pages 511–68 in *Evangelica II, 1982–1991: Collected Essays.* Edited by F. Van Segbroeck. BETL 99. Leuven: Leuven University Press, 1991.

———. "Saving/Losing One's Life: Luke 17,33 (Q?) and Mark 8,35." Pages 480–503 in *Evangelica III, 1992–2000: Collected Essays.* BETL 150. Leuven: Leuven University Press, 2001.

Neisser, Ulric. *Cognitive Psychology.* New York: Appleton-Century-Crofts, 1967.

———. "John Dean's Memory: A Case Study." *Cognition* 9 (1981): 1–22.

Neisser, Ulric, et al. "Remembering the Earthquake: Direct Experience vs. Hearing the News." *Memory* 4 (1996): 337–57.

Neubauer, A. "Where Are the Ten Tribes?" *JQR* 1 (1988–1989): 14–28, 95–114, 185–201, 408–23.

Neusner, Jacob. "The Kingdom of Heaven in Kindred Systems, Judaic and Christian." *BBR* 15 (2005): 279–305.

Neusner, Jacob, William Scott Green, and Ernest S. Frerichs, eds. *Judaisms and Their Messiahs at the Turn of the Christian Era.* New York: Cambridge University Press, 1987.

Nevin, Alfred. *Popular Expositor of the Gospels and Acts.* Philadelphia: Ziegler & McCurdy, 1872.

New, David S. *Old Testament Quotations in the Synoptic Gospels, and the Two-Document Hypothesis.* SBLSCS 37. Atlanta: Scholars Press, 1993.

Newman, Barclay M., Jr. "Translating 'the Kingdom of God' and 'the Kingdom of Heaven' in the New Testament." *BT* 25 (1974): 401–4.

Newman, Carey C., James R. Davila, and Gladys S. Lewis, eds. *The Jewish Roots of Christological Monotheism: Papers from the St. Andrews Conference on the Historical Origins of the Worship of Jesus.* JSJSup 63. Leiden: Brill, 1999.

Newsom, Carol. *Songs of the Sabbath Sacrifice: A Critical Edition.* HSS. Atlanta: Scholars Press, 1985.

Nickelsburg, George W. E. *1 Enoch 1: A Commentary on the Book of 1 Enoch, Chapters 1–36; 81–108.* Hermeneia. Minneapolis: Fortress, 2001.

———. "The Qumranic Transformation of a Cosmological and Eschatological Tradition (1QH 4:29–40)." Pages 649–59 in vol. 2 of *The Madrid Qumran Congress: Proceedings of the International Congress on the Dead Sea Scrolls, Madrid, 18–21 March, 1991.* Edited by Julio Trebolle Barrera and Luis Vegas Montaner. 2 vols. STDJ 11. Leiden: Brill, 1992.

———. "Son of Man." *ABD* 6:137–50.

Nickerson, Raymond S. "Confirmation Bias: A Ubiquitous Phenomenon in Many Guises." *Review of General Psychology* 2 (1998): 175–230.

Nie, Giselle de. "History and Miracle: Gregory's Use of Metaphor." Pages 261–79 in *The World of Gregory of Tours.* Edited by Kathleen Mitchell and Ian Wood. CBT 8. Leiden: Brill, 2002.

Niebuhr, Karl-Wilhelm. *Gesetz und Paränese: Katechismusartige Weisungsreihen in der frühjüdischen Literatur.* WUNT 2/28. Tübingen: Mohr Siebeck, 1987.

———. "4Q521, 2 II—Ein eschatologischer Psalm." Pages 151–68 in *Mogilany 1995: Papers on the Dead Sea Scrolls Offered in Memory of Aleksy Klawek.* Edited by Z. J. Kapera. Qumranica Mogilanensia 15. Kraków: Enigma, 1998.

Niederwimmer, Kurt. *Askese und Mysterium: Über Ehe, Ehescheidung und Eheverzicht in den Anfängen des christlichen Glaubens.*

FRLANT 113. Göttingen: Vandenhoeck & Ruprecht, 1975.

———. *The Didache: A Commentary.* Translated by Linda M. Maloney. Hermeneia. Minneapolis: Fortress, 1998.

Nietzsche, Friedrich. *The Antichrist.* Translated by H. L. Mencken. New York: Alfred A. Knopf, 1920.

Nihan, Christophe. *From Priestly Torah to Pentateuch: A Study in the Composition of the Book of Leviticus.* FAT 2/25. Tübingen: Mohr Siebeck, 2007.

Nilsson, Lars-Göran. "Remembering Actions and Words." Pages 137–48 in *The Oxford Handbook of Memory.* Edited by Endel Tulving and Fergus I. M. Craik. Oxford: Oxford University Press, 2000.

Nineham, D. E. *Saint Mark.* WPC. Philadelphia: Westminster, 1963.

Nitzan, Bilhah. "The Laws of Reproof in 4QBerakhot (4Q286–290) in Light of Their Parallels in the Damascus Covenant and Other Texts from Qumran." Pages 149–65 in *Legal Texts and Issues: Proceedings of the Second Meeting of the International Organization for Qumran Studies, Cambridge 1995.* Edited by Moshe Bernstein, Florentino García Martínez, and John Kampen. STDJ 23. Leiden: Brill, 1997.

———. "4QBerakhot$^{a–e}$ (4Q286–290): A Covenantal Ceremony in the Light of Related Texts." *RevQ* 16 (1995): 487–506.

Nolan, Brian M. *The Royal Son of God: The Christology of Matthew 1–2 in the Setting of the Gospel.* OBO 23. Fribourg: Éditions Universitaires; Göttingen: Vandenhoeck & Ruprecht, 1979.

Nolland, John. *The Gospel of Matthew: A Commentary on the Greek Text.* NIGTC. Grand Rapids: Eerdmans, 2005.

———. *Luke 1–9:20.* WBC 35A. Dallas: Word, 1989.

Norden, Eduard. *Agnostos Theos: Untersuchungen zur Formengeschichte religiöser Rede.* Leipzig: B. G. Teubner, 1913.

———. "Josephus und Tacitus über Jesus Christus und eine messianische Prophetie." *NJahrb* 31 (1913): 636–66.

Notopoulos, James A. "Mnemosyne in Oral Literature." *TAPA* 69 (1938): 465–93.

Novakovic, Lidija. *Messiah, the Healer of the Sick: A Study of Jesus as the Son of David in the Gospel of Matthew.* WUNT 2/170. Tübingen: Mohr Siebeck, 2003.

Noy, David, and Hanswulf Bloedhorn. *Syria and Cyprus.* Vol. 3 of *Inscriptiones Judaicae Orientis.* TSAJ 102. Tübingen: Mohr Siebeck, 2004.

Nützel, J. M. "Zum Schicksal der eschatologischen Propheten." *BZ* 20 (1976): 59–94.

Nygren, Anders. *Commentary on Romans.* Philadelphia: Muhlenberg, 1949.

Oakman, Douglas E. "The Lord's Prayer in Social Perspective." Pages 137–86 in *Authenticating the Words of Jesus.* Edited by Bruce Chilton and Craig A. Evans. NTTS 28/1. Leiden: Brill, 1998.

Oberman, Heiko A. *The Reformation: Roots and Ramifications.* Grand Rapids: Eerdmans, 1994.

O'Brien, Peter T. *Colossians, Philemon.* WBC 33. Waco, TX: Word, 1982.

Oegema, Gerbern S. "The Historical Jesus and Judaism." Pages 449–69 in *Jüdische Schriften in ihrem antik-jüdischen und urchristlichen Kontext.* Edited by Hermann Lichtenberger and Gerbern S. Oegema. SJSHRZ 1. Gütersloh: Gütersloher Verlagshaus, 2002.

Öhler, Markus. *Elia im Neuen Testament: Untersuchung zur Bedeutung des alttestamentlichen Propheten im frühen Christentum.* BZNW 88. Berlin: de Gruyter, 1997.

———. "The Expectation of Elijah and the Presence of the Kingdom of God." *JBL* 118 (1999): 461–76.

———. "Jesus as Prophet: Remarks on Terminology." Pages 125–42 in *Jesus, Mark, and Q: The Teaching of Jesus and Its Earliest Records.* Edited by Michael Labahn and Andreas Schmidt. JSNTSup 214. Sheffield: Sheffield Academic Press, 2001.

O'Leary, Stephen D. "When Prophecy Fails and When It Succeeds: Apocalyptic Prediction and the Re-entry into Ordinary Time." Pages 341–62 in *Apocalyptic Time.* Edited

by Albert I. Baumgarten. SHR 86. Leiden: Brill, 2000.

Olick, Jeffrey K., and Joyce Robbins. "Social Memory Studies: From 'Collective Memory' to the Historical Sociology of Mnemonic Practices." *Annual Review of Sociology* 24 (1998): 105–40.

Olson, Daniel C. "Enoch and the Son of Man in the Epilogue of the Parables." *JSP* 18 (1998): 27–38.

O'Neill, J. C. *Jesus the Messiah: Six Lectures on the Ministry of Jesus.* London: Cochrane, 1980.

———. "The Kingdom of God." *NovT* 34 (1993): 130–41.

———. *The Point of It All: Essays on Jesus Christ.* TSS 1. Leiden: Deo Publications, 2000.

———. *Who Did Jesus Think He Was?* BIS 11. Leiden: Brill, 1995.

Ong, Walter J. *Orality and Literacy: The Technologizing of the Word.* London: Methuen, 1982.

Oosthuizen, G. C. "Isaiah Shembe and the Zulu World View." *HR* 8 (1968): 1–30.

Oppenheimer, Aharon. Review of Peter Schäfer, *Der Bar Kokhba Aufstand: Studien zum zweiten jüdischen Krieg gegen Rom.* *JSJ* 14 (1983): 218–19.

Orlov, Andrei A. *The Enoch-Metatron Tradition.* TSAJ 107. Tübingen: Mohr Siebeck, 2005.

———. "The Face as the Heavenly Counterpart of the Visionary in the Slavonic *Ladder of Jacob.*" Pages 399–419 in *From Apocalypticism to Merkabah Mysticism: Studies in the Slavonic Pseudepigrapha.* JSJSup 114. Leiden: Brill, 2007.

———. "God's Face in the Enochic Tradition." Pages 179–93 in *Paradise Now: Essays on Early Jewish and Christian Mysticism.* Edited by April D. DeConick. SBLSymS 11. Atlanta: Scholars Press, 2006.

———. "In the Mirror of the Divine Face: The Enochic Features of the *Exagoge* of Ezekiel the Tragedian." Pages 183–99 in *The Significance of Sinai: Traditions about Sinai and Divine Revelation in Judaism and Christianity.* Edited by George J. Brooke, Hindy

Najman, and Loren T. Stuckenbruck. TBN 12. Leiden: Brill, 2008.

———. "Moses' Heavenly Counterpart in the Book of Jubilees and the *Exagoge* of Ezekiel the Tragedian." *Bib* 88 (2007): 326–50.

Ort, L. J. R. *Mani: A Religio-Historical Description of His Personality*. DHRP 1. Leiden: Brill, 1967.

Orwell, George. "Benefit of Clergy: Some Notes on Salvador Dali." Pages 170–84 in *Dickens, Dali, and Others: Studies in Popular Culture*. Edited by George Orwell. Cornwall, NY: Cornwall Press, 1946.

Otto, Rudolf. *The Kingdom of God and the Son of Man*. Translated by Floyd V. Filson and Bertram Lee Woolf. Rev. ed. London: Lutterworth, 1943.

Owen, Paul, and David Shepherd. "Speaking Up for Qumran, Dalman and the Son of Man: Was *Bar Enasha* a Common Term for 'Man' in the Time of Jesus?" *JSNT* 81 (2001): 81–122.

Pagels, Elaine. *The Gnostic Gospels*. New York: Random House, 1979.

Paget, James Carleton. "Egypt." Pages 183–97 in *Redemption and Resistance: The Messianic Hopes of Jews and Christians in Antiquity*. Edited by Markus Bockmuehl and James Carleton Paget. London: T & T Clark, 2007.

Pahl, Michael W. *Discerning the "Word of the Lord": The "Word of the Lord" in 1 Thessalonians 4:15*. LNTS 389. London: T & T Clark, 2009.

Palmer, Susan J., and Natalie Finn. "Coping with Apocalypse in Canada: Experiences of Endtime in la Mission de l'Esprit Saint and the Institute of Applied Metaphysics." *Sociological Analysis* 53 (1992): 397–415.

Park, David M. "Paul's σκόλοψ τῇ σαρκί: Thorn or Stake?" *NovT* 22 (1980): 179–83.

Parkes, Murray. *Bereavement: Studies of Grief in Adult Life*. New York: International Universities Press, 1972.

Partridge, Christopher. "The End Is Nigh: Failed Prophecy, Apocalypticism, and the Rationalization of Violence in New Religious Eschatologies." Pages 191–212 in *The Oxford Handbook of Eschatology*. Edited by Jerry L. Walls. Oxford: Oxford University Press, 2008.

Pate, C. Marvin, and Douglas W. Kennard. *Deliverance Now and Not Yet: The New Testament and the Great Tribulation*. New York: Peter Lang, 2003.

Patterson, Stephen J. "Con: Jesus Was Not an Apocalyptic Prophet." Pages 69–82 in *The Apocalyptic Jesus: A Debate*. Edited by Robert J. Miller. Santa Rosa, CA: Polebridge, 2001.

———. "The End of Apocalypse: Rethinking the Historical Jesus." *ThTo* 52 (1995): 29–58.

———. *The God of Jesus: The Historical Jesus and the Search for Meaning*. Harrisburg, PA: Trinity Press International, 1998.

———. *The Gospel of Thomas and Jesus*. Sonoma, CA: Polebridge, 1993.

———. "Q: The Lost Gospel." *BRev* 9, no. 5 (1993): 34–41, 61–62.

———. Review of Dale C. Allison Jr., *Jesus of Nazareth: Millenarian Prophet*. JBL 119 (2000): 357–60.

———. "An Unanswered Question." *JSHJ*, forthcoming.

———. "Understanding the *Gospel of Thomas* Today." Pages 33–76 in *The Fifth Gospel: The Gospel of Thomas Comes of Age*. By Stephen J. Patterson and James M. Robinson. Harrisburg, PA: Trinity Press International, 1998.

———. "Why Did Christians Say: 'God Raised Jesus from the Dead'?" *Forum* 10 (1994): 135–60.

Pazarro, David A., et al. "Ripple Effects in Memory: Judgments of Moral Blame Can Distort Memory for Events." *Memory and Cognition* 34 (2006): 550–55.

Peabody, Francis Greenwood. *The Christian Life in the Modern World*. New York: Macmillan, 1914.

———. "New Testament Eschatology and New Testament Ethics." Pages 305–12 in *Transactions of the Third International Congress for the History of Religions*. Oxford: Clarendon, 1908.

Pearson, Birger A. *Ancient Gnosticism: Traditions and Literature*. Minneapolis: Fortress, 2007.

——— "The Gospel according to the 'Jesus Seminar.'" Pages 23–57 in *The Emergence of the Christian Religion: Essays on Early Christianity*. Harrisburg, PA: Trinity Press International, 1997.

———. "A Q Community in Galilee?" *NTS* 50 (2004): 476–94.

———. "1 Thessalonians 2:14–16: A Deutero-Pauline Interpolation." *HTR* 64 (1971): 79–94.

Peels, H. G. L. *The Vengeance of God: The Meaning of the Root NQM and the Function of the NQM-Texts in the Context of Divine Revelation in the Old Testament*. OtSt 31. Leiden: Brill, 1995.

Pennington, Jonathan T. *Heaven and Earth in the Gospel of Matthew*. NovTSup 126. Leiden: Brill, 2007. Repr., Grand Rapids: Baker Academic, 2009.

———. "Heaven, Earth, and a New Genesis: Theological Cosmology in Matthew." Pages 28–44 in *Cosmology and the New Testament*. Edited by Jonathan T. Pennington and Sean M. McDonough. London: T & T Clark, 2008.

Penton, M. James. *Apocalypse Delayed: The Story of Jehovah's Witnesses*. 2nd ed. Toronto: University of Toronto Press, 1997.

Perrin, Nicholas. "Recent Trends in *Gospel of Thomas* Research (1991–2006): Part I, The Historical Jesus and the Synoptic Gospels." *CBR* 5 (2007): 183–206.

Perrin, Norman. *The Kingdom of God in the Teaching of Jesus*. NTL. Philadelphia: Westminster, 1963.

Perry, T. A. *Wisdom Literature and the Structure of Proverbs*. University Park: Pennsylvania State University Press, 1993.

Pervo, Richard I. "The Ancient Novel Becomes Christian." Pages 685–712 in *The Novel in the Ancient World*. Edited by Gareth Schmeling. Leiden: Brill, 1996.

———. *Profit with Delight: The Literary Genre of the Acts of the Apostles*. Philadelphia: Fortress, 1987.

Pesce, Mauro. *Paolo e gli arconti a Corinto: Storia della ricerca (1888–1975) ed esegesi di 1 Cor. 2,6.8*. TRSR 13. Brescia: Paideia Editrice, 1977.

Pesch, Rudolf. *Das Abendmahl und Jesu Todesverständnis*. QD 80. Freiburg: Herder, 1978.

———. *Das Markusevangelium: Teil 2, Einleitung und Kommentar zu Kap. 8,27–16,20*. HTKNT 2/2. Freiburg: Herder, 1977.

———. "Zur Entstehung des Glaubens an die Auferstehung Jesu." *TQ* 153 (1973): 222–26.

Peterson, David G. *Hebrews and Perfection: An Examination of the Concept of Perfection in the Epistle to the Hebrews*. SNTSMS 47. Cambridge: Cambridge University Press, 1982.

Peterson, Jeffrey. "Christ Our Pasch: Shaping Christian Identity in Corinth." Pages 133–44 in *Renewing Tradition: Studies in Honor of James W. Thompson*. Edited by Mark W. Hamilton, Thomas H. Olbricht, and Jeffrey Peterson. PTMS 65. Eugene, OR: Pickwick, 2007.

———. "The Extent of Christian Theological Diversity: Pauline Evidence." *RestQ* 47 (2005): 1–12.

Phillips, Helen. "Mind Fiction: Why Your Brain Tells Tall Tales." *New Scientist* 2572 (October 7, 2008): 32–36.

Phillips, Thomas E. "The Genre of Acts: Moving toward a Consensus?" *CBR* 4 (2006): 365–96.

Pines, Shlomo. "'Israel, My Firstborn' and the Sonship of Jesus." Pages 177–90 in *Studies in Mysticism and Religion, Presented to Gershom G. Scholem on His Seventieth Birthday*. Edited by E. E. Urbach, R. J. Zwi Werblowsky, and Ch. Wirszubski. Jerusalem: Magnes, 1967.

Piper, John. "*Love Your Enemies*": Jesus' Love Command in the Synoptic Gospels and in the Early Christian Paraenesis; A History of the Tradition and Interpretation of Its Uses*. SNTSMS 38. Cambridge: Cambridge University Press, 1979.

Piper, Ronald A. *Wisdom in the Q-Tradition: The Aphoristic Teaching of Jesus*. SNTSMS

61. Cambridge: Cambridge University Press, 1989.

Pitre, Brant. *Jesus, the Tribulation, and the End of the Exile: Restoration Eschatology and the Origin of the Atonement.* WUNT 2/204. Tübingen: Mohr Siebeck; Grand Rapids: Baker Academic, 2005.

Poirier, John C. "Jesus as an Elijanic Figure in Luke 4:16–30." *CBQ* 71 (2009): 349–63.

———. "Montanist Pepuza-Jerusalem and the Dwelling Place of Wisdom." *JECS* 7 (1999): 491–507.

Pokorný, Petr. *Der Brief des Paulus an die Epheser.* THKNT 10/2. Leipzig: Evangelische Verlagsanstalt, 1992.

Poole, Matthew. *Annotations on the Holy Bible.* 3 vols. London: Henry G. Bohn, 1846.

Popkes, Enno Edzard. "Von der Eschatologie zur Protologie: Transformationen apokalyptiker Motive im Thomasevangelium." Pages 211–33 in *Apokalyptik als Herausforderung neutestamentlicher Theologie.* Edited by Michael Becker and Markus Öhler. WUNT 2/214. Tübingen: Mohr Siebeck, 2006.

Popkes, Wiard. *Christus Traditus: Eine Untersuchungen zum Begriff der Dahingabe im Neuen Testament.* ATANT 49. Zürich: Zwingli, 1967.

Popper, Karl. "Normal Science and Its Dangers." Pages 51–58 in *Criticism and the Growth of Knowledge.* Edited by Imre Lakatos and Alan Musgrave. London: Cambridge University Press, 1970.

Porter, Stephen, and Kristine A. Peace. "The Scars of Memory: A Prospective, Longitudinal Investigation of the Consistency of Traumatic and Positive Memories in Adulthood." *Psychological Science* 18 (2007): 435–41.

Powell, Mark Allan. "Authorial Intention and Historical Reporting: Putting Spong's Literalization Thesis to the Test." *JSHJ* 1 (2003): 225–49.

Price, Robert M. *The Incredible Shrinking Son of Man: How Reliable Is the Gospel Tradition?* Amherst, NY: Prometheus Books, 2003.

Puech, Émile. *La croyance des Esséniens en la vie future: Immortalité, résurrection, vie éternelle? Histoire d'une croyance dans le judaïsme ancien.* 2 vols. EBib 21, 22. Paris: Gabalda, 1993.

———. "Some Remarks on 4Q246 and 4Q521 and Qumran Messianism." Pages 545–65 in *The Provo International Conference on the Dead Sea Scrolls: Technological Innovations, New Texts, and Reformulated Issues.* Edited by Donald W. Parry and Eugene Ulrich. STDJ 30. Leiden: Brill, 1999.

Puech, H.-C. "Un logion de Jésus sur bandelette funéraire." *RHR* 147 (1955): 126–29.

Quispel, Gilles. "Das ewige Ebenbild des Menschen zur Begegnung mit dem Selbst in der Gnosis." Pages 140–57 in *Gnostic Studies 1.* Istanbul: Nederlands Historisch-Archaeologisch Instituut, 1974.

Radcliffe, Timothy. "'The Coming of the Son of Man': Mark's Gospel and the Subversion of 'the Apocalyptic Imagination.'" Pages 176–89 in *Language, Meaning and God: Essays in Honour of Herbert McCabe.* Edited by Brian Davies. London: Geoffrey Chapman, 1987.

Radday, Yehuda T. "Chiastic Patterns in Biblical Hebrew Poetry." Pages 50–117 in *Chiasmus in Antiquity: Structures, Analyses, Exegesis.* Edited by John W. Welch. Provo, UT: Research Press, 1999.

Radl, Walter. "Der Tod Jesu in der Darstellung der Evangelien." *ThGl* 72 (1982): 432–46.

Rainbow, Paul A. "Jewish Monotheism as a Matrix for New Testament Christology: A Review Article." *NovT* 33 (1991): 78–91.

Räisänen, Heikki. "Did Paul Expect an Earthly Kingdom?" Pages 2–20 in *Paul, Luke and the Graeco-Roman World: Essays in Honour of Alexander J. M. Wedderburn.* Edited by Alf Christophersen et al. JSNTSup 217. New York: Sheffield Academic Press, 2002.

———. "Exorcisms and the Kingdom: Is Q 11:20 a Saying of the Historical Jesus?" Pages 119–42 in *Symbols and Strata: Essays on the Sayings Gospel Q.* Edited by Risto Uro. SESJ 45. Helsinki: Finnish Exegetical Society; Göttingen: Vandenhoeck & Ruprecht, 1996.

———. "Last Things First: 'Eschatology' as the First Chapter in an Overall Account of Early Christian Ideas." Pages 444–87 in *Moving beyond New Testament Theology? Essays in Conversation with Heikki Räisänen*. Edited by Todd Penner and Caroline Vander Stichele. SESJ 88. Helsinki: Finnish Exegetical Society; Göttingen: Vandenhoeck & Ruprecht, 2005.

———. *Paul and the Law*. 2nd ed. WUNT 29. Tübingen: Mohr Siebeck, 1987.

Rapp, Peter R. "Visual Discrimination and Reversal Learning in the Aged Monkey (*Macca mulatta*)." *Behavioral Neuroscience* 104 (1990): 876–84.

Rau, Eckhard. *Jesus—Freund von Zöllnern und Sündern: Eine methodenkritische Untersuchung*. Stuttgart: Kohlhammer, 2000.

———. "Q-Forschung und Jesusforschung: Versuch eines Brückenschlags." *ETL* 82 (2006): 373–403.

———. "Wie entstehen unechte Jesusworte?" Pages 159–85 in *Gemeinschaft am Evangelium: Festschrift für Wiard Popkes zum 60. Geburtstag*. Edited by Edwin Brandt, Paul S. Fiddes, and Joachim Molthagen. Leipzig: Evangelische Verlagsanstalt, 1996.

Ravitzky, Aviezer. *Messianism, Zionism, and Jewish Religious Radicalism*. Chicago: University of Chicago, 1996.

Rawlinson, A. E. J. "The Kingdom of God in the Apostolic Age." *Theology* 14 (1927): 262–66.

———. *The New Testament Doctrine of the Christ*. London: Green, 1926.

Reed, Graham. *The Psychology of Anomalous Experience: A Cognitive Approach*. Rev. ed. Buffalo, NY: Prometheus Books, 1988.

Reif, Stefan C. "Codicological Aspects of Jewish Liturgical History." *BJRL* 75 (1993): 117–31.

Reimarus, Hermann Samuel. *Reimarus: Fragments*. Edited by Charles Talbert. Philadelphia: Fortress, 1970.

Reinbold, Wolfgang. *Der älteste Bericht über den Tod Jesu: Literarische Analyse und historische Kritik der Passionsdarstellungen der Evangelien*. BZNW 69. Berlin: de Gruyter, 1994.

———. *Der Prozess Jesu*. BTSc 28. Göttingen: Vandenhoeck & Ruprecht, 2006.

Reinhartz, Adele. "Rabbinic Perceptions of Simeon Bar Kosiba." *JSJ* 20 (1989): 171–94.

Reisberg, Daniel, and Friderike Heuer. "Remembering the Details of Emotional Events." Pages 162–90 in *Affect and Accuracy in Recall: Studies of "Flashbulb" Memories*. Edited by Eugene Winograd and Ulric Neisser. Cambridge: Cambridge University Press, 1992.

Reiser, Marius. *Jesus and Judgment: The Eschatological Proclamation in Its Jewish Context*. Translated by Linda M. Maloney. Minneapolis: Fortress, 1997.

Renkema, Johan. *Lamentations*. Translated by Brian Doyle. HCOT. Leuven: Peeters, 1998.

Resch, Alfred. *Agrapha: Aussercanonische Evangelienfragmente*. TU 5/4. Leipzig: J. C. Hinrichs, 1889.

Reuss, Joseph, ed. *Matthäus-Kommentare aus der grieschen Kirche*. TU 61. Berlin: Akademie-Verlag, 1957.

Revell, E. J. *The Designation of the Individual: Expression Usage in Biblical Narrative*. CBET 14. Kampen: Kok Pharos, 1996.

Reyna, Valerie F., and C. J. Brainerd. "Fuzzy-Trace Theory: An Interim Synthesis." *Learning and Individual Differences* 7 (1995): 1–75.

Reyna, Valerie F., and Farrell Lloyd. "Theories of False Memory in Children and Adults." *Learning and Individual Differences* 9 (1997): 95–123.

Reynolds, Benjamin E. *The Apocalyptic Son of Man in the Gospel of John*. WUNT 2/249. Tübingen: Mohr Siebeck, 2008.

———. "The 'One Like a Son of Man' according to the Old Greek of Daniel 7,13–14." *Bib* 89 (2008): 70–80.

Rhodes, Matthew G., and Larry L. Jacoby. "Toward Analyzing Cognitive Illusions: Past, Present, and Future." Pages 379–93 in *The Foundations of Remembering: Essays in Honor of Henry L. Roediger III*. Edited by James S. Nairne. New York: Psychology Press, 2007.

Richardson, Christopher. "The Passion: Re-considering Hebrews 5.7–8." Pages 51–67 in *A Cloud of Witnesses: The Theology of Hebrews in Its Ancient Contexts*. Edited by Richard Bauckham et al. London: T & T Clark, 2008.

Riches, John. *Jesus and the Transformation of Judaism*. New York: Seabury, 1982.

Riesner, Rainer. "Back to the Historical Jesus through Paul and His School (The Ransom Logion—Mark 10.45; Matthew 20.28)." *JSHJ* 1 (2003): 171–99.

———. *Jesus als Lehrer: Eine Untersuchung zum Ursprung der Evangelien-Überlieferung*. WUNT 2/7. Tübingen: Mohr Siebeck, 1981.

Ring, Kenneth. *Life at Death: A Scientific Investigation of the Near-Death Experience*. New York: Coward, McCann & Geoghegan, 1980.

Riniker, Christian. *Die Gerichtsverkündigung Jesu*. EH 23/653. Bern: Peter Lang, 1999.

Rivkin, Ellis. *What Crucified Jesus?* Nashville: Abingdon, 1984.

Robbins, C. Michael. *The Testing of Jesus in Q*. SBL 108. New York: Peter Lang, 2007.

Roberts, Colin H. "The Kingdom of Heaven (Lk. XVII.21)." *HTR* 41 (1948): 1–8.

Robertson, Archibald, and Alfred Plummer. *A Critical and Exegetical Commentary on the First Epistle of St Paul to the Corinthians*. ICC. Edinburgh: T & T Clark, 1914.

Robinson, James M. "Building Blocks in the Social History of Q." Pages 87–112 in *Reimagining Christian Origins: A Colloquium Honoring Burton L. Mack*. Edited by Elizabeth A. Castelli and Hal Taussig. Valley Forge, PA: Trinity Press International, 1996.

———. "The Critical Edition of Q and the Study of Jesus." Pages 27–52 in *The Sayings Source Q and the Historical Jesus*. Edited by A. Lindemann. BETL 158. Leuven: Leuven University Press, 2001.

———. "Foreword: A Down-to-Earth Jesus." Pages xiii–xviii in *Jesus and His World: An Archaeological and Cultural Dictionary*. By John J. Rousseau and Rami Arav. Minneapolis: Fortress, 1995.

———. "Galilean Upstarts: A Sot's Cynical Disciples?" Pages 223–49 in *Sayings of Jesus: Canonical and Non-Canonical; Essays in Honour of Tjitze Baarda*. Edited by William L. Petersen, Johan S. Vos, and Henk J. de Jonge. NovTSup 89. Leiden: Brill, 1997.

———. *The Gospel of Jesus: In Search of the Original Good News*. San Francisco: HarperSanFrancisco, 2005.

———. "Jesus' Theology in the Sayings Source Q." Pages 25–43 in *Early Christian Voices in Texts, Traditions, and Symbols: Essays in Honor of François Bovon*. Edited by David H. Warren, Ann Graham Brock, and David W. Pao. BIS 66. Boston: Brill, 2003.

———. "Kerygma and History in the New Testament." Pages 20–70 in *Trajectories through Early Christianity*. By James M. Robinson and Helmut Koester. Philadelphia: Fortress, 1971.

———. "The Q Trajectory: Between John and Matthew via Jesus." Pages 173–94 in *The Future of Early Christianity: Essays in Honor of Helmut Koester*. Edited by Birger A. Pearson. Minneapolis: Fortress, 1991.

———. "Theological Autobiography." Pages 117–50 in *The Craft of Religious Studies*. Edited by Jon R. Stone. New York: Palgrave, 2000.

Robinson, James M., Paul Hoffmann, and John S. Kloppenborg, eds. *The Critical Edition of Q: Synopsis*. Hermeneia. Minneapolis: Fortress; Leuven: Peeters, 2000.

Robinson, John A. "Perspective, Meaning, and Remembering." Pages 199–217 in *Remembering Our Past: Studies in Autobiographical Memory*. Edited by David C. Rubin. Cambridge: Cambridge University Press, 1996.

Robinson, John A. T. "Elijah, John and Jesus: An Essay in Detection." Pages 28–52 in *Twelve New Testament Studies*. SBT 34. London: SCM Press, 1962.

———. *Jesus and His Coming*. 2nd ed. Philadelphia: Westminster, 1979.

———. "The New Look on the Fourth Gospel." Pages 94–106 in *Twelve New Testament Studies*. SBT 34. London: SCM Press, 1962.

————. *The Priority of John*. Edited by J. F. Coakley. London: SCM Press, 1985.

Robinson, S. E. "Apocalypticism in the Time of Hillel and Jesus." Pages 121–36 in *Hillel and Jesus: Comparisons of Two Major Religious Leaders*. Edited by James H. Charlesworth and Loren L. Johns. Minneapolis: Fortress, 1997.

Rochford, E. Burke, Jr. "The Sociology of New Religious Movements." Pages 267–69 in *American Sociology of Religion: Histories*. Edited by Anthony J. Blasi. RSO 13. Leiden: Brill, 2007.

Rodríguez, Rafael. "Authenticating Criteria: The Use and Misuse of a Critical Method." *JSHJ* 7 (2009): 152–67.

————. "Structuring Early Christian Memory: Jesus in Tradition, Performance, and Text." PhD diss., University of Sheffield, 2007.

Roediger, Henry L., III, and Kathleen B. McDermott. "Creating False Memories: Remembering Words Not Presented in Lists." *Journal of Experimental Psychology: Learning, Memory, and Cognition* 21 (1995): 803–14.

————. "Distortions of Memory." Pages 149–63 in *The Oxford Handbook of Memory*. Edited by Endel Tulving and Fergus I. M. Craik. Oxford: Oxford University Press, 2000.

Roediger, Henry L., III, Michelle L. Meade, and Erik T. Bergman. "Social Contagion of Memory." *Psychonomic Bulletin and Review* 8, no. 2 (2001): 365–71.

Roetzel, Calvin J. *Paul: The Man and the Myth*. Minneapolis: Fortress, 1999.

Rohrbaugh, Richard L. *The New Testament in Cross-Cultural Perspective*. Eugene, OR: Cascade Books, 2007.

Rollmann, H., and W. Zager. "Unveröffentliche Briefe William Wredes zur Problematisierung des messianischen Selbstbewußtseins Jesu." *ZNTh/JHMT* 8 (2001): 274–322.

Roose, Hanna. *Eschatologische Mitherrschaft: Entwicklungslinien einer urchristlichen Erwartung*. NTOA/SUNT 54. Göttingen: Vandenhoeck & Ruprecht; Fribourg: Academic Press, 2004.

Rordorf, Willy. "Does the Didache Contain Jesus Tradition Independently of the Synoptic Gospels?" Pages 394–423 in *Jesus and the Oral Gospel Tradition*. Edited by Henry Wansbrough. JSNTSup 64. Sheffield: JSOT Press, 1991.

Rose, Steven. *The Making of Memory: From Molecules to Mind*. New York: Doubleday, 1992.

Rosenfield, Israel. *The Invention of Memory*. New York: Basic Books, 1988.

Rosenthal, Joel T. "Bede's Use of Miracles in 'The Ecclesiastical History.'" *Traditio* 31 (1975): 328–35.

Ross, Michael. "Relation of Implicit Theories to the Construction of Personal Histories." *Psychological Review* 96 (1989): 341–57.

Ross, Michael, and Roger Buehler. "Creative Remembering." Pages 205–35 in *The Remembering Self: Construction and Accuracy in the Self-Narrative*. Edited by Ulric Neisser and Robyn Fivush. Cambridge: Cambridge University Press, 1994.

Rothschild, Clare K. *Baptist Traditions and Q*. WUNT 190. Tübingen: Mohr Siebeck, 2005.

————. *Luke-Acts and the Rhetoric of History: An Investigation of Early Christian Historiography*. WUNT 2/175. Tübingen: Mohr Siebeck, 2004.

Rowe, C. Kavin. "Acts 2:36 and the Continuity of Lukan Christology." *NTS* 53 (2007): 37–56.

Rowe, Robert D. *God's Kingdom and God's Son: The Background to Mark's Christology from Concepts of Kingship in the Psalms*. AGJU 50. Leiden: Brill, 2002.

Rowland, Christopher. *Christian Origins: An Account of the Setting and Character of the Most Important Messianic Sect of Judaism*. London: SPCK, 1989.

Rubin, David C. Introduction to *Remembering Our Past: Studies in Autobiographical Memory*. Edited by David C. Rubin. Cambridge: Cambridge University Press, 1996.

————. *Memory in Oral Traditions: The Cognitive Psychology of Epic, Ballads, and Counting-Out Rhymes*. New York: Oxford University Press, 1995.

Rubin, David C., and Marc Kozin. "Vivid Memories." *Cognition* 16 (1984): 81–95.

Rubin, David C., Tamara A. Rahhal, and Leonard W. Poon. "Things Learned in Early Adulthood Are Remembered Best." *Memory and Cognition* 26 (1998): 3–19.

Rüger, Hans Peter. "'Mit welchem Maß ihr meßt, wird euch gemessen werden.'" *ZNW* 60 (1969): 174–82.

Russell, Bertrand. *The Problems of Philosophy.* Oxford: Oxford University Press, 1959.

Rynearson, Edward K. *Retelling Violent Death.* Philadelphia: Brunner-Routledge, 2001.

Sabourin, Leopold. *The Gospel according to St. Matthew.* 2 vols in 1. Bombay: St. Paul Publications, 1982.

Sachs, J. D. S. "Recognition Memory for Syntactic and Semantic Aspects of Connected Discourse." *Perception and Psychophysics* 2 (1967): 437–42.

Saiedi, Nader. *Gate of the Heart: Understanding the Writings of the Báb.* Waterloo, ON: Wilfrid Laurier University Press, 2008.

Sanday, W. *Outlines of the Life of Christ.* 2nd ed. Edinburgh: T & T Clark, 1906.

Sanders, E. P. *The Historical Figure of Jesus.* London: Penguin, 1993.

———. *Jesus and Judaism.* Philadelphia: Fortress, 1985.

———. "Jesus: His Religious Type." *Reflections* 87 (1992): 4–12.

———. *Judaism: Practice and Belief, 63 BCE–66 CE.* London: SCM Press; Philadelphia: Trinity Press International, 1992.

———. "Paul." Pages 112–29 in *Early Christian Thought in Its Jewish Context.* Edited by John Barclay and J. P. Sweet. Cambridge: Cambridge University Press, 1996.

Sanders, E. P., and Margaret Davies. *Studying the Synoptic Gospels.* London: SCM Press; Philadelphia: Trinity Press International, 1989.

Sanders, Jack T. *Charisma, Converts, Competitors: Societal and Sociological Factors in the Success of Early Christianity.* London: SCM Press, 2000.

———. "The Criterion of Coherence and the Randomness of Charisma: Poring through

Some Aporias in the Jesus Tradition." *NTS* 44 (1998): 1–25.

Sanders, James A. "From Isaiah 61 to Luke 4." Pages 46–69 in *Luke and Scripture: The Function of Sacred Traditions in Luke-Acts.* By Craig A. Evans and James A. Sanders. Minneapolis: Fortress, 1993.

Sandnes, Karl Olav. "*Imitatio Homeri?* An Appraisal of Dennis R. MacDonald's 'Mimesis Criticism.'" *JBL* 124 (2005): 715–32.

———. *Paul—One of the Prophets? A Contribution to the Apostle's Self-Understanding.* WUNT 2/43. Tübingen: Mohr Siebeck, 1991.

Sandt, Huub van de, and David Flusser. *The Didache: Its Jewish Sources and Its Place in Early Judaism and Christianity.* CRINT 3/5. Assen: Royal Van Gorcum; Minneapolis: Fortress, 2002.

Sänger, Dieter. "'Auf Betreiben der Vornehmsten unseres Volkes' (Iosephus ant. Iud. XVIII 64): Zur Frage einer jüdische Beteiligung an der Kreuzigung Jesus." Pages 1–25 in *Das Urchristentum in seiner literarischen Geschichte: Festschrift für Jürgen Becker zum 65. Geburtstag.* Edited by Ulrich Mell and Ulrich B. Müller. BZNW 100. Berlin: de Gruyter, 1999.

Sauer, J. "Traditionsgeschichtliche Erwägungen zu den synoptischen und paulinischen Aussagen über Feindesliebe und Wiedervergeltungsverzicht." *ZNW* 76 (1985): 1–28.

Schacter, Daniel L. "Memory Distortion: History and Current Status." Pages 1–43 in *Memory Distortion: How Minds, Brains, and Societies Reconstruct the Past.* Edited by Daniel L. Schacter. Cambridge, MA: Harvard University Press, 1995.

———. *The Seven Sins of Memory: How the Mind Forgets and Remembers.* Boston: Houghton Mifflin, 2001.

Schacter, Daniel L., and Donna Rose Addis. "Constructive Memory: The Ghosts of Past and Future." *Nature* 445 (2007): 27.

Schacter, Daniel L., David A. Gallo, and Elizabeth A. Kensinger. "The Cognitive Neuroscience of Implicit and False Memories: Perspectives on Processing Specificity." Pages

353–77 in *The Foundations of Remembering: Essays in Honor of Henry L. Roediger III.* Edited by James S. Nairne. New York: Psychology Press, 2007.

Schade, Hans-Heinrich. *Apokalyptische Christologie bei Paulus: Studien zum Zusammenhang von Christologie und Eschatologie in den Paulusbriefen.* GTA 18. Göttingen: Vandenhoeck & Ruprecht, 1981.

Schäfer, Peter. "Bar Kokhba and the Rabbis." Pages 1–22 in *The Bar Kokhba War Reconsidered: New Perspectives on the Second Jewish Revolt against Rome.* Edited by Peter Schäfer. TSAJ 100. Tübingen: Mohr Siebeck, 2003.

———. *The History of the Jews in the Greco-Roman World.* London: Routledge, 2003.

Schechter, Solomon. *Aspects of Rabbinic Theology.* New York: Schocken Books, 1961.

Schenk, Wolfgang. "Sekundäre jesuanisierungen von primären Paulus-Aussagen bei Markus." Pages 877–904 in vol. 2 of *The Four Gospels, 1992: Festschrift Frans Neirynck.* Edited by F. Van Segbroeck et al. 3 vols. BETL 100. Leuven: Leuven University Press, 1992.

Schenker, Adrian. *Das Neue am neuen Bund und das Alte am alten: Jer 31 in der hebräischen und griechischen Bibel, von der Textgeschichte zu Theologie, Synagoge und Kirche.* FRLANT 212. Göttingen: Vandenhoeck & Ruprecht, 2006.

Schlatter, Adolf. *Der Evangelist Matthäus: Seine Sprache, seine Ziel, seine Selbständigkeit.* Stuttgart: Calwer, 1948.

Schleritt, Frank. *Der vorjohanneische Passionsbericht: Eine historisch-kritische und theologische Untersuchung zu Joh 2,13–22; 11,47–14,31 und 18,1–20,29.* BZNW 154. Berlin: de Gruyter, 2007.

Schlosser, Jacques. "La composition du document Q." Pages 123–48 in *La source des paroles de Jésus (Q): Aux origines du christianisme.* Edited by Andreas Dettwiler and Daniel Marguerat. Paris: Labor et Fides, 2008.

———. *Le Dieu de Jésus: Étude exégétique.* LD 129. Paris: Cerf, 1987.

———. *Le règne de Dieu dans les dits de Jésus.* 2 vols. EB. Paris: Gabalda, 1980.

———. "Q et la christologie implicite." Pages 289–316 in *The Sayings Source Q and the Historical Jesus.* Edited by A. Lindemann. BETL 158. Leuven: Leuven University Press, 2001.

Schlueter, Carol J. *Filling Up the Measure: Polemical Hyperbole in 1 Thessalonians 2.14–16.* JSNTSup 98. Sheffield: JSOT Press, 1994.

Schmeller, Thomas. "Das Reich Gottes im Gleichnis." *TLZ* 119 (1994): 599–608.

Schmidt, Daryl. "1 Thess 2:13–16: Linguistic Evidence for an Interpolation." *JBL* 102 (1993): 269–79.

Schmidt, Nathaniel. *The Prophet of Nazareth.* New York: Macmillan, 1905.

Schmithals, Walter. "Gibt es Kriterien für die Bestimmung echter Jesusworte?" *ZNT* 1 (1998): 59–64.

———. "Jesus, Apocalypticism, and the Origins of Christianity." Pages 1–20 in *The Theology of the First Christians.* Louisville: Westminster John Knox, 1997.

———. *The Office of Apostle in the Early Church.* Translated by John E. Steely. Nashville: Abingdon, 1969.

Schmitt, J. "L'oracle d'Is., LXI, 1 SS. et sa relecture par Jésus." *RSR* 54 (1980): 97–108.

Schmolck, H., E. A. Buffalo, and L. R. Squire. "Memory Distortions Develop over Time: Recollections of the O. J. Simpson Trial Verdict after 15 and 32 Months." *Psychological Science* 11 (2000): 39–45.

Schnackenburg, Rudolf. *Der Brief an die Epheser.* EKKNT 10. Zürich: Benziger; Neukirchen-Vluyn: Neukirchener Verlag, 1982.

———. "Der eschatologische Abschnitt Lk 17,20–37." Pages 213–34 in *Mélanges bibliques: En homage au R. P. Béda Rigaux.* Edited by Albert Descamps and André de Halleux. Gembloux: Duculot, 1970.

———. *God's Rule and Kingdom.* Translated by John Murray. 2nd ed. London: Burns & Oates; New York: Herder & Herder, 1968.

————. *The Gospel of Matthew*. Translated by Robert R. Barr. Grand Rapids: Eerdmans, 2002.

Schneider, Gerhard. "Imitatio Dei als Motiv der 'Ethik Jesu.'" Pages 155–67 in *Jesusüberlieferung und Christologie: Neutestamentliche Aufsätze, 1970–1990*. NovTSup 67. Leiden: Brill, 1992.

Schneider, Johannes. *Die Passionsmystik des Paulus: Ihr Wesen, ihr Hintergrund und ihre Nachwirkungen*. UNT 15. Leipzig: J. C. Hinrichs, 1929.

Schnider, Franz. *Jesus der Prophet*. OBO 2. Fribourg: Universitätsverlag; Göttingen: Vandenhoeck & Ruprecht, 1973.

Schniewind, Julius. "Die Archonten dieses Äons, 1 Kor. 2,6–8." Pages 104–9 in *Nachgelassene Reden und Aufsätze*. ThBT 1. Berlin: Töpelmann, 1952.

Schoeps, Hans Joachim. "Von der imitation dei zur Nachfolge Christi." Pages 286–301 in *Aus frühchristlicher Zeit: Religionsgeschichtliche Untersuchungen*. Tübingen: Mohr Siebeck, 1950.

Scholem, Gershom. *The Messianic Idea in Judaism and Other Essays on Jewish Spirituality*. New York: Schocken Books, 1971.

————. *Sabbatai Sevi: The Mystical Messiah*. Princeton, NJ: Princeton University Press, 1973.

Schrage, Wolfgang. "Leid, Kreuz und Eschaton: Die Peristasen Katologe als Merkmale paulinischer Theologia Crucis und Eschatologie." *EvT* 34 (1974): 141–75.

Schrauf, Robert W. "¡Costalero Quiero Ser! Autobiographical Memory and the Oral Life Story of a Holy Week Brother in Southern Spain." *Ethos* 25 (1997): 428–53.

Schreiber, Johannes. *Theologie des Vertrauens: Eine redaktionsgeschichtliche Untersuchung des Markusevangeliums*. Hamburg: Furche, 1967.

Schreiber, Stefan. *Gesalbter und König: Titel und Konzeptionen der königlichen Gesalbtenerwartung in frühjüdischen und urchristlichen Schriften*. BZNW 105. Berlin: de Gruyter, 2000.

————. "Henoch als Menschensohn: Zur problematischen Schlußidentifikation in den Bilderreden des äthiopischen Henochbuches (äthHen 71,14)." *ZNW* 91 (2000): 1–17.

Schröter, Jens. "Die Frage nach dem historischen Jesus und der Charakter historischer Erkenntnis." Pages 207–54 in *The Sayings Source Q and the Historical Jesus*. Edited by A. Lindemann. BETL 158. Leuven: Leuven University Press, 2001.

————. "The Historical Jesus and the Sayings Tradition: Comments on Current Research." *Neot* 30 (1996): 151–68.

————. "The Son of Man as the Representative of God's Kingdom: On the Interpretation of Jesus in Mark and Q." Pages 34–68 in *Jesus, Mark and Q: The Teaching of Jesus and Its Earliest Records*. Edited by Michael Labahn and Andreas Schmidt. JSNTSup 214. Sheffield: Sheffield Academic Press, 2001.

Schudson, Michael. "Dynamics of Distortion in Collective Memory." Pages 346–64 in *Memory Distortion: How Minds, Brains, and Societies Reconstruct the Past*. Edited by Daniel L. Schacter. Cambridge, MA: Harvard University Press, 1995.

————. "The Present in the Past and the Past in the Present." *Communication* 11 (1989): 105–13.

Schulz, Siegfried. *Q: Die Spruchquelle der Evangelisten*. Zürich: Theologischer Verlag, 1972.

Schürmann, Heinz. *Das Lukasevangelium: Erster Teil: Kommentar zu Kap. 1,1–9,50*. HTKNT 3/1. Freiburg: Herder, 1969.

————. *Das Lukasevangelium: Zweiter Teil, Erste Folge: Kommentar zu Kap. 9,51–11,54*. HTKNT 3/2. Freiburg: Herder, 1994.

————. "Der Jüngerkreis Jesu als Zeichen für Israel (und als Urbild des kirchlichen Rätestandes)." Pages 45–60 in *Ursprung und Gestalt: Erörterungen und Besinnungen zum Neuen Testament*. KBANT. Düsseldorf: Patmos-Verlag, 1970.

————. "Die vorösterlichen Anfänge der Logientradition: Versuch eines formgeschichtlichen Zugangs zum Leben Jesu." Pages 342–70 in *Der historische Jesus und der kerygmatische Christus*. Edited by H. Ristow and K. Matthiae. Berlin: Evangelische Verlagsanstalt, 1962.

———. "Wie hat Jesus seinen Tod bestanden und verstanden? Eine methodenkritische Besinnung." Pages 325–63 in *Orientierung an Jesus: Zur Theologie der Synoptiker; Für Josef Schmid.* Edited by Paul Hoffmann with Norbert Brox and Wilhelm Pesch. Freiburg: Herder, 1973.

Schüssler Fiorenza, Elisabeth. *Jesus and the Politics of Interpretation.* New York: Continuum, 2000.

Schwartz, Barry. *Abraham Lincoln and the Forge of National Memory.* Chicago: University of Chicago Press, 2000.

———. "Social Change and Collective Memory: The Democratization of George Washington." *American Sociological Review* 56 (1991): 221–36.

Schwartz, Bennett L., et al. "Event Memory and Misinformation Effects in a Gorilla." *Animal Cognition* 7 (2004): 93–100.

Schwartz, Daniel R. "'Judean' or 'Jew'? How Should We Translate *Ioudaios* in Josephus?" Pages 3–28 in *Jewish Identity in the Greco-Roman World = Jüdische Identität in der griechisch-römischen Welt.* Edited by Jörg Frey, Daniel R. Schwartz, and Stephanie Gripentrog. AJEC/AGJU 71. Leiden: Brill, 2007.

Schwartz, Seth. *Imperialism and Jewish Society, 200 B.C.E. to 640 C.E.* Princeton, NJ: Princeton University Press, 2001.

Schwarz, Hillel. "Millenarianism: An Overview." Pages 6028–38 in vol. 9 of *Encyclopedia of Religion.* Edited by Lindsay Jones. 10 vols. Detroit: Macmillan Reference, 2005.

Schweitzer, Albert. *The Mystery of the Kingdom of God: The Secret of Jesus' Messiahship and Passion.* New York: Macmillan, 1950.

———. *The Psychiatric Study of Jesus: Exposition and Criticism.* Boston: Beacon, 1948.

———. *The Quest of the Historical Jesus.* Minneapolis: Fortress, 2001.

Schweitzer, Ursula. *Das Wesen des Ka im Diesseits und Jenseits der alten Ägypter.* Glückstadt: J. J. Augustin, 1956.

Schweizer, Eduard. *The Good News according to Mark.* Translated by Donald H. Madvig. Atlanta: John Knox, 1976.

———. *Jesus, the Parable of God. What Do We Really Know about Jesus?* Allison Park, PA: Pickwick, 1994.

———. Review of Klaus Berger, *Die Auferstehung des Propheten und die Erhöhung des Menschensohnes. TLZ* 103 (1978): 874–78.

Schwemer, Anna Maria. "Gott als König und seine Königsherrschaft in den Sabbatliedern aus Qumran." Pages 45–118 in *Königsherrschaft Gottes und himmlischer Kult im Judentum, Urchristentum und in der hellenistischen Welt.* Edited by Martin Hengel and Anna Maria Schwemer. WUNT 2/55. Tübingen: Mohr Siebeck, 1991.

Scott, B. B. "How Did We Get Here?" Pages 47–64 in *Jesus Reconsidered: Scholarship in the Public Eye.* Edited by B. B. Scott. Santa Rosa, CA: Polebridge, 2007.

Scott, E. F. "Life." Pages 30–32 in vol. 2 of *A Dictionary of Christ and the Gospels.* Edited by James Hastings. 2 vols. Edinburgh: T & T Clark, 1908.

———. "The Place of Apocalyptical Conceptions in the Mind of Jesus." *JBL* 41 (1922): 137–42.

Scott, James M. *On Earth as in Heaven: The Restoration of Sacred Time and Sacred Space in the Book of Jubilees.* JSJSup 91. Leiden: Brill, 2005.

Scott, R. B. Y. "A Kingdom of Priests (Exodus xix 6)." *OtSt* 8 (1950): 213–19.

Scott, Thomas. *The Holy Bible: Containing the Old and New Testaments, according to the Authorized Version, with Explanatory Notes, Practical Observations, and Copious Marginal References.* 6 vols. Boston: Crocker & Brewster, 1844.

Sedulius Scottus. *Kommentar zum Evangelium nach Matthäus.* Vol. 2. Edited by Bengt Löfstedt. Freiburg: Herder, 1991.

Seeley, David. "Jesus' Temple Act." *CBQ* 55 (1993): 263–83.

Segal, Alan F. "Jesus and First-Century Judaism." Pages 59–65 in *Jesus at 2000.* Edited by Marcus J. Borg. Boulder, CO: Westview, 1997.

Seidel, Anna K. "The Image of the Perfect Ruler in Early Taoist Messianism: Lao-Tzu and Li Hung." *HR* 9 (1969–1970): 216–47.

Seitz, O. J. F. "Love Your Enemies: The Historical Setting of Matthew v.43f.; Luke vi.27f." *NTS* 16 (1969): 39–54.

Sellew, Philip. "The Gospel of Thomas: Prospects for Future Research." Pages 327–46 in *The Nag Hammadi Library after Fifty Years: Proceedings of the 1995 Society of Biblical Literature Commemoration.* Edited by John D. Turner and Anne McGuire. NHMS 44. Leiden: Brill, 1997.

Sellin, Gerhard. *Der Brief an die Epheser.* KEK 8. Göttingen: Vandenhoeck & Ruprecht, 2008.

Senior, Donald. *The Passion according to Matthew: A Redactional Study.* BETL 29. Leuven: Leuven University Press, 1975.

Seper, F. H. "ΚΑΙ ΤΙ ΘΕΛΩ ΕΙ ΗΔΗ ΑΝΗΦΘΗ (Lc 12,49b)." *VD* 36 (1958): 147–53.

Sevrin, Jean-Marie. "Thomas, Q et le Jésus de l'histoire." Pages 461–76 in *The Sayings Source Q and the Historical Jesus.* Edited by A. Lindemann. BETL 158. Leuven: Leuven University Press, 2001.

Shaffir, William. "Interpreting Adversity: Dynamics of a Commitment in a Messianic Redemption Campaign." *JJSoc* 36 (1994): 43–53.

———. "Jewish Messianism Lubavitch-Style: An Interim Report." *JJSoc* 35 (1993): 115–28.

———. "When Prophecy Is Not Validated: Explaining the Unexpected in a Messianic Campaign." *JJSoc* 37 (1995): 119–36.

Sharman, Stefanie J., Maryanne Garry, and Carl J. Beuke. "Imagination or Exposure Causes Imagination Inflation." *American Journal of Psychology* 117 (2004): 157–68.

Sharot, Stephen. *Messianism, Mysticism, and Magic: A Sociological Analysis of Jewish Religious Movements.* Chapel Hill: University of North Carolina Press, 1982.

Shils, Edward. *Tradition.* London: Faber, 1981.

Shupe, Anson D., Jr. *Six Perspectives on New Religions: A Case Study Approach.* New York: Edwin Mellen, 1981.

Sider, John W. "Rediscovering the Parables: The Logic of the Jeremias Tradition." *JBL* 102 (1983): 61–83.

Silver, Abba Hillel. *A History of Messianic Speculation in Israel from the First through the Seventeenth Centuries.* New York: Macmillan, 1927.

Sim, David C. *Apocalyptic Eschatology in the Gospel of Matthew.* SNTSMS 88. Cambridge: Cambridge University Press, 1996.

Simon, Ernst. "The Neighbor (*Re'a*) Whom We Shall Love." Pages 29–56 in *Modern Jewish Ethics: Theory and Practice.* Edited by Marvin Fox. Columbus: Ohio State University Press, 1975.

Simons, Daniel J., and Christopher F. Chabris. "Gorillas in Our Midst: Sustained Inattentional Blindness for Dynamic Events." *Perception* 28 (1999): 1059–74.

Singelenberg, Richard. "The '1975' Prophecy and Its Impact among Dutch Jehovah's Witnesses." *Sociological Analysis* 50 (1989): 23–40.

Sjöberg, Erik. *Die Menschensohn im äthiopischen Henochbuch.* Lund: Gleerup, 1946.

Small, Jocelyn P. *Wax Tablets of the Mind: Cognitive Studies of Memory and Literacy in Classical Antiquity.* New York: Routledge, 1997.

Smit, Peter-Ben. *Fellowship and Food in the Kingdom: Eschatological Meals and Scenes of Utopian Abundance in the New Testament.* WUNT 2/234. Tübingen: Mohr Siebeck, 2008.

Smith, Daniel A. *The Post-Mortem Vindication of Jesus in the Sayings Gospel Q.* LNTS 338. London: T & T Clark, 2006.

Smith, D. Moody. *John among the Gospels.* 2nd ed. Columbia: University of South Carolina Press, 2001.

Smith, Jonathan Z. "The Prayer of Joseph." Pages 253–94 in *Religions in Antiquity: Essays in Memory of Erwin Randsell Goodenough.* Edited by Jacob Neusner. SHR 14. Leiden: Brill, 1968.

Smith, Morton. "Ascent to the Heavens and Deification in 4QMᵃ." Pages 181–88 in *Archaeology and History in the Dead Sea Scrolls: The New York University Conference in Memory of Yigael Yadin*. Edited by Lawrence H. Schiffman. JSPSup 8. Sheffield: JSOT Press, 1990.

———. "Two Ascended to Heaven—Jesus and the Author of 4Q491." Pages 290–301 in *Jesus and the Dead Sea Scrolls*. Edited by James H. Charlesworth. New York: Doubleday, 1992.

Smoller, Laura A. "Miracle, Memory, and Meaning in the Canonization of Vincent Ferrer, 1453–1454." *Speculum* 73 (1998): 429–54.

Snow, David A., and Richard Machalek. "On the Presumed Fragility of Unconventional Beliefs." *JSSR* 21 (1982): 15–26.

Spence, Jonathan D. *God's Chinese Son: The Taiping Heavenly Kingdom of Hong Xiuquan*. New York: W. W. Norton, 1996.

Spencer, F. A. M. *The Theory of Christ's Ethics*. London: Allen & Unwin, 1929.

Spilka, Bernard, et al. *The Psychology of Religion: An Empirical Approach*. 3rd ed. New York: Guilford, 2003.

Spong, John Shelby. *Born of a Woman: A Bishop Rethinks the Birth of Jesus*. San Francisco: HarperSanFrancisco, 1992.

———. *Liberating the Gospels: Reading the Bible with Jewish Eyes; Freeing Jesus from 2,000 Years of Misunderstanding*. San Francisco: HarperSanFrancisco, 1996.

———. *Resurrection: Myth or Reality? A Bishop's Search for the Origins of Christianity*. San Francisco: HarperSanFrancisco, 1994.

Sproston, Wendy E. "Satan in the Fourth Gospel." Pages 307–11 in *Papers on the Gospels*. Vol. 2 of *Studia Biblica 1978: Sixth International Congress on Biblical Studies*. Edited by E. A. Livingstone. JSNTSup 2. Sheffield: JSOT Press, 1980.

Sproston North, Wendy E. *The Lazarus Story within Johannine Tradition*. JSNTSup 212. Sheffield: Sheffield Academic Press, 2001.

Stancliffe, Clare. *St. Martin and His Hagiographer: History and Miracle in Sulpicius Severus*. Oxford: Clarendon, 1983.

Stanton, Graham. *The Gospels and Jesus*. 2nd ed. Oxford: Oxford University Press, 2002.

———. "Jesus of Nazareth: A Magician and a False Prophet Who Deceived God's People." Pages 164–80 in *Jesus of Nazareth: Lord and Christ; Essays on the Historical Jesus and New Testament Christology*. Edited by Joel B. Green and Max Turner. Grand Rapids: Eerdmans, 1994.

———. "Matthew as a Creative Interpreter of the Sayings of Jesus." Pages 257–72 in *The Gospel and the Gospels*. Edited by Peter Stuhlmacher. Grand Rapids: Eerdmans, 1991.

Stark, Rodney, and Roger Finke. *Acts of Faith: Explaining the Human Side of Religion*. Berkeley: University of California Press, 2000.

Stark, Rodney, and Laurence R. Iannaccone. "Why the Jehovah's Witnesses Grow So Rapidly: A Theoretical Application." *JCR* 12 (1997): 133–57.

Starr, Joshua. "Le movement messianique au début du VIIIᵉ siècle." *REJ* 102 (1937): 81–92.

Stauffer, Ethelbert. *Jesus and His Story*. Translated by Richard and Clara Wilson. New York: Alfred A. Knopf, 1970.

Stayer, James M. *Anabaptists and the Sword*. 2nd ed. Lawrence, KS: Coronado, 1876.

Steck, Odil Hannes. *Israel und das gewaltsame Geschick der Propheten: Untersuchungen zur Überlieferung des deuteronomistischen Geschichtsbildes im Alten Testament*. WMANT 23. Neukirchen-Vluyn: Neukirchener Verlag, 1967.

Stegemann, Ekkehard, and Wolfgang Stegemann. "König Israels, nicht König der Juden? Jesus als König im Johannesevangelium." Pages 41–56 in *Messias-Vorstellungen bei Juden und Christen*. Edited by Ekkehard Stegemann. Stuttgart: Kohlhammer, 1993.

Stegemann, Hartmut. "Some Remarks to *1QSa*, to *1QSb*, and to Qumran Messianism." *RevQ* 17 (1996): 479–505.

———. "The 'Teacher of Righteousness' and Jesus: Two Types of Religious Leadership in Judaism at the Turn of the Era." Pages 196–213 in *Jewish Civilization in the Hellenistic-Roman Period*. Edited by Shemaryahu Talmon. Philadelphia: Trinity Press International, 1991.

Stegman, Thomas. *The Character of Jesus: The Linchpin to Paul's Argument in 2 Corinthians*. AnBib 158. Rome: Pontifical Biblical Institute, 2005.

Steiner, Richard C. "Incomplete Circumcision in Egypt and Edom: Jeremiah (9:24–25) in the Light of Josephus and Jonckheere." *JBL* 118 (1999): 497–505.

Stephen, Michele. "Cargo Cults, Cultural Creativity, and Autonomous Imagination." *Ethos* 25 (1997): 333–58.

Sterling, Greg. "*Mors philosophi*: The Death of Jesus in Luke." *HTR* 94 (2001): 383–402.

Stern, David. "The Alphabet of Ben Sira and the Early History of Parody in Jewish Literature." Pages 423–48 in *The Idea of Biblical Interpretation: Essays in Honor of James L. Kugel*. Edited by Hindy Najman and Judith H. Newman. JSJSup 83. Leiden: Brill, 2004.

Stern, Menahem. "A. Schalit's Herod." *JJS* 11 (1960): 55–56.

Stettler, Hanna. *Die Christologie der Pastoralbriefe*. WUNT 2/105. Tübingen: Mohr Siebeck, 1998.

Steudel, Annette. "The Development of Essenic Eschatology." Pages 79–86 in *Apocalyptic Time*. Edited by Albert I. Baumgarten. SHR 86. Leiden: Brill, 2000.

———. "The Eternal Reign of the People of God—Collective Expectations in Qumran Texts (4Q246 and 1QM)." *RevQ* 17 (1996): 507–25.

———. "Die Heiligung des Gottesnamens im Vaterunser: Erwägungen zum antikjüdischen Hintergrund." Pages 242–56 in *Judaistik und neutestamentliche Wissenschaft: Standorte, Grenzen, Beziehungen*. Edited by Lutz Doering, Hans-Günther Waubke, and Florian Wilk. FRLANT 226. Göttingen: Vandenhoeck & Ruprecht, 2008.

———. "אחרית הימים" in the Texts from Qumran." *RevQ* 16 (1993): 225–46.

Stimpfle, Alois. *Blinde sehen: Die Eschatologie im traditionsgeschichtlichen Prozess des Johannes-evangeliums*. BZNW 57. Berlin: de Gruyter, 1990.

Stone, Jon R., ed. *Expecting Armageddon: Essential Readings in Failed Prophecy*. New York: Routledge, 2000.

Stone, Michael E. *Adam's Contract with Satan: The Legend of the Cheirograph of Adam*. Bloomington: Indiana University Press, 2002.

———. "Lists of Revealed Things in Apocalyptic Literature." Pages 415–52 in *Magnalia Dei: The Mighty Acts of God; Essays on the Bible and Archaeology in Memory of G. Ernest Wright*. Edited by Frank Moore Cross, Werner E. Lemke, and Patrick D. Miller Jr. Garden City, NY: Doubleday, 1976.

Straub, Werner. *Die Bildersprache des Apostels Paulus*. Tübingen: Mohr Siebeck, 1937.

Strauss, David Friedrich. *The Life of Jesus Critically Examined*. Edited by Peter C. Hodgson. Translated by George Eliot. Philadelphia: Fortress, 1972.

———. *A New Life of Jesus*. 2 vols. London: Williams & Norgate, 1865.

Strauss, Mark L. *The Davidic Messiah in Luke-Acts: The Promise and Its Fulfillment in Lukan Christology*. JSNTSup 110. Sheffield: Sheffield Academic Press, 1995.

Strecker, Georg. *Theology of the New Testament*. Translated by M. Eugene Boring. New York: de Gruyter; Louisville: Westminster John Knox, 2000.

Streeter, B. H. "Professor Burkitt and the Parables of the Kingdom." *The Interpreter* 7 (1910–1911): 241–47.

———. "Synoptic Criticism and the Eschatological Problem." Pages 425–36 in *Oxford Studies in the Synoptic Problem*. Edited by W. Sanday. Oxford: Clarendon, 1911.

Strobel, August. "Die Passa-Erwartung als urchristliches Problem in Lc 17 20f." *ZNW* 49 (1958): 157–96.

Stroker, William Dettwiller. "The Formation of Secondary Sayings of Jesus." PhD diss., Yale University, 1970.

Stuckenbruck, Loren. *1 Enoch 91–108.* CEJL. Berlin: de Gruyter, 2007.

Stuhlmacher, Peter. "Eighteen Theses on Paul's Theology of the Cross." Pages 155–68 in *Reconciliation, Law, and Righteousness: Essays in Biblical Theology.* Philadelphia: Fortress, 1986.

Stuhlmann, Rainer. *Das eschatologische Maß im Neuen Testament.* FRLANT 132. Göttingen: Vandenhoeck & Ruprecht, 1983.

Stuhlmueller, Carroll. *Creative Redemption in Deutero-Isaiah.* AnBib 43. Rome: Biblical Institute Press, 1970.

Subramanian, J. Samuel. *The Synoptic Gospels and the Psalms as Prophecy.* LNTS 351. London: T & T Clark, 2007.

Sullivan, Clayton. *Rethinking Realized Eschatology.* Macon, GA: Mercer University Press, 1988.

Sullivan, Lawrence E. *Icanchu's Drum: An Orientation to Meaning in South American Religions.* New York: Macmillan; London: Collier Macmillan, 1988.

Sundermann, Werner. "Der Paraklet in der ostmanichäischen Überlieferung." Pages 201–12 in *Manichaean Studies: Proceedings of the First International Conference on Manichaeism, August 5–9, 1987, Department of History of Religions, Lund University, Sweden.* Edited by P. Bryder. LSAAR 1. Lund: Lund Plus Ultra, 1988.

Sundkler, Bengt G. M. *Bantu Prophets in South Africa.* London: Oxford University Press, 1961.

Surprenant, Aimée M., Tamra J. Bireta, and Lisa A. Farley. "A Brief History of Memory and Aging." Pages 107–23 in *The Foundations of Remembering: Essays in Honor of Henry L. Roediger III.* Edited by James S. Nairne. New York: Psychology Press, 2007.

Swetnam, James. "The Crux at Hebrews 5,7–8." *Bib* 81 (2000): 347–61.

Tabbernee, William. "Revelation 21 and the Montanist 'New Jerusalem.'" *ABR* 37 (1989): 52–60.

Tabor, James D. "Are You the One? The Textual Dynamics of Messianic Self-Identity." Pages 179–89 in *Knowing the End from the Beginning: The Prophetic, the Apocalyptic,* and Their Relationships. Edited by Lester L. Grabbe and Robert D. Haak. London: T & T Clark International, 2003.

Takaaki, Sanada. "A Prophecy Fails: A Reappraisal of a Japanese Case." *JJRS* 6 (1979): 217–37.

Talarico, Jennifer M., and David C. Rubin. "Confidence, Not Consistency, Characterizes Flashbulb Memories." *Psychological Science* 14 (2003): 455–61.

———. "Flashbulb Memories Result from Ordinary Memory Processes and Extraordinary Event Characteristics." Pages 79–97 in *Flashbulb Memories: New Issues and New Perspectives.* Edited by Olivier Luminet and Antonietta Curci. New York: Psychology Press, 2009.

Talbert, Charles H. *Literary Patterns, Theological Themes, and the Genre of Luke-Acts.* SBLMS 20. Missoula, MT: Scholars Press, 1974.

———. "What Is Meant by the Historicity of Acts?" Pages 197–217 in *Reading Luke-Acts in Its Mediterranean Milieu.* NovTSup 107. Leiden: Brill, 2003.

Talmon, Shemaryahu, ed. *Jewish Civilization in the Hellenistic-Roman Period.* Philadelphia: Trinity Press, 1991.

Tannehill, Robert C. *Luke.* ANTC. Nashville: Abingdon, 1996.

Tardieu, Michel. *Manichaeism.* Urbana: University of Illinois Press, 2008.

Tatum, W. Barnes. "The Jewish Jesus: Apocalyptic Prophet or Subversive Sage?" *The Fourth R* 14, no. 1 (2001): 8–10.

———. *John the Baptist and Jesus: A Report of the Jesus Seminar.* Sonoma, CA: Polebridge, 1994.

Taubes, Jacob. "The Price of Messianism." *JJS* 33 (1982): 595–600.

Taylor, C. *The Teaching of the Twelve Apostles.* Cambridge: Deighton, Bell, 1886.

Taylor, Joan E. *The Immerser: John the Baptist within Second Temple Judaism.* Grand Rapids: Eerdmans, 1997.

Taylor, N. H. "Palestinian Christianity and the Caligula Crisis, Part II: The Markan Eschatological Discourse." *JSNT* 62 (1996): 13–41.

Taylor, Vincent. *The Gospel according to St. Mark: The Greek Text with Introduction, Notes, and Indexes.* 2nd ed. London: Macmillan; New York: St. Martin's Press, 1966.

———. *The Life and Ministry of Jesus.* Nashville: Abingdon, n.d.

Taylor, W. S. "Memory and the Gospel Tradition." *ThTo* 15 (1959): 470–79.

Teeple, Howard M. *The Mosaic Eschatological Prophet.* SBLMS 10. Philadelphia: Society of Biblical Literature, 1957.

Thackery, Henry St. John. *The Relation of St. Paul to Contemporary Jewish Thought.* London: Macmillan, 1900.

Theisohn, Johannes. *Der auserwählte Richter: Untersuchungen zum traditionsgeschichtlichen Ort der Menschensohngestalt der Bilderreden des Äthiopischen Henoch.* SUNT 12. Göttingen: Vandenhoeck & Ruprecht, 1974.

Theissen, Gerd. "Die Goldene Regel (Matthäus 7:12//Lukas 6:31): Über den Sitz im Leben ihrer positiven und negativen Form." *BibInt* 11 (2003): 386–99.

———. *The Gospels in Context: Social and Political History in the Synoptic Tradition.* Translated by Linda M. Maloney. Minneapolis: Fortress, 1991.

———. "Jesus—Prophet einer millenaristischen Bewegung? Sozialgeschichtliche Überlegungen zu einer sozialanthropologischen Deutung der Jesusbewegung." Pages 197–228 in *Jesus als historische Gestalt: Beiträge zur Jesusforschung.* Edited by Annette Merz. FRLANT 202. Göttingen: Vandenhoeck & Ruprecht, 2003.

———. "A Major Narrative Unit (the Passion Story) and the Jerusalem Community in the Years 40–50 C.E." Pages 166–99 in *The Gospels in Context: Social and Political History in the Synoptic Tradition.* Translated by Linda M. Maloney. Minneapolis: Fortress, 1991.

———. *Psychological Aspects of Pauline Theology.* Translated by John P. Galvin. Philadelphia: Fortress, 1987.

———. "Vom historischen Jesus zum kerygmatischen Gottessohn." *EvT* 68 (2008): 285–304.

Theissen, Gerd, and Annette Merz. "The Delay of the Parousia as a Test Case for the Criterion of Coherence." *LS* 32 (2007): 49–66.

———. *The Historical Jesus: A Comprehensive Guide.* Minneapolis: Fortress, 1998.

Theissen, Gerd, and Dagmar Winter. *The Quest for the Plausible Jesus: The Question of Criteria.* Louisville: Westminster John Knox, 2002.

Thiselton, Anthony C. *The First Epistle of the Corinthians: A Commentary on the Greek Text.* NIGTC. Grand Rapids: Eerdmans, 2000.

Tholuck, A. *Commentary on the Sermon on the Mount.* Edinburgh: T & T Clark, 1874.

Thoma, Clemens. "Die gegenwärtige und kommende Herrschaft Gottes als fundamentals jüdisches Anliegen im Zeitalter Jesu." Pages 57–77 in *Zukunft in der Gegenwart: Wegweisungen in Judentum und Christentum.* Edited by Clemens Thoma. JC 1. Bern: Herbert Lang, 1976.

Thomas, Ayanna K., and Elizabeth Loftus. "Creating Bizarre False Memories through Imagination." *Memory and Cognition* 30 (2002): 423–31.

Thomas, Christine M. *The Acts of Peter, Gospel Literature, and the Ancient Novel: Rewriting the Past.* Oxford: Oxford University Press, 2003.

Thomas, Johannes. *Der jüdische Phokylides: Formgeschichtliche Zugänge zu Pseudo-Phokylides und Vergleich mit der neutestamentlichen Paränese.* NTOA 23. Freiburg: Universitätsverlag; Vandenhoeck & Ruprecht, 1992.

Thompson, Charles P., et al. *Autobiographical Memory: Remembering What and Remembering When.* Mahwah, NJ: Lawrence Erlbaum Associates, 1996.

Thompson, Michael. *Clothed with Christ: The Example and Teaching of Jesus in Romans 12.1–15.13.* JSNTSup 59. Sheffield: JSOT Press, 1991.

Thrall, Margaret. *The Second Epistle to the Corinthians.* 2 vols. ICC. Edinburgh: T & T Clark, 1994–2000.

Tiller, Patrick A. *A Commentary on the Animal Apocalypse of 1 Enoch*. SBLEJL 4. Atlanta: Scholars Press, 1993.

Tindal, Matthew. *Christianity as Old as the Creation; or, The Gospel, a Republication of the Religion of Nature*. London, 1730.

Tindall, William York. *John Bunyan: Mechanick Preacher*. New York: Columbia University Press, 1934.

Tödt, H. E. *The Son of Man in the Synoptic Tradition*. NTL. London: SCM Press, 1965.

Tollestrup, Patricia A., John W. Turtle, and John C. Yuille. "Actual Victims and Witnesses to Robbery and Fraud: An Archival Analysis." Pages 144–59 in *Adult Eyewitness Testimony: Current Trends and Developments*. Edited by David Frank Ross, J. Don Read, and Michael P. Toglia. Cambridge: Cambridge University Press, 1994.

Tomasino, Anthony J. "Oracles of Insurrection: The Prophetic Catalyst of the Great Revolt." *JJS* 59 (2008): 86–111.

Topel, John. "The Tarnished Golden Rule (Luke 6:31): The Inescapable Radicalness of Christian Ethics." *TS* 59 (1998): 475–85.

Torrey, Charles C. *The Apocryphal Literature: A Brief Introduction*. New Haven: Yale University Press, 1945.

———. "The Aramaic Texts." Pages 261–76 in *The Excavations at Dura-Europos: Final Report VIII, Part 1: The Synagogue*. By Carl H. Kraeling. New Haven: Yale University Press, 1956.

Trapp, John. *A Commentary or Exposition upon All the Books of the New Testament*. Edited by W. Webster. London: Richard D. Dickinson, 1865.

Trilling, Wolfgang. "Zur Entstehung des Zwölferkreises: Eine geschichtskritische Überlegung." Pages 185–208 in *Studien zur Jesusüberlieferung*. SBA 1. Stuttgart: Katholisches Bibelwerk, 1988.

Trocmé, Étienne. *The Childhood of Christianity*. Translated by John Bowden. London: SCM Press, 1997.

———. *The Formation of the Gospel according to Mark*. Translated by Pamela Gaughan. Philadelphia: Westminster, 1975.

Trumbower, Jeffrey A. "The Historical Jesus and the Speech of Gamaliel (Acts 5.35–9)." *NTS* 39 (1993): 500–517.

———. "The Role of Malachi in the Career of John the Baptist." Pages 28–41 in *The Gospels and the Scriptures of Israel*. Edited by Craig A. Evans and W. Richard Stegner. JSNTSup 104. Sheffield: Sheffield Academic Press, 1994.

Tuckett, Christopher M. "The *Didache* and the Writings That Later Formed the New Testament." Pages 83–128 in *The Reception of the New Testament in the Apostolic Fathers*. Edited by Andrew F. Gregory and Christopher M. Tuckett. Oxford: Oxford University Press, 2005.

———. "Isaiah in Q." Pages 51–61 in *Isaiah in the New Testament*. Edited by Steve Moyise and Maarten J. J. Menken. London: T & T Clark, 2005.

———. "Luke 4:16–30 and Q." Pages 343–54 in *Logia: Les Paroles de Jésus—The Sayings of Jesus*. Edited by Joël Delobel. BETL 59. Leuven: Leuven University Press, 1982.

———. "Q and the Historical Jesus." Pages 215–41 in *Der historische Jesus: Tendenzen und Perspektiven der gegenwärtigen Forschung*. Edited by Jens Schröter and Ralph Brucker. BZNW 114. Berlin: de Gruyter, 2002.

———. *Q and the History of Early Christianity: Studies on Q*. Edinburgh: T & T Clark, 1996.

———. "Scripture in Q." Pages 3–26 in *The Scriptures in the Gospels*. Edited by C. M. Tuckett. BETL 131. Leuven: Leuven University Press, 1997.

———. "The Son of Man and Daniel 7: Inclusive Aspects of Early Christologies." Pages 164–90 in *Christian Origins: Worship, Belief and Society; The Milltown Institute and the Irish Biblical Association Millennium Conference*. Edited by Kieran J. O'Mahony. JSNTSup 241. Sheffield: Sheffield Academic Press, 2003.

———. "The Son of Man and Daniel 7: Q and Jesus." Pages 371–94 in *The Sayings Source Q and the Historical Jesus*. Edited by A. Lindemann. BETL 158. Leuven: Leuven University Press, 2001.

————. "Sources and Methods." Pages 121–37 in *The Cambridge Companion to Jesus*. Edited by Markus Bockmuehl. Cambridge: Cambridge University Press, 2001.

————. "Synoptic Tradition in the Didache." Pages 197–230 in *The New Testament in Early Christianity*. Edited by Jean-Marie Sevrin. BETL 86. Leuven: Leuven University Press, 1989.

Tumminia, Diana. "How Prophecy Never Fails." *SocRel* 59 (1998): 157–70.

Turner, David L. *Matthew*. BECNT. Grand Rapids: Baker Academic, 2008.

Turner, H. E. W. *Jesus, Master and Lord: A Study in the Historical Truth of the Gospels*. London: Mowbray; New York: Morehouse-Gorham, 1953.

Turner, Victor. *The Ritual Process: Structure and Anti-Structure*. Ithaca, NY: Cornell University Press, 1969.

Urbach, Ephraim E. *The Sages: Their Concepts and Beliefs*. 2 vols. Jerusalem: Magnes, 1975.

Uro, Risto. "John the Baptist and the Jesus Movement: What Does Q Tell Us?" Pages 231–57 in *The Gospel behind the Gospels: Current Studies in Q*. Edited by Ronald A. Piper. NovTSup 75. Leiden: Brill, 1995.

————. *Sheep among the Wolves: A Study of the Mission Instructions in Q*. AASF 47. Helsinki: Suomalainen Tiedeakatemia, 1987.

————. "*Thomas* and the Oral Gospel Tradition." Pages 8–32 in *Thomas at the Crossroads: Essays on the Gospel of Thomas*. Edited by Risto Uro. Edinburgh: T & T Clark, 1998.

————. *Thomas: Seeking the Historical Context of the Gospel of Thomas*. London: T & T Clark, 2003.

Vaage, Leif E. "Bird-Watching at the Baptism of Jesus: Early Christian Mythmaking in Mark 1:9–11." Pages 280–94 in *Reimagining Christian Origins: A Colloquium Honoring Burton L. Mack*. Edited by Elizabeth A. Castelli and Hal Taussig. Valley Forge, PA: Trinity Press International, 1996.

————. "Composite Texts and Oral Mythology: The Case of the 'Sermon' in Q (6:20–49)." Pages 75–97 in *Conflict and Invention: Literary, Rhetorical, and Social Studies on the Sayings Gospel Q*. Edited by John S. Kloppenborg. Valley Forge, PA: Trinity Press International, 1995.

————. *Galilean Upstarts: Jesus' First Followers according to Q*. Valley Forge, PA: Trinity Press International, 1994.

————. "The Son of Man Sayings in Q: Stratigraphical Location and Significance." *Semeia* 55 (1991): 103–29.

VanderKam, James C. "Righteous One, Messiah, Chosen One, and Son of Man in 1 Enoch 37–71." Pages 182–83 in *The Messiah: Developments in Earliest Judaism and Christianity*. Edited by James H. Charlesworth. Minneapolis: Fortress, 1992.

————. "Studies in the Apocalypse of Weeks." *CBQ* 46 (1984): 511–23.

Van der Watt, J. G. "The Use of αἰώνιος in the Concept ζωὴ αἰώνιος in John's Gospel." *NovT* 31 (1989): 217–28.

Van Oyen, Geert, and Tom Shepherd, eds. *The Trial and Death of Jesus: Essays on the Passion Narrative in Mark*. Leuven: Peeters, 2006.

Vaughan, William, and Sharon L. Greene. "Pigeon Visual Memory Capacity." *Journal of Experimental Psychology: Animal Behavior Processes* 10 (1984): 256–71.

Vena, Osvaldo D. *The Parousia and Its Rereadings: The Development of the Eschatological Consciousness in the Writings of the New Testament*. SBL 27. New York: Peter Lang, 2001.

Verheyden, J. "The Conclusion of Q: Eschatology in Q 22,28–30." Pages 695–718 in *The Sayings Source Q and the Historical Jesus*. Edited by A. Lindemann. BETL 158. Leuven: Leuven University Press, 2001.

Vermès, Géza. *The Complete Dead Sea Scrolls in English*. New York: Penguin, 1997.

————. *The Resurrection: History and Myth*. New York: Doubleday, 2008.

Veyne, Paul. *Did the Greeks Believe in Their Myths? An Essay on the Constitutive Imagination*. Chicago: University of Chicago Press, 1988.

Vielhauer, Philipp. "Gottesreich und Menschensohn in der Verkündigung Jesu." Pages

55–91 in *Aufsätze zum Neuen Testament*. TB 31. Munich: Kaiser, 1965.

Vielhauer, Philipp, and Georg Strecker. "Apocalyptic in Early Christianity." Pages 569–602 in vol. 2 of *New Testament Apocrypha*. Edited by Edgar Hennecke, Wilhelm Schneemelcher, and R. McL. Wilson. Rev. ed. 2 vols. Cambridge: James Clarke; Louisville: Westminster John Knox, 1992.

Vinson, Richard B. *Luke*. SHBC. Macon, GA: Smyth & Helwys, 2008.

Viviano, Benedict T. *The Kingdom of God in History*. GNS 27. Wilmington, DE: Michael Glazier, 1988.

Vögtle, Anton. *Das Neue Testament und die Zukunft des Kosmos*. KBANT. Düsseldorf: Patmos-Verlag, 1970.

———. "Wie kam es zum Osterglauben?" Pages 11–131 in *Wie kam es zum Osterglauben?* By Anton Vögtle and Rudolf Pesch. Düsseldorf: Patmos-Verlag, 1975.

Völter, Daniel B. *Polykarp und Ignatius und die ihnen zugeschriebenen Briefe*. Leiden: Brill, 1910.

Volz, Paul. *Die Eschatologie der jüdischen Gemeinde im neutestamentlichen Zeitalter, nach dem Quellen der rabbinischen, apokalyptischen und apokryphen Literatur*. 2nd ed. Tübingen: Mohr Siebeck, 1934.

Vorster, W. S. "Eschatological Prophet and/or Wisdom Teacher?" *HvTSt* 47 (1991): 526–42.

Vos, Johannes Sijko. *Traditionsgeschichtliche Untersuchungen zur paulinischen Pneumatologie*. Assen: Van Gorcum, 1973.

Vriezen, Th. C. "Prophecy and Eschatology." Pages 199–229 in *Congress Volume: Copenhagen 1953*. VTSup 1. Leiden: Brill, 1953.

Vusco, Vittorio. "'Point of View' and 'Implicit Reader' in Two Eschatological Texts: Lk 19,11–28; Acts 1,6–8." Pages 1677–96 in *The Four Gospels, 1992: Festschrift Frans Neirynck*. Edited by F. Van Segbroeck et al. 3 vols. BETL 100. Leuven: Leuven University Press, 1992.

Wacholder, Ben Zion. *Essays on Jewish Chronology and Chronography*. New York: Ktav, 1976.

———. *Messianism and Mishnah: Time and Place in the Early Halakah*. Cincinnati: Hebrew Union College Press, 1979.

Wagner, J. Ross. *Heralds of the Good News: Isaiah and Paul "In Concert" in the Letter to the Romans*. NovTSup 101. Leiden: Brill, 2002.

Wailes, Stephen L. *Medieval Allegories of Jesus' Parables*. Berkeley: University of California Press, 1987.

Walker, William O. *Interpolations in the Pauline Letters*. JSNTSup 213. London: Sheffield Academic Press, 2001.

Wallis, Ian G. *The Faith of Jesus Christ in Early Christian Traditions*. SNTSMS 84. Cambridge: Cambridge University Press, 1984.

Wanke, Daniel. "Vorläufer, Typus und Asket: Bemerkungen zur Gestalt des Elia in der altchristlichen Literatur." Pages 102–14 in *Was suchst du hier, Elia? Ein hermeneutisches Arbeitsbuch*. Edited by Klaus Grüwaldt and Harald Schroeter. Hermeneutica 4. Rheinbach-Merzbach: CMZ-Verlag, 1995.

Wanke, Joachim. *"Bezugs- und Kommentarworte" in den synoptischen Evangelien: Beobachtungen zur Interpretationsgeschichte der Herrenworte in der vorevangelischen Überlieferung*. ETS 44. Leipzig: St. Benno-Verlag, 1981.

Ward, Benedicta. *Miracles and the Medieval Mind: Theory, Record, and Event, 1000–1215*. Philadelphia: University of Pennsylvania Press, 1982.

Ward, R. B. "Partiality in the Assembly: James 2:2–4." *HTR* 62 (1969): 87–97.

Wardi, Emmanuel. "Cognitive Dissonance and Proselytism: An Application of Festinger's Model to Thirteenth-Century Joachites." Pages 269–82 in *Apocalyptic Time*. Edited by Albert I. Baumgarten. SHR 86. Leiden: Brill, 2000.

Warner, Martin. *The Formation of Christian Dogma: An Historical Study of Its Problems*. New York: Harper & Row, 1957.

Waterman, Leroy. *The Religion of Jesus: Christianity's Unclaimed Heritage of Prophetic Religion*. New York: Harper & Brothers, 1952.

Watson, Francis. "'I Received from the Lord . . .': Paul, Jesus, and the Last Supper." Pages 102–24 in *Jesus and Paul Reconnected: Fresh Pathways into an Old Debate*. Edited by Todd D. Still. Grand Rapids: Eerdmans, 2007.

Watts, Rikki E. *Isaiah's New Exodus and Mark*. WUNT 2/88. Tübingen: Mohr Siebeck, 1997.

Weatherly, John A. "The Authenticity of 1 Thessalonians 2.13–16: Additional Evidence." *JSNT* 42 (1991): 79–98.

Webb, Robert L. "John the Baptist and His Relationship to Jesus." Pages 179–229 in *Studying the Historical Jesus: Evaluations of the State of Current Research*. Edited by Bruce Chilton and Craig A. Evans. NTTS 19. Leiden: Brill, 1994.

———. *John the Baptizer and Prophet: A Socio-Historical Study*. Eugene, OR: Wipf & Stock, 2006.

Weeden, Theodore J. "Two Jesuses, Jesus of Jerusalem and Jesus of Nazareth: Provocative Parallels and Imagination Imitation." *Forum* 6 (2003): 137–341.

Wehnert, Jürgen. *Die Reinheit des "christlichen Gottesvolkes" aus Juden und Heiden: Studien zum historischen und theologischen Hintergrund des sogenannten Aposteldekrets*. FRLANT 173. Göttingen: Vandenhoeck & Ruprecht, 1997.

Weinfeld, Moshe. "The Day of the Lord: Aspirations for the Kingdom of God in the Bible and Jewish Liturgy." Pages 341–72 in *Studies in Bible 1986*. ScrHier 31. Jerusalem: Magnes, 1986.

Weinstein, Donald. "Millenarianism in a Civic Setting: The Savonarola Movement in Florence." Pages 187–203 in *Millennial Dreams in Action: Studies in Revolutionary Religious Movements*. Edited by Sylvia L. Thrupp. New York: Schocken Books, 1970.

Weiser, Neil. "The Effects of Prophetic Disconfirmation of the Committed." *RRelRes* 16 (1974): 19–30.

Weiss, Johannes. *Der erste Korintherbrief*. 9th ed. KEK 5. Göttingen: Vandenhoeck & Ruprecht, 1910.

———. *Jesus' Proclamation of the Kingdom of God*. Translated and edited by Richard Hyde Hiers and David Larrimore Holland. Philadelphia: Fortress, 1971.

———. *Die Predigt Jesu vom Reiche Gottes*. Göttingen: Vandenhoeck & Ruprecht, 1900.

———. "Das Problem der Entstehung des Christentums." *AR* 16 (1913): 468–71.

Welborn, L. L. *Paul, the Fool of Christ: A Study of 1 Corinthians 1–4 in the Comic-Philosophic Tradition*. JSNTSup 293. London: T & T Clark, 2005.

Wenell, Karen J. *Jesus and Land: Sacred and Social Space in Second Temple Judaism*. LNTS 334. London: T & T Clark, 2007.

Wenham, David. "The Kingdom of God and Daniel." *ExpTim* 98 (1987): 132–34.

———. *Paul: Follower of Jesus or Founder of Christianity?* Grand Rapids: Eerdmans, 1995.

———. *The Rediscovery of Jesus' Eschatological Discourse*. GP 4. Sheffield: JSOT Press, 1984.

———. "The Rock on Which to Build: Some Mainly Pauline Observations about the Sermon on the Mount." Pages 187–206 in *Built upon the Rock: Studies in the Gospel of Matthew*. Edited by Daniel M. Gurtner and John Nolland. Grand Rapids: Eerdmans, 2008.

Werman, Cana. "Epochs and End-Time: The 490-Year Scheme in Second Temple Literature." *DSD* 13 (2006): 229–55.

Wernle, Paul. *The Rise of the Religion*. Vol. 1 of *The Beginnings of Christianity*. Translated by G. A. Bienemann. Edited by W. D. Morrison. London: Williams & Norgate; New York: Putnam, 1903.

Wesley, John. *Explanatory Notes upon the New Testament*. London: Epworth, 1950.

Westcott, B. F. *Saint Paul's Epistle to the Ephesians*. London: Macmillan, 1906.

Wheeldon, M. J. "'True Stories': The Reception of 'Historiography' in Antiquity." Pages 33–63 in *History as Text: The Writing of Ancient History*. Edited by Averil Cameron. Chapel Hill: University of North Carolina Press, 1989.

Wiebe, Ben. "The Focus of Jesus' Eschatology." Pages 121–46 in *Self-Definition and Self-Discovery in Early Christianity: A Study in Changing Horizons.* Edited by David J. Hawkin and Tom Robinson. Lewiston, NY: Edwin Mellen, 1990.

Wigner, Eugene P. "Remarks on the Mind-Body Question." Pages 167–81 in *Quantum Theory and Measurement.* Edited by John Archibald Wheeler and Wojciech Hubert Zurek. Princeton: Princeton University Press, 1983.

Wilckens, Ulrich. *Geschichte des Wirkens Jesu in Galiläa.* Part 1 of *Geschichte der urchristlichen Theologie,* vol. 1 of *Theologie des Neuen Testaments.* Neukirchen-Vluyn: Neukirchener Verlag, 2002.

———. *Röm 6–11.* Vol. 2 of *Der Brief an die Römer.* EKKNT 6/2. Zürich: Benzinger; Neukirchen-Vluyn: Neukirchener Verlag, 1978.

———. *Röm 12–16.* Vol. 3 of *Der Brief an die Römer.* EKKNT 6/3. Zürich: Benziger; Neukirchen Vluyn: Neukirchener-Verlag, 1982.

Williams, George Huntston. *The Radical Reformation.* Kirksville, MO: Sixteenth Century Journal Publishers, 1992.

Williams, Helen L., Martin A. Conway, and Gillian Cohen. "Autobiographical Memory." Pages 63–70 in *Memory in the Real World.* Edited by Gillian Cohen and Martin Conway. 3rd ed. New York: Psychology Press, 2008.

Williams, Margaret H. "The Meaning and Function of *Ioudaios* in Graeco-Roman Inscriptions." ZPE 116 (1997): 249–62.

Williams, Sam K. *Jesus' Death as Saving Event: The Background and Origin of a Concept.* HDR 2. Missoula, MT: Scholars Press, 1975.

Willitts, Joel. *Matthew's Messianic Shepherd-King: In Search of "The Lost Sheep of the House of Israel."* BZNW 147. Berlin: de Gruyter, 2007.

Wills, Lawrence M., and Benjamin G. Wright III, eds. *Conflicted Boundaries in Wisdom and Apocalypticism.* SBLSymS 35. Atlanta: Society of Biblical Literature, 2005.

Wilson, Anne E., and Michael Ross. "The Identity Function of Autobiographical Memory: Time Is on Our Side." *Memory* 11 (2003): 137–49.

Wilson, John. "What Does Thucydides Claim for His Speeches?" *Phoenix* 36 (1982): 95–103.

Wilson, Walter T. *Love without Pretense: Romans 12.9–21 and Hellenistic-Jewish Wisdom Literature.* WUNT 2/46. Tübingen: Mohr Siebeck, 1991.

Wilson, William P. "How Religious or Spiritual Miracle Events Happen Today." Pages 264–79 in *Religious and Spiritual Events.* Vol. 1 of *Miracles: God, Science, and Psychology in the Paranormal.* Edited by J. Harold Ellens. Westport, CT: Praeger, 2008.

Windisch, Hans. *Der zweite Korintherbrief.* KEK 6. Göttingen: Vandenhoeck & Ruprecht, 1924.

———. "Die Sprüche vom Eingehen in das Reich Gottes." ZNW 27 (1928): 163–92.

———. *The Meaning of the Sermon on the Mount.* Translated by S. MacLean Gilmour. Philadelphia: Westminster, 1951.

Windischmann, Friedrich Heinrich Hugo. *Erklärung des Briefes an die Galater.* Mainz: Kirchheim, Schott & Thielmann, 1843.

Winger, Michael. "Word and Deed." *CBQ* 62 (2000): 679–92.

Wink, Walter. "Jesus' Reply to John: Matt 11:2–6/Luke 7:18–23." *Forum* 5 (1989): 121–28.

———. *Naming the Powers: The Language of Power in the New Testament.* Philadelphia: Fortress, 1984.

Winograd, Eugene, and Ulric Neisser, eds. *Affect and Accuracy in Recall: Studies of "Flashbulb" Memories.* Cambridge: Cambridge University Press, 1992.

Winston, David. *The Wisdom of Solomon.* AB 43. Garden City, NY: Doubleday, 1979.

Winter, Paul. *On the Trial of Jesus.* 2nd rev. ed. SJ 1. Berlin: de Gruyter, 1974.

Wise, Michael Owen. "Thunder in Gemini (4Q318)." Pages 39–48 in *Thunder in Gemini and Other Essays on the History, Language and Literature of Second Temple Palestine.* JSPSup 15. Sheffield: Sheffield Academic Press, 1994.

———. "To Know the Times and the Seasons: A Study of the Aramaic Chronograph 4Q599." *JSP* 15 (1997): 3–51.

Witherington, Ben, III. *The Christology of Jesus*. Minneapolis: Fortress, 1990.

———. *Jesus, Paul, and the End of the World: A Comparative Study in New Testament Eschatology*. Downers Grove, IL: InterVarsity, 1992.

———. *Jesus the Sage: The Pilgrimage of Wisdom*. Minneapolis: Fortress, 1994.

Wolff, Christian. *Der zweite Brief des Paulus an die Korinther*. THKNT 8. Berlin: Evangelische Verlagsanstalt, 1989.

———. "Humility and Self-Denial in Jesus' Life and Message and in the Apostolic Existence of Paul." Pages 145–60 in *Paul and Jesus: Collected Essays*. Edited by A. J. M. Wedderburn. JSNTSup 37. Sheffield: Sheffield Academic Press, 1989.

Wolter, Michael. *Das Lukasevangelium*. HNT 5. Tübingen: Mohr Siebeck, 2008.

———. *Der Brief an die Kolosser; Die Brief an Philemon*. ÖTKNT 12. Gütersloh: Gütersloher Verlagshaus; Würzburg: Echter, 1993.

———. "Was heisset nu Gottes reich?" *ZNW* 86 (1995): 5–19.

Woude, A. S. van der. *Die messianischen Vorstellungen der Gemeinde von Qumrân*. SSN 3. Assen: Van Gorcum, 1957.

Woude, A. S. van der, and M. de Jonge. "11QMelchizedek and the New Testament." *NTS* 12 (1966): 301–26.

Wrede, William. *The Messianic Secret*. Translated by J. C. G. Greig. LTT. Cambridge: James Clarke, 1971.

Wright, Lawrence. *Remembering Satan*. New York: Alfred A. Knopf, 1995.

Wright, N. T. *Jesus and the Victory of God*. Minneapolis: Fortress, 1996.

———. "Romans." Pages 393–770 in vol. 10 of *The New Interpreter's Bible*. Edited by Leander E. Keck. Nashville: Abingdon, 2002.

Wünsch, August. "Die Zahlensprüche in Talmud und Midrasch." *ZDMG* 65 (1911): 395–412.

Xeravits, Géza G. *King, Priest, Prophet: Positive Eschatological Protagonists of the Qumran Library*. STDJ 47. Leiden: Brill, 2003.

———. "Wisdom Traits in the Qumranic Presentation of the Eschatological Prophet."

Pages 183–92 in *Wisdom and Apocalypticism in the Dead Sea Scrolls and in the Biblical Tradition*. Edited by F. García Martínez. BETL 148. Leuven: Leuven University Press, 2003.

Yardeni, Ada. "8. XHev/Se papDeed of Sale B ar and heb." Pages 26–33 in *Aramaic, Hebrew, and Greek Documentary Texts from Nahal Hever and Other Sites*. By Hannah M. Cotton and Ada Yardeni. DJD 27. Oxford: Clarendon, 1997.

Yates, Roy. "Colossians 2,14: Metaphor of Forgiveness." *Bib* 71 (1990): 248–59.

———. *The Epistle to the Colossians*. EC. London: Epworth, 1993.

Yu-wen, Jen. *The Taiping Revolutionary Movement*. New Haven: Yale University Press, 1973.

Zager, Werner. *Gottesherrschaft und Endgericht in der Verkündigung Jesu: Eine Untersuchung zur markinischen Jesusüberlieferung einschließlich der Q-Parallelen*. BZNW 82. Berlin: de Gruyter, 1996.

Zehnle, Richard F. *Peter's Pentecost Discourse: Tradition and Lukan Reinterpretation in Peter's Speeches of Acts 2 and 3*. SBLMS 15. Nashville: Abingdon, 1971.

Zeilinger, Franz. *Der Erstegeborene der Schöpfung: Untersuchungen zur Formalstruktur und Theologie des Kolosserbriefes*. Vienna: Herder, 1974.

Zeller, Dieter. *Der Brief an die Römer*. RNT. Regensburg: Friedrich Pustet, 1985.

———. "Die Entstehung des Christentums." Pages 15–123 in *Christentum I: Von den Anfängen bis zur Konstantinischen Wende*. Edited by Dieter Zeller. RM 28. Stuttgart: Kohlhammer, 2002.

———. *Die weisheitlichen Mahnsprüche bei den Synoptikern*. FB 17. Würzburg: Echter, 1977.

———. "Eine weisheitliche Grundschrift in der Logienquelle?" Pages 389–401 in vol. 1 of *The Four Gospels, 1992: Festschrift Frans Neirynck*. Edited by F. Van Segbroeck et al. 3 vols. BETL 100. Leuven: Leuven University Press, 1992.

Zerubavel, Eviatar. *Social Mindscapes: An Invitation to Cognitive Sociology*. Cambridge, MA: Harvard University Press, 1997.

Zerubavel, Yael. *Recovered Roots: Collective Memory and the Making of Israeli National Tradition*. Chicago: University of Chicago Press, 1995.

Zias, Joe. "Crucifixion in Antiquity: The Evidence." Online: www.centuryone.org/crucifixion2.html. Cited 18 November 2009.

Zimmerli, Walter. "Das 'Gnadenjahr des Herrn.'" Pages 321–32 in *Archäologie und Altes Testaments: Festschrift für Kurt Galling zum 8 Januar 1970*. Edited by Arnulf Kuschke and Ernst Kutsch. Tübingen: Mohr Siebeck, 1970.

Zimmermann, Johannes. *Messianische Texte aus Qumran: Königliche, priesterliche, und prophetische Messiasvorstellung in den Schriftfunden von Qumran*. WUNT 2/104. Tübingen: Mohr Siebeck, 1998.

———. "Observations on 4Q246—The 'Son of God.'" Pages 175–90 in *Qumran-Messianism: Studies on the Messianic Expectations in the Dead Sea Scrolls*. Edited by James H. Charlesworth, Hermann Lichtenberger, and Gerbern S. Oegema. Tübingen: Mohr Siebeck, 1998.

Zmijewski, Josef. *Die Eschatologiereden des Lukas-Evangeliums: Eine traditions- und redaktionsgeschichtliche Untersuchung zu Lk 21,5–36 und Lk 17,20–37*. BBB 40. Bohn: Peter Hanstein, 1972.

Zöckler, Otto. *The Cross of Christ: Studies in the History of Religion and the Inner Life of the Church*. Translated by Maurice J. Evans. London: Hodder & Stoughton, 1877.

Zöckler, Thomas. *Jesu Lehren im Thomasevangelium*. NHMS 47. Leiden: Brill, 1999.

Zwiep, Arie W. *Judas and the Choice of Matthias: A Study on Context and Concern of Acts 1:15–26*. WUNT 2/187. Tübingen: Mohr Siebeck, 2004.

Zwi Werblowsky, R. J. "Messiah and Messianic Movements." Page 1019 in Macropaedia 11 of *The New Encyclopedia Britannica*. 15th ed. Chicago: Encyclopedia Britannica, 1983.

———. "Mysticism and Messianism: The Case of Hasidism." Pages 305–14 in *Man and His Salvation: Studies in Memory of S. G. F. Brandon*. Edited by Eric J. Sharpe and John R. Hinnells. Manchester: Manchester University Press; Totowa, NJ: Rowman & Littlefield, 1973.

Zygmunt, Joseph F. "Prophetic Failure and Chiliastic Identity: The Case of Jehovah's Witnesses." *American Journal of Sociology* 75 (1970): 926–48.

———. "When Prophecies Fail: A Theoretical Perspective on the Comparative Evidence." *American Behavioral Scientist* 16 (1972): 245–68.

Ancient Writings Index

Old Testament

Genesis

4:15 394n33
4:17–18 222
4:23–24 295n310
5:1 362
5:18–24 222
5:27 449
6–9 441
7:4 375n199
13:15 181n641
14 252n118
15:7 192
18:3 295n310
19 383
19:2 295n310
19:17 383n224, 384
19:19 295n310,
    383n224, 384
19:20 384
19:26 383n224
24:3 108
24:7 108
25:7 449
32:29 299
35:10 355n141
47:3 295n310
47:12 365
48:16 298n320
49:1 51n91
49:10 253
49:28 71n172
50:20 365
50:21 365

Exodus

2:11–12 286
4:22 300
7–12 286
8:19 229, 271
12:2 192n674
12:11 133
12:25 180, 192
13:18 260
14:26–29 286
15:2 369
15:18 106, 107n338
16 271
16:8 105
19:6 203, 290n290
19:8 192n674
19:16–18 457
19:17 192n674
20:2 353n134
20:3 353n134
20:7 353n134
20:8 353n134
20:12 353n134, 357
20:13 353n134
20:14 353n134
20:18 192n674
22:25–27 332
23:4–5 362n168
23:20 80, 130, 139
23:30 192
24:4 71n172
24:8 272

Leviticus

11:44 356, 375n201
11:45–46 356n143

17–18 359n156
17–26 353n138
18–20 371
18:6 371n185
19 x, 272, 315–16,
    347n110, 351–54,
    356n144, 358, 361,
    364, 368, 370–73,
    374nn192–93,
    378–80
19:2 353n138, 355–
    56, 358, 371n185,
    373, 375n201
19:3 352–53n134,
    371n185, 371n187
19:4 352–53n134,
    372n189
19:5–8 371n185
19:8 371n186
19:9–10 371n185,
    372n189, 379n209
19:11 352–53n134,
    371nn185–86,
    371n189
19:11–12 379n209
19:12 352–53n134,
    371nn187–88,
    371–2n189
19:13 358,
    371nn186–87
19:13–14 371n185,
    371n188, 379n209
19:14 372n190
19:15 351, 357, 363–
    64, 370, 371n186,
    371n188, 372n189

19:15–16 379n209
19:15–17 357, 365
19:15–18 357–58,
    363–65, 371n185,
    371n187
19:16 352–53n134,
    371n186, 371n188
19:17 351, 353n134,
    355, 357, 362–66,
    371n186, 371n188,
    372n189, 373
19:17–18 347n110,
    351, 354–55,
    362n167,
    364, 366–68,
    371nn185–86,
    379n209
19:18 352–55,
    356n144, 358–63,
    365–68, 371nn185–
    86, 371nn188–89,
    372nn189–90, 380
19:19 379n209
19:22 371n186
19:23 180, 192
19:26 371n189
19:26–28 379n209
19:29 379n209
19:31 371n189,
    379n209
19:32 379n209
19:33 353n138
19:33–34 361,
    371n185, 371n187,
    372n190, 379n209

19:34 354, 359, 361,
   371nn186–87
19:35 370
19:35–36 371n187,
   379n209
19:37 373n192
20:10 353n134
20:24 192
20:25 371n185
20:26 356, 368, 373,
   375n201
22 370
22:28 369–70
25 366
25:35–36 366
25:35–38 367
25:36 353n134, 365–67
26:4 375n199

Numbers

1:4 232
1:44 71n172, 232
11 271
13:18 181n641
14:23 181n641
14:25–35 192
15:2 180, 192
16 286
18:20 192
20:24 180
22 444n25
24:14 51n91
24:15–17 296
24:17 77n204, 111,
   253, 258–59n150
24:17–19 284
25:6–16 285n272
27:12 181n641
31:2 355
32:33 177
33:54 181
33:55 375n202, 416
34:17 192

Deuteronomy

1:8 180–81, 192
1:21 192
1:23 71n172, 232
1:35 181n641, 272
3:4 177
3:10 177

3:13 177
4:9 27n109
4:21 180
4:23 27n109
4:31 27n109
4:38 192
5:16 357
6:12 27n109
6:18 181
8:11 27n109
8:14 27n109
8:19 27n109
9:7 27n109
10:9 192
11:14 375n199
14:27 192
16:20 181
17:18 173n618
18:15 84n234, 260,
   274n217
18:15–18 270–71,
   273, 274n218
18:18 84n234, 260,
   274n217
18:18–20 296
21:20 212n739
23:2–3 180n637
24:12–13 332
25:19 27n109
26:1 192
27:3 192
29:28 72
30:1–5 72n177
30:3–4 43
30:7 343
30:11 447n39
30:11–14 99n307
30:12 447n39
30:20 181n641
32:8 298n320
32:43 409
32:47 181n641
33:8–11 296
34:10 260, 274n217

Joshua

1:6 181
3:12 71n172, 233
4:8 233
6 260
13:12 177

13:21 177
13:27 177
13:30 177
13:31 177
14:4 192
15:13 192
19:9 192
23:13 375n202
24 315

Judges

5:31 368
9:53 425
18:9 180

Ruth

1:1 363

1 Samuel

1:11 27n109
8:7 105
9:27–10:8 292n297
12:17–18 375n199
16:1–13 292n297
16:13 289n288
16:14–23 246n91
17:32 295n310
20:8 295n310
20:13 295n310
22:15 295n310
24:14 235n55
25:8 295n310
25:22 295n310
27:5 295n310
29:8 295n310

2 Samuel

2:4 289n288
3:9 295n310
7:10–14 238
7:11–14 253
7:12 284
7:12–14 284n260
7:12–16 287
7:13 173n618
7:19–29 295n310
15 387
19:12 295n310
19:20 295n310
20:6 295n310
24:23 295n310

1 Kings

1:33 295n310
2:45 295n310
17:8–16 269n195
17:8–24 267n185
17:17–24 269n195
17:21 415n101
18:40 285
19:16 266n178
19:16–21 268
19:19–21 267n183

2 Kings

1:8 53n97
1:9–12 269, 285
2–13 268
4:1–7 268, 269n195
4:8–37 269n195
4:29 268
4:42–44 268n192
9:1–10 292n297
9:35 425n140
10:18 295n310
17:38 27n109
23:30 289n288

1 Chronicles

12:23 177
16:35 72n177
17:14 170, 186n660
28:5 171, 173n618,
   186n660
29:11 106
29:23 186n660
29:30 201n691

2 Chronicles

1:1 398n52
13:8 186n660, 201n691
15:10 177
19:2 361
20:30 173n619

Ezra

4:5 177
4:6 177
4:24 177
6:17 71

Nehemiah

1:8–9 72n177

Esther

3:6 177
9:30 177

Job

19:26 248n102
42:17 248n102

Psalms

1:3 217n754
1:5 39–40n40
2 279, 397
2:7 292n297
3 378
4 378
LXX 4:3 418n114
5:2 106n333
6 378
LXX 6:4 410
7 378
9 378
10 378
10:16 106n333
11:4 172, 173n618
LXX 15:3 360n156
LXX 16:6 418n114
LXX 17 411
LXX 17:6 418n114
18:49 409, 411
18:50 411
LXX 21 411
LXX 21:2 410
LXX 21:23 410
22 411n88
22:1 426n147, 427,
   432
22:28 106n333,
   170n602
22:29 170
24 180n637
24:7–10 106n333
29:10 106n333
29:29 170n602
LXX 30 411
LXX 30:6 410
LXX 31:3 418n114
34:7 298n320
37:11 181–82, 183n647
LXX 37:12 389
LXX 39 411

40:6–7 411
LXX 40:10 410
LXX 41 411
LXX 41:6 410
41:9 68n163
LXX 41:12 410
LXX 42:5 410
42:5–6 427
42:11 427
43:5 427
44:4 106n333
47:2–3 106n333
47:7–8 106n333
48:2 106n333, 244
55:17 415
66:10–12 276n225
LXX 68 407, 411
LXX 68:5 408, 410
LXX 68:8 408
LXX 68:10 408, 410
LXX 68:11 408
LXX 68:20 408
LXX 68:21 408
LXX 68:22 407–408,
   410
68:24 106n333
69 407–409,
   411nn88–89
69:9 407
69:10 410–11
69:22–23 407
69:25 407
74:12 106n333
LXX 77:2 409
78 411
78:24 273n213
84:3 106n333
91:11–12 298n320
93:1–2 106n333
95:3 106n333
LXX 95:10 234n51
96:10 106n333
97:1 106n333
99:1 106n333
102:22 202
103:19 106, 172–73,
   170
104:13 375n199
105:13 203
105:15 266n178
106:47 72n177
110 243, 247, 250, 286

110:1 230, 250,
   292n298
116:10 411n86
117:1 409
136:4–7 340n85
139:21 361
139:21–22 355
145:1 106n333
145:11–13 170
147:2 72n177
149:2 106n333

Proverbs

1:1 235n55, 398n52
1:31 217n754
3:1 27n109
3:12 375n200
4:5 27n109
14:9 375n197
15:3 375n197
24:17–18 362n168
25:21 346
30:11–14 341n86

Ecclesiastes

1:1 398n52

Isaiah

2:2 51n91
3:10 217n754
6:5 106n333
6:13 217n756
7:14 454
8:19 106n333
9:5 200n684
9:7 284n259
10:7 106n333
10:10 106n333
10:25 131n449
10:33–34 217n756
11:1–2 284n259
11:1–5 280n244
11:1–10 266n178
11:3–4 252
11:4 284
11:10–12 232n42
11:11–13 72n177
13:22 149n528
16:5 284n259
24–27 40

24:18 35n19
24:21 47n71
24:23 37n26, 174
25:6 124
25:6–8 41n47
25:8 124n421
26:2–3 180n637
26:19 42, 248n102,
   275
26:20 131n449
27:12–13 72n177
29:17 131n449
29:18 275
29:18–19 42
29:19 275
30:27–28 276n225
30:30 276n225
32:1–2 292n296
32:15 49n81
33:22 106n333
34:4 43
34:16 49n81
35:4 37n27
35:5 192n674, 275
35:5–6 42, 229
35:6 192n674, 275
35:10 124n421
40–55 33, 108,
   113n364
40–66 113
40:3 53n97
40:9–10 37n27
41:14–16 217n754
41:21 106n333
42:1–4 78
42:7 275
42:18 42, 275
43:2 276n225
43:5–6 72n177
43:14–21 72n177
43:15 106n333
44:3–4 49n81
44:6 106n333
49:6 72n177, 267n184
49:24–25 278
50:6 414n98
50:8 45n67
51:1–2 214
51:5 45n67
52 113, 115

52:7 37n26, 100n309,
    113–15, 196,
    268n190, 274
52:7–8 113–14
52:7–9 113
52:9 113
52:15 414n98
53 414
53:5 402
53:6 414n98
53:7 414n98
53:9 414n98
53:12 278, 402,
    414n98
55:1–2 41n47
56:1 45n67
56:8 72n177
60–62 51
60:3–7 72n177
60:20 124n421
60:21 181n641, 192
60:22 191n672
61 42, 53n97, 80, 113,
    230, 265, 273,
    279n239, 312n17
61:1 42, 49n81, 113–
    15, 265–66, 268,
    275, 279n239
61:1–2 113n364, 114,
    229, 274
61:1–3 114–15,
    229n34, 264–66,
    268, 287
61:2 113
61:3 113
61:7 181
63:10–14 378
65:13–14 41n47
65:19 124n421
66:1 172
66:14 82
66:18–24 72n177
66:24 276n230

Jeremiah

3:19 375n200
7:22–23 105
9:24–25 214n748
15:7 217n754
23:5 280n244

23:5–6 253n124,
    280n244, 284n259
23:8 72n177
23:20 51n91
26 237n64
26:1 177
27:1 177
28:1 177
29:10–14 72n177
30:9 284n259
31:1 72n177
31:8 72n177
31:10 72n177
31:13 124n421
31:31 79
32:37–41 72n177
33:14–16 253n124
33:15 280n244
33:15–17 284n259
33:17–22 280n244
51:33 217n754

Ezekiel

5:5 51n90
7:7 45n67
9:4 394n33
11:17–20 72n177
11:19 49n81
13:9 180
20:33 37
20:33–44 72n177
28:25 72n177
30:3 45n67
34:11–16 72n177
34:23 280n244
34:24 284n259
34:27 41n48, 124n421
36:21–38 41n48,
    124n421
36:24 72n177
36:25–27 49n81
37 56n111, 62
37:1–14 49n81,
    248n102
37:11–28 72n177
37:15 56n111
37:19 56n111
37:24 280n244
37:24–25 284n259
37:25 111n354
38–39 40

38:12 51n90
39:26–27 72n177
39:29 49n81
40–48 51
45:7 192
48:31 71n172

Daniel

2:31–45 381n216
2:44 201n691
3 217
3:54 173
4:11 217n756
4:19–23 217n756
4:31 37n26
4:37 172
6:10 415
6:26 37n26
6:28 177
7 39, 40n42, 80–81,
    87, 228n31, 294,
    301, 302n340
7:7–27 381n216
7:9 302n338
7:9–11 249
7:9–14 82
7:10 276n225
7:13 230
7:13–14 81, 248n100,
    295, 302n338
7:14 37n26, 81
7:18 37n26
7:27 37n26, 290n290
8:9–26 381n216
8:14 161
9 40n42
9:24–27 77n204,
    381n216
9:25 114
9:25–26 280n244
9:27 81
10:13 298n320
10:14 51n91
10:20–21 298n320
11:1 298n320
11:21–12:4(13)
    381n216
11:31 81
12:1 40
12:2 116, 125, 188n666
12:2–3 301n336

12:5–12 144n510
12:7 161
12:11 81
12:11–12 161

Hosea

6:11 217n754
10:1 217n754
10:8 82
11:1 375n200
11:11 72n177
12:13 274n217

Joel

2:1 45n67
2:28 49
2:28–29 49n81
2:28–32 78
3:13 217n754
3:14 45n67

Amos

1–2 341n88
2:10 260
4:7 375n199
4:13 280n244,
    292n297
8:9–10 387
9:11 253n124,
    284n259
9:13 41n48, 124n421

Obadiah

15 45n67
19–21 170
21 170, 174n622

Jonah

4:6 29

Micah

4:7 37n26, 174
4:8 37n27
4:12–13 217n754
5:2 253n124
7:6 80, 129, 229

Nahum

1:2 354–55

Habakkuk

1:2 149n528
2:3 45n67, 149

Zephaniah

1:14 45n67
3:15 106n333
3:20 72n177

Haggai

2:6 131n449

Zechariah

1:12 149n528
3:8 280n244, 284n259
6:12 238, 280n244, 284n259
8:7 72n177
9–14 61
9:9 245, 253n124, 287
9:11 272n208
10:6–12 72n177
12:7–8 284n259
12:10 49n81
13:7 42, 81, 391
14:4–5 62, 261n156
14:5 37n27, 81
14:9 37n26, 107, 174
14:16 174n622
14:16–17 37n26

Malachi

1:14 106n333
3:1 41–42, 80–81, 130, 139, 269n196, 274n218
3:2 37n27
3:19 276n230
4:4–5 269n196, 274n218
4:5 53n97, 267n187, 274n218
4:5–6 42, 267n184, 269
4:6 270

New Testament

Matthew

1–2 453–54
1:18–23 451
1:18–25 154
2 448
2:2 234, 245, 301n336
2:6 245
2:9–10 301n336
2:13–23 154
3:2 83, 124n424, 204n701, 206–7
3:7 83, 277n232
3:7–10 53n97, 206–7
3:8 218
3:8–9 214, 216
3:8–10 215
3:9 214
3:10 83, 215–18, 277
3:11 34, 40n43, 100n311, 207, 216, 218, 277
3:11–12 42, 53n97, 206–7, 219, 274
3:12 215, 217, 277
3:14 90n252, 206
3:15 22
4:1 212n737
4:1–11 17, 246
4:8 173n619, 178
4:17 83, 124n424
4:23 37n26, 113n365, 307n3
5 329, 334, 337
5–7 305, 309–10, 312n20
5:1–2 309
5:1–7:28 306–7, 453
5:3 42, 80, 124n421, 165, 179, 182, 184n655, 193, 196, 201, 310
5:3–12 265, 309
5:4 42, 80
5:5 181n641, 183n647
5:6 42, 80, 310
5:7 310, 324n48
5:8 310
5:9 310
5:10 166, 179, 193–94, 196, 310, 326
5:10–12 130, 310
5:11–12 42, 310
5:12 36, 310
5:16 310
5:17 42
5:17–20 310
5:18 307
5:19 36, 136n469, 166, 193, 195, 310
5:20 39, 166, 180, 193, 310
5:21–22 136n469
5:21–26 271
5:21–37 308n5
5:21–48 264n168, 373
5:22 34
5:25–26 331n66
5:26 310
5:27–28 212n734
5:27–30 271
5:29–30 130
5:31–32 271, 307, 405n69
5:33 310
5:33–36 271
5:35 244
5:37–42 271
5:38–39 360
5:38–42 336
5:38–48 309, 329–31, 333n72, 341
5:39 316, 329, 331, 334n73
5:39–42 338, 341–42, 344
5:40 316, 329, 333n72
5:41 316, 322, 329, 331–32, 344, 376
5:42 316, 330, 332, 367
5:43 352n131, 361, 374n193
5:43–48 93, 271, 343
5:44 285, 310, 328nn63–64, 329–31, 342
5:44–45 349
5:44–48 349n120
5:45 310, 320, 330–31, 350n123
5:45–48 349n121
5:46 320, 329, 332, 343n94, 346
5:46–47 330, 337–38, 342, 345
5:47 320, 329, 331, 346, 367
5:48 310, 321, 329, 331, 333, 349, 350nn122–23
6:1 310
6:1–18 310
6:2–4 136n469
6:3 22
6:4 310
6:6 310
6:9 38, 310
6:9–13 377
6:10 36, 37n26, 93, 165, 190
6:11 271
6:14 310
6:18 310
6:19–21 36, 136n469
6:24 307
6:24–33 212n735
6:26 310
6:32 310
6:33 166, 180n636, 193, 310
7:1 136n469, 309, 327
7:1–2 47n71, 347n111, 370n184
7:2 325n50, 327
7:3–5 309
7:5 347n111
7:6 313
7:11 310
7:12 309, 324n49, 329–30
7:13 39, 179n636
7:13–14 130
7:16–18 309
7:16–21 216
7:19 34, 83, 216, 217n755
7:21 39, 166, 181n638, 193, 228, 309–10
7:22 17
7:22–23 47n71, 246
7:24–27 47n71, 228, 309
7:28 93
7:28–8:1 309
8:11–12 38n28, 42, 43n56, 51, 74n186, 166, 178–79, 186, 193, 196
8:12 194

8:16 17
8:17 409n79
8:18–22 267n183,
    424n136
8:20 212, 294n307
8:21–22 212n736
8:22 93, 168
9:32–34 18
9:34 396–97n43
9:35 37n26, 113n365,
    196, 307n3
9:37–38 217
10 13, 305
10:1 71
10:1–23 25
10:1–42 306–7
10:5–42 382
10:7 38, 165, 190
10:7–8 188
10:9–11 212n735
10:10 13, 405n69
10:14 168
10:14–15 136n469
10:15 34, 62n136, 228
10:23 33, 44n60, 227,
    264n168, 293n303
10:24–25 26, 296,
    309, 312n18
10:28 34, 56n112
10:32–33 39, 80, 129,
    136n469, 228, 246
10:34–36 40, 80, 129,
    229, 270, 424n136
10:34–37 212n736
10:37 272, 424n136
10:37–38 384n224
10:38 384n224,
    425n138, 428
10:38–39 212n738
10:39 36, 384n224,
    428
10:40 228
10:42 136n469
11:2–3 206
11:2–4 42, 90n252,
    229, 265–66
11:2–6 80, 219, 275–
    76, 278
11:2–19 305
11:7–9 140n490, 204–5
11:7–10 130
11:7–11 139, 206

11:7–19 54n100, 306–7
11:9 139, 263
11:10 41, 80–81, 139,
    269n196, 274n218
11:11 137–39, 165,
    184n655, 195, 205
11:12 165n596, 166,
    180n636, 194
11:12–13 40, 206, 307
11:14 269n196
11:16–19 83, 139–40,
    206, 428
11:18–19 205, 212
11:19 294n307
11:20–24 93, 141n493
11:21–24 228
11:22 34, 62n136
11:24 34
11:25–27 226, 295
12:18–21 78
12:22–23 17–18
12:23 246
12:24 93, 396–97n43
12:25–26 112–13, 178
12:25–27 17
12:28 17, 38, 49n80,
    93, 99–101, 104,
    112–13, 166,
    181n640, 190,
    202, 229
12:29 17, 219,
    271n204, 278
12:30 93
12:32 39, 200
12:33–34 312n19
12:33–35 216
12:34 83
12:36 34, 62n136
12:38–39 84n233
12:38–40 271n201
12:39–40 272
12:41 271n201
12:41–42 39, 40n40
13 117
13:1–52 306
13:10–52 307
13:12 36
13:19 166
13:24 166, 184n655
13:24–30 35, 118n392,
    217
13:31 166, 202

13:33 166, 184n655,
    202
13:34–35 409, 411
13:36–43 35,
    118n392, 133
13:37 293n303
13:38 166, 203,
    375n197
13:40 216, 217n755
13:41 35, 37n26,
    38n28, 166,
    183n652, 196, 230,
    246–47, 293n303
13:41–42 178
13:43 166, 197
13:44 167, 184n655,
    197
13:44–45 133n456
13:45 167, 184n655
13:45–46 197
13:47 167
13:47–48 133
13:49–50 133
13:52 167
13:54 93, 307n3
13:57 93
14:1–12 226
14:3 83
14:5 83
14:12 83
14:13–21 273
14:26 56n112
14:28–31 438, 454n64
15:14 309, 312n18
15:17–18 211
15:22 246
15:32–39 273
16 288
16:1–4 84n233
16:13 293n303
16:13–20 287, 302
16:17 288
16:17–19 287n276,
    292n295
16:18 194
16:19 167, 179,
    180n636, 197
16:27 293n303
16:28 37n26,
    183n652, 247,
    293n303
17:24–27 245

18:1 204n701
18:1–35 306
18:3 165n595, 188n664
18:4 136n469, 167, 195
18:6–7 34
18:8–9 34, 130, 343n93
18:9 187
18:10 298n320,
    300n331
18:10–14 184n655
18:12–14 307
18:23 167
18:23–35 244
19:3–9 405n69
19:8 271n201
19:12 167, 184n655,
    197, 212n733
19:16 36
19:17 179n636, 187,
    454
19:19 352n131
19:25 93
19:27–28 80
19:28 21, 42, 68,
    73, 74n186, 168,
    183n650, 186, 229,
    246, 251, 293n303
19:29 36, 181n639
20:1 167
20:21 173n618,
    183n652, 204n701
21:4–5 287
21:5 245
21:11 263
21:28–32 54n100
21:31 167, 179n636
21:43 167, 196
21:46 83, 263
22:1–14 245
22:2 167, 193
22:13 35
22:31 58n121
22:33 93
22:39 358
23 93, 382
23:1–39 306–7
23:3 105
23:8–10 164
23:10 41, 226, 286, 295
23:12 36, 53n97,
    212n738
23:13 39, 167, 179

23:15 34
23:33 34
23:34–35 33
23:37–39 227
24:1–25:46 306–7
24:7 178
24:14 113n365, 167, 196
24:17–18 383–84n224
24:23–24 286n273
24:26 385nn227–28
24:26–27 127, 383n223
24:27 227
24:27–28 384n226
24:30 127, 293n303
24:37 227
24:37–39 35, 384n224
24:38 385n229
24:39 227, 293n303, 386n230
24:40–41 35
24:42–40 149
24:42–44 40
24:43 129
24:43–44 227
24:44 100n311
24:45–51 35, 147, 227
24:47 264n168
24:51 35
25:1 167, 180n636, 193
25:1–13 40, 147, 179, 228
25:10 179n636
25:10–12 130, 246
25:13 149
25:21 179n636
25:23 179n636
25:26–28 307
25:29 36
25:30 35
25:31 293n303
25:31–46 36, 81, 136n469, 187, 230, 246
25:34 167, 179, 181, 187, 191, 193, 194n677
25:37–41 307
25:41 47n71
25:46 187
26:2 293n303
26:26–29 377

26:28 272
26:38 410
26:41 419
26:51–54 429
26:64 287
26:67 421
27:2 83
27:15–26 239n76
27:19 240
27:24–25 454n64
27:27–31 409n79
27:33 425n140
27:34 389n10, 407–8
27:37 413n94
27:39–41 409n79
27:40 408n79
27:42 408n79
27:44 408, 411
27:46 410, 432n160
27:48 407–8
27:50 427n147
27:51–53 58n123, 61, 437, 452–53
27:53 61n132
27:57 414n98
27:57–61 83
28:11–15 455n68, 456
28:16–20 50, 211, 246n93, 248
28:17 147
28:18 248
28:18–20 22
28:19 71

Mark

1:1–8 53n97
1:2 274n218
1:4–6 206
1:7–8 206–7
1:8 49n80
1:9–11 53n98, 450
1:11 226, 279n242
1:12–13 17
1:14–15 113n365, 153, 188, 196, 265
1:15 38, 43–44, 112–13, 165, 180n636, 190, 215
1:16–20 50, 212nn735–36, 267n183, 424n136

1:21 307n3
1:21–28 17
1:22 93
1:27 93
1:32 17
1:34 17
1:35 212n737
1:39 17, 307n3
1:45 212n737
2:10 293n303
2:13–14 212n735
2:14 212n736
2:18–20 205
2:28 293n303
3:6 83
3:14 69
3:14–19 67
3:15 17
3:21 93, 254n129
3:22 17, 254n129, 397n43
3:23 47n71
3:23–26 17
3:24 178
3:24–26 112–13
3:26 47n71
3:27 17, 219, 278
3:28 264n168
3:35 184n655
4:1–9 217
4:1–34 306–7
4:3–9 341
4:10 67
4:11 165
4:15 166
4:24 325n53, 327
4:25 36
4:26 165, 201n690
4:30–31 165–66, 184n655
4:31–32 139n484
5:1–20 17
6 13
6:2 307n3
6:3 93, 302n342
6:4 92n271, 222, 264, 296
6:7 17, 67
6:7–10 382
6:7–12 25
6:8–9 13
6:12 83

6:13 17
6:14–16 56n111, 83–84
6:14–29 206, 226
6:15 263, 268n188
6:17 83
6:19 83
6:20 83
6:23 178
6:27–29 83
6:30–44 273
6:31–44 212n737
7:9–13 93
7:15 210–11
7:24–30 18
8:1–10 212n737, 273
8:11–13 84n233
8:27–28 83–84, 263
8:27–30 41, 133, 279n241, 280, 292
8:28 92n271, 268n188
8:29 229, 292n295
8:30 287
8:31 123n418, 293n303, 382n221
8:31–33 428
8:33 292n295
8:34 212n738, 384n224, 425n138, 428
8:34–35 384n224
8:35 36, 382n221, 428
8:36 136n469
8:38 80, 228, 241, 293n303
9:1 33, 44, 66, 126, 142, 154, 165, 181n641, 190, 197, 227n26, 264n168
9:7 226, 270n200
9:9 293n303
9:10 150
9:11 267n187
9:12 81, 267n187, 293n303
9:12–13 269
9:13 42, 206
9:14–18 25
9:14–29 18
9:22 277
9:31 123n418, 293n303, 382n221, 428

9:35 93, 139n484
9:37 105
9:38–41 18
9:40 93
9:41 41, 286, 295
9:42 34–35
9:43 179n636, 186
9:43–45 34
9:43–47 39, 186
9:43–48 35, 130,
    136n469, 212n734,
    212n738, 343n93
9:45 179n636, 186
9:47 38n28, 165, 179,
    181n638, 184n655,
    186–87, 194, 197,
    201n690
9:47–48 34
9:47–50 216–17
9:48 81
9:49 40, 277
10:2–12 405n69
10:5 271n201
10:14 165, 179,
    184n655, 196, 201
10:15 39, 126, 165,
    180n636, 184n655,
    188n664, 215,
    264n168
10:17 36, 181n639,
    200
10:17–25 187
10:17–27 136n469,
    195, 212n735
10:17–31 201n686
10:18 454
10:19 93
10:23 39, 165, 181
10:23–25 39, 197,
    202n696
10:24 165
10:25 165, 181n638
10:27 457
10:28–30 193
10:28–31 212n736
10:29 168
10:29–30 36
10:30 39, 187, 191, 200
10:31 36, 93, 139n484
10:33 293n303
10:33–34 382n221, 428
10:34 123n418

10:35–40 229, 246, 251
10:38–39 276
10:45 81, 293n303,
    407n72, 428
10:46–52 229
10:47–48 246, 281
11:1–10 281
11:9–10 41, 229
11:10 186n660,
    190n671
11:12–14 264
11:13–14 218n758
11:15–16 264
11:15–17 236
11:18 93
11:20–21 218n758
11:27–33 54n100, 206
12:1–12 22, 167
12:18–27 39, 123n418,
    212n734
12:28–34 194n675,
    380
12:31 352n131
12:33 352n131
12:34 165, 180n636
12:35 246
12:35–37 242n84, 281,
    286
12:37 83
12:38–40 136n469
12:40 47n71
13 31n2, 40n44, 44,
    60, 123n418,
    132n450, 142, 153,
    381, 383nn223–24
13–16 78
13:1–37 306–7
13:2 43, 60, 230,
    236n63
13:3–23 40
13:5 132n450
13:5–8 381n216
13:8 132n450, 178
13:9 60, 132n450, 149
13:9–10 132n450
13:10 152, 167
13:11 60, 132n450
13:12 40, 60, 132n450
13:12–16 381n216
13:13 132n450,
    136n469
13:14 81, 383–84n224

13:14–16 60
13:15–16 383n224
13:16 383n224
13:19–22 381n216
13:20 132n450
13:21 383n223
13:21–22 286n273
13:21–23 127
13:22 132n450
13:23 132n450, 149
13:24 60
13:24–27 381n216
13:26 39, 132n450,
    293n303
13:26–27 81, 227
13:27 35, 42, 132n450
13:28–29 218n758
13:29 168
13:30 33, 44n60, 66,
    227n26
13:31 128
13:32 150, 295
13:33–37 40, 149,
    427n152
13:35 60, 422n129
13:35–36 60
14 283, 416
14–15 414
14–16 60, 388, 404
14:1 83
14:1–2 412
14:3–9 290
14:7–8 404
14:9 163n592
14:10 60, 68, 404,
    414n96
14:10–11 426n144
14:11 60, 414n96
14:12–16 412
14:17 60, 415
14:17–21 414,
    426n144, 429
14:17–31 415
14:18 60, 414n96, 415
14:18–21 404
14:20 60
14:21 60, 293n303,
    414n96, 415
14:22–24 405n69
14:22–25 377, 404,
    406, 415, 430
14:24 272, 414n98

14:25 41, 146n518,
    165, 178, 190, 193
14:26–31 415,
    426n146
14:27 42, 81, 391, 404
14:28 123n418
14:30 415
14:32 419
14:32–42 417n110,
    418–19, 426n145,
    427, 429, 432–33
14:33–34 418
14:33–35 418
14:34 60, 410, 411n87,
    418–19, 427
14:35 419
14:36 416, 418
14:37 60, 419
14:38 416, 418–19
14:39 419
14:41 60, 293n303,
    414n96, 416
14:42 60, 414n96
14:43 60, 68
14:43–46 426n144
14:43–49 404, 406
14:43–50 429
14:44 60, 414n96
14:46 83
14:48–49 404
14:50 236n60, 390–91
14:50–52 60
14:53 60
14:53–65 404, 429
14:53–15:1 60
14:54 426n146
14:57 39n40
14:58 43, 230, 236n63,
    238
14:60–61 406
14:61 404, 414n98
14:61–62 230, 302
14:62 39, 142, 246,
    247n94, 249, 251,
    293n303
14:65 60, 264n169,
    406, 414n98, 421
14:66–72 426n146
14:72 60
15 408
15:1 60, 83, 404,
    414n96

15:1–5 239, 404, 406
15:1–15 60, 429
15:1–39 404
15:2 41, 234, 246
15:2–5 230
15:4 83
15:5 414n98
15:6–15 239n76, 240,
    414n98
15:9 41, 234, 246
15:9–10 83
15:9–14 83
15:10 60, 414n96
15:12 234, 246
15:14–15 83
15:15 60, 404, 414n96
15:16 60, 235n58
15:16–20 230
15:16–32 406
15:16–47 83
15:18 41, 234, 246
15:19 414n98
15:21 425n138, 454
15:22 425n140
15:23 389n10, 407
15:25 404
15:26 41, 234, 235n54,
    246, 404, 413n94
15:27 412, 414n98
15:29–32 391n20
15:32 41, 246, 408,
    409n79, 411–12
15:33 60, 437, 450
15:34 410, 411n87,
    426n147, 427, 432
15:35 391n20
15:36 407–8
15:38 60
15:39 414n98
15:40 389
15:40–41 390, 425n141
15:42–46 425n142
15:42–47 404
15:43 77, 204n701
15:47 390
16:1 390
16:1–8 123n418, 416
16:7 50
16:14 147
16:19 247n94, 248n101

Luke

1–2 449, 453–54
1:1–4 451
1:5–25 83
1:16–17 267n187
1:17 269n196
1:19 248n99
1:26–38 83
1:32–33 245
1:33 183n652,
    201n691, 204n701
1:48 295n310
1:57–80 83
2:1–52 83
2:25 77
2:29–30 295n310
2:41–51 154
3 53n97, 210n724
3:1–2 451
3:7 277n232
3:7–9 53n97, 206–7
3:8 214, 216, 218
3:8–9 215
3:9 215–18, 277
3:10–14 206, 208
3:15–18 53n97
3:16 34, 40n43,
    100n311, 207, 216,
    218, 277
3:16–17 129, 207, 219,
    274
3:16–18 206
3:17 215, 217, 230, 277
3:23–38 281
4:1 212n737
4:1–13 17, 246
4:5 178
4:15–16 307n3
4:16–19 42, 230
4:16–30 265
4:27 268
4:32 93
4:43 113n365, 168,
    196
4:44 307n3
6 x, 310, 312n20, 329,
    334, 337, 380–81,
    453
6:6 307n3
6:17–49 306, 307n2

6:20 124n421, 165,
    179, 184n655, 193,
    196, 201, 309
6:20–21 80
6:20–23 42, 194, 265,
    309
6:20–49 309, 312
6:22–23 130
6:23 36
6:24–26 309, 341
6:27 285, 310, 323n45,
    329, 332, 343, 350,
    360
6:27–28 316, 329–30,
    334, 337–38,
    341–42
6:27–36 309, 329–30,
    377n206
6:27–37 350
6:27–38 331, 346
6:27–42 272, 312n20,
    328, 334, 336,
    340–41, 342n90,
    348–51, 374n193
6:28 328nn63–64,
    329, 332
6:29 316, 329, 331–
    32, 333n72, 360
6:29–30 334, 337–38,
    341–44
6:30 316, 330, 332,
    367
6:31 324n49, 329–30
6:32 320, 323n45,
    329, 331, 346, 350
6:32–34 321, 330,
    332, 345
6:32–35 93
6:33 311, 320, 329,
    331, 343n94, 346
6:34 320, 329, 331, 367
6:35 136n469, 311,
    320, 325, 348n115,
    350
6:35–36 330–31, 349
6:36 321, 325n52,
    349n120, 350
6:37 136n469,
    325n54, 327,
    347n111, 350,
    357n148

6:37–38 47n71, 309,
    342, 344–45
6:38 311, 325n51, 327
6:39 309, 312n18
6:39–40 309
6:40 26, 309
6:41–42 309
6:42 347n111
6:43–45 216, 309
6:46 166, 228n33, 309
6:46–49 228
6:47–49 47n71, 309
7:1 309
7:11–17 267n185
7:16–17 42
7:18–19 206
7:18–23 42, 80,
    90n252, 219, 229,
    275–76, 278
7:18–35 305
7:22–23 265–66
7:24–26 204–5
7:24–27 130, 140n490
7:24–28 139, 206
7:24–35 54n100, 306
7:26 139, 263
7:27 41, 80–81, 139,
    269n196
7:28 137–39, 165,
    184n655, 195, 205
7:31–35 83, 139–40,
    206
7:33–34 205, 212
7:34 294n307
7:36–50 290n289
7:39 263, 264n169
8:1 113n365, 196
8:1–3 212n735
8:4–18 307
9–10 13
9:1–10 25
9:3–5 382
9:10–17 273
9:23–24 384n224
9:27 142
9:50 93n274
9:52 25
9:52–56 269
9:57–60 267n183,
    424n136
9:58 212, 294n307
9:59–60 212n736

9:60 93, 168
9:61–62 212n736,
    267n183, 383n224,
    424n136
9:62 168, 180n636,
    195, 197, 383n224
10:1–16 307
10:1–17 25
10:2 217
10:2–16 382
10:4 212n735, 268
10:7 405n69
10:7–8 212n735
10:9 38, 165, 188, 190
10:10–11 168
10:10–12 136n469
10:11 190
10:12 34, 228
10:13–15 93,
    141n493, 228
10:14 34, 62n136
10:16 26, 164, 228
10:18 18, 47n71,
    112–13
10:19–20 17
10:21–22 226, 295
10:25 36, 181n639
10:29 362
11 382
11:1–4 204
11:2 36, 37n26, 38, 93,
    165, 190
11:2–4 311, 377
11:3 271
11:13 49n80
11:14–15 17–18
11:15 93, 397
11:16 84n233
11:17–18 112–13, 178
11:17–19 17
11:20 17, 38, 93, 99–
    101, 104, 112–13,
    166, 181n640, 190,
    202, 229, 271
11:21–22 17, 219, 278
11:22 219, 278
11:23 93
11:29–30 272
11:29–32 271n201
11:31–32 39, 40n40
11:32 271n201

11:37–54 307
11:39–52 93
11:49–51 33
11:52 167
12:2–3 128
12:5 34
12:8–9 39, 80,
    136n469, 228, 241,
    246, 295n308,
    300n331
12:13–21 136n469
12:22–31 212n735
12:31 166, 180n636,
    193
12:32 168, 196, 201
12:33–34 36, 136n469,
    212n735
12:35 133
12:35–38 40, 146n518,
    228
12:35–40 35
12:39 129
12:39–40 40, 149, 227
12:40 100n311
12:41–46 227
12:42–46 35, 147
12:44 264n168
12:49 34
12:49–50 40n43, 129,
    216, 218–19, 230,
    276–78
12:51–53 40, 80, 129,
    212n736, 229, 270,
    424n136
12:54–56 84n233
12:58–59 331n66
13:6–9 216–18
13:7 218
13:10 307n3
13:10–17 18
13:18 202
13:18–19 166
13:20–21 166,
    184n655, 202
13:23–24 130
13:24 39, 179n636
13:24–27 246
13:25 47n71
13:27 47n71
13:28 194

13:28–29 38n28, 42,
    43n56, 51, 74n186,
    166, 178–79, 186,
    193, 196
13:31–33 429
13:32 18
13:33 92n271, 264, 296
13:34–35 227
14:1 101–2
14:11 36, 53n97,
    136n469, 212n738
14:12–14 40, 137n469
14:15 41, 178, 204n701
14:16 167
14:16–24 245
14:24 41
14:26 93, 212n736,
    272, 424n136
14:26–27 384n224
14:27 212n738,
    409n79, 425n138,
    428
15:3–7 184n655
15:3–32 307
16:1–31 307
16:8 200
16:13 212n735
16:16 40, 54n100,
    113n365, 165n596,
    166, 180n636, 194,
    196, 206, 210
16:17 105n328, 310
16:18 405n69
16:19–31 22, 36,
    56n112, 137n469
17:1–2 34
17:20 106, 204n701
17:20–21 93, 98–104,
    106, 168, 184n655,
    190, 202
17:21 106, 127
17:22 102, 293n303,
    382
17:22–37 100, 127,
    307, 382
17:23 385
17:23–24 127, 383
17:23–33 386
17:24 227, 293n303,
    385
17:25 382
17:26 227, 385

17:26–27 382, 385
17:26–30 35, 276n225
17:27 385–86
17:28 385
17:28–29 382–83
17:28–30 385
17:29 386
17:30 227, 293n303,
    385
17:31 383n224, 385–86
17:31–32 383, 385
17:31–33 383–84n224
17:32 384
17:33 36, 212n738,
    384n224, 384, 386,
    428
17:34–35 35, 384
17:37 384
18:8 33, 227, 293n303
18:14 36
18:18 36
18:29–30 168, 193, 197
18:30 36
19 175
19:10 293n303
19:11 44, 51, 65–67,
    146n518, 147, 154,
    175, 204n701
19:11–27 150, 246
19:12 178
19:12–27 65
19:15 178
19:26 36
19:44 43, 236n63
20:34–35 39, 195, 200
21:5–38 307
21:10 178
21:31 168
21:34–36 40, 137n469
21:36 293n303
22:14 68
22:15–20 377
22:16 168, 178
22:17–20 405n69
22:18 38, 190
22:19 163n592
22:20 79, 101–2, 272
22:28–30 42, 68, 73,
    80, 183n650,
    194n676, 229,
    246, 251
22:29 196

22:29–30 168, 178, 186, 193, 197
22:30 41, 247
22:37 414n98
22:39–46 416–17
22:47–48 404
22:48 293n303
22:55 277
22:69 142, 150n531
22:70 287
23:6–12 429
23:17–25 239n76
23:30 81–82
23:33 425n140
23:34 397n48, 420n120
23:36 407–8
23:38 413n94
23:42 37n26, 183, 184n654, 204n701
23:42–43 198, 291n292
23:43 56n112
23:46 410, 411n87, 420n120, 427n147
24:6 163n592
24:7 293n303
24:8 163n592
24:11 456
24:19 263
24:21 85
24:26 248, 286
24:36–37 147
24:46 286

Q (Sayings Source; Lukan numbering)

6 342
6:17–49 307
6:20 124n422, 313
6:20–23 123–24, 279n239, 311–13, 341
6:20–26 315
6:20–49 315
6:21–23 314
6:22 293n303
6:23 125
6:24–26 313
6:27 316, 320, 353, 373, 375
6:27–28 311, 313–14, 316, 318, 321–22, 343, 346, 378–79

6:27–29 354
6:27–30 316, 320–21, 328, 334, 348n115, 360, 373, 377, 379
6:27–31 321
6:27–35 314, 378
6:27–36 315, 321, 328, 334
6:27–38 313
6:27–42 313n21, 314, 316, 322–25, 342, 346, 348, 351, 362, 368, 370–75, 377–82
6:27–47 346
6:28 316, 328, 375
6:28–30 348n115
6:29 313, 328, 376
6:29–30 311, 314, 316, 318–22, 344, 378–79
6:29–49 315
6:30 313, 320, 368, 373, 376
6:31 311, 313–14, 318–19, 322, 334, 358, 373, 376
6:31–34 377–78
6:31–36 316
6:31–38 379
6:31–42 379
6:32 311, 320, 322, 376
6:32–33 313–14, 346
6:32–34 321, 323, 368, 373
6:32–35 321–22
6:32–36 334, 362
6:34 311, 313, 320, 367–68, 376
6:35 311, 313–14, 321, 368, 376
6:36 311, 313, 321–24, 355–56, 369, 373, 376
6:36–42 365
6:37 124, 313, 321–22, 325, 347, 348n115, 363, 370, 373, 376
6:37–38 311, 321–22, 324–26, 328, 345, 347, 357–58

6:37–42 315–16, 347, 377
6:38 124, 313, 325, 360, 370, 376
6:39 311, 313, 322
6:39–45 313
6:40 311, 313
6:41 321, 376
6:41–42 311, 313, 321–22, 347, 363–65, 373, 379
6:42 321, 323, 376
6:43–44 313
6:43–45 311, 315
6:44 313
6:45 313
6:46 311
6:46–49 313, 315, 374n192
6:47–49 311
7:18–23 53, 279n239, 312
7:24–25 140n488
7:24–35 307
7:28 210
7:33 294n307
7:33–34 140n488
7:34 211, 293n303
9:58 293n303, 294n307
10:1–16 307
10:9 124
11:2 124
11:20 39n36
11:30 293n303
11:31–32 383n222
11:37–54 307
12:5 124
12:8 293n303
12:10 293n303
12:33 125
12:40 293n303
13:28 124n422
13:29 124n422
14:26 357
14:26–27 384n224
14:34–35 384n224
17:3 365
17:3–4 357
17:22–37 307
17:23–33 386
17:24 293n303, 384n226

17:26 293n303
17:26–30 384n224
17:28–29 384n224
17:31 384n224
17:31–32 384n224
17:37 384n226

John

1:7–8 139n484
1:15 207
1:20 139n484
1:20–23 207n716
1:26–27 207
1:29 90n252
1:29–34 207n716
1:30 139n484, 207
1:41 41
1:43 50
1:43–51 288n281
1:49 235n55
1:51 293n303
2:1–11 437
2:13–22 237n66
2:14–16 236
2:17 407, 410, 411n88
2:18 84n233
2:19 43, 236n63, 238
2:19–22 147
2:22 150, 154, 163n592
3:1 396n43
3:3 142n501, 181n641, 188
3:3–16 188
3:5 142n501, 179n636, 188
3:5–8 49n80
3:13 293n303
3:14 293n303
3:15 188
3:15–16 188
3:16 188
3:17 295
3:18 105
3:22 212n737
3:27–30 207n716
3:28 139n484
3:30 139n484
3:35–36 295
3:36 101n318, 188
4:2 210–11
4:19 90n271

4:25 41
4:25–26 286
4:29 41
4:35–38 217
4:48 84n233
5:19–27 295
5:19–47 307
5:21 188
5:24 188
5:27 39, 82, 293n303
5:28–29 40, 125
5:29 188
5:36 139n484
5:40 188
6 268n192, 272
6:1–15 273
6:9 268n192
6:14 90n271
6:14–15 41, 288n281
6:15 288n284
6:25–34 273
6:27 188, 293n303
6:30 84n233
6:30–34 272
6:33 188
6:39–40 34
6:40 36, 188
6:44 34
6:47 188
6:52–58 272
6:53 293n303, 404,
    405n69
6:54 34
6:59 307n3
6:61 93
6:62 293n303
6:63 188
6:66 147
6:67 67
6:70–71 67
7:20 93
7:27 292n296
7:37–39 49n80
7:46 93
8:28 293n303
8:48 93, 254n129
8:51–52 33n10,
    227n26
8:52 93
9:22 41
9:35 293n303
10:10 188

10:11–18 429
10:20 93
10:24 41
10:28 188
10:41 139n484
11:16 302n342
11:24 34
11:25 188
11:27 41
12:1–8 290n289
12:15 245, 287
12:16 154, 163n592
12:23 293n303
12:23–27 429
12:25 200, 428
12:27 409n82, 410,
    411n87, 417n111,
    426n145
12:27–38 417n110
12:31 18, 62, 396,
    397n43
12:31–32 47n71
12:31–33 62
12:33 417n110
12:34 199n680,
    293n303
13:16 26, 312
13:18 409n82, 410,
    411n87
13:21–26 404
13:21–30 426n144,
    429
13:30 404
13:31 293n303
14:1–16:33 307
14:2–3 36
14:3 35, 179n634
14:16–17 49n80
14:19 404
14:22 302n342
14:26 49n80, 161n578,
    163n592
14:30 18, 396, 397n43
14:30–31 62, 417n110
15:1–16 216, 217n755
15:6 34
15:12–13 430
15:19 132n450
15:20 312
15:20 26, 163n592
15:20–21 132n450

15:25 408, 409n82,
    410, 411n87
15:26 49n80, 161n578
15:26–27 132n450
16:1 132n450
16:2 132n450
16:4 132n450, 163n592
16:5–10 430
16:7 132n450
16:7–14 132n450
16:8–11 62
16:11 18, 396, 397n43
16:12–13 161n578
16:13 49n80
16:16 404
16:16–17 132n450
16:16–24 147
16:18 147
16:21 132n450
16:21–22 62
16:22 82
16:33 132n450
17:1–26 307
17:3 295
18:1–9 429
18:1–11 404
18:2–3 426n144
18:6–11 404
18:10–12 430
18:11 426n145
18:12–14 404
18:13–24 429
18:15–18 426n146
18:19–24 404
18:20 307n3
18:25–27 426n146
18:28–19:16 429
18:28–19:30 404
18:30 404
18:31 395
18:33 234
18:35–36 404
18:36 183n652,
    188n664
18:38–40 239n76
18:39 234
19:1 404, 414n98
19:3 234
19:11 404
19:13 235n58

19:17 409n79,
    425n138, 425n140,
    454
19:18 404, 412
19:19 234, 404,
    413n94
19:20 391n20
19:21 234
19:25 425n141
19:28–29 408, 410,
    411n87
19:30 427n147
19:32 411–12
19:34 393n26, 404,
    420n120
19:38–42 404, 425n142
20:24 67
20:25 404
20:27 404
20:31 187
21 66
21:1–25 50
21:20–23 66–67, 147
21:20–24 150
21:23 154

Acts

1 42n55, 175
1–15 50
1:5 49n80
1:6 44, 66, 154,
    155n557, 175
1:7 66, 175
1:8 49n80
1:9 296n315
1:12–26 67–68
1:20 407
2 78
2–3 279
2:4 49n80
2:17 49, 51n91
2:22–36 248
2:29–36 150n531
2:30–35 247n94
2:32–36 243
2:33 250
2:36 279n241, 280,
    290
2:38 49n80
3 274n218
3:13 238n72

3:17 396n43, 397
3:17–26 288n281
3:18 280
3:19–21 50n88, 152
3:20 280
3:22 270n200
3:22–23 92n271, 263
4:2 58n121
4:25–26 279n242, 397
4:27 238n72
5:4 105
5:31 247n94
5:35–39 84
6:14 43, 236n63
6:15 301n336
7:37 263, 270n200
7:54–60 420n120
7:55 247–48
7:55–56 247n94
7:59 56n112
8:12 19n80, 113n365, 196
9:24 102
9:31 50n86
10:36 114n368
10:36–38 114
10:38 114n368
11:16 163n592
12 42n55, 298n320
12:12–15 298
13:14–15 307n3
13:28–29 238n72
13:32–33 290
13:33 279n242
14:12 304n348
14:22 40n44, 179n636, 194n676
15:20 359n156
16:23 393n30
16:39 240n77
17:6–9 240n77
18:12–17 240n77
19:1–7 74n188
19:37–41 240n77
20:35 163n592, 325n51
21:32 393n30
21:38 85n237, 260
23:6 58n121
23:6–8 39
23:29 240n77
24–26 238
24:15 125, 375n198

25:25 240n77
26:6–7 72n178
26:8 58n122
26:23 452
26:31–32 240n77

Romans

1:2–3 243
1:3 398, 404
1:3–4 58n122, 279, 281, 284n260, 291
1:4 49n80, 58n121, 398, 404
1:7 399
2:1 348n115
3:21–26 431
3:22 430
3:25 393, 404
3:26 430–31
4:17 59n124
4:25 402, 414
5:1 399
5:5 49n80
5:6 279n241
5:8 279n241, 402
5:9 393, 404
5:18–19 430
5:18–21 430
6:3–11 411
6:4 403–4, 420
6:5–6 420
6:6 392, 403, 411
6:17 105n327
6:22 217n754
8:1–5 419n115
8:8–16 419n115
8:14 419n115
8:15 417–18
8:17 394n36, 411, 420
8:20–22 63n142
8:23–24 49n80
8:29 58n123, 452
8:32 402, 414
8:34 247n94
9:5 398, 404
9:27 418
10:14–17 115n372
11:9–10 407
11:26 51
12–14 346–48, 372n190

12:2 200n684
12:9 352n131
12:13 372n190
12:14 316n29, 332, 346–47
12:17 327n58, 347n113, 348n115
12:17–21 346, 372n190
12:19 347n113
12:21 347n113
13:3 396
13:9 352n131, 372n190
13:9–10 360n156
13:11 50n88, 96
13:12 124n424
13:14 348
14:3 347
14:10–13 347
14:13 372n190
14:15 279n241
14:17 101n318, 104, 115
15 409
15:1 409n79
15:1–3 380, 406, 411n89, 430
15:2–3 399, 406, 419
15:3 402, 407–9, 411–12
15:8 401
15:8–9 409
15:9 411
15:11 409
15:12 398

1 Corinthians

1:13 392
1:17 392
1:17–18 404
1:18 392
1:20 200n684, 397
1:23 392
2:2 392
2:6 397
2:6–8 200n684, 396
2:8 392, 394n35, 396–98, 404
3:13 277
3:18 200n684
4 313
4:5 313, 348n115
4:8 313

4:11 420
4:11–12 314
4:12 348n115
4:12–13 314
4:20 19n80, 104, 115
5:7 412, 413n93, 423
6:2 252
6:9 185n659
6:9–10 39, 104, 115, 181, 191
7:10–11 405n69
7:25 264
7:26–29 63n142
7:29–30 50n88
8:11 279n241
10:1–5 272
10:11 51n91
10:16 393, 404
10:33–11:1 406, 419
11:1 394n36, 420
11:2 405
11:23 401–2, 404, 405n69, 414–15, 421
11:23–25 377, 403–5, 415
11:23–26 163, 430
11:24–25 163n592, 415
11:25 79, 272, 404
11:26 41n47
11:27 404
12:1–13 49n80
15 67, 70
15:3 279, 398, 404, 405n69
15:3–7 55, 78, 163
15:4 403–4
15:5 68
15:11 49n84
15:12–13 58n121
15:20 58n123, 63
15:23 58n123
15:24 104, 115
15:24–25 398, 404
15:24–26 47n71
15:25 150n531
15:25–27 63n141
15:50 19n80, 39, 104, 115, 181, 191
16:3 419
16:22 48, 50n88

2 Corinthians

1:5 394n36
1:9 59n124
4:4 200n684, 396
4:8–10 395
4:10 395, 420
4:13–14 411n86
5:5 49n80
5:14 279n241
5:17 215n751
6:5 393
8:9 406
10:1 380, 399, 406,
    407n72
11 400
11:23–24 393
12:1–4 295
12:3 56n112
12:5 416
12:7 416, 419n115
12:7–9 415–16, 420
12:8 416
12:9 416
12:10 416
13:4 392, 406n71, 416

Galatians

1–2 49
1:3 399
1:3–4 414, 430
1:4 402, 404
1:17 50n85
1:18 422n126
1:18–19 50n85, 422
1:18–2:10 50
1:18–2:14 55
1:20 414
2 426n146
2:1–10 69–70
2:2–10 49
2:9 162n584, 422
2:15–21 431
2:16 431
2:19 392, 403, 411,
    420
2:20 402, 404, 414,
    430–31
3:1 392
3:22 431
4:4 51n91

4:6 49n80, 417–18,
    419n115
4:19 394n35
5:11 392
5:14 352n131
5:19–21 39, 181, 191
5:21 104, 115
5:24 392, 420
6:12 392, 394, 404
6:14 392, 404, 420
6:17 393, 395, 404,
    409n79, 420

Ephesians

1:20 247n94
1:21 200
2:5–6 151n541
2:7 191, 200
4:10 247n94
4:31–5:1 348–49
4:32 350
4:32–5:2 349–50
5:1 349–50
5:1–2 349n121, 350
5:2 350, 414, 430
5:5 183n652
5:25 414
6:12 396

Philippians

1:21–24 56n112
2:7–8 380, 406–7, 430
2:8 392, 399, 404,
    431n156
2:9–11 247n94
3:5 405n69
3:7–11 431
3:9 431
3:10 394n36, 411, 420
3:18 392, 404
4:5 33

Colossians

1:13 398, 404
1:18 58n123, 452
1:20 392–93, 404
1:24 63n142, 394n36
2:10 398, 404
2:12 403–4, 411, 420
2:12–13 151n541

2:13–14 393, 413–14
2:14 392
2:14–15 397
2:15 396
2:20 411
3:1 247n94
3:3 411
3:15 399
4:2 419

1 Thessalonians

1:1 226
1:3 226
1:5–6 49n80
1:6 393n26, 420
1:10 48n77, 226
2:14–16 399–401, 404
2:16 63n142, 100
3:3–4 63n142
3:11 226
3:11–13 226
3:13 48n77, 226
4–5 148
4:8 49n80
4:13–18 226–27
4:13–5:11 48n77
4:14 229
4:15–17 81n223
4:17 35
5:1–7 149
5:2 129, 227n28
5:6 419
5:9 226
5:9–10 279n241
5:10 419
5:15 327n58, 348n115
5:23 48n77, 226

2 Thessalonians

1:5 62n136, 195
2 142
2:7 63n142

1 Timothy

2:5–6 431
2:6 407n72, 414
6:12–13 431
6:13 238, 395
6:15 247n94
6:17 200n684

2 Timothy

2:8 163n592, 281
2:12 228n31, 290n290
2:14 163n592
2:17–18 101n318
2:18 151n541
3:1 51n91
3:1–5 34n12
4:10 200n684
4:18 172n613

Titus

2:12 200n684
2:14 407n72, 414, 431

Hebrews

1:2 51n91
1:3 247n94
1:5 279n242, 281
1:10–12 43
1:14 298n320
2:10–11 410
2:12 411n88
5:5 279n242
5:7 417n110
5:7–8 417–18
5:7–10 431
6:5 200n684
6:6 391n20
7 252n118
7:14 281
8:1 173n618, 247n94
9:26 51n91
10:5–7 411
10:12 247n94
10:37 50n88, 131n449
12:1–2 431
12:2 247n94, 431n156
13:12 391n20

James

1 378
1:2–5 378
2:1 371n188
2:2–4 371n188
2:5 124n421, 181
2:8 352n131, 371n188
2:9 371n188
3:18 217n754
4:11 357n148, 358,
    371n188

4:11–12 357
5:3 51n91
5:4 371n188
5:6 357n148
5:8 50n88, 124n424
5:9 357n148, 371n188
5:12 244, 371n188
5:20 371n188

1 Peter

1:1–3 380
1:2 49n80
1:3 58n121
1:6 131n449
1:12 49n80
1:13 133
1:19 412n92
1:20 51n91
2:20 420
2:20–24 421, 431
3:9 327, 348n115
3:18 375n198
3:18–19 56n112
3:22 247n94
4:7 124n424
4:17 50n88
5:10 131n449

2 Peter

1:11 179n636
2:5 35n19
2:6 35n19
2:9 62n136
3 66
3:1–10 148
3:3 51n91
3:3–4 131
3:6–7 35n19
3:7 62n136
3:10 129, 227n28
3:11–12 152

1 John

3:10–12 199n682
3:18 105–6
3:24 49n80

Jude

6 62n136
7 35n19
18 51n91

Revelation

1:1 50n88
1:3 50n88
1:4 100n310
1:5 58n123, 396n43,
  431n156, 452
1:6 203
1:7 100n310, 127
1:8 100n310
1:13 248n99
2–3 298n320
2:5 100n310
2:16 100n310
2:26–27 279n242
3:3 129, 227n28
3:5 228n31
3:7 281
3:10 40
3:11 100n310
3:14 431n156
3:21 247n94, 249n105,
  290n290
4:2 173n618
4:8 100n310
5:5 281
5:6–14 412
5:10 203
6:10 148
6:14 43
7:2–4 394n33
7:4–8 71n175
7:14 100n310
7:17 124n421, 247n94
8:2 248n99
9:12 100n310
11 242
11:3–12 56n111
11:12 296n315
11:14 100n310
11:15 19n80, 183n652
12:5 247n94
14:7 34n13, 62n136
14:14 248n99, 296n315
14:14–20 217n754
16:15 100n310, 129,
  149, 227n28
17:12 201n691
17:17 201n691
17:18 201n691
19:7–9 41n47

19:15 279n242
19:20 217n755,
  276n225
20 175
20:1–15 47n71
20:4 249n105, 252,
  290n290
20:4–6 252
20:10 217n755,
  276n225
20:14–15 217n755,
  276n225
21:4 124n421
21:8 276n225
21:12 72n178
21:12–13 179n633
21:15 179n633
21:21 179n633
21:25 179n633
22:1 247n94
22:2 126
22:3 247n94
22:5 290n290
22:7 100n310
22:10 33
22:12 33, 100n310
22:14 179–80n636
22:16 281
22:20 49n79, 50n88,
  100n310

**Apocrypha and
Septuagint**

Baruch

2:17 56n112
4:37 72n177
5:5 51, 72n177

1 Esdras

1:24 203
4:46 172
4:58 172
5:73 177

Judith

1:1 177
8:31 375n199
16:17 34n13, 276n230

1 Maccabees

2:26 285n272
4:46 267n187
7:4 173n618
10:53 173n618
10:55 173n618
11:52 173n618
14:41 267n187

2 Maccabees

1:24 106n333
1:27 72n177
2:7 72n177
2:18 72n177
7 56n111
7:9 188n666
7:9–23 248n102
7:36 57
12:43–44 57
12:44 248n102

3 Maccabees

2:2 172
2:4 35n19

4 Maccabees

2:23 172n612
9:9 277n231
12:12 277n231
13:12 402n65
14:6 56n112
15:3 188n666
17:5 301n336

Sirach

4:10 375n200
12:5–7 361n165
13:15 352n132
16:7 35n19
17:17 298n320
19:13–17 364
23:25 217n754
31:15 318n32, 358
36:1–17 95–96
36:13 72n177
37:6 27n109
45:23 285n272
46:1 274n217
47:12–23 378

48:1–3 378
48:1–12 378
48:4–11 378
48:10 72n177, 267
48:11 268n187
48:12 378

Tobit

1:18 172
4:12 181
4:14–15 358
4:15 318n32
12:15 248n99
13:1 106n333, 201n691
13:5 72n177
13:13 72n177, 172
13:15–16 174
13:16–18 236n63
13:17 172
14:5 43n57, 51, 72n177, 236n63

Wisdom of Solomon

2:18 375n200
5:5 301n336
6:4 106n333
10:10 106n333, 172
11:1 274n217
15:8 56n112
18:15 172

Old Testament Pseudepigrapha

Ahiqar

8:30 (Arabic) 217
8:35 (Syriac) 217
8:88 (Armenian) 318n32

Apocalypse of Abraham

18:3 172
21:6 198
29:14 108
31:2–5 34

Apocalypse of Adam

3:3 35n19
6:1 217n754

Apocalypse of Elijah

4:7–13 285
4:7–19 56n111
4:7–20 267n187
4:27–29 249n105
5:4 35

Assumption of Moses

3:11 274n217
10:9 301n336
11:16 274n217

2 Baruch (Syriac Apocalypse)

29:3 108, 280n244, 292n297
29:4–6 41n47
29:5–7 41n48
29:5–8 124n421
30:1 280n244
30:1–2 248n102
30:25 56n112
32:1 217n754
37:1 277n231
39:7 37n26, 280n244, 284n266, 292n297
40:1 252, 280n244
40:2–4 174
44:12 37n27, 191
44:13 191, 196
44:15 194, 196, 277n231
50:2–51:5 248n102
51:5 301n336
51:8 197
51:10 301n336
59:2 277n231
59:4–11 274n217
70:2 47n71
70:9 252, 280n244, 284n266

72:2 280n244, 284n266
72:2–6 252
73:1 37n26, 174
73:1–2 124n421
78:1 71n174
78:1–7 71n175, 72n178
82:20 33
85:10 33
85:13 34

3 Baruch (Greek Apocalypse)

4:16 277n231
11:2 172, 179n633
12–13 298n320

4 Baruch (Paraleipomena Jeremiou)

9:20 71

1 Enoch (Ethiopic Apocalypse)

1–16 35n19
1:3–9 37n27
1:7 62n136
1:9 62n136
5:6–8 181n641
10:4–6 47n71
10:6 34, 277n231
10:12 34n13, 62n136
10:13 47n71
10:18–19 41n48, 124n421
14:8 296n315
14:18–24 172
14:19 276n225
15:4 188n666
15:6 188n666
17:5 276n225
20:5 298n320
22:3–13 56n112
25:3 37n27
26:1 51n90
27:4 34n13
36–71 288n283, 301
37:4 188n666
40:1–2 248n99
40:9 181n639, 188n666

46:3–5 39
46:4–6 252n119
48:10 280n244
49:3 49n81
49:4 252n119
51:3 249
52:4 280n244
54:1–2 34, 277n231
54:2–6 217
54:4–6 47n71
54:6 277n231
55:4 252n119
57:1 72n178
58:3 188n666
61:8 252n119
61:12 198
62:2 49n81
62:2–16 39
62:3–5 252n119
62:7 292n296
62:14 41n47, 199n680
62:15–16 248n102
67:10–11 35n19
67:13 276n225
69:26–29 39, 252n119
71:15 200
71:15–16 192
84:2 37n26, 106n333
89:72 71n174
90:24 34
90:24–25 34, 277n231
90:25 217
90:28–29 236n63
90:28–36 43n57
90:31 267n187
90:33 72n178
91:5–7 34n12
91:9 217, 277n231
91:12–13 43
91:12–17 40n42, 45n68, 109
92:1 252n119
93 40n42, 45n68, 109
93:4 35n19
93:7 173n619
93:9 34n12
94:1 40
94:6–7 40
95:6 40
98:3 217
100:4 34n13, 62n136
100:5 298n320

100:7 375n198
100:9 34, 277n231
102:1 277n231
103:1 37n26
104:1–6 301n336
104:2–7 301n336
108:12–15 249n105

2 Enoch (Slavonic Apocalypse)

10:2 276n225
20:3 172
42:3 198
42:5 41n47
42:10 188n666
50:2 191
50:5 196n678
61:1–2 318n32
61:2–3 191
63:4 217
66:6 124n421, 194
70:10 35n19

3 Enoch (Hebrew Apocalypse)

4 222
45:3 35n19
48A:10 41n47

4 Ezra

2:10 185
4:2 200
4:26 33
4:27 200
4:30 47n71, 217n754
4:38–39 217n754
4:39 47n71
6:9 200
6:24 40
6:25–26 267n187
7:12–13 200
7:13 197
7:28 292n297
7:28–29 280n244
7:29 282n252
7:30–31 126
7:32 56n112, 125
7:32–44 248n102
7:36 198
7:36–38 34, 277n231

7:47 199n681, 200
7:50 200
7:112–13 200
7:123 198
8:1–2 200
8:1–3 193
8:52 194n677, 198, 200
12:31–32 252
12:32 280n244,
    284n259, 292n296
12:34 34n13
13:1–4 39n39
13:10–11 34,
    276n225, 277n231
13:12–13 232n42
13:32 292n297, 398n52
13:32–50 72n178
13:39–50 232n42
13:40 71n174
13:40–47 72
16:52 131n449

Greek Apocalypse of Ezra

1:9 34
2:18–19 35n19
4:37 35
7:12 35n19

Joseph and Aseneth

8:11 188n666
20:7 59n124
23:9 327n58
28:5 327n58
28:10 327n58
28:14 327n58
29:3 327n58

Jubilees

1:15 72n178
1:22–28 37n27
1:23–25 49n81
1:27 43n57
1:28 37n26
4:19 34n13
4:23 252n119
7:20 352n132
8:9 51n90
9:15 277n231

10:17 252n119
16:6 35n19
16:9 35n19
16:18 203
20:2 352n132
20:5–6 35n19
22:22 35n19
23 109–10, 251n115
23:11–25 34n12
23:29 47n71, 124n421
23:31 56n112, 57
24:30 34n13
33:20 203
35:16–17 298n320
36:4 352n132, 358n152
36:8 352n132
36:10 35n19

Letter of Aristeas

47–51 71n175
188 375n201
207 318n32, 322–23,
    358n153, 361
210 375n201
281 375n201

Liber antiquitatum bibliocarum (Pseudo–Philo)

3:1–3 35n19
3:9–10 35n19
3:10 248n102
11:10 318n32, 359n156
11:12 298n320
15:5 298n320
19:12–13 248n102
23:13 188n666
32:2–3 402n65
32:9 57n116
33:1 298n320
33:5 301n336
48:1 267n187
48:1–2 285n272
59–60 246n91
59:4 298n320

Life of Adam and Eve

(Greek)

13:2 51n91
13:6 56n112

26:4 34n13
28:4 248n102
31:4 56n112
32:4 56n112
37:1–38:4 57n116
39:2–3 249n105

(Latin)

49:3 276n225
51:2 107n335

Lives of the Prophets

3:13 200n684
21:12 267n187

Martyrdom and Ascension of Isaiah

3:8 274n217
3:17–18 71
9:24–26 249n105
10:14 247n94
11:32–33 247n94
11:40 249n105

Prayer of Joseph

3 299n326

Psalms of Solomon

2:30 106n333, 172
2:32 106n333
3:12 188n666,
    248n102
5:19 106n333
8:28 72n178
11:1–9 51
11:2–3 72n178
14:10 181n639
15:3–6 375n198
15:4–5 277n231
15:12 34n13, 62n136
15:18–19 106n333
17 252, 284
17–18 280n244
17:1 106n333
17:3 37n26, 106n333
17:3–21 186n660
17:4 72n178, 199n680

17:21 72n178,
    253n122, 398n52
17:21–44 285
17:26–28 72n178
17:32 253
17:37 49n81
17:44 72n178

Pseudo-Phocylides

8 371n187
9–10 371n187
11 371n187
14–15 371n187
16–17 371n187
19 371n187
39 371n187
40 371n187
152 362n165

**Sentences of the
Syriac Menander**

250–51 318n32

Sybilline Oracles

1:367–68 407n75
1:435 260n155
2:170–73 72n178
2:187–89 267n187
2:243 247n94
2:288–90 290n290
2:305–6 35
2:344–47 173
3:1–7 172n614
3:46–48 37n26
3:47–48 173n616
3:49 199n680
3:50 199n680
3:53–54 34, 277n231
3:54 276n225
3:81–82 43
3:84 276n225
3:175–95 34n12
3:689–91 276n225
3:766 199n680
3:767 37n26
3:767–73 174
4:152–61 34n12
4:159–60 277n231
4:165–70 277n232
4:179–90 125
4:181–92 248n102

4:186 34
5:250 51n90
5:397–433 43, 236n63
5:414 302n338
5:422 238
6:24 407n75
8:104–5 35
8:205–8 42
8:208 124n421
8:231 35
8:233 43
8:303 407n75
8:350 35
8:413 43
8:481 352n131
12:289–99 173
frg. 3 47 181n639

**Syriac Apocalypse
of Daniel**

30 296n315

**Testament of
Abraham**

(Long Recension)

1:4 248n99
4:5 248n99
7:7 172
8:1 248n99
9:7 248n99
11:10 198
13:6 73n184
14:8 198
15:11 248n99
20 420n120
20:8–14 56n112
20:10–11 57n116
20:14 198

(Short Recension)

11:3–4 252n119

Testament of Adam

4:1 298n320

Testament of Asher

4:3 375n201
4:5 375n201
5:2 188n666

6:6 188n666
7:3 72n178

**Testament of
Benjamin**

3:3–4 352n132
3:8 47n71
9:2 72n178
10:6 248
10:7 74
10:8 125
10:11 72n178
12:2 71n174

Testament of Dan

5:4 51n91
5:8–9 72n178
5:10–11 47n71
5:10–13 40
5:13 37n26
6:1–4 47n71

Testament of Gad

4:2 352n132, 371n186
4:3 371n186
6:1 371n186
6:3 371n186
6:5 371n186
6:7 371n186

Testament of Isaac

4:43–48 301n336
8:5 185

**Testament of
Issachar**

5:2 352n132
6:2–4 72n178
7:6 361

Testament of Jacob

2:5 298n320
5:9 35

Testament of Job

33:9 172
39–40 56n111, 242
43:10 298n320

**Testament of
Joseph**

6:7 298n320
19:3–8 72n178
19:10 51n91

**Testament of
Judah**

18:1 51n91
21:6 375n198
22:2–3 37n26
24:1 111n356
24:3 49n81
24:4–5 37n26
25:1–2 74
25:1–3 248
25:3 47n71, 277n231
25:4 36

Testament of Levi

1:1 34n13, 62n136
2:17 295n310
3:3 47n71
5:2 37n27
5:3 298n320
12:5 180
13:9 290n290
18:3 111n356
18:10–11 126, 198
18:11 49n81
18:12 47n71

**Testament of
Moses**

1:5 274n217
2:1 180
3:11 274n217
4:2 106n333
10:1 37n26, 112
10:1–3 47n71, 107
10:1–12 37n27
11:16 274n217
12:7 274n217

**Testament of
Naphtali**

1:6 318n32
4:2–5 72n178

Testament of Reuben

6:9 352n132

Testament of Solomon

3:5 295
12:3 425n140
26:4 173n619

Testament of Zebulun

6:6 361n162
8:2 51n91
8:3 361n162
9:5 51n91
9:8 47n71
10:3 277n231

Dead Sea Scrolls and Related Texts

CD-A (*Damascus Document*ᵃ)

2:12 266n178
3:20 188n666
6:1 266n178
6:14–7:5 371
6:16 371n185
6:18 371n185
6:20 352n132, 371n185
6:21 371n185
7:1 371n185
7:2–3 371n185
7:4 371n185
7:15–21 253, 284n266
7:18–21 111n356, 259n150
8:5–6 371n185
9:2–8 354
12:23–13:1 280n244
14:18–19 280n244

CD-B (*Damascus Document*ᵇ)

19:10–11 280n244, 284n266
20:1 280n244

1QH (*Hodayot*)

3:29–36 276n225
4:11 295n310
4:21–24 295n310
4:29–40 107n335
5:20 298n320
5:25 49n81
6:8–12 295n310
8:16–26 295n310
11:19–36 107n335
19:3–35 107n335
19:27–33 295n310
23:10–15 266n181
23:12–24 114
25–26 261

1QM (*War Scroll*)

2:2–3 71n172
6:6 37n26
11:7 266n178
12:7 37n26
12:7–8 37n26
12:16 37n26

1QpHab (*Pesher to Habakkuk*)

2:5–10 34n12
7:5–8 149
7:9–14 149

1QS (*Rule of the Community*)

1:10 361n165
4:7 188n666
4:17–19 47n71
4:21–22 49n81
4:26 49n81
5:24–25 364n174
5:25 49n81, 352n132
6:25 49n81
9:9–11 280n244, 296
9:11 270n199

1Q28a (1QSa) (*Rule of the Congregation*)

2:2–22 41n47
2:11–14 292n97
2:11–15 280n244

1Q28b (1QSb) (*Rule of Benedictions*)

3:5 37n26
4:25–26 37n26, 174
5:20–22 252
5:21 37n26, 203, 253n122
5:24–29 284n266

4Q161 (4QpIsaᵃ) (*Isaiah Pesher*ᵃ)

3:11–25 280n244
3:18–25 284n266
frgs. 8–10 284n259
frgs. 8–10 col. III 20–21 253n122

4Q164 (4QpIsaᵈ) (*Isaiah Pesher*ᵈ)

frg. 1 74
frg. 1 4 68n160
frg. 1 7 68n160

4Q174 (4QFlor) (*Florilegium*)

1:1–3 43n57, 236n63
1:10–13 280n244
1:11–13 253

4Q175 (4QTest) (*Testimonia*)

in toto 111n356, 270n199, 296

4Q181 (4QAgesCreat B) (*Ages of Creation B*)

frg. 1 col. II 4 188n666

4Q185 (*Sapiential Work*)

in toto 94

4Q203 (4QEnGiantsᵃ ar) (*Book of Giants*ᵃ ar)

frg. 9 37n26

4Q225 (4QpsJubᵃ) (*Pseudo-Jubilees*ᵃ)

frg. 2 col. II 5 248n99

4Q242 (4QPrNab ar) (Prayer of Nabonidus ar)

in toto 76n199

4Q243 (4QpsDanᵃ ar) (*Pseudo-Daniel*ᵃ ar)

in toto 76n199

4Q244 (4QpsDanᵇ ar) (*Pseudo-Daniel*ᵇ ar)

in toto 76n199

4Q245 (4QpsDanᶜ ar) (*Pseudo-Daniel*ᶜ ar)

in toto 76n199

4Q246 (*Aramaic Apocalypse*)

in toto 37n26
2:5–6 252n117

4Q252 (4QcommGen A) (*Commentary on Genesis A*)

5:1–4 253, 284
5:1–7 280n244
5:3 280n244

4Q264 (4QSⁱ) (*Rule of the Community*ⁱ)

1–4 295n310

4Q285 (4QSM) (*Sefer ha-Milḥamah*)

frg. 5 280n244
5:4 284n266

**4Q286 (4QBer^a)
(Blessings^a)**

frg. 7 col. I 172
frg. 7 col. II 2–13 378

**4Q287 (4QBer^b)
(Blessings^b)**

frg. 2 11 172n611

**4Q300 (4QMyst^b)
(Mysteries^b)**

frg. 3 47n71

**4Q377 (4Qapocr-
Pent B) (Apocry-
phon Pentateuch B)**

in toto 266n178
frg. 1 recto col. II 5
   274n219

**4Q381 (Non-Ca-
nonical Psalms B)**

frg. 19 1 172n611

**4Q385 (4QpsEzek^a)
(Pseudo-Ezekiel^a)**

frg. 3 6 131n449

**4Q386
(4QpsEzek^b)
(Pseudo-Ezekiel^b)**

frg. 1 col. 2 72n178

**4Q398 (4QMMT^e)
(Halakhic Letter^e)**

frgs. 14–17 col. II 6 94

**4Q399 (4QMMT^f)
(Halakhic Letter^f)**

col. II 3 94

**4Q400
(4QShirShabb^a)
(Songs of the Sab-
bath Sacrifice^a)**

in toto 172
frg. 1 col. II 1–4 171
2 106n333

**4Q403
(4QShirShabb^d)
(Songs of the Sab-
bath Sacrifice^d)**

frg. 1 I 106n333

**4Q405
(4QShirShabb^f)
(Songs of the Sab-
bath Sacrifice^f)**

in toto 172
frg. 20 col. II 21–22 2
   248n99
frg. 23 II 106n333

**4Q417
(Instruction^c)**

frg. 1 col. I 1–4 365

**4Q427 (4QH^a)
(Hodayot^a)**

frg. 7 261

**4Q471b (Self-
Glorification
Hymn^a)**

in toto 261

**4Q491 (4QM^a)
(War Scroll^a)**

in toto 262n164
frg. 11 261

**4Q504 (4QDib-
Ham^a) (Words of
the Luminaries^a)**

frgs. 1–2 col. VI
   12–14 72n178
frg. 4 10 203

**4Q509+4Q505
(4QpapPrFêtesc)
(Festival Prayers^c)**

3 72n178

**4Q511 (4QShir^b)
(Songs of the Sage^b)**

frg. 35 301n336

**4Q521 (Messianic
Apocalypse)**

in toto 37n26, 42,
   47n71, 249n105,
   265–66, 268, 290
frg. 2 49n81
frg. 2 col. II 1 280n244
frg. 2 col. II 12 59n124
frgs. 7 + 5 col. II 6
   59n124

**4Q525 (4QBéat)
(Beatitudes)**

in toto 94

**4Q554 (4QNj^a ar)
(New Jerusalem^a
ar)**

in toto 72n178

4Q558 (Vision^b ar)

frg. 1 col. II 4 267n187

**4Q559 (4Qpap-
BibChronology
ar) (Biblical
Chronology)**

in toto 444n24

**11Q5 (11QPs^a)
(Psalms^a)**

in toto 246n91

**11Q13 (11QMelch)
(Melchizedek)**

in toto 80, 115,
   252n118, 265, 274
2:13 252
2:15–20 114
2:18 280n224
18 266n178

**11Q19 (11QT^a)
(Temple^a)**

29:8–10 43, 236n63
57:5–6 72n178
59:17–18 173n618

Targumic Texts

**Fragmentary
Targum**

on Gen 38:26
   124n423
on Gen 49:10–12
   284n266
P on Exod 15:18
   146n518
V on Exod 12:42
   146n518, 253n122
on Num 11:26
   284n266
on Num 24:7 232n42
on Num 24:17–19
   284n266

Targum Canticles

1:1 232n42
1:8 274n217
4:4 288n281
7:4 288n281
8:5 51n89

Targum Esther

1:1 46n69

Targum Ezekiel

13:9 188n666
20:11 188n666
20:13 188n666
20:21 188n666

Targum Hosea

2:2 72n178
14:10 188n666

Targum Isaiah

on 6:13 72n178
on 9:5 280n244
on 10:27 280n244
on 11:1 280n244
on 11:1–2 273n216
on 16:5 249
on 31:4 37n26, 174
on 40:9 37n26
on 42:1–4 49n81
on 52:7 37n26

on 53:5 238
on 53:8 72n178

Targum Lamentations

2:22 288n281

Targum Micah

4:7 37n26
4:7–8 174n621
4:8 292n296
5:3 72n178

Targum Neofiti I

on Gen 4:8 172n613, 193
on Gen 19:26 384n225
on Gen 38:25 124n423
on Exod 2:12 197
on Exod 12:42 146n518
on Lev 19:18 361
on Num 24:7 72n178
on Deut 32:35 199n681

Targum Onqelos

on Gen 28:13–16 299n325
on Gen 49:11 260n154
on Exod 24:8 272n208
on Lev 18:5 188n666
on Deut 33:6 188n666

Targum Psalms

1:1 40n40
45:3 253n122, 273
80:16 253n122

Targum Pseudo-Jonathan

on Gen 4:1 199n682
on Gen 11:1 402n65
on Gen 11:10 402n65
on Gen 15:1 193
on Gen 19:26 384n225
on Gen 28:13–17 299n325

on Gen 33:10 298n320
on Gen 38:27 124n423
on Gen 48:16 298n320
on Gen 49:10–12 284n266
on Gen 49:15 197
on Exod 4:13 267n187
on Exod 6:18 267n187, 285n272
on Exod 13:17 56n111
on Exod 15:18 107
on Exod 24:8 272n208
on Exod 40:10 267n187
on Exod 40:11 284n266
on Lev 18:5 188n666
on Lev 19:18 318n32
on Lev 22:28 369, 370n182, 375n201
on Num 24:17–19 284n266
on Num 25:12 269n196, 274n218
on Deut 30:4 267n184
on Deut 33:5 260n155
on Isa 28:28 217n754
on Isa 33:11 217n754

Targum Ruth

2:13 191

Targum 1 Samuel

2:6 188n666
25:29 188n666

Targum 2 Samuel

22:28 124n421
23:5 199n680

Targum Zechariah

2:14–15 37n27
3:8 292n297
4:7 292n297
6:12 292n297
6:12–13 238
9:11 272n208
14:4–5 51
14:9 37n26, 107

Mishnah, Talmud, and Related Literature

Mishnah

'Abot

1:1 405n69
1:3 405n69
2:7 191
2:10 318n32
2:16 193
3:12 192
3:16 96
3:17 41n47, 193
4:16 188n666, 193
4:17 197
5:10 341n89
5:19 191, 193–94, 198
6:7 191

Berakot

1:5 199n680, 280n244
2:2 106n333, 180n636
5:3 370n181
5:22 59n124

Baba Meṣiʿa

2:11 189

'Edduyot

28n115, 267n187

Megillah

4:9 370n181

Nedarim

9:4 366

Pe'ah

1:1 193

Pesaḥim

8:6 240n78

Qiddušin

1:10 181n641
4:14 34, 193–94

Roš Haššanah

4:5 59n124

Sanhedrin

9:15 40
10:1 39, 58n121, 181n641, 192, 213
10:1–4 192
10:2 191
10:3 40n40, 72n178, 75, 192

Šeqalim

2:5 267n187

Soṭah

1:9 274n217
9:15 34n12, 80, 129, 267–68n187, 280n244

Taʿanit

1:1 59n124

Tamid

7:4 188n666

Yoma (= Kippurim)

4:1–2 106n333
6:2 106n333

Tosefta

Berakot

3:6 415
3:24 58n121
7:21 193

Pe'ah

4:18–19 195

Sanhedrin

6:2 371n188
9:11 355n140
12:9–13:12 192
12:11 189
13:1 191, 198
13:1–5 194

13:2 189, 191
13:6–8 191
13:10 191, 192n674
13:12 72n178, 75, 191

Soṭah

5:11 366
9:11 359, 362
13:2 49n81

Taʿanit

1:13 106n333

Yoma (= Kippurim)

4:10–11 194

Jerusalem Talmud

'Abodah Zarah

3:1 439

Berakot

2c (1:1) 248n99
4a (2:1) 180n636
4b (2:1) 180n636
5a (2:3) 253n122
6a (3:1) 188n666
7a (4:1) 415
9b (5:2) 58n121
9c (5:3) 369
11d (7:3) 191, 195
12c (8:6) 34n13
13d (9:2) 194

Ḥagigah

77a (2:1) 34n13, 190,
   195

Kelim

32b (9:4) 189n666

Ketubim

35a (12:3) 196
35b (12:4) 51n89

Kilʾayim

32b (9:4) 51n89, 196

Maʿaśerot

51a (3:10) 198

Megillah

75c (4:10) 369

Moʿed Qaṭan

81c–d (3:1) 446n38
83b (3:7) 190

Nedarim

38a (3:8) 191
41c (9:4) 352n133,
   359, 362

Peʾah

15b (1:1) 195, 369
15c (1:1) 34, 198
15d (1:1) 193
16b (1:1) 192–93, 199

Pesaḥim

33a (6:1) 191

Qiddušin

61b (1:7) 198
61d (1:9) 194

Šabbat

3c (1:3) 191

Sanhedrin

18a (1:1) 396n39
23c (6:4) 355n140
25d (7:13) 446
27c (10:1) 198
29b (10:3) 194
29b–c (10:3) 197
29c (10:6) 72n178

Šeqalim

47c (3:3) 194, 196,
   268n187

Soṭah

17a (1:5) 355n140

Taʿanit

68d (4:5) 110n353,
   111, 253n122,
   258n150

**Babylonian
Talmud**

'Abodah Zarah

3b 190, 284n266
7a 375n200
9a–b 259
17a 189n666

'Arakin

16b 363–64, 365n175,
   373

Baba Batra

10b 195
11a 195
15a 443
15b 196, 199, 363–64
17b 375n200
75a 193
134a 139n484

Berakot

3a 37n25
4b 194
9b 194
10b 180n636
13a–b 180n636
14b 180n636
16b 198
21a 188n666
28b 194n675
34a 195
47a 215n750
51a 191
57a 194
57b 107n335
61b 180n636

Baba Meṣiʿa

59a 192
59b 446
85b 195

Baba Qamma

51a 355n140

'Erubin

43a–b 267n187
54a 24
54b 195

Giṭṭin

36b 368
57b 189
68b 195

Ḥagigah

14a 249, 302n338
14b 194n677, 195
15a 196, 199, 248n99
15b 191, 198

Ḥullin

83a 375n200

Ketubim

37b 355n140
111a 195

Megillah

28b 195

Menaḥot

44a 193

Pesaḥim

50a 36, 195
75a 355n140
119b 41n47, 193

Qiddušin

39b 193
40a 217n754
40b 191, 193–96

Roš Haššanah

17b 375n199

Šabbat

30b 198
31a 318n32
88b 368
127a 193
133b 369
153a 195

Sanhedrin

37a 51n90
38b 249

41a 396n39
45a 355n140
52a–b 355n140
91a–b 56n112
92b 56n111
93b 110n353,
259n150
94a–b 284n266
96b–99a 267n187
97a 80, 129
97a–98a 398n52
98a 115, 296n315,
302
98b 181, 192
99a 192, 195
99a–b 24
101b 191, 198
102b 191
104b 191
105a 191, 194
108a 35n19
110b 72n178, 191,
192n674

Soṭah

7b 189, 191
8b 355n140
9a 33
35a 191
49a 37n25

Sukkah

28a 139n484

Ta'anit

7a 375n197
7b 362n165
11a 298n320
22a 195
24b–25a 375n200

Temurah

16a 198

Yebamot

22a 215
48b 215n750
62a 215n750
97b 215n750

Yoma (= Kippurim)

4a 296n315
23a 367–68
76a 446n37
87a 415
88a 195

Zebaḥim

102a 260n155
116a 276n225

Other Rabbinic Works

'Abot de Rabbi Nathan

A 1 107n335
A 2 189n666
A 12 57n114, 199
A 14 191, 198
A 15 318n32,
373n191
A 16 318n32, 355,
356n144, 361,
362n169
A 19 189n666, 195
A 21 190, 191n672,
199n681
A 25 193–94, 198
A 26 366
A 28 193–94
A 35 51
A 36 189, 192n674
A 39 194
A 40 191, 194,
199n681
B 10 191, 193,
194n675, 198
B 22 189
B 25 57n114
B 26 318n32, 359, 362
B 27 178n632, 191,
193
B 28 139n484
B 29 189n666, 191,
195–96, 199
B 32 197
B 33 197, 199
B 34 199

B 43 191
B 44 193–94, 199n681
B 45 189n666, 191

Mekilta

on Exod 12:42
146n518
on Exod 13:18
353n134, 365
on Exod 13:19 367
on Exod 14:24
199n681
on Exod 14:31
72n178, 191
on Exod 15:1 56n112
on Exod 15:2 369
on Exod 15:18 37n26,
43n57, 236n63
on Exod 16:14 446n37
on Exod 17:16 37n26
on Exod 18:1 35n19,
276n225
on Exod 18:12
375nn197–98
on Exod 18:14
260n155
on Exod 20:20
188–89n666

Mekilta de Rabbi Simeon ben Yoḥai

36:2 on Exod 15:18
37n26

Midrash on Proverbs

13 194
13:4 196
17 195

Midrash on Psalms

1:2 260n155
10:1 368
11:6 195, 197
14:6 193
18:30 196
23:5 446n37
31:3 194
31:6 198
37:3 193

49:3 191
55:3 298n320
78:12 195
90:17 75n196

Midrash Petirat Moshe (Midrash on the Death of Moses)

in toto 360
BHM 1:125–28
57n114
BHM 6:75–77
57n114

Midrash Rabbah

Genesis Rabbah

9:3 197
9:8 189, 194
9:13 172n613
11:10 189n666
12:10 199n680
14:3 189
17:5 107n335
20:1 199n681
24:7 352n133, 359,
362
28:8 194
33:1 193
44:4 193
47:6 299n325
51:8 193
55:3 355
62:2 193
68:12 299n325
69:3 299n325
73:11 193
78:3 298n320
82:6 299n325
87:6 199n681
90:6 191
96:5 51n89
98:9 232n42

Exodus Rabbah

1:26 288n281
7:4 198
15:13 260n155
15:15 199n682
18:12 146n518

30:24 193
31:3 194
31:5 193
50:5 194
52:3 193

Leviticus Rabbah

3:1 197
3:2 191, 198
4:5 193
9:6 284n266
13:3 193
24:4 356
24:5 352, 353n134
27:1 193
30:2 197
34:4 191, 196n678

Numbers Rabbah

9:17 189, 191
13:14 302
16:23 191
18:13 194
21:20 196

*Deuteronomy
Rabbah*

1:10 274n217
3:17 267n187
5:6 371n188
7:9 193
11:10 57

Ruth Rabbah

5:6 288n281

Ecclesiastes Rabbah

1:28 288n281
2:1 197
4:5 197
8.4.1 355n140

Canticles Rabbah

1.1.9 191
2.5.3 193
2:12 75n195

*Lamentations
Rabbah*

2.2.4 258n150
2:4 111n357

Pesiqta de Rab Kahana

6:2 196
7:10 193
8:1 197
12:19 193

Pesiqta Rabbati

1:6 51n89
4 71n172
15:10 288n281
15:22 192n674
16:6 196
18:1 197
20:4 296n315
31:10 51n89
35:3 267n187
41:5 193
50:1 198
50:3 195

Sipra

on Leviticus

121 on Lev 11:44 356,
    375n201
193 on Lev 18:5 191
195 on Lev 19:1 352
200 on Lev 19:15–16
    371n188
200 on Lev 19:17–18
    364, 367–68, 373
200 on Lev 19:18
    352n133, 359,
    361–62
205 on Lev 19:33–34
    361
263 on Lev 26:12 193
263 on Lev 26:13 193

Sipre

on Deuteronomy

1 on Deut 1:1 364
9 on Deut 1:10 197
10 on Deut 1:10 195,
    198
32 on Deut 6:5 194
47 on Deut 11:21 197
48 on Deut 11:22
    196, 199

49 on Deut 11:22
    356n144, 375n201
53 on Deut 11:26 194
89 on Deut 13:9 361
186/7 on Deut 19:10–
    11 366
235 on Deut 22:13 366
305 on Deut 31:14
    57n114
310 on Deut 32:7 196
313 on Deut 32:10
    108
339 on Deut 32:50
    57n114
356 on Deut 33:29
    193–94
357 on Deut 34:1
    57n114
357 on Deut 34:5
    248n99

Soperim

3:13 369

Tanḥuma

'Eqeb

7 75n196
7b 288n281

Tanḥuma Buber

Ki-Tavo

4 189n666

Lekh-Lekha

1 180n636
12 190

Metsora'

1 192, 194

Mishpatim

12 267n187

Pequde

7 193, 194n677

Qedoshim

1 197
2 355n141
7:3 353n134

Shelah

25 191
28 188n666, 189, 191

Wayehi

12:6 51n89

Wayyera

11 199n681

Tanḥuma Yelameddenu

Tsaw

13 193
14 195

Tanna debe Eliyahu

18 193
26 194n675
28 194n675

Yalqut

on 1 Kgs 18:26
    199n682
on Isa 46:23 75n195

Apostolic Fathers

Barnabas

4:9 51n91
6:13 126
8:5 234n51
12:9 51n91
12:10 247n94
16:5 51n91
18–20 332n68
19:4 365
19:4–5 363
21:3 47n71

1 Clement

11:1–2 384n225
13 325
13:1 325
13:1–2 323, 327

13:2 316, 324–27,
   328n60, 328n62,
   338, 341–42, 345,
   348, 351
16:7 414
23:3–5 148
24:1 58n123
31:2–4 402n65
36:4 279n242
36:5 247n94
46:8 34
50:4 131n449
52:2 407n73

2 Clement

3:2 228n31
5:5 191n672
6:9 179n636
11:1–7 148
12:6 152
13:4 323n45
14:2 51n91
16:3 62n136
17:6 62n136
18:2 62n136

Didache

1–2 333
1–6 332n68
1:2 329–30, 332,
   352n131, 359,
   371n189
1:2–5 316
1:2–6 329–30
1:2–2:2 359n156
1:3 329–32, 340–41
1:3–5 341, 351
1:3–2:1 332–34
1:4 329–33, 339,
   341–42
1:5 330–32
1:6 330–31
2:2 371n189
2:3 371n189
2:5 371n189
2:7 372n189
3:4 372n189
3:5 372n189
3:7 183n647
4:1 405n69
4:3 372n189

4:4 372n189
4:8 372n189
6:2 333n73
8:2 36, 377
8:3 415
9:4 35n16, 185
10:5 35n16, 179n634,
   185, 194n677
10:6 41n47, 48
16:3 51n91
16:6 58n121

Diognetus

10:2 172n613

Ignatius

To the Ephesians
16:1 181

To the Magnesians
11:1 238n72

To Polycarp
2:1 330

To the Romans
6:3 420

To the Smyrnaeans
1:2 238n72
10:2 228n31

To the Trallians
9:1 238n72

Martyrdom of
Polycarp

1:1–2 420n120
16:1 420n120
22:3 172n613

Polycarp

To the Philippians
2:1 247n94
2:2–3 326
2:3 316, 324n48, 326–
   28, 337, 341–42,
   345n107, 351
5:2 200n684, 290n290

5:3 185
7:1 62n136
8:2 420n120
12:3 328n63

Shepherd of
Hermas

Similitude
9.12.8 179n636
9.15.2 179n636
9.16.2 179n636
9.20.2–3 179n636

Nag Hammadi
Codices

I,4 Treatise on the
Resurrection
1.43.25–50.18 101n318
1.49 151n541

II,3 Gospel of
Philip
61:5–10 199n682

II,7 Book of
Thomas the
Contender
138 302n342

III,5 Dialogue of
the Savior
50 130

New Testament
Apocrypha and
Pseudepigrapha

Acts of Andrew
and Matthias
21 296n315

Acts of John
81 327n58

Acts of Paul
7 455n69

Acts of Pilate
4(20):1 426n145

Acts of Thomas

1 302n342
11 302n342
12 130
27 38n31
31 302n342
33 100
34–35 302n342
39 302n342
45 302n342
57 302n342
136 181
147–53 302n342

Apocalypse of Paul
7–10 298n320

Apocalypse of
Peter
6:1 247n94

Apostolic Con-
stitutions and
Canons
7.2 359n156
7.26.5 48–49

Epistula
Apostolorum
3 247n94
18 359n156
51 296n315

Gospel of
Nicodemus
Latin B 10(26):1
   452n59

Gospel of Peter

1:1 238n72
2 (E) 218n758
2:3 425n142
2:3–5 238n72
4:11 235n55, 413n94
5:16 407–8

5:19 410, 426n147
6:21 404
6:23–24 425n142
8:29 238n72
8:31 238n72
11:43–49 238n72

Gospel of the Nazarenes

5 47n71
frg. 16 352n131

Gospel of the Savior

107:43–48 276n228

Gospel of Thomas

1 126n431, 302n342
3 38n34, 98n296, 98n300, 99, 130, 184n655
4 36, 184
5 128
6 373n191
8 35, 133
10 219, 230, 276–77
11 128
12 130
13 133, 161n578, 279n239
16 40, 129–30, 230
18 126, 130
19 36, 126
20 184, 192
21 40, 129, 133
22 130, 179n636, 184, 188n664
25 352n131
27 184n655
31 130, 264
34 312
35 17, 219, 278
37 126
42 212n735
45 312
46 54n100, 130, 137–39, 184n655, 188n664, 210
49 38n34, 184
50 184

51 99, 102, 126, 151n541, 155, 184
52 155
54 184n655
55 212n738, 425n138, 428
56 130
57 35, 126–27, 133, 184, 192, 217
60 184
61 35
64 184
67 130
68–69 130
69 130
71 43, 236n63
75 130
76 36, 133n456, 184, 192
78 130
82 40n44, 184, 230, 276n228
85 126n431
86 125n426, 293n303
91 130
96 184
96–98 192
97 184
98 184
99 184
103 130, 133
105 130
107 184, 192
109 130, 133n456, 184, 192, 197
111 43, 126
113 38n34, 98–99, 101n318, 102–3, 126–27, 181n641, 184, 202
114 36, 161n578, 179n636, 184, 187n662

Infancy Gospel of Thomas

in toto 448
2–19 154

Pistis Sophia

21 303n342

Protevangelium of James

9–18 154
21 154

Pseudo-Clementine Homilies

3:19 332
7:4 359–60n156
11:4–5 359–60n156
12:26 349n120
12:32 330, 359
18:16 322n44

Pseudo-Clementine Recognitions

1:60 139n484
8:56 360n156

Transitus Mariae

B 17 296n315

Greek and Latin Works

Adamantius

Dialogue (De recta in Deum fide) (On True Faith in God)

5.22 394n34

Ambrose

Espositio Evangelii secundum Lucam

407n74

Ambrosiaster

Commentary on Romans

15:2–3 420n117

Aristides

Apology

15 359n156

Aristophanes

Ranae (Frogs)

1177 415n101

Artemidorus

Onirocritica

2:53 403n67
2:56 409n79
4:49 403n67

Athanasius

Vita Antonii (Life of Antony)

20.1 384n225
60 57n115

Augustine

De civitate Dei (The City of God)

10.8 384n225
16.30 384n225
20.9 175n627

De doctrina christiana (Christian Instruction)

4.10.24 28n116

Epistulae (Letters)

75.21–22 29n119
82.35 29n119

Expositio in epistulam ad Galatas

64 394n31

De sermone Domini in monte (Sermon on the Mount)

2.22.75 359n156

De Trinitate

15.17.30 408n77

Basil of Caesarea

Commentary on Isaiah

51 354n139

Regulae brevius tractatae (Shorter Rules)

276 349n120

Bede

Commentary on Acts

1:6 175n624
12:12–15 298n320

Cassiodorus

Expositio psalmorum

68:10 408n76

Chrysostom and Pseudo-Chrysostom

Homiliae in epistulam ad Ephesios

5:1 349n120

Homiliae in epistulam ad Romanos

27.2 408n79

Homiliae in epistulam i ad Corinthios

2:6–8 397n45

Homiliae in Joannem

42 268n192

Homiliae in Matthaeum

26.5 172n613
38.1 105n327
87.1 407n75

De legislatore

296n315

Cicero

De oratore

2.353–54 375n202

Clement of Alexandria

Paedagogus (Christ the Educator)

2.2.32.2–3 212n739
3.12 359n156

Protrepticus (Exhortation to the Greeks)

10(103) 384n225

Quis dives salvetur (Salvation of the Rich)

40.2 41

Stromata (Miscellanies)

2.91.2 324n46
6.15.132 57n114

Commodian

Instructiones adversus gentium deos pro christiana disciplina

42 (2.1) 72n178

Cyprian

De dominica oratione

28 359n156

Cyril of Alexandria

Commentary on Isaiah

52.8 112n362

Commentary on Luke

48 273n213
96 218n759

Homilies on Luke

73 38n30
117 99n307

Didymus of Alexandria

Fragmenta in Psalmos

frg. 883 276n228

Dio Cassius

Roman History

54.3.7 235n53

Diogenes Laertius

Vitae philosophorum (Lives of Eminent Philosophers)

1.9 318n32
5.21 318n32

Ephraem

Commentary on Exodus

20.2 359n156

Epiphanius

Panarion (Refutation of All Heresies)

40.5.3 199n682
48.14.1 51n92
49.1.3 51n92
64.70.5–17 56n112

Eusebius

Demonstratio evangelica (Demonstration of the Gospel)

3.2 (92b–c) 273n213

Historia ecclesiastica (Ecclesiastical History)

1.13.11 302n342
3.19–20.5 185
3.20 283n255
3.28.2 185
3.39 156
3.39.12 185
3.39.14–16 445
4.2.5 259n151
4.6.2 111n357, 259n150
4.14.9 327n58
5.1.43–44 235n53
5.1.44 235n54
5.1.57–63 403n67
5.18.2 51n92

De martyribus Palaestinae (The Martyrs of Palestine)

9.9–10 403n67

Onomasticon

365/74:19 425n140

Praeparatio evangelica (Preparation for the Gospel)

8.7.6 318n32, 359n156
8.7.12–13 307n3
8.10.4 274n217
8.14.50 451n54
9.28–29 260n155
9.29.4–5 249n106
10.8 457n76

Gregory of Nyssa

Vita Mosis

2.91–93 443n23

Haymo of Halberstadt

Expositio in epistulam ad Romanos

8:15 418n113
13:3 397n45

Herodotus

Historiae (Histories)

1.128 416n107
2.27–28 443
2.68–72 443
3.142 318n32
7.136 318n32

Hippolytus

Commentarium in Danielem

3.29 455n69

Refutatio omnium haeresium (Refutation of All Heresies)

5.8.23–24 40

Horace

Epistulae (Epistles)
1.16.48 403n67

Irenaeus

*Adversus Haereses
(Against Heresies)*
1.23.5 151n541
2.31.2 151n541
3.2.1–2 156n559
3.13.2 156n560
3.16.4 172n613
4.13.3 323n45, 354
4.16.3 360n156
5.31.1 57n117
5.32.1 175n626
5.33.3 41, 124n421,
    185
5.35 51

*Epideixis tou apo-
stolikou kerygmatos
(Demonstration
of the Apostolic
Preaching)*
87 360n156

Isho'dad of Merv

*Commentary on
Luke*
19:12–27 65n153

Isocrates

*Ad Demonicum
(Or. 1)*
14 318n32

Ad Nicoclem (Or. 2)
49 318n32
61 318n32

Aegineticus (Or. 19)
51 318n32

Jerome

*Commentariorum in
epistulam ad Ephe-
sios libri III*
5:1 349n120

*Commentariorum in
epistulam ad Galatas
libri III*
6:17 394n31

*Commentariorum in
Matthaeum libri IV*
3:11 218n761,
    278n236
25:6 146n518
27:34 407n74
27:51–53 453n60

*Vita S. Pauli, primi
eremitae*
14 57n115

Josephus

Against Apion
1.15–52 444n24

Jewish Antiquities
1–9 444n24
1.70 276n225
1.72–76 35n19
1.80–88 444n24
1.232 402n65
2.102 236n62
2.129 236n62
2.327 274n217
4.108–109 444n25
4.165 274n217
4.329 274n217
6.166–168 246n91
6.307 375n197
8.314 375n197
10.268 76n199
11.133 71n175
12.100 455n69
14.36 235n56
15.373 235n56
16.311 235n56
17.204 240n78
17.271–272 261n158
17.273 261n158
17.273–277 398
17.278–284 398
17.278–285 261n158
18.3–10 84n234

18.23–25 84n234
18.53 162
18.56 239
18.60–62 239
18.63 238n71
18.64 238, 391
18.85–87 261n157,
    399
18.116–119 53n97,
    205
18.117 206
19.64 401n61
20.48 217n754
20.97–99 84,
    261n157, 399
20.102 84n234
20.167–168 261n157,
    399
20.169–172 85n237,
    260, 398
20.170 260
20.188 261n157, 399
20.208–209 240n78

Jewish War
2.56 261n158
2.57–59 261n158, 398
2.60–65 261n158, 398
2.118 84n234
2.139 362n165
2.154 56n112
2.169 239
2.175–176 239
2.253 236n62
2.258–260 261n157,
    399
2.261–263 260, 398
2.305–306 236n62
2.433 84n234
2.433–438 261n158,
    398
3.362 56n112
4.389–393 261n158
4.503–544 398
4.503–584 261n158
4.564–566 261n158
6.104 235n56
6.288–300 451n54
6.300–309 237–38
6.301–302 207
6.305 240

6.309 401
6.312–313 76–77
7.21–36 398
7.153–157 398
7.171 235n56
7.253 84n234

Julius Caesar

Gallic Wars
6.14 27n106

Justin

*Apologia i (First
Apology)*
13.3 238n72
15.9 330, 332, 340–41
15.13 350n122
31.6 110n353,
    259n150
61.4–5 179n636

*Apologia ii (Second
Apology)*
3.1 433n162

*Dialogus cum Try-
phone (Dialogue
with Trypho)*
5.22 394n34
8.4 267n187,
    292n296, 292n298
32 302n338
73.1 234n51
80.4 175n626
93.2–3 359n156
96.3 330, 350n122
99 426n145
106 445
117.3 172n613
125.3 300n329
133.6 330, 332

Lactantius

*Epitome divinarum
institutionum (Epit-
ome of the Divine
Institutes)*
71(66) 34n12

Livy

History of Rome

5.13.5–8 240n78

Longinus

De sublimitate (On the Sublime)

379n210

Marius Victorinus

Commentary on Galatians

6:17 394n32

Oecumenius of Trikka

Fragmenta in epistulam i ad Corinthios

2:6–8 397n45

Origen

Commentarii in evangelium Joannis

2.31 299n324
6.16 77n204
10.2 445n28
10.4 445n28
10.17–18 445n35
10.222 410n85
13.11(67) 299n322
13.27 57n118

Commentarii in evangelium Matthaei

11.5–6 445n30
13.8 414n99
frg. 134 445n29

Contra Celsum (Against Celsus)

1.40–48 445n29
1.57 84n234
1.58–60 445n29
2.11 426n144
2.15 426n146

2.24 426n145
2.55 416
2.68 416
2.69 445n29
3.25 445n29
6.63 349n120, 355n142

Exhortatio ad martyrium (Exhortation to Martyrdom)

37 276n225

Homiliae in Jeremiam

14.6 426n145
18.5 218n759
50.1(3).3 40n44, 276n228

Homiliae in Josuam

8.7 443n23

Homiliae in Lucam

23 210n724
23.1 53n97
25.4 84n234
26.1 218n76, 277n233

Homiliae in Numeros

18.3(4) 445n29

De Principiis (Peri archon) (First Principles)

1.8.1 298n320
2.8.5 426n145
4.2.5 443n23
4.2.9 443n23
4.3.1 443n23
4.3.4 446n35
4.3.5 443n23
4.3.12 299n326

Selecta in Psalmos

in toto 218n761, 277n233

Paschasius Radbertus

Expositio in evangelium Matthaei Libri XII

27:48 407n75

Pelagius

Commentary on 1 Corinthians

2:6–8 397n45

Commentary on Ephesians

4:31–5:1 349n120

Commentary on Romans

15:3 408n79

Petronius

Satyricon

111 403n67

Philo

Allegorical Interpretation

3.213 384n225

Hypothetica

307n3, 318n32, 359n156

On Dreams

1.171 299n326
2.123–28 307n3

On Drunkenness

164 384n225

On Flight and Finding

208 299n326

On Giants

12 298n320

On God

443n23

On Rewards and Punishments

95 285
98–105 124n421
163–168 75
163–172 72
164–165 72n178
168 72n178

On the Confusion of Tongues

2–3 443

On the Embassy to Gaius

302 235n58

On the Life of Abraham

261 172n612

On the Life of Moses

1.148–149 260n155
1.158 260n155

On the Posterity of Cain

7 443n23
61 416n107

On the Special Laws

2.62 307n3

On the Virtues

5.1 274n217

Questions and Answers on Genesis

1.23 298n320
1.86 274n217
4.29 274n217
4.52 384n225

That Every Good Person Is Free

81–82 307n3

That the Worse At-
tacks the Better

95 443n23

Photius

Fragmenta in epistu-
lam ad Galatas

6.17 394n32

Plato

Phaedo

114d 455n67

Phaedrus

274e–275a 27n106

Theaetetus

142d 380n214

Pliny the Younger

Epistulae

10.31 240n78

Plutarch

Alexander

2–3 443

Moralia

397C 12

Pompeius

45.5 235n56

Pseudo-Justin

Quaestiones et
responsiones ad
orthodoxos

58n121
120 185

Quintilian

Institutio oratoria

8.6.67–76 400
11.2.39 377

Rhetorica ad
Herennium

3.30–40 375n202
3.35 375n203

Sedulius Scottus

Commentary on
Matthew

27:34 407n74
27:48 408n75

Seneca

De beneficiis

2.1.1 318n32

Epistulae morales

47.11 318n32

Severian of Gabala

Fragmenta in epistu-
lam i ad Corinthios

2:6–8 397n45

Sextus

Sentences

87–90 318n32
105 37n26

Socrates
Scholasticus

Historia ecclesia-
stica (Ecclesiastical
History)

7.38 260n152

Suetonius

Divus Augustus

13.1–2 403n67

Domitianus

10.1 235nn53–54

Gaius Caligula

32.2 235n53

Vespasianus

4.5 77

Tacitus

Annales

6.29 403n67
15.44 238

Historiae

5.13 77

Tertullian

Ad Scapulam

1 353n138, 362

Adversus Mar-
cionem (Against
Marcion)

1.23 354
4.3 156n559
4.16 323n45,
   353n138, 362
4.26 38n32
4.35 99n307
5.4 394n34
5.10 185
5.14 347n110
19.1 234n51

Adversus Praxean
(Against Praxeas)

30 427n147

De anima

50 66–67

Apologeticus
(Apology)

2.20 235n53
39 38n32

De baptismo
(Baptism)

20 40n44, 172n613

De carne Christi
(The Flesh of Christ)

17.5–6 199n682

De oratione (Prayer)

5 38n30

De patientia
(Patience)

5.15 199n682

De praescriptione
haereticorum (Pre-
scription against
Heretics)

22.3 156n560

Theodore of
Heraclea

Commentary on
Matthew

frg. 18 218n761,
   277n233

Theodoret of
Cyrus

Commentary on
Colossians

2:13–14 393n28

Commentary on
1 Corinthians

2:6–8 397n45

Commentary on
Galatians

6:17 394n31

Commentary on
Hebrews

5:7–8 417n110

Commentary on
Romans

12:14 346n110
15:2–3 419–20
15:3 408n79

Theophylact

Commentary on
Luke

19:11 175n624

Commentary on Matthew

6:10 38n30
10:1 71
27:50 427n147

Exposition of 1 Corinthians

2:6–8 397n45

Exposition of Ephesians

4:32 350n124

Exposition of Romans

15:3 408n79

Thomas Aquinas

Commentary on Ephesians

4:32 350n123

Commentary on Galatians

6:17 394n32

Thucydides

History of the Peloponnesian War

1.20 304
1.22 1–2, 28
1.23.3 451n54
2.8.3 451n54

2.97.4 325n51
3.89.2–4 451n54

Xenophon

Hellenica

2.4.19 69
2.4.23 69

Other Ancient Works

Cologne Mani Codex

17–20 297n318
17:15–16 297
23:5 297n318
24:12–15 298

32:8 297n318
66:4–69:8 258n146
69:15 297n318
72:21 297n318
94 217n757

The Kephalaia of the Teacher

1 297n318
7 36:6–7 297n318
14:3–7 257n144
15:19–23 258n146
258:26–259:23 258n146

Author Index

Aarde, Andries van 68n161
Abbott, Edwin A. 154–56
Abbott, T. K. 349n120
Abegg, Martin G. 111n354,
    261n160, 262n162
Abravanel, Isaac 116, 358n150
Achtemeier, Paul J. 143n502,
    412n92
Adam, Karl 41n46
Adams, Edward 33n7,
    129n439
Adas, Michael 255n134
Addis, Donna Rose 12
Adeyemi, M. E. 396n40
Adler, Alfred 6
Ådna, Jostein 43n57, 236n63,
    237n66
Aešcoly, A. Z. 75n193
Ahearne-Kroll, Stephen P.
    408n75, 427n149
Aichele, George 10n52
Aitken, Ellen Bradshaw
    405n70, 422n128
Aland, Kurt 455n66
Aleksandrov, G. S. 258n150
Alexander, Loveday C. A. 451
Alexander, Philip S. 51n90
Alford, Henry 278n238,
    393n28, 395n38
Allberry, C. R. C. 303n343
Allen, Willoughby C. 143n502
Allison, Dale C., Jr. 10n51,
    16n75, 18n77, 23n94,
    24n97, 25n102, 31nn2–3,

32n7, 33n10, 36n24,
    39n39, 40n41, 40n44,
    42n56, 43n57, 44n63,
    45n65, 47n71, 48n74,
    55n106, 60n130, 61nn130–
    32, 62n133, 63n143,
    64nn144–45, 65n149,
    65n151, 73n181, 80nn215–
    16, 80n218, 85n236,
    87nn244–45, 88n247,
    91n262, 98n300, 109n348,
    117n385, 119n397,
    120n405, 125n427,
    129n441, 132n453,
    132n455, 134n458,
    134n460, 135n464,
    136n468, 142n499,
    146n520, 149n529,
    150n531, 152n546,
    153nn554–55, 161n581,
    165n595, 181n640,
    212n732, 212n734,
    214n745, 215n749,
    216n752, 223n10, 225n18,
    226n19, 228nn29–31,
    237n67, 249n107, 260n153,
    265nn176–77, 267n183,
    268n193, 269n197,
    270n199, 270n201,
    271nn203–5, 272nn206–7,
    272n209, 274n218,
    277n234, 279n239,
    285n271, 287n276,
    288n281, 300n332,

301n336, 310nn7–8,
    319n36, 321n40, 326n55,
    336nn78–79, 343n97,
    348nn116–17, 352n129,
    353nn136–37, 357n146,
    365n176, 367n177,
    384n224, 389n12, 420n120,
    422n130, 425n142, 448n45,
    450n52, 452n58, 461n89
Amanat, Abbas 163n591
Anderson, Eric 148n525
Anderson, Hugh 279n238
Anderson, Michael C. 2n5
Andrews, B. 4n22
Ansbacher, Heinz L. 6n33
Ansbacher, Rowena R. 6n33
Applebaum, Shim'on 259n151
Arav, Rami 37n26
Arnal, William 53nn97–98,
    124n422
Arnold, Matthew 155n557
Asgeirsson, Jon Ma. 122n413,
    229n33
Ashton, John 188n665
Assmann, Jan 6n30, 7n37
Atkinson, Kenneth 285n269
Attridge, Harold A. 49,
    417n110
Aune, David E. 20n82, 49n79,
    85n237, 107n335, 148n526,
    188n664, 247n98, 252n121,
    263n166, 264n168,
    298n320, 412n92
Aus, Roger David 438–39

Avery-Peck, Alan J. 269n194
Avigad, N. 425n138

Baarda, T. J. 40n43
Baasland, Ernst 190n669,
    198n679
Bacchiocchi, Samuele 107n335
Bacher, Wilhelm 358n150
Backhaus, Knute 10n52
Baddeley, Alan 2n5, 5n25,
    12n60
Bader, Chris 148n526
Bailey, Lloyd R. 302n342
Baillet, Maurice 261, 262n161
Baker, Aelred 41n45
Baker, John A. 175n626
Balch, Robert W. 148n526,
    149n529, 150n535,
    151n536, 254n127
Baldermann, Ingo 280n247
Balota, David A. 24n98
Bammel, Ernst 19n80, 234n50,
    396n39
Barbel, Joseph 301n337
Barbour, Robin 89n250,
    107n334
Barclay, Craig R. 3n12
Barclay, John 93n275, 392n23
Barnard, Leslie W. 91n265
Barnett, P. W. 273n212
Barr, Robert R. 452n57
Barrett, C. K. 62n135,
    279n241
Barth, Karl 64n144
Barth, Markus 349n120
Bartlett, F. C. 2n7, 4n20, 9n48,
    13n65
Barton, Stephen C. 6n30,
    29n117, 390n14
Bartsch, Hans-Werner 62n134
Barzilay, Isaac E. 116n381
Bashear, Suliman 144n510,
    161n582
Bauckham, Richard 1n1,
    9n46, 9n48, 17n75,
    63n142, 122n414, 162n584,
    218n758, 241n81, 245n89,
    249n106, 259n150,
    283n255, 417n110
Bauer, Patricia J. 8n46
Bauer, Ulrich 383n223
Baum, Armin Daniel 9n48

Baumeister, Roy F. 1n2
Baumgarten, Albert I. 85n237,
    94, 95n282, 116n379,
    124n422, 145n514,
    149n526, 152n550, 447n41
Beale, G. K. 76n199
Beasley-Murray, G. R. 31n2,
    99, 101n314, 276n229,
    279n238
Beavis, Mary Ann 75n195
Beck, D. M. 360n156
Becker, Hans-Jürgen 320n37
Becker, Jürgen 19n81, 54n101,
    54n103, 58n124, 72n176,
    108n343, 208, 234n50,
    265n171, 273n215,
    291n291, 293n301
Becker, Michael 31n2, 127n434
Beckford, James A. 64n148
Beckwith, Roger T. 77n204
Beker, J. Christiaan 63n142,
    96n286
Belfiore, Elizabeth 456n70
Bell, G. K. A. 264n166
Belle, G. van 62n138
Bellinger, William H., Jr.
    414n97
Bellinzoni, Arthur J. 324n46,
    340n83
Ben-Amos, Dan 457n74
Bengel, Johann Albrecht
    175, 349n120, 415n102,
    417n110
Benoit, P. 111n358, 453n60
Berding, Kenneth 328n60
Berger, Abraham 254n126
Berger, David 282n252,
    292n293
Berger, Klaus 10n52, 56n111,
    180n637, 246n91, 361n160
Bergman, Erik T. 4n20
Bergman, Jan 181n640,
    271n204
Berkey, Robert F. 99n302,
    124n424
Berkhof, Hendrikus 60n130
Bermejo, Fernando 137n473,
    213n740, 213n742
Bernhardsson, Magnus
    163n591
Bernstein, Daniel M. 3n18
Bernstein, Moshe 363n170

Best, Ernest 63nn142–43,
    348n119
Betz, Hans Dieter 310n10,
    320n39, 394n32
Betz, Otto 115n373, 264n171,
    287, 394n33
Beuke, Carl J. 4n19
Beuken, W. A. M. 113n366
Beutler, Johannes 132n451
Bietenhard, Hans 175n626
Bird, Michael F. 29n118,
    42n56, 264n171
Bireta, Tamra J. 28n110
Bittner, Wolfgang 302n340
Black, Mark 61n131
Black, Matthew 377n206
Blackman, E. C. 176n628
Blank, Josef 62n138
Blankea, Olaf 297n317
Blasi, Anthony J. 147n522
Bleeker, C. Jouco 145n511,
    243n86
Blenkinsopp, Joseph 245n90,
    274n218
Blinzler, J. 212n733
Bloedhorn, Hanswulf 193n675
Boccaccini, Gabriele 43n57,
    300nn330–31
Bockmuehl, Markus 6n30,
    9n48, 27n108, 76n203, 94,
    123n417, 259n151, 399n56
Boer, M. C. de 49n83
Boers, Hendrikus 224, 399n55
Bohannan, Laura 284n261
Böhlemann, Peter 218n759,
    218n761, 277n233
Bohlen, Maren 170n600,
    180n636
Böhlig, Alexander 257n143,
    258n146, 300n327
Boismard, M.-É. 140, 349n121
Bolin, Thomas M. 459n83
Bolt, Peter G. 60n130
Bolten, Johann Adrian
    294n305
Bonanno, George A. 3n15
Bond, Helen 391n19, 401n61
Borg, Marcus 44–45, 52–
    53n96, 59, 73, 86n238, 89,
    96, 134–35, 136n468, 141,
    156, 157n564, 223, 253–54,
    355n142, 437–41, 444–45

Borgen, Peder 272n210,
285n268
Borges, Jorge Luis 12n62
Borgnet, A. 218n759, 277n233,
360n158, 408n78
Bornkamm, Günther 44n63,
405n69, 426n145
Borsch, Frederick Houk
90n255, 289n285, 294n304
Borse, Udo 394n34
Böttrich, Christfried 129n442,
300n330
Bousset, Wilhelm 46, 297n317
Bovon, François 267n185,
276n229, 312n20, 334n74,
355n142, 367n177
Bowie, Fiona 57n113, 292n293,
304n350
Bowman, John Wick 155n557
Box, G. H. 91n267
Boyd, Gregory A. 9n47, 27n108
Braaten, Carl E. 428n153
Braden, Marcia 148n526
Bradshaw, John 11n55, 14n66
Brainerd, C. J. 3n18, 13n63
Brandenburger, Stefan H.
383n223
Brandt, Edwin 121n409
Brandt, Sigrid 402n65
Branscomb, B. Harvie 54n102
Bransford, John D. 3n15, 11n56
Brant, Joann A. 444n27
Breech, James 78n209
Brenner, Michael 254n130
Brettler, Marc Zvi 245n88,
289n288
Brewer, William F. 2n8, 5n25
Brewin, C. R. 4n22
Bridge, Steven L. 384n224
Broad, C. D. 1n2
Brock, Ann Graham 53n97,
120n405
Broek, R. van den 298n319
Broer, Ingo 399n56, 401n61
Brooke, George J. 95n283,
297n317
Brown, Norman R. 5n27
Brown, R. 7n40
Brown, Raymond E. 62n135,
132n450, 240n78, 268n191,
283n255, 388, 396n39,
403n67, 417n111, 450n53

Brox, Norbert 242n84
Bruce, A. B. 155n557
Bruce, Darryl 381n215
Brucker, Ralph 53n97,
120n406, 235n55, 278n235
Bruner, Frederick Dale 452n57
Bryan, Christopher 396n39
Bryan, Steven M. 73–74n186
Buchanan, George Wesley
169n600, 171
Buck, Christopher 258n149
Bucur, Bogdan G. 151n538
Budick, Sanford 447n40
Buehler, Roger 30n121
Buffalo, E. A. 5n26
Bultmann, Rudolf 32n5, 44n60,
52, 64n144, 68n161, 87,
99, 102n324, 143, 150n531,
156, 159n569, 160n577,
201n688, 221, 224, 242,
280n247, 292n295, 293,
302, 308–9, 312n20, 388,
427n147, 428
Bundy, Walter E. 47, 251n114
Burchard, Christoph 72n176,
93n275, 441n14
Burke, Trevor J. 295n309
Burkett, Delbert 293n302
Burridge, Richard A. 355n142,
443n20
Burrows, Millar 355n142,
368n178
Butler, Jonathan M. 128n438,
146n519, 148n525
Byrskog, Samuel 445n33

Cahill, Michael 296n312
Caird, G. B. 39n40, 45n65,
73n183
Calvin, John 155n557, 172n613,
305–6, 397n45
Cameron, Averil 459n82
Cameron, Ron 48n76,
119n404, 120n408,
122n414, 124n422,
127n433, 131, 158n567,
159n570, 250n109,
279n240, 279n243
Campbell, J. Y. 124n424
Camponovo, Odo 37n26,
172n612
Capes, David B. 226n20

Caragounis, Chrys C.
100n309, 186n660
Carlebach, Elisheva 112n360,
152n545
Carlston, Charles E. 123n419
Carmignac, Jean 176n628
Carr, Wesley 396n41, 397n44,
398n50
Carrington, Philip 353n138,
357n145
Carroll, John T. 60n130
Carroll, Marie 9n48, 30n124
Carroll, Robert P. 144n510
Carson, D. A. 168n597,
214n743
Casey, Maurice 44n59, 80n220,
294n305
Castelli, Elizabeth A.
53nn97–98
Catchpole, David 21n86,
139n485, 227n27, 234n50,
300n331, 301n333, 320n38,
322n43, 333n72, 343n93,
343n95, 345, 346n109,
351–52, 355n142, 357n145
Ceci, Stephen J. 3n19, 11n57
Chabris, Christopher F. 8n44
Chalippe, Candide 437n3
Chalmers, Thomas 347n111
Chamberlin, T. C. 87–88n246
Chandler, Christopher N.
370n184
Chapman, David W. 392n24
Charles, R. H. 91n259,
91n267, 92n270, 109,
141n492
Charlesworth, James H. ix,
32nn4–5, 56n110, 59n127,
76n198, 111n354, 238n70,
261n158, 262–63n164,
271n201, 279–80n244,
280n247, 284n265,
300n330, 302n339
Chazon, Esther G. 72n179
Chenderlin, Fritz 413n93
Chester, Andrew 239n75,
243n86, 280n244, 282n251,
287n275, 288n280,
288n284
Chilton, Bruce 18n77, 40n44,
80n219, 141n492, 168n597,
174n621, 205n710,

254n129, 265n175,
    271n201, 347n113,
    378n208
Christianson, Sven-Ake
    424n136
Christophersen, Alf 63n141
Clark, K. W. 124n424
Clarke, Andrew D. 396n41
Clivaz, Claire 417n110
Coakley, J. F. 131n449, 308n4
Coan, James A. 3n17
Cockerill, Gareth Lee 252n118
Cohen, Gillian 7n40, 8n46
Cohen, Mark 255n133
Cohick, Lynn H. 237n68
Collins, Adela Yarbro 54n102,
    78n209, 81n223, 229n36,
    234n50, 293n301
Collins, John J. 32n4, 37n26,
    43n57, 47n71, 49n83,
    54n102, 76n199, 76nn201–
    2, 106n331, 110n351, 172,
    173nn615–16, 233, 234n49,
    243n86, 249n108, 261n160,
    262n162, 266, 267n186,
    268n189, 280n244, 284,
    285n267, 300n330,
    301nn333–35, 302nn338–
    39, 304n349
Collins, Raymond F. 400n56
Colpe, Carsten 298n319
Connerton, Paul 163n592
Connolly, R. H. 359n156
Conway, Martin A. 7n40,
    8n46, 424n136
Conzelmann, Hans 49n82, 79,
    97n294, 117, 169n600
Cook, David 161n582
Cooper, J. 298n320
Corley, Kathleen E. 290n289
Cotton, Hannah M. 111n355,
    111n358
Craffert, Pieter F. 256n136,
    283n255
Craik, Fergus I. M. 3n16,
    163n592
Cranfield, C. E. B. 51n88,
    408n76
Craven, Toni 449n48
Crawford, Barry S. 44n60,
    279n243
Crenshaw, James L. 355n142

Crompton, Robert 64n148
Crook, Zeba A. 148n526
Cross, F. L. 19n80
Cross, Frank Moore 110n352
Crossan, John Dominic 9n48,
    14n67, 38n34, 44, 55, 70,
    98, 121n410, 130n443,
    132, 137–40, 144, 146–48,
    172n612, 204–5, 222n5,
    237n65, 239n77, 246n91,
    303n345, 342n90, 387–91,
    426n146, 437–38
Cullmann, Oscar 139n481,
    398n49
Curci, Antonietta 7–8n40
Curtis, John Briggs 260n156

Dahl, Nils A. 15n73, 160n576,
    234–35, 238n70, 243n86
Dalman, Gustaf 39,
    169n597, 170, 176, 182,
    189–90, 200n684, 204n699,
    289n287
Daly-Denton, Margaret
    283n256, 408nn77–78
Dan, Joseph 293n300
Daniélou, Jean 175n626
Daube, David 212n739, 214,
    264n170
Davenport, G. L. 109n347
Davies, Brian 61n130
Davies, Margaret 227n23
Davies, W. D. 73n185, 142,
    165n595, 173n620,
    212n734, 228n29, 287n276,
    326n55, 336n79, 367n177,
    384n224
Davila, James R. 241n81,
    242n82, 243n85, 249n106,
    288n283
Davis, Deborah 4n21, 30n123,
    30n125
Davis, Michael Thomas
    111n354
Davis, P. G. 252n116
Dawes, R. M. 4n22
Dawkins, Richard 8n43
Dawson, Lorne L. 145n513,
    148n526, 152n547
Deacy, Christopher 57n113,
    292n293, 304n350

DeConick, April D. 9n48,
    125n425, 126n430,
    129n440, 130–31, 151n538,
    297n317, 298n321
Deignan, Kathleen 128n437
Dein, Simon 57n113, 148n526,
    152n549, 163n590
Deissmann, D. Adolf 264n166,
    427n151
Delling, Gerhard 63n143,
    416n103
Deming, Will 212n734
Denis, John 62n138, 63n139
Denney, James 415n102
Deppe, Dean B. 60n130,
    124n421
Deppermann, Klaus 52n93
Derrett, J. Duncan M.
    351n128
Descamps, Albert 382n221
Desroch, Henri 289n286
Dettwiler, Andreas 120n405
Dewar, Frances 60–61n130
Dewey, Arthur J. 127
Dewick, E. C. 155n557
Dibelius, Martin 15n73,
    16n75, 139n484, 221,
    235, 239, 308n5, 413n94,
    426n145, 427n150
Dihle, Albrecht 318n33,
    358n154
Dimant, Devorah 55n109,
    131n449, 261n160,
    262n161
Dinkler, Eric 292n295
Dobschütz, Ernst von 141, 143
Dodd, C. H. 17n76, 23, 61n131,
    62, 73n183, 89n248, 117,
    132n450, 132n452, 141,
    147, 151n540, 200n683,
    263–64n166, 268n192,
    417n109
Doering, Lutz 37n25
Doeve, J. W. 351n128, 357n145,
    360n159, 374n192
Dohrmann, Natalie B. 199n682
Donfried, Karl Paul 115n376,
    323n45, 400n56
Donnelly, Doris 280n248
Dougall, Lily 211n729
Douglas, Claude C. 105n328
Draisma, Sipke 291n291

Draper, Jonathan A. 119n405, 315n27, 333n70
Drewery, Benjamin 91n266
Dronke, Peter 297n317
Dubis, Mark 63n143
Duchek, Janet M. 24n98
Duling, Dennis C. 98n300, 107n337, 246n91, 284n260, 291n292
Dungan, David L. 311n11
Dunn, James D. G. 16n73, 19n81, 29n117, 49n82, 54n102, 58n123, 63n143, 106n331, 120n406, 122n414, 160n576, 190n669, 265n171, 270n201, 277n233, 280n247, 347, 360n156, 393, 394n31, 418n112, 418n114, 422n126, 431n155
Dupont, Jacques 80n219, 343n93
Dyer, Keith D. 381n217

Easton, Burton Scott 25n103
Ebersohn, Michael 361n162
Ebner, Martin 89n250, 138n477
Eddy, Paul Rhodes 9n47, 27n108
Edelman, Diana Vikander 442n16
Edmonds, Ennis Barrington 58n120
Edwards, Derek 163n592
Egger, Peter 234n50
Ego, Beate 107n338
Ehrman, Bart 54n102, 280n246
Einstein, Albert 91, 92n268, 460
Elam, Yigal 6n30
Elgvin, Torleif 95n284
Elledge, C. D. 56n110, 111n354
Ellens, J. Harold 23n94
Elliott, J. Keith 295n309
Elliott, John H. 401n62
Ellis, Andrew W. 29n120, 380n213
Emmerick, Ronald E. 257n144
Emmet, Cyril W. 52n96, 211n729
Engel, Susan 6–7

Epstein, Ya'akov Nahum 320n37
Ernst, Joseph 275n223
Eshel, Esther 261n160, 262n162
Eskola, Timo 241n81, 247n96, 247n98, 248–49
Esler, Philip F. 401n62
Etkes, Immanuel 457n75
Evans, Craig A. 18n77, 20n83, 37n26, 40n44, 42n52, 61n131, 76n199, 80n219, 106nn330–31, 111n354, 141n492, 168n597, 204n699, 205n710, 215n749, 254n129, 259n150, 261n160, 265n173, 266n180, 269n196, 271n201, 273n216, 347n113, 378n208, 425n138
Eve, Eric 21n87
Eysenck, Michael W. 2n5

Fabry, Heinz-Josef 266n178
Falk, Daniel K. 95n284
Farley, Lisa A. 28n110
Farmer, William R. 414n97
Farnsworth, Gwen 148n526, 151n536
Farrer, Austin 61n130
Fee, Gordon 49n82, 396n41
Feeney, D. C. 459n85
Feldmeier, Richard 417n111, 426n145
Fenton, J. C. 408n76
Fentress, James 7n37, 11n55
Ferguson, Everett 184nn657–58
Festinger, Leon 152
Fiddes, Paul S. 121n409
Filson, Floyd V. 452n57
Findlay, G. G. 413n93
Finegan, Jack 234n50, 441
Finke, Roger 145n512
Finkelstein, Louis 362n169
Finn, Natalie 146n517, 149n526
Fitzmyer, Joseph A. 49n79, 279n244, 312n20, 334n73, 355n142, 396n41, 413n93
Fivush, Robyn 6n32, 30n121
Fleddermann, Harry T. 120n405, 343, 344n100, 345n103, 346n109

Fletcher-Louis, Crispin H. T. 301n337
Flew, Antony G. N. 55n107
Flint, Peter W. 37n26, 76n199, 106n331, 261n160
Flusser, David 74n188, 109n348, 145n511, 243n86, 283n254, 333n70
Foakes-Jackson, F. J. 42n55
Folger, Tim 8n43
Fornberg, Tord 100n312
Fossum, J. E. 241n81
Foster, Lawrence 128n438
Fotopoulos, John 184n656
Fox, Marvin 361n164
Frame, James Everett 100n312
France, R. T. 168n597, 355n142
Frankemölle, Hubert 265n171, 265n176, 357n149, 383n224
Franks, Jeffery J. 3n15, 11n56
Franzmann, Majella 257n144, 297n318, 303n343
Frayer-Griggs, Dan F. 40n43, 277n234
Fredriksen, Paula 50n87, 54n102, 59n126, 73–74, 136n468, 143, 236nn60–61, 237n66
Frenschkowski, Marco 50n86, 122nn413–14, 228n33, 302n342
Frerichs, Ernest S. 45n67, 279–80n244
Frey, Jörg 25n100, 31n2, 54n102, 59n129, 66n156, 95n284, 131n449, 132nn451–52, 188n665, 235n55, 280n245, 302n342, 401n62
Frick, Robert 184n658
Friedlander, Gerald 358n150
Friedman, Theodore 107n335
Friedrich, Gerhard 57n116
Froitzheim, Franzjosef 63n142
Frye, Northrop 456n71
Fuller, Michael E. 74
Fuller, Reginald H. 100n309, 224, 241
Funk, Robert W. 15n72, 69–70, 74n187, 98n298, 101n318, 116–17, 125n428,

138n475, 143n506, 155–56, 222, 225, 231, 234n50, 239n73, 305, 425n141

Gabba, Emilio 457n77
Gager, John G. 85n236, 124n422, 151n537, 152n551, 255n133
Gallo, David A. 5n25
García Martínez, Florentino 95n284, 114n369, 114n371, 261n160, 262n161, 274n219, 363n170
Garrod, Heathcote William 54n102, 136n468
Garrow, Alan J. P. 333n69
Garry, Maryanne 4n19, 13n64
Gaskell, George D. 5n27
Gathercole, Simon 47n71, 81n222
Gaupner, Axel 266n178, 271n202
Gaventa, Beverly Roberts 286n274, 402n64
Geddert, Timothy J. 61n130
Gedi, Noa 6n30
Geiger, Ruthild 101n317, 382n220
Georgi, Dieter 32n6
Gerhardsson, Birger 26n105
Gerstenberger, Erhard S. 351n127
Gibson, Marion 423n133
Gieschen, Charles A. 301n337
Giesen, Heinz 51n88
Giezen, Anne E. van 424n136
Gill, Christopher 459nn84–85
Gill, John 393n28, 413n94
Gilliard, Frank D. 401n63
Glasson, T. Francis 39n40, 89n250, 155n557, 176n628, 273n214
Glazier-McDonald, Beth 274n218
Glover, Richard 328n62, 333n70
Gnilka, Joachim 234n50, 383n224, 408n75
Godet, F. 346n110
Goethals, George R. 4n22
Goff, Lynn M. 3n19
Goffman, Erving 7n36

Goguel, Maurice 140n486, 289n287, 388n5, 426n146
Goldin, Judah 447n40
Goldstein, Jonathan A. 45
Golitzin, Alexander 151n538
Gomulicki, B. R. 3n14
Goodacre, Mark 388–89, 391n18
Goodman, Martin 76n203
Goold, G. P. 451n56
Gotlib, I. H. 4n22
Goulder, Michael 265n171, 265n175, 266n178, 285n267, 295n309, 334n74, 347n113, 351n128, 355–56n142, 360, 453–54
Gourgues, Michel 247n95
Grabbe, Lester L. 77n204, 82n227
Grant, Frederick C. 221, 223n9
Grappe, Christian 37n26, 265n171
Grässer, Erich 146n521, 149n528
Grätz, Sebastian 271n202
Gray, Patrick 61n131
Gray, Timothy C. 61n130
Green, Joel B. 60n130, 264n169, 417n109
Green, William Scott 45n67, 279–80n244
Greene, Gayle 2n9
Greene, Sharon L. 28n112
Gregg, Brian Han 35n15, 36n24, 42n56
Gregory, Andrew F. 324n46, 326n56, 333n71, 372n189, 420n120
Greshake, Gisbert 15n73, 124n422
Gressmann, Hugo 297n317
Grimm, Werner 265n171
Grinnell, George Bird 457n73
Gripentrog, Stephanie 401n62
Grotius, Hugo 346n110, 347n111, 349n120, 355n142, 397n45, 408n79, 415n102, 417n110, 418n113
Grüwaldt, Klaus 268nn187–88
Gundry, Robert H. 57n112, 81n224, 344n100, 356n142,

437, 438n7, 446n34, 450n51, 453–54
Gunther, John J. 302n342
Gurtner, Daniel M. 312n20
Gustafson, Henry 63n143
Guthrie, W. K. C. 23n95
Gutmann, Joseph 199–200n682
Güttgemanns, Erhardt 393n30
Guy, H. A. 52n96

Haak, Robert D. 82n227
Habermas, Gary R. 55n107
Haenchen, Ernst 268n192
Häfner, Gerd 10n52
Hagedorn, Anselm C. 148n526
Hagner, Donald 27n108, 324n46, 324n49, 325n52, 328n62, 452n57
Hahn, Ferdinand 9n48, 18n79, 25n100, 52n95, 58n123, 102n323, 160n576, 169n599, 234n50, 250n112, 279n240, 284n264, 382n218
Halbwachs, Maurice 5n30
Halleux, André de 382n221
Halpern, Sue 2n3, 2n10
Hamerton-Kelly, R. G. 318n33
Hamidović, David 282n252
Hamp, Vinzenz 276n230
Hampl, Patricia 387
Hanks Harwood, Ginger 148n526
Hannah, Darrell D. 249n108, 298n320, 301n337
Hanson, Paul D. 61n131
Hardyck, Jane 148n526
Harkness, Georgia 155n557
Harnack, Adolf 176
Harrington, Daniel 269n194
Harris, J. Rendell 297n317, 302n342
Harrison, P. N. 328n60
Harrisville, Roy A. 428n153
Hartin, Patrick J. 353n138, 357n148
Hartman, Geoffrey H. 447n40
Hartman, Lars 381n216
Harvey, A. E. 15n73, 265n171
Hastie, Reid 4n21, 424n136
Hastings, James 188n665
Hatina, Thomas R. 61n131

Hatton, Peter T. H. 90n257
Häusser, Detlef 279n241
Hawkin, David J. 54n102
Hawkins, Scott A. 4n21
Hay, David M. 247n96,
    255n131
Hayes, John H. 247n97
Hayman, Peter 253n124
Hays, Richard B. 286n274,
    409, 410n85, 411n86,
    420nn118–19, 431n155
Hayward, Robert 285–86n272
Head, Peter M. 225n17
Heard, Richard 155n557
Heckel, Ulrich 282n251,
    415n100, 415n102, 416n108
Hedrick, Charles 19n80,
    444n27, 451n56
Heil, Christoph 384n224
Heinemann, Joseph 37n25, 75,
    111n359, 282n252
Heinrichs, A. 297n318
Hellholm, David 100n312
Henderson, John 2n5, 11n54
Henderson, Suzanne Watts
    290n290
Hengel, Martin 27n108,
    37n25, 49n79, 80n215, 84,
    90n254, 107n336, 107n338,
    171n609, 181n640,
    203n698, 223n6, 234n50,
    243n86, 247nn95–96,
    248n103, 250n112,
    256n136, 259n151,
    265n171, 265n176,
    271n201, 271n204,
    282n251, 291n291,
    358n154, 392n24, 394n34,
    413n93, 422n123
Hennecke, Edgar 142n497
Henry, Matthew 218, 277n233,
    418
Henten, Jan Willem van
    403n66
Henze, Matthias 95
Herman, C. Peter 424n136
Herrmann, Douglas J. 424n136
Hertz, J. H. 352n130,
    352n134, 358n150
Heskett, Randall 266n178
Heuer, Friderike 5n25
Hewitt, Joseph William 392n25

Hexham, Irving 256n138
Heyworth, P. L. 297n317
Hieke, Thomas 275n222,
    383n223
Hiers, Richard H. 97n293,
    100n309, 127n434
Higgins, A. J. B. 139n481,
    382n222
Higgins, E. Tory 424n136
Hill, H. Erskine 155n557
Himmelfarb, Martha 43n57
Hinnells, John R. 128n436
Hinterberger, Martin 295n310
Hirstein, William 2n4
Hittman, Michael 160n575
Hobsbawm, Eric 6n30
Hodge, Charles 176n628,
    346n110
Hoffmann, Paul 68n159,
    119n403, 119n405,
    214n744, 242n84, 311n12,
    346n108
Hofius, Otfried 280n247
Hogdson, Peter C. 25n100,
    289n286, 312n20, 388n4,
    440n12
Holladay, William L. 271n202
Holleman, Joost 56n111
Hollenbach, Paul W. 138n477,
    219
Hollerna, J. Warren 417n109
Holmberg, Bengt 290n290
Holmén, Tom 10n52, 20,
    101n319, 153n555,
    164n593, 290n290, 401n61
Holmes, Michael W. 326n56,
    327n58, 420n120
Holmstrand, Jonas 400n56
Holt, P. M. 57n119, 150n530
Holtz, Traugott 81n223,
    400n56
Holtzmann, Oscar 288n284
Holzbrecher, Frank 392n22
Hook, S. H. 58n122
Hooker, Morna D. 81n222,
    264n167, 414n97
Hoover, Roy W. 15n72,
    101n318, 116n382,
    138n475, 143n506
Horbury, William 232n44,
    240n79, 280n244, 302n339
Horn, Friedrich W. 180n636

Horsley, Richard 15n71,
    76n198, 78n208, 86n239,
    119–20n405, 261n158,
    270n198, 271n201,
    283n258, 303n346, 315–16,
    351–52n128, 375n204
Horst, Pieter W. van der
    192n673, 352–53, 427n152
Hoskyns, E. C. 132n450
Hultgren, Arland J. 122n414
Hultgren, Stephen 237n66
Hunt, Earl 9n46
Hunter, Ian M. L. 29n120,
    380n213
Hurd, John C. 400nn56–57
Hurtado, Larry W. 122n414,
    224n15, 241n81, 252n116,
    255n132

Iannaccone, Laurence R.
    145n512, 145n515,
    146n519
Idel, Moshe 116n379, 300n331
Infeld, Leopold 460
Inge, W. R. 88n247
Isenberg, Sheldon R. 85n237
Isser, Stanley Jerome 273n212

Jackson, A. V. Williams
    258n148
Jacobsen, Howard 318n32
Jacoby, Larry L. 8n41
Jaffé, Dan 283n257
James, Montague Rhodes
    76n200
Janssen, Martina 302n342
Japhet, Sara 170n605
Jefford, Clayton N. 333n70
Jellinek, Adolph 116n379,
    360n157
Jeremias, Joachim 24n96,
    41n45, 44n60, 62n134,
    68–69, 99, 102n320, 109,
    117, 168n597, 203n698,
    204, 218n758, 243n86,
    276nn225–26, 342n91,
    345n106, 383n224, 405n69,
    417n110
Jervell, Jacob 175n625
Jervis, L. Ann 421n121

Jewett, Robert 48n77, 58n122, 59n124, 279n241, 347n111, 396n42, 398n51, 400n56, 402n65, 430n154
Johanson, Bruce C. 100n312
Johns, Loren L. 76n198
Johnson, Luke Timothy 357–58n149, 371n188, 431n156
Johnson, Nancy S. 7n38
Johnson, P. Benton 280n247
Johnson, Sara R. 451n56
Johnson-DeBaufre, Melanie 48n75
Jones, C. P. 394n32
Jones, Lindsay 85n236
Jonge, Henk J. de 123n420, 212n739
Jonge, Marinus de 16n73, 274n219, 291n291
Jónsson, Jakob 448n44, 448n47
Joyce, Paul 107n334
Juel, Donald H. 15n73, 160n576, 235n52
Jülicher, Adolf 117
Jüngel, Eberhard 190n669

Kaestli, J. D. 125n425
Kammen, Michael 6n30
Kampen, John 363n170
Kansteiner, Wulf 6n30
Kapera, Z. J. 266n179
Käsemann, Ernst 58n122, 138n477, 409n79
Kasher, Rimon 296n314
Kassin, Saul M. 4n20
Katz, Steven T. 250n110
Kaufmann, David 74n191, 75n192
Kazen, Thomas 290n290
Keck, Leander E. 419n116
Kee, H. C. 74n188
Kegel, Günter 58n123
Keith, Chris 422n130
Kelber, Werner 24n96, 459n82
Kellermann, Ulrich 56n111, 268n187
Kennard, Douglas W. 63n142
Kensinger, Elizabeth A. 5n25
Kerrigan, Anthony 12n62
Kertelge, Karl 265n171, 347n113, 383n224

Kiechel, Katherine L. 4n20
Kieffer, René 181n640, 271n204
Kihlstrom, John F. 2n9, 424n136
Kimelman, Reuven 282n251
King, George Brockwell 358n150
Kirk, Alan 6n30, 15n71, 18–19n79, 120n405, 131n445, 313n21, 318–19, 379n210, 382n219
Kirsch, Irving 4n19
Kister, Menahem 320n37, 356n144
Klausner, Joseph 70n169, 244n87
Klein, Günter 68n161
Klein, Kerwin Lee 6n30
Klein, Michael L. 114n367
Klein, Ralph W. 170n605
Kleinhenz, Christopher 110n351
Kloppenborg, John 43n58, 53n97, 55n107, 118n396, 119n397, 119nn403–5, 120–21, 122nn414–15, 123n418, 161n579, 214n744, 311n12, 311n14, 314, 315n26, 322n43, 327n59, 333nn71–72, 344n99, 345n104, 346n108, 353n138, 356n142, 357n148, 372n189, 378, 383n222, 383n224
Knauf, Ernst Axel 442n16
Knibb, Michael A. 300n330
Knohl, Israel 199n682, 262n162, 382n252
Knox, John 15n73, 223, 251
Knox, Wilfred L. 138n478
Kobelski, Paul J. 274n219
Koch, Klaus 31n2, 54n102, 106n332, 174n621, 300n331, 381n217
Koenen, Ludwig 297n318
Koenig, Jean 114n367
Koester, Helmut 41n47, 47n71, 52, 118n397, 120n405, 123n420, 126n429, 129n442, 183n648, 228n29, 313n22,

324nn46–47, 328n60, 333n71, 348, 405, 417n110, 422n123
Köhler, Wolf-Dietrich 328n62
Kollmann, Bernd 228n30
Konradt, Matthias 100n312
Kosch, Daniel 122n413, 140n487, 160n576
Kovacs, Judith L. 62n138
Kozin, Marc 424n136
Kraeling, Carl H. 193n675, 200n682
Kraemer, Ross Shepard 299n323
Kramer, Werner 279n241
Kratz, Reinhard G. 382n217
Kraus, Christina Shuttleworth 459n83
Kreitzer, L. Joseph 226n20, 416n106
Kremer, Jacob 415n102
Kreplin, Matthias 263n165, 294n305
Kreyenbroek, Philip G. 163n591
Krüger, Thomas 382n217
Kruse, H. 105n327
Kugel, James L. 203n697, 299, 361n165, 362n167, 363n170, 364n173, 371n186, 444n24, 444n26, 448n43
Kugler, Robert A. 304n349
Kuhn, Heinz-Wolfgang 107n335, 236n62, 392n24, 398n53, 412n90, 416n107
Kuhn, Karl A. 252n117
Kuhn, Karl Georg 168n597, 417n109
Kulik, J. 7n40
Kümmel, Werner Georg 34n13, 99, 100n313, 112n361
Kurosawa, Akira 7n35
Kuschke, Arnulf 113n364
Kutsch, Ernst 113n364
Kvalbein, Hans 75n195, 169n600, 184n656, 188n664
Kvanvig, Helge S. 300nn330–31

Laaksonen, Jari 42n56,
180n636
Laato, Antti 111n356
Labahn, Michael 122n414,
264n166
Labib, Pahor 300n327
Lakatos, Imre 87, 88n246
Lake, Kirsopp 42n55
Lampe, G. W. H. 185n658
Lampe, Peter 61n132, 452n58
Landes, Richard 115n375,
143n505, 148n524,
149n526, 157
Lane, William 278n238
Lang, Friedrich 276n230
Langer, Ellen 27n107
Lanternari, Vittorio 258n147
Larsen, Steen F. 25n101
Laufen, Rudolf 123n419
Layton, Bentley 333n71
Leatham, Miguel C. 145n511
Leckie, J. H. 89
Le Donne, Anthony 6n30,
7n39, 246n91, 285n269,
287n275, 389n11, 389n14
Lee, Aquila H. I. 279n242
Leene, Henk 109n345
Le Goff, Jacques 6n30
Lehtipuu, Outi 36n21, 91n263,
184n654
Leivestad, Ragnar 15n73,
289n287
Lemke, Werner E. 110n352
LeMoine, Frannie J. 110n351
Lenowitz, Harris 31, 75n193,
259n151, 292n294
Leske, Adrian M. 290n290
Levenson, Jon Douglas 45n68,
87n241
Levine, Lee I. 51n90
Levine, Linda J. 4n21, 6n34
Levy, Becca 27n107
Lewin, B. M. 28n114
Lewis, C. S. 251n113
Lewis, Gladys S. 241n81,
242n82, 249n106
Lewis, James R. 115n375
Lewis, Michael 1n2
Lewis, Sarah M. 304n350
Licht, Jacob 110n350
Lichtenberger, Hermann
111n354, 302n339, 353n138

Liddon, H. P. 346n110
LiDonnici, Lynn 72n179
Liebenberg, Jacobus 117n386,
118nn392–93
Lieber, Andrea 72n179
Liebes, Yehuda 289n285
Lietzmann, Hans 394n34
Lieu, Samuel N. C. 257n142
Lightfoot, J. B. 327n57, 397n47
Lightfoot, R. H. 61n130
Lindars, Barnabas 33n10,
62n138, 77, 79n211,
215n751, 251n116,
293n301, 303, 407n73
Lindberg, Carter 96n288
Lindemann, A. 42n54, 43n58,
47n71, 50n86, 118n397,
119n405, 122n414,
131n446, 139n483,
164n593, 294n306
Linton, Marigold 3n12
Lips, Hermann von 97n294,
396n41
Littlewood, Jane 423n134
Llewellyn, Russ 23n94
Lloyd, Farrell 13n63
Loewenstamm, Samuel E.
57n114
Loftus, Elizabeth 3n13,
3nn17–18, 4nn19–21, 8,
30n123, 30n125, 424n136
Logan, Jessica M. 24n98
Lohfink, Gerhard 15n73,
59n126, 62n134, 124n422
Lohmeyer, Ernst 169n600,
186n661
Lohse, Eduard 346n110, 393
Lona, Horacio E. 324n49
Löning, Karl 383n224
Loofs, Friedrich 16n73
Loubser, J. A. 256n138
Loughborough, J. N. 64n147
Louw, Johannes P. 169n598
Love, Tom 9n46
Lovering, Eugene H., Jr.
237n66
Lövestam, Evald 34n12,
272n206
Lowe, Malcolm 401n62
Luckensmeyer, David 48n77,
81n223, 400n56

Lüdemann, Gerd 96n287,
400n56
Luftig, Richard 3n14
Lührmann, Dieter 312n20,
316n29, 353n138, 378n207
Lull, David J. 353n138
Luminet, Olivier 7–8n40
Lupieri, Edmondo F. 207n717
Luther, Martin 395n38
Luz, Ulrich 183n648, 190n669,
202, 228n29, 228n33,
278n235, 279n238, 310n9,
344n101, 443n21, 454n64,
456n72
Lyons, William John 425n138

Macaskill, Grant 110n352
MacDonald, Dennis R.
442n17, 442n19
Machalek, Richard 145n513
MacIntyre, Alisdair 422n124
Mack, Burton 55n107,
96n285, 118n397, 119,
121n411, 159nn570–71,
279n240
Maclean, A. J. 298n320
Madigan, Kevin J. 87n241
Magness, Jodi 425n142
Maldonatus, Juan 306n1
Malherbe, Abraham J. 400n56
Mandel, Barrett J. 4n21
Mandler, Jean M. 7n38
Manson, T. W. 41n46, 89n248,
168n597, 270n198,
275n224, 364n172,
378n207, 384n224
Manuchehri, Sepehr 304n350
Marcus, Joel 22n92, 61n131,
83, 96n289, 112n362,
115n374, 116n378,
141n492, 142n496,
168n597, 181n638,
184n654, 235n57, 236n60,
269n194, 269n196,
279n238, 286n274,
287n279, 292n293, 408n75,
412n91, 414nn98–99
Marguerat, Daniel 120n405,
125n425, 265n171
Markus, Gregory B. 4nn21–22

Marshall, I. Howard 190n669, 218n761, 223n11, 277n233, 367n177, 431n157
Martin, David 135n462
Martin, Edwin 9n46
Martin, Marie-Louise 256n137
Martin, Ralph P. 415n102
Martin, Raymond A. 377n206
Martin, Troy W. 422n129
Martineau, James 31n1, 294n305
Martyn, J. Louis 49n83, 63, 394n35
März, Claus-Peter 228n30, 347n113
Mason, Eric F. 252n118
Mason, Steve 9n49, 91n264
Massaux, Édouard 324n46, 328n62, 333n71, 338n80
Mathews, Shailer 102n324
Matthiae, K. 26n105
Mayordomo, Moisés 61n132, 452n58
Mazzoni, Giuliana A. L. 4n19
McAfee Moss, Charlene 61n131
McCant, Jerry W. 415n102
McCown, C. C. 94n276
McDermott, Kathleen B. 2n6, 3n11, 3n16, 4n20
McDonough, Sean M. 183n650
McGhee, Glen S. 124n422, 161n582
McGuire, Anne 95n284
McIver, Robert K. 9n48, 30n124
McKnight, Scot 27n108, 87n242, 113n363, 214n747, 219n762, 237n68, 270n201, 271n203, 272n211, 273n215, 445n33, 461n88
McNamara, Martin 200n684, 370n182
McNeile, A. H. 270n198
McNicol, Allan J. 311n11
Meade, Michelle L. 4n20
Mearns, C. L. 141
Meeks, Wayne A. 91
Mees, Michael 323n45
Meggitt, Justin J. 236n60, 433

Meier, John P. 20n82, 38n30, 44n60, 47n72, 53n97, 68, 70n169, 70n171, 73n181, 83n230, 140n489, 169n597, 206nn713–14, 208n720, 209n723, 211n727, 267, 270, 275n223, 280–84, 286
Meinhold, Arndt 314n25
Meir, Samuel ben 362n166
Melamed, Ezra Tsiyon 320n37
Mell, Ulrich 426n146
Melton, Arthur W. 9n46
Melton, J. Gordon 59n128, 144–45, 149n526, 149n529, 150n533
Menahem, R. 214n748
Mendels, Doron 286n274, 458n81
Menken, Maarten J. J. 80n215, 229n34
Merkel, Helmut 37n25, 153n553, 445n32
Merklein, Helmut 169n597, 174n622, 190n669, 202n695, 206n713
Merz, Annette 15n73, 20n82, 79n212, 85n236, 99n304, 137n472, 140n491, 206–11, 213, 218n759, 234n50, 239n74, 244n86, 275n221, 292n295
Meshorer, Ya'akov 111n358
Mettinger, Tryggve N. D. 289–90n288
Metzler, April E. 6n32
Meye, Robert P. 70
Meyer, Ben F. 41, 45n66, 54n102, 271n201
Meyer, Eduard 69
Meyer, Marvin W. 122n413, 229n33
Meyvaert, Paul 254n128, 457n78
Michaud, Jean-Paul 122n414
Michel, Otto 248n100
Michelon, Pascale 424n136
Middleton, David 163n592
Milavec, Aaron 333n70
Mildenberg, Leo 111n356
Milgrom, Jacob 353n134, 356n143, 358n152, 361n160, 368

Milik, J. T. 111n358
Milikowsky, Chaim 267n187, 444, 446n36, 455n66
Millard, Alan 374n195, 380n214
Miller, David M. 268n189
Miller, Gene 396n41
Miller, James F. 39n40
Miller, Merrill P. 48n76, 124n422, 127n433, 131n447, 158nn566–67, 159n570, 250, 265n172, 279n240, 279n243
Miller, Patrick D., Jr. 110n352
Miller, Robert J. 31n2, 44n61, 44n63, 48n74, 98n300, 132n455, 135n464, 144n508, 237n66, 438n7
Miller, Timothy 59n128
Mintz, Jerome R. 457n74
Miscall, Peter 10n52
Mitchell, David C. 282n252
Mitchell, Kathleen 457n78
Mitchell, Margaret M. 421n121
Mitton, C. Leslie 24n96
Modica, Joseph B. 237n68
Mohr, Christine 297n317
Molthagen, Joachim 121n409
Montefiore, C. G. 353n138
Moo, Douglas J. 61n131, 393n28, 409n79, 414n98
Mooney, James 152n544
Moore, Carey A. 450n49
Moore, George Foot 94n276
Morgan, Robert 89n250
Morgan, Thomas 155n557
Morrison, W. D. 46n70, 141n492
Moscovitch, Morris 5n28, 8n41
Moses, L. G. 222n3
Moss, Mark B. 28n111
Moule, C. F. D. 103, 224–25, 234n50
Moulton, James Hope 297n317, 298n320, 394n34
Mounce, William 431n157
Mournet, T. 27n108, 445n33
Mowinckel, Sigmund 292n296
Moyise, Steve 80n215, 229n34, 265n171
Muddiman, John 349n120

Muggeridge, Malcom 1n2
Muirhead, Lewis A. 155n557
Mullen, Mary K. 27n107
Müller, Mogens 293n302
Müller, Ulrich B. 50n87,
    54n103, 59n126, 294n305,
    295n308, 426n146
Mullins, Terence Y. 416n104
Münsterberg, Hugo 3n18
Murphy-O'Connor, Jerome
    432n159
Musgrave, Alan 88n246
Myers, Ched 61n130

Nagel, Peter 212n735
Nairne, James S. 5n25, 8n41,
    25n98, 28n110
Najman, Hindy 95n283,
    297n317, 448n43
Neimeyer, Greg J. 6n32
Neirynck, Franz 347n112,
    384n224
Neisser, Ulric 2n10, 3n12,
    5n25, 6n32, 7n40, 25n101,
    30n121, 381
Neubauer, A. 71n175, 74n190
Neusner, Jacob 45n67,
    107n333, 190n669,
    269n194, 279–80n244,
    299n324
Nevin, Alfred 218
New, David S. 80n217
Newman, Barclay M., Jr.
    179n635
Newman, Carey C. 32n7,
    241n81, 242n82, 249n106
Newman, Judith H. 448n43
Newsom, Carol 171n610
Nickelsburg, George W. E.
    44n59, 45n68, 57n114,
    107n335, 110n351,
    293n304, 301n334
Nickerson, Raymond S. 88n246
Nicklas, Tobias 298n320
Nicoll, W. Robertson 413n93,
    415n102
Nida, Eugene A. 169n598
Nie, Giselle de 457n78, 458n80
Niebuhr, Karl-Wilhelm
    266n179, 371n187
Niederwimmer, Kurt 212n734,
    332nn67–68, 339n82

Nihan, Christophe 351n125
Nilsson, Lars-Göran 163n592
Nineham, D. E. 70, 206n715,
    408n76
Nitzan, Bilhah 363n170,
    364n174
Nolan, Brian M. 283n256,
    398n52
Nolland, John 312n20, 318n33,
    356n142, 452n57
Norden, Eduard 77n205,
    342n92
Norelli, E. 125n425, 265n171
Notley, R. Steven 109n348
Notopoulos, James A. 13n65
Novakovic, Lidija 283n256
Noy, David 193n675
Numbers, Ronald L. 128n438,
    146n519, 148n525
Nützel, J. M. 56n111
Nygren, Anders 346n111

Oakman, Douglas E. 378n208
Oberman, Heiko A. 96n288
O'Brien, Peter T. 214n743,
    413n94
O'Day, Gail R. 61n131
Oegema, Gerbern S. 111n354,
    302n339, 353n138
Öhler, Markus 31n2, 81n221,
    127n434, 264n166,
    267n187, 269n196,
    286n272
O'Leary, Stephen D. 124n422,
    149n526, 161n582
Olick, Jeffrey K. 6n30, 8n42
Olson, Daniel C. 300n330
O'Mahony, Kieran J. 294n306,
    432n159
O'Muircheartaigh, Colm A.
    5n27
O'Neill, J. C. 138n480,
    169n600, 202n692,
    288n282, 292n298
Ong, Walter J. 30n120, 374–75
Oosthuizen, G. C. 256n138
Oppenheimer, Aharon 14n70
Orlov, Andrei A. 296n317
Ort, L. J. R. 257n141,
    257n145, 297n318
Orwell, George 426

Otto, Rudolf 93–94, 97,
    169n600, 172n612,
    295n310, 298n320
Owen, Paul 294n305

Pagels, Elaine 445n31
Paget, James Carleton 76n203,
    94n279, 259n151
Pahl, Michael W. 81n223,
    421n122
Painchaud, Louis 257n142
Palmer, Susan J. 146n517,
    148–49n526
Pao, David W. 53n97, 120n405
Park, David M. 416n107
Parkes, Murray 423n132
Parry, Donald W. 252n117,
    261n160
Partridge, Christopher 65n149
Pate, C. Marvin 63n142
Patterson, Stephen J. 48,
    55n108, 90n252, 98n300,
    99n301, 117, 118n392,
    119n398, 125nn427–28,
    132, 134n460, 289n285
Pazarro, David A. 4n24
Peabody, David B. 311n11
Peabody, Francis Greenwood
    89n250, 97
Peace, Kristine A. 424n136
Pearson, Birger A. 44n59,
    50n86, 54n102, 118n397,
    121n412, 131n445,
    293n304, 399n55
Peels, H. G. L. 351n126
Peltier, A. C. 270n197
Penner, Todd 50n87
Pennington, Jonathan T.
    181–82, 183n650
Penton, M. James 144n509
Perani, Mauro 446n36
Perrin, Nicholas 125n425
Perrin, Norman 98n300,
    102n323
Perry, T. A. 340n84
Pervo, Richard I. 442n17,
    442n19, 448n46
Pesce, Mauro 396n41
Pesch, Rudolf 56n111, 234n50,
    273n211, 404n68, 422n127
Pesch, Wilhelm 242n84
Peters, Alan 28n111

Petersen, William L. 123n420,
    212n739
Peterson, David G. 417n110
Peterson, Jeffrey 50n84, 413n93
Phillips, Helen 2n4
Phillips, Thomas E. 442n18
Pickrell, Jacqueline E. 3n17,
    4n19
Pines, Shlomo 38
Piper, John 356n144
Piper, Ronald A. 140n488,
    319n35, 345n103, 378n207
Pitre, Brant 40n44, 42n56,
    87n242, 194n676
Pleydell-Pearce, Christopher
    W. 424n136
Plummer, Alfred 413n93
Poffet, J.-M. 125n425, 265n171
Poirier, John C. 52n92,
    265n174, 268n190
Poirier, Paul-Hubert 257n142
Pokorný, Petr 349n120
Polaschek, Devon 13n64
Poole, Matthew 71, 103n326,
    298n320, 346n110,
    350n123, 355n142,
    359n156, 417n110,
    418n113
Poon, Leonard W. 381n215,
    424n136
Popkes, Enno Edzard 127n434,
    302n342
Popkes, Wiard 61n130
Popper, Karl 88n246
Porter, Stanley E. 10n52,
    153n555, 215n749
Porter, Stephen 424n136
Powell, Mark Allan 438n7,
    445n31, 450n51
Price, Robert M. 159n573
Puech, Émile 56n110, 252n117
Puech, H.-C. 40n41

Quispel, Gilles 297n318

Radcliffe, Timothy 61n130
Radday, Yehuda T. 352n130
Radl, Walter 61n130
Rahhal, Tamara A. 424n136
Raich, J. M. 306n1
Rainbow, Paul A. 303–4n347

Räisänen, Heikki 39n36,
    50n87, 52n95, 54n102,
    55n104, 59n126, 63n141,
    91n258, 101
Ranger, Terence 6n30
Rapp, Peter R. 28n111
Rau, Eckhard 22n91, 121n409,
    130n444, 141n492,
    160n576, 161n578
Ravitzky, Aviezer 96n289,
    115n377, 293n299
Rawlinson, A. E. J. 108n340,
    244
Read, J. Don 11n59
Reckman, Richard F. 4n22
Reder, Lynne M. 3n17
Reed, Graham 297n317
Reif, Stefan C. 374n194
Reimarus, Hermann Samuel
    49n69, 432n160, 455n68
Reinbold, Wolfgang 234n50,
    390n16, 400n56, 400n60,
    425n139, 425n142,
    426n144
Reinhartz, Adele 258–59n150
Reisberg, Daniel 5n25
Reiser, Marius 44n60, 47n71,
    62n137, 94, 135n465,
    216n753
Reiterer, Friedrich V. 298n320
Renkema, Johan 341n87
Resch, Alfred 349n121
Reuss, J. 218n761, 277n233
Revell, E. J. 295nn310–11
Reyna, Valerie 3n18, 13n63
Reynolds, Benjamin E.
    294n306, 302n338
Rhodes, Matthew G. 8n41
Richardson, Christopher
    417n110
Richardson, Peter 400n56,
    421n121
Riches, John 16n73, 285n270
Riecken, Henry W. 152
Riesner, Rainer 26n104, 407n72
Ring, Kenneth 297n317
Riniker, Christian 35n17,
    216n753
Rips, Lance J. 5n27
Ristow, H. 26n105
Rivkin, Ellis 240n79
Robbins, C. Michael 246n93

Robbins, Joyce 6n30, 8n42
Robbins, Thomas 148n526
Roberts, Colin H. 99n307
Robertson, Archibald 413n93
Robinson, James M. 37n26,
    53n97, 118n397, 119,
    124n422, 125n428, 137,
    212n739, 214n744, 222n4,
    228, 292n295, 311n12,
    313n22, 346n108
Robinson, John 4n23
Robinson, John A. T. 48,
    131n449, 138n477, 141–42,
    270n198, 277n233, 305, 308
Robinson, S. E. 76n198
Robinson, Tom 54n102
Rochford, E. Burke, Jr. 147n522
Rodríguez, Rafael 6n30,
    15n71, 95n284, 163n589
Roediger, Henry L. III 2n6,
    3n11, 3n16, 3n19, 4n20
Roetzel, Calvin J. 422
Rohrbaugh, Richard L. 222n1
Rollmann, H. 291n291
Roose, Hanna 73n184,
    290n290
Rordorf, Willy 333n70
Rose, Steven 5n29
Rosene, Douglas L. 28n111
Rosenfield, Israel 10n53
Rosenthal, Joel T. 457n78
Ross, David Frank 11n59
Ross, Michael 3n11, 4n21,
    6n31, 6–7n34, 30n121
Rothschild, Clare K. 213n741,
    275n222, 442n18
Rousseau, John J. 37n26
Rowe, C. Kavin 291n291
Rowe, Robert D. 106n333,
    186n660
Rowland, Christopher 85n236
Rubin, David C. 2n8, 3n12,
    4n23, 7n38, 8n40, 11n55,
    375n196, 375n202,
    377n205, 381n215, 424n136
Rüger, Hans Peter 124n423,
    370n183
Ruiten, J. van 109n345
Russell, Bertrand 5n25
Ruzer, Serge 320n37
Rynearson, Edward K.
    423n134, 424n135

Saarni, Carolyn 1n2
Sabourin, Leopold 279n238
Sachs, J. D. S. 11n56
Saiedi, Nader 304n350
Sanday, W. 52n96, 141n495
Sanders, E. P. 13n63, 19n81,
    21–22, 44n60, 48–49, 54,
    71n171, 72–74, 76, 87n241,
    93, 101, 155n558, 214–15,
    227n23, 232n43, 236n63,
    237n64, 237n69, 280n247,
    293n299, 352n132,
    426n144
Sanders, Jack T. 85n236,
    92–93
Sanders, James A. 42n52,
    265n173
Sandt, Huub van de
    333nn70–71
Sänger, Dieter 294n305,
    300n330, 426n146
Saperstein, Marc 254n126
Sato, Migaku 61n132, 452n58
Sauer, J. 380n212
Schachter, Stanley 152
Schacter, Daniel L. 2n5, 3n16,
    5nn25–26, 5n28, 7n37,
    11n57, 12
Schade, Hans-Heinrich
    63n142, 400n56
Schäfer, Peter 14n70, 111n354,
    255n133, 259n150
Schenk, Wolfgang 412n91
Schenker, Adrian 79n214
Schiffman, Lawrence H.
    262n161
Schlatter, Adolf 364n172
Schlegel, Unliane 25n100
Schleritt, Frank 390n16,
    417n111
Schlosser, Jacques 37n27,
    47n71, 102n322, 105–6,
    120n405, 139n481,
    357n148, 380n212
Schlueter, Carol J. 400
Schmeller, Thomas 118n392
Schmidt, Andreas 122n414,
    264n166
Schmidt, B. 407n74
Schmidt, Daryl 399n55
Schmidt, Nathaniel 294n305

Schmithals, Walter 16n73,
    54n102, 58n123, 59n129,
    65n152, 68–69, 97n290
Schmitt, J. 265n171
Schmolck, H. 5n26
Schnackenburg, Rudolf
    115n373, 136n468,
    349n120, 382n221, 452n57
Schneemelcher, Wilhelm
    142n497
Schneider, Gerhard 356n142
Schneider, Johannes 394n34
Schnider, Franz 264n166
Schniewind, Julius 396n41,
    397n46, 397n48
Schoeps, Hans Joachim
    356n142
Scholem, Gershom 65n150,
    75n194, 112n360, 159n574,
    233, 254, 255n135,
    259n151, 289n285
Schöpflin, Karin 298n320
Schrage, Wolfgang 63n142
Schrauf, Robert W. 423n131
Schreiber, Johannes 61n130
Schreiber, Stefan 169n599,
    266n178, 285n268,
    300n330
Schroeter, Harald
    268nn187–88
Schröter, Jens 17n75, 53n97,
    120n406, 121n410,
    122n414, 139n483, 235n55,
    278n235, 302–3n342
Schudson, Michael 5n26,
    6n30, 161n583, 162n586
Schuller, Eileen M. 95n284,
    261n160
Schulz, Siegfried 120, 143n502,
    352n128
Schürmann, Heinz 26n105,
    73n181, 242n84, 313–14,
    323, 348, 356n142,
    383n224
Schüssler Fiorenza, Elisabeth
    86n239
Schwartz, Barry 161n580,
    162n586
Schwartz, Bennett L. 28n112
Schwartz, Daniel R. 401n62
Schwartz, Hillel 85n236
Schwartz, Seth 76n198

Schweitzer, Albert 31, 44n60,
    59, 87n241, 88, 89n249,
    97, 116, 134, 157, 243n86,
    251n114, 255n133,
    289n287
Schweitzer, Ursula 297n317
Schweizer, Eduard 16n73,
    54n102, 56n111, 169n600
Schwemer, Anna Maria
    37n25, 107n336, 107n338,
    171n609
Scott, B. B. 33n8, 43n58, 98,
    119n399
Scott, E. F. 155n557, 188n665
Scott, James M. 46n68,
    71n171, 109n346, 268n187
Scott, R. B. Y. 203n697
Scott, Thomas 359n156
Segal, Alan F. 52n96
Seidel, Anna K. 258n147
Seifrid, Mark A. 214n743
Seitz, O. J. F. 343n96, 352n128
Seland, Torrey 188n664
Sellew, Philip 95n284
Sellin, Gerhard 349n120
Senior, Donald 452n57
Seper, F. H. 276n227
Shaffir, William 57n113,
    150n535, 152n545,
    152n549, 296n313
Shanks, Hershel 425n142
Sharman, Stefanie J. 4n19
Sharon, Moshe 258n149
Sharot, Stephen 112n360
Sharpe, Eric J. 26n105,
    128n436
Shea, Chris 444n27, 451n56
Shepherd, David 294n305
Shepherd, Tom 388n8
Shevell, Steven K. 5n27
Shils, Edward 6n30, 162n585
Shupe, Anson D., Jr. 146n516
Sider, John W. 136n467
Silberman, Neil Asher
    303n346
Silver, Abba Hillel 222n2,
    259n151
Sim, David C. 135n463
Simon, Ernst 361n164
Simons, Daniel J. 8n44
Singelenberg, Richard 149n526
Sjöberg, Erik 292n296

Small, Jocelyn 27n110
Smit, Peter-Ben 41n48
Smith, Daniel A. 227n25
Smith, D. Moody 390n15
Smith, Jonathan Z. 299n324,
    300n328
Smith, Morton 261–62
Smoller, Laura A. 5n29
Snow, David A. 145n513
Soards, Marion L. 112n362
Spence, Jonathan D. 256n139,
    257n140
Spencer, F. A. M. 141n492
Spilka, Bernard 153n551
Spong, John Shelby 438n7
Sproston North, Wendy E.
    33n10, 63n138
Squire, L. R. 5n26
Stancliffe, Clare 440n13
Stanton, Graham 160n576,
    170n600, 202n693,
    202n696, 264n169
Stark, Rodney 145n512,
    146n519
Starr, Joshua 116n380
Stauffer, Ethelbert 138n477,
    155n557
Stayer, James M. 233n46
Stegemann, Ekkehard 246n92
Stegemann, Hartmut 226n21,
    262n162
Stegemann, Wolfgang 246n92
Stegman, Thomas 406n71
Stegner, W. Richard 269n196
Steiner, Richard C. 214n748
Stephen, Michele 256n136
Sterling, Greg 403n66
Stern, David 199n682, 448n43
Stern, Menahem 284n262
Stettler, Hanna 281n249,
    407n72
Steudel, Annette 37n25,
    38n29, 51n91, 77n204,
    145n514, 262n162,
    290n290
Stewart, Eric 148n526
Stimpfle, Alois 131n448,
    169n599
Stone, Jon R. 149n526, 222n4
Stone, Michael 110, 413n95
Straub, Werner 394n34

Strauss, David Friedrich
    25n100, 30n122,
    289n286, 312n20, 388,
    437n5, 440n12, 454n65,
    456nn70–72
Strauss, Mark L. 283n256
Strawn, Brent A. 111n354
Strecker, Georg 142n497,
    190n669
Streeter, B. H. 141, 143
Strobel, August 101n317
Stroker, William Dettwiller
    327n58
Stuckenbruck, Loren T. 6n30,
    29n117, 34n12, 95n283,
    297n317, 390n14
Stuhlmacher, Peter 115n373,
    160n576, 264n171, 404n68
Stuhlmann, Rainer 63n143
Stuhlmueller, Carroll 274n219
Subramanian, J. Samuel 410n83
Sullivan, Clayton 100n309,
    170n600
Sullivan, Lawrence E. 152n543
Sundermann, Werner 257n144,
    297n318
Sundkler, Bengt G. M. 256n137
Surprenant, Aimée M. 28n110
Sweet, J. P. 93n275
Swetnam, James 417n110

Tabbernee, William 51n92
Tabor, James D. 82n227
Takaaki, Sanada 153n551
Talarico, Jennifer M. 8n40
Talbert, Charles 14n69, 83n229,
    158n568, 432n160, 455n68
Talmon, Shemaryahu 227n21,
    266n180
Tannehill, Robert C. 218n759,
    334n74
Tardieu, Michel 297n318
Tatum, W. Barnes 53n97,
    208–9n721
Taubes, Jacob 151
Taussig, Hal 53nn97–98
Taylor, C. 360n156
Taylor, Joan E. 139n482,
    213n741, 214n748
Taylor, N. H. 142n496
Taylor, Vincent 70n169,
    312n20, 437

Taylor, W. S. 9n48
Teeple, Howard M. 270n200,
    271n201
Thackeray, Henry St. John
    91n259
Thatcher, Tom 6n30, 9n48,
    15n71, 19n79, 131n445,
    422–23n130
Theisohn, Johannes 252n120
Theissen, Gerd 10n50, 14n68,
    15–16n73, 20n82, 22n93,
    79n212, 85n236, 92n269,
    99n304, 137n472, 140n491,
    142n496, 206–11, 213,
    218n759, 234n50, 239n74,
    243–44n86, 275n221,
    292n295, 292n298,
    296n316, 373n191, 396n39,
    398n49, 422n127
Thiselton, Anthony C. 397n45
Tholuck, A. 312n20
Thoma, Clemens 108n340
Thomas, Ayanna K. 4n19
Thomas, Christine M. 455n69
Thomas, Johannes 371n187
Thompson, Charles P. 5n26,
    5n28
Thompson, Michael 347,
    348n114, 372n190, 407n72
Thornton, Claus-Jürgen
    49n79, 394n34
Thrall, Margaret 416nn104–5
Thrupp, Sylvia L. 138n479
Tigchelaar, Eibert J. C.
    114n369, 114n371
Tiller, Patrick A. 43n57
Tindal, Matthew 270n197
Tindall, William York 389n13
Toglia, Michael P. 4n21, 11n59
Tollestrup, Patricia A. 11n59
Tomasino, Anthony J. 77n204
Topel, John 319n35, 373n191
Torrey, Charles C. 193n675,
    449
Towner, Philip H. 431n157
Trapp, John 80n219, 175n624,
    359n156
Trebolle Barrera, Julio
    107n335
Trilling, Wolfgang 71n171
Trocmé, Étienne 156n561,
    233n45

Troyer, Kristin de 122n413, 229n33
Trumbower, Jeffrey A. 84n235, 269n196
Tuckett, Christopher M. 33, 53n97, 80n215, 120nn405–6, 122n416, 123n417, 123n420, 124n421, 229n34, 265n174, 265n176, 294n306, 324n46, 326n56, 330n65, 333nn71–73, 352n128, 372n189, 420n120
Tulving, Endel 3n16, 163n592
Tumminia, Diana 149n526, 152n542
Turner, David L. 356n142
Turner, H. E. W. 99n303
Turner, John D. 95n284
Turner, Max 264n169
Turner, Victor 153n552
Turtle, John W. 11n59

Udoh, Fabian E. 237n66
Ulrich, Eugene 252n117, 261n160
Ulrichsen, Jarl Henning 188n664
Urbach, Ephraim E. 38n33, 370n181
Uro, Risto 39n36, 125n425, 129n442, 140n488, 382n218

Vaage, Leif E. 53n98, 118n397, 314–15, 379n210
VanderKam, James C. 110n351, 300n330
Vander Stichele, Caroline 50n87
Van der Watt, J. G. 188n663
Van Segbroeck, F. 66n154, 120n405, 347n112, 412n91
Vaughan, William 28n112
Vaux, R. de 111n358
Vegas Montaner, Luis 107n335
Vena, Osvaldo D. 143n502
Verheyden, J. 42n54
Vermaseren, M. J. 298n319
Vermes, Geza 55, 171n608, 201n689
Vermeylen, Jacques 113n366

Vervenne, M. 109n345
Veyne, Paul 458n80
Vielhauer, Philipp 68n161, 142n497, 190n669, 203n698
Vinson, Richard B. 334n74
Viviano, Benedict T. 175n623
Vögtle, Anton 56n111, 58n122, 201n686, 203n698
Völter, Daniel B. 327n57
Volz, Paul 109n347, 172n613, 190n669
Vos, Johannes Sijko 49n81, 123n420, 212n739
Vriezen, Th. C. 90
Vusco, Vittorio 66n154

Wacholder, Ben Zion 77n204, 95
Wagner, J. Ross 115n372
Wailes, Stephen L. 117n387
Walker, William O. 399n55
Wallis, Ian G. 431n155
Wallis, Roy 254n127
Walls, Jerry L. 65n149
Walsh, Richard 10n52
Wanke, Daniel 268n188
Wanke, Joachim 164, 312n18
Wansbrough, Henry 20n82, 333n70
Ward, Benedicta 458n79
Ward, R. B. 371n188
Wardi, Emmanuel 152n550
Warner, Martin 52n95
Warren, David H. 53n97, 120n405
Waterman, Leroy 155n557
Watson, Francis 405n69
Watts, Fraser 433n163
Watts, Rikki E. 265n175
Waubke, Hans-Günther 37n25
Weatherly, John 100n312, 400nn56–57, 401n62
Webb, Robert L. 205n710, 209n723, 261n157, 264n170, 275n223
Webster, W. 80n219, 359n156
Wedderburn, A. J. M. 394n34
Weeden, Theodore J. 237n67
Wehnert, Jürgen 359n156
Weinfeld, Moshe 38n29
Weinstein, Donald 138n479

Weiser, Neil 149n526, 149n529, 152n542
Weiss, Johannes 31, 88, 97, 112, 141n492, 157, 169n600, 201, 243n86, 396n40
Welborn, L. L. 397n43
Welch, John W. 352n130
Wenell, Karen J. 71n172, 73n181
Wenham, David 204n699, 312n20, 333n70, 381n216, 394n34, 405n68, 416n108
Weren, Wim 62n133
Werman, Cana 77n204
Wernle, Paul 141n492
Wesley, John 71n173
Westcott, B. F. 349n120
Wheeldon, M. J. 459n82
Wheeler, John Archibald 462n90
Wickham, Chris 7n37, 11n55
Wiebe, Ben 54n102
Wigner, Eugene P. 462n90
Wilckens, Ulrich 25n100, 63n142, 314n25, 346n110
Wilk, Florian 37n25
Wilkins, Sue 148n526, 151n536
Williams, Ann 57n119
Williams, George Huntston 233n46
Williams, Helen L. 7n40
Williams, Margaret H. 401n62
Williams, Sam K. 431n156
Willis, John T. 355n142
Willis, Wendell 115n376, 172n612, 184n657
Willitts, Joel 183n650, 283n256
Wills, Lawrence M. 95n284
Wilson, A. E. 4n21, 6–7n34
Wilson, Barbara A. 381n215
Wilson, John 28n113
Wilson, R. McL. 142n497
Wilson, Walter T. 347n112
Wilson, William P. 23n94
Windisch, Hans 180n637, 190n669, 201n687, 201n689, 415n102
Windischmann, Friedrich Heinrich Hugo 394n34
Winger, Michael 9n48, 15n71, 25n99, 121n412
Wink, Walter 275n223, 398n49

Winninge, Mikael 290n290
Winograd, Eugene 5n25, 7n40,
  25n101
Winston, David 172n612
Winter, Dagmar 10n50, 14n68,
  15–16n73, 22n93, 92n269
Winter, Paul 234n50
Wirszubski, C. 38n33
Wise, Michael Owen 77n204,
  444n24
Wiseman, T. P. 459n85
Witherington, Ben, III 41n46,
  118, 184n654, 396n41
Wold, Benjamin G. 6n30,
  29n117, 390n14
Wolff, Christian 394n34,
  415n102
Wolter, Michael 202n695,
  266n178, 271n202,
  379n211, 413n94
Wood, Ian 457n78
Woude, A. S. van der 199n270,
  273n214, 274n219

Wrede, William 242, 289n287,
  291
Wright, Benjamin G., III
  95n284
Wright, Daniel B. 5n27
Wright, Lawrence 4n20
Wright, N. T. 33n7, 45n65,
  223n8, 419
Wünsch, August 341n89

Xeravits, Géza G. 268n189,
  274n219

Yardeni, Ada 111n358
Yates, Roy 393n28, 413n95
Yuille, John C. 11n59
Yu-wen, Jen 255n135, 256n139

Zager, Werner 216n753,
  291n291
Zanna, Mark P. 424n136
Zehnle, Richard F. 274n218
Zeilinger, Franz 63n143

Zeller, Dieter 56n111, 347n112,
  356n142, 373n191
Zerubavel, Eviatar 163n587
Zerubavel, Yael 161n583,
  163n592
Zias, Joe 392n25
Zieme, Peter 257n144
Zimmerli, Walter 113n364
Zimmermann, Johannes
  114n370, 265n172,
  302n339
Zmijewski, Josef 102n322
Zöckler, Otto 235n53
Zöckler, Thomas 100n308
Zwi Werblowsky, R. J. 38n33,
  48n75, 128n436, 145n511,
  243n86
Zwiep, Arie W. 67n158
Zygmunt, Joseph F. 144n509,
  149nn526–27, 149n529,
  150nn532–33, 151n536,
  152n542

Subject Index

abba 215, 417–18
Abba Saul 369–70
Abraham
  in the Apocalypse of Weeks
    109–10
  descent from 213–16
  enthronement of 248
  as king 108
  and the kingdom of God
    178, 185
  and the land of Israel 75
  less than John the Baptist
    54, 139n485
  and the sacrifice of Isaac
    454
  in the *Testament of Abraham* 449
Abravanel, Isaac 116
Abulafia, Abraham 116, 254,
  259, 301n331
Adam 109, 129, 183, 208, 362,
  425n140
Akiba
  and bar Kokhba 77, 110–11,
    258n150, 279
  and the golden rule 359
  and Leviticus 19 352, 358–
    59, 362, 366
  and the messianic age 75–76
  and paradox 96
  and two thrones in heaven
    302n338

antitheses (supertheses) in
  the Sermon on the Mount
  271, 310
apocalyptic eschatology. *See*
  also eschatology
  definition of 32–33
  in early Christianity 48–53,
    141–43, 303
  explanatory scope of 134–37
  and irrational thought 93–97
  popularity of 76–78
apocryphal gospels 447–48
authenticity, criteria of x,
  9–10, 15n73, 20–22, 153,
  231. *See also* dissimilarity,
  criterion of; method for
  constructing the historical
  Jesus

Baal Shem Tov 16n74, 457
Bab, the 304n350
Bahai Faith, the 148n526, 150,
  258n149, 304n350
Bahaullah 222, 258n149
Barabbas 239–40
Bar Kokhba 75, 77, 110–12,
  258, 279, 282n252, 283
beatitudes 42, 53n97, 80, 123–
  24, 182–83, 194, 229n34,
  265, 310–11
Bokelson, Jan 233
Buddha 222, 257, 280n247

Cain 199n682
charisma 86, 92–93, 135, 291
children, becoming like 126–
  27, 129, 201, 203, 214–15
cognitive dissonance 146, 148
collective messianism 290n290
"common Judaism" 76, 214
"coming one, the" 42, 80, 219,
  229, 240–41, 274–78. *See*
  also John the Baptist
context and interpretation
  103–4
continuity, argument from
  43n58, 48–55, 79, 137
contradictions in the Jesus
  tradition 88–97
covenant renewal 79, 272,
  315–16
covenantal nomism 213–16
crucifixion. *See also* Jesus,
  crucifixion of
  and baptism 403
  as coronation 230
  in John's Gospel 62–63, 147
  parodic nature of 235
  in Paul 392–98, 416
  as public deterrent 391
  as Roman punishment
    235–36, 398–99
  stories about, the need for
    421–24
cry from the cross 426–27, 432

darkness at noon 387, 437,
    445, 450–51, 459
David. *See also* messiah; Son
    of David
    descent from 252–53, 281–
        85, 398
    kingdom of 186, 245–46,
        286–87
    as prophet 273n216
    and Psalms 411
    throne of 51, 171, 249
    typology 283, 387, 427n150
day of judgment 34
decalogue 352–53, 359n156,
    371
devil. *See* Satan
dissimilarity, criterion of x,
    19, 88n247, 205. *See also*
    authenticity, criteria of;
    method for reconstructing
    the historical Jesus
divorce, prohibition of 22,
    122, 136n468, 308n5
dove at the baptism 440, 445,
    450

Eden, garden of; paradise 126,
    183–84, 190n669, 198
Egyptian, the 260–61, 398
Eliezer, Rabbi 75, 446–47
Elijah
    ascension of 57, 244
    eschatological role of 95,
        267–68, 292
    Jesus as 83, 133, 267–70,
        283n253, 285–86
    John the Baptist as 53n97,
        81, 241
    and the prophets of Baal
        199n682
    in rabbinic legends 446–47
    and violence 285
Elisha 268–70
end, the. *See also* eschatology
    denial of nearness of 65–67
    nearness of 33, 38–41, 45,
        48–50
Enoch 57, 109, 159, 222, 244,
    248, 252, 300–301
entering into or inheriting the
    land of Israel 179–81

eschatological discourse in Q
    382–86
eschatological figures in Juda-
    ism 251–53
eschatology. *See also* apoca-
    lyptic eschatology; end,
    the; eschatological figures
    in Judaism; eternal life;
    exile, return of tribes
    from; fire; Gehenna;
    Hades; John the Baptist;
    kingdom of God; messiah;
    parousia, delay of; realized
    eschatology; resurrection
    in the Apocalypse of Weeks
        109–10
    in *2 Baruch* 95
    "consistent" 134–35
    in Daniel 106
    in Deutero-Isaiah 108–9
    ethics and 97
    future reward
        and alms 196n678
        and apocalyptic eschatol-
            ogy 32
        and eternal life 36
        and the *Gospel of Thomas*
            130
        in the Jesus tradition 34,
            36, 136n469
        in Judaism 34
        and the kingdom of God
            193
        in the Sermon on the Plain
            322
        and the world to come 193
    great tribulation, end-time
        woes
        and apocalyptic eschatol-
            ogy 32
        in the Dead Sea Scrolls 94
        and the historical Jesus
            87, 277
        in the Jesus tradition 40,
            194n676
        in Judaism 34, 40
        in Paul 63
        as present experience 151
        as realized eschatology
            65, 146
        and Jerusalem 50–52, 186

Jewish prayers and 45–46,
    107
    in John 62–63, 131–32,
        188–89
    in *Jubilees* 109
    judgment, final. *See also* fire;
        Sodom
        in early Christianity 55, 226
        in Jesus tradition 33–36,
            38–39, 41–42, 80–82,
            135–37, 216–19,
            228–30, 276–78
        and John the Baptist 53,
            55, 204, 208, 215–18,
            276–77
        in John's Gospel 62–63
        in Judaism 252, 285, 301
        and the messiah 285
        as near 44–47, 210
        in the parables 117
        in Q 123–25, 208
        in Mark 60–61
        in Matthew 61–62
        miraculous abundance 41
        of Paul 63, 48–49, 90–91,
            142
        at Qumran 94–95
        reversal of fates 36
eternal life 36, 56n111, 57,
    181n639, 186–91, 200–201
Eve 183
exile, return of tribes from
    35n11, 42–43, 51, 71–76,
    186–90, 267n184, 293n299

failed prophecy 57, 64–67,
    128–32, 144–53, 250
fasting 137, 205, 211–12
feeding of the five thousand
    268n192, 272–73
fiction in the Tanak 443–44
fire 34–35, 40, 80–81, 83, 129,
    178, 194, 215–19, 230, 269,
    274–78

Galilee 50–51, 122, 141, 203,
    268
Gehenna 34–35, 44, 81, 87,
    124–25, 130, 179, 184, 194,
    199. *See also* Hades
Gethsemane 387, 415–21,
    426–27, 432–33

golden rule
  canonical placement of 309
  in *1 Clement* 324, 326
  as conventional maxim 321,
    358–60, 375
  in the *Didache* 329–32, 334
  and Leviticus 19 358–59,
    373
  and love of enemy 318–19
  structure of 319, 322
gospels (canonical)
  as biography 443
  as fiction 437–46
  form criticism of 16,
    304n350, 306
  genre of 441–46
  as haggadah 438–39, 441
  humor in 446–49
  infancy narratives of 438,
    440, 445, 448–49, 451,
    453–54
  intentions of authors of
    436–37, 455–56
  metaphorical narratives in
    437–41, 443, 445–56, 458
  redaction criticism of 306,
    453–55

Hades 36. *See also* Gehenna
haggadah 438–39, 441, 446–
  48, 451, 455
Herod Antipas 82–84, 432–33,
  451
Herod the Great 448n47
Hoffman, Melchior 51–52

imagination 2, 460
imitatio Dei 311, 320–22, 325,
  349, 355–56, 358, 368, 375
Isaac 166, 178, 185–86, 248,
  299, 355n141, 403n65, 454

Jacob 74, 166, 172, 178, 248,
  299–300
Jehovah's Witnesses 151
Jesus. *See also* crucifixion;
  John the Baptist; "King of
  the Jews"
  aphorisms of 14, 16, 20n82,
    21, 24–25, 116–17, 119,
    305–6, 308, 322
  arrest, cause of 398–402

and asceticism 205, 211–13
baptism of 21–22, 53–54,
  138, 141n492, 204, 220,
  226, 242n84, 440, 445,
  450. *See also* dove at the
  baptism
baptismal practice of 210–
  11, 213–14
burial of 390, 403, 414n98,
  425
character of 407–8
christological traditions attributed to 227–30
as "the coming one" 80, 138,
  219, 274–78
comparison to others 82–85
crucifixion of 50, 235–36,
  389–95, 411–14, 419, 425
death of 233–40, 392–403,
  427–33
and Deutero-Isaiah 113–15,
  263–66, 275
disciples of 25–26, 145–46
discourses attributed to
  305–9, 381–86
enthronement of 247–51
entry into Jerusalem 286–87
eschatological traditions attributed to 33–43
exorcisms of 17–19, 133–34
family of 283n255
generation of 33–34, 272
and Gentiles 42n56, 186,
  368, 373
handing over of 414–15
as itinerant 24–25
and John the Baptist 53–55,
  82–85, 204–20
as judge 42, 186, 219, 228–
  29, 246, 252, 263, 303
and kingship 233–40, 244–47
as messiah 41, 222, 242–44,
  266–67, 279–93, 301–2
miracles of 23n94
misunderstanding of 154–56
parables of 116–18
as prophet 222, 263–67
as prophet like Moses
  270–74
and purity 211
resurrection of 55–59, 63,
  240–44

self-conception of 221–304
as Son of man 39, 80, 222,
  227–30, 241–42, 293–303
as teacher 24–25
trial of 235n58, 287
as a twin 160n578, 296–303
willingness to die 427–33
Jesus Seminar ix, 15, 53n97,
  69–70, 74, 98–99, 101n318,
  117, 143n506, 209n721,
  234n50, 425n141
Jesus son of Ananias 207, 238,
  240, 400–401
John the Baptist
  baptismal practice of 210–11
  differences from Jesus 137–
    41, 206–13, 428
  disciples of 74n188, 80
  as Elijah 81, 241, 269
  eschatology of 53–55, 81,
    206–8, 210, 219
  and the kingdom of God
    40n42, 166, 180n636, 204,
    206–8
  and Malachi 130, 269
  messianic preaching of 42,
    209–10, 274–78
  parallels with, likeness to
    Jesus 82–85, 204–10
  as risen from the dead
    56n111
  sources for 122, 205, 207–8
Joseph, father of Jesus 154,
  440, 451
Joseph of Arimathea 77,
  391n19, 425
Joseph the patriarch 299,
  352n134, 356–57
Judas the Galilean 84–85, 238
Judas Iscariot 42n55, 60,
  62n138, 67–69, 123, 298,
  402, 414, 426–27
Judith, book of 449–50

Kimbangu, Simon 256, 258
"King of the Jews" 230–31,
  233–40, 245–46, 279n243,
  282, 404, 429, 460
kingdom of God
  in Christian texts outside the
    canonical gospels 184–85
  coming of 191–92

in the Dead Sea Scrolls
171–72
and eternal life 186–91
entering 179, 191–92
futurity of 39
as dynamic activity 168–69,
201–2
as God's people 202–3
as "good news" 196–97
inheriting 191
in Jewish literature 37
and kingship 244–47
in Matthew 181–82
parables and 192–93
presence of 98–116
in rabbinic texts 189–90,
201n691
as realm, territory, or state
of affairs 168–99
relative value of 197
"sons of" 194–95
and suffering 194
in the synoptics 164–68
and the world to come
188–201
Kook, Abraham 115
Krishnamurti 280n247

Last Supper of Jesus 41, 79,
178, 403
Lord's Prayer 36–38, 271

Mani, Manichaeism 233n48,
257–58, 296–98, 303
maranatha 48–49
memorable formulations 24
memory
aids to 374–76
ancient and modern 27–28
communal, social 7, 25n101,
28–29, 161–64
as construction 2–3, 30
cross-cultural differences in
27–29
death and 423–24
deterioration with time 5
and emotion 424n136
eyewitness testimony 1–2
"flashbulb" memories 7–8
general impressions 10–14,
28
personal interests and 5–7, 30

reliability of 1–17, 22, 423,
460–61
"reminiscence bump"
424n136
and repetition 24–25
repisodic 381
and scriptural language 389
sequential reordering of 5
and storytelling 7
messiah. See also Abravanel,
Isaac; Abulafia, Abraham;
Akiba; Bar Kokhba; Kook,
Abraham; Sabbatai Sevi;
Schneerson, Menachem;
Scholem, Gershom; Son
of David; Yudghan of
Hamadan
death of 282n252
and Elijah 95, 274
as hidden 289–93
and Isaiah 61 266
Jesus as 222–23, 242, 279–93
and John the Baptist 209
in Judaism 75–77, 84, 175,
252–53, 258–60, 279n244,
282n251
and Lubavitchers 152, 296
and Passover 146n518,
228n30
as present 115–16
as priestly 262
as prince 111
as prophet 273
reign of 111
and resurrection 242–43
revelation of 108, 292–93
at right hand of God 249
and Son of man 302
and temple 238
and twelve tribes 232n42
two advents of 150
messianic secret 293
method for constructing the
historical Jesus 14–20,
153–54, 231–32, 460–61.
See also authenticity, criteria of; tradition histories
millenarianism; messianic
movements
characteristics of 40,
58n122, 85–86, 133
and eschatology 134–35

logic and 115–16
and prophecy 64–65, 143–
53, 160, 250
and social concern 208
Miller, William; Millerites 64,
146, 148n525, 150
miracles
and Elijah 267
and Elisha 268
and fiction 437–39, 447–48,
456–58
and Isaiah 61 266
and Jesus 20n82, 37n72,
267–68, 276, 406
and messianic figures 23n94
and skepticism 23n94
and worldview 456–58
missionary activity 25–26,
152–53
missionary discourse 25–26,
211–12, 382
Montanism 51–52, 136n467
Moses of Crete 259–60
Muhammad 57, 94, 159, 222

Noah and Noah's flood 35,
109, 227, 382, 385–86

Origen 53n97, 77n204, 84, 91,
175, 210n724, 426nn144–
46, 443–46, 456

paradise. See Eden, garden of
parousia, delay of 65, 101,
140n491, 144–53, 208
passion narrative
as eschatological discourse
60–65
historicity of 387–92,
423–27
as "history scripturalized"
389–92
and Paul 392–403, 405–23
pre-Markan origin of 403–5
as "prophecy historicized"
387–92
Psalms in 407–11
Passover 146n518, 228–30,
240, 391, 412–13, 423
Paul
christology of 226, 231, 247,
281–82, 293–304

"conversion" of 138, 389
development in 90–91
eschatology of 39, 48–50,
    55, 63, 91, 103–4, 115, 142,
    208n721
his imitation of Jesus Christ
    420
inconsistency in 90–92, 96,
    103–4
and Jerusalem 50n85
Jesus tradition in 22, 25,
    44n59, 70, 81n223, 313–14,
    346–48, 372n190, 380,
    392–423
kingdom of God in 103–4,
    288n284
passion traditions in
    392–423
and the resurrection of
    Jesus 55
self-conception of 138, 389
as source for earliest Chris-
    tianity 158
his "stigmata" 393–95
his "thorn in the flesh"
    415–16
and the twelve disciples
    69–70
Peter 280, 298, 426–27
Pilate 236–40, 391, 395–96,
    425
prophecy, fulfillment of 41–42,
    78–82, 127–32, 149–50,
    250
prophecy, reinterpretation of
    64–65, 144–53, 250
prophet like Moses 270–74,
    296

Q (sayings source)
    eschatology of 123–25, 208
    and the *Gospel of Thomas*
        132–33
    stratification of 118–25

rabbinic memorization 26n105
realized eschatology 127–32
recurrent attestation 17–21
resurrection
    and Elijah 268n187
    and exaltation 247–48, 250

in the Jesus tradition and
    early Christianity 39–40,
    44, 55–59, 146, 157, 226,
    240–44, 290–91
in Judaism 55–56, 58, 282
in Mark 123n418
parallels to Jesus' resurrec-
    tion 57–58
as present reality 151
Reuben, David 75

Sabbatai Sevi 75, 112n360,
    159–60, 233, 255n135, 259,
    289n285, 458
Sabbath 107n335, 136n468,
    236
Satan
    and eschatology 112–13, 136
    as father of Cain 199n682
    as "the god of this world"
        278
    in *Gospel of Thomas*
        133–34
    in the Jesus tradition 17–20,
        47
    in John's Gospel 62
    as "the strong one" 278
Savonarola 138
Schneerson, Menachem 57,
    96, 115, 163, 291–92, 296
Scholem, Gershom 254
Semitic idiom of relative nega-
    tion 105–6
Sermon on the Mount, the
    182, 305, 309–11, 336,
    374n193
Sermon on the Plain, the
    "brother" in 365
    compositional history of in
        contemporary scholarship
        313–16
    content of in Q 311–13
    Gentiles in 368
    good and bad in 368
    hypocrisy in 364–65
    judging others in 357–58
    lending in 365–68
    Leviticus 19 in 351–74
    love of neighbor and enemy
        in 353–55
    measuring in 370
    mercy in 369–70

neighbor in 353–55, 361–62
origin of 380–81
parallelism in 316–23, 334–
    46, 375–37
parallels to in Clement of
    Rome 323–26
parallels to in the *Didache*
    329–34, 372–74
parallels to in Ephesians
    348–51
parallels to in the *Epistle of
    Aristeas* 322–23
parallels to in Paul 346–48
parallels to in Polycarp
    326–28
quadripartite structures in
    334–46
relation to the Sermon on
    the Mount 309–11
as stable composition
    374–77
unity of 316–23, 378–80
vengeance in 360
Shakers, the 128, 151
Shembe, Isaiah 256n138
sign prophets in Josephus
    260–61, 271, 273, 398–99
Simon of Cyrene 388, 391n19,
    425, 454
Society of Biblical Literature
    Seminar on Ancient Myths
    and Modern Theories of
    Christian Origins 157–58
Socrates 16, 23n95, 308, 380,
    399, 433
Sodom 35, 382–84, 386
Son of David 115, 209, 238,
    249, 252, 259, 279–93. *See
    also* David; messiah
speck and log saying 363–64
Spirit of God 38, 49, 132n450,
    160n578, 264, 266n178,
    271n204, 417–18
"strong one, the" 209–10, 230,
    275, 278
Sun Myung Moon 304n350

temple
    as center of world 186
    destruction of 60
    entering into 180n637
    in heaven 171, 173

incident in the 136–37, 236–
  38, 264, 283n253, 388
kingdom and 170–71, 174,
  201n689
new temple 43, 51, 76, 110,
  290n290
sayings about 43, 45, 147,
  230, 236n63, 287
tax for 245
Testament of Abraham
  57n114, 249, 420n120,
  448–49
theological commitments of
  historians 221–25
Theudas 84–85, 261n157, 399
third quest 461
Thomas, Gospel of
  "Christ," absence of from
    279
  eschatology of 125–34, 143,
    151, 155–56, 184, 187–88

kingdom in 98, 184, 187
origin of apocryphal ma-
  terials 160n578
parables in 117
and Q 14n67, 132–33
relationship to Luke 101–3
"Son of man" in 293
as source for Jesus and earliest Christianity 157–58,
  160n578, 306, 432
and the Twelve 69–70
tradition histories 14n67,
  16–17, 21, 121, 153, 231
Twelve, the
  and Daniel 7 80
  fate after Easter 147
  historicity of 21, 67–70
  as judges 197
  meaning of 71–76, 232–33,
    267
  parallels to 74–75, 232–33

and return of Israel from
  exile 42–43, 71–76, 186
twelve tribes of Israel 67–76,
  80, 186, 197. *See also* exile,
  return of tribes from
twins, celestial 296–303

Valentinians 298–99

women at the cross 389–91,
  425
world/age to come 39,
  189–204
Wovoka 159–60, 222

Xiuquan, Hong 256–57

Yudghan of Hamadan 222